USA BASEBALL

CONNECT WITH US!

/USABaseball

Join the more than 130,000 fans who like us on Facebook.

@USABaseball

More than 40,000 people receive breaking news and special offers by following us on Twitter.

@USABaseball

Follow us on Instagram for a behind-the-scenes look at USA Baseball's events.

OUR PASTIME'S FUTURE.sm

usabaseball.com

BaseBall america
2014 DIRECTORY

Editor
JOSH LEVENTHAL

Assistant Editors
BEN BADLER, ALEXIS BRUDNICKI J.J. COOPER, AARON FITT, VINCE LARA-CINISOMO
JOSH NORRIS JIM SHONERD, BILL WOODWARD

Database and Application Development
BRENT LEWIS

Photo Editor
JIM SHONERD

Design & Production
SARA HIATT MCDANIEL, LINWOOD WEBB

Programming & Technical Development
BRENT LEWIS

Cover Photo
ANDREW WOOLLEY

DISTRIBUTED BY SIMON & SCHUSTER ISBN-13: 978-1-932391-51-0

BaseBall america

PRESIDENT/PUBLISHER Lee Folger
DIRECTOR OF EDITORIAL AND OPERATIONS Will Lingo

EDITORIAL
EDITOR IN CHIEF John Manuel
MANAGING EDITOR J.J. Cooper
NEWS EDITOR Josh Leventhal
ASSOCIATE EDITOR Matt Eddy
WEB EDITOR Vincent Lara-Cinisomo
NATIONAL WRITERS Ben Badler, Aaron Fitt
ASSISTANT EDITORS Clint Longenecker, Josh Norris, Jim Shonerd

PRODUCTION
DESIGN & PRODUCTION DIRECTOR Sara Hiatt McDaniel
MULTIMEDIA MANAGER Linwood Webb
PRODUCTION MANAGER Christina Ponce

ADVERTISING
ADVERTISING DIRECTOR George Shelton
DIRECT MARKETING MANAGER Ximena Caceres
MARKETPLACE MANAGER Kristopher M. Lull
ADVERTISING ACCOUNT EXECUTIVE Abbey Langdon

BUSINESS
CUSTOMER SERVICE Melissa Hales, Ronnie McCabe
ACCOUNTING/OFFICE MANAGER Hailey Carpenter
TECHNOLOGY MANAGER Brent Lewis
ADMINISTRATIVE ASSISTANT Shannon Tuohey

WHERE TO DIRECT QUESTIONS
ADVERTISING: advertising@baseballamerica.com
BUSINESS BEAT: joshleventhal@baseballamerica.com
COLLEGES: aaronfitt@baseballamerica.com
DESIGN/PRODUCTION: production@baseballamerica.com
DRAFT: johnmanuel@baseballamerica.com
HIGH SCHOOLS: clintlongenecker@baseballamerica.com
INDEPENDENT LEAGUES: jjcooper@baseballamerica.com
MAJOR LEAGUES: matteddy@baseballamerica.com
MINOR LEAGUES: joshleventhal@baseballamerica.com
PHOTOS: photos@baseballamerica.com
PROSPECTS: benbadler@baseballamerica.com
REPRINTS: production@baseballamerica.com
SUBSCRIPTIONS/CUSTOMER SERVICE:
customerservice@baseballamerica.com
WEBSITE: customerservice@baseballamerica.com

GrindMedia

GRINDMEDIA MANAGEMENT
SVP, GROUP PUBLISHER Norb Garrett
norb.garrett@grindmedia.com
VP, DIGITAL Greg Morrow
greg.morrow@grindmedia.com
PRODUCTION DIRECTOR Kasey Kelley
kasey.kelley@grindmedia.com
EDITORIAL DIRECTOR—DIGITAL Chris Mauro
chris.mauro@grindmedia.com
FINANCE DIRECTOR Adam Miner
adam.miner@grindmedia.com
VP, MANUFACTURING & ADVERTISING OPERATIONS
Greg Parnell greg.parnell@sorc.com
SENIOR DIRECTOR, AD OPERATIONS
Pauline Atwood pauline.atwood@sorc.com
DIRECTOR, PUBLISHING TECHNOLOGIES
Dale Bryson dale.bryson@sorc.com
DIRECTOR OF EVENTS Scott Desiderio
scott.desiderio@transworld.net

ADVERTISING SALES
SALES STRATEGY MGR/PRINT & EVENTS
Chris Engelsman
chris.engelsman@grindmedia.com
SALES STRATEGY MGR/DIGITAL Elisabeth Murray
elisabeth.murray@grindmedia.com

DIGITAL
DIRECTOR OF ENGINEERING Jeff Kimmel
jeff.kimmel@grindmedia.com
SENIOR PRODUCT MANAGER Rishi Kumar
rishi.kumar@grindmedia.com
SENIOR PRODUCT MANAGER Marc Bartell
marc.bartell@grindmedia.com
CREATIVE DIRECTOR Peter Tracy
peter.tracy@grindmedia.com

MARKETING AND EVENTS
DIRECTOR OF EVENT SALES Sean Nielsen
sean.nielsen@grindmedia.com

FACILITIES
MANAGER Randy Ward randy.ward@grindmedia.com
OFFICE COORDINATOR Ruth Hosea
ruth.hosea@grindmedia.com
ARCHIVIST Thomas Voehringer
thomas.voehringer@sorc.com

SOURCE INTERLINK MEDIA

OFFICERS OF SOURCE INTERLINK COMPANIES, INC.
PRESIDENT AND CHIEF EXECUTIVE OFFICER /
Michael Sullivan
EVP, CHIEF ADMINISTRATIVE OFFICER
Stephanie Justice
EVP, CHIEF PROCUREMENT OFFICER Kevin Mullan

SOURCE INTERLINK MEDIA, LLC
PRESIDENT Chris Argentieri
GENERAL MANAGER David Algire
CHIEF CREATIVE OFFICER Alan Alpanian
SVP, FINANCE Dan Bednar
VP, SINGLE COPY SALES AND MARKETING Chris Butler
EVP, ENTHUSIAST AUTOMOTIVE Doug Evans
CHIEF CONTENT OFFICER Angus MacKenzie
CHIEF ANALYTICS OFFICER John Marriott
SVP, BUSINESS DEVELOPMENT Tyler Schulze
EVP, SALES AND MARKETING Eric Schwab

CONSUMER MARKETING, ENTHUSIAST MEDIA SUBSCRIPTION COMPANY, INC.
VP, CONSUMER MARKETING Tom Slater
VP, RETENTION AND OPERATIONS FULFILLMENT
Donald T. Robinson III

2014 National Baseball Hall of Fame Commemorative Coin Program

2014 National Baseball Hall of Fame
Commemorative Coins
Coming Spring 2014

Visit *www.usmint.gov* or call
1-800 –USA-MINT (6468) for more information.

 /UnitedStatesMint   /USMINT   /USMINT

UNITED STATES MINT

TABLE OF CONTENTS

Medlar Field at Lubrano Park, State College, Pa.

STATE COLLEGE SPIKES

Dodger Stadium

BILL NICHOLS

WHAT'S NEW IN 2014

TRIPLE-A
Franchise Move: El Paso (Texas) Chihuahuas replace Tucson Padres in Pacific Coast League.
Ballpark: Charlotte Knights (International)—BB&T Ballpark.

DOUBLE-A
Name: Akron Aeros (Eastern) become Akron RubberDucks.

ROOKIE
Affiliation: Bristol (Appalachian) changes from White Sox to Pirates.
Affiliation: Chicago White Sox replace Kansas City Royals in Arizona League.

Map illustrations by Paul Trap

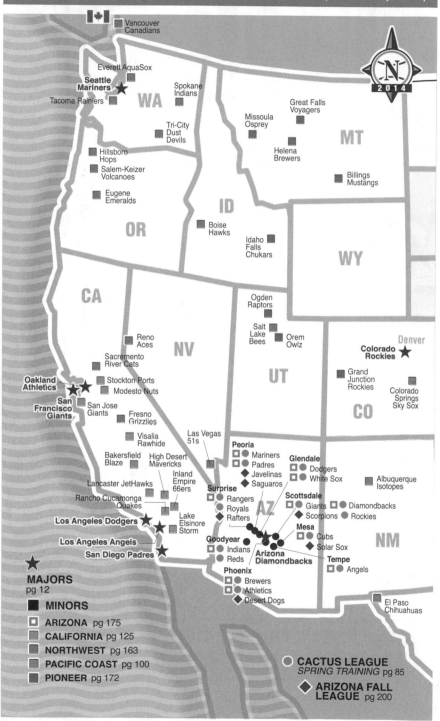

Vancouver Canadians

Everett AquaSox

Seattle Mariners

Tacoma Rainiers

WA

Spokane Indians

Tri-City Dust Devils

Hillsboro Hops

Salem-Keizer Volcanoes

Eugene Emeralds

OR

MT

Great Falls Voyagers

Missoula Osprey

Helena Brewers

Billings Mustangs

ID

Boise Hawks

Idaho Falls Chukars

WY

CA

Reno Aces

NV

Sacramento River Cats

Oakland Athletics

Stockton Ports

Modesto Nuts

San Francisco Giants

San Jose Giants

Fresno Grizzlies

Visalia Rawhide

Bakersfield Blaze

High Desert Mavericks

Lancaster JetHawks

Rancho Cucamonga Quakes

Los Angeles Dodgers

Los Angeles Angels

San Diego Padres

Las Vegas 51s

Inland Empire 66ers

Lake Elsinore Storm

Ogden Raptors

Salt Lake Bees

Orem Owlz

UT

Denver

Colorado Rockies

Grand Junction Rockies

Colorado Springs Sky Sox

CO

Albuquerque Isotopes

Peoria
○ Mariners
○ Padres
◆ Javelinas
◆ Saguaros

Glendale
○ Dodgers
○ White Sox

Scottsdale
○ Giants
◆ Scorpions

○ Diamondbacks
○ Rockies

Surprise
○ Rangers
○ Royals
◆ Rafters

AZ

Mesa
○ Cubs
◆ Solar Sox

NM

Goodyear
○ Indians
○ Reds

Arizona Diamondbacks

Tempe
○ Angels

Phoenix
○ Brewers
○ Athletics
◆ Desert Dogs

El Paso Chihuahuas

★ **MAJORS**
pg 12

■ **MINORS**

□ **ARIZONA** pg 175

□ **CALIFORNIA** pg 125

□ **NORTHWEST** pg 163

□ **PACIFIC COAST** pg 100

□ **PIONEER** pg 172

○ **CACTUS LEAGUE**
SPRING TRAINING pg 85

◆ **ARIZONA FALL LEAGUE** pg 200

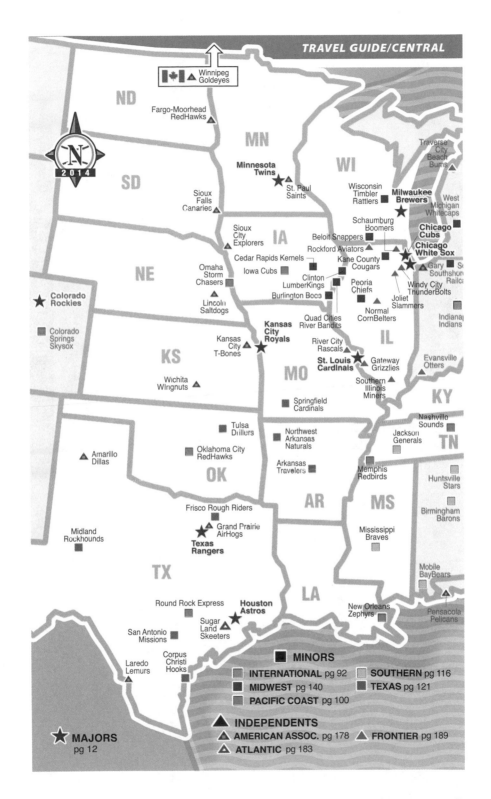

ND

Winnipeg Goldeyes

Fargo-Moorhead RedHawks

MN

Traverse City Beach Bums

SD

Minnesota Twins

St. Paul Saints

Wisconsin Timber Rattlers

Milwaukee Brewers

West Michigan Whitecaps

WI

Sioux Falls Canaries

Schaumburg Boomers

Chicago Cubs

Sioux City Explorers

IA

Beloit Snappers

Chicago White Sox

Rockford Aviators

Cedar Rapids Kernels

Kane County Cougars

Gary Southshore Railca

NE

Omaha Storm Chasers

Iowa Cubs

Clinton LumberKings

Peoria Chiefs

Windy City ThunderBolts

Colorado Rockies

Lincoln Saltdogs

Burlington Bees

Quad Cities River Bandits

Normal CornBelters

Joliet Slammers

Indianap Indians

Colorado Springs Skysox

Kansas City Royals

IL

Kansas City T-Bones

River City Rascals

St. Louis Cardinals

Gateway Grizzlies

Evansville Otters

KS

MO

Southern Illinois Miners

KY

Wichita Wingnuts

Springfield Cardinals

Nashville Sounds

Tulsa Drillers

Northwest Arkansas Naturals

Jackson Generals

TN

Amarillo Dillas

Oklahoma City RedHawks

OK

Arkansas Travelers

Memphis Redbirds

Huntsville Stars

AR

MS

Birmingham Barons

Frisco Rough Riders

Grand Prairie AirHogs

Mississippi Braves

Midland Rockhounds

Texas Rangers

Mobile BayBears

TX

LA

Round Rock Express

Houston Astros

New Orleans Zephyrs

Pensacola Pelicans

San Antonio Missions

Sugar Land Skeeters

Laredo Lemurs

Corpus Christi Hooks

■ **MINORS**

■ INTERNATIONAL pg 92	□ SOUTHERN pg 116
■ MIDWEST pg 140	■ TEXAS pg 121
■ PACIFIC COAST pg 100	

▲ **INDEPENDENTS**

| ▲ AMERICAN ASSOC. pg 178 | △ FRONTIER pg 189 |
| △ ATLANTIC pg 183 | |

★ **MAJORS**
pg 12

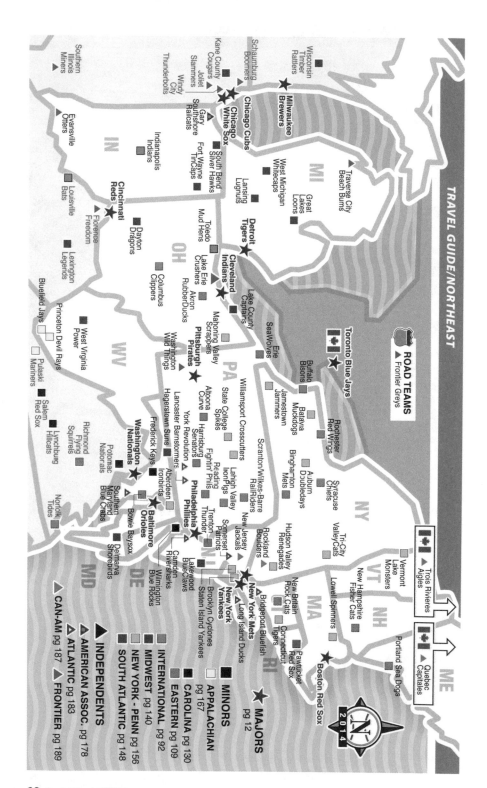

ROAD TEAMS
▲ Frontier Greys

Southern Illinois Miners
Wisconsin Timber Rattlers
Schaumburg Boomers
Kane County Cougars
Joliet Slammers
Windy City Thunderbolts
Milwaukee Brewers
Chicago White Sox
Chicago Cubs
Gary Southshore Railcats
Evansville Otters
Indianapolis Indians
South Bend Silver Hawks
Fort Wayne TinCaps
West Michigan Whitecaps
Great Lakes Loons
Traverse City Beach Bums
Cincinnati Reds
Lansing Lugnuts
Detroit Tigers
Louisville Bats
Florence Freedom
Dayton Dragons
Toledo Mud Hens
Cleveland Indians
Lexington Legends
Columbus Clippers
Akron RubberDucks
Lake Erie Crushers
Lake County Captains
Erie SeaWolves
Bluefield Jays
Princeton Devil Rays
West Virginia Power
Mahoning Valley Scrappers
Pittsburgh Pirates
Washington Wild Things
Pulaski Mariners
Williamsport Crosscutters
State College Spikes
Altoona Curve
Salem Red Sox
Richmond Flying Squirrels
Lynchburg Hillcats
Washington Nationals
Potomac Nationals
Frederick Keys
Hagerstown Suns
Harrisburg Senators
Lancaster Barnstormers
York Revolution
Reading Fightin Phils
Philadelphia Phillies
Trenton Thunder
Norfolk Tides
Southern Maryland Blue Crabs
Bowie Baysox
Baltimore Orioles
Aberdeen Ironbirds
Camden Riversharks
Somerset Patriots
New Jersey Jackals
Delmarva Shorebirds
Wilmington Blue Rocks
Lakewood BlueClaws
New York Mets
New York Yankees
Rockland Boulders
Bridgeport Bluefish
Long Island Ducks
Brooklyn Cyclones
Staten Island Yankees
Hudson Valley Renegades
Connecticut Tigers
New Britain Rock Cats
Pawtucket Red Sox
Buffalo Bisons
Batavia Muckdogs
Jamestown Jammers
Scranton/Wilkes-Barre RailRiders
Lehigh Valley IronPigs
Rochester Red Wings
Binghamton Mets
Auburn Doubledays
Syracuse Chiefs
Tri-City ValleyCats
Vermont Lake Monsters
New Hampshire Fisher Cats
Lowell Spinners
Portland Sea Dogs
Boston Red Sox

▲ Trois Rivieres Aigles
▲ Quebec Capitales

Toronto Blue Jays

MI
IN
OH
WV
PA
NY
NJ
MD
DE
MA
VT
NH
RI
ME

MAJORS pg 12

MINORS
INTERNATIONAL pg 140
EASTERN pg 109
MIDWEST pg 167
CAROLINA pg 130
NEW YORK - PENN pg 156
SOUTH ATLANTIC pg 148
APPALACHIAN pg 92

INDEPENDENTS
AMERICAN ASSOC. pg 178
ATLANTIC pg 183
CAN-AM pg 187
FRONTIER pg 189

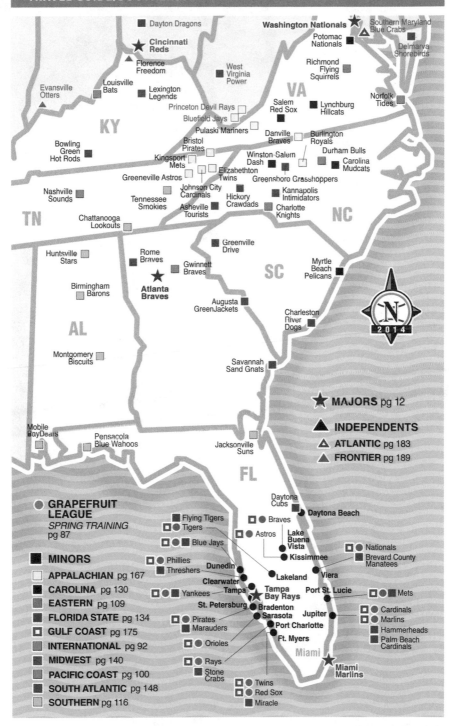

Dayton Dragons
Washington Nationals
Southern Maryland Blue Crabs
Cincinnati Reds
Potomac Nationals
Delmarva Shorebirds
Florence Freedom
West Virginia Power
Richmond Flying Squirrels
Evansville Otters
Louisville Bats
Lexington Legends
KY
VA
Salem Red Sox
Lynchburg Hillcats
Norfolk Tides
Princeton Devil Rays
Bluefield Jays
Pulaski Mariners
Danville Braves
Burlington Royals
Bowling Green Hot Rods
Bristol Pirates
Kingsport Mets
Winston-Salem Dash
Durham Bulls
Carolina Mudcats
Greeneville Astros
Elizabethton Twins
Greensboro Grasshoppers
Nashville Sounds
Johnson City Cardinals
Hickory Crawdads
Kannapolis Intimidators
Tennessee Smokies
Asheville Tourists
Charlotte Knights
NC
TN
Chattanooga Lookouts
Huntsville Stars
Rome Braves
Greenville Drive
SC
Myrtle Beach Pelicans
Birmingham Barons
Gwinnett Braves
Atlanta Braves
Augusta GreenJackets
Charleston River Dogs
AL
Montgomery Biscuits
Savannah Sand Gnats

★ **MAJORS** pg 12
▲ **INDEPENDENTS**
△ **ATLANTIC** pg 183
▲ **FRONTIER** pg 189

Mobile BayBears
Pensacola Blue Wahoos
Jacksonville Suns
FL

● **GRAPEFRUIT LEAGUE**
SPRING TRAINING pg 87

Daytona Cubs
Braves
Daytona Beach
Flying Tigers
Tigers
Astros
Lake Buena Vista
Nationals
Brevard County Manatees

■ **MINORS**
□ **APPALACHIAN** pg 167
■ **CAROLINA** pg 130
■ **EASTERN** pg 109
■ **FLORIDA STATE** pg 134
□ **GULF COAST** pg 175
■ **INTERNATIONAL** pg 92
■ **MIDWEST** pg 140
■ **PACIFIC COAST** pg 100
■ **SOUTH ATLANTIC** pg 148
□ **SOUTHERN** pg 116

Blue Jays
Kissimmee
Phillies
Threshers
Dunedin
Lakeland
Viera
Clearwater
Port St. Lucie
Yankees
Tampa
Tampa Bay Rays
Mets
St. Petersburg
Bradenton
Cardinals
Pirates
Marauders
Sarasota
Port Charlotte
Jupiter
Marlins
Orioles
Ft. Myers
Hammerheads
Palm Beach Cardinals
Rays
Miami
Stone Crabs
Twins
Red Sox
Miami Marlins
Miracle

MAJOR LEAGUES

MAJOR LEAGUE BASEBALL

Mailing Address: 245 Park Ave. New York, NY 10167.
Telephone: (212) 931-7800. **Website:** www.mlb.com.
Commissioner: Allan H. "Bud" Selig.
Chief Operating Officer: Robert Manfred. **Executive Vice President, Business:** Tim Brosnan. **Executive VP, Labor Relations:** Dan Halem. **Executive VP, Finance/Chief Financial Officer:** Jonathan Mariner. **Executive VP, Administration/Chief Information Officer:** John McHale. **Executive VP, Baseball Development:** Frank Robinson. **Executive VP, Baseball Operations:** Joe Torre.

Baseball Operations

Special Assistant to the Commissioner: Tony La Russa.
Senior VP, Baseball Operations: Joe Garagiola Jr., Kim Ng, Peter Woodfork.
Senior Director, Major League Operations: Roy Krasik. **Consultant:** Lou Melendez.
Director, International Baseball Operations: Chris Haydock. **Director, Baseball Operations:** Jeff Pfeifer. **Senior Manager, Minor League Operations:** Fred Seymour. **Manager, Amateur Player Administration:** Chuck Fox. **Specialist, Umpire Administration:** Cathy Davis. **Manager, International Talent Development:** Joel Araujo.
Coordinator, Major League Operations: Gina Liento. **Coordinator, On Field Operations:** Stephen Mara. **Administrator, International Baseball Operations:** Shane Barclay. **Senior Coordinator, International Baseball Operations:** Rebecca Seesel. **Senior Administrative Assistant:** Llubia Bussey, Ana Rivas. **Manager, International Baseball Operations:** Giovanni Hernandez.
Director, Major League Umpiring: Randy Marsh. **Director, Replay:** Justin Klemm. **Director, Umpiring Development:** Rich Rieker. **Director, Umpire Administration:** Matt McKendry. **Director, Umpire Medical Services:** Mark Letendre. **Umpiring Supervisors:** Cris Jones, Tom Leppard, Chuck Meriwether, Ed Montague, Steve Palermo, Charlie Reliford, Larry Young. **Umpire Evaluator:** Ed Rapuano. **Special Assistant, Umpiring:** Bruce Froemming. **Sure Administrator:** Raquel Wagner.
Video Coordinator: Freddie Hernandez. **Baseball Systems:** Nancy Crofts. **Director, Dominican Operations:** Rafael Perez. **Assistant Manager:** Osiris Ramirez. **Director, Arizona Fall League:** Steve Cobb. **Senior Director, Major League Scouting Bureau:** Frank Marcos. **Assistant Director, Scouting Bureau:** Rick Oliver.

Baseball Development

VP, Youth/Facilities Development: Darrell Miller.
Director, Baseball Initiatives: Sylvia Lind. **Senior Manager, Baseball Development/Urban Youth Academies:** Ben Baroody.

Security

VP, Security/Facility Management: Bill Bordley.
Director, Security Operations: John Skinner. **Supervisor, Executive Protection:** Charles Hargrove. **Director, Facility Operations:** Paul Hanlon. **Senior Manager, Security Operations:** José Gonzalez. **Manager, Latin America Security Operations:** Tom P. Reilly. **Supervisor, Executive Offices Security Operations:** William Diaz. **Senior Manager, Facility Operations:** Harold Brantley. **Senior Manager:** Shelagh Dillon. **Supervisor, Security/Facility Management:** Yenifer Fauche. **Security Analyst:** Christopher Ellis. **Assistant to VP, Security/Facility Management:** Danielle Beckom.

Investigations

Senior VP, Investigations: Dan Mullin.
VP, Investigations: George Hanna. **VP, Educational Programming/Investigative Services:** Earnell Lucas. **Managers, Investigations:** Nancy Zamudio, Ed Dominguez. **Manager, Investigations/DR-DOI Office:** Nelson Tejada. **Senior Investigators:** Ricardo Burnham, Awilda Santana, Tom J. Reilly, Ed Maldonado. **Senior Analyst:** Kevin Cepelak. **Research Analyst:** Ariadne Bonano. **Research Coordinators:** Kendall Barreiro, Natalie Romine.

Public Relations

Telephone: (212) 931-7878. **Fax:** (212) 949-5654.
Senior VP, Public Relations: Patrick Courtney.
VP, Business Public Relations: Matt Bourne. **Senior Director, Public Relations:** Michael Teevan. **Senior Director, Public Relations:** John Blundell. **Director, Business Public Relations:** Jeff Heckelman. **Manager, Public Relations:** Donald Muller. **Managers, Business Public Relations:** Steven Arocho, Daniel Queen, Lauren Verrusio. **Specialists, Public Relations:** Lydia Panayotidis, Jen Zudonyi. **Coordinator, Business Public Relations:** Sarah Leer. **Senior Administrative Assistant:** Ginger Dillon.

Club Relations

Senior VP, Scheduling/Club Relations: Katy Feeney.
Administrative Assistant, Scheduling/Club Relations: Ana Cruz. **Coordinator, Club Relations:** Bennett Shields. **Senior VP, Club Relations:** Phyllis Merhige. **Senior Administrative Assistant, Club Relations:** Angelica Cintron. **Administrator, Club Relations:** Ian Johns.

Licensing

Senior VP, Licensing: Howard Smith.
VP, Domestic Licensing: Steve Armus. **VP, Hard Goods:** Mike Napolitano. **Senior Director, Consumer Products/Retail Marketing:** Adam Blinderman. **Director, Licensing/Minor Leagues:** Eliot Runyon. **Senior Director, Non-**

MAJOR LEAGUES

Authentics: Greg Sim. **Senior Director, Authentic Collection:** Ryan Samuelson. **Senior Manager, Presence Marketing:** Robin Jaffe.

Publishing/Photographs
VP, Publishing/Photographs: Don Hintze. **Editorial Director:** Mike McCormick. **Art Director, Publications:** Faith Rittenberg. **MLB Photographs:** Jessica Foster.

Special Events
Senior VP, Special Events: Marla Miller.
Senior Directors, Special Events: Brian O'Gara, Eileen Buser. **Directors, Special Events:** Jacqueline Secaira-Cotto, Rob Capilli. **Senior Manager, Special Events:** Jeremiah Yolkut. **Managers, Special Events:** Bernie Goon, Ashley Scherer.

Broadcasting
Senior VP, Broadcasting: Chris Tully.
VP, Broadcast Administration/Operations: Bernadette McDonald. **Senior Director, Broadcasting Business Affairs:** Susanne Hilgefort. **Director, Broadcast Administration/Operations:** Chuck Torres. **Manager, Broadcasting:** Dewey Gong.

Corporate Sales/Marketing
VP, Partnership Marketing: Jeremy Cohen. **VP, National Sales:** Chris Marciani.

Advertising
Senior VP/Chief Marketing Officer: Jacqueline Parkes.
VP, Research/Strategic Planning: Dan Derian. **VP, Design Services:** Anne Occi. **VP, Brand Marketing/Advertising:** Dan Kelleher. **Director, Brand Marketing/Advertising:** Rita O'Neill. **Director, Research:** Marc Beck. **Director, Brand Marketing/Advertising:** Lance Gitlin. **Senior Manager, Brand Marketing/Advertising:** Felicia Principe.

Community Affairs
VP, Community Affairs: Tom Brasuell.
Director, Community Affairs: Celia Bobrowsky. **Director, Reviving Baseball in Inner Cities:** David James.

General Administration
Senior VP, Accounting/Treasurer: Bob Clark. **Senior VP/General Counsel, Business:** Ethan Orlinsky. **Senior VP/General Counsel, BOC:** Tom Ostertag. **Senior VP, Finance:** Kathleen Torres. **Senior VP, Chief Technology Officer:** Mike Morris. **VP, Deputy General Counsel:** Domna Candido. **Senior VP, Diversity/Strategic Alliances:** Wendy Lewis. **VP, Human Resources:** Ray Scott. **VP/Deputy General Counsel:** Jennifer Simms. **Director, Baseball Assistance Team:** Erik Nilsen. **VP, Office Operations:** Donna Hoder. **Senior Director, Quality Control:** Peggy O'Neill-Janosik. **VP, Recruitment:** John Quinones. **Director, Risk Management/Financial Reporting:** Anthony Avitabile. **Senior Manager, Records:** Mildred Delgado. **Director, Retirement Services:** Rich Hunt. **Director, Benefits/HRIS:** Diane Cuddy. **Director, Organizational Development/Employee Relations:** Ron Rydell.

International
Mailing Address: 245 Park Ave., 31st Floor, New York, NY 10167. **Telephone:** (212) 931-7500. **Fax:** (212) 949-5795.
Senior VP, International Business Operations: Paul Archey.
VP, International Licensing: Denis Nolan. **VP/Executive Producer, International Broadcasting:** Russell Gabay. **VP, Sponsorship/Market Development:** Dominick Balsamo. **VP, World Baseball Classic:** James Pearce. **VP, International Broadcast Sales:** Frank Uddo. **VP, Asia/Managing Director, MLB Japan:** Jim Small. **Managing Director, MLB China:** Leon Xie. **Senior Manager, MLB Europe, Middle East/Africa:** Jason Holowaty. **Director, MLB Australia/Oceania:** Thomas Nicholson. **CEO, Australian Baseball League:** Peter Wermuth.

MLB Western Operations
Office Address: 2415 East Camelback Rd., Suite 850, Phoenix, AZ 85016. **Telephone:** (602) 281-7300. **Fax:** (602) 281-7313.
VP, Western Operations/Special Projects: Laurel Prieb. **Office Coordinator:** Valerie Dietrich.

Major League Baseball Productions
Office Address: One MLB Network Plaza, Secaucus, NJ 07094-2403. **Telephone:** (201) 751-8500. **Fax:** (201) 751-8568.
VP, Executive In Charge of Production: David Gavant.
Executive Producer: David Check. **Senior Director, Operations:** Shannon Valine. **Senior Manager, Media Management/Tech Ops:** Chris Monico. **Director, Programming:** Jon O'Sheal. **Director, Library Licensing:** Nick Trotta. **Senior Writer:** Jeff Scott. **Coordinating Producer, Field Production:** Robert Haddad. **Coordinating Producer:** Adam Schlackman. **Managing Producer:** Kristen Wendland.

Umpires
Jordan Baker, Lance Barksdale, Lance Barrett, Ted Barrett, Dan Bellino, Cory Blaser, C.B. Bucknor, Vic Carapazza, Mark Carlson, Gary Cederstrom, Eric Cooper, Fieldin Culbreth, Phil Cuzzi, Kerwin Danley, Gary Darling, Bob Davidson, Gerry Davis, Dana DeMuth, Laz Diaz, Mike DiMuro, Rob Drake, Bruce Dreckman, Doug Eddings, Paul Emmel, Mike Estabrook, Mike Everitt, Chad Fairchild, Andy Fletcher, Marty Foster, Greg Gibson, Manny Gonzalez, Brian Gorman, Chris Guccione, Tom Hallion, Angel Hernandez, Ed Hickox, John Hirschbeck, Sam Holbrook, James Hoye, Marvin Hudson, Dan Iassogna, Adrian Johnson, Jim Joyce, Jeff Kellogg, Brian Knight, Ron Kulpa, Jerry Layne, Alfonso Marquez, Tim McClelland, Jerry Meals, Bill Miller, Mike Muchlinski, Paul Nauert, Jeff Nelson, Brian O'Nora, Alan Porter, David Rackley, Tony Randazzo, DJ Reyburn, Jim Reynolds, Brian Runge, Paul Schrieber, Dale Scott, Todd Tichenor, Tim Timmons, Larry Vanover, Mark Wegner, Bill Welke, Tim Welke, Hunter Wendelstedt, Joe West, Mike Winters, Jim Wolf.

Events
2014 All-Star Game: July 15 at Target Field, Minnesota. **2014 World Series:** Unavailable.

AMERICAN LEAGUE

Year League Founded: 1901.
2014 Opening Date: March 31. **Closing Date:** Sept. 28.
Regular Season: 162 games.
Division Structure: East—Baltimore, Boston, New York, Tampa Bay, Toronto. **Central**—Chicago, Cleveland, Detroit, Kansas City, Minnesota. **West**—Houston, Los Angeles, Oakland, Seattle, Texas.
Playoff Format: Two non-division winners with best records meet in one-game wildcard playoff. Wildcard winner and three division champions meet in two best-of-five Division Series. Winners meet in best-of-seven Championship Series.
All-Star Game: July 15, Target Field, Minneapolis, Minn. (National League vs. American League).
Roster Limit: 25, through Aug 31, when rosters expand to 40.
Brand of Baseball: Rawlings.
Statistician: MLB Advanced Media, 75 Ninth Ave., 5th Floor, New York, NY 10011.

STADIUM INFORMATION

Team	Stadium	Dimensions			Capacity	2013 Att.
		LF	CF	RF		
Baltimore	Oriole Park at Camden Yards	333	410	318	45,971	2,357,561
Boston	Fenway Park	310	390	302	37,493	2,833,333
Chicago	U.S. Cellular Field	330	400	335	40,615	1,768,413
Cleveland	Progressive Field	325	405	325	43,345	1,572,926
Detroit	Comerica Park	345	420	330	41,782	3,083,397
Houston	Minute Maid Park	315	435	326	40,976	1,651,883
Kansas City	Kauffman Stadium	330	410	330	37,903	1,750,754
Los Angeles	Angel Stadium	333	404	333	45,050	3,019,505
Minnesota	Target Field	339	404	328	39,504	2,477,644
New York	Yankee Stadium	318	408	314	50,291	3,279,589
Oakland	O.co Coliseum	330	400	367	35,067	1,809,302
Seattle	Safeco Field	331	401	326	47,447	1,761,546
Tampa Bay	Tropicana Field	315	404	322	41,315	1,510,300
Texas	Rangers Ballpark in Arlington	332	400	325	49,170	3,178,273
Toronto	Rogers Centre	328	400	328	50,598	2,536,562

NATIONAL LEAGUE

Year League Founded: 1876.
2014 Opening Date: March 22. **Closing Date:** Sept. 28.
Regular Season: 162 games.
Division Structure: East—Atlanta, Miami, New York, Philadelphia, Washington. **Central**—Chicago, Cincinnati, Milwaukee, Pittsburgh, St. Louis. **West**—Arizona, Colorado, Los Angeles, San Diego, San Francisco.
Playoff Format: Two non-division winners with best records meet in one-game wildcard playoff. Wildcard winner and three division champions meet in two best-of-five Division Series. Winners meet in best-of-seven Championship Series.
All-Star Game: July 15, Target Field, Minneapolis, Minn. (National League vs. American League).
Roster Limit: 25, through Aug. 31 when rosters expand to 40.
Brand of Baseball: Rawlings.
Statistician: MLB Advanced Media, 75 Ninth Ave., 5th Floor, New York, NY 10011.

STADIUM INFORMATION

Team	Stadium	Dimensions			Capacity	2013 Att.
		LF	CF	RF		
Arizona	Chase Field	330	407	334	49,033	2,134,795
Atlanta	Turner Field	335	400	330	49,743	2,548,679
Chicago	Wrigley Field	355	400	353	41,160	2,642,682
Cincinnati	Great American Ball Park	328	404	325	42,319	2,534,369
Colorado	Coors Field	347	415	350	50,499	2,793,828
Los Angeles	Dodger Stadium	330	395	330	56,000	3,743,527
Miami	Marlins Park	344	422	335	37,000	1,586,322
Milwaukee	Miller Park	344	400	345	41,900	2,531,105
New York	Citi Field	335	408	330	42,200	2,135,657
Philadelphia	Citizens Bank Park	329	401	330	43,647	3,012,403
Pittsburgh	PNC Park	325	399	320	38,496	2,256,862
St. Louis	Busch Stadium	336	400	335	46,681	3,369,769
San Diego	Petco Park	336	396	322	42,685	2,166,691
San Francisco	AT&T Park	339	399	309	41,503	3,326,796
Washington	Nationals Park	336	402	335	41,888	2,652,422

Arizona Diamondbacks

Office Address: Chase Field, 401 E. Jefferson St, Phoenix, AZ 85004.
Mailing Address: P.O. Box 2095, Phoenix, AZ 85001.
Telephone: (602) 462-6500. **Fax:** (602) 462-6599. **Website:** www.dbacks.com

Ownership
Managing General Partner: Ken Kendrick. **General Partners:** Mike Chipman, Jeff Royer.

BUSINESS OPERATIONS

President/CEO: Derrick Hall. **Executive Vice President, Business Operations:** Cullen Maxey. **Special Assistants to President/CEO:** Luis Gonzalez, Roland Hemond. **Military Affairs Specialist:** Captain Jack Ensch. **Executive Assistant to President/CEO:** Brooke Mitchell. **Executive Assistant to Executive VP, Business Operations:** Katy Bernham.

Broadcasting
VP, Broadcasting: Scott Geyer. **Senior Director, Game Operations/Multi-Media Productions:** Rob Weinheimer. **Senior Manager, Multi-Media Productions:** Jon Willey.

Corporate Partnerships/Marketing
VP, Corporate Partnerships: Judd Norris. **Director, Corporate Partnership Services:** Kerri White. **VP, Marketing:** Karina Bohn. **Senior Manager, Marketing/Promotions:** Dustin Payne. **Senior Marketing Media Specialist:** Rayme Lofgren.

Ken Kendrick

Finance/Legal
Executive VP/CFO: Tom Harris. **VP, Finance:** Craig Bradley. **Director, Financial Management/Purchasing:** Jeff Jacobs. **Director, Accounting:** Chris James. **Executive Assistant to Managing General Partner/CFO:** Sandy Cox. **Senior VP/General Counsel:** Nona Lee. **Senior Director, Legal Affairs/Associate General Counsel:** Caleb Jay.

Community Affairs
VP, Corporate/Community Impact: Debbie Castaldo. **Manager, Community Programs:** Tara Trzinski. **Manager, Community Events:** Robert Itzkowitz. **Manager, Multicultural/Partner Programs:** Julie Romero.

Communications/Media Relations
Senior VP, Communications: Josh Rawitch. **Director, Publications:** Josh Greene. **Director, Player/Media Relations:** Casey Wilcox. **Manager, Player/Media Relations:** Patrick O'Connell. **Manager, Corporate Communications:** Katie Krause. **Coordinator, Communications:** Jim Myers. **Social Media Specialist:** John Prewitt.

Special Projects/Fan Experience
VP, Special Projects: Graham Rossini. **Director, Baseball Outreach/Development:** Jeff Rodin. **Manager, Spring Training Operations/GM, Salt River Fields:** David Dunne.

2014 SCHEDULE
Standard Game Times: 6:40 p.m.; Sun. 1:10.

MARCH		MAY	
22 . . . . Los Angeles		2-4 . . . . .at San Diego	
(in Sydney, Australia)		5-7 . . . . . . at Milwaukee	
22 . . . . Los Angeles		9-11 . . . .at Chicago (AL)	
(in Sydney, Australia)		12-14 . . . . . . Washington	
31 . . . . San Francisco		16-18 . . . Los Angeles (NL)	
		20-22 . . . . . . at St. Louis	
APRIL		23-25 . . . at New York (NL)	
1-3 . . . . San Francisco		26-28 . . . . San Diego	
4-6 . . . . at Colorado		29-31 . . . . Cincinnati	
8-10 . . . . at San Francisco			
11-13 . . . Los Angeles (NL)		**JUNE**	
14-16 . . . . . New York (NL)		1 . . . . Cincinnati	
18-20 . at Los Angeles (NL)		3-5 . . . . at Colorado	
21-24 . . . . at Chicago (NL)		6-8 . . . . Atlanta	
25-27 . . . . . . Philadelphia		9-10 . . . . Houston	
28-30 . . . . Colorado		11-12 . . . . . .at Houston	
		13-15 . at Los Angeles (NL)	

JULY		SEPTEMBER	
16-19 . . . . . . Milwaukee		5-7 . . . . .Kansas City	
20-22 . . . . San Francisco		8-10 . . . . Colorado	
24-25 . . . . . . .Cleveland		12-13 . . . . .at Cleveland	
27-29 . . . .at San Diego		14-17 . . . . . . at Miami	
		18-21 . . . .at Washington	
JULY		22-24 . . . . . . San Diego	
1-3 . . . . . . .at Pittsburgh		26-27 . . . Los Angeles (NL)	
4-6 . . . . .at Atlanta		29-31 . . . . Colorado	
7-9 . . . . Miami			
11-13 . . . at San Francisco		**SEPTEMBER**	
18-20 . . . . .Chicago (NL)		1-4 . . . . .at San Diego	
21-23 . . . . Detroit		5-7 . . . at Los Angeles (NL)	
25-27 . . . . at Philadelphia		9-11 . . . . at San Francisco	
28-30 . . . . .at Cincinnati		12-14 . . . . San Diego	
31 . . . . Pittsburgh		15-17 . . . . . San Francisco	
		18-21 . . . . . . at Colorado	
AUGUST		22-24 . . . . . at Minnesota	
1-3 . . . . Pittsburgh		26-28 . . . . .St. Louis	

GENERAL INFORMATION
Stadium (year opened): Chase Field (1998).
Team Colors: Sedona Red, Sonoran Sand and Black.

Player Representative: Brad Ziegler.
Home Dugout: Third Base.
Playing Surface: Grass.

Human Resources/Information Technology
Senior VP, Chief Human Resources/Diversity Officer: Marian Rhodes. **VP, Chief Information Officer:** Bob Zweig.

Stadium Operations
VP, Facility Operations/Event Services: Russ Amaral. **Senior Director, Security:** Sean Maguire. **Senior Manager, Security:** Greg Green. **Director, Facility Services:** Jose Montoya. **Director, Engineering:** Jim White. **Director, Event Services:** Bryan White. **Event Coordinator:** Jeff Gomez. **Head Groundskeeper:** Grant Trenbeath.

Ticket Sales
Telephone: (602) 514-8400. **Fax:** (602) 462-4141.
Senior VP, Ticket Sales/Marketing: John Fisher. **Senior Director, Business Strategy/Operations:** Kenny Farrell. **Senior Director, Ticket Sales:** Ryan Holmstedt.

Travel/Clubhouse
Senior Director, Team Travel/Home Clubhouse Manager: Roger Riley. **Manager, Equipment/Visiting Clubhouse:** Bob Doty.

BASEBALL OPERATIONS
Executive VP/General Manager: Kevin Towers. **Assistant GM:** Billy Ryan. **VP/Special Assistant to GM:** Bob Gebhard. **Special Assistant to GM/Major League Scout:** Bill Bryk. **Special Assistant to GM:** Barry Axelrod, Craig Shipley, David Duncan, Jerry Krause. **VP, Latin America Operations:** Junior Noboa. **Director, Baseball Operations:** Ryan Isaac. **Coordinator, Baseball Operations:** Sam Eaton. **Major League Video Coordinator:** Allen Campbell. **Administrative Assistant:** Kristyn Pierce.

Kevin Towers

Major League Staff
Manager: Kirk Gibson.
Coaches: Bench—Alan Trammell; **Pitching**—Mike Harkey; **Batting**—Turner Ward; **First Base**—Dave McKay; **Third Base**—Glenn Sherlock; **Bullpen**—Mel Stottlemyre, Jr.

Medical/Training
Club Physicians: Dr. Michael Lee, Dr. Roger McCoy. **Head Trainer:** Ken Crenshaw. **Assistant Trainer:** Ryan DiPanfilo. **Strength/Conditioning Coordinator:** Nate Shaw. **Manual/Performance Therapist:** Neil Rampe.

Minor Leagues
Telephone: (602) 462-6500. **Fax:** (602) 462-6425.
Director, Player Development: Mike Bell. **Assistant to Player Development:** TJ Lasita. **Director, Minor League Administration:** Susan Webner. **Coordinators:** Tony Perezchica (field/infield), Dan Carlson (pitching), Chris Cron (hitting), Joel Youngblood (outfield/baserunning), Bill Plummer (catching), Hatuey Mendoza (Latin Liaison), Wilfredo Tejada (Dominican field), Brad Arnsberg (rehab), Andrew Hauser (medical), David Rivera (assistant medical), Vaughn Robinson (strength), Kyle Torgerson (manual performance), Jim Currigan (video), Bob Bensinger (complex).

Farm System

Class	Club (League)	Manager	Hitting Coach	Pitching Coach
Triple-A	Reno (PCL)	Phil Nevin	Greg Gross	Mike Parrott
Double-A	Mobile (SL)	Andy Green	Jacob Cruz	Wellington Cepeda
High A	Visalia (CAL)	Robby Hammock	Bobby Smith	Gil Heredia
Low A	South Bend (MWL)	Mark Haley	Jason Camilli	Doug Bochtler
Short-season	Hillsboro (NWL)	JR House	Mark Grace	Doug Drabek
Rookie	Missoula (PIO)	Audo Vicente	Vince Harrison	Jeff Bajenaru
Rookie	Diamondbacks (AZL)	Luis Urueta	Javier Colina	Larry Pardo

Scouting
Telephone: (602) 462-6500. **Fax:** (602) 462-6425.
Director, Scouting: Ray Montgomery.
Director, Pacific Rim Operations: Mack Hayashi. **Special Assistant, Pacific Rim Operations:** Jim Marshall. **Assistant Director, Scouting:** Brendan Domaracki. **Major League Scouts/Special Assistants to GM:** Bill Bryk (Schererville, IN), Todd Greene (Alpharetta, GA), Mike Piatnik (Winter Haven, FL). **Pro Scouts:** Brian Boehringer (Fenton, MO), Mike Brown (Naples, FL), Bob Cummings (Oak Lawn, IL), Clay Daniel (Jacksonville, FL), Jeff Gardner (Costa Mesa, CA), Brad Kelley (Scottsdale, AZ), Bill Gayton (San Diego, CA), Pat Murtaugh (West Lafayette, IN), Tom Romenesko (Santee, CA), John Vander Wal (Grand Rapids, MI). **Independent Leagues, Coordinator:** Chris Carminucci (Southbury, CT).
Regional Supervisors: Todd Donovan (East Lyme, CT), Spencer Graham (Gresham, OR), Greg Lonigro (Connellsville, PA), Steve McAllister (Chillicothe, IL), Howard McCullough (Greenville, NC).
Area Scouts: John Bartsch (Rocklin, CA), Nathan Birtwell (Nashville, TN), Hal Kurtzman (Lake Balboa, CA), TR Lewis (Marietta, GA), Joe Mason (Millbrook, AL), Rick Matsko (Davidsville, PA), Jeff Mousser (Huntington Beach, CA), Rusty Pendergrass (Missouri City, MO), Donnie Reynolds (Portland, OR), Joe Robinson (St Louis, MO), Tony Piazza (Springfield, MO), JR Salinas (Dallas, TX), Mike Serbalik (Clifton Park, NY), Rick Short (Peoria, IL), Doyle Wilson (Phoenix, AZ), George Swain (Wilmington, NC), Frankie Thon Jr (Miami, FL), Luke Wrenn (Lakeland, FL). **Part-Time Scouts:** Doug Mathieson (Aldergrove, BC), Homer Newlin (Tallahassee, FL), Steve Oleschuk (Verdun, QC).
International Scouting Supervisor: Luis Baez (Santo Domingo, DR). **International Scouts: Dominican Republic**—Gabriel Berroa, José Ortiz, Rafael Mateo; **Panama**—José Díaz Perez; **Nicaragua**—Julio Sanchez; **Colombia**—Luis Gonzalez; **Venezuela**—Marlon Urdaneta.

Atlanta Braves

Office Address: 755 Hank Aaron Dr., Atlanta, GA 30315.
Mailing Address: PO Box 4064, Atlanta, GA 30302.
Telephone: (404) 522-7630. **Website:** www.braves.com.

Ownership
Operated/Owned By: Liberty Media.
Chairman/CEO: Terry McGuirk. **Chairman Emeritus:** Bill Bartholomay. **President:** John Schuerholz. **Senior Vice President:** Henry Aaron.

BUSINESS OPERATIONS
Executive VP, Business Operations: Mike Plant. **Senior VP/General Counsel:** Greg Heller.

Finance
Chief Financial Officer: Chip Moore.

Marketing/Sales
Executive VP, Sales/Marketing: Derek Schiller. **VP, Marketing:** Gus Eurton. **VP, Ticket Sales:** Paul Adams. **VP, Corporate Sales:** Jim Allen.

Media Relations/Public Relations
Telephone: (404) 614-1556. **Fax:** (404) 614-1391.
Director, Media Relations: Brad Hainje. **Director, Public Relations:** Beth Marshall.
Publications Manager: Andy Pressley. **Public Relations Coordinator:** Mackenzie Anderson.
Media Relations Manager: Adrienne Midgley. **Media Relations Coordinator:** Jim Misudek.

Terry McGuirk

Stadium Operations
Senior Director, Stadium Operations/Security: Larry Bowman. **Field Director:** Ed Mangan. **Director, Game Entertainment:** Scott Cunningham. **PA Announcer:** Casey Motter. **Official Scorers:** Mike Stamus, Jack Wilkinson.

Ticketing
Telephone: (404) 577-9100. **Fax:** (404) 614-2480.
Director, Ticket Operations: Anthony Esposito.

Travel/Clubhouse
Director, Team Travel/Equipment Manager: Bill Acree. **Visiting Clubhouse Manager:** John Holland.

2014 SCHEDULE
Standard Game Times: 7:10 p.m.; Fri. 7:35; Sun. 1:35.

MARCH	5-7 . . . . St. Louis	19-22 . . . . at Washington	8-10 . . . . . . Washington
31 . . . . at Milwaukee	9-11 . . . . . . Chicago (NL)	24-26 . . . . . . .at Houston	11-14 . . . Los Angeles (NL)
	12-14 . . . at San Francisco	27-29 . . . . at Philadelphia	15-17 . . . . Oakland
APRIL	16-18 . . . . .at St. Louis	30 . . . . . . .New York (NL)	18-20 . . . . . at Pittsburgh
1-2 . . . . . . at Milwaukee	19-22 . . . . . .Milwaukee		21-24 . . . . . .at Cincinnati
4-6 . . . . . at Washington	23-25 . . . . . . .Colorado	**JULY**	26-28 . . . at New York (NL)
8-10 . . . . .New York (NL)	26-27 . . . . Boston	1-2 . . . . . . .New York (NL)	29-31 . . . . .Miami
11-13 . . . . .Washington	28-29 . . . . . .at Boston	4-6 . . . . .Arizona	
14-17 . . . at Philadelphia	30-31 . . . . at Miami	7-10 . . . at New York (NL)	**SEPTEMBER**
18-20 . . . . . . at N.Y Mets		11-13 . . . .at Chicago (NL)	1-3 . . . . . . .Philadelphia
21-23 . . . . .Miami	**JUNE**	18-20 . . . . . .Philadelphia	5-7 . . . . at Miami
25-27 . . . . . . Cincinnati	1 . . . . at Miami	21-24 . . . . .Miami	8-10 . . . . . at Washington
29-30 . . . . at Miami	3-4 . . . . Seattle	25-28 . . . . . San Diego	12-14 . . . . .at Texas
	6-8 . . . . at Arizona	29-31. at Los Angeles (NL)	15-17 . . . . . Washington
MAY	9-12 . . . . . . at Colorado		19-21 . . . . .New York (NL)
1 . . . . at Miami	13-15 . . . Los Angeles (AL)	**AUGUST**	22-25 . . . . . . Pittsburgh
2-4 . . . . . . San Francisco	16-18 . . . . . .Philadelphia	1-3 . . . . at San Diego	26-28 . . . . at Philadelphia
		5-6 . . . . .at Seattle	

GENERAL INFORMATION
Stadium (year opened):
Turner Field (1997).
Team Colors: Red, white and blue.
Player Representative: Brandon Beachy.
Home Dugout: First Base.
Playing Surface: Grass.

BASEBALL OPERATIONS

Telephone: (404) 522-7630. **Fax:** (404) 614-3308.
Executive VP/General Manager: Frank Wren.
VP/Assistant GM, Player Development: Bruce Manno. **Executive Assistants:** Annie Lee, Chris Rice.

Frank Wren

Major League Staff
Manager: Fredi Gonzalez.
Coaches: Bench—Carlos Tosca; **Pitching**—Roger McDowell; **Hitting**—Greg Walker; **First Base**—Terry Pendleton; **Third Base**—Doug Dascenzo; **Bullpen**—Eddie Perez.

Medical/Training
Head Team Physician: Dr. Xavier Duralde.
Trainer: Jeff Porter. **Assistant Trainer:** Jim Lovell.
Director, Strength/Conditioning: Rick Slate. **Major League Strength/Conditioning Coach:** Phil Falco.

Player Development
Telephone: (404) 522-7630. **Fax:** (404) 614-1350.
Director, Minor League Operations: Ronnie Richardson. **Special Assistants to the GM, Player Development:** Jose Martinez, Lee Elia. **Baseball Operations Assistants:** Matt Grabowski, Ron Knight.
Minor League Field Coordinator: Dave Bialas. **Pitching Coordinator:** Rich Dubee. **Hitting Coordinator:** Ronnie Ortegon. **Roving Instructors:** Joe Breeden (catching), Bobby Mitchell (outfield/baserunning), Luis Lopez (infield), James Gonzalez (assistant strength/conditioning), Derek Botelho (Pitching Rehabilitation Instructor).

Farm System

Class	Club (League)	Manager	Coach	Pitching Coach
Triple-A	Gwinnett (IL)	Brian Snitker	Garey Ingram	Marty Reed
Double-A	Mississippi (SL)	Aaron Holbert	Jamie Dismuke	Dennis Lewallyn
High A	Lynchburg (CL)	Luis Salazar	John Moses	Derrick Lewis
Low A	Rome (SAL)	Jonathan Schuerholz	Bobby Moore	Gabe Luckett
Rookie	Danville (APP)	Randy Ingle	Carlos Mendez	Dan Meyer
Rookie	Braves (GCL)	Rocket Wheeler	Rick Albert	William Martinez
Rookie	Braves (DSL)	Francisco Santiesteban	Tommy Herrera	Mike Alvarez

Scouting
Telephone: (404) 522-7630. **Fax:** (404) 614-1350.
Assistant GM: John Coppolella.
Special Assistants to GM/Major League Scouts: Matt Carroll (Erdenheim, PA), Jim Fregosi (Tarpon Springs, FL), Dave Holliday (Bixby, OK), Jeff Schugel (Highlands Ranch, CO) Brad Sloan (Brimfield, IL), Rick Williams (Tampa, FI) Jeff Wren (Senoia, GA). **Professional Scouts:** Rod Gilbreath (Lilburn, GA), Lloyd Merritt (Myrtle Beach, SC), John Stewart (Granville, NY).
Director, Scouting: Tony DeMacio. **Office Coordinator, Scouting:** Dixie Keller.
National Crosscheckers: John Flannery (Austin, TX), Deron Rombach (Arlington, TX). **Regional Crosscheckers: West**—Tom Davis (Ripon, CA), **Southwest**—James "Bump" Merriweather (Glendale, AZ), **East**—Steve Fleming (Louisa, VA), **Midwest**—Terry R. Tripp (Harrisburg, IL), **Southeast**—Brian Bridges (Rome, GA).
Area Scouts: Kevin Barry (Kinmundy, IL), Billy Best (Holly Spings, NC), Bill Bliss (Phoenix, AZ), Hugh Buchanan (Snellville, GA), Brett Evert (Salem, OR), Ralph Garr (Richmond, TX), Buddy Hernandez (Orlando, FL), Gene Kerns (Hagerstown, MD), Chris Knabenshue (Fort Collins, CO), Steve Leavitt (Huntington Beach, CA), Rick Sellers (Remus, MI), Dennis Sheehan (Glasco, NY), Don Thomas (Geismar, LA), Terry C. Tripp (Norris, IL), Gerald Turner (Bedford, TX), Darin Vaughan (Kingwood, TX). **Part-Time Scouts:** Dick Adams (Lincoln, CA), Stu Cann (Bradley, IL), Dewayne Kitts (Moncks Corner, SC), Abraham Martinez (Santa Isabel, PR), Lou Sanchez (Miami, FL).
Director, International Scouting/Operations: Johnny Almaraz.
Assistant Director, International Scouting/Operations: Jose Martinez. **International Coordinators: Central American Supervisor**—Luis Ortiz (San Antonio, TX); **Eastern Rim**—Phil Dale (Victoria, Australia).
International Area Supervisors: Matias Laureano (Dominican Republic), Hiroyuki Oya (Japan), Rolando Petit (Venezuela), Manuel Samaniego (Mexico). **Part-Time Scouts:** Neil Burke (Australia), Nehomar Caldera (Venezuela), Junior Carrion (Dominican Republic), Jeremy Chou (Taiwan), Carlos Garcia Roque (Colombia), Raul Gonzalez (Panama), Remmy Hernandez (Dominican Republic), Hyun-Sung Kim (South Korea), Dargello Lodowica (Curacao), Alfredo Molina (Ecuador), Rafael Motooka (Brazil), Nestor Perez (Spain), Carlos Rodriguez (Venezuela), Jefferson Romero D'Lima (Venezuela), Miguel Theran (Colombia), Marvin Throneberry (Nicaragua), Carlos Torres (Venezuela).

Baltimore Orioles

Office Address: 333 W Camden St., Baltimore, MD 21201.
Telephone: (888) 848-BIRD. **Fax:** (410) 547-6272.
E-mail Address: birdmail@orioles.com. **Website:** www.orioles.com.

Ownership
Operated By: The Baltimore Orioles Limited Partnership Inc.
Chairman/CEO: Peter Angelos.

BUSINESS OPERATIONS
Executive Vice President: John Angelos. **VP/Special Liaison to Chairman:** Lou Kousouris.
General Legal Counsel: Russell Smouse. **Director, Human Resources:** Lisa Tolson. **Director, Information Systems:** James Kline.

Finance
VP/CFO: Robert Ames. **VP, Finance:** Michael D. Hoppes, CPA.

Public Relations/Communications
Telephone: (410) 547-6150. **Fax:** (410) 547-6272.
VP, Communications/Marketing: Greg Bader. **Director, Public Relations:** Monica Barlow.
Manager, Media Relations: Jeff Lantz. **Coordinator, Baseball Information:** Jay Moskowitz.
Coordinator, Public Relations/New Media: Amanda Sarver. **Director, Promotions/Community Relations:** Kristen Schultz.

Peter Angelos

Ballpark Operations
Director, Ballpark Operations: Kevin Cummings. **Head Groundskeeper:** Nicole McFadyen.
PA Announcer: Ryan Wagner. **Official Scorers:** Jim Henneman, Marc Jacobson, Ryan Eigenbrode.

Ticketing
Telephone: (888) 848-BIRD. **Fax:** (410) 547-6270.
VP, Ticketing/Fan Services: Neil Aloise. **Assistant Director, Sales:** Mark Hromalik. **Ticket Manager:** Audrey Brown.

Travel/Clubhouse
Coordinator, Team Travel: Kevin Buck.
Equipment Manager (Home): Chris Guth. **Equipment Manager (Road):** Fred Tyler.

2014 SCHEDULE
Standard Game Times: 7:05 p.m; Sun. 1:35

MARCH		
MARCH		
31 . . . . Boston		

APRIL
2-3. . . . . Boston
4-6. . . . . .at Detroit
7-9. . . . at New York (AL)
11-13 . . . . . . .Toronto
14-16 . . . . . . .Tampa Bay
18-21 . . . . .at Boston
22-24 . . . . . at Toronto
25-27 . . . . . Kansas City
29-30 . . . . Pittsburgh

MAY
2-4. . . . . . . at Minnesota
6-8. . . . . . . at Tampa Bay

9-11 . . . . Houston
12-14 . . . . Detroit
15-18 . . . . .at Kansas City
20-21 . . . at Pittsburgh
22-25 . . . . . . Cleveland
26-28 . . . . . at Milwaukee
29-31 . . . . . .at Houston

JUNE
1 . . . . .at Houston
3-5. . . . . .at Texas
6-8. . . . . Oakland
9-11 . . . . Boston
12-15 . . . . .Toronto
16-18 . . . . at Tampa Bay
20-22 . . at New York (AL)
23-25 . . . . . Chicago (AL)

27-29 . . . . . .Tampa Bay
30 . . . . Texas

JULY
1-3. . . . . Texas
4-6. . . . . .at Boston
7-8. . . . at Washington
9-10 . . . . . . Washington
11-13 . . . . .New York (AL)
18-20 . . . . . .at Oakland
21-23 . at Los Angeles (AL)
24-27 . . . . . . .at Seattle
29-31 . . . Los Angeles (AL)

AUGUST
1-3. . . . . Seattle
5-7. . . . . at Toronto
8-10 . . . . St. Louis

11-13 . . . . .New York (AL)
15-17 . . . . .at Cleveland
18-20 . . . .at Chicago (AL)
22-24 . . . .at Chicago (NL)
25-28 . . . . . .Tampa Bay
29-31 . . . . . . .Minnesota

SEPTEMBER
1 . . . . Minnesota
2-4. . . . . Cincinnati
5-7. . . . . at Tampa Bay
8-10 . . . . .at Boston
12-14 . . . .New York (AL)
15-17 . . . . .Toronto
19-21 . . . . Boston
22-25 . . . at New York (AL)
26-28 . . . . at Toronto

GENERAL INFORMATION
Stadium (year opened): Oriole Park at Camden Yards (1992).
Team Colors: Orange, black and white.

Player Representative: Darren O'Day.
Home Dugout: First Base.
Playing Surface: Grass.

BASEBALL OPERATIONS

Telephone: (410) 547-6107. **Fax:** (410) 547-6271.

Executive Vice President, Baseball Operations: Dan Duquette. **VP, Baseball Operations:** Brady Anderson. **Special Assistant to the Executive VP, Baseball Operations:** Lee Thomas. **Director, Baseball Administration:** Tripp Norton. **Director, Major League Administration:** Ned Rice. **Director, Player Personnel:** John Stockstill. **Assistant Director, Player Personnel:** Mike Snyder. **Coordinator, Baseball Analytics:** Sarah Gelles. **Manager, Baseball Operations:** Bill Wilkes. **Coordinator, Baseball Operations:** Pat DiGregory. **Video Coordinator:** Michael Silverman. **Advance Scouting Coordinator:** Ben Werthan. **Coordinator, Pro Scouting:** Matt Koizim.

Dan Duquette

Major League Staff

Manager: Buck Showalter.

Coaches: Bench—John Russell; **Pitching**—Dave Wallace; **Batting**—Jim Presley; **Assistant Hitting**—Einar Diaz; **First Base**—Wayne Kirby; **Third Base**—Bobby Dickerson; **Bullpen**—Dom Chiti.

Medical/Training

Club Physician: Dr. William Goldiner. **Club Physician, Orthopedics:** Dr. John Wilckens. **Head Athletic Trainer:** Richie Bancells. **Assistant Athletic Trainers:** Brian Ebel, Chris Correnti. **Strength/Conditioning Coach:** Joe Hogarty.

Player Development

Telephone: (410) 547-6120. **Fax:** (410) 547-6298.

Director, Player Development: Brian Graham. **Director, Minor League Operations:** Kent Qualls. **Coordinator, Minor League Administration:** J. Maria Arellano. **Coordinator, Player Development:** Cale Cox. **Director, Pitching Development:** Rick Peterson. **Coordinator, Minor League Hitting:** Jeff Manto. **Coordinator, Organizational Hitting Instructor/Evaluator:** Terry Crowley. **Coordinator, Minor League Catching:** Don Werner. **Coordinator, Minor League Infield:** Dave Anderson. **Roving Instructor, Outfield/Baserunning/Strength:** Scott Beerer.

Medical Coordinator: Dave Walker. **Latin American Medical Coordinator:** Manny Lopez. **Coordinator, Minor League Strength/Conditioning:** Ryan Crotin. **Coordinator, Strength/Conditioning—Sarasota:** Ryan Driscoll. **Coordinator, Minor League Rehab Pitching:** Scott McGregor. **Minor League Equipment Manager:** Jake Parker. **Pitching Administrator, Florida/DSL:** Dave Schmidt. **Administrator, Sarasota Operations:** Len Johnston.

Farm System

Class	Club (League)	Manager	Hitting Coach	Pitching Coach
Triple-A	Norfolk (IL)	Ron Johnson	Denny Walling	Mike Griffin
Double-A	Bowie (EL)	Gary Kendall	Butch Davis	Blaine Beatty
High A	Frederick (CL)	Luis Pujols	Torre Tyson	Kennie Steenstra
Low A	Delmarva (SAL)	Ryan Minor	Paco Figueroa	Alan Mills
Short-season	Aberdeen (NYP)	Matt Merullo	Unavailable	Justin Lord
Rookie	Orioles (GCL)	Orlando Gomez	Milt May	Wilson Alvarez
Rookie	Orioles (DSI)	Elvis Morel	D. Pascual/R. Perez	R. Caraballo/M. Jabalera

Scouting

Telephone: (410) 547-6212. **Fax:** 410-547-6928.

Director, Scouting: Gary Rajsich. **Scouting Administrator:** Brad Ciolek. **National Supervisor:** Danny Haas (Fort Myers, FL). **National Crosschecker:** Matt Haas (Cincinnati, OH). **West Coast Supervisor:** David Blume (Elk Grove, CA). **Midwest Supervisors:** Jim Richardson (Marlow, OK), Ernie Jacobs (Wichita, KS).

Area Scouts: Dean Albany (Baltimore, MD), Kelvin Colon (Miami, FL), Adrian Dorsey (Nashville, TN), Thom Dreier (Houston, TX), Kirk Fredriksson (Torrington, CT), John Gillette (Gilbert, AZ), David Jennings (Spanish Fort, AL), Arthur McConnehead (Atlanta, GA), Rich Morales (Pacifica, CA), Mark Ralston (Carlsbad, CA), Jim Thrift (Sarasota, FL), Brandon Verley (White Salmon, WA), Scott Walter (Manhattan Beach, CA).

Major League Scouts: Dave Engle (San Diego, CA), Jim Howard (Clifton Park, NY), Bruce Kison (Bradenton, FL). **Professional Scouts:** Todd Frohwirth (Waukesha, WI), Fred Uhlman Sr. (Baltimore, MD).

Executive Director, International Recruiting: Fred Ferreira. **Director, Baseball Operations for the Dominican Republic:** Nelson Norman. **Academy Director, Dominican Republic:** Felipe Rojas Alou. **International Scouts:** Joel Bradley, Enrique Constante, Ronnie Deck, Calvin Maduro, Brett Ward.

Boston Red Sox

Office Address: Fenway Park, 4 Yawkey Way, Boston, MA 02215.
Telephone: (617) 226-6000. **Fax:** (617) 226-6416. **Website:** www.redsox.com

Ownership
Principal Owner: John Henry.
Chairman: Thomas C. Werner. **President/CEO:** Larry Lucchino. **Vice Chairmen:** David Ginsberg, Phillip H. Morse.
Executive Vice President, Corporate Strategy/General Counsel: Ed Weiss.

BUSINESS OPERATIONS
Executive VP/Chief Operating Officer: Sam Kennedy. **Executive VP, Business Affairs:**
Jonathan Gilula. **Executive VP/Senior Advisor to the President/CEO:** Charles Steinberg.
Senior VP, Fenway Affairs: Larry Cancro. **Financial Advisor to the President/CEO:** Jeff White.
Senior Advisor, Baseball Projects: Jeremy Kapstein. **VP, Business Development:** Tim Zue.

Larry Lucchino

Finance
Senior VP/CFO: Steve Fitch. **VP/Controller:** Mark Solitro.

Human Resources/Information Technology
VP, Human Resources: Amy Waryas. **VP, Information Technology:** Brian Shield.

Sales/Corporate Partnerships/Marketing
Senior VP, Corporate Partnerships: Troup Parkinson. **VP, Client Services:** Marcell Bhangoo.
Senior VP, Marketing/Brand Development: Adam Grossman.

Public Affairs/Media
Senior Director, Public Affairs: Pam Kenn. **VP/Team Historian:** Dick Bresciani.

Legal
Senior VP/Assistant General Counsel: Jennifer Flynn. **Senior VP/Special Counsel:** David Friedman. **VP/Club Counsel:** Elaine Weddington Steward.

Foundation
Honorary Chairman: Tim Wakefield. **Interim Executive Director/Director, Special Events:** Gena Borson.

Ballpark Operations
VP, Fan Services/Entertainment: Sarah McKenna. **Senior Director, Ballpark Operations:** Pete Nesbit. **Senior Director, Florida Business Operations:** Katie Haas.

Ticketing Services/Operations
Senior VP, Ticketing/Fenway Enterprises: Ron Bumgarner. **VP, Ticketing:** Richard Beaton. **VP, Fenway Enterprises:** Carrie Campbell.

2014 SCHEDULE
Standard Game Times: 7:10 p.m.; Sun. 1:35

MARCH		
31 . . . . .at Baltimore		

APRIL
2-3 . . . . .at Baltimore
4-6 . . . . .Milwaukee
7-9 . . . . Texas
10-13 . . at New York (AL)
15-17 . . .at Chicago (AL)
18-21 . . . . . . Baltimore
22-24 . . . . New York (AL)
25-27 . . . . . at Toronto
29-30 . . . . . . .Tampa Bay

MAY
1 . . . . .Tampa Bay
2-4 . . . . Oakland
6-7 . . . . Cincinnati

9-11 . . . . .at Texas
13-15 . . . . . at Minnesota
16-18 . . . . Detroit
20-22 . . . . .Toronto
23-25 . . . . . at Tampa Bay
26-27 . . . . . . at Atlanta
28-29 . . . . Atlanta
30-31 . . . . . . .Tampa Bay

JUNE
1 . . . . .Tampa Bay
2-4 . . . . . .at Cleveland
6-8 . . . . .at Detroit
9-11 . . . . . .at Baltimore
12-15 . . . . Cleveland
16-18 . . . . . . Minnesota
19-22 . . . . . .at Oakland

23-25 . . . . . . .at Seattle
27-29 . . . at New York (AL)
30 . . . . Chicago (NL)

JULY
1-2 . . . . Chicago (NL)
4-6 . . . . Baltimore
8-10 . . . . . Chicago (AL)
11-13 . . . . . .at Houston
18-20 . . . . . Kansas City
21-24 . . . . at Toronto
25-27 . . . . . at Tampa Bay
28-30 . . . . .Toronto

AUGUST
1-3 . . . . . .New York (AL)
5-7 . . . . .at St. Louis
8-10 . . at Los Angeles (AL)

12-13 . . . . .at Cincinnati
14-17 . . . . Houston
18-21 . . . Los Angeles (AL)
22-24 . . . . Seattle
25-27 . . . . . . at Toronto
29-31 . . . . . at Tampa Bay

SEPTEMBER
1 . . . . at Tampa Bay
2-4 . . . . at New York (AL)
5-7 . . . . .Toronto
8-10 . . . . Baltimore
11-14 . . . .at Kansas City
16-18 . . . . .at Pittsburgh
19-21 . . . . . .at Baltimore
23-25 . . . . . . .Tampa Bay
26-28 . . . . .New York (AL)

GENERAL INFORMATION
Stadium (year opened):
Fenway Park (1912).
Team Colors: Navy blue, red and white.

Player Representative: Unavailable.
Home Dugout: First Base.
Playing Surface: Grass.

BASEBALL OPERATIONS

Executive VP/General Manager: Ben Cherington.
VP/Assistant GM: Mike Hazen. **VP/Assistant GM:** Brian O'Halloran. **VP, Player Personnel:** Allard Baird. **Traveling Secretary:** Jack McCormick. **Director, Player Personnel:** Dave Finley. **Director, Major League Operations:** Zack Scott. **Senior Baseball Analyst:** Tom Tippett. **Baseball Operations Analyst:** Greg Rybarczyk. **Coordinator, Baseball Operations:** Mike Murov, Mike Regan. **Coordinator Baseball Systems Development:** Shawn O'Rourke. **Executive Assistant:** Erin Cox. **Senior Advisor:** Bill James. **Special Assistants to GM:** Pedro Martinez, Jason Varitek.

Ben Cherington

Major League Staff

Manager: John Farrell.
Coaches: Bench—Torey Lovullo; **Pitching**—Juan Nieves; **Hitting**—Greg Colbrunn; **First Base**—Arnie Beyeler; **Third Base**—Brian Butterfield; **Bullpen**—Dana LeVangie; **Assistant Hitting Coach**—Victor Rodriguez; **Staff Assistant**—Brian Abraham; **Bullpen Catcher**—Mani Martinez; **BP Thrower**—Matt Noone.

Medical/Training

Medical Director: Larry Ronan. **Head Team Orthopedist:** Dr. Peter Asnis. **Director, Sports Medicine Services:** Dan Dyrek. **Head Athletic Trainer:** Rick Jameyson. **Medical Operations Coordinator:** Jim Rowe. **Assistant Trainers:** Brad Pearson, Masai Takahashi. **Strength/Conditioning Coach:** Pat Sandora. **Massage Therapist:** Russell Nua, Shinichiro Uchikubo. **Physical Therapist:** Ray Mattfeld. **Head Minor League Physician:** Brian Busconi.

Player Development

Senior Director, Minor League Operations: Raquel Ferreira. **Director, Player Development:** Ben Crockett. **Assistant Director, Player Development:** Duncan Webb. **Assistant Director, Florida Baseball Operations:** Ethan Faggett. **Minor League Equipment Manager:** Mike Stelmach. **Field Coordinator:** David Howard. **Latin American Pitching Coordinator:** Goose Gregson. **Minor League Athletic Training Coordinator:** Paul Buchheit. **Latin Medical Coordinator:** Mauricio Elizondo. **Minor League Strength/Conditioning Coordinator:** Mike Roose. **Minor League Physical Therapist:** Chip Simpson. **Coordinator, Player Development Programs:** Laz Gutierrez. **Roving Instructors:** Andy Fox (infield), Chad Epperson (catching), Tim Hyers (hitting), Ralph Treuel (pitching), George Lombard (outfield/baserunning).

Farm System

Class	Club (League)	Manager	Coach(es)	Pitching Coach
Triple-A	Pawtucket (IL)	Kevin Boles	Bruce Crabbe/Dave Joppie	Rich Sauveur
Double-A	Portland (EL)	Billy McMillon	Rich Gedman	Bob Kipper
High A	Salem (CL)	Carlos Febles	UL Washington	Kevin Walker
Low A	Greenville (SAL)	Darren Fenster	Nelson Paulino	Paul Abbott
Short-season	Lowell (NYP)	Unavailable	Noah Hall	Walter Miranda
Rookie	Red Sox (GCL)	Tom Kotchman	Raul Gonzalez/Dave Tomlin	Dick Such
Rookie	Red Sox (DSL)	Jose Zapata	Junior Zamora	Amaury Telemaco/Óscar Lira

Scouting

Director, Amateur Scouting: Amiel Sawdaye. **Director, Professional Scouting:** Jared Porter. **Director, International Scouting:** Eddie Romero.
Special Assistant, Player Personnel: Eddie Bane. **Assistant Director, Amateur Scouting:** Gus Quattlebaum. **Assistant Director, Player Personnel:** Jared Banner. **Coordinator, International/Amateur Scouting:** Steve Sanders. **Advance Scouting Assistant:** Harrison Slutsky. **Special Assignment Scouts:** Galen Carr (Burlington, VT), Steve Peck (Scottsdale, AZ) Mark Wasinger (El Paso, TX). **Major League Advance Scout:** Steve Langone (Reading, MA). **Major League Scouts:** Jaymie Bane (Parrish, FL), Bob Hamelin (Charlotte, NC), Dave Klipstein (Roanoke, TX). **Professional Scouts:** Nate Field (Denver, CO), Gary Hughes (Aptos, CA), David Keller (Houston, TX), John Lombardo (Grand Prairie, TX), Matt Mahoney (Scottsdale, AZ), Joe McDonald (Lakeland, FL), Anthony Turco (Tampa, FL).
National Scouting Coordinator: Mike Rikard (Durham, NC). **National Crosschecker:** John Booher (Buda, TX). **Regional Crosscheckers: South East**—Fred Petersen (Lincoln, NE), **South West**—Jim Robinson (Arlington, TX). **North East**—Quincy Boyd (Harrisburg, NC). **West**—Dan Madsen (Murrieta, CA). **Area Scouts:** Jon Adkins (Wayne, WV), Tom Battista (Thousand Oaks, CA), Chris Calciano (Ocean View, DE), Tim Collinsworth (McKinney, TX), Raymond Fagnant (East Granby, CT), Blair Henry (Naperville, IL), Tom Kotchman (Seminole, FL), Chris Mears (Oklahoma City, OK), Brian Moehler (Marietta, GA), Edgar Perez (Vega Baja, PR), Pat Portugal (Wake Forest, NC), Chris Pritchett (Vancouver, BC), John Pyle (Frankfort IL), Willie Romay (Miami Springs, FL), Demond Smith (Sacramento, CA), Danny Watkins (Tuscaloosa, AL), Vaughn Williams (Phoenix, AZ), Jim Woodward (Claremont, CA). **Part Time Scouts:** Buzz Bowers (Orleans, MA), Rob English (Duluth, GA), Stephen Hargett (St. Augustine, FL), Jay Oliver (Texarkana, TX), Keith Prager (La Verne, CA), Adam Stern (London, Ontario), Terry Sullivan (La Grange, IL).
Coordinator, Latin American Scouting: Todd Claus. **Coordinator, Venezuela Scouting/Venezuela Scout:** Manny Padron. **International Crosschecker:** Rolando Pino. **Director, Dominican Academy:** Jesus Alou. **Assistant Director, Dominican Academy:** Javier Hernandez. **Dominican Republic Scouting Supervisor:** Manny Nanita. **Dominican Republic Crosschecker:** Victor Rodriguez, Jr. **Coordinator, Pacific Rim Scouting:** Jon Deeble. **International Scouts:** Jonathan Cruz (Dominican Republic), Angel Escobar (Venezuela), Franco Faveli (Panama), Steve Fish (Australia), Cris Garibaldo (Panama), Ernesto Gomez (Venezuela), John Kim (Korea), Louie Lin (Taiwan), Carlos Lugo (Dominican Republic), Wilder Lobo (Venezuela), Ramon Mora (Venezuela), Rafael Mendoza (Nicaragua), Dennis Neuman (Aruba/Curacao), Santiago Prada (Colombia), Alex Requena (Venezuela), Rene Saggiadi (Europe), David Tapia (Mexico), Victor Torres (Dominican Republic), Sotero Torres (Mexico). **International Pro Scouts:** David Cortes (Mexico), Toshi Kato (Japan).

Chicago Cubs

Office Address: Wrigley Field, 1060 W. Addison St., Chicago, IL 60613.
Telephone: (773) 404-2827. **Website:** www.cubs.com.

Ownership
Chairman: Tom Ricketts. **Board of Directors:** Laura Ricketts, Pete Ricketts, Todd Ricketts and Tribune Company.

BUSINESS OPERATIONS

President, Business Operations: Crane Kenney. **Executive Vice President, Business Operations:** Mark McGuire. **Executive VP, Community Affairs/General Counsel:** Michael Lufrano. **Senior VP, Strategy/Development:** Alex Sugarman. **VP, Sales/Partnerships:** Colin Faulkner. **VP, Communications/Community Affairs:** Julian Green. **VP/CFO:** Jon Greifenkamp. **VP, Ballpark Operations:** Carl Rice. **VP, Human Resources:** Bryan Robinson. **Executive Assistant to the Chairman:** Lorraine Swiatly. **Executive Coordinator, Business Operations:** Sarah Poontong.

Ballpark Operations
Senior Director, Wrigley Field Event Operations: Matt Kenny. **Director, Fan Experiences:** Jahaan Blake. **Director, Facilities:** Tim Owens. **Director, Security/Safety Operations:** James Reynolds. **Head Groundskeeper:** Roger Baird. **Public Address Announcer:** Andrew Belleson. **Organist:** Gary Pressy.

Tom Ricketts

Marketing/Communications
Senior Director, Marketing: Alison Miller. **Manager, Communications:** Kevin Saghy. **Assistant, Social Media/Public Relations:** Mary Reisert.

Corporate Partnerships
Senior Director, Corporate Partnerships: Allen Hermeling. **Assistant Director, Corporate Partnerships Sales Operations:** Brian O'Connor. **Director, Procurement/Sourcing:** Patrick Meenan.

Information Technology/Human Resources
Senior Director, Information Technology: Andrew McIntyre. **HR Manager, Organization/Staffing:** Marisol Widmayer. **HR Manager, Ballpark Operations:** Danielle Alexa. **HR Manager, Program Development:** Rachel Rush.

Legal/Community Affairs
Assistant General Counsel: Lydia Wahlke. **Counsel:** Mike Feldman. **Director, Community Affairs:** Connie Falcone.

Ticket Sales/Service/Operations
Director, Ticket Sales: Andy Blackburn. **Director, Ticket Services:** Brian Garza. **Director, Ticket Operations:** Cale Vennum.

2014 SCHEDULE
Standard Game Times: 7:05 p.m., Sun. 1:20.

MARCH		
31 . . . . at Pittsburgh		

APRIL
2-3. . . . . . . at Pittsburgh
4-6. . . . . . . .Philadelphia
8-10 . . . . Pittsburgh
11-13 . . . . . . .at St. Louis
15-16 . . . . .New York (AL)
18-20 . . . . Cincinnati
21-24 . . . . .Arizona
25-27 . . . . . at Milwaukee
28-30 . . . . . .at Cincinnati

MAY
2-4. . . . . St. Louis
5-6. . . . . . . Chicago (AL)

7-8. . . . . .at Chicago (AL)
9-11. . . . . at Atlanta
12-15 . . . . . . .at St. Louis
16-18 . . . . .Milwaukee
20-21 . . . . .New York (AL)
22-25 . . . . . at San Diego
26-28 . . . at San Francisco
30-31 . . . . . at Milwaukee

JUNE
1 . . . . at Milwaukee
3-5. . . . . .New York (NL)
6-8. . . . . .Miami
9-12 . . . . . . at Pittsburgh
13-15 . . . . at Philadelphia
16-18 . . . . .at Miami
20-22 . . . . Pittsburgh

23-25 . . . . Cincinnati
26-29 . . . . . .Washington
30 . . . . .at Boston

JULY
1-2. . . . . .at Boston
4-6. . . . . . at Washington
7-10 . . . . . .at Cincinnati
11-13 . . . . Atlanta
18-20 . . . . . . at Arizona
22-24 . . . . . . San Diego
25-27 . . . . St. Louis
28-31 . . . . .Colorado

AUGUST
1-3. . . at Los Angeles (NL)
5-7. . . . . . . at Colorado

8-10 . . . . .Tampa Bay
11-14 . . . . . . .Milwaukee
15-17 . . . at New York (NL)
19-21 . . . . . San Francisco
22-24 . . . . Baltimore
26-28 . . . . . .at Cincinnati
29-31 . . . . . . .at St. Louis

SEPTEMBER
1-3. . . . . .Milwaukee
5-7. . . . . Pittsburgh
8-10 . . . . at Toronto
12-14 . . . . . at Pittsburgh
15-17 . . . . Cincinnati
18-21 . . .Los Angeles (NL)
22-24 . . . . St. Louis
26-28 . . . . . at Milwaukee

GENERAL INFORMATION
Stadium (year opened): Wrigley Field (1914).
Team Colors: Royal blue, red and white.
Player Representative: Unavailable.
Home Dugout: Third Base.
Playing Surface: Grass.

BASEBALL OPERATIONS

Telephone: (773) 404-2827. **Fax:** (773) 404-4147.
President, Baseball Operations: Theo Epstein.
Executive VP/General Manager: Jed Hoyer. **Assistant GMs:** Randy Bush, Shiraz Rehman.
Special Assistant to President/GM: Tim Wilken. **Special Assistant to GM/Director, Video/Advance Scouting:** Kyle Evans. **Director, Baseball Operations:** Scott Harris. **Director, Research/Development:** Chris Moore. **Traveling Secretary:** Vijay Tekchandani. **Executive Assistant to President/GM:** Hayley DeWitte. **Assistant Director, Advance Scouting/Strategy:** Bobby Basham. **Coordinator, Baseball Operations:** Jeff Greenberg. **Analyst, Research/Development:** Jeremy Greenhouse. **Coordinator, Major League Video/Pacific Rim Liaison:** Naoto Masamoto. **Coordinator, Advance Scouting:** Nate Halm. **Coordinator, Player Development/Scouting Video:** Mitch Duggins. **Assistant, Research/Development:** Sean Ahmed.

Theo Epstein

Major League Staff

Manager: Rick Renteria.
Coaches: Bench—Brandon Hyde; **Pitching**—Chris Bosio; **Hitting**—Bill Mueller; **Assistant Hitting**—Mike Brumley; **Third Base**—Gary Jones; **First Base**—Eric Hinske; **Bullpen**—Lester Strode; **Quality Assurance**—Jose Castro; **Staff Assistants**—Mike Borzello, Franklin Font; **Bullpen Catcher**—Chad Noble.

Medical/Training

Team Physician: Dr. Stephen Adams. **Team Orthopedist:** Dr. Stephen Gryzlo.
Director, Medical Administration: Mark O'Neal. **Head Athletic Trainer:** P.J. Mainville. **Assistant Athletic Trainers:** Ed Halbur, Matt Johnson. **Strength/Conditioning Coach:** Tim Buss. **Physical Therapist:** Ryan Mertz. **Massage Therapist:** Slavic Kodryan.

Media Relations

Director, Media Relations: Peter Chase. **Assistant Director, Media Relations:** Jason Carr. **Coordinator, Media Relations:** Dusty Harrington. **Assistant, Media Relations:** Safdar Khan.

Player Development

Telephone: (773) 404-4035. **Fax:** (773) 404-4147.
Senior VP, Scouting/Player Development: Jason McLeod. **Director, Player Development:** Jaron Madison. **Assistant Director, Player Development/International Scouting:** Alex Suarez. **Coordinator, Minor League Administration:** Derrick Fong. **Field Coordinator:** Tim Cossins. **Coordinators:** Derek Johnson (pitching), Anthony Iapoce (hitting), Jose Flores (infield), Carmelo Martinez (Latin American field), Mike Mason (assistant pitching), Rick Tronerud (rehab pitching). **Coordinator, Minor League Athletic Training:** Nick Frangella. **Assistant Coordinator, Minor League Athletic Training:** Chuck Baughman. **Coordinator, Minor League Physical Development:** Doug Jarrow. **Coordinator, Cultural Programs:** Rey Fuentes. **Manager, Mesa Baseball Administration:** Gil Passarella. **Clubhouse Manager:** Dana Noeltner. **Assistant Clubhouse Manager:** Sam DeChristopher.

Farm System

Class	Club (League)	Manager	Hitting Coach	Pitching Coach
Triple-A	Iowa (PCL)	Marty Pevey	Brian Harper	Bruce Walton
Double-A	Tennessee (SL)	Buddy Bailey	Desi Wilson	Storm Davis
High A	Daytona (FSL)	Dave Keller	Mariano Duncan	Ron Villone
Low A	Kane County (MWL)	Mark Johnson	Tom Beyers	Dave Rosario
Short-season	Boise (NWL)	Gary Van Tol	Unavailable	Brian Lawrence
Rookie	Cubs (AZL)	Jimmy Gonzalez	Ricardo Medina	Anderson Tavarez
Rookie	Cubs (DSL)	Juan Cabreja	O. Bernard/Y. Ozorio	Leo Hernandez
Rookie	Cubs (VSL)	Pedro Gonzalez	Franklin Blanco	Angel Guzman

Scouting

Director, Amateur Scouting: Matt Dorey (Vancouver, WA). **Assistant Director, Amateur Scouting:** Lukas McKnight (Gurnee, IL). **Director, Professional Scouting:** Joe Bohringer (Western Springs, IL). **Coordinator, Pro Scouting:** Andrew Bassett (Chicago, IL). **Major League Scouts:** Dave Littlefield (Sewickley, PA), Jason Karegeannes (De Pere, WI), Adam Wogan (Brooklyn, NY). **Pro Scouts:** Billy Blitzer (Brooklyn, NY), Steve Boros (Kingwood, TX), Jake Ciarrachi (Chicago, IL), Jason Cooper (Kirkland, WA), Denny Henderson (Orange, CA), Steve Hinton (Mather, CA), Terry Kennedy (Chandler, AZ), Mark Kiefer (Hunt, TX), Ken Kravec (Sarasota, FL), Bob Lofrano (Woodland Hills, CA), Mark Servais (LaCrosse, WI), Keith Stohr (Viera, FL). **Amateur Scouting Assistant:** Shane Farrell (Chicago, IL).
National Crosscheckers: Sam Hughes (Atlanta, GA), Ron Tostenson (El Dorado Hills, CA). **Crosscheckers: Southeast**—Bobby Filotei (Daphne, GA); **Central**—Steve Riha (Houston, TX); **West**—Mark Adair (Sherman Oaks, CA); **Midwest/Northeast**—Lukas McKnight (Gurnee, IL). **Area Scouts:** Tim Adkins (Huntington, WV), Tom Clark (Lake City, FL), Chris Clemons (Robinson, TX), Ramser Correa (Caguas, PR), Jim Crawford (Madison, MS), Jonathan Davis (Nashville, TN), Scott Fairbanks (Issaquah, WA), Trey Forkerway (Houston, TX), Al Geddes (Canby, OR), John Koronka (Clairmont, FL), Keith Lockhart (Dacula, GA), Alex Lontayo (Chula Vista, CA), Steve McFarland (Scottsdale, AZ), Tom Myers (Santa Barbara, CA), Ty Nichols (Broken Arrow, OK), Luis Raffan (Miami, FL), Keith Ryman (Jefferson City, TN), Eric Servais (St. Louis Park, MN), Matt Sherman (Norwell, MA), Billy Swoope (Norfolk, VA), Gabe Zappin (Walnut Creek, CA), Stan Zielinski (Winfield, IL).
International Crosschecker/Pacific Rim Supervisor: Paul Weaver (Phoenix, AZ). **Coordinator, Pacific Rim/Mexico:** Steve Wilson. **International Scouts:** Hector Ortega (Venezuela), Jose Serra (Dominican Republic), Steve Wilson (Pacific Rim), Brent Phelan (Australia), Manny Esquivia (Colombia), Cirilo Cumberbatch (Panama), Gian Guzman (Dominican Republic), Julio Figueroa (Venezuela) and Min Kyu Sung (Korea).

Chicago White Sox

Office Address: U.S. Cellular, Field, 333 W. 35th St., Chicago, IL 60616.
Telephone: (312) 674-1000. **Fax:** (312) 674-5116. **Website:** www.whitesox.com and orgullosox.com

Ownership
Chairman: Jerry Reinsdorf. **Vice Chairman:** Eddie Einhorn.
Board of Directors: Robert Judelson, Judd Malkin, Robert Mazer, Allan Muchin, Jay Pinsky, Lee Stern, Burton Ury, Charles Walsh.
Special Assistant to Chairman: Dennis Gilbert. **Assistant to Chairman:** Barb Reincke. **Coordinator, Administration/Investor Relations:** Katie Hermle.

BUSINESS OPERATIONS
Senior Executive Vice President: Howard Pizer.
Senior Director, Information Services: Don Brown. **Senior Director, Human Resources:** Moira Foy. **Senior Coordinator, Human Resources:** Leslie Gaggiano.

Jerry Reinsdorf

Finance
Senior VP, Administration/Finance: Tim Buzard. **Senior Director, Finance:** Bill Waters. **Accounting Manager:** Chris Taylor.

Marketing/Sales
Senior VP, Sales/Marketing: Brooks Boyer. **Senior Director, Business Development/Broadcasting:** Bob Grim. **Senior Director, Game Operations:** Nichole Manning. **Senior Manager, Scoreboard Operations/Production:** Jeff Szynal. **Manager, Game Operations:** Amy Sheridan. **Manager, In-Game Entertainment:** Dan Mielke. **Senior Coordinator, Graphic Apparel/Design:** Lauren Markiewicz.
Director, Corporate Partnerships Sales Development: George McDoniel. **Director, Corporate Partnerships Activation:** Gail Tucker. **Manager, Corporate Partnerships Development:** Jeff Floerke. **Coordinators, Corporate Partnership Activation:** Arden Reed, Kat Claeys.
Director, Ticket Sales: Tom Sheridan. **Manager, Premium Seating Sales:** Rob Boaz.

Media Relations/Public Relations
Telephone: (312) 674-5300. **Fax:** (312) 674-5116.
Senior VP, Communications: Scott Reifert.
Director, Media Relations: Bob Beghtol. **Director, Public Relations:** Lou Hernandez. **Manager, Media Relations:** Ray Garcia. **Manager, Public Relations:** Marty Maloney. **Coordinators, Media Relations/Services:** Joe Roti, Leni Depoister.
Senior Director, Community Relations/Executive Director, CWS Charities: Christine O'Reilly. **Managers, Community Relations:** Sarah Marten, Laura Visin. **Manager, Youth Baseball Initiatives:** Kevin Coe.
Director, Mass Communications: Nicole Saunches. **Director, Advertising/Design Services:** Gareth Breunlin. **Manager, Online Communications:** Dakin Dugaw.

2014 SCHEDULE
Standard Game Times: 7:10 p.m.; Sun. 1:10.

MARCH			
31 . . . . .Minnesota	7-8. . . . . . . Chicago (NL)	23-25 . . . . . .at Baltimore	7-10 . . . . .at Seattle
	9-11 . . . . .Arizona	26-29 . . . . . at Toronto	12-13 . . . at San Francisco
APRIL	12-14 . . . . . .at Oakland	30 . . . . . Los Angeles (AL)	15-17 . . . . .Toronto
2-3 . . . . .Minnesota	16-18 . . . . . .at Houston		18-20 . . . . Baltimore
4-6. . . . . .at Kansas City	19-21 . . . .at Kansas City	**JULY**	22-24 . . . at New York (AL)
7-9. . . . . . . at Colorado	22-25 . . . .New York (AL)	1-2. . . . . Los Angeles (AL)	26-28 . . . . Cleveland
10-13 . . . . . . Cleveland	26-28 . . . . Cleveland	4-6. . . . . Seattle	29-31 . . . . Detroit
15-17 . . . . Boston	30-31 . . . . San Diego	7-10 . . . . .at Boston	
18-20 . . . . .at Texas		11-13 . . . . . .at Cleveland	**SEPTEMBER**
21-24 . . . . . . .at Detroit	**JUNE**	18-20 . . . . Houston	2-3. . . . . . at Minnesota
25-28 . . . . . .Tampa Bay	1 . . . . San Diego	21-23 . . . . . . Kansas City	5-7. . . . . . .at Cleveland
29-30 . . . . Detroit	2-4. . . at Los Angeles (NL)	24-27 . . . . . at Minnesota	8-11. . . . . Oakland
	6-8. . . at Los Angeles (AL)	29-31 . . . . . . .at Detroit	12-14 . . . . . . .Minnesota
MAY	9-12 . . . . Detroit		15-17 . . . .at Kansas City
2-4. . . . . . . .at Cleveland	13-15 . . . . . Kansas City	**AUGUST**	19-21 . . . at Tampa Bay
5-6. . . . . .at Chicago (NL)	17-18 . . . . .San Francisco	1-3. . . . . Minnesota	22-24 . . . . .at Detroit
	19-22 . . . . . at Minnesota	4-6. . . . . Texas	25-28 . . . . . Kansas City

GENERAL INFORMATION
Stadium (year opened):
U.S. Cellular Field (1991).
Team Colors: Black, white and silver.
Player Representative: Unavailable.
Home Dugout: Third Base.
Playing Surface: Grass.

Stadium Operations
    Senior VP, Stadium Operations: Terry Savarise. **Senior Director, Event Operations:** Troy Brown. **Senior Director, Park Operations:** Greg Hopwood. **Senior Director, Guest Services/Diamond Suite Operations:** Julie Taylor. **Head Groundskeeper:** Roger Bossard. **PA Announcer:** Gene Honda. **Official Scorers:** Bob Rosenberg, Don Friske.

Ticketing
    Telephone: (312) 674-1000. **Fax:** (312) 674-5102.
    Director, Ticket Operations: Mike Mazza. **Manager, Ticket Accounting Administration:** Ken Wisz.

Travel/Clubhouse
    Director, Team Travel: Ed Cassin.
    Manager, White Sox Clubhouse: Vince Fresso. **Manager, Visiting Clubhouse:** Gabe Morell. **Manager, Umpires Clubhouse:** Joe McNamara Jr.

BASEBALL OPERATIONS

Rick Hahn

    Executive Vice President: Ken Williams.
    Senior VP/General Manager: Rick Hahn.
    VP/Assistant GM: Buddy Bell. **Assistant to GM:** Jeremy Haber. **Special Assistants:** Bill Scherrer, Dave Yoakum, Marco Paddy. **Executive Assistant to GM:** Nancy Nesnidal. **Senior Director, Baseball Operations:** Dan Fabian. **Assistant Director, Baseball Operations:** Daniel Zien. **Coordinator, Baseball Information:** Dan Strittmatter.

Major League Staff
    Manager: Robin Ventura.
    Coaches: Bench—Mark Parent; **Pitching**—Don Cooper; **Batting**—Todd Steverson; **First Base**—Daryl Boston; **Third Base**—Joe McEwing; **Bullpen**—Bobby Thigpen; **Assistant Hitting Coach**—Harold Baines; **Manager, Cultural Development**—Lino Diaz.

Medical/Training
    Senior Team Physician: Dr. Charles Bush-Joseph. **Head Athletic Trainer:** Herm Schneider. **Assistant Athletic Trainer:** Brian Ball. **Director, Strength/Conditioning:** Allen Thomas.

Player Development
    Senior Director, Minor League Operations: Grace Guerrero Zwit. **Director, Player Development:** Nick Capra. **Assistant Director, Player Development/Scouting:** Del Matthews. **Senior Coordinator, Minor League Administration:** Kathy Potoski. **Player Development Assistant:** Robbie Cummings. **Manager, Clubhouse/Equipment:** Dan Flood.
    Minor League Field Coordinator: Kirk Champion. **Pitching Coordinator:** Curt Hasler. **Hitting Coordinator:** Tim Laker. **Assistant Hitting Coordinator:** Vance Law. **Instructors:** Doug Sisson (outfield/baserunning), Everado Magallanes (infield), John Orton (catching), Dale Torborg (conditioning coordinator). **Latin Liaison:** Bobby Magallanes. **Minor League Medical/Rehabilitation Coordinator:** Scott Takao. **Physical Therapist:** Brett Walker. **Coaching Assistants:** Jerry Hairston, Chet DiEmidio. **Dominican Republic Academy Coordinator:** Rafael Santana. **Dominican Field Coordinator:** Julio Valdez.

Farm System

Class	Club (League)	Manager	Coach	Pitching Coach
Triple-A	Charlotte (IL)	Joel Skinner	Andy Tomberlin	Richard Dotson
Double-A	Birmingham (SL)	Julio Vinas	Brandon Moore	Britt Burns
High A	Winston-Salem (CL)	Tommy Thompson	Gary Ward	J.R. Perdew
Low A	Kannapolis (SAL)	Pete Rose Jr.	Robert Sasser	Jose Bautista
Rookie	Great Falls (PIO)	Charles Poe	Greg Briley	Brian Drahman
Rookie	White Sox (AZL)	Mike Gellinger	Unavailable	Felipe Lira
Rookie	White Sox (DSL)	Guillermo Reyes	Domingo Michel	Efrain Valdez

Scouting
    Telephone: (312) 674-1000. **Fax:** (312) 674-5105.
    Pro Scouts: Bruce Benedict (Atlanta, GA), Kevin Bootay (Sacramento, CA), Joe Butler (Long Beach, CA), Chris Lein (Jacksonville, FL), Paul Provas (Arlington, TX), Alan Regier (Gilbert, AZ), Daraka Shaheed (Vallejo, CA), John Tumminia (Newburgh, NY), Bill Young (Scottsdale, AZ).
    Director, Amateur Scouting: Doug Laumann (Florence, KY).
    Assistant Director, Scouting/Player Development: Nick Hostetler. **National Crosscheckers:** Nathan Durst (Sycamore, IL), Ed Pebley (Brigham City, UT). **Regional Crosscheckers: East**—Joe Siers (Wesley Chapel, FL), **Midwest**—Mike Shirley (Anderson, IN), **West**—Derek Valenzuela (Temecula, CA). **Advisor to Baseball Department:** Larry Monroe (Schaumburg, IL).
    Area Scouts: Asaad Ali (Phoenix, AZ), Mike Baker (Santa Ana, CA), Kevin Burrell (Sharpsburg, GA), Ryan Dorsey (Carmel, IN), Abe Fernandez (Ft. Mill, SC), Joel Grampietro (Tampa, FL), Phil Gulley (Morehead, KY), Warren Hughes (Mobile, AL), JJ Lally (Denison, IA), George Kachigian (Coronado, CA), John Kazanas (Phoenix, AZ), Steve Nichols (Mount Dora, FL), Glenn Murdock (Livonia, MI), Jose Ortega (Fort Lauderdale, FL), Clay Overcash (Oologan, OK), Keith Staab (College Station, TX), Noah St. Urbain (Stockton, CA), Adam Virchis (Modesto, CA), Chris Walker (Houston, TX), Gary Woods (Solvang, CA).
    International Scouts: Amador Arias (Venezuela), Marino DeLeon (Dominican Republic), Robinson Garces (VZ), Tomas Herrera (Mexico), Miguel Peguero (Dominican Republic), Guillermo Peralta (Dominican Republic), Omar Sanchez (Venezuela), Fermin Ubri (Dominican Republic).

Cincinnati Reds

Office Address: 100 Joe Nuxhall Way, Cincinnati, OH 45202.
Telephone: (513) 765-7000. **Fax:** (513) 765-7342.
Website: www.reds.com.

Ownership

Operated by: The Cincinnati Reds LLC.
President/CEO: Robert Castellini. **Chairman:** Joseph Williams Jr. **Vice Chairman/Treasurer:** Thomas Williams. **COO:** Phillip Castellini. **Executive Assistant to COO:** Diana Busam. **Secretary:** Christopher Fister.

BUSINESS OPERATIONS

Senior Vice President, Business Operations: Karen Forgus. **VP, Event Services/Merchandising:** Lauren Werner. **Business Operations Assistant/Speakers Bureau:** Emily Mahle. **Business Operations Assistant:** Alex Heekin. **Senior Advisor, Business Operations:** Joe Morgan.

Finance/Administration

VP, Finance/CFO: Doug Healy. **VP/General Counsel:** James Marx. **Controller:** Bentley Viator. **Assistant to General Counsel/CFO:** Teena Schweier. **Director, Human Resources:** Garry McGuire. **Senior Manager, Human Resources:** Allison Stortz. **VP, Technology:** Brian Keys.

Sales/Ticketing

VP, Corporate Sales: Bill Reinberger. **Director, Sponsorship Development:** Dave Collins. **VP, Ticketing/Business Development:** Aaron Eisel. **Senior Director, Ticket Sales/Service:** Mark Schueler. **Director, Premium Sales/Service:** Chris Bausano. **Director, Client Services:** Craig Warman. **Senior Director, Ticket Marketing/Development:** Sarah Contardo. **Director, Ticket Initiatives:** David Ziegler. **Senior Director, Ticket Operations:** John O'Brien. **Assistant Director, Ticket Operations:** Ken Ayer. **Season Ticket Manager:** Bev Bonavita.

Media Relations

Director, Media Relations: Rob Butcher. **Assistant Director, Media Relations:** Larry Herms. **Assistant Director, Media Relations/Digital Content:** Jamie Ramsey.

Communications/Marketing

VP, Communications/Marketing: Ralph Mitchell. **Director, Digital Media:** Lisa Braun. **Director, Marketing:** Audra Sordyl. **Senior Manager, Communications/Web Content:** Jarrod Rollins. **Public Relations Manager:** Michael Anderson. **Communications Coordinator:** Brendan Hader. **Senior Director, Entertainment/Productions:** Adam Lane. **Director, Creative Operations:** Jansen Dell. **Senior Director, Promo Events/Player Relations:** Zach Bonkowski.

Community Relations

Executive Director: Charley Frank. **Director, Community Relations:** Lindsey Lander. **Manager, Finance/Operations:**

Bob Castellini

2014 SCHEDULE

Standard Game Times: 7:10 p.m.; Sun. 1:10

MARCH		
31 . . . . St. Louis		

APRIL		
2-3 . . . . St. Louis		
4-6 . . . . . at New York (NL)		
7-9 . . . . .at St. Louis		
11-13 . . . . . . .Tampa Bay		
14-16 . . . . Pittsburgh		
18-20 . . .at Chicago (NL)		
21-24 . . . . at Pittsburgh		
25-27 . . . . at Atlanta		
28-30 . . . . . Chicago (NL)		

MAY		
1-4 . . . . .Milwaukee		
6-7 . . . . .at Boston		

9-11 . . . . .Colorado
13-15 . . . . San Diego
16-18 . . . . at Philadelphia
19-21 . . . at Washington
23-25 . . . . St. Louis
26-28 . at Los Angeles (NL)
29-31 . . . . at Arizona

JUNE		
1 . . . . at Arizona		
3-5 . . . . . . San Francisco		
6-8 . . . . .Philadelphia		
9-12 . . .Los Angeles (NL)		
13-15 . . . . . at Milwaukee		
17-19 . . . . . at Pittsburgh		
20-22 . . . . .Toronto		
23-25 . . . .at Chicago (NL)		

26-29 . . . at San Francisco
30 . . . . at San Diego

JULY		
1-2 . . . . . . at San Diego		
4-6 . . . . .Milwaukee		
7-10 . . . . . Chicago (NL)		
11-13 . . . . Pittsburgh		
18-20 . . . at New York (AL)		
21-23 . . . . at Milwaukee		
25-27 . . . . . Washington		
28-30 . . . . Arizona		
31 . . . . at Miami		

AUGUST		
1-3 . . . . at Miami		
4-5 . . . . . . .at Cleveland		
6-7 . . . . Cleveland		

8-10 . . . . .Miami
12-13 . . . . Boston
14-17 . . . . . at Colorado
18-20 . . . . . .at St. Louis
21-24 . . . . Atlanta
26-28 . . . . . Chicago (NL)
29-31 . . . . . at Pittsburgh

SEPTEMBER		
2-4 . . . . .at Baltimore		
5-7 . . . . . .New York (NL)		
8-11 . . . . St. Louis		
12-14 . . . . . at Milwaukee		
15-17 . . .at Chicago (NL)		
19-21 . . . . . .at St. Louis		
23-25 . . . . . .Milwaukee		
26-28 . . . . Pittsburgh		

GENERAL INFORMATION

Stadium (year opened): Great American Ball Park (2003). **Home Dugout:** First Base.

Player Representative: Mike Leake. **Playing Surface:** Grass. **Team Colors:** Red, white and black.

Matthew Wagner. **Executive Director, Reds Hall of Fame:** Rick Walls. **Operations Manager/Chief Curator, Reds Hall of Fame:** Chris Eckes.

Ballpark Operations
VP, Ballpark Operations: Tim O'Connell. **Senior Director, Ballpark Operations:** Sean Brown. **Director, Ballpark Administration:** Colleen Rodenberg. **Ballpark Operations Superintendent:** Bob Harrison. **Guest Relations Manager:** Jan Koshover. **Manager, Technology Business Center:** Chris Campbell. **Director, Safety/Security:** Kerry Rowland. **Chief Engineer:** Roger Smith. **Assistant Chief Engineer:** Gary Goddard. **Head Groundskeeper:** Doug Gallant. **Assistant Head Groundskeeper:** Derrik Grubbs. **Grounds Supervisor:** Robbie Dworkin. **Manager, Home Clubhouse/Equipment:** Rick Stowe. **Visiting Clubhouse Manager:** Mark Stowe. **Clubhouse Assistant:** Josh Stewart.

BASEBALL OPERATIONS
President, Baseball Operations/General Manager: Walt Jocketty. **Executive Assistant to GM:** Melissa Hill.
VP, Assistant GM: Bob Miller. **VP, Scouting/Player Development/International Operations:** Bill Bavasi. **VP/Special Assistant:** Jerry Walker. **VP, Baseball Operations:** Dick Williams. **Senior Advisor:** Joe Morgan. **Special Assistants:** Eric Davis, Mario Soto. **Director, Baseball Operations:** Nick Krall. **Manager, Baseball Systems Development:** Brett Elkins. **Director, Baseball Research/Analysis:** Sam Grossman. **Manager, Video Scouting:** Rob Coughlin.

Walt Jocketty

Medical/Training
Medical Director: Dr. Timothy Kremchek. **Head Athletic Trainer:** Paul Lessard. **Assistant Athletic Trainer:** Steve Baumann. **Stength/Conditioning Coordinator:** Sean Marohn. **Assistant Athletic Trainer:** Tomas Vera.

Major League Staff
Manager: Bryan Price.
Coaches: Bench—Jay Bell; **Batting**—Don Long; **Pitching**—Jeff Pico; **First Base**—Billy Hatcher; **Third Base**—Steve Smith; **Bullpen**—Mack Jenkins; **Catching**—Mike Stefanski; **Coach**—Freddie Benavides.

Player Development
Director, Player Development: Jeff Graupe. **Director, Minor League Administration:** Lois Hudson. **Arizona Operations Manager:** Mike Saverino. **Assistant to Arizona Operations Manager:** Charlie Rodriguez. **Minor League Video Coordinator:** Mike Persichilli. **Minor League Equipment Manager:** Jonathan Snyder. **Field Coordinator:** Bill Doran. **Latin America Field Coordinator:** Joel Noboa. **Roving Instructor:** Ken Griffey Sr. **Coordinators:** Ryan Jackson (hitting), Mark Riggins (pitching), Darren Bragg (outfield/baserunning), Richard Stark (medical), Patrick Serbus (athletic training). **Director, Dominican Republic Academy:** Juan Peralta. **Physical Therapist/Rehab Coordinator:** Brad Epstein.

Farm System

Class	Club (League)	Manager	Coach	Pitching Coach
Triple-A	Louisville (IL)	Jim Riggleman	Tony Jaramillo	Ted Power
Double-A	Pensacola (SL)	Delino DeShields	Alex Pelaez	Jeff Fassero
High A	Bakersfield (CAL)	Pat Kelly	Ray Martinez	Tom Browning
Low A	Dayton (MWL)	Jose Miguel Nieves	Luis Bolivar	Tony Fossas
Rookie	Billings (PIO)	Dick Schofield	Kevin Mahar	Dick Ebert
Rookie	Reds (AZL)	Eli Marrero	Jolbert Cabrera	Elmer Dessens
Rookie	Reds 1 (DSL)	Luis Saturria	Unavailable	Luis Montano
Rookie	Reds 2 (DSL)	Unavailable	Cristobal Rodriguez	Luis Andujar

Scouting
Senior Director, Professional/Global Scouting: Terry Reynolds. **Senior Director, Amateur Scouting:** Chris Buckley. **Assistant Director, Amateur Scouting:** Paul Pierson. **Special Assistants:** Cam Bonifay, J. Harrison, Marty Maier, John Morris, Mike Squires, Jeff Taylor. **Major League Advance Scout:** Shawn Pender. **Professional Scouts:** Will Harford, Jeff Morris, Steve Roadcap, Dominic Viola.
Crosscheckers: Jeff Barton (Gilbert, AZ), Bill Byckowski (Ontario, Canada), Jerry Flowers (Cypress, TX), Mark McKnight (Tega Cay, SC), Mark Snipp (Humble, TX). **Scouting Supervisors:** Tony Arias (Miami Lakes, FL), Rich Bordi (Rohnert Park, CA), Jeff Brookens (Chambersburg, PA), Clark Crist (Tucson, AZ), Rex De La Nuez (Burbank, CA), Byron Ewing (Haslet, TX), Rick Ingalls (Long Beach, CA), Ben Jones (Alexandria, LA), Joe Katuska (Cincinnati, OH), Mike Keenan (Manhattan, KS), Brad Meador (Cincinnati, OH), Mike Misuraca (Murrieta, CA), John Poloni (Tarpon Springs, FL), Lee Seras (Flanders, NJ), Perry Smith (Charlotte, NC), Andy Stack (Hartford, WI), Greg Zunino (Cape Coral, FL). **Scouts:** Nick Carrier (Hemlock, NY), Jim Grief (Paducah, KY), Bill Killian (Stanwood, MI), David Lander (Los Angeles, CA), Denny Nagel (Cincinnati, OH), Marlon Styles (Cincinnati, OH), Sammy Torreira (Aiea, HI), Mike Wallace (Escondido, CA), John Walsh (Windsor, CT), Roger Weberg (Bemidji, MN).
Director, Latin America Scouting: Tony Arias. **Assistant Director, Latin America Scouting:** Miguel Machado. **Coordinator, Global Scouting:** Jim Stoeckel. **Scouting Coordinator, Dominican Republic:** Richard Jimenez. **Special Assistant:** Jay Shindo. **Scouting Administrator, Venzuela:** Jose Fuentes.
International Scouts: Edward Bens (Dominican Republic), Geronimo Blanco (Colombia), Emmanuel Cartegena (Dominican Republic), Cesar Castro (Dominican Republic), Aguido Gonzalez (Venezuela), Eury Luis Haslen (Dominican Republic), Victor Nova (Dominican Republic), Victor Oramas (Venezuela), Camilo Pina (Dominican Republic), Anibal Reluz (Panama), Jose Valdelamar (Colombia).

Cleveland Indians

Office Address: Progressive Field, 2401 Ontario St., Cleveland, OH 44115.
Telephone: (216) 420-4200. **Fax:** (216) 420-4396.
Website: www.indians.com.

Ownership
Owner: Lawrence Dolan. **Chairman/Chief Executive Officer:** Paul Dolan.

BUSINESS OPERATIONS
President: Mark Shapiro.
Senior Vice President, Strategy/Business Analytics: Andrew Miller. **Executive Administrative Assistant:** Marlene Lehky. **Executive VP, Business:** Dennis Lehman. **Executive VP, Sales/Marketing:** Brian Barren. **Executive Administrative Assistant, Business:** Dru Kosik.

Corporate Partnerships/Finance
Director, Corporate Partnerships: Ted Baugh. **Partnership Manager:** Bryan Hoffart. **Manager, Corporate Partnership Services:** Sam Zelasko. **Senior Account Executives, Corporate Partnerships:** Penny Forster, Seamus Carr, Dominic Polito. **Senior VP, Finance/CFO:** Ken Stefanov. **VP/General Counsel:** Joe Znidarsic. **Controller:** Sarah Taylor. **Senior Director, Planning/Analysis/Reporting:** Rich Dorffer. **Manager, Accounting:** Karen Menzing. **Manager, Payroll Accounting:** Mary Forkapa. **Concessions Accounting Manager:** Nicole Parker.

Larry Dolan

Human Resources
VP, Human Resources/Chief Diversity Officer: Sara Lehrke. **Manager, Training:** Mailynh Vu. **Manager, Training/Development:** Jennifer Gibson. **Coordinator, Benefits:** Crystal Basile. **Human Resource Generalist:** David Mraz.

Marketing
VP, Marketing/Brand Management: Alex King. **Assistant Director, In-Game Experience Operations:** Jason Kidik. **Manager, In-Game Entertainment:** Annie Merovich. **Manager, Productions:** Nick Gambone. **Assistant Director, Brand Management:** Nicole Schmidt. **Coordinator, Creative Services:** Ashley Churchill. **VP, Concessions:** Kurt Schloss.

Communications/Baseball Information
Telephone: (216) 420-4380. **Fax:** (216) 420-4430.
Senior VP, Public Affairs: Bob DiBiasio. **Senior Director, Communications:** Curtis Danburg. **Director, Baseball Information:** Bart Swain. **Assistant Director, Communications:** Anne Keegan. **Assistant Director, Baseball Information:** Court Berry-Tripp. **Coordinator, Communications:** Joel Hammond. **Team Photographer:** Dan Mendlik.

Ballpark Operations
VP, Ballpark Operations: Jim Folk. **Director, Facility Maintenance:** Chris Donahoe. **Head Groundskeeper:** Brandon Koehnke. **Senior Director, Ballpark Operations:** Jerry Crabb. **Assistant Director, Ballpark Operations:** Brad Mohr. **Director, Facility Maintenance:** Seth Cooper. **Coordinator, Game Day Staff:** Renee VanLaningham. **Coordinator,**

2014 SCHEDULE
Standard Game Times: 7:05 p.m.; Sun. 1:05.

MARCH		
31 . . . . .at Oakland		

APRIL
1-2. . . . . .at Oakland
4-6. . . . . .Minnesota
7-9. . . . . San Diego
10-13 . . . .at Chicago (AL)
15-17 . . . . .at Detroit
18-20 . . . . . . .Toronto
21-24 . . . . . . Kansas City
25-27 . . . at San Francisco
28-30. . .at Los Angeles (AL)

MAY
2-4. . . . . . . Chicago (AL)
5-8. . . . . Minnesota

9-11 . . . . . . at Tampa Bay
13-15 . . . . at Toronto
16-18 . . . . Oakland
19-21 . . . . Detroit
22-25 . . . . . at Baltimore
26-28 . . . at Chicago (AL)
30-31 . . . . . . .Colorado

JUNE
1 . . . . .Colorado
2-4. . . . . Boston
6-9. . . . . .at Texas
10-11 . . . .at Kansas City
12-15 . . . . . . .at Boston
16-19 . . . Los Angeles (AL)
20-22 . . . . Detroit
24-25 . . . . . . at Arizona

27-29 . . . . .at Seattle
30 . . . at Los Angeles (NL)

JULY
1-2. . . at Los Angeles (NL)
4-6. . . . . Kansas City
7-10 . . . . . .New York (AL)
11-13 . . . . . Chicago (AL)
18-20 . . . . .at Detroit
21-23 . . . . at Minnesota
24-27 . . . . .at Kansas City
29-31 . . . . Seattle

AUGUST
1-3. . . . . Texas
4-5. . . . . Cincinnati
6-7. . . . . . . .at Cincinnati

8-10 . . . . at New York (AL)
12-13 . . . . .Arizona
15-17 . . . . . . Baltimore
19-21 . . . . . at Minnesota
22-24 . . . . Houston
26-28 . . . .at Chicago (AL)
29-31 . . . . .at Kansas City

SEPTEMBER
1-4. . . . . Detroit
5-7. . . . . . Chicago (AL)
9-11 . . . . . . .Minnesota
12-14 . . . . . . .at Detroit
15-18 . . . . . .at Houston
19-21 . . . . . at Minnesota
22-24 . . . . . Kansas City
26-28 . . . . . .Tampa Bay

GENERAL INFORMATION
Stadium (year opened):
Progressive Field (1994).
Team Colors: Navy blue, red and silver.

Player Representative: Justin Masterson.
Home Dugout: Third Base.
Playing Surface: Grass.

Ballpark Services: Steve Walters. **Dockmaster:** Omar Jufko.

Information Systems
Senior VP, Technology/Chief Information Officer: Neil Weiss. **Director, Software Development/Support:** Matt Tagliaferri. **Manager, End-User Support:** Matthew Smith. **Director, Information Technology:** Whitney Kuszmaul.

Ticketing
Telephone: (216) 420-4487. **Fax:** (216) 420-4481.
Director, Ticket Services: Gene Connelly. **Manager, Ticket Services:** Andrea Zaggar. **Manager, Ticket Office:** Katie Walters. **Ticket Operations Manager:** Nate Thompson. **Director, Fan Services:** Angel Jefferson.

Spring Training/Arizona Operations
Manager, Arizona Operations: Ryan Lantz. **Manager, Arizona Clubhouse:** Fletcher Wilkes. **Director, Team Travel:** Mike Seghi. **Home Clubhouse Manager:** Tony Amato. **Assistant Home Clubhouse Manager:** Marty Bokovitz. **Manager, Video Operations:** Bob Chester. **Visiting Clubhouse Manager:** Willie Jenks.

BASEBALL OPERATIONS

Telephone: (216) 420-4200. **Fax:** (216) 420-4321.
Executive VP/General Manager: Chris Antonetti.
VP, Baseball Operations/Assistant GM: Mike Chernoff.
Director, Baseball Administration: Wendy Hoppel. **Director, Baseball Operations:** Derek Falvey. **Director, Baseball Analytics:** Keith Woolner. **Executive Administrative Assistant:** Marlene Lehky. **Sports Psychologist:** Dr. Charles Maher. **Assistant, Baseball Operations:** Matt Forman. **Senior Baseball Analyst:** Sky Andrecheck.

Major League Staff
Manager: Terry Francona.
Coaches: Bench—Brad Mills; **Pitching**—Mickey Callaway; **Hitting**—Ty Van Burkleo; **First Base**—Sandy Alomar Jr.; **Third Base**—Mike Sarbaugh; **Bullpen**—Kevin Cash; **Assistant Hitting Coach**—Matt Quatraro. **Assistant, Major League Staff:** Armando Camacaro, Ricky Pacione.

Chris Antonetti

Medical/Training
Head Team Physician: Dr. Mark Schickendantz. **Senior Director, Medical Services:** Lonnie Soloff. **Head Athletic Trainer:** James Quinlan. **Assistant Athletic Trainers:** Jeff Desjardins, Michael Salazar. **Strength/Conditioning Coach:** Joe Kessler.

Player Development
Telephone: (216) 420-4308. **Fax:** (216) 420-4321.
VP, Player Development: Ross Atkins.
Assistant Director, Player Development: Carter Hawkins. **Assistant, Player Development:** Eric Binder. **Administrative Assistant:** Nilda Taffanelli. **Advisors, Player Development:** Johnny Goryl, Tim Tolman. **Director, Latin America Operations:** Ramon Pena. **Field Coordinator:** Tom Wiedenbauer. **Coordinators:** Ruben Niebla (pitching), Alan Zinter (hitting), Todd Kubacki (strength/conditioning), Thomas Albert (rehabilitation), Julio Rangel (lower level pitching/mental skills), Luis Ortiz (lower level hitting/cultural development). **Advisor, Latin America:** Minnie Mendoza. **Latin America Strength/Conditioning Coordinator:** Nelson Perez.

Farm System

Class	Club	Manager	Coach	Pitching Coach
Triple-A	Columbus (IL)	Chris Tremie	Jim Rickon	Tony Arnold
Double-A	Akron (EL)	David Wallace	Rouglas Odor	Jeff Harris
High A	Carolina (CL)	Scooter Tucker	Tony Mansolino	Steve Karsay
Low A	Lake County (MWL)	Mark Budzinski	Shaun Larkin	Rigo Beltran
Short-season	Mahoning Valley (NYP)	Ted Kubiak	Phil Clark	Greg Hibbard
Rookie	Indians (AZL)	Anthony Medrano	J. Betances/D. Malave	M. Allen/D. Swanson
Rookie	Indians (DSL)	Jose Mejia	D. Bautista/C. Fermin	J. Sanchez/C. Yan

Scouting
Telephone: (216) 420-4200. **Fax:** (216) 420-4321.
Senior Director, Scouting Operations: John Mirabelli.
Director, Amateur Scouting: Brad Grant. **Assistant Director, Scouting:** Paul Gillispie. **Director, Pro Scouting:** Steve Lubratich. **Assistant Director, Pro Scouting:** Victor Wang. **Advance Scouting Coordinator:** Alex Eckelman. **Assistant Director, International Scouting:** Jason Lynn. **International Crosschecker:** Koby Perez. **Latin America Crosschecker/South Florida Area Scout:** Juan Alvarez.
Senior Major League Scouts: Dave Malpass (Huntington Beach, CA), Don Poplin (Norwood, NC). **Pro Scouts:** Mike Calitri (Tampa, FL), Doug Carpenter (North Palm Beach, FL), Jim Cuthbert (Breinigsville, PA), Trey Hendricks (Cleveland, OH), Dave Miller (Wilmington, NC), Chris Gale (Austin, TX), Bryan Corey (Mesa, AZ). **Scouting Advisor/Crosschecker:** Paul Cogan (Rocklin, CA). **National Crosscheckers:** Scott Barnsby (Huntsville, AL), Bo Hughes (Sherman Oaks, CA). **Regional Crosscheckers:** Kevin Cullen (Frisco, TX), Scott Meaney (Apex, NC), Jason Smith (Long Beach, CA). **Area Scouts:** Steve Abney (Lawrence, KS), Mark Allen (Lake Kiowa, TX), Chuck Bartlett (Starkville, MS), Mike Bradford (Pensacola, FL) Jon Heuerman (Chandler, AZ), Don Lyle (Sacramento, CA), Bob Mayer (Somerset, PA), Junie Melendez (North Ridgeville, OH), Carlos Muniz (San Pedro, CA), Les Pajari (Angora, MN), Mike Soper (Tampa, FL), Ryan Thompson (Huntington Beach, CA), Brad Tyler (Bishop, GA), Jack Uhey (Vancouver, WA), Brent Urcheck (Philadelphia, PA), Kyle Van Hook (Brenham, TX). **Part-Time Scouts:** Bob Malkmus (Union, NJ), Ryan Perry (Rocklin, CA), Bill Schudlich (Dearborn, MI), Adam Stahl (Ballwin, MO), Jose Trujillo (Bayamon, PR).

Colorado Rockies

Office Address: 2001 Blake St., Denver, CO 80205.
Telephone: (303) 292-0200. **Fax:** (303) 312-2116.
Website: www.coloradorockies.com.

Ownership
Operated by: Colorado Rockies Baseball Club Ltd.
Owner/General Partner: Charles K. Monfort. **Owner/Chairman/Chief Executive Officer:** Richard L. Monfort.
Executive Assistant to the Owner/General Partner: Patricia Penfold. **Executive Assistant to the Owner/Chairman/Chief Executive Officer:** Terry Douglass.

BUSINESS OPERATIONS
Executive Vice President/Chief Operating Officer: Greg Feasel. **Assistant to Executive VP/Chief Operating Officer:** Kim Olson. **VP, Human Resources:** Elizabeth Stecklein.

Richard Monfort

Finance
Executive VP/CFO/General Counsel: Hal Roth. **VP, Finance:** Michael Kent. **Senior Director, Purchasing:** Gary Lawrence. **Coordinator, Purchasing:** Gloria Giraldi. **Senior Director, Accounting:** Phil Emerson. **Accountants:** Joel Binfet, Laine Campbell. **Payroll Administrator:** Juli Daedelow.

Marketing/Sales
Director, Corporate Sales: Walker Monfort. **Assistant to Director, Corporate Sales:** Nicole Ortiz. **Assistant Director, Corporate Sales:** Kari Anderson. **Account Executives:** Dan Lentz, Nate VanderWal. **VP, Community/Retail Operations:** James P. Kellogg. **Director, Retail Operations:** Aaron Heinrich. **Senior Director, Information Systems:** Bill Stephani. **Director, Promotions/Special Events:** Jason Fleming.
Director, In-Game Entertainment/Broadcasting: Kent Krosbakken. **Senior Director, Advertising/Marketing/Publications:** Jill Campbell. **Supervisor, Advertising/Marketing:** Sarah Topf. **Assistant Editor, Interactive Marketing/Publications:** Julian Valentin. **Coordinator, Multicultural Marketing/Advertising:** Marisol Villagomez.

Communications
Telephone: (303) 312-2325. **Fax:** (303) 312-2319.
VP, Communications: Jay Alves. **Assistant Director, Communications:** Nick Piburn. **Manager, Communications:** Matt Whewell. **Assistant, Communications/Baseball Operations:** Irma Castaneda.

Ballpark Operations
VP, Ballpark Operations: Kevin Kahn. **Senior Director, Food Service Operations/Development:** Albert Valdes. **Senior Director, Guest Services:** Steven Burke. **Head Groundskeeper:** Mark Razum. **Assistant Head Groundskeeper:** James Sowl. **Senior Director, Engineering/Facilities:** James Wiener. **Director, Engineering:** Randy Carlill. **Director,**

2014 SCHEDULE
Standard Game Times: 6:40 p.m.; Sat. 6:10; Sun. 1:10.

MARCH			
31 . . . . at Miami	7-8 . . . . .at Texas	23-25 . . . . St. Louis	8-10 . . . . at Arizona
	9-11 . . . . . . .at Cincinnati	26-29 . . . . at Milwaukee	11-13 . . . . . at San Diego
APRIL	13-14 . . . . .at Kansas City	30 . . . . . at Washington	14-17 . . . . . . Cincinnati
1-3 . . . . at Miami	16-18 . . . . . . San Diego		19-20 . . . . . . Kansas City
4-6 . . . . Arizona	20-22 . . . . San Francisco	**JULY**	22-24 . . . . .Miami
7-9 . . . . . . Chicago (AL)	23-25 . . . . . at Atlanta	1-2 . . . . . . at Washington	25-28 . . . at San Francisco
11-13 . . . at San Francisco	26-28 . . . at Philadelphia	3-6 . . . . Los Angeles (NL)	29-31 . . . . at Arizona
14-17 . . . . . at San Diego	30-31 . . . . . .at Cleveland	7-9 . . . . San Diego	
18-20 . . . . .Philadelphia		11-13 . . . . . . Minnesota	**SEPTEMBER**
21-23 . . . . . San Francisco	**JUNE**	18-20 . . . at Pittsburgh	1-3 . . . . . . San Francisco
25-27 . at Los Angeles (NL)	1 . . . . .at Cleveland	21-23 . . . . . Washington	5-7 . . . . San Diego
28-30 . . . . at Arizona	3-5 . . . . Arizona	25-27 . . . . . . Pittsburgh	8-10 . . . . at New York (NL)
	6-8 . . . . . Los Angeles (NL)	28-31 . . . .at Chicago (NL)	12-14 . . . . . .at St. Louis
MAY	9-12 . . . . Atlanta		15-17 . . . Los Angeles (NL)
1-4 . . . . . . .New York (NL)	13-15 . . . at San Francisco	**AUGUST**	18-21 . . . . .Arizona
5-6 . . . . Texas	16-18 . at Los Angeles (NL)	1-3 . . . . .at Detroit	22-24 . . . . . at San Diego
	20-22 . . . . . . .Milwaukee	5-7 . . . . . . Chicago (NL)	26-28 . at Los Angeles (NL)

GENERAL INFORMATION
Stadium (year opened):
Coors Field (1995).
Team Colors: Purple, black and silver.

Player Representative: Unavailable.
Home Dugout: First Base.
Playing Surface: Grass.

Facilities: Oly Olsen. **Official Scorers:** Dave Einspahr, Dave Plati. **Public Address Announcer:** Reed Saunders.

Ticketing
Telephone: (303) 762-5437, (800) 388-7625. **Fax:** (303) 312-2115.
VP, Ticket Operations/Sales/Services: Sue Ann McClaren.
Senior Director, Ticket Services/Finance/Technology: Kent Hakes. **Assistant Director, Ticket Operations:** Kevin Flood. **Senior Director, Season Tickets/Renewals/Business Strategy:** Jeff Benner. **Director, Groups/Outbound Sales/ Suites:** Matt Haddad. **Manager, Suites/Party Facilities:** Traci Abeyta. **Senior Account Executive:** Todd Thomas.

Travel/Clubhouse
Director, Major League Operations: Paul Egins. **Director, Clubhouse Operations:** Alan Bossart. **Assistant to the Director, Clubhouse Operations:** Mike Pontarelli. **Manager, Visiting Clubhouse:** Keith Schulz

BASEBALL OPERATIONS

Telephone: (303) 292-0200. **Fax:** (303) 312-2320.
Executive VP/Chief Baseball Officer/General Manager: Dan O'Dowd. **Assistant to Executive VP/Chief Baseball Officer/GM:** Adele Armagost. **Senior VP, Major League Operations/Assistant GM:** Bill Geivett. **Director, Baseball Operations/Assistant General Counsel:** Zack Rosenthal. **Coordinator, Baseball Administration:** Kent McKendry. **Assistant, Baseball Operations:** Matt Obernauer. **Special Assistant to Baseball Operations:** Pat Daugherty.

Major League Staff
Manager: Walt Weiss.
Coaches: Bench—Tom Runnells; **Pitching**—Jim Wright; **Hitting**—Blake Doyle; **Third Base**—Stu Cole; **Baserunning/Outfield/First Base**—Eric Young; **Bullpen**—Bo McLaughlin; **Catching/Defensive Positioning**—Rene Lachemann; **Bullpen Catcher**—Pat Burgess; **Strength/Conditioning**—Brian Jordan; **Video**—Brian Jones.

Dan O'Dowd

Medical/Training
Senior Director, Medical Operations/Special Projects: Tom Probst. **Medical Director:** Dr. Thomas Noonan. **Club Physicians:** Dr. Allen Schreiber, Dr. Douglas Wyland. **Head Trainer:** Keith Dugger. **Assistant Athletic Trainer:** Scott Gehret.

Player Development
Telephone: (303) 292-0200. **Fax:** (303) 312-2320.
Senior Director, Player Development: Jeff Bridich. **Director, Pitching Operations:** Mark Wiley. **Assistant Director, Player Development:** Zach Wilson. **Head Pitching Coordinator:** Doug Linton. **Assistant Pitching Coordinator:** Bob Apodaca. **Catching Coordinator:** Mark Strittmatter. **Strength/Conditioning Coordinator:** Gabe Bauer. **Assistant Video Coordinator:** Scott Alves. **Peak Performance Coordinator:** Andy McKay.
Rehabilitation Coordinator: Scott Murayama. **Assistant Rehabilitation Coordinator:** Andy Stover. **Equipment Manager:** Jerry Bass.
Supervisors, Development: Duane Espy (Tulsa), Fred Nelson (Modesto), Marv Foley (Asheville), Ron Gideon (Tri City), Tony Diaz (Grand Junction).

Farm System

Class	Club (League)	Manager	Coach	Pitching Coach
Triple-A	Colorado Springs (PCL)	Glenallen Hill	Dave Hajek	Dave Schuler
Double-A	Tulsa (TL)	Kevin Riggs	Darin Everson	Darryl Scott
High A	Modesto (CAL)	Don Sneddon	Jon Stone	Dave Burba
Low A	Asheville (SAL)	Fred Ocasio	Mike Devereaux	Unavailable
Short-season	Tri-City (NWL)	Drew Saylor	Warren Schaeffer	Frank Gonzales
Rookie	Grand Junction (PIO)	Anthony Sanders	Lee Stevens	Ryan Kibler
Rookie	Rockies (DSL)	Mauricio Gonzalez	F. Nunez/E. Jose	Edison Lora

Scouting
Telephone: (303) 292-0200. **Fax:** (303) 312-2320.
VP, Scouting: Bill Schmidt. **Assistant Director, Scouting:** Danny Montgomery. **Senior Director, Scouting Operations:** Marc Gustafson. **Director, Pro Scouting:** Jon Weil.
Advance Scout: Chris Warren. **Pro Scouts:** Ty Coslow (Louisville, KY), Will George (Woolwich Township, NJ), Jack Gillis (Sarasota, FL), Mike Hamilton (Dallas, TX), Joey Housey (Hollywood, FL), Rick Mathews (Centerville, IA), Mike Paul (Tucson, AZ). **Part-Time Pro Scout:** Fred Wright (Harrisburg, NC). **Special Assignment Scout:** Terry Wetzel (Overland Park, KS).
National Crosschecker: Mike Ericson (Phoenix, AZ), Damon Iannelli (Brandon, MS), Jay Matthews (Concord, NC).
Area Scouts: Julio Campos (Guaynabo, PR) John Cedarburg (Fort Myers, FL), Scott Corman (Lexington, KY), Jordan Czarniecki (Nashville, TN), Jeff Edwards (Missouri City, TX), Chris Forbes (Phoenix, AZ), Mike Garlatti (Edison, NJ), Mark Germann (Atkins, IA), Matt Hattabaugh (Westminster, CA), Darin Holcomb (Seattle, WA), Jon Lukens (Dana Point, CA), Alan Matthews (Atlanta, GA), Jesse Retzlaff (Dallas, TX), Rafeal Reyes (Miami, FL), Ed Santa (Powell, OH), Gary Wilson (Sacramento, CA). **Part-Time Scouts:** Norm DeBriyn (Fayetteville, AR), Dave McQueen (Bossier City, LA), Greg Pullia (Plymouth, MA).
Senior Director, International Operations: Rolando Fernandez. **Manager, Dominican Operations:** Jhonathan Leyba. **Supervisor, Venezuelan Scouting:** Orlando Medina. **International Scouts:** Phil Allen (Australia), Martin Cabrera (Dominican Republic), Carlos Gomez (Venezuela), Frank Roa (Dominican Republic), Josher Suarez (Venezuela).

Detroit Tigers

Office Address: 2100 Woodward Ave, Detroit, MI 48201.
Telephone: (313) 471-2000. **Fax:** (313) 471-2138. **Website:** www.tigers.com

Ownership
Operated By: Detroit Tigers Inc. **Owner:** Michael Ilitch.
President/CEO/General Manager: David Dombrowski.
Special Assistants to President: Al Kaline, Willie Horton. **Special Assistants to the General Manager:** Jim Leyland, Dick Egan. **Executive Assistant to President/CEO/GM:** Marty Lyon. **Senior VP:** Jim Devellano

BUSINESS OPERATIONS
Executive Vice President, Business Operations: Duane McLean.
Executive Assistant to Executive VP, Business Operations: Peggy Thompson.

Finance/Administration
VP/CFO: Stephen Quinn.
Senior Director, Finance: Kelli Kollman. **Director, Purchasing/Supplier Diversity:** DeAndre Berry. **Accounting Manager:** Sheila Robine.
Financial Analyst: Kristin Jorgensen. **Accounts Payable Coordinator:** Debbi Sword. **Accounts Receivable Coordinator:** Sharon Szkarlat. **Administrative Assistant:** Tracy Rice.
Senior Director, Human Resources: Karen Gruca. **Director, Payroll Administration:** Maureen Kraatz. **Associate Counsel:** Amy Peterson. **Internal Audit Manager:** Candice Lentz.

Mike Ilitch

Public/Community Affairs
VP, Community/Public Affairs: Elaine Lewis.
Director, Tigers Foundation: Jordan Field. **Manager, Player Relations:** Sam Abrams. **Manager, Community Affairs:** Alexandra Thrubis. **Community Affairs Coordinator:** Garnet Conerway. **Administrative Assistants:** Audrey Zielinski/Donna Bernardo.

Sales/Marketing
VP, Corporate Partnerships: Steve Harms.
Director, Corporate Sales: Steve Cleary. **Senior Director, Corporate Sales:** Kurt Buhler. **Corporate Sales Managers:** Soula Burns, John Wolski. **Sponsorship Services Manager:** Angelita Hernandez. **Sponsorship Services Coordinator:** Keri Gallagher.
VP, Marketing: Ellen Hill Zeringue.
Director, Marketing: Ron Wade. **Marketing Coordinator:** Mac Slavin. **Marketing/Promotions Coordinator:** Angela Perez. **Director, Promotions/Special Events:** Eli Bayles. **Promotions Coordinator:** Haley Kolff. **Director, Broadcasting/In-Game Entertainment:** Stan Fracker. **VP, Ticket/Suite Sales:** Scot Pett.

2014 SCHEDULE
Standard Game Times: 7:08 p.m.; Sun. 1:08.

MARCH
31 . . . . Kansas City

APRIL
2-3 . . . . Kansas City
4-6 . . . . Baltimore
8-9 . . . at Los Angeles (NL)
11-13 . . . . . at San Diego
15-17 . . . . Cleveland
18-20 . . . Los Angeles (AL)
21-24 . . . . . Chicago (AL)
25-27 . . . . . at Minnesota
29-30 . . . .at Chicago (AL)

MAY
2-4 . . . . . . .at Kansas City
5-8 . . . . Houston

9-11 . . . . Minnesota
12-14 . . . . . at Baltimore
16-18 . . . . . .at Boston
19-21 . . . . .at Cleveland
22-25 . . . . Texas
26-29 . . . . . .at Oakland
30-31 . . . . . .at Seattle

JUNE
1 . . . . .at Seattle
3-5 . . . . .Toronto
6-8 . . . . Boston
9-12 . . . .at Chicago (AL)
13-15 . . . . . . Minnesota
16-18 . . . . . Kansas City
20-22 . . . . .at Cleveland
24-26 . . . . . . .at Texas

27-29 . . . . . .at Houston
30 . . . . Oakland

JULY
1-2 . . . . Oakland
3-6 . . . . .Tampa Bay
8-9 . . . . Los Angeles (NL)
10-13 . . . . .at Kansas City
18-20 . . . . Cleveland
21-23 . . . . . at Arizona
24-27 . at Los Angeles (AL)
29-31 . . . . . Chicago (AL)

AUGUST
1-3 . . . . .Colorado
4-7 . . . . at New York (AL)
8-10 . . . . at Toronto

11-12 . . . . . at Pittsburgh
13-14 . . . . . . .Pittsburgh
15-17 . . . . Seattle
19-21 . . . . . at Tampa Bay
22-24 . . . . . at Minnesota
26-28 . . . .New York (AL)
29-31 . . .at Chicago (AL)

SEPTEMBER
1-4 . . . . .at Cleveland
5-7 . . . . San Francisco
8-10 . . . . . . Kansas City
12-14 . . . . Cleveland
15-17 . . . . . at Minnesota
19-21 . . . .at Kansas City
22-24 . . . . . Chicago (AL)
25-28 . . . . Minnesota

GENERAL INFORMATION
Stadium (year opened): Comerica Park (2000).
Team Colors: Navy blue, orange and white.

Player Representative: Alex Avila.
Home Dugout: Third Base.
Playing Surface: Grass.

Media Relations/Communications
   Telephone: (313) 471-2114. **Fax:** (313) 471-2138.
   VP, Communications: Ron Colangelo. **Director, Baseball Media Relations:** Aileen Villarreal. **Manager, Baseball Media Relations:** Chad Crunk. **Coordinator, Baseball Media Relations:** Kate Ready.

BASEBALL OPERATIONS
   Telephone: (313) 471-2000. **Fax:** (313) 471-2099.
   General Manager: David Dombrowski.
   VP/Assistant GM: Al Avila. **VP/Legal Counsel:** John Westhoff. **VP, Player Personnel:** Scott Reid. **Special Assistant:** David Chadd, Dick Egan. **Director, Baseball Operations:** Mike Smith. **Statistical Analyst Coordinator:** Sam Menzin. **Executive Assistant to President/GM:** Marty Lyon. **Executive Assistant:** Eileen Surma.

Dave Dombrowski

Major League Staff
   Manager: Brad Ausmus.
   Coaches: Pitching—Jeff Jones; **Batting**—Wally Joyner; **First Base**—Omar Vizquel; **Third Base**—Dave Clark; **Bullpen**—Mick Billmeyer; **Bench:** Gene Lamont; **Assistant Hitting:** Darnell Coles.

Medical/Training
   Director, Medical Services/Head Athletic Trainer: Kevin Rand. **Assistant Athletic Trainers:** Matt Rankin, Doug Teter. **Strength/Conditioning Coordinator:** Javair Gillett. **Team Physicians:** Dr. Michael Workings, Dr. Stephen Lemos, Dr. Louis Saco (Florida). **Coordinator, Medical Services:** Gwen Keating.

Player Development
   Director, Minor League Operations: Dan Lunetta. **Director, Player Development:** Dave Owen. **Director, Minor League/Scouting Administration:** Cheryl Evans. **Director, Latin American Player Development:** Manny Crespo. **Coordinator, Minor League Operations:** Avi Becher. **Administrative Assistant, Minor League Operations:** Marilyn Acevedo. **Minor League Field Coordinator:** Bill Dancy. **Minor League Medical Coordinator:** Corey Tremble. **Minor League Strength/Conditioning Coordinator:** Chris Walter. **International Medical Coordinator:** Steve Melendez. **Assistant Minor League Strength/Conditioning Coordinator:** Steve Chase. **Minor League Video Operations Assistant:** RJ Burgess.
   Roving Instructors: Bruce Fields (hitting), Kevin Bradshaw (infield), AJ Sager (pitching), Joe DePastino (catching), Gene Roof (outfield/baserunning), Brian Peterson (performance enhancement), Robert "Ghost" Frutchey (minor league clubhouse manager).

Farm System

Class	Club	Manager	Coach	Pitching Coach
Triple-A	Toledo (IL)	Larry Parrish	Leon Durham	Al Nipper
Double-A	Erie (EL)	Unavailable	Gerald Perry	Jaime Garcia
High A	Lakeland (FSL)	Dave Huppert	Larry Herndon	Mike Maroth
Low A	West Michigan (MWL)	Andrew Graham	Nelson Santovenia	Mike Henneman
Short-season	Connecticut (NYP)	Mike Rabelo	Scott Dwyer	Mark Johnson
Rookie	Tigers (GCL)	Basilio Cabrera	Unavailable	Jorge Cordova

Scouting
   Telephone: (863) 413-4112. **Fax:** (863) 413-1954.
   VP, Amateur Scouting/Special Assistant to GM: David Chadd. **Director, Amateur Scouting:** Scott Pleis. **Assistant, Amateur Scouting:** Julian Shabazz.
   Director, Pro Scouting: Scott Bream. **Major League Scouts:** Jim Olander (Vail, AZ), Mike Russell (Gulf Breeze, FL), Bruce Tanner (New Castle, PA), Jeff Wetherby (Wesley Chapel, FL).
   National Crosscheckers: Ray Crone (Cedar Hill, TX), Tim Hallgren (Cape Girardeau, MO). **Regional Crosscheckers: Southeast**—James Orr (Orlando, FL); **Central/Northeast**—Tom Osowski (Franklin, WI); **Midwest**—Mike Hankins (Lee's Summit, MO); **West**—Tim McWilliam (San Diego, CA).
   Area Scouts: Bryson Barber (Pensacola, FL), Grant Brittain (Hickory, NC), Bill Buck (Manassas, VA), Rolando Casanova (Miami, FL), Scott Cerny (Rocklin, CA), Murray Cook (Orlando, FL), Tim Grieve (New Braunfels, TX), Garrett Guest (Lockport, IL), Ryan Johnson (Oregon City, OR), Matt Lea (Burbank, CA), Marty Miller (Chicago, IL), Steve Pack (San Marcos, CA), Brian Reid (Gilbert, AZ), Jim Rough (Sharpsburg, GA), Chris Wimmer (Yukon, OK), Harold Zonder (Louisville, KY).
   Director, International Operations: Tom Moore. **Director, Latin American Development:** Manny Crespo. **Director, Latin American Scouting:** Miguel Garcia. **Coordinator, Pacific Rim Scouting:** Kevin Hooker. **Director, Dominican Operations:** Ramon Perez. **Coordinator, Dominican Academy:** Oliver Arias. **Venezuelan Scouting Supervisor:** Alejandro Rodriguez. **Coordinator, Venezuelan Academy:** Oscar Garcia. **Scouting Assistant, International Operations:** Eric Nieto.

Houston Astros

Office Address: Minute Maid Park, Union Station, 501 Crawford, Suite 400, Houston, TX 77002.
Mailing Address: PO Box 288, Houston, TX 77001.
Telephone: (713) 259-8000. **Fax:** (713) 259-8981.
Email Address: fanfeedback@astros.mlb.com. **Website:** www.astros.com.

Ownership
Owner/Chairman: Jim Crane.

BUSINESS OPERATIONS
President, Business Operations: Reid Ryan. **Executive Assistant:** Eileen Colgin.
Senior Vice President, Premium Sponsorships: Jamie Hildrith. **Senior VP, Business Operations:** Marcel Braithwaite. **Senior VP, Corporate Partnerships:** Matt Brand. **Senior VP, Ticket Sales/Marketing:** Jason Howard. **Senior VP, Finance:** Jonathan Germer. **VP, Community Relations/Executive Director, Astros Foundation:** Meg Vallaincourt. **VP, Stadium Operations:** Bobby Forrest. **VP, Finance:** Doug Seckel. **VP, Foundation Development:** Marian Harper. **VP, Marketing/Strategy:** Michael Dillon. **VP, Human Resources:** Vivan Mora.

Jim Crane

Media Relations/Community Relations
Telephone: (713) 259-8900. **Fax:** (713) 259-8025.
Senior Director, Media Relations: Gene Dias. **Managers, Media Relations:** Steve Grande, Dena Propis. **Coordinator, Media Relations:** Chris Peixoto. **Manager, Broadcasting:** Lowell Matheny. **Director, CSN Business Development:** Samir Mayur. **Manager, Community Relations:** Dairanetta Spain. **Manager, Urban Youth Academy:** Daryl Wade.

Marketing
Director, Brand Engagement: Christie Miller. **Manager, Marketing:** Chris Hunsaker. **Manager, Creative Services:** Chris David Garcia. **Manager, Grass Roots Marketing:** Stephen Richards. **Senior Manager, Marketing Entertainment:** Kyle Hamsher. **Director, Business Strategy/Analytics:** Jay Verrill.

Corporate Partnerships
Senior Director, Corporate Partnerships: Creighton Kahoalli. **Director, Activation/Strategy:** Jacqueline Uram. **Account Executives, Corporate Sponsorships:** Keshia Dupas, Jessica Schmidt, Jeff Stewart.

Events/Human Resources
Director, Special Events/Tours: Jonathan Sterchy. **Director, Event Booking/Sales:** Stephanie Stegall. **Assistant Director, Special Events:** Allison White. **Manager, Special Events Operations:** Cara Lewanda.
Senior Director, Payroll/Employee Benefits: Ruth Kelly. **Manager, Payroll:** Jessica Horton. **Managers, HR:** Chanda Lawdermilk, Edna Chan, Jennifer Springs. **Coordinator, HR:** Heather Kuehn. **Receptionist:** Helen Washington.

2014 SCHEDULE
Standard Game Times: 7:10 p.m.; Sat. 6:10; Sun. 1:10.

APRIL
1-3	New York (AL)
4-7	Los Angeles (AL)
8-10	at Toronto
11-13	at Texas
15-17	Kansas City
18-20	at Oakland
21-23	at Seattle
24-27	Oakland
29-30	Washington

MAY
2-4	Seattle
5-8	at Detroit
9-11	at Baltimore
12-14	Texas
16-18	Chicago (AL)
19-21	at Los Angeles (AL)
22-25	at Seattle
26-28	at Kansas City
29-31	Baltimore

JUNE
1	Baltimore
3-5	Los Angeles (AL)
6-8	at Minnesota
9-10	at Arizona
11-12	Arizona
13-15	Tampa Bay
17-18	at Washington
19-22	at Tampa Bay
24-26	Atlanta
27-29	Detroit

30	Seattle

JULY
1-2	Seattle
3-6	at Los Angeles (AL)
7-9	at Texas
11-13	Boston
18-20	at Chicago (AL)
22-24	at Oakland
25-27	Miami
28-30	Oakland
31	Toronto

AUGUST
1-3	Toronto
5-7	at Philadelphia
8-10	Texas

11-13	Minnesota
14-17	at Boston
19-21	at New York (AL)
22-24	at Cleveland
25-27	Oakland
28-31	Texas

SEPTEMBER
2-3	Los Angeles (AL)
5-7	at Oakland
8-10	at Seattle
12-14	at Los Angeles (AL)
15-18	Cleveland
19-21	Seattle
22-24	at Texas
26-28	at New York (NL)

GENERAL INFORMATION
Stadium (year opened):
Minute Maid Park (2000).
Team Colors: Navy and orange.

Player Representative: Unavailable.
Home Dugout: First Base.
Playing Surface: Grass.

Stadium Operations

Director, Safety/Security: Chad Ludkey. **Senior Director, Major League Field Operations:** Dan Bergstrom. **Director, Guest Services:** Michael Kenny. **Manager, Engineering:** Michael Seighman. **Supervisor, Engineering:** Brian Hayward.

Ticketing

Senior Director, Ticket Operations/Strategy: Brooke Ellenberger. **Senior Director, Group Sales/Inside Sales:** P.J. Keene. **Director, Box Office Operations:** Bill Cannon. **Director, Premium Sales/Service:** Clay Kowalski. **Director, Season Ticket Services:** Alan Latkovic. **Director, Season Ticket Sales:** Duane Haring.

BASEBALL OPERATIONS

General Manager: Jeff Luhnow.
Assistant General Manager: David Stearns. **Special Assistants to the GM:** Craig Biggio, Roger Clemens, Enos Cabell, Doug Brocail.
Baseball Analyst: Brandon Taubman. **Coordinator, Baseball Operations:** Pete Putila. **Director, Decision Sciences:** Sig Mejdal. **Analyst:** Mike Fast. **Mathematical Modeler:** Colin Wyers. **Senior Technical Architect:** Ryan Hallahan. **Analytics Developer:** Darren DeFreeuw.

Jeff Luhnow

Major League Staff

Manager: Bo Porter.
Coaches: Bench—Dave Trembley; **Pitching**—Brent Strom; **Hitting**—John Mallee; **First Base**—Iarrik Brock; **Third Base**—Pat Listach; **Bullpen**—Craig Bjornson; **Assistant Hitting Coach**—Ralph Dickenson; **Bullpen Catcher**—Javier Bracamonte.

Team Operations/Clubhouse

Manager, Team Operations: Dan O'Neill. **Coordinator, Advance Information:** Tom Koch-Weser. **Clubhouse Manager:** Carl Schneider. **Visiting Clubhouse Manager:** Steve Perry. **Umpire Attendant/Clubhouse Assistant:** Chuck New. **Clubhouse Attendants:** David Burd, Stacy Gallagher. **Video Coordinator:** Jim Summers.

Medical/Training

Medical Director: Dr. David Lintner. **Team Physicians:** Dr. Thomas Mehlhoff, Dr. James Muntz, Dr. Pat McCulloch. **Medical Risk Manager/Analyst:** Bill Firkus. **Head Trainer:** Nate Lucero. **Assistant Trainer:** Rex Jones. **Strength/ Conditioning Coach:** Jacob Beiting.

Player Development

Telephone: (713) 259-8920. **Fax:** (713) 259-8600.
Director, Player Development: Quinton McCracken. **Assistant Director, Player Development:** Allen Rowin. **Special Assistant, Player Development:** Dan Radison. **Director, Florida Operations:** Jay Edminston. **Field Coordinator:** Paul Runge. **Minor League Coordinators:** Jamey Snodgrass (medical), Brendan Verner (strength/conditioning), Daniel Roberts (rehab), Jeff Albert (hitting), Dyar Miller (pitching), Doug White (pitching rover). **Development Specialists:** Jeff Murphy (Triple-A), Tom Lawless (Double-A), Mark Bailey (High A), Vince Coleman (Low A). **Infield Instructor:** Adam Everett. **Special Assignment Coach:** Morgan Ensberg. **GCL Coach:** Gordy MacKenzie. **DSL Coach:** Melvi Ortega. **ESL/ Player Acculturation Coordinator:** Doris Gonzales. **Dominican Republic Academy Administrator:** Caridad Cabrera.

Farm System

Class	Club	Manager	Hitting Coach	Pitching Coach
Triple-A	Oklahoma City (PCL)	Tony DeFrancesco	Leon Roberts	Steve Webber
Double-A	Corpus Christi (TL)	Keith Bodie	Tim Garland	Gary Ruby
High A	Lancaster (CAL)	Rodney Linares	Darryl Robinson	Don Alexander
Low A	Quad Cities (SAL)	Omar Lopez	Joel Chimelis	Dave Borkowski
Short-season	Tri-City (NYP)	Ed Romero	Russ Steinhorn	Chris Holt
Rookie	Greeneville (APP)	Josh Bonifay	Cesar Cedeno	Josh Miller
Rookie	Astros (GCL)	Marty Malloy	Ramon Vasquez	Hector Mercado
Rookie	Astros (DSL)	Johan Maya	Luis Mateo	Rick Aponte

Scouting

Telephone: (713) 259-8925. **Fax:** (713) 259-8600.
Director, Amateur Scouting: Mike Elias. **Director, Pro Scouting:** Kevin Goldstein. **Coordinator, Amateur Scouting:** Paul Cusick. **Professional Scouts:** Charles Aliano (Land O' Lakes, FL), Hank Allen (Upper Marlboro, MD), Ruben Amaro Sr. (Weston, FL), Ken Califano (Stafford, VA), Alex Jacobs (Lakeland, FL), Jason Lefkowitz (Dallas, TX), Spike Lundberg (Murrieta, CA), Tim Moore (Sacramento, CA), Paul Ricciarini (Pittsfield, MA), Tom Shafer (Lockport, IL), Will Sharp (Athens, GA), Aaron Tassano (Phoenix, AZ). **National Crosschecker:** David Post (Canton, GA). **Regional Supervisors: Midwest**— Ralph Bratton (Dripping Springs, TX); **East**—JD Alleva (Charlotte, NC); **West**—Kris Gross (Newport Beach, CA); **FL/PR/ Northeast**—Evan Brannon. **Area Scouts:** Tim Bittner (Mechanicsville, VA), Bryan Byrne (Walnut Creek, CA), Brad Budzinski (Huntington Beach, CA), Tim Costic (Stevenson Ranch, CA), Justin Cryer (Oxford, MS), Gavin Dickey (Atlanta, GA), Paul Gale (Keizer, OR), Noel Gonzales (Houston, TX), Troy Hoerner (Middleton, WI), John Martin (Tampa, FL), Mark Ross (Tucson, AZ), Bobby St. Pierre (Port Washington, NY), Jim Stevenson (Tulsa, OK), Nick Venuto (Newton Falls, OH). **Senior Advising Scouts:** Bob King (La Mesa, CA), Bob Poole (Redwood City, CA). **Part-Time Scouts:** Joey Sola (Caguas, PR), Robert Gutierrez (Miami Gardens, FL), Ross Smith (Tallahassee, FL).
Director, International: Oz Ocampo (New York, NY). **Specialist, International Operations/Associate Counsel:** Stephanie Wilka. **Advisor, Latin American Development:** Julio Linares. **International Field Coordinator:** Carlos Alfonso. **International Crosschecker:** Marc Russo (Clearwater Beach, FL). **International Scouts:** **Venezuela**—Oscar Alvarado, Daniel Acuna, Jose Palacios; **Dominican Republic**—Roman Ocumarez, Rafael Belen, Jose Lima, Francis Mojica, Jose Ortiz; **Panama**—Carlos Gonzalez; **Colombia**—Neder Horta; **Nicaragua**—Leocadio Guevara; **Australia**—Greg Morriss.

Kansas City Royals

Office Address: One Royal Way, Kansas City, MO 64129.
Mailing Address: PO Box 419969, Kansas City, MO 64141.
Telephone: (816) 921-8000. **Fax:** (816) 924-0347. **Website:** www.royals.com

Ownership
Operated By: Kansas City Royals Baseball Club, Inc.
Chairman/CEO: David Glass. **President:** Dan Glass. **Board of Directors:** Ruth Glass, Don Glass, Dayna Martz, Julia Irene Kauffman. **Executive Administrative Assistant (Executive Staff):** Ginger Salem.

BUSINESS OPERATIONS
Senior Vice President, Business Operations: Kevin Uhlich. **Executive Administrative Assistant:** Cindy Hamilton. **Director, Royals Hall of Fame:** Curt Nelson. **Director, Authentic Merchandise Sales:** Justin Villarreal.

David Glass

Finance/Administration
VP, Finance/Administration: David Laverentz. **Director, Finance:** Adam Tyhurst. **Director, Human Resources:** Johnna Meyer. **Director, Risk Management:** Patrick Fleischmann. **Senior Director, Payroll:** Tom Pfannenstiel. **Senior Director, Information Systems:** Brian Himstedt. **Director, Information Systems Operations:** Scott Novak. **Senior Director, Ticket Operations:** Anthony Blue. **Director, Ticket Operations:** Chris Darr.

Communications/Broadcasting
VP, Communications/Broadcasting: Mike Swanson. **Assistant Director, Communications:** Mike Cummings. **Coordinator, Media Relations/Alumni:** Dina Blevins. **Coordinator, Communications/Broadcasting:** Colby Curry.

Publicity/Community Relations
VP, Community Affairs/Publicity: Toby Cook. **Senior Director, Community Relations:** Ben Aken. **Senior Director, Publicity:** Lora Grosshans. **Director, Royals Charities:** Marie Dispenza. **Director, Community Outreach:** Betty Kaegel.

Ballpark Operations
VP, Ballpark Operations/Development: Bob Rice. **Senior Director, Groundskeeping/Landscaping:** Trevor Vance. **Senior Director, Stadium Engineering:** Todd Burrow. **Director, Ballpark Services:** Johnny Williams. **Director, Event Operations:** Isaac Riffel. **Director, Guest Services/Experience:** Anthony Mozzicato.

Marketing/Business Development
VP, Marketing/Business Development: Michael Bucek.
Senior Director, Event Presentation/Production: Don Costante. **Director, Marketing/Advertising:** Brad Zollars. **Director, Digital/Social Media:** Erin Sleddens. **Senior Director, Corporate Sponsorships/Broadcast Sales:** Wes Engram. **Senior Director, Client Services:** Michele Kammerer. **Senior Director, Sales/Service:** Steve Shiffman. **Director,**

2014 SCHEDULE
Standard Game Times: 7:10 p.m.; Sat. 6:10; Sun. 1:10.

MARCH		
31 . . . . .at Detroit	5-7 . . . . . . at San Diego	20-22 . . . . Seattle	8-10 . . . . . San Francisco

MARCH
31 . . . . .at Detroit

APRIL
2-3 . . . . .at Detroit
4-6 . . . . . . Chicago (AL)
7-9 . . . . .Tampa Bay
11-13 . . . . . at Minnesota
15-17 . . . . . .at Houston
18-20 . . . . . . Minnesota
21-24 . . . . . .at Cleveland
25-27 . . . . . .at Baltimore
29-30 . . . . .Toronto

MAY
1 . . . . .Toronto
2-4 . . . . Detroit

5-7 . . . . . . at San Diego
8-11 . . . . .at Seattle
13-14 . . . . . . .Colorado
15-18 . . . . . . Baltimore
19-21 . . . . Chicago (AL)
23-25 . at Los Angeles (AL)
26-28 . . . . Houston
29-31 . . . . . . at Toronto

JUNE
1 . . . . at Toronto
2-3 . . . . .at St. Louis
4-5 . . . . St. Louis
6-9 . . . . . .New York (AL)
10-11 . . . . Cleveland
13-15 . . .at Chicago (AL)
16-18 . . . . .at Detroit

20-22 . . . . Seattle
23-25 . . .Los Angeles (NL)
27-29 . . .Los Angeles (AL)
30 . . . . at Minnesota

JULY
1-2 . . . . at Minnesota
4-6 . . . . .at Cleveland
7-9 . . . . . . at Tampa Bay
10-13 . . . . Detroit
18-20 . . . . .at Boston
21-23 . . . .at Chicago (AL)
24-27 . . . . . . Cleveland
29-31 . . . . . . .Minnesota

AUGUST
1-3 . . . . .at Oakland
5-7 . . . . . . at Arizona

8-10 . . . . . San Francisco
11-14 . . . . Oakland
15-18 . . . . . at Minnesota
19-20 . . . . . at Colorado
22-24 . . . . .at Texas
26-28 . . . . . . Minnesota
29-31 . . . . . . Cleveland

SEPTEMBER
1-3 . . . . Texas
5-7 . . . . . at New York (AL)
8-10 . . . . .at Detroit
11-14 . . . . Boston
15-17 . . . . . Chicago (AL)
19-21 . . . . Detroit
22-24 . . . . .at Cleveland
25-28 . . . .at Chicago (AL)

GENERAL INFORMATION
Stadium (year opened):
Ewing M. Kauffman Stadium (1973).
Team Colors: Royal blue and white.
Player Representative: Aaron Crow.
Home Dugout: First Base.
Playing Surface: Grass.

Sales/Analytics: Theodore Hodges. **Director, Ticket Services:** Scott Wadsworth.

BASEBALL OPERATIONS

Dayton Moore

Telephone: (816) 921-8000. **Fax:** (816) 924-0347.
Senior VP, Baseball Operations/General Manager: Dayton Moore.
VP, Baseball Operations/Assistant GM: Dean Taylor. **Assistant GM, Player Personnel:**
J.J. Picollo. **Assistant GM, International Operations:** Rene Francisco. **Senior Advisor to GM/
Scouting/Player Development:** Mike Arbuckle. **Director, Baseball Administration:** Jin Wong.
Director, Pro Scouting: Gene Watson.
Director, Baseball Analytics: Mike Groopman. **Assistant Director, Baseball Analytics:**
John Williams. **Manager, Arizona Operations:** Nick Leto. **Systems Architect, Baseball
Analytics:** Jared Macke. **Analyst, Baseball Analytics:** Daniel Mack. **Executive Assistant to
the GM:** Emily Penning. **Senior Advisors:** Art Stewart, Donnie Williams, John Boles. **Special
Assistant, Player Personnel:** Louie Medina.
VP, Baseball Operations: George Brett. **Special Assistants to GM:** Pat Jones, Mike Toomey,
Mike Pazik, Jim Fregosi, Jr., Tim Conroy. **Team Travel:** Jeff Davenport. **Video Coordinator:** Mark
Topping.

Major League Staff
Manager: Ned Yost.
Coaches: Bench—Don Wakamatsu; **Pitching**—Dave Eiland; **Hitting**—Pedro Grifol; **First Base**—Rusty Kuntz; **Third
Base**—Dale Sveum; **Bullpen**—Doug Henry; **Coach**—Mike Jirschele.

Medical/Training
Team Physician: Dr. Vincent Key. **Head Athletic Trainer:** Nick Kenney. **Assistant Athletic Trainer:** Kyle Turner.
Strength/Conditioning: Ryan Stoneberg.

Player Development
Telephone: (816) 921-8000. **Fax:** (816) 924-0347.
Director, Player Development: Scott Sharp.
Assistant Director, Player Development: Kyle Vena.
Special Assistant: Steve Foster (pitching), Jack Maloof (hitting). **Special Assistant, Player Development:** Chino
Cadahia, John Wathan. **Senior Pitching Advisor:** Bill Fischer. **Coordinators:** Tony Tijerina (field), Terry Bradshaw (hitting),
Glenn Hubbard (infield), Milt Thompson (bunting/baserunning), Chris DeLucia (medical), Tony Medina (Latin America
medical), Garrett Sherrill (strength/conditioning), Luis Perez (Latin America strength/conditioning), Justin Hahn (rehab),
Carlos Reyes (rehab pitching), Jeff Diskin (cultural development), Freddy Sandoval (mental skills).

Farm System

Class	Club (League)	Manager	Hitting Coach	Pitching Coach
Triple-A	Omaha (PCL)	Brian Poldberg	Tommy Gregg	Larry Carter
Double-A	Northwest Arkansas (TL)	Vance Wilson	Andre David	Jim Brower
High A	Wilmington (CL)	Darryl Kennedy	Milt Thompson	Steve Luebber
Low A	Lexington (SAL)	Brian Buchanan	Abraham Nunez	Steve Merriman
Rookie	Idaho Falls (PIO)	Omar Ramirez	Damon Hollins	Mark Davis
Rookie	Burlington (APP)	Tommy Shields	Nelson Liriano	Carlos Martinez
Rookie	Royals (DSL)	Jose Gualdron	Onil Joseph	Rafael Roque

Scouting
Telephone: (816) 921-8000. **Fax:** (816) 924-0347.
Director, Scouting: Lonnie Goldberg.
Manager, Scouting Operations: Linda Smith. **Assistant to Amateur Scouting:** Jack Monahan.
Major League Scouts: Charles Bolton (Indianapolis, IN), Dennis Cardoza (Munds Park, AZ), Mike Pazik (Bethesda, MD),
Jon Williams (Imperial, MO), Ron Toenjes (Georgetown, TX), Mitch Webster (Kansas City, MO), Alec Zumwalt (Winston-
Salem, NC).
National Supervisors: Paul Gibson (Center Moriches, NY), Junior Vizcaino (Raleigh, NC). **Regional Supervisors:**
Midwest—Gregg Miller (Meeker, OK), **Southeast**—Gregg Kilby (Tampa, FL), **West**—Dan Ontiveros (Laguna Niguel, CA),
Northeast—Sean Rooney (Apex, NC).
Area Scouts: Rich Amaral (Huntington Beach, CA), Jim Buckley (Tampa, FL), Travis Ezi (Baton Rouge, LA), Casey Fahy
(Apex, NC), Jim Farr (Williamsburg, VA), Mike Farrell (Indianapolis, IN), Bobby Gandolfo (King of Prussia, PA), Sean Gibbs
(Canton, GA), Colin Gonzales (Dana Point, CA), Buddy Gouldsmith (Reno, NV), Josh Hallgren (Vancouver, WA), Chad Lee
(Norman, OK), Justin Lehr (Spring, TX), Scott Melvin (Quincy, IL), Alex Mesa (Miami, FL), Ken Munoz (Scottsdale, AZ), Matt
Price (Overland Park, KS).
Part-Time Scouts: Kirk Barclay (Wyoming, ON), Eric Briggs (Bolivar, MO), Rick Clendenin (Clendenin, WV), Louis Collier
(Chicago, IL), Corey Eckstein (Chilliwack, BC), Brian Hiler (Cincinnati, OH), Josh Labandeira (Fresno, CA), Jerry Lafferty
(Kansas City, MO), Brittan Motley (Grandview, MO), Chad Raley (Baton Rouge, LA), Johnny Ramos (Carolina, PR).
Latin America Supervisor: Orlando Estevez. **International Scouts:** Richard Castro (Venezuela), Alberto Garcia
(Venezuela) Juan Indriago (Venezuela), Jose Gualdron (Venezuela), Joelvis Gonzalez (Venezuela), Edson Kelly (Aruba),
Juan Lopez (Nicaragua), Nathan Miller (Taiwan), Rafael Miranda (Colombia), Fausto Morel (Dominican Republic), Ricardo
Ortiz (Panama), Edis Perez (Dominican Republic), Rafael Vasquez (Dominican Republic), Franco Wawoe (Curacao).

Los Angeles Angels

Office Address: 2000 Gene Autry Way, Anaheim, CA 92806.
Mailing Address: PO Box 2000, Anaheim, CA 92803.
Telephone: (714) 940-2000. **Fax:** (714) 940-2205.
Website: www.angels.com.

Ownership
Owner: Arte Moreno. **Chairman:** Dennis Kuhl. **President:** John Carpino.

BUSINESS OPERATIONS

Arte Moreno

Chief Financial Officer: Bill Beverage. **Senior Vice President, Finance/Administration:** Molly Jolly. **Director, Legal Affairs/Risk Management:** Alex Winsberg. **Controller:** Cris Lacoste. **Accountants:** Lorelei Largey, Kylie McManus, Jennifer Whynott. **Financial Analyst:** Jennifer Jeanblanc. **Assistant, Accounting:** Linda Chubak. **Assistant, Payroll:** Alison Kelso. **Benefits Manager:** Cecilia Schneider.

Director, Human Resources: Deborah Johnston. **Human Resources Generalist:** Brittany Johnson. **Human Resources Representative:** Mayra Trinidad. **Staffing Analyst:** Kristin Talamantes. **Director, Information Services:** Al Castro. **Senior Network Engineer:** Neil Fariss. **Senior Desktop Support Analyst:** David Yun. **Technology Integration Specialist:** Paramjit 'Tiny' Singh. **Helpdesk Assistant:** Kim Davis.

Marketing/Corporate Sales
Senior Director, Corporate Sponsorship: Neil Viserto. **Senior Director, Business Development:** Mike Fach. **Corporate Sales Account Executives:** Nicole Provansal, Rick Turner, Matt Wiech, Drew Zinser. **Sponsorship Services Managers:** Maria Dinh, Bobby Kowan. **Sponsorship Services Coordinators:** Rosanne Tarrant, Vanessa Vega. **Sponsorship Research Analyst:** Michael Sylvan.

VP, Marketing/Ticket Sales: Robert Alvarado. **Marketing Managers:** John Rozak, Kevin Shaw, Ryan Vance. **Marketing Coordinator/Graphic Designer:** Jeff Lee. **Director, Ticket Sales/Services:** Tom DeTemple. **Manager, Ticket Sales:** Josh Hunhoff. **Manager, Client Services:** Justin Hallenbeck. **Client Services Representatives:** Shawn Meyer, Alisa Mitry, Adriana Ryan. **Event Sales/Service Manager:** Courtney Wallace.

Public/Media Relations/Communications
Telephone: (714) 940-2014. **Fax:** (714) 940-2205.
VP, Communications: Tim Mead. **Director, Communications:** Eric Kay. **Media Relations Representative:** Adam Chodzko. **Communications Administrative Assistant:** Matt Birch. **Senior Director, Community Relations:** Jenny Price. **Community Relations Coordinator:** Chrissy Vaughn. **Photo Editor:** Jordan Murph. **Team Photographer:** Matt Brown.

Ballpark Operations/Facilities
Senior Director, Ballpark Operations: Brian Sanders. **Director, Ballpark Operations:** Sam Maida. **Event Manager:**

2014 SCHEDULE
Standard Game Times: 7:05 p.m.; Sun. 12:35.

MARCH		
31 . . . . Seattle	9-12 . . . . at Toronto	27-29 . . . . .at Kansas City	8-10 . . . . Boston

MARCH
31 . . . . Seattle

APRIL
1-2 . . . . Seattle
4-7 . . . . .at Houston
8-9 . . . . .at Seattle
11-13 . . . . .New York (NL)
14-16 . . . . Oakland
18-20 . . . . . . .at Detroit
21-23 . . . . at Washington
25-27 . . at New York (AL)
28-30 . . . . Cleveland

MAY
2-4 . . . . Texas
5-7 . . . . . .New York (AL)

9-12 . . . . at Toronto
13-14 . . . . at Philadelphia
15-18 . . . . . . .Tampa Bay
19-21 . . . . Houston
23-25 . . . . . Kansas City
26-29 . . . . . . .at Seattle
30-31 . . . . . . .at Oakland

JUNE
1 . . . . .at Oakland
3-5 . . . . .at Houston
6-8 . . . . . . Chicago (AL)
9-11 . . . . Oakland
13-5 . . . . at Atlanta
16-19 . . . . .at Cleveland
20-22 . . . . Texas
24-26 . . . . Minnesota

27-29 . . . . .at Kansas City
30 . . . . . .at Chicago (AL)

JULY
1-2 . . . . . .at Chicago (AL)
3-6 . . . . Houston
7-9 . . . . .Toronto
10-13 . . . . .at Texas
18-20 . . . . Seattle
21-13 . . . . Baltimore
24-27 . . . . Detroit
29-31 . . . . .at Baltimore

AUGUST
1-3 . . . . . . at Tampa Bay
4-5 . . at Los Angeles (NL)
6-7 . . . . .Los Angeles (NL)

8-10 . . . . Boston
12-13 . . . . .Philadelphia
15-17 . . . . .at Texas
18-21 . . . . .at Boston
22-24 . . . . . .at Oakland
25-27 . . . . .Miami
28-31 . . . . Oakland

SEPTEMBER
2-3 . . . . .at Houston
4-7 . . . . . . at Minnesota
9-11 . . . . .at Texas
12-14 . . . . Houston
15-18 . . . . Seattle
19-21 . . . . Texas
22-24 . . . . . .at Oakland
26-28 . . . . . . .at Seattle

GENERAL INFORMATION

Stadium (year opened):
Angel Stadium of Anaheim (1966).
Team Colors: Red, dark red, blue and silver.

Player Representative: C.J. Wilson.
Home Dugout: Third Base.
Playing Surface: Grass.

Calvin Ching. **Security Manager:** Mark Macias. **Field/Ground Maintenance Manager:** Barney Lopas. **Turf Grass Managers:** Michael Clark, Greg Laesch. **Receptionists:** Sandy Sanford, Margie Walsh.
　　Director, Facility Services: Mike McKay. **Manager, Facility Services:** Linda Fitzgerald. **Purchasing Manager:** Suzanne Peters. **Asset Coordinator:** Daniel Angulo. **Manager, Facility Maintenance:** Steve Preston. **Housekeeping Manager:** Robert Donovan. **Custodial Supervisors:** Nathan Bautista, Pedro Del Castillo, Ray Nells. **Office Assistant:** Jose Padilla. **Manager, Entertainment/Production:** Peter Bull. **Producer, Video Operations:** David Tsuruda. **Associate Producer:** Danny Pitts. **Entertainment Coordinator:** Emily Cabrera.

Ticketing
　　Director, Ticketing Operations: Sheila Brazelton. **Manager, Ticket Office:** Susan Weiss. **Director, Ticket Services:** Johnny Mendez.

Travel/Clubhouse
　　Clubhouse Manager: Keith Tarter. **Assistant Clubhouse Manager:** Shane Demmitt. **Visiting Clubhouse Manager:** Brian 'Bubba' Harkins. **Senior Video Coordinator:** Diego Lopez. **Video Coordinator:** Ruben Montano. **Traveling Secretary:** Tom Taylor.

BASEBALL OPERATIONS
　　General Manager: Jerry Dipoto.
　　Assistant GM, Baseball Operations: Matt Klentak. **Assistant GM, Player Development/Scouting:** Scott Servais. **Special Advisor:** Bill Stoneman. **Special Assistants to GM:** Marcel Lachemann, Tim Huff, Rico Brogna. **Director, Baseball Operations:** Justin Hollander. **Coordinator, Baseball Operations:** Jonathan Strangio. **Coordinator, Scouting:** Nate Horowitz. **Coordinator, Advance Scouting:** Jeremy Zoll. **Coordinator, Major League Player Information:** Nick Francona. **Baseball Administration Coordinator:** Kathy Mair

Jerry Dipoto

Major League Staff
　　Manager: Mike Scioscia. **Coaches: Bench**—Dino Ebel; **Pitching**—Mike Butcher; **Batting**—Don Baylor; **First Base**—Alfredo Griffin; **Third Base**—Gary DiSarcina; **Bullpen**—Steve Soliz; **Bullpen Catcher**—Tom Gregorio; **Assistant Hitting:** Dave Hansen; **Major League Player Information:** Rick Eckstein.

Medical/Training
　　Team Physician: Dr. Craig Milhouse. **Team Orthopedists:** Dr. Robert Grumet, Dr. Michael Shepard. **Head Athletic Trainer:** Adam Nevala. **Assistant Athletic Trainer:** Rick Smith. **Strength/Conditioning Coach:** T.J. Harrington.

Player Development
　　Director, Player Development: Bobby Scales. **Manager, Minor League Operations:** Mike LaCassa. **Minor League Equipment Manager, Arizona:** Brett Crane. **Field Coordinator:** Mike Micucci. **Roving Instructors:** Paul Sorrento (Hitting), Jim Eppard (Assistant Hitting), Bill Lachemann (Catching/Special Assignment), Tyrone Boykin (Outfield/Baserunning/Bunting), Jim Gott (Pitching), Kernan Ronan (Rehab Pitching), Pete Harnisch (Special Assignment Pitching), Bobby Knoop (Special Assignment Infield), Geoff Hostetter (Training Coordinator), Al Sandoval (Strength/Conditioning), Eric Munson (Rehab).

Farm System

Class	Club	Manager	Hitting Coach	Pitching Coach
Triple-A	Salt Lake (PCL)	Keith Johnson	Francisco Matos	Erik Bennett
Double-A	Arkansas (TL)	Phillip Wellman	Tom Tornincasa	Pat Rice
High A	Inland Empire (CAL)	Denny Hocking	Brenton Del Chiaro	Matt Wise
Low A	Burlington (MWL)	Bill Richardson	Nathan Haynes	Ethan Katz
Rookie	Orem (PIO)	Unavailable	Ryan Barba/Paul Mcanulty	Chris Gissell
Rookie	Angels (AZL)	Elio Sarmiento	Brian Betancourth	Mike Hampton/Ryan O'Malley
Rookie	Angels (DSL)	Carson Vitale	Anel De Los Santos	Hector Astacio

Scouting
　　Director, Pro Scouting: Hal Morris.
　　Major League/Special Assignment Scout: Timothy Schmidt (San Bernardino, CA).
　　Professional Scouts: Jeff Cirillo (Medina, WA), Chris Fetter (Carmel, IN), Mike Koplove (Philadelphia, PA), Tim McIntosh (Stockton, CA), Ken Stauffer (Katy, TX), Gary Varsho (Chili, WI), Bobby Williams (Sarasota, FL).
　　Director, Amateur Scouting: Ric Wilson.
　　National Crosscheckers: Jeff Malinoff (Lopez, WA), Greg Morhardt (S. Windsor, CT). **Regional Supervisors: Northeast**—Jason Baker (Lynchburg, VA); **Southeast**—Chris McAlpin (Moultrie, GA); **Northern Midwest**—Joel Murrie (Evergreen, CO); **Southern Midwest**—Kevin Ham (Cypress, TX); **Northwest**—Scott Richardson (Sacramento, CA); **Southwest**—Jayson Durocher (Phoenix, AZ).
　　Area Scouts: Don Archer (Canada), Jared Barnes (South Bend, IN), John Burden (Fairfield, OH), Drew Chadd (Wichita, KS), Tim Corcoran (LaVerne, CA), Dan Cox (Huntington Beach, CA), Jason Ellison (Issaquah, WA), Nick Gorneault (Springfield, MA), John Gracio (Mesa, AZ), Chad Hermansen (Henderson, NV), Todd Hogan (Dublin, GA), Brandon McArthur (Kennesaw, GA), Dan Radcliff (Palmyra, VA), Ralph Reyes (Miami, FL), Omar Rodriguez (Puerto Rico), Rudy Vasquez (San Antonio, TX), Rob Wilfong (San Dimas, CA), J.T. Zink (Hoover, AL).
　　Director, International Scouting: Carlos Gomez.
　　International Scouting Supervisors: Alfredo Ulloa (Dominican Republic), Lebi Ochoa (Venezuela). **International Scouts:** Jochy Cabrera (Dominican Republic), Jason Dunn (Asia), Domingo Garcia (Dominican Republic), Carlos Ramirez (Venezuela), Rene Rojas (Dominican Republic), Mauro Zerpa (Venezuela).

Los Angeles Dodgers

Office Address: 1000 Elysian Park Ave., Los Angeles, CA 90090.
Telephone: (323) 224-1500. **Fax:** (323) 224-1269. **Website:** www.dodgers.com

Ownership
Chairman: Mark Walter.
President/CEO: Stan Kasten. **Partner:** Earvin 'Magic' Johnson, Peter Guber, Todd Boehly, Robert 'Bobby' Patton, Jr.
Special Advisors to Chairman: Tommy Lasorda, Sandy Koufax, Dr. Frank Jobe, Don Newcombe.

BUSINESS OPERATIONS

Executive Vice President: Bob Wolfe. **Executive VP/Chief Marketing Officer:** Lon Rosen.
CFO: Tucker Kain. **Senior VP/General Counsel:** Sam Fernandez. **Senior VP, Planning/Development:** Janet Marie Smith. **Senior VP, External Affairs:** Renata Simril. **Senior VP, Corporate Partnerships:** Michael Young. **Senior VP, Stadium Operations:** Steve Ethier. **Controller:** Eric Hernandez. **Director, Finance:** Paige Bobbitt.

Sales/Partnership
VP, Ticket Sales: David Siegel. **Director, Season Sales:** David Kirkpatrick. **Senior Director, Partnership Administration:** Jenny Oh. **Senior Director, Corporate Partnerships:** Lorenzo Sciarrino. **Account Director, Corporate Partnerships:** Greg Morrison, Walker Fletcher. **Account Director, International Partnerships:** Martin Kim. **Director, Partnership Sales Administration:** Paige Kirkpatrick. **Director, Premium Sales/Services:** Antonio Morici.

Mark Walter

Marketing/Broadcasting
VP, Marketing/Broadcasting: Erik Braverman. **Director, Advertising/Promotions:** Shelley Wagner. **Director, Production:** Greg Taylor. **Director, Graphic Design:** Ross Yoshida. **Director, Broadcast Engineering:** Tom Darin.

Human Resources/Legal
Senior Director, Human Resources: Leonor Romero. **Senior Counsel:** Chad Gunderson.

Communications/Community Relations
Director, Public Relations: Joe Jareck. **Assistant Director, Public Relations:** Yvonne Carrasco. **Director, Digital/Print Content:** Jon Weisman.

Information Technology/Stadium Operations/Security
VP, Information Technology: Ralph Esquibel. **VP, Security:** William Woodward. **Director, Safety/Security:** Michael Betzler. **Director, Fan Services:** Eric George. **Director, Facility Operations:** Estella Flores.

Ticketing
Telephone: (323) 224-1471. **Fax:** (323) 224-2609.
VP, Ticket Operations: Billy Hunter. **VP, Ticket Development:** Seth Bluman. **Director, Ticket Operations:** Aaron Dubner.

2014 SCHEDULE
Standard Game Times: 7:10 p.m.; Sun. 1:10

MARCH		MAY		
22 . . . . vs Arizona		1 . . . . at Minnesota	16-18 . . . . Colorado	6-7. . . .at Los Angeles (AL)
(in Sydney, Australia)		2-4. . . . . at Miami	20-22 . . . . . .at San Diego	8-10 . . . . . . at Milwaukee
22 . . . . vs Arizona		5-7. . . . . .at Washington	23-25 . . . at Kansas City	11-14 . . . . . . .at Atlanta
(in Sydney, Australia)		8-11 . . . . . San Francisco	26-29 . . . . .St. Louis	15-17 . . . . . . Milwaukee
30 . . . . . . .at San Diego		12-14 . . . . Miami	30 . . . . .Cleveland	19-21 . . . . San Diego
		16-18 . . . . at Arizona		22-24 . . . . .New York (NL)
APRIL		20-22 . . at New York (NL)	JULY	26-27 . . . . at Arizona
1-2. . . . . .at San Diego		23-25 . . . at Philadelphia	1-2. . . . . . . .Cleveland	29-31 . . . . .at San Diego
4-6. . . . . . San Francisco		26-28 . . . . . . Cincinnati	3-6. . . . . at Colorado	
8-9. . . . . Detroit		29-31 . . . . Pittsburgh	8-9. . . . . .at Detroit	SEPTEMBER
11-13 . . . . . at Arizona			10-13 . . . . . . San Diego	1-3. . . . . Washington
15-17 . . . at San Francisco		JUNE	18-20 . . . . . at St. Louis	5-7. . . . . Arizona
18-20 . . . . Arizona		1 . . . . Pittsburgh	21-23 . . . . .at Pittsburgh	8-10 . . . . San Diego
21-24 . . . . . .Philadelphia		2-4. . . . . . .Chicago (AL)	25-27 . . . at San Francisco	12-14 . . . at San Francisco
25-27 . . . . . . Colorado		6-8. . . . . . . at Colorado	29-31 . . . . Atlanta	15-17 . . . . . at Colorado
29-30 . . . . . at Minnesota		9-12 . . . . .at Cincinnati	AUGUST	18-21 . . . . at Chicago (NL)
		13-15 . . . . Arizona	1-3. . . . . . . .Chicago (NL)	22-24 . . . . . San Francisco
			4-5. . . . Los Angeles (AL)	26-28 . . . . Colorado

GENERAL INFORMATION
Stadium (year opened): Dodger Stadium (1962).
Team Colors: Dodger blue and white.
Player Representative: Clayton Kershaw.
Home Dugout: Third Base.
Playing Surface: Grass

BASEBALL OPERATIONS
Telephone: (323) 224-1500. **Fax:** (323) 224-1463.
General Manager: Ned Colletti.
Special Advisor to the GM: Gerry Hunsicker. **Special Assistant to the GM:** Pat Corrales.
Director, Baseball Administration: Ellen Harrigan. **Director, Baseball Contracts/Research/
Operations:** Alex Tamin. **Director, Team Travel:** Scott Akasaki. **Director, International/Minor
League Relations:** Joseph Reaves. **Advisor, Team Travel:** Billy DeLury. **Major League Video
Coordinator:** John Pratt. **Manager, Baseball Research/Operations:** Matt Marks. **Coordinator,
Baseball Operations:** Jordan Peikin.

Ned Colletti

Major League Staff
Manager: Don Mattingly.
Coaches: Bench—Tim Wallach; **Pitching**—Rick Honeycutt; **Hitting**—Mark McGwire; **First
Base**—Davey Lopes; **Third Base**—Lorenzo Bundy; **Bullpen**—Chuck Crim. **Assistant Pitching
Coach:** Ken Howell. **Assistant Hitting Coach:** John Valentin. **Instructors:** Manny Mota, Steve Yeager. **Bullpen Catcher:**
Rob Flippo.
Manager, Dodger Clubhouse: Mitch Poole. **Assistant Manager, Dodger Clubhouse:** Alex Torres. **Clubhouse
Attendant:** Jose Castillo. **Manager, Visiting Clubhouse:** Jewwrry Turner.

Medical/Training
VP, Medical Services: Stan Conte. **Assistant Athletic Trainers:** Nancy Patterson Flynn, Greg Harrel. **Strength/
Conditioning Coaches:** Brandon McDaniel, Brian Stoneberg. **Physical Therapist:** Steve Smith. **Massage Therapist:**
Ichiro Tani. **Team Physicians:** Dr. Neal ElAttrache, Dr. John Plosay, Dr. Brian Shafer, Dr. Mary Gendy, Dr. Scott Takano.
Administrative Assistant, Medical Services: Andrew Otovic.

Player Development
Telephone: (323) 224-1500. **Fax:** (323) 224-1359.
VP, Player Development: De Jon Watson.
Field Coordinator: Bruce Hines. **Senior Advisors to Player Development:** Gene Clines, Charlie Hough. **Senior
Manager, Player Development:** Chris Madden. **Manager, Minor League Administration:** Adriana Urzua. **Assistant,
Player Development:** Alex Romero. **Instructors:** Maury Wills, Ramon Martinez, Rick Rhoden, Tommy Davis. **Coordinators:**
Eric Owens (hitting), Rick Knapp (pitching), Damon Mashore (outfield/baserunning), Juan Castro (infield), Travis Barbary
(catching), Todd Takayoshi (assistant hitting). **Manager, Baseball Operations-Glendale:** Shawn Marette. **Coordinator,
Minor League Video:** Matt Lawrence. **Latin American Field Coordinator:** Jesus Azujae. **Dominican Field Coordinator:**
Kremlin Martinez.

Farm System

Class	Club (League)	Manager	Coach	Pitching Coach
Triple-A	Albuquerque (PCL)	Damon Berryhill	Franklin Stubbs	Glenn Dishman
Double-A	Chattanooga (SL)	Razor Shines	Shawn Wooten	Scott Radinsky
High A	Rancho Cucamonga (CAL)	P.J. Forbes	Mike Eylward	Matt Herges
Low A	Great Lakes (MWL)	Bill Haselman	Johnny Washington	Bill Simas
Rookie	Ogden (PIO)	Jack McDowell	Leo Garcia	Greg Sabat
Rookie	Dodgers (AZL)	John Shoemaker	Henry Cruz	Hector Berrios
Rookie	Dodgers (DSL)	Pedro Mega	Antonio Bautista	Roberto Giron

Scouting
VP, Amateur Scouting: Logan White.
Special Advisor, Amateur Scouting/National Crosschecker: Gib Bodet (San Clemente, CA). **Special Assistant,
Amateur Scouting:** Larry Barton (Leona Valley, CA). **National Crosscheckers:** Roy Clark (Marietta, GA), Paul Fryer
(Calabasas, CA), John Green (Tucson, AZ). **East Regional Supervisor:** Manny Estrada (Longwood, FL). **Midwest Regional
Supervisor:** Gary Nickels (Naperville, IL). **West Regional Supervisor:** Brian Stephenson (Fullerton, CA). **Manager,
Scouting/Travel Administration:** Jane Capobianco. **Coordinator, Scouting:** Trey Magnuson.
Area Scouts: Clint Bowers (Kingwood, TX), Bobby Darwin (Corona, CA), Rich Delucia (Reading, PA), Scott Hennessey
(Ponte Verde, FL), Orsino Hill (Sacramento, CA), Calvin Jones (Highland Village, TX), Henry Jones (Vancouver, WA), Lon
Joyce (Spartanburg, SC), Jeffrey Lachman (Los Angeles, CA), Marty Lamb (Nicholasville, KY), Scott Little (Cape Girardeau,
MO), Dennis Moeller (Simi Valley, CA), Matthew Paul (Pass Christian, MS), Clair Rierson (Wake Forest, NC), Chet Sergo
(Plano, IL), Rob Sidwell (Windermere, FL), Dustin Yount (Phoenix, AZ). **Scouting Consultant:** George Genovese.
VP, Professional Scouting: Rick Ragazzo. **Special Assistants to the GM:** Ken Bracey, Toney Howell. **Assistant,
Baseball Operations:** Kyle Esecson. **Advance Scouts:** Willie Fraser, Gary Pellant. **Professional Scouts:** Josh Bard, Peter
Bergeron, Greg Booker, Scott Groot, Bill Latham, Ron Mahay, Tydus Meadows, Steve Pope, John Sanders, Chris Smith.
VP, Player Personnel: Vance Lovelace. **Special Assistants, Player Personnel:** Rafael Chaves, Aaron Sele, Jose Vizcaino.
VP, International Scouting: Bob Engle. **Senior Manager, International Scouting Operations:** Hidenori Sueyoshi.
Manager, International Scouting: Roman Barinas. **Special Advisor, International Player Performance:** Rafael Colon.
Senior Scouting Advisor, Dominican Republic: Ralph Avila. **Coordinator, Pacific Rim:** Pat Kelly. **Coordinator, Latin
America:** Patrick Guerrero. **Coordinator, International:** Mike Tosar. **Coordinator, Europe:** Gene Grimaldi.
Supervisor, Dominican Republic: Franklin Taveras. **Supervisor, Venezuela:** Pedro Avila. **Assignment Scout, Pacific
Rim:** Jamey Storvick. **International Scouts:** Rolando Chirino (Curacao), Elvio Jimenez (Dominican), Wilton Guerrero
(Dominican), Bienvenido Tavarez (Dominican), Marco Mazzieri (Europe), Isao O'Jimi (Japan), Byung-Hwan An (Korea), Mike
Brito (Mexico), Nemesio Porras (Nicaragua), Luis Molina (Panama), Juan Garcia-Puig (Spain), Jose Briceno (Venezuela),
Francisco Cartaya (Venezuela), Camilo Pascual (Venezuela), Oswaldo Villalobos (Venezuela).

Miami Marlins

Office Address: Marlins Park, 501 Marlins Way, Miami, FL 33125
Telephone: (305) 480-1300. **Fax:** (305) 480-3012.
Website: www.marlins.com.

Ownership
Owner/CEO: Jeffrey H. Loria. **Vice Chairman:** Joel A. Mael.
President: David P. Samson. **Special Assistants to the Owner:** Bill Beck, Jack McKeon. **Special Assistants to the President:** Jeff Conine, Andre Dawson, Tony Perez.

BUSINESS OPERATIONS

Jeffrey Loria

Executive Vice President/Chief Financial Officer: Michel Bussiere. **Executive VP, Operations/Events:** Claude Delorme.
Executive Assistant to Owner/Vice Chairman/President: Beth McConville. **Executive Assistant to the Executive VP/CFO:** Lisa Milk. **Executive Assistant to the Executive VP, Operations/Events:** Teresita Garcia.

Administration
VP, Human Resources: Ana Hernández. **Manager, Human Resources:** Michelle Casanova. **Administrative Coordinator, Human Resources:** Giselle Lopez. **Director, Risk Management:** Fred Espinoza.

Finance
Senior VP, Finance: Susan Jaison. **Controller:** Alina Trigo. **Administrator, Payroll:** Carolina Calderon. **Coordinator, Payroll:** Edgar Perez. **Staff Accountants:** Diana Jorge, Michael Mullane. **Coordinators, Accounts Payable:** Nick Kautz, Anthony Paneque. **Coordinator, Accounting:** John Cantalupo.

Marketing
Senior VP, Marketing/Event Booking: Sean Flynn. **Director, Multicultural Marketing:** Juan Martinez. **Director, Marketing/Promotions:** Matthew Britten. **Manager, Multicultural Marketing:** Darling Jarquin. **Manager, Marketing:** Boris Menier. **Supervisor, Promotions:** Rafael Capdevila.

Legal
Senior VP/General Counsel: Derek Jackson. **Associate Counsel:** Ashwin Krishnan.

Sales/Ticketing
Senior VP, Corporate Partnerships: Brendan Cunningham. **VP, Business Development:** Dale Hendricks. **Director, Corporate Partnerships:** Tony Tome, Michael Meyers. **VP, Sales/Service:** Ryan McCoy. **Director, Director, Ticket Operations:** Mardi Dilger.

Game Presentation/Events/Ballpark Operations
Senior Director, Game Presentation/Events: Larry Blocker. **Director, Engineering:** Randolph Cousar. **Assistant**

2014 SCHEDULE
Standard Game Times: 7:10 p.m.; Sun. 1:10

MARCH			
31 . . . . .Colorado	5-7 . . . . . . .New York (NL)	19-22 . . . . .New York (NL)	8-10 . . . . . .at Cincinnati
	8-11 . . . . . . at San Diego	23-26 . . . . at Philadelphia	11-13 . . . . St. Louis
APRIL	12-14 . at Los Angeles (NL)	27-29 . . . . Oakland	14-17 . . . . .Arizona
1-3 . . . . .Colorado	15-18 . . . at San Francisco		19-20 . . . . Texas
4-6 . . . . San Diego	20-22 . . . . . .Philadelphia	**JULY**	22-24 . . . . . . at Colorado
8-10 . . . . . at Washington	23-25 . . . . . . .Milwaukee	1-3 . . . . . . .Philadelphia	25-27 . at Los Angeles (AL)
11-13 . . . . at Philadelphia	26-28 . . . . at Washington	4-6 . . . . .at St. Louis	29-31 . . . . at Atlanta
14-16 . . . . . . .Washington	30-31 . . . . Atlanta	7-9 . . . . at Arizona	
18-20 . . . . Seattle		11-13 . . . at New York (NL)	**SEPTEMBER**
21-23 . . . . at Atlanta	**JUNE**	18-20 . . . . . San Francisco	1-3 . . . . . . .New York (NL)
25-27 . . . at New York (NL)	1 . . . . Atlanta	21-24 . . . . at Atlanta	5-7 . . . . Atlanta
29-30 . . . . Atlanta	2-3 . . . . .Tampa Bay	25-27 . . . . . .at Houston	8-11 . . . . . at Milwaukee
	4-5 . . . . . . at Tampa Bay	28-30 . . . . . Washington	12-14 . . . . at Philadelphia
MAY	6-8 . . . . . .at Chicago (NL)	31 . . . . Cincinnati	15-17 . . . at New York (NL)
1 . . . . Atlanta	10-11 . . . . .at Texas	**AUGUST**	18-21 . . . . . . Washington
2-4 . . . . .Los Angeles (NL)	13-15 . . . . . Pittsburgh	1-3 . . . . Cincinnati	23-25 . . . . . .Philadelphia
	16-18 . . . . . Chicago (NL)	5-7 . . . . at Pittsburgh	26-28 . . . . at Washington

GENERAL INFORMATION
Stadium (year opened): Marlins Park (2012).
Team Colors: Red-Orange, Yellow, Blue, Black, White.

Player Representative: Steve Cishek.
Home Dugout: Third Base.
Playing Surface: Grass.

Director, Engineering: Chad Messina. VP, Facilities: Jeffrey King. Senior Director, Ballpark Operations: Michael Hurt. Director, Parking: Michael McKeon. Director, Game Services: Antonio Torres-Roman. Associate Counsel/Director, Special Events: Chelsea Hirschhorn.

Communications/Media Relations
Senior Vice President, Communications and Broadcasting: P.J. Loyello. Director, Media Relations: Matt Roebuck. Director, Business Communications: Carolina Perrina de Diego. Manager, Media Relations: Marty Sewell. Supervisor, Media Relations: Joe Vieira. Coordinator, Media Relations: Jon Erik Alvarez. Administrative Assistant: Maria Armella. Director, Broadcasting: Emmanuel Muñoz. Coordinator, Broadcasting: Kyle Sielaff.
Director, Community Outreach: Angela Smith. Director, Creative Services: Alfred Hernandez. VP/Executive Director, Marlins Foundation: Alfredo Mesa. Director, Foundation Partnerships: Joanne Messing.

Travel/Clubhouse
Director, Team Travel: Manny Colon. Equipment Manager: John Silverman. Visiting Clubhouse Manager: Rock Hughes. Assistant, Clubhouse Attendant: Domenic Camarda. Assistant, Clubhouse Attendant: Lou Assalone.

BASEBALL OPERATIONS
Telephone: (305) 480-1300. Fax: (305) 480-3032.
President, Baseball Operations: Michael Hill. VP/General Manager: Dan Jennings.
Executive Assistant to the President, Baseball Operations/VP/GM: Rita Filbert. VP/Assistant GM: Mike Berger. VP, Player Personnel: Craig Weissmann. Senior Advisor to Player Personnel: Orrin Freeman. Director, Baseball Operations: Dan Noffsinger. Director, Team Travel: Manny Colon. Video Coaching Coordinator: Cullen McRae.

Michael Hill

Major League Staff
Manager: Mike Redmond.
Coaches: Bench—Rob Leary; Pitching—Chuck Hernandez, Hitting—Frank Menechino; First Base/Infield—Perry Hill; Third Base—Brett Butler; Bullpen—Reid Cornelius; Bullpen Coordinator—Jeff Urgelles.

Medical/Training
Head Trainer: Sean Cunningham. Assistant Trainers: Mike Kozak, Dustin Luepker. Strength/Conditioning Coach: Ty Hill. Team Psychologist: Robert Seifer.

Player Development
VP, Player Development: Marty Scott. Director, Player Development: Brian Chattin. Assistant Director, Player Development/International Operations: Marc Lippman. Senior Advisor, Player Development: Tommy Thompson. Supervisor, Player Development: Brett West. Minor League Video Coordinator: Dan Budreika.
Field Coordinator: John Pierson. Pitching Coordinator: Wayne Rosenthal. Hitting Coordinator: Jeff Pentland. Infield Coordinator: Jorge Hernandez. Outfield/Baserunning Coordinator: Unavailable. Catching Coordinator: Clint Sammons. Latin Coordinator: Bobby Ramos. Training/Rehab Coordinator: Gene Basham. Strength/Conditioning Coordinator: Mark Brennan. Rehab Coach: Jeff Schwarz. Minor League Equipment/Clubhouse Manager: Mark Brown.

Farm System

Class	Club (League)	Manager	Hitting Coach	Pitching Coach
Triple-A	New Orleans (PCL)	Andy Haines	Damon Minor	Charlie Corbell
Double-A	Jacksonville (SL)	Andy Barkett	Kevin Randel/Rich Arena	John Duffy
High A	Jupiter (FSL)	Brian Schneider	Corey Hart	Joe Coleman
Low A	Greensboro (SAL)	Dave Berg	Frank Moore	Jeremy Powell
Short-season	Batavia (NYP)	Angel Espada	Rigoberto Silverio	Brendan Sagara
Rookie	Marlins (GCL)	Julio Garcia	Lenny Harris/Daniel Santin	Manny Olivera

Scouting
Telephone: (561) 630-1816/Pro (561) 630-1809.
VP, Scouting: Stan Meek. Assistant Director, Scouting: Gregg Leonard. Director, Pro Scouting: Jeff McAvoy. Advance Scout: Joe Moeller (San Clemente, CA). Manager, Amateur Scouting: Michael Youngberg.
Professional Scouts: Pierre Arsenault (Pierrefonds, QC), Brendan Hause (San Diego, CA), Matt Kinzer (Fort Wayne, IN), Benny Latino (Hammond, LA), Dave Roberts (Fort Worth, TX), Phil Rossi (Jessup, PA), Mickey White (Sarasota, FL).
National Crosschecker: David Crowson (College Station, TX). Regional Supervisors: Southeast—Mike Cadahia (Miami, FL); Northeast—Carmen Carcone (Canton, GA); Central—Steve Taylor (Shawnee, OK); West—Scott Goldby (Yuba City, CA); Canada—Steve Payne (Barrington, RI).
Area Scouts: Eric Brock (Indianapolis, IN), Christian Castorri (Dacula, GA), Robby Corsaro (Victorville, CA), Dave Dangler (Tampa, FL), Matt Gaski (Greensboro, NC), John Hughes (Walnut Creek, CA), Brian Kraft (Bixby, OK), Laz Llanes (Miami, FL), Joel Matthews (Concord, NC), Tim McDonnell (Westminster, CA), Bob Oldis (Iowa City, Iowa), Gabe Sandy (Damascus, OR), Scott Stanley (Peoria, AZ), Ryan Wardinsky (The Woodlands, TX), Mark Willoughby (Hammond, LA), Nick Zumsande (Fairfax, IA).
Director, International Operations: Albert Gonzalez. International Supervisors: Sandy Nin (Santo Domingo, Dominican Republic), Wilmer Castillo (Maracay, VZ). International Scouts: Hugo Aquero (Dominican Republic), Carlos Avila (Venezuela), Luis Cordoba (Panama), Edgarluis J Fuentes (Venezuela), Alvaro Julio (Colombia), Alix Martinez (Dominican Republic), Domingo Ortega (Dominican Republic), Robin Ordonez (Venezuela).

Milwaukee Brewers

Office Address: Miller Park, One Brewers Way, Milwaukee, WI 53214.
Telephone: (414) 902-4400. **Fax:** (414) 902-4053.
Website: www.brewers.com.

Ownership
Operated By: Milwaukee Brewers Baseball Club.
Chairman/Principal Owner: Mark Attanasio.

BUSINESS OPERATIONS
Chief Operating Officer: Rick Schlesinger. **Executive Vice President, Finance/Administration:** Bob Quinn. **VP, General Counsel:** Marti Wronski. **VP, Business Operations:** Teddy Werner. **Executive Assistant:** Adela Reeve. **Executive Assistant, Ownership Group:** Samantha Ernest. **Executive Assistant/Paralegal:** Kate Rock.

Finance/Accounting
VP/Controller: Joe Zidanic. **Accounting Director:** Vicki Wise. **Payroll Manager:** Vickie Gowan. **VP, Human Resources/Office Management:** Sally Andrist.
VP, Technology/Information Systems: Nick Watson. **Director, Network Services:** Corey Kmichik. **Manager, Infrastructure/Information Security:** Adam Bauer. **Manager, Baseball Systems Development:** Josh Krowiorz.

Marketing/Corporate Sponsorships

Mark Attanasio

VP, Corporate Marketing: Tom Hecht. **Senior Director, Corporate Marketing:** Andrew Pauls. **Directors, Corporate Marketing:** Jed Justman, Andrew Lukanich. **VP, Consumer Marketing:** Jim Bathey. **Senior Director, Merchandise Branding:** Jill Aronoff. **Senior Director, Marketing:** Kathy Schwab. **Director, Suite Services:** Kristin Loeser. **Coordinator, Marketing/Promotions:** Brittany Luznicky.
VP, Broadcasting/Entertainment: Aleta Mercer. **Director, Audio/Video Productions:** Deron Anderson. **Manager, Entertainment/Broadcasting:** Andrew Olsen. **Coordinators, Audio/Video Production:** Cory Wilson, Matt Morell.

Media Relations/Communications
VP, Communications: Tyler Barnes. **Senior Director, Media Relations:** Mike Vassallo. **Director, New Media:** Caitlin Moyer. **Senior Manager, Media Relations:** John Steinmiller. **Manager, Media Relations:** Ken Spindler. **Publications Assistant:** Robbin Barnes. **Senior Director, Community Relations:** Katina Shaw. **Director, Alumni Relations:** Dave Nelson. **Coordinator, Community Relations:** Erica Bowring. **Executive Director, Brewers Community Foundation:** Cecelia Gore.

Stadium Operations
VP, Stadium Operations: Bob Hallas. **Director, Grounds:** Michael Boettcher. **Supervisor, Warehouse:** Patrick Rogo.
VP, Brewers Enterprises: Jason Hartlund. **Manager, Event Services:** Matt Lehmann. **Senior Manager, Guest Services:** Jennacy Cruz. **Receptionists:** Jody McBee, Susan Ramsdell.

2014 SCHEDULE
Standard Game Times: 7:10 p.m.; Sun. 1:10.

MARCH		
31 . . . . Atlanta	5-7 . . . . Arizona	20-22 . . . . . . at Colorado
	9-11 . . . . . .New York (AL)	23-25 . . . . . Washington
APRIL	13-15 . . . . Pittsburgh	26-29 . . . . .Colorado
1-2 . . . . Atlanta	16-18 . . . .at Chicago (NL)	
4-6 . . . . .at Boston	19-22 . . . . . . at Atlanta	**JULY**
7 . . . . . . at Philadelphia	23-25 . . . . at Miami	1-2 . . . . at Toronto
9-10 . . . . . at Philadelphia	26-28 . . . . . Baltimore	4-6 . . . . . . .at Cincinnati
11-13 . . . . Pittsburgh	30-31 . . . . . Chicago (NL)	7-10 . . . . . .Philadelphia
14-16 . . . . . . St. Louis		11-13 . . . . St. Louis
17-20 . . . . . at Pittsburgh	**JUNE**	18-20 . . . . at Washington
21-23 . . . . San Diego	1 . . . . Chicago (NL)	21-23 . . . . Cincinnati
25-27 . . . . Chicago (NL)	2-3 . . . . Minnesota	24-27 . . . . .New York (NL)
28-30 . . . . . . .at St. Louis	4-5 . . . . at Minnesota	28-30 . . . . . at Tampa Bay
	6-8 . . . . . . at Pittsburgh	
MAY	10-12 . . . at New York (NL)	**AUGUST**
1-4 . . . . .at Cincinnati	13-15 . . . . Cincinnati	1-3 . . . . .at St. Louis
	16-19 . . . . . . at Arizona	5-7 . . . . . . San Francisco
		8-10 . . . . Los Angeles (NL)

11-14 . . . .at Chicago (NL)	
15-17 . at Los Angeles (NL)	
19-20 . . . . .Toronto	
22-24 . . . . . . Pittsburgh	
25-27 . . . . . at San Diego	
29-31 . . . at San Francisco	
SEPTEMBER	
1-3 . . . . . .at Chicago (NL)	
4-7 . . . . St. Louis	
8-11 . . . . Miami	
12-14 . . . . Cincinnati	
16-18 . . . . . . .at St. Louis	
19-21 . . . . . at Pittsburgh	
23-25 . . . . . .at Cincinnati	
26-28 . . . . . Chicago (NL)	

GENERAL INFORMATION
Stadium (year opened): Miller Park (2001).
Team Colors: Navy blue, gold and white.
Player Representative: Unavailable.
Home Dugout: First Base.
Playing Surface: Grass.

Ticketing
Telephone: (414) 902-4000. **Fax:** (414) 902-4056.
Senior Director, Ticket Operations: Regis Bane. **Senior Director, Ticket Sales:** Billy Friess. **Director, Group Ticket Sales:** Chris Barlow. **Administrative Assistant:** Irene Bolton.

BASEBALL OPERATIONS

Telephone: (414) 902-4400. **Fax:** (414) 902-4515.
President, Baseball Operations/General Manager: Doug Melvin.
VP/Assistant GM: Gord Ash. **Special Assistant to GM/Pro Scouting/Player Personnel:** Dick Groch. **Special Assistant to GM:** Craig Counsell.
Senior Director, Baseball Operations: Tom Flanagan. **Director, Video Scouting/Baseball Research for Pro Scouting:** Karl Mueller. **Manager, Advance Scouting/Baseball Research:** Scott Campbell. **Manager/Coaching Assistant/Digital Media Coordinator:** Joe Crawford. **Senior Administrator, Baseball Operations:** Barb Stark. **Senior Director, Team Travel:** Dan Larrea.

Doug Melvin

Major League Staff
Manager: Ron Roenicke.
Coaches: Bench—Jerry Narron; **Pitching**—Rick Kranitz; **Hitting**—Johnny Narron; **First Base**—Garth Iorg; **Third Base**—Ed Sedar; **Bullpen**—Lee Tunnell; **Outfield Coach**—John Shelby; **Infield Coach**—Mike Guerrero.

Medical/Training
Head Team Physician: Dr. William Raasch. **Head Athletic Trainer:** Dan Wright. **Assistant Athletic Trainer:** Dave Yeager. **Strength/Conditioning Specialist:** Josh Seligman. **Director, Medical Operations:** Roger Caplinger.

Player Development
Special Assistant to GM/Director, Player Development/Training Center: Reid Nichols (Phoenix, AZ). **Special Assistant to GM/Baseball Operations:** Dan O'Brien. **Business Manager, Player Development/Minor League Operations:** Scott Martens. **Manager, Administration/Player Development:** Mark Mueller. **Assistant to Director, Staff/Player Development:** Tony Diggs. **Coordinator, Arizona Complex/Video Operations:** Matt Kerls.
Field/Catching Coordinator: Charlie Greene. **Coordinators:** Frank Neville (athletic training), Rick Tomlin (pitching), Jeremy Reed (hitting), Bob Miscik (infield), Mark Dewey (assistant pitching coordinator). **Special Instructor, Player Development:** Don Money.

Farm System

Class	Club (League)	Manager	Coach	Pitching Coach
Triple-A	Nashville (PCL)	Rick Sweet	Bob Skube	Fred Dabney
Double-A	Huntsville (SL)	Carlos Subero	Sandy Guerrero	Chris Hook
High A	Brevard County (FSL)	Joe Ayrault	Ned Yost IV/Reggie Williams	David Chavarria
Low A	Wisconsin (MWL)	Matt Erickson	K. Dominguez/C. Caufield	Elvin Nina
Rookie	Helena (PIO)	Tony Diggs	Jason Dubois	Rolando Valles
Rookie	Brewers (AZL)	Nestor Corredor	Al LeBoeuf	Steve Cline
Rookie	Brewers (DSL)	Jose Pena	Luis De Los Santos	Jose Nunez

Scouting
Telephone: (414) 902-4400. **Fax:** (414) 902-4059.
Director, Professional Scouting: Zack Minasian. **Director, Amateur Scouting:** Bruce Seid. **Assistant Director, Amateur Scouting/Baseball Research:** Tod Johnson. **Manager, Administration/Amateur Scouting:** Amanda Kropp. **Assistant, Pro Scouting:** Ben McDonough.
National Crosschecker: Joe Ferrone (Grosse Pointe, MI). **National Pitching Crosschecker:** Jim Rooney (Oak Park, IL). **Regional Supervisors:** Corey Rodriguez (Palo Verdes Estates, CA), Doug Reynolds (Tallahassee, FL), Tim McIlvaine (Tampa, FL).
Pro Scouts: Lary Aaron (Fayetteville, GA), Brad Del Barba (Fort Mitchell, KY), Bryan Gale (Wayne, PA), Joe Kowal (Yardley, PA), Cory Melvin (Tampa, FL), Ben McLure (Hummelstown, PA), Tom Mooney (Pittsfield, MA), Andy Pratt (Peoria, AZ), Marv Thompson (West Jordan, UT), Ryan Thompson (Scottsdale, AZ), Derek Watson (Chicago, IL), Tom Wheeler (Martinez, CA), Leon Wurth (Paducah, KY).
Area Scouts: Drew Anderson (Waite Park, MN), Josh Belovsky (Orange, CA), Carlos Dominguez (Cary, NC), KJ Hendricks (Arlington, TX), Manolo Hernandez (Puerto Rico), Dan Huston (Westlake Village, CA), Harvey Kuenn, Jr (New Berlin, WI), Justin McCray (Davis, CA), Mark Muzzi (Dallas, TX), Dan Nellum (Crofton, MD), Scott Nichols (Richland, MS), Brian Sankey (The Hills, TX), Jeff Scholzen (Santa Clara, UT), John T. Shelby III (Tampa, FL), Jeff Simpson (Lexington, KY), Steve Smith (Kennesaw, GA), Charles Sullivan (Weston, FL), Shawn Whalen (Vancouver, WA), Steffan Wilson (Wayne, PA).
Supervisor, Canada: Jay Lapp (London, Ontario, Canada).
Part-Time Scouts: John Bushart (Thousand Oaks, CA), Richard Colpaert (Shelby Township, MI), Don Fontana (Pittsburgh, PA), Joe Hodges (Rockwood, TN), Ernie Rogers (Chesapeake, VA), JP Roy (Saint Nicolas, Quebec, Canada), Lee Seid (Henderson, NV), Brad Stoll (Lawrence, KS), Nathan Trosky (Carmel, CA).
Director, Latin America Operations/Scouting: Eduardo Brizuela (Pembroke Pines, FL). **Director, Latin America Scouting:** Manny Batista (Vega Alta, PR). **Latin America Scout Supervisors:** Eduardo Sanchez (Dominican Republic), Fernando Veracierto (Venezuela). **Latin America Scouts:** Julio De La Cruz (Dominican Republic), Reinaldo Hidalgo (Venezuela), Alcides Melendez (Venezuela), Jose Morales (Dominican Republic), Clifford Nuitter (Central America), Jose Ramos (Dominican Republic), Edgar Suarez (Venezuela).

Minnesota Twins

Office Address: Target Field, 1 Twins Way, Minneapolis, MN 55403.
Telephone: (612) 659-3400. **Fax:** 612-659-4025. **Website:** www.twinsbaseball.com.

Ownership
Operated By: The Minnesota Twins.
Chief Executive Officer: Jim Pohlad.
Chairman, Executive Board: Jerry Bell. **Executive Board:** Jim Pohlad, Bob Pohlad, Bill Pohlad, Dave St. Peter.

BUSINESS OPERATIONS
President, Minnesota Twins: Dave St. Peter. **Executive Vice President, Business Development:** Laura Day. **Executive VP, Business Administration/CFO:** Kip Elliott.
Special Assistant to the President/GM: Bill Smith. **Director, Ballpark Development/Planning:** Dan Starkey. **Executive Assistants:** Danielle Berg, Joan Boeser, Lynette Gittins.

Jim Pohlad

Human Resources/Finance/Technology
VP, Human Resources/Diversity: Raenell Dorn. **Director, Payroll:** Lori Beasley. **Director, Benefits:** Leticia Silva. **Human Resources Generalist:** Holly Corbin. **Senior Director, Finance:** Andy Weinstein. **Senior Manager, Ticket Accounting:** Jerry McLaughlin. **Senior Manager, Accounting:** Lori Windschitl. **Senior Manager, Financial Planning/Analysis:** Mike Kramer. **Senior Director, Procurement:** Bud Hanley. **Manager, Procurement:** Mike Sather.
VP, Technology: John Avenson. **Senior Director, Technology:** Wade Navratil.

Marketing
VP, Brand Marketing: Nancy O'Brien. **Senior Manager, Marketing/Promotions Manager:** Julie Okland. **Director, Emerging Markets:** Miguel Ramos. **Director, Productions/Creative Services:** Joe Pohlad. **Senior Manager, Twins Productions:** Sam Henschen. **Manager, Creative Services:** Matt Semke.

Corporate Partnerships
Senior Director, Corporate Partnership: Jeff Jurgella. **Senior Account Executives:** Doug Beck, Karen Cleary, Jordan Woodcroft. **Coordinators, Corporate Client Services:** Kayleen Alexson, Paulette Cheatham, Amelia Johnson, Joe Morin.

Communications
Telephone: (612) 659-3471. **Fax:** (612) 659-4029.
Director, Baseball Communications/Player Relations: Dustin Morse. **Manager, Baseball Communications:** Mitch Hestad. **Coordinator, Publications/Baseball Communications:** Mike Kennedy. **Coordinator, Player Relations/Media Service:** Andrew Heydt. **Senior Director, Corporate Communications/Broadcasting:** Kevin Smith.

Community Relations
Senior Director, Community Affairs: Bryan Donaldson. **Manager, Community Relations:** Stephanie Johnson. **Manager, Community Programs:** Josh Ortiz. **Coordinator, Community Relations:** Gloria Westerdahl.

2014 SCHEDULE
Standard Game Times: 7:10 p.m.; Sun 1:10.

MARCH		
31 . . . . . .at Chicago (AL)		

APRIL		
2-3 . . . . .at Chicago (AL)		
4-6 . . . . . . .at Cleveland		
7 . . . . Oakland		
9-10 . . . . Oakland		
11-13 . . . . . Kansas City		
15-17 . . . . .Toronto		
18-20 . . .at Kansas City		
22-24 . . . at Tampa Bay		
25-27 . . . . Detroit		
29-30 . . . Los Angeles (NL)		

MAY		
1 . . . . . .Los Angeles (NL)		
2-4 . . . . Baltimore		

5-8 . . . . . . .at Cleveland
9-11 . . . . .at Detroit
13-15 . . . . Boston
16-18 . . . . Seattle
20-21 . . . . at San Diego
23-25 . . at San Francisco
26-29 . . . . Texas
30-31 . . . at New York (AL)

JUNE
1 . . . . . . at New York (AL)
2-3 . . . . . . at Milwaukee
4-5 . . . . .Milwaukee
6-8 . . . . Houston
9-11 . . . . .at Toronto
13-15 . . . . . . .at Detroit
16-18 . . . . . . .at Boston
19-22 . . . . Chicago (AL)

24-26 . at Los Angeles (AL)
27-29 . . . . .at Texas
30 . . . . Kansas City

JULY
1-2 . . . . Kansas City
3-6 . . . . . .New York (AL)
7-10 . . . . .at Seattle
11-13 . . . . . . at Colorado
18-20 . . . . . .Tampa Bay
21-23 . . . . . . Cleveland
24-27 . . . . Chicago (AL)
29-31 . . . .at Kansas City

AUGUST
1-3 . . . . . .at Chicago (AL)
5-6 . . . . San Diego
7-10 . . . . .at Oakland

11-13 . . . . . .at Houston
15-18 . . . . . Kansas City
19-21 . . . . . . Cleveland
22-24 . . . . Detroit
26-28 . . . .at Kansas City
29-31 . . . . . .at Baltimore

SEPTEMBER
1 . . . . .at Baltimore
2-3 . . . . . . Chicago (AL)
4-7 . . . . Los Angeles (AL)
9-11 . . . . . .at Cleveland
12-14 . . . .at Chicago (AL)
15-17 . . . . Detroit
19-21 . . . . Cleveland
22-24 . . . . .Arizona
25-28 . . . . .at Detroit

GENERAL INFORMATION
Stadium (year opened): Target Field (2010). **Home Dugout:** First Base.
Team Colors: Red, navy blue and white. **Playing Surface:** Four-way blend
Player Representative: Glen Perkins. of Kentucky Bluegrass.

Ticket Sales/Service

Telephone: 1-800-33-TWINS. **Fax:** (612) 659-4030.
VP, Ticket Sales/Service: Mike Clough. **Director, Suite/Premium Seat Sales/Service:** Scott O'Connell. **Director, Season Sales/Service:** Eric Hudson.

Ticket Operations/Target Field Events

VP, Ticket Operations: Paul Froehle. **Director, Box Office:** Mike Stiles. **Director, Target Field Events/ Tours:** David Christie.

Ballpark Operations

Senior VP, Operations: Matt Hoy. **Senior Director, Ballpark Operations:** Dave Horsman. **Senior Director, Ballpark Systems:** Gary Glawe. **Director, Guest Services:** Patrick Forsland.
Head Groundskeeper: Larry DiVito. **Manager, Grounds:** Al Kuehner. **Manager, Field Maintenance:** Jared Alley. **Senior Manager, Ballpark Maintenance:** Dana Minion. **Senior Manager, Ballpark Operations:** John McEvoy. **Senior Manager, Premium Services:** Jeffrey Kroll. **Manager, Building Security:** Jeff Reardon. **Manager, Event Security:** Dick Dugan. **PA Announcer:** Adam Abrams. **Equipment Manager:** Rod McCormick. **Visitors Clubhouse:** Jason Lizakowski. **Director, Major League Video:** Sean Harlin.

BASEBALL OPERATIONS

Executive VP/General Manager: Terry Ryan
VP, Player Personnel: Mike Radcliff. **VP/Assistant GM:** Rob Antony. **Special Assistant:** Tom Kelly. **Manager, Major League Administration/Baseball Research:** Jack Goin. **Administrative Assistant to the GM:** Lizz Downey. **Director, Team Travel:** Mike Herman. **Baseball Operations Assistant:** Nick Beauchamp. **Coordinator, Baseball Research:** Andrew Ettel.

Major League Staff

Manager: Ron Gardenhire.
Coaches: Bench—Terry Steinbach; **Pitching**—Rick Anderson; **Batting**—Tom Brunansky; **First Base**—Scott Ullger; **Third Base**—Joe Vavra; **Bullpen**—Bobby Cuellar, **Coach**—Paul Molitor.

Terry Ryan

Medical/Training

Club Physicians: Dr. John Steubs, Dr. Vijay Eyunni, Dr. Tom Jetzer, Dr. Jon Hallberg, Dr. Diane Dahm, Dr. Amy Stromwall, Dr. Pearce McCarty, Dr. Rick Aberman. **Head Trainer:** Dave Pruemer. **Assistant Trainers:** Tony Leo, Lanning Tucker. **Strength/Conditioning Coach:** Perry Castellano.

Player Development

Telephone: (612) 659-3480. **Fax:** (612) 659-4026.
Director, Minor League Operations: Brad Steil. **Senior Manager, Minor League Administration:** Kate Townley. **Minor League Coordinators:** Joel Lepel (field), Eric Rasmussen (pitching), Bill Springman (hitting), Sam Perlozzo (infield/baserunning).

Farm System

Class	Club (League)	Manager	Coach	Pitching Coach
Triple-A	Rochester (IL)	Gene Glynn	Tim Doherty	Marty Mason
Double-A	New Britain (EL)	Jeff Smith	Chad Allen	Stu Cliburn
High A	Fort Myers (FSL)	Doug Mientkiewicz	Jim Dwyer	Gary Lucas
Low A	Cedar Rapids (MWL)	Jake Mauer	Tommy Watkins	Ivan Arteaga
Rookie	Elizabethton (APP)	Ray Smith	Unavailable	Henry Bonilla
Rookie	Twins (GCL)	Ramon Borrego	R. Ingram/R. Hernandez	E. Wassermann/L. Rivera
Rookie	Twins (DSL)	Jimmy Alvarez	Ramon Nivar	Manuel Santana
Rookie	Twins (VSL)	Asdrubal Estrada	Pablo Torres	Unavailable

Scouting

Telephone: (612) 659-3491. **Fax:** (612) 659-4026.
Director, Scouting: Deron Johnson.
Coordinator, Professional Scouting: Vern Followell. **Senior Manager, Scouting/International Administration:** Amanda Daley. **Administrative Assistant to Scouting:** Rafael Yanez.
Major League Scouts: Ken Compton, Wayne Krivsky. **Pro Scouts:** Larry Corrigan, Bill Harford, Bob Hegman, Bill Mele, Bill Milos, Earl Winn. **Special Assignment Scout:** Earl Frishman
National Crosschecker: Tim O'Neil. **Scouting Supervisors: East**—Mark Quimuyog; **West**—Sean Johnson; **Southeast**—Billy Corrigan; **Midwest**—Mike Ruth. **Area Scouts:** Trevor Brown (WA), Taylor Cameron (CA), JR DiMercurio (KS), Brett Dowdy (FL), Marty Esposito (TX), John Leavitt (CA), Jeff Pohl (IN), Jack Powell (GA), Greg Runser (TX), Alan Sandberg (TN), Elliott Strankman (CA), Ricky Taylor (NC), Freddie Thon (FL), Jay Weitzel (PA), Ted Williams (AZ), John Wilson (NJ), Mark Wilson (MN).
Coordinator, International Scouting: Howard Norsetter.
Coordinator, Latin American Scouting: Fred Guerrero
International Scouts—Full-Time: Cary Broder (Taiwan), Glenn Godwin (Europe, Africa), David Kim (Pacific Rim), Luis Lajara (Dominican Republic), Jose Leon (Supervisor-Venezuela, Panama), Manuel Luciano (Dominican Republic), Marlon Nava (Venezuela), Eduardo Soriano (Dominican Republic).
International Scouts—Part-Time: Gavin Bennett (South Africa), John Cortese (Italy), Andy Johnson (Europe), Juan Padilla (Venezuela), Franklin Parra (Venezuela), Yan-Yu "Kenny" Su (Taiwan), Koji Takahashi (Japan), Pablo Torres (Venezuela), Lester Victoria (Curacao), Troy Williams (Germany).

New York Mets

Office Address: Citi Field, 126th Street, Flushing, NY 11368.
Telephone: (718) 507-6387. **Fax:** (718) 507-6395.
Website: www.mets.com, www.losmets.com. **Twitter:** @mets, @losmets.

Ownership
Operated By: Sterling Mets LP.
Chairman/Chief Executive Officer: Fred Wilpon. **President:** Saul Katz. **Chief Operating Officer:** Jeff Wilpon. **Board of Directors:** Fred Wilpon, Saul Katz, Jeff Wilpon, Richard Wilpon, Michael Katz, David Katz, Tom Osterman, Steve Greenberg, Stuart Sucherman.

BUSINESS OPERATIONS
Executive Vice President/Chief Revenue Officer: Lou DePaoli. **Executive VP/General Counsel:** David Cohen. **VP/Deputy General Counsel:** Neal Kaplan.

Finance
CFO: Mark Peskin. **VP/Controller:** Len Labita. **Assistant Controller/Director:** John Ventimiglia.

Marketing/Sales
Senior VP, Marketing/Communications: David Newman. **Executive Director, Marketing Productions:** Tim Gunkel. **Senior Director, Marketing:** Mark Fine. **Senior Director, Broadcasting:** Lorraine Hamilton. **Director, Entertainment Marketing/Production:** Vito Vitiello. **Director, Social Media:** Will Carafello. **Director, Marketing:** Jon Kars. **Senior VP, Corporate Sales/Services:** Paul Asencio.

Fred Wilpon

Media Relations
Telephone: (718) 565-4330. **Fax:** (718) 639-3619.
VP, Media Relations: Jay Horwitz. **Senior Director, Media Relations:** Shannon Forde. **Director, Communications:** Danielle Parillo. **Assistant Director, Media Relations:** Ethan Wilson. **Coordinator, Media Relations:** Jonathan Kerber. **Assistant, Media Relations:** Melissa Rodriguez.

Ticketing
Telephone: (718) 507-8499. **Fax:** (718) 507-6369.
VP, Ticket Sales/Services: Leigh Castergine. **Senior Director, Group Sales:** Kirk King. **Senior Director, Season Ticket Account Services:** Jamie Ozure. **Senior Director, Ticket Sales:** Katie Mahon. **Senior Director, Premium Sales:** Roberto Beltramini. **Senior Director, Sales Strategy/Operations:** John Morris. **Director, Ticket Fulfillment/Services:** Jarett Parver. **Director, Ticket Operations:** Michael Berman. **Director, Tickets Sales/Services:** Brian Towers.

Venue Services/Operations
Senior VP, Venue Services/Operations: Mike Landeen. **VP, Metropolitan Hospitality:** Heather Collamore. **Executive**

2014 SCHEDULE
Standard Game Times: 7:10 p.m.; Sun. 1:10.

MARCH	9-11 . . . . . . .Philadelphia	24-25 . . . . Oakland	8-11 . . . . at Philadelphia
31 . . . . Washington	12-13 . . at New York (AL)	26-29 . . . . . at Pittsburgh	12-14 . . . . . Washington
	14-15 . . . . .New York (AL)	30 . . . . at Atlanta	15-18 . . . . . Chicago (NL)
APRIL	16-18 . . . . at Washington		19-20 . . . . . . .at Oakland
2-3 . . . . Washington	20-22 . . . Los Angeles (NL)	**JULY**	22-24 . at Los Angeles (NL)
4-6 . . . . Cincinnati	23-25 . . . . .Arizona	1-2 . . . . at Atlanta	26-28 . . . . Atlanta
8-10 . . . . at Atlanta	26-28 . . . . . . Pittsburgh	4-6 . . . . Texas	29-31 . . . . .Philadelphia
11-13 . at Los Angeles (AL)	29-31 . . . at Philadelphia	7-10 . . . . Atlanta	
14-16 . . . . . . at Arizona		11-13 . . . . .Miami	**SEPTEMBER**
18-20 . . . . Atlanta	**JUNE**	18-20 . . . . at San Diego	1-3 . . . . at Miami
21-24 . . . . St. Louis	1 . . . . . . at Philadelphia	21-23 . . . . . . .at Seattle	4-6 . . . . . . .at Cincinnati
25-27 . . . . .Miami	3-5 . . . . .at Chicago (NL)	24-27 . . . . at Milwaukee	8-10 . . . . .Colorado
29-30 . . . . at Philadelphia	6-8 . . . . at San Francisco	28-30 . . . . .Philadelphia	11-14 . . . . . Washington
	10-12 . . . . . . .Milwaukee		15-17 . . . . .Miami
MAY	13-15 . . . . . . San Diego	**AUGUST**	19-21 . . . . . . at Atlanta
1-4 . . . . . . at Colorado	16-18 . . . . .at St. Louis	1-4 . . . . . .San Francisco	23-25 . . . . . at Nationals
5-7 . . . . at Miami	19-22 . . . . at Miami	5-7 . . . . . at Washington	26-28 . . . . Houston

GENERAL INFORMATION
Stadium (year opened): Citi Field (2009).   **Player Representative:** Unavailable.
Team Colors: Blue and orange.   **Home Dugout:** First Base.
Playing Surface: Grass.

Director, Venue Services: Paul Schwartz. Manager, Venue Services: Taryn Donovan. Director, Sales—Metropolitan Hospitality: Gina Pizzutello. Executive Director, Ballpark Operations: Sue Lucchi. Senior Director, Building Operations: Peter Cassano. Director, Ballpark Operations: Mike Dohnert. Director, Landscaping/Field Operations: Bill Deacon. VP, Technology: Tom Festa. Executive Director, Guest Experience: Chris Brown.

Travel/Clubhouse

Clubhouse Manager: Kevin Kierst. Assistant Equipment Manager: Dave Berni. Visiting Clubhouse Manager: Tony Carullo. Director, Team Travel: Brian Small.

BASEBALL OPERATIONS

Sandy Alderson

Telephone: (718) 803-4013, (718) 565-4339. Fax: (718) 507-6391.
General Manager: Sandy Alderson.
VP/Assistant GM: John Ricco. Special Assistant to GM: J.P. Ricciardi.
Executive Assistant to GM: June Napoli. Director, Baseball Operations: Adam Fisher.
Manager, Baseball Analytics: Ian Levin. Coordinator, Baseball Systems Development: Joe Lefkowitz. Assistant, Baseball Operations: Jeffrey Lebow. Assistant, Advance Scouting: Jim Kelly. Manager, Player Relations: Donovan Mitchell.

Major League Staff

Manager: Terry Collins.
Coaches: Bench—Bob Geren; Pitching—Dan Warthen; Batting—Dave Hudgens; First Base—Tom Goodwin; Third Base—Tim Teufel; Bullpen—Ricky Bones.

Medical/Training

Medical Director: Dr. David Altchek. Physician: Dr. Struan Coleman. Trainer: Ray Ramirez. Assistant Trainer: Brian Chicklo. Strength/Conditioning Coordinator: Jim Malone. Physical Therapist: John Zajac. Massage Therapist: Yoshihiro Nishio.

Player Development

Telephone: (718) 565-4302. Fax: (718) 205-7920.
VP, Scouting/Player Development: Paul DePodesta.
Director, Minor League Operations: Jon Miller. Manager, Minor League Operations/Baseball Information: T.J. Barra. Coordinator, International Operations: Ronny Reyes. Assistant, Minor League Operations: Jennifer Wolf. Director, Player Development: Dick Scott. Coordinator, Instruction/Infield: Kevin Morgan. Hitting Coordinator: Lamar Johnson. Short-Season Hitting Coordinator: Luis Rivera. Pitching Coordinator: Ron Romanick. Short-Season Pitching Coordinator: Miguel Valdes. Catching Coordinator: Bob Natal. Outfield/Baserunning Coordinator: Jack Voigt. Rehab Pitching Coordinator: Jon Debus. Medical Coordinator: Mike Herbst. Rehab/Physical Therapist: Dave Pearson. Strength/Conditioning: Jason Craig. Senior Advisor: Guy Conti. Pitching Consultant: Al Jackson. Special Instructor: Bobby Floyd. International Field Coordinator: Rafael Landestoy. International Catching Instructor: Ozzie Virgil. Equipment/Operations Manager: John Mullin. Director, Latin American Operations: Juan Henderson.

Farm System

Class	Club	Manager	Coach(es)	Pitching Coach
Triple-A	Las Vegas (PCL)	Wally Backman	George Greer	Frank Viola
Double-A	Binghamton (EL)	Pedro Lopez	Luis Natera	Glenn Abbott
High A	St. Lucie (FSL)	Ryan Ellis	Joel Fuentes	Phil Regan
Low A	Savannah (SAL)	Luis Rojas	Val Pascucci	Marc Valdes
Short-season	Brooklyn (NYP)	Unavailable	Benny Distefano	Tom Signore
Rookie	Kingsport (APP)	Jose Leger	Yunir Garcia	Jonathan Hurst
Rookie	Mets (GCL)	Jose Carreno	Ender Chavez	Josh Towers
Rookie	Mets 1 (DSL)	Alberto Castillo	B. Marte/L. Hernandez	Lilian Castro
Rookie	Mets 2 (DSL)	David Davalillo	F. Martinez/M. Martinez	Carlos Capellan

Scouting

Telephone: (718) 565-4311. Fax: (718) 205-7920.
Director, Amateur Scouting: Tommy Tanous. Assistant, Amateur Scouting: Bryan Hayes. Director, Pro Scouting: Jim D'Aloia. Professional Scouts: Bryn Alderson (New York, NY), Mack Babitt (Richmond, CA), Conor Brooks (Plymouth, MA), Thomas Clark (Shrewsbury, MA), Tim Fortugno (Elk Grove, CA), Roland Johnson (Newington, CT), Ashley Lawson (Athens, TN), Shaun McNamara (Worcester, MA), Art Pontarelli (Lincoln, RI), Roy Smith (Chicago, IL), Rudy Terrasas (Santa Fe, TX). Assistant Scouting Director: Marc Tramuta (Fredonia, NY). Regional Supervisors: Southeast—Steve Barningham (Land O'Lakes, FL), West—Doug Thurman (San Jose, CA), Northeast—Marlin McPhail (Irmo, SC), Midwest—Mac Seibert (Cantonment, FL). Area Supervisors: Cesar Aranguren (Clermont, FL), Jim Blueberg (Carson City, NV), Jim Bryant (Macon, GA), Ray Corbett (College Station, TX), Jarrett England (Murfreesboro, TN), Steve Gossett (Fremont, NE), Tyler Holmes (Forest Park, IL), Tommy Jackson (Birmingham, AL), Fred Mazuca (Tustin, CA), Claude Pelletier (St. Lazare, Quebec), Jim Reeves (Camas, WA), Kevin Roberson (Scottsdale, AZ), Max Semler (Allen, TX), Jim Thompson (Philadelphia, PA), Andrew Toussaint (Los Angeles, CA).
Director, International Scouting: Chris Becerra (Ventura, CA). International Crosschecker: Mike Silvestri (Davie, FL). International Supervisors: Gerardo Cabrera (Dominican Republic), Hector Rincones (Venezuela). Crosschecker: Hilario Soriano (Dominican Republic). International Scouts: Modesto Abreu (Dominican Republic), Marciano Alvarez (Dominican Republic), Lionel Chattele (Europe), Alexis De La Cruz (Dominican Republic), Robert Espejo (Venezuela), Harold Herrera (Colombia Supervisor), Gabriel Low (Mexico), Nestor Moreno (Venezuela), Daurys Nin (Dominican Republic), Ismael Perez (Venezuela), Sendly Reina (Curacao), Carlos Perez (Venezuela).

New York Yankees

Office Address: Yankee Stadium, One East 161st St., Bronx, NY 10451.
Telephone: (718) 293-4300. **Fax:** (718) 293-8431.
Website: www.yankees.com, www.yankeesbeisbol.com. **Twitter:** @Yankees, @YankeesPR, @LosYankees.

Ownership
Managing General Partner/Co-Chairperson: Harold Z. (Hal) Steinbrenner. **General Partner/Co-Chairperson:** Henry G. (Hank) Steinbrenner. **General Partner/Vice Chairperson:** Jennifer Steinbrenner Swindal. **General Partner/ Vice Chairperson:** Jessica Steinbrenner. **Vice Chairperson:** Joan Steinbrenner. **Executive Vice President/Chief International Officer:** Felix Lopez.

BUSINESS OPERATIONS
President: Randy Levine, Esq.
Chief Operating Officer/General Counsel: Lonn A. Trost, Esq.
Senior VP, Strategic Ventures: Marty Greenspun. **Senior VP, Chief Security Officer:** Sonny Hight. **Senior VP, Yankee Global Enterprises/CFO:** Anthony Bruno. **Senior VP, Corporate/ Community Relations:** Brian Smith. **Senior VP, Corporate Sales/Sponsorship:** Michael Tusiani. **Senior VP, Marketing:** Deborah Tymon. **VP/Chief Financial Officer, Accounting:** Robert Brown. **VP, Financial Operations:** Scott Krug. **Deputy General Counsel/VP, Legal Affairs:** Alan Chang. **Controller:** Derrick Baio. **VP, Stadium Operations:** Doug Behar.

Harold Steinbrenner

Communications/Media Relations
Telephone: (718) 579-4460. **Fax:** (718) 293-8414.
Director, Communications/Media Relations: Jason Zillo. **Assistant Director, Baseball Information/Public Communications:** Michael Margolis. **Manager, Baseball Information:** Lauren Moran. **Manager, Communications/Media Relations, Yankee Stadium Events:** Kenny Leandry. **Coordinator, Media Services:** Alexandra Trochanowski. **Assistant, Communications/Media Relations:** Justin Long. **Administrative Assistant, Media Relations:** Dolores Hernandez.

Ticket Operations
Telephone: (718) 293-6000. **Fax:** (718) 293-4841.
Senior Director, Ticket Operations: Irfan Kirimca. **Executive Director, Ticket Service/Operations:** Kevin Dart.

2014 SCHEDULE
Standard Game Times: 7:05 p.m.; Sat.-Sun. 1:05.

APRIL
1-3 . . . . at Houston
4-6 . . . . at Toronto
7-9 . . . . Baltimore
10-13 . . . . Boston
15-16 . . . . . Chicago (NL)
17-20 . . . . . at Tampa Bay
22-24 . . . . .at Boston
25-27 . . . Los Angeles (AL)
29-30 . . . . Seattle

MAY
1 . . . . Seattle
2-4 . . . . .Tampa Bay
5-7 . . . at Los Angeles (AL)
9-11 . . . . . at Milwaukee

12-13 . . . . .New York (NL)
14-15 . . at New York (NL)
16-18 . . . . . . Pittsburgh
20-21 . . .at Chicago (NL)
22-25 . . . .at Chicago (AL)
26-28 . . . . . .at St. Louis
30-31 . . . . . . Minnesota

JUNE
1 . . . . Minnesota
3-5 . . . . Oakland
6-9 . . . . . .at Kansas City
10-12 . . . . . . .at Seattle
13-15 . . . . . .at Oakland
17-19 . . . . .Toronto
20-22 . . . . . . Baltimore
23-25 . . . . . . at Toronto

27-29 . . . . Boston
30 . . . . .Tampa Bay

JULY
1-2 . . . . .Tampa Bay
3-6 . . . . . . at Minnesota
7-10 . . . . .at Cleveland
11-13 . . . . . .at Baltimore
18-20 . . . . . Cincinnati
21-24 . . . . Texas
25-27 . . . . .Toronto
28-30 . . . . .at Texas

AUGUST
1-3 . . . . .at Boston
4-7 . . . . Detroit
8-10 . . . . Cleveland

11-13 . . . . . .at Baltimore
15-17 . . . . at Tampa Bay
19-21 . . . . Houston
22-24 . . . . Chicago (AL)
26-28 . . . . . . .at Detroit
29-31 . . . . . . at Toronto

SEPTEMBER
2-4 . . . . Boston
5-7 . . . . Kansas City
9-11 . . . . Tampa Bay
12-14 . . . . . .at Baltimore
15-17 . . . . at Tampa Bay
18-21 . . . . .Toronto
22-25 . . . . . . Baltimore
26-28 . . . . . . .at Boston

GENERAL INFORMATION
Stadium (year opened): Yankee Stadium (2009).
Team Colors: Navy blue and white.
Player Representative: Unavailable.
Home Dugout: First Base.
Playing Surface: Grass.

BASEBALL OPERATIONS

Telephone: (718) 293-4300. **Fax:** (718) 293-0015.
Senior VP/General Manager: Brian Cashman.
Senior VP/Assistant GM: Jean Afterman, Esq. **Assistant GM, Pro Player Personnel:** Billy Eppler. **Senior VP/Special Advisor:** Gene Michael. **Special Advisors:** Yogi Berra, Reggie Jackson. **Special Assistant to the GM:** Stump Merrill.
Director, Quantitative Analysis: Michael Fishman. **Assistant, Baseball Operations:** Steve Martone. **Systems Architect:** Brian Nicosia. **Coordinator, Baseball Operations:** Stephen Swindal Jr. **Analysts, Baseball Operations:** David Grabiner, Jim Logue, Alex Rubin. **Administrative Assistant:** Mary Pellino.
Director, Mental Conditioning: Chad Bohling. **Coordinator, Mental Conditioning:** Chris Passarella.

Brian Cashman

Major League Staff

Manager: Joe Girardi.
Coaches: Bench—Tony Pena; **Pitching**—Larry Rothschild; **Batting**—Kevin Long; **First Base**—Mick Kelleher; **Third Base**—Rob Thomson; **Bullpen**—Gary Tuck; **Bullpen Catcher**—Roman Rodriguez.

Medical/Training

Team Physician, New York: Dr. Christopher Ahmad.
Head Athletic Trainer: Steve Donohue. **Assistant Athletic Trainer:** Mark Littlefield. **Strength/Conditioning Coordinator:** Matthew Krause. **Assistant Athletic Trainer/Physical Therapist:** Michael Schuk.

Player Development

Senior Vice President, Baseball Operations: Mark Newman.
Director, Player Personnel: John Kremer. **Director, Player Development:** Pat Roessler. **Hitting Coordinator:** James Rowson. **Special Assistant, Major/Minor League Operations:** Trey Hillman. **Assistant Director, Baseball Operations:** Billy Hart. **Assistants, Baseball Operations:** Yunior Tabares, Leonel Vinas. **Analyst, Baseball Operations:** Scott Benecke. **Administrative Assistant:** Jackie Williams. **Senior Pitching Instructors:** Nardi Contreras, Greg Pavlik. **Pitching Coordinator:** Gil Patterson. **Hitting Instructor:** Tom Slater. **Field Coordinator:** Jody Reed. **Infield Coordinator:** Carlos Mendoza. **Catching Coordinator:** Julio Mosquera. **Outfield/Baserunning Coordinator:** Mike Quade. **Head Athletic Trainer, Player Development:** Tim Lentych. **Strength/Conditioning Coordinator:** Mike Kicia.
Medical Coordinator, Player Development/Scouting: Mike Wickland. **Equipment Manager, Player Development:** David Hays. **Clubhouse Manager, Player Development:** Chris Root.

Farm System

Class	Club (League)	Manager	Hitting Coach	Pitching Coach
Triple-A	Scranton/WB (IL)	Dave Miley	Butch Wynegar	Scott Aldred
Double-A	Trenton (EL)	Tony Franklin	Marcus Thames	Tommy Phelps
High A	Tampa (FSL)	Al Pedrique	PJ Pilittere	Danny Borrell
Low A	Charleston (SAL)	Luis Dorante	Edwar Gonzalez	Carlos Chantres
Short-season	Staten Island (NYP)	Mario Garza	Ty Hawkins	Tim Norton
Rookie	Yankees I (GCL)	Travis Chapman	Caonabo Cosme	Cory Arbiso
Rookie	Yankees II (GCL)	Patrick Osborn	Drew Henson	Jose Rosado
Rookie	Yankees I (DSL)	Raul Dominguez	Roy Gomez	Gabriel Tatis
Rookie	Yankees II (DSL)	Sonder Encarnacion	Edwin Beard	Gerardo Casadiego

Scouting

Telephone: (813) 875-7569. **Fax:** (813) 873-2302.
VP, Amateur Scouting: Damon Oppenheimer.
Assistant Director, Amateur Scouting: Eric Schmitt. **Manager, Professional Scouting:** Will Kuntz. **Professional Scouts:** Joe Caro, Kendall Carter, Jay Darnell, Dave DeFreitas, Gary Denbo, Bill Emslie, Abe Flores, Jalal Leach, Pete MacKanin, Bill Mele, Bob Miske, Tim Naehring, Greg Orr, Josh Paul, Kevin Reese, Dennis Twombley, Rick Williams, Tom Wilson. **Special Assignment Scout:** Jim Hendry. **Pitching Analyst:** Scott Lovekamp.
Amateur Scouting, National Crosscheckers: Brian Barber, Tim Kelly, Jeff Patterson, D.J. Svihlik. **Area Scouts:** Troy Afenir (Escondido, CA), Denis Boucher (Montreal), Steve Breen (Glen Ellyn, IL), Andy Cannizaro (Mandeville, LA), Adam Czajkowski (Tampa, FL), Jeff Deardorff (Clermont, FL), Bobby DeJardin (San Clemente, CA), Phil Geisler (Mount Horeb, WI), Mike Gibbons (Liberty Township, OH), Matt Hyde (Canton, MA), Dave Keith (Anaheim, CA), Steve Kmetko (Phoenix, AZ), Steve Lemke (Geneva, IL), Mike Leuzinger (Canton, TX), David List, Carlos Marti (Miramar, FL), Oscar Martinez (Guanica, Puerto Rico), Darryl Monroe (Decatur, GA), Bill Pintard (Carpinteria, CA), Cesar Presbott (Bronx, NY), Matt Ranson (Topeka, KS), Brian Rhees (Live Oak, TX), Stewart Smothers (Los Angeles, CA), Mike Thurman (West Linn, OR).
Coordinator, International Player Development: Pat McMahon. **Assistant Director, International Operations:** Alex Cotto. **Director, Latin Baseball Academy:** Joel Lithgow. **Manager, Latin Baseball Academy:** Aniuska Sanchez. **Cultural Development Coordinator:** Hector Gonzalez. **Director, International Scouting:** Donny Rowland. **International Crosscheckers:** Dennis Woody, Steve Wilson, Gordon Blakeley. **Latin American Crosscheckers:** Victor Mata, Ricardo Finol. **Supervisor, Dominican Republic:** Raymon Sanchez. **Scouting Development Coaches:** Luis Brito, Francisco Santana. **Dominican Republic Scouts:** Esteban Castillo, Raymi Dicent, Arturo Pena, Juan Rosario, Jose Sabino. **Venezuela Scouts:** Alan Atacho, Darwin Bracho, Roney Calderon, Jose Gavidia, Borman Landaeta, Cesar Suarez. **Mexico Scouts:** Lee Sigman, Leobardo Figueroa, Humberto Soto. **International Scouts:** Carlos Levy (Panama), Edgar Rodriguez (Nicaragua), Luis Sierra (Colombia), Ken Su (Taiwan), Ji-Eun Lee (Korea), John Wadsworth (Australia), Doug Skiles (Europe, Netherland Antilles).

Oakland Athletics

Office Address: 7000 Coliseum Way, Oakland, CA 94621.
Telephone: (510) 638-4900. **Fax:** (510) 562-1633. **Website:** www.oaklandathletics.com.

Ownership
Owner/Managing Partner: Lew Wolff.

BUSINESS OPERATIONS
President: Michael Crowley. **Vice President, Venue Development:** Keith Wolff. **Executive Assistant:** Carolyn Jones. **General Counsel:** Neil Kraetsch. **Senior Counsel:** Ryan Horning.

Finance/Administration
Vice President, Finance: Paul Wong. **Senior Director, Finance:** Kasey Jarcik. **Accounting Manager:** Ling Ding. **Payroll Manager:** Rose Dancil. **Senior Accountant, Accounts Payable:** Isabelle Mahaffey.

Director, Human Resources: Kim Kubo. **Human Resources Assistant:** Erica Sahli. **Director, Information Technology:** Nathan Hayes. **IT Manager:** David Frieberg. **Desktop Administrator:** Chris Jio. **Office Services Coordinator:** Julie Vasconcellos. **Executive Offices Receptionist:** Maggie Baptist.

Lew Wolff

Sales/Marketing
VP, Sales/Marketing: Jim Leahey. **Assistant, Sales/Marketing:** Sarina Madnick. **Senior Director, Marketing:** Troy Smith. **Senior Manager, Digital Marketing:** Travis LoDolce. **Manager, Advertising/ Marketing:** Amy MacEwen. **Creative Services Manager:** Mike Ono. **Advertising Assistant:** Jessica Christian. **Senior Director, Corporate Partnerships:** Steve Pastorino. **Director, Partnership Services:** Franklin Lowe. **Senior Account Manager, Corporate Partnerships:** Jill Golden. **Corporate Account Manager:** Jessica Scott. **Corporate Service Assistant:** Mitch Tom. **Senior Manager, Promotion/Events:** Heather Rajeski. **Special Events Coordinator:** Sandy Karbel.

Public Relations/Communications
VP, Communications/Broadcasting: Ken Pries. **Director, Public Relations:** Bob Rose. **Baseball Information Manager:** Mike Selleck. **Media Services Manager:** Debbie Gallas. **Manager, Player/Media Relations:** Adam Loberstein. **Coordinator, Media Relations/Broadcasting:** Zak Basch. **Team Photographer:** Michael Zagaris.

Director, Community Relations: Detra Paige. **Coordinator, Community Relations:** Melissa Guzman. **Manager, Authentication:** Erik Farrell. **Senior Director, Multimedia Services:** David Don. **Stadium Entertainment Production Manager:** Matt Shelton. **Multimedia Services Manager:** Jon Martin. **Public Address Announcer:** Dick Callahan.

Stadium Operations
VP, Stadium Operations: David Rinetti. **Senior Director, Stadium Operations:** Paul La Veau. **Senior Manager, Stadium Operations Events:** Kristy Ledbetter. **Stadium Services Manager:** Randy Duran. **Guest Services Manager:** Whitney Smith.

2014 SCHEDULE
Standard Game Times: 7:05 p.m.; Sat./Sun. 1:05.

MARCH		
31 . . . . Cleveland		

APRIL		
1-2 . . . . Cleveland		
3-6 . . . . Seattle		
7 . . . . at Minnesota		
9-10 . . . . . at Minnesota		
11-13 . . . . . . .at Seattle		
14-16 . at Los Angeles (AL)		
18-20 . . . . Houston		
21-23 . . . . Texas		
24-27 . . . . . .at Houston		
28-30 . . . . .at Texas		

MAY		
2-4 . . . . .at Boston		

| 5-7 . . . . Seattle |
| 9-11 . . . . . . Washington |
| 12-14 . . . . . Chicago (AL) |
| 16-18 . . . . . .at Cleveland |
| 20-22 . . . . . at Tampa Bay |
| 23-25 . . . . . at Toronto |
| 26-29 . . . . Detroit |
| 30-31 . . . Los Angeles (AL) |

JUNE
1 . . . . . . Los Angeles (AL)
3-5 . . . . at New York (AL)
6-8 . . . . . . .at Baltimore
9-11 . . at Los Angeles (AL)
13-15 . . . . .New York (AL)
16-18 . . . . Texas
19-22 . . . . Boston

| 24-25 . . at New York (NL) |
| 27-29 . . . . at Miami |
| 30 . . . . .at Detroit |

JULY
1-2 . . . . .at Detroit
3-6 . . . . .Toronto
7-8 . . . . . . San Francisco
9-10 . . . . at San Francisco
11-13 . . . . .at Seattle
18-20 . . . . . . Baltimore
22-24 . . . . Houston
25-27 . . . . .at Texas
28-30 . . . . . .at Houston

AUGUST
1-3 . . . . Kansas City
4-6 . . . . .Tampa Bay

| 7-10 . . . . Minnesota |
| 11-14 . . . . .at Kansas City |
| 15-17 . . . . . . at Atlanta |
| 19-20 . . . . .New York (NL) |
| 22-24 . . Los Angeles (AL) |
| 25-27 . . . . .at Houston |
| 28-31 . at Los Angeles (AL) |

SEPTEMBER
1-3 . . . . Seattle
5-7 . . . . Houston
8-11 . . . . .at Chicago (AL)
12-14 . . . . .at Seattle
16-18 . . . . Texas
19-21 . . . . .Philadelphia
22-24 . . Los Angeles (AL)
25-28 . . . . .at Texas

GENERAL INFORMATION
Stadium (year opened): O.co Coliseum (1968). **Team Colors:** Kelly green and gold.

Player Representative: Unavailable. **Home Dugout:** Third Base. **Playing Surface:** Grass.

Ticket Sales/Operations/Services
 Executive Director, Ticket Sales/Operations: Steve Fanelli. **Senior Director, Ticket Services:** Josh Ziegenbusch. **Director, Ticket Operations:** David Adame. **Ticket Services Manager:** Catherine Glazier. **Suite Services Manager:** Moti Bycel. **Premium Services Manager:** David King. **Ticket Operations Manager:** Anuj Patel.
 Director, Ticket Sales: Brian DiTucci. **Manager, Group Sales:** Josh Feinberg. **Manager, Season Ticket Sales:** Aaron Dragomir. **Manager, Inside Sales:** Aaron Dragomir.

Travel/Clubhouse
 Director, Team Travel: Mickey Morabito. **Equipment Manager:** Steve Vucinich. **Visiting Clubhouse Manager:** Mike Thalblum. **Assistant Equipment Manager:** Brian Davis. **Umpire/Clubhouse Assistant:** Matt Weiss. **Arizona Clubhouse Manager:** James Gibson. **Arizona Assistant Clubhouse Managers:** Thomas Miller, Chad Yaconetti.

BASEBALL OPERATIONS

 VP/General Manager: Billy Beane.
 Assistant GM: David Forst. **Director, Baseball Operations:** Farhan Zaidi. **Director, Pro Scouting/Baseball Development:** Dan Feinstein. **Director, Player Personnel:** Billy Owens. **Special Assistants to GM:** Grady Fuson, Chris Pittaro. **Executive Assistant:** Betty Shinoda. **Director, Baseball Administration:** Pamela Pitts. **Video Coordinator:** Adam Rhoden. **Special Assistant to Baseball Operations:** Scott Hatteberg. **Architect/Baseball Systems:** Rob Naberhaus. **Baseball Operations Analyst:** Michael Schatz.

Major League Staff
 Manager: Bob Melvin.
 Coaches: Bench—Chip Hale; **Pitching**—Curt Young; **Batting**—Chili Davis; **First Base**—Tye Waller; **Third Base**—Mike Gallego; **Bullpen**—Darren Bush. **Coach**—Ariel Prieto.

Billy Beane

Medical/Training
 Head Athletic Trainer: Nick Paparesta. **Assistant Athletic Trainers:** Walt Horn, Brian Schulman. **Strength/ Conditioning Coach:** Michael Henriques. **Major League Massage Therapist:** Ozzie Lyles. **Team Physicians:** Dr. Allan Pont, Dr. Elliott Schwartz. **Team Orthopedist:** Dr. Jon Dickinson. **Associate Team Orthopedist:** Dr. Will Workman. **Arizona Team Physicians:** Dr. Fred Dicke, Dr. Doug Freedberg.

Player Development
 Telephone: (510) 638-4900. **Fax:** (510) 563-2376.
 Director, Player Development: Keith Lieppman. **Director, Minor League Operations:** Ted Polakowski. **Administrative Assistant, Player Development:** Valerie Vander Heyden. **Minor League Roving Instructors:** Juan Navarrete (infield), Scott Emerson (pitching), Marcus Jensen (hitting). **Minor League Video Coordinator:** Mark Smith. **Minor League Medical Coordinator:** Jeff Collins. **Coordinator, Medical Services:** Larry Davis. **Minor League Strength/ Conditioning Coordinator:** Josh Cutte. **Minor League Strength/Conditioning Assistant Coordinator:** Sean Doran. **Special Instructor, Pitching/Rehabilitation:** Garvin Alston. **Minor League Rehabilitation Coordinator:** Nate Brooks.

Farm System

Class	Club (League)	Manager	Coach	Pitching Coach
Triple-A	Sacramento (PCL)	Steve Scarsone	Greg Sparks	Rick Rodriguez
Double-A	Midland (TL)	Aaron Nieckula	Webster Garrison	Don Schulze
High A	Stockton (CAL)	Ryan Christenson	Brian McArn	John Wasdin
Low A	Beloit (MWL)	Rick Magnante	Lloyd Turner	Craig Lefferts
Short-season	Vermont (NYP)	David Newhan	Tommy Everidge	Steve Connelly
Rookie	Athletics (AZL)	Ruben Escalera	Juan Dilone	Carlos Chavez
Rookie	Athletics (DSL)	Carlos Casimiro	Rahdames Perez	Gabriel Ozuna

Scouting
 Telephone: (510) 638-4900. **Fax:** (510) 563-2376.
 Director, Scouting: Eric Kubota (Rocklin, CA).
 Assistant Director, Scouting: Michael Holmes (Winston Salem, NC). **Director, Pro Scouting/Baseball Development:** Dan Feinstein (Lafayette, CA). **Scouting Assistant:** Kate Greenthal (San Francisco, CA). **West Coast Supervisor:** Scott Kidd (Folsom, CA). **Midwest Supervisor:** Ron Marigny (Cypress, TX). **East Coast Supervisor:** Marc Sauer (Tampa, FL). **Northeast Supervisor:** Sean Rooney (Apex, NC). **Pro Scouts:** Jeff Bittiger (Saylorsburg, PA), Dan Freed (Lexington, IL), John McLaren (Peoria, AZ), Will Schock (Oakland, CA), Steve Sharpe (Kansas City, MO), Tom Thomas (Phoenix, AZ), Mike Ziegler (Orlando, FL).
 Area Scouts: Neil Avent (Greensboro, NC), Yancy Ayres (Topeka, KS), Armann Brown (Houston, TX), Jermaine Clark (Discovery Bay, CA), Jim Coffman (Portland, OR), Ruben Escalera (Carolina, PR), Matt Higginson (Burlington, ON), , Eric Martins (Diamond Bar, CA), Kevin Mello (Chicago, IL), Kelcey Mucker (Baton Rouge, LA), Trevor Ryan (Tempe, AZ), Trevor Schaffer (Belleair, FL), Rich Sparks (Sterling Heights, MI), Jemel Spearman (Lithonia, GA), JT Stotts (Moorpark, CA), Ron Vaughn (Windsor, CT).
 Director, Latin American Operations: Raymond Abreu (Santo Domingo, DR). **Coordinator, International Scouting:** Sam Geaney (Oakland, CA). **Coordinator, Latin American Scouting:** Julio Franco (Carrizal, VZ).
 International Scouts: Ruben Barradas (Venezuela), Juan Carlos De La Cruz (Dominican Republic), Angel Eusebio (Dominican Republic), Andri Garcia (Venezuela), Adam Hislop (Taiwan), Lewis Kim (South Korea), Pablo Marmol (Dominican Republic), Juan Mosquera (Panama), Tito Quintero (Colombia), Amaurys Reyes (Dominican Republic), Oswaldo Troconis (Venezuela), Juan Villanueva (Venezuela).

Philadelphia Phillies

Office Address: Citizens Bank Park, One Citizens Bank Way, Philadelphia, PA 19148.
Telephone: (215) 463-6000. **Website:** www.phillies.com.

Ownership
Operated By: The Phillies.
President/CEO: David Montgomery. **Chairman:** Bill Giles.

BUSINESS OPERATIONS

Vice President/General Counsel: Rick Strouse. **VP, Phillies Enterprises:** Richard Deats. **VP, Employee/Customer Services:** Kathy Killian. **Director, Ballpark Enterprises/Business Development:** Joe Giles. **Director, Information Systems:** Brian Lamoreaux. **Director, Employee Benefits/Services:** JoAnn Marano.

Ballpark Operations
Senior VP, Administration/Operations: Michael Stiles. **Director, Operations/Facility:** Mike DiMuzio. **Director, Operations/Events:** Eric Tobin. **Director, Operations/Security:** Sal DeAngelis. **Manager, Concessions Development:** Bruce Leith. **Head Groundskeeper:** Mike Boekholder. **PA Announcer:** Dan Baker. **Official Scorers:** Jay Dunn, Mike Maconi, Joseph Bellina.

David Montgomery

Communications
Telephone: (215) 463-6000. **Fax:** (215) 389-3050.
VP, Communications: Bonnie Clark. **Director, Baseball Communications:** Greg Casterioto. **Coordinator, Baseball Communications:** Craig Hughner. **Communications Assistant:** Deanna Sabec. **Baseball Communications Assistant:** Chris Ware.

Finance
VP/CFO: John Nickolas. **Director, Payroll Services:** Karen Wright.

Marketing/Promotions
Senior VP, Marketing/Sales: David Buck. **Manager, Client Services/Alumni Relations:** Debbie Nocito. **Director, Corporate Partnerships:** Rob MacPherson. **Director, Advertising Sales:** Brian Mahoney. **Director, Corporate Sales:** Scott Nickle. **Manager, Advertising Sales:** Tom Sullivan.
Director, Marketing Programs/Events: Kurt Funk. **Director, Entertainment:** Chris Long. **Manager, Broadcasting:** Rob Brooks. **Manager, Advertising/Internet Services:** Jo-Anne Levy-Lamoreaux.

Sales/Tickets
Telephone: (215) 463-1000. **Fax:** (215) 463-9878.
VP, Sales/Ticket Operations: John Weber. **Director, Ticket Department:** Dan Goroff. **Director, Ticket Technology/Development:** Chris Pohl. **Director, Season Ticket Sales:** Derek Schuster. **Manager, Suite Sales/Services:** Tom Mashek.

2014 SCHEDULE

Standard Game Times: 7:05 p.m.; Sun. 1:35

MARCH			
31 . . . . .at Texas	5-6 . . . . .Toronto	19-22 . . . . . .at St. Louis	8-11 . . . . at New York (NL)
	7-8 . . . . at Toronto	23-26 . . . . .Miami	12-13 . at Los Angeles (AL)
APRIL	9-11 . . . at New York (NL)	27-29 . . . . Atlanta	15-17 . . . at San Francisco
1-2 . . . . .at Texas	13-14 . . . Los Angeles (AL)		18-20 . . . . Seattle
4-6 . . . . . .at Chicago (NL)	16-18 . . . . . . Cincinnati	**JULY**	22-24 . . . . St. Louis
7 . . . . .Milwaukee	20-22 . . . . . . at Miami	1-3 . . . . at Miami	25-27 . . . . . Washington
9-10 . . . . . . .Milwaukee	23-25 . . . Los Angeles (NL)	4-6 . . . . at Pittsburgh	29-31 . . . at New York (NL)
11-13 . . . . Miami	26-28 . . . . Colorado	7-10 . . . . . at Milwaukee	
14-17 . . . . Atlanta	29-31 . . . .New York (NL)	11-13 . . . . Washington	**SEPTEMBER**
18-20 . . . . . at Colorado		18-20 . . . . . . at Atlanta	1-3 . . . . at Atlanta
21-24 . at Los Angeles (NL)	**JUNE**	21-24 . . . San Francisco	5-7 . . . . . at Washington
25-27 . . . . . . at Arizona	1 . . . . . . .New York (NL)	25-27 . . . . .Arizona	8-11 . : . . . . . . Pittsburgh
29-30 . . . .New York (NL)	3-5 . . . . . at Washington	28-30 . . . at New York (NL)	12-14 . . . . .Miami
	6-8 . . . . . . .at Cincinnati	31 . . . . . . at Washington	15-18 . . . at San Diego
MAY	10-12 . . . . . . San Diego		19-21 . . . . . .at Oakland
2-4 . . . . Washington	13-15 . . . . . Chicago (NL)	**AUGUST**	23-25 . . . . at Miami
	16-18 . . . . . . at Atlanta	1-3 . . . . . . at Washington	26-28 . . . . Atlanta
		5-7 . . . . Houston	

GENERAL INFORMATION

Stadium (year opened): Citizens Bank Park (2004).
Team Colors: Red, white and blue.

Player Representative: Unavailable.
Home Dugout: First Base.
Playing Surface: Natural Grass.

Director, Ticket Services/Intern Program: Phil Feather. **Manager, Season Ticket Services:** Mike Holdren.

Travel/Clubhouse
Director, Team Travel/Clubhouse Services: Frank Coppenbarger.
Manager, Visiting Clubhouse: Kevin Steinhour. **Manager, Home Clubhouse:** Phil Sheridan. **Manager, Equipment/Umpire Services:** Dan O'Rourke.

BASEBALL OPERATIONS

Senior VP/General Manager: Ruben Amaro Jr.
Senior Advisor to the President/GM: Pat Gillick. **Assistant GM:** Scott Proefrock. **Assistant GM, Player Personnel:** Benny Looper. **Senior Advisor to GM:** Dallas Green. **Senior Advisor to GM:** Charlie Manuel. **Special Assistants to GM:** Bart Braun, Charley Kerfeld. **Special Consultant, Baseball Operations:** Ed Wade. **Director, Baseball Administration:** Susan Ingersoll Papaneri. **Director, Professional Scouting:** Mike Ondo. **Baseball Information Analyst:** Jay McLaughlin. **Manager, Baseball Analytics:** Scott Freedman. **Administrative Assistant, Baseball Operations:** Adele MacDonald. **Baseball Operations Representative:** Chris Cashman.

Ruben Amaro Jr.

Major League Staff
Manager: Ryne Sandberg.
Coaches: Bench—Larry Bowa; **Pitching**—Bob McClure; **Hitting**—Steve Henderson; **First Base**—Juan Samuel; **Third Base**—Pete Mackanin; **Assistant Hitting**—John Mizerock; **Bullpen**—Rod Nichols; **Bullpen Catcher**—Jesus Tiamo.

Medical/Training
Director, Medical Services: Dr. Michael Ciccotti. **Head Athletic Trainer:** Scott Sheridan. **Assistant Athletic Trainer:** Shawn Fcasni. **Strength/Conditioning Coordinator:** Paul Fournier. **Manual Therapy Specialist:** Ichiro Kitano. **Employee Assistance Professional:** Dickie Noles.

Player Development
Telephone: (215) 463-6000. **Fax:** (215) 755-9324.
Assistant GM, Player Personnel: Benny Looper. **Director, Player Development:** Joe Jordan.
Director, Minor League Operations: Lee McDaniel. **Assistant Director, Player Development:** Steve Noworyta. **Special Assistant, Player Personnel:** Jorge Velandia. **Director, Florida Operations/GM. Clearwater Threshers:** John Timberlake. **Assistant Director, Minor League Operations/Florida Operations:** Joe Cynar. **Coordinator, International Operations:** Ray Robles.
Field Coordinator: Doug Mansolino. **Senior Advisor, Player Development:** Mike Compton. **Assistant Field Coordinator/Hitting:** Andy Tracy. **Pitching Coordinator:** Carlos Arroyo. **Infield Coordinator:** Chris Truby. **Outfield/base running:** Andy Abad. **Catching:** Ernie Whitt. **Athletic Trainer coordinator:** James Ready. **Strength/Conditioning Coordinator:** Jason Meredith.

Farm System

Class	Club (League)	Manager	Coach	Pitching Coach
Triple-A	Lehigh Valley (IL)	Dave Brundage	Sal Rende/Mickey Morandini	Ray Burris
Double-A	Reading (EL)	Dusty Wathan	Rob Ducey	Dave Lundquist
High A	Clearwater (FSL)	Ramon Henderson	Frank Cacciatore	Bob Milacki
Low A	Lakewood (SAL)	Greg Legg	Lino Connell	Les Lancaster
Short-season	Williamsport (NYP)	Nelson Prada	Shawn Williams	Aaron Fultz
Rookie	Clearwater (GCL)	Roly DeArmas	Rafael DeLima	Steve Schrenk
Rookie	Phillies (DSL)	Manny Amador	L. Garcia/C. Henriquez	Alex Conception
Rookie	Phillies (VSL)	Trino Aguilar	S. Navas/H. Ovalles	Les Straker

Scouting
Assistant GM, Amateur Scouting: Marti Wolever (Scottsdale, AZ).
Director, Amateur Scouting Administration: Rob Holiday (Philadelphia, PA). **Coordinators, Scouting:** Mike Ledna (Arlington Heights, IL), Bill Moore (Alta Loma, CA).
Regional Supervisors: Gene Schall (Mid-Atlantic/Harleysville, PA), Eric Valent (Southeast/Wernersville, PA), Scott Trcka (Central/Hobart, IN), Darrell Conner (West/Riverside, CA).
Area Scouts: Alex Agostino (Quebec), Shane Bowers (La Verne, CA), Steve Cohen (Spring, TX), Joey Davis (Rocklin, CA), Nate Dion (West Chester, OH), Mike Garcia (Moreno Valley, CA), Brad Holland (Gilbert, AZ), Eric Jacques (Bellevue, WA), Aaron Jersild (Alpharetta, GA), Brian Kohlscheen (Norman, OK), Alan Marr (Sarasota, FL), Paul Murphy (Wilmington, DE), Demerius Pittman (Corona, CA), Paul Scott (Rockwall, TX), David Seifert (Paw Paw, IL), Mike Stauffer (Brandon, MS).
Director International Scouting: Sal Agostinelli (Kings Park, NY). **International Scouts:** Norman Anciani (Panama), Rafael Alvarez (Venezuela), Nathan Davison (Australia), Franklin Felida (Dominican Republic), Tomas Herrera (Mexico), Andres Hiraldo (Dominican Republic), Ferenc Jongejan (Netherlands), Gregory Manuel (Aruba), Jesus Mendez (Venezuela), Jairo Morelos (Colombia), Romulo Oliveros (Venezuela), Bernardo Perez (Dominican Republic), Carlos Salas (Dominican Republic), Claudio Scerrato (Italy), Darryn Smith (South Africa), Everth Valazuez (Venezuela).
Director, Major League Scouting: Gordon Lakey (Barker, TX). **Special Assignment Scouts:** Howie Frieling (Apex, NC), Dave Hollins (Orchard Park, NY). **Major League Advance Scout:** Craig Colbert (Portland, OR). **Professional Scouts:** Sonny Bowers (Hewitt, TX), Steve Jongewaard (Napa, CA), Jesse Levis (Fort Washington, PA), Jon Mercurio (Coraopolis, PA), Roy Tanner (Palatka , FL), Del Unser (Scottsdale, AZ), Dan Wright (Cave Springs, AR).

Pittsburgh Pirates

Office Address: PNC Park at North Shore, 115 Federal St., Pittsburgh, PA, 15212.
Mailing Address: PO Box 7000, Pittsburgh, PA 15212.
Telephone: (412) 323-5000. **Fax:** (412) 325-4412. **Website:** www.pirates.com. **Twitter:** @Pirates.

Ownership
Chairman of the Board: Robert Nutting.
Board of Directors: Donald Beaver, Eric Mauck, G. Ogden Nutting, Robert Nutting, William Nutting, Duane Wittman.

BUSINESS OPERATIONS
President: Frank Coonelly. **Executive Vice President/CFO:** Jim Plake. **Executive VP/ General Manager, PNC Park:** Dennis DaPra. **Senior VP, Community/Public Affairs:** Patty Paytas. **VP/General Counsel:** Bryan Stroh.

Finance/Administration/Information Technology
Director, Human Resources: Jamie Holewski. **Senior Director, IT:** Terry Zeigler. **Director, Employee Services:** Patti Mistick. **Senior Director, Business Analytics:** Jim Alexander.

Communications
Fax: (412) 325-4413.
Senior Director, Communications: Brian Warecki. **Director, Baseball Communications:** Jim Trdinich. **Director, Broadcasting:** Marc Garda. **Director, Media Relations:** Dan Hart.

Community Relations
Director, Community Relations: Michelle Mejia. **Manager, Diversity Initiatives:** Chaz Kellem.

Marketing
Senior Director, Marketing/Special Events: Brian Chiera. **Director, Alumni Affairs/Promotions/Licensing:** Joe Billetdeaux. **Director, Advertising/Creative Services:** Kiley Cauvel. **Director, Special Events:** Christine Serkoch. **Director, PNC Park Events:** Ann Elder.

Corporate Sponsorships
Senior Director, Corporate Sponsorship Sales/Service: Aaron Cohn.

Stadium Operations
Senior Director, Ballpark Operations: Chris Hunter. **Senior Director, Security/Contract Services:** Jeff Podobnik. **Director, Field Operations:** Manny Lopez. **Senior Director, Florida Operations:** Trevor Gooby.

Ticketing
Telephone: (800) 289-2827. **Fax:** (412) 325-4404.

Frank Coonelly

2014 SCHEDULE
Standard Game Times: 7:05 p.m.; Sun. 1:35.

MARCH		
31 . . . . Chicago (NL)		

APRIL		
2-3 . . . . Chicago (NL)		
4-6 . . . . St. Louis		
8-10 . . . . at Chicago (NL)		
11-13 . . . . . at Milwaukee		
14-16 . . . . . .at Cincinnati		
17-20 . . . . . .Milwaukee		
21-24 . . . . . . Cincinnati		
25-27 . . . . . .at St. Louis		
29-30 . . . . . .at Baltimore		

MAY		
2-4 . . . . .Toronto		
5-7 . . . . . . San Francisco		

9-11 . . . . St. Louis
13-15 . . . . . at Milwaukee
16-18 . . . at New York (AL)
20-21 . . . . . . Baltimore
22-25 . . . . . Washington
26-28 . . . at New York (NL)
29-31 . at Los Angeles (NL)

JUNE
1 . . . . at Los Angeles (NL)
2-4 . . . . . . at San Diego
6-8 . . . . .Milwaukee
9-12 . . . . . Chicago (NL)
13-15 . . . . . . at Miami
17-19 . . . . . . Cincinnati
20-22 . . .at Chicago (NL)
23-25 . . . . at Tampa Bay

26-29 . . . . .New York (NL)

JULY
1-3 . . . . .Arizona
4-6 . . . . . . .Philadelphia
7-10 . . . . . . .at St. Louis
11-13 . . . . .at Cincinnati
18-20 . . . . . . .Colorado
21-23 . . . Los Angeles (NL)
25-27 . . . . . . at Colorado
28-30 . . . at San Francisco
31 . . . . at Arizona

AUGUST
1-3 . . . . at Arizona
5-7 . . . . .Miami
8-10 . . . . San Diego

11-12 . . . . Detroit
13-14 . . . . .at Detroit
15-17 . . . . at Washington
18-20 . . . . Atlanta
22-24 . . . . at Milwaukee
25-27 . . . . St. Louis
29-31 . . . . . . Cincinnati

SEPTEMBER
1-3 . . . . .at St. Louis
5-7 . . . . .at Chicago (NL)
8-11 . . . . . at Philadelphia
12-14 . . . . . Chicago (NL)
16-18 . . . . Boston
19-21 . . . . . .Milwaukee
22-25 . . . . . . at Atlanta
26-28 . . . . . .at Cincinnati

GENERAL INFORMATION
Stadium (year opened): PNC Park (2001).
Team Colors: Black and gold.

Player Representative: Neil Walker.
Home Dugout: Third Base.
Playing Surface: Grass.

Senior Director, Ticket Sales/Service: Christopher Zaber. Director, Suite Sales/Service: Terri Smith. Director, New Business Development: Nick McNeill. Director, Season Ticket Service/Retention: Jim Popovich. Director, Ticket Operations: Andrew Bragman.

BASEBALL OPERATIONS

Senior VP/General Manager: Neal Huntington. Assistant GM, Scouting: Greg Smith. Assistant GM, Development: Kyle Stark. Director, Player Personnel: Tyrone Brooks. Director, Baseball Operations: Kevan Graves. Director, Baseball Systems Development: Dan Fox. Special Assistants to GM: Jim Benedict, Marc DelPiano, Jax Robertson, Doug Strange.

Major League Scouts: Mike Basso, Bob Minor, Steve Williams. Pro Scouts: Ricky Bennett, Carlos Berroa, Jamie Brewington, Jim Dedrick, Ron Hopkins, John Kosciak, Alvin Rittman, Gary Robinson, Lewis Shaw. Coordinator, Baseball Operations: Alex Langsam. Baseball Operations Assistant: Will Lawton. Quantitative Analyst: Mike Fitzgerald. Data Architect: Josh Smith. Video Coordinator: Kevin Roach. Advance Scouting Coordinator: Wyatt Toregas.

Neal Huntington

Major League Staff

Manager: Clint Hurdle.

Coaches: Bench—Jeff Banister; Pitching—Ray Searage; Hitting—Jeff Branson; First Base—Rick Sofield; Third Base—Nick Leyva; Bullpen—Euclides Rojas; Coach—David Jauss; Coach—Jeff Livesey.

Medical/Training

Medical Director: Dr. Patrick DeMeo. Team Physician: Dr. Edward Snell. Head Major League Athletic Trainer: Todd Tomczyk. Assistant Major League Athletic Trainer: Ben Potenziano. Head Major League Strength/Conditioning Coach: Brendon Huttmann. Assistant Major League Strength/Conditioning Coach/Latin American Strength/Conditioning Coordinator: Kiyoshi Momose. Physical Therapist/Rehab Coordinator: Jeremiah Randall.

Minor Leagues

Director, Minor League Operations: Larry Broadway.

Coordinator, Minor League Operations: Diane DePasquale. Coordinator, Florida Baseball Operations: Juan Rodriguez. Field Coordinator: Brad Fischer. Assistant Field Coordinator: Dave Turgeon. Outfield/Baserunning Coordinator: Kimera Bartee. Pitching Coordinator: Scott Mitchell. Infield Coordinator: Gary Green. Hitting Coordinator: Larry Sutton. Senior Advisor, Minor League Operations: Woody Huyke.

Dominican Field Coordinator: Gera Alvarez. Senior Advisor, Latin American Operations: Luis Silverio. Special Assistant to Player Development: Frank Kremblas. Athletic Training Coordinator: Carl Randolph. Minor League Rehab Coordinator: Wes Eberlin. Sport Performance Coordinator: Carlo Alvarez. Athletic Development Coordinator: Joe Hughes. Director, Mental Conditioning: Bernie Holliday. Mental Conditioning Coordinator: Tyson Holt. Assistant Coordinator, Mental Conditioning: Hector Morales. Minor League Equipment Manager: Pat Hagerty. Dominican Academy Administrator: Juan Carlos Mendoza.

Farm System

Class	Club (League)	Manager	Coach(es)	Pitching Coach
Triple-A	Indianapolis (IL)	Dean Treanor	Mike Pagliarulo	Tom Filer
Double-A	Altoona (EL)	Carlos Garcia	Ryan Long	Stan Kyles
High A	Bradenton (FSL)	Tom Prince	Kory DeHaan	Justin Meccage
Low A	West Virginia (SAL)	Michael Ryan	Keoni De Renne	Jeff Johnson
Short-season	Jamestown (NYP)	Brian Esposito	Orlando Merced	Mark DiFelice
Rookie	Bristol (APP)	Edgar Varela	Terry Alexander	Miguel Bonilla
Rookie	Bradenton (GCL)	Milver Reyes	Mike Lum	Scott Elarton
Rookie	Pirates (DSL1)	Gera Alvarez	Jonathan Prieto/Cecilio Beltre	Dan Urbina
Rookie	Pirates (DSL2)	Mendy Lopez	Johe Acosta/Osiel Flores	Jairo Cuevas

Scouting

Fax: (412) 325-4414.

Director, Scouting: Joe Delli Carri.

Coordinator: Jim Asher. National Supervisors: Jack Bowen (Bethel Park, PA), Jimmy Lester (Columbus, GA), Matt Ruebel (Oklahoma City, OK). Regional Supervisors: Jesse Flores (Sacramento, CA), Rodney Henderson (Lexington, KY), Everett Russell (Thibodaux, LA), Greg Schilz (Washington D.C.). Area Supervisors: Rick Allen (Agoura Hills, CA), Matt Bimeal (Baldwin City, KS), Jerome Cochran (Slidell, LA), Trevor Haley (Houston, TX), Sean Heffernan (Florence, SC), Phil Huttmann, (Plano, TX), Jerry Jordan (Kingsport, TN), Max Kwan (Kent, WA) Darren Mazeroski (Panama City Beach, FL), Nick Presto (Palm Beach Gardens, FL), Mike Sansoe (Walnut Creek, CA), Brian Selman (Washington, DC), Steve Skrinar (East Chatham, NY), Mike Steele (Phoenix, AZ), Brian Tracy (Orange, CA), Anthony Wycklendt (Brookfield, WI). Part-Time Scout: Enrique Hernandez (Puerto Rico).

Director, Latin American Scouting: Rene Gayo. Full-Time Scouts: Orlando Covo (Colombia), Nelson Llenas (Dominican Republic), Juan Mercado (Dominican Repuplic), Rodolfo Petit (Venezuela), Victor Santana (Dominican Republic), Cristino Valdez (Dominican Republic), Jesus Chino Valdez (Mexico). Part-Time Scouts: Esteban Alvarez (Dominican Republic), Pablo Csorgi (Venezuela), David De La Cruz (Dominican Republic), Denny Diaz (Dominican Republic), Daniel Espitia Garcia (Colombia), Jhoan Hidalgo (Venezuela), Jose Lavagnino (Mexico), Javier Magdaleno (Venezuela), Juan Morales (Venezuela), Robinson Ortega (Colombia), Rogelio Osuna (Mexico), Jose Pineda (Panama), Juan Pinto (Mexico), Cesar Saba (Dominican Republic), Cristobal Santoya (Colombia), Gary Sewell (Jamaica), Leon Taylor (Jamaica), Ruben Tinoco (Mexico), Marc Van Zanten (Netherlands Antilles), Darryl Yrausquin (Aruba). International Scouts: Fu-Chun Chiang (Korea, Taiwan), Tom Gillespie (Europe), Tony Harris (Australia).

St. Louis Cardinals

Office Address: 700 Clark Street, St. Louis MO 63102.
Telephone: (314) 345-9600. **Fax:** (314) 345-9523. **Website:** www.cardinals.com.

Ownership

Operated By: St. Louis Cardinals, LLC.
Chairman/Chief Executive Officer: William DeWitt, Jr.
President: Bill DeWitt III.
Senior Administrative Assistant to Chairman: Grace Kell. **Senior Administrative Assistant to President:** Julie Laningham.

BUSINESS OPERATIONS

Bill DeWitt III

Finance

Fax: (314) 345-9520.
Senior VP/Chief Financial Officer: Brad Wood. **Director, Finance:** Rex Carter. **Director, Human Resources:** Ann Seeney.
VP, Event Services/Merchandising: Vicki Bryant. **Director, Special Events:** Julia Row.

Marketing/Sales/Community Relations

Fax: (314) 345-9529.
Senior VP, Sales/Marketing: Dan Farrell. **Administrative Assistant, VP Sales/Marketing:** Gail Ruhling. **VP, Corporate Marketing/Stadium Entertainment:** Thane van Breusegen. **Director, Scoreboard Operations/Fan Entertainment/Senior Account Executive:** Tony Simokaitis. **Director, Publications:** Steve Zesch.
VP, Community Relations/Executive Director, Cardinals Care: Michael Hall. **Administrative Assistant:** Bonnie Parres.

Communications

Fax: (314) 345-9530.
VP, Communications: Ron Watermon. **Director, Media Relations:** Brian Bartow. **Manager, Media Relations:** Melody Yount. **Media Relations Specialist:** Chris Tunno. **Public Relations Specialist:** Lindsey Weber. **PA Announcer:** John Ulett. **Official Scorers:** Gary Muller, Jeff Durbin, Mike Smith.

Stadium Operations

Fax: (314) 345-9535.
VP, Stadium Operations: Joe Abernathy.
Administrative Assistant: Hope Baker. **Director, Security/Special Services:** Joe Walsh. **Director, Quality Assurance/ Guest Services:** Mike Ball. **Head Groundskeeper:** Bill Findley.

2014 SCHEDULE

Standard Game Times: 7:15 p.m.; Sun. 1:15.

MARCH		JULY	SEPTEMBER

MARCH
31 . . . . .at Cincinnati

APRIL
2-3 . . . . .at Cincinnati
4-6 . . . . at Pittsburgh
7-9 . . . . Cincinnati
11-13 . . . . . Chicago (NL)
14-16 . . . . . at Milwaukee
17-20 . . . at Washington
21-24 . . . at New York (NL)
25-27 . . . . . . Pittsburgh
28-30 . . . . . . .Milwaukee

MAY
2-4 . . . . . .at Chicago (NL)
5-7 . . . . at Atlanta

9-11 . . . . . . at Pittsburgh
12-15 . . . . . Chicago (NL)
16-18 . . . . Atlanta
20-22 . . . . .Arizona
23-25 . . . . . .at Cincinnati
26-28 . . . . .New York (AL)
29-31 . . . . . San Francisco

JUNE
1 . . . . .San Francisco
2-3 . . . . Kansas City
4-5 . . . . . .at Kansas City
6-8 . . . . at Toronto
10-11 . . . . . at Tampa Bay
13-15 . . . . . . Washington
16-18 . . . . .New York (NL)
19-22 . . . . . .Philadelphia

23-25 . . . . . . at Colorado
26-29 . at Los Angeles (NL)

JULY
1-3 . . . . . at San Francisco
4-6 . . . . .Miami
7-10 . . . . Pittsburgh
11-13 . . . . .at Milwaukee
18-20 . . Los Angeles (NL)
22-23 . . . . . .Tampa Bay
25-27 . . .at Chicago (NL)
29-31 . . . . . at San Diego

AUGUST
1-3 . . . . .Milwaukee
5-7 . . . . Boston
8-10 . . . . . . .at Baltimore

11-13 . . . . at Miami
14-17 . . . . San Diego
18-20 . . . . Cincinnati
22-24 . . . at Philadelphia
25-27 . . . . . at Pittsburgh
29-31 . . . . . Chicago (NL)

SEPTEMBER
1-3 . . . . .Pittsburgh
4-7 . . . . at Milwaukee
8-11 . . . . . .at Cincinnati
12-14 . . . . .Colorado
16-18 . . . . . . .Milwaukee
19-21 . . . . Cincinnati
22-24 . . .at Chicago (NL)
26-28 . . . . at Arizona

GENERAL INFORMATION

Stadium (year opened): Busch Stadium (2006).
Team Colors: Red and white.

Player Representative: Jon Jay.
Home Dugout: First Base.
Playing Surface: Grass.

Ticketing
Fax: (314) 345-9522.
VP, Ticket Sales/Service: Joe Strohm.
Director, Ticket Sales/Marketing: Martin Coco. **Director, Ticket Sales/Services:** Rob Fasoldt. **Director, Client Relations:** Delores Scanlon.

Travel/Clubhouse
Fax: (314) 345-9523.
Traveling Secretary: C.J. Cherre. **Equipment Manager:** Rip Rowan. **Assistant Equipment Manager:** Ernie Moore. **Visiting Clubhouse Manger:** Jerry Risch. **Video Coordinator:** Chad Blair.

BASEBALL OPERATIONS

Senior VP/General Manager: John Mozeliak.
Assistant GM: Mike Girsch. **Senior Executive Assistant:** Linda Brauer. **Senior Special Assistant to GM:** Mike Jorgensen. **Special Assistant to GM:** Cal Eldred, Willie McGee. **Director, Player Personnel:** Matt Slater. **Director, Major League Administration:** Judy Carpenter-Barada. **Director, Baseball Administration:** John Vuch. **Director, Baseball Development:** Chris Correa. **Manager, Baseball Information:** Jeremy Cohen. **Quantitative Analysts:** Matt Bayer, Patrick Casanta, Dane Sorensen.

Major League Staff
Telephone: (314) 345-9600.
Manager: Mike Matheny.
Coaches: Bench—Mike Aldrete; **Pitching**—Derek Lilliquist; **Hitting**—John Mabry; **Assistant Hitting Instructor**—David Bell; **First Base**—Chris Maloney; **Third Base**—Jose Oquendo; **Bullpen**—Blaise Ilsley; **Bullpen Coach**—Jamie Pogue.

John Mozeliak

Medical/Training
Head Team Physician: Dr. Jason Hand. **Head Trainer:** Greg Hauck. **Assistant Trainer:** Chris Conroy. **Assistant Trainer/Rehabilitation Coordinator:** Adam Olsen. **Strength/Conditioning Coach:** Pete Prinzi.

Player Development
Director, Player Development: Gary LaRocque.
Baseball Operations Assistant, Player Development: Tony Ferreira.
Minor League Field Coordinator: Mark DeJohn. **Coordinators:** Tim Leveque (pitching), Derrick May (hitting), Luis Aguayo (international infield/infield instructor), Barry Weinberg (senior medical advisor), Geoff Gabler (minor league medical). **Minor League Equipment Manager:** Dave VondarHaar

Farm System

Class	Club (League)	Manager	Hitting Coach	Pitching Coach
Triple-A	Memphis (PCL)	Ron Warner	Mark Budaska	Bryan Eversgerd
Double-A	Springfield (TL)	Mike Shildt	Erik Pappas	Randy Niemann
High A	Palm Beach (FSL)	Dann Bilardello	Roger LaFrancois	Ace Adams
Low A	Peoria (MWI)	Joe Kruzel	Jobel Jimenez	Jason Simontacchi
Short-season	State College (NYP)	Oliver Marmol	Ramon Ortiz	Dernier Orozco
Rookie	Johnson City (APP)	Johnny Rodriguez	Roberto Espinoza	Paul Davis
Rookie	Cardinals (GCL)	Steve Turco	Kleininger Teran	Darwin Marrero
Rookie	Cardinals (DSL)	Fray Peniche	Unavailable	John Matos

Scouting
Fax: (314) 345-9519.
Director, Scouting: Dan Kantrovitz.
Special Assistant to Amateur Scouting: Mike Roberts. **Baseball Operations Assistant, Scouting:** Jared Odom.
Professional Scouts: Ryan Franklin (Shawnee, OK), Jeff Ishii (Chino, CA), Mike Jorgensen (Fenton, MO), Marty Keough (Scottsdale, AZ), Deric McKamey (Bluffton, OH), Joe Rigoli (Parsippany, NJ), Kerry Robinson (Ballwin, MO). **Crosscheckers:** Joe Almaraz (San Antonio, TX), Fernando Arango (Davie, FL), Brian Hopkins (Brunswick, OH), Jeremy Schied (Aliso Viejo, CA), Roger Smith (Eastman, GA), Jamal Strong (Vacaville, CA), Matt Swanson (Round Rock, TX). **Area Scouts:** Matt Blood (Durham, NC), Nicholas Brannon (Baton Rouge, LA), Jason Bryans (Windsor, Ontario), Dominic "Ty" Boyles (Atlanta, GA), Mike Dibiase (Irvine, CA), Rob Fidler (Seattle, WA), Mike Garciaparra (Orange, CA), Ralph Garr Jr. (Houston, TX), Charlie Gonzalez (Weston, FL), Dirk Kinney (Kansas City, MO), Aaron Krawiec (Gilbert, AZ), Aaron Looper (Shawnee, OK), Sean Moran (Levittown, PA), Zach Mortimer (Sacramento, CA), Charles Peterson (St Cloud, MN), Juan Ramos (Carolina, PR).
Part-Time Scouts: Scott Cooper (St Louis, MO), Jimmy Matthews (Athens, GA), Andre Miller (Santa Barbara, CA), Jared Odom (St Louis, MO), Todd Stein (St. Louis, MO).
Director, International Operations: Moises Rodriguez. **Baseball Operations Assistant, International:** Luis Morales. **International Crosschecker:** Cesar Geronimo, Jr. **Scouting Supervisor, Dominican Republic:** Angel Ovalles. **Administrator, Dominican Republic Operations:** Aaron Rodriguez.
International Scouts: Jean Carlos Alvarez (Dominican Republic), Rodny Jimenez (Dominican Republic), Omar Rogers (Dominican Republic), Jose Gregorio Gonzalez (Venezuela), Estuar Ruiz (Venezuela), Carlos Balcazar (Colombia), Crysthiam Blanco (Nicaragua).

San Diego Padres

Office Address: Petco Park, 100 Park Blvd, San Diego, CA 92101.
Mailing Address: PO Box 122000, San Diego, CA 92112.
Telephone: (619) 795-5000. **E-mail address:** comments@padres.com. **Website:** www.padres.com.
Twitter: @padres. **Facebook:** www.facebook.com/padres. **Instagram:** www.instagram.com/padres

Ownership
Operated By: Padres LP. **Executive Chairman:** Ron Fowler. **President/CEO:** Mike Dee.

BUSINESS OPERATIONS
Senior Vice President, Business Administration/General Counsel: Erik Greupner.
Manager, Business Strategy/Analytics: Ryan Gustafson.

Finance/Administration/Information Technology/Human Resources
Senior VP/CFO: Ronda Sedillo. **Director, Accounting:** Todd Bollman. **Director, Information Technology:** Ray Chan. **Director, Human Resources:** Sara Greenspan.

Public Affairs/ Community Relations/Military Affairs
Telephone: (619) 795-5265. **Fax:** (619) 795-5266.
Senior VP, Public Affairs: Sarah Farnsworth. **VP, Community Relations:** Sue Botos. **Director, Military Affairs:** Michael Berenston. **Manager, Community Affairs/Padres Foundation:** Nhu Tran. **Manager, Latino Affairs:** Alex Montoya. **Manager, Community Relations:** Veronica Nogueira.

Ron Fowler

Entertainment/Partnerships/Marketing/ Communications/Creative Services
Senior VP/Chief Marketing Officer: Wayne Partello. **VP, Corporate Partnerships:** Jarrod Dillon. **Director, Entertainment/Production:** Erik Meyer. **Director, Partnership Development:** Joe Mulford. **Director, Communications:** Dave Holtzman. **Manager, Promotions/Merchandising:** Michael Babida. **Manager, In-Park Entertainment:** Mike Grace. **Manager, Entertainment/Production Engineer:** Hendrik Jaehn. **Manager, Game Presentation/Production:** Jennifer Cota. **Manager, Player/Media Relations:** Josh Ishoo. **Manager, Communications/Broadcasting:** Shana Wilson.

Ballpark Operations
VP, Ballpark Operations/GM, Petco Park: Mark Guglielmo. **VP, Concessions/Retail:** Scott Marshall. **VP, Petco Park Events:** Jeremy Horowitz. **Director, Security:** John Leas. **Director, Event Operations:** Ken Kawachi. **Director, Field Operations:** Luke Yoder. **Director, Guest Services:** Kameron Durham. **Director, Petco Park Events:** Nick Maranda. **Official Scorers:** Jack Murray, Bill Zavestoski.

Ticketing
Telephone: (619) 795-5500. **Fax:** (619) 795-5034.
Senior VP, Sales/Services: Steve Ziff. **Senior Director, Padres Premium Plus:** Gordon Cooke. **Director, Ticket Operations:** Jim Kiersnowski. **Director, Sales Administration:** Robert Davis. **Director, Group Tickets/Hospitality:** Eric

2014 SCHEDULE
Standard Game Times: 7:10 p.m.; Sat. 5:40; Sun. 1:10

MARCH		JULY	SEPTEMBER
MARCH	8-11 . . . . .Miami	23-25 . . . at San Francisco	11-13 . . . . .Colorado
30 . . . . . Los Angeles (NL)	13-15 . . . . . .at Cincinnati	27-29 . . . . .Arizona	14-17 . . . . . . .at St. Louis
	16-18 . . . . at Colorado	30 . . . . Cincinnati	19-21 . at Los Angeles (NL)
APRIL	20-21 . . . . . .Minnesota		22-24 . . . . at Arizona
1-2. . . . . Los Angeles (NL)	22-25 . . . . . Chicago (NL)	**JULY**	25-27 . . . . . .Milwaukee
4-6. . . . . .at Miami	26-28 . . . . at Arizona	1-2. . . . . Cincinnati	29-31 . . .Los Angeles (NL)
7-9. . . . . . .at Cleveland	30-31 . . . .at Chicago (AL)	4-6. . . . . .San Francisco	
11-13 . . . . Detroit		7-9. . . . . . . at Colorado	**SEPTEMBER**
14-17 . . . . .Colorado	**JUNE**	10-13 . at Los Angeles (NL)	1-4. . . . . .Arizona
18-20 . . . . .San Francisco	1 . . . . . .at Chicago (AL)	18-20 . . . .New York (NL)	5-7. . . . . at Colorado
21-23 . . . . . at Milwaukee	2-4. . . . . .Pittsburgh	22-24 . . .at Chicago (NL)	8-10 . at Los Angeles (NL)
24-27 . . . . at Washington	6-8. . . . . Washington	25-28 . . . . . at Atlanta	12-14 . . . . at Arizona
28-30 . . at San Francisco	10-12 . . . at Philadelphia	29-31 . . . . St. Louis	15-18 . . . . . .Philadelphia
	13-15 . . at New York (NL)		19-21 . . . . .San Francisco
MAY	16-17 . . . . .at Seattle	**AUGUST**	22-24 . . . . .Colorado
2-4. . . . . .Arizona	18-19 . . . . Seattle	1-3. . . . . Atlanta	25-28 . . . at San Francisco
5-7. . . . . . . Kansas City	20-22 . . .Los Angeles (NL)	5-6. . . . . . at Minnesota	
		8-10 . . . . . at Pittsburgh	

GENERAL INFORMATION
Stadium (year opened): Petco Park (2004).
Team Colors: Blue, white, tan and gray

Player Representative: Chase Headley.
Home Dugout: First Base.
Playing Surface: Grass.

McKenzie. **Director, CRM/Ticket Analytics:** Ben Roller. **Director, Membership Services:** Sindi Schug.

Travel/Clubhouse
    Director, Team Travel/Equipment Manager: Brian Prilaman. **Assistant Equipment Manager/Umpire Room Attendant:** Tony Petricca. **Assistant to Equipment Manager:** Spencer Dallin. **Visiting Clubhouse Manager:** David Bacharach.

BASEBALL OPERATIONS
Telephone: (619) 795-5077. **Fax:** (619) 795-5361.
    Executive VP/General Manager: Josh Byrnes.
    Senior VP, Baseball Operations: Omar Minaya. **VP/Assistant GM:** Fred Uhlman Jr. **VP/Assistant GM:** AJ Hinch. **VP/Assistant GM, Player Personnel:** Chad MacDonald.
    Assistant GM: Josh Stein. **Special Assistants, Baseball Operations:** Mark Kotsay, Mark Loretta. **Manager, Baseball Operations:** Nick Ennis. **Director, Team Travel/Equipment Manager:** Brian Prilaman. **Assistant, Baseball Operations/Professional Scouting:** Alex Slater. **Assistant, Baseball Operations:** Mark Prior. **Architect, Baseball Systems:** Wells Oliver. **Developer, Baseball Systems:** Brian McBurney. **Advance Scout, Baseball Operations:** Ben Sestanovich. **Major League Advance Scout:** Eric Junge. **Video Coordinator, Clubhouse:** Mike Tompkins. **Executive Assistant:** Julie Myers.

Josh Byrnes

Major League Staff
    Manager: Bud Black.
    Coaches: Bench—Dave Roberts; **Pitching**—Darren Balsley; **Hitting**—Phil Plantier; **Assistant Hitting**—Alonzo Powell; **First Base**—Jose Valentin; **Third Base**—Glenn Hoffman; **Bullpen**—Willie Blair.

Medical/Training
    Club Physician: Scripps Clinic Medical Staff. **Head Athletic Trainer:** Todd Hutcheson. **Assistant Athletic Trainer:** Paul Navarro. **Physical Therapist:** Rick Stauffer. **Therapist/Sports Massage:** Philip Kerr. **Strength/Conditioning Coach:** Brett McCabe.

Player Development
    Telephone: (619) 795-5343. **Fax:** (619) 795-5036.
    VP, Player Development: Randy Smith.
    Manager, Player Development/International Operations: Juan Lara. **Manager, Minor Leagues Operations:** Warren Miller. **Equipment Manager, Minor Leagues:** Zach Nelson.
    Coordinator, Dominican Republic Operations: Cesar Rizik. **Assistant Administrator, Dominican Republic Operations:** Jesus Negrette. **Roving Instructors:** Randy Johnson (Field Coordinator), Gorman Heimueller (Pitching Coordinator), Sean Berry (Hitting Coordinator), Eddie Rodriguez (Infield Coordinator), Glen Barker (Outfield/Baserunning Coordinator), Evaristo Lantigua (Coordinator, Latin American Instruction), Joseph Tarantino (Medical Coordinator), Jordan Wolf (Strength/Conditioning Coordinator), Ryan Bitzel (Rehab Coordinator).

Farm System

Class	Farm Club (League)	Manager	Coach	Pitching Coach
Triple-A	El Paso (PCL)	Pat Murphy	Jacque Jones	Mike Cather
Double-A	San Antonio (TL)	Rich Dauer	Francisco Morales	Jimmy Jones
High A	Lake Elsinore (CAL)	Jamie Quirk	Jody Davis	Bronswell Patrick
Low A	Fort Wayne (MWL)	Michael Collins	Morgan Burkhart	Burt Hooton
Short-season	Eugene (NWL)	Robbie Wine	Homer Bush	Nelson Cruz
Rookie	Padres (AZL)	Rod Barajas	Carlos Sosa	Dave Rajsich
Rookie	Padres (DSL)	Jose Guillen	J. Ramirez/J. Pozo	M. Rojas/J. Quezada

Scouting
    Director, Scouting: Billy Gasparino (Venice, CA).
    Assistant to Director, Scouting: Eddie Ciafardini (San Diego, CA). **Advisor to Amateur Scouting:** Dan Cholowsky (Chandler, AZ). **Video Coordinator, Scouting/Player Development:** Matt Schaffner (San Diego, CA). **National Crosscheckers:** Sean Campbell (Nashville, TN), Kurt Kemp (Peachtree City, GA).
    Supervisors: Mark Conner (Hendersonville, TN), Pete DeYoung (Carlsbad, CA), Tim Holt (Allen, TX), Chip Lawrence (Palmetto, FL). **Amateur Scouts:** Justin Baughman (Seattle, WA), Willie Bosque (Winter Garden, FL), Jim Bretz (South Windsor, CT), Tom Burns (Harrisburg, PA), Jeff Curtis (Arlington, TX), Lane Decker (Piedmont, OK), Kevin Ellis (Katy, TX), Josh Emmerick (Oceanside, CA), Chris Kelly (Sarasota, FL), Dave Lottsfeldt (Denver, CO), Brent Mayne (Costa Mesa, CA), Sam Ray (Clayton, CA), Andrew Salvo (Pelham, AL), Jeff Stewart (Normal, IL), Tyler Stubblefield (Acworth, GA), Matt Thomas (Lexington, KY). **Part-Time Scouts:** Willie Ronda (Las Lomas Rio Piedras, PR), Murray Zuk (Souris, Manitoba).
    Special Assignment Scouts: Chris Bourjos (Scottsdale, AZ), Kevin Jarvis (Franklin, TN), Steve Lyons (San Antonio, TX), Jeff Pickler (Chandler, AZ). **Professional Scouts:** Joe Bochy (Plant City, FL), Jim Elliot (Winston-Salem, NC), Al Hargesheimer (Arlington Heights, IL), Matt Smith (Surprise, AZ), Mike Venafro (Fort Myers, FL), Chris Young (Austin, TX). **Coordinator, Latin American Scouting:** Felix Feliz. **Supervisor, Venezuela:** Yfrain Linares. **Supervisor, Central America/Mexico:** Robert Rowley. **International Crosschecker:** Trevor Schumm. **International Crosschecker:** Chip Lawrence.
    International Scouts: Antonio Alejos (Venezuela), Milton Croes (Aruba), Marcial Del Valle (Colombia), Emenegildo Diaz (Dominican Republic), Mayron Isenia (Curacao), Elvin Jarquin (Nicaragua), Martin Jose (Dominican Republic), Victor Magdaleno (Venezuela), Ricardo Montenegro (Panama), Luis Prieto (Venezuela), Ysrael Rojas (Dominican Republic), Jose Salado (Dominican Republic). **Part-time Scouts:** Andres Cabadias (Colombia), Ryan Drees (Japan), Hoon NamGung (South Korea), Damian Shanahan (Australia)

San Francisco Giants

Office Address: AT&T Park, 24 Willie Mays Plaza, San Francisco, CA 94107.
Telephone: (415) 972-2000. **Fax:** (415) 947-2800. **Website:** sfgiants.com, sfgigantes.com.

Ownership
Operated by: San Francisco Baseball Associates L.P.

BUSINESS OPERATIONS
President/Chief Executive Officer: Laurence M. Baer. **Special Assistant:** Willie Mays. **Senior Advisor:** Willie McCovey.

Finance
Senior Vice President Finance/Treasurer: Lisa Pantages. **Senior VP/Chief Information Officer:** Bill Schlough. **Senior Director, Information Technology:** Ken Logan.

Human Resources/Legal
Chief People Officer: Leilani Gayles. **VP, Human Resources:** Joyce Thomas. **Senior VP/ General Counsel:** Jack F. Bair. **VP/Deputy General Counsel:** Elizabeth R. Murphy.

Communications
Telephone: (415) 972-2445. **Fax:** (415) 947-2800.

Laurence M. Baer

Senior VP, Communications/Senior Advisor to the CEO: Staci Slaughter. **Senior Director, Broadcast Services:** Maria Jacinto. **Senior Director, Media Relations:** Jim Moorehead. **Director, Baseball Information:** Matt Chisholm. **Manager, Hispanic Marketing/Media Relations:** Erwin Higueros. **Coordinator, Baseball Information/ Media Relations:** Liam Connolly. **VP, Public Affairs/Community Relations:** Shana Daum. **VP, Creative Services/Visual Identity:** Nancy Donati. **Director, Photography/Archives:** Missy Mikulecky.

Business Operations
Senior VP, Business Operations: Mario Alioto. **Managing VP, Sponsorship/New Business Development:** Jason Pearl. **VP, Sponsor/Special Event Support:** Danny Dann. **Director, Special Events:** Valerie McGuire. **Director, Sponsorship Sales:** Bill Lawrence. **VP, Retail Operations:** Dave Martinez.

Ticketing
Telephone: (415) 972-2000. **Fax:** (415) 972-2500.
Managing VP, Ticket Sales/Services: Russ Stanley. **VP, Sales:** Jeff Tucker. **VP, Strategic Revenue Services:** Jerry Drobny. **Senior Director, Ticket Services:** Devin Lutes. **Senior Box Office Manager:** Todd Pierce. **VP, Client Relations:** Annemarie Hastings. **Senior Director, Suite/Group Sales:** Rocky Koplik.

Marketing
Senior VP, Consumer Marketing: Tom McDonald. **Senior Director, SFG Productions/Entertainment:** Chris Gargano. **Director, Executive Producer:** Paul Hodges.

2014 SCHEDULE
Standard Game Times: 7:15 p.m.; Sun. 1:05

MARCH	8-11 . . at Los Angeles (NL)	26-29 . . . . Cincinnati
31 . . . . at Arizona	12-14 . . . . Atlanta	
	15-18 . . . . .Miami	**JULY**
APRIL	20-22 . . . . . at Colorado	1-3 . . . . St. Louis
1-3 . . . . at Arizona	23-25 . . . . . . Minnesota	4-6 . . . . . . at San Diego
4-6 . . . at Los Angeles (NL)	26-28 . . . . . Chicago (NL)	7-8 . . . . .at Oakland
8-10 . . . . Arizona	29-31 . . . . . .at St. Louis	9-10 . . . . Oakland
11-13 . . . . . . .Colorado		11-13 . . . . .Arizona
15-17 . . .Los Angeles (NL)	**JUNE**	18-20 . . . . at Miami
18-20 . . . . . at San Diego	1 . . . . .at St. Louis	21-24 . . . at Philadelphia
21-23 . . . . . at Colorado	3-5 . . . . . .at Cincinnati	25-27 . . . Los Angeles (NL)
25-27 . . . . . . Cleveland	6-8 . . . . . .New York (NL)	28-30 . . . . Pittsburgh
28-30 . . . . . . San Diego	9-12 . . . . Washington	
	13-15 . . . . .Colorado	**AUGUST**
MAY	17-18 . . . .at Chicago (AL)	1-4 . . . . . at New York (NL)
2-4 . . . . at Atlanta	20-22 . . . . at Arizona	5-7 . . . . . . at Milwaukee
5-7 . . . . at Pittsburgh	23-25 . . . . San Diego	8-10 . . . . . .at Kansas City

12-13 . . . . . Chicago (AL)
15-17 . . . . . .Philadelphia
19-21 . . . .at Chicago (NL)
22-24 . . . . at Washington
25-28 . . . . .Colorado
29-31 . . . . . . .Milwaukee
SEPTEMBER
1-3 . . . . at Colorado
5-7 . . . . .at Detroit
9-11 . . . . .Arizona
12-14 . . . Los Angeles (NL)
15-17 . . . . . . at Arizona
19-21 . . . . . at San Diego
22-24 . at Los Angeles (NL)
25-28 . . . . San Diego

GENERAL INFORMATION
Stadium (year opened): AT&T Park (2000). **Player Representative:** Matt Cain.
Team Colors: Black, orange and cream. **Home Dugout:** Third Base.
Playing Surface: Grass.

Administration/Ballpark Operations/Clubhouse
Senior VP, Administration: Alfonso G. Felder. Senior VP, Ballpark Operations: Jorge Costa. VP, Ballpark Operations: Gene Telucci. Senior Director, Security: Tinie Roberson. VP, Guest Services: Rick Mears. Head Groundskeeper: Greg Elliott. PA Announcer: Renel Brooks-Moon. Giants Equipment Manager: Miguel Murphy. Home Clubhouse Assistants: Brandon Evans, Ron Garcia, David Lowenstein. Visitors Clubhouse Manager: Harvey Hodgerney. Director, Team Travel: Brett Alexander. Coordinator, Organizational Travel: Michael Scardino.

BASEBALL OPERATIONS

Telephone: (415) 972-1922. Fax: (415) 947-2929.
Senior VP/General Manager: Brian R. Sabean.
VP/Assistant GM, Player Personnel: Dick Tidrow. VP/Assistant GM: Bobby Evans. Special Assistant to GM: Felipe Alou. VP, Pro Scouting/Player Evaluation: Jeremy Shelley. Senior Advisor, Baseball Operations: Tony Siegle. Director, Minor League Operations/Quantitative Analysis: Yeshayah Goldfarb. Executive Assistant to GM: Karen Sweeney. Coordinator, Video Coaching System: Danny Martin, Yo Miyamoto.

Major League Staff
Manager: Bruce Bochy.
Coaches: Bench—Ron Wotus; Pitching—Dave Righetti; Hitting—Hensley Meulens/Joe Lefebvre; First Base—Roberto Kelly; Third Base—Tim Flannery; Bullpen—Mark Gardner/Bill Hayes.

Brian Sabean

Medical/Training
Team Physicians: Dr. Robert Murray, Dr. Ken Akizuki, Dr. Anthony Saglimbeni. Head Trainer: Dave Groeschner. Assistant Trainers: Anthony Reyes, Eric Ortega. Strength/Conditioning Coach: Carl Kochan. Coordinator, Medical Administration: Chrissy Yuen.

Player Development
Director, Player Development: Shane Turner.
Senior Consultant, Player Personnel: Jack Hiatt. Special Assistants, Player Development: Joe Amalfitano, Jim Davenport, Fred Stanley. Director, Arizona Operations: Alan Lee. Coordinator, Instruction/Minor League Hitting: Steve Decker. Coordinator, Minor League Pitching: Bert Bradley. Coordinator, Infield Instruction: Jose Alguacil. Coordinator, Baserunning/Outfield Instruction: Henry Cotto. Coordinator, Catching Instruction: Jeff Tackett. Minor League Coach: Tom Trebelhorn. Minor League Roving Instructors: Lee Smith (pitching), Kirt Manwaring (catching). Manager, Player Personnel Administration: Clara Ho. Coordinator, Minor League Operations: Eric Flemming. Arizona Minor League Operations Assistant: Gabriel Alvarez.

Farm System

Class	Farm Club (League)	Manager	Coach(es)	Pitching Coach
Triple-A	Fresno (PCL)	Bob Mariano	Andy Skeels	Dwight Bernard
Double-A	Richmond (EL)	Russ Morman	Ken Joyce	Ross Grimsley
High A	San Jose (CAL)	Lenn Sakata	Lipso Nava	Michael Couchee
Low A	Augusta (SAL)	Mike Goff	Hector Borg/Todd Linden	Steve Kline
Short-season	Salem Keizer (NWL)	Gary Davenport	Ricky Ward	Jerry Cram/Matt Yourkin
Rookie	Giants (AZL)	Nestor Rojas	Billy Horton	L. McCall/M. Rodriguez
Rookie	Giants (DSL)	Carlos Valderrama	Juan Parra/Hector Ortiz	Marcos Aguasvivas

Scouting
Telephone: (415) 972-2360. Fax: (415) 947-2929.
VP/Assistant GM, Scouting/International Operations: John Barr (Haddonfield, NJ).
Coordinator, Scouting Administration: Adam Nieting. Scouting Assistant: Jose Bonilla. Senior Advisors, Scouting: Ed Creech (Moultrie, GA), Lee Elder (Scottsdale, AZ), Doug Mapson (Chandler, AZ), Matt Nerland (Clayton, CA), Paul Turco Sr (Sarasota, FL). Special Assignment Scouts: Pat Burrell (Scottsdale, AZ), Tom Korenek (Houston, TX), Darren Wittcke (Sherwood, OR). Advance Scouts: Steve Balboni (Murray Hill, NJ), Keith Champion (Ballwin, MO). Major League Scouts: Brian Johnson (Detroit, MI), Michael Kendall (Rancho Palos Verde, CA), Stan Saleski (Dayton, OH), Paul Turco Jr (Tampa, FL), Tom Zimmer (Seminole, FL). Senior Consultants, Scouting: Dick Cole (Costa Mesa, CA).
Supervisors: East—John Castleberry (High Point, NC); Midwest—Arnold Brathwaite (Grand Prairie, TX); West—Joe Strain (Englewood, CO).
Territorial Scouts: East Region—Jose Alou (Boynton, FL), Ray Callari (Cote Saint Luc, Quebec), Kevin Christman (Noblesville, IN), John DiCarlo (Glenwood, NJ), Donnie Suttles (Marion, NC), Andrew Jefferson (Atlanta, GA), Mike Metcalf (Sarasota, FL), Glenn Tufts (Bridgewater, MA); Midwest Region—Jim Gabella (Burlington, IA), Daniel Murray (Prairie Village, KS), Todd Thomas (Dallas, TX), Hugh Walker (Jonesboro, AR); West Region—Brad Cameron (Los Alamitos, CA), Chuck Hensley (Mesa, AZ), Gil Kubski (Los Angeles, CA), Keith Snider (Stockton, CA), Matt Woodward (Camas, WA). West Coast Video/Area Scout: Colin Sabean (San Francisco, CA). Part-Time Scouts: Bob Barth (Williamstown, NJ), Jim Chapman (Langley, BC), Jorge Posada Sr (San Juan, PR), Tim Rock (Orlando, FL).
Director, Dominican Operations: Pablo Peguero. Coordinator, Pacific Rim Scouting: John Cox. International Crosschecker: Joe Salermo (Hallandale Beach, FL). Latin America Crosschecker: Junior Roman (San Sebastian, PR). Venezuela Supervisor: Ciro Villalobos. Assistant Director, Dominican Operations: Felix Peguero.
International Scouts: Jonathan Arraiz (Venezuela), Jonathan Bautista (Dominican Republic), Phillip Elhage (Curacao/Bonaire/Aruba), Gabriel Elias (Dominican Republic), Edgar Fernandez (Venezuela), Ricardo Heron (Panama), Jeff Kusumoto (Japan), Juan Marquez (Venezuela), Daniel Mavarez (Colombia), Oscar Montero (Venezuela), Sandy Moreno (Nicaragua), Ruddy Moretta (Dominican Republic), Jim Patterson (Australia), Luis Pena (Mexico), Jesus Stephens (Dominican Republic).

Seattle Mariners

Office Address: 1250 First Ave. South, Seattle, WA 98134.
Mailing Address: PO Box 4100, Seattle, WA 98194.
Telephone: (206) 346-4000. **Fax:** (206) 346-4400. **Website:** www.mariners.com.

Ownership
Board of Directors: Minoru Arakawa, John Ellis, Buck Ferguson, Chris Larson, Howard Lincoln, Wayne Perry, Frank Shrontz.
Chair/CEO: Howard Lincoln.
President/Chief Operating Officer: Unavailable.

BUSINESS OPERATIONS

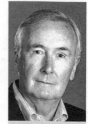

Howard Lincoln

Finance
Executive Vice President, Finance/Ballpark Operations: Kevin Mather. **VP, Finance:** Tim Kornegay. **Controller:** Greg Massey. **Senior VP, Human Resources:** Marianne Short.

Corporate Business/Marketing
Executive VP, Business/Operations: Bob Aylward. **VP, Corporate Business/Community Relations:** Joe Chard. **Senior Director, Corporate Business:** Ingrid Russell-Narcisse. **Senior Director, Community Relations:** Gina Hasson. **Manager, Community Programs:** Sean Grindley. **VP, Marketing:** Kevin Martinez. **Director, Marketing:** Gregg Greene.

Sales
VP, Sales: Frances Traisman. **Director, Group Business Development:** Bob Hellinger. **Director, Ticket Sales:** Cory Carbary.

Baseball Information/Communications
Telephone: (206) 346-4000. **Fax:** (206) 346-4400.
Senior VP, Communications: Randy Adamack.
Senior Director, Baseball Information: Tim Hevly. **Assistant Director, Baseball Information:** Jeff Evans. **Manager, Baseball Information:** Kelly Munro. **Manager, Baseball Information:** Fernando Alcala.
Director, Public Information: Rebecca Hale. **Director, Graphic Design:** Carl Morton.

Ticketing
Telephone: (206) 346-4001. **Fax:** (206) 346-4100.
Senior Director, Ticketing/Parking Operations: Malcolm Rogel. **Director, Ticket Services:** Jennifer Sweigert.

Stadium Operations
VP, Ballpark Operations: Scott Jenkins. **Senior Director, Safeco Field Operations:** Tony Pereira. **Senior Director, Engineering/Maintenance:** Joe Myhra. **Security:** Sylvester Servance. **Director, Events:** Jill Hashimoto.
VP, Information Services: Dave Curry. **Director, PBX/Retail Systems:** Oliver Roy. **Director, Database/Applications:**

2014 SCHEDULE
Standard Game Times: 7:10 p.m.; Sun. 1:10.

MARCH			
31 . . . at Los Angeles (AL)	5-7 . . . . .at Oakland	20-22 . . . . .at Kansas City	7-10 . . . . . Chicago (AL)
	8-11 . . . . . . Kansas City	23-25 . . . . Boston	11-13 . . . . .Toronto
APRIL	12-14 . . . . . .Tampa Bay	27-29 . . . . Cleveland	15-17 . . . . .at Detroit
	16-18 . . . . . at Minnesota	30 . . . . .at Houston	18-20 . . . . at Philadelphia
1-2. . . at Los Angeles (AL)	20-21 . . . . .at Texas		22-24 . . . . .at Boston
3-6. . . . . .at Oakland	22-25 . . . . Houston	**JULY**	25-27 . . . . Texas
8-9. . . . Los Angeles (AL)	26-29 . . . Los Angeles (AL)	1-2. . . . . .at Houston	29-31 . . . . . . .Washington
11-13 . . . . Oakland	30-31 . . . . Detroit	4-6. . . . . at Chicago (AL)	
14-17 . . . . .at Texas		7-10 . . . . . . .Minnesota	**SEPTEMBER**
18-20 . . . . at Miami	**JUNE**	11-13 . . . . Oakland	1-3 . . . . .at Oakland
21-23 . . . . Houston	1 . . . . Detroit	18-20 . at Los Angeles (AL)	4-7 . . . . .at Texas
25-27 . . . . Texas	3-4. . . . . at Atlanta	21-23 . . . . .New York (NL)	8-10. . . . . Houston
29-30 . . . at New York (AL)	6-9. . . . . at Tampa Bay	24-27 . . . . . . Baltimore	12-14 . . . . Oakland
	10-12 . . . . .New York (AL)	29-31 . . . . .at Cleveland	15-18 . at Los Angeles (AL)
MAY	13-15 . . . . Texas		19-21 . . . . . . .at Houston
1 . . . . . at New York (AL)	16-17 . . . . San Diego	**AUGUST**	22-25 . . . . . . at Toronto
2-4. . . . . .at Houston	18-19 . . . . . at San Diego	1-3. . . . . . . .at Baltimore	26-28 . . . Los Angeles (AL)
		5-6. . . . . Atlanta	

GENERAL INFORMATION
Stadium (year opened): Safeco Field (1999).
Team Colors: Northwest green, silver and navy blue.
Player Representative: Charlie Furbush
Home Dugout: First Base.
Playing Surface: Grass.

Justin Stolmeier. **Director, Procurement:** Norma Cantu. **Head Groundskeeper:** Bob Christofferson. **Assistant Head Groundskeepers:** Tim Wilson, Leo Liebert. **PA Announcer:** Tom Hutyler. **Official Scorer:** Eric Radovich.

Merchandising
Senior Director, Merchandise: Jim LaShell. **Director, Retail Merchandising:** Julie McGillivray.

Travel/Clubhouse
Director, Team Travel: Ron Spellecy.
Clubhouse Manager: Ryan Stiles. **Visiting Clubhouse Manager:** Ted Walsh. **Video Coordinator:** Jimmy Hartley. **Assistant Video Coordinator:** Craig Manning.

BASEBALL OPERATIONS
Executive VP/General Manager: Jack Zduriencik
Assistant GM: Jeff Kingston. **Special Assistants:** Roger Hansen, Ken Madeja, Joe McIlvaine, Ted Simmons, Pete Vuckovich. **Administrator, Baseball Operations:** Debbie Larsen.

Jack Zduriencik

Major League Staff
Manager: Lloyd McClendon
Coaches: Bench—Trent Jewett; **Pitching**—Rick Waits; **Hitting**—Howard Johnson; **First Base**—Andy Van Slyke; **Third Base**—John Stearns; **Infield Coach**—Chris Woodward; **Bullpen**—Mike Rojas; **Bullpen Catcher**—Jason Phillips.

Medical/Training
Medical Director: Dr. Edward Khalfayan. **Club Physician:** Dr. Mitchel Storey. **Head Trainer:** Rick Griffin. **Assistant Trainers:** Rob Nodine, Matt Toth. **Strength/Conditioning:** James Clifford.

Player Development
Telephone: (206) 346-4316. **Fax:** (206) 346-4300.
Director, Player Development: Chris Gwynn. **Administrator, Minor League Operations:** Jan Plein. **Assistant, Minor League Operations:** Jack Mosimann. **Coordinator, Minor League Instruction:** Jack Howell. **Coordinator, Athletic Trainers:** James Southard. **Latin Athletic Trainer Coordinator:** Javier Alvidrez. **Assistant Athletic Trainer:** Ben Fraser. **Rebab Pitching Coordinator:** Gary Wheelock. **Performance Specialist Coordinator:** Rob Fumagalli. **Roving Instructors:** Terry Clark (pitching), Dan Wilson (catching), Lee May Jr. (hitting), Jim Pankovits (infield), Brant Brown (outfield), Daren Brown (bunting/baserunning), Alvin Davis (special assignment), Jose Moreno (Latin America field), Nasusel Cabrera (Latin America pitching).

Farm System

Class	Club (League)	Manager	Coach	Pitching Coach
Triple-A	Tacoma (PCL)	Rich Donnelly	Cory Snyder	Jaime Navarro
Double-A	Jackson (SL)	James Horner	Roy Howell	Lance Painter
High A	High Desert (CAL)	Eriberto Menchaca	Max Venable	Andrew Lorraine
Low A	Clinton (MWL)	Chris Prieto	Mike Kinkade	Cibney Bello
Short-season	Everett (NWL)	Unavailable	Scott Steinmann	Nasusel Cabrera
Rookie	Pulaski (APP)	Rob Mummau	Brent Johnson	Jason Blanton
Rookie	Peoria (AZL)	Darrin Garner	A. Bottin/J. Umbria	Rich Dorman
Rookie	Mariners (DSL)	Claudio Almonte	F. Gerez/M. Pimentel	Danielin Acevedo
Rookie	Mariners (VSL)	Russell Vasquez	A. Delgado/R. Paz	Carlos Hernandez

Scouting
Telephone: (206) 346-4314. **Fax:** (206) 346-4300.
Director, Professional Scouting: Tom Allison. **Director, Amateur Scouting:** Tom McNamara. **Assistant Scouting Director/Senior National Crosschecker:** Mark Lummus. **Scouting Administrator:** Hallie Larson.
Major League Scouts: Micah Franklin (Gilbert, AZ), Roger Hansen (Stanwood, WA), Bob Harrison (Long Beach, CA), Greg Hunter (Seattle, WA), Bill Kearns (Milton, MA), Lee MacPhail (Shaker Heights, OH), Ken Madeja (Novi, MI), Bill Masse (Manchester, CT), Joe McIlvaine (Newtown Square, PA), John McMichen (Tampa, FL), Joe Nelson (West Palm Beach, FL), Joe Nigro (Staten Island, NY), Duane Shaffer (Goodyear, AZ), Ted Simmons (Chesterfield, MO), Todd Vecchio (Canonsburg, PA), Pete Vuckovich (Johnstown, PA), Woody Woodward (Palm Coast, FL)
National Crosschecker: Butch Baccala (Auburn, CA). **Territorial Supervisors: West**—Jeremy Booth (Katy, TX); **Midwest**—Jesse Kapellusch (Emporia, KS); **Canada**—Brian Nichols (Taunton, MA); **Northeast**—Alex Smith (Abingdon, MD); **Southeast**—Garrett Ball (Atlanta, GA).
Area Supervisors: Dave Alexander (Lafayette, IN), Jay Catalano (Nashville, TN), Ben Collman (Austin, TX), Dustin Evans (Taylorsville, GA), Ryan Holmes (Frisco, TX), Steve Markovich (Highlands, NJ), Devitt Moore (Durham, NC), Mike Moriarty (Marlton, NJ), Rob Mummau (Palm Harbor, FL), Gary Patchett (LaHabra, CA), Chris Pelekoudas (Mesa, AZ), Stacey Pettis (Antioch, CA), Myron Pines (Garden Grove, CA), Joe Ross (Kirkland, WA), Tony Russo (Montgomery, IL), Noel Sevilla (Miami, FL), Bob Steinkamp (Beatrice, NE), Greg Whitworth (Los Angeles, CA).
International Scouting Director: Tim Kissner (Kirkland, WA). **Supervisor, Dominican Republic:** Eddy Toledo (Santo Domingo, DR). **Coordinator, Pacific Rim/Mexico:** Ted Heid (Glendale, AZ). **Administrative Director, Dominican Operations:** Martin Valerio (Santo Domingo, Dominican Republic). **Coordinator, Venezuelan Operations:** Emilio Carrasquel (Barquisimeto, Venezuela). **International Crosschecker:** Scott Hunter (Mt. Laurel, NJ). **Canada/Europe Coordinator:** Wayne Norton.
International Scouts: Tristan Loetzsch (QLD, Australia), Yasushi Yamamoto (Kanagawa, Japan).

Tampa Bay Rays

Office Address: Tropicana Field, One Tropicana Drive, St. Petersburg, FL 33705.
Telephone: (727) 825-3137. **Fax:** (727) 825-3111. **Website:** www.raysbaseball.com.

Ownership
Principal Owner: Stuart Sternberg. **President:** Matt Silverman.

BUSINESS OPERATIONS

Senior Vice President, Administration/General Counsel: John Higgins. **Senior VP, Business Operations:** Brian Auld. **Senior VP:** Mark Fernandez. **Senior VP, Development/Business Affairs:** Michael Kalt. **VP, Development:** Melanie Lenz. **Senior Director, Development:** William Walsh. **Senior Director, Procurement/Business Services:** Bill Wiener, Jr. **Senior Director, Information Technology:** Juan Ramirez. **Director, Human Resources:** Jennifer Tran. **Director, Partner/VIP Relations:** Cass Halpin.

Finance
VP, Finance: Rob Gagliardi. **Controller:** Patrick Smith.

Marketing/Community Relations
VP, Branding/Fan Experience: Darcy Raymond. **Director, Marketing:** Carey Cox. **Senior Director, Community Relations:** Suzanne Luecke.

Stuart Sternberg

Communications/Broadcasting
Phone: (727) 825-3242.
VP, Communications: Rick Vaughn. **Director, Communications:** Dave Haller. **Senior Director, Broadcasting:** Larry McCabe.

Corporate Partnerships
Senior Director, Corporate Partnerships: Josh Bullock. **Director, Corporate Partnerships:** Richard Reeves.

Ticket Sales
Phone: (888) FAN-RAYS. **VP, Sales/Service:** Brian Richeson. **Senior Director, Season Ticket Sales/Service:** Jeff Tanzer. **Director, Ticket Operations:** Robert Bennett. **Assistant Director, Ticket Operations:** Ken Mallory.

Stadium Operations
VP, Operations/Facilities: Rick Nafe. **Senior Director, Stadium Operations:** Scott Kelyman. **Senior Director, Stadium Operations:** Tom Karac. **Director, Stadium Operations:** Chris Raineri. **Director, Audio/Visual Services:** Ron Golick. **Head Groundskeeper:** Dan Moeller. **Director, Customer Service/Stadium Experience:** Eric Weisberg.

Travel/Clubhouse
Director, Team Travel/Clubhouse Operations: Chris Westmoreland. **Manager, Home Clubhouse:** Jose Fernandez. **Manager, Visitors Clubhouse:** Guy Gallagher. **Video Coordinator:** Chris Fernandez.

2014 SCHEDULE

Standard Game Times: 7:10 p.m.; Sun. 1:40.

MARCH		
31 . . . . .Toronto		

APRIL		
1-3 . . . . .Toronto		
4-6 . . . . Texas		
7-9 . . . . . .at Kansas City		
11-13 . . . . . .at Cincinnati		
14-16 . . . . . .at Baltimore		
17-20 . . . . .New York (AL)		
22-24 . . . . . . .Minnesota		
25-28 . . . .at Chicago (AL)		
29-30 . . . . . . .at Boston		

MAY		
1 . . . . .at Boston		
2-4 . . . . . at New York (AL)		
6-8 . . . . Baltimore		

JUNE		
9-11 . . . . Cleveland		
12-14 . . . . .at Seattle		
15-18 . at Los Angeles (AL)		
20-22 . . . . Oakland		
23-25 . . . . Boston		
26-28 . . . . . . at Toronto		
30-31 . . . . . . .at Boston		
1 . . . . .at Boston		
2-3 . . . . at Miami		
4-5 . . . . .Miami		
6-9 . . . . Seattle		
10-11 . . . . St. Louis		
13-15 . . . . . . .at Houston		
16-18 . . . . Baltimore		
19-22 . . . . Houston		

JULY		
23-25 . . . . . . Pittsburgh		
27-29 . . . . . .at Baltimore		
30 . . . . . at New York (AL)		
1-2 . . . . at New York (AL)		
3-6 . . . . .at Detroit		
7-9 . . . . Kansas City		
11-13 . . . . .Toronto		
18-20 . . . . . at Minnesota		
22-23 . . . . . .at St. Louis		
25-27 . . . . Boston		
28-30 . . . . . .Milwaukee		

AUGUST		
1-3 . . . . . Los Angeles (AL)		
4-6 . . . . .at Oakland		
8-10 . . . . .at Chicago (NL)		

11-14 . . . . .at Texas		
15-17 . . . . .New York (AL)		
19-21 . . . . Detroit		
22-24 . . . . . . at Toronto		
25-28 . . . . . .at Baltimore		
29-31 . . . . Boston		

SEPTEMBER		
1 . . . . Boston		
2-4 . . . . .Toronto		
5-7 . . . . Baltimore		
9-11 . . . . at New York (AL)		
12-14 . . . . at Toronto		
15-17 . . at New York (AL)		
19-21 . . . . . Chicago (AL)		
23-25 . . . . .at Boston		
26-28 . . . . . .at Cleveland		

GENERAL INFORMATION

Stadium (year opened): Tropicana Field (1998).
Team Colors: Dark blue, light blue, yellow.
Player Representative: Matt Moore.

Home Dugout: First Base.
Playing Surface: AstroTurf
Game Day Grass 3D-60 H.

BASEBALL OPERATIONS

Executive VP, Baseball Operations: Andrew Friedman.
Director, Baseball Operations: Chaim Bloom, Erik Neander. **Director, Major League Administration:** Sandy Dengler. **Senior Baseball Advisor:** Don Zimmer. **Special Assistant, Baseball Operations:** Rocco Baldelli.
Architect, Baseball Systems: Brian Plexico. **Director, Baseball Research/Development:** James Click. **Assistant, Baseball Operations Systems:** Matt Hahn. **Developer, Baseball Systems:** Dan Turkenkopf. **Coordinator, Baseball Research/Development:** Peter Bendix. **Analysts, Baseball Research/Development:** Joshua Kalk, Shawn Hoffman. **Assistant, Baseball Operations:** Graham Tyler. **Assistant, Baseball Research/Development:** Jonathan Erlichman.

Andrew Friedman

Major League Staff

Manager: Joe Maddon.
Coaches: Bench—Dave Martinez; **Pitching**—Jim Hickey; **Hitting**—Derek Shelton; **First Base**—George Hendrick; **Third Base**—Tom Foley; **Bullpen**—Stan Boroski; **Hitting/Catching**—Jamie Nelson.

Medical/Training

Medical Director: Dr. James Andrews. **Medical Team Physician:** Dr. Michael Reilly. **Orthopedic Team Physician:** Dr. Koco Eaton. **Head Athletic Trainer:** Ron Porterfield. **Assistant Athletic Trainers:** Paul Harker, Mark Vinson. **Strength/Conditioning Coach:** Kevin Barr.

Player Development

Telephone: (727) 825-3267. **Fax:** (727) 825-3493.
Director, Minor League Operations: Mitch Lukevics.
Assistant, Minor League Operations: Jeff McLerran. **Administrator, International/Minor League Operations:** Giovanna Rodriguez. **Field Coordinators:** Jim Hoff, Bill Evers. **Minor League Coordinators:** Skeeter Barnes (outfield/baserunning), Dick Bosman (pitching), Steve Livesey (hitting), Paul Hoover (catching), Chad Mottola (hitting), Dewey Robinson (pitching), Kyle Snyder (pitching), Joe Benge (medical), Joel Smith (rehabilitation), Trung Cao (strength/conditioning). **Equipment Manager:** Tim McKechney. **Assistant Equipment Manager:** Shane Rossetti. **Video Coordinator, Baseball Operations:** Ryan Bristow.

Farm System

Class	Club (League)	Manager	Coach	Pitching Coach
Triple-A	Durham (IL)	Charlie Montoyo	Dave Myers	Neil Allen
Double-A	Montgomery (SL)	Brady Williams	Ozzie Timmons	R.C. Lichtenstein
High A	Charlotte (FSL)	Jared Sandberg	Joe Szekely	Steve Watson
Low A	Bowling Green (MWL)	Michael Johns	Dan Dement	Bill Moloney
Short-season	Hudson Valley (NYP)	Tim Parenton	Manny Castillo	Jorge Moncada
Rookie	Princeton (APP)	Danny Sheaffer	Reinaldo Ruiz	Jose Gonzalez
Rookie	Rays (GCL)	Jim Morrison	W. Rincones/H. Torres	Marty DeMerritt
Rookie	Rays (DSL)	Julio Zorrilla	A. DeFreites/R. Guerrero	R. Yil/W. Hernandez
Rookie	Rays (VSL)	German Melendez	A. Freire/G. Omaña	E. Ramos/A. Bastardo

Scouting

Director, Scouting: R.J. Harrison (Phoenix, AZ).
Assistant Director, Amateur Scouting: Rob Metzler. **Administrator, Scouting:** Nancy Berry.
Director, Pro Scouting: Matt Arnold. **Special Assignment Scouts:** Mike Cubbage (Keswick, VA), Larry Doughty (Leawood, KS), Bobby Heck (Kingwood, TX), Mike Juhl (Indian Train, NC), Fred Repke (Carson City, NV). **Major League Scouts:** Bob Cluck (San Diego, CA). **Professional Scouts:** Michael Brown (Chandler, AZ), Jason Cole (Austin, TX), Jason Grey (Mesa, AZ), Kevin Ibach (Geneva, IL), Brian Keegan (Matthews, NC), Jim Pransky (Davenport, IA).
National Crosschecker: Chuck Ricci (Greencastle, PA). **Eastern Regional Supervisor:** Kevin Elfering (Wesley Chapel, FL). **Midwest Regional Supervisor:** Jeff Cornell (Lee's Summitt, MO). **Western Regional Supervisor:** Jake Wilson (Ramona, CA). **Scout Supervisors:** Tim Alexander (Jamesville, NY), Josh Arhart (Solano Beach, CA), James Bonnici (Auburn Hills, MI), Jack Cressend (Mandeville, LA), Rickey Drexler (New Iberia, LA), J.D. Elliby (Mansfield, TX), Brett Foley (Chicago, IL), Brian Hickman (Fort Mill, SC), Ryan Henderson (Gilbert, AZ), Milt Hill (Cumming, GA), Paul Kirsch (Wilsonville, OR), Ronnie Merrill (Tampa, FL), Robbie Moen (El Segundo, CA), Brian Morrison (Fairfield, CA), Pat Murphy (Marble Falls, TX), Lou Wieben (Little Ferry, NJ). **Part-Time Area Scouts:** Tom Couston (Sarasota, FL), Jose Hernandez (Miami, FL), Gil Martinez (San Juan, PR), Graig Merritt (Pitts Meadow, Canada), Casey Onaga (Honolulu, HI), Jack Sharp (Dallas, TX), Donald Turley (Spring, TX), John Wiedenbauer (Ormond Beach, FL).
Director, Latin America Scouting: Carlos Rodriguez (Tampa, FL). **Coordinator, International Operations:** Patrick Walters (Tampa, FL). **International Crosschecker:** Steve Miller (Tampa, FL). **Director, Venezuela Operations:** Ronnie Blanco. **Coordinator, Pacific Rim:** Tim Ireland. **Coordinator, Colombia:** Angel Contreras. **Scouting Supervisor, Mexico:** Eddie Diaz. **Scouting Supervisor, Dominican Republic:** Danny Santana. **Scouting Supervisor, Venezuela:** Marlon Roche. **Consultant, International Operations:** John Gilmore. **International Scouts:** Aaron Acosta (Mexico), Guillermo Armenta (Mexico), Carlos Batista (Dominican Republic), William Bergolla (Venezuela), Orlando Cabrera (Brazil), Juan Francisco Castillo (Venezuela), Alfredo Celestin (Dominican Republic), Adriano De Souza (Brazil), Mario Gonzalez (Venezuela), Braly Guzman (Dominican Republic), Keith Hsu (Taiwan), Chairon Isenia (Curacao), Raul Lopez (Mexico), Grimaldo Martinez (Mexico), Miguel Richardson (Dominican Republic), Drew Samuelson (Australia), Tateki Uchibori (Japan), Euclides Vargas (Venezuela), Jiri Vitt (Czech Republic), Gustavo Zapata (Panama).

Texas Rangers

Office Address: 1000 Ballpark Way, Arlington, TX 76011.
Mailing Address: PO Box 90111, Arlington, TX 76011.
Telephone: (817) 273-5222. **Fax:** (817) 273-5110. **Website:** www.texasrangers.com.

Ownership
Co-Chairman: Ray C. Davis, Bob R. Simpson. **Chairman, Ownership Committee:** Neil Leibman.

BUSINESS OPERATIONS

Executive VP, Business Operations: Rob Matwick. **Senior Executive Vice President:** Jim Sundberg. **Executive VP/Chief Financial Officer:** Kellie Fischer. **Executive VP, Communications:** John Blake. **Executive VP, Business Partnerships/Development:** Joe Januszewski. **Executive VP, Rangers Enterprises/Customer Service/Sales:** Jay Miller. **Executive VP, Entertainment/ Productions:** Chuck Morgan. **Executive Assistant to Co-Chairman:** Keli West. **Executive Assistant to Business Operations/Finance:** Gabrielle Stokes. **Executive Assistant:** Leslie Dempsey. **Manager, Ownership Concierge Services:** Amy Beam.

Ray Davis

Finance/Accounting
VP/Controller: Starr Gulledge. **Assistant Controller:** Brian Thompson.

Human Resources/Legal/Information Technology
Senior VP, Human Resources/Risk Management: Terry Turner. **Associate Counsel:** Kate Cassidy. **VP, Information Technology:** Mike Bullock.

Ballpark/Event Operations
VP, Security/Parking: Blake Miller. **Assistant VP, Customer Service:** Donnie Pordash.

Communications/Community Relations/Social Media
Assistant VP, Player Relations: Taunee Paur Taylor. **Senior Director, Broadcasting/Communications:** Angie Swint. **Senior Director, Media Relations:** Rich Rice. **Director, Social Media:** Kaylan Eastepp. **Manager, Player Relations:** Rebecca Starkey. **Manager, Photography:** Kelly Gavin. **Manager, Media Services:** Brian SanFilippo. **Manager, Publications/Media Relations:** Rob Morse. **Coordinator, Communications:** Madison Pelletier. **VP, Community Outreach/Executive Director, Foundation:** Karin Morris. **Assistant VP, Community Outreach:** Breon Dennis.

Facilities
Senior Director, Maintenance: Mike Call. **Director, Grounds:** Dennis Klein. **Director, Complex Grounds:** Steve Ballard. **Director, Facility Operations:** Duane Arber. **Special Assistant, Ballpark Operations:** Tim Purpura.

Marketing/Game Presentation
VP, Marketing: Becky Kimbro. **Creative Director:** Jerod Couch. **Graphics Director:** Tracy Benck. **Senior Director, Promotions/Special Events:** Sherry Flow. **Senior Director, Game Entertainment/Productions:** Chris DeYuyscher.

2014 SCHEDULE
Standard Game Times: 7:05 p.m.; Sun. 2:05.

MARCH
31 . . . . .Philadelphia

APRIL
1-2 . . . . . . .Philadelphia
4-6 . . . . . . at Tampa Bay
7-9 . . . . . . .at Boston
11-13 . . . . Houston
14-17 . . . . Seattle
18-20 . . . . . Chicago (AL)
21-23 . . . . . .at Oakland
25-27 . . . . . .at Seattle
28-30 . . . . Oakland

MAY
2-4 . . . at Los Angeles (AL)
5-6 . . . . at Colorado

7-8 . . . . .Colorado
9-11 . . . . Boston
12-14 . . . . . .at Houston
16-18 . . . . .Toronto
20-21 . . . . Seattle
22-25 . . . . . . .at Detroit
26-29 . . . . at Minnesota
30-31 . . . . at Washington

JUNE
1 . . . . at Washington
3-5 . . . . Baltimore
6-9 . . . . Cleveland
10-11 . . . . .Miami
13-15 . . . . .at Seattle
16-18 . . . . . .at Oakland
20-22 . at Los Angeles (AL)

24-26 . . . . Detroit
27-29 . . . . . .Minnesota
30 . . . . at Baltimore

JULY
1-3 . . . . .at Baltimore
4-6 . . . at New York (NL)
7-9 . . . . Houston
10-13 . . . Los Angeles (AL)
18-20 . . . . . . at Toronto
21-24 . . . at New York (AL)
25-27 . . . . Oakland
28-30 . . . . .New York (AL)

AUGUST
1-3 . . . . .at Cleveland
4-6 . . . . . .at Chicago (AL)

8-10 . . . . . . .at Houston
11-14 . . . . . .Tampa Bay
15-17 . . . Los Angeles (AL)
19-20 . . . . . . at Miami
22-24 . . . . . Kansas City
25-27 . . . . . . .at Seattle
28-31 . . . . . .at Houston

SEPTEMBER
1-3 . . . . .at Kansas City
4-7 . . . . Seattle
9-11 . . . Los Angeles (AL)
12-14 . . . . Atlanta
16-18 . . . . . .at Oakland
19-21 . at Los Angeles (AL)
22-24 . . . . Houston
25-28 . . . . Oakland

GENERAL INFORMATION
Stadium (year opened): Rangers Ballpark in Arlington (1994). **Team Colors:** Royal blue and red.
Player Representative: Derek Holland. **Home Dugout:** First Base. **Playing Surface:** Grass.

BASEBALL OPERATIONS

Telephone: (817) 273-5222. **Fax:** (817) 273-5285.
General Manager: Jon Daniels.
Assistant GM: Thad Levine, AJ Preller. **Senior Special Assistant to the GM, Scouting:** Don Welke. **Senior Advisor to GM:** Tom Giordano. **Director, Baseball Operations:** Matt Vinnola.
Executive Assistant to GM: Barbara Pappenfus. **Special Assistants to the GM:** Tony Fernandez, Greg Maddux, Ivan Rodriguez. **Major League Special Assistant:** Scott Littlefield. **Special Assistant, Major League Scout:** Greg Smith.

Jon Daniels

Major League Staff

Manager: Ron Washington.
Coaches: Bench—Tim Bogar; **Pitching**—Mike Maddux; **Hitting**—Dave Magadan; **First Base**—Bengie Molina; **Third Base**—Gary Pettis; **Bullpen**—Andy Hawkins; **Assistant Hitting Coach**—Bobby Jones.

Medical/Training

Team Physician: Dr. Keith Meister. **Team Internist:** Dr. David Hunter.
Spine Consultant: Dr. Andrew Dossett. **Senior Director, Medical Operations:** Jamie Reed. **Head Trainer:** Kevin Harmon. **Assistant Trainer:** Matt Lucero. **Director, Strength/Conditioning:** Jose Vazquez.

Player Development

Telephone: (817) 436-5999. **Fax:** (817) 273-5285.
Mike Daly: Senior Director, Minor League Operations
Special Assistants, Player Development: Harry Spilman, Mark Connor. **Manager, Cultural Enhancement:** Bill McLaughlin. **Special Assistant:** Dave Oliver. **Coordinator, Minor League/International Operations:** Paul Kruger. **Field Coordinator:** Jayce Tingler. **Coordinators:** Danny Clark (pitching), Scott Coolbaugh (hitting), Brook Jacoby (assistant hitting), Hector Ortiz (catching), Riley Westman (assistant catching), Keith Comstock (rehab pitching), Casey Candaele (infield/baserunning), Brian Dayette (special assignment coach), Napoleon Pichardo (strength/conditioning), Dale Gilbert (medical), Jeff Bodenhamer (rehab). **Assistant, Arizona Operations:** Josh Shelton. **Minor League Equipment Manager:** Chris Ackerman

Farm System

Class	Club (League)	Manager	Coach	Pitching Coach
Triple-A	Round Rock (PCL)	Steve Buechele	J. Mashore/S. Owen	Brad Holman
Double-A	Frisco (TL)	Jason Wood	Jason Hart	Jeff Andrews
High A	Myrtle Beach (CL)	Joe Mikulik	Josue Perez	Steve Mintz
Low A	Hickory (SAL)	Corey Ragsdale	Bobby Rose	Oscar Marin
Short-season	Spokane (NWL)	Tim Hulett	Unavailable	Jose Jaimes
Rookie	Rangers (AZL)	Kenny Holmberg	D. McDonald/B. Shouse	J. Seaver/K. Hook
Rookie	Rangers (DSL)	Aaron Levin	A. Infante/G. Mercedes	P. Blanco/H. Lugo

Scouting

Assistant General Manager: A.J. Preller.
Director, Amateur Scouting: Kip Fagg. **Director, Pro Scouting:** Josh Boyd.
Director, International Scouting: Mike Daly. **ML Special Assistant:** Scott Littlefield. **Special Assistant/Major League Scout:** Greg Smith. **Manager, Amateur Scouting:** Matt Klotsche. **Senior Advisor to the GM:** Tom Giordano (Orlando, FL). **Major League Scouts:** Russ Ardolina (Rockville, MD), Keith Boeck (Chandler, AZ).
Pro Scouts: Mike Anderson (Austin, TX), Chris Briones (Reno, NV), Scot Engler (Montgomery, IL), Jay Eddings (Plano, TX), Ross Fenstermaker (Granite Bay, CA), Mike Grouse (Lee's Summit, MO), Todd Walther (Hurst, TX).
National Crosschecker: Clarence Johns (Atlanta, GA). **Special Assistant to the General Manager:** James Keller (Sacramento, CA). **Crosscheckers: West Coast Crosschecker:** Casey Harvie (Lake Stevens, WA). **Midwest Crosschecker:** Randy Taylor (Katy, TX). **Eastern Crosschecker:** Ryan Coe (Acworth, GA). **Southeast Crosschecker:** Brian Williams (Cincinnati, OH). **Special Assignment Crosschecker:** Jake Krug (Flower Mound, TX).
Area Scouts: Doug Banks (Scottsdale, AZ), Roger Coryell (Ypsilanti, MI), Bobby Crook (Fort Worth, TX), Steve Flores (Temecula, CA), Jonathan George (North Huntingdon, PA), Todd Guggiana (Long Beach, CA), Jay Heafner (Katy, TX), Chris Kemp (Charlotte, NC), Gary McGraw (Gaston, OR), Michael Medici (Aurora, IL), Butch Metzger (Sacramento, CA), Takeshi Sakurayama (Manchester, CT), Dustin Smith (Olathe, KS), Cliff Terracuso (Jupiter, FL), Frankie Thon (Guaynabo, Puerto Rico), Derrick Tucker (Woodstock, GA), Jeff Wood (Birmingham, AL).
Part-Time Scouts: Chris Collias (Oak Park, MI), Buzzie Keller (Seguin, TX), Bob Laurie (Plano, TX), James Vilade (Frisco, TX). **Amateur Video Scouting Coordinator:** Matt Simonetti.
Senior Advisor, Pacific Rim Operations: Jim Colborn. **Coordinator, Pacific Rim Operations:** Joe Furukawa (Japan). **Director, International Scouting:** Gil Kim. **Director, Latin American Scouting:** Rafic Saab. **Dominican Program Coordinator/Scout:** Danilo Troncosco. **Manager, Pacific Rim Operations:** Curtis Jung. **Manager, Cultural Enhancement/International Scout (Mexico):** Bill McLaughlin. **Assistant, International Operations:** Stosh Hoover. **Latin America Crosscheckers:** Roberto Aquino.
International Scouts: Rogel Andrade (Venezuela), Willy Espinal (Dominican Republic), Jose Felomina (Curacao), Jose Fernandez (Florida), Johnny Gomez (Venezuela), Carlos Gonzalez (Venezuela), Chu Halabi (Aruba), Jung-Hua Liu (Taiwan), Rodolfo Rosario (Dominican Republic), Joel Ronda (Puerto Rico), Hamilton Sarabia (Colombia), Eduardo Thomas (Panama), Manuel Velez (Mexico), Hajime Watabe (Japan).

Toronto Blue Jays

Office/Mailing Address: 1 Blue Jays Way, Suite 3200, Toronto, Ontario M5V 1J1.
Telephone: (416) 341-1000. **Fax:** (416) 341-1250. **Website:** www.bluejays.com.

Ownership
Operated by: Toronto Blue Jays Baseball Club. **Principal Owner:** Rogers Communications Inc.

BUSINESS OPERATIONS

Paul Beeston

Vice Chairman, Rogers Communications: Phil Lind. **President, Rogers Media:** Keith Pelley. **President/CEO, Toronto Blue Jays/Rogers Centre:** Paul Beeston.
Vice President, Special Projects: Howard Starkman. **Special Assistant to the Organization:** Roberto Alomar, Pat Hentgen.

Finance/Administration
Senior VP, Business Operations: Stephen R. Brooks. **Executive Assistant:** Donna Kuzoff. **Senior Director, Finance:** Lynda Kolody. **Director, Payroll/Benefits:** Brenda Dimmer. **Director, Risk Management:** Suzanne Joncas. **Senior Manager:** Ciaran Keegan. **Accounting Manager:** Tanya Proctor. **Financial Business Manager:** Leslie Galant-Gardiner. **Manager, Revenue Reporting/Analysis:** Craig Whitmore. **Manager, Stadium Payroll:** Sharon Dykstra. **Manager, Ticket Receipts/Vault Services:** Joseph Roach.
Director, Human Resources: Paulette Soper. **Manager, Human Resources:** Matthew Dusureault. **Senior Manager, Information Technology:** Anthony Miranda. **VP, Business Affairs/Legal Counsel:** Matthew Shuber. **Director, Business Affairs/Legal Counsel:** Jessica Fingerhut. **Executive Assistant, Business Affairs:** Suey Lau.

Marketing/Community Relations
VP, Marketing/Merchandising: Anthony Partipilo. **Executive Assistant, Marketing:** Maria Cresswell. **Director, Game Entertainment/Promotions:** Marnie Starkman. **Manager, Community Marketing/Player Relations:** Holly Gentemann. **Executive Director, Jays Care Foundation:** Danielle Bedasse. **VP, Corporate Partnerships:** Mark Ditmars. **Directors, Corporate Partnership/Business Development:** John Griffin, David O'Reilly. **Director, Marketing Services:** Natalie Agro. **Senior Manager, Corporate Partnerships/Business Development:** Mark Palmer. **Senior Manager, Marketing Services:** Honsing Leung. **Executive Assistant:** Darla McKeen.

Communications
VP, Communications: Jay Stenhouse. **Manager, Baseball Information:** Mal Romanin. **Coordinator, Baseball Information:** Erik Grosman. **Coordinator, Communications:** Sue Mallabon.

Stadium Operations
VP, Stadium Operations/Security: Mario Coutinho. **Executive Assistant:** June Sym. **Director, Guest Experience:** Carmen Day. **Manager, Event Services:** Julie Minott. **Manager, Game Operations:** Karyn Gottschalk.

2014 SCHEDULE
Standard Game Times: 7:07 p.m.; Sat/Sun: 1:07

MARCH		
31 . . . . at Tampa Bay	7-8 . . . . Philadelphia	23-25 . . . . New York (AL)
	9-12 . . . Los Angeles (AL)	26-29 . . . . . Chicago (AL)
APRIL	13-15 . . . . Cleveland	
1-3 . . . . at Tampa Bay	16-18 . . . . at Texas	**JULY**
4-6 . . . . New York (AL)	20-22 . . . . at Boston	1-2 . . . . Milwaukee
8-10 . . . . Houston	23-25 . . . . Oakland	3-6 . . . . at Oakland
11-13 . . . . . at Baltimore	26-28 . . . . . . Tampa Bay	7-9 . . at Los Angeles (AL)
15-17 . . . at Minnesota	29-31 . . . . . Kansas City	11-13 . . . at Tampa Bay
18-20 . . . . . at Cleveland		18-20 . . . . Texas
22-24 . . . . . . Baltimore	**JUNE**	21-24 . . . . Boston
25-27 . . . . Boston	1 . . . . Kansas City	25-27 . . at New York (AL)
29-30 . . . . at Kansas City	3-5 . . . . at Detroit	28-30 . . . . at Boston
	6-8 . . . . St. Louis	31 . . . . at Houston
MAY	9-11 . . . . Minnesota	
1 . . . . at Kansas City	12-15 . . . . . at Baltimore	**AUGUST**
2-4 . . . . . . at Pittsburgh	17-19 . . at New York (AL)	1-3 . . . . at Houston
5-6 . . . . . at Philadelphia	20-22 . . . . . at Cincinnati	5-7 . . . . Baltimore
		8-10 . . . . Detroit

11-13 . . . . at Seattle	
15-17 . . . at Chicago (AL)	
19-20 . . . . at Milwaukee	
22-24 . . . . Tampa Bay	
25-27 . . . . Boston	
29-31 . . . . New York (AL)	
SEPTEMBER	
2-4 . . . . . . at Tampa Bay	
5-7 . . . . at Boston	
8-10 . . . . . Chicago (NL)	
12-14 . . . . . Tampa Bay	
15-17 . . . . . at Baltimore	
18-21 . . . at New York (AL)	
22-25 . . . . Seattle	
26-28 . . . . Baltimore	

GENERAL INFORMATION

Stadium (year opened): Rogers Centre (1989).
Team Colors: Blue and white.
Player Representative: Unavailable.
Home Dugout: Third Base.
Playing Surface: AstroTurf Gameday 3D Synthetic Turf.

Ticket Operations
Director, Ticket Operations: Justin Hay. **Director, Ticket Services:** Sheila Stella. **Manager, Box Office:** Christina Dodge.

Ticket Sales/Service
VP, Ticket Sales/Service: Jason Diplock. **Executive Assistant:** Stacey Jackson. **Director, Luxury Suite Sales/Service:** Michael Hook. **Director, Ticket Sales:** Franc Rota. **Manager, Group Sales:** Ryan Gustavel. **Manager, Season Ticket Services:** Erik Bobson. **Manager, Ticket Sales:** John Santana.

Travel/Clubhouse
Director, Team Travel/Clubhouse Operations: Mike Shaw. **Equipment Manager:** Jeff Ross. **Clubhouse Manager:** Kevin Malloy. **Visiting Clubhouse Manager:** Len Frejlich. **Video Operations:** Robert Baumander. **Coordinator, Advance Scouting/Video:** Ryan Mittleman. **Director, Team Employee Assistance Program:** Ray Karesky.

BASEBALL OPERATIONS

Senior VP, Baseball Operations/General Manager: Alex Anthopoulos. **VP, Baseball Operations/Assistant GM:** Tony LaCava. **Assistant GM:** Andrew Tinnish. **Special Assistant to the GM:** Dana Brown. **Consultants:** George Bell, Cito Gaston, Fred McGriff, Paul Quantrill. **Administrator, Baseball Operations:** Heather Connolly. **Baseball Information Analyst:** Jason Sheehan. **Baseball Operations Analyst:** Joe Pare. **Executive Assistant to GM:** Anna Coppola.

Alex Anthopoulos

Major League Staff
Manager: John Gibbons.
Coaches: Bench—DeMarlo Hale; **Pitching**—Pete Walker; **Hitting**—Kevin Seitzer; **First Base**—Tim Leiper; **Third Base**—Luis Rivera; **Bullpen**—Bob Stanley. **Bullpen Catcher:** Alex Anreopoulos.

Medical/Training
Medical Advisor: Dr. Bernie Gosevitz. **Consulting Physician:** Dr. Ron Taylor. **Consulting Team Physicians:** Dr. Irv Feferman, Dr. Noah Forman. **Head Trainer:** George Poulis. **Assistant Trainer:** Mike Frostad. **Strength/Conditioning Coordinator:** Chris Joyner.

Player Development
Telephone: (727) 734-8007. **Fax:** (727) 734-8162.
Director, Minor League Operations: Charlie Wilson. **Senior Advisor:** Rich Miller. **Coordinator, Instruction:** Clayton McCullough. **Minor League Field Coordinator:** Doug Davis. **Coordinators:** Dane Johnson (pitching), Mike Barnett (hitting), Mike Mordecai (infield), Tim Raines (outfield/baserunning), Sal Fasano (catching), Rick Langford (rehab pitching), Donovan Santas (strength/conditioning). **Hitting Instructor:** Steve Springer. **Athletic Training/Rehab Coordinator:** Jeff Stevenson. **Assitant Athletic Training/Rehab Coordinator:** Scott Weberg. **Consultant:** Sandy Alomar Sr. **Equipment Coordinator:** Billy Wardlow. **Assistants, Player Development:** Megan Evans, Mike Nielsen. **Administrative Assistant:** Kim Marsh.

Farm System

Class	Club (League)	Manager	Hitting Coach	Pitching Coach
Triple-A	Buffalo (IL)	Gary Allenson	Richie Hebner	Randy St. Claire
Double-A	New Hampshire (EL)	Bobby Meacham	Jon Nunnally	Jim Czajkowski
High A	Dunedin (FSL)	Omar Malave	Stubby Clapp	Darold Knowles
Low A	Lansing (MWL)	John Tamargo Jr.	Ken Huckaby	Vince Horsman
Short-season	Vancouver (NWL)	John Schneider	Dave Pano	Jeff Ware
Rookie	Bluefield (APP)	Dennis Holmberg	Cesar Martin	Antonio Caceres
Rookie	Blue Jays (GCL)	Kenny Graham	Paul Elliott	Willie Collazo
Rookie	Blue Jays (DSL)	Jose Mateo	Carlos Villalobos	R. Lazo/O. Peraza

Scouting
Director, Professional Scouting: Perry Minasian. **Director, Amateur Scouting:** Brian Parker.
Special Assistant, Amateur Scouting: Chuck LaMar. **Coordinator, Professional Scouting:** David Haynes. **Coordinator, Amateur Scouting:** Harry Einbinder. **Special Assignment Scout:** Russ Bove. **Major League Scouts:** Jim Beattie, Sal Butera, Ed Lynch, Jim Skaalen. **Senior Advisor/Professional Scout:** Mel Didier. **Professional Crosscheckers:** Kevin Briand, Dan Decillis, Dan Evans, Jon Lalonde. **Professional Scouts:** Matt Anderson, Jon Bunnell, Steve Connelly, Kimball Crossley, Bob Fontaine, Kevin Fox, Bryan Lambe, Ted Lekas, Nick Manno, Brad Matthews, David May Jr, Steve Springer. **Independent League Scout:** Ryan Lakey.
National Crosscheckers: Blake Davis, Mike Mangan. **Regional Crosscheckers:** Blake Crosby, C.J. Ebarb, Tim Rooney, Rob St Julien. **Area Scouts:** Mike Alberts (Leominster, MA), Joey Aversa (Fountain Valley, CA), Coulson Barbiche (Columbus, OH), Matt Bishoff (Tampa, FL), Dallas Black (Conway, AZ), Darold Brown (Elk Grove, CA), Mike Burns (Houston, TX), Ryan Fox (Yakima, WA), Pete Holmes (Phoenix, AZ), Jeff Johnson (Indianapolis, IN), Brian Johnston (Baton Rouge, LA), Chris Kline (Tarboro, NC), Randy Kramer (Aptos, CA), Jim Lentine (San Clemente, CA), Nate Murrie (Bowling Green, KY), Dan Norris (Gainesville, FL), Matt O'Brien (Clermont, FL), Wes Penick (Clive, IA), Jorge Rivera (Puerto Nuevo, PR), Bud Smith (Lakewood, CA), Mike Tidick (Statesboro, GA), Michael Wagner (Addison, TX), Doug Witt (Brooklyn, MD). **Special Assistant, Latin American Operations:** Ismael Cruz. **Director, Dominican Republic:** Jose Rosario. **Director, Venezuela:** Luis Marquez. **Canada Scouts:** Don Cowan (Delta, BC), Jamie Lehman (Brampton, ON). **International Scouts:** Jairo Castillo (San Pedro, DR), Lionel Chattelle (Wiesbaden, DE), Jose Contreras (Oriente, VZ), Ruban Contreras (Santo Domingo, DR), Luciano del Rosario (Bani, DR), Juan Garcia (Oriente, VZ), Rafael Moncada (San Diego Valencia, VZ), Lorenzo Perez (Manoguayabo, DR), Henry Sandoval (Valencia, VZ), Daniel Sotelo (Managua, Nicaragua), Marino Tejada (Santo Domingo, DR), Alex Zapata (Panama City, PA).

Washington Nationals

Office Address: 1500 South Capitol Street SE, Washington, DC 20003.
Telephone: (202) 640-7000. **Fax:** (202) 547-0025.
Website: www.nationals.com.

Ownership
Managing Principal Owner: Theodore Lerner.
Principal Owners: Annette Lerner, Mark Lerner, Marla Lerner Tanenbaum, Debra Lerner Cohen, Robert Tanenbaum, Edward Cohen, Judy Lenkin Lerner.

BUSINESS OPERATIONS

Ted Lerner

Chief Operating Officer, Lerner Sports: Alan Gottlieb. **Chief Revenue/Marketing Officer:** Valerie Camillo. **Senior Vice President, Administration:** Elise Holman. **VP, Government/ Municipal Affairs:** Gregory McCarthy. **Senior Director, Client Services/Business Operations:** Britton Stackhouse Miller.

Business Affairs/Legal
VP, Ballpark Enterprises/Guest Services: Catherine Silver. **Senior Director, Ballpark Enterprises:** Maggie Gessner. **Senior Director, Guest Services/Hospitality Operations:** Jonathan Stahl. **Senior Manager, Guest Experience:** Maurice Ruffin. **Senior Manager, Guest Experience Operations:** Billy Langenstein. **Senior Manager, Operations:** Lisa Marie Czop. **VP/ Managing Director, Corporate Partnerships/Business Development:** John Knebel. **Director, Corporate Partnerships:** Mike Berry. **Director, Sponsorship Activation:** Kevin Hill.
VP/General Counsel: Damon Jones. **Deputy General Counsel:** Amy Inlander Minniti.

Finance/Human Resources
CFO: Lori Creasy. **VP, Finance:** Ted Towne. **Senior Director, Accounting:** Kelly Pitchford. **Director, Financial Reporting:** Ross Hollander. **Manager, Baseball/Dream Foundation Accounting:** Michael Page. **Senior Accountants:** Rachel Proctor, Michael Sullivan. **VP, Human Resources:** Alexa Herndon. **Director, Benefits:** Stephanie Giroux.

Media Relations/Communications
VP/Managing Director, Communications/Brand Development: Lara Potter. **Senior Director, Corporate Communications:** Joanna Warner. **Senior Manager, Corporate Communications:** Alexandra Schauffler. **Manager, New Media:** Noah Frank. **Senior Director, Baseball Media Relations:** John Dever. **Director, Baseball Media Relations/ New Media:** Amanda Comak. **Coordinator, Baseball Media Relations:** Kyle Brostowitz.

Community Relations
Senior Director, Community Relations: Shawn Bertani. **Manager, Community Relations:** Nicole Murray. **Coordinator, Community Relations:** London Hitchman.

2014 SCHEDULE
Standard Game Times: 7:05 p.m.; Sun. 1:35

MARCH		
31 . . . . . at New York (NL)		

APRIL		
2-3 . . . . . at New York (NL)		
4-6 . . . . Atlanta		
8-10 . . . . Miami		
11-13 . . . . at Atlanta		
14-16 . . . . at Miami		
17-20 . . . . . . St. Louis		
21-23 . . . Los Angeles (AL)		
24-27 . . . . San Diego		
29-30 . . . . . . .at Houston		

MAY		
2-4 . . . . . . at Philadelphia		
5-7 . . . . . Los Angeles (NL)		

9-11 . . . . .at Oakland
12-14 . . . . at Arizona
16-18 . . . . . .New York (NL)
19-21 . . . . Cincinnati
22-25 . . . . . at Pittsburgh
26-28 . . . . .Miami
30-31 . . . . Texas

JUNE		
1 . . . . Texas		
3-5 . . . . .Philadelphia		
6-8 . . . . at San Diego		
9-12 . . . . at San Francisco		
13-15 . . . . . . .at St. Louis		
17-18 . . . . Houston		
19-22 . . . . Atlanta		
23-25 . . . . . at Milwaukee		

26-29 . . . .at Chicago (NL)
30 . . . . .Colorado

JULY		
1-2 . . . . .Colorado		
4-6 . . . . Chicago (NL)		
7-8 . . . . Baltimore		
9-10 . . . . . . at Baltimore		
11-13 . . . . at Philadelphia		
18-20 . . . . . .Milwaukee		
21-23 . . . . . . at Colorado		
25-27 . . . . . .at Cincinnati		
28-30 . . . . at Miami		
31 . . . . .Philadelphia		

AUGUST		
1-3 . . . . .Philadelphia		
5-7 . . . . . .New York (NL)		

8-10 . . . . at Atlanta
12-14 . . . at New York (NL)
15-17 . . . . Pittsburgh
18-21 . . . . .Arizona
22-24 . . . . . San Francisco
25-27 . . . . at Philadelphia
29-31 . . . . .at Seattle

SEPTEMBER		
1-3 . . at Los Angeles (NL)		
5-7 . . . . .Philadelphia		
8-10 . . . . Atlanta		
11-14 . . . at New York (NL)		
15-17 . . . . at Atlanta		
18-21 . . . . at Miami		
23-25 . . . . .New York (NL)		
26-28 . . . . .Miami		

GENERAL INFORMATION
Stadium (year opened): Nationals Park (2008).
Team Colors: Red, white and blue.

Player Representative: Unavailable.
Home Dugout: First Base.
Playing Surface: Grass.

Marketing/Broadcasting
VP, Marketing/Broadcasting: John Guagliano. Executive Director, Production/Entertainment/Promotions: Jacqueline Coleman. Director, Consumer Marketing: Scott Lewis. Senior Director, Creative/Digital/Brand Strategy: Chad Kurz. Manager, Promotions/Events: Amanda Hauge. Manager, Production/Operations: Dave Lundin.

Ticketing/Sales
VP/Managing Director, Sales/Client Services: Chris Gargani. Senior Director, Ticket Sales: David McElwee. Senior Account Executive, Ticket Sales: Kevin Nawrocki. Manager, Group Sales: Brian Beck. Senior Account Executive, Group Sales: Katherine Mitchell. Senior Director, Premium Sales/Service: Michael Shane. Director, Ticket Services: Andy Burns. Senior Director, Ticket Operations: Tom Jackson. Director, Ticket Operations: Derek Younger.

Ballpark Operations
VP, Facilities: Frank Gambino. Director, Ballpark Operations: Adam Lasky. Director, Security: Stewart Branam. Assistant Manager, Security: Kathleen Costello. Head Groundskeeper: John Turnour.

BASEBALL OPERATIONS

Mike Rizzo

President, Baseball Operations/General Manager: Mike Rizzo.
Assistant GM: Bryan Minniti. Special Assistant to the GM/Major League Administration: Harolyn Cardozo. Senior Advisor to the GM: Phillip Rizzo. VP, Clubhouse Operations/Team Travel: Rob McDonald. Assistant, Team Travel: Ryan Wiebe. Director, Baseball Operations: Adam Cromie. Manager, Baseball Analytics: Sam Mondry-Cohen. Baseball Operations Analyst: Michael DeBartolo. Assistant, Baseball Operations: Aron Weston. Consultant, Baseball Operations: Davey Johnson. Assistant, Scouting: Eddie Longosz. Coordinator, Advance Scouting/Video: Erick Dalton. Assistant, Advance Scouting: Christopher Rosenbaum. Assistant, International Scouting: Taisuke Sato. Clubhouse/Equipment Manager: Mike Wallace. Visiting Clubhouse Manager: Matt Rosenthal. Equipment Coordinator: Dan Wallin. Clubhouse Attendant: Andrew Melnick.

Major League Staff
Manager: Matt Williams.
Coaches: Bench—Randy Knorr; Pitching—Steve McCatty; Hitting—Rick Schu; First Base—Tony Tarasco; Third Base—Bob Henley; Bullpen—Matt LeCroy; Defensive Coordination/Advance Coach: Mark Weidemaier.

Medical/Training
Medical Director/Head Team Physician: Dr. Wiemi Douoguih. Head Athletic Trainer: Lee Kuntz. Assistant Athletic Trainer: Steve Gober. Strength/Conditioning Coach: John Philbin. Assistant, Strength/Conditioning Coach: Matt Eiden. Medical Staff Assistant: John Hsu.

Player Development
VP, Player Personnel: Bob Boone.
Assistant GM/VP, Player Development: Doug Harris. Director, Player Development: Mark Scialabba. Assistant Director, Minor League Operations: Ryan Thomas. Assistant, Player Development: JJ Estevez. Director, Florida Operations: Thomas Bell. Senior Manager, Florida Operations: Jonathan Tosches. Administrative Assistant, Florida Operations: Dianne Wiebe. Dominican Republic Academy Administrator: Fausto Severino. Coordinators: Tony Beasley (field), Jeff Garber (field), Spin Williams (pitching), Troy Gingrich (hitting), Gary Thurman (outfield/baserunning), Gary Cathcart (AUB Manager/instruction), Mark Grater (rehab pitching), Jon Kotredes (medical and rehab), Landon Brandes (strength and conditioning). Coordinator, Minor League Equipment/Clubhouse: Calvin Minasian.

Farm System

Class	Club	Manager	Coach(es)	Pitching Coach
Triple-A	Syracuse (IL)	Billy Gardner Jr.	Joe Dillon	Paul Menhart
Double-A	Harrisburg (EL)	Brian Daubach	Mark Harris	Chris Michalak
High A	Potomac (CL)	Tripp Keister	Brian Rupp	Franklin Bravo
Low A	Hagerstown (SAL)	Patrick Anderson	Luis Ordaz	Sam Narron
Short-season	Auburn (NYP)	Gary Cathcart	Amaury Garcia	Tim Redding
Rookie	Nationals (GCL)	Michael Barrett	Jorge Mejia	Micheal Tejera

Scouting
Assistant GM/VP, Scouting Operations: Kris Kline.
Director, Pro Scouting: Bill Singer. Director, Player Procurement: Kasey McKeon. Special Assistants to the GM: Chuck Cottier, Mike Daughtry, Bob Johnson, Deric Ladnier, Ron Rizzi, Jay Robertson, Bob Schaefer. National Supervisor: Mark Baca. Special Assistant to the GM/National Crosschecker, East: Jeff Zona. National Crosschecker, Central: Jimmy Gonzales. National Crosschecker, West: Fred Costello.
Area Supervisors: Steve Arnieri (Barrington, IL), Ray Blanco (Miami, FL), Reed Dunn (Nashville, TN), Paul Faulk (Myrtle Beach, SC), Ben Gallo (Encinitas, CA) Ed Gustafson (Denton, TX), John Malzone (Needham, MA), Alex Morales (Wellington, FL), Bobby Myrick (Colonial Heights, VA), Tim Reynolds (Irvine, CA), Eric Robinson (Acworth, GA), Mitch Sokol (Phoenix, AZ), Everett Stull (Elk Grove, CA), Paul Tinnell (Bradenton, FL), Tyler Wilt (Willis, TX).
Director, Latin American Operations: Johnny DiPuglia. Dominican Republic Scouting Supervisor: Moises De La Mota. Venezuela Scouting Supervisor: German Robles. Coordinator, Pacific Rim: Marty Brown. International Scouts: Modesto Ulloa (Dominican Republic), Carlos Ulloa (Dominican Republic). Part-Time Scouts: Pablo Arias (Dominican Republic), Virgilio De Leon (Dominican Republic), Juan Munoz (Venezuela), Salvador Donadelli (Venezuela), Eduardo Rosario (Venezuela), Ronald Morillo (Venezuela), Caryl Van Zanten (Curacao), Miguel Ruiz (Panama), Eduardo Cabrera (Colombia).

MEDIA
INFORMATION

LOCAL MEDIA INFORMATION

AMERICAN LEAGUE

BALTIMORE ORIOLES
Radio Announcers: Joe Angel, Fred Manfra. **Flagship Station:** WBAL 1090 AM.
TV Announcers: Mike Bordick, Jim Hunter, Jim Palmer, Gary Thorne. **Flagship Station:** Mid-Atlantic Sports Network (MASN).

BOSTON RED SOX
Radio Announcers: Joe Castiglione, Dave O'Brien. **Flagship Station:** WEEI (93.7 FM/850 AM).
TV Announcers: Don Orsillo, Jerry Remy. **Flagship Station:** New England Sports Network (regional cable).

CHICAGO WHITE SOX
Radio Announcers: Ed Farmer, Darrin Jackson, Chris Rongey (pre/post). **Flagship Station:** WSCR The Score 670-AM.
TV Announcers: Ken Harrelson, Steve Stone. **Flagship Stations:** WGN TV-9, WCIU-TV, Comcast SportsNet Chicago (regional cable).

CLEVELAND INDIANS
Radio Announcers: Tom Hamilton, Jim Rosenhaus. **Flagship Station:** WTAM 1100-AM.
TV Announcers: Rick Manning, Matt Underwood, Al Pawlowski. **Flagship Station:** SportsTime Ohio.

DETROIT TIGERS
Radio Announcers: Dan Dickerson, Jim Price. **Flagship Station:** WXYT 97.1 FM and AM 1270.
TV Announcers: Rod Allen, Mario Impemba. **Flagship Station:** FOX Sports Detroit (regional cable).

HOUSTON ASTROS
Radio Announcers: Steve Sparks, Robert Ford. **Spanish:** Alex Trevino, Francisco Romero. **Flagship Stations:** KBME 790-AM, KLAT 1010-AM (Spanish).
TV Announcers: Bill Brown, Alan Ashby, Geoff Blum. **Flagship Station:** Comcast Sports Net Houston.

KANSAS CITY ROYALS
Radio Announcers: Denny Matthews, Steve Physioc, Steve Stewart. **Kansas City affiliate:** KCSP 610-AM.
TV Announcers: Ryan Lefebvre, Rex Hudler, Joel Goldberg. **Flagship Station:** FOX Sports Kansas City.

LOS ANGELES ANGELS
Radio Announcers: Terry Smith, Mark Langston. **Spanish:** Jose Mota, Amaury Pi-Gonzalez. **Flagship Station:** AM 830, 1330 KWKW (Spanish).
TV Announcers: Victor Rojas, Mark Gubicza. **Flagship Stations:** Fox Sports West (regional cable).

MINNESOTA TWINS
Radio Announcers: Cory Provus, Dan Gladden. **Radio Network Studio Host:** Kris Atteberry. **Radio Engineer:** Kyle Hammer. **Spanish Radio Play-by-Play:** Alfonso Fernandez. **Spanish Radio Analyst:** Tony Oliva. **Flagship Station:** 1500 ESPN.
TV Announcers: Bert Blyleven, Dick Bremer. **Flagship Station:** Fox Sports North.

NEW YORK YANKEES
Radio Announcers: John Sterling, Suzyn Waldman. **Flagship Station:** WFAN 660-AM, WADO 1280-AM. **Spanish Radio Announcers:** Francisco Rivera, Unavailable.
TV Announcers: David Cone, Jack Curry, John Flaherty, Michael Kay, Al Leiter, Bob Lorenz, Meredith Marakovits, Paul O'Neill, Ken Singleton. **Flagship Station:** YES Network (Yankees Entertainment & Sports).

OAKLAND ATHLETICS
Radio Announcers: Vince Cotroneo, Ken Korach. **Flagship Station:** KGMZ 95.7 The Game, FM.
TV Announcers: Ray Fosse, Glen Kuiper. **Flagship Stations:** Comcast Sports Net California.

SEATTLE MARINERS
Radio Announcers: Rick Rizzs, Aaron Goldsmith. **Flagship Station:** KOMO 1000-AM.
TV Announcers: Mike Blowers, Dave Simms. **Flagship Station:** FOX Sports Net Northwest.

TAMPA BAY RAYS
Radio Announcers: Andy Freed, Dave Wills. **Flagship Station:** Sports Animal WDAE 620 AM.
TV Announcers: Brian Anderson, Dewayne Staats, Todd Kalas. **Flagship Station:** Sun Sports.

TEXAS RANGERS
Radio Announcers: Eric Nadel, Matt Hicks; Spanish-Eleno Ornelas, Benji Gil. **Flagship Station:** KESN 103.3 FM, KZMP 1540 AM (Spanish).
TV Announcers: Steve Busby, Tom Grieve, Mark McLemore, Emily Jones; Spanish-Victor Villalba, Jose Guzman. **Flagship Stations:** FOX Sports Southwest (regional cable), TXA 21 (Fridays), Time Warner (Spanish).

TORONTO BLUE JAYS
Radio Announcers: Jerry Howarth, Jack Morris, Mike Wilner. **Flagship Station:** SportsNet Radio Fan 590-AM.
TV Announcers: Buck Martinez, Pat Tabler. **Flagship Station:** Rogers Sportsnet.

NATIONAL LEAGUE

ARIZONA DIAMONDBACKS
Radio Announcers: Greg Schulte, Tom Candiotti, Jeff Munn, Rodrigo Lopez (Spanish), Oscar Soria (Spanish), Richard Saenz (Spanish). **Flagship Stations:** KTAR 620-AM & ESPN DEPORTES 710-AM (Spanish).
TV Announcers: Steve Berthiaume, Bob Brenly, Luis Gonzalez, Joe Garagiola Sr. **Flagship Stations:** FOX Sports Arizona (regional cable).

ATLANTA BRAVES
Radio Announcers: Jim Powell, Don Sutton. **Flagship Stations:** WCNN-AM 680, The Fan (93.7 FM), WNNX-FM (100.5).
TV Announcers: Chip Caray, Joe Simpson. **Flagship Stations:** FS South and SportSouth (regional cable).

CHICAGO CUBS
Radio Announcers: Pat Hughes, Ron Coomer. **Flagship Station:** WGN 720-AM.
TV Announcers: Len Kasper, Jim Deshaies. **Flagship Stations:** WGN Channel 9 (national cable), Comcast SportsNet Chicago (regional cable), WCIU-TV Channel 26.

CINCINNATI REDS
Radio Announcers: Marty Brennaman, Thom Brennaman, Jeff Brantley, Jim Kelch. **Flagship Station:** WLW 700-AM.
TV Announcers: Chris Welsh, Thom Brennaman, Jeff Brantley. **Flagship Station:** Fox Sports Ohio (regional cable).

COLORADO ROCKIES
Radio Announcers: Jack Corrigan, Jerry Schemmel. **Flagship Station:** KOA 850-AM.
TV Announcers: Drew Goodman, George Frazier, Jeff Huson.

LOS ANGELES DODGERS
Radio Announcers: Vin Scully, Rick Monday, Charley Steiner, Nomar Garciaparra. **Spanish:** Jaime Jarrín, Fernando Valenzuela, Pepe Yñiguez. **Flagship Stations:** AM570 Fox Sports LA, KTNQ 1020-AM (Spanish).
TV Announcers: Vin Scully, Charley Steiner, Orel Hershiser, Nomar Garciaparra, Alanna Rizzo, John Hartung, Jerry Hairston, Jr. **Spanish:** Jorge Jarrin, Manny Mota. **Flagship Stations:** SportsNet LA (regional cable).

MIAMI MARLINS
Radio Announcers: Dave Van Horne, Glenn Geffner. **Flagship Stations:** WINZ 940-AM, WAQI 710-AM (Spanish). **Spanish Radio Announcers:** Felo Ramirez, Yiky Quintana.
TV Announcers: Tommy Hutton, Rich Waltz, Jeff Conine, Frank Forte, Craig Minervini, Allison Williams, Preston Wilson, Cliff Floyd. **Spanish TV Announcers:** Cookie Rojas, Raul Striker Jr. **Flagship Stations:** FSN Florida (regional cable).

MILWAUKEE BREWERS
Radio Announcers: Bob Uecker, Joe Black. **Flagship Station:** WTMJ 620-AM.
TV Announcers: Bill Schroeder, Brian Anderson. **Flagship Station:** Fox Sports Net North.

NEW YORK METS
Radio Announcers: Unavailable. **Flagship Station:** WOR 710-AM.
TV Announcers: Gary Cohen, Keith Hernandez, Ron Darling, Ralph Kiner, Kevin Burkhardt. **Flagship Stations:** PIX11-TV, Sports Net New York (regional cable).

PHILADELPHIA PHILLIES
Radio Announcers: Larry Andersen, Scott Franzke, Jim Jackson. **Flagship Stations:** WPHT 1210-AM.
TV Announcers: Tom McCarthy. **Flagship Stations:** WPHL PHL17, Comcast SportsNet (regional cable).

PITTSBURGH PIRATES
Radio Announcers: Steve Blass, Greg Brown, Tim Neverett, Bob Walk, John Wehner. **Flagship Station:** Sports Radio 93.7 FM The Fan.
TV Announcers: Steve Blass, Greg Brown, Tim Neverett, Bob Walk, John Wehner. **Flagship Station:** ROOT SPORTS (regional cable).

ST. LOUIS CARDINALS
Radio Announcers: Mike Shannon, John Rooney. **Flagship Station:** KMOX 1120 AM.
TV Announcers: Rick Horton, Al Hrabosky, Dan McLaughlin. **Flagship Stations:** Fox Sports Midwest.

SAN DIEGO PADRES
Radio Announcers: Ted Leitner, Bob Scanlan. **Flagship Station:** The Mighty 1090-AM/ESPN 1700-AM.
TV Announcers: Dick Enberg, Mark Grant, Tony Gwynn, Mike Pomeranz, Mark Sweeney. **Flagship Station:** Fox Sports San Diego.

SAN FRANCISCO GIANTS
Radio Announcers: Mike Krukow, Duane Kuiper, Jon Miller, Dave Flemming. **Spanish:** Tito Fuentes, Erwin Higueros. **Flagship Station:** KNBR 680-AM (English); ESPN Deportes-860AM (Spanish).
TV Announcers: CSN Bay Area—Mike Krukow, Duane Kuiper; KNTV-NBC 11—Jon Miller, Mike Krukow. **Flagship Stations:** KNTV-NBC 11, CSN Bay Area (regional cable).

WASHINGTON NATIONALS
Radio Announcers: Charlie Slowes, Dave Jageler. **Flagship Station:** WJFK 106.7 FM.
TV Announcers: Bob Carpenter, FP Santangelo. **Flagship Station:** Mid-Atlantic Sports Network (MASN).

NATIONAL MEDIA INFORMATION

BASEBALL STATISTICS

ELIAS SPORTS BUREAU INC. NATIONAL MEDIA BASEBALL STATISTICS
Official Major League Statistician
Mailing Address: 500 Fifth Ave., Suite 2140, New York, NY 10110. Telephone: (212) 869-1530. Fax: (212) 354-0980.
Website: www.esb.com.
President: Seymour Siwoff.
Executive Vice President: Steve Hirdt. Vice President: Peter Hirdt. Data Processing Manager: Chris Thorn.

MLB ADVANCED MEDIA
Official Minor League Statistician
Mailing Address: 75 Ninth Ave., New York, NY 10011. Telephone: (212) 485-3444. Fax: (212) 485-3456. Website: MiLB.com.
Assistant Director, Stats: Chris Lentine. Manager, Stats: Shawn Geraghty. Stats Supervisors: Jason Rigatti, Ian Schwartz. Stats Coordinators: Lawrence Fischer, Jake Fox, Dominic French, Kelvin Lee.

MILB.COM
Official Website of Minor League Baseball
Mailing Address: 75 Ninth Ave, New York, NY 10011. Telephone: (212) 485-3444. Fax: (212) 485-3456. Website: MiLB.com.
Director, Minor League Club Initiatives: Nathan Blackmon. Managing Producer, MiLB.com: Brendon Desrochers. Club Producers: Dan Marinis, Danny Wild. Columnist: Ben Hill.

STATS
Mailing Address: 2775 Shermer Road, Northbrook, IL 60062. Telephone: (847) 583-2100. Fax: (847) 470-9140. Website: www.stats.com. Email: sales@stats.com. Twitter: twitter.com/STATSBiznews, twitter.com/STATS_MLB. CEO: Gary Walrath. Co-Chief Operating Officers: Steve Byrd, Robert Schur. Senior Vice President, Sales: Greg Kirkorsky. Senior Vice President, Sports Solutions: Brian Kopp. Assistant Vice President, Sports Operations: Allan Spear. Manager, Baseball Operations: Jeff Chernow. Director, Marketing and Communications: Nick Stamm.

TELEVISION NETWORKS

ESPN/ESPN2
Mailing Address, ESPN Connecticut: ESPN Plaza, Bristol, CT 06010. Telephone: (860) 766-2000. Fax: (860) 766-2213.
Mailing Address, ESPN New York Executive Offices: 77 W 66th St, New York, NY, 10023. Telephone: (212) 456-7777. Fax: (212) 456-2930.
Executive Chairman, ESPN, Inc.: George Bodenheimer.
President: John Skipper. Executive VP, Administration: Ed Durso. Executive VP, Programming and Production: John Wildhack. Executive VP, Program Scheduling/Development: Norby Williamson. Executive VP, News/Talent/Content Operations: Steve Anderson. Senior VP/Executive Producer, Production: Jed Drake. Senior VP Production/Remote Events, Mark Gross. SVP Programming Acquisitions, Burke Magnus. VP, Production: Mike McQuade. Coordinating Producer, Baseball Tonight: Fernando Lopez.
Email: Kristen.M.Hudak@espn.com Kristen Hudak, Senior Publicist, Communications

ESPN CLASSIC, ESPNEWS
VP, Strategic Program Planning: John Papa.

ESPN INTERNATIONAL, ESPN DEPORTES
Executive VP/Managing Director, ESPN International: Russell Wolff.
Senior VP, ESPN Deportes: Traug Keller. General Manager, ESPN Deportes: Lino Garcia. VP, ESPN Deportes, Programming: Freddy Rolon.

FOX SPORTS/FOX SPORTS 1
Mailing Address, Los Angeles: Fox Network Center, Building 101, Fifth floor, 10201 West Pico Blvd., Los Angeles, CA 90035. Telephone: (310) 369-6000. Fax: (310) 969-6700.
Mailing Address, New York: 1211 Avenue of the Americas, 20th Floor, New York, NY 10036. Telephone: (212) 556-2500. Fax: (212) 354-6902. Website: www.foxsports.com.
President/COO: Eric Shanks. Executive Vice President/Executive Producer: John Entz. General Manager/COO, FOX Sports 1: David Nathanson. Executive VP, News: Scott Ackerson. Executive VP, Field Operations/Engineering: Ed Delaney. Executive VP/Creative Director: Gary Hartley. Executive VP, Programming/Research: Bill Wanger. Senior VP, Production: Jack Simmons. VP, Production: Judy Boyd. VP, Field Operations/Engineering: Mike Davies. Coordinating Producer, MLB on FOX: Pete Macheska. Game Director, MLB on FOX: Bill Webb. Senior VP, Communications/Media Relations: Lou D'Ermilio. VP, Communications: Dan Bell. Director, Communications: Ileana Pena. Manager: Eddie Motl. Publicist: Valerie Krebs.

MLB NETWORK
Mailing Address: One MLB Network Plaza, Secaucus, NJ 07094. Telephone: (201) 520-6400.
President/CEO: Tony Petitti. Executive VP: Rob McGlarry. Executive VP, Advertising/Sales: Bill Morningstar. Senior VP, Marketing/Promotion: Mary Beck. Senior VP, Finance/Administration: Tony Santomauro. Senior VP, Operations/Engineering: Susan Stone. VP, Programming: Andy Butters. VP, Engineering/IT: Mark Haden. VP, Distribution/

Affiliate Sales/Marketing: Brent Fisher. **VP, Studio/Broadcast Operations:** Bob Mincieli. **VP, Business Public Relations, Major League Baseball:** Matt Bourne. **Director, Media Relations, MLB Network:** Lorraine Fisher. **Specialist, Media Relations, MLB Network:** Lou Barricelli.

TURNER SPORTS

Mailing Address: 1015 Techwood Drive, Atlanta, GA 30318.
Telephone: (404) 827-1700. **Fax:** (404) 827-1339. **Website:** www.tbs.com/sports/mlb.
President: David Levy.
Executive VP, Chief Operating Officer: Lenny Daniels. **Senior VP, Production/Executive Creative Director:** Craig Barry. **Senior VP, Turner Sports Strategy, Marketing/Programming:** Christina Miller. **VP/Executive Producer, Content:** Albert "Scooter" Vertino. **VP/Executive Producer, Production:** Tim Kiely. **VP, Sports Programming:** John Vandegrift. **Executive VP, Turner Sports Ad Sales/Marketing:** Jon Diament. **Senior VP, Communications:** Sal Petruzzi. **VP, Communications:** Nate Smeltz. **Senior Publicist, Communications:** Eric Welch.

OTHER TELEVISION NETWORKS

CBS SPORTS

Mailing Address: 51 W 52nd St., New York, NY 10019. **Telephone:** (212) 975-5230. **Fax:** (212) 975-4063.
Chairman: Sean McManus. **President:** David Berson. **Executive VP, Programming:** Rob Correa. **Executive Producer/ VP, Production:** Harold Bryant. **Senior VP, Communications:** Jennifer Sabatelle.

CNN SPORTS

Mailing Address: One CNN Center, Atlanta, GA 30303. **Telephone:** (404) 878-1600. **Fax:** (404) 878-0011.
Vice President, Production: Jeffrey Green.

HBO SPORTS

Mailing Address: 1100 Avenue of the Americas, New York, NY 10036. **Telephone:** (212) 512-1000. **Fax:** (212) 512-1751.
President, HBO Sports: Ken Hershman.

NBC SPORTS GROUP

Mailing Address: 1 Blachley Rd., Stamford, CT 06902. **Telephone:** (203) 356-7000.
Chairman: Mark Lazarus. **Group President:** Jon Litner. **President, Programing:** Jon Miller. **CMO:** John Miller. **EVP, Sales/Marking:** Seth Winter. **SVP/GM, Digital Media:** Rick Cordella. **Executive Producer:** Sam Flood. **Senior VP, Communications:** Greg Hughes.

ROGERS SPORTSNET (Canada)

Mailing Address: 9 Channel Nine Court, Toronto, ON M1S 4B5. **Telephone:** (416) 332-5600. **Fax:** (416) 332-5629.
Website: www.sportsnet.ca.
President, Rogers Media: Keith Pelley. **President, Rogers Sportsnet:** Scott Moore. **Director, Communications/ Promotions:** Dave Rashford.

THE SPORTS NETWORK (Canada)

Mailing Address: 9 Channel Nine Court, Toronto, ON M1S 4B5. **Telephone:** (416) 384-5000. **Fax:** (416) 332-4337.
Website: www.tsn.ca.

RADIO NETWORKS

ESPN RADIO

Address: ESPN Plaza, 935 Middle St., Bristol, CT 06010.
Telephone: (860) 766-2000, (800) 999-9985. **Fax:** (860) 766-4505.
Website: http://espn.go.com/espnradio.
GM, ESPN Radio Network: Mo Davenport. **Vice President, Network Content:** David Roberts. **VP, Deportes Programming/Business Initiatives:** Freddy Rolon. **Senior Director II, Affiliate/Syndicated Content:** Scott Masteller. **Senior Director, Radio Programming:** Peter Gianesini. **Senior Director, Digital Audio Content:** Keith Goralski. **Executive Producer II:** John Martin.

SIRIUS XM SATELLITE RADIO

Mailing Address: 1500 Eckington Place NE, Washington, DC 20002. **Telephone:** (202) 380-4000. **Fax:** 202-380-4500.
Hotline: (866) 652-6696. **E-Mail Address:** mlb@siriusxm.com. **Website:** www.siriusxm.com.
President/Chief Content Officer: Scott Greenstein. **Senior VP, Sports:** Steve Cohen. **VP, Sports:** Brian Hamilton. **Director, MLB programming:** Chris Eno. **Senior Director, Communications/Sports Programming:** Andrew Fitzpatrick.

SPORTS BYLINE USA

Mailing Address: 300 Broadway, Suite 8, San Francisco, CA 94133. **Telephone:** (415) 434-8300. **Guest Line:** (800) 358-4457. **Studio Line:** (800) 878-7529. **Fax:** (415) 391-2569. **E-Mail Address:** editor@sportsbyline.com. **Website:** www. sportsbyline.com. **President:** Darren Peck. **Executive Producer:** Ira Hankin.

YAHOO SPORTS RADIO

Mailing Address: 5353 West Alabama St., Suite 415, Houston, TX 77056. **Telephone:** (800) 224-2004. **Fax:** (713) 479-5333. **Website:** www.yahoosportsradio.com.

GENERAL INFORMATION

MAJOR LEAGUE BASEBALL PLAYERS ASSOCIATION

Mailing Address: 12 E. 49th St., 24th Floor, New York, NY 10017. **Telephone:** (212) 826-0808. **Fax:** (212) 752-4378.
E-Mail Address: feedback@mlbpa.org. **Website:** www.mlbplayers.com.
Year Founded: 1966. **Twitter:** @MLB_Players. @MLBPlayersTrust @MLBPAClubhouse
Executive Director: Tony Clark.
Chief Operating Officer: Kevin McGuiness. **General Counsel:** David Prouty. **Senior Advisor:** Rick Shapiro. **Assistant General Counsels:** Heather Chase, Robert Guerra, Bob Lenaghan, Matt Nussbaum, Michael Stival. **Senior Labor Counsel:** Ian Penny. **Special Counsel:** Steve Fehr.
Chief Administrative Officer: Martha Child. **Chief Financial Officer:** Marietta DiCamillo. **Special Assistants to the Executive Director:** Bobby Bonilla, Phil Bradley, Jose Cruz, Jr. Rick Helling, Mike Myers, Steve Rogers. **Special Advisor to the Executive Director:** Dave Winfield. **Special Assistant, Player Programs and Initiatives:** Jeffrey Hammonds.
Player Services: Leonor Barua, Virginia Carballo, Allyne Price. **Director of Player Development:** Bob Tewksbury. **Contract Administrator:** Cindy Abercrombie. **Director, Communications:** Greg Bouris. **Director, Players Trust:** Melissa Persaud. **Players Trust Program Coordinator:** Hillary Caffarone. **Accounting Assistants:** Jennifer Cooney, Terri Hinkley, Yolanda Largo. **Administrative Assistants:** Aisha Hope, Melba Markowitz, Sharon O'Donnell, Lisa Pepin. **Accounting Assistant:** Deirdre Sweeney. **Receptionist:** Rebecca Rivera.
Director, Business Affairs/Licensing/Senior Counsel, Business: Timothy Slavin. **General Manager, Business Affairs/Media/International:** Richard White. **Director, Licensing/Business Development:** Evan Kaplan. **Senior Category Director, Retail Development/Apparel/Events Director:** Nancy Willis. **Category Director, Interactive Media:** Michael Amin. **New Media Content Director:** Chris Dahl. **Licensing Manager, Hard Goods/Collectibles:** Tom Cerabino. **Licensing Manager, Apparel/Retail Development:** Danielle Lopez. **Business Services Manager:** Heather Gould. **Executive Assistant, Business Affairs:** Gretchen Mueller. **Licensing Manager:** Paul Zickler. **Licensing Assistant:** Eric Rivera. **Office Services Clerk:** Victor Lugo.
Executive Board: Player representatives of the 30 major league clubs.
MLBPA Association Representatives: Curtis Granderson, Jeremy Guthrie. **Alternate Association Representatives:** Justin Masterson, Carlos Villanueva. **MLBPA Pension Representatives:** Chris Capuano, Craig Breslow. **Alternate Pension Representatives:** Ross Ohlendorf, Kevin Slowey

SCOUTING

MAJOR LEAGUE BASEBALL SCOUTING BUREAU

Mailing Address: 3500 Porsche Way, Suite 100, Ontario, CA 91764. **Telephone:** (909) 980-1881. **Fax:** (909) 980-7794.
Year Founded: 1974.
Senior Director: Frank Marcos. **Assistant Director:** Rick Oliver. **Office Coordinator:** Debbie Keedy. **Supervisor-Scouting Operations:** Adam Cali.
Scouts: Rick Arnold (Spring Mills, PA), Andy Campbell (Gilbert, AZ), Adrian Casanova (Miami, FL), Mike Childers (Lexington, KY), Craig Conklin (Malibu, CA), Dan Dixon (Temecula, CA), Brad Fidler (Douglassville, PA), Rusty Gerhardt (New London, TX), Dennis Haren (San Diego, CA), Chris Heidt (Rockford, IL), Don Kohler (Asbury, NJ), Mike Larson (Waseca, MN), Johnny Martinez (St Louis, MO), Paul Mirocke (Land O Lakes, FL), Carl Moesche (Gresham, OR), Tim Osborne (Woodstock, GA), Gary Randall (Rock Hill, SC), Kevin Saucier (Pensacola, FL), Harry Shelton (Ocoee, FL), Pat Shortt (South Hempstead, NY), Craig Smajstrla (Pearland, TX), Jim Walton (Shattuck, OK).
Supervisor-Canada: Walt Burrows (Brentwood Bay, BC).
Canadian Scouts: Jason Chee-Aloy (Toronto), Ken Lenihan (Bedford, Nova Scotia), Jasmin Roy (Longueuil, Quebec), Bob Smyth (Ladysmith, BC), Tony Wylie (Anchorage, AK).
Supervisor-Latin America, Puerto Rico: Pepito Centeno (Cidra, PR).
Latin American Scouts: Fabio Herrera (Dominican Republic), Raul Gomez (Dominican Republic), Luis Perez (Venezuela), Julio Cordido (Venezuela).
Video Technicians: Jabari Barnett (Phoenix, AZ), Matt Barnicle (Long Beach, CA), Rafael Castellanos (Dominican Republic), Wayne Mathis (Cuero, TX), Christie Wood (Raleigh, NC).

PROFESSIONAL BASEBALL SCOUTS FOUNDATION

Mailing Address: 5010 N. Parkway Calabasas, Suite 201, Calabasas, CA 91302.
Telephone: (818) 224-3906 / Fax (818) 267-5516
Email: cindy.pbsf@yahoo.com
Website: www.pbsfonline.com
Chairman: Dennis J. Gilbert. **Executive Director:** Cindy Picerni
Board of Directors: Bill "Chief" Gayton, Pat Gillick, Derrick Hall, Roland Hemond, Gary Hughes, Jeff Idelson, Dan Jennings, J.J. Lally, Tommy Lasorda, Frank Marcos, Roberta Mazur, Harry Minor, Bob Nightengale, Damon Oppenheimer, Tracy Ringolsby, John Scotti, Tom Sherak, Dale Sutherland, Kevin Towers, Dave Yoakum, John Young.

SCOUT OF THE YEAR FOUNDATION

Mailing Address: P.O. Box 211585, West Palm Beach, FL 33421. **Telephone:** (561) 798-5897, (561) 818-4329. **E-mail Address:** bertmazur@aol.com.
President: Roberta Mazur. **Vice President:** Tracy Ringolsby. **Treasurer:** Ron Mazur II.
Board of Advisers: Pat Gillick, Roland Hemond, Gary Hughes, Tommy Lasorda.
Scout of the Year Program Advisory Board: Tony DeMacio, Joe Klein, Roland Hemond, Gary Hughes, Dan Jennings, Linda Pereira.

UMPIRES

JIM EVANS ACADEMY
Mailing Address: 200 South Wilcox St., #508, Castle Rock, CO 80104. **Telephone:** (303) 290-7411. **E-mail Address:** jim@umpireacademy.com. **Website:** www.umpireacademy.com.
Operator: Jim Evans.

PROFESSIONAL BASEBALL UMPIRE CORP
Street Address: 9550 16th Street North, St Petersburg, FL 33716. **Mailing Address:** P.O. Box A, St. Petersburg, FL 33731-1950. **Telephone:** (727) 822-6937. **Fax:** (727) 821-5819.
President/CEO: Pat O'Conner. **Secretary/VP, Legal Affairs/General Counsel:** D. Scott Poley. **Executive Director, PBUC:** Justin Klemm. **Chief, Instruction/PBUC Evaluator:** Mike Felt. **Field Evaluators/Instructors:** Jorge Bauza, Dusty Dellinger, Tyler Funneman, Larry Reveal, Darren Spagnardi. **Medical Coordinator:** Mark Stubblefield. **Special Assistant, PBUC:** Lillian Patterson.

THE UMPIRE SCHOOL
Mailing Address: P.O. Box A, St. Petersburg, FL, 33731-1950. **Telephone:** (877) 799-UMPS. **Fax:** (727) 821-5819.
Email: info@therightcall.net. **Website:** www.therightcall.net.
Executive Director: Justin Klemm. **Chief of Instruction:** Mike Felt. **Curriculum Coordinator:** Larry Reveal. **Lead Rules Instructor:** Jorge Bauza. **Field Leaders:** Dusty Dellinger, Tyler Funneman, Darren Spagnardi. **Medical Coordinator:** Mark Stubblefield. **Administrator:** Andy Shultz.

WENDELSTEDT UMPIRE SCHOOL
Mailing Address: P.O. Box 1079 Albion, MI, 49224. **Telephone:** 800-818-1690. **Fax:** 888-881-9801.
Email Address: admin@umpireschool.com. **Website:** www.umpireschool.com.

WORLD UMPIRES ASSOCIATION
Mailing Address: P.O. Box 394, Neenah, WI 54957. **Telephone:** (920) 969-1580. **Fax:** (920) 969-1892. **Email Address:** worldumpiresassn@aol.com.
Year Founded: 2000.
President: Joe West. **Vice President:** Fielden Culbreth. **Secretary/Treasurer:** Jerry Layne. **Labor Counsel:** Brian Lam. **Administrator:** Phil Janssen.

TRAINERS

PROFESSIONAL BASEBALL ATHLETIC TRAINERS SOCIETY
Mailing Address: 1201 Peachtree St., 400 Colony Square, Suite 1750, Atlanta, GA 30361. **Telephone:** (404) 875-4000, ext. 1. **Fax:** (404) 892-8560. **E-mail Address:** rmallernee@mallernee-branch.com. **Website:** www.pbats.com.
Year Founded: 1983.
President: Mark O'Neal (Chicago Cubs). **Secretary:** Ron Porterfield (Tampa Bay Rays). **Treasurer:** Tom Probst (Colorado Rockies). **American League Head Athletic Trainer Representative:** Nick Kenney (Kansas City Royals). **American League Assistant Athletic Trainer Representative:** Rob Nodine (Seattle Mariners). **National League Head Athletic Trainer Representative:** Keith Dugger (Colorado Rockies). **National League Assistant Athletic Trainer Representative:** Mike Kozak (Miami Marlins). **Immediate Past President:** Richie Bancells (Baltimore Orioles).
General Counsel: Rollin Mallernee II.

MUSEUMS

BABE RUTH BIRTHPLACE
Office Address: 216 Emory St., Baltimore, MD 21230. **Telephone:** (410) 727-1539. **Fax:** (410) 727-1652. **E-mail Address:** info@baberuthmuseum.com. **Website:** www.baberuthmuseum.com.
Year Founded: 1973.
Executive Director: Mike Gibbons. **Deputy Director:** John Ziemann. **Chief Curator:** Shawn Herne. **Communications:** Katy Fincham/Steph Deisher.
Hours: Museum open Tuesday-Sunday: 10 a.m. to 5 p.m. Gift shop open daily, 10 a.m. to 5 p.m. **Closed:** New Year's Day, Thanksgiving and Christmas.

CANADIAN BASEBALL HALL OF FAME AND MUSEUM
Museum Address: 386 Church St., St. Marys, Ontario N4X 1C2. **Mailing Address:** P.O. Box 1838, St. Marys, Ontario N4X 1C2. **Telephone:** (519) 284-1838. **Fax:** (519) 284-1234. **E-mail Address:** baseball@baseballhalloffame.ca. **Website:** www.baseballhalloffame.ca.
Year Founded: 1983.
Director, Operations: Scott Crawford.
Museum Hours: May—weekends only; June 1-Oct. 8—Monday-Saturday, 10:30-4; Sunday, noon-4.

FIELD OF DREAMS MOVIE SITE
Address: 28995 Lansing Rd., Dyersville, IA 52040. **Telephone:** (563) 875-8404; (888) 875-8404. **Fax:** (563) 875-7253. **E-mail Address:** info@fodmoviesite.com. **Website:** www.fodmoviesite.com.
Year Founded: 1989. **Office/Business Manager:** Betty Boeckenstedt. **Hours:** April-November, 9 a.m.-6 p.m.

WORLD OF LITTLE LEAGUE: PETER J. McGOVERN MUSEUM AND OFFICIAL STORE
Office Address: 525 Route 15, South Williamsport, PA 17702. **Mailing Address:** P.O. Box 3485, Williamsport, PA 17701. **Telephone:** (570) 326-3607. **Fax:** (570) 326-2267. **E-mail Address:** museum@littleleague.org. **Website:** www. LittleLeagueMuseum.org.

Year Founded: 1982.
Vice President/Executive Director: Lance Van Auken. **Director, Public Programming/Outreach:** Janice Ogurcak.
Curator: Adam Thompson.
Museum Hours: Open 9 a.m. to 5 p.m., Monday-Sunday. **Closed:** Easter, Thanksgiving, Christmas and New Year's Day

LOUISVILLE SLUGGER MUSEUM AND FACTORY
Office Address: 800 W. Main St., Louisville, KY 40202.
Telephone: (502) 588-7228, (877) 775-8443. **Fax:** (502) 585-1179. **Website:** www.sluggermuseum.org.
Year Founded: 1996.
Executive Director: Anne Jewell.
Museum Hours: Jan. 1-June 30/Aug. 11-Dec. 31—Mon-Sat 9 a.m.-5 p.m., Sun. 11 a.m.-5 p.m.; July 1-Aug. 10—Sun-Thurs 9 a.m.-6 p.m., Fri-Sat 9 a.m.-8 p.m. **Closed:** Thanksgiving/Christmas Day.

NATIONAL BASEBALL HALL OF FAME AND MUSEUM
Address: 25 Main St., Cooperstown, NY 13326. **Telephone:** (888) 425-5633, (607) 547-7200. **Fax:** (607) 547-2044.
E-mail Address: info@baseballhalloffame.org. **Website:** www.baseballhall.org.
Year Founded: 1939.
Chairman: Jane Forbes Clark. **Vice Chairman:** Joe Morgan. **President:** Jeff Idelson.
Museum Hours: Open daily, year-round, closed only Thanksgiving, Christmas and New Year's Day. 9 a.m.-5 p.m.
Summer hours, 9 a.m.-9 p.m. (Memorial Day weekend through the day before Labor Day.)
2014 Hall of Fame Induction Weekend: July 25-28, Cooperstown, NY.

NEGRO LEAGUES BASEBALL MUSEUM
Mailing Address: 1616 E. 18th St., Kansas City, MO 64108. **Telephone:** (816) 221-1920. **Fax:** (816) 221-8424. **E-mail
Address:** bkendrick@nlbm.com. **Website:** www.nlbm.com.
Year Founded: 1990.
President: Bob Kendrick. **Executive Director Emeritus:** Don Motley.
Museum Hours: Tues.-Sat. 9 a.m.-6 p.m.; Sun. noon-6 p.m.

NOLAN RYAN FOUNDATION AND EXHIBIT CENTER
Mailing Address: 2925 South Bypass 35, Alvin, TX 77511. **Telephone:** (281) 388-1134. **FAX:** (281) 388-1135. **Website:**
www.nolanryanfoundation.org.
Hours: Mon.-Fri. 9 a.m.-4 p.m. The exhibit is closed Saturdays and Sundays.

RESEARCH

SOCIETY FOR AMERICAN BASEBALL RESEARCH
Mailing Address: 4455 East Camelback Rd., Suite D-140, Phoenix, AZ 85018. **Telephone:** (800) 969-7227. **Fax:** (602)
595-5690. **Website:** www.sabr.org
Year Founded: 1971.
President: Vince Gennaro. **Vice President:** Bill Nowlin. **Secretary:** Todd Lebowitz. **Treasurer:** F.X. Flinn. **Directors:**
Ty Waterman, Fred Worth, Emily Hawks, Leslie Heaphy. **Executive Director:** Marc Appleman. **Web Content Editor/
Producer:** Jacob Pomrenke.

ALUMNI ASSOCIATION

MAJOR LEAGUE BASEBALL PLAYERS ALUMNI ASSOCIATION
Mailing Address: 1631 Mesa Ave., Copper Building, Suite D, Colorado Springs, CO 80906. **Telephone:** (719) 477-1870.
Fax: (719) 477-1875. **E-mail Address:** postoffice@mlbpaa.com. **Website:** www.baseballalumni.com. **Facebook:** face-
book.com/majorleaguebaseballplayersalumniassociation. **Twitter:** @MLBPAA.
Chief Executive Officer: Dan Foster (dan@mlbpaa.com). **Chief Operating Officer:** Geoffrey Hixson (geoff@mlbpaa.
com). **Vice President, Operations:** Mike Groll (mikeg@mlbpaa.com). **Director, Administration:** Mary Russell Baucom
(maryrussell@mlbpaa.com). **Director, Communications:** Nikki Warner (nikki@mlbpaa.com). **Development Coordinator:**
Elaine Riebow (elaine@mlbpaa.com). **Membership Development Coordinator:** Kate Hutchinson (Kate@mlbpaa.com).
Memorabilia Coordinator: Greg Thomas (greg@mlbpaa.com). **Special Events Coordinator:** Rene Vizcarra (Rene@mlb-
paa.com). **Special Events Coordinator:** Eric Kronebusch (eric@mlbpaa.com). **Special Events Coordinator:** Justin Sutton
(Justin@mlbpaa.com). **Public Relations Assistant:** Rachel Levitsky (Rachel@mlbpaa.com). **Special Projects Assistant:**
Tyler Kuch (tkuch@mlbpaa.com). **Database Administrator:** Chris Burkeen (cburkeen@mlbpaa.com)

MAJOR LEAGUE ALUMNI MARKETING
Chief Executive Officer: Dan Foster (dan@mlbpaa.com). **Chief Operating Officer:** Geoffrey Hixson (geoff@mlb-
paa.com). **Vice President, Legends Entertainment Group:** Chris Torgusen (chris@mlbpaa.com). **Vice President of
Operations:** Mike Groll (mikeg@mlbpaa.com). **Director, Administration:** Mary Russell Baucom (maryrussell@mlbpaa.
com). **Marketing Coordinator, Legends Entertainment Group:** Ryan Thomas (rthomas@mlbpaa.com). **Director of
New Business Development:** Pete Kelly (pete@mlbpaa.com). **Memorabilia Coordinator:** Matt Tissi (mtissi@mlbpaa.
com). **Account Executive:** Jennifer Gulino (Jennifer@mlbpaa.com). **Memorabilia Coordinator:** Chris Spomer (cspomer@
mlbpaa.com). **Sales Manager:** Kyle Matthews (kyle@mlbpaa.com). **Sales Manager:** Amy Wagner (Amy@mlbpaa.com).

MINOR LEAGUE BASEBALL ALUMNI ASSOCIATION
Mailing Address: P.O. Box A, St. Petersburg, FL 33731-1950. **Telephone:** (727) 822-6937. **Fax:** (727) 821-5819. **E-Mail
Address:** alumni@MiLB.com. **Website:** www.milb.com.

ASSOCIATION OF PROFESSIONAL BALL PLAYERS OF AMERICA

Mailing Address: 101 S. Kraemer Ave., Suite 112, Placentia, CA 92870. **Telephone:** (714) 528-2012. **Fax:** (714) 528-2037. **E-mail Address:** ballplayersassn@aol.com. **Website:** www.apbpa.org.
Year Founded: 1924.
President: Roland Hemond. **First Vice President:** Tal Smith. **Second VP:** Stephen Cobb. **Third VP:** Tony Siegle. **Secretary/Treasurer:** Dick Beverage. **Membership Services Administrator:** Jennifer Joost. **Membership Services Manager:** Patty Joost.
Directors: Tony Gwynn, Dusty Baker, Tony La Russa, Tom Lasorda, Brooks Robinson, Nolan Ryan, Terry Francona, James Leyland, Mike Scioscia, Ryne Sandberg.

BASEBALL ASSISTANCE TEAM (B.A.T.)

Mailing Address: 245 Park Ave., 31st Floor, New York, NY 10167.
Telephone: (212) 931-7822, Fax: (212) 949-5433. **Website:** www.baseballassistanceteam.com.
Year Founded: 1986.
To Make a Donation: (866) 605-4594.
President: Randy Winn.
Vice President: Bob Watson.
Board of Directors: Sal Bando, Dick Freeman, Steve Garvey, Luis Gonzalez, Adam Jones, Mark Letendre, Alan Nahmias, Christine O'Reilly, Ted Sizemore, Staci Slaughter, Gary Thorne, Bob Watson, Greg Wilcox, Randy Winn.
Director: Erik Nilsen. **Secretary:** Thomas Ostertag. **Treasurer:** Scott Stamp. **Consultant:** Sam McDowell. **Consultant:** Dr. Genoveva Javier. **Operations:** Dominique Correa, Michelle Fucich.

MINISTRY

BASEBALL CHAPEL

Mailing Address: P.O. Box 302, Springfield, PA 19064. **Telephone:** (610) 999-3600.
E-mail Address: office@baseballchapel.org. **Website:** www.baseballchapel.org.
Year Founded: 1973.
President: Vince Nauss.
Hispanic Ministry: Cali Magallanes, Gio Llerena. **Director, Ministry Operations:** Rob Crose.
Board of Directors: Don Christensen, Greg Groh, Dave Howard, Vince Nauss, Bill Sampen, Walt Wiley.

TRADE/EMPLOYMENT

BASEBALL WINTER MEETINGS

Mailing Address: P.O. Box A, St. Petersburg, FL 33731. **Telephone:** (727) 822-6937. **Fax:** (727) 821-5819. **E-Mail Address:** BaseballWinterMeetings@milb.com. **Website:** www.baseballwintermeetings.com.
2014 Convention: Dec. 8-11, Hilton San Diego Bayfront, San Diego, Calif.

BASEBALL TRADE SHOW

Mailing Address: P.O. Box A, St. Petersburg, FL 33731-1950. **Telephone:** (866) 926-6452. **Fax:** (727) 683-9865.
E-Mail Address: TradeShow@MiLB.com. **Website:** www.BaseballTradeShow.com.
Contact: Noreen Brantner, Sr. **Asst. Director, Exhibition Services & Sponsorships.**
2014 Show: Dec. 8-10, San Diego Convention Center, San Diego, CA.

PROFESSIONAL BASEBALL EMPLOYMENT OPPORTUNITIES

Mailing Address: P.O. Box A, St. Petersburg, FL 33731-1950. **Telephone:** 866-WE-R-PBEO. **Fax:** 727-821-5819. **Website:** www.PBEO.com. **Email:** info@PBEO.com. **Contact:** Mark Labban, Manager, Business Development.

BASEBALL CARD MANUFACTURERS

PANINI AMERICA INC.

Mailing Address: Panini America, 5325 FAA Blvd., Suite 100, Irving TX 75061. **Telephone:** (817) 662-5300, (800) 852-8833. **Website:** www.paniniamerica.net. **Email:** Marketing@paniniamerica.net. **Marketing Manager:** Scott Prusha.

GRANDSTAND CARDS

Mailing Address: 22647 Ventura Blvd., #192, Woodland Hills, CA 91364. **Telephone:** (818) 992-5642. **Fax:** (818) 348-9122. **E-mail Address:** gscards1@pacbell.net.

BRANDT SPORTS MARKETING (FORMERLY MULTIAD SPORTS)

Mailing Address: 8914 N. Prairie Pointe Ct., Peoria, IL 61615. **Telephone:** (800) 720-9740. **Fax:** (563) 386-4817. **Website:** http://www.brandtco.com/sports.
Contact: Jim Dougas, jim.douglas@brandtco.com. **Phone:** 309-215-9243. **Fax:** 563-386-4817.
Contact: Dave Mateer, dave.mateer@brandtco.com. **Phone:** 309-215-9248. **Fax:** 563-386-4817.

TOPPS

Mailing Address: One Whitehall St., New York, NY 10004. **Telephone:** (212) 376-0300. **Fax:** (212) 376-0573. **Website:** www.topps.com.

UPPER DECK

Mailing Address: 2251 Rutherford Rd., Carlsbad, CA 92008. **Telephone:** (800) 873-7332. **Fax:** (760) 929-6548.
E-mail Address: customer_service@upperdeck.com. **Website:** www.upperdeck.com.

SPRING TRAINING

CACTUS LEAGUE

For spring training schedules, see page 239

ARIZONA DIAMONDBACKS

Major League
   Complex Address: Salt River Fields at Talking Stick, 7555 N. Pima Road, Scottsdale, AZ 85256.
   Telephone: (480) 270-5000.
   Seating Capacity: 11,000 (7,000 fixed seats, 4,000 lawn seats).
   Location: From Loop-101, use exit 44 (Indian Bend Road) and proceed west for approximately one-half mile; turn right at Pima Road to travel north and proceed one-quarter mile; three entrances to Salt River Fields will be available on the right-hand side.

Minor League
   Complex Address: Same as major league club.

CHICAGO CUBS

Major League
   Complex Address: Cubs Park, 2330 W. Rio Salado Pkwy., Mesa, AZ 85201.
   Telephone: (480) 668-0500. **Seating Capacity:** 15,000.
Location: on the land of the former Riverview Golf Course, bordered by the 101 and 202 interchange in Mesa.

Minor League
   Complex Address: Same as major league club.

CHICAGO WHITE SOX

Major League
   Complex Address: Camelback Ranch—Glendale, 10710 West Camelback Road, Phoenix, AZ 85037.
Telephone: (623) 302-5200. **Seating Capacity:** 13,000.
   Hotel Address: Comfort Suites Glendale, 9824 W. Camelback Rd, Glendale, AZ 85305. **Telephone:** (623) 271-9005. **Hotel Address:** Renaissance Glendale Hotel & Spa, 9495 W. Coyotes Blvd., Glendale, AZ 85305. **Telephone:** 629-937-3700.

Minor League
   Complex/Hotel Address: Same as major league club.

CINCINNATI REDS

Major League
   Complex Address: Cincinnati Reds Player Development Complex, 3125 S. Wood Blvd, Goodyear, AZ 85338. **Telephone:** (623) 932-6590. **Ballpark Address:** Goodyear Ballpark, 1933 S. Ballpark Way, Goodyear, AZ 85338. **Telephone:** (623) 882-3120.
   Hotel Address: Marriott Residence Inn, 7350 N. Zanjero Blvd., Glendale, AZ 85305. **Telephone:** (623) 772-8900. **Fax:** (623) 772-8905.

Minor League
   Complex/Hotel Address: Same as major league club.

CLEVELAND INDIANS

Major League
   Complex Address: Surprise Stadium, 15754 N. Bullard Ave., Surprise, AZ 85374. **Telephone:** (623) 266-8100. **Seating Capacity:** 10,714. **Location:** I-10 West to Route 101 North, 101 North to Bell Road, left at Bell for seven miles, stadium on left.

Minor League
   Complex Address: Same as major league club.
   Hotel Address: Holiday Inn Express, 16540 N. Bullard Ave., Surprise, AZ 85374. **Telephone:** (623) 975-5540.

COLORADO ROCKIES

Major League
   Complex Address: Salt River Fields at Talking Stick, 7555 N. Pima Rd., Scottsdale, AZ 85258. **Telephone:** (480) 270-5800. **Seating Capacity:** 11,000. **Location:** From Loop 101 northbound, Take exit 44 (Indian Bend Rd) and turn left, proceeding west for approximately a half mile, turn right at Pima and the ballpark will be located on the right; From Loop 101 southbound, take exit 43 (Via De Ventura) and turn left, proceeding west for a half mile, turn left at the Via De Ventura entrance into the ballpark parking lot. **Visiting Team Hotel:** The Scottsdale Plaza Resort, 7200 North Scottsdale Road, Scottsdale, AZ 85253. **Telephone:** (480) 948-5000. **Fax:** (480) 951-5100.

Minor League
   Complex/Hotel Address: Same as major league club.

KANSAS CITY ROYALS

Major League
   Complex Address: Surprise Stadium, 15946 N. Bullard Ave., Surprise, AZ 85374. **Telephone:** (623) 222-2222. **Seating Capacity:** 10,700. **Location:** I-10 West to Route 101 North, 101 North to Bell Road, left on Bell for five miles, stadium on left.
   Hotel Address: Wigwam Resort, 300 East Wigwam Blvd., Litchfield Park, Arizona 85340. **Telephone:** (623)-935-3811 Minor League

Minor League
   Complex Address: Same as major league club. **Hotel Address:** Comfort Hotel and Suites, 13337 W. Grand Ave., Surprise, AZ 85374. **Telephone:** (623) 583-3500.

LOS ANGELES ANGELS

Major League
   Complex Address: Tempe Diablo Stadium, 2200 W. Alameda, Tempe, AZ 85282. **Telephone:** (480) 858-7500. **Fax:** (480) 438-7583. **Seating Capacity:** 9,558. **Location:** I-10 to exit 153B (48th Street), south one mile on 48th Street to Alameda Drive, left on Alameda.

Minor League
   Complex Address: Tempe Diablo Minor League Complex, 2225 W. Westcourt Way, Tempe, AZ 85282. **Telephone:** (480) 858-7558.
   Hotel Address: Sheraton Phoenix Airport, 1600 South 52nd Street, Tempe, AZ 85281. **Telephone:** (480) 967-6600.

LOS ANGELES DODGERS

Major League

Complex Address: Camelback Ranch, 10710 West Camelback Rd., Phoenix, AZ 85037. **Seating Capacity:** 13,000, plus standing room.
Location: I-10 or I-17 to Loop 101 West or North, Take Exit 5, Camelback Road West to ballpark. **Telephone:** (623) 302-5000. **Hotel:** Unavailable.

Minor League

Complex/Hotel Address: Same as major league club.

MILWAUKEE BREWERS

Major League

Complex Address: Maryvale Baseball Park, 3600 N. 51st Ave., Phoenix, AZ 85031. **Telephone:** (623) 245-5555. **Seating Capacity:** 9,000. **Location:** I-10 to 51st Ave., north on 51st Ave.
Hotel Address: Unavailable.

Minor League

Complex Address: Maryvale Baseball Complex, 3805 N. 53rd Ave., Phoenix, AZ 85031. **Telephone:** (623) 245-5600. **Hotel Address:** Unavailable.

OAKLAND ATHLETICS

Major League

Complex Address: Phoenix Municipal Stadium, 5999 E. Van Buren, Phoenix, AZ 85008. **Telephone:** (602) 225-9400. **Seating Capacity:** 8,500. **Location:** I-10 to exit 153 (48th Street), HoHoKam Expressway to Van Buren Street (US Highway 60), right on Van Buren. **Hotel Address:** Doubletree Suites Hotel, 320 N 44th St, Phoenix, AZ 85008. **Telephone:** (602) 225-0500.

Minor League

Complex Address: Papago Park Baseball Complex, 1802 N. 64th St, Phoenix, AZ 85008. **Telephone:** (480) 949-5951. **Hotel Address:** Crowne Plaza, 4300 E. Washington, Phoenix, AZ 85034. **Telephone:** (602) 273-7778.

SAN DIEGO PADRES

Major League

Complex Address: Peoria Sports Complex, 8131 W. Paradise Lane, Peoria, AZ 85382. **Telephone:** (623) 486-7000. **Fax:** (623) 486-7154. **Seating Capacity:** 11,333. **Location:** I-17 to Bell Road exit, west on Bell to 83rd Ave.
Hotel Address: La Quinta Inn & Suites (623) 487-1900, 16321 N 83rd Avenue, Peoria, AZ 85382.

Minor League

Complex/Hotel: Country Inn and Suites (623) 879-9000, 20221 N 29th Avenue, Phoenix, AZ 85027.

SAN FRANCISCO GIANTS

Major League

Complex Address: Scottsdale Stadium, 7408 E. Osborn Rd., Scottsdale, AZ 85251. **Telephone:** (480) 990-7972. **Fax:** (480) 990-2643. **Seating Capacity:** 11,500. **Location:** Scottsdale Road to Osborne Road, east on Osborne for a 1/2 mile. **Hotel Address:** Hilton Garden Inn Scottsdale Old Town, 7324 East Indian School Rd, Scottsdale, AZ 85251. **Telephone:** (480) 481-0400.

Minor League

Complex Address: Giants Minor League Complex 8045 E. Camelback Road, Scottsdale, AZ 85251. **Telephone:** (480) 990-0052. **Fax:** (480) 990-2349.

SEATTLE MARINERS

Major League

Complex Address: Peoria Sports Complex, 15707 N. 83rd Ave., Peoria, AZ 85382. **Telephone:** (623) 776-4800. **Fax:** (623) 776-4829. **Seating Capacity:** 11,000. **Location:** I-17 to Bell Road exit, west on Bell to 83rd Ave.
Hotel Address: LaQuinta Inn & Suites, 16321 N. 83rd Ave., Peoria, AZ 85382. **Telephone:** (623) 487-1900.

Minor League

Complex Address: Peoria Sports Complex (1993), 15707 N. 83rd Ave., Peoria, AZ 85382. **Telephone:** (623) 776-4800. **Fax:** (623) 776-4828. **Hotel Address:** Hampton Inn, 8408 W Paradise Lane, Peoria, AZ 85382. **Telephone:** (623) 486-9918.

TEXAS RANGERS

Major League

Complex Address: Surprise Stadium, 15754 N. Bullard Ave., Surprise, AZ 85374. **Telephone:** (623) 266-8100. **Seating Capacity:** 10,714. **Location:** I-10 West to Route 101 North, 101 North to Bell Road, left at Bell for seven miles, stadium on left. **Hotel Address:** Residence Inn Surprise, 16418 N. Bullard Ave., Surprise, AZ 85374. **Telephone:** (623) 249-6333.

Minor League

Complex Address: Same as major league club. **Hotel Address:** Holiday Inn Express and Suites Surprise, 16549 N. Bullard Ave., Surprise AZ 85374. **Telephone:** (800) 939-4249.

GRAPEFRUIT LEAGUE

For spring training schedules, see page 241

ATLANTA BRAVES

Major League
Stadium Address: Champion Stadium at ESPN Wide World of Sports Complex, 700 S Victory Way, Kissimmee, FL 34747. **Telephone:** (407) 939-1500.
Seating Capacity: 9,500. **Location:** I-4 to exit 25B (Highway 192 West), follow signs to Magic Kingdom/Wide World of Sports Complex, right on Victory Way.
Hotel Address: World Center Marriott, World Center Drive, Orlando, FL 32821. **Telephone:** (407) 239-4200.

Minor League
Complex Address: Same as major league club. **Telephone:** (407) 939-2232. **Fax:** (407) 939-2225.
Hotel Address: Marriot Village at Lake Buena Vista, 8623 Vineland Ave., Orlando, FL 32821. **Telephone:** (407) 938-9001.

BALTIMORE ORIOLES

Major League
Complex Address: Ed Smith Stadium, 2700 12th Street, Sarasota, FL 34237. **Telephone:** (941) 893-6300. **Fax:** (941) 893-6377. **Seating Capacity:** 7,500. **Location:** I-75 to exit 210, West on Fruitville Road, right on Tuttle Avenue. **Hotel Address:** Residence Inn, 1040 University Blvd, Sarasota, FL 34234. **Telephone:** (941) 358 1468.

Minor League
Complex Address: Buck O'Neil Baseball Complex at Twin Lakes Park, 6700 Clark Rd., **Sarasota, FL 34241. Telephone:** (941) 923-1996. **Hotel Address:** Days Inn, 5774 Clark Rd., Sarasota, FL 34233. **Telephone:** (941) 921-7812. **Hotel Address:** AmericInn, 5931 Fruitville Rd., **Sarasota, FL 34232. Telephone:** (941) 342-8778.

BOSTON RED SOX

Major League
Complex Address: JetBlue Park at Fenway South, 11500 Fenway South Drive, Fort Myers, FL 33913.
Telephone: (239) 334 4799. **Directions:** From the North: Take I-75 South to Exit 131 (Daniels Parkway); Make a left off the exit and go east for approximately two miles; JetBlue Park will be on your left. From the South: Take I-75 North to Exit 131 (Daniels Parkway); Make a right off exit and go east for approximately two miles; JetBlue Park will be on your left.

Minor League
Complex/Hotel Address: Fenway South, 11500 Fenway South Drive, Fort Myers, FL 33913.

DETROIT TIGERS

Major League
Complex Address: Joker Marchant Stadium, 2301 Lakeland Hills Blvd., Lakeland, FL 33805. **Telephone:** (863) 686-8075. **Seating Capacity:** 9,000. **Location:** I-4 to exit 33 (Lakeland Hills Boulevard).

Minor League
Complex: Tigertown, 2125 N. Lake Ave., Lakeland, FL 33805. **Telephone:** (863)686-8075.

HOUSTON ASTROS

Major League
Complex Address: Osceola County Stadium, 631 Heritage Park Way, Kissimmee, FL 34744. **Telephone:** (321) 697-3200. **Fax:** (321) 697-3197.
Seating Capacity: 5,300. **Location:** From Florida Turnpike South, take exit 244, west on US 192, right on Bill Beck Blvd.
Hotel Address: Embassy Suites Orlando-Lake Buena Vista South, 4955 Kyngs Heath Rd., Kissimmee, FL 34746. **Telephone:** (407) 597-4000.

Minor League
Complex Information: Same as Major League club.
Hotel Address: Holiday Inn Main Gate East, 5711 W. Irlo Bronson Memorial Hwy., Kissimmee, FL 34746. **Telephone:** (407) 396-4222.

MIAMI MARLINS

Major League
Complex Address: Roger Dean Stadium, 4751 Main St., Jupiter, FL 33458. **Telephone:** (561) 775-1818. **Telephone:** (561) 799-1346. **Seating Capacity:** 7,000.
Location: I-95 to exit 83, east on Donald Ross Road for one mile to Central Blvd., left at light, follow Central Boulevard to circle and take Main Street to Roger Dean Stadium.
Hotel Address: Palm Beach Gardens Marriott, 4000 RCA Boulevard, Palm Beach Gardens, FL 33410. **Telephone:** (561) 622-8888. **Fax:** (561) 622-0052.

Minor League
Complex/Hotel Address: Same as major league club.

MINNESOTA TWINS

Major League
Complex Address: Lee County Sports Complex/Hammond Stadium, 14100 Six Mile Cypress Pkwy., Fort Myers, FL 33912. **Telephone:** (239) 533-7610. **Seating Capacity:** 8,100. **Location:** Exit 21 off I-75, west on Daniels Parkway, left on Six Mile Cypress Parkway.
Hotel Address: Four Points by Sheraton, 13600 Treeline Avenue South, Ft. Myers, FL 33913. **Telephone:** (239) 322-1399.

Minor League
Complex/Hotel Address: Same as major league club.

NEW YORK METS

Major League
Complex Address: Tradition Field, 525 NW Peacock Blvd., Port St. Lucie, FL 34986. **Telephone:** (772) 871-2100. **Seating Capacity:** 7,000. **Location:** Exit 121C (St Lucie West Blvd.) off I-95, east 1/4 mile, left onto NW Peacock.
Hotel Address: Hilton Hotel, 8542 Commerce Centre Drive, Port St. Lucie, FL 34986. **Telephone:** (772) 871-6850.

Minor League
Complex Address: Same as major league club. **Hotel Address:** Main Stay Suites, 8501 Champions Way, Port St. Lucie, FL 34986. **Telephone:** (772) 460-8882.

NEW YORK YANKEES

Major League

Complex Address: George M. Steinbrenner Field, One Steinbrenner Dr., Tampa, FL 33614. **Telephone:** (813) 879-2244.
Seating Capacity: 11,076. **Hotel:** Unavailable.

Minor League

Complex Address: Yankees Player Development/Scouting Complex, 3102 N. Himes Ave., Tampa, FL 33607. **Telephone:** (813) 875-7569. **Hotel:** Unavailable.

PHILADELPHIA PHILLIES

Major League

Complex Address: Bright House Networks Field, 601 N. Old Coachman Rd., Clearwater, FL 33765. **Telephone:** (727) 467-4457. **Fax:** (727) 712-4498. **Seating Capacity:** 8,500. **Location:** Route 60 West, right on Old Coachman Road, ballpark on right after Drew Street.
Hotel Address: Holiday Inn Express, 2580 Gulf to Bay Blvd., Clearwater, FL 33765. **Telephone:** (727) 797-6300. **Hotel Address:** La Quinta Inn, 21338 US 19 North, Clearwater, FL 33765. **Telephone:** (727) 799-1565.

Minor League

Complex Address: Carpenter Complex, 651 N. Old Coachman Rd., Clearwater, FL 33765. **Telephone:** (727) 799-0503. **Fax:** (727) 726-1793. **Hotel Addresses:** Hampton Inn, 21030 US Highway 19 North, Clearwater, FL 34625. **Telephone:** (727) 797-8173. **Hotel Address:** Econolodge, 21252 US Hwy. 19, Clearwater, FL 34625. **Telephone:** (727) 799-1569.

PITTSBURGH PIRATES

Major League

Stadium Address: McKechnie Field, 17th Ave. West and Ninth Street West, Bradenton, FL 34205. **Seating Capacity:** 8,500.
Location: US 41 to 17th Ave., west to 9th Street. **Telephone:** (941) 747-3031. **Fax:** (941) 747-9549.

Minor League

Complex/Hotel Address: Pirate City, 1701 27th St. E., Bradenton, FL 34208.

ST. LOUIS CARDINALS

Major League

Complex Address: Roger Dean Stadium, 4795 University Dr., Jupiter, FL 33458. **Telephone:** (561) 775-1818. **Fax:** (561) 799-1380. **Seating Capacity:** 6,864. **Location:** I-95 to exit 58, east on Donald Ross Road for 1/4 mile.

Hotel Address: Embassy Suites, 4350 PGA Blvd., Palm Beach Gardens, FL 33410. **Telephone:** (561) 622-1000.

Minor League

Complex: Same as major league club. **Hotel:** Double Tree Palm Beach Gardens. **Telephone:** (561) 622-2260.

TAMPA BAY RAYS

Major League

Stadium Address: Charlotte Sports Park, 2300 El Jobean Road, Port Charlotte, FL 33948. **Telephone:** (941) 235-5025. **Seating Capacity:** 6,823 (5,028 fixed seats). **Location:** I-75 to US-17 to US-41, turn left onto El Jobean Rd.
Hotel Address: The Rays do not retain a club hotel.

Minor League

Complex/Hotel Address: Same as major league club.

TORONTO BLUE JAYS

Major League

Stadium Address: Florida Auto Exchange Stadium, 373 Douglas Ave., Dunedin, FL 34698. **Telephone:** (727) 733-0429. **Seating Capacity:** 5,509. **Location:** US 19 North to Sunset Point; west on Sunset Point to Douglas Avenue; north on Douglas to Stadium; ballpark is on the southeast corner of Douglas and Beltrees.

Minor League

Complex Address: Bobby Mattick Training Center at Englebert Complex, 1700 Solon Ave., Dunedin, FL 34698. **Telephone:** (727) 733-9302. **Hotel Address:** Baymont Inn & Suites 26508 US 19 North, Clearwater, FL 33761. **Telephone:** (727) 796-1234.

WASHINGTON NATIONALS

Major League

Complex Address: Space Coast Stadium, 5800 Stadium Pkwy., Viera, FL 32940. **Telephone:** (321) 633-9200. **Seating Capacity:** 8,100. **Location:** I-95 southbound to Fiske Blvd (exit 74), south on Fiske/Stadium Parkway to stadium; I-95 northbound to State Road #509/Wickham Road (exit 73), left off exit, right on Lake Andrew Drive; turn right on Stadium Parkway, stadium is 1/2 mile on left.
Hotel Address: Hampton Inn, 130 Sheriff Drive, Viera, FL. **Telephone:** (321) 255-6868.

Minor League

Complex Address: Carl Barger Complex, 5600 Stadium Pkwy., **Viera, FL 32940. Telephone:** (321) 633-8119.
Hotel: Same as major league club.

MINOR
LEAGUES

MINOR LEAGUE BASEBALL

THE NATIONAL ASSOCIATION OF PROFESSIONAL BASEBALL LEAGUES

MINOR LEAGUE BASEBALL ™

Street Address: 9550 16th St. North, St. Petersburg, FL 33716. **Mailing Address:** PO Box A, St. Petersburg, FL 33731-1950. **Telephone:** (727) 822-6937. **Fax:** (727) 821-5819. **Fax/Marketing:** (727) 894-4227. **Fax/Licensing:** (727) 825-3785. **President/CEO:** Pat O'Conner.

Vice President: Stan Brand. **Senior VP, Legal Affairs/General Counsel:** D. Scott Poley. **VP, Baseball/Business Operations:** Tim Brunswick. **VP, Business Development:** Tina Gust. **Special Counsel:** George Yund. **Chief Marketing Officer/President, MiLB Enterprises:** Michael Hand. **Executive Director, Communications:** Steve Densa. **Director, Finance/Accounting:** Sean Brown. **Director, Security/Facility Operations:** Earnell Lucas. **Assistant Director, Legal Affairs:** Louis Brown. **Manager, Baseball Operations/Executive Assistant to the President:** Mary Wooters.

Pat O'Conner

AFFILIATED MEMBERS/COUNCIL OF LEAGUE PRESIDENTS

Triple-A

League	President	Telephone	Fax Number
International	Randy Mobley	(614) 791-9300	(614) 791-9009
Mexican	Plinio Escalante	011-52-555-557-1007	011-52-555-395-2454
Pacific Coast	Branch Rickey	(512) 310-2900	(512) 310-8300

Double-A

League	President	Telephone	Fax Number
Eastern	Joe McEacharn	(207) 761-2700	(207) 761-7064
Southern	Lori Webb	(770) 321-0400	(770) 321-0037
Texas	Tom Kayser	(210) 545-5297	(210) 545-5298

High Class A

League	President	Telephone	Fax Number
California	Charlie Blaney	(805) 985-8585	(805) 985-8580
Carolina	John Hopkins	(336) 691-9030	(336) 464-2737
Florida State	Chuck Murphy	(386) 252-7479	(386) 252-7495

Low Class A

League	President	Telephone	Fax Number
Midwest	George Spelius	(608) 364-1188	(608) 364-1913
South Atlantic	Eric Krupa	(727) 538-4270	(727) 499-6853

Short-Season

League	President	Telephone	Fax Number
New York-Penn	Ben Hayes	(727) 289-7112	(727) 683-9691
Northwest	Mike Ellis	(406) 541 9301	(406) 543-9463

Rookie Advanced

League	President	Telephone	Fax Number
Appalachian	Lee Landers	(704) 252-2656	Unavailable
Pioneer	Jim McCurdy	(509) 456-7615	(509) 456-0136

Rookie

League	President	Telephone	Fax Number
Arizona	Bob Richmond	(208) 429-1511	(208) 429-1525
Dominican Summer	Orlando Diaz	(809) 532-3619	(809) 532-3619
Gulf Coast	Operated by MiLB	(727) 456-1734	(727) 821-5819
Venezuela Summer	F. Moreno/R. Fereira	011-58-241-823-8101	011-58-241-823-8101

NATIONAL ASSOCIATION BOARD OF TRUSTEES

TRIPLE-A

At-large: Ken Young (Norfolk). **International League:** Ken Schnacke (Columbus). **Pacific Coast League:** Sam Bernabe, Chairman (Iowa). **Mexican League:** Cuauhtemoc Rodriguez (Quintana Roo).

DOUBLE-A

Eastern League: Joe Finley (Trenton). **Southern League:** Stan Logan (Birmingham). **Texas League:** Reid Ryan (Corpus Christi).

CLASS A

California League: Tom Volpe (Stockton). **Carolina League:** Chuck Greenberg (Myrtle Beach). **Florida State League:** Ken Carson, Secretary (Dunedin). **Midwest League:** Tom Dickson (Lansing). **South Atlantic League:** Chip Moore (Rome).

SHORT-SEASON

New York-Penn League: Marv Goldklang (Hudson Valley). **Northwest League:** Bobby Brett (Spokane).

ROOKIE

Appalachian League: Mitch Lukevics (Princeton). **Pioneer League:** Dave Baggott, Vice Chairman (Ogden). **Gulf Coast League:** Bill Smith (Twins).

PROFESSIONAL BASEBALL PROMOTION CORP.

President/CEO: Pat O'Conner.

Senior Vice President, Legal Affairs/General Counsel: D. Scott Poley.

Chief Marketing Officer/President, MiLB Enterprises: Michael Hand. **VP, Baseball/Business Operations:** Tim Brunswick. **VP, BIRCO/Business Services:** Brian Earle. **VP, Business Development:** Tina Gust. **VP, Sales/Marketing:** Rod Meadows. **Executive Director, Communications:** Steve Densa. **Director, Finance/Accounting:** Sean Brown. **Director, Information Technology:** Rob Colamarino. **Director, Licensing:** Sandie Hebert. **Director, Business Development:** Scott Kravchuk. **Director, Security/Facility Operations:** Earnell Lucas. **Senior Assistant Director, Exhibition Services/Sponsorships:** Noreen Brantner. **Senior Assistant Director, Event Services:** Kelly Butler. **Assistant Director, Licensing:** Carrie Adams. **Assistant Director, Legal Affairs:** Louis Brown. **Assistant Director, Business Development:** Jill Dedene. **Assistant Director, Accounting:** James Dispanet. **Senior Manager, Corporate Communications:** Mary Marandi. **Senior Account Manager:** Heather Raburn.

Associate Counsel: Robert Fountain. **Manager, Business Development:** Mark Labban. **Contract Manager:** Jeannette Machicote. **Manager, Baseball/Business Operations:** Andy Shultz. **Manager, Baseball Operations/Executive Assistant to President:** Mary Wooters. **Graphic Designer:** Ashley Allphin. **Staff Accountant:** Michelle Heystek. **Marketing Coordinator:** Jessica Merrick. **Sales/Account Coordinator:** Gabe Rendón. **Coordinator, Trademarks/Intellectual Properties:** Jess Vera. **Coordinator, Business Services:** Jessica Watts.

PROFESSIONAL BASEBALL UMPIRE CORP.

President/CEO: Pat O'Conner.

Secretary/Vice President, Legal Affairs/General Counsel: D. Scott Poley.

Executive Director, PBUC: Justin Klemm. **Chief, Instruction/PBUC Evaluator:** Mike Felt. **Field Evaluators/Instructors:** Jorge Bauza, Dusty Dellinger, Tyler Funneman, Larry Reveal, Darren Spagnardi. **Medical Coordinator:** Mark Stubblefield. **Special Assistant, PBUC:** Lillian Patterson.

GENERAL INFORMATION

					Regular Season		All-Star Games	
		Teams	Games	Opening Day	Closing Day		Date	Host
International		14	144	April 3	Sept. 1		*July 16	Durham
Pacific Coast		16	144	April 3	Sept. 1		*July 16	Durham
Eastern		12	142	April 3	Sept. 1		July 16	Altoona
Southern		10	140	April 3	Sept. 1		June 17	Chattanooga
Texas		8	140	April 3	Sept. 1		June 24	Arkansas
California		10	140	April 3	Sept. 1		#June 17	Wilmington
Carolina		8	140	April 3	Sept. 1		#June 17	Wilmington
Florida State		12	140	April 3	Aug. 31		June 14	Bradenton
Midwest		16	140	April 3	Sept. 1		June 17	West Michigan
South Atlantic		14	140	April 3	Sept. 1		June 17	Hickory
New York-Penn		14	76	June 13	Sept. 1		Aug. 19	Brooklyn
Northwest		8	76	June 13	Sept. 1		Aug. 5	Eugene
Appalachian		10	68	June 19	Aug. 29		None	
Pioneer		8	76	June 16	Sept. 4		None	
Arizona		13	56	June 20	Aug. 29		None	
Gulf Coast		16	60	June 20	Aug. 28		None	

*Triple-A All-Star Game. #California League vs. Carolina League.

INTERNATIONAL LEAGUE

Office Address: 55 South High St., Suite 202, Dublin, Ohio 43017.
Telephone: (614) 791-9300. **Fax:** (614) 791-9009.
E-Mail Address: office@ilbaseball.com. **Website:** www.ilbaseball.com.
Years League Active: 1884-

President/Treasurer: Randy Mobley.
Vice Presidents: Dave Rosenfield, Tex Simone. **Assistant to the President:** Chris Sprague.
Corporate Secretary: Max Schumacher.
Directors: Don Beaver (Charlotte), Rob Crain (Scranton/Wilkes-Barre), Joe Finley (Lehigh Valley), George Habel (Durham), North Johnson (Gwinnett), Joe Napoli (Toledo), Bob Rich Jr (Buffalo), Dave Rosenfield (Norfolk), Ken Schnacke (Columbus), Max Schumacher (Indianapolis), Naomi Silver (Rochester), Bill Dutch (Syracuse), Mike Tamburro (Pawtucket), Gary Ulmer (Louisville).
Office Manager: Gretchen Addison.
Division Structure: North—Buffalo, Lehigh Valley, Pawtucket, Rochester, Scranton/Wilkes-Barre, Syracuse. West—Columbus, Indianapolis, Louisville, Toledo. South—Charlotte, Durham, Gwinnett, Norfolk.
Regular Season: 144 games. **2014 Opening Date:** April 3. **Closing Date:** Sept 1.
All-Star Game: July 16 at Durham (IL vs Pacific Coast League).
Playoff Format: South winner meets West winner in best of five series; wild card (non-division winner with best winning percentage) meets North winner in best of five series. Winners meet in best-of-five series for Governors' Cup championship.
Gildan Triple-A Championship Game: Sept. 16 at Charlotte (IL vs Pacific Coast League).
Roster Limit: 25. **Player Eligibility:** No restrictions.
Official Baseball: Rawlings ROM-INT.
Umpires: Sean Barber (Lakeland, FL), Toby Basner (Snellville, GA), Ryan Blakney (Wenatchee, WA), Seth Buckminster (Fort Worth, TX), Kelvin Bultron (Canovanas, Puerto Rico), Jon Byrne (Charlotte, NC), Travis Carlson (Lakeland, FL), Chris Conroy (North Adams, MA), Andy Dudones (Uniontown, OH), Mike Estabrook (Boynton Beach, FL), Ian Fazzio (Springfield, MO), Jeff Gosney (Lakeland, FL), Max Guyll (Fort Wayne, IN), Adam Hamari (Marquette, MI), Anthony Johnson (McComb, MS), Will Little (Fall Branch, TN), Ben May (Racine, WI), Brad Myers (Holland, OH), David Rackley (Matthews, NC), Jonathan Saphire (Centerville, OH), David Soucy (Bluffton, SC), Carlos Torres (Acarigua, Venezuela), John Tumpane (Chicago, IL), Chris Vines (Canton, GA), Chad Whitson (Dublin, OH).

Randy Mobley

STADIUM INFORMATION

| Club | Stadium | Opened | Dimensions | | | Capacity | 2013 Att. |
			LF	CF	RF		
Buffalo	Coca-Cola Field	1988	325	404	325	18,025	537,747
Charlotte	BB&T Ballpark	2014	325	400	315	10,002	254,834
Columbus	Huntington Park	2009	325	400	318	10,100	635,613
Durham	Durham Bulls Athletic Park	1995	305	400	327	10,000	512,648
Gwinnett	Coolray Field	2009	335	400	335	10,427	323,799
Indianapolis	Victory Field	1996	320	402	320	14,500	648,906
Lehigh Valley	Coca-Cola Park	2008	336	400	325	10,000	613,075
Louisville	Louisville Slugger Field	2000	325	400	340	13,131	581,114
Norfolk	Harbor Park	1993	333	400	318	12,067	382,195
Pawtucket	McCoy Stadium	1946	325	400	325	10,031	559,933
Rochester	Frontier Field	1997	335	402	325	10,840	429,338
Scranton/WB	PNC Field	2013	330	408	330	10,000	435,839
Syracuse	NBT Bank Stadium	1997	330	400	330	11,671	345,047
Toledo	Fifth Third Field	2002	320	408	315	10,300	560,080

BUFFALO BISONS

Office Address: Coca-Cola Field, One James D Griffin Plaza, Buffalo, NY 14203.
Telephone: (716) 846-2000. **Fax:** (716) 852-6530.
E-Mail Address: info@bisons.com. **Website:** www.bisons.com.
Affiliation (2nd year): Toronto Blue Jays (2013).
Years in League: 1886-90, 1912-70, 1998-

OWNERSHIP/MANAGEMENT

Operated By: Rich Products Corp.
Principal Owner/President: Robert Rich Jr. **President, Rich Entertainment Group:** Melinda Rich. **President, Rich Baseball Operations:** Jon Dandes.
Vice President/General Manager: Mike Buczkowski. **VP/COO, Rich Entertainment Group:** Joseph Segarra. **VP/Secretary:** William Gisel. **Corporate Counsel:** Jill Bond, William Grieshober.

Director, Sales: Anthony Sprague. Director, Stadium Operations: Tom Sciarrino. Controller: Kevin Parkinson. Senior Accountants: Rita Clark. Accountants: Amy Delaney, Tori Dwyer. Director, Ticket Operations: Mike Poreda. Director, Public Relations: Brad Bisbing. Director, Entertainment/Marketing Services: Matt La Sota. Creative Services/Website Marketing Coordinator: Ashley Beamish. Group Sales Manager: Geoff Lundquist. Sales Coordinators: Rachel Osucha, Mike Simoncelli. Account Executives: Jeffrey Erbes, Mark Gordon, Jim Harrington, Robert Kates, Geoff Lundquist, Burt Mirti, Frank Mooney, Beth Potozniak. Ticket Sales Representatives: Nicholas Iacona Coordinator, Merchandise: Victoria Rebmann. Manager, Office Services: Margaret Russo. Executive Assistant: Tina Lesher. Community Relations: Gail Hodges. Director, Food Services: Robert Free. General Manager, Pettibones Grille: Sean Regan. Food Service Operations Supervisor: Curt Anderson. Head Groundskeeper: Chad Laurie. Chief Engineer: Pat Chella. Home Clubhouse/Baseball Operations Coordinator: Scott Lesher. Visiting Clubhouse Manager: Steve Morris.

FIELD STAFF

Manager: Gary Allenson. Hitting Coach: Richie Hebner. Pitching Coach: Randy St. Claire. Athletic Trainer: Voon Chong. Strength/Conditioning Coach: Armando Gutierrez.

GAME INFORMATION

Radio Announcers: Ben Wagner, Duke McGuire. No. of Games Broadcast: 144. Flagship Station: WWKB-1520. PA Announcer: Jerry Reo. Official Scorers: Kevin Lester, Jon Dare. Stadium Name: Coca-Cola Field. Location: From north, take I-190 to Elm St. exit, left onto Swan St.; From east, take I-190 West to exit 51 (Route 33) to end, exit at Oak Street, right onto Swan St.; From west, take I-190 East, exit 53 to I-90 North, exit at Elm St., left onto Swan St. Standard Game Times: 7:05 pm, Sun 1:05. Ticket Price Range: $6-13 Visiting Club Hotel: Adams Mark Hotel, 120 Church St, Buffalo, NY 14202. Telephone: (716) 845-5100. Visiting Club Hotel: Hyatt Hotel, 2 Fountain Plaza, Buffalo, NY 14202. Telephone: (716) 856-1234.

CHARLOTTE KNIGHTS

Office Address: BB&T Ballpark 324 S. Mint St., Charlotte, NC 28202.
Telephone: (704) 357-8071. Fax:
E-Mail Address: knights@charlotteknights.com. Website: www.charlotteknights.com.
Affiliation (first year): Chicago White Sox (1999). Years in League: 1993-

OWNERSHIP/MANAGEMENT

Operated by: Knights Baseball, LLC.
Principal Owners: Don Beaver, Bill Allen.
Executive Vice President/Chief Operating Officer: Dan Rajkowski. General Manager, Baseball Operations: Scott Brown. VP, Marketing: Mark Smith. VP, Sales: Chris Semmens.
Director, Special Programs/Events: Julie Clark. Director, Media Relations: Tommy Viola. Director, Broadcasting/Team Travel: Matt Swierad. Director, Stadium Operations: Mark McKinnon. Facility Manager: Tom Gorter. Director, Merchandising: Karen Schieber. Business Manager: Michael Sanger. Senior Account Executive: Brett Butler. Director, Ticket Sales/Hospitality: Sean Owens. Director, Ticket Operations: Matt Millward. Director, Community/Team Relations: Lindsey Roycraft. Video Director: David Ruckman. Creative Director: Bill Walker. Account Executives: Kathryn Bobel, Rebekah Boggs, Eric Garvey, Ryan Pittsonberger. Corporate Sales Executive: Jeremy Auker. Special Events Sales Manager: Amber Williams. Special Events Manager: Amber Williams. Manager, Sponsorship Sales: Audrey Stanek. Ticket Sales Associate: Jonathan English.
Head Groundskeeper: Eddie Busque. Assistant Groundskeeper: Justin Fulbright. Operations Coordinator: Nick Braun.

FIELD STAFF

Manager: Joel Skinner. Hitting Coach: Andy Tomberlin. Pitching Coach: Richard Dotson. Assistant Coach: Ryan Newman. Athletic Trainer: Joe Geck. Strength/Conditioning Coach: Chad Efron.

GAME INFORMATION

Radio Announcer: Matt Swierad. No. of Games Broadcast: 144. Flagship Station: ESPN 730 AM. PA Announcer: Unavailable. Official Scorers: Dave Friedman, David McDowell. Stadium Name: BB&T Ballpark. Location: Exit 10 off I 77. Ticket Price Range: $8-18. Visiting Club Hotel: Doubletree by Hilton Charlotte, 895 W. Trade St., Charlotte, NC 28202.

COLUMBUS CLIPPERS

Office Address: 330 Huntington Park Lane, Columbus, OH 43215.
Telephone: (614) 462-5250. Fax: (614) 462-3271. Tickets: (614) 462-2757.
E-Mail Address: info@clippersbaseball.com. Website: www.clippersbaseball.com.
Affiliation (first year): Cleveland Indians (2009). Years in League: 1955-70, 1977-

OWNERSHIP/MANAGEMENT

Operated By: Columbus Baseball Team Inc.
Principal Owner: CBT Inc. Board of Directors: Steven Francis, Tom Fries, Wayne Harer, Thomas Katzenmeyer, David Leland, Cathy Lyttle, Gary Schaeffer, Jeffrey Sopp, McCullough Williams.

President/General Manager: Ken Schnacke. Assistant GM: Mark Warren. Director, Ballpark Operations: Steve Dalin. Assistant Director, Ballpark Operations: Phil Colilla. Director, Ticket Operations: Scott Ziegler. Assistant Director, Ticket Operations: Eddie Langhenry. Director, Marketing/Sales: Mark Galuska. Assistant Director, Marketing: Patrick Thompson. Assistant Director, Promotions: Seth Rhodes. Assistants, Promotions: Emily Poynter, Kaycie Jacobs and Chelsea Gilman. Director, Communications/Media/Team Historian: Joe Santry. Assistant Director, Media Relations: Anthony Slosser. Director, Website Communications: Josh Samuels. Directors, Broadcasting: Ryan Mitchell, Scott Leo. Director, Merchandising: Krista Oberlander. Assistant Director, Merchandising: Robin Vlah. Director, Group Sales: Ben Keller. Assistant Directors, Group Sales: Brett Patton, Steve Kuilder.

Assistants, Tickets: Kevin Daniels, Kevin Smith. Director, Multimedia: Josh Glenn. Assistant Director, Multimedia: Yoshi Ando. Director, Finance: Bonnie Badgley. Executive Assistant to the President/GM: Ashley Held. Office Manager: Melissa Schrader. Director, Sponsor Relationships: Joyce Martin. Director, Event Planning: Micki Shier. Assistant Director, Event Planning: Shannon O'Boyle. Director, Clubhouse Operations: George Robinson. Clubhouse Manager: Matt Pruzinsky. Ballpark Superintendent: Gary Delozier. Head Groundskeeper: Wes Ganobcik. Assistant Groundskeeper: Nick Roe.

FIELD STAFF

Manager: Chris Tremie. Coach: Jim Rickon. Pitching Coach: Tony Arnold. Trainer: Chad Wolfe. Strength/Conditioning Coach: Ed Subel.

GAME INFORMATION

Radio Announcers: Ryan Mitchell, Scott Leo. No. of Games Broadcast: 144. Flagship Station: WMNI 920AM. PA Announcer: Matt Leininger. Official Scorer: Jim Habermehl, Ray Thomas.

Stadium Name: Huntington Park. Location: From north: South on I-71 to I-670 west, exit at Neil Ave., turn left at intersection onto Neil Ave.; From south: North on I-71, exit at Front St. (#100A), turn left at intersection onto Front St., turn left onto Nationwide Blvd.; From east: West on I-70, exit at Fourth St., continue on Fulton St. to Front St., turn right onto Front St., turn left onto Nationwide Blvd.; From west: East on I-70, exit at Fourth St., continue on Fulton St. to Front St., turn right onto Front St., turn left onto Nationwide Blvd. Ticket Price Range: $6-20.

Visiting Club Hotel: Crowne Plaza, 33 East Nationwide Blvd., Columbus, OH 43215. Telephone: (877) 348-2424. Visiting Club Hotel: Drury Hotels Columbus Convention Center, 88 East Nationwide Blvd., Columbus, OH 43215. Telephone: (614) 221-7008. Visiting Club Hotel: Hyatt Regency Downtown, 350 North High Street, Columbus, OH 43215. Telephone: (614) 463-1234.

DURHAM BULLS

Office Address: 409 Blackwell St., Durham, NC 27701. Mailing Address: PO Box 507, Durham, NC 27702.
Telephone: (919) 687-6500. Fax: (919) 687-6560.
Website: www.durhambulls.com. Twitter: @DurhamBulls
Affiliation (first year): Tampa Bay Rays (1998). Years in League: 1998-

OWNERSHIP/MANAGEMENT

Operated By: Capitol Broadcasting Company, Inc.
President/CEO: Jim Goodmon. Vice President: George Habel.

General Manager: Mike Birling. Director, Corporate Partnerships: Chip Allen. Director, Marketing: Scott Carter. Director, Ticket Sales and Service: Peter Wallace. Director, Promotions: Krista Boyd. Manager, Multimedia: Walmer Medina. Manager, Corporate Partnerships: Morgan Weber. Account Executives, Sponsorship: Nick Bavin, Patrick Kinas, Stephanie Rogers. Coordinator, Mascot/Community Relations: Nicholas Tennant. Coordinator, Media Relations: Matt Sutor. Director, Ticket Operations: Tim Seaton. Manager, Premium Ticket Sales: Eli Starkey. Assistant Manager, Premium Ticket Sales: Tim Campbell. Account Executive, Tickets: Tyler Churchill. Premium Ticket Sales Associates: Paul Friedlander, Virginia Pace, Bryan Smith. Manager, Group Sales: Brian Simorka. Assistant Manager, Group Sales: Andrew Ferrier. Group Sales Consultants: Brett Hamrick, Daniel Nobles, Heather Driskell, Luke Tompkins.

Director, Special Events: Mary Beth Warfford. Director, Merchandise/Team Travel: Bryan Wilson. Director, Stadium Operations: Josh Nance. GM, Concessions: Elise Aronson. Assistant GM, Concessions: Ralph Orona. Head Groundskeeper, DBAP: Scott Strickland. Head Groundskeeper, DAP: Cameron Brendle. Manager, Business: Rhonda Carlile. Supervisor, Accounting: Theresa Stocking. Accountant/Receptionist: NaTasha Jessup. Manager, Home Clubhouse: Colin Saunders. Manager, Visiting/Umpires Clubhouses: Aaron Kuehner. Team Ambassador: Bill Law.

FIELD STAFF

Manager: Charlie Montoyo. Hitting Coach: Dave Myers. Pitching Coach: Neil Allen. Trainer: Mike Sandoval.

GAME INFORMATION

Broadcasters: Patrick Kinas, Ken Tanner. No. of Games Broadcast: 144. Flagship Stations: 620-AM The Buzz, 99.9 FM The Fan.
PA Announcer: Tony Riggsbee. Official Scorer: Brent Belvin.

Stadium Name: Durham Bulls Athletic Park. Location: From Raleigh, I-40 West to Highway 147 North, exit 12B to Willard, two blocks on Willard to stadium; From I-85, Gregson St. exit to downtown, left on Chapel Hill St., right on Mangum St. Standard Game Times: 7:05 pm, Sun 5:05. Ticket Price Range: $6-14.

Visiting Club Hotel: Hilton Durham near Duke University; 3800 Hillsborough Road, Durham, NC 27705. Telephone: (919) 383-8033.

GWINNETT BRAVES

Office Address: 2500 Buford Drive, Lawrenceville, GA 30043.
Mailing Address: PO Box 490310, Lawrenceville, GA 30049.
Telephone: (678) 277-0300. Fax: (678) 277-0338.
E-Mail Address: gwinnettinfo@braves.com. Website: www.gwinnettbraves.com.
Affiliation (first year): Atlanta Braves (2009). Years in League: 2009-

OWNERSHIP/MANAGEMENT

Operated By: Atlanta National League Baseball Club Inc.
General Manager: North Johnson.
Assistant GM: Shari Massengill. Office Manager: Tyra Williams. Corporate Partnerships Manager: Austin Rhodes.
Corporate Partnerships Senior Executive: Ande Sadtler.Corporate Partnerships Coordinator: Tom Caillouette. Ticket
Sales Manager: Tyler Graham. Assistant Ticket Sales Manager: Jerry Pennington. Ticket Operations Manager:
Crystal Tanner. Account Executives: Darah Hensley, Alden Treadway, Mitch Weller, Matt Williams. Manager, Marketing/
Promotions Manager: Brandon Apter. Media Relations Manager: Dave Lezotte. Community Relations Manager:
Shay Marlowe. Creative Services Manager: Andrea Roa. Sports Turf Manager: Chris Ball. Stadium Operations
Manager: Ryan Stoltenberg. Stadium Operations Coordinator: Jonathan Blair. Facilities Maintenance Manager: Gary
Hoopaugh. Clubhouse Manager: Nick Dixon. Aramark General Manager: Mindy Pevzner.

FIELD STAFF

Manager: Brian Snitker. Hitting Coach: Garey Ingram. Pitching Coach: Marty Reed. Trainer: Mike Graus.

GAME INFORMATION

Radio Announcer: Tony Schiavone. No. of Games Broadcast: 144. Flagship Station: Unavailable.
PA Announcer: Kevin Kraus. Official Scorers: Guy Curtright, Jon Schwartz, Frank Barnett, Tim Gaines.
Stadium Name: Coolray Field. Location: I-85 (at Exit 115, State Road 20 West) and I-985 (at Exit 4), follow signs to
park. Ticket Price Range: $5-30.
Visiting Club Hotel: Courtyard by Marriott Buford/Mall of Georgia, 1405 Mall of Georgia Blvd., Buford, GA 30519.
Telephone: (678) 215-8007.

INDIANAPOLIS INDIANS

Office Address: 501 W Maryland St., Indianapolis, IN 46225.
Telephone: (317) 269-3542. Fax: (317) 269-3541.
E-Mail Address: indians@indyindians.com. Website: www.indyindians.com.
Affiliation (first year): Pittsburgh Pirates (2005). Years in League: 1963, 1998-

OWNERSHIP/MANAGEMENT

Operated By: Indians Inc.
President/Chairman of the Board: Max Schumacher. Vice President/General Manager: Cal Burleson. Assistant GM:
Randy Lewandowski. VP, Corporate Affairs: Bruce Schumacher. Director, Business Operations: Brad Morris. Director,
Tickets/Operations: Matt Guay. Director, Corporate Sales/Marketing: Joel Zawacki. Director, Merchandising: Mark
Schumacher. Director, Facilities: Tim Hughes. Director, Broadcasting: Howard Kellman. Senior Manager, Marketing/
Communications: Amanda Bray. Senior Manager, Ticket/Premium Services: Kerry Vick.
Manager, Sponsorship Services: Keri Oberting. Manager, Ticket Sales: Chad Bohm. Manager, Ticket Services:
Bryan Spisak. Manager, Marketing: Jennifer Schwab. Manager, Communications: Brian Bosma. Manager, Stadium
Operations: Andrew Jackson. Manager, Community Relations/Promotions: Brian McLaughlin. Manager, Facilities:
Matt Rapp. Manager, Telecast/Productions: Scott Templin. Manager, Stadium Maintenance: Allan Danehy. Manager,
Merchandise: Missy Weaver. Manager, IT: Sean Couse. Coordinator, Community Relations/Promotions: Hunter Brown.
Coordinator, Communications: Chris Robinson. Coordinator, Sponsorship Services: Drew Donovan. Sponsorship
Sales Account Executives: Chris Inderstrodt, Christina Toler. Senior Ticket Sales Executives: Ryan Barrett, Jonathan
Howard. Ticket Sales Executives: Nathan Butler, Ty Eaton, Noelle Cook, Garrett Rosh.
Graphic Designer: Adam Pintar. Office Manager: Julie Rumschlag. Administrative Assistant: Sarah McKinney.
Head Groundskeeper: Joey Stevenson. Assistant Groundskeeper: Joey Gerking. Operations Support: Ricky Floyd.
Operations Support: Sandra Johnson. Community Relations Assistant: Chelsea Lowman. Marketing Assistant:
Robert Kimes. Web Design: Whitney Alderson. Business Operations Assistant: Sarah Gilfoy. Stadium Operations
Assistant: Jennifer Heard. Sponsorship Assistant: Benjamin Watkins. Video Production Assistant: Nick Guenther.
Merchandise Assistant: Amanda Jones. Ticket Services Assistants: Erin Bailes, Quinn Gruber, Kylie Iadicicco, Eric Meyer,
Sondra Parys, Brian Robak.

FIELD STAFF

Manager: Dean Treanor. Hitting Coach: Mike Pagliarulo. Pitching Coach: Tom Filer. Trainer: Bryan Housand.
Strength/Conditioning Coach: Ricky White.

GAME INFORMATION

Radio Announcers: Howard Kellman, Will Flemming. No. of Games Broadcast: 144. Flagship Station: WNDE 1260-
AM.
PA Announcer: David Pygman. Official Scorers: Bill McAfee, Gary Johnson, Bill Potter, Kim Rogers, Ed Holdaway.

Stadium Name: Victory Field. Location: I-70 to West St. exit, north on West St. to ballpark; I-65 to Martin Luther King and West St. exit, south on West St. to ballpark. Standard Game Times: 7:05 pm; 1:35 (Wed/Sun), 7:15 (Fri). Ticket Price Range: $10-16.

Visiting Club Hotel: Comfort Suites City Centre 515 S. West St., Indianapolis, IN 46225. Telephone: (317) 631-9000.

LEHIGH VALLEY IRONPIGS

Office Address: 1050 IronPigs Way, Allentown, PA 18109.
Telephone: (610) 841-7447. Fax: (610) 841-1509.
E-Mail Address: info@ironpigsbaseball.com. Website: www.ironpigsbaseball.com.
Affiliation (first year): Philadelphia Phillies (2008). Years in League: 2008-

OWNERSHIP/MANAGEMENT

Ownership: LV Baseball LP.
President/General Manager: Kurt Landes.
Assistant GM: Howard Scharf. Director, Media Relations: Matt Provence. Director, New Media: Jon Schaeffer. Director, Community Relations: Kelly Gooley. Director, Merchandise: Adam Fondl. Director, Ticket Sales: Scott Evans. Director, Ticket Operations: Amy Schoch. Director, Group Sales: Don Wilson. Director, Marketing: Ron Rushe. Marketing Services Managers: Courtney Novotnak, Amanda Stout. Director, Creative Services: Terrance Breen. Manager, Creative Services: Justin Vrona. Director, Promotions: Lindsey Knupp. Director, Special Events: Mary Nixon. Director, Concessions and Catering: Alex Rivera. Manager, Concessions: Brock Hartranft. Manager, Catering: Steve Agosti. Executive Chef: Jerry Rogers. Controller: Deb Landes. Manager, Finance: Michelle Perl.
Director, Stadium Operations: Jason Kiesel. Stadium Operations Managers: Ryan Beck, Kyle Walbert. Managers, Sponsorship: Chris Kobela, Gary Nevolis, Jim Taipalus. Manager, Ticket Operations: Brittany Balonis. Ticket Representatives: Kristen Alford, Steve Carhart, Andrew Klein, Bryan Soulard. Group Representatives: Liz DiBerardino, Ryan Hines, Brad Ludwig, Nick Wootsick. Director, Field Operations: Ryan Hills. Receptionist: Pat Golden.

FIELD STAFF

Manager: Dave Brundage. Hitting Coach: Sal Rende. Pitching Coach: Ray Burris. Trainers: Chris Mudd. Strength/ Conditioning: Jason Meredith.

GAME INFORMATION

Radio Announcers: Matt Provence, Jon Schaeffer. No. of Games Broadcast: 144. Flagship Radio Station: ESPN 1240/1320 AM. Television Station: TV2. Television Announcers: Mike Zambelli, Steve Degler, Matt Provence, Doug Heater. No. of Games Televised: 72 (all home games).
PA Announcer: Unavailable. Official Scorers: Mike Falk, Jack Logic, David Sheriff, Dick Shute.
Stadium Name: Coca-Cola Park. Location: Take US 22 to exit for Airport Road South, head south, make right on American Parkway, left into stadium. Standard Game Times: 7:05 pm, Sat 6:35, Sun 1:35 (April-June), 5:35 (July-Aug).

LOUISVILLE BATS

Office Address: 401 E Main St., Louisville, KY 40202.
Telephone: (502) 212-2287. Fax: (502) 515-2255.
E-Mail Address: info@batsbaseball.com. Website: www.batsbaseball.com.
Affiliation (first year): Cincinnati Reds (2000). Years in League: 1998-

OWNERSHIP/MANAGEMENT

Chariman: Dan Ulmer Jr.
Board of Directors: Edward Glasscock, Gary Ulmer, Kenny Huber, Steve Trager, Michael Brown.
President/CEO: Gary Ulmer. Senior Vice President: Greg Galiette.
VP, Business Operations: James Breeding. VP, Operations/Technology: Scott Shoemaker. Director, Baseball Operations: Josh Hargreaves. Controller: Michele Anderson. Director, Ticket Operations: Brian Knight. Director, Media/Public Relations: Chadwick Fischer. Media Relations Assistant: Chris Gehring. Director, Group Sales: Bryan McBride. Director, Broadcasting: Matt Andrews. Director, Corporate Suites: Malcolm Jollie. Assistant Director, Stadium Operations: Randy Williams. Director, Online Media/Design: Tony Brown. Director, Sponsorships: Sarah Nordman. Senior Account Executives: Hal Norwood, Evan Patrick, Michael Harmon, Brad Wagner. Account Executives: Kevin Gamm. Corporate Sales Consultant: Tom Sabin. Assistant Director, Ticket Operations: Andrew Siers. Groundskeeper: Tom Nielsen. Assistant Groundskeeper: Craig Sampsell. Clubhouse Manager: Derrick Jewell.

FIELD STAFF

Manager: Jim Riggleman. Hitting Coach: Tony Jaramillo. Pitching Coach: Ted Power. Trainer: Jimmy Mattocks.

GAME INFORMATION

Radio Announcers: Matt Andrews, Nick Curran. No. of Games Broadcast: 144. Flagship Station: WKRD 790-AM.
PA Announcer: Charles Gazaway. Official Scorer: Nick Evans. Organist: Bob Ramsey.
Stadium Name: Louisville Slugger Field. Location: I-64 and I-71 to I-65 South/North to Brook Street exit, right on Market St., left on Jackson St.; stadium on Main St. between Jackson and Preston. Ticket Price Range: $7-11.
Visiting Club Hotel: Galt House Hotel, 140 North Fourth Street, Louisville, KY 40202. Telephone: (502) 589-5200.

NORFOLK TIDES

Office Address: 150 Park Ave, Norfolk, VA 23510.
Telephone: (757) 622-2222. **Fax:** (757) 624-9090.
E-Mail Address: receptionist@norfolktides.com. **Website:** www.norfolktides.com.
Affiliation (first year): Baltimore Orioles (2007). **Years in League:** 1969-

OWNERSHIP/MANAGEMENT

Operated By: Tides Baseball Club Inc.
President: Ken Young.
General Manager: Joe Gregory.
Executive Vice President/Senior Adviser to President: Dave Rosenfield. **Assistant GM:** Ben Giancola. **Director, Media Relations:** Ian Locke. **Director, Community Relations:** Heather McKeating. **Director, Ticket Operations:** Gretchen Todd. **Director, Group Sales:** Stephanie Hierstein. **Director, Stadium Operations:** Mike Zeman. **Business Manager:** Andrew Garrelts. **Manager, Merchandising:** Ann Marie Piddisi. **Corporate Sponsorships/Promotions:** Jonathan Mensink. **Corporate Sponsorships/Promotions:** Mike Watkins. **Corporate Sponsorships/Promotions:** Desiree Ellison. **Director, Military Affairs:** John Muszkewycz. **Assistant Director, Stadium Operations:** Mike Cardwell. **Assistant to the Director, Tickets:** Sze Fong. **Media Relations Assistant:** John Rogerson. **Administrative Assistant:** Lisa Blocker. **Community Relations Assistant:** Sarah Taylor. **Group Sales Representative:** Aubrie Ewell. **Group Sales Representative:** Josh Wilson. Box Office Assistant: Diego Betts.
Head Groundskeeper: Kenny Magner. **Assistant Groundskeeper:** Derek Trueblood. **Home Clubhouse Manager:** Kevin Casey. **Visiting Clubhouse Manager:** Mark Bunge.

FIELD STAFF

Manager: Ron Johnson. **Hitting Coach:** Denny Walling. **Pitching Coach:** Mike Griffin. **Coach:** Jose Hernandez.

GAME INFORMATION

Radio Announcers: Pete Michaud, Dave Rosenfield. **No. of Games Broadcast:** 144. **Flagship Station:** ESPN 94.1 FM.
PA Announcer: Jack Ankerson. **Official Scorers:** Mike Holtzclaw, Dave Lewis.
Stadium Name: Harbor Park. **Location:** Exit 9, 11A or 11B off I-264, adjacent to the Elizabeth River in downtown Norfolk. **Standard Game Times:** 7:15 pm, Sun 1:15. **Ticket Price Range:** $11-14.
Visiting Club Hotel: Sheraton Waterside, 777 Waterside Dr, Norfolk, VA 23510. **Telephone:** (757) 622-6664.

PAWTUCKET RED SOX

Office Address: One Ben Mondor Way, Pawtucket, RI 02860.
Mailing Address: PO Box 2365, Pawtucket, RI 02861.
Telephone: (401) 724-7300. **Fax:** (401) 724-2140.
E-Mail Address: info@pawsox.com. **Website:** www.pawsox.com.
Affiliation (first year): Boston Red Sox (1973). **Years in League:** 1973-

OWNERSHIP/MANAGEMENT

Operated by: Pawtucket Red Sox Baseball Club, Inc.
President: Mike Tamburro.
Vice President/General Manager: Lou Schwechheimer. **VP/Chief Operating Officer:** Matt White. **VP, Sales/Marketing:** Michael Gwynn. **VP, Stadium Operations:** Mick Tedesco. **VP, Public Relations:** Bill Wanless. **Director, Community Relations:** Jeff Bradley. **Manager, Sales:** Augusto Rojas. **Director, Merchandising:** Eric Petterson. **Director, Media Creation:** Kevin Galligan. **Director, Ticket Sales:** John Wilson. **Director, Warehouse Operations:** Dave Johnson. **Director, Hospitality:** Lauren Dincecco.
Account Executives: Tom Linehan, Sam Sousa, Mike Lyons, Geoff Sinnott. **AJ Lewis Field Superintendant:** Matt McKinnon. **Assistant Groundskeeper:** Kyle Carney. **Director, Security:** Rick Medeiros. **Director, Clubhouse Operations:** Carl Goodreau. **Executive Chef:** Ken Bowdish.

FIELD STAFF

Manager: Kevin Boles. **Hitting Coach:** Dave Joppie. **Pitching Coach:** Rich Sauveur. **Coach:** Bruce Crabbe. **Trainer:** Jon Jochim.

GAME INFORMATION

Radio Announcers: Jeff Levering. **No. of Games Broadcast:** 144. **Flagship Station:** WHJJ 920-AM.
PA Announcer: Scott Fraser. **Official Scorer:** Bruce Guindon.
Stadium Name: McCoy Stadium. **Location:** From north, 95 South to exit 2A in Massachusetts (Newport Ave.), **follow Newport Ave. for 2 miles, right on Columbus Ave., follow** one mile, stadium on right. From south, 95 North to exit 28 (School St.), right at bottom of exit ramp, through two sets of lights, left onto Pond St., right on Columbus Ave., stadium entrance on left; From west (Worcester), 295 North to 95 South and follow directions from north; From east (Fall River), 195 West to 95 North and follow directions from south. **Standard Game Times:** 7 pm, Sat 6, Sun 1. **Ticket Price Range:** $5-11.
Visiting Club Hotel: Marriott Courtyard Providence Downtown, 32 Exchange Terrace at Memorial Blvd, Providence, RI 02903. **Telephone:** (401) 272-1191.

ROCHESTER RED WINGS

Office Address: One Morrie Silver Way, Rochester, NY 14608.
Telephone: (585) 454-1001. **Fax:** (585) 454-1056.
E-Mail: info@redwingsbaseball.com. **Website:** www.redwingsbaseball.com.
Affiliation (first year): Minnesota Twins (2003). **Years in League:** 1885-89, 1891-92, 1895-

OWNERSHIP/MANAGEMENT:

Operated by Rochester Community Baseball, Inc.
President/CEO/COO: Naomi Silver. **Chairman:** Gary Larder.
General Manager: Dan Mason. **Assistant GM:** Will Rumbold. **Controller:** Darlene Giardina. **Director, Human Resources:** Paula LoVerde. **Manager, Ticket Office:** Dave Welker. **Manager, Executive Services:** Marcia DeHond. **Director, Communication:** Tim Doohan. **Director, Corporate Development:** Nick Sciarratta. **Director, Group Sales/Promotions:** Bob Craig. **Director, Marketing:** Matt Cipro. **Director, Ticket Operations:** Rob Dermody. **Director, Video Production:** John Blotzer. **Director, Merchandising/Community Relations:** Danielle Barone. **Assistant, Merchandising/Administration:** Kathy Bills. **Character Coordinator/Account Executive:** Josh Britt.
Head Groundskeeper: Gene Buonomo. **Assistant Groundskeeper:** Geno Buonomo. **Account Executives:** Eric Friedman, Derek Swanson. **Administrative Assistant:** Gini Darden. **General Manager, Food/Beverage:** Jeff Dodge. **Business Manager, Food/Beverage:** Dave Bills. **Manager, Concessions:** Jeff DeSantis. **Director, Catering:** Courtney Trawitz. **Sales Manager, Catering:** Jeremy Armison. **Executive Chef:** Mark Feiock. **Manager, Warehouse:** Rob Burgett.

FIELD STAFF

Manager: Gene Glynn. **Hitting Coach:** Tim Doherty. **Pitching Coach:** Marty Mason. **Trainer:** Larry Bennese.

GAME INFORMATION

Radio Announcer: Josh Whetzel. **No. of Games Broadcast:** 144. **Flagship Stations:** WHTK 1280-AM, WYSL 1040-AM. **PA Announcers:** Kevin Spears, Rocky Perrotta. **Official Scorers:** Warren Kozireski, Brendan Harrington.
Stadium Name: Frontier Field. **Location:** I-490 East to exit 12 (Brown/Broad Street) and follow signs; I-490 West to exit 14 (Plymouth Ave) and follow signs. **Standard Game Times:** 7:05 pm, Sun 1:05. **Ticket Price Range:** $7-11.
Visiting Club Hotel: Rochester Plaza, 70 State St, Rochester, NY 14608. **Telephone:** (585) 546-3450.

SCRANTON/WILKES-BARRE RAILRIDERS

Office Address: 235 Montage Mountain Rd., Moosic, PA 18507.
Telephone: (570) 969-2255. **Fax:** (570) 963-6564.
E-Mail Address: info@swbrailriders.com. **Website:** www.swbrailriders.com.
Affiliation (first year): New York Yankees (2007). **Years in League:** 1989-

OWNERSHIP/MANAGEMENT

Owned/Operated By: SWB Yankees LLC.
President/General Manager: Rob Crain. **Executive VP, Operations:** Jeremy Ruby. **Executive VP, Business Operations:** Paul Chilek. **VP, Marketing/Corporate Services:** Katie Beekman. **VP, Stadium Operations:** Curt Camoni. **VP, Sales:** Mike Trudnak. **Director, Media Relations/Broadcasting:** John Sadak. **Media Relations/Broadcasting Assistant:** Unavailable. **Director, Gameday Operations:** William Steiner. **Corporate Partnerships Executive:** Curtis Phair. **Director, Corporate Services/Special Events:** Kristina Knight. **Community Relations Manager:** Rachel Mark. **Corporate Services Managers:** Karen Luciano, Lindsey Graham. **Fan Experience Manager:** Victor Sweet. **Director, Ticket Operations:** Seth Atkinson. **Assistant Ticket Operations Manager:** Bryant Guilmette.
Director, Ticket Sales: Robert McLane. **Regional Sales Managers:** Holly Norton, Giovanni Fricchione, Mike Poplaski, Alyssa Novick, Noelle Richard. **Senior Inside Sales Representative:** Kelly Cusick. **Inside Sales Representative:** Amanda Zuzik. **Operations Manager:** Rob Galdieri. **Director, Field Operations:** Steve Horne. **Director, Facility Operations:** Joe Villano. **Receptionist/Office Manager:** Maggie Rowlands.

FIELD STAFF

Manager: Dave Miley. **Hitting Coach:** Butch Wynegar. **Pitching Coach:** Scott Aldred. **Coach:** Luis Sojo. **Trainer:** Darren London. **Strength/Conditioning Coach:** Lee Tressel.

GAME INFORMATION

Radio Announcer: John Sadak. **No. of Games Broadcast:** 144. **Flagship Stations:** 100.7 FM, 1340 WYCK-AM, 1400 WICK-AM, 1440 WCDL-AM, 106.7 FM. **TV Announcer:** John Sadak. **No. of Games Broadcast:** 20. **Flagship Station:** WQMY-TV.
PA Announcer: Dean Corwin. **Official Scorers:** Dave Lauriha, John Errico.
Stadium Name: PNC Field. **Location:** From Interstate 18 North take Exit 182; from I-81 South take Exit 182-A; stadium is on Montage Mountain Road. **Standard Game Times:** 6:35 pm (April/May) 7:05 pm (June-August), Sun 1:05 pm. **Ticket Price Range:** $7-$12.
Visiting Club Hotel: Radisson Lackawanna Station. **Telephone:** (570) 342-8300.

SYRACUSE CHIEFS

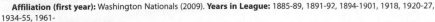

Office Address: One Tex Simone Drive, Syracuse, NY 13208.
Telephone: (315) 474-7833. **Fax:** (315) 474-2658.
E-Mail Address: baseball@syracusechiefs.com. **Website:** www.syracusechiefs.com.
Affiliation (first year): Washington Nationals (2009). **Years in League:** 1885-89, 1891-92, 1894-1901, 1918, 1920-27, 1934-55, 1961-

OWNERSHIP/MANAGEMENT

Operated By: Community Owned Baseball Club of Central New York, Inc.
Chairman: Robert Julian. **President:** William Dutch. **First Executive Vice President:** Paul Solomon.
General Manager: Jason Smorol. **Assistant GM:** Jason Horbal. **Director, Sales/Marketing:** Kathleen McCormick. **Director, Finance:** Frank Santoro. **Assistant Director, Finance:** Joseph Persia. **Director, Group Sales/Graphic Design Coordinator:** Brandon Massey. **Director, Broadcasting/Public Relations:** Jason Benetti. **Assistant Director, Broadcasting/Public Relations:** Kevin Brown. **Director, Ticket Sales:** Greg Dietz. **Director, Multimedia Production:** Anthony Cianchetta. **Manager, Corporate Sales:** Julie Cardinali. **Manager, Luxury Suites/Guest Relations:** Erin Stancick. **Manager, Community Relations/Social Media:** Jeffrey Irizarry. **Head Groundskeeper:** John Stewart. **Team Historian:** Ron Gersbacher.

FIELD STAFF

Manager: Billy Gardner Jr. **Hitting Coach:** Joe Dillon. **Pitching Coach:** Paul Menhart. **Trainer:** Jeff Allred. **Strength Coordinator:** Brett Henry.

GAME INFORMATION

Radio Announcers: Jason Benetti/Kevin Brown. **No. of Games Broadcast:** 144. **Flagship Station:** The Score 1260 AM.
PA Announcers: Nick Aversa, Roger Mirabito. **Official Scorer:** Dom Leo.
Stadium Name: NBT Bank Stadium. **Location:** New York State Thruway to exit 36 (I-81 South), to 7th North St. exit, left on 7th North, right on Hiawatha Blvd. **Standard Game Times:** 7 pm, Sun 2pm. **Ticket Price Range:** $5-12.
Visiting Club Hotel: Crowne Plaza Syracuse, 701 E Genesee St, Syracuse, NY 13210. **Telephone:** (315) 479-7000.

TOLEDO MUD HENS

Office Address: 406 Washington St., Toledo, OH 43604.
Telephone: (419) 725-4367. **Fax:** (419) 725-4368.
E-Mail Address: mudhens@mudhens.com. **Website:** www.mudhens.com.
Affiliation (first year): Detroit Tigers (1987). **Years in League:** 1889, 1965-

OWNERSHIP/MANAGEMENT

Operated By: Toledo Mud Hens Baseball Club, Inc.
Chairman of the Board: Michael Miller.
Vice President: David Huey. **Secretary/Treasurer:** Charles Bracken.
President/General Manager: Joseph Napoli.
Chief Marketing Officer: Kim McBroom. **Assistant GM/Director, Corporate Partnerships:** Neil Neukam. **Assistant GM, Ticket Sales/Operations:** Erik Ibsen. **Assistant GM, Food/Beverage:** Craig Nelson. **CFO:** Pam Alspach. **Manager, Promotions:** Michael Keedy. **Communications Director:** Andi Roman. **Director, Ticket Sales/Services:** Thomas Townley. **Accounting:** Sheri Kelly, Brian Leverenz. **Manager, Gameday Operations:** Greg Setola.
Corporate Sales Associate: Ed Sintic. **Season Ticket/Group Sales Associates:** Frank Kristie, Kyle Moll, John Mulka. **Manager, Digital Communications:** Nathan Steinmetz. **Game Plan Advisor:** Colleen Rerucha. **Special Events Coordinator:** Emily Croll. **Director, Broadcast Services:** Greg Tye. **Graphic Designer:** Dan Royer. **Manager, Souvenir Sales:** Craig Katz. **Manager, Swamp Shop:** Stephanie Miller. **Manager, Ballpark Operations:** Ken Westenkirchner. **Office Manager:** Carol Hamilton. **Executive Assistant:** Tracy Evans. **Turf Manager:** Jake Tyler. **Clubhouse Manager:** Joe Sarkisian. **Team Historian:** John Husman.

FIELD STAFF

Manager: Larry Parrish. **Coach:** Leon Durham. **Pitching Coach:** Al Nipper. **Trainer:** Chris McDonald.

GAME INFORMATION

Radio Announcer: Jim Weber. **No. of Games Broadcast:** 144. **Flagship Station:** WCWA 1230 AM. **TV Announcers:** Jim Weber, Matt Melzak. **No. of Games Broadcast:** 72 (all home games). **TV Flagship:** Buckeye Cable Sports Network.
PA Announcer: Unavailable. **Official Scorers:** Jeff Businger, Ron Kleinfelter, Guy Lammers, John Malkoski Sr.
Stadium Name: Fifth Third Field. **Location:** From Ohio Turnpike 80/90, exit 54 (4A) to I-75 North, follow I-75 North to exit 201-B, left onto Erie Street, right onto Washington Street; From Detroit, I-75 South to exit 202-A, right onto Washington Street; From Dayton, I-75 North to exit 201-B, left onto Erie Street, right on Washington Street; From Ann Arbor, Route 23 South to I-475 East, I-475 east to I-75 South, I-75 South to exit 202-A, right onto Washington Street. **Ticket Price Range:** $10.
Visiting Club Hotel: Park Inn, 101 North Summit, Toledo, OH 43604. **Telephone:** (419) 241-3000.

PACIFIC COAST LEAGUE

PACIFIC COAST LEAGUE

Address: One Chisholm Trail, Suite 4200, Round Rock, Texas 78681.
Telephone: (512) 310-2900. **Fax:** (512) 310-8300.
E-Mail Address: office@pclbaseball.com. **Website:** www.pclbaseball.com.
President: Branch B. Rickey.

Vice President: Don Logan (Las Vegas).

Directors: Don Beaver (New Orleans), Sam Bernabe (Iowa), John Pontius (Memphis), Chris Cummings (Fresno), Dave Elmore (Colorado Springs), Aaron Artman (Tacoma), Don Logan (Las Vegas), Chris Almendarez (Round Rock), Marc Amicone (Salt Lake), Gary Green (Omaha), Art Matin (Oklahoma), Josh Hunt (Tucson), Jeff Savage (Sacramento), John Traub (Albuquerque), Frank Ward (Nashville), Stuart Katzoff (Reno).

Director, Business: Melanie Fiore. **Director, Baseball Operations:** Dwight Hall. **Media/Operations Assistant:** Matt Lundgren.

Division Structure: American Conference—Northern: Colorado Springs, Iowa, Omaha, Oklahoma City. **Southern:** Memphis, Nashville, New Orleans, Round Rock. Pacific Conference—Northern: Fresno, Reno, Sacramento, Tacoma. Southern: Fresno, Albuquerque, El Paso, Las Vegas, Salt Lake.

Regular Season: 144 games. **2014 Opening Date:** April 3. **Closing Date:** Sept 1.

Branch Rickey

All-Star Game: July 16 at Durham Bulls, Durham, N.C. (PCL vs International League).

Playoff Format: Pacific Conference/Northern winner meets Southern winner, and American Conference/Northern winner meets Southern winner in best-of-five semifinal series. Winners meet in best-of-five series for league championship.

Triple-A Championship Game: Sept 16 at Charlotte Knights (PCL vs International League).
Roster Limit: 24. **Player Eligibility Rule:** No restrictions.
Brand of Baseball: Rawlings ROM.

Umpires: Nick Bailey (Big Spring, TX), Jordan Baker (Shawnee, OK), Lance Barrett (Fort Worth, TX), Ryan Blakney (Wenatchee, WA), Cory Blaser (Westminster, CO), Blake Davis (Englewood, CO), Jordan Ferrell (Clarksville, TN), Spencer Flynn, (Plymouth, MN), Hal Gibson (Marysville, WA), Brian Hertzog (Lake Stevens, WA), Patrick Hoberg (Urbandale, IA), Joel Hospodka (Omaha, NE), Kolin Kline (Arvada, CO), Shaun Lampe (Phoenix, AZ), Patrick Mahoney (Pittsburg, CA), Brandon Misun (Edmond, OK), Gabriel Morales (Livermore, CA), Jeffrey Morrow (Fenton, MO) Michael Muchlinski (Ephrata, WA), Alex Ortiz (Los Angeles, CA), Marcus Pattillo (Jonesboro, AR), Daniel Reyburn (Franklin, TN), Mark Ripperger (Carlsbad, CA), Stuart Scheurwater (Regina, Saskatchewan, Canada), Adam Schwarz (Riverside, CA), Chris Segal (Burke, VA), Gregory Stanzak (Phoenix, AZ), Quinn Wolcott (Puyallup, WA), Thomas Woodring (Boulder, NV).

STADIUM INFORMATION

Club	Stadium	Opened	Dimensions			Capacity	2013 Att.
			LF	CF	RF		
Albuquerque	Isotopes Park	2003	340	400	340	13,279	568,417
Colorado Springs	Security Service Field	1988	350	410	350	8,400	334,245
* El Paso	N/A	2014	N/A	N/A	N/A	10,000	200,077
Fresno	Chukchansi Park	2002	324	402	335	12,500	471,686
Iowa	Principal Park	1992	335	400	335	11,000	509,798
Las Vegas	Cashman Field	1983	328	433	328	9,334	311,516
Memphis	AutoZone Park	2000	319	400	322	14,300	493,706
Nashville	Herschel Greer Stadium	1978	327	400	327	10,700	321,042
New Orleans	Zephyr Field	1997	333	405	332	10,000	329,942
Oklahoma City	RedHawks Field at Bricktown	1998	325	400	325	11,455	399,965
Omaha	Werner Park	2011	310	402	315	9,023	415,650
Reno	Aces Ballpark	2009	339	410	340	9,100	389,860
Round Rock	The Dell Diamond	2000	330	400	325	10,000	595,584
Sacramento	Raley Field	2000	330	405	325	14,014	586,090
Salt Lake	Spring Mobile Ballpark	1994	345	420	315	15,500	515,633
Tacoma	Cheney Stadium	1960	325	425	325	8000	352,032

* Team played in Tucson in 2013

ALBUQUERQUE ISOTOPES

Office Address: 1601 Avenida Cesar Chavez SE, Albuquerque, NM 87106.
Telephone: (505) 924-2255. **Fax:** (505) 242-8899.
E-Mail Address: info@abqisotopes.com. **Website:** www.abqisotopes.com.
Affiliation (first year): Los Angeles Dodgers (2009). **Years in League:** 1972-2000, 2003-

OWNERSHIP/MANAGEMENT

President: Ken Young. **Vice President/Secretary/Treasurer:** Emmett Hammond. **General Manager:** John Traub. **Assistant GM, Sales/Marketing:** Nick LoBue. **Director, Box Office/Retail Operations:** Chrissy Baines. **Director,**

Sales/Promotions: Adam Beggs. **Director, Media Relations:** Laura Verillo. **Director, Stadium Operations:** Bobby Atencio. **Manager, Community Relations/Promotions:** Kim Stoebick. **Manager, Suite Relations:** Paul Hartenberger. **Manager, Creative Services:** Kris Shepard. **Season Ticket/Group Sales Representatives:** Bryan Pruitt, Jason Buchta, Dylan Storm Jordan Vicain. **Director, Accounting/Human Resources:** Cynthia DiFrancesco. **Assistant Director, Retail Operations:** Patrick Westrick. **Assistant Director, Box Office Operations:** Kyle Hamman.

Stadium Operations Assistant: Nathan McNair. **Director, Field Operations:** Casey Griffin. **Manager, Field Operations:** Clint Belau. **Home Clubhouse Manager:** Unavailable. **Visiting Clubhouse Manager:** Rick Pollack. **Front Office Assistant:** Mark Otero. **GM, Ovations Foodservices:** Patrick Queeney. **Catering Manager, Ovations Foodservices:** Amanda Baca. **Concession Manager, Ovations Foodservices:** Matt Butler. **Head Chef:** Mario D'Elia.

FIELD STAFF

Manager: Damon Berryhill. **Hitting Coach:** Franklin Stubbs. **Pitching Coach:** Glenn Dishman. **Trainer:** Yosuke Nakajima.

GAME INFORMATION

Radio Announcer: Josh Suchon. **No. of Games Broadcast:** 144. **Flagship Station:** KNML 610-AM.

PA Announcer: Stu Walker. **Official Scorers:** Gary Herron, James Hilchen.

Stadium Name: Isotopes Park. **Location:** From I-25, exit east on Avenida Cesar Chavez SE to University Boulevard; From I-40, exit south on University Boulevard SE to Avenida Cesar Chavez. **Standard Game Times:** 7:05 pm, Sun 6:05. **Ticket Price Range:** $7-$25.

Visiting Club Hotel: Sheraton Albuquerque Airport Hotel, 2910 Yale Blvd SE, Albuquerque, NM 87106. **Telephone:** (505) 843-7000.

COLORADO SPRINGS SKY SOX

Office Address: 4385 Tutt Blvd., Colorado Springs, CO 80922.
Telephone: (719) 597-1449. **Fax:** (719) 597-2491.
E-Mail address: info@skysox.com. **Website:** www.skysox.com.
Affiliation (first year): Colorado Rockies (1993). **Years in League:** 1988-

OWNERSHIP/MANAGEMENT

Operated By: Colorado Springs Sky Sox Inc.
Principal Owner: David Elmore.

President/General Manager: Tony Ensor. **Assistant GM/Director, Public Relations:** Mike Hobson. **Assistant GM/Director, Corporate Sales:** Chris Phillips. **Senior Director, Ticketing:** Whitney Shellem. **Senior Director, Group Sales:** Keith Hodges. **Director, Broadcasting:** Dan Karcher. **Director, Accounting:** Kelly Hanlon. **Director, Marketing/Promotions:** Jon Eddy. **Vice President, Field Operations:** Steve DeLeon. **Manager, Graphics/Merchandise:** Rebecca Lynch. **Manager, Stadium Operations:** Eric Martin. **Manager, Corporate Sales:** Drew Trujillo. **Assistant Director, Group Sales:** Jim Rice. **Manager, Community Relations/Ticketing:** Alyce Bofferding. **Manager, Group Sales:** Mike Marsoe, Charles Mushin. **Manager, Ticketing:** Cole Chisholm. **Event Manager:** Brien Smith. **GM, Diamond Creations:** Don Giuliano. **Executive Chef:** Chris Evans.

Public Relations Assistant: Derek Blalock. **Stadium Operations Assistant:** Austin Ingersoll. **Corporate Sales/On-field Emcee Assistant:** Kristen Rheinlander. **Marketing/Production Assistant:** Brian Paneral. **Ticketing Assistant:** Andrew Gallant. **Group Sales Assistant:** Steve Reedy. **Receptionist:** Marianne Paine. **Home Clubhouse Manager:** Ricky Grima. **Visiting Clubhouse Manager:** Steve Martin.

FIELD STAFF

Manager: Glenallen Hill. **Coach:** Dave Hajek. **Pitching Coach:** Dave Schuler.

GAME INFORMATION

Radio Announcer: Dan Karcher. **No. of Games Broadcast:** 144. **Flagship Station:** AM 1300 The Animal.

PA Announcer: Josh Howe. **Official Scorer:** Marty Grantz, Rich Wastler.

Stadium Name: Security Service Field. **Location:** I-25 South to Woodmen Road exit, east on Woodmen to Powers Blvd., right on Powers to Barnes Road. **Standard Game Times:** 7:05 pm, Sat 6:05, Sun 1:35. **Ticket Price Range:** $5-13.

Visiting Club Hotel: Hilton Garden Inn, 1810 Briargate Parkway, Colorado Springs, CO 80920. **Telephone:** (719) 598-6866.

FRESNO GRIZZLIES

Office Address: 1800 Tulare St., Fresno, CA 93721.
Telephone: (559) 320-4487. **Fax:** (559) 264-0795.
E-Mail Address: info@fresnogrizzlies.com. **Website:** www.FresnoGrizzlies.com.
Social Media: Facebook.com/wherechampionsaregrown, Twitter.com/FresnoGrizzlies, Instagram.com/instagrizz_FG.
Affiliation (first year): San Francisco Giants (1998). **Years in League:** 1998-

OWNERSHIP/MANAGEMENT

Operated By: Fresno Baseball Club, LLC.
President: Chris Cummings.

Vice President, Sales: Derek Franks. **VP, Marketing/Operations:** Drew Vertiz. **Director, Client Services:** Andrew Melrose. **Director, Corporate Partnerships/Community Fund:** Jerry James. **Director, Stadium Operations:** Harvey Kawasaki. **Director, Human Resources:** Ashley Tennell. **Director, Sales:** Andrew Milios. **Director, Stadium Events/ Baseball Operations:** Joe Castillo. **Grizzlies Community Fund Manager:** Whitney Campbell. **Marketing Creative Manager:** Sam Hansen. **Operations Manager:** Ira Calvin. **Group Sales Manager:** Adam Gleich. **Finance Manager:** Monica Delacerda. **Staff Accountant:** Landon Hollman. **Event Staff Manager:** Steve Sodini. **Team Store Manager:** Lalonnie Calderon. **Graphic Designer:** Jennifer Rose. **Box Office Manager:** Cody Holden.

Assistant Manager, Ticket Sales: Brian Boden. **Community Relations Coordinator:** Risa Isard. **Coordinator, Marketing/Promotions:** Nick Haas. **Media Relations Coordinator:** Ryan Young. **Ticket Sales Coordinator:** Eric Moreno. **Entertainment/Mascot Coordinator:** Troy Simeon. **Community Relations Assistant:** Chris Wilson. **Corporate Partnerships/New Business Development:** Ray Ortiz. **Partnership Account Executive:** Phillip Kasparian. **Ticket Account Executives:** Chris Cox, Andrew Hacnik, Jon Stockton. **Group Sales Account Executive:** Kyle Kleiman. **Ticket Sales Assistant:** Andrea Renfro. **Client Services Executive:** Camille Moultrie. **Head Groundskeeper:** David Jacinto. **GM, Ovations Concessions:** Tim Dickert.

FIELD STAFF

Manager: Bob Mariano. **Hitting Coach:** Andy Skeels. **Pitching Coach:** Dwight Bernard. **Athletic Trainer:** James Petra. **Strength/Conditioning Coach:** Brad Lawson.

GAME INFORMATION

Radio Announcer: Doug Greenwald. **No. of Games Broadcast:** 144. **Flagship Radio Station:** Unavailable. **Flagship TV Station:** ABC 30.1.

PA Announcer: Unavailable. **Official Scorer:** Matt Pena.

Stadium Name: Chukchansi Park, 1800 Tulare St., Fresno, CA 93721. **Directions:** From 99 North, take Fresno St. exit, left on Fresno St., left on Inyo or Tulare to stadium; From 99 South, take Fresno St. exit, left on Fresno St., right on Broadway to H St.; From 41 North, take Van Ness exit toward Fresno, left on Van Ness, left on Inyo or Tulare, stadium is straight ahead; From 41 South, take Tulare exit, stadium is located at Tulare and H Streets, or take Van Ness exit, right on Van Ness, left on Inyo or Tulare, stadium is straight ahead. **Ticket Price Range:** $9-19.

Visiting Club Hotel: Holiday Inn Downtown Fresno, 1055 Van Ness, Fresno, CA 93721. **Telephone:** (888) 465-4329.

EL PASO CHIHUAHUAS

Office Address: 123 West Mills, Suite 300, El Paso, TX 79901.
Telephone: (915) 533-2273. **Fax:** (915) 242-2031.
E-Mail Address: info@epchihuahuas.com. **Website:** www.epchihuahuas.com.
Affiliation (first year): San Diego Padres (2014). **Years in League:** 2014-

OWNERSHIP/MANAGEMENT

Owner/Chairman of the Board: Paul Foster. **Owner/CEO/Vice Chairman:** Josh Hunt. **Owners:** Alejandra de la Vega Foster, Woody Hunt.

President: Alan Ledford. **General Manager:** Brad Taylor.

Account Executive, Ticket Sales: Dana Argo. **Head Groundskeeper:** Andy Beggs. **Manager, Finance/Administration:** Pamela De La O. **Assistant Manager, Ticket Operations:** Adam Dolezal. **Director, Ballpark Operations:** Douglas Galeano. **Manager, Broadcasting/Media Relations:** Tim Hagerty. **Manager, Retail Operations:** Kara Hayes. **Account Executive, Ticket Sales:** Ryan Knox. **Manager, Ticket Operations:** Rebecca Jacobsen. **Director, Corporate Partnerships:** Becky Lee. **Senior Account Executive, Ticket Sales:** Colby Miller. **Account Executive, Ticket Sales:** Primo Martinez. **Manager, Marketing Communications:** Angela Olivas. **Director, Ticket Sales:** Nathan Reilly. **Account Executive, Corporate Partnerships:** Judge Scott. **Account Executive, Ticket Sales:** Nick Seckerson. **Marketing Database Coordinator:** Jon Staub. **Manager, Promotions:** Tori Stein.

FIELD STAFF

Manager: Pat Murphy. **Hitting Coach:** Jacque Jones. **Pitching Coach:** Mike Cather. **Trainer:** Nathan Stewart.

GAME INFORMATION

Radio Announcer: Tim Hagerty. **No. of Games Broadcast:** 144. **Flagship Station:** ESPN 600 AM El Paso.
PA Announcer: Unavailable. **Official Scorer:** Unavailable.
Stadium Name: Unavailable. **Standard Game Times:** 7:05 pm, Sun 1:05. **Ticket Price Range:** $5-10.50.
Visiting Club Hotel: Unavailable.

IOWA CUBS

Office Address: One Line Drive, Des Moines IA 50309.
Telephone: (515) 243-6111. **Fax:** (515) 243-5152.
Website: www.iowacubs.com.
Affiliation (first year): Chicago Cubs (1981). **Years in League:** 1969-

OWNERSHIP/MANAGEMENT

Operated By: Raccoon Baseball Inc.

Chairman/Principal Owner: Michael Gartner. **Executive Vice President:** Michael Giudicessi. **President/General**

Manager: Sam Bernabe. **Shareholder:** Mike Gartner. **Executive VP/Assistant GM:** Nate Teut. **VP/Assistant GM:** Jim Nahas. **VP/CFO:** Sue Tollefson. **VP/Director, Broadcast Operations:** Deene Ehlis. **Director, Media Relations:** Randy Wehofer. **Director, Communications:** Scott Sailor. **Director, Marketing/Video Presentation:** Blake Havard. **Director, Multimedia Arts:** Justin Walters. **Director, Ticket Operations:** Kenny Houser. **Director, Luxury Suites:** Brent Conkel. **Assistant Ticket Manager:** Eric Hammes. **Director, Group Sales:** Aaron Roland. **Director, Stadium Operations:** Jeff Tilley. **Manager, Stadium Operations:** Jake Samo. **Assistant, Stadium Operations:** Jerod Davey. **Nic Peters. Corporate Relations:** Red Hollis. **Head Groundskeeper:** Chris Schlosser. **Director, Merchandise:** Rick Giudicessi. **Director, Special Events:** Chelsie Rohrs. **Accountant:** Lori Auten. **Manager, Cub Club:** Derek Hickey. **Director, Information Technology:** Ryan Clutter. **Landscape Coordinator:** Shari Kramer.

FIELD STAFF

Manager: Marty Pevey. **Hitting Coach:** Brian Harper. **Pitching Coach:** Bruce Walton. **Athletic Trainer:** Scott Barringer. **Strength/Conditioning:** Ryan Clausen.

GAME INFORMATION

Radio Announcers: Deene Ehlis, Randy Wehofer. **No. of Games Broadcast:** 144. **Flagship Station:** AM 940 KPSZ. **PA Announcers:** Aaron Johnson, Mark Pierce, Corey Coon, Rick Stageman, Joe Hammen. **Official Scorers:** Jayme Adam, Michael Pecina, James Hilchen. **Stadium Name:** Principal Park. **Location:** I-80 or I-35 to I-235, to Third St. exit, south on Third St., left on Line Drive. **Standard Game Times:** 7:05 pm, Sun 1:05. **Ticket Price Range:** $4-14. **Visiting Club Hotel:** Embassy Suites, 101 East Locust St., Des Moines, IA 50309. **Telephone:** (515) 244-1700.

LAS VEGAS 51S

Office Address: 850 Las Vegas Blvd. North, Las Vegas, NV 89101.
Telephone: (702) 943-7200. **Fax:** (702) 943-7214.
E-Mail Address: info@lv51.com. **Website:** www.lv51.com.
Affiliation (first year): New York Mets (2013). **Years in League:** 1983-

OWNERSHIP/MANAGEMENT

Summerlin Las Vegas Baseball Club LLC President/COO: Don Logan. **General Manager/VP of Sales/Marketing:** Chuck Johnson. **VP, Ticket Operations:** Mike Rodriguez. **VP, Operations/Security:** Nick Fitzenreider. **Director, Sponsorships:** James Jensen. **Chief Financial Officer:** Tim Colbert. **Controller:** Araxi Demirjian. **Director, Broadcasting:** Russ Langer. **Director, Ticket Sales:** Erik Eisenberg. **Director, Community Relations/Customer Service:** Melissa Harkavy. **Sponsorship Services Manager/Travel Coordinator:** William Graham. **Business Development:** Larry Brown. **Media Relations Director:** Jim Gemma. **Ticket Operations Assistant:** Michelle Taggart. **Administrative Assistants:** Jan Dillard, Pat Dressel. **Account Executives, Ticket Sales:** Bryan Frey, Tyler Johnson, Josh Rusnak, TJ Thedinga. **Retail Operations Manager:** Jason Weber. **Operations Manager:** Chip Vespe.

FIELD STAFF

Manager: Wally Backman. **Hitting Coach:** George Greer. **Pitching Coach:** Frank Viola. **Athletic Trainer:** Joe Golia. **Strength/Conditioning Coach:** Dustin Clarke.

GAME INFORMATION

Radio Announcer: Russ Langer. **No. of Games Broadcast:** 144. **Flagship Station:** Sports 920 AM The Game. **PA Announcer:** Dan Bickmore. **Official Scorer:** Mark Wasik. **Stadium Name:** Cashman Field. **Location:** I-15 to US 95 exit (downtown), east to Las Vegas Blvd. North exit, one-half mile north to stadium. **Standard Game Time:** 7:05 pm. **Ticket Price Range:** $10-14. **Visiting Club Hotel:** Golden Nugget Hotel & Casino, 129 Fremont Street, Las Vegas, NV 89101. **Telephone:** (702) 385-7111.

MEMPHIS REDBIRDS

Office Address: 175 Toyota Plaza, Suite 300, Memphis, TN 38103.
Stadium Address: 200 Union Ave., Memphis, TN 38103.
Telephone: (901) 721-6000. **Fax:** (901) 842-1222.
Website: www.memphisredbirds.com.
Affiliation (first year): St. Louis Cardinals (1998). **Years in League:** 1998-

OWNERSHIP/MANAGEMENT

Ownership: Memphis Redbirds Baseball Foundation, Inc. **Managed by:** Global Spectrum.
General Manager: Ben Weiss. **Assistant GM/Director, Sales:** Derek Goldfarb. **Director, Operations:** Mark Anderson. **Coordinator, Operations:** Kevin Rooney. **Director, Finance:** Art Davis. **Director, Marketing:** Adam Goldberg. **Ticket Operations Manager:** Travis Trumitch. **Ticket Sales Manager:** Jason Mott. **Marketing Manager:** Erin O'Donnell. **Media Relations Manager:** Michael Whitty. **Graphic Designer/Photographer:** Allison Rhoades. **Special Event Coordinator:** Kellie Grabert. **Corporate Sales Executive:** Corey Bush. **Corporate Sales Coordinator:** Leigh Eisenberg. **Sales Coordinator:** Shannon Comerford. **Ticket Sales Executives:** Corey Gilden, Alex Sides. **Staff Accountant:** Cindy Neal. **Office Coordinator:** Linda Smith. **Head Groundskeeper:** Ed Collins. **Chief Engineer:** Danny Abbott. **Maintenance:** Spencer Shields. **Groundskeeper:** Andrew Strong.

FIELD STAFF

Manager: Ron Warner. **Coach:** Mark Budaska. **Pitching Coach:** Bryan Eversgerd. **Trainer:** Jeremy Clipperton. **Strength/Conditioning Coach:** Sean Johnson.

GAME INFORMATION

Radio Announcer: Steve Selby. **No. of Games Broadcast:** 144. **Flagship Station:** WHBQ 560-AM.
PA Announcer: Unavailable. **Official Scorer:** JJ Guinozzo.
Stadium Name: AutoZone Park. **Location:** North on I-240, exit at Union Ave. West, one and half mile to park.
Standard Game Times: 7:05 pm, Sat 6:05, Sun 1:35. **Ticket Price Range:** $6-23.
Visiting Club Hotel: Sleep Inn at Court Square, 40 N Front, Memphis, TN 38103. **Telephone:** (901) 522-9700.

NASHVILLE SOUNDS

Office Address: 534 Chestnut St., Nashville, TN 37203.
Telephone: (615) 690-HITS. **Fax:** (615) 256-5684.
E-Mail address: info@nashvillesounds.com. **Website:** www.nashvillesounds.com
Affiliation (first year): Milwaukee Brewers (2005). **Years in League:** 1998-

OWNERSHIP/MANAGEMENT

Operated By: MFP Baseball.
Owners: Frank Ward, Masahiro Honzawa.
Vice President/General Manager: Brad Tammen. **Assistant GM:** Brandon Yerger. **VP, Baseball Operations/ Communications:** Doug Scopel. **VP, Corporate Partnerships/Marketing:** Jason Franke. **VP, Ticket Sales/Service:** Eric Rowley. **Director, Accounting:** Barb Walker. **Director, Community Relations:** Shannon Lapsley.
Executive Assistant to Vice President/General Manager: Shauna Holman. **Manager, Merchandise:** Katie Ward. **Manager, Group Sales:** Justin Fenlon. **Manager, Stadium Operations:** Chad Green. **Manager, Community Relations/ Mascot Coordinator:** Buddy Yelton. **Manager, Media Relations:** Alex Wassel. **Manager, Advertising:** Ryan Madar. **Manager, Corporate Partnerships/Promotions:** Andi Grindley. **Account Executives:** Justin Webster, Rob Koch, Chris Day, Tim Nemes. **Head Groundskeeper:** Thomas Trotter. **Assistant Groundskeeper:** Alex Norman. **Clubhouse Managers:** Unavailable.

FIELD STAFF

Manager: Rick Sweet. **Coach:** Bob Skube. **Pitching Coach:** Fred Dabney. **Trainer:** Aaron Hoback. **Strength/ Conditioning Coach:** Andrew Emmick.

GAME INFORMATION

Radio Announcer: Jeff Hem. **No. of Games Broadcast:** 144. **Flagship Station:** 102.5 FM WPRT.
PA Announcers: Eric Berner, Jim Kiser. **Official Scorers:** Eric Jones, Trevor Garrett, Robert Hernberger, Kyle Parkinson. **Stadium Name:** Herschel Greer Stadium. **Location:** I-65 to Wedgewood exit, west to Eighth Ave., right on Eighth to Chestnut St., right on Chestnut. **Standard Game Times:** 7:05 pm, Sat 6:35, Sun 2:05 (April-June 15), 6:35 (June 29-Sept). **Ticket Price Range:** $8-15.
Visiting Club Hotel: Holiday Inn Hotel Nashville Opryland Airport, 2200 Elm Hill Pike, Nashville, TN 37214. **Telephone:** (615) 883-9770.

NEW ORLEANS ZEPHYRS

Office Address: 6000 Airline Drive, Metairie, LA 70003.
Telephone: (504) 734-5155. **Fax:** (504) 734-5118.
E-Mail Address: zephyrs@zephyrsbaseball.com. **Website:** www.zephyrsbaseball.com.
Affiliation (first year): Miami Marlins (2009). **Years in League:** 1998-

OWNERSHIP/MANAGEMENT

Managing Partner/President: Don Beaver.
Minority Owner/Vice President/General Counsel: Walter Leger. **Executive Director/General Manager:** Mike Schline. **VP, Sales/Marketing/Community Relations:** Jeff Booker. **Director, Broadcasting/Team Travel:** Tim Grubbs. **Color Analyst/Speakers Bureau:** Ron Swoboda. **Director, Media Relations:** Dave Sachs. **Director, Promotions/ Community Relations:** Brandon Puls. **Director, Ticket Operations:** Kathy Kaleta. **Assistant, Community Relations/ Promotions:** Rachel Whitley. **Director, Finance/Accounting:** Donna Light. **Director, Stadium Operations:** Jose Avila. **Assistant, Stadium Operations:** Timmy Hinds. **Director, Clubhouse:** Brett Herbert. **Group Outings Coordinators:** Jonathan Christensen, Alex Sides, Jonathan Jones, Katie Boland. **Marketing:** Sarah Wasser. **Head Groundskeeper:** Thomas Marks. **Maintenance Coordinator:** Craig Shaffer. **Receptionist:** Susan Radkovich.

FIELD STAFF

Manager: Andy Haines. **Hitting Coach:** Damon Minor. **Pitching Coach:** Charlie Corbell. **Trainer:** Chris Olson.

GAME INFORMATION

Radio Announcers: Tim Grubbs, Ron Swoboda. **No. of Games Broadcast:** 144. **Flagship Station:** WMTI 106.1 FM.
PA Announcer: Doug Moreau. **Official Scorer:** JL Vangilder.
Stadium Name: Zephyr Field. **Location:** I-10 West toward Baton Rouge, exit at Clearview Pkwy (exit 226) and contin-

ues south, right on Airline Drive (US 61 North) for 1 mile, stadium on left; From airport, take Airline Drive (US 61) east for 4 miles, stadium on right. **Standard Game Times:** 7 pm, Sat 6, Sun 2 (April-May), 6 (June-Sept). **Ticket Price Range:** $6-10.

Visiting Club Hotel: Sheraton Four Points, 6401 Veterans Memorial Blvd, Metairie, LA 70003. **Telephone:** (504) 885-5700.

OKLAHOMA CITY REDHAWKS

Office Address: 2 S Mickey Mantle Drive, Oklahoma City, OK 73104.
Telephone: (405) 218-1000. **Fax:** (405) 218-1001.
E-Mail Address: info@okcredhawks.com. **Website:** www.okcredhawks.com.
Affiliation (first year): Houston Astros (2011). **Years in League:** 1963-1968, 1998-

OWNERSHIP/MANAGEMENT

Operated By: OKC Athletic Club LLC.
Principal Owner: Mandalay Baseball Properties. **President/General Manager:** Michael Byrnes. **VP, Ticketing:** Jenna Byrnes. **Director, Ticket Operations:** Armando Reyes. **Director, Finance/Accounting:** Jon Shaw. **Director, Corporate Partnerships:** Matt Taylor. **Director, Facility Operations:** Harlan Budde. **Director, Operations:** Mitch Stubenhofer. **Director, Entertainment:** Shannon Landers. **Director, Food /Beverage:** Travis Johnson. **Manager, Media Relations/ Broadcasting:** Alex Freedman. **Manager, Sponsor Services:** Jennifer Van Tuyl. **Manager, Merchandise:** Nancy Simmons. **Office Manager:** Travis Hunter. **Head Groundskeeper:** Monte McCoy.

FIELD STAFF

Manager: Tony DeFrancesco. **Hitting Coach:** Leon Roberts. **Pitching Coach:** Steve Webber. **Catching Coach:** Mark Bailey. **Athletic Trainer:** Mike Freer. **Strength/Conditioning Coach:** Alex Pounds.

GAME INFORMATION

Radio Announcer: Alex Freedman No. of Games Broadcast: 144. **Station:** KGHM-AM 1340.
PA Announcer: Tom Travis. **Official Scorers:** Jim Byers, Ryan McGhee, Rich Tortorelli.
Stadium Name: Chickasaw Bricktown Ballpark. **Location:** Bricktown area in downtown Oklahoma City, near interchange of I-235 and I-40, off I-235 take Sheridan exit to Bricktown; off I-40 take Shields exit, north to Bricktown. **Standard Game Times:** 7:05 pm, Sun 2:05 (April-May), 6:05 (June-Aug). **Ticket Price Range:** $7-17.
Visiting Club Hotel: Unavailable.

OMAHA STORM CHASERS

Office Address: Werner Park, 12356 Ballpark Way, Papillion, NE 68046.
Telephone: (402) 734-2550. **Ticket Office Telephone:** (402) 738-5100. **Fax:** (402) 734-7166.
E-mail Address: info@omahastormchasers.com. **Website:** www.omahastorm-chasers.com.
Affiliation (first year): Kansas City Royals (1969). **Years in League:** 1998-

OWNERSHIP/MANAGEMENT

Operated by: Alliance Baseball
Managing Partners: Gary Green, Larry Botel, Eric Foss, Brian Callaghan, Stephen Alepa.
Chief Executive Officer: Gary Green. **President/General Manager:** Martie Cordaro.
Assistant GM: Laurie Schlender. **Assistant GM, Operations:** Andrea Stava. **Director, Broadcasting:** Mark Nasser. **Director, Business Development:** Dave Endress. **Director, Ticket Sales:** Sean Olson. **Broadcaster/Director, Baseball Operations:** Brett Pollock. **Director, Marketing:** Ben Hemmen. **Director, Special Events:** Ben Kratz. **Corporate Sales Executive:** Jason Kinney. **Group Sales Manager:** Andrew Madden. **Group Sales Executives:** Ryan Worthen, Austin Duren, Alex Beck. **Ticket Operations Manager:** Zach Daw. **Client Services Manager:** Kaci Long. **Ballpark Operations Manager:** Brett Myers. **Community Relations Manager:** Caitlyn Brown. **Media Relations Manager:** Andrew Mitchell. **Creative Services Manager:** Mark Kuhlmann. **Finance Assistant:** Meredith Daniels. **Ballpark Operations Assistant:** Matt Owen. **Head Groundskeeper:** Noah Diercks. **Assistant Groundskeeper:** Adam Basinger. **Front Office Assistant:** Donna Kostal.

FIELD STAFF

Manager: Brian Poldberg. **Hitting Coach:** Tommy Gregg. **Pitching Coach:** Larry Carter. **Athletic Trainer:** Dave Iannicca. **Strength Coach:** David Kathmann

GAME INFORMATION

Radio Announcers: Mark Nasser, Brett Pollock. **No. of Games Broadcast:** 144. **Flagship Station:** KOIL-AM 1180.
PA Announcers: Craig Evans, Jake Ryan, Matt Siegel. **Official Scorers:** Frank Adkisson, Steve Pivovar, Ryan White.
Stadium Name: Werner Park. **Location:** Highway 370, just east of I-80 (exit 439). **Standard Game Times:** 6:35 pm (April-May), 7:05 (June-Sept), Fri/Sat 7:05, Sun 2:05.
Visiting Club Hotel: Courtyard Omaha La Vista, 12560 Westport Parkway, La Vista, NE 68128. **Telephone:** (402) 339-4900. **Fax:** (402) 339-4901.

RENO ACES

Office Address: 250 Evans Ave., Reno, NV 89501.
Telephone: (775) 334-4700. Fax: (775) 334-4701.
Website: www.renoaces.com
Affiliation (first year): Arizona Diamondbacks (2009). Years in League: 2009-

OWNERSHIP/MANAGEMENT

President/Managing Partner: Stuart Katzoff.
Partners: Jerry Katzoff, Herb Simon, Steve Simon.
Chief Financial Officer: Kevin Bower. General Counsel: Brett Beecham. Executive Vice President/Chief Operating Officer: Eric Edelstein. General Manager: Rick Parr.
Director, Broadcasting: Ryan Radtke. Manager, Communications: Shannon Siders. Director, Marketing: Brett McGinness. Manager, Promotions/Community Relations: Audrey Hill. Director, Business Development: Brian Moss. Account Executive, Marketing Partnerships: Emily Jaenson. Marketing Partnerships Service Coordinator: Michael D'Olivo. Vice President, Ticket Sales: Todd Pund. Manager, Ticket Operations: Sarah Bliss.
Account Executives: Kris Morrow, Brian McMillen, Lorenzo Taormina, Niko Saladis, Jeff Turner, Matt Jex. Representative, Client Services: Cody Lyford. Sales Coordinator: Michael Baum. Director, Ballpark Operations: Tara O'Connor. Manager, Grounds: Eric Blanton. Assistant Groundskeeper: Lane Pickel. Coordinator, Operations: Daniel Mulligan. Manager, Facilities: Mark Link. Assistant, Facilities: Adam Mercado. Director, Merchandise: Taylor Russo. Retail Buyer: Stacey Little. Controller: Jerry Meyer. Senior Staff Accountant: Melinda Jessee. Junior Staff Accountant: Jacquie Menicucci.

FIELD STAFF

Manager: Phil Nevin. Hitting Coach: Greg Gross. Pitching Coach: Mike Parrott. Trainer: Joe Metz. Strength/ Conditioning Coordinator: Mike Schofield.

GAME INFORMATION

Radio Announcer: Ryan Radtke. No. of Games Broadcast: 144. Flagship Station: Fox Sports 630 AM.
PA Announcer: Unavailable. Official Scorer: Jack Kuestermeyer.
Stadium Name: Aces Ballpark. Location: From Carson City (south of Reno): 395 North to I-80 West, Exit 14 (Wells Ave.), left on Wells, right at Kuenzli St., ballpark on right; From East, I-80 West to exit 14 (Wells Ave.), left on Wells, right on Kuenzli, right at East 2nd St.; From West, I-80 East to Exit 13 (Virginia St.), right on Virginia, left on Second, ballpark on left; From North, 395 South to I-80 West, Exit 14 (Wells Ave.), left on Wells, right on Kuenzli. Standard Game Times: 7:05 pm, 6:35, 1:05. Ticket Price Range: $7-30.
Visiting Club Hotel: Silver Legacy Resort Casino. Telephone: 775-325-7401.

ROUND ROCK EXPRESS

Office Address: 3400 East Palm Valley Blvd., Round Rock, TX 78665.
Telephone: (512) 255-2255. Fax: (512) 255-1558.
E-Mail Address: info@rrexpress.com. Website: www.roundrockexpress.com.
Affiliation (first year): Texas Rangers (2011). Year in League: 2005-

OWNERSHIP/MANAGEMENT

Operated By: Ryan Sanders Baseball, LP.
Principal Owners: Nolan Ryan, Don Sanders.
CEO/Owner: Reese Ryan. Owners: Reid Ryan, Brad Sanders, Bret Sanders, Jay Miller, Eddie Maloney. Executive Vice President, Ryan Sanders Baseball: JJ Gottsch. Executive Assistants, Ryan Sanders Baseball: Debbie Bowman, Rebecca Gustafson.
President: Dave Fendrick. General Manager: Chris Almendarez. Senior VP, Marketing: Laura Fragoso. VP, Corporate Sales: Henry Green. VP, Ticket Sales: Gary Franke. VP, Business Development: Gregg Miller. VP, Administration/ Accounting: Debbie Coughlin.
Senior Director, Stadium Operations: David Powers. Senior Director, United Heritage Center: Scott Allen. Senior Director, Ticket Operations: Ross Scott. Director, Broadcasting: Mike Capps. Director, Communications: Jill Cacic. Director, Community Relations: Tim Jackson. Director, Entertainment/Promotions: Rob Runnels Director, Stadium Maintenance: Aurelio Martinez. Retail Manager: Debbie Goodman. Marketing Coordinator: Whitney Rhoden. Client Services: Cade Richardson. IT Manager, Sam Isham. Stadium Maintenance Manager: Corey Woods.
Senior Account Executive: Stuart Scally. Account Executives: Julia Benavides, Luke Crum, Andy Berger, Melissa Schmalbach. Head Groundskeeper: Garrett Reddehase. Assistant Groundskeeper: Phillip Grefrath. Clubhouse Manager: Kenny Bufton. Maintenance Staff: Raymond Alemon, Ofelia Gonzalez. Event Staff Coordinator: Randy Patterson. Office Manager: Wendy Abrahamsen.

FIELD STAFF

Manager: Steve Buechele. Hitting Coach: Justin Mashore. Pitching Coach: Brad Holman. Coach: Spike Owen. Trainer: Jason Roberts. Strength Coach: Ric Mabie.

GAME INFORMATION

Radio Announcers; Mike Capps. No. of Games Broadcast: 144. Flagship Station: The Horn 104.9 FM Austin.

PA Announcer: Derrick Grubbs. **Official Scorer:** Tommy Tate.
Stadium Name: Dell Diamond. **Location:** US Highway 79, 3.5 miles east of Interstate 35 (exit 253) or 1.5 miles west of Texas Tollway 130. **Standard Game Times:** 7:05 pm, 6:05, 1:05. **Ticket Price Range:** $7-$14.
Visiting Club Hotel: Hilton Garden Inn, 2310 North IH-35, Round Rock, TX 78681. **Telephone:** (512) 341-8200.

SACRAMENTO RIVER CATS

Office Address: 400 Ballpark Drive, West Sacramento, CA 95691.
Telephone: (916) 376-4700. **Fax:** (916) 376-4710.
E-Mail address: reception@rivercats.com. **Website:** www.rivercats.com.
Affiliation (first year): Oakland Athletics (2000). **Years in League:** 1903, 1909-11, 1918-60, 1974-76, 2000-

OWNERSHIP/MANAGEMENT

Owner/CEO: Susan Savage.
General Manager: Jeff Savage. **Executive VP/CFO:** Dan Vistica. **Senior VP, Business Operations:** Chip Maxson. **Director, Corporate Partnerships:** Greg Coletti. **Coordinator, Partnership Acitvation:** Kelly O'Brien. **Human Resources Manager:** Grace Bailey. **Director, Event Operations:** Ryan Von Sossan. **Manager, Marketing:** Leslie Lindsey. **Coordinator, Marketing:** Kelly Cassidy. **Manager, Entertainment/Promotions:** Dane Lund. **Coordinator, Multimedia/Graphic Design:** Mike Villareal. **Coordinator, Events/Entertainment:** Brittney Broberg. **Mascot Coordinator:** Rhett Holland. **Coordinator, Public Relations/Baseball Operations:** Mark Ling.
Public Relations Assistant/New Media Editor: Matt Lundgren. **Manager, Merchandise:** Rose Holland. **Assistant Manager, On Deck Shop:** Erin Kilby. **Coordinator, Website/Research:** Brent Savage. **Head Groundskeeper:** Chris Shastid. **Coordinator, Grounds:** Marcello Clamar. **Facility Engineer:** Mike Gossen. **Director, Ticket Operations:** John Krivacic. **Manager, Season Tickets/Senior Corporate Account Executive:** Katie Krivacic. **Ticket Operations Assistant:** Khimberly Marshall. **Director, Ticket Sales:** Adam English. **Manager, Inside Sales:** Jordan Cannon. **Senior Corporate Account Executive:** John Watts. **Corporate Account Executives:** Mychal Baker, Cooper Farrer, Andrew Dean. **Senior Group Events Account Executive:** Meagan Schreiner. **Group Events Account Executives:** Michele Bello, Eddie Eixenberger, Eric Esposito, Megan Hinde, Alejandro Lacayo, Joey Van Cleave. **Controller:** Maddie Strika. **Accounting Assistant:** Michelle Agurto. **Receptionist:** Leah Larot.

FIELD STAFF

Manager: Steve Scarsone. **Hitting Coach:** Greg Sparks. **Pitching Coach:** Rick Rodriguez. **Trainer:** Brad LaRosa. **Strength Coach:** Derek Cantieni.

GAME INFORMATION

Radio Announcer: Johnny Doskow. **No. of Games Broadcast:** Home-72 Road-72. **Flagship Station:** Talk 650 KSTE.
PA Announcer: Greg Lawson. **Official Scorers:** Brian Bergei, Ryan Bjork, Mark Honbo.
Stadium Name: Raley Field. **Location:** I-5 to Business-80 West, exit at Jefferson Boulevard. **Standard Game Time:** 7:05 pm. **Ticket Price Range:** $8-60.
Visiting Club Hotel: Holiday Inn.

SALT LAKE BEES

Office Address: 77 W 1300 South, Salt Lake City, UT 84115.
Telephone: (801) 325-BEES (2337). **Fax:** (801) 485-6818.
E-Mail Address: info@slbees.com. **Website:** www.slbees.com.
Affiliation (first year): Los Angeles Angels (2001). **Years in League:** 1915-25, 1958-65, 1970-84, 1994-.

OWNERSHIP/MANAGEMENT

Operated by: Larry Miller Baseball Inc.
Principal Owner: Gail Miller.
CEO, Larry Miller Group of Companies: Greg Miller.
President, Miller Sports Properties: Steve Miller. **Chief Operating Officer:** Jim Olson. **Chief Revenue Officer:** Don Stirling. **Vice President/General Manager:** Marc Amicone. **Senior VP, Corporate Partnerships:** Chris Baum. **Senior VP, Marketing:** Craig Sanders. **Senior VP, Ticket Sales:** Clay Jensen. **General Counsel:** Robert Tingey. **VP, Communications:** Frank Zang. **Director, Broadcasting:** Steve Klauke. **VP, Corporate Partnerships:** Greg Tanner.
Director, Game Operations: Chance Fessler. **Director, Ticket Sales/Services:** Casey Patterson. **Director, Corporate Partnerships:** Brian Prutch. **Director, Marketing:** Kevin Dalton. **Box Office Manager:** Laura Russell. **Ticket/Group Sales Manager:** Brad Jacoway. **VP, Public Safety:** Jim Bell. **VP, Food Services:** Mark Stedman. **Director, Food Services:** Dave Dalton. **Youth Programs Coordinator:** Nate Martinez. **Clubhouse Manager:** Eli Rice.

FIELD STAFF

Manager: Keith Johnson. **Hitting Coach:** Francisco Matos. **Pitching Coach:** Erik Bennett. **Trainer:** Brian Reinker.

GAME INFORMATION

Radio Announcer: Steve Klauke. **No. of Games Broadcast:** 144. **Flagship Station:** 1280-AM The Zone.
PA Announcer: Jeff Reeves. **Official Scorers:** Howard Nakagama, Terry Harward.
Stadium Name: Spring Mobile Ballpark. **Location:** I-15 North/South to 1300 South exit, east to ballpark at West

Temple. **Standard Game Times:** 6:35 (April-May), 7:05 (June-Sept), Sun 1:05. **Ticket Price Range:** $8-24.
   Visiting Club Hotel: Sheraton City Centre, 150 W 500 South, Salt Lake City, UT 84101. **Telephone:** (801) 401-2000.

TACOMA RAINIERS

Office Address: 2502 South Tyler St., Tacoma, WA 98405.
Telephone: (253) 752-7707. **Fax:** (253) 752-7135.
Website: www.tacomarainiers.com.
Affiliation: Seattle Mariners (1995). **Years in League:** 1904-1905, 1960-

OWNERSHIP/MANAGEMENT

Owners: The Baseball Club of Tacoma.
President: Aaron Artman.
Director, Administration/Assistant to President: Patti Stacy. **Vice President, Business Development:** Jim Flavin.
Creative Director: Tony Canepa. **Senior Director, Marketing/Corporate Partner Services:** Audrey Berglund. **Senior Director, Ballpark Operations:** Ryan Schutt. **Director, Partner Development:** Julia Falvey. **Director, Communications:** Ben Spradling. **Director, Ticket Sales:** Shane Santman. **Director, Event/Tickets Services:** Nicole Strunks. **Director, Baseball Operations/Merchandise:** Ashley Roth. **Director, Ticket Operations:** Cameron Badgett. **Manager, Corporate Partner Services:** Betsy Hechtner. **Manager, Stadium Operations:** Nick Cherniske. **Coordinator, Box Office:** Necia Borba. **Coordinator, Game Entertainment:** Max Fosberg. **Coordinator:** Event Sales: Byron Pullen. **Corporate Sales Managers:** Ben Nelson, Jon Luke, Tim O'Hollaren, Ross Richards. **Group Event Coordinator:** Chris Aubertin, Karleen Cordova, Taryn Duncan, Haley Harshaw, Ainsley O'Keefe. **Controller:** Brian Coombe.
Accounting: Elise Schorr. **Head Groundskeeper:** David Schutt. **Home Clubhouse Manager:** Shane Hickenbottom.

FIELD STAFF

Manager: Rich Donnelly. **Coach:** Cory Snyder. **Pitching Coach:** Jaime Navarro. **Trainer:** Tom Newberg. **Trainer:** B.J. Downie. **Performance Coach:** Gabe Bourland

GAME INFORMATION

Radio Broadcaster: Mike Curto. **No. of Games Broadcast:** 144. **Flagship Station:** KHHO 850-AM.
PA Announcer: Derek Stansbury. **Official Scorers:** Kevin Kalal, Gary Brooks, Michael Jessee.
Stadium Name: Cheney Stadium. **Location:** From I-5, take exit 132 (Highway 16 West) for 1.2 miles to 19th St. East exit, merge right onto 19th Street, right onto Clay Huntington Way and follow into the parking lot of the ballpark. **Standard Game Times:** 7:05, Sun 1:35. **Ticket Price Range:** $7-$25.
   Visiting Club Hotel: Hotel Murano, 1320 Broadway Plaza, Tacoma, WA 98402. **Telephone:** (253) 238-8000.

EASTERN LEAGUE

Office Address: 30 Danforth St, Suite 208, Portland, ME 04101.
Telephone: (207) 761-2700. **Fax:** (207) 761-7064.
E-Mail Address: elpb@easternleague.com. **Website:** www.easternleague.com.
Years League Active: 1923-.

President/Treasurer: Joe McEacharn.

Vice President/Secretary: Charles Eshbach. **VP:** Chuck Domino. **Assistant to President:** Bill Rosario.

Directors: Ken Babby (Akron), Rick Brenner (New Hampshire), Lou DiBella (Richmond), Josh Solomon (New Britain), Charlie Eshbach (Portland), Joe Finley (Trenton), Bob Lozinak (Altoona), Art Matin (Erie), Michael Reinsdorf (Harrisburg), Brian Shallcross (Bowie), Craig Stein (Reading), Mike Urda (Binghamton).

Division Structure: Eastern—Binghamton, New Britain, New Hampshire, Portland, Reading, Trenton. Western—Akron, Altoona, Bowie, Erie, Harrisburg, Richmond.

Regular Season: 142 games. **2014 Opening Date:** April 3. **Closing Date:** Sept 1.

All-Star Game: July 16 at Altoona. **Playoff Format:** Top two teams in each division meet in best-of-five series. Winners meet in best-of-five series for league championship.

Roster Limit: 25. **Player Eligibility Rule:** No restrictions. **Brand of Baseball:** Rawlings.

Umpires: John Bacon (Sherrodsville, OH), Joe Born (Lafayette, IN), Ryan Clark (McDonough, GA), Billy Cunha (Fort Jones, CA), Ramon De Jesus (Santo Domingo, DR), Brian DeBrauwere (Hummelstown, PA), Blake Felix (Fort Worth, TX), Eric Gillam (Roscoe, IL), Chris Gonzalez (Campbell, CA), Nick Mahrley (Scottsdale, AZ), Dan Merzel (Philadelphia, PA), Roberto Moreno (Cumana, VZ), Roberto Ortiz (Hopkinsville, KY), Brian Reilly (Grand Rapids, MI), Tim Rosso (Saddle Brook, NJ), Chris Tipton (Orlando, FL), Junior Valentine (Maryville, TN), Jansen Visconti (Latrobe, PA).

Joe McEacharn

STADIUM INFORMATION

Club	Stadium	Opened	Dimensions			Capacity	2013 Att.
			LF	CF	RF		
Akron	Canal Park	1997	331	400	337	9,097	295,459
Altoona	Peoples Natural Gas Field	1999	325	405	325	7,210	286,227
Binghamton	NYSEG Stadium	1992	330	400	330	6,012	185,093
Bowie	Prince George's Stadium	1994	309	405	309	10,000	252,593
Erie	Jerry Uht Park	1995	312	400	328	6,000	206,780
Harrisburg	Metro Bank Park	1987	325	400	325	6,300	284,361
New Britain	New Britain Stadium	1996	330	400	330	6,146	307,097
New Hampshire	Northeast Delta Dental Stadium	2005	326	400	306	6,500	353,639
Portland	Hadlock Field	1994	315	400	330	7,368	341,420
Reading	FirstEnergy Stadium	1951	330	400	330	9,000	436,134
Richmond	The Diamond	1985	330	402	330	9,560	434,769
Trenton	Arm & Hammer Park	1994	330	407	330	6,150	360,010

AKRON RUBBERDUCKS

Office Address: 300 S Main St., Akron, OH 44308.
Telephone: (330) 253-5151. **Fax:** (330) 253-3300.
E-Mail address: information@akronrubberducks.com. **Website:** www.akronrubberducks.com.

Affiliation (first year): Cleveland Indians (1989). **Years in League:** 1989-

OWNERSHIP/MANAGEMENT

Operated By: Akron Baseball LLC.

Principal Owner: Ken Babby. **General Manager/COO:** Jim Pfander.

Assistant General Manager: Scott Riley. **Director, Promotions:** Christina Shisler. **Director, Public/Media Relations:** Adam Liberman. **Director, Broadcasting/Baseball Information:** Dave Wilson. **Director, Merchandise:** Courtney Campbell. **Director, Creative Services:** Chris Thomas. **Director, Stadium Operations:** Adam Horner. **Head Groundskeeper:** Chris Walsh. **Assistant Director, Ballpark Operations:** Ryan Olszewski. **Director, Food/Beverage:** Brian Manning. **Assistant Director, Food/Beverage:** Sam Dankoff. **Director, Suites/Community Relations:** Sierra Sawtelle. **Executive Assistant, CEO/Office Manager:** Emily Ray. **Box Office Manager:** Brock Cline. **Director, Ticketing:** Brian Flenner. **Assistant Director, Ticketing:** Jeremy Heit. **Senior Group Sales Manager:** Mitch Cromes. **Ticket Sales Executives:** Pete Nugent, Dee Shilling, Craig Wilson. **Director, Corporate Partnerships:** Brent DeCoster. **Sponsorship Sales Coordinator:** Juli Donlen.

FIELD STAFF

Manager: Dave Wallace. **Hitting Coach:** Rouglas Odor. **Pitching Coach:** Jeff Harris. **Trainer:** Jeremy Heller. **Strength/Conditioning Coach:** Jake Sankal.

GAME INFORMATION

Radio Announcers: Jim Clark, Dave Wilson. **No. of Games Broadcast:** 142. **Flagship Station:** Fox Sports Radio 1350-AM.

PA Announcer: Leonard Grabowski. **Official Scorer:** Tom Giffen.

Stadium Name: Canal Park. **Location:** From I-76 East or I-77 South, exit onto Route 59 East, exit at Exchange/Cedar, right onto Cedar, left at Main Street; From I-76 West or I-77 North, exit at Main Street/Downtown, follow exit onto Broadway Street, left onto Exchange Street, right at Main Street. **Standard Game Time:** 7:05 pm, Sun 1:05. **Ticket Price Range:** $5-9.

Visiting Club Hotel: Unavailable.

ALTOONA CURVE

Office Address: Peoples Natural Gas Field, 1000 Park Avenue, Altoona, PA 16602.
Telephone: (814) 943-5400. **Fax:** (814) 942-9132.
E-Mail Address: frontoffice@altoonacurve.com. **Website:** www.altoonacurve.com.
Affiliation (first year): Pittsburgh Pirates (1999). **Years in League:** 1999-

OWNERSHIP/MANAGEMENT

Operated By: Lozinak Professional Baseball.

Managing Members: Bob and Joan Lozinak. **COO:** David Lozinak. **CFO:** Mike Lozinak. **Chief Administrative Officer:** Steve Lozinak. **General Manager:** Rob Egan. **Senior Adviser:** Sal Baglieri.

Assistant GM, Marketing/Promotions: Matt Hoover. **Assistant GM, Communications:** Mike Passanisi. **Director, Finance:** Mary Lamb. **Director, Ticket Operations:** Chris Keefer. **Director, Group Sales:** Corey Homan. **Director, Merchandising:** Claire Hoover. **Director, Ballpark Operations:** Doug Mattern. **Head Groundskeeper:** Ben Young. **Manager, Concessions:** Glenn McComas. **Assistant Manager, Concessions:** Michelle Anna. **Director, Creative Services:** Mark Milligan. **Manager, Community Relations:** Courtney Simpson. **Manager, Special Events/All-Star Game Coordinator:** Emily Erickson. **Development/Operations:** Tim Lozinak. **Sponsorship Sales Account Executive:** Chuck Griswold. **Box Office Manager:** Steffan Langguth. **Senior Associate, Ticket:** Nathan Bowen. **Associate, Ticketing:** Luke Johnson. **Administrative Assistant:** Carol Schmittle.

FIELD STAFF

Manager: Carlos Garcia. **Hitting Coach:** Ryan Long. **Pitching Coach:** Stan Kyles. **Trainer:** Mike Zalno.

GAME INFORMATION

Radio Announcers: Mike Passanisi. **No. of Games Broadcast:** 142. **Flagship Station:** WVAM 1430-AM.

PA Announcer: Rich DeLeo. **Official Scorers:** Ted Beam, Dick Wagner.

Stadium Name: Peoples Natural Gas Field. **Location:** Just off Frankstown Road Exit off I-99. **Standard Game Times:** 7 pm, 6:30 (April-May); Sat 6, Sun 6. **Ticket Price Range:** $5-12.

Visiting Club Hotel: Super 8, 3535 Fairway Drive, Altoona, PA 16602. **Telephone:** (814) 942-5350.

BINGHAMTON METS

Office Address: 211 Henry St., Binghamton, NY 13901. **Mailing Address:** PO Box 598, Binghamton, NY 13902.
Telephone: (607) 723-6387. **Fax:** (607) 723-7779.
E-Mail Address: bmets@bmets.com. **Website:** www.bmets.com.
Affiliation (first year): New York Mets (1992). **Years in League:** 1923-37, 1940-63, 1966-68, 1992-

OWNERSHIP/MANAGEMENT

Principal Owners: Bill Maines, David Maines, George Scherer, Michael Urda.

General Manager: Jim Weed. **Assistant GM:** Heith Tracy.

Director, Stadium Operations: Richard Tylicki. **Box Office Manager:** Joe Pascarella. **Director, Video Production:** Jstin Cohen. **Corporate Sales Executive:** Josh Patton. **Director, Community Relations:** Connor Gates. **Special Event Coordinator:** Erica Folli. **Director, Food/Beverage:** Bob Urda. **Scholastic Programs Coordinator:** Lou Ferraro. **Accountant:** Karen Micalizzi. **Director, Merchandise:** Lisa Shattuck. **Director, Broadcast/Media Relations:** Tim Heiman. **Sports Turf Manager:** EJ Folli. **Home Clubhouse Manager:** Jacob Polovchak.

FIELD STAFF

Manager: Pedro Lopez. **Coach:** Luis Natera. **Pitching Coach:** Glenn Abbott.

GAME INFORMATION

Radio Announcer: Tim Heiman. **No. of Games Broadcast:** 142. **Flagship Station:** WNBF 1290-AM.

PA Announcer: Chris Schmidt. **Official Scorer:** Steve Kraly.

Stadium Name: NYSEG Stadium. **Location:** I-81 to exit 4S (Binghamton), Route 11 exit to Henry Street. **Standard Game Times:** 6:35, 7:05 (Fri-Sat), 1:05 (Day Games). **Ticket Price Range:** $7-22.

Visiting Club Hotel: Best Western, 569 Harry L Drive, Johnson City, NY 13790. **Telephone:** (607) 729-9194.

BOWIE BAYSOX

Office Address: Prince George's Stadium, 4101 NE Crain Hwy, Bowie, MD 20716.
Telephone: (301) 805-6000. **Fax:** (301) 464-4911.
E-Mail Address: info@baysox.com. **Website:** www.baysox.com.
Affiliation (first year): Baltimore Orioles (1993). **Years in League:** 1993-

OWNERSHIP/MANAGEMENT
Owned By: Bowie Baysox Baseball Club LLC.
President: Ken Young.
General Manager: Brian Shallcross. **Assistant GM:** Phil Wrye. **Director, Marketing:** Brandan Kaiser. **Director, Field/Facility Operations:** Matt Parrott. **Director, Ticket Operations:** Charlene Fewer. **Director, Sponsorships:** Matt McLaughlin. **Promotions Manager:** Chris Rogers. **Communications Manager:** Matt Wilson. **Sponsorship Account Manager:** Adam Pohl. **Group Events Managers:** Jake Seils, Ted Elsasser, Ashley Nalley, Murray Waller. **Box Office Manager:** Ryan Barber. **Community Programs Manager:** Joe Miller. **Stadium Operations Manager:** Brandon Rolfe. **Director, Gameday Personnel:** Darlene Mingioli. **Clubhouse Manager:** Andy Maalouf. **Bookkeeper:** Carol Terwilliger.

FIELD STAFF
Manager: Gary Kendall. **Coach:** Butch Davis. **Pitching Coach:** Blaine Beatty.

GAME INFORMATION
Radio Announcer: Adam Pohl. **No. of Games Broadcast:** 71 (all home games). **Flagship Station:** www.baysox.com.
PA Announcer: Adrienne Roberson. **Official Scorers:** Bill Hay, Carl Smith, Ted Black, Herb Martinson.
Stadium Name: Prince Georges Stadium. **Location:** 1/4 mile south of US 50/Route 301 Interchange in Bowie.
Standard Game Times: 6:35 pm, Sun 2:05 (April-June), 6:05 (July Aug). **Ticket Price Range:** $7-17.
Visiting Club Hotel: Best Western Annapolis, 2520 Riva Rd, Annapolis, MD 21401. **Telephone:** (410) 224-2800.

ERIE SEAWOLVES

Office Address: 110 E 10th St., Erie, PA 16501.
Telephone: (814) 456-1300. **Fax:** (814) 456-7520.
E-Mail Address: seawolves@seawolves.com. **Website:** www.seawolves.com.
Affiliation (first year): Detroit Tigers (2001). **Years in League:** 1999-

OWNERSHIP/MANAGEMENT
Principal Owners: Mandalay Baseball Properties, LLC.
President: Greg Coleman. **Assistant GM, Communications:** Greg Gania. **Assistant GM, Sales:** Mark Pirrello. **Director, Accounting/Finance:** Amy McArdle. **Director, Ticket Sales:** Cody Herrick. **Account Executive:** Garrett Hickey. **Director, Group Sales:** Dan Torf. **Group Sales Coordinator:** Kevin Forte. **Ticket Operations Assistant:** Kelsey Brown. **Director, Food/Beverage (Pro Sports Catering):** Austin Punzel.

FIELD STAFF
Manager: Unavailable. **Coach:** Gerald Perry. **Pitching Coach:** Jaime Garcia. **Trainer:** T.J. Jaunders.

GAME INFORMATION
Radio Announcer: Greg Gania. **No. of Games Broadcast:** 142. **Flagship Station:** WFNN 1330-AM.
PA Announcer: Bob Shreve. **Official Scorer:** Les Caldwell.
Stadium Name: Jerry Uht Park. **Location:** US 79 North to East 12th Street exit, left on State Street, right on 10th Street.
Standard Game Times: 7:05 pm, 6:35 (April), Sun 1:35. **Ticket Prices:** $8-12.
Visiting Club Hotel: Clarion Lake Erie, 2800 West 8th St., Erie, PA 16505.

HARRISBURG SENATORS

Office Address: Metro Bank Park, City Island, Harrisburg, PA 17101. **Mailing Address:** PO Box 15757, Harrisburg, PA 17105.
Telephone: (717) 231-4444. **Fax:** (717) 231-4445.
E-Mail address: information@senatorsbaseball.com. **Website:** www.senators-baseball.com.
Affiliation (first year): Washington Nationals (2005). **Years in League:** 1924-35, 1987-

OWNERSHIP, MANAGEMENT
Operated By: Senators Partners, LLC.
Chairman: Michael Reinsdorf. **CEO:** Bill Davidson. **President:** Kevin Kulp. **General Manager:** Randy Whitaker. **Assistant GM:** Aaron Margolis. **Accounting Manager:** Donna Demczak. **Accounting Intern:** Jon Garber. **Senior Corporate Sales Executive:** Todd Matthews. **Director, Merchandise:** Ann Marie Naumes. **Director, Ticket Sales:** Nate DeFazio. **Senior Account Executives:** Jonathan Boles, Jessica Kauffman. **Account Executive:** Kevin Dougherty, Tom Kronenberger. **Director, Stadium Operations:** Tim Foreman. **Head Groundskeeper:** Brandon

Forsburg. **Stadium Operations Coordinator:** Ben Moyer. **Stadium Operations Interns:** Tyler Maghery, Marcus Miller. **Director, Broadcasting/Media Relations:** Terry Byrom. **Broadcaster/Media Relations Intern:** Perry Mattern. **Director, Community Relations/Box Office Operations:** Emily Winslow. **Community Relations Coordinator:** Mary Kate Holder.
Director, Digital/New Media: Ashley Grotte. **Game Entertainment Coordinator:** Sean Purcell. **Ticket Sales Interns:** Dan Ampthor, Katie Evans, Chuck Heisley, Matt McGrady, Brendan Porter. **Box Office Intern:** Nick DeMarco. **Community Relations/Mascot Intern:** Grant Gorham.

FIELD STAFF

Manager: Brian Daubach. **Hitting Coach:** Mark Harris. **Pitching Coach:** Chris Michalak. **Coach:** Melvin Dorta. **Trainer:** Eric Montague. **Strength Coach:** Tony Rogowski.

GAME INFORMATION

Radio Announcers: Terry Byrom, Perry Mattern. **No. of Games Broadcast:** 142. **Flagship Station:** 1460-AM.
PA Announcer: Chris Andre. **Official Scorers:** Terry Walters, Bruce Bashore, Jeff McGaw.
Stadium Name: Metro Bank Park. **Location:** I-83, exit 23 (Second Street) to Market Street, bridge to City Island. **Ticket Price Range:** $5-13.50.
Visiting Club Hotel: Park Inn by Radisson, 5401 Carlisle Pike, Mechanicsburg, PA 17050. **Telephone:** (800) 772-7829.

NEW BRITAIN ROCK CATS

Office Address: 230 John Karbonic Way, New Britain, CT 06051. **Mailing Address:** PO Box 1718, New Britain, CT 06050.
Telephone: (860) 224-8383. **Fax:** (860) 225-6267.
E-Mail Address: rockcats@rockcats.com. **Website:** www.rockcats.com.
Affiliation (first year): Minnesota Twins (1995). **Years in League:** 1983-

OWNERSHIP/MANAGEMENT

Operated By: New Britain Double Play LLC.
Directors: Josh Solomon, Jim Solomon, Jennifer Goorno. **General Manager:** Tim Restall. **Vice President, Corporate Partnerships/Marketing:** Mike Ambramson. **VP, Business Development:** Derek Sharp. **Director, Broadcasting/Media Relations:** Jeff Dooley. **Director, Stadium Operations:** Eric Fritz. **Director, Corporate Tickets:** Steve Given. **Director, Group Sales:** Josh Montinieri. **Senior Manager, Hospitality:** Andres Levy. **Ticket Operations Manager:** Dylan Conway. **Group Sales Managers:** Kristin Zemke, Scott Casten. **Manager, Media/Group Sales:** Pat O'Sullivan. **Community Relations Manager:** Ali Gochman. **Corporate Sales Manager:** Andrew Vallejo. **Client Services Manager:** Amanda Goldsmith. **Merchandise Manager:** Ben Cecil. **Marketing Coordinator:** Lori Soltis. **Controller:** Jim Bonfiglio. **Director, Creative Services:** Ted Seavey.

FIELD STAFF

Manager: Jeff Smith. **Coach:** Chad Allen. **Pitching Coach:** Stu Cliburn. **Trainer:** Chris Johnson.

GAME INFORMATION

Radio Announcer: Jeff Dooley. **No. of Games Broadcast:** 142. **Flagship Station:** Fox Sports Radio 1410, WMRD 1150-AM.
PA Announcer: John Sheatsley. **Official Scorer:** Ed Smith.
Stadium Name: New Britain Stadium. **Location:** From I-84, take Route 72 East (exit 35 of Route 9 South (exit 39A), left at Ellis St. (exit 25), left at South Main St., stadium one mile on right; From Route 91 or Route 5, take Route 9 North to Route 71 (exit 24), first exit. **Ticket Price Range:** $6-20.
Visiting Club Hotel: Holiday Inn Express, 120 Laning St, Southington, CT 06489. **Telephone:** (860) 276-0736.

NEW HAMPSHIRE
FISHER CATS

Office Address: 1 Line Drive, Manchester, NH 03101.
Telephone: (603) 641-2005. **Fax:** (603) 641-2055.
E-Mail Address: info@nhfishercats.com. **Website:** www.nhfishercats.com.
Affiliation (first year): Toronto Blue Jays (2004). **Years in League:** 2004-

OWNERSHIP/MANAGEMENT

Operated By: DSF Sports.
Owner: Art Solomon. **President:** Rick Brenner.
President: Rick Brenner. **Vice President, Sales:** Mike Ramshaw. **VP, Business Operations:** Steve Pratt. **Corporate Controller:** Karl Stone. **Director, Box Office Operations:** Tim Hough. **Director, Facilities/Turf:** Shawn Meredith. **Director, Marketing/Public Affairs:** Jenna Raizes. **Director, Broadcast/Media Relations:** Tom Gauthier. **Stadium Operations Manager:** DJ White. **Merchandise Manager:** Justin Stecz. **Community Relations Manager:** Megan Shea. **Sports Turf Manager:** Dan Boyle. **Production/Graphic Design Manager:** Sean Hladick. **Corporate Sales Manager:**

Jason Corbeil. **Ticket Sales Account Executives:** Chris Aubertin, Stephanie Fournier, Chris Wall, Matt Labossiere, Kirby Wade. **Ticket Sales Account Executive/On-Field Promotions:** Jeff Martin. **Executive Assistant/Office Manager:** Kayla Hines. **President, Advantage Food/Beverage:** Tim Restall. **Director, Food/Beverage Operations:** Chris Carlisle. **Executive Chef:** Alan Foley.

FIELD STAFF

Manager: Bobby Meacham. **Hitting Coach:** Jon Nunnally. **Pitching Coach:** Jim Czajkowski. **Trainer:** Bob Tarpey. **Strength/Conditioning:** Brian Pike.

GAME INFORMATION

Radio Announcers: Tom Gauthier, Bob Lipman, Dick Lutsk, Charlie Sherman. **No. of Games Broadcast:** 142. **Flagship Station:** WGIR 610-AM.

PA Announcer: Alex James. **Official Scorers:** Chick Smith, Lenny Parker, Greg Royce, Pete Dupuis.

Stadium Name: Northeast Delta Dental Stadium. **Location:** From I-93 North, take I-293 North to exit 5 (Granite Street), right on Granite Street, right on South Commercial Street, right on Line Drive. **Ticket Price Range:** $6-12.

Visiting Club Hotel: Comfort Inn, 298 Queen City Ave, Manchester, NH 03102. **Telephone:** (603) 668-2600.

PORTLAND SEA DOGS

Office Address: 271 Park Ave., Portland, ME 04102. **Mailing Address:** PO Box 636, Portland, ME 04104.

Telephone: (207) 874-9300. **Fax:** (207) 780-0317.

E-Mail Address: seadogs@seadogs.com. **Website:** www.seadogs.com.

Affiliation (first year): Boston Red Sox (2003). **Years in League:** 1994-

OWNERSHIP/MANAGEMENT

Operated By: Portland, Maine Baseball, Inc.

Chairman: Bill Burke.

Treasurer: Sally McNamara. **President:** Charles Eshbach. **Executive Vice President/General Manager:** Geoff Iacuessa. **Senior VP:** John Kameisha. **VP, Financial Affairs/Game Operations:** Jim Heffley. **Assistant GM, Media Relations:** Chris Cameron. **Assistant GM, Marketing/Promotions:** Liz Riley. **Executive Director, Ticket Sales:** Dennis Meehan. **Ticket Office Manager:** Dennis Carter. **Account Executive, Corporate Sales:** Ashley Montgomery. **Account Executive, Ticket Sales:** Courtney Rague, Justin Phillips. **Account Executive, Season Tickets/Merchandise Manager:** Lindsay Oliver. **Director, Broadcasting:** Mike Antonellis. **Director, Food Services:** Mike Scorza. **Assistant Director, Food Services:** Greg Moyes. **Office Manager:** Lyndsey Berry. **Clubhouse Managers:** Craig Candage Sr., Nick Fox. **Head Groundskeeper:** Rick Anderson.

FIELD STAFF

Manager: Billy McMillon. **Coach:** Rich Gedman. **Pitching Coach:** Bob Kipper. **Trainer:** Brandon Henry.

GAME INFORMATION

Radio Announcer: Mike Antonellis. **No. of Games Broadcast:** 142. **Flagship Station:** WPEI 95.9 FM.

PA Announcer: Paul Coughlin. **Official Scorer:** Thom Hinton.

Stadium Name: Hadlock Field. **Location:** From South, I-295 to exit 5, merge onto Congress Street, left at St John Street, merge right onto Park Ave; From North, I-295 to exit 6A, right onto Park Ave. **Ticket Price Range:** $5-10.

Visiting Club Hotel: DoubleTree by Hilton Portland Maine, 363 Maine Mall Rd, South Portland, ME 04106. **Telephone:** (207) 775-6161.

READING FIGHTIN PHILS

Office Address: Route 61 South/1900 Centre Ave., Reading, PA 19605. **Mailing Address:** PO Box 15050, Reading, PA 19612.

Telephone: (610) 370-BALL (2255). **Fax:** (610) 373-5868.

E-Mail Address: info@fightins.com. **Website:** www.fightins.com.

Affiliation (first year): Philadelphia Phillies (1967). **Years in League:** 1933-35, 1952-61, 1963-65, 1967-

OWNERSHIP/MANAGEMENT

Operated By: E&J Baseball Club, Inc.

Principal Owner: Reading Baseball LP. **Managing Partner:** Craig Stein.

General Manager: Scott Hunsicker. **Assistant GM:** Ashley Peterson.

Director, Sales: Joe Bialek. **Controller:** Kristyne Haver. **Head Groundskeeper:** Dan "Dirt" Douglas. **Director, Baseball Operations/Merchandise:** Kevin Sklenarik. **Director, Graphic Arts/Game Entertainment:** Matt Jackson. **Director, Food/Beverage:** Eric Freeman. **Director, Community Relations/Internship Coordinator:** Mike Robinson. **Video Director:** Andy Kauffman. **Office Manager:** Deneen Giesen. **Assistant Director, Sales:** Anthony Pignetti. **Director, Group Sales:** Jon Muldowney. **Director, Ticket Operations:** Tim McGee. **Director, Business Development:** Tonya Petrunak. **Director, Educational Programs/Game Presentation:** Todd Hunsicker. **Director, PR/Media Relations:** Eric Scarcella. **Manager, Fundraising:** Andrew Nelson. **Manager, Group Sales:** Jon Nally. **Manager, Concessions:** Travis Hart. **Manager, Group Operations:** Zach Haas. **Manager, Operations:** Brian Hoeper.

FIELD STAFF

Manager: Dusty Wathan. **Coach:** Rob Ducey. **Pitching Coach:** Dave Lundquist.

GAME INFORMATION

Radio Announcer: Mike Ventola. **No. of Games Broadcast:** 142. **Flagship Station:** WRAW 1340-AM.
PA Announcer: Justin Choate. **Official Scorers:** Paul Jones, Brian Kopetsky, Josh Leiboff, Dick Shute.
Stadium Name: FirstEnergy Stadium. **Location:** From east, take Pennsylvania Turnpike West to Morgantown exit, to 176 North, to 422 West, to Route 12 East, to Route 61 South exit; From west, take 422 East to Route 12 East, to Route 61 South exit; From north, take 222 South to Route 12 exit, to Route 61 South exit; From south, take 222 North to 422 West, to Route 12 East exit at Route 61 South. **Standard Game Times:** 7:05 pm, 6:35 (April-May), Sun 1:05. **Ticket Price Range:** $6-11.
Visiting Club Hotel: Crowne Plaza Reading Hotel, 1741 Papermill Road, Wyomissing, PA 19610. **Telephone:** (610) 376-3811.

RICHMOND FLYING SQUIRRELS

Office Address: 3001 N Blvd., Richmond, VA 23230.
Telephone: (804) 359-3866. **Fax:** (804) 359-1373.
E-Mail Address: info@squirrelsbaseball.com. **Website:** www.squirrelsbaseball.com.
Affiliation: San Francisco Giants (2009). **Years in League:** 2009-

OWNERSHIP/MANAGEMENT

Operated By: Navigators Baseball LP.
President/Managing Partner: Lou DiBella. **CEM:** Chuck Domino. **Vice President/COO:** Todd "Parney" Parnell. **General Manager:** Bill Papierniak. **Controller:** Faith Casey. **Assistant Controller:** Jessica Miller. **Director, Corporate Sales:** Ben Terry. **Corporate Sales Executives:** Mike Murphy, Jerrine Lee. **Director, Tickets:** Brendon Porter. **Box Office Manager:** Patrick Flower. **Director, Broadcasting:** Jon Laaser. **Manager, Media Relations:** Jay Burnham. **Creative Services Manager:** Jason Grohoske. **Director, Promotions/In-Game Entertainment:** Kellye Semonich. **Community Relations Manager:** Stefanie Sacks. **Director, Group Sales:** Brandon Greene. **Group Sales Executives:** Megan Angstadt, Camp Peery, Chris Walker, Garrett Erwin. **Suites/Group Sales Executive:** Elyse Holben.
Executive Director, Food/Beverage/Merchandise: Ben Rothrock. **Assistant Directors, Food/Beverage:** Mike Caddell, Tyler Callahan. **Chef/Catering/Banquet Services:** Gavin Edmunds. **Director, Field Operations:** Steve Ruckman. **Assistant Director, Field Operations:** Cody Harvey. **Director, Stadium Operations:** Steve Pump.

FIELD STAFF

Manager: Russ Morman. **Coach:** Ken Joyce. **Pitching Coach:** Ross Grimsley. **Athletic Trainer:** David Getsoff. **Strength/Conditioning Coach:** Adam Vish.

GAME INFORMATION

Radio Announcers: Jon Laaser, Jay Burnham. **No. of Games Broadcast:** 142. **Flagship Station:** Sports Radio 910 WRNL-AM.
PA Announcer: Jimmy Barrett. **Official Scorer:** Scott Day.
Stadium Name: The Diamond. **Capacity:** 9,560. **Location:** Right off I-64 at the Boulevard exit. **Standard Game Times:** 7:05 pm, Sat 6:35, Sun 5:05. **Ticket Price Range:** $7-11.
Visiting Club Hotel: Comfort Suites at Virginia Center Commons, 10601 Telegraph Road, Glen Allen, VA. **Telephone:** (804) 262-2000.

TRENTON THUNDER

Office Address: One Thunder Road, Trenton, NJ 08611.
Telephone: (609) 394-3300. **Fax:** (609) 394-9666.
E-Mail address: fun@trentonthunder.com. **Website:** www.trentonthunder.com.
Affiliation (first year): New York Yankees (2003). **Years in League:** 1994-

OWNERSHIP/MANAGEMENT

Operated By: Garden State Baseball LLP.

General Manager/COO: Will Smith. **Senior VP, Corporate Sales/Partnerships:** Eric Lipsman. **VP, Stadium Operations:** Ryan Crammer. **Director, Public Relations:** Bill Cook. **Director, Merchandising:** Joe Pappalardo. **Director, Finance/Baseball Operations:** Jeff Hurley. **Director, Ticket Operations:** Matt Pentima. **Director, Creative/Audiovisual Services:** Greg Lavin. **Director, Ticket Sales/Corporate Partnerships:** Patrick McMaster. **Director, Community Relations/Database Management:** TJ Jahn. **Director, Broadcasting:** Josh Maurer. **Director, Food/Beverage:** Chris Champion. **Director, Group Sales:** Nate Schneider.

Manager, Stadium Operations: Steve Brokowsky. **Office Manager:** Susanna Hall. **Production Manager:** Chris Foster. **Manager, Corporate Sales/Partnerships:** Seth Cantor. **Group Sales Account Executive:** Lindsey Ravior. Tom Henninger. **Ticket Sales Account Executives:** Janelle Alfano, John Belfiore, Michael Heberlein. **Business Development Executive:** Brad McNamara, Katie Esselman. **Group Sales Account Representative:** Matt Mango, Logan Miller, Andy Marshall. **Group Sales Coordinator:** Lisa Szymendera. **Assistant, Broadcast/Media Relations:** Adam Giardino. **Assistant. Tickets:** Matt Heineman. **Assistant, Stadium Operations:** Nick Beers. **Head Groundskeeper:** Unavailable. **Building Superintendent:** Scott Ribsam.

FIELD STAFF

Manager: Tony Franklin. **Hitting Coach:** Marcus Thames. **Pitching Coach:** Tommy Phelps. **Coach:** Orlando Mercado. **Trainer:** Lee Meyer. **Strength/Conditioning Coach:** Orlando Crance.

GAME INFORMATION

Radio Announcers: Josh Maurer, Adam Giardino. **No. of Games Broadcast:** 142. **Flagship Station:** WTSR 91.3 FM. **PA Announcer:** Unavailable. **Official Scorers:** Jay Dunn, Greg Zak.

Stadium Name: Arm & Hammer Park. **Location:** From I-95, take Route 1 North to Route 29 South, stadium entrance just before tunnel; From NJ Turnpike, take Exit 7A and follow I-195 West, Road will become Rte 29, Follow through tunnel and ballpark is on left. **Standard Game Times:** 7:05 pm, Sun 1:05pm. **Ticket Price Range:** $10-13.

Visiting Club Hotel: Unavailable.

SOUTHERN LEAGUE

Mailing Address: 2551 Roswell Rd., Suite 330, Marietta, GA 30062.
Telephone: (770) 321-0400. **Fax:** (770) 321-0037.
E-Mail Address: loriwebb@southernleague.com. **Website:** www.southernleague.com.
Years League Active: 1964-
Mailing Address: 2551 Roswell Rd, Suite 330, Marietta, GA 30062.
Telephone: (770) 321-0400. **Fax:** (770) 321-0037.
E-Mail Address: loriwebb@southernleague.com. **Website:** www.southernleague.com.
Years League Active: 1964-
President: Lori Webb.
Vice President: Steve DeSalvo. **Directors:** Jonathan Nelson (Birmingham), Rich Mozingo (Chattanooga), Miles Prentice (Huntsville), Reese Smith (Jackson), Peter Bragan, Jr. (Jacksonville), Steve DeSalvo (Mississippi), Mike Savit (Mobile), Tom Dickson (Montgomery), Quinton Studer (Pensacola), Doug Kirchhofer (Tennessee). **Operations Director:** Peter Webb.
Division Structure: North: Birmingham, Chattanooga, Huntsville, Jackson, Tennessee. **South:** Jacksonville, Mississippi, Mobile, Montgomery, Pensacola.
Regular Season: 140 games (split schedule). **2014 Opening Date:** April 3. **Closing Date:** Sept 1. **All-Star Game:** June 17, at Chattanooga Lookouts.

Lori Webb

Playoff Format: First-half division winners meet second-half division winners in best-of-five series for league championship. **Roster Limit:** 25. **Player Eligibility Rule:** No restrictions. **Brand of Baseball:** Rawlings. **Umpires:** Jonathan Bailey, John Bostwick, Jose Esteras, Blake Felter, Ryan Goodman, Brandon Henson, Javerro January, Benjamin Leake, Shane Livensparger, Matthew McCoy, Derek Mollica, Thomas Newsom III, Garrett Patterson, Alex Ransom, Jeremy Riggs.

STADIUM INFORMATION

Club	Stadium	Opened	Dimensions LF	CF	RF	Capacity	2013 Att.
Birmingham	Regions Field	2013	320	400	325	8,500	396,820
Chattanooga	AT&T Field	2000	325	400	330	6,362	220,854
Huntsville	Joe W. Davis Municipal Stadium	1985	345	405	330	10,488	123,904
Jackson	Ballpark at Jackson	1998	310	395	320	6,000	119,202
Jacksonville	Baseball Grounds of Jacksonville	2003	321	420	317	11,000	295,258
Mississippi	Trustmark Park	2005	335	402	332	7,416	200,268
Mobile	Hank Aaron Stadium	1997	325	400	310	6,000	149,675
Montgomery	Riverwalk Stadium	2004	314	380	332	7,000	258,532
Pensacola	Bayfront Stadium	2012	325	400	335	6,000	307,094
Tennessee	Smokies Park	2000	330	400	330	6,000	244,984

BIRMINGHAM BARONS

Office Address: 1401 1st Ave. South, Birmingham, AL, 35233. **Mailing Address:** PO Box 877, Birmingham, AL, 35201.
Telephone: (205) 988-3200. **Fax:** (205) 988-9698.
E-Mail Address: barons@barons.com. **Website:** www.barons.com.
Affiliation (first year): Chicago White Sox (1986). **Years in League:** 1964-65, 1967-75, 1981-

OWNERSHIP/MANAGEMENT
Principal Owners: Don Logan, Jeff Logan, Stan Logan.
General Manager: Jonathan Nelson.
Director, Broadcasting: Curt Bloom. **Director, Media Relations:** Nick Dobreff. **Director, Sales:** John Cook. **Director, Tickets:** David Madison. **Director, Production:** Mike Ferko. **Director, Stadium Operations:** Nick Lampasona. **Director, Customer Service:** George Chavous. **Corporate Sales Manager:** Don Leo. **Director, Group Sales:** Charlie Santiago.
Group Sales Managers: Steve Bayko, Brett Oates. **Assistant Director, Ticket Operations:** Jarrod Johnson Director, Retail Sales: Joseph Cooper. **General Manager, Parkview Catering:** Eric Crook.Concessions Manager: Brian DiciaccioCorporate Event Planner: Sydney WilbanksCorporate Event Planner: Emily Stuenkel Office Manager: Shaunte Bailey. **Accountant:** Jo Ann Bragan. **Chief Financial Officer:** Randy Prince. **Head Groundskeeper:** Daniel Ruggiero. **Assistant Groundskeeper:** Andrew Batts.

FIELD STAFF
Manager: Julio Vinas. **Hitting Coach:** Brandon Moore. **Pitching Coach:** Britt Burns. **Trainer:** Scott Johnson. **Strength/ Conditioning:** Shawn Powell.

GAME INFORMATION
Radio Announcer: Curt Bloom. **No. of Games Broadcast:** 140. **Flagship Station:** News Radio 105.5 WERC-FM.
PA Announcer: Derek Scudder. **Official Scorers:** AA Moore, Grant Martin.

Stadium Name: Regions Field. **Location:** I-65 (exit 259B) in downtown Birmingham. **Standard Game Times:** 7:05 pm, Sat 6:30, Sun 2:05. **Ticket Price Range:** $7-14.

Visiting Club Hotel: Sheraton Birmingham Hotel, 2101 Richard Arrington Junior Boulevard North, Birmingham, AL 35203. **Telephone:** (205) 324-5000.

CHATTANOOGA LOOKOUTS

Office Address: 201 Power Alley, Chattanooga, TN 37402. **Mailing Address:** PO Box 11002, Chattanooga, TN 37401.

Telephone: (423) 267-2208. **Fax:** (423) 267-4258.

E-Mail Address: lookouts@lookouts.com. **Website:** www.lookouts.com.

Affiliation (first year): Los Angeles Dodgers (2009). **Years in League:** 1964-65, 1976-

OWNERSHIP/MANAGEMENT

Operated By: Scenic City Baseball LLC.

Principal Owner: Frank Burke.

President/General Manager: Rich Mozingo. **Director, Group Sales:** Morgan Billups, Andrew Zito, Jennifer Crum. **Director, Merchandising/Ticketing:** Chrysta Jorgensen. **Manager, Media Relations:** Dan Kopf. **Director, Concessions:** Steve Sullivan. **Director, Broadcasting:** Larry Ward. **Director, Corporate Sales:** Harold Craw. **Business Administration/Accounting:** Anastacia McCowan. **Head Groundskeeper:** Brandon Moore. **Corporate Sales Manager:** Alex Tanish.

FIELD STAFF

Manager: Razor Shines. **Hitting Coach:** Shawn Wooten. **Pitching Coach:** Scott Radinsky.

GAME INFORMATION

Radio Announcers: Larry Ward, Jim Reynolds. **No. of Games Broadcast:** 140. **Flagship Station:** 105.1 FM ESPN Chattanooga (WALV-FM).

PA Announcer: Unavailable. **Official Scorers:** Wirt Gammon, Andy Paul.

Stadium Name: AT&T Field. **Location:** From I-24, take US 27 North to exit 1C (4th Street), first left onto Chestnut Street, left onto Third Street. **Ticket Price Range:** $5-9.

Visiting Club Hotel: Holiday Inn, 2232 Center Street, Chattanooga, TN 37421. **Telephone:** (423) 485-1185.

HUNTSVILLE STARS

Office Address: 3125 Leeman Ferry Rd., Huntsville, AL 35801.

Telephone: (256) 882-2562. **Fax:** (256) 880-0801.

E-Mail Address: starsinfo@huntsvillestars.com. **Website:** www.huntsvillestars.com.

Affiliation (first year): Milwaukee Brewers (1999). **Years in League:** 1985-

OWNERSHIP/MANAGEMENT

Operated By: Huntsville Stars LLC.

President: Miles Prentice. **General Manager:** Buck Rogers. **Assistant GM:** Babs Rogers. **Manager, Media:** Nicole Collins. **Broadcaster:** Steve Jarnicke. **Corporate Sales Manager:** Renee Ducote. **Director, Merchandising/Sales:** Jessica McQueen. **Director, StadiumOperations/Head Groundkeeper:** Mike Stowe. **Office Manager:** Earl Grilliot.

FIELD STAFF

Manager: Carlos Subero. **Coach:** Sandy Guerrero. **Pitching Coach:** Chris Hook. **Athletic Trainer:** Steve Patera. **Strength/Conditioning Coach:** Nate Dine.

GAME INFORMATION

PA Announcer: Matt Mitchell. **Official Scorer:** Don Rizzardi.

Stadium Name: Joe Davis Municipal Stadium. **Location:** I-65 to I-565 East,south on Memorial Parkway to Drake Avenue exit, right on Don Mincher Drive. **Ticket Price Range:** $5-$20.

Visiting Club Hotel: Unavailable.

JACKSON GENERALS

Office Address: 4 Fun Place, Jackson, TN 38305.

Telephone: (731) 988-5299. **Fax:** (731) 988-5246.

E-Mail Address: sarge@jacksongeneralsbaseball.com. **Website:** www.jacksongeneralsbaseball.com.

Affiliation (first year): Seattle Mariners (2007). **Years in League:** 1998-

OWNERSHIP/MANAGEMENT

Operated by: Jackson Baseball Club LP.

Chairman: David Freeman. **President:** Reese Smith.

General Manager: Jason Compton. **Vice President, Sales/Marketing:** Mike Peasley.

Accounting Manager: Charles Ferrell. **Turf Manager:** Marty Wallace. **Manager, Media Relations/Broadcasting:** Chris Harris. **Manager, Ticket Operations:** Clay Fowler. **Manager, Stadium Operations:** Chris Turpin. **Manager, Catering/Concessions:** Eric Kormanik. **Manager, Promotions/Merchandise:** Nick Hall. **Manager, Corporate Sales:** Mark Kaufman. **Manager, Group Ticket Sales:** Chris Freeman. **Manager, Publications/Design:** Patrick Wallace. **Manager, Stadium Security:** Robert Jones. **Manager, Home Clubhouse Operations:** CJ Fedewa.

FIELD STAFF
Manager: Jim Horner. **Coach:** Roy Howell. **Pitching Coach:** Lance Painter. **Trainer:** Eddie Tamez.

GAME INFORMATION
Radio Announcer: Chris Harris. **No. of Games Broadcast:** 140. **Flagship Station:** WBFG 96.5-FM. **PA Announcer:** Dan Reeves. **Official Scorer:** Mike Henson.
Stadium Name: The Ballpark in Jackson. **Location:** From I-40, take exit 85 South on FE Wright Drive, left onto Ridgecrest Road. **Standard Game Times:** 7:05 pm, Sat 6:05, Sun 2:05 or 6:05. **Ticket Price Range:** $6-10.
Visiting Club Hotel: Doubletree Hotel, 1770 Hwy 45 Bypass, Jackson, TN 38305. **Telephone:** (731) 664-6900.

JACKSONVILLE SUNS

Office Address: 301 A Philip Randolph Blvd., Jacksonville, FL 32202. **Mailing Address:** PO Box 4756, Jacksonville, FL 32201.
Telephone: (904) 358-2846. **Fax:** (904) 358-2845.
E-Mail Address: info@jaxsuns.com. **Website:** www.jaxsuns.com.
Affiliation (first year): Miami Marlins (2009). **Years In League:** 1970-

OWNERSHIP/MANAGEMENT
Operated by: Baseball Jax Inc.
Senior Madame Chairman: Mary Frances Bragan.
President: Peter Bragan Jr. **General Manager:** Chris Peters. **Director, Field Operations:** Christian Galen. **Director, Merchandise:** Brett Andrews. **Assistant GM:** Casey Nichols. **Senior Director, Business Administration:** Barbara O'Berry. **Director, Video Services:** Brian Delettre. **Director, Group Sales:** January Putt. **Manager, Group Sales:** Trevor Johnson. **Director, Ticket Operations:** Amy Delettre. **Director, Stadium Operations:** JD Metrie. **Director, Community Relations:** Jarrod Simmons. **Director, Broadcasting:** Roger Hoover. **Manager, Box Office:** Theresa Viets. **General Manager, Ballpark Foods:** Jamie Davis. **Assistant GM, Ballpark Foods/Finance:** Mitch Buska. **Manager Account Executives:** Amy Arnette, Corey Kernan, Stephen Unser, Tyler Souza.

FIELD STAFF
Manager: Andy Barkett. **Hitting Coach:** Kevin Randel. **Pitching Coach:** John Duffy. **Coach:** Rich Arena.

GAME INFORMATION
Radio Announcer: Roger Hoover. **No. of Games Broadcast:** 140. **Flagship Station:** 94.1 FM-WSOS. **Official Scorer:** Jason Eliopulos.
Stadium Name: Bragan Field at The Baseball Grounds of Jacksonville. **Location:** I-95 South to Martin Luther King Parkway exit, follow Gator Bowl Blvd around Everbank Field; I-95 North to Exit 347 (Emerson Street), go right to Hart Bridge Expressway, take Sports Complex exit, left at light to stop sign, take left and follow around Everbank Field; From Mathews Bridge, take A Philip Randolph exit, right on A Philip Randolph, straight to stadium. **Standard Game Times:** 7:05 pm, Sun 3:05/6:05. **Ticket Price Range:** $7.50-$22.50.
Visiting Club Hotel: Hyatt Regency Jacksonville Riverfront, 225 Coastline Dr, Jacksonville, FL 32202. **Telephone:** (904) 633-9095.

MISSISSIPPI BRAVES

Office Address: Trustmark Park, 1 Braves Way, Pearl, MS 39208. **Mailing Address:** PO Box 97389, Pearl, MS 39288.
Telephone: (601) 932-8788. **Fax:** (601) 936-3567.
E-Mail Address: mississippibraves@braves.com. **Website:** www.mississippibraves.com.
Affiliation (first year): Atlanta Braves (2005). **Years in League:** 2005-

OWNERSHIP/MANAGEMENT
Operated By: Atlanta National League Baseball Club Inc.
General Manager: Steve DeSalvo. **Assistant GM:** Jim Bishop. **Ticket Manager:** Nick Anderson. **Merchandise Manager:** Sarah Banta. **Media Relations Manager:** Miranda Black. **Director, Sales:** Dave Burke. **Sales Associates:** Joe Crocker, Sean Guillotte, Destin Smith, Gerrod Speer, Marrieo Stovall. **Head Chef:** Tina Funches.
Suites/Catering Manager: Debbie Herrington. **Stadium Operations Manager:** Matt McCoy. **Promotions/Entertainment Manager:** Brian Prochilo. **Concessions Manager:** Felicia Thompson. **Office Manager:** Christy Shaw. **Restaurant Manager:** Gene Slaughter. **Director, Field/Facility Operations:** Matt Taylor. **Receptionist:** Katie Patterson.

FIELD STAFF
Manager: Aaron Holbert. **Coach:** Jamie Dismuke. **Pitching Coach:** Dennis Lewallyn. **Trainer:** Ricky Alcantara.

GAME INFORMATION
Radio Announcer: Kyle Tate. **No. of Games Broadcast:** 140. **Flagship Station:** WYAB 103.9 FM.
PA Announcer: Derrel Palmer. **Official Scorer:** Mark Beason. **Stadium Name:** Trustmark Park. **Location:** I-20 to exit 48/Pearl (Pearson Road). **Ticket Price Range:** $6-$20.
Visiting Club Hotel: Holiday Inn Trustmark Park, 110 Bass Pro Drive, Pearl, MS 39208. **Telephone:** (601) 939-5238.

MOBILE BAYBEARS

Office Address: Hank Aaron Stadium, 755 Bolling Bros Blvd., Mobile, AL 36606.
Telephone: (251) 479-2327. **Fax:** (251) 476-1147.
E-Mail Address: info@mobilebaybears.com. **Website:** www.mobilebaybears.com.
Affiliation (first year): Arizona Diamondbacks (2007). **Years in League:** 1966, 1970, 1997-

OWNERSHIP/MANAGEMENT
Operated by: HWS Baseball Group.
Principal Owner: Mike Savit.
President/COO: Bill Shanahan. **Vice President:** Mike Gorrasi. **Assistant GM, Finance:** Betty Adams. **Assistant GM, Corporate Sales:** Mike Callahan. **Director, Communications:** Ari Rosenbaum. **Director, Sales:** Bradley Reynolds. **Director, Business Development:** Kyne Sheehy. **Concessions Manager:** Tara Crawford. **Coordinator, Stadium Operations:** Nathan Breiner. **Director, Broadcasting:** Justin Baker. **Account Executives:** Eric Yager, Kevin Knott. **Team Chaplain:** Lorin Barr.

FIELD STAFF
Manager: Andy Green. **Hitting Coach:** Jacob Cruz. **Pitching Coach:** Wellington Cepeda.

GAME INFORMATION
Radio Announcer: Justin Baker. **No. of Games Broadcast:** 140. **Website Broadcast:** www.baybearsradio.com.
PA Announcer: Unavailable. **Official Scorers:** Unavailable.
Stadium Name: Hank Aaron Stadium. **Location:** I-65 to exit 1 (Government Blvd East), right at Satchel Paige Drive, right at Bolling Bros Blvd. **Standard Game Times:** 7:05 pm, Sat 6:05 Sun 2:05. **Ticket Price Range:** $6-16.
Visiting Club Hotel: Riverview Plaza, 64 S Water St, Mobile, AL 36602. **Telephone:** (251) 438-4000.

MONTGOMERY BISCUITS

Office Address: 200 Coosa St., Montgomery, AL 36104.
Telephone: (334) 323-2255. **Fax:** (334) 323-2225.
E-Mail address: info@biscuitsbaseball.com. **Website:** www.biscuitsbaseball.com.
Affiliation (first year): Tampa Bay Rays (2004). **Years in League:** 1965-1980, 2004-

OWNERSHIP/MANAGEMENT
Operated By: Montgomery Professional Baseball LLC.
Principal Owners: Tom Dickson, Sherrie Myers.
President/General Manager: Greg Rauch. **Assistant General Manager:** Scott Trible. **Director, Marketing:** Staci Wilkenson. **Director, Client Services/Media Partnerships:** Jonathan Vega.
Corporate Account Executives: Ross Winkler, Bill Bixon. **Group Sales Representatives:** Greg Liebbe, Sean Porter. **Events Coordinator:** Jordan Thomas. **Manager, Special Events:** Molly Johnson. **Sales/Marketing Assistant:** Sarah Stephan. **Fan Engagement Coordinator:** Kailey Mizelle. **Production Assistant:** Branden Roth. **Broadcaster, Media Relations:** Aaron Vargas. **Director, Retail Operations:** Steve Keller. **Director, Stadium Operations:** Steve Blackwell. **Box Office Manager:** Kyle Kreutzer. **Head Groundskeeper:** Alex English. **Catering Managers:** Marissa Gordon. **Director, Food/Beverage:** Dave Parker. **Executive Chef:** Chris Micci. **Concessions Manager:** Beau Combs. **Executive Director, Business Operations:** Linda Fast. **Business Manager:** Tracy Mims. **Administrative Assistant:** Bill Sisk. **Season Ticket Concierge:** Bob Rabon.

FIELD STAFF
Manager: Brady Williams. **Hitting Coach:** Ozzie Timmons. **Pitching Coach:** RC Lichtenstein.

GAME INFORMATION
Radio Announcer: Aaron Vargas. **No of Games Broadcast:** 140. **Flagship Station:** WLWI 1440-AM.
PA Announcer: Rick Hendrick. **Official Scorer:** DJ Watkins.
Stadium Name: Montgomery Riverwalk Stadium. **Location:** I-65 to exit 172, east on Herron Street, left on Coosa Street. **Ticket Price Range:** $8-12.
Visiting Club Hotel: Candlewood Suites, 9151 Boyd-Cooper Pkwy, Montgomery, AL 36117. **Telephone:** (334) 277-0677.

PENSACOLA BLUE WAHOOS

Office Address: 351 West Cedar St., Pensacola, FL 32502. **Mailing Address:** 351 West Cedar St., Pensacola, FL 32502.
Telephone: (850) 934-8444. **Fax:** (850) 791-6256.
E-Mail Address: info@bluewahoos.com. **Website:** www.bluewahoos.com.
Affiliation (third year): Cincinnati Reds (2012). **Years in League:** 2012-

OWNERSHIP/MANAGEMENT

Operated by: Northwest Florida Professional Baseball LLC. **Principal Owners:** Quint Studer, Rishy Studer.
President: Bruce Baldwin. **Executive Vice President:** Jonathan Griffith. **Receptionist:** Linda Aguado. **Stadium Operations Manager:** Ryan Long. **Creative Services Manager:** Adam Waldron. **Director, Sports Turf Management:** Ray Sayre. **Sales Manager:** Chuck Arnold. **Director, Human Relations:** Dick Baker. **Media Relations Coordinator/Broadcaster:** Tommy Thrall. **Director, Promotions/Community Relations:** Donna Kirby. **Director, Merchandise:** Denise Richardson. **Box Office Manager:** Eric Kroll. **Director, Food/Beverage:** Mark Micallef. **Finance Director:** Amber McClure. **Groups Sales Executives:** Leroy Williams, Michael Taylor.

FIELD STAFF

Manager: Delino DeShields. **Hitting Coach:** Alex Pelaez. **Pitching Coach:** Jeff Fassero. **Trainer:** Charles Leddon.

GAME INFORMATION

Radio Announcers: Tommy Thrall. **No. of Games Broadcast:** 140. **Flagship Stations:** WBSR Pensacola 1450 AM/101.1 FM.
PA Announcer: Josh Gay. **Official Scorer:** Brenton Goebel.
Stadium Name: Pensacola Bayfront Stadium. **Standard Game Times:** 6:30 pm, Sat 6:30, Sun 4 pm. **Ticket Price Range:** $9-$18.
Visiting Club Hotels: Hilton Garden Inn, Hampton Inn, Homewood Suites.

TENNESSEE SMOKIES

Office Address: 3540 Line Drive, Kodak, TN 37764.
Telephone: (865) 286-2300. **Fax:** (865) 523-9913.
E-Mail Address: info@smokiesbaseball.com. **Website:** www.smokiesbaseball.com.
Affiliation (first year): Chicago Cubs (2007). **Years in League:** 1964-67, 1972-

OWNERSHIP/MANAGEMENT

Owner: Randy Boyd.
President: Doug Kirchhofer. **Vice President:** Chris Allen. **General Manager:** Brian Cox. **Assistant GM:** Jeff Shoaf.
Director, Corporate Sales: Jeremy Boler. **Senior Director, Corporate Marketing:** Craig Jenkins. **Director, Ticket/Group Sales:** Tim Volk. **Director, Community Relations:** Lauren Chesney. **Director, Food/Beverage:** Tony DaSilveira. **Director, Stadium Operations:** Bryan Webster. **Director, Box Office/Retail Operations:** Robby Scheuermann. **Senior Account Executive, Groups:** Jason Moody. **Manager, Marketing Development:** Nathan Horn. **Business Manager:** Suzanne French. **Account Executives:** Tyler Castro, Baylor Love, Michael McMullen, Brad Putch, Matt Strutner. **Receptionist:** Tolena Trout.

FIELD STAFF

Manager: Buddy Bailey. **Hitting Coach:** Desi Wilson. **Pitching Coach:** Storm Davis. **Trainer:** Shane Nelson.

GAME INFORMATION

Radio Announcer: Mick Gillispie. **No. of Games Broadcast:** 140. **Flagship Station:** WNML 99.1-FM/990-AM.
PA Announcer: Unavailable. **Official Scorers:** Jack Tate, Jared Smith, Bernie Reimer.
Stadium Name: Smokies Park. **Location:** I-40 to exit 407, Highway 66 North. **Standard Game Times:** 7:15 pm, Sat 6:15 pm, Sun 2/5. **Ticket Price Range:** $6-11.
Visiting Club Hotel: Hampton Inn & Suites Sevierville, 105 Stadium Drive, Kodak, TN 37764. **Telephone:** (865) 465-0590.

TEXAS LEAGUE

TEXAS LEAGUE OF PROFESSIONAL BASEBALL CLUBS

Mailing Address: 2442 Facet Oak, San Antonio, TX 78232.
Telephone: (210) 545-5297. **Fax:** (210) 545-5298.
E-Mail Address: texasleague@sbcglobal.net. **Website:** www.texas-league.com.

Tom Kayser

Years League Active: 1888-1890, 1892, 1895-1899, 1902-1942, 1946-

President/Treasurer: Tom Kayser. **Vice Presidents:** Burl Yarbrough, Bill Valentine.

Corporate Secretary: Matt Gifford. **Assistant to the President:** John Harris.

Directors: Jon Dandes (Northwest Arkansas), Ken Schrom (Corpus Christi), William DeWitt III (Springfield), Dale Hubbard (Tulsa), Scott Sonju (Frisco), Miles Prentice (Midland), Russ Meeks (Arkansas), Burl Yarbrough (San Antonio).

Division Structure: North—Arkansas, Northwest Arkansas, Springfield, Tulsa. South—Corpus Christi, Frisco, Midland, San Antonio. **Regular Season:** 140 games (split schedule).

2014 Opening Date: April 3. **Closing Date:** Sept 1. **All-Star Game:** June 24 at Arkansas.

Playoff Format: First-half division winners play second-half division winners In best-of-five series. Winners meet in best-of-five series for league championship.

Roster Limit: 25. **Player Eligibility Rule:** No restrictions. **Brand of Baseball:** Rawlings.

Umpires: Mike Cascioppo (Escondido, CA), Matt Czajak (Flower Mound, TX), Derek Eaton (Tracy, CA), Travis Eggert (Gilbert, AZ), Bryan Fields (Lincoln, NE), Ramon Hernandez (Columbia, MD), Lee Meyers (Madera, CA), Clayton Park (Georgetown, TX), Alberto Ruis (San Antonio, TX), Ronnie Teague (Cypress, TX), Brett Terry (Beaverton OR), Nate White (Reno, NV).

STADIUM INFORMATION

				Dimensions			
Club	**Stadium**	**Opened**	**LF**	**CF**	**RF**	**Capacity**	**2013 Att.**
Arkansas	Dickey-Stephens Park	2007	332	413	330	5,842	293,749
Corpus Christi	Whataburger Field	2005	325	400	315	5,362	379,395
Frisco	Dr Pepper Ballpark	2003	335	409	335	10,216	479,873
Midland	Citibank Ballpark	2002	330	410	322	4,669	317,233
NW Arkansas	Arvest Ballpark	2008	325	400	325	6,500	318,592
San Antonio	Nelson Wolff Municipal Stadium	1994	310	402	340	6,200	294,346
Springfield	John Q. Hammons Field	2003	315	400	330	6,750	338,345
Tulsa	ONEOK Field	2010	330	400	307	7,833	393,600

ARKANSAS TRAVELERS

Office Address: Dickey-Stephens Park, 400 West Broadway, North Little Rock, AR 72114.
Mailing Address: PO Box 55066, Little Rock, AR 72215.
Telephone: (501) 664-1555. **Fax:** (501) 664-1834.
E-Mail Address: travs@travs.com. **Website:** www.travs.com.
Affiliation (first year): Los Angeles Angels (2001). **Years in League:** 1966-

OWNERSHIP/MANAGEMENT

Ownership: Arkansas Travelers Baseball Club, Inc.

President: Russ Meeks.

General Manager: Paul Allen.

Director, Broadcasting/Media Relations: Phil Elson. **Director, Finance:** Patti Clark. **Director, In-Game Entertainment:** Tommy Adam. **Director, Merchandise/Licensing/Corporate Sales:** Rusty Meeks. **Park Superintendent:** Greg Johnston. **Assistant Park Superintendent:** Reggie Temple. **Director, Luxury Suites/Account Executive:** Jared Schein. **Director, Tickets/Corporate Sales:** Drew Williams. **Director, Marketing:** Lance Restum. **Director, Stadium Operations/Account Executive:** Jeff Daley. **Corporate Event Planners:** Ben Harrington, Eric Schrader, J Keith.

FIELD STAFF

Manager: Phillip Wellman. **Coach:** Tom Tornincasa. **Pitching Coach:** Pat Rice. **Trainer:** Greg Spence. **Strength/Conditioning Coach:** Joe Griffin.

GAME INFORMATION

Radio Announcers: Phil Elson. **No. of Games Broadcast:** 140. **Flagship Station:** KARN 920 AM.

PA Announcer: Russ McKinney. **Official Scorers:** Tim Cooper, Todd Traub.

Stadium Name: Dickey-Stephens Park. **Location:** I-30 to Broadway exit, proceed west to ballpark, located at Broadway Avenue and the Broadway Bridge. **Standard Game Time:** 7:10 pm. **Ticket Price Range:** $3-12.

Visiting Club Hotel: Clarion Little Rock, 925 S University Avenue, Little Rock, AR 72204. **Telephone:** (501) 664-5020.

CORPUS CHRISTI HOOKS

Office Address: 734 East Port Ave., Corpus Christi, TX 78401.
Telephone: (361) 561-4665. **Fax:** (361) 561-4666.
E-Mail Address: info@cchooks.com. **Website:** www.cchooks.com.
Affiliation (first year): Houston Astros (2005). **Years in League:** 1958-59, 2005-

OWNERSHIP/MANAGEMENT

Owned/Operated By: Houston Astros.
President: Ken Schrom. **Vice President/General Manager:** Michael Wood.
Director, Sponsor Services: Elisa Macias. **Controller:** Christy Lockard. **Director, Communications:** Matt Rogers.
Director, Stadium Operations: Jeremy Sturgeon. **Director, Sales/Marketing:** Andy Steavens. **Director, Ballpark Entertainment:** JD Davis. **Director, Season Ticket Services:** Bryan Mayhood. **Director, Group Sales:** Amanda Pruett. **Media Relations Coordinator:** Chris Blake. **Media Relations Manager:** Michael Coffin. **Community Outreach Coordinator:** Courtney Merritt. **Ticket Operations Coordinator:** Danielle Norris. **Social Media Coordinator:** Gil Perez. **Retail Manager:** Daniel Sanchez. **Maintenance Manager:** Daniel Castillo. **Stadium Operations:** Mike Shedd. **Clubhouse Manager:** Brad Starr. **Game Day Staff Coordinator:** Brad Crabtree. **Field Superintendent:** Josh Brewer.

FIELD STAFF

Manager: Keith Bodie. **Hitting Coach:** Tim Garland. **Pitching Coach:** Gary Ruby. **Development Specialist:** Tom Lawless. **Athletic Trainer:** Bryan Baca. **Strength Coach:** Trey Wiedman.

GAME INFORMATION

Radio Announcers: Michael Coffin, Chris Blake, Gene Kasprzyk. **No. of Games Broadcast:** 140. **Flagship Station:** KKTX-AM 1360.
PA Announcer: Lon Gonzalez.
Stadium Name: Whataburger Field. **Location:** I-37 to end of interstate, left at Chaparral, left at Hirsh Ave. **Ticket Price Range:** $5-14.
Visiting Club Hotel: Holiday Inn Corpus Christi Downtown Marina, 707 North Shoreline Blvd., Corpus Christi, Texas, 78401. **Telephone:** (361) 882-1700.

FRISCO ROUGHRIDERS

Office Address: 7300 RoughRiders Trail, Frisco, TX 75034.
Telephone: (972) 731-9200. **Fax:** (972) 731-5355.
E-Mail Address: info@ridersbaseball.com. **Website:** www.ridersbaseball.com.
Affiliation (first year): Texas Rangers (2003). **Years in League:** 2003-

OWNERSHIP/MANAGEMENT

Operated by: Mandalay Baseball Properties.
President: Scott Sonju.
Vice President, Partnerships/Communications: Scott Burchett. **VP, Operations:** Mike Poole. **VP, Accounting/Finance:** Dustin Alban. **Senior Director, Corporate Partnerships:** Steven Nelson. **Director, Operations:** Scott Arnold. **Director, Partner Services:** Matt Ratliff. **Director, Partner/Event Services:** Kristin Russell. **Director, Group Sales:** Andy Benedict. **Director, Outside Sales:** Andrew Sidney. **Director, Ticket Operations:** Jason Brayman. **Director, Game Entertainment:** Gina Pierce. **Director, Community Development:** LaShawn Moore. **Head Groundskeeper:** David Bicknell. **Director, Maintenance:** Alfonso Bailon. **Assistant Director, Maintenance:** Gustavo Bailon. **Manager, Broadcasting/Media:** Alex Vispoli. **Ticket Operations Manager:** Rob Miles. **Partner Services Manager:** David Kosydar.

FIELD STAFF

Manager: Jason Wood. **Coach:** Jason Hart. **Pitching Coach:** Jeff Andrews. **Trainer:** Carlos Olivas. **Strength/Conditioning:** Eric McMahon.

GAME INFORMATION

Broadcaster: Alex Vispoli. **No. of Games Broadcast:** 140. **Flagship Station:** Unavailable.
PA Announcer: John Clemens. **Official Scorer:** Larry Bump.
Stadium Name: Dr Pepper Ballpark. **Location:** Dallas North Tollway to State Highway 121. **Standard Game Times:** 7 pm, Sun 4 (April-June), 6 (July-Sept).
Visiting Club Hotel: Comfort Suites at Frisco Square, 9700 Dallas Parkway, Frisco, TX 75033. **Phone:** (972) 668-9700. **Fax:** (972) 668-9701.

MIDLAND ROCKHOUNDS

Office Address: Security Bank Ballpark, 5514 Champions Drive, Midland, TX 79706.
Telephone: (432) 520-2255. **Fax:** (432) 520-8326.
Website: www.midlandrockhounds.org.
Affiliation (first year): Oakland Athletics (1999). **Years in League:** 1972-

OWNERSHIP/MANAGEMENT

Operated By: Midland Sports, Inc. **Principal Owners:** Miles Prentice, Bob Richmond.
President: Miles Prentice. **Executive Vice President:** Bob Richmond. **General Manager:** Monty Hoppel.
Assistant GM: Jeff VonHolle. **Assistant GM, Marketing/Tickets:** Jamie Richardson. **Assistant GM, Merchandise/Facilities:** Ray Fieldhouse. **Assistant GM, Media Relations:** Greg Bergman. **Director, Broadcasting/Publications:** Bob Hards. **Director, Business Operations:** Eloisa Galvan. **Head Groundskeeper:** Eric Campbell. **Office Manager:** Frances Warner. **Director, Public Relations:** Brian Smith. **Director, Group Sales:** Morgan Halpert. **Director, Client Services:** Shelley Haenggi. **Director, Ticket Operations:** Andrew Brown. **Sales/Marketing Executive:** John English. **Coordinator, Community Relations:** Courtnie Golden. **Complex Coordinator:** Sarah Jones. **Coordinator, Game Entertainment:** Russ Pinkerton. **Home Clubhouse Manager:** Derek Smith. **Visiting Clubhouse Manager:** TJ Leonard. **Complex Operations Manager:** CJ Bahr. **Assistant Groundskeeper:** Levi Driesen.

FIELD STAFF

Manager: Aaron Nieckula. **Hitting Coach:** Webster Garrison. **Pitching Coach:** Don Schulze. **Trainer:** Justin Whitehouse. **Strength/Conditioning:** Terrence Brannic.

GAME INFORMATION

Radio Announcer: Bob Hards. **No. of Games Broadcast:** 140. **Flagship Station:** KCRS 550 AM.
PA Announcer: Wes Coles. **Official Scorer:** Steve Marcum.
Stadium Name: Security Bank Ballpark. **Location:** From I-20, exit Loop 250 North to Highway 191 intersection. **Standard Game Times:** 7 pm. **Ticket Price Range:** $7-16.
Visiting Club Hotel: Sleep Inn and Suites, 5612 Deauville Blvd, Midland, TX 79706. **Telephone:** (432) 694-4200.

NORTHWEST ARKANSAS
NATURALS

Office Address: 3000 S 56th St., Springdale, AR 72762.
Telephone: (479) 927-4900. **Fax:** (479) 756-8088.
E-Mail Address: tickets@nwanaturals.com. **Website:** www.nwanaturals.com.
Affiliation (first year): Kansas City Royals (2008). **Years in League:** 2008-

OWNERSHIP/MANAGEMENT

Principal Owner: Rich Products Corp.
Chairman: Robert Rich Jr. **President, Rich Entertainment:** Melinda Rich.
President, Rich Baseball. Jon Dandes. **General Manager:** Justin Cole. **Sales Manager:** Mark Zaiger. **Business Manager:** Morgan Helmer. **Marketing/PR Manager:** Dustin Dethlefs. **Stadium Operations Director:** Jeff Windle. **Head Groundskeeper:** Brock White. **Ticket Office Coordinator:** Sam Ahern. **Promotions Coordinator:** Julie Maletto. **Production Coordinator:** Rob Sternberg. **Special Events Coordinator:** Adam Wright. **Operations Coordinator:** Marshall Schellhardt. **Gameday Staff Coordinator:** Rebekah Carpenter. **Merchandise Coordinator:** Shelby Huff. **Equipment Manager:** Danny Helmer.

FIELD STAFF

Manager: Vance Wilson. **Hitting Coach:** Andre David. **Pitching Coach:** Jim Brower. **Trainer:** Masa Koyanagi.

GAME INFORMATION

Radio Announcers: Unavailable. **No. of Games Broadcast:** 140. **Flagship:** KQSM-FM 92.1 The Ticket.
PA Announcer: Bill Rogers. **Official Scorer:** Chris Ledeker.
Stadium Name: Arvest Ballpark. **Location:** I-540 to US 412 West (Sunset Ave); Left on 56th St. **Ticket Price Range:** $7-13. **Standard Game Times:** 7:05 pm, Sun 2:05 pm (April/May), 6:05 pm (June-August).
Visiting Club Hotel: Holiday Inn Springdale, 1500 S 48th St, Springdale, AR 72762. **Telephone:** (479) 751-8300.

SAN ANTONIO MISSIONS

Office/Mailing Address: 5757 Highway 90 West, San Antonio, TX 78227.
Telephone: (210) 675-7275. **Fax:** (210) 670-0001.
E-Mail Address: sainfo@samissions.com. **Website:** www.samissions.com.
Affiliation (first year): San Diego Padres (2007). **Years in League:** 1888, 1892, 1895-99, 1907-42, 1946-64, 1968-

OWNERSHIP/MANAGEMENT

Operated by: Elmore Sports Group. **Principal Owner:** David Elmore.
President: Burl Yarbrough. **General Manager:** Dave Gasaway. **Assistant GMs:** Mickey Holt, Jeff Long, Bill Gerlt. **GM, Diamond Concessions:** Mike Lindal. **Controller:** Ivan Molina. **Director, Broadcasting:** Mike Saeger. **Office Manager:** Delia Rodriguez. **Box Office Manager:** Rob Gusick. **Director, Operations:** John Hernandez. **Director, Group Sales:** George Levandoski. **Director, Public Relations:** Rich Weimert. **Field Superintendent:** Rob Gladwell. **Assistant Field Superintendent:** Kevin Coyne.

FIELD STAFF

Manager: Rich Dauer. **Hitting Coach:** Francisco Morales. **Pitching Coach:** Jimmy Jones. **Trainer:** Daniel Turner.

GAME INFORMATION

Radio Announcer: Mike Saeger. **No. of Games Broadcast:** 140. **Flagship Station:** KKYX 680-AM.
PA Announcer: Roland Ruiz. **Official Scorer:** David Humphrey.
Stadium Name: Nelson Wolff Stadium. **Location:** From I-10, I-35 or I-37, take US Hwy 90 West to Callaghan Road exit.
Standard Game Times: 7:05 pm, Sun 4:05/6:05.
Visiting Club Hotel: Holiday Inn Northwest/Sea World. **Telephone:** (210) 520-2508.

SPRINGFIELD CARDINALS

Office Address: 955 East Trafficway, Springfield, MO 65802.
Telephone: (417) 863-0395. **Fax:** (417) 832-3004.
E-Mail Address: springfield@cardinals.com. **Website:** springfieldcardinals.com.
Affiliation (first year): St. Louis Cardinals (2005). **Years in League:** 2005-

OWNERSHIP/MANAGEMENT

Operated By: St. Louis Cardinals.
Vice President/General Manager: Matt Gifford. **VP, Baseball/Business Operations:** Scott Smulczenski. **VP, Facility Operations:** Bill Fischer. **Director, Ticket Operations:** Angela Deke. **VP, Sales/Marketing:** Dan Reiter. **Manager, Promotions/Productions:** Kent Shelton. **Manager, Market Development:** Scott Bailes. **Manager, Stadium/Game Day Operations:** Aaron Lowrey. **Manager, Public Relations/Broadcaster:** Andrew Buchbinder. **Coordinator, Fan Interaction:** Faith Lorhan. **Box Office Supervisor/Office Assistant:** Ayrica Batson. **Head Groundskeeper:** Brock Phipps. **Assistant Head Groundskeeper:** Derek Edwards.

FIELD STAFF

Manager: Mike Shildt. **Hitting Coach:** Erik Pappas. **Pitching Coach:** Randy Niemann. **Trainer:** Scott Ensell. **Strength Coach:** Josh Cue.

GAME INFORMATION

Radio Announcer: Andrew Buchbinder. **No. of Games Broadcast:** 140. **Flagship Station:** JOCK 98.7 FM.
PA Announcer: Unavailable. **Official Scorers:** Mark Stillwell, Tim Tourville.
Stadium Name: Hammons Field. **Location:** Highway 65 to Chestnut Expressway exit, west to National, south on National, west on Trafficway. **Standard Game Time:** 7:10 pm. **Ticket Price Range:** $6-27.
Visiting Club Hotel: University Plaza Hotel, 333 John Q Hammons Parkway, Springfield, MO 65806. **Telephone:** (417) 864-7333.

TULSA DRILLERS

Office Address: 201 N. Elgin, Tulsa, OK 74120.
Telephone: (918) 744-5998. **Fax:** (918) 747-3267.
E-Mail Address: mail@tulsadrillers.com. **Website:** www.tulsadrillers.
com.
Affiliation (first year): Colorado Rockies (2003). **Years in League:** 1933-42, 1946-65, 1977-

OWNERSHIP/MANAGEMENT

Operated By: Tulsa Baseball Inc.
Co-Chairmen: Dale Hubbard, Jeff Hubbard.
General Manager: Mike Melega. **Assistant GM:** Jason George. **Bookkeeper:** Cheryll Couey. **Executive Assistant:** Kara Biden. **Director, Stadium Operations:** Mark Hilliard. **Director, Media/Public Relations:** Brian Carroll. **Director, Marketing/Business Development:** Rob Gardenhire. **Director, Merchandise:** Tom Jones. **Director, Group Ticket Sales:** Geoff Beaty. **Manager, Promotions/Game Entertainment:** Justin Gorski. **Head Groundskeeper:** Gary Shepherd.
Manager, Group Sales: Matt Larson. **Manager, Business Development:** Kevin Butcher. **Assistant Bookkeeper:** Jenna Savill. **Account Executive:** Joanna Hubbard. **Mascot Coordinator:** Vincent Pace. **Marketing Assistant:** Jordan Suskind. **Ticket Office Assistant:** Ethan Hooker. **Group Sales Assistant:** Spencer Hurst. **Stadium Operations Assistant:** Beau Chisholm. **Merchandise Assistant:** TK Worley. **Media Assistant:** Chris Fisher. **Director, Food Services:** Carter Witt. **Director, Concessions:** Wayne Campbell. **Clubhouse Manager:** Sam Salabura.

FIELD STAFF

Manager: Kevin Riggs. **Hitting Coach:** Darin Everson. **Pitching Coach:** Darryl Scott. **Trainer:** Chris Dovey. **Strength Coach:** Brian Buck. **Supervisor, Double-A Development:** Ron Gideon.

GAME INFORMATION

Radio Announcer: Dennis Higgins. **No. of Games Broadcast:** 140. **Flagship Station:** KTBZ 1430-AM.
PA Announcer: Kirk McAnany. **Official Scorers:** Bruce Howard, Duane DaPron, Larry Lewis, Barry Lewis.
Stadium Name: ONEOK Field. **Location:** I-244 to Cincinnati/Detroit Exit (6A); north on Detroit Ave, right onto John Hope Franklin Blvd, right on Elgin Ave. **Standard Game Times:** 7:05 pm, Sun 2:05 (April-June), 7:05 (July-Aug).
Visiting Club Hotel: Hyatt Regency, 100 E 2nd St, Tulsa, OK 74103. **Telephone:** (918) 582-9000.

CALIFORNIA LEAGUE

Office Address: 3600 South Harbor Blvd, Suite 122, Oxnard, CA 93035.
Telephone: (805) 985-8585. **Fax:** (805) 985-8580.
Website: www.californialeague.com. **E-Mail:** info@californialeague.com.
Years League Active: 1941-1942, 1946-
President: Charlie Blaney. **Vice President:** Tom Volpe.

Directors: Bobby Brett (Rancho Cucamonga), Brad Seymour (Lancaster), Dave Elmore (Inland Empire), D.G. Elmore (Bakersfield), Dave Heller (High Desert), Gary Jacobs (Lake Elsinore), Mike Savit (Modesto), Tom Seidler (Visalia), Tom Volpe (Stockton), Dan Orum (San Jose).

Director, Operations/Marketing: Matt Blaney. **Historian:** Chris Lampe. **Legal Counsel:** Jonathan Light. **CPA:** Jeff Hass.

Regular Season: 140 games (split schedule).

2014 Opening Date: April 3. **Closing Date:** Sept 1.

Playoff Format: Six teams. First-half winners in each division earn first-round bye; second-half winners meet wild cards with next best overall records in best-of-three quarterfinals. Winners meet first-half champions in best-of-five semifinals. Winners meet in best-of-five series for league championship.

All-Star Game: vs Carolina League, June 17 at Wilmington.

Roster Limit: 25 active (35 under control). **Player Eligibility:** No more than two players and one player/coach on active list may have more than six years experience. **Brand of Baseball:** Rawlings.

Umpires: Nestor Ceja, Paul Clemons, Ben Guttenberger, Clayton Hamm, David Marcoe, Blake Mickleson, Charles Ramos, Clint Vondrak, Jacob Wilburn, Lewis Williams III.

Charlie Blaney

| | | | | Dimensions | | | | |
Club	Stadium	Opened	LF	CF	RF	Capacity	2012 Att.
Bakersfield	Sam Lynn Ballpark	1941	328	354	328	2,700	56,345
High Desert	Mavericks Stadium	1991	340	401	340	3,808	92,379
Inland Empire	San Manuel Stadium	1996	330	410	330	5,000	192,549
Lake Elsinore	The Diamond	1994	330	400	310	7,866	217,869
Lancaster	Clear Channel Stadium	1996	350	410	350	4,500	158,266
Modesto	John Thurman Field	1952	312	400	319	4,000	177,700
R Cucamonga	LoanMart Field	1993	335	400	335	6,615	172,306
San Jose	Municipal Stadium	1942	320	390	320	5,208	201,011
Stockton	Banner Island Ballpark	2005	300	399	326	5,200	199,742
Visalia	Rawhide Ballpark	1946	320	405	320	2,468	115,321

BAKERSFIELD BLAZE

Office Address: 4009 Chester Ave., Bakersfield, CA 93301. **Mailing Address:** PO Box 10031, Bakersfield, CA 93389.
Telephone: (661) 716-4487. **Fax:** (661) 322-6199.
E-Mail Address: blaze@bakersfieldblaze.com. **Website:** www.bakersfieldblaze.com.
Affiliation (first year): Cincinnati Reds (2011). **Years In League:** 1941-42, 1946-75, 1978-79, 1982-

OWNERSHIP/MANAGEMENT

Principal Owner: Elmore Sports Group (David Elmore).

General Manager: Elizabeth Martin. **Assistant GM, Operations:** Philip Guiry. **Assistant GM, Media/Marketing:** Dan Besbris. **Assistant GM, Ticketing/Groups:** Mike Candela. **Director, Merchandise:** Dale Billodeaux. **Ticket Sales Manager:** Brianne Gidcumb. **Head Groundskeeper:** Eric Dye.

FIELD STAFF

Manager: Pat Kelly. **Hitting Coach:** Ray Martinez. **Pitching Coach:** Tom Browning.

GAME INFORMATION

Radio Announcer: Dan Besbris. **Flagship Station:** 1230-AM.

PA Announcer: Mike Cushine. **Official Scorer:** Tim Wheeler.

Stadium Name: Sam Lynn Ballpark. **Location:** Highway 99 to California Avenue, east two miles to Chester Avenue, north two miles to stadium. **Standard Game Time:** 7:30 pm. **Ticket Price Range:** $7-12

Visiting Club Hotel: Marriott at the Convention Center, 801 Truxtun Ave, Bakersfield, CA 93301. **Telephone:** (661) 323-1900.

HIGH DESERT MAVERICKS

Stadium/Office Address: 12000 Stadium Way, Adelanto, CA 92301.
Telephone: (760) 246-6287.
E-Mail Address: rcook@hdmavs.com. **Website:** www.hdmavs.com.
Affiliation (first year): Seattle Mariners (2007). **Years in League:** 1991-

OWNERSHIP/MANAGEMENT
Operated By: Main Street California.
Managing Partner: Dave Heller. **President:** Jim Coufos. **General Manager:** Ryan Cook. **Controller:** Deb Niemann. **Director, Marketing:** Zach Osadche. **Director, Tickets Sales:** Clinton Jorth.

FIELD STAFF
Manager: Eriberto Menchaca. **Hitting Coach:** Max Venable. **Pitching Coach:** Andrew Lorraine.

GAME INFORMATION
Radio Announcer: Unavailable.
PA Announcer: Unavailable. **Official Scorer:** Unavailable.
Stadium Name: Stater Bros Stadium. **Location:** I-15 North to Highway 395 to Adelanto Road. **Standard Game Times:** 7:05 pm; Sun 1:05 1st half 2nd half 5:05. **Ticket Price Range:** $5-$15.
Visiting Club Hotel: Unavailable.

INLAND EMPIRE 66ERS

Office Address: 280 South E St., San Bernardino, CA 92401.
Telephone: (909) 888-9922. **Fax:** (909) 888-5251.
Website: www.66ers.com.
Affiliation (first year): Los Angeles Angels (2011). **Years in League:** 1941, 1987-

OWNERSHIP/MANAGEMENT
Operated by: Inland Empire 66ers Baseball Club of San Bernardino.
Principal Owners: David Elmore, Donna Tuttle. **President:** David Elmore. **Chairman:** Donna Tuttle.
General Manager: Joe Hudson. **Assistant GM:** Ryan English. **Director, Group Sales:** Steve Pelle. **Director, Marketing/Promotions:** Matt Kowallis. **Director, Operations/Security:** Jordan Smith. **Assistant Director, Group Sales:** Adam Franey. **Community Groups Sales Manager:** Ashley Anderson. **Manager, Ticket Sales/Operations:** Sean Peterson. **Corporate Groups Sales Manager:** Andrew Pittman. **Graphics/In-Game Entertainment Manager:** Jason Sargent. **Promotions Manager:** Emily Adams. **Administrative Assistant:** Angie Geibel. **Head Groundskeeper:** Dominick Guerrero. **CFO:** John Fonseca.

FIELD STAFF
Manager: Denny Hocking. **Hitting Coach:** Brent Del Chiaro. **Pitching Coach:** Matt Wise. **Trainer:** Omar Uribe. **Strength/Conditioning Coach:** Unavailable.

GAME INFORMATION
Radio Announcer: Sam Farber. **Flagship Station:** 66ers Radio on TuneIn.
PA Announcer: JJ Gould. **Official Scorer:** Bill Maury-Holmes.
Stadium Name: 66ers Stadium. **Location:** From south, I-215 to 2nd Street exit, east on 2nd, right on G Street; from north, I-215 to 3rd Street exit, left on Rialto, right on G Street. **Standard Game Times:** 7:05 pm; Sun 2:05 (April-June), 5:05 (July-Aug). **Ticket Price Range:** $5.50-12.
Visiting Club Hotel: Hampton Inn & Suite Highland: 27959 Highland Avenue, Highland, California, 92346. **Telephone:** (909) 862-8000.

LAKE ELSINORE STORM

Office Address: 500 Diamond Drive, Lake Elsinore, CA 92530. **Mailing Address:** PO Box 535, Lake Elsinore, CA 92531.
Telephone: (951) 245-4487. **Fax:** (951) 245-0305.
E-Mail Address: info@stormbaseball.com. **Website:** www.stormbaseball.com.
Affiliation (first year): San Diego Padres (2001). **Years in League:** 1994-

OWNERSHIP/MANAGEMENT
Owners: Gary Jacobs, Len Simon.
President: Dave Oster. **Assistant GM:** Raj Narayanan. **Director, Stadium Operations:** Patrick Kennedy. **Assistant Director:** Casey Scott. **Director, Broadcasting:** Sean McCall. **Group Sales Representatives:** Kasey Rawitzer, Eric Theiss. **Senior Graphics/Animation Designer:** Mark Beskid. **Director, Ticketing:** Eric Colunga. **Assistant Director, Ticketing:** Sara Dugan. **Partnership Coordinator:** Dave Barnick. **Director, Mascot Operations:** Stephen Webster. **Director, Administration/Human Resources:** Rick Riegler. **Director, Merchandise:** Donna Grunow. **Assistant Director,**

Merchandise: Leah Kelley. **Director, Food/Beverage:** Andrew Nelson. **Director, Concession Operations:** Chris Kidder. **Director, Grounds/Maintenance:** Joe Jimenez. **Maintenance Supervisor:** Jassiel Reza. **Office Manager:** Peggy Mitchell. **Clubhouse Manager:** Terrance Tucker.

FIELD STAFF
Manager: Jamie Quirk. **Hitting Coach:** Jody Davis. **Pitching Coach:** Bronswell Patrick. **Trainer:** Will Sinon. **Strength Coach:** Pat Trainor.

GAME INFORMATION
Radio Announcer: Sean McCall. **No. of Games Broadcast:** 140. **Flagship Station:** KMYT 94.5.
PA Announcer: Joe Martinez. **Official Scorer:** Lloyd Nixon.
Stadium Name: The Diamond. **Location:** From I-15, exit at Diamond Drive, west one mile to stadium. **Standard Game Times:** 6:05 pm, Thurs/Fri 7:05 pm, Sun 2:05 (first half), 5:05 (second half). **Ticket Price Range:** $10-14.
Visiting Club Hotel: Lake Elsinore Hotel and Casino, 20930 Malaga St, Lake Elsinore, CA 92530. **Telephone:** (951) 674-3101.

LANCASTER JETHAWKS

Office Address: 45116 Valley Central Way, Lancaster, CA 93536.
Telephone: (661) 726-5400. **Fax:** (661) 726-5406.
E-Mail Address: Will@jethawks.com. **Website:** www.jethawks.com.
Affiliation (first year): Houston Astros (2009). **Years in League:** 1996-

OWNERSHIP/MANAGEMENT
Operated By: Hawks Nest LLC.
President: Pete Carfagna. **Vice President:** Brad Seymour.
General Manager: William Thornhill. **Assistant GM, Tickets/Merchandise:** Will Murphy. **Director, Facility/Baseball Operations:** John Laferney. **Director, Food/Beverage:** Adam Fillenworth. **Community Relations Manager/Account Executive:** Jennifer Adamczyk. **Graphic Designer:** Andy Inman. **Director, Media Relations:** Jason Schwartz. **Ticket Account Executives:** Brandon Capelo, Dylan Baker.

FIELD STAFF
Manager: Rodney Linares. **Coach:** Darryl Robinson. **Pitching Coach:** Don Alexander. **Infield Coach:** Morgan Ensberg. **Trainer:** Grant Hufford.

GAME INFORMATION
Radio Announcer: Jason Schwartz. **No. of Games Broadcast:** 140. **Flagship Station:** www.jethawks.com.
PA Announcer: John Tyler. **Official Scorer:** David Guenther.
Stadium Name: The Hangar. **Location:** Highway 14 In Lancaster to Avenue I exit, west one block to stadium. **Standard Game Times:** 7 pm, Sun 2 (April-June), 5 (July-Sept). **Ticket Price Range:** $6-12.
Visiting Club Hotel: Comfort Inn, 1825 W. Avenue J-12, Lancaster CA 93534. **Telephone:** (661) 723-2001.

MODESTO NUTS

Office Address: 601 Neece Drive, Modesto, CA 95351. **Mailing Address:** PO Box 883, Modesto, CA 95353.
Telephone: (209) 572-4487. **Fax:** (209) 572-4490.
E-Mail Address: fun@modestonuts.com. **Website:** www.modestonuts.com.
Affiliation (first year): Colorado Rockies (2005). **Years in League:** 1946-64,1966-

OWNERSHIP/MANAGEMENT
Operated by: HWS Group IV.
Principal Owner: Mike Savit.
President: Bill Shanahan. **Executive Vice President:** Michael Gorrasi. **General Manager:** Tyler Richardson. **Vice President, HWS Beverage:** Ed Mack. **Director, Brand Management:** Robert Moullette. **Director, Group Sales:** Peter Billups. **Director, In-Game Entertainment:** Joe Tichy. **Manager, Tickets:** Austin Weltner.

FIELD STAFF
Manager: Unavailable. **Coach:** Jon Stone. **Pitching Coach:** Dave Burba.

GAME INFORMATION
Radio Announcer: Unavailable.
PA Announcer: Unavailable. **Official Scorer:** Unavailable.
Stadium Name: John Thurman Field. **Location:** Highway 99 in southwest Modesto to Tuolomne Boulevard exit, west on Tuolomne for one block to Neece Drive, left for 1/4 mile to stadium. **Standard Game Times:** 7:05 pm, Sun 1:05pm/6:05 pm. **Ticket Price Range:** $6-13.
Visiting Club Hotel: Park Inn By Radisson, 1720 Sisk Rd, Modesto, CA 95350. **Telephone:** (209) 577-3825.

RANCHO CUCAMONGA
QUAKES

Office Address: 8408 Rochester Ave., Rancho Cucamonga, CA 91730. **Mailing Address:** P.O. Box 4139, Rancho Cucamonga, CA 91729.
Telephone: (909) 481-5000. **Fax:** (909) 481-5005.
E-Mail Address: info@rcquakes.com. **Website:** www.rcquakes.com.
Affiliation (first year): Los Angeles Dodgers (2011). **Years in League:** 1993-

OWNERSHIP/MANAGEMENT
Operated By: Brett Sports & Entertainment.
Principal Owner: Bobby Brett. **President:** Brent Miles.
Vice President/General Manager: Grant Riddle. **VP, Tickets:** Monica Ortega. **Assistant GM, Group Sales:** Linda Rathfon. **Director, Sponsorships:** Chris Pope. **Sponsorship Account Executive:** Andrew Canales. **Promotions Manager:** Kristen Vella. **Promotions Coordinator:** Jon Hall. **Director, Group Sales:** Kyle Burleson. **Group Sales Manager:** Matt Sirios. **Ticket Sales Managers:** Melinda Balandra, Art Torres. **Account Executive:** Carly Nicola. **Director, Accounting:** Amara McClellan. **Director, Public Relations:** Mike Lindskog. **Office Manager:** Shelley Scebbi. **Director, Food/Beverage:** Jose Reyna.

FIELD STAFF
Manager: P.J. Forbes. **Hitting Coach:** Mike Eylward. **Pitching Coach:** Matt Herges. **Trainer:** Unavailable.

GAME INFORMATION
Radio Announcer: Mike Lindskog.
PA Announcer: Chris Albaugh. **Official Scorer:** Ryan Wilson.
Stadium Name: LoanMart Field. **Location:** I-10 to I-15 North, exit at Foothill Boulevard, left on Foothill, left on Rochester to Stadium. **Standard Game Times:** 7:05 p.m.; Sun. 2:05 (April-June), 5:05 (July-Sept.). **Ticket Price Range:** $8-12.
Visiting Club Hotel: Best Western Heritage Inn, 8179 Spruce Ave, Rancho Cucamonga, CA 91730. **Telephone:** (909) 466-1111.

SAN JOSE GIANTS

Office Address: 588 E Alma Ave., San Jose, CA 95112. **Mailing Address:** PO Box 21727, San Jose, CA 95151.
Telephone: (408) 297-1435. **Fax:** (408) 297-1453.
E-Mail Address: info@sjgiants.com. **Website:** www.sjgiants.com.
Affiliation (first year): San Francisco Giants (1988). **Years in League:** 1942, 1947-58, 1962-76, 1979-

OWNERSHIP/MANAGEMENT
Operated by: Progress Sports Management.
Principal Owners: San Francisco Giants, Heidi Stamas, Richard Beahrs.
President/CEO: Daniel Orum. **Chief Operating Officer/General Manager:** Mark Wilson. **Chief Marketing Officer:** Juliana Paoli. **Vice President, Food/Beverage/Stadium Events:** Zach Walter. **VP, Sales:** Ainslie Walter. **VP, Ballpark Operations:** Lance Motch. **VP, Finance/Human Resources:** Tyler Adair. **Director, Player Personnel:** Linda Pereira. **Director, Broadcasting:** Joe Ritzo. **Director, Ticketing:** Kellen Minteer. **Senior Sales Executive/Youth Development Program Manager:** Taylor Wilding. **Manager, Marketing/Media Relations:** Ben Taylor. **Manager, Human Resources/Food/Beverage:** Elizabeth Espinoza. **Coordinator, Retail/Community Relations:** Ashley Chapin. **Coordinator, Ticket Services:** John Rally. **Assistant, Marketing:** Matt Alongi. **Account Executive:** Alex Bost. **Groundskeeper:** Cody Cimino.

FIELD STAFF
Manager: Lenn Sakata. **Hitting Coach:** Lipso Nava. **Pitching Coach:** Michael Couchee. **Trainer:** Garret Havig. **Strength/Conditioning Coach:** Mike Lidge.

GAME INFORMATION
Radio Announcers: Joe Ritzo, Rocky Koplik. **No. of Games Broadcast:** 140. **Flagship:** www.sjgiants.com. **Television Announcers:** Joe Ritzo, Joe Castellano, Rocky Koplik. **No. of Games Broadcast:** 20 on Comcast Hometown Network, 70 on MiLB.TV.
PA Announcer: Russ Call. **Official Scorer:** Mike Hohler.
Stadium Name: Municipal Stadium. **Location:** South on I-280, Take 10th/11th Street Exit, Turn right on 10th Street, Turn left on Alma Ave; North on I-280: Take the 10th/11th Street Exit, Turn left on 10th Street, Turn Left on Alma Ave. **Standard Game Times:** 7 pm, Sat 5, Sun 1 (5 after June 30). **Ticket Price Range:** $7-16.
Visiting Club Hotel: DoubleTree Hotel San Jose, 2050 Gateway Place, San Jose, CA 95110. **Telephone:** (408) 453-4000.

STOCKTON PORTS

Office Address: 404 W Fremont St., Stockton, CA 95203.
Telephone: (209) 644-1900. **Fax:** (209) 644-1931.
E-Mail Address: info@stocktonports.com. **Website:** www.stocktonports.com.
Affiliation (first year): Oakland Athletics (2005). **Years in League:** 1941, 1946-72, 1978-

OWNERSHIP/MANAGEMENT

Operated By: 7th Inning Stretch LLC.
President: Pat Filippone. **Assistant General Manager:** Bryan Meadows. **Director, Tickets:** Tim Pollack. **Director, Marketing:** Taylor McCarthy. **Manager, Corporate Sales:** Aaron Morales. **Account Executives:** Lisa Peterson, Glenn Sides. **Community Relations Manager:** Kellie Ryan. **Sponsorship/Ticket Sales Executive:** Greg Bell. **Box Office Manager:** Dustin Coder. **Manager, Graphics/Social Media:** Mark Fanta. **Bookkeeper:** Vang Hang. **Front Office Manager:** Deborah Pelletier. **Ovations General Manager:** Mike Bristow.

FIELD STAFF

Manager: Ryan Christenson. **Hitting Coach:** Brian McArn. **Pitching Coach:** John Wasdin. **Trainer:** Travis Tims.

GAME INFORMATION

Radio Announcer: Zack Bayrouty. **No. of Games Broadcast:** 140. **Flagship Station:** KWSX 1280-AM. **Television:** Comcast Hometown Network.
PA Announcer: Mike Conway. **Official Scorer:** Paul Muyskens.
Stadium Name: Banner Island Ballpark. **Location:** From I-5/99, take Crosstown Freeway (Highway 4) exit El Dorado Street, north on El Dorado to Fremont Street, left on Fremont. **Standard Game Times:** 7:05 pm. **Ticket Price Range:** $6-$12.
Visiting Club Hotel: Hampton Inn Stockton, 5045 South State Route 99 East, Stockton, CA 95215. **Telephone:** (209) 946-1234.

VISALIA RAWHIDE

Office Address: 300 N Giddings St., Visalia, CA 93291.
Telephone: (559) 732-4433. **Fax:** (559) 739-7732.
E-Mail Address: info@rawhidebaseball.com. **Website:** www.rawhidebaseball.com.
Affiliation (first year): Arizona Diamondbacks (2007). **Years in League:** 1946-62, 1968-75, 1977-

OWNERSHIP/MANAGEMENT

President: Tom Seidler.
General Manager: Jennifer Pendergraft. **Executive Assistant:** Erin O'Brien.
Director, Ticketing/Group Events: Charlie Saponara. **Manager, Ticketing:** Dan Makela. **Event Coordinator:** Jessica Massart. **Coordinator, Client Servicing:** Charlie Bennett. **Director, Broadcasting:** Donny Baarns. **Manager, Media Relations:** Josh Jackson. **Manager, Hispanic Marketing/Community Relations:** Jesus Romero. **Director, Ballpark Operations:** Cody Gray. **Head Groundskeeper:** Jason Smith. **Operations Assistant, Food/Beverage:** Chris Lukasiewicz. **Ballpark Operations Assistant:** Les Kissick.

FIELD STAFF

Manager: Robby Hammock. **Hitting Coach:** Bobby Smith. **Pitching Coach:** Gil Heredia. **Trainer:** Takashi Onuki.

GAME INFORMATION

Radio Announcers: Donny Baarns, Josh Jackson. **No. of Games Broadcast:** 140. **Flagship Station:** KJUG 1270-AM.
PA Announcer: Brian Anthony. **Official Scorer:** Harry Kargenian.
Stadium Name: Rawhide Ballpark. **Location:** From Highway 99, take 198 East to Mooney Boulevard exit, left at second signal on Giddings; four blocks to ballpark. **Standard Game Times:** 7 pm, Sun 2 (first half), 6 (second half). **Ticket Price Range:** $5-20.
Visiting Club Hotel: Lamp Liter Inn, 3300 W Mineral King Ave, Visalia, CA 93291. **Telephone:** (559) 732-4511.

CAROLINA LEAGUE

Office Address: 1806 Pembroke Rd., Suite 2-B, Greensboro, NC 27408.
Telephone: (336) 691-9030. **Fax:** (336) 464-2737.
E-Mail Address: office@carolinaleague.com. **Website:** www.carolinaleague.com.
Years League Active: 1945-.
President/Treasurer: John Hopkins.

John Hopkins

Vice President: Art Silber (Potomac). **Corporate Secretary:** Ken Young (Frederick). **Directors:** Tim Zue (Salem), Paul Sunwall (Lynchburg), Chuck Greenberg (Myrtle Beach), Dave Ziedelis (Frederick), Steve Bryant (Carolina), Jack Minker (Wilmington), Billy Prim (Winston-Salem), Art Silber (Potomac). **Administrative Assistant:** Marnee Larkins.

Division Structure: North—Frederick, Lynchburg, Potomac, Wilmington. South—Carolina, Myrtle Beach, Salem, Winston-Salem.

Regular Season: 140 games (split schedule). **2014 Opening Date:** April 3. **Closing Date:** Sept 1.

All-Star Game: June 17 at Wilmington (Carolina League vs California League).

Playoff Format: First-half division winners play second-half division winners in best-of-three series; if a team wins both halves, it plays a wild card (team in that division with next-best second-half record). Division series winners meet in best-of-five series for Mills Cup.

Roster Limit: 25 active. **Player Eligibility Rule:** No age limit. No more than two players and one player/coach on active list may have six or more years of prior minor league service.

Brand of Baseball: Rawlings.

Umpires: Doug Del Bello (Hamburg, NY), Travis Godec (Roanoke, VA), Jimmie Hollingsworth (Irmo SC), Brian Miller (Cleveland, OH), Brian Peterson (Manchester, NJ), Jeremie Rehak (Murrysville, PA), Jorge Teran (Barquisimeto, Lara, Venezuela), Ryan Willis (Fredericksburg, VA).

STADIUM INFORMATION

			Dimensions				
Club	**Stadium**	**Opened**	**LF**	**CF**	**RF**	**Capacity**	**2013 Att.**
Carolina	Five County Stadium	1991	330	400	309	6,500	224,736
Frederick	Harry Grove Stadium	1990	325	400	325	5,400	324,311
Lynchburg	City Stadium	1939	325	390	325	4,281	160,537
Myrtle Beach	TicketReturn.com Field	1999	308	405	328	5,200	222,406
Potomac	Pfitzner Stadium	1984	315	400	315	6,000	236,772
Salem	Salem Memorial Stadium	1995	325	401	325	5,502	172,293
Wilmington	Frawley Stadium	1993	325	400	325	6,532	292,319
Winston-Salem	BB&T Ballpark	2010	315	399	323	5,500	301,366

CAROLINA MUDCATS

Office Address: 1501 NC Hwy 39, Zebulon, NC 27597. **Mailing Address:** PO Drawer 1218, Zebulon, NC 27597.

Telephone: (919) 269-2287. **Fax:** (919) 269-4910.

E-Mail Address: muddy@carolinamudcats.com. **Website:** www.carolinamudcats.com.

Affiliation (first year): Cleveland Indians (2012). **Years in League:** 2012-

OWNERSHIP/MANAGEMENT

Operated by: Mudcats Baseball, LLC. **Majority Owner/President:** Steve Bryant.

General Manager: Joe Kremer. **Assistant GM:** Eric Gardner. **Office Manager:** Jackie DiPrimo. **Director, Stadium Operations:** Daniel Spence. **Director, Food/Beverage:** Dwayne Lucas. **Director, Merchandise:** Janell Bullock. **Director, Game Productions/Creative Services:** Aaron Bayles. **Director, Promotions:** Duke Sanders. **Director, External Affairs/ Corporate Development:** Ricky Ray. **Associate, Group Sales/Community Relations:** Jordan Buck. **Associates, Group Sales:** Juan Toro, Aaron Freeman, Max Marshall. **Director, Field Operations:** John Packer. **Director, Broadcasting/Media Relations:** Darren Headrick.

FIELD STAFF

Manager: Scooter Tucker. **Hitting Coach:** Tony Mansolino. **Pitching Coach:** Steve Karsay. **Trainer:** Bobby Ruiz.

GAME INFORMATION

Radio Announcer: Darren Headrick. **No. of Games Broadcast:** 140. **Flagship Station:** WGWD 98.5 FM.

PA Announcer: Ricky Ray. **Official Scorer:** John Hobgood.

Stadium Name: Five County Stadium. **Location:** From Raleigh, US 64 East to 264 East, exit at Highway 39 in Zebulon. **Standard Game Times:** 7 pm, Sat 6, Sun 2. **Ticket Price Range:** $7-12.

Visiting Club Hotel: Hampton Inn Wake Forest NC, 12318 Wake Union Church Road, Wake Forest, NC 27587. **Telephone:** (919) 554-0222. **Fax:** (919) 554-1499.

FREDERICK KEYS

Office Address: 21 Stadium Dr., Frederick, MD 21703.
Telephone: (301) 662-0013. **Fax:** (301) 662-0018.
E-Mail Address: info@frederickkeys.com. **Website:** www.frederickkeys.com.
Affiliation (first year): Baltimore Orioles (1989). **Years in League:** 1989-

OWNERSHIP/MANAGEMENT

Ownership: Maryland Baseball Holding LLC.
President: Ken Young. **General Manager:** Dave Ziedelis. **Assistant GM:** Branden McGee. **Director, Ticket Operations:** Felicia Adamus. **Director, Marketing:** Bridget McCabe. **Promotions Manager:** Christine Roy. **Group Sales Manager:** Matt Miller. **Account Managers:** Donny Lawson, Ben Sealy, Amanda Kostolansky. **Account Manager/Broadcaster:** Doug Raftery. **Box Office Assistants:** David Damerell, Derek Tellinghuisen. **Stadium Operations Manager:** Kari Collins. **Head Groundskeeper:** Mike Soper. **Office Manager:** Barb Freund. **Finance Manager:** Tami Hetrick.

FIELD STAFF

Manager: Luis Pujols. **Hitting Coach:** Torre Tyson. **Pitching Coach:** Kennie Steenstra. **Athletic Trainer:** Pat Wesley.

GAME INFORMATION

Radio Announcer: Doug Raftery.
PA Announcer: Andy Redmond. **Official Scorers:** Bob Roberson, Dennis Hetrick, Dave Musil.
Stadium Name: Harry Grove Stadium. **Location:** From I-70, take exit 54 (Market Street), left at light; From I-270, take exit 32 (I-70 Baltimore/Hagerstown) toward Baltimore (I-70), to exit 54 at Market Street. **Ticket Price Range:** $9-12.
Visiting Club Hotel: Comfort Inn—Frederick, 7300 Executive Way, Frederick, MD 21704. **Telephone:** (301) 668-7272.

LYNCHBURG HILLCATS

Office Address: Lynchburg City Stadium, 3180 Fort Ave., Lynchburg, VA 24501. **Mailing Address:** PO Box 10213, Lynchburg, VA 24506.
Telephone: (434) 528-1144. **Fax:** (434) 846-0768.
E-Mail address: info@lynchburg-hillcats.com. **Website:** www.Lynchburg-hillcats.com.
Affiliation (first year): Atlanta Braves (2011). **Years in League:** 1966-

OWNERSHIP/MANAGEMENT

Operated By: Lynchburg Baseball Corp.
President/General Manager: Paul Sunwall. **Assistant GM:** Ronnie Roberts. **Head Groundskeeper/Sales:** Darren Johnson. **Director, Broadcasting:** Erik Wilson. **Director, Food/Beverage:** Zach Willis. **Director, Promotions:** Ashley Stephenson. **Director, Group Sales:** Brad Goodale. **Ticket Manager:** John Hutt. **Office Manager:** Diane Arrington.

FIELD STAFF

Manager: Luis Salazar. **Hitting Coach:** John Moses. **Pitching Coach:** Derek Lewis. **Trainer:** Joe Toenjes.

GAME INFORMATION

Radio Announcer: Erik Wilson. **No. of Games Broadcast:** 70 (all home games). **Flagship Station:** WZZU-97.9FM.
PA Announcer: Chuck Young. **Official Scorers:** Malcolm Haley, Chuck Young.
Stadium Name: Calvin Falwell Field at Lynchburg City Stadium. **Location:** US 29 Business South to Lynchburg City Stadium (exit 6); US 29 Business Notth to Lynchburg City Stadium (exit 4). **Ticket Price Range:** $7-10.
Visiting Club Hotel: Best Western, 2815 Candlers Mountain Rd, Lynchburg, VA 24502. **Telephone:** (434) 237-2986.

MYRTLE BEACH PELICANS

Office Address: 1251 21st Ave. N., Myrtle Beach, SC 29577.
Telephone: (843) 918-6002. **Fax:**(843) 918-6001.
E-Mail Address: info@myrtlebeachpelicans.com. **Website:** www.myrtlebeachpelicans.com.
Affiliation (first year): Texas Rangers (2011). **Years in League:** 1999-

OWNERSHIP/MANAGEMENT

Operated By: Myrtle Beach Pelicans LP. **Managing Partner:** Chuck Greenberg.
General Manager: Andy Milovich. **Senior Director, Business Development:** Guy Schuman. **Senior Director, Ticket Sales:** Zach Brockman. **Box Office Manager:** Shannon Samanka. **Group Sales Managers:** Glenn Goodwin, Justin Bennett. **Corporate Sales Manager:** Katelyn Guild. **Account Executives:** Gandy Henry, Todd Chapman. **Director, Broadcasting/Media Relations:** Nathan Barnett. **Senior Director, Marketing:** Kristin Call. **Senior Director, Community Development :** Jen Borowski. **Executive Producer, In-Game Entertainment:** Kyle Guertin. **Facility Operations Manager:** Mike Snow. **Merchandise Manager:** Dan Bailey. **Director, Food/Beverage:** Brad Leininger. **Director, Sports Turf Management:** Corey Russell. **Assistant Director, Sports Turf Management:** Kevin Schmidt. **Clubhouse Manager:** Stan Hunter. **Senior Director, Finance:** Anne Frost. **Administrative Assistant:** Beth Freitas.

FIELD STAFF

Manager: Joe Mikulik. **Hitting Coach:** Josue Perez. **Pitching Coach:** Steve Mintz. **Athletic Trainer:** Joshua Newburn. **Strength/Conditioning:** Anthony Miller.

GAME INFORMATION

PA Announcer: Unavailable. **Official Scorer:** Steve Walsh.
Stadium Name: Ticketreturn.com Field at Pelicans Ballpark. **Location:** US Highway 17 Bypass to 21st Ave. North, half mile to stadium. **Standard Game Times:** Unavailable. **Ticket Price Range:** $7-$13.
Visiting Club Hotel: Hampton Inn-Broadway at the Beach, 1140 Celebrity Circle, Myrtle Beach, SC 29577. **Telephone:** (843) 916-0600.

POTOMAC NATIONALS

Office Address: 7 County Complex Ct., Woodbridge, VA 22192. **Mailing Address:** PO Box 2148, Woodbridge, VA 22195.
Telephone: (703) 590-2311. **Fax:** (703) 590-5716.
E-Mail Address: info@potomacnationals.com. **Website:** www.potomacnationals.com.
Affiliation (first year): Washington Nationals (2005). **Years in League:** 1978-

OWNERSHIP/MANAGEMENT

Operated By: Potomac Baseball LLC.
Principal Owner: Art Silber. **President:** Lani Silber Weiss.
Vice President/General Manager: Josh Olerud. **Assistant GM, Promotions:** Zach Prehn. **Ticket Director:** Brett Adams. **Director, Media Relations/Broadcasting:** Bryan Holland. **Senior Executive, Corporate Partnerships:** Seth Distler. **Director, Food Services/Merchandise Director:** Aaron Johnson. **Director, Stadium Operations:** Arthur Bouvier. **Senior Group Sales Director:** Andrew Stinson. **Group Sales Executive:** Julie Goldberg. **Group Sales Executive:** Jacob Martinez. **Director, Community Relations/Creative Design:** Alexis Deegan. **Head Groundskeeper:** Stephen King, Jr. **Manager, Business Operations:** Shawna Hooke.

FIELD STAFF

Manager: Tripp Keister. **Hitting Coach:** Brian Rupp. **Pitching Coach:** Franklin Bravo.

GAME INFORMATION

Radio Announcer: Bryan Holland. **No. of Games Broadcast:** 140. **Flagship:** www.potomacnationals.com.
Official Scorer: David Vincent, Ben Trittipoe.
Stadium Name: Pfitzner Stadium. **Location:** From I-95, take exit 158B and continue on Prince William Parkway for five miles, right into County Complex Court. **Standard Game Times:** 7:05 pm, Sat 6:35, Sun 1:05 (first half), Sun 6:05 (second half). **Ticket Price Range:** $8-15.
Visiting Club Hotel: Country Inn and Suites, Prince William Parkway, Woodbridge, VA 22192. **Telephone:** (703) 492-6868.

SALEM RED SOX

Office Address: 1004 Texas St., Salem, VA 24153. **Mailing Address:** PO Box 842, Salem, VA 24153.
Telephone: (540) 389-3333. **Fax:** (540) 389-9710.
E-Mail Address: info@salemsox.com. **Website:** www.salemsox.com.
Affiliation (first year): Boston Red Sox (2009). **Years in League:** 1968-

OWNERSHIP/MANAGEMENT

Operated By: Carolina Baseball LLC/Fenway Sports Group.
President: Sam Kennedy. **General Manager:** Ryan Shelton.
VP/Senior Assistant GM: Allen Lawrence. **Director, Corporate Sponsorships:** Steven Elovich. **Marketing/Promotions Manager:** Matt Hoffman. **VP, Operations:** Tim Anderson. **Stadium Operations Coordinator:** Matt Bird. **Group Sales Account Executive:** Casey Eliff. **Ticketing Manager:** Dustin Davis. **Food/Beverage Manager:** Patrick Pelletier. **Accounting/Office Manager:** Robin Griffin. **Head Groundskeeper:** Ross Groenevelt. **Office Assistant:** Susan Norris. **Clubhouse Manager:** Tom Wagner.

FIELD STAFF

Manager: Carlos Febles. **Hitting Coach:** U.L. Washington. **Pitching Coach:** Kevin Walker. **Trainer:** David Herrera.

GAME INFORMATION

Radio Announcer: Evan Lepler. **No. of Games Broadcast:** 140. **Flagship Station:** WFIR 960-AM.
PA Announcer: Travis Jenkins. **Official Scorer:** Billy Wells.
Stadium Name: Salem Memorial Ballpark. **Location:** I-81 to exit 141 (Route 419), follow signs to Salem Civic Center Complex. **Standard Game Times:** 7:05 pm, Sat/Sun 4:05. **Ticket Price Range:** $7-13.
Visiting Club Hotel: Comfort Inn Airport, 5070 Valley View Blvd, Roanoke, VA 24012. **Telephone:** (540) 527-2020.

WILMINGTON BLUE ROCKS

Office Address: 801 Shipyard Drive, Wilmington, DE 19801.
Telephone: (302) 888-2015. **Fax:** (302) 888-2032.
E-Mail Address: info@bluerocks.com. **Website:** www.bluerocks.com.
Affiliation (first year): Kansas City Royals (2007). **Years in League:** 1993-

OWNERSHIP/MANAGEMENT

Operated by: Wilmington Blue Rocks LP.
Honorary President: Matt Minker. **President:** Tom Palmer. **Vice President:** Jack Minker. **Secretary/Treasurer:** Bob Stewart. **General Manager:** Chris Kemple. **Assistant GM:** Andrew Layman. **Director, Broadcasting/Media Relations:** Matt Janus. **Broadcasting/Media Relations Assistant:** Seth Bernstein. **Director, Merchandise:** Jim Beck. **Merchandise Assistant:** Amanda Pecota.
Director, Marketing: Joe Valenti. **Assistant Director, Marketing:** Jake Schrum. **Marketing Assistant:** Danielle Cedeno. **Director, Community Affairs:** Kevin Linton. **Box Office Manager:** Mark Cunningham. **Director, Group Sales:** Stefani Rash. **Group Sales Executives:** Megan Holloway. **Director, Field Operations:** Steve Gold. **Office Manager:** Elizabeth Kolodziej. **Director, Advertising Sales:** Brian Radle. **Manager, Game Entertainment:** Mike Diodati.

FIELD STAFF

Manager: Darryl Kennedy. **Coach:** Milt Thompson. **Pitching Coach:** Steve Luebber. **Athletic Trainer:** James Stone. **Strength/Conditioning Coach:** Joe Greany.

GAME INFORMATION

Radio Announcers: Matt Janus. **No. of Games Broadcast:** 140. **Flagship Station:** 89.7 WGLS-FM.
PA Announcer: Kevin Linton. **Official Scorers:** Dick Shute, Eric Rhew.
Stadium Name: Judy Johnson Field at Daniel Frawley Stadium. **Location:** I-95 North to Maryland Ave (exit 6), right on Maryland Ave, and through traffic light onto Martin Luther King Blvd, right at traffic light on Justison St, follow to Shipyard Dr; I-95 South to Maryland Ave (exit 6), left at fourth light on Martin Luther King Blvd, right at fourth light on Justison St, follow to Shipyard Dr. **Standard Game Times:** 7:05 pm, 6:35 (April-May), Sat 6:05, Sun 1:35. **Ticket Price Range:** $4-12.
Visiting Club Hotel: Clarion Belle, 1612 N DuPont Hwy, New Castle, DE 19720. **Telephone:** (302) 299-1408.

WINSTON-SALEM DASH

Office Address: 926 Brookstown Ave., Winston-Salem, NC 27101.
Stadium Address: 951 Ballpark Way, Winston-Salem, NC 27101.
Telephone: (336) 714-2287. **Fax:** (336) 714-2288.
E-Mail Address: info@wsdash.com. **Website:** www.wsdash.com.
Affiliation (first year): Chicago White Sox (1997). **Years in League:** 1945-

OWNERSHIP/MANAGEMENT

Operated by: Sports Menagerie LLC.
Principal Owner: Billy Prim.
President: Geoff Lassiter. **Vice President/Chief Financial Officer:** Kurt Gehsmann. **VP, Baseball Operations:** Ryan Manuel. **VP, Ticket Sales:** CJ Johnson. **VP, Corporate Partnerships:** Chris Wood. **VP, Sponsor Services:** Andrew Beattie.
Accounting Manager: Anita Jasso. **Staff Accountant:** Amanda Elbert. **Associate Director, Creative Services:** Kristin DiSanti. **Sponsor Services Account Assistants:** Mimi Driscoll, Nick Jones. **Director, Entertainment:** Gabriel Wilhelm. **Director, Media Relations/Broadcasting:** Brian Boesch. **Business Development Manager:** Darren Hill. **Business Development Representatives:** Taylor Boyle, Bryan Ferrer. **Group Sales Manager:** Russell Parmele. **Group Sales Representatives:** Tommy Grant, Matt Satterfield, Paul Stephens. **Sales Coordinator:** Kyerra Carter. **Box Office Manager:** Kenny Lathan. **Box Office Supervisor:** Andy Webb. **Head Groundskeeper:** Doug Tanis.

FIELD STAFF

Manager: Tommy Thompson. **Hitting Coach:** Gary Ward. **Pitching Coach:** JR Perdew. **Athletic Trainer:** Josh Fallin. **Strength/Conditioning Coach:** Raymond Smith.

GAME INFORMATION

Radio Announcer: Brian Boesch. **No. of Games Broadcast:** 140. **Flagship Station:** 600 AM-WSJS (Thursday games) or wsdash.com (all games).
PA Announcer: Unavailable. **Official Scorers:** Bill Grainger, Todd Bess.
Stadium Name: BB&T Ballpark. **Stadium Location:** I-40 Business to Peters Creek Parkway exit (exit 5A). **Standard Game Times:** 7 pm, Sun 2/5.
Visiting Club Hotel: Ramada Plaza Hotel and Spa. **Telephone:** (336) 723-2911.

FLORIDA STATE LEAGUE

Office Address: 104 E Orange Ave Daytona Beach, FL 32114.
Mailing Address: PO Box 349, Daytona Beach, FL 32115.
Telephone: (386) 252-7479. **Fax:** (386) 252-7495.
E-Mail Address: fslbaseball@cfl.rr.com. **Website:** www.floridastateleague.com.
Years League Active: 1919-1927, 1936-1941, 1946-.

President/Treasurer: Chuck Murphy.
Executive VP: Ken Carson. **VPs:** North Division—Ken Carson. South Division—Paul Taglieri.
Corporate Secretary: C. David Hood. **Special Advisor:** Ben Hayes.
Directors: Mike Bauer (Jupiter/Palm Beach), Ken Carson (Dunedin), Jared Forma (Port Charlotte), Marvin Goldklang (Fort Myers), Trevor Gooby (Bradenton), Ron Myers (Lakeland), Josh Lawther (Daytona), Kyle Smith (Brevard County), Vance Smith (Tampa), Paul Taglieri (St. Lucie), John Timberlake (Clearwater).
Office Manager: Laura LeCras.
Division Structure: North—Brevard County, Clearwater, Daytona, Dunedin, Lakeland, Tampa. South—Fort Myers, Jupiter, Palm Beach, Port Charlotte, St. Lucie, Bradenton.
Regular Season: 140 games (split schedule). **2014 Opening Date:** April 3. **Closing Date:** August 31. **All-Star Game:** June 14 at Bradenton.
Playoff Format: First-half division winners meet second-half winners in best-of-three series. Winners meet in best-of-five series for league championship.
Roster Limit: 25. **Player Eligibility Rule:** No age limit. No more than two players and one player-coach on active list may have six or more years of prior minor league service.
Brand of Baseball: Rawlings.
Umpires: Ryan Additon (Davie, FL), Ryan Benson (Stamford, CT), Jeffrey Carnahan(Crystal River, FL), Scott Costello (Barrie, Ontario), John Libka (Mayville, MI), James Rackley (Lady Lake, FL), Sean Ryan (Waunakee, WI), Ryan Simmons (Morton, IL), Charles Tierney (Louisville, KY), Alexander Tosi (Lake Villa , IL), Samuel Vogt (Pittsburgh, PA), Alex Ziegler (Metairie, LA).

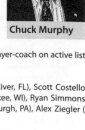

Chuck Murphy

STADIUM INFORMATION

Club	Stadium	Opened	Dimensions LF	CF	RF	Capacity	2013 Att.
Bradenton	McKechnie Field	1923	335	400	335	8,654	109,845
Brevard County	Space Coast Stadium	1994	340	404	340	7,500	97,238
Charlotte	Charlotte Sports Park	2009	343	413	343	5,028	107,995
Clearwater	Bright House Field	2004	330	400	330	8,500	172,151
Daytona	Jackie Robinson Ballpark	1930	317	400	325	4,200	146,049
Dunedin	Florida Auto Exchange Stadium	1977	335	400	327	5,509	50,695
Fort Myers	Hammond Stadium	1991	330	405	330	7,900	121,832
Jupiter	Roger Dean Stadium	1998	330	400	325	6,871	64,813
Lakeland	Joker Marchant Stadium	1966	340	420	340	7,828	60,011
Palm Beach	Roger Dean Stadium	1998	330	400	325	6,871	64,121
St. Lucie	Mets Stadium	1988	338	410	338	7,000	98,664
Tampa	Steinbrenner Field	1996	318	408	314	11,026	118,770

BRADENTON MARAUDERS

Mailing Address: 1701 27th St. East, Bradenton, FL 34208.
Telephone: (941) 747-3031. **Fax:** (941) 747-9442.
E-Mail Address: maraudersinfo@pirates.com. **Website:** www.bradentonmarauders.com.
Affiliation (first year): Pittsburgh Pirates (2010). **Years in League:** 1919-20, 1923-24, 1926, 2010-

OWNERSHIP/MANAGEMENT

Operated By: Pittsburgh Associates.
Senior Director, Florida Operations: Trevor Gooby. **Manager, McKechnie Operations:** A.J. Grant. **Manager, Florida Operations:** Juan Rodriguez. **Concessions Manager:** Jon Kerstetter. **Manager, Sales/Marketing:** Rachelle Madrigal. **Coordinator, Concessions:** Liz King. **Coordinator, Sales/Marketing:** Stacy Morgan. **Coordinator, Sales/ Marketing:** Mike Warren. **Coordinator, Ticket Operations:** Justin Kristich. **Coordinator, Sales/Business:** Anne Putnam. **Coordinator, Florida Operations:** Zach DeCicco. **Coordinator, Communication/Broadcasting:** Nate March. **Head Groundskeeper:** Victor Madrigal.

FIELD STAFF
　　Manager: Tom Prince. **Coach:** Kory DeHaan. **Pitching Coach:** Justin Meccage. **Coach:** Greg Picart. **Athletic Trainer:** Dru Scott. **Strength/Conditioning Coach:** Cole Durham.

GAME INFORMATION
　　PA Announcer: Art Ross. **Official Scorer:** Dave Taylor.
　　Stadium Name: McKechnie Field. **Location:** I-75 to exit 220 (220B from I-75N) to SR 64 West/Manatee Ave, Left onto 9th St. West, McKechnie Field on the left. **Standard Game Times:** 6:30 pm, Sun 1 (1st half), 5 (second half). **Ticket Price Range:** $6-10.
　　Visiting Club Hotel: Courtyard by Marriott Bradenton Sarasota Waterfront, 100 Riverfront Drive West, Bradenton, FL 34205. **Telephone:** (941) 747-3727.

BREVARD COUNTY MANATEES

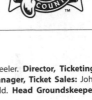

　　Office Address: 5800 Stadium Pkwy, Suite 101, Viera, FL 32940.
　　Telephone: (321) 633-9200. **Fax:** (321) 633-4418.
　　E-Mail Address: info@spacecoaststadium.com. **Website:** www.manateesbaseball.com.
　　Affiliation (first year): Milwaukee Brewers (2005). **Years in League:** 1994-

OWNERSHIP/MANAGEMENT
　　Operated By: Central Florida Baseball Group LLC.
　　Chairman: Tom Winters. **Vice Chairman:** Dwight Titus. **President:** Charlie Baumann.
　　General Manager: Kyle Smith.
　　Assistant GM: Chad Lovitt. **Director, Business Operations/Merchandise:** Kelley Wheeler. **Director, Ticketing/Media:** Frank Longobardo. **Director, Promotions/Community Relations:** Kevin Soto. **Manager, Ticket Sales:** John Manzoian. **Director, Broadcasting:** Dave Walkovic. **Clubhouse Manager:** Ryan McDonald. **Head Groundskeeper:** Doug Lopas.

FIELD STAFF
　　Manager: Joe Ayrault. **Coaches:** Ned Yost IV, Reggie Williams. **Pitching Coach:** Dave Chavarria. **Trainer:** Tommy Craig. **Strength/Conditioning Coordinator:** Jonah Mergen.

GAME INFORMATION
　　PA Announcer: JC Meyerholz. **Official Scorer:** Unavailable.
　　Stadium Name: Space Coast Stadium. **Location:** I-95 North to Wickham Rd (exit 191), left onto Wickham, right at traffic circle onto Lake Andrew Drive for 1 1/2 miles through the Brevard County government office complex to the four-way stop, right on Stadium Parkway, Space Coast Stadium 1/2 mile on the left; I-95 South to Rockledge exit (exit 195), left onto Stadium Parkway, Space Coast Stadium is 3 miles on right. **Standard Game Times:** 6:35 pm, Sun 5:05. **Tickets:** $6 - $10.
　　Visiting Club Hotel: Unavailable.

CHARLOTTE STONE CRABS

　　Office Address: 2300 El Jobean Rd., Port Charlotte, FL 33948. **Mailing Address:** 2300 El Jobean Rd, Building A, Port Charlotte, FL 33948.
　　Telephone: (941) 206-4487. **Fax:** (941) 206-3599.
　　E-Mail Address: info@stonecrabsbaseball.com. **Website:** www.stonecrabsbaseball.com.
　　Affiliation (first year): Tampa Bay Rays (2009). **Years in League:** 2009-

OWNERSHIP/MANAGEMENT
　　Operated By: Ripken Baseball.
　　General Manager: Jared Forma.
　　Assistant General Manager: Holly Jones. **Marketing Manager:** Mary Hegley. **Community Relations Manager:** Sammy DiTonno. **Full Charge Bookkeeper:** Lori Engleman. **Accounting Clerk:** Sue Denny. **Director, Food/Beverage:** Matt Vanderhoff. **Manager, Food/Beverage:** Marshall Clapper. **Manager, Corporate Sponsorship Sales:** Bill Holohan. **Account Representatives:** Jeff Cook, Hallie Rubins, Patrick Wondrak.

FIELD STAFF
　　Manager: Jared Sandberg. **Coach:** Joe Szekely. **Pitching Coach:** Steve Watson.

GAME INFORMATION
　　PA Announcer: Josh Grant. **Official Scorer:** Rich Spedaliere.
　　Stadium Name: Charlotte Sports Park. **Location:** I-75 to Exit 179, turn left onto Toldeo Blade Blvd then right on El Jobean Rd. **Ticket Price Range:** $9-11.
　　Visiting Club Hotel: Days Inn, 1941 Tamiami Trail, Port Charlotte, FL 33948. **Telephone:** 941-627-8900.

CLEARWATER THRESHERS

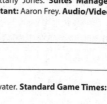

Office Address: 601 N Old Coachman Road, Clearwater, FL 33765.
Telephone: (727) 712-4300. **Fax:** (727) 712-4498.
Website: www.threshersbaseball.com.
Affiliation (first year): Philadelphia Phillies (1985). **Years in League:** 1985-

OWNERSHIP/MANAGEMENT

Operated by: Philadelphia Phillies.
Chairman: Bill Giles. **President:** David Montgomery.
Director, Florida Operations/General Manager: John Timberlake. **Business Manager:** Dianne Gonzalez. **Assistant GM/Director, Sales:** Dan McDonough. **Assistant GM, Ticketing:** Jason Adams. **Office Administration:** DeDe Angelillis. **Manager, Group Sales:** Dan Madden. **Senior Sales Associate:** Bobby Mitchell. **Manager, Ballpark Operations:** Jerry Warren. **Operations Assistant:** Sean McCarthy. **Coordinator, Facility Maintenance:** Cory Sipe. **Manager, Special Events:** Doug Kemp. **Manager, Community Relations/Promotions:** Amanda Koch. **Clubhouse Manager:** Mark Meschede. **Manager, Food/Beverage:** Brad Dudash. **Assistant, Food/Beverage:** Brittany Jones. **Suites Manager:** Wendy Armstrong. **Ticket Office Managers:** Pat Privelege, Kyle Webb. **Group Sales Assistant:** Aaron Frey. **Audio/Video:** Nic Repper. **Buyer/Manager, Merchandise:** Robin Warner. PR Assistant: Rob Stretch.

FIELD STAFF

Manager: Ramon Henderson. **Coach:** Frank Cacciatore. **Pitching Coach:** Bob Milacki.

GAME INFORMATION

PA Announcer: Don Guckian. **Official Scorer:** Larry Wiederecht. **Stadium Name:** Bright House Field. **Location:** US 19 North and Drew Street in Clearwater. **Standard Game Times:** 7 pm, Fri/Sat 6:30. **Ticket Price Range:** $5-10.
Visiting Club Hotel: La Quinta Inn, 3301 Ulmerton Road, Clearwater, FL, 33762. **Telephone:** (800) 753-3757.

DAYTONA CUBS

Office Address: 110 E Orange Ave., Daytona Beach, FL 32114.
Telephone: (386) 257-3172. **Fax:** (386) 523-9490.
E-Mail Address: info@daytonacubs.com. **Website:** www.daytonacubs.com.
Affiliation (first year): Chicago Cubs (1993). **Years in League:** 1920-24,1928, 1936-41, 1946-73, 1977-87, 1993-

OWNERSHIP/MANAGEMENT

Operated By: Big Game Florida LLC.
Principal Owner/President: Andrew Rayburn.
General Manager: Josh Lawther. **Assistant GMs:** Clint Cure, Jim Jaworski. **Director, Broadcasting/Media Relations:** Robbie Aaron. **Assistant GM, Stadium Operations:** JR Laub. **Director, Ticket Operations:** Erin Killian. **Director, Special Events/Community Relations:** Kasey Blair. **Manager, Food/Beverage:** Kevin Dwyer. **Manager, Merchandise/Box Office:** Corey Brothers. **Manager, Corporate Sales:** Corey Eirich. **Office Manager:** Tammy Devine. **Head Groundskeeper:** Mike Geiger.

FIELD STAFF

Manager: Dave Keller. **Hitting Coach:** Mariano Duncan. **Pitching Coach:** Ron Villone. **Trainer:** Peter Fagan.

GAME INFORMATION

Radio Announcer: Robbie Aaron. **No. of Games Broadcast:** 140. **Flagship Station:** AM-1230 WSBB.
PA Announcer: Tim Lecras. **Official Scorer:** Don Roberts.
Stadium Name: Jackie Robinson Ballpark. **Location:** I-95 to International Speedway Blvd Exit (Route 92), east to Beach Street, south to Magnolia Ave to ballpark; A1A North/South to Orange Ave west to ballpark. **Standard Game Time:** 7:05 p.m. **Ticket Price Range:** $6-12.
Visiting Club Hotel: Holiday Inn Resort Daytona Beach Oceanfront, 1615 S Atlantic Ave Daytona Beach, FL 32118. **Telephone:** (386) 255-0921.

DUNEDIN BLUE JAYS

Office Address: 373 Douglas Ave. Dunedin, FL 34698.
Telephone: (727) 733-9302. **Fax:** (727) 734-7661.
E-Mail Address: dunedin@bluejays.com. **Website:** dunedinbluejays.com.
Affiliation (first year): Toronto Blue Jays (1987). **Years in League:** 1978-79, 1987-

OWNERSHIP/MANAGEMENT

Director/General Manager, Florida Operations: Shelby Nelson. **Assistant GM:** Janette Donoghue.

Accounting Manager: Gayle Gentry. **Manager, Group Sales/Retail/Community Relations:** Kathi Beckman. **Manager, Sales:** Mike Liberatore. **Community Relations Coordinator:** Tim Vieira. **Ticket Operations Coordinator:** Hunter Haas. **Administrative Assistant/Receptionist:** Michelle Smith. **Stadium Operations Supervisor:** Leon Harrell. **Stadium Operations Supervisor:** Zac Phelps. **Senior Advisor:** Ken Carson. **Head Superintendent:** Patrick Skunda. **Assistant Superintedent:** Matt Johnson.

FIELD STAFF
Manager: Omar Malavé. **Hitting Coach:** Stubby Clapp. **Pitching Coach:** Darold Knowles. **Trainer:** Shawn McDermott.

GAME INFORMATION
Radio Announcer: Tyler Murray.
PA Announcer: Bill Christie. **Official Scorer:** Unavailable.
Stadium Name: Florida Auto Exchange Stadium. **Location:** From I-275, north on Highway 19, left on Sunset Point Rd for 4.5 miles, right on Douglas Ave; stadium is on right. **Standard Game Times:** 6:30 pm, Sun 5. **Ticket Price Range:** $7.
Visiting Club Hotel: La Quinta, 21338 US Highway 19 North, Clearwater, Fl. **Telephone:** (727) 799-1565.

FORT MYERS MIRACLE

Office Address: 14400 Six Mile Cypress Pkwy, Fort Myers, FL 33912.
Telephone: (239) 768-4210. **Fax:** (239) 768-4211.
E-Mail Address: miracle@miraclebaseball.com. **Website:** www.miraclebaseball.com.
Affiliation (first year): Minnesota Twins (1993). **Years in League:** 1926, 1978-87, 1991

OWNERSHIP/MANAGEMENT
Operated By: Greater Miami Baseball Club LP.
Principal Owner/Chairman: Marvin Goldklang. **Executive Adviser To Chairman:** Mike Veeck.
President: Steve Gliner. **Vice President/General Manager:** Andrew Seymour.
Senior Director, Corporate Sales/Marketing: Terry Simon. **Senior Director, Business Operations:** Suzanne Reaves. **Senior Director, Business Development:** John Kuhn. **Director, Food/Beverage:** Phillip Busch. **Manager, Broadcasting/Multimedia:** Brice Zimmerman. **Broadcasting/Multimedia Assistant:** Adam MacDonald. **Community Relations:** Ashley Adams. **Administrative Assistant/Operations:** Chris Thompson. **Head Groundskeeper:** Keith Blasingim. **Clubhouse Manager:** Brock Rasmussen.

FIELD STAFF
Manager: Doug Mientkiewicz. **Coach:** Jim Dwyer. **Pitching Coach:** Gary Lucas. **Trainer:** Alan Rail.

GAME INFORMATION
Radio Announcers: Brice Zimmerman, Adam MacDonald. **No. of Games Broadcast:** 140. **Flagship:** miraclebaseball.com.
PA Announcer: Jay Wyse. **Official Scorer:** Scott Pedersen.
Stadium Name: Hammond Stadium. **Location:** Exit 131 off I-75, west on Daniels Parkway, left on Six Mile Cypress Parkway. **Standard Game Times:** 7:05 pm, Sat 6:05; Sun 4:05. **Ticket Price Range:** $5-11.
Visiting Club Hotel: Fairfield Inn by Marriot, 7090 Cypress Terrace, Fort Myers, FL 33907. **Telephone:** (239) 437-5600.

JUPITER HAMMERHEADS

Office Address: 4751 Main St., Jupiter, FL 33458.
Telephone: (561) 775-1818. **Fax:** (561) 691-6886.
E-Mail Address: f.desk@rogerdeanstadium.com. **Website:** www.jupiterhammerheads.com.
Affiliation (first year): Miami Marlins (2002). **Years in League:** 1998-

OWNERSHIP/MANAGEMENT
Owned By: Miami Marlins. **Operated By:** Jupiter Stadium LTD.
General Manager, Jupiter Stadium LTD: Mike Bauer. **Executive Assistant:** Carol McAteer.
Assistant GM, Jupiter Stadium LTD/GM, Jupiter Hammerheads: Ryan Moore. **Assistant GM, Jupiter Stadium:** Alex Inman. **Director, Accounting:** John McCahan. **Corporate Partnerships Manager:** Ryan Moore. **Group Sales Manager:** Jason Cantone. **Marketing/Media Relations Manager:** Kristen Cummins. **Manager, Event Services:** Alex Inman. **Director, Grounds:** Jordan Treadway. **Assistant Directors, Grounds:** Matt Eggerman, Cory Wilder. **Stadium Building Manager:** Walter Herrera. **Merchandise Manager:** Linda Hanson. **Press Box:** Zac Vierra. **Office Manager:** Yolanda Rodriguez.

FIELD STAFF
Manager: Brian Schneider. **Coach:** Corey Hart. **Pitching Coach:** Joe Coleman.

GAME INFORMATION
PA Announcers: Dick Sanford, John Frost, Lou Palmer. **Official Scorer:** Brennan McDonald.
Stadium Name: Roger Dean Stadium. **Location:** I-95 to exit 83, east on Donald Ross Road for ¼ mile. **Standard Game Times:** 6:35 pm, Sun 1:05 or 5:05 p.m.. **Ticket Price Range:** $6.50-8.50.
Visiting Club Hotel: Fairfield Inn by Marriot, 6748 Indiantown Rd., Jupiter, FL 33458.

LAKELAND FLYING TIGERS

Office Address: 2125 N Lake Ave., Lakeland, FL 33805.
Telephone: (863) 686-8075. **Fax:** (863) 688-9589.
Website: www.lakelandflyingtigers.com.
Affiliation (first year): Detroit Tigers (1967). **Years in League:** 1919-26, 1953-55, 1960, 1962-64, 1967-.

OWNERSHIP/MANAGEMENT

Owned By: Detroit Tigers, Inc.
Principal Owner: Mike Ilitch. **President:** David Dombrowski. **Director, Florida Operations:** Ron Myers.
General Manager: Zach Burek. **Manager, Administration/Operations:** Shannon Follett. **Ticket Manager:** Ryan Eason. **Group Sales Manager:** Dan Lauer. **Receptionist:** Maria Walls.

FIELD STAFF

Manager: Dave Huppert. **Coach:** Larry Herndon. **Pitching Coach:** Mike Maroth. **Trainer:** TJ Obergefell. **Clubhouse Manager:** Bo Bianco.

GAME INFORMATION

PA Announcer: Unavailable . **Official Scorer:** Ed Luteran.
Stadium Name: Joker Marchant Stadium. **Location:** Exit 33 on I-4 to 33 South, 1.5 miles on left. **Standard Game Times:** 6:30, Fri 7:11, Sat 6, Sun 1. **Ticket Price Range:** $4-7.
Visiting Club Hotel: Imperial Swan Hotel & Suites, 4141 South Florida Ave., Lakeland, FL 33813. **Telephone:** (863) 647-3000.

PALM BEACH CARDINALS

Office Address: 4751 Main St., Jupiter, FL 33458.
Telephone: (561) 775-1818. **Fax:** (561) 691-6886.
E-Mail Address: f.desk@rogerdeanstadium.com. **Website:** www.palmbeachcardinals.com.
Affiliation (first year): St. Louis Cardinals (2003). **Years in League:** 2003-

OWNERSHIP/MANAGEMENT

Owned By: St. Louis Cardinals.
Operated By: Jupiter Stadium LTD. **General Manager, Jupiter Stadium LTD:** Mike Bauer. **Executive Assistant:** Carol McAteer.
Assistant GM, Jupiter Stadium LTD/GM, Palm Beach Cardinals: Alex Inman. **Assistant GM, Jupiter Stadium:** Ryan Moore. **Director, Accounting:** John McCahan. **Corporate Partnerships Manager:** Ryan Moore. **Group Sales Manager:** Jason Cantone. **Manager, Marketing/Media Relations:** Kristen Cummins. **Manager, Event Services:** Alex Inman. **Director, Grounds:** Jordan Treadway. **Assistant Directors, Grounds:** Matt Eggerman, Cory Wllder. **Stadium Building Manager:** Walter Herrera. **Merchandise Manager:** Linda Hanson. **Ticket Manager:** Jason Cantone. **Press Box:** Brian Newton. **Office Manager:** Yolanda Rodriguez.

FIELD STAFF

Manager: Dann Bilardello. **Hitting Coach:** Roger LaFrancois. **Pitching Coach:** Arthur "Ace" Adams. **Athletic Trainer:** Keith Joynt.

GAME INFORMATION

PA Announcers: John Frost, Dick Sanford, Lou Palmer. **Official Scorer:** Lou Villano.
Stadium Name: Roger Dean Stadium. **Location:** I-95 to exit 83, east on Donald Ross Road for ¼ mile. **Standard Game Times:** 6:30 pm; Sun 5. **Ticket Price Range:** $6.50-8.50.
Visiting Club Hotel: Fairfield Inn by Marriott, 6748 Indiantown Rd., Jupiter, FL 33458.

ST. LUCIE METS

Office Address: 525 NW Peacock Blvd., Port St Lucie, FL 34986.
Telephone: (772) 871-2100. **Fax:** (772) 878-9802.
Website: www.stluciemets.com
Affiliation (first year): New York Mets (1988). **Years in League:** 1988-

OWNERSHIP/MANAGEMENT

Operated by: Sterling Mets LP.
Chairman/CEO: Fred Wilpon. **President:** Saul Katz. **COO:** Jeff Wilpon.
Executive Director, Minor League Facilities: Paul Taglieri.
General Manager: Traer Van Allen. **Executive Assistant:** Cynthia Malaspino. **Staff Accountant:** Shannon Krause Manager. **Food/Beverage Operations:** Sheldon Dodson Manager. **Ticketing/Merchandise:** Stephen Fox Manager. **Group Sales/Community Relations:** Cassie Younce. **Assistant Manager, Corporate Partnerships:** Lauren Mahoney.

Assistant Manager, Ticketing/Merchandise: Kyle Gleockler. **Assistant Manager, Food/Beverage Operations:** John Gallagher.

FIELD STAFF

Manager: Ryan Ellis. **Hitting Coach:** Joel Fuentes. **Pitching Coach:** Phil Regan. **Trainer:** Matt Hunter. **Strength Coach:** Dane Inderrieden.

GAME INFORMATION

PA Announcer: Evan Nine. **Official Scorer:** Bob Adams.
Stadium Name: Tradition Field. **Location:** Exit 121 (St Lucie West Blvd) off I-95, east 1/2 mile, left on NW Peacock Blvd. **Standard Game Times:** 6:30 pm, Sun 1. **Ticket Price Range:** $5-8.50.
Visiting Club Hotel: SpringHill Suites, 2000 NW Courtyard Circle, Port St Lucie, FL 34986. **Telephone:** (772) 871-2929.

TAMPA YANKEES

Office Address: One Steinbrenner Drive, Tampa, FL 33614.
Telephone: (813) 875-7753. **Fax:** (813) 673-3174.
E-Mail Address: vsmith@yankees.com. **Website:** tybaseball.com.
Affiliation (first year): New York Yankees (1994). **Years in League:** 1919-27, 1957-1988, 1994-

OWNERSHIP/MANAGEMENT

Operated by: New York Yankees LP.
Principal Owner: Harold Steinbrenner.
General Manager: Vance Smith.
Assistant GM, Sales/Marketing: Matt Gess. **Community Relations Coordinator:** AmySue Manzione. **Ticket Operations:** Jennifer Magliocchetti. **Head Groundskeeper:** Ritchie Anderson.

FIELD STAFF

Manager: Al Pedrique. **Hitting Coach:** PJ Pilittere. **Pitching Coach:** Danny Borrell. **Coach:** JD Closser. **Trainer:** Michael Becker. **Strength/Conditioning:** Joe Siara.

GAME INFORMATION

PA Announcer: Unavailable. **Official Scorer:** Unavailable.
Stadium Name: George Steinbrenner Field. **Location:** I-275 to Dale Mabry Hwy, North on Dale Mabry Hwy (Facility is at corner of West Dr. Martin Luther King Blvd/Dale Mabry Hwy). **Standard Game Times:** 7 pm, Sat 6 pm, Sun 1 pm. **Ticket Price Range:** $4-6.

MIDWEST LEAGUE

Office Address: 1118 Cranston Rd., Beloit, WI 53511.
Mailing Address: PO Box 936, Beloit, WI 53512.
Telephone: (608) 364-1188. **Fax:** (608) 364-1913.
E-Mail Address: mwl@midwestleague.com. **Website:** www.midwestleague.com.

Years League Active: 1947-.
President/Treasurer: George H. Spelius.
Vice President/Legal Counsel/Secretary: Richard A. Nussbaum II. **Directors:** Andrew Berlin (South Bend), Stuart Katzoff (Bowling Green), Chuck Brockett (Burlington), Lew Chamberlin (West Michigan), Dennis Conerton (Beloit), Paul Davis (Clinton), Tom Dickson (Lansing), Jason Freier (Fort Wayne), David Heller (Quad Cities), Gary Keoppel (Cedar Rapids), Gary Mayse (Dayton), Brad Seymour (Lake County), Paul Barbeau (Great Lakes), Rocky Vonachen (Peoria), Mike Woleben (Kane County), Rob Zerjav (Wisconsin). **League Administrator:** Holly Voss.

Division Structure: East—Bowling Green, Dayton, Fort Wayne, Lake County, Lansing, South Bend, Great Lakes, West Michigan. West—Beloit, Burlington, Cedar Rapids, Clinton, Kane County, Peoria, Quad Cities, Wisconsin.

Regular Season: 140 games (split schedule). **2013 Opening Date:** April 3. **Closing Date:** Sept 1.

All-Star Game: June 17 at West Michigan.

Playoff Format: Eight teams qualify. First-half and second-half division winners and wild-card teams meet in best-of-three quarterfinal series. Winners meet in best-of-three series for division championships. Division champions meet in best-of-five final for league championship.

Roster Limit: 25 active. **Player Eligibility Rule:** No age limit. No more than two players and one player-coach on active list may have more than five years experience.

Brand of Baseball: Rawlings ROM-MID.

Umpires: Unavailable.

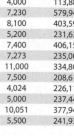

George Spelius

STADIUM INFORMATION

Club	Stadium	Opened	Dimensions LF	CF	RF	Capacity	2013 Att.
Beloit	Pohlman Field	1982	325	380	325	3,500	61,045
Bowling Green	Bowling Green Ballpark	2009	312	401	325	4,559	216,301
Burlington	Community Field	1947	338	403	318	3,200	62,932
Cedar Rapids	Veterans Memorial Stadium	2000	315	400	325	5,300	180,688
Clinton	Ashford University Field	1937	335	390	325	4,000	113,880
Dayton	Fifth Third Field	2000	338	402	338	7,230	579,946
Fort Wayne	Parkview Field	2009	336	400	318	8,100	403,596
Great Lakes	Dow Diamond	2007	332	400	325	5,200	231,639
Kane County	Fifth Third Bank Ballpark	1991	335	400	335	7,400	406,152
Lake County	Classic Park	2003	320	400	320	7,273	235,002
Lansing	Cooley Law School Stadium	1996	305	412	305	11,000	334,806
Peoria	Peoria Chiefs Stadium	2002	310	400	310	7,500	208,616
Quad Cities	Modern Woodmen Park	1931	343	400	318	4,024	226,112
South Bend	Coveleski Regional Stadium	1987	336	405	336	5,000	237,448
West Michigan	Fifth Third Ballpark	1994	317	402	327	10,051	377,948
Wisconsin	Fox Cities Stadium	1995	325	400	325	5,500	241,938

BELOIT SNAPPERS

Office Address: 2301 Skyline Drive, Beloit, WI 53511. **Mailing Address:** PO Box 855, Beloit, WI 53512.
Telephone: (608) 362-2272. **Fax:** (608) 362-0418.
E-Mail Address: snappy@snappersbaseball.com. **Website:** www.snappersbaseball.com.

Affiliation (first year): Oakland Athletics (2013). **Years in League:** 1982-

OWNERSHIP/MANAGEMENT

Operated by: Beloit Professional Baseball Association Inc. **Chairman:** Dennis Conerton. **President:** Dennis Conerton. **Corporate Sales/Promotions:** Bill Czaja. **Director, Media Relations/Marketing:** Robert Coon. **Director, Tickets:** Kelvin Long. **Director, Community Relations/Merchandise:** Natalie Tobey. **Head Groundskeeper:** Zach Ricketts.

FIELD STAFF

Manager: Rick Magnante. **Hitting Coach:** Lloyd Turner. **Pitching Coach:** Craig Lefferts. **Trainer:** Brian Thorson.

GAME INFORMATION

Radio Announcer: Corey Gloor. **No. of Games Broadcast:** 35. **Flagship Station:** 1380-AM ESPN.

PA Announcer: Unavailable. **Official Scorer:** Unavailable.
Stadium Name: Pohlman Field. **Location:** I-90 to exit 185-A, right at Cranston Road for 1 1/2 miles; I-43 to Wisconsin 81 to Cranston Road, right at Cranston for 1 ½ miles. **Standard Game Times:** 7 pm, 6:30 (April-May), Sun 2. **Ticket Price Range:** $7-9.
Visiting Club Hotel: Rodeway Inn, 2956 Milwaukee Rd, Beloit, WI 53511. **Telephone:** (608) 364-4000.

BOWLING GREEN HOT RODS

Office Address: Bowling Green Ballpark, 300 8th Ave., Bowling Green, KY 42101.
Telephone: (270) 901-2121. **Fax:** (270) 901-2165.
E-Mail Address: fun@bghotrods.com. **Website:** www.bghotrods.com.
Affiliation (first year): Tampa Bay Rays (2009). **Years in League:** 2010-

OWNERSHIP/MANAGEMENT

Operated By: Manhattan Sports Capital Acquisition.
President/Managing Partner: Stuart Katzoff. **Partner:** Jerry Katzoff.
General Manager/COO: Adam Nuse. **Senior Vice President, Operations:** Ken Clary. **Assistant GM:** Ben Hemmen. **Director, Sales:** Eric Leach. **Director, Creative Services:** Atlee McHeffey. **Director, Marketing/ Promotions:** Jennifer Johnson. **Broadcast/Media Relations Manager:** Unavailable. **Sports Turf Manager:** John Gides. **Box Office/Season Ticket Manager:** Matt Ingram. **Merchandise/Community Affairs Manager:** Michelle Gravert. **Group Sales Manager:** Don DiBastiani. **Account Executive:** Connor King.

FIELD STAFF

Manager: Michael Johns. **Hitting Coach:** Dan Dement. **Pitching Coach:** Bill Moloney.

GAME INFORMATION

Radio Announcer: Unavailable. **No. of Games Broadcast:** 140. **Flagship Station:** WBGN 1340-AM.
PA Announcer: Chris Kelly.
Stadium Name: Bowling Green Ballpark. **Location:** From I-65, take Exit 26 (KY-234/Cemetery Road) into Bowling Green for 3 miles, left onto College Street for .2 miles, right onto 8th Avenue. **Standard Game Times:** 7:05 pm, Sun 2:05. **Ticket Price Range:** $7-12.
Visiting Club Hotel: Unavailable.

BURLINGTON BEES

Office Address: 2712 Mt Pleasant St., Burlington, IA 52601. **Mailing Address:** PO Box 824, Burlington, IA 52601.
Telephone: (319) 754-5705. **Fax:** (319) 754-5882.
E-Mail Address: staff@gobees.com. **Website:** www.gobees.com.
Affiliation (first year): Los Angeles Angels (2013). **Years in League:** 1962-

OWNERSHIP/MANAGEMENT

Operated By: Burlington Baseball Association Inc.
President: Dave Walker. **General Manager:** Chuck Brockett. **Director, Group Outings:** Kim Brockett. **Director, Community Relations:** Nick Waterman. **Director, Tickets/Merchandising:** Jill Mason. **Media Relations:** Michael Broskowski. **Groundskeeper:** TJ Brewer.

FIELD STAFF

Manager: Bill Richardson. **Hitting Coach:** Nathan Haynes. **Pitching Coach:** Ethan Katz. **Trainer:** Chris Wells. **Strength/ Conditioning:** Adam Auer.

GAME INFORMATION

Radio Announcer: Michael Broskowski. **No. of Games Broadcast:** 140. **Flagship Station:** KBUR 1490-AM.
PA Announcer: Sean Cockrell . **Official Scorer:** Ted Gutman.
Stadium Name: Community Field. **Location:** From US 34, take US 61 North to Mt Pleasant Street, east 1/8 mile. **Standard Game Times:** 6:30 pm, Sun 2. **Ticket Price Range:** $4-8.
Visiting Club Hotel: Pzazz Best Western FunCity, 3001 Winegard Dr, Burlington, IA 52601. **Telephone:** (319) 753-2223.

CEDAR RAPIDS KERNELS

Office Address: 950 Rockford Road SW, Cedar Rapids, IA 52404. **Mailing Address:** PO Box 2001, Cedar Rapids, IA 52406.
Telephone: (319) 363-3887. **Fax:** (319) 363-5631.
E-Mail Address: kernels@kernels.com. **Website:** www.kernels.com.
Affiliation (first year): Minnesota Twins (2013). **Years in League:** 1962-

OWNERSHIP/MANAGEMENT

Operated by: Cedar Rapids Ball Club Inc.
President: Gary Keoppel. **General Manager:** Doug Nelson.
Assistant GM: Scott Wilson. **Sales:** Morgan Hawk. **IT/Communications Manager:** Andrew Pantini. **Sports Turf Manager:** Jesse Roeder. **Director, Ticket/Group Sales:** Andrea Brommelkamp. **Director, Finance:** Charlie Patrick. **Manager, Entertainment/Community Relations:** Ryne George. **Director, Corporate Sales/Marketing:** Jessica Fergesen. **Director, Food/Beverage:** Debra Maier. **Coordinator, History:** Marcia Moran. **Manager, Ticket Office:** Lauren Perry. **Manager, Stadium Operations:** Joe Krumm. **Receptionist:** Sue Stack.

FIELD STAFF

Manager: Jake Mauer. **Hitting Coach:** Tommy Watkins. **Pitching Coach:** Ivan Arteaga. **Trainer:** Curtis Simondet.

GAME INFORMATION

Radio Announcer: Morgan Hawk. **No. of Games Broadcast:** 140. **Flagship Station:** KMRY 1450-AM/93.1-FM.
PA Announcers: Bob Hoyt, Josh Paulson. **Official Scorers:** Steve Meyer, Josh Schroeder, Shane Severson.
Stadium Name: Veterans Memorial Stadium. **Location:** From I-380 North, take the Wilson Ave exit, turn left on Wilson Ave, after the railroad tracks, turn right on Rockford Road, proceed .8 miles, stadium is on left; From I-380 South, exit at First Avenue, proceed to Eighth Avenue (first stop sign) and turn left, stadium entrance is on right (before tennis courts).
Standard Game Times: 6:35 pm, Sun 2:05. **Ticket Price Range:** $7-11 in advance, $8-12 day of game.
Visiting Club Hotel: Best Western Cooper's Mill, 100 F Ave NW, Cedar Rapids, IA 52405. **Telephone:** (319) 366-5323.

CLINTON LUMBERKINGS

Office Address: Ashford University Field, 537 Ball Park Drive, Clinton, IA 52732.
Mailing Address: PO Box 1295, Clinton, IA 52733.
Telephone: (563) 242-0727. **Fax:** (563) 242-1433.
E-Mail Address: lumberkings@lumberkings.com. **Website:** www.lumberkings.com.
Affiliation (first year): Seattle Mariners (2009). **Years in League:** 1956-

OWNERSHIP/MANAGEMENT

Operated By: Clinton Baseball Club Inc.
President: Paul Davis.
General Manager: Ted Tornow. **Director, Broadcasting/Media Relations:** Chad Seely. **Director, Operations:** Jason Wright. **Director, Concessions:** Kathy Ward. **Manager, Stadium/Sportsturf:** Unavailable. **Accountant:** Ryan Marcum. **Assistant Director, Operations:** Morty Kriner. **Director, Facility Compliance:** Tom Whaley. **Office Procurement Manager:** Les Moore. **Clubhouse Manager:** Unavailable.

FIELD STAFF

Manager: Chris Prieto. **Coach:** Mike Kinkade. **Pitching Coach:** Cibney Bello. **Trainer:** Geoff Swanson. **Strength/Conditioning:** Taylor Nakamura.

GAME INFORMATION

Radio Announcer: Chad Seely. **No. of Games Broadcast:** 140. **Flagship Station:** Unavailable.
PA Announcer: Brad Seward. **Official Scorer:** Unavailable.
Stadium Name: Ashford University Field. **Location:** Highway 67 North to Sixth Ave. North, right on Sixth, cross railroad tracks, stadium on right. **Standard Game Times:** 6:30 pm, Sun 2. **Ticket Price Range:** $5-8.
Visiting Club Hotel: Oak Tree Inn, 2300 Valley W Ct., Clinton, IA 52732. **Telephone:** (563) 243-1000.

DAYTON DRAGONS

Office Address: Fifth Third Field, 220 N Patterson Blvd., Dayton, OH 45402. **Mailing Address:** PO 2107, Dayton, OH 45401.
Telephone: (937) 228-2287. **Fax:** (937) 228-2284.
E-Mail Address: dragons@daytondragons.com. **Website:** www.daytondragons.com.
Affiliation (first year): Cincinnati Reds (2000). **Years in League:** 2000-

OWNERSHIP/MANAGEMENT

Operated By: Dayton Professional Baseball Club LLC/Mandalay Baseball Properties LLC. **Owners:** Mandalay Baseball Properties LLC, Earvin "Magic" Johnson, Archie Griffin.
President: Robert Murphy.
Executive Vice President: Eric Deutsch. **Executive VP/General Manager:** Gary Mayse.
VP, Accounting/Finance: Mark Schlein. **VP, Corporate Partnerships:** Jeff Webb, Brad Eaton. **VP, Sponsor Services:** Brandy Guinaugh. **Director, Media Relations:** Tom Nichols. **Director, Group Sales:** Mike Vujea. **Director, Entertainment:** Kaitlin Rohrer. **Marketing Managers:** Lindsey Huerter, Nisha Jaga, Greg Lees, Jason McKendry, Amanda Spakes, Samantha Weaver. **Box Office Manager:** Stefanie Mitchell. **Corporate Marketing Managers:** Jose de la Vega, Evan Elkins, Trafton Eutsler, Travis Green, Matt Heithaus, Carl Hertzberg, Maurice Hillman, Viterio Jones, Jake Miller, Jacob Swartz. **Senior Operations Director:** Joe Eaglowski. **Facilities Operations Manager:** Joe Elking. **Baseball Operations Manager:** John Wallace. **Entertainment Assistant:** Chelsie Cooper. **Manager, Retail Operations:** Zack Spencer.

Assistant Manager, Retail Operations: Amber Mingus. **Office Manager/Executive Assistant to the President:** Leslie Stuck. **Staff Accountant:** Dorothy Day. **Administrative Secretary:** Barbara Van Schaik. **Sports Turf Manager:** Britt Barry. **Event Operations Manager:** Cody Oakes.

FIELD STAFF
Manager: Jose Miguel Nieves. **Coach:** Luis Bolivar. **Pitching Coach:** Tony Fossas. **Trainer:** Tyler Steele.

GAME INFORMATION
Radio Announcers: Tom Nichols. **No. of Games Broadcast:** 140. **Flagship Station:** WONE 980 AM. **Television Announcer:** Tom Nichols. **No. of Games Broadcast:** 25. **Flagship Station:** WHIO 7.2.
PA Announcer: Ben Oburn. **Official Scorers:** Matt Lindsay, Mike Lucas, Matt Zircher.
Stadium Name: Fifth Third Field. **Location:** I-75 South to downtown Dayton, left at First St.; I-75 North, right at First St. exit. **Ticket Price Range:** $7-$15.
Visiting Club Hotel: Courtyard by Marriott, 100 Prestige Place, Miamisburg, OH 45342. **Telephone:** (937) 433-3131.

FORT WAYNE TINCAPS

Office Address: 1301 Ewing Street, Fort Wayne, IN 46802.
Telephone: (260) 482-6400. **Fax:** (260) 471-4678.
E-Mail Address: info@tincaps.com. **Website:** www.tincaps.com.
Affiliation (first year): San Diego Padres (1999). **Years in League:** 1993-

OWNERSHIP/MANAGEMENT
Operated By: Hardball Capital.
Owner: Jason Freier.
President/General Manager: Mike Nutter. **Vice President, Sales/Finance:** Brian Schackow. **VP, Corporate Partnerships:** David Lorenz. **VP, Marketing/Promotions:** Michael Limmer. **Director, Group Sales:** Brad Shank. **Assistant Director, Group Sales:** Jared Parcell. **Director, Ticketing:** Pat Ventura. **Assistant Director, Ticketing/Reading Program Director:** Paige Salway. **Director, Food/Beverage:** Bill Lehn. **Culinary Director:** Scott Kammerer. **Catering Director:** Brandon Tinkle. **Manager, Food/Beverage Operations:** Dan Krleski. **Coordinators, Special Events:** Holly Raney, Jen Walters.
Director, Facilities: Tim Burkhart. **Assistant Director, Maintenance:** Donald Miller. **Head Groundskeeper:** Keith Winter. **Assistant Groundskeeper:** Andrew Burnette. **Creative Director:** Tony DesPlaines. **Video Production Manager:** Melissa Darby. **Managers, Ticket Sales:** Tyler Baker, Brent Harring, Austin Allen, Justin Shurley, Erik Lose. **Manager, Corporate Partnerships:** Tom Baxter. **Director, Broadcasting/Media Relations:** Mike Couzens. **Office Manager:** Cathy Tinney. **Manager, Merchandise:** Karen Schieber. **Assistant Director, Marketing/Community Relations:** Abby Naas.

FIELD STAFF
Manager: Michael Collins. **Hitting Coach:** Morgan Burkhart. **Pitching Coach:** Burt Hooton. **Trainer:** Ricky Huerta. **Strength/Conditioning Coach:** Dan Byrne.

GAME INFORMATION
Radio Announcers: Mike Couzens, Mike Maahs, John Nolan. **No. of Games Broadcast:** 140. **Flagship Station:** WKJG 1380-AM.
PA Announcers: Jared Parcell, Jim Shovlin. **Official Scorers:** Rich Tavierne, Bill Salyer, Bill Scott, Chris Bauman.
Stadium Name: Parkview Field. **Location:** Downtown Fort Wayne off of Jefferson Blvd. **Ticket Price Range:** $5-12.50.
Visiting Club Hotel: Downtown Courtyard by Marriott, 1150 S Harrison St., Fort Wayne, IN 46802. **Telephone:** (260) 490-3629.

GREAT LAKES LOONS

Office Address: 825 East Main St, Midland, MI 48640.
Telephone: (989) 837-2255. **Fax:** (989) 837-8780.
E-Mail Address: info@loons.com. **Website:** www.loons.com.
Affiliation (first year): Los Angeles Dodgers (2007). **Years in League:** 2007-

OWNERSHIP/MANAGEMENT
Operated By: Michigan Baseball Operations. **Stadium Ownership:** Michigan Baseball Foundation.
Founder/Foundation President: William Stavropoulos.
President: Paul Barbeau.
Vice President/General Manager: Scott Litle. **VP, Facilities/Operations:** Matt McQuaid. **VP, Finance:** Jana Chotivkova. **VP Marketing/Entertainment:** Chris Mundhenk. **General Manager, Dow Diamond Events:** Dave Gomola. **Assistant GM, Corporate Partnerships/Director, Development:** Emily Schafer. **Assistant GM, Event Operations:** Ann Craig. **Production Coordinator:** Trent Elliott. **Assistant GM, Ticket Sales:** Tiffany Seward. **Director, Accounting:** Jamie Start. **Assistant GM, Food/Beverage:** Jenny Smart. **Director, Group Sales:** Tara Bergeron. **Programming:** Jared Sandler. **Director, Ticket Sales:** Kevin Schunk. **Assistant to MBF President:** Marge Parker. **Accounting Manager:** Kathleen Cifuentes. **Communications Director:** Bruce Gunther.
Business Development Manager: Tim Jacques. **Concessions Manager:** James Reed. **Corporate Partnerships Manager:** Eric Ramseyer. **Group Sales Coordinators:** Nick Knieling, James Cahilellis. **Retail Manager:** Jenean Clarkson.

Promotions Manager: Amber Ferris. **Stadium Operations Manager:** Dan Straley. **Catering Coordinator:** Amanda Colmus. **Executive Chef:** Andrea Noonan. **Head Groundskeeper:** Nick Wolcott. **Administrative Assistant:** Melissa Kehoe.

FIELD STAFF

Manager: Bill Haselman. **Hitting Coach:** Johnny Washington. **Pitching Coach:** Bill Simas.

GAME INFORMATION

Play-by-Play Broadcaster: Brad Golder. **No. of Games Broadcast:** 140. **Flagship Station:** WLUN-FM 100.9.
PA Announcer: Jerry O'Donnell. **Official Scorers:** Terry Wilczek, Larry Loiselle
Stadium Name: Dow Diamond. **Location:** I-75 to US-10 W, Take the M-20/US-10 Business exit on the left toward downtown Midland, Merge onto US-10 W/MI-20 W (also known as Indian St.), turn left onto State St., The entrance to the stadium is at the intersection of Ellsworth and State St. **Standard Game Times:** 6:05 pm (April), 7:05 (May-Sept), Sun 2:05. **Ticket Price Range:** $6-9.
Visiting Club Hotel: Holiday Inn, 810 Cinema Dr, Midland, MI 48642. **Telephone:** (989) 794-8500.

KANE COUNTY COUGARS

Office Address: 34W002 Cherry Lane, Geneva, IL 60134
Telephone: (630) 232-8811. **Fax:** (630) 232-8815.
E-Mail Address: info@kanecountycougars.com. **Website:** www.kccougars.com.
Affiliation (first year): Chicago Cubs (2013). **Years in League:** 1991-

OWNERSHIP/MANAGEMENT

Operated By: Cougars Baseball Partnership/American Sports Enterprises, Inc.
Managing Partners: Mike Woleben, Mike Murtaugh. **Vice President/General Manager:** Curtis Haug. **Senior Director, Finance/Administration:** Douglas Czurylo. **Finance/Accounting Manager:** Lance Buhmann. **Senior Director, Ticketing:** R. Michael Patterson. **Senior Ticket Sales Representative:** Alex Miller. **Sales Representatives:** Joe Golota, Derek Weber, Sean Freed. **Director, Ticket Services/Community Relations:** Amy Mason. **Senior Ticket Operations Representative:** Paul Quillia. **Ticket Operations Representative:** Jack Luse. **Director, Security:** Dan Klinkhamer. **Director, Promotions:** Jenni Brechtel. **Promotions Assistant:** Derek Harrigan. **Director, Public Relations:** Shawn Touney. **Design/Graphics:** Emmet Broderick. **Media Placement Coordinator:** Bill Baker. **Webmaster:** Kevin Sullivan. **Director, Food/Beverage:** Geoff Wentzel. **Director, Catering:** Jon Williams. **Business Manager:** Robin Hull. **Concessions Manager:** Dan McIntosh. **Catering Manager:** Trevor Parnell. **Kitchen Manager:** Kristan Arnold. **Senior Director, Stadium Operations:** Mike Klafehn. **Head Groundskeeper:** Jake Hannes. **Stadium Maintenance Supervisor:** Jeff Snyder.

FIELD STAFF

Manager: Mark Johnson. **Hitting Coach:** Tom Beyers. **Pitching Coach:** Dave Rosario. **Trainer:** Jonathan Fiero.

GAME INFORMATION

Radio Announcer: Wayne Randazzo. **No. of Games Broadcast:** 140. **Flagship Station:** WBIG 1280-AM.
PA Announcer: Kevin Sullivan. **Official Scorer:** Wayne Randazzo.
Stadium Name: Fifth Third Bank Ballpark. **Location:** From east or west, I-88 Ronald Reagan Memorial Tollway) to Farnsworth Ave. North exit, north five miles to Cherry Lane, left into stadium; from northwest, I-90 (Jane Addams Memorial Tollway) to Randall Rd. South exit, south to Fabyan Parkway, east to Kirk Rd., north to Cherry Lane, left into stadium complex. **Standard Game Times:** 6:30 pm, Sundays 1. **Ticket Price Range:** $9-15.
Visiting Club Hotel: Pheasant Run Resort, 4051 E Main St., St. Charles, IL 60174. Telephone: (630) 584-6300.

LAKE COUNTY CAPTAINS

Office Address: Classic Park, 35300 Vine St., Eastlake, OH 44095-3142.
Telephone: (440) 975-8085. **Fax:** (440) 975-8958.
E-Mail Address: bseymour@captainsbaseball.com. **Website:** www.captainsbaseball.com.
Affiliation (first year): Cleveland Indians (2003). **Years in League:** 2010-

OWNERSHIP/MANAGEMENT

Operated By: Cascia LLC. **Owners:** Peter and Rita Carfagna, Ray and Katie Murphy.
Chairman/Secretary/Treasurer: Peter Carfagna. **Vice Chairman:** Rita Carfagna. **Vice President:** Ray Murphy. **VP, General Manager:** Brad Seymour. **Assistant GM, Sales:** Neil Stein. **Director, Media Relations:** Craig Deas. **Manager, Promotions:** Drew LaFollette. **Director, Captains Concessions:** John Klein. **Director, Stadium Operations:** Josh Porter. **Director, Turf Operations:** Dan Stricko. **Director, Finance:** Rob Demko. **Director, Ticket Operations/Merchandise:** Jen Yorko. **Director, Ticket Sales:** Amy Gladieux. **Director, Community Relations:** Andrew Grover. **Ticket Sales Account Executives:** Christy Buchar, Nick Dobrinich, Brian Fisher. **Office Assistant:** Jim Carfagna.

FIELD STAFF

Manager: Mark Budzinski. **Coach:** Shaun Larkin. **Pitching Coach:** Rigo Beltran.

GAME INFORMATION

Radio Announcer: Craig Deas. **No. of Games Broadcast:** 140. **Flagship Station:** WELW 1330-AM.
PA Announcer: Ray Milavec. **Official Scorers:** Glen Blabolil, Mike Mohner.
Stadium Name: Classic Park. **Location:** From Ohio State Route 2 East, exit at Ohio 91, go left and the stadium is 1/4 mile north on your right; From Ohio State Route 90 East, exit at Ohio 91, go right and the stadium in approximately five miles north on your right. **Standard Game Times:** 6:30 pm (April-May), 7 (May-Sept), Sat 1 (April-May), 7 (May-Sept), Sun 1;30.
Visiting Club Hotel: Holiday Inn, 7701 Reynolds Road, Mentor, OH 44060. **Telephone:** (440) 951-7333.

LANSING LUGNUTS

Office Address: 505 E Michigan Ave., Lansing, MI 48912.
Telephone: (517) 485-4500. **Fax:** (517) 485-4518.
E-Mail Address: info@lansinglugnuts.com. **Website:** www.lansinglugnuts.com.
Affiliation (first year): Toronto Blue Jays (2005). **Years in League:** 1996-

OWNERSHIP/MANAGEMENT

Operated By: Take Me Out to the Ballgame LLC.
Principal Owners: Tom Dickson, Sherrie Myers.
General Manager: Nick Grueser. **Assistant GM:** Nick Brzezinski. **Community Relations Manager:** Angela Sees. **Director, Business Operations:** Heather Viele. **Business Coordinator:** Brianna Pfeil. **Corporate Sales Manager:** Kohl Tyrrell. **Corporate Account Executive:** Bill Adler. **Senior Senior Group Sales Representative:** Faith Brooks. **Group Sales Representative:** Adam Paschen. **Sales Assistant:** Clifford Sims. **Box Office/Team Relations Manager:** Josh Calver.
Season Ticket Specialist: Greg Kruger. **Retail Manager:** Matt Hicks. **Stadium Operations Manager:** Dennis Busse. **Stadium Operations Assistant:** Vince Giancana. **Head Groundskeeper:** Mike Kacsor. **Senior Food/Beverage Director:** Brett Telder. **Concessions Manager:** Andrew Creswell. **Director, Marketing:** Jeremy Smoker. **Marketing Assistant:** Ben Owen. **Corporate Partnerships Manager:** Michaela Vryhof. **Corporate Partnerships Representative:** Ashley Moore.

FIELD STAFF

Manager: John Tamargo Jr. **Hitting Coach:** Ken Huckaby. **Pitching Coach:** Vince Horsman. **Athletic Trainer:** Drew Macdonald.

GAME INFORMATION

Radio Announcer: Jesse Goldberg-Strassler. **No of Games Broadcast:** 140. **Flagship Station:** WQTX 92.1-FM.
PA Announcer: Unavailable. **Official Scorer:** Unavailable.
Stadium Name: Cooley Law School Stadium. **Location:** I-96 East/West to US 496, exit at Larch Street, north of Larch, stadium on left. **Ticket Price Range:** $8-$23.50 Visiting Club.
Visiting Club Hotel: Crowne Plaza Hotel, 925 S Creyts Rd, Lansing Charter Township, MI 48917. **Telephone:** (877) 227-6963.

PEORIA CHIEFS

Office Address: 730 SW Jefferson, Peoria, IL 61605.
Telephone: (309) 680-4000. **Fax:** (309) 680-4080.
E-Mail Address: feedback@chiefsnet.com. **Website:** www.peoriachiefs.com.
Affiliation (first year): St. Louis Cardinals (2013). **Years in League:** 1983-

OWNERSHIP/MANAGEMENT

Operated By: Peoria Chiefs Community Baseball Club LLC.
President: Rocky Vonachen. **Manager, Box Office:** Ryan Sivori. **Director, Media/Baseball Operations:** Nathan Baliva. **Director, Corporate Partnerships:** Brendan Kelly. **Manager, Corporate Partnerships:** Kevin McClelland. **Merchandise Manager:** Paige Peugh. **Manager, Entertainment/Community Relations:** Katie Nichols. **Marketing Manager:** Hannah Wolfe. **Ticket Sales Manager:** Mike Schulte. **Merchandise Manager:** Paige Peugh. **Account Executives:** Paul Adelman, Lauren Kenney, Mike Schulte. **Head Groundskeeper:** Mike Reno. **Director, Food/Beverage:** Pat Delaney.

FIELD STAFF

Manager: Joe Kruzel. **Hitting Coach:** Jobel Jimenez. **Pitching Coach:** Jason Simontacchi. **Trainer:** Michael Petrarca.

GAME INFORMATION

Radio Announcer: Nathan Baliva. **No. of Games Broadcast:** 140. **Flagship Station:** www.peoriachiefs.com, Peoria Chiefs App in iTunes.
PA Announcer: Unavailable. **Official Scorers:** Bryan Moore, Nathan Baliva.
Stadium Name: Dozer Park. **Location:** From South/East, I-74 to exit 93 (Jefferson St.), continue one mile, stadium is one block on left; From North/West, I-74 to Glen Oak Exit, turn right on Glendale, which turns into Kumpf Blvd., turn right on Jefferson, stadium on left. **Standard Game Times:** 7 pm, 6:30 (April-May, after Aug 18), Sat 6:30, Sun 2. **Ticket Price Range:** $7-11.
Visiting Club Hotel: Quality Inn & Suites, 4112 Brandywine Dr, Peoria, IL, 61614. **Telephone:** (309) 685-2556.

QUAD CITIES RIVER BANDITS

Office Address: 209 S Gaines St., Davenport, IA 52802.
Telephone: (563) 324-3000. **Fax:** (563) 324-3109.
E-Mail Address: bandit@riverbandits.com. **Website:** www.riverbandits.com.
Affiliation (first year): Houston Astros (2013). **Years in League:** 1960-

OWNERSHIP/MANAGEMENT

Operated by: Main Street Iowa LLC; David Heller, Bob Herrfeldt.
General Manager: Andrew Chesser. **VP, Sales:** Shawn Brown. **Assistant GM, Baseball Operations:** Travis Painter. **Assistant GM, Special Events:** Taylor Satterly. **Finance Manager:** Dustin Miller. **Director, Community Relations:** Brittany Carter. **Director, Media Relations:** Marco LaNave. **Director, Stadium Operations:** Elliott Sweitzer. **Director, Ticket Operations:** Andrea Williams. **Manager, Production:** Stacy Issen. **Manager, Special Events:** Alli Costello. **Account Executives:** Amanda Henzen, Paul Kleinhans-Schulz. **Director, Food/Beverage:** Patrick Glackin. **Director, Concessions:** Peter Neubert. **Chef:** Teresa Willis.

FIELD STAFF

Manager: Omar Lopez. **Hitting Coach:** Joel Chimelis. **Pitching Coach:** Dave Borkowski. **Athletic Trainer:** Michael Rendon. **Strength/Conditioning Coach:** James McNichol. **Development Specialist:** Vince Coleman.

GAME INFORMATION

Radio Announcer: Marco LaNave. **No. of Games Broadcast:** 140. **Flagship Station:** www.riverbandits.com.
PA Announcer: Scott Werling. **Official Scorer:** Unavailable.
Stadium Name: Modern Woodmen Park. **Location:** From I-74, take Grant St. exit left, west onto River Dr., left on South Gaines St. from I-80, take Brady Street exit south, right on River Dr., left on South Gaines St. **Standard Game Times:** 7 pm; Sat 6 pm; Sun 1:15 pm (April-June 15, after Aug. 10), 5 pm (June 22-Aug. 10). **Ticket Price Range:** $5-13.
Visiting Club Hotel: Clarion Hotel, 5202 Brady St., Davenport, IA 52806. **Telephone:** (563) 391-1230.

SOUTH BEND
SILVER HAWKS

Office Address: 501 W South St., South Bend, IN 46601. **Mailing Address:** PO Box 4218, South Bend, IN 46634.
Telephone: (574) 235-9988. **Fax:** (574) 235-9950.
E-Mail Address: hawks@silverhawks.com. **Website:** www.silverhawks.com.
Affiliation (first year): Arizona Diamondbacks (1997). **Years in League:** 1988-.

OWNERSHIP/MANAGEMENT

Owner: Andrew Berlin.
President: Joe Hart.
Assistant General Manager, Tickets: Andy Beuster. **Vice President/Business Development:** Nick Brown. **Assistant GM, Operations:** Peter Argueta. **Director, Finance/Human Resources:** Cheryl Carlson. **Box Office Manager:** Devon Hastings. **Director, Marketing/Promotions:** Kelly Knutson. **Account Executives:** Mike Frissore, Dave Webster, Mitch McKamey, Alex Withorn. **Director, Production:** Chris Hagstrom. **Director, Food/Beverage:** Nick Barkley. **Head Groundskeeper:** TJ Wohlever.

FIELD STAFF

Manager: Mark Haley. **Hitting Coach:** Jason Camilli. **Pitching Coach:** Doug Bochtler. **Trainer:** Rafael Freitas. **Strength Coach:** Skyler Zarndt.

GAME INFORMATION

Radio Announcer: Unavailable. **Flagship Station:** www.silverhawks.com.
PA Announcer: Unavailable. **Official Scorer:** Unavailable.
Stadium Name: Four Winds Field. **Location:** I-80/90 toll road to exit 77, take US 31/33 south to South Bend to downtown (Main Street), to Western Ave. right on Western, left on Taylor. **Standard Game Times:** 7:05 pm; Fri 7:35, Sun 2:05. **Ticket Price Range:** $9-11.
Visiting Club Hotel: DoubleTree by Hilton Hotel South Bend. **Telephone:** (574) 234-2000.

WEST MICHIGAN WHITECAPS

Office Address: 4500 West River Drive, Comstock Park, MI 49321. **Mailing Address:** PO Box 428, Comstock Park, MI 49321.
Telephone: (616) 784-4131. **Fax:** (616) 784-4911.
E-Mail Address: playball@whitecapsbaseball.com. **Website:** www.whitecapsbaseball.com.
Affiliation (first year): Detroit Tigers (1997). **Years in League:** 1994-

OWNERSHIP/MANAGEMENT

Operated By: Whitecaps Professional Baseball Corp. **Principal Owners:** Denny Baxter, Lew Chamberlin. **President:** Scott Lane. **Vice President:** Jim Jarecki. **VP, Sales:** Steve McCarthy. **Facility Events Manager:** Mike Klint. **Operations Manager:** Tyler Edema. **Director, Food/Beverage:** Matt Timon. **Community Relations Coordinator:** Jessica Muzevuca. **Director, Marketing/Media:** Mickey Graham. **Promotions Manager:** Keith Roelfsema. **Multimedia Manager:** Elaine Cunningham. **Box Office Manager:** Shaun Pynnonen. **Groundskeeper:** Michael Huie. **Facility Maintenance Manager:** John Passarelli. **Director, Ticket Sales:** Chad Sayen.

FIELD STAFF

Manager: Andrew Graham. **Coach:** Nelson Santovenia. **Pitching Coach:** Mike Henneman. **Trainer:** TJ Obergefell.

GAME INFORMATION

Radio Announcers: Ben Chiswick, Dan Elve. **No. of Games Broadcast:** 140. **Flagship Station:** WBBL 107.3-FM. **PA Announcers:** Mike Newell, Bob Wells. **Official Scorers:** Mike Dean, Don Thomas. **Stadium Name:** Fifth Third Ballpark. **Location:** US 131 North from Grand Rapids to exit 91 (West River Drive). **Ticket Price Range:** $6-14. **Visiting Club Hotel:** Holiday Inn Express-GR North, 358 River Ridge Dr NW, Walker, MI 49544. **Telephone:** (616) 647-4100.

WISCONSIN TIMBER RATTLERS

Office Address: 2400 N Casaloma Drive, Appleton, WI 54913. **Mailing Address:** PO Box 7464, Appleton, WI 54912.
Telephone: (920) 733-4152. **Fax:** (920) 733-8032.
E-Mail Address: info@timberrattlers.com. **Website:** www.timberrattlers.com.
Affiliation (first year): Milwaukee Brewers (2009). **Years in League:** 1962-

OWNERSHIP/MANAGEMENT

Operated By: Appleton Baseball Club, Inc.
Chairman: Doug Westemeier.
President/General Manager: Rob Zerjav.
Vice President/Assistant GM: Aaron Hahn. **Controller:** Cathy Spanbauer. **Director, Food/Beverage:** Ryan Grossman. **Director, Stadium Operations/Security:** Ron Kaiser. **Director, Community Relations:** Dayna Baitinger. **Director, Media Relations:** Chris Mehring. **Corporate Partnerships:** Ryan Cunniff, Jerrad Radocay. **Director, Merchandise:** Jay Grusznski. **Director, Tickets:** Ryan Moede. **Banquet Facilities Manager:** Jenny Smith. **Executive Chef:** Tim Hansen. **Assistant, Food/Beverage Director:** Chumley Hodgson. **Assistant Stadium Operations Manager:** Aaron Johnson. **Director, Group Sales:** Seth Merrill. **Group Sales:** Brittany Ezre, Rebecca Sievers. **Creative Director:** Ann Mollica. **Marketing Coordinator:** Hilary Dauer. **Entertainment Coordinator:** Kevin Ross. **Production Manager:** Scot Frassetto. **Clubhouse Manager:** Travis Voss. **Office Manager:** Mary Robinson. **Groundskeeper:** Eddie Warczak.

FIELD STAFF

Manager: Matt Erickson. **Coaches:** Ken Dominguez, Chuckie Caufield. **Pitching Coach:** Elvin Nina. **Trainer:** Jeff Paxson.

GAME INFORMATION

Radio Announcer: Chris Mehring. **No. of Games Broadcast:** 140. **Flagship Station:** WNAM 1280-AM. **Television Announcers:** Bob Brainerd, John Maino, Ted Stefaniak, Brad Woodall. **Television Affiliates:** Time Warner Cable SportsChannel, WACY-TV. **No. of Games Broadcast:** 40. **PA Announcer:** Joey D. **Official Scorer:** Jay Grusznski. **Stadium Name:** Neuroscience Group Field at Fox Cities Stadium. **Location:** Highway 41 to Highway 15 (00) exit, west to Casaloma Dr., left to stadium. **Standard Game Times:** 7:05 pm, 6:35 (April-May), Sat 6:35, Sun 1:05. **Ticket Price Range:** $6-25. **Visiting Club Hotel:** Microtel Inn & Suites, 321 Metro Dr, Appleton, WI 54913. **Telephone:** (920) 997-3121.

SOUTH ATLANTIC LEAGUE

Office Address: 13575 58th Street North, Suite 141, Clearwater, FL 33760-3721.
Telephone: (727) 538-4270. **Fax:** (727) 499-6853.
E-Mail Address: office@saloffice.com. **Website:** www.southatlanticleague.com.
Years League Active: 1904-1964, 1979-.
President/Secretary/Treasurer: Eric Krupa.
First Vice President: Chip Moore (Rome). **Second VP:** Craig Brown (Greenville).
Directors: Don Beaver (Hickory), Cooper Brantley (Greensboro), Craig Brown (Greenville), Brian DeWine (Asheville), Joseph Finley (Lakewood), Jason Freier (Savannah), Marvin Goldklang (Charleston), Chip Moore (Rome), Bruce Quinn (Hagerstown), Brad Smith (Kannapolis), Bill Shea (Lexington), Jeff Eiseman (Augusta), Tom Volpe (Delmarva), Tim Wilcox (West Virginia).
Division Structure: North—Delmarva, Greensboro, Hagerstown, Hickory, Kannapolis, Lakewood, West Virginia. South—Asheville, Augusta, Charleston, Greenville, Lexington, Rome, Savannah.
Regular Season: 140 games (split schedule). **2014 Opening Date:** April 3. **Closing Date:** Sept 1.

Eric Krupa

All-Star Game: June 17 at Hickory.
Playoff Format: First-half and second-half division winners meet in best-of-three semifinal series. Winners meet in best-of-five series for league championship.
Roster Limit: 25 active. **Player Eligibility Rule:** No age limit. No more than two players and one player-coach on active list may have more than five years of experience.
Brand of Baseball: Rawlings.
Umpires: Jordan Albarado (Scott, LA), David Arrieta (Maracaibo, Venezuela), Erich Bacchus (Germantown, MD), Adam Beck (Winter Springs, FL), Jonathan Felczak (Bonney Lake, WA), Tyler Ferguson (Stayton, OR), Andrew Freed (Cary, NC), Derek Gonzalez (Orem, UT), Jeffrey Gorman (Hayward, CA), Richard Grassa (Lindenhurst, NY), Ben Levin (Cincinnati, OH), Brennan Miller (Fairfax Station, VA), Michael Provine (Newtown, PA), Skyler Shown (Owensboro, KY).

STADIUM INFORMATION

| Club | Stadium | Opened | Dimensions | | | Capacity | 2013 Att. |
			LF	CF	RF		
Asheville	McCormick Field	1992	326	373	297	4,000	163,664
Augusta	Lake Olmstead Stadium	1995	330	400	330	4,322	176,762
Charleston	Joseph P. Riley Jr. Ballpark	1997	306	386	336	5,800	283,274
Delmarva	Arthur W. Perdue Stadium	1996	309	402	309	5,200	206,772
Greensboro	NewBridge Bank Park	2005	322	400	320	7,599	362,274
Greenville	Fluor Field	2006	310	400	302	5,000	300,402
Hagerstown	Municipal Stadium	1931	335	400	330	4,600	65,606
Hickory	I.P. Frans Stadium	1993	330	401	330	5,062	143,157
Kannapolis	CMC-NorthEast Stadium	1995	330	400	310	4,700	125,811
Lakewood	FirstEnergy Park	2001	325	400	325	6,588	400,299
Lexington	Whitaker Bank Ballpark	2001	320	401	318	6,033	274,805
Rome	State Mutual Stadium	2003	335	400	330	5,100	168,026
Savannah	Historic Grayson Stadium	1941	290	410	310	8,000	131,763
West Virginia	Appalachian Power Park	2005	330	400	320	4,300	149,198

ASHEVILLE TOURISTS

Office Address: McCormick Field, 30 Buchanan Place, Asheville, NC 28801.
Telephone: (828) 258-0428. **Fax:** (828) 258-0320.
E-Mail Address: info@theashevilletourists.com. **Website:** www.theashevilletourists.com.
Affiliation (first year): Colorado Rockies (1994). **Years in League:** 1976-

OWNERSHIP/MANAGEMENT

Operated By: DeWine Seeds Silver Dollar Baseball, LLC.
President: Brian DeWine.
General Manager: Larry Hawkins.
Senior Sales Executive: Chris Smith. **Box Office Manager:** Neil Teitelbaum. **Business Manager:** Ryan Straney. **Promotions/Merchandise Manager:** Jon Clemmons. **Community Relations Manager:** Michelle Buss. **Media Relations/Broadcasting Manager:** Doug Maurer. **Group Sales Associates:** Chris Zolli, Dave McKurth. **Outside Sales Associate:** Bob Jones. **Stadium Operations Director:** Patrick Spence. **Senior Director of Food/Beverage:** Craig Phillips (Pro Sports Catering). **Publications/Website:** Bill Ballew.

FIELD STAFF

Manager: Fred Ocasio. **Hitting Coach:** Mike Devereaux. **Pitching Coach:** Unavailable. **Development Supervisor:** Marv Foley.

GAME INFORMATION

Radio Announcer: Doug Maurer. **No. of Games Broadcast:** 140. **Flagship Station:** WRES 100.7-FM.
PA Announcer: Rick Rice. **Official Scorer:** Jim Baker, Larry Pope
Stadium Name: McCormick Field. **Location:** I-240 to Charlotte St. South exit, south one mile on Charlotte, left on McCormick Place. **Ticket Price Range:** $6-11.
Visiting Club Hotel: Quality Inn, 1 Skyline Drive, Arden, NC 28704. **Telephone:** (828) 684-6688.

AUGUSTA GREENJACKETS

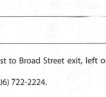

Office Address: 78 Milledge Rd., Augusta, GA 30904. **Mailing Address:** PO Box 3746 Hill Station, Augusta, GA 30914.
Telephone: (706) 736-7889. **Fax:** (706) 736-1122.
E-Mail Address: info@greenjacketsbaseball.com. **Website:** www.greenjacketsbaseball.com.
Affiliation (first year): San Francisco Giants (2005). **Years in League:** 1988-

OWNERSHIP/MANAGEMENT

Ownership Group: AGON Sports & Entertainment.
Owner: Chris Schoen **President:** Jeff Eiseman. **General Manager:** Tom Denlinger. **Assistant GM:** Brian Marshall.
Director, Ticket Sales: Mike Van Hise. **Accounting:** Debbie Brown. **Corporate Sales Executive:** Dan Szatkowski.
Stadium Operations Manager: Kyle Titus. **Marketing Manager:** Lindsey McGuire. **Account Executives:** Keaton Kovacs, Anthony Laurendi, Cam Caddell. **Operations Coordinator:** David Onusko.

FIELD STAFF

Manager: Mike Goff. **Coaches:** Hector Borg, Todd Linden. **Pitching Coach:** Steve Kline.

GAME INFORMATION

PA Announcer: Unavailable.
Stadium Name: Lake Olmstead Stadium. **Location:** I-20 to Washington Road exit, east to Broad Street exit, left on Milledge Road. **Standard Game Times:** 7 pm; Sun 2 pm. **Ticket Price Range:** $7-15.
Visiting Club Hotel: Quality Inn, 1455 Walton Way, Augusta, GA 30901. **Telephone:** (706) 722-2224.

CHARLESTON RIVERDOGS

RIVERDOGS

Office Address: 360 Fishburne St., Charleston, SC 29403. **Mailing Address:** PO Box 20849, Charleston, SC 29413.
Telephone: (843) 723-7241. **Fax:** (843) 723-2641.
E-Mail Address: admin@riverdogs.com. **Website:** www.riverdogs.com.
Affiliation (first year): New York Yankees (2005). **Years in League:** 1973-78, 1980-

OWNERSHIP/MANAGEMENT

Operated by: The Goldklang Group/South Carolina Baseball Club LP.
Chairman: Marv Goldklang. **President:** Mike Veeck. **Director of Fun:** Bill Murray. **Co-Owners:** Peter Freund, Dr. Gene Budig, Al Phillips.
Executive Vice President/General Manager: Dave Echols. **VP, Corporate Sales:** Andy Lange. **VP, Special Events:** Melissa Azevedo. **Assistant GM:** Ben Abzug. **Director, Stadium Operations:** John Schumacher. **Director, Marketing:** Noel Blaha. **Director, Promotions:** Joey Cain. **Director, Broadcasting/Media Relations:** Sean Houston. **Director, Food/Beverage:** Josh Shea. **Director, Merchandise:** Mike DeAntonio. **Director, Community Relations:** Lauren Allio. **Director, Ticket Sales:** Jake Terrell. **Business Manager:** Dale Stickney.
Box Office Manager: Ryan Stewart. **Special Events Manager:** Kristen Wolfe. **Food/Beverage Manager:** Peter Parker. **Sales Representative:** David Cullins. **Operations Assistant:** Harris Seletsky. **Special Events/Promotions Assistant:** Haley Kirschner. **Head Groundskeeper:** Mike Williams. **Clubhouse Manager:** Kenneth Bassett.

FIELD STAFF

Manager: Luis Dorante. **Hitting Coach:** Edwar Gonzalez. **Pitching Coach:** Carlos Chantres. **First-Base Coach:** Justin Tordi. **Trainer:** Jimmy Downam. **Strength/Conditioning Coach:** Anthony Velazquez.

GAME INFORMATION

Radio Announcer: Sean Houston. **No. of Games Broadcast:** 140. **Flagship Station:** WTMZ 910-AM.
PA Announcer: Ken Carrington. **Official Scorer:** Mike Hoffman.
Stadium Name: Joseph Riley Jr. Ballpark. **Location:** 360 Fishburne St, Charleston, SC 29403, From US 17, take Lockwood Dr. North, right on Fishburne St. **Standard Game Times:** 7:05pm, Sat 6:05pm, Sun 5:05. **Ticket Price Range:** $5-18.
Visiting Club Hotel: Crowne Plaza Charleston, 4381 Tanger Outlet Blvd, North Charleston, SC 29418. **Telephone:** (843) 744-4422.

DELMARVA SHOREBIRDS

Office Address: 6400 Hobbs Rd., Salisbury, MD 21804. **Mailing Address:** PO Box 1557, Salisbury, MD 21802.
Telephone: (410) 219-3112. **Fax:** (410) 219-9164.
E-Mail Address: info@theshorebirds.com. **Website:** www.theshorebirds.com.
Affiliation (first year): Baltimore Orioles (1997). **Years in League:** 1996-

OWNERSHIP/MANAGEMENT

Operated By: 7th Inning Stretch, LLP.
Directors: Tom Volpe, Pat Filippone. **General Manager:** Chris Bitters.
Assistant GM: Jimmy Sweet. **Director, Community Relations/Marketing:** Shawn Schoolcraft. **Business Development Executive:** Alyssa Dooyema. **Director, Tickets:** Brandon Harris. **Group Sales Manager:** Andrew Bryda. **Box Office Manager:** Ryan Muller. **Ticket Sales Account Executive:** Zac Penman. **Director, Stadium Operations:** Matt Bernhardt. **Head Groundskeeper:** Tim Young. **Director, Broadcasting/Graphic Design:** Bret Lasky. **Accounting Manager:** Gail Potts. **Office Manager:** Audrey Vane.

FIELD STAFF

Manager: Ryan Minor. **Hitting Coach:** Paco Figueroa. **Pitching Coach:** Alan Mills. **Athletic Trainer:** Trek Schuler.

GAME INFORMATION

Radio Announcer: Bret Lasky. **No of Games Broadcast:** 140. **Flagship Station:** 960 WTGM.
PA Announcer: Dustin Mills. **Official Scorer:** Gary Hicks.
Stadium Name: Arthur Perdue Stadium. **Location:** From US 50 East, right on Hobbs Rd.; From US 50 West, left on Hobbs Road. **Standard Game Time:** 7:05 pm. **Ticket Price Range:** $4-12.
Visiting Club Hotel: Downtown Holiday Inn, 300 South Salisbury Boulevard, Salisbury, MD 21801. **Telephone:** (410) 546-4400.

GREENSBORO GRASSHOPPERS

Office Address: 408 Bellemeade St., Greensboro, NC 27401.
Telephone: (336) 268-2255. **Fax:** (336) 273-7350.
E-Mail Address: info@gsohoppers.com. **Website:** www.gsohoppers.com.
Affiliation (first year): Miami Marlins (2003). **Years in League:** 1979-

OWNERSHIP/MANAGEMENT

Operated By: Greensboro Baseball LLC.
Principal Owners: Cooper Brantley, Wes Elingburg, Len White.
President/General Manager: Donald Moore.
Vice President, Baseball Operations: Katie Dannemiller. **CFO:** Benjamin Martin. **Assistant GM/Head Groundskeeper:** Jake Holloway. **Assistant GM, Sales/Marketing:** Tim Vangel. **Director, Ticket Sales:** Erich Dietz. **Coordinator, Ticket Services:** Kyle Smith. **Director, Promotions/Community Relations:** Courtney Campbell.
Director, Production/Entertainment: Shawn Russell. **Director, Creative Services:** Amanda Williams. **Office Administrator:** Hillary Overmyer. **Executive Director, Business Development:** John Redhead. **Group Sales Associates:** Todd Olson. **Sales Associate:** Rosalee Brewer. **Director, Stadium Operations:** Tim Hardin. **Assistant Groundskeeper:** Kaid Musgrave.

FIELD STAFF

Manager: David Berg. **Coach:** Frank Moore. **Pitching Coach:** Jeremy Powell. **Trainer:** Ben Cates.

GAME INFORMATION

Radio Announcer: Andy Durham. **No. of Games Broadcast:** 70 (all home games). **Flagship Station:** WPET 950-AM.
PA Announcer: Jim Scott. **Official Scorer:** Wayne Butler/Wilt Browning.
Stadium Name: NewBridge Bank Park. **Location:** From I-85, take Highway 220 South (exit 36) to Coliseum Blvd, continue on Edgeworth Street, ballpark at corner of Edgeworth and Bellemeade Streets. **Standard Game Times:** 7 pm, Sun 4. **Ticket Price Range:** $6-10.
Visiting Club Hotel: Days Inn 6102 Landmark Center Blvd., Greensboro, NC 27407. **Telephone:** (336) 553-2763.

GREENVILLE DRIVE

Office Address: 945 South Main St., Greenville, SC 29601.
Telephone: (864) 240-4500. **Fax:** (864) 240-4501
E-Mail Address: info@greenvilledrive.com. **Website:** www.greenvilledrive.com
Affiliation (first year): Boston Red Sox (2005). **Years in League:** 2005-

OWNERSHIP/MANAGEMENT

Operated By: Greenville Drive, LLC.
Co-Owner/President: Craig Brown. **Co-Owners:** Roy Bostock, Paul Raether.
General Manager: Eric Jarinko. **Executive Vice President:** Nate Lipscomb. **VP, Finance:** Eric Blagg. **VP, Ticket Sales:** Kyle Krebs. **Senior Director, Business Development:** Emily Walker. **Director, Game Entertainment:** Sam LoBosco. **Sponsor Services Manager:** Jennifer Brown. **Special Events/Community Relations Manager:** Samantha Bauer. **Media Relations Manager:** Cameron White. **Corporate Sales/Marketing Coordinator:** Alex Fiedler. **Creative Services Manager:** Clint Boyleston. **Creative Services Manager:** James Fowler. **Account Executives:** Josh Funderburg, Coleman Hornaday, Rachel Prindle, Aaron Smith. **Retail Manager:** Wade Mann. **Merchandise Manager:** Steve Seman. **Facilities Manager:** Eric Anastasi. **Head Groundskeeper:** Greg Burgess. **General Accountant:** Connie Pynne. **Office Manager:** Jamie Schafer.

FIELD STAFF

Manager: Darren Fenster. **Hitting Coach:** Nelson Paulino. **Pitching Coach:** Paul Abbott. **Head Athletic Trainer:** Satoshi Kajiyama.

GAME INFORMATION

Radio Announcer: Ed Jenson. **No. of Games Broadcast:** 70 (all home games). **Flagship Station:** www.greenville-drive.com.
PA Announcer: Doug Mayer. **Official Scorer:** Sanford Rogers.
Stadium Name: Fluor Field. **Location:** From south, I-85N to exit 42 toward downtown Greenville, turn left onto Augusta Rd., stadium is two miles on the left; From north, I-85S to I-385 toward Greenville, turn left onto Church St., turn right onto University Ridge. **Standard Game Times:** 7 pm, Sun 4. **Ticket Price Range:** $6-9.
Visiting Club Hotel: Baymont Inn and Suites, 246 Congaree Rd., Greenville, SC 29607. **Telephone:** (864) 288-1200.

HAGERSTOWN SUNS

HAGERSTOWN SUNS

Office Address: 274 E Memorial Blvd., Hagerstown, MD 21740.
Telephone: (301) 791-6266. **Fax:** (301) 791-6066.
E-Mail Address: info@hagerstownsuns.com. **Website:** www.hagerstownsuns.com.
Affiliation (first year): Washington Nationals (2007). **Years in League:** 1993-

OWNERSHIP/MANAGEMENT

Principal Owner/Operated by: Hagerstown Baseball LLC.
President: Bruce Quinn. **General Manager:** Bill Farley. **Director, Marketing/Community Relations:** Kyle MacBain. **Director, Media Relations:** Eli Pearlstein. **Director, Group Sales:** Josh Mastin. **Stadium Operations/Account Executive:** Andrew Houston. **Director, Human Resources/Promotions/Entertainment:** Lori Kendall. **Director, Sales/Community Affairs:** Bob Bruchey. **Director, Ticket Operations:** Paul Krenzer. **Assistant, Promotions:** Rachel Hawkins. **Assistant, Marketing:** Hannah Wolfe.

FIELD STAFF

Manager: Patrick Anderson. **Hitting Coach:** Luis Ordaz. **Pitching Coach:** Sam Narron. **Trainer:** TD Swinford.

GAME INFORMATION

Radio Announcer: Eli Pearlstein. **No. of Games Broadcast:** 140. **Flagship Station:** WJEJ 1240-AM.
PA Announcer: Unavailable. **Official Scorer:** Will Kauffman.
Stadium Name: Municipal Stadium. **Location:** Exit 32B (US 40 West) on I-70 West, left at Eastern Blvd.; Exit 6A (US 40 East) on I-81, right at Eastern Blvd. **Standard Game Times:** 7:05 pm, Sun 1:05. **Ticket Price Range:** $9-12.
Visiting Club Hotel: Clarion Hotel, 901 Dual Highway, Hagerstown, MD, 21740. **Telephone:** (301) 733-5100.

HICKORY CRAWDADS

Office Address: 2500 Clement Blvd. NW, Hickory, NC 28601.
Mailing Address: PO Box 1268, Hickory, NC 28603.
Telephone: (828) 322-3000. **Fax:** (828) 322-6137.
E-Mail Address: crawdad@hickorycrawdads.com. **Website:** www.hickorycrawdads.
com.
Affiliation (first year): Texas Rangers (2009). **Years in League:** 1952, 1960, 1993-

OWNERSHIP/MANAGEMENT

Operated by: Hickory Baseball Inc. **Principal Owners:** Don Beaver, Luther Beaver, Charles Young.
President: Don Beaver. **General Manager:** Mark Seaman. **Assistant GM:** Charlie Downs. **Director, Promotions:** Pete Subsara. **Director, Broadcasting/Media Relations:** Aaron Cox. **Business Manager:** Donna White. **Director, Community Relations/Events:** Megan Meade. **Clubhouse Manager:** Unavailable. **Director, Group Sales:** Travis Gortman. **Director, Ticket Operations/Merchandising:** Douglas Locascio. **Head Groundskeeper:** Zach Van Voorhees. **Director, Food/ Beverage:** Teddy Ingraham. **Group Sales Executive:** Stephen Johnson.

FIELD STAFF

Manager: Corey Ragsdale. **Hitting Coach:** Bobby Rose. **Pitching Coach:** Oscar Marin. **Trainer:** Sean Fields. **Strength/ Conditioning:** Wade Lamont.

GAME INFORMATION

Radio Announcer: Aaron Cox. **No. of Games Broadcast:** 140. **Flagship Station:** hickorycrawdads.com.
PA Announcers: Ralph Mangum, Jason Savage, Steve Jones. **Official Scorers:** Mark Parker, Paul Fogelman.
Stadium Name: LP Frans Stadium. **Location:** I-40 to exit 123 (Lenoir North), 321 North to Clement Blvd, left for ½ mile.
Standard Game Times: 7 pm, Sun 5 p.m.
Visiting Club Hotel: Crowne Plaza, 1385 Lenior-Rhyne Boulevard SE, Hickory, NC 28602. **Telephone:** (828) 323-1000.

KANNAPOLIS INTIMIDATORS

Office Address: 2888 Moose Road, Kannapolis, NC 28083. **Mailing Address:** PO Box 64, Kannapolis, NC 28082.
Telephone: (704) 932-3267. **Fax:** (704) 938-7040. **E-Mail Address:** info@intimidators-baseball.com. **Website:** www.intimidatorsbaseball.com.
Affiliation (first year): Chicago White Sox (2001). **Years in League:** 1995-

OWNERSHIP/MANAGEMENT

Operated by: Smith Family Baseball Inc.
President: Brad Smith. **General Manager:** Randy Long. **Head Groundskeeper:** Billy Ball. **Director, Stadium Operations:** Darren Cozart. **Director, Broadcasting/Media Relations:** Josh Feldman. **Director, Ticket Operations:** Brandon Wilson. **Director, Promotions:** Unavailable. **Sales Executive:** Jacob Newman. **Assistant Groundskeeper:** Mitchell Hooten.

FIELD STAFF

Manager: Pete Rose Jr. **Hitting Coach:** Robert Sasser. **Pitching Coach:** Jose Bautista. **Trainer:** Unavailable. **Strength/ Conditioning Coach:** Unavailable.

GAME INFORMATION

Radio Announcer: Josh Feldman. **No. of Games Broadcast:** 70 (all home games). **Flagship Station:** www.intimida-torsbaseball.com.
PA Announcer: Sean Fox. **Official Scorer:** Unavailable.
Stadium Name: CMC-NorthEast Stadium. **Location:** Exit 63 on I-85, west on Lane Street to Stadium Drive. **Standard Game Times:** 7:05 pm, Sun 5:05. **Ticket Price Range:** $5-$12.
Visiting Club Hotel: Spring Hill Suites. **Address:** 7811 Gateway Lane NW, Concord, NC 28027. **Telephone:** (704) 979-2500.

LAKEWOOD BLUECLAWS

Office Address: 2 Stadium Way, Lakewood, NJ 08701.
Telephone: (732) 901-7000. Fax: (732) 901-3967.
E-mail Address: info@blueclaws.com. Website: www.blueclaws.com
Affiliation (first year): Philadelphia Phillies (2001). Years in League: 2001-

OWNERSHIP/MANAGEMENT

Operated By: American Baseball Company, LLC.
President: Joseph Finley.
General Manager: Brandon Marano. Assistant GM, Tickets: Joe Harrington. Controller: Bob Halsey. Director, Marketing: Mike Ryan. Director, Promotions: Hal Hansen. Director, Community Relations: Jim DeAngelis. Director, Sponsorship: Zack Rosenberg. Director, Business Development: Dan DeYoung. Director, Group Sales: Jim McNamara. Director, New Client Development: Mike Van Hise. Director, Special Events: Steve Farago. Director, Inside Sales: Lisa Carone. Director, Corporate Sponsorship: Chris Tafrow. Director, Regional Sales: John Fierko. Director, Retail Operations: Lisa Carone.
Senior Manager, Media/Public Relations: Greg Giombarrese. Senior Manager, Ticket Sales: Rob Vota. Senior Manager, Ticket Sales: Kevin Fenstermacher. Senior Manager, Ticket Sales: Andrew Granozio. Ticket Sales Managers: Justin Campbell, Annmarie Clifford, Sean MacLeary, Rob McGillick. Manager, BlueClaws Baseball Academy: Joe Agnello. Regional Sales Manager: Sara Lamont. Corporate Sales Manager: Dave Ricci. Sponsorship Manager: Amy DeMichele. Ticket Sales Coordinator: Libby Rowe. Premium Services Manager: Maria Cervino. Ticket Operations Coordinator: Paige Selle. Concourse Operations Manager: Robert Van Praag. Manager, Food/Beverage: Mike Barry. Executive Administrator: Lindsay Lubeck. Clubhouse Manager: Russ Schaffer. Head Groundskeeper: Ryan Radcliffe.

FIELD STAFF

Manager: Mickey Morandini. Hitting Coach: Greg Legg. Pitching Coach: Aaron Fultz.

GAME INFORMATION

Radio Announcers: Greg Giombarrese, Dan Acheson. No. of Games Broadcast: 140. Flagship Station: WOBM 1160-AM.
PA Announcers: Kevin Clark, Mike Stoughton. Official Scorers: Joe Bellina, Jared Weiss.
Stadium Name: FirstEnergy Park. Location: Route 70 to New Hampshire Avenue, North on New Hampshire for 2.5 miles to ballpark. Standard Game Times: 7:05 pm, 6:35 pm (April-May); Sun 1:05, 5:05 (July-Aug). Ticket Price Range: $7-12.
Visiting Team Hotel: Clarion Hotel Toms River, 815 Route 37 West, Toms River, NJ 08755. Telephone: (732) 341-3400.

LEXINGTON LEGENDS

Office Address: 207 Legends Lane, Lexington, KY 40505.
Telephone: (859) 252-4487. Fax: (859) 252-0747.
E-Mail Address: webmaster@lexingtonlegends.com. Website: www.lexingtonle-gends.com.
Affiliation (first year): Kansas City Royals (2013). Years in League: 2001-

OWNERSHIP/MANAGEMENT

Operated By: Ivy Walls Management Co.
Principal Owner: Bill Shea. President/COO: Andy Shea.
General Manager: Unavailable. Assistant GM: Unavailable. Vice President, Facilities: Gary Durbin.
Director, Stadium Operations/Manager, Human Resource: Shannon Kidd. Business Manager: Tina Wright. Corporate Sales Manager: Jeremy Dixon. Box Office Manager: David Barry. Director, Ticket Sales: Ty Cobb. Director, Broadcasting/Media Relations: Keith Elkins. Senior Account Executive: Ron Borkowski. Director, Community Relations/Special Events: Sarah Bosso. Promotions Coordinator: Brent Billings. Production Manager: Nick Juhasz. Head Groundskeeper: Jason Boston. Facility Specialist: Steve Moore.

FIELD STAFF

Manager: Brian Buchanan. Hitting Coach: Abraham Nunez. Pitching Coach: Steve Merriman. Bench Coach: Glenn Hubbard. Athletic Trainer: Mark Keiser. Strength/Conditioning Coach: Aaron Reis.

GAME INFORMATION

Radio Announcer: Keith Elkins. No. of Games Broadcast: 140. Flagship Station: WLXG 1300-AM.
PA Announcer: Ty Cobb. Official Scorer: Unavailable.
Stadium Name: Whitaker Bank Ballpark. Location: From I-64/75, take exit 113, right onto North Broadway toward downtown Lexington for 1.2 miles, past New Circle Road (Highway 4), right into stadium, located adjacent to Northland Shopping Center. Standard Game Times: 7:05 pm, Wed 12:05, Sun 1:35. Ticket Price Range: $4-$24.
Visiting Club Hotel: Ramada Inn and Conference Center, 2143 N Broadway, Lexington, KY 40505. Telephone: (859) 299-1261.

ROME BRAVES

Office Address: State Mutual Stadium, 755 Braves Blvd., Rome, GA 30161. **Mailing Address:** PO Box 1915, Rome, GA 30162-1915.
  Telephone: (706) 378-5100. **Fax:** (706) 368-6525.
  E-Mail Address: rome.braves@braves.com. **Website:** www.romebraves.com.
  Affiliation (first year): Atlanta Braves (2003). **Years in League:** 2003-

OWNERSHIP MANAGEMENT

Operated By: Atlanta National League Baseball Club Inc.
  General Manager: Michael Dunn. **Assistant GM:** Jim Jones.
  Director, Stadium Operations: Eric Allman. **Director, Ticket Manager:** Jeff Fletcher. **Director, Culinary Director:** Owen Reppert. **Director, Food/Beverage:** Brad Smith. **Special Projects Manager:** Erin White. **Administrative Manager:** Christina Shaw. **Account Representatives:** John Layng, Kyle Allen. **Head Groundskeeper:** Unavailable. **Retail Manager:** Starla Roden. **Warehouse Operations Manager:** Terry Morgan. **Neighborhood Outreach Coordinator:** Laura Harrison.

FIELD STAFF

Manager: Jonathan Schuerholz. **Coach:** Bobby Moore. **Pitching Coach:** Gabe Luckert. **Trainer:** Kyle Damschroder.

GAME INFORMATION

Radio Announcer: Ben Poplin. **No. of Games Broadcast:** 140. **Flagship Station:** WATG 95.7 FM. **Television:** www.romebraves.com (home games).
  PA Announcer: Tony McIntosh. **Official Scorers:** Jim O'Hara, Lyndon Huckaby.
  Stadium Name: State Mutual Stadium. **Location:** I-75 North to exit 190 (Rome/Canton), left off exit and follow Highway 411/Highway 20 to Rome, right at intersection on Highway 411 and Highway 1 (Veterans Memorial Highway), stadium is at intersection of Veterans Memorial Highway and Riverside Parkway. **Ticket Price Range:** $4-10.
  Visiting Club Hotel: Days Inn, 840 Turner McCall Blvd, Rome, GA 30161. **Telephone:** (706) 295-0400.

SAVANNAH SAND GNATS

Office Address: 1401 E Victory Dr., Savannah, GA 31404. **Mailing Address:** PO Box 3783, Savannah, GA 31414.
  Telephone: (912) 351-9150. **Fax:** (912) 352-9722.
  E-Mail Address: info@sandgnats.com. **Website:** www.sandgnats.com.
  Affiliation (first year): New York Mets (2007). **Years in League:** 1904-1915, 1936-1960, 1962, 1984-

OWNERSHIP/MANAGEMENT

Operated By: Savannah Professional Baseball, LLC.
  President: John Katz.
  Vice President: Scott Burton. **Director, Stadium Operations:** Evan Christian. **Director, Business Development:** Brittany Petersen. **Director, Marketing/Promotions:** Jonathan Mercier. **Director, Communications:** Vince Caffiero. **Director, Ticketing Operations:** Joe Shepard. **Finance Manager:** Evan DeCamp. **Head Groundskeeper:** Andy Rock. **Account Executives:** Maggie McGavin, Kyle Williamson, Josh Andrews, Cameron Richardson.

FIELD STAFF

Manager: Luis Rojas. **Hitting Coach:** Valentino Pascucci. **Pitching Coach:** Marc Valdes. **Trainer:** Eric Velazquez. **Strength/Conditioning Coach:** Jason Griffin.

GAME INFORMATION

Radio Announcer: Toby Hyde. **No. of Games Broadcast:** 140. **Flagship Station:** WBMQ 960-AM.
  PA Announcer: Sean Brown. **Official Scorer:** Steven Linsday.
  Stadium Name: Historic Grayson Stadium. **Location:** From I-16 E to 37th St. exit, left on 37th, right on Abercorn St., left on Victory Drive; From I-95 to exit 16, east on 204, right on Victory Drive, Stadium is on right in Daffin Park. **Standard Game Times:** 7:05 pm, Sat 6:05, Sun 2:05. **Ticket Price Range:** $7-10.
  Visiting Club Hotel: Fairfield Inn & Suites, 2 Lee Blvd., Savannah, GA 31405. **Telephone:** (912) 351-9150.

WEST VIRGINIA POWER

Office Address: 601 Morris St., Suite 201, Charleston, WV 25301.
Telephone: (304) 344-2287. **Fax:** (304) 344-0083.
E-Mail Address: info@wvpower.com. **Website:** www.wvpower.com.
Affiliation (first year): Pittsburgh Pirates (2009). **Years in League:** 1987-

OWNERSHIP/MANAGEMENT

Operated By: West Virginia Baseball, LLC.
Managing Partner: Tim Wilcox. **General Manager:** Tim Mueller. **Assistant GM, Marketing:** Kristin Call. **Assistant GM, Operations:** Jeremy Taylor. **Accountant:** Darren Holstein. **Box Office Manager:** Nikki Mirth. **Director, Food/Beverage:** Nate Michel. **Director, Media Relations:** Adam Marco. **Director, Tickets:** Kevin Buffalino. **Event Planner:** Will Bell. **Groundskeeper:** Brent Szarka. **Production Manager:** Jay Silverman.

FIELD STAFF

Manager: Michael Ryan. **Coach:** Keoni De Renne. **Pitching Coach:** Jeff Johnson. **Trainer:** Phillip Mastro.

GAME INFORMATION

Radio Announcer: Adam Marco. **No. of Games Broadcast:** 140. **Flagship Stations:** ESPN 104.5 FM, WSWW 1490-AM. **PA Announcer:** Unavailable. **Official Scorer:** Unavailable.
Stadium Name: Appalachian Power Park. **Location:** I-77 South to Capitol Street exit, left on Lee Street, left on Brooks Street. **Standard Game Times:** 7:05 pm, Sun 2:05. **Ticket Price Range:** $6-9.
Visiting Club Hotel: Holiday Inn and Suites-Charleston West, 400 Second Avenue SW, South Charleston, WV 25303. **Telephone:** (304) 744-4641.

NEW YORK-PENN LEAGUE

Mailing Address: 204 37th Ave. North, #366, St. Petersburg, Florida 33704.
Telephone: (727) 289-7112. **Fax:** (727) 683-9691.
Website: www.newyork-pennleague.com.
Years League Active: 1939-

President: Ben Hayes.
President Emeritus: Robert Julian. **Treasurer:** Jon Dandes (Jamestown). **Secretary:** Doug Estes (Williamsport).
Directors: Tim Bawmann (Lowell), Steve Cohen (Brooklyn), Jon Dandes (Jamestown), Glenn Tilley (Aberdeen), David Daum (Auburn), Bill Gladstone (Tri-City), Marvin Goldklang (Hudson Valley), Chuck Greenberg (State College), Kyle Bostick (Vermont), Michael Savit (Mahoning Valley), Miles Prentice (Connecticut), Naomi Silver (Batavia), Glenn Reicin (Staten Island), Paul Velte (Williamsport).

Office Manager: Laurie Hayes. **League Historian:** Charles Wride.
Division Structure: McNamara—Aberdeen, Brooklyn, Hudson Valley, Staten Island. **Pinckney**—Auburn, Batavia, Jamestown, Mahoning Valley, State College, Williamsport. **Stedler**—Lowell, Connecticut, Tri-City, Vermont.
Regular Season: 76 games. **2014 Opening Date:** June 13. **Closing Date:** Sept 1.
All-Star Game: Aug 19 at Brooklyn.
Playoff Format: Division winners and wild-card team meet in best-of-three semifinals. Semifinal winners meet in best-of-three series for league championship.
Roster Limit: 30 active, but only 25 may be in uniform and eligible to play in any given game.

Ben Hayes

Player Eligibility Rule: No more than four players 23 or older; no more than three players on active list may have four or more years of prior service.
Brand of Baseball: Rawlings.
Umpires: Unavailable.

STADIUM INFORMATION

| Club | Stadium | Opened | Dimensions | | | Capacity | 2013 Att. |
			LF	CF	RF		
Aberdeen	Ripken Stadium	2002	310	400	310	6,000	189,879
Auburn	Falcon Park	1995	330	400	330	2,800	39,381
Batavia	Dwyer Stadium	1996	325	400	325	2,600	33,909
Brooklyn	KeySpan Park	2001	315	412	325	7,500	232,224
Connecticut	Dodd Stadium	1995	309	401	309	6,270	68,757
Hudson Valley	Dutchess Stadium	1994	325	400	325	4,494	164,230
Jamestown	Russell E. Diethrick Jr. Park	1941	335	410	353	3,324	38,728
Lowell	Edward LeLacheur Park	1998	337	400	301	4,842	156,358
Mahoning Valley	Eastwood Field	1999	335	405	335	6,000	114,598
State College	Medlar Field at Lubrano Park	2006	325	399	320	5,412	133,637
Staten Island	Richmond County Bank Ballpark	2001	325	400	325	6,500	128,441
Tri-City	Joseph L. Bruno Stadium	2002	325	400	325	5,000	156,712
Vermont	Centennial Field	1922	323	405	330	4,000	81,683
Williamsport	Bowman Field	1923	345	405	350	4,200	64,188

ABERDEEN IRONBIRDS

Office Address: 873 Long Dr., Aberdeen, MD 21001.
Telephone: (410) 297-9292. **Fax:** (410) 297-6653.
E-Mail Address: info@ironbirdsbaseball.com. **Website:** www.ironbirdsbaseball.com.
Affiliation (first year): Baltimore Orioles (2002). **Years in League:** 2002-

OWNERSHIP/MANAGEMENT

Operated By: Ripken Professional Baseball LLC.
Principal Owner: Cal Ripken Jr. **Co-Owner/Executive Vice President:** Bill Ripken.
General Manager: Joe Harrington. **Assistant GM:** Brad Cox. **Director, Ticket Operations:** Ian Clark. **Group Sales Manager:** Lee Greely. **Director, Retail Merchandising:** Don Eney. **Video Production Manager:** Mike Zapalowicz. **Manager, Facilities:** Steve Fairbaugh. **Head Groundskeeper:** Patrick Coakley.

FIELD STAFF

Manager: Matt Merullo. **Hitting Coach:** Unavailable. **Pitching Coach:** Justin Lord. **Trainer:** Chris Poole. **Strength/Conditioning Coach:** Kevin Clark.

GAME INFORMATION
Radio Announcer: Paul Taylor. **No. of Games Broadcast:** 76. **Flagship Station:** www.ironbirdsbaseball.com.
PA Announcer: Danny Mays. **Official Scorer:** Joe Stetka.
Stadium Name: Ripken Stadium. **Location:** I-95 to exit 85 (Route 22), west on 22 West, right onto Long Drive. **Ticket Price Range:** $9-15.50.

AUBURN DOUBLEDAYS

Office Address: 130 N Division St., Auburn, NY 13021.
Telephone: (315) 255-2489. **Fax:** (315) 255-2675.
E-Mail Address: info@auburndoubledays.com. **Website:** www.auburndoubledays.com.
Affiliation (first year): Washington Nationals (2011). **Years in League:** 1958-80, 1982-

OWNERSHIP/MANAGEMENT
Operated by: Auburn Community Non-Profit Baseball Association Inc.
President: David Daum. **General Manager:** Michael Voutsinas.

FIELD STAFF
Manager: Gary Cathcart. **Coach:** Amaury Garcia. **Pitching Coach:** Tim Redding.

GAME INFORMATION
Radio Announcer: Unavailable. **No of Games Broadcast:** Unavailable. **Flagship Station:** Unavailable.
Stadium Name: Falcon Park. **Location:** I-90 to exit 40, right on Route 34 South for 8 miles to York Street, right on York, left on North Division Street. **Standard Game Times:** 7 pm. **Ticket Price Range:** $5-8.
Visiting Club Hotel: Unavailable.

BATAVIA MUCKDOGS

Office Address: Dwyer Stadium, 299 Bank St., Batavia, NY 14020.
Telephone: (585) 343-5454. **Fax:** (585) 343-5620.
E-Mail Address: tslck@muckdogs.com. **Website:** www.muckdogs.com.
Affiliation (first year): Miami Marlins (2013). **Years in League:** 1939-53, 1957-59, 1961-

OWNERSHIP/MANAGEMENT
Operated By: Red Wings Management, LLC.
General Manager: Travis Sick. **Assistant GM:** Mike Ewing. **Director, Stadium Operations:** Don Rock. **Director, Merchandise:** Danielle Barone. **Clubhouse Manager:** John Versage.

FIELD STAFF
Manager: Angel Espada. **Hitting Coach:** Rigoberto Silverio. **Pitching Coach:** Brendan Sagara. **Trainer:** Michael Bibbo.

GAME INFORMATION
Radio Announcer: Matthew Coller. **No. of Games Broadcast:** 58 (all home games, 20 away games). **Flagship Station:** WBTA 1490-AM.
PA Announcer: Wayne Fuller. **Official Scorer:** Paul Bisig.
Stadium Name: Dwyer Stadium. **Location:** I-90 to exit 48, left on Route 98 South, left on Richmond Avenue, left on Bank Street. **Standard Game Times:** 7:05 pm, Sun 1:05/5:05. **Ticket Price Range:** $5.50-7.50.
Visiting Club Hotel: Days Inn of Batavia, 200 Oak St, Batavia, NY 14020. **Telephone:** (585) 344-6000

BROOKLYN CYCLONES

Office Address: 1904 Surf Ave., Brooklyn, NY 11224.
Telephone: (718) 37-BKLYN. **Fax:** (718) 449-6368.
E-Mail Address: info@brooklyncyclones.com. **Website:** www.brooklyncyclones.com.
Affiliation (first year): New York Mets (2001). **Years in League:** 2001-

OWNERSHIP/MANAGEMENT
Chairman, CEO: Fred Wilpon. **President:** Saul Katz. **COO:** Jeff Wilpon.
Vice President: Steve Cohen. **General Manager:** Kevin Mahoney. **Assistant GM:** Gary Perone. **Director, Communications:** Billy Harner. **Manager, Ticket Operations:** Greg Conway. **Graphics Manager:** Kevin Jimenez. **Operations Manager:** Vladimir Lipsman. **Community Relations Manager:** Josh Mevorach. **Head Groundskeeper:** Mike Meola. **Community Outreach/Promotions:** King Henry. **Account Executives:** Brett Hood, Nicole Kneessy, Sal LaMonica, Craig Coughlin, Josh Hernandez, Angelina Tennis, Ricky Viola. **Staff Accountant:** Tatiana Isdith. **Administrative Assistant, Community Relations:** Sharon Lundy-Ross.

FIELD STAFF

Manager: Unavailable. **Coach:** Benny Distefano. **Pitching Coach:** Tom Signore.

GAME INFORMATION

Radio Announcer: David Greenwald. **No. of Games Broadcast:** 76. **Flagship Station:** WKRB 90.3-FM.
PA Announcer: Mark Frotto. **Official Scorer:** Alex Freeman.
Stadium Name: MCU Park. **Location:** Belt Parkway to Cropsey Ave. South, continue on Cropsey until it becomes West 17th St., continue to Surf Ave., stadium on south side of Surf Ave.; By subway, west/south to Stillwell Ave./Coney Island station. **Ticket Price Range:** $8-17.
Visiting Club Hotel: Holiday Inn Express, 279 Butler Street, Brooklyn, NY 11217. **Telephone:** (718) 855-9600.

CONNECTICUT TIGERS

Office Address: 14 Stott Ave., Norwich, CT 06360.
Telephone: (860) 887-7962. **Fax:** (860) 886-5996.
E-Mail Address: info@cttigers.com. **Website:** www.cttigers.com.
Affiliation (first year): Detroit Tigers (2010). **Years in League:** 2010-

OWNERSHIP/MANAGEMENT

Operated By: Oneonta Athletic Corp.
President: Miles Prentice. **Senior Vice President:** CJ Knudsen. **VP/General Manager:** Eric Knighton. **Assistant GM:** Dave Schermerhorn. **Director, Concessions/Merchandise:** Heather Bartlett. **Director, Sales:** Brent Southworth. **Box Office Manager:** Josh Postler. **Group Sales Manager:** Jack Kasten.

FIELD STAFF

Manager: Mike Rabelo. **Hitting Coach:** Scott Dwyer. **Pitching Coach:** Mark Johnson. **Trainer:** Unavailable.

GAME INFORMATION

Radio: Unavailable.
PA Announcer: Ed Weyant. **Official Scorer:** Chris Cote.
Stadium Name: Dodd Stadium. **Location:** Exit 82 off I-395. **Standard Game Times:** 7:05 pm, Sun 4:05. **Ticket Price Range:** $7-20.

HUDSON VALLEY RENEGADES

Office Address: Dutchess Stadium, 1500 Route 9D, Wappingers Falls, NY 12590.
Mailing Address: PO Box 661, Fishkill, NY 12524.
Telephone: (845) 838-0094. **Fax:** (845) 838-0014.
E-Mail Address: info@hvrenegades.com. **Website:** www.hvrenegades.com.
Affiliation (first year): Tampa Bay Rays (1996). **Years in League:** 1994-

OWNERSHIP/MANAGEMENT

Operated by: Keystone Professional Baseball Club Inc.
Principal Owner: Marv Goldklang. **President:** Jeff Goldklang.
Senior Vice President/General Manager: Eben Yager.
VP: Rick Zolzer. **Assistant GM:** Kristen Huss. **Director, Stadium Operations:** Tom Hubmaster. **Director, Baseball Communications:** Joe Ausanio. **Director, Business Operations:** Vicky DeFreese. **Director, Corporate Partnerships:** Rob Bell. **Director, Promotions:** Sean Kammerer. **Director, Marketing/Communications:** Corinne Adams. **Manager, New Business Development:** Dave Neff. **Manager, Director, Food/Beverage:** Teri Bettencourt. **Head Groundskeeper:** Tim Merante. **Community Relations Specialist:** Bob Outer. **Box Office Manager:** Morgan Powell. **Director, Ticket Sales:** DJ Constantino.

FIELD STAFF

Manager: Tim Parenton. **Hitting Coach:** Manny Castillo. **Pitching Coach:** Jorge Moncada.

GAME INFORMATION

Radio Announcer: Unavailable. **No. of Games Broadcast:** 38 (all home games). **Flagship Stations:** WBNR 1260-AM/WLNA 1420-AM.
PA Announcer: Rick Zolzer. **Official Scorers:** Unavailable.
Stadium Name: Dutchess Stadium. **Location:** I-84 to exit 11 (Route 9D North), north one mile to stadium. **Standard Game Times:** 7:05 pm, Sun 5:05.
Visiting Club Hotel: Days Inn, 20 Schuyler Blvd and Route 9, Fishkill, NY 12524. **Telephone:** (845) 896-4995.

JAMESTOWN JAMMERS

Office Address: 485 Falconer St., Jamestown, NY 14701.
Mailing Address: PO Box 638, Jamestown, NY 14702.
Telephone: (716) 664-0915. Fax: (716) 664-4175.
E-Mail Address: email@jamestownjammers.com. Website: www.jamestownjammers.com.
Affiliation (first year): Pittsburgh Pirates (2013). Years in League: 1939-57, 1961-73, 1977-.

OWNERSHIP/MANAGEMENT
Operated By: Rich Baseball Operations.
President: Robert Rich Jr. Chief Operating Officer: Jonathan Dandes.
General Manager: Matthew Drayer. Assistant GM: John Pogorzelski. Head Groundskeeper: Josh Waid.

FIELD STAFF
Manager: Brian Esposito. Coach: Orlando Merced. Pitching Coach: Mark DiFelice.

GAME INFORMATION
Radio: Unavailable.
PA Announcer: Unavailable. Official Scorer: Jim Riggs.
Stadium Name: Russell E Diethrick Jr Park. Location: From I-90, south on Route 60, left on Buffalo St., left on Falconer St. Standard Game Times: 7:05 pm, Sun 6:05. Ticket Price Range: $6-8.
Visiting Club Hotel: Red Roof Inn, 1980 Main St., Falconer, NY 14733. Telephone: (716) 665-3670.

LOWELL SPINNERS

Office Address: 450 Aiken St., Lowell, MA 01854.
Telephone: (978) 459-2255. Fax: (978) 459-1674.
E-Mail Address: info@lowellspinners.com. Website: www.lowellspinners.com.
Affiliation (first year): Boston Red Sox (1996). Years in League: 1996-

OWNERSHIP/MANAGEMENT
Operated By: Diamond Action Inc.
Owner/CEO: Drew Weber.
President/General Manager: Tim Bawmann. Executive Vice President, Sales: Brian Lindsay. VP/Controller: Patricia Harbour. Executive VP, Communications: Jon Goode. VP, Stadium Operations: Dan Beaulieu. Director, Facility Management: Gareth Markey. Assistant GM/Media Relations: Jon Boswell. Director, Merchandising: Jeff Cohen. VP, Group Ticketing: Jon Healy. Director, Ticket Operations: Justin Williams. Director, Game Day Entertainment: Matt Steinberg. Head Groundskeeper: Jeff Paolino. Director, Creative Services: Jarrod FitzGerald. Clubhouse Manager: Del Christman. Marketing Assistant: Matt Berthiaume. Assistant Comptroller: Taylor Gillette. Concession Assistant: Ronnie Wallace.

FIELD STAFF
Manager: Unavailable. Hitting Coach: Noah Hall. Pitching Coach: Walter Miranda. Athletic Trainer: Nick Faciana.

GAME INFORMATION
Radio Announcer: John Leahy. No. of Games Broadcast: 76. Flagship Station: WCAP 980-AM.
PA Announcers: Mike Riley, George Brown. Official Scorer: David Rourke.
Stadium Name: Edward LeLacheur Park. Location: From Route 495 and 3, take exit 35C (Lowell Connector), follow connector to exit 5B (Thorndike St.) onto Dutton Street, left onto Father Morrissette Blvd., right on Aiken St. Standard Game Times: 7:05 pm. Ticket Price Range: $7-10 (Advance); $9-$12 (Day of Game).
Visiting Club Hotel: Radisson of Chelmsford, 10 Independence Dr, Chelmsford, MA 01879. Telephone: (978) 356-0800.

MAHONING VALLEY SCRAPPERS

Office Address: 111 Eastwood Mall Blvd., Niles, OH 44446.
Telephone: (330) 505-0000. Fax: (303) 505-9696.
E-Mail Address: info@mvscrappers.com. Website: www.mvscrappers.com.
Affiliation (first year): Cleveland Indians (1999). Years in League: 1999-

OWNERSHIP/MANAGEMENT
Operated By: HWS Baseball Group.
Managing General Partner: Michael Savit.

General Manager: Jordan Taylor. **Assistant GM, Marketing:** Heather Sahil. **Assistant GM, Sales:** Matt Thompson. **Manager, Box Office/Merchandise:** Stephanie Novak. **Assistant GM, Operations:** Brad Hooser. **Group Sales Manager:** Chris Sumner. **Head Groundskeeper:** Chris Mason. **Manager, Accounting:** Courtney Perrino. **Manager, Community Relations:** Annie Stoltenberg.

FIELD STAFF

Manager: Ted Kubiak. **Coach:** Phil Clark. **Pitching Coach:** Greg Hibbard.

GAME INFORMATION

Radio Announcer: Unavailable. **No. of Games Broadcast:** 76. **Flagship Station:** Unavailable.
PA Announcer: Unavailable. **Official Scorer:** Craig Antush.
Stadium Name: Eastwood Field. **Location:** I-80 to 11 North to 82 West to 46 South; stadium located behind Eastwood Mall. **Ticket Price Range:** $8-12.
Visiting Club Hotel: Days Inn & Suites, 1615 Liberty St, Girard, OH 44429. **Telephone:** (330) 759-9820.

STATE COLLEGE SPIKES

Office Address: 112 Medlar Field, Lubrano Park, University Park, PA 16802.
Telephone: (814) 272-1711. **Fax:** (814) 272-1718.
Website: www.statecollegespikes.com.
Affiliation (first year): St. Louis Cardinals (2013). **Years in League:** 2006-

OWNERSHIP/MANAGEMENT

Operated By: Spikes Baseball LP. **Chairman/Managing Partner:** Chuck Greenberg.
Senior Vice President/General Manager: Jason Dambach. **VP, Sales:** Scott Walker. **Senior Director, Ballpark Operations:** Dan Petrazzolo. **Accounting Manager:** Karen Mahon. **Business/Box Office Manager:** Steve Christ. **Manager, Ticket Sales:** Brian DeAngelis. **Manager, Entertainment/Promotions:** Ben Love. **Ticket Account Executives:** Erik Hoffman, Steve Kettler. **Senior Sales Executive:** Steve Kassimer. **Sports Turf Manager:** Matt Neri. **Community Relations/Promotions Assistant:** Amy Hudzik.

FIELD STAFF

Manager: Oliver Marmol. **Hitting Coach:** Ramon Ortiz. **Pitching Coach:** Dernier Orozco. **Trainer:** Dan Martin.

GAME INFORMATION

Radio Announcers: Steve Jones, Joe Putnam. **No of Games Broadcast:** 76. **Flagship Station:** WZWW 95.3-FM.
PA Announcer: Jeff Brown. **Official Scorers:** Dave Baker, John Dixon.
Stadium Name: Medlar Field at Lubrano Park. **Location:** From west, US 322 to Mount Nittany Expressway, I-80 to exit 158 (old exit 23/Milesburg), follow Route 150 South to Route 26 South; From east, I-80 to exit 161 (old exit 24/Bellefonte) to Route 26 South or US 220/I-99 South. **Standard Game Times:** 7:05 pm, Sun 6:05. **Ticket Price Range:** $6-14.
Visiting Club Hotel: Ramada Conference Center State College, 1450 Atherton St, State College, PA 16801. **Telephone:** (814) 238-3001

STATEN ISLAND YANKEES

Stadium Address: 75 Richmond Terrace, Staten Island, NY 10301.
Telephone: (718) 720-9265. **Fax:** (718) 273-5763.
Website: www.siyanks.com.
Affiliation (first year): New York Yankees (1999). **Years in League:** 1999-

OWNERSHIP/MANAGEMENT

Principal Owners: Nostalgic Partners.
CEO: Steven Violetta. **President/General Manager:** Jane Rogers.
Director, Corporate Partnerships: Jill Wright. **Director, Entertainment:** Michael Katz. **Finance Manager:** Anthony Di Flaurio. **Vice President, Ticket Sales:** Brian Levine. **Ticket Operations Manager:** Steve McCann. **Senior Sales Executive:** Tim Holder. **Sales Executives:** Steven Liss, Andrew Lupo, Joseph Mola. **Manager, Stadium Operations:** Mike Rogers. **Stadium Operations:** Bobby Brown. **Clubhouse Manager:** Nate Six.

FIELD STAFF

Manager: Mario Garza. **Hitting Coach:** Ty Hawkins. **Pitching Coach:** Tim Norton. **Coach:** Luis Figueroa. **Trainer:** Anthony Moon. **Strength/Conditioning Coach:** Jake Dunning.

GAME INFORMATION

Radio Announcer: Unavailable. **No. of Games Broadcast:** 76. **Flagship Station:** Unavailable.
PA Announcer: Unavailable. **Official Scorer:** Unavailable.
Stadium Name: Richmond County Bank Ballpark at St. **George. Location:** From I-95, take exit 13E (1-278 and Staten Island), cross Goethals Bridge, stay on I-278 East and take last exit before Verrazano Narrows Bridge, north on Father Capodanno Boulevard, which turns into Bay Street, which goes to ferry terminal; ballpark next to Staten Island Ferry Terminal. **Standard Game Times:** 7 pm, Sun 4.

TRI-CITY VALLEYCATS

Office Address: Joseph Bruno Stadium, 80 Vandenburg Ave., Troy, NY 12180. **Mailing Address:** PO Box 694, Troy, NY 12181.
Telephone: (518) 629-2287. **Fax:** (518) 629-2299.
E-Mail Address: info@tcvalleycats.com. **Website:** www.tcvalleycats.com.
Affiliation (first year): Houston Astros (2002). **Years in League:** 2002-

OWNERSHIP/MANAGEMENT

Operated By: Tri-City ValleyCats Inc.
Principal Owners: Martin Barr, John Burton, William Gladstone, Rick Murphy, Alfred Roberts, Stephen Siegel.
President: William Gladstone.
Vice President/General Manager: Rick Murphy. **Assistant GM:** Matt Callahan. **Fan Development/Community Relations Manager:** Michelle Skinner. **Business Development Manager:** Jason Lecuyer. **Stadium Operations Manager:** Keith Sweeney. **Media Relations Manager:** Chris Chenes. **Account Executives:** Ryan Burke, Chris Dawson, Ben Whitehead. **Food/Beverage Coordinator:** Dianna Blanchard. **Box Office Manager:** Jessica Kaszeta. **Accountant:** Dan LaLonde.

FIELD STAFF

Manager: Ed Romero. **Hitting Coach:** Russ Steinhorn. **Pitching Coach:** Chris Holt.

GAME INFORMATION

Radio Announcer: Unavailable. **No. of Games Broadcast:** 38 (all homes games). **Flagship Station:** www.tcvalleycats.com.
PA Announcer: Anthony Pettograsso. **Official Scorer:** Unavailable.
Stadium Name: Joseph Bruno Stadium. **Location:** From north, I-87 to exit 7 (Route 7), go east 1 1/2 miles to I-787 South, to Route 378 East, go over bridge to Route 4, right to Route 4South, one mile to Hudson Valley Community College campus on left; From south, I-87 to exit 23 (I-787), I-787 north six miles to exit for Route 378 east, over bridge to Route 4, right to Route 4 South, one mile to campus on left; From east, Massachusetts Turnpike to exit B-1 (I-90), nine miles to Exit 8 (Defreestville), left off ramp to Route 4 North, five miles to campus on right; From west, I-90 to exit 24 (I-90 East), I-90 East for six miles to I-787 North (Troy), 2.2 miles to exit for Route 378 East, over bridge to Route 4, right to Route 4 south for one mile to campus on left. **Standard Game Times:** 7 pm, Sun 5. **Ticket Price Range:** $5.50-$10.50
Visiting Club Hotel: Travelodge, 831 New Loudon Road, Latham, NY 12110. **Telephone:** (518) 785-6626.

VERMONT LAKE MONSTERS

Office Address: 1 King Street Ferry Dock, Burlington, VT 05401.
Telephone: (802) 655-4200. **Fax:** (802) 655-5660.
E-Mail Address: info@vermontlakemonsters.com. **Website:** www.vermontlakemonsters.com.
Affiliation (first year): Oakland Athletics (2011). **Years in League:** 1994-

OWNERSHIP/MANAGEMENT

Operated by: Vermont Expos Inc.
Principal Owner/President: Ray Pecor Jr. **Vice President:** Kyle Bostwick. **General Manager:** Nate Cloutier. **Assistant GM:** Joe Doud. **Accounts Manager/Merchandise Director:** Kate Echo. **Director, Manager, Box Office:** Adam Matth. **Director, Fan Development/Promotions:** Unavailable. **Director, Media Relations:** Paul Stanfield. **Clubhouse Operations:** Phil Schelzo.

FIELD STAFF

Manager: David Newhan. **Hitting Coach:** Tommy Everidge. **Pitching Coach:** Steve Connelly.

GAME INFORMATION

Radio Announcers: George Commo. **No. of Games Broadcast:** 50 (all home games; 12 away games). **Flagship Station:** 960 The Zone.
PA Announcer: Unavailable.
Stadium Name: Centennial Field. **Location:** I-89 to exit 14W, right on East Ave. for one mile, right at Colchester Ave. **Standard Game Times:** 7:05 pm, Sat 6:05, Sun 5:05. **Ticket Price Range:** $5-8.
Visiting Club Hotel: Sheraton Hotel & Conference Center. **Telephone:** (802) 865-6600.

WILLIAMSPORT CROSSCUTTERS

Office Address: Bowman Field, 1700 W Fourth St., Williamsport, PA 17701. **Mailing Address:** PO Box 3173, Williamsport, PA 17701.
Telephone: (570) 326-3389. **Fax:** (570) 326-3494.
E-Mail Address: mail@crosscutters.com. **Website:** www.crosscutters.com.
Affiliation (first year): Philadelphia Phillies (2007). **Years in League:** 1968-72, 1994-

OWNERSHIP/MANAGEMENT
Operated By: Geneva Cubs Baseball Inc.
Principal Owners: Paul Velte, John Schreyer Family Trust.
President: Paul Velte.
Vice President/General Manager: Doug Estes. **VP, Marketing/Public Relations:** Gabe Sinicropi. **Director, Concessions:** Bill Gehron. **Director, Ticket Operations/Community Relations:** Sarah Budd. **Director, Partner Services:** Jennifer Lorson.

FIELD STAFF
Manager: Nelson Prada. **Coach:** Shawn Williams. **Pitching Coach:** Aaron Fultz. **Trainer:** Michael Hefta.

GAME INFORMATION
Radio Announcer: Todd Bartley. **No. of Games Broadcast:** 76. **Flagship Station:** WLYC 1050-AM, 104.1-FM.
PA Announcer: Rob Thomas. **Official Scorer:** Ken Myers.
Stadium Name: Bowman Field. **Location:** From south, Route 15 to Maynard Street, right on Maynard, left on Fourth Street for one mile; From north, Route 15 to Fourth Street, left on Fourth. **Ticket Price Range:** $5-$9.
Visiting Club Hotel: Best Western, 1840 E Third St, Williamsport, PA 17701. **Telephone:** (570) 326-1981.

NORTHWEST LEAGUE

Mike Ellis

Office Address: 140 N Higgins Ave., No. 211, Missoula, MT, 59802.
Telephone: (406) 541-9301. **Fax:** (406) 543-9463.
E-Mail Address: mellisnwl@aol.com. **Website:** www.northwestleague.com.
Years League Active: 1954-.
President/Treasurer: Mike Ellis.
Vice President: Dave Elmore (Eugene). **Corporate Secretary:** Jerry Walker (Salem-Keizer).
Directors: Dave Elmore (Eugene), Bobby Brett (Spokane), Tom Volpe (Everett), Jake Kerr (Vancouver), Mike McMurray (Hillsboro), Brent Miles (Tri-City), Jerry Walker (Salem-Keizer), Neil Leibman (Boise).
Administrative Assistant: Judy Ellis.
Division Structure: South—Boise, Hillsboro, Eugene, Salem-Keizer. North—Everett, Spokane, Tri-City, Vancouver.
Regular Season: 76 games (split schedule). **2014 Opening Date:** June 14. **Closing Date:** Sept. 2.
All-Star Game: Aug. 6, in Everett.
Playoff Format: First-half division winners meet second-half division winners in best-of-three series. Winners meet in best-of-three series for league championship.
Roster Limit: 30 active, 35 under control. **Player Eligibility Rule:** No more than three players on active list may have four or more years of prior service.
Brand of Baseball: Rawlings.
Umpires: Unavailable.

STADIUM INFORMATION

| Club | Stadium | Opened | Dimensions | | | Capacity | 2013 Att. |
			LF	CF	RF		
Boise	Memorial Stadium	1989	335	400	335	3,426	91,324
Eugene	PK Park	2010	335	400	325	4,000	112,028
Everett	Everett Memorial Stadium	1984	324	380	330	3,682	92,489
Hillsboro	Hillsboro Ballpark	2013	325	400	325	N/A	135,167
Salem-Keizer	Volcanoes Stadium	1997	325	400	325	4,100	98,024
Spokane	Avista Stadium	1958	335	398	335	7,162	187,371
Tri-City	Dust Devils Stadium	1995	335	400	335	3,700	83,987
Vancouver	Nat Bailey Stadium	1951	335	395	335	6,500	184,042

BOISE HAWKS

Office Address: 5600 N. Glenwood St. Boise, ID 83714.
Telephone: (208) 322-5000. **Fax:** (208) 322-6846.
Website: www.boisehawks.com.
Affiliation (first year): Chicago Cubs (2001). **Years in League:** 1975-76, 1978, 1987-

OWNERSHIP/MANAGEMENT
Operated by: Boise Baseball LLC.
CEO: Neil Leibman.
President/General Manager: Todd Rahr.
Vice President/Business Operations: Dina Rahr. **VP, Development:** Jinny Giery. **Assistant GM/Sales Manager:** Bryan Beban. **Assistant GM/Director of Fun:** Britt Talbert. **Development/Communications Manager:** Courtney Garner. **Manager, Broadcast/Baseball Information:** Mike Safford. **Director, Stadium Operations:** Jeff Israel. **Director, Food/Beverage:** Jake Lutz.

FIELD STAFF
Manager: Gary Van Tol. **Hitting Coach:** Unavailable. **Pitching Coach:** Brian Lawrence. **Trainer:** Toby Williams.

GAME INFORMATION
Radio Announcer: Mike Safford. **No. of Games Broadcast:** 76. **Flagship Station:** KTIK 1350-AM.
PA Announcer: Unavailable. **Official Scorer:** Curtis Haines.
Stadium Name: Memorial Stadium. **Location:** I-84 to Cole Rd., north to Western Idaho Fairgrounds at 5600 North Glenwood St. **Standard Game Time:** 7:15 pm. **Ticket Price Range:** $7-14.
Visiting Club Hotel: Unavailable.

EUGENE EMERALDS

Office Address: 2760 Martin Luther King Jr Blvd., Eugene, OR 97401. **Mailing Address:** PO Box 10911, Eugene, OR 97440.
Telephone: (541) 342-5367. **Fax:** (541) 342-6089.
E-Mail Address: info@emeraldsbaseball.com. **Website:** www.emeraldsbaseball.com.
Affiliation (first year): San Diego Padres (2001). **Years in League:** 1955-68, 1974-

OWNERSHIP/MANAGEMENT
Operated By: Elmore Sports Group Ltd.
Principal Owner: David Elmore.
General Manager: Allan Benavides. **Assistant GMs:** Sarah Heth, Matt Dompe. **Director, Food/Beverage:** Nikki Ochs. **Director, Mascot Operations:** Gatlin Neuman. **Director, Tickets:** Fei Li. **Assistant Director, Tickets:** Chris Bowers. **Assistant Director, Corporate Events:** Casey Quirke. **Graphic Designer:** Danny Crowley.

FIELD STAFF
Manager: Robbie Wine. **Hitting Coach:** Homer Bush. **Pitching Coach:** Nelson Cruz.

GAME INFORMATION
Radio Announcer: Matt Dompe. **No. of Games Broadcast:** 76. **Flagship Station:** 95.3-The Score.
PA Announcer: Ted Welker. **Official Scorer:** George McPherson.
Stadium Name: PK Park. **Standard Game Time:** 7:05 pm, Sun 5:05. **Ticket Price Range:** $6-12.
Visiting Club Hotel: Holiday Inn, 919 Kruse Way, Springfield, OR, 97477. **Telephone:** (541) 284-0707.

EVERETT AQUASOX

Mailing Address: 3802 Broadway, Everett, WA 98201.
Telephone: (425) 258-3673. **Fax:** (425) 258-3675.
E-Mail Address: info@aquasox.com. **Website:** www.aquasox.com.
Affiliation (first year): Seattle Mariners (1995). **Years in League:** 1984-

OWNERSHIP/MANAGEMENT
Operated by: 7th Inning Stretch, LLC. **Directors:** Tom Volpe, Pat Filippone.
Executive Vice President: Tom Backemeyer. **Assistant GM:** Katie Crawford Woods. **VP, Corporate Sponsorships:** Brian Sloan. **Director, Corporate Partnerships/Broadcasting:** Pat Dillon. **Group Sales/Merchandise Manager:** Erica Fensterbush. **Director, Food/Beverage:** Nick Reuter. **Director, Tickets:** Not Available. **Account Executives:** Duncan Jensen, Andrew Garrison, Greg Bell. **Finance Manager:** Tony Ackerman.

FIELD STAFF
Manager: Unavailable. **Hitting Coach:** Scott Steinmann. **Pitching Coach:** Nasusel Cabrera.

GAME INFORMATION
Radio Announcer: Pat Dillon. **No. of Games Broadcast:** 76. **Flagship Station:** KRKO 1380-AM.
PA Announcer: Iom Lafferty. **Official Scorer:** Pat Castro.
Stadium Name: Everett Memorial Stadium. **Location:** I-5, exit 192. **Standard Game Times:** 7:05 pm, Sun 4:05. **Ticket Price Range:** $7-17.
Visiting Club Hotel: Holiday Inn, Downtown Everett, 3105 Pine St, Everett, WA 98201. **Telephone:** (425) 339-2000.

HILLSBORO HOPS

Office Address: 4460 NW 229th Ave., Hillsboro, OR, 97124.
Telephone: (503) 640-0887.
E-Mail Address: info@hillsborohops.com. **Website:** www.hillsborohops.com.
Affiliation (first year): Arizona Diamondbacks (2013). **Years in League:** 2013-

OWNERSHIP/MANAGEMENT
Operated by: Short Season LLC.
Managing Partners: Mike McMurray, Mark Mays, Josh Weinman, Myron Levin. **President:** Mike McMurray.
General Manager: KL Wombacher. **Chief Financial Officer:** Laura McMurray. **Director, Ballpark Operations:** Juan Huitron. **Director, Tickets:** Jason Gavigan. **Director, Merchandise:** Lauren Wombacher. **Director, Media Relations/Broadcasting:** Rich Burk.

FIELD STAFF
Manager: JR House. **Hitting Coach:** Mark Grace. **Pitching Coach:** Doug Drabek.

GAME INFORMATION
PA Announcer: Unavailable.
Stadium Name: Hillsboro Ballpark. **Location:** 4460 NW 229th, Hillsboro, OR, 97124. **Standard Game Times:** 7:05 pm, Sun 1:35. **Ticket Price Range:** $7-$16.
Visiting Club Hotel: Comfort Inn, Hillsboro, OR. **Telephone:** (503) 648-3500.

SALEM-KEIZER VOLCANOES

Street Address: 6700 Field of Dreams Way, Keizer, OR 97303. **Mailing Address:** PO Box 20936, Keizer, OR 97307.
Telephone: (503) 390-2225. **Fax:** (503) 390-2227.
E-Mail Address: Volcanoes@volcanoesbaseball.com. **Website:** www.volcanoesbaseball.com.
Affiliation (first year): San Francisco Giants (1997). **Years in League:** 1997-

OWNERSHIP/MANAGEMENT
Operated By: Sports Enterprises Inc. **Principal Owners:** Jerry Walker, Bill Tucker.
President/General Manager: Jerry Walker. **President, Stadium Operations:** Rick Nelson. **President, Business Operations:** Tom Leip. **Senior Account Executive/Game Day Operations:** Jerry Howard. **Director, Broadcasting/Media Relations:** Rob Schreier. **Director, Ticket Office Operations:** Bea Howard. **Director, Business Development:** Justin Lacche.

FIELD STAFF
Manager: Gary Davenport. **Hitting Coach:** Ricky Ward. **Pitching Coach:** Jerry Cram. **Coach:** Matt Yourkin.

GAME INFORMATION
Radio Announcer: Rob Schreier. **No. of Games Broadcast:** 76. **Flagship Station:** KBZY AM-1490.
PA Announcer: Unavailable. **Official Scorer:** Scott Sepich.
Stadium Name: Volcanoes Stadium. **Location:** I-5 to exit 260 (Chemawa Road), west one block to Stadium Way NE, north six blocks to stadium. **Standard Game Times:** 6:35 pm, Sun 5:05. **Ticket Price Range:** $7-30.
Visiting Club Hotel: Comfort Suites, 630 Hawthorne Ave SE, Salem, OR 97301. **Telephone:** (503) 585-9705.

SPOKANE INDIANS

Office Address: Avista Stadium, 602 N. Havana, Spokane, WA 99202. **Mailing Address:** PO Box 4758, Spokane, WA 99220.
Telephone: (509) 535-2922. **Fax:** (509) 534-5368.
E-Mail Address: mail@spokaneindiansbaseball.com. **Website:** www.spokaneindiansbaseball.com.
Affiliation (first year): Texas Rangers (2003). **Years in League:** 1972, 1983

OWNERSHIP/MANAGEMENT
Operated By: Longball Inc.
Principal Owner: Bobby Brett. **Co-Owner/Senior Adviser:** Andrew Billig.
Vice President/General Manager: Chris Duff. **Senior VP:** Otto Klein. **VP, Tickets:** Josh Roys. **Director, Business Operations:** Lesley DeHart. **Assistant GM/Sponsorships:** Kyle Day. **Promotions Coordinators:** Yvette Yzaguirre, Elise Rooney. **Director, Group Sales:** Nick Gaebe. **Group Sales Coordinators:** Cara Paganini, Caleb Debois. **Director, Concessions/Operations:** Justin Stottlemyre. **Director, Public Relations:** Dustin Toms. **Account Executives:** Alex Reed, Mike Boyle, Chris Combo, Jared Munson. **CFO:** Greg Sloan. **Director, Accounting:** Dawnelle Shaw. **Head Groundskeeper:** David Yearout. **Assistant Director, Stadium Operations:** Larry Blummer.

FIELD STAFF
Manager: Tim Hulett. **Hitting Coach:** Unavailable. **Pitching Coach:** Jose Jaimes. **Strength/Conditioning Coach:** Ed Yong. **Trainer:** Zach Jones.

GAME INFORMATION
Radio Announcer: Mike Boyle. **No. of Games Broadcast:** 76. **Flagship Station:** 1510 KGA.
PA Announcer: Unavailable. **Official Scorer:** Unavailable.
Stadium Name: Avista Stadium at the Spokane Fair and Expo Center. **Location:** From west, I-90 to exit 283B (Thor/Freya), east on Third Ave., left onto Havana; From east, I-90 to Broadway exit, right onto Broadway, left onto Havana. **Standard Game Time:** 6:30 pm, Sun 3:30 pm. **Ticket Price Range:** $5-13.
Visiting Club Hotel: Mirabeau Park Hotel & Convention Center, N 1100 Sullivan Rd, Spokane, WA 99037. **Telephone:** (509) 924-9000.

TRI-CITY DUST DEVILS

Office Address: 6200 Burden Blvd., Pasco, WA 99301.
Telephone: (509) 544-8789. **Fax:** (509) 547-9570.
E-Mail Address: info@dustdevilsbaseball.com. **Website:** www.dustdevilsbaseball.com.
Affiliation (first year): Colorado Rockies (2001). **Years in League:** 1955-1974, 1983-1986, 2001-

OWNERSHIP/MANAGEMENT

Operated by: Northwest Baseball Ventures.
Principal Owners: George Brett, Hoshino Dreams Corp, Brent Miles. **President:** Brent Miles.
Vice President/General Manager: Derrel Ebert. **VP, Business Operations:** Tim Gittel. **Assistant GM, Tickets:** Dan O'Neill Director, Sponsorships: Anne Brenner. **Ticket Sales Manager:** Andy Wood. **Sponsorships Coordinator:** Ann Shaffer. **Account Executive:** Jason Bravo. **Account Executive:** Brennan McIntire. **Account Executive:** Erik Roach. **Head Groundskeeper:** Michael Angel.

FIELD STAFF

Manager: Drew Saylor. **Hitting Coach:** Warren Schaeffer. **Pitching Coach:** Frank Gonzales. **Trainer:** Casey Papas. **Development Supervisor:** Duane Espy.

GAME INFORMATION

Radio Announcer: Chris King. **No. of Games Broadcast:** 76. **Flagship Station:** Newstalk 870 AM KFLD.
PA Announcer: Patrick Harvey. **Official Scorers:** Tony Wise, Scott Tylinski.
Stadium Name: Gesa Stadium. **Location:** I-182 to exit 9 (Road 68), north to Burden Blvd, right to stadium. **Standard Game Time:** 7:15 pm. **Ticket Price Range:** $7-10.
Visiting Club Hotel: Red Lion Hotel-Columbia Center, 1101 N Columbia Center Blvd, Kennewick, WA 99336. **Telephone:** (509) 783-0611.

VANCOUVER CANADIANS

Office Address: Scotiabank Field at Nat Bailey Stadium, 4601 Ontario St, Vancouver, British Columbia V5V 3H4.
Telephone: (604) 872-5232. **Fax:** (604) 872-1714.
E-Mail Address: staff@canadiansbaseball.com. **Website:** www.canadiansbaseball.com.
Affiliation (first year): Toronto Blue Jays (2011). **Years in League:** 2000-

OWNERSHIP/MANAGEMENT

Operated by: Vancouver Canadians Professional Baseball LLP.
Managing General Partner: Jake Kerr. **Partner:** Jeff Mooney. **President:** Andy Dunn.
General Manager: JC Fraser. **Assistant GM:** Allan Bailey. **Financial Controller:** Andrew Remedios. **VP, Sales/Marketing:** Graham Wall. **Director, Ballpark Operations:** Trevor Sheffield. **Director, Communications/Broadcast:** Rob Fai. **Director, Community Relations/Social Media:** Jeff Holloway. **Director, Sales/Community Relations:** Alex Dachis. **Manager, Sales/Marketing Services:** Jennifer Wilcock. **Coordinator, Sales/Community Relations:** Andrew Forsyth. **Coordinator, Sales/Promotions:** Michael Richardson. **Coordinator, Sales:** Sam Jacobs. **Head Groundskeeper:** Tom Archibald.

FIELD STAFF

Manager: John Schneider. **Hitting Coach:** Dave Pano. **Pitching Coach:** Jeff Ware. **Trainer:** Reggie Mungrue.

GAME INFORMATION

Radio Announcer: Rob Fai. **No. of Games Broadcast:** 76. **Flagship Station:** The Team 1040-AM.
PA Announcer: Don Andrews/John Ashbridge. **Official Scorer:** Mike Hanafin.
Stadium Name: Nat Bailey Stadium. **Location:** From downtown, take Cambie Street Bridge, left on East 25th Ave./ King Edward Ave, right on Main Street, right on 33rd Ave, right on Ontario St to stadium; From south, take Highway 99 to Oak Street, right on 41st Ave, left on Main Street to 33rd Ave, right on Ontario St to stadium. **Standard Game Times:** 7:05 pm, Sun 1:05. **Ticket Price Range:** $9-20.
Visiting Club Hotel: Accent Inns, 10551 Edwards Dr, Richmond, BC V6X 3L8. **Telephone:** (604) 273-3311.

APPALACHIAN LEAGUE

APPALACHIAN LEAGUE
of professional baseball clubs

ROOKIE ADVANCED

Mailing Address: 759 182nd Ave. E., Redington Shores, FL 33708.
Telephone: 704-252-2656.
E-Mail Address: office@appyleague.net. **Website:** www.appyleague.com.

Years League Active: 1921-25, 1937-55, 1957-
President/Treasurer: Lee Landers. **Corporate Secretary:** David Lane (Greeneville).
Directors: Charlie Wilson (Bluefield), Larry Broadway (Bristol), Scott Sharp (Burlington), Ronnie Richardson (Danville), Brad Steil (Elizabethton), Quinton McCracken (Greeneville), Gary LaRocque (Johnson City), Jon Miller (Kingsport), Mitch Lukevics (Princeton), Chris Gwynn (Pulaski).
Executive Committee: Wayne Carpenter (Pulaski), Ronnie Richardson (Atlanta), David Lane (Greeneville), Dan Moushon (Burlington), Jon Vuch (St. Louis), Charlie Wilson (Toronto).
Board of Trustees Representative: Mitch Lukevics (Tampa Bay).
League Administrator: Bobbi Landers.
Division Structure: East—Bluefield, Burlington, Danville, Princeton, Pulaski. West—Bristol, Elizabethton, Greeneville, Johnson City, Kingsport.
Regular Season: 68 games. **2014 Opening Date:** June 19. **Closing Date:** Aug 29.
All-Star Game: None.
Playoff Format: East winner plays East second-place team, and West winner plays West second-place team in best-of-three series. Winners meet in best-of-three series for league championship.
Roster Limit: 30 active, 35 under control. **Player Eligibility Rule:** No more than three players on the active roster may have three or more years of prior minor league service.
Brand of Baseball: Rawlings.
Umpires: Unavailable

Lee Landers

STADIUM INFORMATION

Club	Stadium	Opened	Dimensions			Capacity	2013 Att.
			LF	CF	RF		
Bluefield	Bowen Field	1939	335	400	335	2,250	28,232
Bristol	DeVault Memorial Stadium	1969	325	400	310	2,000	20,309
Burlington	Burlington Athletic Stadium	1960	335	410	335	3,000	32,200
Danville	Dan Daniel Memorial Park	1993	330	400	330	2,588	25,152
Elizabethton	Joe O'Brien Field	1974	335	414	326	1,500	24,725
Greeneville	Pioneer Park	2004	331	400	331	2,400	45,261
Johnson City	Howard Johnson Field	1956	320	410	320	2,500	25,612
Kingsport	Hunter Wright Stadium	1995	330	410	330	2,500	23,476
Princeton	Hunnicutt Field	1988	330	396	330	1,950	24,610
Pulaski	Calfee Park	1935	335	405	310	2,500	25,842

BLUEFIELD BLUE JAYS

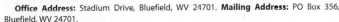

Office Address: Stadium Drive, Bluefield, WV 24701. **Mailing Address:** PO Box 356, Bluefield, WV 24701.
Telephone: (304) 324-1326. **Fax:** (304) 324-1318.
E-Mail Address: babybirds1@comcast.net. **Website:** www.bluefieldjays.com.
Affiliation (first year): Toronto Blue Jays (2011). **Years in League:** 1946-55, 1957-

OWNERSHIP/MANAGEMENT

Director: Charlie Wilson (Toronto Blue Jays).
Vice President: Bill Looney. **Secretary:** MK Burton. **Counsel:** David Kersey.
President: George McGonagle. **General Manager:** Jeff Gray. **Director, Field Operations/Grounds:** Mike White.

FIELD STAFF

Manager: Dennis Holmberg. **Coach:** Cesar Martin. **Pitching Coach:** Antonio Caceres.

GAME INFORMATION

PA Announcer: Unavailable.
Stadium Name: Bowen Field. **Location:** I-77 to Bluefield exit 1, Route 290 to Route 460 West, fourth light right onto Leatherwood Lane, left at first light, past Chevron station and turn right, stadium quarter-mile on left. **Ticket Price Range:** $4.
Visiting Club Hotel: Quality Inn Bluefield, 3350 Big Laurel Highway/460 West, Bluefield, WV 24701. **Telephone:** (304) 325-6170.

BRISTOL PIRATES

Ballpark Location: 1501 Euclid Ave., Bristol, VA 24201. **Mailing Address:** PO Box 1434, Bristol, VA 24203.
Telephone: (276) 206-9946. **Fax:** (276) 669-7686.
E-Mail Address: gm@bristolbaseball.com. **Website:** www.bristolpiratesbaseball.com
Affiliation (first year): Pittsburgh Pirates (2014). **Years in League:** 1921-25, 1940-55, 1969-

OWNERSHIP/MANAGEMENT
Owned by: Pittsburgh Pirates
Operated by: Bristol Baseball Inc.
Director: Larry Broadway (Pittsburgh Pirates). **President/General Manager:** Mahlon Luttrell. **Vice Presidents:** Lucas Hobbs, Tim Johnston, Mark Young. **Treasurer:** Dorothy Cox. **Secretary:** Perry Hustad

FIELD STAFF
Manager: Edgar Varela. **Hitting Coach:** Terry Alexander. **Pitching Coach:** Miguel Bonilla. **Trainer:** Lee Slagle.

GAME INFORMATION
Radio: Internet broadcast through milb.com.
PA Announcer: Tim Johnston. **Official Scorer:** Perry Hustad.
Stadium Name: DeVault Memorial Stadium. **Location:** I-81 to exit 3 onto Commonwealth Ave., right on Euclid Ave for half-mile. **Standard Game Time:** 7 pm. **Ticket Price Range:** $3-6.
Visiting Club Hotel: Holiday Inn, 3005 Linden Drive Bristol, VA 24202. **Telephone:** (276) 466-4100.

BURLINGTON ROYALS

Office Address: 1450 Graham St., Burlington, NC 27217. **Mailing Address:** PO Box 1143, Burlington, NC 27216.
Telephone: (336) 222-0223. **Fax:** (336) 226-2498.
E-Mail Address: info@burlingtonroyals.com. **Website:** www.burlingtonroyals.com.
Affiliation (first year): Kansas City Royals (2007). **Years in League:** 1986-

OWNERSHIP/MANAGEMENT
Operated by: Burlington Baseball Club Inc.
Director: Scott Sharp (Kansas City Royals).
President: Miles Wolff. **Vice President:** Dan Moushon.
General Manager: Ryan Keur. **Assistant GM:** Jared Orton. **Director, Stadium Operations:** Mike Thompson.

FIELD STAFF
Manager: Tommy Shields. **Hitting Coach:** Nelson Liriano. **Pitching Coach:** Carlos Martinez.

GAME INFORMATION
Radio Announcer: Matt Krause. **No. of Games Broadcast:** 44 (all home games, 10 away games). **Flagship:** www.burlingtonroyals.com.
PA Announcer: Tyler Williams. **Official Scorer:** Unavailable.
Stadium Name: Burlington Athletic Stadium. **Location:** I-40/85 to exit 145, north on Route 100 (Maple Avenue) for 1 1/2 miles, right on Mebane Street for 1 1/2 miles, right on Beaumont, left on Graham. **Standard Game Time:** 7 pm. **Ticket Price Range:** $5-9.

DANVILLE BRAVES

Office Address: Dan Daniel Memorial Park, 302 River Park Drive, Danville, VA 24540. **Mailing Address:** PO Box 378, Danville, VA 24543.
Telephone: (434) 797-3792. **Fax:** (434) 797-3799.
E-Mail Address: info@dbraves.com. **Website:** www.dbraves.com.
Affiliation (first year): Atlanta Braves (1993). **Years in League:** 1993-

OWNERSHIP/MANAGEMENT
Operated by: Atlanta National League Baseball Club Inc.
Director: Ronnie Richardson (Atlanta Braves).
General Manager: David Cross. **Assistant GM:** Bob Kitzmiller. **Operations Manager:** Will Sanford. **Head Groundskeeper:** Jon Hall.

FIELD STAFF
Manager: Randy Ingle. **Coach:** Carlos Mendez. **Pitching Coach:** Dan Meyer. **Athletic Trainer:** Joe Luat.

GAME INFORMATION
Radio Announcer: Nick Pierce. **No. of Games Broadcast:** 34 (all home games). **Flagship Station:** www.dbraves.com.

PA Announcer: Jay Stephens. **Official Scorer:** Mark Bowman.
Stadium Name: American Legion Field Post 325 Field at Dan Daniel Memorial Park. **Location:** US 29 Bypass to River Park Drive/Dan Daniel Memorial Park exit; follow signs to park. **Standard Game Times:** 7 pm, Sun 4. **Ticket Price Range:** $5-8.

ELIZABETHTON TWINS

Office Address: 300 West Mill St., Elizabethton, TN 37643. **Stadium Address:** 208 N Holly Lane, Elizabethton, TN 37643. **Mailing Address:** 136 S Sycamore St., Elizabethton, TN 37643. **Telephone:** (423) 547-6441. **Fax:** (423) 547-6442.
E-Mail Address: etwins@cityofelizabethton.org. **Website:** www.elizabethtontwins.com.
Affiliation (first year): Minnesota Twins (1974). **Years in League:** 1937-42, 1945-51, 1974-

OWNERSHIP/MANAGEMENT
Operator: City of Elizabethton.
Director: Brad Steil.
President: Harold Mains.
General Manager: Mike Mains. **Clubhouse Operations/Head Groundskeeper:** David McQueen.

FIELD STAFF
Manager: Ray Smith. **Coach:** Unavailable. **Pitching Coach:** Henry Bonilla. **Trainer:** Steven Taylor.

GAME INFORMATION
Radio Announcer: Nick Hyder. **No. of Games Broadcast:** 40 (all home games, six away games). **Flagship Station:** WBEJ 1240-AM.
PA Announcer: Tom Banks. **Official Scorer:** Unavailable.
Stadium Name: Joe O'Brien Field. **Location:** I-81 to Highway I-26, exit at Highway 321/67, left on Holly Lane. **Standard Game Time:** 7 pm. **Ticket Price Range:** $3-6.
Visiting Club Hotel: Holiday Inn, 101 W Springbrook Dr, Johnson City, TN 37601. **Telephone:** (423) 282-4611.

GREENEVILLE ASTROS

Office Address: 135 Shiloh Road, Greeneville, TN 37743. **Mailing Address:** PO Box 5192, Greeneville, TN 37743.
Telephone: (423) 638-0411. **Fax:** (423) 638-9450.
E-Mail Address: greeneville@astros.com. **Website:** www.greenevilleastros.com.
Affiliation (first year): Houston Astros (2004). **Years in League:** 2004-

OWNERSHIP/MANAGEMENT
Operated by: Houston Astros Baseball Club.
Director: Quinton McCracken (Houston Astros).
General Manager: David Lane. **Assistant GM:** Hunter Reed. **Account Executive:** Ben Spillner, Kelsey Thompson. **Head Groundskeeper:** Kelly Rensel. **Clubhouse Operations:** Unavailable.

FIELD STAFF
Manager: Josh Bonifay. **Hitting Coach:** Cesar Cedeno. **Pitching Coach:** Josh Miller. **Trainer:** Unavailable.

GAME INFORMATION
Internet Radio: Steve Wilhoit.
PA Announcer: Bobby Rader. **Official Scorer:** Johnny Painter.
Stadium Name: Pioneer Park. **Location:** On the campus of Tusculum College, 135 Shiloh Rd Greeneville, TN 37743.
Standard Game Time: 7 pm, Sat/Sun 6 pm. **Ticket Price Range:** $6-8.
Visiting Club Hotel: Quality Inn, 3160 E Andrew Johnson Hwy, Greeneville, TN 37745. **Telephone:** (423) 638-7511.

JOHNSON CITY CARDINALS

Office Address: 111 Legion St., Johnson City, TN 37601. **Mailing Address:** PO Box 179, Johnson City, TN 37605.
Telephone: (423) 461-4866. **Fax:** (423) 461-4864.
E-Mail Address: contact@jccardinals.com. **Website:** www.jccardinals.com.
Affiliation (first year): St. Louis Cardinals (1975). **Years in League:** 1911-13, 1921-24, 1937-55, 1957-61, 1964-

OWNERSHIP/MANAGEMENT
Owned by: St. Louis Cardinals.
Operated by: Johnson City Sports Foundation Inc. **President:** Lee Sowers.

Director: John Vuch (St. Louis Cardinals).
General Manager: Tyler Parsons. **Assistant GM:** Unavailable.

FIELD STAFF

Manager: Johnny Rodriguez. **Coach:** Roberto Espinoza. **Pitching Coach:** Paul Davis.

GAME INFORMATION

PA Announcer: Unavailable. **Official Scorer:** Gene Renfro.
Stadium Name: Howard Johnson Field at Cardinal Park. **Location:** I-26 to exit 23, left on East Main, through light onto Legion Street. **Standard Game Time:** 7 pm. **Ticket Price Range:** $4-$6.
Visiting Club Hotel: Holiday Inn, 101 W Springbrook Dr, Johnson City, TN 37601. **Telephone:** (423) 282-4611.

KINGSPORT METS

Office Address: 800 Granby Rd., Kingsport, TN 37660.
Telephone: (423) 224-2626. **Fax:** (423) 224-2625.
E-Mail Address: info@kmets.com. **Website:** www.kmets.com
Affiliation (first year): New York Mets (1980). **Years in League:** 1921-25, 1938-52, 1957, 1960-63, 1969-82, 1984-

OWNERSHIP/MANAGEMENT

Operated By: New York Mets. **Director:** Jon Miller.
General Manager: Brian Paupeck.

FIELD STAFF

Manager: Jose Leger. **Coach:** Yunir Garcia. **Pitching Coach:** Jonathan Hurst

GAME INFORMATION

Radio: Internet only (www.kmets.com). **PA Announcer:** Unavailable. **Official Scorer:** Jon Moorehouse.
Stadium Name: Hunter Wright Stadium, 800 Granby Road, Kingsport, TN 37660 Directions: I-26, Exit 1 (Stone Drive), left on West Stone Drive (US 11W), right on Granby Road. **Game Time:** 7 pm, 5 (Sat/Sun). **Ticket Price Range:** $4-7.
Visiting Club Hotel: Quality Inn, 3004 Bays Mountain Plaza, Kingsport, TN 37664. **Telephone:** (423) 230-0534.

PRINCETON RAYS

Office Address: 205 Old Bluefield Rd., Princeton, WV 24739. **Mailing Address:** PO Box 5646, Princeton, WV 24740.
Telephone: (304) 487-2000. **Fax:** (304) 487-8762.
E-Mail Address: princetonrays@frontier.com . **Website:** www.princetonrays.net.
Affiliation (first year): Tampa Bay Rays (1997). **Years in League:** 1988-

OWNERSHIP/MANAGEMENT

Operated By: Princeton Baseball Association Inc.
Director: Mitch Lukevics (Tampa Bay Rays). **President:** Mori Williams.
General Manager: Jim Holland. **Director, Stadium Operations:** Mick Bayle. **Official Scorer:** Bob Redd. **Graphic Designer:** Warren Hypes. **Clubhouse Manager:** Anthony Dunagan. **Administrative Assistant:** Tommy Thomason. **Chaplain:** Craig Stout.

FIELD STAFF

Manager: Danny Sheaffer. **Coach:** Reinaldo Ruiz. **Pitching Coach:** Jose Gonzalez. **Athletic Trainer:** Unavailable.

GAME INFORMATION

Radio Announcer: Unavailable. **No. of Games Broadcast:** 68. **Flagship Station:** Unavailable.
Official Scorer: Bob Redd.
Stadium Name: Hunnicutt Field. **Location:** Exit 9 off I-77, US 460 West to downtown exit, left on Stafford Dr., stadium located behind Mercer County Technical Education Center. **Standard Game Times:** 7:05 pm, Sun 6:05 pm. **Ticket Price Range:** $4-6.
Visiting Club Hotel: Days Inn, I-77 and Ambrose Lane, Princeton, WV 24740. **Telephone:** (304) 425-8100.

PULASKI MARINERS

Shipping Address: 700 South Washington Ave., Pulaski VA 24301. **Mailing Address:** PO Box 676, Pulaski, VA 24301.
Telephone: (540) 980-1070. **Fax:** (540) 980-1850.
E-Mail Address: info@pulaskimariners.net.
Affiliation (first year): Seattle Mariners (2008). **Years in League:** 1946-50, 1952-55, 1957-58,

1969-77, 1982-92, 1997-2006, 2008-

OWNERSHIP/MANAGEMENT

Operated By: Pulaski Baseball Inc.
Director: Chris Gwynn (Seattle Mariners). **President:** Tom Compton.
General Manager: Lois Dittirch. **Office Manager:** John Dittrich.

FIELD STAFF

Manager: Rob Mummau. **Hitting Coach:** Brent Johnson. **Pitching Coach:** Jason Blanton.

GAME INFORMATION

PA Announcer: Unavailable. **Official Scorer:** Charles Altizer.
Stadium Name: Calfee Park. **Location:** Interstate 81 to Exit 89-B (Route 11), north to Pulaski, right on Pierce Avenue.
Standard Game Times: 7 p.m. **Ticket Price Range:** $4-6.
Visiting Club Hotel: Comfort Inn, 4424 Cleburne Blvd, Dublin, VA 24084. **Telephone:** (540) 674-1100.

PIONEER LEAGUE

Office Address: 2607 S. Southeast Blvd., Building B, Suite 115, Spokane, WA 99223.
Mailing Address: PO Box 2564, Spokane, WA 99220.
Telephone: (509) 456-7615. **Fax:** (509) 456-0136.
E-Mail Address: fanmail@pioneerleague.com. **Website:** www.pioneerleague.com.
Years League Active: 1939-42, 1946-

President: Jim McCurdy.
Directors: Dave Baggott (Ogden), Matt Ellis (Missoula), DG Elmore (Helena), Kevin Greene (Idaho Falls), Michael Baker (Grand Junction), Jeff Katofsky (Orem), Vinny Purpura (Great Falls), Jim Iverson (Billings).
League Administrator: Teryl MacDonald. **Executive Director:** Mary Ann McCurdy.
Division Structure: North—Billings, Great Falls, Helena, Missoula. South—Grand Junction, Idaho Falls, Ogden, Orem.
Regular Season: 76 games (split schedule). **2014 Opening Date:** June 26. **Closing Date:** Sept 4.
All-Star Game: None.
Playoff Format: First-half division winners meet second-half division winners in best-of-three series. Winners meet in best-of-three series for league championship.
Roster Limit: 35 active, 30 dressed for each game. **Player Eligibility Rule:** No player on active list may have three or more years of prior minor league service.
Brand of Baseball: Rawlings.
Umpires: Unavailable.

Jim McCurdy

STADIUM INFORMATION

Club	Stadium	Opened	Dimensions LF	CF	RF	Capacity	2013 Att.
Billings	Dehler Park	2008	329	410	350	3,071	105,417
Grand Junction	Sam Suplizio Field	1949	302	400	333	7,014	87,436
Great Falls	Centene Stadium at Legion Park	1956	335	414	335	3,800	58,386
Helena	Kindrick Field	1939	335	400	325	1,700	33,515
Idaho Falls	Melaleuca Field	1976	340	400	350	3,400	96,367
Missoula	Ogren Park at Allegiance Field	2004	309	398	287	3,500	81,686
Ogden	Lindquist Field	1997	335	396	334	5,000	124,687
Orem	Home of the Owlz	2005	305	408	312	4,500	85,630

BILLINGS MUSTANGS

Office Address: Dehler Park, 2611 9th Ave. North, Billings, MT 59101. **Mailing Address:** PO Box 1553, Billings, MT 59103.
Telephone: (406) 252-1241. **Fax:** (406) 252-2968.
E-Mail Address: mustangs@billingsmustangs.com. **Website:** www.billingsmustangs.com .
Affiliation (first year): Cincinnati Reds (1974). **Years in League:** 1948-63, 1969-

OWNERSHIP/MANAGEMENT
Operated By: Billings Pioneer Baseball Club.
President: Woody Hahn.
General Manager: Gary Roller. **Senior Director, Corporate Sales/Partnerships:** Chris Marshall. **Senior Director, Stadium Operations:** Matt Schoonover. **Senior Director, Broadcasting/Media Relations:** Ryan Schuiling. **Senior Director, Food Services:** Curt Prchal. **Senior Director, Field Maintenance/Facilities:** John Barta.

FIELD STAFF
Manager: Dick Schofield. **Hitting Coach:** Kevin Mahar. **Pitching Coach:** Derrin Ebert. **Athletic Trainer:** Andrew Cleves.

GAME INFORMATION
Radio Broadcaster: Ryan Schuiling. **No. of Games Broadcast:** 76. **Flagship Station:** ESPN 910 AM KBLG.
PA Announcer: Kyle Riley. **Official Scorer:** George Kimmet.
Stadium Name: Dehler Park. **Location:** I-90 to Exit 450, north on 27th Street North to 9th Avenue North. **Standard Game Times:** 7:05 pm, Sun 2:05. **Ticket Price Range:** $4-$10.
Visiting Club Hotel: Crowne Plaza, 27 North 27th Street, Billings, MT, 59101. **Telephone:** (406) 252-7400.

GRAND JUNCTION ROCKIES

Office Address: 1315 North Ave, Grand Junction, CO 81501.
Telephone: (970) 255-7625. **Fax:** (970) 241-2374.
E-Mail Address: timray@gjrockies.com. **Website:** www.gjrockies.com.
Affiliation (3rd year): Colorado Rockies (2001). **Years in League:** 2001-

OWNERSHIP/MANAGEMENT
Principal Owners/Operated by: GJR LLC.
General Manager: Tim Ray. **Assistant GM:** Mike Ruvolo. **Business Manager:** Matt Coakley.

FIELD STAFF
Manager: Anthony Sanders. **Hitting Coach:** Lee Stevens. **Pitching Coach:** Ryan Kibler. **Developmental Supervisor:** Tony Diaz. **Trainer:** John Duff

GAME INFORMATION
Radio Announcer: Adam Spolane. **No. of Games Broadcast:** 76. **Flagship Station:** The Vault 100.7 FM.
Official Scorer: Dan Kenyon.
Stadium Name: Suplizio Field. **Location:** 1315 North Ave, Grand Junction, CO 81501. **Standard Game Times:** 7:05 pm, Sun 4:05pm. **Ticket Price Range:** $7-10.
Visiting Club Hotel: Double Tree by Hilton.

GREAT FALLS VOYAGERS

Office Address: 1015 25th St. N., Great Falls, MT 59401.
Telephone: (406) 452-5311. **Fax:** (406) 454-0811.
E-Mail Address: voyagers@gfvoyagers.com. **Website:** www.gfvoyagers.com.
Affiliation (first year): Chicago White Sox (2003). **Years in League:** 1948-1963, 1969-

OWNERSHIP/MANAGEMENT
Operated By: Great Falls Baseball Club, Inc.
President: Vinney Purpura.
General Manager: Kattie Meyer. **Assistant GM:** Scott Reasoner. **Ticket Sales Manager:** Kelly Wombacher. **Account Executive:** Nathan Davis.

FIELD STAFF
Manager: Charles Poe. **Coach:** Greg Briley. **Pitching Coach:** Brian Drahman.

GAME INFORMATION
Radio Announcer: Unavailable. **No. of Games Broadcast:** 76. **Flagship Station:** KXGF-1400 AM.
PA Announcer: Lance DeHaan. **Official Scorer:** Mike Lewis.
Stadium Name: Centene Stadium located at Legion Park. **Location:** From I-15 to exit 281 (10th Ave S), left on 26th, left on Eighth Ave North, right on 25th, ballpark on right, past railroad tracks. **Ticket Price Range:** $4-9.
Visiting Club Hotel: Townhouse Inn of Great Falls, 1411 10th Ave S, Great Falls, MT 59405. **Telephone:** (406) 761-4600.

HELENA BREWERS

Office Address: 1300 N. Ewing, Helena, MT 59601. **Mailing Address:** PO Box 6756, Helena, MT 59604.
Telephone: (406) 495-0500. **Fax:** (406) 495-0900.
E-Mail Address: info@helenabrewers.net. **Website:** www.helenabrewers.net.
Affiliation (first year): Milwaukee Brewers (2003). **Years in League:** 1978-2000, 2003-

OWNERSHIP/MANAGEMENT
Operated by: Helena Baseball Club LLC.
Principal Owner: David Elmore.
General Manager: Paul Fetz. **Director, Operations/Ticketing:** Travis Hawks. **Director, Group Sales/Marketing:** Dylan LaPlante . **Radio Announcer/Director, Broadcasting/Media Relations:** Steve Wendt.

FIELD STAFF
Manager: Tony Diggs. **Hitting Coach:** Jason Dubois. **Pitching Coach:** Rolando Valles . **Trainer:** Unavailable.

GAME INFORMATION

Radio Announcer: Steve Wendt. **No. of Games Broadcast:** 76. **Flagship Station:** KCAP 1340-AM.
PA Announcer: Randy Bowsher. **Official Scorers:** Kevin Higgens, Craig Struble, Jim Shope, Andrew Gideon.
Stadium Name: Kindrick Field. **Location:** Cedar Street exit off I-15, west to Last Chance Gulch, left at Memorial Park.
Standard Game Time: 7:05 pm, Sun 1:05. **Ticket Price Range:** $6-9.
Visiting Club Hotel: Red Lion Colonial. **Telephone:** 406-443-2100.

IDAHO FALLS CHUKARS

Office Address: 900 Jim Garchow Way, Idaho Falls, ID 83402. **Mailing Address:** PO 2183, Idaho, ID 83403.
Telephone: (208) 522-8363. **Fax:** (208) 522-9858.
E-Mail Address: chukars@ifchukars.com. **Website:** www.ifchukars.com.
Affiliation (first year): Kansas City Royals (2004). **Years in League:** 1940-42, 1946-

OWNERSHIP/MANAGEMENT

Operated By: The Elmore Sports Group.
Principal Owner: David Elmore.
President/General Manager: Kevin Greene. **Assistant GM, Merchandise:** Andrew Daugherty. **Account Manager/ Food Service Specialist:** Paul Henderson. **Clubhouse Manager:** Jared Troescher. **Head Groundskeeper:** Chris Sundvold.

FIELD STAFF

Manager: Omar Ramirez. **Hitting Coach:** Damon Hollins. **Pitching Coach:** Mark Davis. **Bench Coach:** Julio Bruno.

GAME INFORMATION

Radio Announcers: John Balginy, Chris Lewis. **No. of Games Broadcast:** 76. **Flagship Station:** KUPI/ESPN 980-AM.
Official Scorer: John Balginy.
Stadium Name: Melaleuca Field. **Location:** I-15 to West Broadway exit, left onto Memorial Drive, right on Mound Avenue, 1/4 mile to stadium. **Standard Game Times:** 7:15 pm, Sun 4. **Ticket Price Range:** $8-11.
Visiting Club Hotel: Guesthouse Inn & Suites, 850 Lindsay Blvd, Idaho Falls, ID 83402. **Telephone:** (208) 522-6260.

MISSOULA OSPREY

Office Address: 140 N. Higgins, Suite 201, Missoula, MT 59802.
Telephone: (406) 543-3300. **Fax:** (406) 543-9463.
E-Mail Address: info@missoulaosprey.com. **Website:** www.missoulaosprey.com.
Affiliation (first year): Arizona Diamondbacks (1999). **Years in League:** 1956-60, 1999-

OWNERSHIP/MANAGEMENT

Operated By: Mountain Baseball LLC.
President: Mike Ellis. **Vice President:** Judy Ellis.
Executive VP: Matt Ellis. **VP/General Manager:** Jeff Griffin. **Retail Manager:** Kim Klages Johns. **Office Manager:** Nola Hunter. **Account Executive:** Grant Warner.

FIELD STAFF

Manager: Audo Vicente. **Hitting Coach:** Vince Harrison. **Pitching Coach:** Jeff Bajenaru. **Strength/Conditioning:** Sean Light. **Trainer:** Jeremy Fradin.

GAME INFORMATION

Radio Announcer: Nolan Alexander. **No. of Games Broadcast:** Home-38, Away-38. **Flagship Station:** ESPN 97.5 FM.
PA Announcer: Tom Schultz. **Official Scorer:** Dan Hunter.
Stadium Name: Ogren Park Allegiance Field. **Location:** 700 Cregg Lane. **Directions:** Take Orange St. to Cregg Ln., west on Cregg Ln., stadium west of McCormick Park. **Standard Game Times:** 7:05 pm, Sun 5:05. **Ticket Price Range:** $6-12.
Visiting Club Hotel: Comfort Inn-University, 1021 E. Broadway, Missoula, MT 59802. **Telephone:** (406) 549-7600.

OGDEN RAPTORS

Office Address: 2330 Lincoln Ave., Ogden, UT 84401.
Telephone: (801) 393-2400. **Fax:** (801) 393-2473.
E-Mail Address: homerun@ogden-raptors.com. **Website:** www.ogden-raptors.com.
Affiliation (first year): Los Angeles Dodgers (2003). **Years in League:** 1939-42, 1946-55, 1966-74, 1994-

OWNERSHIP/MANAGEMENT

Operated By: Ogden Professional Baseball, Inc.
Principal Owners: Dave Baggott, John Lindquist.
President/General Manager: Dave Baggott.

Director, Media Relations/Broadcaster: Brandon Hart. **Director, Stadium Operations/Merchandise:** Geri Kopinski. **Director, Food Service Personnel:** Louise Hillard. **Director, Security:** Mark Ramsey. **Director, Ticket Operations:** Kylie Johnson. **Director, Information Technology:** Chris Greene. **Public Relations:** Pete Diamond. **Groundskeeper:** Kenny Kopinski. **Assistant Groundkeeper:** Bob Richardson.

FIELD STAFF

Manager: Lee Tinsley. **Hitting Coach:** Leo Garcia. **Pitching Coach:** Greg Sabat.

GAME INFORMATION

Radio Announcer: Brandon Hart. **No. of Games Broadcast:** 76. **Flagship Station:** 97.5 FM.
PA Announcer: Pete Diamond. **Official Scorer:** Dennis Kunimura.
Stadium Name: Lindquist Field. **Location:** I-15 North to 21th Street exit, east to Lincoln Ave., south three blocks to park. **Standard Game Times:** 7 pm, 4 pm (Sun). **Ticket Price Range:** $4-10.

OREM OWLZ

Office Address: 970 W. University Parkway, Orem, UT 84058.
Telephone: (801) 377-2255. **Fax:** (801) 377-2345.
E-Mail Address: fan@oremowlz.com. **Website:** www.oremowlz.com.
Affiliation: Los Angeles Angels (2001). **Years in League:** 2001-

OWNERSHIP/MANAGEMENT

Operated By: Bery Bery Gud To Me LLC.
Principal Owner: Jeff Katofsky.
General Manager: Justo Vazquez. **Assistant GM:** Jillian Dingee. **IT Manager:** Julie Hatch. **Director, Sales/ Marketing:** Abby Lyman.

FIELD STAFF

Manager: Unavailable. **Coaches:** Ryan Barba, Paul Mcanulty. **Pitching Coach:** Chris Gissell.

GAME INFORMATION

Radio Announcer: Trevor Amicone. **No. of Games Broadcast:** 76. **Flagship Station:** Unavailable.
PA Announcer: Unavailable. **Official Scorer:** Rachel Hartgrove.
Stadium Name: Home of the Owlz. **Location:** Exit 269 (University Parkway) off I-15 at Utah Valley University campus. **Ticket Price Range:** $4-12.
Visiting Club Hotel: Holiday Inn & Suites, 1290 W. University Parkway, Orem, UT 8405.

ARIZONA LEAGUE

Office Address: 620 W Franklin St., Boise, ID 83702. **Mailing Address:** PO Box 1645, Boise, ID 83701.
Telephone: (208) 429-1511. **Fax:** (208) 429-1525.
E-Mail Address: bobrichmond@qwestoffice.net
Years League Active: 1988-
President/Treasurer: Bob Richmond.
Vice President: Tim Purpura (Rangers). **Corporate Secretary:** Ted Polakowski (Athletics).
Administrative Assistant: Rob Richmond.
Divisional Alignment: East—Angels, Athletics, Cubs, Diamondbacks, Giants. Central—Brewers, Dodgers, Indians, Reds. West—Mariners, Padres, Rangers, White Sox.
2014 Opening Date: June 20. **Closing Date:** Aug 29. **Regular Season:** 56 games.
Playoff Format: Division champions from the first and second half qualify. Two teams with best overall records receive first-round bye and will meet first-round winners in semifinals. Winners advance to one-game championship.
All-Star Game: None.
Roster Limit: 35 active.
Player Eligibility Rule: No player may have three or more years of prior minor league service.

Clubs	Playing Site	Manager	Coach	Pitching Coach
Angels	Angels complex, Tempe	Elio Sarmiento	Brian Betancourth	M. Hampton/R. O'Malley
Athletics	Papago Park Baseball Complex, Phoenix	Ruben Escalera	Juan Dilone	Carlos Chavez
Brewers	Maryvale Baseball Complex, Phoenix	Nestor Corredor	Al LeBoeuf	Steve Cline
Cubs	Fitch Park, Mesa	Jimmy Gonzalez	Ricardo Medina	Anderson Tavarez
D-backs	Salt River Fields at Talking Stick	Luis Urueta	Javier Colina	Larry Pardo
Dodgers	Camelback Ranch, Glendale	John Shoemaker	Henry Cruz	Hector Berrios
Giants	Giants complex, Scottsdale	Nestor Rojas	Billy Horton	L. McCall/M. Rodriguez
Indians	Goodyear Ballpark	Anthony Medrano	J. Betances/D. Malave	M. Allen/D. Swanson
Mariners	Peoria Sports Complex	Darrin Garner	A. Bottin/J. Umbria	Rich Dorman
Padres	Peoria Sports Complex	Rod Barajas	Carlos Sosa	Dave Rajsich
Rangers	Surprise Recreation Campus	Kenny Holmberg	D. McDonald/B. Shouse	J. Seaver/K. Hook
Reds	Goodyear Ballpark	Eli Marrero	Jolbert Cabrera	Elmer Dessens
White Sox	Camelback Ranch, Glendale	Mike Gellinger	Unavailable	Felipe Lira

GULF COAST LEAGUE

Operated By: Minor League Baseball.
Office Address: 9550 16th St. North, St. Petersburg, FL 33716.
Telephone: 727-456-1734. **Fax:** 727-821-5819.
Website: www.milb.com. **E-Mail Address:** gcl@milb.com.
Vice President, Baseball & Business Operations: Tim Brunswick.
Manager, Baseball & Business Operations: Andy Shultz.
Regular Season: 60 games. **2014 Opening Date:** June 20. **Closing Date:** Aug 28.
Divisional Alignment: East—Cardinals, Marlins, Mets, Nationals. Northeast—Astros, Braves, Tigers, Yankees 2. Northwest—Blue Jays, Phillies, Pirates, Yankees 1. South—Orioles, Rays, Red Sox, Twins.
Playoff Format: Division winner with best record plays division winner with fourth-best record, division winners with Nos. 2 and 3 records play one-game semifinals. Winners meet in best-of-three series for championship.
All-Star Game: None.
Roster Limit: 35 active, only 30 of whom may be in uniform and eligible to play in any given game. At least 10 must be pitchers as of July 1.
Player Eligibility Rule: No player may have three or more years of prior minor league service.
Brand of Baseball: Rawlings.

Clubs	Playing Site	Manager	Coach(es)	Pitching Coach
Astros	Astros Complex, Kissimmee	Marty Malloy	Ramon Vasquez	Hector Mercado
Blue Jays	Mattick Training Center, Dunedin	Kenny Graham	Paul Elliott/Danny Solano	Willie Collazo
Braves	ESPN Wide World of Sports, Orlando	Rocket Wheeler	Rick Albert/Barbaro Garbey	Willie Martinez
Cardinals	Cardinals Complex, Jupiter	Steve Turco	Kleininger Teran	Darwin Marrero
Marlins	Roger Dean Stadium Complex, Jupiter	Julio Garcia	Danny Santin/Lenny Harris	Manny Olivera
Mets	Mets Complex, Port St Lucie	Jose Carreno	Ender Chavez	Josh Towers
Nationals	Nationals Complex, Viera	Michael Barrett	Jorge Mejia	Michael Tejera
Orioles	Ed Smith Stadium Complex, Sarasota	Orlando Gomez	Ramon Sambo	Wilson Alvarez
Phillies	Carpenter Complex, Clearwater	Roly de Armas	Rafael DeLima	Steve Schrenk
Pirates	Pirate City, Bradenton	Milver Reyes	Mike Lum	Scott Elarton
Rays	Charlotte Sports Park, Port Charlotte	Jim Morrison	W. Rincones/H. Torres	Marty DeMerritt
Red Sox	Jet Blue Park, Fort Myers	Tom Kotchman	Raul Gonzalez/Dave Tomlin	Dick Such
Tigers	Tigertown, Lakeland	Basilio Cabrera	Unavailable	Jorge Cordova
Twins	Lee County Sports Complex, Fort Myers	Ramon Borrego	R. Hernandez/R. Ingram	E. Wassermann
Yankees 1	Himes Complex, Tampa	Travis Chapman	C. Cosme/M. Hernandez	Cory Arbiso
Yankees 2	Himes Complex, Tampa	Patrick Osborn	D. Henson/H. Rabago	Jose Rosado

INDEPENDENT LEAGUES

AMERICAN ASSOCIATION

Office Address: 1415 Hwy 54 West, Suite 210, Durham, NC 27707.
Telephone: (919) 401-8150. **Fax:** (919) 401-8152. **Website:** www.americanassociationbaseball.com.
Year Founded: 2005.
Commissioner: Miles Wolff. **President:** Dan Moushon.
Director, Umpires: Kevin Winn.
Division Structure—North Division: Fargo-Moorhead RedHawks, St. Paul Saints, Sioux Falls Canaries, Winnipeg Goldeyes. Central Division—Gary SouthShore RailCats, Kansas City T-Bones, Lincoln Saltdogs, Sioux City Explorers. South Division—Amarillo Sox, Grand Prairie AirHogs, Laredo Lemurs, Wichita Wingnuts.
Regular Season: 100 games.
2014 Opening Date: May 15. **Closing Date:** Sept. 1.
Playoff Format: Three division winners and one wild card play in best-of-five series. Winners play for best-of-five American Association championship.
Roster Limit: 22.
Eligibility Rule: Minimum of four first-year players; maximum of five veterans (at least six or more years of professional service).
Brand of Baseball: Rawlings.
Statistician: Pointstreak.com, 602-1595 16th Avenue, Richmond Hill, ON Canada L4B 3N9.

STADIUM INFORMATION

Club	Stadium	Opened	LF	CF	RF	Capacity	2013 Att.
Amarillo	Amarillo National Bank Sox Stadium	1949	355	429	355	7,500	105,798
Fargo-Moorhead	Newman Outdoor Field	1996	318	408	314	4,513	186,091
Gary SouthShore	U.S. Steel Yard	2002	320	400	335	6,139	165,024
Grand Prairie	QuikTrip Park at Grand Prairie	2008	330	400	330	5,445	111,195
Kansas City	CommunityAmerica Ballpark	2003	300	396	328	6,537	265,596
Laredo	Uni-Trade Stadium	2012	335	405	335	6,000	151,055
Lincoln	Haymarket Park	2001	335	395	325	4,500	177,982
St. Paul	Midway Stadium	1982	320	400	320	6,069	239,399
Sioux City	Lewis and Clark Park	1993	330	400	330	3,630	52,052
Sioux Falls	Sioux Falls Stadium	1964	312	410	312	4,656	161,131
Wichita	Lawrence-Dumont Stadium	1934	344	401	312	6,055	147,119
Winnipeg	Shaw Park	1999	325	400	325	7,481	276,359

Dimensions column spans LF, CF, RF.

AMARILLO SOX

Office Address: 801 S Polk St, Amarillo, TX 79101.
Telephone: (806) 242-4653. **Fax:** (806) 322-1839.
Email Address: mark.lee@amarillosox.com. **Website:** www.amarillosox.com.
VP/General Manager: Mark Lee. **Assistant GM:** Russell Johnson. **Director, Sales/Marketing:** Adam Cox.
Field Manager: Bobby Brown.

GAME INFORMATION

Stadium Name: Amarillo National Bank Sox Stadium. **Location:** Take Grand Street exit and proceed north on Grand Street; turn left onto SE 3rd Ave.
Standard Game Times: 7:05 pm, Sun 6:05.

FARGO-MOORHEAD
REDHAWKS

Office Address: 1515 15th Ave N, Fargo, ND 58102.
Telephone: (701) 235-6161. **Fax:** (701) 297-9247.
Email Address: redhawks@fmredhawks.com. **Website:** www.fmredhawks.com.
Operated by: Fargo Baseball LLC.
President: Bruce Thom. **Chief Executive Officer:** Brad Thom.
General Manager: Josh Buchholz. **Senior Accountant:** Rick Larson. **Director, Promotions:** Karl Hoium. **Director, Ticket Sales/Assistant Director, Marketing:** Michael Larson. **Director,. Director, Food/Beverage:** Sean Kiernan. **Head Groundskeeper:** Sam Petersen. **Group Sales Coordinators:** Corey Eidem, Anna Rasmussen.
Manager/Director, Player Procurement: Doug Simunic. **Player Procurement Consultant:** Jeff Bittiger. **Pitching Coach:** Freddy Flores. **Coaches:** Bucky Burgau, Kole Zimmerman. **Trainer:** Craig Brandenburger. **Home Clubhouse**

Manager: Isaac Olson. **Visiting Clubhouse Manager:** Chris Krick.

GAME INFORMATION
   Radio Announcer: Scott Miller. **No. of Games Broadcast:** 100. **Flagship Station:** 740-AM The FAN.
   Stadium Name: Newman Outdoor Field. **Location:** I-29 North to exit 67, east on 19th Ave North, right on Albrecht Boulevard. **Standard Game Times:** 7:02 pm, Sat 6, Sun 1.

GARY SOUTHSHORE RAILCATS

Office Address: One Stadium Plaza, Gary, IN 46402.
Telephone: (219) 882-2255. **Fax:** (219) 882-2259.
Email Address: info@railcatsbaseball.com. **Website:** www.railcatsbaseball.com.
Operated by: PLS Holdings.
Owner/CEO: Pat Salvi. **Owner:** Lindy Salvi.
   General Manager: Pete Laven. **Vice President/General Counsel:** Beth Heffernan. **Assistant GM/Box Office Manager:** David Kay. **Assistant GM/Director, Sales:** Brian Lyter. **VP, Marketing/Promotions:** Natalie Kirby. **Director, Stadium Operations/Head Groundskeeper:** Michele Pickering. **Manager, Merchandise/Community Relations:** Amy Baran. **Senior Account Executive:** Percy Thornbor Jr. **Executive Assistant:** Arcella Moxley.
   Manager: Greg Tagert.

GAME INFORMATION
   No. of Games Broadcast: 100. **Flagship Station:** WLPR 89.1-FM.
   Stadium Name: US Steel Yard. **Location:** I-80/94 to Broadway Exit (Exit 10), north on Broadway to Fifth Avenue, east one block to stadium. **Standard Game Times:** 7:10 pm, Sat 6:10, Sun 2:10.

GRAND PRAIRIE AIRHOGS

Office Address: 1600 Lone Star Parkway, Grand Prairie, TX 75050.
Telephone: (972) 504-9383. **Fax:** (972) 504-2288.
Websites: www.airhogsbaseball.com/www.quiktrippark.com.
Operated By: Southern Independent Baseball, LLC.
Owner: Gary Elliston.. **Vice President/General Manager:** John Bilbow. **Assistant GM & Director of Ticket Operations:** Katy White. **VP, Communications:** David Hatchett. **Manager, Finance/Merchandise:** Trista Earlston. **Director, Director, Ballpark Operations:** TD Taylor. **Events Coordinator:** Matt Raffaele. **Director, Food/Beverage:** Chris Moriarty.Director, Sales: Karen Lucchesi.
   Manager: Ricky VanAsselberg. **Coach:** Jeff Russell, Eric Champion.

GAME INFORMATION
   No of Games Broadcast: 100. **Webcast:** www.airhogsbaseball.com.
   Stadium Name: QuikTrip Park at Grand Prairie. **Location:** From I-30, take Beltline Road exit going north, take Lone Star Park entrance towards the stadium.
   Standard Game Times: 7:05 pm, Sun 2:05.

KANSAS CITY T-BONES

Office Address: 1800 Village West Parkway, Kansas City, KS 66111.
Telephone: (913) 328-5618. **Fax:** (913) 328-5674.
Email Address: tickets@tbonesbaseball.com.
Website: www.tbonesbaseball.com.
Operated By: T-Bones Baseball Club, LLC; Ehlert Development.
Owner: John Ehlert. **President:** Adam Ehlert.
   VP/General Manager: Chris Browne. **Senior Director, Corporate Sales:** Seth Alberg. **Assistant GM, Group Sales:** Kurt Sieker. **Director, Media Relations/Press Box:** Matt Fulks. **Director, Promotions:** Ashley Goodrich. **Director, Ticket Operations/Box Office Manager:** Crystal McQuain. **Sales Executive:** Ryan Stos. **Bookkeeper:** Sherrie Stover. **Account Executive, Group Sales:** Jared Reid. **Director, Stadium Operations:** Rylan D. Brody. **Head Groundskeeper:** Glen Averson.
   Manager: John Massarelli. **Coaches:** Frank White, Bill Sobbe, Dave Schaub. **Trainer:** Josh Adams. **Bullpen Catcher:** Jimmie Wade. **Equipment Manger:** john west. **Clubhouse Manager:** Andrew Hornbeck.

GAME INFORMATION
   Radio Announcer: Nathan Moore.. **No. of Games Broadcast:** 100. **Flagship Station:** KUDL 1660-AM.
   Stadium Name: CommunityAmerica Ballpark. **Location:** State Avenue West off I-435 and State Avenue. **Standard Game Times:** 7:05 pm, 5:05 pm (Sun).

LAREDO LEMURS

Office Address: 6320 Sinatra Drive, Laredo, TX 78045.
Telephone: (956) 753-6877. **Fax:** (956) 791-0672.
Website: www.laredolemurs.com.
Managing Partner: Mark Schuster.
President: Ruben Navas.
Director, Operations: Chuy Vela-Cuellar. **Corporate Sales:** Susan Gusman, Juan Salinas. **Office Manager/Receptionist:** Victoria Cardenas. **Group Sales:** Monica Mendiola. **Promotions Coordinator:** Tanyn Walters. **Clubhouse Manager:** Gibby Vela-Cuellar.
Manager: Pete Incaviglia.

GAME INFORMATION

Announcer: Unavailable. **No. of Games Broadcast:** 100. **Webcast:** www.laredolemurs.com.
Stadium Name: Uni-Trade Stadium. **Location:** From North: I-35 to Exit 9 turn left onto Loop 20/Bob Bullock Blvd, south on Loop 20 for 3 miles, make right onto Sinatra Blvd, stadium on left; From South: I-35 to Exit 2 turn right onto Hwy 59 for 4 miles, turn left onto Loop 20 North for 2 miles, turn left onto Sinatra Drive, stadium on left.
Standard Game Times: 7:30 pm.

LINCOLN SALTDOGS

Office Address: 403 Line Drive Circle, Suite A, Lincoln, NE 68508.
Telephone: (402) 474-2255. **Fax:** (402) 474-2254.
Email Address: info@saltdogs.com. **Website:** www.saltdogs.com.
Owner: Jim Abel. **President:** Charlie Meyer.
Vice President/General Manager: Tim Utrup. **Assistant GM/Director, Sales/Marketing:** Bret Beer. **Director, Broadcasting/Communications:** Drew Bontadelli. **Director, Merchandising/Promotions:** Anne Duchek. **Director, Season Tickets/Ticket Packages:** Toby Antonson. **Director, Stadium Operations:** Dave Aschwege. **Assistant Director, Stadium Operations:** Jeff Koncaba. **Office Manager:** Alicia Oakeson. **Athletic Turf Manager:** Josh Klute. **Assistant Turf Manager:** Jen Roeber.
Manager: Ken Oberkfell. **Coaches:** John Harris, Dan Reichert

GAME INFORMATION

Radio Announcer: Drew Bontadelli. **No. of Games Broadcast:** 100. **Flagship Station:** KFOR 1240-AM. **Webcast Address:** www.kfor1240.com.
Stadium Name: Haymarket Park. **Location:** I-80 to Cornhusker Highway West, left on First Street, right on Sun Valley Boulevard, left on Line Drive.
Standard Game Times: 7:05 pm, Sun 5:05 pm.

ST. PAUL SAINTS

Office Address: 1771 Energy Park Dr, St Paul, MN 55108.
Telephone: (651) 644-3517. **Fax:** (651) 644-1627.
Email Address: funisgood@saintsbaseball.com.
Website: www.saintsbaseball.com.
Principal Owners: Marv Goldklang, Bill Murray, Mike Veeck. **Chairman:** Marv Goldklang. **President:** Mike Veeck. **Vice-President/Owner:** Jeff Goldklang
Executive Vice President/General Manager: Derek Sharrer. **Executive VP:** Tom Whaley. **Assistant GMs:** Scott Bush, Chris Schwab. **VP, Customer Service/Community Partnerships:** Annie Huidekoper. **Director, Broadcast/Media Relations:** Sean Aronson. **Coordinator Director, Promotions Manager:** Sierra Bailey. **Box Office Manager:** Alex Harkaway. **Corporate Activation Manager:** Tyson Jeffers
Director, Food/Beverage: Curtis Nachtsheim. **Business Manager:** Leesa Anderson. **Office Manager:** Gina Kray. **Stadium Operations:** Bob Klepperich. **Groundskeeper:** Connie Rudolph.
Manager: George Tsamis. **Coach:** Kerry Ligtenerg.

GAME INFORMATION

Radio Announcer: Sean Aronson. **No. of Games Broadcast:** 100. **Flagship Station:** Club 1220 AM. **Webcast Address:** www.saintsbaseball.com.
Stadium Name: Midway Stadium. **Location:** From I-94, take Snelling Avenue North exit, west onto Energy Park Drive.
Standard Game Times: 7:05 pm, Sun 1:05.

SIOUX CITY EXPLORERS

Office Address: 3400 Line Drive, Sioux City, IA 51106.
Telephone: (712) 277-9467. **Fax:** (712) 277-9406.
Email Address: promotions@xsbaseball.com. **Website:** www.xsbaseball.com.
President: Matt Adamski.
VP/General Manager: Shane M Tritz. **Assistant GM:** Ashley Schoenrock. **Office Manager:** Julie Stinger.
Field Manager: Steve Montgomery

GAME INFORMATION

Radio Announcer: Dave Nitz. **No. of Games Broadcast:** 100. **Flagship Station:** KSCJ 1360-AM. **Webcast Address:** www.xsbaseball.com.
Stadium Name: Lewis and Clark Park. **Location:** I-29 to Singing Hills Blvd, North, right on Line Drive.
Standard Game Times: 7:05 pm, Sun 6:05.

SIOUX FALLS CANARIES

Office Address: 1001 N West Ave, Sioux Falls, SD 57104.
Telephone: (605) 333-0179. **Fax:** (605) 333-0139.
Email Address: info@canaries.com. **Website:** www.sfcanaries.com.
Operated by: Sioux Falls Sports, LLC.
CEO/President/Managing Partner: Tom Garrity.
Vice President, Operations: Nate Welch. **Director, Stadium Operations:** Larry McKenney. **Office/Ticketing Manager:** Kim Hipple. **VP, Media/Public Relations:** Jim Olander. **VP, Sales:** Matt Ferguson.
Manager: Steve Shirley.

GAME INFORMATION

Radio Announcer: Scott Beatty. **No. of Games Broadcast:** 100. **Flagship Station:** KWSN 1230-AM. **Webcast Address:** www.kwsn.com.
Stadium Name: Sioux Falls Stadium. **Location:** I 29 to Russell Street, east one mile, south on West Avenue.
Standard Game Times: 7:05 pm, Sat 6:05 pm, Sun 4:05.

WICHITA WINGNUTS

Office Address: 300 South Sycamore, Wichita, KS 67213.
Telephone: (316) 264-6887. **Fax:** (316) 264-2129.
Website: www.wichitawingnuts.com.
Owners: Steve Ruud, Dan Waller, Gary Austerman, Nick Easter, Nate Robertson.
President/General Manager: Josh Robertson. **Assistant GM/Director, Corporate Sales:** Ben Keiter. **Ticket Sales & Community Relations Manager:** Robert Slaughter. **Communications Manager:** Jason Kempf Operations Manager, NBC: Kevin Jenks. **Director, Stadium Operations:** Jeff Kline. **Director, Operations, Group Sales & Promotions Manager:** Drew Hays. **Manager, Media Relations & Game Operations Manager:** Scott Johnson. **Game Day Staff & Merchandise Manager:** Meryl Loop. **Clubhouse Manager:** Cleo Welch. **Assistant Clubhouse Manager:** Caleb Beeson.
Manager: Kevin Hooper. **Coaches:** Jose Amado, Luke Robertson.

GAME INFORMATION

No. of Games Broadcast: 100. **Games Broadcast:** KWME 92.7-FM.
Webcast Address: www.wichitawingnuts.com.
Stadium Name: Lawrence-Dumont Stadium. **Location:** 135 North to Kellogg (54) West, Take Seneca Street exit North to Maple, Go East on Maple to Sycamore, Stadium is located on corner of Maple and Sycamore.
Standard Game Times: 7:05 pm, Sun 2:05 pm.

WINNIPEG GOLDEYES

Office Address: One Portage Ave E, Winnipeg, Manitoba R3B 3N3.
Telephone: (204) 982-2273. **Fax:** (204) 982-2274.
Email Address: goldeyes@goldeyes.com. **Website:** www.goldeyes.com.
Operated by: Winnipeg Goldeyes Baseball Club, Inc.
Principal Owner/President: Sam Katz.
General Manager: Andrew Collier. **Assistant GM:** Regan Katz. **Media Relations Manager:** Scott Unger.
Administrative Assistant: Bonnie Benson. **Chief Financial Officer:** Jason McRae-King. **Controller:** Judy Jones.

Director, Sales/Marketing: Dan Chase. **Sales/Marketing Coordinator:** Angela Sanche. **Account Representatives:** Dennis McLean, Jamie Sparks, Scott Taylor. **Promotions Coordinator:** Allison Pattison. **Box Office Manager:** Kevin Arnst. **Retail Manager:** Sean Seywright. **Facility Manager/Head Groundskeeper:** Don Ferguson. **Manager/Director, Player Procurement:** Rick Forney. **Coach:** Tom Vaeth. **Clubhouse Manager:** Jamie Samson.

GAME INFORMATION

Radio Announcer: Unavailable. **No. of Games Broadcast:** 100. **Flagship Station:** The Jewel 100.7 FM Television Announcers: Scott Taylor. **No. of Games Telecast:** Home-20, Away-0. **Station:** Shaw TV Channel 9.

Stadium Name: Shaw Park. **Location:** North on Pembina Highway to Broadway, East on Broadway to Main Street, North on Main Street to Water Avenue, East on Water Avenue to Westbrook Street, North on Westbrook Street to Lombard Avenue, East on Lombard Avenue to Mill Street, South on Mill Street to ballpark. **Standard Game Times:** 7 pm, Sat 6, Sun 1:30.

ATLANTIC LEAGUE

Mailing Address: Clipper Magazine Stadium, 650 N. Prince St., Lancaster, Pa., 17603.
Telephone: (717) 509-4487. **Fax:** (717) 509-8476.
Email Address: info@atlanticleague.com. **Website:** www.atlanticleague.com.
Year Founded: 1998-
Chief Executive Officer/Founder: Frank Boulton. **President:** Peter Kirk. **Vice President:** Steven Kalafer.
Executive Director: Joe Klein.
Directors: Frank Boulton (Long Island, Bridgeport), Steve Kalafer (Somerset), Peter Kirk (Lancaster, York, Southern Maryland, Sugar Land), Frank Boulton/Peter Kirk (Camden).
Coordinator, League Operations/Latin: Ellie Rodriguez. **League Office:** Jasson Read.
Division Structure: Liberty Division—Bridgeport, Camden, Long Island, Somerset. Freedom Division—Lancaster, Somerset, Southern Maryland, Sugar Land, York.
Regular Season: 140 games (split-schedule).
2014 Opening Date: April 24. **Closing Date:** Sept 21.
All-Star Game: July 16 at Sugar Land, Texas.
Playoff Format: First-half division winners meet second-half winners in best of five series. Winners meet in best-of-five final for league championship.
Roster Limit: 25. Teams may keep 27 players from start of season until May 31.
Eligibility Rule: No restrictions.
Brand of Baseball: Rawlings.
Statistician: Statistician: Pointstreak.com, 602 - 1595 16th Avenue, Richmond Hill, ON, Canada L4B 3N9.

STADIUM INFORMATION

Club	Stadium	Opened	Dimensions LF	CF	RF	Capacity	2013 Att.
Bridgeport	The Ballpark at Harbor Yard	1998	325	405	325	5,300	157,267
Camden	Campbell's Field	2001	325	405	325	6,425	217,145
Lancaster	Clipper Magazine Stadium	2005	372	400	300	6,000	290,165
Long Island	Citibank Park	2000	325	400	325	6,002	371,186
Somerset	Commerce Bank Ballpark	1999	317	402	315	6,100	339,468
So. Maryland	Regency Stadium	2008	305	400	320	6,000	242,894
Sugar Land	Constellation Field	2012	348	405	325	7,500	382,059
York	Sovereign Bank Stadium	2007	300	400	325	5,000	254,370

BRIDGEPORT BLUEFISH

Office Address: 500 Main St, Bridgeport, CT 06604. **Telephone:** (203) 345-4800.
Fax: (203) 345-4830. **Website:** www.bridgeportbluefish.com.
Operated by: Past Time Partners, LLC.
Principal Owner/CEO, Past Time Partners: Frank Boulton. **Senior VP, Past Time Partners:** Mike Pfaff. **Partners, Past Time Partners:** Tony Rosenthal, Fred Heyman, Jeffrey Serkes.
General Manager: Ken Shepard. **Assistant GM, Corporate Partnership Development:** Jamie Toole. **Director, Public Relations/Baseball Operations:** Paul Herrmann. **Director, Operations:** Tom Farruggio. **Director, Community Relations/Promotions:** Marisa Marvin. **Ticket Manager:** Drew LaBov. **Head Groundkeeper/Operations Coordinator:** Geremy Grate. **Partnership Development/Project Manager:** Dan Gregory.
Manager: Willie Upshaw. **Pitching Coach:** Pat Ahearne. **Trainer:** Ericka Ventura.

GAME INFORMATION
Radio Announcer: RJ Garcea. **No. of Games Broadcast:** 70 (webcast). **Flagship Station:** 1490 WGCH. **PA Announcer:** Bill Jensen. **Official Scorer:** Chuck Sadowski.
Stadium Name: The Ballpark at Harbor Yard. **Location:** I-95 to exit 27, Route 8/25 to exit 1. **Standard Game Times:** 7:05 pm, Sat 6:05, Sun 1:05.
Visiting Club Hotel: Holiday Inn Bridgeport, 1070 Main St, Bridgeport, CT 06604. **Telephone:** (203) 334-1234.

CAMDEN RIVERSHARKS

Office Address: 401 N Delaware Ave, Camden, NJ 08102.
Telephone: (856) 963-2600. **Fax:** (856) 963-8534.
Email Address: riversharks@riversharks.com. **Website:** www.riversharks.com.
Operated by: Camden Baseball, LLC. **Principal Owners:** Frank Boulton, Peter Kirk.
President: Jon Danos.
Controller: Emily Merrill. **President/General Manager:** Adam Lorber. **Assistant GM:** Lindsay Rosenberg. **Director, Group Events:** Bob Nehring.

Director, Group Sales: Mark Schieber. **Director, Business Operations:** Tony Conte. **Director, Corporate Partnerships:** Drew Nelson. **Marketing Manager:** Mike Barone. **Creative Services Manager:** Kirsten Boye. **Broadcasting/Media Relations Manager:** Joe Tordy. **Group Sales Managers:** Ross Anderson, David Koehler, Joe Bartlett. **Box Office Manager:** Chris Zabady. **Stadium Operations Manager:** Frank Slavinski.

Manager: Ron Karkovice. **Bench Coach:** Brett Bonvechio. **Pitching Coach:** Chris Widger.

GAME INFORMATION

Radio: www.riversharks.com / Z88.9 FM. **Riversharks**

Broadcaster: Joe Tordy. **PA Announcer:** Kevin Casey. **Official Scorer:** Dick Shute. **Stadium Name:** Campbell's Field.

Location: From Philadelphia, right on Sixth Street, right after Ben Franklin Bridge toll booth, right on Cooper Street until it ends at Delaware Ave; From Camden, I-676 to exit 5B, follow signs to field.

Standard Game Times: 7:05 pm, Sat 5:35, Sun 1:35. Gates open one hour prior to game time.

Visiting Club Hotel: Holiday Inn, Route 70 and Sayer Avenue, Cherry Hill, NJ 08002. **Telephone:** (856) 663-5300.

LANCASTER BARNSTORMERS

Office Address: 650 North Prince St, Lancaster, PA 17603.

Telephone: (717) 509-4487. **Fax:** (717) 509-4486.

Email Address: info@lancasterbarnstormers.com. **Website:** www.lancasterbarnstormers.com.

Operated by: Lancaster Barnstormers Baseball Club, LLC.

Principal Owners: Opening Day Partners.

CEO: Jon Danos. **General Manager:** Kristen Simon. **Vice President, Fan Experience:** Anthony DeMarco. **VP, Business Development:** Vince Bulik. **VP, Sales:** Rob Armbruster. **Controller:** Emily Merrill. **Director, Stadium Operations:** Don Pryer. **Assistant GM:** Ed Synder. **Director, Sky Boxes/Ticket Services:** Maureen Wheeler. **Director, Business Development:** Bob Ford. **Accounting Manager:** Leanne Beaghan. **Stadium Operations Manager:** Andrew Wurst.

Public Relations/Brand Coordinator: Alexy Posner. **Creative Services Coordinator:** John Brennan. **Promotions/Events Coordinator:** Rachel Miller. **Business Development Representatives:** Terry Christopher, Philip Benigno, Quinton Collins, Pam Nelson. **Client Services Representatives:** Liz Welch, Amber Guinther.

Manager: Butch Hobson. **Clubhouse Manager:** John Thomas

GAME INFORMATION

Radio Announcer: Dave Collins. **No. of Games Broadcast:** Home-70, Away-70. **Flagship Stations:** WLAN 1390 AM, WPDC 1600 AM. **PA Announcer:** John Witwer. **Official Scorer:** Joel Schreiner.

Stadium Name: Clipper Magazine Stadium. **Location:** From Route 30, take Fruitville Pike or Harrisburg Pike toward downtown Lancaster, stadium on North Prince between Clay Street and Frederick Street. **Standard Game Times:** 7 pm, Sun 1.

LONG ISLAND DUCKS

Mailing Address: 3 Court House Dr, Central Islip, NY 11722.

Telephone: (631) 940-3825. **Fax:** (631) 940-3800.

Email Address: info@liducks.com. **Website:** www.liducks.com.

Operated by: Long Island Ducks Professional Baseball, LLC.

Founder/CEO: Frank Boulton. **Owner/Chairman:** Seth Waugh.

Owner/Senior VP, Baseball Operations: Bud Harrelson.

President/General Manager: Michael Pfaff. **Assistant GM/Senior VP, Sales:** Doug Cohen. **Director, Administration:** Gerry Anderson. **Director, Group Sales:** John Wolff. **Director, Season Sales:** Brad Kallman. **Manager, Box Office:** Ben Harper. **Manager, Merchandise/Client Services:** Jay Randall. **Manager, Media Relations/Broadcasting:** Michael Polak. **Manager, Promotions/Community Outreach:** Jordan Schiff. **Manager, Operations:** Scott Marshall. **Manager, Corporate Sales:** Chris Burns. **Staff Accountant:** Annemarie DeMasi.

Account Executives: Brian Leavy, Anthony Rubino. **Coordinator, Administration:** Megan Gordon. **Ticket Assistant:** Justin McClafferty. **Group Sales Assistant:** Jonathan Cruz.

Manager: Kevin Baez. **Coaches:** Steve Foucault, Bud Harrelson. **Trainers:** Tony Amin, Adam Lewis, Dorothy Pitchford.

GAME INFORMATION

Radio Announcers: Michael Polak, Chris King, David Weiss. **No. of Games Broadcast:** 140 on www.liducks.com. **Flagship Station:** 103.9-FM LI News Radio. **PA Announcer:** Bob Ottone. **Official Scorer:** Michael Polak.

SOMERSET PATRIOTS

Office Address: One Patriots Park, Bridgewater, NJ 08807.
Telephone: (908) 252-0700. **Fax:** (908) 252-0776.
Website: www.somersetpatriots.com.
Operated by: Somerset Baseball Partners, LLC.
Principal Owners: Steve Kalafer, Josh Kalafer, Jonathan Kalafer.
Chairman: Steve Kalafer.
President/General Manager: Patrick McVerry. **Senior Vice President, Marketing:** Dave Marek. **VP, Public Relations:** Marc Russinoff. **VP, Operations:** Bryan Iwicki. **VP, Ticket Operations:** Matt Kopas. **Director, Tickets:** Brian Cahill. **Director, Merchandise:** Rob Crossman. **Corporate Sales Manager:** Kevin Fleming. **Group Sales Manager:** Tom McCartney.
Account Executives: Nick Cherrillo, Katherine Hunton, Deanna Liotard. **Account Executive/Operations Manager:** Joshua Malakoff. **Group Sales Manager:** Emily Forsythe. **Executive Assistant to GM:** Michele DaCosta. **Controller:** Ron Schulz. **Accountant:** Stephanie DePass. **Receptionist:** Lorraine Ott. **GM, Centerplate:** Mike McDermott. **Head Groundskeeper:** Dan Purner.
Manager: Brett Jodie. **Hitting:** Shane Spencer. **Pitching Coach:** Cory Domel. **Trainer:** Unavailable. **Manager Emeritus:** Sparky Lyle.

GAME INFORMATION

Radio Announcer: Justin Antweil. **No. of Games Broadcast:** Home-70, Away-70. **Flagship Station:** WCTC 1450-AM. **PA Announcer:** Paul Spychala.
Official Scorer: John Nolan.
Ballpark Name: TD Bank Ballpark. **Location:** Route 287 North to exit 13B/Route 287 South to exit 13 (Somerville Route 28 West); follow signs to ballpark. **Standard Game Times:** 7:05 pm, Sun 1:35/5:05.
Visiting Club Hotel: Hotel Somerset-Bridgewater.

SOUTHERN MARYLAND
BLUE CRABS

Office Address: 11765 St Linus Dr, Waldorf, MD 20602.
Telephone: 301-638-9788. **Fax:** 301-638-9788.
Email address: info@somdbluecrabs.com. **Website:** www.somdbluecrabs.com.
Principal Owners: Opening Day Partners LLC, Brooks Robinson.
Chairman: Peter Kirk. **President:** Jon Danos. **Controller:** Emily Merrill.
General Manager: Patrick Day.
Assistant GM, Marketing/Special Events: Courtney Knichel. **Assistant GM, Operations:** Sean Maher. **Finance Manager:** Theresa Coffey.
Group Sales Manager: Matt Ammerman. **Sales Account Executives:** Sara Naar, Justin Miller, Del Baxter, Chantell Williams. **Director, Corporate Sales:** Candace Gick. **Creative Services:** Kevin Dove. **Corporate Partnerships Coordinator:** Sara Armiger. **Community Relations:** Kevin Kelley. **Stadium Operations:** Steve Bowden. **GM, Centerplate Concessions/Merchandise:** Tim McGuire.
Manager: Lance Burkhart. **Hitting Coach:** Jeremy Owens (player/coach). **Pitching Coach:** Joe Gannon

GAME INFORMATION

Radio: All Home Games, www.somdbluecrabs.com. **Stadium:** Regency Furniture Stadium. **Standard Game Times:** 7:05 pm, Sat 6:35, Sun 2:05.

SUGAR LAND SKEETERS

Office Address: 1 Stadium Drive, Sugar Land Texas 77498.
Telephone: (281) 240-4487.
General Manager: Chris Jones. **Assistant GM:** Lindsay Kirk. **Assistant GM:** JT Onyett. **Special Assistant:** Deacon Jones. **Accounting Manager:** Debra Primmer. **Director, Human Resources:** Kimberly Ciszewski. **Senior Director, Community Development:** Kyle Dawson.
Director, Operations: Michael Kirk. **Sponsorship Services Director:** Jacqueline Holm. **Sponsorship Services Manager:** Ryan Derr. **Group Services Manager:** Chris Parsons. **Senior Sales Managers:** Ira Liebman, Tyler Stamm.
Sales Account Executives: Teneisha Hall, Taylor Galipp, Randy Koch, Sunny Okpon. **Ticket Sales Director:** Colt Riley. **Box Office Manager:** Jennifer Schwarz. **Customer Service Manager:** Adam Mettler. **Director, Entertainment:** Dan Ford. **Director, Marketing/Communications:** MJ Burns. **Manager, Marketing/Communications:** Molly Hughes. **Manager, Graphic Design/Web:** Todd Blair. **Head Groundskeeper:** Brad Detmore. **Assistant Groundskeeper:** Chris Smith. **Operations Manager:** Donnie Moore. **Special Events Manager:** Justin Roque. **Special Events Sales Manager:** Nikki Welsh. **Legends Hospitality General Manager:** Matt Coonrad. **Legends Merchandise Manager:** Jackie Beers. **Legends Warehouse Manager:** George Wasai, Jr.

Manager: Gary Gaetti. **Pitching Coach:** Jeff Scott.

GAME INFORMATION

Radio Announcer: Ira Liebman. **No. of Games Broadcast:** 140. **Flagship Station:** KBRZ 1460 AM.
Standard Game Times: 7:05 pm, Sat/Sun 6:05/2:05. **Directions to Ballpark:** Southbound HWY 59 - Take the exit toward Corporate Dr/US-90/Stafford/Sugar Land. Turn right onto HWY 6. Travel northbound to Imperial Blvd. Turn right onto Imperial Blvd from HWY 6.
Visiting Club Hotel: Sugar Land Marriott Town Square

YORK REVOLUTION

Office Address: 5 Brooks Robinson Way, York, PA 17401.
Telephone: (717) 801-4487. **Fax:** (717) 801-4499.
Email Address: info@yorkrevolution.com. **Website:** www.yorkrevolution.com.
Operated by: York Professional Baseball Club, LLC.
Principal Owners: York Professional Baseball Club, LLC.
President/General Manager: Eric Menzer. **Vice President, Business Development:** Nate Tile. **Assistant GM, Business Operations:** John Gibson. **Finance Manager:** Lori Brunson. **Director, Ticketing:** Cindy Brown. **Box Office Manager:** Michael Foster. **Manager, Promotions/Communications:** Paul Braverman. **Director, Group Sales:** Mike Chatburn. **Senior Account Executives:** Kaylee Swanson, John Hunt. **Account Executives:** Deidre Geroni, Caitlin Burke, Ben Smith, Wade Johnson, Brandon Tesuluk. **Client Services Coordinator:** Reed Gunderson. **Special Events Coordinator:** Adam Nugent.
Stadium Operations Manager: Lewis LaBar. **Head Groundskeeper:** Mike Urich. **Creative Director:** Corey Shaud. **Legends Hospitality GM, Concessions/Merchandise/Catering:** Patrick Bluso. **Legends Hospitality Catering Manager:** Adam Baumbach. **Legends Hospitality Chef:** Tiffany Eger.
Manager: Mark Mason. **Pitching Coach:** Paul Fletcher. **Bench/Third-Base Coach:** Enohel Polanco.

GAME INFORMATION

Radio Announcer: Darrell Henry. **No. of Games Broadcast:** 140. **Flagship Station:** WOYK 1350 AM. **PA Announcer:** Ray Jensen, Merrill Spahn. **Official Scorer:** Brian Wisler.
Stadium Name: Santander Stadium. **Location:** Take Route 30 West to North George Street. **Directions:** Turn left onto North George Street; follow that straight for four lights, Santander Stadium is on left. **Standard Game Times:** 6:30 pm, Sun 5 pm, 2 pm (April/Sept).
Visiting Club Hotel: The Yorktowne Hotel, 48 E Market Street, York, PA 17401. **Telephone:** (717) 848-1111.

CAN-AM LEAGUE

Office Address: 1415 Hwy 54 West, Suite 210, Durham, NC 27707.
Telephone: (919) 401-8150. **Fax:** (919) 401-8152. **Website:** www.canamleague.com.
Year Founded: 2004.
Commissioner: Miles Wolff. **President:** Dan Moushon.
Director, Umpires: Kevin Winn.
Regular Season: 96 games.
2014 Opening Date: May 22. **Closing Date:** Sept 1.
Playoff Format: Two teams with the best winning percentage meet in best-of-7 championship series.
Roster Limit: 22.
Eligibility Rule: Minimum of five and maximum of eight first-year players; minimum of five players must be an LS-4 or higher; a maximum of four may be veterans.
Brand of Baseball: Rawlings.
Statistician: Pointstreak.com.

STADIUM INFORMATION

Club	Stadium	Opened	Dimensions LF	CF	RF	Capacity	2013 Att.
New Jersey	Yogi Berra Stadium	1998	308	398	308	3,784	76,883
Quebec	Stade Municipal	1938	315	385	315	4,500	141,396
Rockland	Provident Bank Park	2011	323	403	313	4,750	143,231
Trois-Rivieres	Stade Fernand-Bedard	1938	342	372	342	4,500	71,568

NEW JERSEY JACKALS

Office Address: One Hall Dr, Little Falls, NJ 07424.
Telephone: (973) 746-7434. **Fax:** (973) 655-8006.
Email Address: info@jackals.com. **Website:** www.jackals.com.
Operated by: Floyd Hall Enterprises, LLC.
Chairman: Floyd Hall.
President: Greg Lockard.
General Manager: Larry Hall. **Business Manager:** Jennifer Fertig. **Director, Group Sales:** Jordan Cascino. **Group Sales Representatives:** Michael Berhang, Shannon Koop. **Facilities Manager:** Aldo Licitra. **Concessions Manager:** Michelle Guarino.
Clubhouse Manager: Wally Brackett.
Manager: Joe Calfapietra. **Coaches:** Ed Ott, Ani Ramos

GAME INFORMATION

Webcast Announcer: No. **of Games Broadcast:** 96. **Webcast Address:** www.jackals.com.
Stadium Name: Yogi Berra Stadium. **Location:** On the campus of Montclair State University; Route 80 or Garden State Parkway to Route 46, take Valley Road exit to Montclair State University.
Standard Game Times: 7:05 pm, Sat 6:35, Sun 2:05.

QUEBEC CAPITALES

Office Address: 100 Rue du Cardinal Maurice-Roy, Quebec City, QC G1K8Z1.
Telephone: (418) 521-2255. **Fax:** (418) 521-2266.
Email Address: info@capitalesdequebec.com. **Website:** www.capitalesdequebec.com.
Owner: Jean Tremblay.
President: Michel Laplante.
Assistant GM: Julie Lefrancois. **Director, Media/Marketing:** Marc-Antoine Gariepy. **Sales Director:** Pier-luc Nappert.
Assistant, Media/Marketing: Maxime Aubry.
Manager: Patrick Scalabrini. **Coaches:** TJ Stanton, Goefrey Tomlinson

GAME INFORMATION

Webcast Address: www.capitalesdequebec.com.
Stadium Name: Stade Municipal de Quebec. **Location:** Highway 40 to Highway 173 (Centre-Ville) exit 2 to Parc Victoria.
Standard Game Times: 7:05 pm, Sat 6:05 pm, Sun 1:05.

ROCKLAND BOULDERS

Office Address: 1 Provident Bank Park Drive, Pomona, NY 10970.†
Telephone: (845) 364-0009. **Fax:** (845) 364-0001.
E-Mail Address: info@rocklandboulders.com. **Website:** www.rocklandboulders.com.
President: Ken Lehner. **Executive Vice President:** Shawn Reilly. **Counsel:** Jonathan Fine. **Director of First Impressions:** Kristi Saporito. **Ticket Manager:** Brett Kaufman. **Operations Manager:** Dave Schenkel..
Manager: Jamie Keefe. **Trainer:** Lori Rahim.

GAME INFORMATION
Stadium Name: Provident Bank Park. **Location:** Take Exit 12 towards Route 45, make left at stop sign on Conklin Road, make left on Route 45, turn right on Pomona Road, take 1st right on Fireman's Memorial Drive.
Standard Game Times: 7:05 p.m., **Sun 2:**05/5:05.

TROIS-RIVIERES AIGLES

Office Address: 1760 Avenue Gilles-Villeneuve, Trois-Rivieres, QC G9A 5K8.
Telephone: (819) 379-0404. **Fax:** (819) 379-5087.
Email Address: info@lesaiglestr.com. **Website:** www.lesaiglestr.com
President: Jean-Francois Picard. **General Manager:** Bob McDuff. **Director, Stadium Facilities:** Real Lajoie. **Finance Director:** Steven Belanger. **Account Representatives:** Bobby Baril, Ben Chaput
Manager: Pete LaForest. **Coach:** Max Poulin

GAME INFORMATION
Stadium Name: Stade Fernand-Bedard. **Location:** Take Hwy 40 West, exit Boul. des forges/Centre-ville, keep right, turn right at light, turn right at stop sign.
Standard Game Times: 7:05 p.m., **Sun 1:**35

FRONTIER LEAGUE

Office Address: 2041 Goose Lake Rd Suite 2A, Sauget, IL 62206.
Telephone: (618) 215-4134. **Fax:** (618) 332-2115.
Email Address: office@frontierleague.com. **Website:** www.frontierleague.com.
Year Founded: 1993.
Commissioner: Bill Lee.
Deputy Commissioner: Steve Tahsler.
President: Rich Sauget (Gateway). **Executive Committee:** Clint Brown (Florence), Steven Edelson (Lake Erie), Stu Williams (Washington), Leslye Wuerfel (Traverse City).
Board of Directors: Tim Arseneau (Southern Illinois), Bill Bussing (Evansville), Steve Malliet (Normal/River City), Pat Salvi (Schaumburg), Josh Schaub (Joliet), Mike Stranczek (Windy City), Bryan Wickline (Rockford).
Division Structure: East—Evansville, Florence, Frontier Greys, Lake Erie, Southern Illinois, Traverse City, Washington. West—Gateway, Joliet, Normal, River City, Rockford, Schaumburg, Windy City.
Regular Season: 96 games. **2014 Opening Date:** May 15. **Closing Date:** Sept 4.
All-Star Game: July 16 at Gateway.
Playoff Format: Top 4 non-division winners have a single-game series, with winners advancing to a best-of-3 Divisional Round. Championship Series is best-of-5.
Roster Limit: 24. **Eligibility Rule:** Minimum of eleven Rookie 1/Rookie 2 players. No player may be 27 prior to Jan. 1 of current season with the exception of one player that may not be 30 years of age prior to Jan. 1 of the current season.
Brand of Baseball: Wilson.
Statistician: Pointstreak, 602-1595 16th Avenue, Richmond Hill, ONT L4B 3N9.

STADIUM INFORMATION

| Club | Stadium | Opened | Dimensions | | | Capacity | 2013 Att. |
			LF	CF	RF		
Evansville	Bosse Field	1915	315	415	315	5,110	140,786
Florence	UC Health Stadium	2004	325	395	325	4,200	112,270
Gateway	GCS Ballpark	2002	318	395	325	5,500	162,572
Joliet	Silver Cross Field	2002	330	400	327	6,229	93,875
Lake Erie	All-Pro Freight	2009	325	400	325	5,000	122,097
Normal	The Corn Crib	2010	356	400	344	7,000	126,367
River City	T.R. Hughes Ballpark	1999	320	382	299	4,989	92,652
Rockford	Aviators Stadium	2006	315	393	312	3,279	87,612
Schaumburg	Schaumburg Stadium	1999	355	400	353	8,107	150,254
So. Illinois	Rent One Park	2007	325	400	330	4,500	126,084
Traverse City	Wuerfel Park	2006	320	400	320	4,600	164,915
Washington	CONSOL Energy Park	2002	325	400	325	3,200	87,076
Windy City	Standard Bank Stadium	1999	335	390	335	2,598	74,609

EVANSVILLE OTTERS

Mailing Address: 23 Don Mattingly Way, Evansville, IN 47711.
Telephone: (812) 435-8686.
Operated by: Evansville Baseball, LLC.
President: Bill Bussing. **Senior Vice President:** Bix Branson. **General Manager:** Joel Padfield. **Director, Operations:** Jake Riffert. **Account Executive/Director, Media Relations/Broadcasting:** Mike Radomski. **Controller:** Casie Williams. **Sports Turf Manager:** Lance Adler.
Manager: Andy McCauley.

GAME INFORMATION
Radio Announcer: Mike Radomski. **No. of Games Broadcast:** Home-51, Away-45. **Flagship Station:** WUEV 91.5-FM.
PA Announcer: Zane Clodfelter.
Stadium Name: Bosse Field. **Location:** US 41 to Lloyd Expressway West (IN-62), Main St Exit, Right on Main St, ahead 1 mile to Bosse Field. **Standard Game Times:** 6:35 pm, Sun 5:05; Doubleheaders 5:05 p.m.
Visiting Club Hotel: Comfort Inn & Suites, 3901 Hwy 41 N, Evansville, IN 47711.

FLORENCE FREEDOM

Office Address: 7950 Freedom Way, Florence, KY, 41042.
Telephone: (859) 594-4487. **Fax:** (859) 594-3194.
Email Address: info@florencefreedom.com.
Operated by: Canterbury Baseball, LLC.
President: Clint Brown. **General Manager:** Josh Anderson. **Assistant GM, Operations:** Kim Brown. **Assistant GM, Marketing/Promotions:** Sarah Eichenberger. **Director, Community Relations/Special Events:** Shaun Birindelli.

Director, Broadcasting/Media Relations: Aaron Morse. **Business Manager:** Shelli Bitter. **Director, Amateur Baseball:** Tyler Brake. **Box Office Manager:** Chanel Lessing.
  Manager: Fran Riordan. **Pitching Coach:** Chris Homer.

GAME INFORMATION
  Official Scorer: Joe Gall.
  Stadium: UC Health Stadium. **Location:** I71/75 South to exit 180, left onto US 42, right on Freedom Way; I-71/75 North to exit 180. **Standard Game Times:** 6:35 pm, Sat 6:05, Sun 5:05.
  Visting Club Hotel: Quality Inn.

FRONTIER GREYS

Mailing Address: 2041 Goose Lake Road, Suite 2A, Sauget, IL 62206.
Telephone: (618) 215-4134.
Operated by: Frontier League Baseball Travel Team, LLC.
President: Steve Tahsler. **Secretary:** Bill Lee.
Field manager: Brent Metheny. **Bench Coach:** Cliff Howe.

GATEWAY GRIZZLIES

Telephone: (618) 337-3000. **Fax:** (618) 332-3625. **Email Address:** info@gatewaygrizzlies.com.
  Website: www.gatewaygrizzlies.com.
  Operated by: Gateway Baseball, LLC. **Managing Officer:** Richard Sauget.
  General Manager: Steven Gomric. **Director, Stadium Operations:** Brent Pownall.
Director, Corporate Sales: CJ Hendrickson. **Events Manager:** Jason Heinzmann. **Radio Broadcaster/Media Relations Director:** Adam Young. **Director, Marketing/Graphics:** Alex Wilson. **Ticket Director:** Brett Perkins. **Assistant Director, Stadium Operations:** Kurt Ringkamp. **Director, Merchandise:** Monica Rodriguez. **Sales Associate:** Anna Grimm. **Director, Promotions:** Hannah Harres.
  Manager: Phil Warren. **Pitching Coach:** Randy Martz. **Hitting Coach:** Zach Borowiak. **Trainer:** Geof Manzo.

GAME INFORMATION
  Radio Announcer: Adam Young. **No of Games Broadcast:** Home-48, Away-48. **Flagship Station:** 590-AM KFNS. **Affiliate Station:** 1400-AM KJFF. **PA Announcer:** Tom Calhoun.
  Stadium Name: GCS Ballpark. **Location:** I-255 at exit 15 (Mousette Lane). **Standard Game Times:** 7:05 pm, Sun 6:05/3:05.
  Visiting Club Hotel: Ramada Inn, 6900 N Illinois St, Fairview Heights, IL 62208. **Telephone:** (618) 632-4747.

LAKE ERIE CRUSHERS

Mailing Address: 2009 Baseball Blvd, Avon, OH, 44011.
Telephone: (440) 934-3636. **Fax:** (440) 934-2458.
Email Address: info@lakeeriecrushers.com. **Website:** www.lakeeriecrushers.com.
Operated by: Avon Pro Baseball LLC.
Managing Officer: Steven Edelson.
Assistant GM, Operations: Paul Siegwarth. **Accountant:** Kathleen Hudson. **Box Office Manager:** Unavailable.
Director, Group Sales: Michael Link. **Director, Concessions/Catering:** Kevin Dailey. **Account Executives:** Matt Kendeigh, Andrew Pfifer, Mike Hyde. **Director, Broadcasting:** Andy Barch.
  Manager: Unavailable.

GAME INFORMATION
  Stadium Name: All Pro Freight Stadium. **Location:** Intersection of I-90 and Colorado Ave in Avon, OH. **Standard Game Times:** 7:05 pm, Sun 5:05.

NORMAL CORNBELTERS

Mailing Address: 1000 West Raab Road, Normal, IL 61761.
Telephone: 309-454-2255 (BALL). **Fax:** 309- 454-2287 (BATS).
Ownership: Normal Baseball Group.
President: Steve Malliet.
  General Manager: Kyle Kreger. **Vice President, Ticket Sales:** Joe Rejc. **Corporate Partnerships Director:** Lori Johnson. **Box Office Manager:** Justin Cartor. **In-Game Entertainment Coordinator:** Jeff Holtke. **Community, Public/Media Relations Manager:** Mike Rains. **Group Sales Manager:** Brendan O'Neill. **Stadium**

Operations Manager: Jacob Seeger.
Field Manager: Brooks Carey

GAME INFORMATION

Radio Announcer: Greg Halbleib.
Flagship Station: Online only at www.Normalbaseball.com
No. of Games Broadcast: All 51 games streaming online at www.normalbaseball.com
Stadium Name: The Corn Crib.
Location: From I-55 North, go south on I-55 and take the 165 exit, turn left at light, turn right on Raab Road to ballpark on right; From I-55 South, go north on I-55 and take the 165 exit, merge onto Route 51 (Main Street), turn right on Raab Road to ballpark on right. **Standard Game Times:** 7 pm, Sun 6.

RIVER CITY RASCALS

Office Address: 900 TR Hughes Blvd, O'Fallon, MO 63366.
Telephone: (636) 240-2287. **Fax:** (636) 240-7313.
Email Address: info@rivercityrascals.com. **Website:** www.rivercityrascals.com.
Operated by: PS and J Professional Baseball Club LLC.
Owners: Tim Hoeksema, Jan Hoeksema, Fred Stratton, Anne Stratton, Pam Malliet, Steve Malliet, Michael Veeck, Greg Wendt.
President/General Manager: Dan Dial. **Assistant GM:** Lisa Fegley. **Senior Director, Ticket Operations:** Courtney Oakley. **Director, Stadium Operations:** Tom Bauer. **Director, Food/Beverage:** Maureen Stranz. **Business Manager:** Sheri Livingston. **Senior Account Executive:** Tim McConkey
Team Manager: Steve Brook. **Assistant Coach:** Caleb Curry. **Assistant Coach:** Todd Worrell

GAME INFORMATION

No. of Games Broadcast: Home-51, Away-45. **PA Announcer:** Randy Moehlman.
Stadium Name: TR Hughes Ballpark. **Location:** I-70 to exit 219, north on TR Hughes Road, follow signs to ballpark. **Standard Game Times:** 7:05 pm, Sun 6:05.
Visiting Club Hotel: America's Best Value Inn 1310 Bass Pro Drive St. **Charles, MO. Telephone:** (636) 947-5900.

ROCKFORD AVIATORS

Office Address: 4503 Interstate Blvd Loves Park, IL 61111.
Telephone: (815) 885-2255. **Fax:** (815) 885-2204.
Website: www.rockfordaviators.com
Owned by: Rock River Valley Baseball **CEO:** W Chris Hanners. **President:** Bryan Wickline.
General Manager: Brad Sholes. **Director, Group Sales:** Evan Diece. **Head Groundskeeper:** Jesse Blake.
Field Manager: James Frisbie. **Hitting Coach:** Patrick O'Sullivan. **Pitching Coach:** Dan Grybash

GAME INFORMATION

Radio Announcer: Unavailable. **No. of Games Broadcast:** 96. **Flagship Station:** 100.5 NTA-FM. **PA Announcer:** Brett Myhres. **Official Scorer:** Unavailable.
Stadium Name: Aviators Stadium. **Location:** I-90 (Jane Addams Tollway) to Riverside Blvd exit (automatic toll booth), east to Interstate Dr, north on Interstate Drive to dead end. **Standard Game Times:** 7:05 pm, Sun 5:05.
Visiting Club Hotel: Clock Tower Resort, 7801 East State Street Rockford, Ill, 61108. **Telephone:** (800) 358-7666.

SCHAUMBURG BOOMERS

Office Address: 1999 Springsguth Road, Schaumburg, IL 60193
Email Address: info@boomersbaseball.com Website: www.boomersbaseball.com
Owned by: Pat and Lindy Salvi
President/General Manager: Andy Viano.
VP, Corporate Sales: Jeff Ney. **Director, Marketing/Media:** Ed McCaskey.
Business Manager: Todd Fulk. **Director, Facilities:** Mike Tlusty. **Creative Marketing Manager:** Dan Tomaszewski. **Community Relations Manager/Account Executive:** Sara Romano. **Promotions Manager/Account Executive:** Mike Kline. **Broadcaster:** Tim Calderwood. **Manager/Client Services:** Kate Kleiva.
Manager: Jamie Bennett. **Hitting Coach:** CJ Thieleke. **Pitching Coach:** TJ Nall. **First Base Coach:** Bill Frato.

GAME INFORMATION

Broadcaster: Tim Calderwood. **No. of Games Broadcast:** Home-51, Away-45. **Flagship Station:** WRMN 1410 AM Elgin. **Official Scorer:** Ken Trendel.
Stadium: Schaumburg Boomers Stadium. **Location:** I-290 to Thorndale Ave Exit, head West on Elgin-O'Hare Expressway until Springsguth Road Exit, second left at Springsguth Road (shared parking lot with Schaumburg Metra Station). **Visiting Club Hotel:** Sonesta ES Suites, 901 E Woodfield Office Ct, Schaumburg IL 60173.

SOUTHERN ILLINOIS MINERS

Office Address: Rent One Park, 1000 Miners Drive, Marion, IL 62959.
Telephone: (618) 998-8499. **Fax:** (618) 969-8550.
Email Address: info@southernillinoisminers.com. **Website:** www.southernillinoisminers.com.
Operated by: Southern Illinois Baseball Group. **Owner:** Jayne Simmons.
Vice President: Tim Arseneau. **General Manager:** Jody Sellers. **Director, Ticket Operations:** Billy Leitner. **Director, Video Production/Creative Services:** Heath Hooker. **Director, Finance:** Cathy Perry. **Director, Extra Events/Stadium Operations:** Casey Petermeyer. **Client Services Manager:** Grant Davis. **Account Executives:** Eric Pionk, Jon Basil.
Manager: Mike Pinto. **Hitting Coach:** Stephen Holdren. **Coach/Advance Scout:** John Lakin.

GAME INFORMATION

No. of Games Broadcast: 96. **Flagship Station:** 97.7 WHET-FM.
Stadium Name: Rent One Park. **Location:** US 57 to Route 13 East, right at Halfway Road to Fairmont Drive. **Standard Game Times:** 7:05 pm, Sun 5:05.
Visiting Club Hotel: America's Best Value Inn 1802 Bittle Place, Marion, IL 62959.

TRAVERSE CITY BEACH BUMS

Office Address: 333 Stadium Dr, Traverse City, MI 49685.
Telephone: (231) 943-0100. **Fax:** (231) 943-0900.
Email Address: info@tcbeachbums.com. **Website:** www.tcbeachbums.com.
Operated by: Traverse City Beach Bums, LLC.
Managing Partners: John Wuerfel.
President/CEO: John Wuerfel. **Member/CFO:** Leslye Wuerfel. **Vice President/Director, Baseball Operations:** Jason Wuerfel. **Director, Ticketing:** Ben Holcomb. **Director, Food/Beverage:** Tom Goethel. **Director, Stadium Operations:** Josh Wuerfel. **Director, Promotions:** Tonya Wuerfel. **Director, Broadcasting/Media:** Joe Brand.
Manager: Gregg Langbehn. **Infield Coach:** Matt Pulley. **Bench Coach:** Dan Rohn.

GAME INFORMATION

No. of Games Broadcast: 96. **Flagship Stations:** WLDR 101.9-FM.
PA Announcer: Joe Brand.
Stadium Name: Wuerfel Park. **Location:** Three miles south of the Grand Traverse Mall just off US-31 and M-37 in Chums Village. Stadium is visible from the highway. **Standard Game Times:** 7:05 pm, Sun 5:05 pm

WASHINGTON WILD THINGS

Office Address: One Washington Federal Way, Washington, PA 15301.
Telephone: (724) 250-9555. **Fax:** (724) 250-2333.
Email Address: info@washingtonwildthings.com. **Website:** www.washingtonwildthings.com.
Owned by: Sports Facility, LLC. **Operated by:** Washington Frontier League Baseball, LLC.
President/Chief Executive Officer: Stuart Williams. **General Manager:** Francine Williams. **Director, Marketing/Communications/Corporate Relations:** Christine Blaine. **Assistant GM:** Steve Zavacky. **Corporate Partnership Account Executives:** Zack Kaminski, Tom Harcarik. **Ticket Manager:** Brian King. **Account Executives:** Jackie Fawcett, Matt Banghart. **Promotions/Community Relations:** Liz Steig. **Special Events/Operations:** Wayne Herrod.
PR/Social Media Manager: Deb Hilton. **Box Office/Client Services Manager:** Kelly Williams. **Controller:** JJ Heider. **Assistant Controller:** Jordan Millorino. **Administrative Assistant/Office Manager:** Malcolm Smith. **Creative Services:** Bryan Leones.
Manager: Bart Zeller. **Coach:** Bob Bozutto.

GAME INFORMATION

Official Scorer: John Sacco. **Stadium Name:** CONSOL Energy Park.
Location: I-70 to exit 15 (Chestnut Street), right on Chestnut Street to Washington Crown Center Mall, right at mall entrance, right on to Mall Drive to stadium. **Standard Game Times:** 7:05 Sunday 5:05 p.m.
Visiting Club Hotel: Red Roof Inn.

WINDY CITY THUNDERBOLTS

Office Address: 14011 South Kenton Avenue, Crestwood, IL 60445-2252.
Telephone: (708) 489-2255. **Fax:** (708) 489-2999.
Email Address: info@wcthunderbolts.com. **Website:** www.wcthunderbolts.com.
Owned by: Crestwood Professional Baseball, LLC.
General Manager: Mike Lucas. **Assistant GM:** Mike VerSchave. **Director, Community Relations:** Marissa Miller.
Field Manager: Ron Biga. **Pitching Coach:** Brian Smith. **Hitting Coach:** Pete Pirman.

GAME INFORMATION

Radio Announcer: Terry Bonadonna. **No. of Games Broadcast:** 96. **Flagship Station:** WXAV, 88.3 FM. **Official Scorer:** Steve Trotto.

Stadium Name: Standard Bank Stadium. **Location:** I-294 to South Cicero Ave, exit (Route 50), south for 1 1/2 miles, left at Midlothian Turnpike, right on Kenton Ave; I-57 to 147th Street, west on 147th to Cicero, north on Cicero, right on Midlothian Turnpike, right on Kenton. **Standard Game Times:** 7:05 pm, Sat 6:05, Sun 5:05.

Visiting Club Hotel: Georgioís Comfort Inn, 8800 W 159th St, Orland Park, IL 60462. **Telephone:** (708) 403-1100.

ADDITIONAL LEAGUES

FREEDOM PRO BASEBALL LEAGUE

Mailing Address: PO B0X 5403 Scottsdale, AZ 85261.
Telephone: (480) 255-5696. **Fax:** (480) 947-4099.
E-Mail Address: info@FreedomProBaseballLeague.com. **Website:**
www.FreedomProfessionalBaseballLeague.com
Year Founded: 2012.
President/Founder: Joe Sperle.
Teams: Goodyear Centennials, Tucson CopperState Prospectors, Phoenix Explorers, Prescott Valley Federals.
Regular Season: 80 games. **2014 Opening Date:** May 31. **Closing Date:** Sept 4.
Playoff Format: Best-of-five series.
Roster limit: 22.

PACIFIC ASSOCIATION OF PROFESSIONAL BASEBALL CLUBS

Mailing address: 86 Granada Drive, Corte Madera, CA, 94904.
Telephone: (415) 485-1563. **Email:** info@pacificsbaseball.com. **Website:** www.pacificsbaseball.com.
Year Founded: 2013.
Ownership Group: Redwood Sports & Entertainment Group.
Teams: San Rafael Pacifics, Sonoma Stompers, East Bay Lumberjacks, Hawaii Stars, Maui Na Koa Ikaika, Vallejo Admirals.
Roster Limit: 22. **Eligibility Rules:** None.
Brand of Baseball: Rawlings.
Statistician: Pointstreak.

PECOS LEAGUE

Website: http://www.PecosLeague.com
Address: PO Box 271489, Houston, Tx 77277. **Telephone:** 575.680.2212.
E-mail: info@pecosleague.com
Divisions: South Divison–Alpine Cowboys (Alpine Texas); Bisbee Blue (Bisbee Arizona); Douglas Diablos (Douglas Arizona); Roswell Invaders (Roswell New Mexico); White Sands Pupfish (Alamogordo New Mexico). **Northern Division–Las Vegas Train Robbers (Las Vegas New Mexico); Raton Osos (Raton New Mexico); Santa Fe Fuego (Santa Fe Fuego); Taos Blizzard (Taos New Mexico); Trinidad Triggers (Trinidad Triggers).**
Year Founded: 2010.
Regular Season: 70 games. **Playoff Format:** Best of 3.
Roster Limit: 22.
Eligibility Rules: 25 and under/
Brand of Baseball: National League.
Statistician: Sara Galano

UNITED LEAGUE

Mailing Address: 801 E Campbell Road Suite 638, Richardson, Texas 75081.
Telephone: (972) 792-8873. **Fax:** 972.792.8876. **E-Mail Address:**
txproball@aol.com. **Website:** www.unitedleaguebaseball.com.
Year Founded: 2006 (Operated as part of North American League in 2011-2012).
CEO/Founder: Reunion Sports Group. **Vice President:** Craig Brasfield.
Teams: Fort Worth Cats, San Angelo Colts, Rio Grande Valley Whitewings, Edinburg Roadrunners.
Regular Season: 96 games. **Playoff Format:** Top four teams. **Roster Limit:** 22 man roster. **Eligibility Rules:** Over 18 years old, no roster restrictions.
Brand of Baseball: Brett Baseballs. **Statistician:** Pointstreak.

INTERNATIONAL

AMERICAS

MEXICO

MEXICAN LEAGUE

Member, National Association

NOTE: The Mexican League is a member of the National Association of Professional Baseball Leagues and has a Triple-A classification. However, its member clubs operate largely independent of the 30 major league teams, and for that reason the league is listed in the international section.

Address: Av Insurgentes Sur #797 3er. piso. Col. Napoles. C.P. 03810, Benito Juarez, Mexico, D.F. **Telephone:** 52-55-5557-1007. **Fax:** 52-55-5395-2454. **E-Mail Address:** oficina@lmb.com.mx. **Website:** www.lmb.com.mx.

Years League Active: 1955-.

President: Plinio Escalante Bolio. **Operations Manager:** Nestor Alba Brito.

Division Structure: North—Aguascalientes, Laguna, Mexico City, Monclova, Monterrey, Puebla, Reynosa, Saltillo. South—Campeche, Ciudad del Carmen, Minatitlan, Oaxaca, Quintana Roo, Tabasco, Veracruz, Yucatan.

Regular Season: 110 games (split-schedule). **2014 Opening Date:** April 1. **Closing Date:** Aug 14.

All-Star Game: May 30-June 1, Cancun, Quintana Roo.

Playoff Format: Eight teams qualify, including first- and second-half division winners plus wild-card teams with best overall records; Quarterfinals, semifinals and finals are all best-of-seven series.

Roster Limit: 28. **Roster Limit, Imports:** 6.

AGUASCALIENTES RAILROADMEN

Office Address: López Mateos # 101 Torre "A" Int 214 y 215, Plaza Cristal, Colonia San Luis, CP 20250. **Telephone:** (52) 449-915-1596. **Fax:** (52) 614-459-0336. **E-Mail Address:** Not available. **Website:** http://www.rielerosags.com.

President: Mario Rodriguez. **General Manager:** Iram Campos Lara.

Manager: Leo Rodriguez.

CAMPECHE PIRATES

Office Address: Calle Filiberto Qui Farfan No. 2, Col. Camino Real, CP 24020, Campeche, Campeche. **Telephone:** (52) 981-827-4759. **Fax:** (52) 981-827-4767. **E-Mail Address:** piratas@prodigy.net.mx. **Website:** www.piratasdecampeche.mx.

President: Gabriel Escalante Castillo.

Manager: Roque Sanchez.

CIUDAD DEL CARMEN DOLPHINS

E-Mail Address: Not available. **Website:** http://www.delfinesbeisbol.com.

President: Carlos Mejía Berrio.

Manager: Felix Fermin.

LAGUNA COWBOYS

Office Address: Juan Gutenberg s/n, Col Centro, CP 27000, Torreon, Coahuila. **Telephone:** (52) 871-718-5515. **Fax:** (52) 871-717-4335. **E-Mail Address:** Not available. **Website:** www.clubvaqueroslaguna.com.

President: Ricardo Martin Bringas. **General Manager:** Luis Dovalina.

Manager: Orlando Sanchez.

MEXICO CITY RED DEVILS

Office Address: Av Cuauhtemoc #451-101, Col Narvarte, CP 03020, Mexico DF. **Telephone:** (52) 555-639-8722. **Fax:** (52) 555-639-9722. **E-Mail Address:** diablos@sportsya.com. **Website:** www.diablos.com.mx.

President: Roberto Mansur Galán. **General Manager:** Roberto Castellon.

Manager: Miguel Ojeda.

MINATITLAN OILERS

Office Address: Pancardo S / N COL OIL, Minatitlán, Veracruz, CP 96850. **Telephone:** (52) 951-515-5522. **Fax:** (52) 922-225-8772. **E-Mail Address:** webmaster@petrolerosdeminatitlan.com.mx. **Website:** www.petrolerosdeminatitlan.mx.

President: Ranulfo Marquez Hernandez. **General Manager:** Gustavo Marquez Del Rio.

Manager: Jose Angel Chavez.

MONCLOVA STEELERS

Office Address: Cuauhtemoc #299, Col Ciudad Deportiva, CP 25750, Monclova, Coahuila. **Telephone:** (52) 866-636-2650. **Fax:** (52) 866-636-2688. **E-Mail Address:** acererosdelnorte@prodigy.net.mx. **Website:** www.acereros.com.mx.

President: Donaciano Garza Gutierrez. **General Manager:** Carlos de la Garza Barajas.

Manager: Willie Romero.

MONTERREY SULTANS

Office Address: Av Manuel Barragan s/n, Estadio Monterrey, Apartado Postal 870, Monterrey, Nuevo Leon, CP 66460. **Telephone:** (52) 81-8351-0209. **Fax:** (52) 81-8351-8022. **E-Mail Address:** sultanes@sultanes.com.mx. **Website:** www.sultanes.com.mx.

President: José Maiz García. **General Manager:** Roberto Magdaleno Ramírez.

Manager: Miguel Flores.

OAXACA WARRIORS

Office Address: M Bravo 417 Col Centro 68000, Oaxaca, Oaxaca. **Telephone:** (52) 951-515-5522. **Fax:** (52) 951-515-4966. **E-Mail Address:** oaxacaguerreros@gmail.com. **Website:** www.guerrerosdeoaxaca.com.mx.

President: Luis Narchi Karam. **General Manager:** Guillermo Spindola Morales.

Manager: Hector Estrada.

PUEBLA PARROTS

Office Address: Calz Zaragoza S/N, Unidad Deportiva 5 de Mayo, Col Maravillas, CP 72220, Puebla, Puebla. **Telephone:** (52) 222-222-2116. **Fax:** (52) 222-222-2117. **E-Mail Address:** oficina@pericosdepuebla.com.mx. **Website:** www.pericosdepuebla.com.mx.

President: Rafael Moreno Valle Sanchez. **General Manager:** Edgar Ramirez Salazar.

Manager: Houston Jimenez.

QUINTANA ROO TIGERS

Office Address: Av Mayapan Mz 4 Lt 1 Super Mz 21, CP 77500, Cancun, Quintana Roo. **Telephone:** (52) 998-887-3108. **Fax:** (52) 998-887-1313. **E-Mail Address:** tigres@tigrescapitalinos.com.mx. **Website:** www.tigresqr.com.

President: Cuauhtémoc Rodriguez. **General Manager:** Francisco Minjarez Garcia.

Manager: Roberto Vizcarra.

SALTILLO SARAPE MAKERS

Office Address: Blvd Nazario Ortiz Esquina con Blvd Jesus Sanchez, CP 25280, Saltillo, Coahuila. **Telephone:** (52) 844-416-9455. **Fax:** (52) 844-439-1330. **E-Mail Address:** aley@grupoley.com. **Website:** www.saraperos.com.mx.

President: Alvaro Ley Lopez. **General Manager:**

Eduardo Valenzuela Guajardo.
Manager: Juan Rodriguez.

TABASCO OLMECS
Office Address: Av Circuito Deportiva S/N, Col Atasta, Villahermosa, Tabasco, CP 86100. **Telephone:** (52) 993-352-2787. **Fax:** (52) 993-352-2788. **E-Mail Address:** club@olmecastabasco.com. **Website:** www.olmecastabasco.com.
President: Raul Gonzalez Rodriguez. **General Manager:** Luis Guzman Ramos.
Manager: Raul Cano.

REYNOSA BRONCOS
Office Address: Paris 511, Esq c/ Tiburcio Garza Zamora Altos, Locales 6 y 7, Col Beatty, Reynosa, Tamps. **Telephone:** (52) 922-3462. **Fax:** (52) 925-7118. **E-Mail Address:** broncosdereynosa@gmail.com. **Website:** www.broncosreynosa.com.mx.
President: Eliud Villarreal Garza. **General Manager:** Leonardo Clayton Rodríguez.
Manager: Leonardo Clayton.

VERACRUZ RED EAGLES
Office Address: Av Jacarandas S/N, Esquina España, Fraccionamiento Virginia, CP 94294, Boca del Rio, Veracruz. **Telephone:** (52) 229-935-5004. **Fax:** (229) 935-5008. **E-Mail Address:** rojosdelaguila@terra.com.mx. **Website:** www.aguiladeveracruz.com.
President: Jose Antonio Mansur Beltran. **General Manager:** Grimaldo Martinez Gonz.
Manager: Eddy Castro.

YUCATAN LIONS
Office Address: Calle 50 #406-B, Entre 35 y 37, Col Jesus Carranza, CP 97109, Merida, Yucatán. **Telephone:** (52) 999-926-3022. **Fax:** (52) 999-926-3631. **E-Mail Addresses:** leones@prodigy.net.mx. **Website:** www.leonesdeyucatan.com.mx.
President: Ricalde Gustavo Durán. **General Manager:** Jose Rivero.
Manager: Matias Carrillo.

MEXICAN ACADEMY

Rookie Classification
Mailing Address: Angel Pola No 16, Col Periodista, CP 11220, Mexico, DF Telephone: (52) 555-557-1007. **Fax:** (52) 555-395-2454. **E-Mail Address:** mbl@prodigy.net.mx. **Website:** www.lmbacademia.com.mx.
President: C.P. Plinio Escalante Bolio. **Director General:** Raul Martinez.
Regular Season: 50 games. **Opening Date:** Oct 9. **Closing Date:** Dec 21.

DOMINICAN REPUBLIC
DOMINICAN SUMMER LEAGUE

Member, National Association
Rookie Classification
Mailing Address: Calle Segunda No 64, Reparto Antilla, Santo Domingo, Dominican Republic. **Telephone/Fax:** (809) 532-3619. **Website:** www.dominicansummerleague.com. **E-Mail Address:** ligadeverano@codetel.net.do.
Years League Active: 1985-.
President: Orlando Diaz.
Member Clubs/Division Structure: Boca Chica North—Angels, Marlins, Mets 2, Phillies, Pirates 1, Rangers, Rockies, Yankees 2. **Boca Chica South**—Cubs, Cardinals, Diamondbacks/Reds, Mets 1, Nationals, Orioles 2, Pirates 2, Yankees 1. **Boca Chica Northwest**—Astros, Athletics, Dodgers, Indians, Mariners, Rays, Red Sox, Royals. **Boca Chica Baseball City**—Diamondbacks, Giants, Orioles 1, Padres, Reds, Twins, White Sox. **San Pedro de Macoris**—Blue Jays, Braves, Brewers, Tigers.
Regular Season: 72 games. **2014 Opening Date:** Unavailable. **Closing Date:** Unavailable.
Playoff Format: Six teams qualify for playoffs, including four division winners and two wild-card teams. Teams with two best records receive a bye to the semifinals; four other playoff teams play best-of-three series. Winners advance to best-of-three semifinals. Winners advance to best-of-five championship series.
Roster Limit: 35 active. **Player Eligibility Rule:** No player may have four or more years of prior minor league service. No draft-eligible player from the U.S. or Canada (not including players from Puerto Rico) may participate in the DSL. No age limits apply.

VENEZUELA
VENEZUELAN SUMMER LEAGUE

Member, National Association
Rookie Classification
Mailing Address: Torre Movilnet, Oficina 10, Piso 9, Valencia, Carabobo, Venezuela. **Telephone:** (58) 241-823-8101. **Fax:** (58) 241-824-3340. **Website:** www.vsl.com.ve.
Years League Active: 1997-.
Administrator: Franklin Moreno, Ramon Feriera Jr. **Coordinator:** Ramon Feriera.
Participating Organizations: Cubs, Mariners, Phillies, Rays, Tigers.
Regular Season: 70 games. **2014 Opening Date:** May 12. **Closing Date:** Aug 2.
Playoffs: Best-of-three series between top two teams in regular season.
Roster Limit: 35 active. **Player Eligibility Rule:** No player may have four or more years of prior minor league service. No draft-eligible player from the U.S. or Canada (not including players from Puerto Rico) may participate in the VSL. No age limits apply.

CHINA
CHINA BASEBALL LEAGUE

Mailing Address: 5, Tiyuguan Road, Beijing 100763, China. **Telephone:** (86) 10-6716-9082. **Fax:** (86) 10-6716-2993. **E-Mail Address:** cga_cra@263.net.
Years League Active: 2002-.

Chairman: Hu Jian Guo. **Vice Chairmen:** Tom McCarthy, Shen Wei. **Executive Director:** Yang Jie. **General Manager, Marketing/Promotion:** Lin Xiao Wu.
Member Clubs: Beijing Tigers, Guangdong Leopards, Henan Elephants, Jiangsu Hopestars, Shanghai Golden Eagles, Sichuan Dragons, Tianjin Lions.
Regular Season: 28 games.
Playoff Format: Top two teams meet in one-game championship.

JAPAN
NIPPON PROFESSIONAL BASEBALL

Mailing Address: Mita Bellju Building, 11th Floor, 5-36-7 Shiba, Minato-ku, Tokyo 108-0014. **Telephone:** 03-6400-1189. **Fax:** 03-6400-1190.
Website: www.npb.or.jp, www.npb.or.jp/eng
Commissioner: Katsuhiko Kumazaki.
Executive Secretary: Atsushi Ihara. **Secretaries:** Shoji Numazawa, Shinya Isomura. **Director, Baseball Operations:** Nobby Ito. **Director, Public Relations:** Katsuhisa Matsuzaki.
Director, Central League Operations: Kazunori Ogaki.
Director, Pacific League Operations: Kazuo Nakano.
Nippon Series: Best-of-seven series between Central and Pacific League champions, begins Oct. 25.
All-Star Series: July 18 at Seibu Dome; July 19 at Koshien Stadium.
Roster Limit: 70 per organization (one major league club, one minor league club). Major league club is permitted to register 28 players at a time, though just 25 may be available for each game.
Roster Limit, Imports: Four in majors (no more than three position players or pitchers); unlimited in minors.

CENTRAL LEAGUE
Regular Season: 144 games.
2014 Opening Date: March 28. **Closing Date:** Sept 25.
Playoff Format: Second-place team meets third-place team in best-of-three series. Winner meets first-place team in best-of-seven series to determine representative in Japan Series (first-place team has one-game advantage to begin series).

CHUNICHI DRAGONS
Mailing Address: Chunichi Bldg 6F, 4-1-1 Sakae, Naka-ku, Nagoya 460-0008. **Telephone:** 052-261-8811. **Fax:** 052-263-7696.
Chairman: Bungo Shirai. **President:** Takao Sasaki.
General Manager: Hiromitsu Ochiai. **Field Manager:** Motonobu Tanishige.
2014 Foreign Players: Daniel Cabrera, Alexis Gomez, Anderson Hernandez, Hector Luna, Nelson Payano.

HANSHIN TIGERS
Mailing Address: 2-33 Koshien-cho, Nishinomiya-shi, Hyogo-ken 663-8152. **Telephone:** 0798-46-1515. **Fax:** 0798-46-3555.
Chairman: Shinya Sakai. **President:** Nobuo Minami.
General Manager: Katsuhiro Nakamura. **Field Manager:** Yutaka Wada.
2014 Foreign Players: Mauro Gomez, Randy Messenger, Matt Murton, Seung-Hwan Oh, Tom O'Malley (Coach).

HIROSHIMA TOYO CARP
Mailing Address: 2-3-1 Minami Kaniya, Minami-ku, Hiroshima 732-8501. **Telephone:** 082-554-1000. **Fax:** 082-568-1190.
President: Hajime Matsuda. **General Manager:** Kiyoaki Suzuki. **Field Manager:** Kenjiro Nomura.
2014 Foreign Players: Bryan Bullington, Brad Eldred, Kila Ka'aihue, Kam Mickolio, Zach Phillips.

TOKYO YAKULT SWALLOWS
Mailing Address: Seizan Bldg, 4F, 2-12-28 Kita Aoyama, Minato-ku, Tokyo 107-0061. **Telephone:** 03-3405-8960. **Fax:** 03-3405-8961.
Chairman: Sumiya Hori. **President:** Tsuyoshi Klnugasa.
General Manager: Junsei Atarashi. **Field Manager:** Junji Ogawa.

2014 Foreign Players: Wladimir Balentien, Tony Barnette, Chris Carpenter, Lastings Milledge, Chris Narveson, Orlando Roman.

YOKOHAMA DeNA BAYSTARS
Mailing Address: Kannai Arai Bldg, 7F, 1-8 Onoe-cho, Naka-ku, Yokohama 231-0015. **Telephone:** 045-681-0811. **Fax:** 045-661-2500.
Chairman: Makoto Haruta. **President:** Jun Ikeda.
General Manager: Shigeru Takada. **Field Manager:** Kiyoshi Nakahata.
2014 Foreign Players: Aarom Baldiris, Tony Blanco, Guillermo Moscoso, Jorge Sosa, Enyelbert Soto.

YOMIURI GIANTS
Mailing Address: Yomiuri Shimbun Bldg, 26F, 1-7-1 Otemachi, Chiyoda-ku, Tokyo 100-8151. **Telephone:** 03-3246-7733. **Fax:** 03-3246-2726.
Chairman: Kojiro Shiraishi. **President:** Tsunekazu Momoi. **General Manager:** Atsushi Harasawa. **Field Manager:** Tatsunori Hara.
2014 Foreign Players: Leslie Anderson, Jose Lopez, Scott Mathieson, Chris Seddon.

PACIFIC LEAGUE
Regular Season: 144 games.
2014 Opening Date: March 28. **Closing Date:** Oct. 2.
Playoff Format: Second-place team meets third-place team in best-of-three series. Winner meets first-place team in best-of-seven series to determine league's representative in Japan Series (first-place team has one-game advantage to begin series).

CHIBA LOTTE MARINES
Mailing Address: 1 Mihama, Mihama-ku, Chiba-shi, Chiba-ken 261-8587. **Telephone:** 03-5682-6341.
Chairman: Takeo Shigemitsu. **President:** Iekuni Nakamura. **Field Manager:** Tsutomu Ito.
2014 Foreign Players: Craig Brazell, Luis Cruz, Seth Greisinger, Chad Huffman, Carlos Rosa.

FUKUOKA SOFTBANK HAWKS
Mailing Address: Fukuoka Yahoo! Japan Dome, Hawks Town, Chuo-ku, Fukuoka 810-0065. **Telephone:** 092-847-1006. **Fax:** 092-844-4600.
Owner: Masayoshi Son. **Chairman:** Sadaharu Oh. **President:** Yoshimitsu Goto. **Field Manager:** Koji Akiyama.
2014 Foreign Players: Edison Barrios, Barbaro Canizares, Dae Ho Lee, Paul Oseguera, Dennis Sarfate, Jason Standridge, Brian Wolfe.

HOKKAIDO NIPPON HAM FIGHTERS
Mailing Address: 1 Hitsujigaoka, Toyohira-ku, Sapporo 062-8655. **Telephone:** 011-857-3939. **Fax:** 011-857-3900.
Chairman: Hiroji Okoso. **President:** Junichi Fujii.
General Manager: Masao Yamada. **Field Manager:** Hideki Kuriyama.
2014 Foreign Players: Michel Abreu, Mike Crotta, Luis Mendoza, Juan Miranda.

ORIX BUFFALOES
Mailing Address: 3-Kita-2-30 Chiyozaki, Nishi-ku, Osaka 550-0023. **Telephone:** 06-6586-0221. **Fax:** 06-6586-0240.
Chairman: Yoshihiko Miyauchi. **President:** Hiroaki Nishina. **General Manager:** Ryuzo Setoyama. **Field Manager:** Hiroshi Moriwaki.
2014 Foreign Players: Brandon Dickson, Esteban German, Alex Maestri, Wily Mo Pena.

SAITAMA SEIBU LIONS
Mailing Address: 2135 Kami-Yamaguchi, Tokorozawa-shi, Saitama-ken 359-1189. **Telephone:** 04-2924-1155.

Fax: 04-2928-1919.
President: Hajime Igo. **Field Manager:** Haruki Ihara.
2014 Foreign Players: Michael Bowden, Cody Ransom, Greg Reynolds, Randy Williams.

TOHOKU RAKUTEN GOLDEN EAGLES
Mailing Address: 2-11-6 Miyagino, Miyagino-ku, Sendai-shi, Miyagi-ken 983-0045. **Telephone:** 022-298-5300. **Fax:** 022-298-5360.
Chairman: Hiroshi Mikitani. **President:** Yozo Tachibana. **Field Manager:** Senichi Hoshino.
2014 Foreign Players: Travis Blackley, Brian Falkenborg, Andruw Jones, Kevin Youkilis.

KOREA

KOREA BASEBALL ORGANIZATION

Mailing Address: 946-16 Dokokdong, Kangnam-gu, Seoul, Korea. **Telephone:** (02) 3460-4600. **Fax:** (02) 3460-4639.
Years League Active: 1982-.
Website: www.koreabaseball.com.
Commissioner: Koo Bon-Neung. **Secretary General:** Yang Hae-Young.
Member Clubs: Doosan Bears, Hanwha Eagles, Kia Tigers, LG Twins, Lotte Giants, NC Dinos, Nexen Heroes, Samsung Lions, SK Wyverns.
Regular Season: 128 games. **2014 Opening Date:** March 29.

Playoffs: Third- and fourth-place teams meet in best-of-three series; winner advances to meet second-place team in best-of-five series; winner meets first-place team in best-of-seven Korean Series for league championship.
Roster Limit: 26 active through Sept 1, when rosters expand to 31. **Imports:** Two active.

TAIWAN

CHINESE PROFESSIONAL BASEBALL LEAGUE

Mailing Address: 2F, No 32, Pateh Road, Sec 3, Taipei, Taiwan 10559. **Telephone:** 886-2-2577-6992. **Fax:** 886-2-2577-2606. **Website:** www.cpbl.com.tw.
Years League Active: 1990-.
Commissioner: Jenn-Tai Hwang. **Deputy Secretary General:** Hueimin Wang. **E-Mail Address:** richard.wang@cpbl.com.tw.
Member Clubs: Brother Elephants, EDA Rhinos, Lamigo Monkeys, Uni Lions.
Regular Season: 120 games. **2014 Opening Date:** Not available. **Playoffs:** Half-season winners are eligible for the postseason. If a non-half-season winner team possesses a higher overall winning percentage than any other half-season winner, then this team gains a wild-card and will play a best-of-five series against the half-season winner with lower winner percentage.
The winner of the playoff series advances to Taiwan Series (best-of-seven).

EUROPE

NETHERLANDS

DUTCH MAJOR LEAGUE

Mailing Address: Koninklijke Nederlandse Baseball en Softball Bond (Royal Dutch Baseball and Softball Association), Postbus 2650, 3430 GB Nieuwegein, Holland. **Telephone:** 31-30-751-3650. **Fax:** 31-30-751-3651. **Website:** www.knbsb.nl.
Member Clubs: ADO, Amsterdam Pirates, Dordrecht, HCAW, Kinheim, Neptunus, Mampaey Hawks, UVV, Vaessen Pioniers.
President: Bob Bergkamp.

ITALY

ITALIAN BASEBALL LEAGUE

Mailing Address: Federazione Italiana Baseball Softball, Viale Tiziano 74, 00196 Roma, Italy. **Telephone:** 39-06-32297201. **Fax:** 39-06-36858201. **Website:** www.fibs.it.
Member Clubs: Bologna, Godo, Grosseto, Nettuno, Novara, Parma, Rimini, San Marino.
President: Riccardo Fraccari.

WINTER BASEBALL

CARIBBEAN BASEBALL CONFEDERATION

Mailing Address: Frank Feliz Miranda No 1 Naco, Santo Domingo, Dominican Republic. **Telephone:** (809) 381-2643. **Fax:** (809) 565-4654.
Commissioner: Juan Francisco Puello. **Secretary:** Benny Agosto.
Member Countries: Colombia, Dominican Republic, Mexico, Nicaragua, Puerto Rico, Venezuela (Colombia and Nicaragua do not play in the Caribbean Series).
2015 Caribbean Series: Puerto Rico, February.

DOMINICAN LEAGUE

Office Address: Estadio Quisqueya, 2da Planta, Ens La Fe, Santo Domingo, Dominican Republic. **Telephone:** (809) 567-6371. **Fax:** (809) 567-5720. **E-Mail Address:** ligadom@hotmail.com. **Website:** www.lidom.com.
Years League Active: 1951-.

President: Leonardo Matos Berrido. **Executive Director:** Jorge Torres Ocumarez. **Press Manager:** Freddy Ortiz Pujols.
Member Clubs: Aguilas Cibaenas, Estrellas de Oriente, Gigantes del Cibao, Leones del Escogido, Tigres del Licey, Toros del Este.
Regular Season: 50 games. **2014 Opening Date:** Unavailable.
Playoff Format: Top four teams meet in 18-game round-robin. Top two teams advance to best-of-nine series for league championship. Winner advances to Caribbean Series.
Roster Limit: 30. **Imports:** 7.

MEXICAN PACIFIC LEAGUE

Mailing Address: Blvd Solidaridad No 335, Plaza las Palmas, Edificio A, Nivel 1, Local 4, Hermosillo, Sonora, Mexico CP 83246. **Telephone:** (52) 662-310-9714. **Fax:** (52) 662-310-9715. **E-Mail Address:** ligadelpacifico@liga-

delpacifico.com.mx. **Website:** www.ligadelpacifico.com.
mx.

    Years League Active: 1958-.
    President: Omar Canizales Soto. **Administration:**
Remigio Valencia. **General Manager:** Christian O. Valencia
Veliz. **Media Manager:** Pedro A. Gutierrez.
    Member Clubs: Culiacan Tomateros, Guasave
Algodoneros, Hermosillo Naranjeros, Los Mochis Caneros,
Mazatlan Venados, Mexicali Aguilas, Navojoa Mayos,
Obregon Yaquis.
    Regular Season: 68 games. **2014 Opening Date:**
Unavailable.
    Playoff Format: Six teams advance to best-of-seven
quarterfinals. Three winners and losing team with best
record advance to best-of-seven semifinals. Winners meet
in best-of-seven series for league championship. Winner
advances to Caribbean Series.
    Roster Limit: 30. **Imports:** 5.

PUERTO RICAN LEAGUE

    Office Address: Avenida Munoz Rivera 1056, Edificio
First Federal, Suite 501, Rio Piedras, PR 00925. **Mailing
Address:** PO Box 191852, San Juan, PR 00019. **Telephone:**
(787) 765-6285, 765-7285. **Fax:** (787) 767-3028. **Website:**
www.ligapr.com.
    Years League Active: 1938-2007; 2008-
    President: Hector Rivera.
    Member Clubs: Caguas Criollos, Carolina Gigantes,
Mayaguez Indios, Ponce Leones, Santurce Canjrejeros.
    Regular Season: 40 games. **2014 Opening Date:**
Unavailable.
    Playoff Format: Top four teams meet in best-of-seven
semifinal series. Winners meet in best-of-nine series for
league championship. Winner advances to Caribbean
Series.
    Roster Limit: 30. **Imports:** 5.

VENEZUELAN LEAGUE

    Mailing Address: Avenida Casanova, Centro Comercial
"El Recreo," Torre Sur, Piso 3, Oficinas 6 y 7, Sabana Grande,
Caracas, Venezuela. **Telephone:** (58) 212-761-6408. **Fax:**
(58) 212-761-7661. **Website:** www.lvbp.com.
    Years League Active: 1946-.
    President: Oscar Prieto Párraga. **Vice Presidents:**
Humberto Angrisano, Domingo Santander. **General
Manager:** Domingo Alvarez.
    Member Clubs: Anzoategui Caribes, Aragua Tigres,
Caracas Leones, La Guaira Tiburones, Lara Cardenales,
Magallanes Navegantes, Margarita Bravos, Zulia Aguilas.
    Regular Season: 64 games. **2014 Opening Date:**
Unavailable.
    Playoff Format: Top two teams in each division, plus
a wild-card team, meet in 16-game round-robin series.
Top two finishers meet in best-of-seven series for league
championship. Winner advances to Caribbean Series.
    Roster Limit: 26. **Imports:** 7.

COLOMBIAN LEAGUE

    Office/Mailing Address: Unavailable. **Telephone:**
Unavailable. **E-mail Address:** mramirez@lcbp.co.
Website: www.teamrenteria.com.
    President: Edinson Renteria. **Vice Presidents:** George
Baladi, Edgar Perez.
    Member Clubs: Barranquilla, Cartagena, Monteria,
Sincelejo.
    Regular season: 65 games. **2014 Opening Date:**
Unavailable.
    Playoff Format: Top two teams meet in best-of-seven
finals for league championship.

AUSTRALIA

AUSTRALIAN BASEBALL LEAGUE

    Mailing Address: 1 Palm Meadows Drive, Carrara,
QLD, 4211, Australia. **Telephone:** 61-7-5510-6819. **Fax:**
61-7-5510-6855. **E-Mail Address:** admin@ableague.com.
au. **Website:** www.theabl.com.
    CEO: Peter Wermuth. **General Manager:** Ben Foster.
    Teams: Adelaide, Brisbane, Canberra, Melbourne,
Perth, Sydney.
    Playoff Format: First-place team plays second-place
team in major semifinal; third-place team plays fourth-
place team in minor semifinal, both best of three series.
Loser of major semifinal plays winner of minor semifinal
in best of three series. Winner of that series plays winner of major semifinal in best of three series for league
championship.

DOMESTIC LEAGUE

ARIZONA FALL LEAGUE

    Mailing Address: 2415 E Camelback Road, Suite 850,
Phoenix, AZ 85016. **Telephone:** (602) 281-7250. **Fax:** (602)
281-7313. **E-Mail Address:** afl@mlb.com. **Website:** www.
mlb.com.
    Years League Active: 1992-.
    Operated by: Major League Baseball.
    Executive Director: Steve Cobb. **Senior
Administrator:** Joan McGrath.
    Teams: Mesa Solar Sox, Peoria Javelinas, Peoria
Saguaros, Phoenix Desert Dogs, Scottsdale Scorpions,
Surprise Rafters.
    2014 Opening Date: Unavailable. Play usually opens
in mid-October. **Playoff Format:** Division champions
meet in one-game championship.
    Roster Limit: 30. Players with less than one year of
major league service are eligible, with one foreign player
and one player below the Double-A level allowed per
team.

MINOR
LEAGUE
SCHEDULES

TRIPLE-A

INTERNATIONAL LEAGUE

BUFFALO BISONS

APRIL	
3-4	Rochester
5-6	at Rochester
7-9	at Lehigh Valley
10-13	Pawtucket
14-17	Scranton/WB
18-19	at Pawtucket
21	at Pawtucket
22-25	at Scranton/WB
26-29	Louisville

MAY	
1-4	Charlotte
5-8	at Gwinnett
9-12	at Charlotte
13-16	Gwinnett
17-20	Lehigh Valley
22-25	at Louisville
26-29	at Indianapolis
30-31	Syracuse

JUNE	
1-2	Syracuse
3-6	Toledo
7-8	Syracuse
9-10	at Syracuse
12-15	at Toledo
16-19	at Columbus
20-23	Rochester

24-27	Columbus
28-30	at Syracuse

JULY	
1	at Syracuse
2-3	Scranton/WB
4-5	at Scranton/WB
6-9	at Rochester
10-13	Durham
17-20	at Pawtucket
21-22	at Lehigh Valley
23-24	Syracuse
25-28	Lehigh Valley
29-31	Indianapolis

AUGUST	
1	Indianapolis
2-5	at Norfolk
7-10	at Durham
11-14	Norfolk
15-17	at Lehigh Valley
19-20	Rochester
21-22	Scranton/WB
23-26	Pawtucket
27-28	at Scranton/WB
29-31	at Syracuse

SEPTEMBER	
1	at Syracuse

CHARLOTTE KNIGHTS

APRIL	
3-6	at Norfolk
7-10	at Durham
11-13	Norfolk
14-15	Durham
16-18	Gwinnett
19-21	at Gwinnett
22-25	Durham
26-29	at Rochester

MAY	
1-4	at Buffalo
5-8	Lehigh Valley
9-12	Buffalo
13-16	at Durham
17-18	at Norfolk
20-21	Norfolk
22-25	Indianapolis
26-29	at Columbus
30-31	at Toledo

JUNE	
1-2	at Toledo
3-6	Rochester
7-10	Columbus
12-15	at Pawtucket
16-19	at Lehigh Valley
20-23	Toledo
24-27	Louisville

28-29	at Gwinnett
30	Gwinnett

JULY	
1	Gwinnett
2-3	at Norfolk
4-5	Norfolk
6-9	at Scranton/WB
10-13	Syracuse
17-20	Scranton/WB
21-24	at Indianapolis
25-28	at Louisville
29-31	Durham

AUGUST	
1	Durham
2-3	at Gwinnett
5-6	Gwinnett
7-10	Pawtucket
11-14	at Syracuse
15-17	at Durham
18-19	Gwinnett
20-21	at Gwinnett
22-25	Norfolk
26-27	at Norfolk
29-30	at Gwinnett
31	Gwinnett

SEPTEMBER	
1	Gwinnett

COLUMBUS CLIPPERS

APRIL	
3-6	Indianapolis
7-9	Louisville
10-13	at Louisville
14-15	at Indianapolis
16-17	at Toledo

18-19	Toledo
21	Toledo
22-25	Gwinnett
26-29	at Norfolk

DURHAM BULLS

APRIL	
3-6	Gwinnett
7-10	Charlotte
11-13	at Gwinnett
14-15	at Charlotte
16-17	Norfolk
18-21	at Norfolk
22-25	at Charlotte
26-29	Scranton/WB

MAY	
1-4	Columbus
5-8	at Syracuse
9-12	at Scranton/WB
13-16	Charlotte
17-20	Louisville
22-25	at Columbus
26-29	at Toledo
30-31	Lehigh Valley

JUNE	
1-2	Lehigh Valley
3-6	Pawtucket
7-8	Norfolk
9-10	at Norfolk
11-14	at Indianapolis
15-18	at Louisville
20-23	Syracuse

GWINNETT BRAVES

APRIL	
3-6	at Durham
7-10	at Norfolk
11-13	Durham
14-15	Norfolk
16-18	at Charlotte
19-21	Charlotte
22-25	at Columbus
26-29	at Toledo

MAY	
1-4	Lehigh Valley
5-8	Buffalo
9-12	at Lehigh Valley
13-16	at Buffalo
17-20	Indianapolis
22-25	Norfolk
26-29	at Pawtucket

MAY	
1-4	at Durham
5-8	Rochester
9-12	Syracuse
13-16	at Rochester
17-20	at Syracuse
22-25	Durham
26-29	Charlotte
30-31	Louisville

JUNE	
1-2	at Louisville
3-6	at Gwinnett
7-10	at Charlotte
12-15	Scranton/WB
16-19	Buffalo
20-23	at Lehigh Valley
24-27	at Buffalo
28-29	at Toledo
30	Louisville

JULY	
1	Louisville

2-3	at Toledo
4-5	Toledo
6-9	Pawtucket
10-13	at Indianapolis
17-20	Indianapolis
21-24	at Louisville
25-28	Norfolk
30-31	Louisville

AUGUST	
1	Lousville
2-5	at Pawtucket
7-10	at Scranton/WB
11-14	Lehigh Valley
15-17	at Toledo
18-20	Toledo
21-22	at Louisville
23-25	Indianapolis
26-27	at Toledo
28-30	at Indianapolis
31	Toledo

SEPTEMBER	
1	Toledo

24-27	Indianapolis
28-30	at Pawtucket

JULY	
1	at Pawtucket
2-3	Gwinnett
4-5	at Gwinnett
6-7	Norfolk
8-9	at Norfolk
10-13	at Buffalo
17-20	at Gwinnett
21-24	Rochester
25-28	Toledo
29-31	at Charlotte

AUGUST	
1	at Charlotte
2-5	at Lehigh Valley
7-10	Buffalo
11-14	at Rohester
15-17	Charlotte
19-21	Norfolk
22-25	Gwinnett
26-27	at Gwinnett
28-30	at Norfolk
31	Norfolk

SEPTEMBER	
1	Norfolk

30-31	at Rochester

JUNE	
1-2	at Rochester
3-6	Columbus
7-10	Rochester
11-14	at Louisville
15-18	at Indianapolis
20-23	Louisville
24-27	Toledo
28-29	Charlotte
30	at Charlotte

JULY	
1	at Charlotte
2-3	at Durham
4-5	Durham
6-9	Syracuse

10-13 . . . . at Norfolk	11-14 . . . . . . .Pawtucket
17-20 . . . . Durham	15-17 . . . . . . at Norfolk
21-24 . . . . . Scranton/WB	18-19 . . . . .at Charlotte
25-28 . . . . at Scranton/WB	20-21 . . . . Charlotte
29-31 . . . . at Scranton/WB	22-25 . . . . . .at Durham
AUGUST	26-27 . . . . Durham
1 . . . . . at Scranton/WB	29-30 . . . . Charlotte
2-3 . . . . Charlotte	31 . . . . .at Charlotte
5-6 . . . . .at Charlotte	**SEPTEMBER**
7-10 . . . . .Norfolk	1 . . . . at Charlotte

INDIANAPOLIS INDIANS

APRIL	28-29 . . . . . at Louisville
3-6 . . . . at Columbus	30 . . . . Toledo
7-9 . . . . .at Toledo	**JULY**
10-12 . . . . Toledo	1 . . . . Toledo
13-15 . . . . .Columbus	2-3 . . . . . . at Louisville
16-18 . . . . . at Louisville	4-5 . . . . Louisville
19-21 . . . . . . Louisville	6-9 . . . . . . Lehigh Valley
22-25 . . . . .at Toledo	10-13 . . . . Columbus
26-29 . . . . Syracuse	17-20 . . . . . at Columbus
MAY	21-24 . . . . Charlotte
1-4 . . . . at Pawtucket	25-28 . . . . . at Rochester
5-8 . . . . . at Scranton/WB	29-31 . . . . . . at Buffalo
9-12 . . . . .Norfolk	**AUGUST**
13-16 . . . . . . .Pawtucket	1 . . . . at Buffalo
17-20 . . . . . . at Gwinnett	2-5 . . . . Toledo
22-25 . . . . . .at Charlotte	7-10 . . . . Rochester
26-29 . . . . Buffalo	12-14 . . . . .at Toledo
30-31 . . . . Scranton/WB	15-16 . . . . at Louisville
JUNE	17-20 . . . . Louisville
1-2 . . . . Scranton/WB	21-22 . . . . Toledo
3-6 . . . . at Syracuse	23-25 . . . . at Columbus
7-10 . . . . at Lehigh Valley	26-27 . . . . . Louisville
11-14 . . . . Durham	28-30 . . . . Columbus
15-18 . . . . . . Gwinnett	31 . . . . . . at Louisville
20-23 . . . . . at Norfolk	**SEPTEMBER**
24-27 . . . . . .at Durham	1 . . . . .at Louisville

LEHIGH VALLEY IRONPIGS

APRIL	**JULY**
3-6 . . . . at Pawtucket	1 . . . . . at Scranton/WB
7-9 . . . . Buffalo	2-3 . . . . Syracuse
10-13 . . . . Rochester	4-5 . . . . at Rochester
14-17 . . . . . . at Syracuse	6-9 . . . . . .at Indianapolis
18-21 . . . . at Scranton/WB	10-13 . . . . . at Louisville
22-25 . . . . . .Norfolk	17-18 . . . . Syracuse
26-29 . . . . . . .Pawtucket	19-20 . . . . . at Syracuse
MAY	21-22 . . . . Buffalo
1-4 . . . . .at Gwinnett	23-24 . . . . . . .Pawtucket
5-8 . . . . .at Charlotte	25-28 . . . . . at Buffalo
9-12 . . . . Gwinnett	29-30 . . . . . at Rochester
13-16 . . . . . Scranton/WB	31 . . . . Rochester
17-20 . . . . . . at Buffalo	**AUGUST**
22-25 . . . . Toledo	1 . . . . Rochester
26-29 . . . . at Norfolk	2-5 . . . . Durham
30-31 . . . . . . .at Durham	7-10 . . . . .at Toledo
JUNE	11-14 . . . . at Columbus
1-2 . . . . .at Durham	15-17 . . . . Buffalo
3-6 . . . . Louisville	19-22 . . . . at Pawtucket
7-10 . . . . . .Indianapolis	23-26 . . . . Syracuse
12-15 . . . . at Rochester	27-28 . . . . . . .Pawtucket
16-19 . . . . . . Charlotte	29-30 . . . . . Scranton/WB
20-23 . . . . . . Columbus	31 . . . . . . at Scranton/WB
24-25 . . . . . at Syracuse	**SEPTEMBER**
26-29 . . . . . Scranton/WB	1 . . . . . . at Scranton/WB
30 . . . . . at Scranton/WB	

LOUISVILLE BATS

APRIL	7-9 . . . . at Columbus
4-6 . . . . .at Toledo	10-12 . . . . Columbus

NORFOLK TIDES

APRIL	24-27 . . . . . at Pawtucket
3-6 . . . . Charlotte	28-30 . . . . . at Rochester
7-10 . . . . Gwinnett	**JULY**
11-13 . . . . at Charlotte	1 . . . . at Rochester
14-15 . . . . . at Gwinnett	2-3 . . . . Charlotte
16-17 . . . . .at Durham	4-5 . . . . . . at Charlotte
18-21 . . . . Durham	6-7 . . . . .at Durham
22-25 . . . at Lehigh Valley	8-9 . . . . Durham
26-29 . . . . Columbus	10-13 . . . . Gwinnett
MAY	17-20 . . . . . . Rochester
1-4 . . . . Scranton/WB	21-24 . . . . Toledo
5-8 . . . . . . .at Louisville	25-28 . . . . at Columbus
9-12 . . . . . .at Indianapolis	29-31 . . . . . . .at Toledo
13-16 . . . . . . Louisville	**AUGUST**
17-18 . . . . Charlotte	1 . . . . .at Toledo
20-21 . . . . at Charlotte	2-5 . . . . Buffalo
22-25 . . . . .at Gwinnett	7-10 . . . . . . at Gwinnett
26-29 . . . . Lehigh Valley	11-14 . . . . . at Buffalo
30-31 . . . . . .Pawtucket	15-17 . . . . Gwinnett
JUNE	19-21 . . . . . .at Durham
1-2 . . . . .Pawtucket	22-25 . . . . .at Charlotte
3-6 . . . . . at Scranton/WB	26-27 . . . . Charlotte
7-8 . . . . . . .at Durham	28-30 . . . . Durham
9-10 . . . . Durham	31 . . . . . . .at Durham
12-15 . . . . . at Syracuse	**SEPTEMBER**
16-19 . . . . . . Syracuse	1 . . . . .at Durham
20-23 . . . . . .Indianapolis	

PAWTUCKET RED SOX

APRIL	**JUNE**
3-6 . . . . . . Lehigh Valley	1-2 . . . . at Norfolk
7-9 . . . . Syracuse	3-6 . . . . .at Durham
10-13 . . . . . . at Buffalo	7-10 . . . . Louisville
14-17 . . . . at Rochester	12-15 . . . . . . Charlotte
18-19 . . . . Buffalo	16-19 . . . . . at Rochester
21 . . . . Buffalo	20-23 . . . . at Scranton/WB
22-25 . . . . . . Rochester	24-27 . . . . . .Norfolk
26-29 . . . . at Lehigh Valley	28-30 . . . . Durham
MAY	**JULY**
1-4 . . . . .Indianapolis	1 . . . . Durham
5-8 . . . . Toledo	2-3 . . . . Rochester
9-12 . . . . . at Louisville	4-5 . . . . . . at Syracuse
13-16 . . . . at Indianapolis	6-9 . . . . . . at Columbus
17-20 . . . . Scranton/WB	10-13 . . . . . . .at Toledo
22-25 . . . . . at Syracuse	17-20 . . . . Buffalo
26-29 . . . . . . Gwinnett	21-22 . . . . . at Syracuse
30-31 . . . . . . at Norfolk	23-24 . . . . at Lehigh Valley

JULY
1 . . . . at Columbus
2-3 . . . . .Indianapolis
4-5 . . . . . .at Indianapolis
6-9 . . . . Toledo
10-13 . . . . Lehigh Valley
17-20 . . . . .at Toledo
21-24 . . . . . . Columbus
25-28 . . . . . . Charlotte
30-31 . . . . at Columbus
AUGUST
1 . . . . at Columbus
2-5 . . . . Rochester
7-10 . . . . . . at Syracuse
11-14 . . . . at Scranton/WB
15-16 . . . . . .Indianapolis
17-20 . . . . at Indianapolis
21-22 . . . . Columbus
23-25 . . . . .at Toledo
26-27 . . . . at Indianapolis
28-30 . . . . Toledo
31 . . . . .Indianapolis
SEPTEMBER
1 . . . . .Indianapolis

25-28 . . . . at Scranton/WB
30-31 . . . . Syracuse

AUGUST
1 . . . . Syracuse
2-5 . . . . Columbus
7-10 . . . . . . .at Charlotte
11-14 . . . . . .at Gwinnett
15-18 . . . . . Scranton/WB

19-22 . . . . . Lehigh Valley
23-26 . . . . at Buffalo
27-28 . . . at Lehigh Valley
29-30 . . . . Syracuse
31 . . . . Rochester

SEPTEMBER
1 . . . . Rochester

ROCHESTER RED WINGS

APRIL
3-4 . . . . at Buffalo
5-6 . . . . Buffalo
7-9 . . . . Scranton/WB
10-13 . . . Lehigh Valley
14-17 . . . . . . .Pawtucket
18-21 . . . . . . at Syracuse
22-25 . . . . at Pawtucket
26-29 . . . . at Charlotte

MAY
1-4 . . . . Louisville
5-8 . . . . at Columbus
9-12 . . . . . . .at Toledo
13-16 . . . . . Columbus
17-20 . . . . Toledo
22-25 . . at Scranton/WB
26-29 . . . . . . Syracuse
30-31 . . . . . Gwinnett

JUNE
1-2 . . . . . . Gwinnett
3-6 . . . . at Charlotte
7-10 . . . . .at Gwinnett
12-15 . . . . Lehigh Valley
16-19 . . . . . .Pawtucket
20-23 . . . . . . at Buffalo
24-25 . . . at Scranton/WB
26-27 . . . at Lehigh Valley

28-30 . . . . .Norfolk

JULY
1 . . . . Norfolk
2-3 . . . . at Pawtucket
4-5 . . . . Lehigh Valley
6-9 . . . . Buffalo
10-11 . . at Scranton/WB
12-13 . . . Scranton/WB
17-20 . . . . at Norfolk
21-24 . . . . . . .at Durham
25-28 . . .Indianapolis
29-30 . . . Lehigh Valley
31 . . . . . at Lehigh Valley

AUGUST
1 . . . . . . at Lehigh Valley
2-5 . . . . . .at Louisville
7-10 . . .at Indianapolis
11-14 . . . . . . Durham
15-18 . . . Syracuse
19-20 . . . at Buffalo
21-22 . . . . at Syracuse
23-25 . . . Scranton/WB
27-28 . . . at Syracuse
29-30 . . . . Buffalo
31 . . . . . . at Pawtucket

SEPTEMBER
1 . . . . . . at Pawtucket

SCRANTON/WILKES-BARRE RAILRIDERS

APRIL
3-6 . . . . at Syracuse
7-9 . . . . . at Rochester
10-13 . . . . Syracuse
14-17 . . . . . . at Buffalo
18-21 . . . Lehigh Valley
22-25 . . . . Buffalo
26-29 . . . . . . .at Durham

MAY
1-4 . . . . . . at Norfolk
5-8 . . . . . .Indianapolis
9-12 . . . . Durham
13-16 . . . at Lehigh Valley
17-20 . . . at Pawtucket
22-25 . . . . Rochester
26-29 . . . .at Louisville
30-31 . . . .at Indianapolis

JUNE
1-2 . . . . . .at Indianapolis
3-6 . . . . .Norfolk
7-10 . . . . . . Toledo
12-15 . . . . at Columbus
16-19 . . . . .at Toledo
20-23 . . . .Pawtucket
24-25 . . . . Rochester
26-27 . . . . at Syracuse
28-29 . . . at Lehigh Valley

30 . . . . Lehigh Valley

JULY
1 . . . . Lehigh Valley
2-3 . . . . at Buffalo
4-5 . . . . Buffalo
6-9 . . . . Charlotte
10-11 . . . . . . Rochester
12-13 . . . at Rochester
17-20 . . . . . .at Charlotte
21-24 . . . . . Gwinnett
25-28 . . . . .Pawtucket
29-31 . . . . . . Gwinnett

AUGUST
1 . . . . Gwinnett
2-3 . . . . Syracuse
4-5 . . . . at Syracuse
7-10 . . . . . . Columbus
11-14 . . . . . . Louisville
15-18 . . . . at Pawtucket
19-20 . . . . . . Syracuse
21-22 . . . . at Buffalo
23-25 . . . at Rochester
27-28 . . . . Buffalo
29-30 . . . at Lehigh Valley
31 . . . . . . Lehigh Valley

SEPTEMBER
1 . . . . Lehigh Valley

SYRACUSE CHIEFS

APRIL
3-6 . . . . Scranton/WB

7-9 . . . . . . at Pawtucket
10-13 . . . at Scranton/WB

14-17 . . . . . Lehigh Valley
18-21 . . . . . . Rochester
22-25 . . . . . .at Louisville
26-29 . . . at Indianapolis

MAY
1-4 . . . . Toledo
5-8 . . . . Durham
9-12 . . . at Columbus
13-16 . . . . .at Toledo
17-20 . . . . Columbus
22-25 . . . . . . .Pawtucket
26-29 . . . . at Rochester
30-31 . . . . at Buffalo

JUNE
1-2 . . . . at Buffalo
3-6 . . . . . .Indianapolis
7-8 . . . . at Buffalo
9-10 . . . . Buffalo
12-15 . . . . . .Norfolk
16-19 . . . . at Norfolk
20-23 . . . . .at Durham
24-25 . . . Lehigh Valley
26-27 . . . Scranton/WB
28-30 . . . . Buffalo

JULY
1 . . . . Buffalo

TOLEDO MUD HENS

APRIL
4-6 . . . . Louisville
7-9 . . . . . .Indianapolis
10-12 . . . .at Indianapolis
13-15 . . . .at Louisville
16-17 . . . . . Columbus
18-19 . . . at Columbus
21 . . . . . . at Columbus
22-25 . . . .Indianapolis
26-29 . . . . Gwinnett

MAY
1-4 . . . . at Syracuse
5-8 . . . . . at Pawtucket
9-12 . . . . . Rochester
13-16 . . . . . Syracuse
17-20 . . . at Rochester
22-25 . . at Lehigh Valley
26-29 . . . . Durham
30-31 . . . . . Charlotte

JUNE
1-2 . . . . . . Charlotte
3-6 . . . . . . at Buffalo
7-10 . . . at Scranton/WB
12-15 . . . . . . Buffalo
16-19 . . . Scranton/WB
20-23 . . . . .at Charlotte
24-27 . . . . at Gwinnett

28-29 . . . . . . .Columbus
30 . . . . at Indianapolis

JULY
1 . . . . . . .at Indianapolis
2-3 . . . . Columbus
4-5 . . . . . . at Columbus
7-9 . . . . . . .at Louisville
10-13 . . . . . .Pawtucket
17-20 . . . . . Louisville
21-24 . . . . at Norfolk
25-28 . . . .at Durham
29-31 . . . . . .Norfolk

AUGUST
1 . . . . .Norfolk
2-5 . . . . . .at Indianapolis
7-10 . . . . Lehigh Valley
12-14 . . . .Indianapolis
15-17 . . . . . Columbus
18-20 . . . at Columbus
21-22 . . . at Indianapolis
23-25 . . . . Louisville
26-27 . . . . . Columbus
28-30 . . . at Louisville
31 . . . . . . at Columbus

SEPTEMBER
1 . . . . . . at Columbus

PACIFIC COAST LEAGUE

ALBUQUERQUE ISOTOPES

APRIL
3-6 . . . . .at Tacoma
7-10 . . . . .at Reno
11-14 . . . . .Tacoma
15-18 . . . . . . El Paso
19-22 . . . . . at Salt Lake
24-27 . . . . .at Fresno
28-30 . . . . .Salt Lake

MAY
1 . . . . . . .Salt Lake
2-5 . . . . . . Fresno
6-9 . . . . .Sacramento
10-13 . . . . . . at El Paso

15-18 . . . . .at Fresno
19-22 . . . . at Salt Lake
23-26 . . . . . . Reno
27-30 . . . at Sacramento
31 . . . . . . Salt Lake

JUNE
1-3 . . . . . . .Salt Lake
5-8 . . . . . .at Tacoma
9-12 . . . . . .Round Rock
13-16 . . . . . New Orleans
17-20 . . . . at Omaha
21-24 . . . . .at Iowa
26-29 . . . . Reno
30 . . . . . . at El Paso

JULY
1-3 . . . . at El Paso
4-6 . . . . Las Vegas
7-10 . . . . El Paso
11-13 . . . . . . at Las Vegas
17-20 . . . . Sacramento
21-24 . . . . Fresno
25-28 . . . . at Reno
29-31 . . . . at Sacramento

AUGUST
1 . . . . at Sacramento

2-5 . . . . Tacoma
7-11 . . . . at Las Vegas
12-15 . . . . . . Memphis
16-19 . . . . Nashville
20-23 . . .at Colorado Springs
24-27 . . . at Oklahoma City
28-29 . . . . . . Las Vegas
31 . . . . Las Vegas

SEPTEMBER
1 . . . . Las Vegas

6-9 . . . . El Paso
10-13 . . . . .at Reno
15-18 . . . . . Albuquerque
19-22 . . . . . . Las Vegas
23-26 . . . . at Salt Lake
27-30 . . . . . . .at Reno
31 . . . . .Salt Lake

JUNE
1-3 . . . . .Sacramento
5-8 . . . . .at Las Vegas
9-12 . . . . Iowa
13-15 . . . . Omaha
17-20 . . . . .at New Orleans
21-24 . . . . at Round Rock
26-29 . . . . Salt Lake
30 . . . . . . at Sacramento

JULY
1-3 . . . . . . at Sacramento

4-6 . . . . Tacoma
7-10 . . . . Sacramento
11-13 . . . . at Tacoma
17-20 . . . . El Paso
21-24 . . . at Albuquerque
25-28 . . . . . at El Paso
29-31 . . . . Reno

AUGUST
1 . . . . Reno
2-5 . . . . Salt Lake
7-11 . . . . at Tacoma
12-15 . . . . Oklahoma City
16-19 . . . Colorado Springs
20-23 . . . . . . at Nashville
24-27 . . . . . .at Memphis
28-31 . . . . .Tacoma

SEPTEMBER
1 . . . . .Tacoma

COLORADO SPRINGS SKY SOX

APRIL
3-6 . . . . . .at New Orleans
7-10 . . . . . at Round Rock
11-14 . . . . . .Round Rock
15-18 . . . . Oklahoma City
19-22 . . . .at New Orleans
24-27 . . . . Iowa
28-30 . . . . at Memphis

MAY
1 . . . . .at Memphis
2-5 . . . . Memphis
6-9 . . . . .Nashville
10-13 . . . at Oklahoma City
15 18 . . . . . New Orleans
19-22 . . . . Memphis
23-26 . . . . . . .at Iowa
27-30 . . . . . at Nashville
31 . . . . New Orleans

JUNE
1-3 . . . . New Orleans
5-8 . . . . .at Iowa
9-12 . . . . . . Las Vegas
12-16 . . . . .Salt Lake
17-20 . . . . at Tacoma

21-24 . . . . Reno
26-29 . . . . Iowa
30 . . . . Oklahoma City

JULY
1-3 . . . . .Oklahoma City
4-6 . . . . at Omaha
7-10 . . . . . at Round Rock
11-13 . . . . .Omaha
17-20 . . . . . .at Memphis
21-24 . . . . . at Nashville
25-28 . . . . . . .Round Rock
29-31 . . . . .Nashville

AUGUST
1 . . . . .Nashville
2-5 . . . at Oklahoma City
7-11 . . . . Omaha
12-15 . . . . at Sacramento
16-19 . . . . .at Fresno
20-23 . . . . . Albuquerque
24-27 . . . . El Paso
28-31 . . . . at Omaha

SEPTEMBER
1 . . . . at Omaha

EL PASO CHIHUAHUAS

APRIL
3-6 . . . . .at Reno
7-10 . . . . at Tacoma
11-14 . . . . Reno
15-18 . . . . at Albuquerque
19-22 . . . . . .at Las Vegas
24-27 . . . . . at Sacramento
28-30 . . . . Fresno

MAY
1 . . . . Fresno
2-5 . . . . .Sacramento
6-9 . . . . .at Fresno
10-13 . . . . . Albuquerque
15-18 . . . . . . Las Vegas
19-22 . . . . at Sacramento
23-26 . . . . . . at Tacoma
27-30 . . . . . Las Vegas
31 . . . . .Tacoma

JUNE
1-3 . . . . .Tacoma
5-8 . . . . .at Reno
9-12 . . . . . . New Orleans
13-16 . . . . .Round Rock
17-20 . . . . at Iowa

21-24 . . . . at Omaha
26 29 . . . . .Tacoma
30 . . . . Albuquerque

JULY
1-3 . . . . Albuquerque
4-6 . . . . at Salt Lake
7-10 . . . . at Albuquerque
11-13 . . . . .Salt Lake
17-20 . . . . . . .at Fresno
21-24 . . . . . .Sacramento
25-28 . . . . Fresno
29-31 . . . . . .at Las Vegas

AUGUST
1 . . . . .at Las Vegas
2-5 . . . . Reno
7-11 . . . . at Salt Lake
12-15 . . . . .Nashville
16-19 . . . . Memphis
20-23 . . . at Oklahoma City
24-27 . . .at Colorado Springs
28-31 . . . . Salt Lake

SEPTEMBER
1 . . . . Salt Lake

FRESNO GRIZZLIES

APRIL
3-6 . . . . .at Las Vegas
7-10 . . . . at Salt Lake
11-14 . . . . . . Las Vegas
15-18 . . . . at Sacramento
19-22 . . . . Reno

24-27 . . . . . Albuquerque
28-30 . . . . at El Paso

MAY
1 . . . . at El Paso
2-5 . . . . . at Albuquerque

IOWA CUBS

APRIL
3-6 . . . . Memphis
7-10 . . . . .Nashville
11-14 . . . . . .at Memphis
15-18 . . . . . . New Orleans
19-22 . . . . . . .Round Rock
24-27 . .at Colorado Springs
28-30 . . . . .Omaha

MAY
1 . . . . .Omaha
2-5 . . . . at Nashville
6-9 . . . . . .at New Orleans
10-13 . . . . .Nashville
15-18 . . . . at Omaha
19-22 . . . . at Round Rock
23-26 . . . Colorado Springs
27-30 . . . . . . at Memphis
31 . . . . at Nashville

JUNE
1-3 . . . . . . at Nashville
5-8 . . . . . Colorado Springs
9-12 . . . . .at Fresno
13-16 . . . . at Sacramento
17-20 . . . . El Paso

21-24 . . . . . Albuquerque
26-29 . .at Colorado Springs
30 . . . . Omaha

JULY
1-3 . . . . .Omaha
4-6 . . . . at Oklahoma City
7-10 . . . . at Omaha
11-13 . . . . Oklahoma City
17-20 . . . . . at Round Rock
21-24 . . . . . New Orleans
25-27 . . . . . . Memphis
29-31 . . . .at New Orleans

AUGUST
1 . . . . .at New Orleans
2-5 . . . . at Omaha
7-11 . . . at Oklahoma City
12-15 . . . . . . Las Vegas
16-19 . . . . . . Salt Lake
20-23 . . . . .at Reno
24-27 . . . . . . at Tacoma
29-31 . . . .Oklahoma City

SEPTEMBER
1 . . . . .Oklahoma City

LAS VEGAS 51S

APRIL
3-6 . . . . Fresno
7-10 . . . . Sacramento
11-14 . . . . . . .at Fresno
15-18 . . . . .at Reno
19-22 . . . . El Paso
24-27 . . . . .Tacoma
28-30 . . . . Reno

MAY
1 . . . . Reno
2-5 . . . . at Tacoma
6-9 . . . . . . at Salt Lake
10-13 . . . . .Tacoma
15-18 . . . . . . at El Paso
19-22 . . . . . .at Fresno
23-26 . . . . . .Sacramento
27-30 . . . . at El Paso
31 . . . . Reno

JUNE
1-3 . . . . Reno
5-8 . . . . Fresno
9-12 . . .at Colorado Springs
13-16 . . . at Oklahoma City
17-20 . . . . .Nashville

21-24 . . . . Memphis
26-29 . . . . at Sacramento
30 . . . . .Salt Lake

JULY
1-3 . . . . .Salt Lake
4-6 . . . . at Albuquerque
7-10 . . . . .at Reno
11-13 . . . . . Albuquerque
17-20 . . . at Salt Lake
21-24 . . . . at Tacoma
25-28 . . . . . Salt Lake
29-31 . . . . El Paso

AUGUST
1 . . . . El Paso
2-5 . . . . . . at Sacramento
7-11 . . . . . Albuquerque
12-15 . . . . .at Iowa
16-19 . . . . . . at Omaha
20-23 . . . . . New Orleans
24-27 . . . . . .Round Rock
28-29 . . . . at Albuquerque
31 . . . . . . at Albuquerque

SEPTEMBER
1 . . . . . . at Albuquerque

MEMPHIS REDBIRDS

APRIL
3-6 . . . . at Iowa
7-10 . . . . at Omaha
11-14 . . . . Iowa
15-18 . . . . . . at Nashville
19-22 . . . Oklahoma City
24-27 . . . at Round Rock
28-30 . . . Colorado Springs

MAY
1 . . . . . Colorado Springs
2-5 . . . at Colorado Springs
6-9 . . . at Oklahoma City
10-13 . . . . . . Round Rock
15-18 . . . . Omaha
19-22 . at Colorado Springs
23-26 . . . . Oklahoma City
27-30 . . . . Iowa
31 . . . at Oklahoma City

JUNE
1-3 . . . . at Oklahoma City
5-8 . . . . Nashville
9-12 . . . . Tacoma
13-16 . . . . Reno
17-20 . . . . . . at Salt Lake

21-24 . . . . . . at Las Vegas
26-29 . . . . . Round Rock
30 . . . . at Nashville

JULY
1-3 . . . . . . at Nashville
4-6 . . . . . New Orleans
7-10 . . . . Nashville
11-13 . . . at New Orleans
17-20 . . . Colorado Springs
21-24 . . . . Omaha
25-27 . . . . at Iowa
29-31 . . . . . . at Omaha

AUGUST
1 . . . . at Omaha
2-5 . . . . at Round Rock
7-11 . . . . . New Orleans
12-15 . . . at Albuquerque
16-19 . . . . . at El Paso
20-23 . . . . Sacramento
24-27 . . . . Fresno
28-31 . . . at New Orleans

SEPTEMBER
1 . . . . at New Orleans

NASHVILLE SOUNDS

APRIL
3-6 . . . . at Omaha
7-10 . . . . at Iowa
11-14 . . . . Omaha
15-18 . . . . Memphis
19-22 . . . . . . at Omaha
24-27 . . . at Oklahoma City
28-30 . . . . . New Orleans

MAY
1 . . . . New Orleans
2-5 . . . . Iowa
6-9 . . . at Colorado Springs
10-13 . . . . at Iowa
15-18 . . . Oklahoma City
19-22 . . . . Omaha
23-26 . . . . at New Orleans
27-30 . . . Colorado Springs
31 . . . . Iowa

JUNE
1-3 . . . . Iowa
5-8 . . . . at Memphis
9-12 . . . . Reno
13-16 . . . . Tacoma
17-20 . . . . at Las Vegas

21-24 . . . . . at Salt Lake
26-29 . . . . . New Orleans
30 . . . . Memphis

JULY
1-3 . . . . Memphis
4-6 . . . . . at Round Rock
7-10 . . . . . at Memphis
11-13 . . . . . Round Rock
17-20 . . . at Oklahoma City
21-24 . . Colorado Springs
25-28 . . . Oklahoma City
29-31 . at Colorado Springs

AUGUST
1 . . . at Colorado Springs
2-5 . . . . . at New Orleans
7-11 . . . . . Round Rock
12-15 . . . . . at El Paso
16-19 . . . at Albuquerque
20-23 . . . . Fresno
24-27 . . . . Sacramento
28-31 . . . at New Orleans

SEPTEMBER
1 . . . . . . at Round Rock

NEW ORLEANS ZEPHYRS

APRIL
3-6 . . . . Colorado Springs
7-10 . . . . at Oklahoma City
11-14 . . . at Oklahoma City
15-18 . . . . at Iowa
19-22 . . . Colorado Springs
24-27 . . . . Omaha
28-30 . . . . . . at Nashville

MAY
1 . . . . at Nashville
2-5 . . . . at Round Rock
6-9 . . . . Iowa
10-13 . . . . . . at Omaha
15-18 . at Colorado Springs
19-22 . . Oklahoma City
23-26 . . . . Nashville
27-30 . . . at Round Rock
31 . . . at Colorado Springs

JUNE
1-3 . . . at Colorado Springs
5-8 . . . . Round Rock
9-12 . . . . . . at El Paso
13-16 . . . at Albuquerque
17-20 . . . . Fresno
21-24 . . . . . Sacramento
26-29 . . . . at Nashville
30 . . . . Round Rock

JULY
1-3 . . . . . . Round Rock
4-6 . . . . . . at Memphis
7-10 . . at Oklahoma City
11-13 . . . . . Memphis
17-20 . . . . . at Omaha
21-24 . . . . . . at Iowa
25-28 . . . . . . Omaha
29-31 . . . . Iowa

AUGUST
1 . . . . Iowa
2-5 . . . . Nashville
7-11 . . at Memphis
12-15 . . . . Tacoma
16-19 . . . . . Reno

AUGUST
1 . . . . Iowa
2-5 . . . . Nashville
7-11 . . . . . at Memphis
12-15 . . . . . . Tacoma
16-19 . . . . Reno

SEPTEMBER
1 . . . . Memphis

OKLAHOMA CITY REDHAWKS

APRIL
3-6 . . . . . at Round Rock
7-10 . . . . at New Orleans
11-14 . . . . . New Orleans
15-18 . at Colorado Springs
19-22 . . . . . at Memphis
24-27 . . . . . . Nashville
28-30 . . . . . Round Rock

MAY
1 . . . . Round Rock
2-5 . . . . at Omaha
6-9 . . . . Memphis
10-13 . . . Colorado Springs
15-18 . . . . at Nashville
19-22 . . at New Orleans
23-26 . . . at Memphis
27-30 . . . . . Omaha
31 . . . . Memphis

JUNE
1-3 . . . . . Memphis
5-8 . . . . at Omaha
9-12 . . . . Salt Lake
13-16 . . . Las Vegas
17-20 . . . . . at Reno

21-24 . . . . . . at Tacoma
26-29 . . . . Omaha
30 . . . at Colorado Springs

JULY
1-3 . . . at Colorado Springs
4-6 . . . . Iowa
7-10 . . . . . New Orleans
11-13 . . . . . . at Iowa
17-20 . . . . . . Nashville
21-24 . . . . . Round Rock
25-28 . . . . . at Nashville
29-31 . . . at Round Rock

AUGUST
1 . . . . . . at Round Rock
2-5 . . . . Colorado Springs
7-11 . . . . Iowa
12-15 . . . . . . at Fresno
16-19 . . . at Sacramento
20-23 . . . . El Paso
24-27 . . . . Albuquerque
29-31 . . . . . . at Iowa

SEPTEMBER
1 . . . . at Iowa

OMAHA STORM CHASERS

APRIL
3-6 . . . . Nashville
7-10 . . . . Memphis
11-14 . . . . . at Nashville
15-18 . . . . . Round Rock
19-22 . . . . . . Nashville
24-27 . . . at New Orleans
28-30 . . . . at Iowa

MAY
1 . . . . at Iowa
2-5 . . . . Oklahoma City
6-9 . . . at Round Rock
10-13 . . . . New Orleans
15-18 . . . . at Memphis
19-22 . . . at Nashville
23-26 . . . . . Round Rock
27-30 . . at Oklahoma City
31 . . . . . . at Round Rock

JUNE
1-3 . . . . . at Round Rock
5-8 . . . . Oklahoma City
9-12 . . . at Sacramento
13-15 . . . . . . at Fresno
17-20 . . . . . Albuquerque

21-24 . . . . El Paso
26-29 . . at Oklahoma City
30 . . . . at Iowa

JULY
1-3 . . . . at Iowa
4-6 . . . . Colorado Springs
7-10 . . . . Iowa
11-13 . at Colorado Springs
17-20 . . . . New Orleans
21-24 . . . . . at Memphis
25-28 . . . at New Orleans
29-31 . . . . . Memphis

AUGUST
1 . . . . Memphis
2-5 . . . . Iowa
7-11 . . at Colorado Springs
12-15 . . . . Salt Lake
16-19 . . . . . . Las Vegas
20-23 . . . . . at Tacoma
24-27 . . . . . . at Reno
28-31 . . . Colorado Springs

SEPTEMBER
1 . . . . . Colorado Springs

RENO ACES

APRIL
3-6 . . . . El Paso
7-10 . . . . Albuquerque
11-14 . . . . . at El Paso
15-18 . . . . . Las Vegas
19-22 . . . . . at Fresno
24-27 . . . . Salt Lake
28-30 . . . . at Las Vegas

MAY
1 . . . . . at Las Vegas
2-5 . . . . at Salt Lake

6-9 . . . . Tacoma
10-13 . . . . Fresno
15-18 . . . . . Salt Lake
19-22 . . . . at Tacoma
23-26 . . . at Albuquerque
27-30 . . . . . . Fresno
31 . . . . . . at Las Vegas

JUNE
1-3 . . . . . at Las Vegas
5-8 . . . . El Paso
9-12 . . . . at Nashville

13-16 . . . . . . at Memphis	29-31 . . . . .at Fresno
17-20 . . . . Oklahoma City	**AUGUST**
21-24 . . . . .Colorado	1 . . . . .at Fresno
26-29 . . . at Albuquerque	2-5 . . . . at El Paso
30 . . . . at Tacoma	7-11 . . . . .Sacramento
JULY	12-15 . . . . at Round Rock
1-3 . . . . at Tacoma	16-19 . . .at New Orleans
4-6 . . . . .Sacramento	20-23 . . . . Iowa
7-10 . . . . Las Vegas	24-27 . . . . Omaha
11-13 . . . . at Sacramento	28-31 . . . . at Sacramento
17-20 . . . . .Tacoma	**SEPTEMBER**
21-24 . . . . . . at Salt Lake	1 . . . . at Sacramento
25-28 . . . . . Albuquerque	

ROUND ROCK EXPRESS

APRIL	21-24 . . . . Fresno
3-6 . . . . . .Oklahoma City	26-29 . . . . . .at Memphis
7-10 . . . Colorado Springs	30 . . . . . .at New Orleans
11-14 . .at Colorado Springs	**JULY**
15-18 . . . . at Omaha	1-3 . . . . . .at New Orleans
19-22 . . . . .at Iowa	4-6 . . . . .Nashville
24-27 . . . . . . Memphis	7-10 . . . Colorado Springs
28-30 . . . at Oklahoma City	11-13 . . . . at Nashville
MAY	17-20 . . . . Iowa
1 . . . . . at Oklahoma City	21-24 . . at Oklahoma City
2-5 . . . . New Orleans	25-28 . .at Colorado Springs
6-9 . . . . .Omaha	29-31 . . .Oklahoma City
10-13 . . . . . at Memphis	**AUGUST**
15-18 . . . . . . .at Iowa	1 . . . . . .Oklahoma City
19-22 . . . . Iowa	2-5 . . . . Memphis
23-26 . . . . . at Omaha	7-11 . . . . . at Nashville
27-30 . . . . . New Orleans	12-15 . . . . Reno
31 . . . . .Omaha	16-19 . . . . .Tacoma
JUNE	20-23 . . . . . at Salt Lake
1-3 . . . . .Omaha	24-27 . . . . . .at Las Vegas
5-8 . . . .at New Orleans	28-31 . . . . .Nashville
9-12 . . . at Albuquerque	**SEPTEMBER**
13-16 . . . . at El Paso	1 . . . . .Nashville
17-20 . . . . . .Sacramento	

SACRAMENTO RIVER CATS

APRIL	**JUNE**
3-6 . . . . at Salt Lake	1-3 . . . . .at Fresno
8-10 . . . . . .at Las Vegas	5-8 . . . . at Salt Lake
11-13 . . . . . . .Salt Lake	9-12 . . . . .Omaha
15-18 . . . . Fresno	13-16 . . . . Iowa
19-22 . . . . . . at Tacoma	17-20 . . . . at Round Rock
24-27 . . . . El Paso	21-24 . . . .at New Orleans
28-30 . . . . .Tacoma	26-29 . . . . . Las Vegas
MAY	30 . . . . Fresno
1 . . . . .Tacoma	**JULY**
2-5 . . . . at El Paso	1-3 . . . . Fresno
6-9 . . . . . at Albuquerque	4-6 . . . . .at Reno
10-13 . . . . Salt Lake	7-10 . . . . .at Fresno
15-18 . . . . .Tacoma	11-13 . . . . Reno
19-22 . . . . El Paso	17-20 . . . . at Albuquerque
23-26 . . . . . Las Vegas	21-24 . . . . . at El Paso
27-30 . . . . . Albuquerque	25-28 . . . . . at Tacoma
31 . . . . .at Fresno	29-31 . . . . . Albuquerque

AUGUST	20-23 . . . . at Memphis
1 . . . . Albuquerque	24-27 . . . . . . at Nashville
2-5 . . . . Las Vegas	28-31 . . . . Reno
7-11 . . . . .at Reno	**SEPTEMBER**
12-15 . . . Colorado Springs	1 . . . . Reno
16-19 . . . . Oklahoma City	

SALT LAKE BEES

APRIL	21-24 . . . . . . .Nashville
3-6 . . . . .Sacramento	26-29 . . . . . .at Fresno
7-10 . . . . Fresno	30 . . . . . . .at Las Vegas
11-13 . . . . at Sacramento	**JULY**
15 18 . . . . at Tacoma	1-3 . . . . .at Las Vegas
19-22 . . . . . Albuquerque	4-6 . . . . El Paso
24-27 . . . . .at Reno	7-10 . . . . .Tacoma
28-30 . . . . at Albuquerque	11-13 . . . . at El Paso
MAY	17-20 . . . . . Las Vegas
1 . . . . . at Albuquerque	21-24 . . . . Reno
2-5 . . . . Reno	25-28 . . . .at Las Vegas
6-9 . . . . Las Vegas	29-31 . . . . .Tacoma
10-13 . . . . at Sacramento	**AUGUST**
15-18 . . . . .at Reno	1 . . . . .Tacoma
19-22 . . . . . Albuquerque	2-5 . . . . .at Fresno
23-26 . . . . Fresno	7-11 . . . . El Paso
27-30 . . . . . at Tacoma	12-15 . . . . . at Omaha
31 . . . . . at Albuquerque	16-19 . . . . .at Iowa
JUNE	20-23 . . . . .Round Rock
1-3 . . . . . at Albqeurque	24-27 . . . . . New Orleans
5-8 . . . . .Sacramento	28-31 . . . . . . at El Paso
9-12 . . . . at Oklahoma City	**SEPTEMBER**
13-16 . .at Colorado Springs	1 . . . . at El Paso
17-20 . . . . Memphis	

TACOMA RAINIERS

APRIL	21-24 . . . . .Oklahoma City
3-6 . . . . Albuquerque	26-29 . . . . . at El Paso
7-10 . . . . El Paso	30 . . . . Reno
11-14 . . . at Albuquerque	**JULY**
15-18 . . . . Salt Lake	1-3 . . . . Reno
19-22 . . . . . .Sacramento	4-6 . . . . .at Fresno
24-27 . . . . .at Las Vegas	7-10 . . . . . . at Salt Lake
28-30 . . . . . at Sacramento	11-13 . . . . Fresno
MAY	17-20 . . . . . . .at Reno
1 . . . . at Sacramento	21-24 . . . . . Las Vegas
2-5 . . . . Las Vegas	25-28 . . . . . .Sacramento
6-9 . . . . .at Reno	29-31 . . . . . . at Salt Lake
10-13 . . . .at Las Vegas	**AUGUST**
15-18 . . . . at Sacramento	1 . . . . at Salt Lake
19-22 . . . . Reno	2-5 . . . . . at Albuquerque
23 26 . . . . El Paso	7-11 . . . . Fresno
27-30 . . . . . . .Salt Lake	12-15 . . . . .at New Orleans
31 . . . . at El Paso	16-19 . . . . at Round Rock
JUNE	20-23 . . . . . . .Omaha
1-3 . . . . at El Paso	24-27 . . . . Iowa
5-8 . . . . Albuquerque	28-31 . . . . .at Fresno
9-12 . . . . . . .at Memphis	**SEPTEMBER**
13-16 . . . . . . at Nashville	1 . . . . .at Fresno
17-20 . . . Colorado Springs	

DOUBLE-A

EASTERN LEAGUE

AKRON RUBBERDUCKS

APRIL		**MAY**	**JUNE**
		2-4 . . . . .at Altoona	1 . . . . .Harrisburg
		5-7 . . . . at Erie	3-5 . . . . . . at New Britain
3-6 . . . . . .at Binghamton	14-16 . . . . Trenton	8-11 . . . . Altoona	6-8 . . . . . . .at Harrisburg
7-9 . . . . .at Altoona	17-19 . . . . .at Bowie	12-14 . . . . . .Harrisburg	9-12 . . . . . . Binghamton
10-13 . . . . .Bowie	21-24 . . . . at Trenton	16-18 . . . . at Erie	13-15 . . . . .Portland
		25-27 . . . . Altoona	19-22 . . . . . .at Altoona	17-19 . . . . . . .at Reading
		28-30 . . . . . Binghamton	23-26 . . . . Reading	20-22 . . . . at Harrisburg
			27-29 . . . . . . at Bowie	23-25 . . . . Erie
			30-31 . . . . . . .Harrisburg	26-29 . . . . . . .Harrisburg

30 . . . . at Erie

JULY
1-3 . . . . at Erie
4-6 . . . . .Bowie
7-10 . . . . at Richmond
11-14 . . . . . at Trenton
17-20 . . . . Erie
21-23 . . . . . . .Richmond
24-27 . . . . .at Reading
28-30 . . . . .Bowie
31 . . . . at Harrisburg

AUGUST
1-3 . . . . . . at Harrisburg
5-7 . . . . New Britain
8-10 . . . . New Hampshire
12-14 . . . . . at Portland
15-17 . . at New Hampshire
19-21 . . . . Altoona
22-24 . . . .at Binghamton
25-28 . . . . . . Trenton
29-31 . . . . Erie

SEPTEMBER
1 . . . . Erie

ALTOONA CURVE

APRIL
3-6 . . . . Erie
7-9 . . . . .Akron
10-13 . . . . . at Richmond
14-16 . . . . at Harrisburg
17-19 . . . . . . .Richmond
21-24 . . . . . . .Harrisburg
25-27 . . . . . at Akron
28-30 . . . . . . at Erie

MAY
1 . . . . at Erie
2-4 . . . . .Akron
5-7 . . . . .Bowie
8-11 . . . . . . at Akron
13-15 . . . .at Binghamton
16-18 . . . . .Richmond
19-22 . . . . . . at Erie
23-26 . . . . . . at Erie
27-29 . . . . at Richmond
30-31 . . . . New Hampshire

JUNE
1 . . . . . New Hampshire
3-5 . . . . Binghamton
6-8 . . . . .at Trenton
10-12 . . . . Portland
13-15 . . . . Reading
17-19 . . at New Hampshire

20-22 . . . . . . at Portland
23-25 . . . at New Britain
26-29 . . . . . Binghamton
30 . . . . at Bowie

JULY
1-3 . . . . at Bowie
4-6 . . . . .Harrisburg
7-10 . . . . Erie
11-14 . . . . at Harrisburg
17-20 . . . . .Bowie
21-23 . . . at New Britain
24-27 . . . . . . at Bowie
28-30 . . . . Erie
31 . . . . Richmond

AUGUST
1-3 . . . . .Richmond
5-7 . . . . at Trenton
8-10 . . . . . . .at Reading
12-14 . . . . Trenton
15-17 . . . . at Erie
19-21 . . . . . . at Akron
22-24 . . . . . New Britain
25-28 . . . . . .Richmond
29-31 . . . . . . at Bowie

SEPTEMBER
1 . . . . at Bowie

BINGHAMTON METS

APRIL
3-6 . . . . .Akron
7-9 . . . . Erie
10-13 . . at New Hampshire
14-16 . . . . . . at Portland
17-19 . . . . New Hampshire
21-24 . . . . Portland
25-27 . . . . at Erie
28-30 . . . . at Akron

MAY
2-4 . . . . Portland
5-7 . . . . at New Hampshire
8-11 . . . . . . .Harrisburg
13-15 . . . . Altoona
16-18 . . at New Hampshire
19-22 . . . . . at Portland
23-26 . . . . . . New Britain
27-29 . . . . . New Hampshire
30-31 . . . . at New Britain

JUNE
1 . . . . at New Britain
3-5 . . . . .at Altoona
6-8 . . . . New Britain
9-12 . . . . at Akron
13-15 . . . . Erie
17-19 . . . . Richmond

20-22 . . . . at Bowie
23-25 . . . . Reading
26-29 . . . . . . .at Altoona
30 . . . . . . at New Britain

JULY
1-3 . . . . . . at New Britain
4-6 . . . . Erie
7-10 . . . . Portland
11-14 . . . . at Erie
17-20 . . . . . . Trenton
21-23 . . . . . at Portland
24-27 . . . . . .at Trenton
28-30 . . . . New Hampshire
31 . . . . .Bowie

AUGUST
1-3 . . . . .Bowie
5-7 . . . . . . at Richmond
8-10 . . . . at Harrisburg
12-14 . . . . Erie
15-17 . . . . . . .at Reading
18-20 . . . . . . at Erie
22-24 . . . . .Akron
25-28 . . . . . New Britain
29-31 . . . . . at Richmond

SEPTEMBER
1 . . . . at Richmond

BOWIE BAYSOX

APRIL
3-6 . . . . .Harrisburg
7-9 . . . . .Richmond
10-13 . . . . at Akron
14-16 . . . . . . at Erie
17-19 . . . . .Akron
21-24 . . . . Erie
25-27 . . at Harrisburg
28-30 . . . . . at Richmond

MAY
1 . . . . at Richmond
2-4 . . . . Erie
5-7 . . . . . . .at Altoona
8-11 . . . . . New Britain
13-15 . . . at Richmond
16-18 . . . .at Reading
19-22 . . . . Erie
23-26 . . . at Harrisburg
27-29 . . . . . . .Akron
30-31 . . . .Richmond

JUNE
1 . . . . .Richmond
3-5 . . . at New Hampshire
6-8 . . . . . . at Portland
10-12 . . . . New Hampshire
13-15 . . . .Harrisburg
16-18 . . . . . at Trenton

20-22 . . . . . Binghamton
23-25 . . . . . . Trenton
26-29 . . . at Richmond
30 . . . . Altoona

JULY
1-3 . . . . Altoona
4-6 . . . . at Akron
7-10 . . at Harrisburg
11-14 . . . . . .Richmond
17-20 . . . .at Altoona
21-23 . . . . . .Harrisburg
24-27 . . . . . . Altoona
28-30 . . . . at Akron
31 . . . . . . at Binghamton

AUGUST
1-3 . . . . . .at Binghamton
5-7 . . . . Portland
8-10 . . . . . at Trenton
12-14 . . . at New Britain
15-17 . . . . . . Trenton
19-21 . . . . . . Reading
22-24 . . . at Richmond
25-28 . . . . . . at Erie
29-31 . . . . . . Altoona

SEPTEMBER
1 . . . . Altoona

ERIE SEAWOLVES

APRIL
3-6 . . . . .at Altoona
7-9 . . . .at Binghamton
10-13 . . . . Trenton
14-16 . . . . . . .Bowie
17-19 . . . . . at Trenton
21-24 . . . . . . at Bowie
25-27 . . . . . Binghamton
28-30 . . . . . Altoona

MAY
1 . . . . Altoona
2-4 . . . . at Bowie
5-7 . . . . .Akron
8-11 . . . . . at Richmond
13-15 . . . .at Trenton
16-18 . . . . . .Akron
19-22 . . . . . . at Bowie
23-26 . . . . . Altoona
27-29 . . . at Harrisburg
30-31 . . . . . . Reading

JUNE
1 . . . . Reading
3-5 . . . . at Portland
6-8 . . at New Hampshire
10-12 . . . . . .Harrisburg
13-15 . . . .at Binghamton
16-18 . . . . Portland

20-22 . . . . . . Richmond
23-25 . . . . . . at Akron
26-29 . . . . . Trenton
30 . . . . .Akron

JULY
1-3 . . . . .Akron
4-6 . . . .at Binghamton
7-10 . . . . . . .at Altoona
11-14 . . . . . Binghamton
17-20 . . . . . at Akron
21-23 . . . . . Reading
24-27 . . . . . .Richmond
28-30 . . . .at Altoona
31 . . . . . at New Britain

AUGUST
1-3 . . . . . at New Britain
5-7 . . . . . New Hampshire
8-10 . . . . . New Britain
12-14 . . . .at Binghamton
15-17 . . . . . . Altoona
18-20 . . . . . Binghamton
22-24 . . . .at Reading
25-28 . . . . . .Bowie
29-31 . . . . . at Akron

SEPTEMBER
1 . . . . at Akron

HARRISBURG SENATORS

APRIL
3-6 . . . . at Bowie
7-9 . . . . at New Britain
10-13 . . . . . Reading
14-16 . . . . . Altoona
18-19 . . . .at Reading
21-24 . . . .at Altoona
25-27 . . . . . .Bowie
28-30 . . . . New Britain

MAY
1 . . . . New Britain
2-4 . . . . .at Reading

5-7 . . . . .Richmond
8-11 . . . . . .at Binghamton
12-14 . . . . . at Akron
16-18 . . . . New Britain
19-22 . . . .at Trenton
23-26 . . . . . .Bowie
27-29 . . . . Erie
30-31 . . . . . at Akron

JUNE
1 . . . . at Akron
3-5 . . . . Reading
6-8 . . . . .Akron

10-12 . . . . at Erie
13-15 . . . . at Bowie
17-19 . . . . . New Britain
20-22 . . . . .Akron
23-25 . . . . . at Richmond
26-29 . . . . . at Akron
30 . . . . Richmond

JULY
1-3 . . . . .Richmond
4-6 . . . . .at Altoona
7-10 . . . . .Bowie
11-14 . . . . Altoona
17-20 . . . . at Richmond
21-23 . . . . . . at Bowie
24-27 . . . . New Hampshire

NEW BRITAIN ROCK CATS

APRIL
3-6 . . . . .Richmond
7-9 . . . . .Harrisburg
10-13 . . . . at Portland
14-16 . . at New Hampshire
17-19 . . . . Portland
21-24 . . . . . New Hampshire
25-27 . . . . . at Richmond
28-30 . . . . . at Harrisburg

MAY
1 . . . . . . at Harrisburg
2-4 . . . . . New Hampshire
5-7 . . . . . Trenton
8-11 . . . . at Bowie
13-15 . . . . Portland
16-18 . . . . at Harrisburg
19-22 . . . . . .Richmond
23-26 . . . .at Binghamton
27-29 . . . . at Portland
30-31 . . . . . Binghamton

JUNE
1 . . . . Binghamton
3-5 . . . . .Akron
6-8 . . . . . .at Binghamton
10-12 . . . . . .at Reading
13-15 . . . . . . Trenton
17-19 . . . . . at Harrisburg

NEW HAMPSHIRE FISHER CATS

APRIL
3-6 . . . . .at Trenton
7-9 . . . . .at Reading
10-13 . . . . . Binghamton
14-16 . . . . . New Britain
17-19 . . . . at Binghamton
21-24 . . . . at New Britain
25-27 . . . . . Reading
28-30 . . . . Trenton

MAY
1 . . . . Trenton
2-4 . . . . . . at New Britain
5-7 . . . . . . Binghamton
8-11 . . . . . at Portland
12-14 . . . . . Reading
16-18 . . . . . Binghamton
19-22 . . . . .at Reading
23-26 . . . . . Portland
27-29 . . .at Binghamton
30-31 . . .at Altoona

JUNE
1 . . . . .at Altoona
3-5 . . . . .Bowie
6-8 . . . . Erie
10-12 . . . . . . at Bowie
13-15 . . . at Richmond
17-19 . . . . . Altoona

28-30 . . . . . at Richmond
31 . . . . .Akron

AUGUST
1-3 . . . . .Akron
4-7 . . . . .at Reading
8-10 . . . . . . Binghamton
12-14 . . . . . . Reading
15-17 . . . at New Britain
19-21 . . . . . . Portland
22-24 . . . . . Trenton
25-28 . . at New Hampshire
29-31 . . . . at Portland

SEPTEMBER
1 . . . . at Portland

20-22 . . . . Reading
23 25 . . . . Altoona
26-29 . . at New Hampshire
30 . . . . Binghamton

JULY
1-3 . . . . Binghamton
4-6 . . . . . . at Portland
7-10 . . . at New Hampshire
11-14 . . . . . . Reading
17-20 . . . .at Reading
21-23 . . . . . . Altoona
24-27 . . . . . Portland
28-30 . . . . . at Trenton
31 . . . . Erie

AUGUST
1-3 . . . . Erie
5-7 . . . . at Akron
8-10 . . . . at Erie
12-14 . . . . .Bowie
15-17 . . . . . . .Harrisburg
19-21 . . . . at Richmond
22-24 . . . .at Altoona
25-28 . . . .at Binghamton
29-31 . . . New Hampshire

SEPTEMBER
1 . . . . . . New Hampshire

20-22 . . . . at Trenton
23-25 . . . . at Portland
26-29 . . . . New Britain
30 . . . . .at Reading

JULY
1-3 . . . . . . .at Reading
4-6 . . . . Trenton
7-10 . . . . . . New Britain
11-14 . . . . at Portland
17-20 . . . . . Portland
21-23 . . . . . Trenton
24-27 . . . . at Harrisburg
28-30 . . . .at Binghamton
31 . . . . Reading

AUGUST
1-3 . . . . Reading
5-7 . . . . at Erie
8-10 . . . . at Akron
12-14 . . . . . . Richmond
15-17 . . . . .Akron
19-21 . . . . . at Trenton
22-24 . . . . . Portland
25-28 . . . . .Harrisburg
29-31 . . . at New Britain

SEPTEMBER
1 . . . . . . at New Britain

PORTLAND SEA DOGS

APRIL
3-6 . . . . .at Reading
7-9 . . . . .at Trenton
10-13 . . . . . New Britain
14-16 . . . . . Binghamton
17-19 . . . . at New Britain
21-24 . . . .at Binghamton
25-27 . . . . . Trenton
28-30 . . . . . Reading

MAY
1 . . . . Reading
2-4 . . . . . at Binghamton
5-7 . . . . .at Reading
8-11 . . . . New Hampshire
13-15 . . . . at New Britain
16-18 . . . . . . Trenton
19-22 . . . . . Binghamton
23-25 . . at New Hampshire
27-29 . . . . . New Britain
30-31 . . . . . at Trenton

JUNE
1 . . . . at Trenton
3-5 . . . . Erie
6-8 . . . . .Bowie
10-12 . . . . . .at Altoona
13-15 . . . . . at Akron
16-18 . . . . . at Erie

READING FIGHTIN PHILS

APRIL
3-6 . . . . Portland
7-9 . . . . . New Hampshire
10-13 . . . . at Harrisburg
14-16 . . . . . at Richmond
18-19 . . . . . .Harrisburg
21-23 . . . . . . .Richmond
25-27 . . at New Hampshire
28-30 . . . . . at Portland

MAY
1 . . . . at Portland
2-4 . . . . .Harrisburg
5-7 . . . . Portland
8-11 . . . . at Trenton
12-14 . . at New Hampshire
16-18 . . . . .Bowie
19-22 . . . New Hampshire
23-26 . . . . . at Akron
27-29 . . . . . Trenton
30-31 . . . . . at Erie

JUNE
1 . . . . at Erie
3-5 . . . . . . at Harrisburg
6-9 . . . . .Richmond
10-12 . . . . . New Britain
13-15 . . . . .at Altoona
17-19 . . . . . . .Akron

RICHMOND FLYING SQUIRRELS

APRIL
3-6 . . . . . . at New Britain
7-9 . . . . at Bowie
10-13 . . . . Altoona
14-16 . . . . Reading
17-19 . . . . . .at Altoona
21-23 . . . . . .at Reading
25-27 . . . . . New Britain
28-30 . . . . .Bowie

MAY
1 . . . . .Bowie
2-4 . . . . at Trenton

20-22 . . . . Altoona
23-25 . . . New Hampshire
26-29 . . . .at Reading
30 . . . . .at Trenton

JULY
1-3 . . . . .at Trenton
4-6 . . . . . . New Britain
7-10 . . . .at Binghamton
11-14 . . . New Hampshire
17-20 . . at New Hampshire
21-23 . . . . . Binghamton
24-27 . . . . at New Britain
28-30 . . . . . Reading
31 . . . . Trenton

AUGUST
1-3 . . . . Trenton
5-7 . . . . at Bowie
8-10 . . . at Richmond
12-14 . . . . . .Akron
15-18 . . . . . .Richmond
19-21 . . . at Harrisburg
22-24 . . at New Hampshire
25-28 . . . . . Reading
29-31 . . . . .Harrisburg

SEPTEMBER
1 . . . . .Harrisburg

20-22 . . . . . at New Britain
23-25 . . . .at Binghamton
26-29 . . . . Portland
30 . . . . . New Hampshire

JULY
1-3 . . . . . New Hampshire
4-6 . . . . at Richmond
7-10 . . . . Trenton
11-14 . . . . at New Britain
17-20 . . . . , New Britain
21-23 . . . . . . at Erie
24-27 . . . . . .Akron
28-30 . . . . . at Portland
31 . . . . at New Hampshire

AUGUST
1-3 . . . . at New Hampshire
4-7 . . . . .Harrisburg
8-10 . . . . Altoona
12-14 . . . .at Harrisburg
15-17 . . . . . Binghamton
19-21 . . . . . at Bowie
22-24 . . . . Erie
25-28 . . . . at Portland
29-31 . . . . . .at Trenton

SEPTEMBER
1 . . . . at Trenton

5-7 . . . . . . at Harrisburg
8-11 . . . . Erie
13-15 . . . . .Bowie
16-18 . . . . . . at Altoona
19-22 . . . . at New Britain
23-26 . . . . . . Trenton
27-29 . . . . . Altoona
30-31 . . . . . at Bowie

JUNE
1 . . . . at Bowie
3-5 . . . . Trenton
6-9 . . . . .at Reading

MINOR LEAGUES

10-12 . . . . at Trenton
13-15 . . . New Hampshire
17-19 . . .at Binghamton
20-22 . . . . at Erie
23-25 . . . . . . .Harrisburg
26-29 . . . . .Bowie
30 . . . . at Harrisburg

JULY
1-3 . . . . . at Harrisburg
4-6 . . . . Reading
7-10 . . . . .Akron
11-14 . . . . . at Bowie
17-20 . . . . . .Harrisburg
21-23 . . . . . at Akron
24-27 . . . . at Erie

28-30 . . . . . . .Harrisburg
31 . . . . .at Altoona

AUGUST
1-3 . . . . at Altoona
5-7 . . . . . . Binghamton
8-10 . . . . Portland
12-14 . . at New Hampshire
15-17 . . . . . at Portland
19-21 . . . . . New Britain
22-24 . . . . . . .Bowie
25-28 . . . . . at Altoona
29-31 . . . . . . Binghamton

SEPTEMBER
1 . . . . Binghamton

TRENTON THUNDER

APRIL
3-6 . . . . . New Hampshire
7-9 . . . . Portland
10-13 . . . . . . at Erie
14-16 . . . . . at Akron
17-19 . . . . Erie
21-24 . . . . .Akron
25-27 . . . . at Portland
28-30 . . at New Hampshire

MAY
1 . . . . at New Hampshire
2-4 . . . . .Richmond
5-7 . . . . . at New Britain
8-11 . . . . Reading
13-15 . . . . Erie
16-18 . . . . . at Portland
19-22 . . . . . .Harrisburg
23-26 . . . at Richmond
27-29 . . . . . .at Reading
30-31 . . . . . . Portland

JUNE
1 . . . . Portland
3-5 . . . . . at Richmond
6-8 . . . . Altoona
10-12 . . . . . .Richmond
13-15 . . . at New Britain
16-18 . . . . .Bowie

20-22 . . . . New Hampshire
23-25 . . . . .at Bowie
26-29 . . . . at Erie
30 . . . . Portland

JULY
1-3 . . . . Portland
4-6 . . . at New Hampshire
7-10 . . . . .at Reading
11-14 . . . . .Akron
17-20 . . . .at Binghamton
21-23 . . at New Hampshire
24-27 . . . . . Binghamton
28-30 . . . . . . New Britain
31 . . . . at Portland

AUGUST
1-3 . . . . . at Portland
5-7 . . . . Altoona
8-10 . . . . .Bowie
12-14 . . . . .at Altoona
15-17 . . . . . .at Bowie
19-21 . . . . New Hampshire
22-24 . . . at Harrisburg
25-28 . . . . . . at Akron
29-31 . . . . . . Reading

SEPTEMBER
1 . . . . Reading

SOUTHERN LEAGUE

BIRMINGHAM BARONS

APRIL
3-7 . . . . . at Montgomery
9-13 . . . . . . .Jacksonville
14-18 . . . . at Mobile
19-23 . . . . . . .Tennessee
24-28 . . . . at Chattanooga
30 . . . . Mobile

MAY
1-4 . . . . Mobile
5-9 . . . . . . at Tennessee
10-14 . . . . Pensacola
15-19 . . . . . at Huntsville
21-25 . . . . . at Pensacola
26-30 . . . . . Chattanooga
31 . . . . at Tennessee

JUNE
1-4 . . . . at Tennessee
5-9 . . . . Jackson
11-15 . . . . . Montgomery
19-23 . . . . at Jacksonville

24-28 . . . . . . .Mississippi
29-30 . . . at Chattanooga

JULY
1-3 . . . . . at Chattanooga
4-8 . . . . .Tennessee
10-14 . . . . . .at Jackson
16-20 . . . . . . .Mississippi
21-25 . . . at Jacksonville
26-30 . . . . . . .Tennessee
31 . . . . . at Chattanooga

AUGUST
1-4 . . . . . at Chattanooga
6-10 . . . . Huntsville
12-16 . . . . . . .at Jackson
17-21 . . . . Chattanooga
22-26 . . . . at Mississippi
28-31 . . . . Pensacola

SEPTEMBER
1 . . . . Pensacola

CHATTANOOGA LOOKOUTS

APRIL
3-7 . . . . Jackson
9-13 . . . . . . at Tennessee
14-18 . . . . . .Jacksonville
19-23 . . . . . .at Jackson
24-28 . . . . . Birmingham
30 . . . . .Tennessee

MAY
1-4 . . . . .Tennessee
5-9 . . . . . . at Pensacola
10-14 . . . . Huntsville
15-19 . . . . . at Mobile
21-25 . . . . . . .Mississippi
26-30 . . .at Birmingham
31 . . . . Mobile

JUNE
1-4 . . . . Mobile
5-9 . . . . . at Mississippi
10-14 . . . . . at Huntsville
19-23 . . . . at Tennessee

24-28 . . . . Pensacola
29-30 . . . . . Birmingham

JULY
1-3 . . . . Birmingham
4-8 . . . . . . at Jacksonville
10-14 . . . . Huntsville
16-20 . . . . . . at Mobile
21-25 . . . . . Montgomery
26-30 . . . . . at Huntsville
31 . . . . Birmingham

AUGUST
1-4 . . . . . . Birmingham
6-10 . . . at Montgomery
12-16 . . . . .Jacksonville
17-21 . . . .at Birmingham
22-26 . . . . . . .at Jackson
28-31 . . . . . . .Tennessee

SEPTEMBER
1 . . . . .Tennessee

HUNTSVILLE STARS

APRIL
3-7 . . . . . . at Jacksonville
9-13 . . . . Pensacola
14-18 . . . . . at Mississippi
19-23 . . . . Mobile
24-28 . . . . at Tennessee
29-30 . . at Montgomery

MAY
1-3 . . . . at Montgomery
5-9 . . . . Jackson
10-14 . . at Chattanooga
15-19 . . . . . Birmingham
21-25 . . at Montgomery
26-30 . . . . . . .Tennessee
31 . . . . .at Jackson

JUNE
1-4 . . . . .at Jackson
5-9 . . . . Mobile
10-14 . . . Chattanooga
19-23 . . . . . at Pensacola

24-28 . . . . . Montgomery
29-30 . . . at Mississippi

JULY
1-3 . . . . . . at Mississippi
4-8 . . . . Jackson
10-14 . . at Chattanooga
16-20 . . . . . . .Tennessee
21-25 . . . . .at Jackson
26-30 . . . Chattanooga
31 . . . . . . .Jacksonville

AUGUST
1-4 . . . . . . .Jacksonville
6-10 . . . .at Birmingham
12-16 . . . . at Tennessee
17-21 . . . . Jackson
22-26 . . . . at Mobile
28-31 . . . . .Mississippi

SEPTEMBER
1 . . . . .Mississippi

JACKSON GENERALS

APRIL
3-7 . . . . . at Chattanooga
9-13 . . . . .Mississippi
14-18 . . . . at Tennessee
19-23 . . . . . Chattanooga
24-28 . . . . at Mobile
30 . . . . Pensacola

MAY
1-4 . . . . . . Pensacola
5-9 . . . . . . at Huntsville
10-14 . . . . . . .Tennessee
15-19 . . . . . Montgomery
21-25 . . . at Jacksonville
26-30 . . . . at Mobile
31 . . . . Huntsville

JUNE
1-4 . . . . Huntsville
5-9 . . . .at Birmingham
11-15 . . . . . .Jacksonville
19-23 . . . . at Mississippi

24-28 . . . . . . .Tennessee
29-30 . . . . Mobile

JULY
1-3 . . . . Mobile
4-8 . . . . at Huntsville
10-14 . . . . . Birmingham
16-20 . . . at Montgomery
21-25 . . . . . Huntsville
26-30 . . . . . at Mobile
31 . . . . Montgomery

AUGUST
1-4 . . . . . . Montgomery
6-10 . . . . . at Pensacola
12-16 . . . . . Birmingham
17-21 . . . . at Huntsville
22-26 . . . . . Chattanooga
28-31 . . . at Montgomery

SEPTEMBER
1 . . . . . . at Montgomery

JACKSONVILLE SUNS

APRIL
3-7 . . . . Huntsville
9-13 . . . . . at Birmingham
14-18 . . . . at Chattanooga
19-23 . . . . Pensacola
24-28 . . . . . Montgomery
30 . . . . at Mississippi

MAY
1-4 . . . . . at Mississippi
5-9 . . . . . at Montgomery
10-14 . . . . Mobile
15-19 . . . . . at Pensacola
21-25 . . . . Jackson
26-30 . . . . . . Montgomery
31 . . . . at Pensacola

JUNE
1-4 . . . . at Pensacola
5-9 . . . . Tennessee
11-15 . . . . . . at Jackson
19-23 . . . . . . Birmingham

24-28 . . . . . . at Mobile
29-30 . . . . at Pensacola

JULY
1-3 . . . . . . at Pensacola
4-8 . . . . . . Chattanooga
10-14 . . . . at Tennessee
16-20 . . . . . . Pensacola
21-25 . . . . . Birmingham
26-30 . . . at Montgomery
31 . . . . at Huntsville

AUGUST
1-4 . . . . . . at Huntsville
6-10 . . . . . . Mississippi
12-16 . . . . at Chattanooga
17-21 . . . . . . Pensacola
22-26 . . . . at Tennessee
28-31 . . . . Mobile

SEPTEMBER
1 . . . . Mobile

MISSISSIPPI BRAVES

APRIL
3-7 . . . . Mobile
9-13 . . . . at Jackson
14-18 . . . . . . Huntsville
19-23 . . . at Montgomery
24-28 . . . . at Pensacola
30 . . . . Jacksonville

MAY
1-4 . . . . Jacksonville
5-9 . . . . at Mobile
10-14 . . . . . Montgomery
15-19 . . . . . . Tennessee
21-25 . . . at Chattanooga
26-30 . . . . . Pensacola
31 . . . . at Montgomery

JUNE
1-4 . . . . at Montgomery
5-9 . . . . . . Chattanooga
11-15 . . . at Tennessee
19-23 . . . . Jackson

24-28 . . . . at Birmingham
29-30 . . . . . Huntsville

JULY
1-3 . . . . Huntsville
4-8 . . . . at Montgomery
10-14 . . . . Mobile
16-20 . . . at Birmingham
21-25 . . . at Tennessee
26-30 . . . . . Pensacola
31 . . . . Mobile

AUGUST
1-4 . . . . Mobile
6-10 . . . . at Jacksonville
12-16 . . . Montgomery
17-21 . . . . . at Mobile
22-26 . . . . Birmingham
28-31 . . . . at Huntsville

SEPTEMBER
1 . . . . at Huntsville

MOBILE BAYBEARS

APRIL
3-7 . . . . . . at Mississippi
9-13 . . . . . Montgomery
14-18 . . . . . Birmingham
19-23 . . . . at Huntsville
24-28 . . . . Jackson
30 . . . . . at Birmingham

MAY
1-4 . . . . . . at Birmingham
5-9 . . . . . . Mississippi
10-14 . . . . at Jacksonville
15-19 . . . . Chattanooga
21-25 . . . . at Tennessee
26-30 . . . . . . Jackson
31 . . . . at Chattanooga

JUNE
1-4 . . . . at Chattanooga
5-9 . . . . . . at Huntsville
11-15 . . . . . Pensacola
19-23 . . . at Montgomery

24-28 . . . . Jacksonville
29-30 . . . . . at Jackson

JULY
1-3 . . . . . . at Jackson
4-8 . . . . Pensacola
10-14 . . . . at Mississippi
16-20 . . . Chattanooga
21-25 . . . at Pensacola
26-30 . . . . . Jackson
31 . . . . at Mississippi

AUGUST
1-4 . . . . . . at Mississippi
6-10 . . . . . Tennessee
12-16 . . . . at Pensacola
17-21 . . . . Mississippi
22-26 . . . . . Huntsville
28-31 . . . at Jacksonville

SEPTEMBER
1 . . . . . . at Jacksonville

MONTGOMERY BISCUITS

APRIL
3-7 . . . . Birmingham
9-13 . . . . at Mobile
14-18 . . . . at Pensacola
19-23 . . . . .Mississippi
24-28 . . . . at Jacksonville
29-30 . . . . . Huntsville

MAY
1-3 . . . . . . Huntsville
5-9 . . . . . Jacksonville
10-14 . . . . at Mississippi
15-19 . . . . .at Jackson
21-25 . . . . . Huntsville
26-30 . . . at Jacksonville
31 . . . . . . .Mississippi

JUNE
1-4 . . . . . .Mississippi
5-9 . . . . . . Pensacola
11-15 . . . at Birmingham
19-23 . . . . . . Mobile

24-28 . . . . at Huntsville
29-30 . . . . at Tennessee

JULY
1-3 . . . . . at Tennessee
4-8 . . . . .Mississippi
10-14 . . . . at Pensacola
16-20 . . . . . . Jackson
21-25 . . . . at Chattanooga
26-30 . . . . .Jacksonville
31 . . . . . .at Jackson

AUGUST
1-4 . . . . . . .at Jackson
6-10 . . . . . Chattanooga
12-16 . . . at Mississippi
17-21 . . . . . .Tennessee
22-26 . . . . at Pensacola
28-31 . . . . . Jackson

SEPTEMBER
1 . . . . Jackson

PENSACOLA BLUE WAHOOS

APRIL
3-7 . . . . .Tennessee
9-13 . . . . . at Huntsville
14-18 . . . . Montgomery
19-23 . . . at Jacksonville
24-28 . . . . .Mississippi
30 . . . . . . .at Jackson

MAY
1-4 . . . . . . .at Jackson
5-9 . . . . . Chattanooga
10-14 . . . .at Birmingham
15-19 . . . . Jacksonville
21-25 . . . . Birmingham
26-30 . . . .at Mississippi
31 . . . . . . .Jacksonville

JUNE
1-4 . . . . . . .Jacksonville
5-9 . . . . . at Montgomery
11-15 . . . . . . at Mobile
19-23 . . . . . . Huntsville

24-28 . . . . at Chattanooga
29-30 . . . . .Jacksonville

JULY
1-3 . . . . . . .Jacksonville
4-8 . . . . . . at Mobile
10-14 . . . . . Montgomery
16-20 . . . at Jacksonville
21-25 . . . . Mobile
26-30 . . .at Mississippi
31 . . . . . at Tennessee

AUGUST
1-4 . . . . . . at Tennessee
6-10 . . . . Jackson
12-16 . . . . . . Mobile
17-21 . . . at Jacksonville
22-26 . . . . Montgomery
28-31 . . . at Birmingham

SEPTEMBER
1 . . . . . . .at Birmingham

TENNESSEE SMOKIES

APRIL
3-7 . . . . . . at Pensacola
9-13 . . . . . Chattanooga
14-18 . . . . Jackson
19-23 . . . at Birmingham
24-28 . . . . . Huntsville
30 . . . . . at Chattanooga

MAY
1-4 . . . . . at Chattanooga
5-9 . . . . . . Birmingham
10-14 . . . . . at Jackson
15-19 . . . at Mississippi
21-25 . . . . . . Mobile
26-30 . . . . at Huntsville
31 . . . . Birmingham

JUNE
1-4 . . . . . Birmingham
5-9 . . . . . at Jacksonville
11-15 . . . . .Mississippi
19-23 . . . . . Chattanooga

24-28 . . . . . . .at Jackson
29-30 . . . . . Montgomery

JULY
1-3 . . . . Montgomery
4-8 . . . . .at Birmingham
10-14 . . . . Jacksonville
16-20 . . . . at Huntsville
21-25 . . . . .Mississippi
26-30 . . .at Birmingham
31 . . . . Pensacola

AUGUST
1-4 . . . . Pensacola
6-10 . . . . . at Mobile
12-16 . . . . Huntsville
17-21 . . . at Montgomery
22-26 . . . . . Jacksonville
28-31 . . . at Chattanooga

SEPTEMBER
1 . . . . . . at Chattanooga

TEXAS LEAGUE

ARKANSAS TRAVELERS

APRIL
- 3-5 . . . at Midland
- 6-8 . . . at Frisco
- 10-12 . . . Midland
- 13-15 . . . Frisco
- 17-20 . . . at Springfield
- 21-24 . . . Tulsa
- 25-28 . . . Springfield
- 29-30 . . . at Tulsa

MAY
- 1-2 . . . at Tulsa
- 3-6 . . . at Northwest Arkansas
- 8-11 . . . Tulsa
- 12-15 . . . Northwest Arkansas
- 16-19 . . . at Springfield
- 21-23 . . . Corpus Christi
- 24-26 . . . San Antonio
- 27-29 . . . at Corpus Christi
- 30-31 . . . at San Antonio

JUNE
- 1 . . . at San Antonio
- 3-6 . . . Springfield
- 7-10 . . . Northwest Arkansas
- 11-14 . . . at Tulsa
- 15-18 at Northwest Arkansas
- 19-22 . . . Springfield
- 25-27 . . . at Frisco
- 28-30 . . . at Midland

JULY
- 2-4 . . . Frisco
- 5-7 . . . Midland
- 9-12 . . . at Tulsa
- 13-16 . . . Springfield
- 17-20 . . . at Tulsa
- 21-23 at Northwest Arkansas
- 24-27 . . . Tulsa
- 28-30 . . . Northwest Arkansas
- 31 . . . at Springfield

AUGUST
- 1-3 . . . at Springfield
- 5-7 . . . San Antonio
- 8-10 . . . Corpus Christi
- 12-14 . . . at San Antonio
- 15-17 . . . at Corpus Christi
- 19-22 . . . Tulsa
- 23-25 . . . Northwest Arkansas
- 26-29 . . . at Springfield
- 30-31 at Northwest Arkansas

SEPTEMBER
- 1 . . . at Northwest Arkansas

CORPUS CHRISTI HOOKS

APRIL
- 3-5 . . . at Tulsa
- 6-8 . . . at Springfield
- 10-12 . . . Tulsa
- 13-15 . . . Springfield
- 17-20 . . . at Frisco
- 21-24 . . . Midland
- 25-28 . . . Frisco
- 29-30 . . . at Midland

MAY
- 1-2 . . . at Midland
- 3-6 . . . San Antonio
- 8-11 . . . at Frisco
- 12-15 . . . at San Antonio
- 16-19 . . . Midland
- 21-23 . . . at Arkansas
- 24-26 at Northwest Arkansas
- 27-29 . . . Arkansas
- 30-31 . . . Northwest Arkansas

JUNE
- 1 . . . Northwest Arkansas
- 3-6 . . . at Midland
- 7-10 . . . San Antonio
- 11-14 . . . Frisco
- 15-18 . . . at San Antonio
- 19-22 . . . Frisco
- 25-27 . . . at Springfield
- 28-30 . . . at Tulsa

JULY
- 2-4 . . . Springfield
- 5-7 . . . Tulsa
- 9-12 . . . at Frisco
- 13-16 . . . Midland
- 17-20 . . . at Frisco
- 21-23 . . . at San Antonio
- 24-27 . . . Midland
- 28-30 . . . San Antonio
- 31 . . . at Midland

AUGUST
- 1-3 . . . at Midland
- 5-7 . . . at Northwest Arkansas
- 8-10 . . . at Arkansas
- 12-14 . . . Northwest Arkansas
- 15-17 . . . Arkansas
- 19-22 . . . at Midland
- 23-25 . . . at San Antonio
- 26-29 . . . Frisco
- 30-31 . . . San Antonio

SEPTEMBER
- 1 . . . San Antonio

FRISCO ROUGHRIDERS

APRIL
- 3-5 . . . Northwest Arkansas
- 6-8 . . . Arkansas
- 10-12 at Northwest Arkansas
- 13-15 . . . at Arkansas
- 17-20 . . . Corpus Christi
- 21-24 . . . San Antonio
- 25-28 . . . at Corpus Christi
- 29-30 . . . at San Antonio

MAY
- 1-2 . . . at San Antonio
- 3-6 . . . Midland
- 8-11 . . . Corpus Christi
- 12-15 . . . at Midland
- 16-19 . . . at San Antonio
- 21-23 . . . Tulsa
- 24-26 . . . Springfield
- 27-29 . . . at Tulsa
- 30-31 . . . at Springfield

JUNE
- 1 . . . at Springfield
- 3-6 . . . San Antonio
- 7-10 . . . Midland
- 11-14 . . . at Corpus Christi
- 15-18 . . . at Midland
- 19-22 . . . at Corpus Christi
- 25-27 . . . Arkansas
- 28-30 . . . Northwest Arkansas

JULY
- 2-4 . . . at Arkansas
- 5-7 . . at Northwest Arkansas
- 9-12 . . . Corpus Christi
- 13-16 . . . at San Antonio
- 17-20 . . . Corpus Christi
- 21-23 . . . at Midland
- 24-27 . . . San Antonio
- 28-30 . . . Midland
- 31 . . . at San Antonio

AUGUST
- 1-3 . . . at San Antonio
- 5-7 . . . Springfield
- 8-10 . . . Tulsa
- 12-14 . . . at Springfield
- 15-17 . . . at Tulsa
- 19-22 . . . San Antonio
- 23-25 . . . at Midland
- 26-29 . . . at Corpus Christi
- 30-31 . . . Midland

SEPTEMBER
- 1 . . . Midland

MIDLAND ROCKHOUNDS

APRIL
- 3-5 . . . Arkansas
- 6-8 . . . Northwest Arkansas
- 10-12 . . . at Arkansas
- 13-15 at Northwest Arkansas
- 17-20 . . . San Antonio
- 21-24 . . . at Corpus Christi
- 25-28 . . . at San Antonio
- 29-30 . . . Corpus Christi

MAY
- 1-2 . . . Corpus Christi
- 3-6 . . . at Frisco
- 8-11 . . . San Antonio
- 12-15 . . . Frisco
- 16-19 . . . at Corpus Christi
- 21-23 . . . Springfield
- 24-26 . . . Tulsa
- 27-29 . . . at Springfield
- 30-31 . . . at Tulsa

JUNE
- 1 . . . at Tulsa
- 3-6 . . . Corpus Christi
- 7-10 . . . at Frisco
- 11-14 . . . at San Antonio
- 15-18 . . . Frisco
- 19-22 . . . at San Antonio
- 25-27 . . . Northwest Arkansas
- 28-30 . . . Arkansas

JULY
- 2-4 . . at Northwest Arkansas
- 5-7 . . . at Arkansas
- 9-12 . . . San Antonio
- 13-16 . . . at Corpus Christi
- 17-20 . . . San Antonio
- 21-23 . . . Frisco
- 24-27 . . . at Corpus Christi
- 28-30 . . . at Frisco
- 31 . . . Corpus Christi

AUGUST
- 1-3 . . . Corpus Christi
- 5-7 . . . Tulsa
- 8-10 . . . Springfield
- 12-14 . . . at Tulsa
- 15-17 . . . at Springfield
- 19-22 . . . Corpus Christi
- 23-25 . . . Frisco
- 26-29 . . . at San Antonio
- 30-31 . . . at Frisco

SEPTEMBER
- 1 . . . at Frisco

NORTHWEST ARKANSAS NATURALS

APRIL
- 3-5 . . . at Frisco
- 6-8 . . . at Midland
- 10-12 . . . Frisco
- 13-15 . . . Midland
- 16-19 . . . at Tulsa
- 21-24 . . . Springfield
- 25-26 . . . at Tulsa
- 27-28 . . . Tulsa
- 29-30 . . . at Springfield

MAY
- 1-2 . . . at Springfield
- 3-6 . . . Arkansas
- 8-11 . . . Springfield
- 12-15 . . . at Arkansas
- 16-17 . . . Tulsa
- 18-19 . . . at Tulsa
- 21-23 . . . San Antonio
- 24-26 . . . Corpus Christi
- 27-29 . . . at San Antonio
- 30-31 . . . at Corpus Christi

JUNE
- 1 . . . at Corpus Christi
- 3-6 . . . Tulsa
- 7-10 . . . at Arkansas
- 11-14 . . . at Springfield
- 15-18 . . . Arkansas
- 19-22 . . . Tulsa
- 25-27 . . . at Midland
- 28-30 . . . at Frisco

JULY
- 2-4 . . . Midland
- 5-7 . . . Frisco
- 9-12 . . . at Springfield
- 13-16 . . . Tulsa
- 17-20 . . . at Springfield
- 21-23 . . . Arkansas
- 24-27 . . . Springfield
- 28-30 . . . at Arkansas
- 31 . . . at Tulsa

AUGUST
- 1-3 . . . at Tulsa
- 5-7 . . . Corpus Christi
- 8-10 . . . San Antonio
- 12-14 . . . at Corpus Christi
- 15-17 . . . at San Antonio
- 19-22 . . . Springfield
- 23-25 . . . at Arkansas
- 26-29 . . . at Tulsa
- 30-31 . . . Arkansas

SEPTEMBER
- 1 . . . Arkansas

SAN ANTONIO MISSIONS

APRIL
3-5 . . . . . . at Springfield
6-8 . . . . at Tulsa
10-12 . . . . . Springfield
13-15 . . . . Tulsa
17-20 . . . . . . at Midland
21-24 . . . . . at Frisco
25-28 . . . . . . Midland
29-30 . . . . Frisco

MAY
1-2 . . . . Frisco
3-6 . . . . . at Corpus Christi
8-11 . . . . . at Midland
12-15 . . . . Corpus Christi
16-19 . . . . Frisco
21-23 at Northwest Arkansas
24-26 . . . . at Arkansas
27 29 . Northwest Arkansas
30-31 . . . . Arkansas

JUNE
1 . . . . Arkansas
3-6 . . . . at Frisco
7-10 . . . . at Corpus Christi
11-14 . . . . . Midland
15-18 . . . . Corpus Christi

19-22 . . . . Midland
25-27 . . . . at Tulsa
28-30 . . . at Springfield

JULY
2-4 . . . . Tulsa
5-7 . . . . . Springfield
9-12 . . . . . at Midland
13-16 . . . . Frisco
17-20 . . . . at Midland
21-23 . . . . Corpus Christi
24-27 . . . . . at Frisco
28-30 . . . at Corpus Christi
31 . . . . Frisco

AUGUST
1-3 . . . . Frisco
5-7 . . . . . at Arkansas
8-10 . at Northwest Arkansas
12-14 . . . . Arkansas
15-17 . Northwest Arkansas
19-22 . . . . . . at Frisco
23-25 . . . . Corpus Christi
26-29 . . . . . . Midland
30-31 . . . at Corpus Christi

SEPTEMBER
1 . . . . . . at Corpus Christi

SPRINGFIELD CARDINALS

APRIL
3-5 . . . . San Antonio
6-8 . . . . . . Corpus Christi
10-12 . . . . at San Antonio
13-15 . . at Corpus Christi
17-20 . . . . Arkansas
21-24 at Northwest Arkansas
26-28 . . . . at Arkansas
29-30 . Northwest Arkansas

MAY
1-2 . . . Northwest Arkansas
3-6 . . . . Tulsa

8-11 . at Northwest Arkansas
12-15 . . . . at Tulsa
16-19 . . . . Arkansas
21-23 . . . . . at Midland
24-26 . . . . . at Frisco
27-29 . . . . . Midland
30-31 . . . . Frisco

JUNE
1 . . . . Frisco
3-6 . . . . at Arkansas
7-10 . . . . Tulsa
11-14 . Northwest Arkansas

TULSA DRILLERS

APRIL
3-5 . . . . . . Corpus Christi
6-8 . . . . San Antonio
10-12 . . at Corpus Christi
13-15 . . . . at San Antonio
16-19 . Northwest Arkansas
21-24 . . . . . at Arkansas
25-26 . Northwest Arkansas
27-28 at Northwest Arkansas
29-30 . . . . . . Arkansas

MAY
1-2 . . . . Arkansas
3 6 . . . . . . at Springfield
8-11 . . . . . at Arkansas
12-15 . . . . . Springfield
16-17 at Northwest Arkansas
18-19 . Northwest Arkansas
21-23 . . . . . at Frisco
24-26 . . . . at Midland
27-29 . . . . Frisco
30-31 . . . . . Midland

JUNE
1 . . . . Midland
3-6 . at Northwest Arkansas
7-10 . . . . . at Springfield
11-14 . . . . . . Arkansas

15-18 . . . . at Tulsa
19-22 . . . . . . at Arkansas
25-27 . . Corpus Christi
28-30 . . . . . San Antonio

JULY
2-4 . . . . at Corpus Christi
5-7 . . . . . at San Antonio
9-12 . Northwest Arkansas
13-16 . . . . . at Arkansas
17-20 . Northwest Arkansas
21-23 . . . . Tulsa
24-27 at Northwest Arkansas
28-30 . . . . at Tulsa

AUGUST
1-3 . . . . Arkansas
5-7 . . . . at Frisco
8-10 . . . . . . at Midland
12-14 . . . . Frisco
15-17 . . . . . . Midland
19-22 at Northwest Arkansas
23-25 . . . . Tulsa
26-29 . . . . . . Arkansas
30-31 . . . . at Tulsa

SEPTEMBER
1 . . . . at Tulsa

31 . . . . Arkansas

AUGUST
1-3 . . . . Arkansas
5-7 . . . . . . at Frisco
8-10 . . . . . . at Midland
12-14 . . . . Frisco
15-17 . . . . . Midland
19-22 at Northwest Arkansas
23-25 . . . . Tulsa
26-29 . . . . . . Arkansas
30-31 . . . . at Tulsa

SEPTEMBER
1 . . . . at Tulsa

15-18 . . . . . Springfield
19-22 at Northwest Arkansas
25-27 . . . . . San Antonio
28-30 . . . . . Corpus Christi

JULY
2-4 . . . . . . at San Antonio
5-7 . . . . at Corpus Christi
9-12 . . . . Arkansas
13-16 at Northwest Arkansas
17-20 . . . . Arkansas
21-23 . . . . at Springfield
24-27 . . . . . at Arkansas
28-30 . . . . . Springfield
31 . . . Northwest Arkansas

AUGUST
1-3 . . . Northwest Arkansas
5-7 . . . . at Midland
8-10 . . . . . . at Frisco
12-14 . . . . . . Midland
15-17 . . . . Frisco
19-22 . . . . . at Arkansas
23-25 . . . . . at Springfield
26-29 . Northwest Arkansas
30-31 . . . . . Springfield

SEPTEMBER
1 . . . . Springfield

8-11 . at Northwest Arkansas
12-15 . . . . at Tulsa
16-19 . . . . Arkansas
21-23 . . . . at Midland
24-26 . . . . at Frisco
27-29 . . . . . Midland
30-31 . . . . Frisco

JUNE
1 . . . . Frisco
3-6 . . . . . . at Arkansas
7-10 . . . . Tulsa
11-14 . Northwest Arkansas

HIGH CLASS A

CALIFORNIA LEAGUE

BAKERSFIELD BLAZE

APRIL
3-6 . . . . Modesto
7-9 . . . . Stockton
10-13 . . . at San Jose
14-16 . . . . at Stockton
17-19 . . . . . San Jose
21-24 . . . . . at Modesto
25-27 . . . . at San Jose
28-30 . . . . Stockton

MAY
1 . . . . Stockton
2-4 . . . . at Modesto
5-8 . . . . . . Inland Empire
9-11 . . . . Visalia
13-15 . . . . . . at Lancaster
16-19 . . . . . at Stockton
20-22 . . . . . . Lancaster
23-26 . . . . . High Desert
27-29 . . . . at Visalia
30-31 . . . . at High Desert

JUNE
1-2 . . . . . at High Desert

3-5 . . . . Stockton
6-9 . . at Rancho Cucamonga
11-14 . . . . Modesto
19-22 . . . . at Stockton
23-25 . . . . . . Visalia
26-29 . . . . . . Stockton

JULY
1-3 . . . . at Visalia
4-7 . . . . Modesto
8-10 . . . . . at San Jose
11-14 . . . . at Modesto
16-18 . . . . . Lake Elsinore
19-22 . Rancho Cucamonga
24-27 . . . . at Lake Elsinore
28-30 . . . . . . Visalia
31 . . at Rancho Cucamonga

AUGUST
1-3 at Rancho Cucamonga
4-6 . . . . San Jose
7-10 . . . . at Visalia
12-14 . . . . at Modesto
15-18 . . . . . . Lancaster
19-21 . . . at Inland Empire

22-24 . . . . . Lake Elsinore
26-28 . . . . . . at Stockton
29-31 . . . . Visalia

HIGH DESERT MAVERICKS

APRIL
3-6 . . . . . . Inland Empire
7-9 . . . . . . Lake Elsinore
10-13 . . . at Inland Empire
14-16 . . . . . . Lancaster
17-19 . . . . . at Lancaster
21-24 . Rancho Cucamonga
25-27 . . . . . at Stockton
28-30 . . . . . at Lancaster

MAY
1 . . . . at Lancaster
2-4 . . . . Visalia
5-8 . at Rancho Cucamonga
9-11 . . . . . . Lancaster
13-15 . . . . . . at Visalia
16-19 . . . . Inland Empire
20-22 . . . at Lake Elsinore
23-26 . . . at Bakersfield
27-29 . Rancho Cucamonga
30-31 . . . . . . Bakersfield

JUNE
1-2 . . . . Bakersfield
3-5 . . . . at San Jose
6-9 . . . . at Stockton
11-14 . . . . Lake Elsinore
19-22 . . . . . at Modesto
23-25 . Rancho Cucamonga
26-29 . . . . . . Modesto

JULY
1-3 . at Rancho Cucamonga
4-7 . . . . . Lake Elsinore
8-10 . . . . . . at Visalia
11-14 . . . at Lake Elsinore
16-18 . . . . . . Stockton
19-22 . . . . . . Visalia
24-27 at Rancho Cucamonga
28-30 . . . . . . Lancaster
31 . . . . . at Inland Empire

AUGUST
1-3 . . . . . at Inland Empire

SEPTEMBER
1 . . . . Visalia

4-6... Rancho Cucamonga
7-10 .... at Lake Elsinore
12-14 ......at Lancaster
15-18 ..... Inland Empire
19-21 ......at Lancaster
22-24 ...... at Modesto
26-28 .... Lancaster
29-31 .... San Jose

SEPTEMBER
1 .... San Jose

INLAND EMPIRE 66ERS

APRIL
3-6...... at High Desert
7-9. .at Rancho Cucamonga
10-13 ......High Desert
14-16 .... at San Jose
17-19 ......Stockton
21-24 .... Lancaster
25-27 .... at Lake Elsinore
28-30 . Rancho Cucamonga

MAY
1.... Rancho Cucamonga
2-4...... Lake Elsinore
5-8...... at Bakersfield
9-11...... at San Jose
13-15 .... Lake Elsinore
16-19 .... at High Desert
20-22 . Rancho Cucamonga
23-26 ......at Lancaster
27-29 ....Modesto
30-31 ....San Jose

JUNE
1-2........ San Jose
3-5........at Lancaster
6-9...... at Lake Elsinore
11-14 .... Visalia
19-22at Rancho Cucamonga
23-25 ..... Lake Elsinore
26-29 . Rancho Cucamonga

JULY
1-3....... at Lake Elsinore
4-7......... Visalia
8-10 ......at Lancaster
11-14 .... at Visalia
16-18 ....Modesto
19-22 ....Stockton
24-27 ...... at Modesto
28-30 ...... at Stockton
31 ....High Desert

AUGUST
1-3.........High Desert
4-6...... at Lake Elsinore
7-10.. Rancho Cucamonga
12-14 ..... Lake Elsinore
15-18 .... at High Desert
19-21 ...... Bakersfield
22-24 .... Lancaster
26-28at Rancho Cucamonga
29-31 ......at Lancaster

SEPTEMBER
1 ....at Lancaster

LAKE ELSINORE STORM

APRIL
3-6........at Lancaster
7-9...... at High Desert
10-13 ..... Lancaster
14-16at Rancho Cucamonga
17-19 ....Modesto
21-24 ..... at Stockton
25-27 ..... Inland Empire
28-30 .... Visalia

MAY
1......... Visalia
2-4.....at Inland Empire
5-8........ Lancaster
9-11 . . Rancho Cucamonga
13-15 ...at Inland Empire
16-19 ....Modesto
20-22 ......High Desert
23-26at Rancho Cucamonga
27-29 ...... Lancaster
30-31 ....at Visalia

JUNE
1-2........at Visalia
3-5...... at Modesto
6-9...... Inland Empire
11-14 .... at High Desert
19-22 .... Lancaster
23-25 ....at Inland Empire
26-29 ......at Lancaster

JULY
1-3........ Inland Empire
4-7...... at High Desert
8-10 .at Rancho Cucamonga
11-14 ......High Desert
16-18 ..... at Bakersfield
19-22 ...... at San Jose
24-27 ...... Bakersfield
28-30 . Rancho Cucamonga
31 ....at Lancaster

AUGUST
1-3.........at Lancaster
4-6....... Inland Empire
7-10 ....High Desert
12-14 ...at Inland Empire
15-18at Rancho Cucamonga
19-21 ....Stockton
22-24 .... at Bakersfield
26-28 ..... San Jose
29-31 . Rancho Cucamonga

SEPTEMBER
1 .... Rancho Cucamonga

LANCASTER JETHAWKS

APRIL
3-6...... Lake Elsinore
7-9.......... San Jose
10-13 .. at Lake Elsinore
14-16 .... at High Desert
17-19 ......High Desert
21-24 ...at Inland Empire
25-27at Rancho Cucamonga
28-30 ....High Desert

MAY
1 ....High Desert
2-4.......... San Jose
5-8...... at Lake Elsinore
9-11..... at High Desert
13-15 ..... Bakersfield
16-19at Rancho Cucamonga
20-22 .....at Bakersfield
23-26 ..... Inland Empire

MODESTO NUTS

APRIL
3-6......at Bakersfield
7-9...... at Visalia
10-13 . Rancho Cucamonga
14-16 .... Visalia
17-19 .... at Lake Elsinore
21-24 ...... Bakersfield
25-27 ......at Visalia
28-30 .... San Jose

MAY
1......... San Jose
2-4...... Bakersfield
5-8...... at San Jose
9-11.........Stockton
13-15at Rancho Cucamonga
16-19 .... at Lake Elsinore
20-22 .... Visalia
23-26 ....Stockton
27-29 ...at Inland Empire
30-31 .... at Stockton

JUNE
1-2...... at Stockton
3-5.... Lake Elsinore
6-9........ San Jose
11-14 .....at Bakersfield
19-22 ......High Desert
23-25 ...... at San Jose
26-29 ..... at High Desert

JULY
1-3......... San Jose
4-7.......at Bakersfield
8-10....... at Stockton
11-14 ...... Bakersfield
16-18 ...at Inland Empire
19-22 ......at Lancaster
24-27 ..... Inland Empire
28-30 ...... San Jose
31 .... at Visalia

AUGUST
1-3.........at Visalia
4-6........ Lancaster
7-10 ...... at Stockton
12-14 ..... Bakersfield
15-18 .... Visalia
19-21 ...... at San Jose
22-24 ......High Desert
26-28 ...... at Visalia
29-31 ....Stockton

SEPTEMBER
1 ....Stockton

RANCHO CUCAMONGA QUAKES

APRIL
3-6.......... San Jose
7-9....... Inland Empire
10-13 ...... at Modesto
14-16 ..... Lake Elsinore
17-19 ...... at Visalia
21-24 ..... at High Desert
25-27 .... Lancaster
28-30 ... at Inland Empire

MAY
1 ......at Inland Empire
2-4...... at Stockton
5-8.........High Desert
9-11..... at Lake Elsinore
13-15 ....Modesto
16-19 .... Lancaster
20-22 ...at Inland Empire
23-26 ..... Lake Elsinore
27-29 ... at High Desert
30-31 .....at Lancaster

JUNE
1-2.......at Lancaster
3-5........... Visalia
6-9........ Bakersfield
11-14 ......at Lancaster
19-22 ..... Inland Empire
23-25 .... at High Desert
26-29 ....at Inland Empire

JULY
1-3.........High Desert
4-7........at Lancaster
8-10....... Lake Elsinore
11-14 .... Lancaster
16-18 ...... at San Jose
19-22 ......at Bakersfield
24-27 ......High Desert
28-30 .... at Lake Elsinore
31 .... Bakersfield

AUGUST
1-3......... Bakersfield
4-6...... at High Desert
7-10 ...at Inland Empire
12-14 .... San Jose
15-18 ..... Lake Elsinore
19-21 ...... at Visalia
22-24 ....Stockton
26-28 ..... Inland Empire
29-31 .... at Lake Elsinore

SEPTEMBER
1 ...... at Lake Elsinore

SAN JOSE GIANTS

APRIL
- 3-6 at Rancho Cucamonga
- 7-9 at Lancaster
- 10-13 Bakersfield
- 14-16 Inland Empire
- 17-19 at Bakersfield
- 21-24 Visalia
- 25-27 Bakersfield
- 28-30 at Modesto

MAY
- 1 at Modesto
- 2-4 at Lancaster
- 5-8 Modesto
- 9-11 Inland Empire
- 13-15 at Stockton
- 16-19 at Visalia
- 20-22 Stockton
- 23-26 Visalia
- 27-29 at Stockton
- 30-31 at Inland Empire

JUNE
- 1-2 at Inland Empire
- 3-5 High Desert
- 6-9 at Modesto
- 11-14 Stockton
- 19-22 at Visalia
- 23-25 Modesto
- 26-29 Visalia

JULY
- 1-3 at Modesto
- 4-7 Stockton
- 8-10 Bakersfield
- 11-14 at Stockton
- 16-18 Rancho Cucamonga
- 19-22 Lake Elsinore
- 24-27 at Visalia
- 28-30 at Modesto
- 31 Stockton

AUGUST
- 1-3 Stockton
- 4-6 at Bakersfield
- 7-10 Lancaster
- 12-14at Rancho Cucamonga
- 15-18 at Stockton
- 19-21 Modesto
- 22-24 Visalia
- 26-28 at Lake Elsinore
- 29-31 at High Desert

SEPTEMBER
- 1 at High Desert

STOCKTON PORTS

APRIL
- 3-6 at Visalia
- 7-9 at Bakersfield
- 10-13 Visalia
- 14-16 Bakersfield
- 17-19 at Inland Empire
- 21-24 Lake Elsinore
- 25-27 High Desert
- 28-30 at Bakersfield

MAY
- 1 at Bakersfield
- 2-4 Rancho Cucamonga
- 5-8 at Visalia
- 9-11 at Modesto
- 13-15 San Jose
- 16-19 Bakersfield
- 20-22 at San Jose
- 23-26 at Modesto
- 27-29 San Jose
- 30-31 Modesto

JUNE
- 1-2 Modesto
- 3-5 at Bakersfield
- 6-9 High Desert
- 11-14 at San Jose
- 19-22 Bakersfield
- 23-25 at Lancaster
- 26-29 at Bakersfield

JULY
- 1-3 Lancaster
- 4-7 at San Jose
- 8-10 Modesto
- 11-14 San Jose
- 16-18 at High Desert
- 19-22 at Inland Empire
- 24-27 Lancaster
- 28-30 Inland Empire
- 31 at San Jose

AUGUST
- 1-3 at San Jose
- 4-6 Visalia
- 7-10 Modesto
- 12-14 at Visalia
- 15-18 San Jose
- 19-21 at Lake Elsinore
- 22-24at Rancho Cucamonga
- 26-28 Bakersfield
- 29-31 at Modesto

SEPTEMBER
- 1 at Modesto

VISALIA RAWHIDE

APRIL
- 3-6 Stockton
- 7-9 Modesto
- 10-13 at Stockton
- 14-16 at Modesto
- 17-19 Rancho Cucamonga
- 21-24 at San Jose
- 25-27 Modesto
- 28-30 at Lake Elsinore

MAY
- 1 at Lake Elsinore
- 2-4 at High Desert
- 5-8 Stockton
- 9-11 at Bakersfield
- 13-15 High Desert
- 16-19 San Jose
- 20-22 at Modesto
- 23-26 at San Jose
- 27-29 Bakersfield
- 30-31 Lake Elsinore

JUNE
- 1-2 Lake Elsinore
- 3-5 at Rancho Cucamonga
- 6-9 Lancaster
- 11-14 at Inland Empire
- 19-22 San Jose
- 23-25 at Bakersfield
- 26-29 at San Jose

JULY
- 1-3 Bakersfield
- 4-7 at Inland Empire
- 8-10 High Desert
- 11-14 Inland Empire
- 16-18 at Lancaster
- 19-22 at High Desert
- 24-27 San Jose
- 28-30 at Bakersfield
- 31 Modesto

AUGUST
- 1-3 Modesto
- 4-6 at Stockton
- 7-10 Bakersfield
- 12-14 Stockton
- 15-18 at Modesto
- 19-21 Rancho Cucamonga
- 22-24 at San Jose
- 26-28 Modesto
- 29-31 at Bakersfield

SEPTEMBER
- 1 at Bakersfield

CAROLINA LEAGUE

CAROLINA MUDCATS

APRIL
- 3-6 Potomac
- 8-10 at Frederick
- 11-14 at Potomac
- 15-17 Salem
- 18-21 Frederick
- 23-25 at Wilmington
- 26-29 at Frederick

MAY
- 1-4 Wilmington
- 5-7 at Lynchburg
- 8-11 at Salem
- 12-14 Lynchburg
- 15-18 Salem
- 20-22 at Wilmington
- 23-26 Myrtle Beach
- 27-29 Wilmington
- 30-31 at Myrtle Beach

JUNE
- 1-2 at Myrtle Beach
- 3-5 Winston-Salem
- 6-8 at Winston-Salem
- 9-11 Potomac
- 12-15 at Wilmington
- 19-21 Frederick
- 22-24 Myrtle Beach
- 25-27 at Salem
- 28-30 at Winston-Salem

JULY
- 1-3 Lynchburg
- 4-6 Salem
- 7-10 at Lynchburg
- 11-14 Winston-Salem
- 16-18 at Lynchburg
- 19-21 at Myrtle Beach
- 22-24 Wilmington
- 25-27 at Potomac
- 29-31 at Salem

AUGUST
- 1-3 Potomac
- 5-7 at Frederick
- 8-10 Myrtle Beach
- 12-14 at Myrtle Beach
- 15-17 at Potomac
- 19-21 Frederick
- 22-25 at Winston-Salem
- 26-29 Lynchburg
- 30-31 Winston-Salem

SEPTEMBER
- 1 Winston-Salem

FREDERICK KEYS

APRIL
- 3-6 at Lynchburg
- 8-10 Carolina
- 11-14 Lynchburg
- 15-17 at Winston-Salem
- 18-21 at Carolina
- 23-25 Myrtle Beach
- 26-29 Carolina

MAY
- 1-4 at Myrtle Beach
- 5-7 at Potomac
- 8-11 Winston-Salem
- 12-14 Potomac
- 15-18 at Winston-Salem
- 20-22 Myrtle Beach
- 23-26 at Wilmington
- 27-29 at Lynchburg
- 30-31 Wilmington

JUNE
- 1-2 Wilmington
- 3-5 at Salem
- 6-8 at Myrtle Beach
- 9-11 Salem
- 12-15 Myrtle Beach
- 19-21 at Carolina
- 22-24 Wilmington
- 25-27 Winston-Salem
- 28-30 at Potomac

JULY
- 1-3 Salem
- 4-6 at Lynchburg
- 7-10 at Salem
- 11-14 Potomac
- 16-18 at Salem
- 19-21 Winston-Salem
- 22-24 at Myrtle Beach
- 25-27 Lynchburg
- 29-31 at Winston-Salem

AUGUST
- 1-3 at Wilmington
- 5-7 Carolina
- 8-10 Wilmington
- 12-14 at Wilmington
- 15-17 Lynchburg
- 19-21 at Carolina
- 22-25 at Potomac
- 26-29 Salem
- 30-31 Potomac

SEPTEMBER
- 1 Potomac

LYNCHBURG HILLCATS

APRIL
- 3-6 Frederick
- 8-10 at Potomac
- 11-14 at Frederick

15-17 . . . . Wilmington
18-21 . . . . .Potomac
23-25 . . . . at Salem
26-29 . . . . at Potomac

MAY

1-4 . . . . .Salem
5-7 . . . . Carolina
8-11 . . . . . at Wilmington
12-14 . . . . . .at Carolina
15-18 . . . . . . Wilmington
20-22 . . . . at Potomac
23-26 . . .Winston-Salem
27-29 . . . . .Frederick
30-31 . . . at Winston-Salem

JUNE

1-2 . . . .Winston-Salem
3-5 . . . . Myrtle Beach
6-8 . . . . .Salem
9-11 . . . at Myrtle Beach
12-15 . . . . . . at Salem
19-21 . . . . Potomac
22-24 . . . .Winston-Salem
25-27 . . . . at Wilmington

28-30 . . . . . Myrtle Beach

JULY

1-3 . . . . .at Carolina
4-6 . . . . .Frederick
7-10 . . . . Carolina
11-14 . . at Myrtle Beach
16-18 . . . . Carolina
19-21 . . . at Wilmington
22-24 . . . . .Salem
25-27 . . . . at Frederick
29-31 . . . . Wilmington

AUGUST

1-3 . . . . at Winston-Salem
5-7 . . . . at Salem
8-10 . . . .Winston-Salem
12-14 . . at Winston-Salem
15-17 . . . .at Frederick
19-21 . . . . . Potomac
22-25 . . . Myrtle Beach
26-29 . . . . .at Carolina
30-31 . . at Myrtle Beach

SEPTEMBER

1 . . . . . . at Myrtle Beach

MYRTLE BEACH PELICANS

APRIL

3-6 . . . . .Salem
8-10 . . . . at Wilmington
11-14 . . . . . . at Salem
15-17 . . . . . Potomac
18-21 . . . . . Wilmington
23-25 . . . . at Frederick
26-29 . . . at Wilmington

MAY

1-4 . . . . .Frederick
5-7 . . . . at Winston-Salem
8-11 . . . . . at Potomac
12-14 . . .Winston-Salem
15-18 . . . . . Potomac
20-22 . . . . at Frederick
23-26 . . . . . .at Carolina
27-29 . . . . .Salem
30-31 . . . . . . Carolina

JUNE

1-2 . . . . Carolina
3-5 . . . . . . at Lynchburg
6-8 . . . . .Frederick
9-11 . . . . . .Lynchburg
12-15 . . . . at Frederick
19-21 . . . . . . Wilmington

22-24 . . . . . . .at Carolina
25-27 . . . . . .Potomac
28-30 . . . . . at Lynchburg

JULY

1-3 . . . . .Winston-Salem
4-6 . . . . . . at Potomac
7-10 . . . at Winston-Salem
11-14 . . . . .Lynchburg
16-18 . . . at Winston-Salem
19-21 . . . . Carolina
22-24 . . . . . . .Frederick
25-27 . . . . at Salem
28-30 . . . . at Potomac

AUGUST

1-3 . . . . .Salem
5-7 . . . . . at Wilmington
8-10 . . . . . . .at Carolina
12-14 . . . . . . Carolina
15-17 . . . . at Salem
19-21 . . . . . Wilmington
22-25 . . . at Lynchburg
26-29 . . . .Winston-Salem
30-31 . . . . .Lynchburg

SEPTEMBER

1 . . . . .Lynchburg

POTOMAC NATIONALS

APRIL

3-6 . . . . .at Carolina
8-10 . . . . . . .Lynchburg
11-14 . . . . Carolina
15-17 . . . at Myrtle Beach
18-21 . . . at Lynchburg
23-25 . . . .Winston-Salem
26-29 . . . . . . .Lynchburg

MAY

1-4 . . . at Winston-Salem
5-7 . . . . .Frederick
8-11 . . . . Myrtle Beach
12-14 . . . . at Frederick
15-18 . . . at Myrtle Beach
20-22 . . . . .Lynchburg
23-26 . . . . . . at Salem
27-29 . . at Winston-Salem
30-31 . . . . . . .Salem

JUNE

1-2 . . . . .Salem

3-5 . . . . . . at Wilmington
6-8 . . . . Wilmington
9-11 . . . . . .at Carolina
12-15 . . . .Winston-Salem
19-21 . . . at Lynchburg
22-24 . . . . .Salem
25-27 . . . at Myrtle Beach
28-30 . . . . . . .Frederick

JULY

1-3 . . . . . at Wilmington
4-6 . . . . . . Myrtle Beach
7-10 . . . . . Wilmington
11-14 . . . at Frederick
16-18 . . . . . Wilmington
19-21 . . . . . at Salem
22-24 . . at Winston-Salem
25-27 . . . . Carolina
28-30 . . . Myrtle Beach

AUGUST

1-3 . . . . . . .at Carolina

SALEM RED SOX

APRIL

3-6 . . . . . at Myrtle Beach
8-10 . . . .Winston-Salem
11-14 . . . Myrtle Beach
15-17 . . . .at Carolina
18-21 . . at Winston-Salem
23-25 . . . . .Lynchburg
26-29 . . .Winston-Salem

MAY

1-4 . . . . . at Lynchburg
5-7 . . . . . . Wilmington
8-11 . . . . Carolina
12-14 . . at Wilmington
15-18 . . . .at Carolina
20-22 . . . .Winston-Salem
23-26 . . . . .Potomac
27-29 . . at Myrtle Beach
30-31 . . . . . at Potomac

JUNE

1-2 . . . . . . at Potomac
3-5 . . . . .Frederick
6-8 . . . . . at Lynchburg
9-11 . . . . . at Frederick
12-15 . . . . .Lynchburg
19-21 . . . at Winston-Salem

22-24 . . . . . at Potomac
25-27 . . . . . Carolina
28-30 . . . . . . Wilmington

JULY

1-3 . . . . at Frederick
4-6 . . . . .at Carolina
7-10 . . . . . . .Frederick
11-14 . . . at Wilmington
16-18 . . . . . .Frederick
19-21 . . . . Potomac
22-24 . . . at Lynchburg
25-27 . . . Myrtle Beach
29-31 . . . . . . Carolina

AUGUST

1-3 . . . . . at Myrtle Beach
5-7 . . . . .Lynchburg
8-10 . . . . .Potomac
12-14 . . . . . at Potomac
15-17 . . . Myrtle Beach
19-21 . . . at Winston-Salem
22-25 . . . . . Wilmington
26-29 . . . . at Frederick
30-31 . . . at Wilmington

SEPTEMBER

1 . . . . at Wilmington

WILMINGTON BLUE ROCKS

APRIL

3-6 . . . . at Winston-Salem
8-10 . . . Myrtle Beach
11-14 . . .Winston-Salem
15-17 . . . at Lynchburg
18-21 . . at Myrtle Beach
23-25 . . . . . Carolina
26-29 . . . . Myrtle Beach

MAY

1 4 . . . . .at Carolina
5-7 . . . . . . at Salem
8-11 . . . . . . .Lynchburg
12-14 . . . . .Salem
15-18 . . . at Lynchburg
20-22 . . . . Carolina
23-26 . . . . . . .Frederick
27-29 . . . .at Carolina
30-31 . . . . . . at Frederick

MAY

1-2 . . . . . . at Frederick
3-5 . . . . .Potomac
6-8 . . . . . at Potomac
9-11 . . . at Winston-Salem
12-15 . . . . Carolina
19-21 . . at Myrtle Beach

22-24 . . . . . . at Frederick
25-27 . . . . .Lynchburg
28-30 . . . . at Salem

JULY

1-3 . . . . .Potomac
4-6 . . . . at Winston-Salem
7-10 . . . . at Potomac
11-14 . . . . .Salem
16-18 . . . . at Potomac
19-21 . . . . .Lynchburg
22-24 . . . .at Carolina
25-27 . . . .Winston-Salem
29-31 . . . at Lynchburg

AUGUST

1-3 . . . . .Frederick
5-7 . . . . Myrtle Beach
8-10 . . . . . . at Frederick
12-14 . . . . . . .Frederick
15-17 . . . .Winston-Salem
19-21 . . . at Myrtle Beach
22-25 . . . . . . at Salem
26-29 . . . . Potamac
30-31 . . . . .Salem

SEPTEMBER

1 . . . . .Salem

WINSTON-SALEM DASH

APRIL

3-6 . . . . Wilmington
8-10 . . . . at Salem
11-14 . . . at Wilmington
15-17 . . . . . .Frederick
18-21 . . . . .Salem
23-25 . . . . . at Potomac
26-29 . . . . at Salem

MAY

1-4 . . . . .Potomac
5-7 . . . . Myrtle Beach
8-11 . . . . . at Frederick
12-14 . . at Myrtle Beach
15-18 . . . . . . .Frederick
20-22 . . . . . . at Salem
23-26 . . . . at Lynchburg
27-29 . . . . .Potomac

30-31 . . . . . . .Lynchburg

JUNE
1-2. . . . . . . .Lynchburg
3-5. . . . . . . .at Carolina
6-8. . . . . Carolina
9-11. . . . . . Wilmington
12-15 . . . . . at Potomac
19-21 . . . . . . .Salem
22-24 . . . . at Lynchburg
25-27 . . . . at Frederick
28-30 . . . . . . Carolina

JULY
1-3. . . . . at Myrtle Beach
4-6. . . . . . .Wilmington
7-10. . . . . Myrtle Beach
11-14 . . . . .at Carolina
16-18 . . . . . Myrtle Beach

19-21 . . . . . at Frederick
22-24 . . . . . .Potomac
25-27 . . . . at Wilmington
29-31 . . . . .Frederick

AUGUST
1-3. . . . . . . .Lynchburg
5-7. . . . . . at Potomac
8-10. . . . . at Lynchburg
12-14 . . . . . .Lynchburg
15-17 . . . . at Wilmington
19-21 . . . . . . .Salem
22-25 . . . . . Carolina
26-29 . . . . at Myrtle Beach
30-31 . . . . . .at Carolina

SEPTEMBER
1 . . . . .at Carolina

FLORIDA STATE LEAGUE

BRADENTON MARAUDERS

APRIL
3-4. . . . . . . .at Charlotte
5-6. . . . . Charlotte
8-10. . . . . . . Palm Beach
11-13 . . . . Jupiter
14-16 . . . . at Palm Beach
17-19 . . . . Jupiter
21-22 . . . . Charlotte
23-24 . . . . . . at Charlotte
25-27 . . . . . . at St. Lucie
28-30 . . . . . at Fort Myers

MAY
1-3. . . . . St. Lucie
4-6. . . . . . . at Fort Myers
7 . . . . Charlotte
8-9. . . . . at Charlotte
10 . . . . Charlotte
12-15 . . . . . . .Lakeland
16-17 . . . . Dunedin
18-19 . . . . . . at Dunedin
20-23 . . . . Daytona
24 . . . . at Charlotte
25 . . . . Charlotte
27-28 . . . . . . .at Tampa
29-30 . . . . Tampa
31 . . . . at Clearwater

JUNE
1-3. . . . . . . at Clearwater
4-7. . . . at Brevard County

8 . . . . Charlotte
9 . . . . at Charlotte
10-12 . . . . . . Palm Beach
16-18 . . . . . at Fort Myers
19-21 . . . . . . at Jupiter
22-24 . . . . . Palm Beach
25-27 . . . . Jupiter
28-30 . . . . . at St. Lucie

JULY
1-3. . . . . .Fort Myers
4-6. . . . . . at Palm Beach
8-10. . . . . . . St. Lucie
11-12 . . . . Tampa
13-14 . . . . . . .at Tampa
16-19 . . . . . . Clearwater
20-21 . . . . . . at Dunedin
22-23 . . . . Dunedin
24-27 . . . . . . at Lakeland
28-31 . . . . . . at Daytona

AUGUST
1-4. . . . . . Brevard County
6-8. . . . . Jupiter
9-11. . . . . . . at St. Lucie
12-14 . . . . . . at Jupiter
15-17 . . . . St. Lucie
19-21 . . . . . . .Fort Myers
22-24 . . . . . at Palm Beach
25-27 . . . . . . .Fort Myers
28-29 . . . . . .at Charlotte
30-31 . . . . Charlotte

BREVARD COUNTY MANATEES

APRIL
3 . . . . Daytona
4 . . . . at Daytona
5 . . . . Daytona
7 . . . . at Daytona
8-10. . . . . . . at Lakeland
11-13 . . . . . . at Dunedin
14-16 . . . . . . .Lakeland
17-19 . . . . Dunedin
21-23 . . . . . . .at Tampa
24-25 . . . . Daytona
26-27 . . . . . . at Daytona
28-30 . . . . . .at Clearwater

MAY
1-3. . . . . Tampa
4-6. . . . . Clearwater
7 . . . . at Daytona
8-9. . . . . at Daytona
10 . . . . at Daytona
12-15 . . . . . . .Fort Myers

16-19 . . . . . . at Jupiter
20-23 . . . . at Palm Beach
24-25 . . . . Tampa
27-28 . . . . . . St. Lucie
29-30 . . . . . . at St. Lucie
31 . . . . .at Charlotte

JUNE
1-3. . . . . . . .at Charlotte
4-7. . . . . .Bradenton
8-9. . . . . Tampa
10-12 . . . . . . at Lakeland
16-18 . . . . Dunedin
19 . . . . Daytona
20 . . . . at Daytona
21-23 . . . . . . at Dunedin
24-26 . . . . . . .Lakeland
27-29 . . . . .at Clearwater

JULY
1 . . . . at Daytona
2 . . . . Daytona

3 . . . . at Daytona
4 . . . . Daytona
5-7. . . . . Clearwater
8-10. . . . . . . at Lakeland
11-14 . . . . Charlotte
16-17 . . . . . . at St. Lucie
18-19 . . . . St. Lucie
20-23 . . . . . at Fort Myers
24-27 . . . . . Palm Beach
28-31 . . . . Jupiter

CHARLOTTE STONE CRABS

APRIL
3-4. . . . . .Bradenton
5-6. . . . . . . at Bradenton
8-10. . . . . . at Fort Myers
11-13 . . . . . . Palm Beach
14-16 . . . . . . .Fort Myers
17-19 . . . . at Palm Beach
21-22 . . . . . at Bradenton
23-24 . . . . . . .Bradenton
25-27 . . . . . . at Jupiter
28-30 . . . . . at St. Lucie

MAY
1-3. . . . . Jupiter
4-6. . . . . St. Lucie
7 . . . . at Bradenton
8-9. . . . . .Bradenton
10 . . . . at Bradenton
12-15 . . . . . . at Daytona
16-19 . . . . . . Clearwater
20-23 . . . . . at Lakeland
24 . . . . Bradenton
25 . . . . at Bradenton
27-30 . . . . Dunedin
31 . . . . . Brevard County

JUNE
1-3. . . . . Brevard County
4-7. . . . . .at Tampa

8 . . . . at Bradenton
9 . . . . .Bradenton
10-12 . . . . . at Fort Myers
16-18 . . . . . . at St. Lucie
19 21 . . . . . . Palm Beach
22-24 . . . . . . .Fort Myers
25-27 . . . . at Palm Beach
28-30 . . . . . at Jupiter

JULY
1-3. . . . . St. Lucie
4-6. . . . . . at Fort Myers
8-10. . . . . Jupiter
11-14 . . .at Brevard County
16-19 . . . . . . .Lakeland
20-23 . . . .at Clearwater
25-27 . . . . . at Dunedin
28-31 . . . . Tampa

AUGUST
1-4. . . . . Daytona
6-8. . . . . . at Palm Beach
9-11. . . . . Jupiter
12-14 . . . . . . Palm Beach
15-17 . . . . . . at Jupiter
18-20 . . . . St. Lucie
22-24 . . . . . . .Fort Myers
25-27 . . . . . at St. Lucie
28-29 . . . . . . .Bradenton
30-31 . . . . . at Bradenton

CLEARWATER THRESHERS

APRIL
3 . . . . at Dunedin
4 . . . . Dunedin
5 . . . . at Dunedin
6 . . . . Dunedin
8-9. . . . . Tampa
10 . . . . .at Tampa
11-13 . . . . . . at Lakeland
14-16 . . . . . . .at Tampa
17-19 . . . . . . .Lakeland
21-23 . . . . Daytona
24 . . . . at Dunedin
25-26 . . . . Dunedin
27 . . . . at Dunedin
28-30 . . . . Brevard County

MAY
1-3. . . . . at Daytona
4-6. . . .at Brevard County
7 . . . . at Daytona
8 . . . . Dunedin
9 . . . . at Dunedin
10 . . . . Dunedin
12-15 . . . . Jupiter
16-19 . . . . . .at Charlotte
20-23 . . . . . at St. Lucie
24-25 . . . . . at Daytona
27-30 . . . . . . .Fort Myers
31 . . . . Bradenton

JUNE
1-3. . . . . .Bradenton

4-7. . . . . . at Palm Beach
8-10. . . . . Tampa
12 . . . . .at Tampa
16-17 . . . . . . .Lakeland
18 . . . . at Lakeland
19 . . . . at Dunedin
20 . . . . Dunedin
21-23 . . . . . . at Lakeland
24-26 . . . . Tampa
27-29 . . . . Brevard County

JULY
1 . . . . Dunedin
2 . . . . at Dunedin
3 . . . . Dunedin
4 . . . . at Dunedin
5-7. . . . .at Brevard County
8 . . . . Tampa
9 . . . . .at Tampa
10 . . . . Tampa
11-14 . . . . . . Palm Beach
16-19 . . . . . at Bradenton
20-23 . . . . Charlotte
24-27 . . . . . . at Jupiter
28-31 . . . . . at Fort Myers

AUGUST
1-4. . . . . St. Lucie
5-8. . . . . Daytona
9-11. . . .at Brevard County
13 . . . . Dunedin
14 . . . . at Dunedin

15-17 . . . . .Lakeland
18-21 . . . . at Daytona
22-24 . . . . Brevard County

26-27 . . . . .at Tampa
28 . . . . Tampa
29-31 . . . . . . at Lakeland

DAYTONA CUBS

APRIL
3 . . . . .at Brevard County
4 . . . . . . .at Brevard County
5 . . . . .at Brevard County
7 . . . . . . Brevard County
8-10 . . . . .Dunedin
11-13 . . . . Tampa
14-16 . . . . . . at Dunedin
17-19 . . . . Tampa
21-23 . . . . .at Clearwater
24-25 . . .at Brevard County
26-27 . . . . Brevard County
28-30 . . . . . . at Lakeland

MAY
1-3 . . . . Clearwater
4-6 . . . . .Lakeland
7 . . . . . . Brevard County
8-9 . . . .at Brevard County
10 . . . . . Brevard County
12-15 . . . . . . Charlotte
16-19 . . . . . at Fort Myers
20-23 . . . . . at Bradenton
24-25 . . . . . Clearwater
27-30 . . . . . . Palm Beach
31 . . . . at St. Lucie

JUNE
1-3 . . . . at St. Lucie
4-7 . . . . Jupiter
8-9 . . . . at Clearwater

DUNEDIN BLUE JAYS

APRIL
3 . . . . Clearwater
4 . . . . .at Clearwater
5 . . . . Clearwater
6 . . . . .at Clearwater
8-10 . . . . . . at Daytona
11-13 . . . . Brevard County
14-16 . . . . . . Daytona
17-19 . .at Brevard County
21-23 . . . . . . at Lakeland
24 . . . . Clearwater
25-26 . . . .at Clearwater
27 . . . . Clearwater
28-30 . . . . . . .at Tampa

MAY
1-2 . . . . .Lakeland
3 . . . . at Lakeland
4-6 . . . . Tampa
7 . . . . Clearwater
8 . . . . . .at Clearwater
9 . . . . Clearwater
10 . . . . . .at Clearwater
12-15 . . . . . at Palm Beach
16-17 . . . . . at Bradenton
18-19 . . . . . .Bradenton
20-23 . . . . . . .Fort Myers
24-25 . . . . . . .Lakeland
27-30 . . . . . .at Charlotte
31 . . . . at Jupiter

JUNE
1-3 . . . . at Jupiter
4-7 . . . . St. Lucie

10-12 . . . . . . at Dunedin
16-18 . . . . Tampa
19 . . . .at Brevard County
20 . . . . Brevard County
21-23 . . . . .at Tampa
24-26 . . . . .Dunedin
27-29 . . . . .Lakeland

JULY
1 . . . . . . Brevard County
2 . . . . .at Brevard County
3 . . . . . Brevard County
4 . . . .at Brevard County
5-7 . . . . at Lakeland
8-10 . . . . .Dunedin
11-14 . . . . . . at Jupiter
16-19 . . . . . . .Fort Myers
20-23 . . . . at Palm Beach
24-27 . . . . . . St. Lucie
28-31 . . . . . . .Bradenton

AUGUST
1-4 . . . . .at Charlotte
5-8 . . . . . .at Clearwater
9-11 . . . . .Lakeland
12 . . . . . Brevard County
14 . . . .at Brevard County
15-17 . . . . .at Tampa
18-21 . . . . . . Clearwater
22-24 . . . . at Lakeland
25-27 . . . . at Dunedin
29-31 . . . . Tampa

8 . . . . at Lakeland
9 . . . . .Lakeland
10-12 . . . . Daytona
16-18 . .at Brevard County
19 . . . . Clearwater
20 . . . . . .at Clearwater
21-23 . . . . Brevard County
24-26 . . . . at Daytona
27-29 . . . . . . .at Tampa

JULY
1 . . . . .at Clearwater
2 . . . . at Clearwater
3 . . . . at Clearwater
4 . . . . Clearwater
5-7 . . . . Tampa
8-10 . . . . . . at Daytona
11-14 . . . . . at Fort Myers
16-19 . . . . Jupiter
20-21 . . . . . . .Bradenton
22-23 . . . . . at Bradenton
24-27 . . . . . . Charlotte
28-31 . . . . . at St. Lucie

AUGUST
1-4 . . . . Palm Beach
5-8 . . . . . . at Lakeland
9-11 . . . . Tampa
13 . . . . . .at Clearwater
14 . . . . Clearwater
15-17 . . . . Brevard County
18-21 . . . . . . .Lakeland
22-24 . . . . . .at Tampa
25-27 . . . . . Daytona
29-31 . . .at Brevard County

FORT MYERS MIRACLE

APRIL
3-4 . . . . at Jupiter
5-6 . . . . Jupiter
8-10 . . . . Charlotte
11-13 . . . . . . St. Lucie
14-16 . . . . . .at Charlotte
17-19 . . . . . . St. Lucie
21-22 . . . . . . at Jupiter
23-24 . . . . Jupiter
25-27 . . . . Palm Beach
28-30 . . . . . . .Bradenton

MAY
1-3 . . . . . at Palm Beach
4-6 . . . . . . .Bradenton
7-8 . . . . at Jupiter
9-10 . . . . .Jupiter
12-15 . .at Brevard County
16-19 . . . . . . Daytona
20-23 . . . . at Dunedin
24-25 . . . . Jupiter
27-30 . . . .at Clearwater
31 . . . . Tampa

JUNE
1-3 . . . . Tampa
4-7 . . . . .Lakeland
8-9 . . . . . at Jupiter

10-12 . . . . Charlotte
16-18 . . . . . .Bradenton
19-21 . . . . . at St. Lucie
22-24 . . . .at Charlotte
25-27 . . . . . . St. Lucie
28-30 . . . . Palm Beach

JULY
1-3 . . . . . . at Bradenton
4-6 . . . . Charlotte
8-10 . . . . at Palm Beach
11-14 . . . . .Dunedin
16-19 . . . . . at Daytona
20-23 . . . Brevard County
24-27 . . . . . . .at Tampa
28-31 . . . . Clearwater

AUGUST
1-4 . . . . at Lakeland
6-8 . . . . . at St. Lucie
9-11 . . . . at Palm Beach
12-14 . . . . . . St. Lucie
15-17 . . . . Palm Beach
19-21 . . . . . at Bradenton
22-24 . . . .at Charlotte
25-27 . . . . at Bradenton
28-29 . . . . Jupiter
30-31 . . . . . at Jupiter

JUPITER HAMMERHEADS

APRIL
3-4 . . . . .Fort Myers
5-6 . . . . . at Fort Myers
8-10 . . . . . . St. Lucie
11-13 . . . . . . .Bradenton
14-16 . . . . at St. Lucie
17-19 . . . . at Bradenton
21-22 . . . . . . .Fort Myers
23-24 . . . at Fort Myers
25-27 . . . . . . Charlotte
28-30 . . . . . . Palm Beach

MAY
1-3 . . . . .at Charlotte
4-6 . . . . Palm Beach
7-8 . . . . . . .Fort Myers
9-10 . . . . at Fort Myers
12-15 . . . . at Clearwater
16-19 . . . . Brevard County
20-23 . . . . . . .at Tampa
24-25 . . . . . at Fort Myers
27-30 . . . . . . .Lakeland
31 . . . . .Dunedin

JUNE
1-3 . . . . .Dunedin
4-7 . . . . at Daytona

8-9 . . . . .Fort Myers
10-12 . . . . . . St. Lucie
16-18 . . . . Palm Beach
19-21 . . . . . . .Bradenton
22-24 . . . . . . St. Lucie
25-27 . . . . at Bradenton
28-30 . . . . Charlotte

JULY
1-3 . . . . Palm Beach
4-6 . . . . . . at St. Lucie
8-10 . . . . . .at Charlotte
11-14 . . . . . . Daytona
16-19 . . . . at Dunedin
20-23 . . . . . . at Lakeland
24-27 . . . . . Clearwater
28-31 . . .at Brevard County

AUGUST
1-4 . . . . Tampa
6-8 . . . . . . at Bradenton
9-11 . . . . . . .at Charlotte
12-14 . . . . . . .Bradenton
15-17 . . . . . . Charlotte
19-21 . . . . . . Palm Beach
28-29 . . . . . at Fort Myers
30-31 . . . . . . .Fort Myers

LAKELAND FLYING TIGERS

APRIL
3 . . . . Tampa
4 . . . . .at Tampa
5 . . . . Tampa
6 . . . . .at Tampa
8-10 . . . . Brevard County
11-13 . . . . Clearwater
14-16 . . .at Brevard County
17-19 . . . at Clearwater
21-23 . . . . . . .Dunedin
24-25 . . . . Tampa
26-27 . . . . . . .at Tampa
28-30 . . . . Daytona

MAY
1-2 . . . . at Dunedin

3 . . . . .Dunedin
4-6 . . . . at Daytona
7 . . . . .at Tampa
8 . . . . Tampa
9-10 . . . . .at Tampa
12-15 . . . . . at Bradenton
16-19 . . . . . . St. Lucie
20-23 . . . . . Charlotte
24-25 . . . . at Dunedin
27-30 . . . . . at Jupiter
31 . . . . Palm Beach

JUNE
1-3 . . . . Palm Beach
4-7 . . . . at Fort Myers
8 . . . . .Dunedin

9 . . . . at Dunedin	11-14 . . . . . . at St. Lucie	4-6 . . . . at Charlotte
10-12 . . . . Brevard County	16-19 . . . . . at Charlotte	7-8 . . . . Palm Beach
16-17 . . . . . at Clearwater	20-23 . . . . Jupiter	9-10 . . . . at Palm Beach
18 . . . . Clearwater	24-27 . . . . . . .Bradenton	12-15 . . . . Tampa
19 . . . . .at Tampa	28-31 . . . . at Palm Beach	16-19 . . . . . at Lakeland
20 . . . . Tampa	**AUGUST**	20-23 . . . . . Clearwater
21 . . . . at Clearwater	1-4 . . . . .Fort Myers	24-25 . . . . at Palm Beach
22-23 . . . . . Clearwater	5-8 . . . . Dunedin	27-28 . . .at Brevard County
24-26 . . .at Brevard County	9-11 . . . . . at Daytona	29-30 . . . Brevard County
27-29 . . . . . at Daytona	13 . . . . .at Tampa	31 . . . . Daytona
JULY	14 . . . . Tampa	**JUNE**
1-2 . . . . Tampa	15-17 . . .at Clearwater	1-3 . . . . Daytona
3 . . . . .at Tampa	18-21 . . . . . at Dunedin	4-7 . . . . at Dunedin
4 . . . . Tampa	22-24 . . . . Daytona	8-9 . . . . Palm Beach
5-7 . . . . Daytona	26-28 . . .at Brevard County	10-12 . . . . . at Jupiter
8-10 . . . . . Brevard County	29-31 . . . . Clearwater	16-18 . . . . . . Charlotte

PALM BEACH CARDINALS

APRIL	10-12 . . . . . at Bradenton	19-21 . . . . . .Fort Myers
3-4 . . . . at St. Lucie	16-18 . . . . Jupiter	22-24 . . . . . at Jupiter
5-6 . . . . St. Lucie	19-21 . . . . .at Charlotte	25-27 . . . . at Fort Myers
8-10 . . . . at Bradenton	22-24 . . . . . at Bradenton	28-30 . . . . . .Bradenton
11-13 . . . . . .at Charlotte	25-27 . . . . . . Charlotte	
14-16 . . . . . .Bradenton	28-30 . . . . . at Fort Myers	
17-19 . . . . . . Charlotte	**JULY**	## TAMPA YANKEES
21-22 . . . . at St. Lucie	1-3 . . . . Jupiter	
23-24 . . . . . . St. Lucie	4-6. . . . . .Bradenton	**APRIL**
25-27 . . . at Fort Myers	8-10 . . . . . . .Fort Myers	3 . . . . at Lakeland
28-30 . . . . Jupiter	11-14 . . . . .at Clearwater	4 . . . . .Lakeland
MAY	16-19 . . . . Tampa	5 . . . . at Lakeland
1-3 . . . . .Fort Myers	20-23 . . . . Daytona	6 . . . . .Lakeland
4-6 . . . . Jupiter	24-27 . . .at Brevard County	8-9 . . . . . .at Clearwater
7-8 . . . . at St. Lucie	28-31 . . . . . . .Lakeland	10 . . . . Clearwater
9-10 . . . . St. Lucie	**AUGUST**	11-13 . . . . Daytona
12-15 . . . . . . .Dunedin	1-4 . . . . at Dunedin	14-16 . . . . . . Clearwater
16-19 . . . . . . .at Tampa	6-8. . . . . Charlotte	17-19 . . . . . at Daytona
20-23 . . . Brevard County	9-11 . . . . . . .Fort Myers	21-23 . . . . Brevard County
24-25 . . . . . . St. Lucie	12-14 . . . . .at Charlotte	24-25 . . . . at Lakeland
27-30 . . . . at Daytona	15-17 . . . . . at Fort Myers	26-27 . . . . . .Lakeland
31 . . . . at Lakeland	19-21 . . . . Jupiter	28-30 . . . . . . Dunedin
JUNE	22-24 . . . . . .Bradenton	**MAY**
1-3 . . . . . . at Lakeland	25-27 . . . . . . Jupiter	1-3 . . . .at Brevard County
4-7 . . . . Clearwater	28-29 . . . . St. Lucie	4-6 . . . . . . at Dunedin
8-9 . . . . at St. Lucie	30-31 . . . . . at St. Lucie	7 . . . . .Lakeland
		8 . . . . at Lakeland

ST. LUCIE METS

APRIL	21-22 . . . . . . Palm Beach	9-10 . . . . Lakeland
3-4 . . . . Palm Beach	23-24 . . . . at Palm Beach	12-15 . . . . . at St. Lucie
5-6 . . . . . at Palm Beach	25-27 . . . . . .Bradenton	16-19 . . . . . Palm Beach
8-10 . . . . at Jupiter	28-30 . . . . . . Charlotte	20-23 . . . . Jupiter
11-13 . . . . . .Fort Myers	**MAY**	24-25 . . .at Brevard County
14-16 . . . . Jupiter	1-3 . . . . at Bradenton	27-28 . . . . . .Bradenton
17-19 . . . . . at Fort Myers		29-30 . . . . . at Bradenton
		31 . . . . at Fort Myers
		JUNE
		1-3 . . . . . . at Fort Myers
		4-7 . . . . Charlotte
		8-9 . . .at Brevard County
		10 . . . . . .at Clearwater
		12 . . . . Clearwater

(Tampa Yankees continued, right column)

JULY	**AUGUST**
1-3 . . . . .at Charlotte	1-4 . . . . at Jupiter
4-6 . . . . Jupiter	5-8 . . . . . Brevard County
8-10 . . . . . . at Bradenton	9-11 . . . . . . at Dunedin
11-14 . . . . . . .Lakeland	13 . . . . .Lakeland
16-17 . . . Brevard County	14 . . . . at Lakeland
18-19 . . .at Brevard County	15-17 . . . . Daytona
20-23 . . . . . .at Tampa	18-19 . . .at Brevard County
24-27 . . . at Daytona	20-21 . . . Brevard County
28-31 . . . . Dunedin	22-24 . . . . . . Dunedin
16-18 . . . . . . at Daytona	26-27 . . . . . . Clearwater
19 . . . . .Lakeland	28 . . . . . .at Clearwater
20 . . . . . . at Lakeland	29-31 . . . . . at Daytona
21-23 . . . . Daytona	
24-26 . . . . .at Clearwater	
27-29 . . . . Dunedin	
JULY	
1-2 . . . . at Lakeland	
3 . . . . .Lakeland	
4 . . . . at Lakeland	
5-7 . . . . at Dunedin	
8 . . . . .at Clearwater	
9 . . . . Clearwater	
10 . . . . .at Clearwater	
11-12 . . . . . at Bradenton	
13-14 . . . . . . .Bradenton	
16-19 . . . . at Palm Beach	
20-23 . . . . St. Lucie	
24-27 . . . . . . .Fort Myers	
28-31 . . . . . .at Charlotte	

LOW CLASS A

MIDWEST LEAGUE

BELOIT SNAPPERS

APRIL	**MAY**	28-30 . . . . . at Quad Cities	8-10 . . . . .Burlington
3-6. . . . . .Burlington	1 . . . . Peoria	31 . . . . .Clinton	11-14 . . . . at Kane County
8-10 . . . . . at South Bend	2-4 . . . . Quad Cities	**JUNE**	16-18 . . . . .Dayton
11-13 . . .at West Michigan	5-7 . . . . .at Peoria	1-2 . . . . .Clinton	19-21 . . . . . Bowling Green
14-16 . . . . . . Great Lakes	8-10 . . . . . at Quad Cities	4-6 . . . . Peoria	23-25 . . . . .at Fort Wayne
17-19 . . . . Lansing	12-14 . . . . . Kane County	7-9 . . . . . . at Burlington	26-28 . . . . .at Lake County
21-24 . . . at Kane County	15-18 . . . . . . at Clinton	10-12 . . . . . at Wisconsin	29-31 . . . . Peoria
25-27 . . . . at Burlington	19-21 . . . . at Cedar Rapids	13-15 . . . . . Kane County	**AUGUST**
28-30 . . . . Peoria	22-24 . . . . Wisconsin	19-22 . . . . .Clinton	1-3 . . . . Cedar Rapids
	25-27 . . . . . . Cedar Rapids	24-26 . . . . . at Burlington	4-6 . . . . at Clinton
		27-30 . . . . . Kane County	7-10 . . at Quad Cities 12-14 Cedar Rapids
		JULY	15-17 . . . . at Clinton
		1-3 . . . . Quad Cities	18-20 . . . . .at Peoria
		4-6 . . . . . at Cedar Rapids	21-23 . . . . . . Quad Cities

24-26 . . . . . at Wisconsin
27-29 . . . . at Peoria
30-31 . . . . Wisconsin

1 . . . . Wisconsin

BOWLING GREEN HOT RODS

APRIL
3-6 . . . . South Bend
8-10 . . . . . . at Burlington
11-13 . . . . at Peoria
14-16 . . . . . Kane County
17-19 . . . . Clinton
21-24 . . . at West Michigan
25-27 . . . . at Lansing
28-30 . . . . South Bend

MAY
1 . . . . South Bend
2-4 . . . . Great Lakes
5-7 . . . . . . at South Bend
8-10 . . . . . at Lake County
12-14 . . . . Lansing
15-18 . . . at Great Lakes
19-21 . . . . . . at Lansing
22-24 . . . . . Lake County
25-27 . . . . West Michigan
28-30 . . . . . Fort Wayne
31 . . . . . . at South Bend

JUNE
1-2 . . . . . at South Bend
4-6 . . . . Dayton
7-9 . . . . Fort Wayne
10-12 . . . . . . at Dayton
13-15 . . . . . at Fort Wayne

19-22 . . . . at Lansing
24-26 . . . . . Lake County
27-30 . . . at West Michigan

JULY
1-3 . . . . . . at Lake County
4-6 . . . . Dayton
8-10 . . . . West Michigan
11-14 . . . . Lansing
16-18 . . . . at Wisconsin
19-21 . . . . . . at Beloit
23-25 . . . . Cedar Rapids
26-28 . . . . Quad Cities
29-31 . . . at South Bend

AUGUST
1-3 . . . . . at Lake County
4-6 . . . . . . South Bend
7-10 . . . . Dayton
12-14 . . . . at Great Lakes
15-17 . . . . . at Dayton
18-20 . . . . Lake County
21-23 . . . . Great Lakes
24-26 . . . at Fort Wayne
27-29 . . . at South Bend
30-31 . . . . . Fort Wayne

SEPTEMBER
1 . . . . Fort Wayne

BURLINGTON BEES

APRIL
3-6 . . . . at Beloit
8-10 . . . . Bowling Green
11-13 . . . . Dayton
14-16 . . . . at Fort Wayne
17-19 . . . at Lake County
21-24 . . . . . Wisconsin
25-27 . . . . Beloit
28-30 . . . . . at Wisconsin

MAY
1 . . . . at Wisconsin
2-4 . . . . at Kane County
5-7 . . . . Clinton
8-10 . . . . . Kane County
12-14 . . . . . . at Clinton
15-18 . . . . Cedar Rapids
19-21 . . . at Quad Cities
22-24 . . . . Peoria
25-27 . . . . Quad Cities
28-30 . . . . . . at Peoria
31 . . . . . at Cedar Rapids

JUNE
1-2 . . . . . at Cedar Rapids
4-6 . . . . . . Quad Cities
7-9 . . . . Beloit
10-12 . . . . . . at Clinton
13-15 . . . at Cedar Rapids

19-22 . . . . . . Wisconsin
24-26 . . . . Beloit
27-30 . . . at Wisconsin

JULY
1-3 . . . . Clinton
4-6 . . . . at Peoria
8-10 . . . . . . at Beloit
11-14 . . . . . . Peoria
16-18 . . . at South Bend
19-21 . . at West Michigan
23-25 . . . . . Great Lakes
26-28 . . . . . . Lansing
29-31 . . at Cedar Rapids

AUGUST
1-3 . . . . Clinton
4-6 . . . . at Quad Cities
7-10 . . . . . . at Clinton
12-14 . . . . . . Peoria
15-17 . . . at Quad Cities
18-20 . . at Kane County
21-23 . . . . Cedar Rapids
24-26 . . . . Kane County
27-29 . . . at Wisconsin
30-31 . . . . Quad Cities

SEPTEMBER
1 . . . . Quad Cities

CEDAR RAPIDS KERNELS

APRIL
3-6 . . . . Clinton
8-10 . . . . at Great Lakes
11-13 . . . . . . at Lansing
14-16 . . . . . South Bend
17-19 . . . West Michigan
21-24 . . . . . . at Peoria
25-27 . . . . . at Clinton

28-30 . . . . . Kane County

MAY
1 . . . . Kane County
2-4 . . . . Peoria
5-7 . . . . at Quad Cities
8-10 . . . at Wisconsin
12-14 . . . . Peoria
15-18 . . . . at Burlington

19-21 . . . . Beloit
22-24 . . . at Quad Cities
25-27 . . . . . at Beloit
28-30 . . . . . . Wisconsin
31 . . . . Burlington

JUNE
1-2 . . . . Burlington
4-6 . . . . . . at Wisconsin
7-9 . . . . at Kane County
10-12 . . . Quad Cities
13-15 . . . . Burlington
19-22 . . . at Kane County
24-26 . . . . . . at Peoria
27-30 . . . . Clinton

JULY
1-3 . . . . . at Wisconsin
4-6 . . . . Beloit
8-10 . . . . . Wisconsin
11-14 . . . . . at Clinton

CLINTON LUMBERKINGS

APRIL
3-6 . . . . at Cedar Rapids
8-10 . . . . . Lake County
11-13 . . . . . Fort Wayne
14-16 . . . . . at Dayton
17-19 . . at Bowling Green
21-24 . . . . Quad Cities
25-27 . . . . Cedar Rapids
28-30 . . . at Quad Cities

MAY
1 . . . . . at Quad Cities
2-4 . . . . . at Wisconsin
5-7 . . . . . at Burlington
8-10 . . . . Peoria
12-14 . . . . . Burlington
15-18 . . . . Beloit
19-21 . . . . . . at Peoria
22-24 . . at Kane County
25-27 . . . . Wisconsin
28-30 . . . Kane County
31 . . . . at Beloit

JUNE
1-2 . . . . . . at Beloit
4-6 . . . . at Kane County
7-9 . . . . Wisconsin
10-12 . . . . . Burlington
13-15 . . . . . . at Peoria

19-22 . . . . at Beloit
24-26 . . . . . Quad Cities
27-30 . . . at Cedar Rapids

JULY
1-3 . . . . . . at Burlington
4-6 . . . . . . Kane County
8-10 . . . . at Peoria
11-14 . . . . Cedar Rapids
16-18 . . . at Great Lakes
19-21 . . . . . at Lansing
23-25 . . . West Michigan
26-28 . . . . South Bend
19-31 . . . at Quad Cities

AUGUST
1-3 . . . . . at Burlington
4-6 . . . . Beloit
7-10 . . . . . Burlington
12-14 . . . at Wisconsin
15-17 . . . . Beloit
18-20 . . . . Wisconsin
21-23 . . at Kane County
24-26 . . . . . . Peoria
27-29 . . . at Quad Cities
30-31 . . . . Cedar Rapids

SEPTEMBER
1 . . . . Cedar Rapids

DAYTON DRAGONS

APRIL
3-6 . . . . . West Michigan
8-10 . . . . at Peoria
11-13 . . . . at Burlington
14-16 . . . . Clinton
17-19 . . . . . Kane County
21-24 . . . at South Bend
25-27 . . . at Great Lakes
28-30 . . . . Lansing

MAY
1 . . . . Lansing
2-4 . . . . at Lake County
5-7 . . . . at Great Lakes
8-10 . . . . . Fort Wayne
12-14 . . . . . South Bend
15-18 . . . . . . at Lansing
19-21 . . . . Great Lakes
22-24 . . . . West Michigan
25-27 . . . at Fort Wayne
28-30 . . at West Michigan
31 . . . . Lansing

JUNE
1-2 . . . . Lansing

4-6 . . . . at Bowling Green
7-9 . . . . . . at Lake County
10-12 . . . . Bowling Green
13-15 . . . . . Lake County
19-22 . . . . at Great Lakes
24-26 . . . at Fort Wayne
27-30 . . . . . Lake County

JULY
1-3 . . . . Fort Wayne
4-6 . . . . at Bowling Green
8-10 . . . . . . South Bend
11-14 . . . . West Michigan
16-18 . . . . . . at Beloit
19-21 . . . . at Wisconsin
23-25 . . . . Quad Cities
26-28 . . . . Cedar Rapids
29-31 . . . . . . at Lansing

AUGUST
1-3 . . . . South Bend
4-6 . . . . Great Lakes
7-10 . . . at Bowling Green
12-14 . . . at Lake County
15-17 . . . . Bowling Green

18-20 . . . . . at South Bend
21-23 . . . at West Michigan
24-26 . . . . . . Great Lakes
27-29 . . . . Lansing

30-31 . . . . . at Lake County

SEPTEMBER
1 . . . . at Lake County

FORT WAYNE TINCAPS

APRIL
3-6 . . . . Great Lakes
8-10 . . . . at Kane County
10-13 . . . . at Clinton
14-16 . . . . . . .Burlington
17-19 . . . . Peoria
21-24 . . . . . at Great Lakes
25-27 . . . at West Michigan
28-30 . . . . . Great Lakes

MAY
1 . . . . Great Lakes
2-4 . . . . South Bend
5 7 . . . . .at Lansing
8-10 . . . . at Dayton
12-14 . . . . . Lake County
15-18 . . . at South Bend
19-21 . . . .at Lake County
22-24 . . . . Lansing
25-27 . . . . .Dayton
28-30 . . . at Bowling Green
31 . . . . West Michigan

JUNE
1-2 . . . . West Michigan
4-6 . . . . . .at Lake County
7-9 . . . . at Bowling Green
10-12 . . . . Lansing
13-15 . . . . . Bowling Green

19 . . . . at West Michigan
21-22 . . . at West Michigan
24-26 . . . . .Dayton
27-30 . . . . at South Bend

JULY
1 3 . . . . at Dayton
4-6 . . . . . . West Michigan
8-10 . . . . at Great Lakes
11-14 . . . . . South Bend
16-18 . . . . at Quad Cities
19-21 . . . at Cedar Rapids
23-25 . . . . .Beloit
26-28 . . . . . . Wisconsin
29-31 . . . . at Great Lakes

AUGUST
1-3 . . . . at West Michigan
4-6 . . . . Lansing
7-10 . . . . . Lake County
12-14 . . . . . .at Lansing
15-17 . . . . . Lake County
18-20 . . . . . . Great Lakes
21-23 . . . .at Lake County
24-26 . . . . . Bowling Green
27-29 . . . . West Michigan
30-31 . . . at Bowling Green

SEPTEMBER
1 . . . . . . at Bowling Green

GREAT LAKES LOONS

APRIL
3-6 . . . . . . .at Fort Wayne
8-10 . . . . . Cedar Rapids
11-13 . . . . . . Quad Cities
14-16 . . . . at Beloit
17-19 . . . . at Wisconsin
21-24 . . . . . Fort Wayne
25-27 . . . . .Dayton
28-30 . . .at Fort Wayne

MAY
1 . . . . .at Fort Wayne
2-4 . . . at Bowling Green
5-7 . . . . .Dayton
8 10 . . . . . at South Bend
12-14 . . . . . West Michigan
15-18 . . . . Bowling Green
19-21 . . . . . . at Dayton
22-24 . . . . . . South Bend
25-27 . . . .at Lake County
28-30 . . . . .at Lansing
31 . . . . Lake County

JUNE
1-2 . . . . . . Lake County
4-6 . . . . at West Michigan
7-9 . . . . .at Lansing
10-12 . . . . West Michigan
13-15 . . . . Lansing

19-22 . . . . .Dayton
24-26 . . . . at South Bend
27-30 . . . . Lansing

JULY
1-3 . . . . South Bend
4-6 . . . . .at Lansing
8-10 . . . . Fort Wayne
11-14 . . . .at Lake County
16-18 . . . . .Clinton
19-21 . . . . . Kane County
23-25 . . . . at Burlington
26-28 . . . . at Peoria
29-31 . . . . . . Fort Wayne

AUGUST
1-3 . . . . Lansing
4-6 . . . . at Dayton
7-10 . . . . at South Bend
12-14 . . . . Bowling Green
15-17 . . . . West Michigan
18-20 . . . .at Fort Wayne
21-23 . . . at Bowling Green
24-26 . . . . at Dayton
27-29 . . . . . Lake County
30-31 . . . at West Michigan

SEPTEMBER
1 . . . . . . at West Michigan

KANE COUNTY COUGARS

APRIL
3-6 . . . . . . at Quad Cities
8-10 . . . . Fort Wayne
11-13 . . . . . Lake County
14-16 . . . at Bowling Green
17-19 . . . . . . at Dayton
21-24 . . . . .Beloit

25-27 . . . . Wisconsin
28-30 . . . . at Cedar Rapids

MAY
1 . . . . . . at Cedar Rapids
2-4 . . . . .Burlington
5-7 . . . . Wisconsin

8-10 . . . . . . at Burlington
12-14 . . . . Beloit
15-18 . . . . . Quad Cities
19-21 . . . at Wisconsin
22-24 . . . . Clinton
25-27 . . . . Peoria
28-30 . . . . at Clinton
31 . . . . at Peoria

JUNE
1-2 . . . . .at Peoria
4-6 . . . . .Clinton
7-9 . . . . . Cedar Rapids
10-12 . . . . at Peoria
13-15 . . . . at Beloit
19-22 . . . . Cedar Rapids
24-26 . . . . . Wisconsin
27-30 . . . . . . at Beloit

JULY
1-3 . . . . Peoria
4-6 . . . . at Clinton

LAKE COUNTY CAPTAINS

APRIL
4-6 . . . . Lansing
8-10 . . . . at Clinton
11-13 . . . at Kane County
14-16 . . . . . . Peoria
17-19 . . . . . .Burlington
21-24 . . . . . .at Lansing
25-27 . . . at South Bend
28-30 . . . West Michigan

MAY
1 . . . . . . West Michigan
2-4 . . . . .Dayton
5-7 . . . at West Michigan
8-10 . . . . Bowling Green
12-14 . . . . .at Fort Wayne
15-18 . . . at West Michigan
19-21 . . . . . . Fort Wayne
22-24 . . . at Bowling Green
25-27 . . . . . Great Lakes
28-30 . . . . . South Bend
31 . . . . . . at Great Lakes

JUNE
1-2 . . . . . at Great Lakes
4-6 . . . . Fort Wayne
7-9 . . . . .Dayton
10 12 . . . . at South Bend
13-15 . . . . at Dayton

19-22 . . . . . . South Bend
24-26 . . . .Bowling Green
27-30 . . . . at Dayton

JULY
1-3 . . . . . .Bowling Green
4-6 . . . . . . at South Bend
8-10 . . . . Lansing
11-14 . . . . . Great Lakes
16-18 . . . . at Cedar Rapids
19-21 . . . . at Quad Cities
23-25 . . . . . . Wisconsin
26-28 . . . . .Beloit
29-31 . . . at West Michigan

AUGUST
1-3 . . . . . . .Bowling Green
4-6 . . . . . . West Michigan
7-10 . . . . . .at Fort Wayne
12-14 . . . . .Dayton
15-17 . . . . .at Fort Wayne
18-20 . . . at Bowling Green
21-23 . . . . . . Fort Wayne
24-26 . . . . . . .at Lansing
27-29 . . . at Great Lakes
30 31 . . . . .Dayton

SEPTEMBER
1 . . . . .Dayton

LANSING LUGNUTS

APRIL
4-6 . . . . . .at Lake County
8-10 . . . . . Quad Cities
11-13 . . . . . . Cedar Rapids
14-16 . . . . at Wisconsin
17-19 . . . . . . at Beloit
21-24 . . . . . Lake County
25-27 . . . .Bowling Green
28-30 . . . . at Dayton

MAY
1 . . . . at Dayton
2-4 . . . . . . West Michigan
5-7 . . . . Fort Wayne
8-10 . . . . at West Michigan
12-14 . . . at Bowling Green
15-18 . . . . .Dayton
19-21 . . . . . Bowling Green
22-24 . . . .at Fort Wayne
25-27 . . . at South Bend
28-30 . . . . . . Great Lakes
31 . . . . at Dayton

JUNE
1-2 . . . . at Dayton
4-6 . . . . South Bend
7-9 . . . . Great Lakes
10-12 . . . .at Fort Wayne
13-15 . . . . . at Great Lakes
19-22 . . . . . Bowling Green
24-26 . . . . . West Michigan
27-30 . . . . at Great Lakes

JULY
1-3 . . . . . at West Michigan
4-6 . . . . Great Lakes
8-10 . . . .at Lake County
11-14 . . . at Bowling Green
16-18 . . . . . Kane County
19-21 . . . . .Clinton
23-25 . . . . at Peoria
26-28 . . . at Burlington
29-31 . . . . .Dayton

AUGUST
1-3 . . . . . . at Great Lakes
4-6 . . . . . . .at Fort Wayne

7-10 . . . . . West Michigan
12-14 . . . . Fort Wayne
15-17 . . . at South Bend
18-20 . . at West Michigan
21-23 . . . . . . South Bend

24-26 . . . . . Lake County
27-29 . . . . at Dayton
30-31 . . . . . South Bend

SEPTEMBER
1 . . . . South Bend

PEORIA CHIEFS

APRIL
3-6 . . . . at Wisconsin
8-10 . . . . Dayton
11-13 . . . Bowling Green
14-16 . . . at Lake County
17-19 . . . at Fort Wayne
21-24 . . . . Cedar Rapids
25-27 . . . . . Quad Cities
28-30 . . . . . . at Beloit

MAY
1 . . . . at Beloit
2-4 . . . . . at Cedar Rapids
5-7 . . . . Beloit
8-10 . . . . at Clinton
12-14 . . . at Cedar Rapids
15-18 . . . . Wisconsin
19-21 . . . . Clinton
22-24 . . . at Burlington
25-27 . . . at Kane County
28-30 . . . . . Burlington
31 . . . . . Kane County

JUNE
1-2 . . . . Kane County
4-6 . . . . . . at Beloit
7-9 . . . at Quad Cities
10-12 . . Kane County
13-15 . . . . . Clinton

19-22 . . . . at Quad Cities
24-26 . . . . Cedar Rapids
27-30 . . . . . Quad Cities

JULY
1-3 . . . . at Kane County
4-6 . . . . Burlington
8-10 . . . . Clinton
11-14 . . . . at Burlington
16-18 . . at West Micigan
19-21 . . . at South Bend
23-25 . . . . . Lansing
26-28 . . . . . Great Lakes
29-31 . . . . . at Beloit

AUGUST
1-3 . . . . . . at Wisconsin
4-6 . . . . . Kane County
7-10 . . . . . Wisconsin
12-14 . . . . at Burlington
15-17 . . at Cedar Rapids
18-20 . . . . Beloit
21-23 . . . . . Wisconsin
24-26 . . . . . at Clinton
27-29 . . . . Beloit
30-31 . . . at Kane County

SEPTEMBER
1 . . . . . at Kane County

QUAD CITIES RIVER BANDITS

APRIL
3-6 . . . . . Kane County
8-10 . . . . . . at Lansing
11-13 . . at Great Lakes
14-16 . . . West Michigan
17-19 . . . . . South Bend
21-24 . . . . . at Peoria
25-27 . . . . . at Clinton

MAY
1 . . . . Clinton
2-4 . . . . . . at Beloit
5-7 . . . . . Cedar Rapids
8-10 . . . . Beloit
12-14 . . . at Wisconsin
15-18 . . . at Kane County
19-21 . . . . . Burlington
22-24 . . . . Cedar Rapids
25-27 . . . at Burlington
28-30 . . . . Beloit
31 . . . . . . at Wisconsin

JUNE
1-2 . . . . at Wisconsin
4-6 . . . . . . at Burlington
7-9 . . . . Peoria
10-12 . . at Cedar Rapids
13-15 . . . . . Wisconsin

19-22 . . . . Peoria
24-26 . . . . . . at Clinton
27-30 . . . . at Peoria

JULY
1-3 . . . . at Beloit
4-6 . . . . Wisconsin
8-10 . . . . . Kane County
11-14 . . . at Wisconsin
16-18 . . . . . Fort Wayne
19-21 . . . . . Lake County
23-25 . . . . . . at Dayton
26-28 . . at Bowling Green
29-31 . . . . Clinton

AUGUST
1-3 . . . . at Kane County
4-6 . . . . Burlington
7-10 . . . . Beloit
12-14 . . . at Kane County
15-17 . . . . . Burlington
18-20 . . at Cedar Rapids
21-23 . . . . . at Beloit
24-26 . . . . . Cedar Rapids
27-29 . . . . . . Clinton
30-31 . . . . at Burlington

SEPTEMBER
1 . . . . at Burlington

SOUTH BEND SILVER HAWKS

APRIL
3-6 . . . . at Bowling Green
8-10 . . . . Beloit
11-13 . . . . . Wisconsin
14-16 . . . at Cedar Rapids
17-19 . . . . at Quad Cities

21-24 . . . . Dayton
25-27 . . . . . Lake County
28-30 . . at Bowling Green

MAY
1 . . . . at Bowling Green
2-4 . . . . . . at Fort Wayne

5-7 . . . . . Bowling Green
8-10 . . . . . . Great Lakes
12-14 . . . . . . at Dayton
15-18 . . . . . Fort Wayne
19-21 . . at West Michigan
22-24 . . . at Great Lakes
25-27 . . . . . . Lansing
28-30 . . at Lake County
31 . . . . . Bowling Green

JUNE
1-2 . . . . Bowling Green
4-6 . . . . . . at Lansing
7-9 . . . at West Michigan
10-12 . . . Lake County
13-15 . . . West Michigan
19-22 . . at Lake County
24-26 . . . . Great Lakes
27-30 . . . . . Fort Wayne

JULY
1-3 . . . . at Great Lakes
4-6 . . . . . Lake County

WEST MICHIGAN WHITECAPS

APRIL
3-6 . . . . at Dayton
8-10 . . . . . . Wisconsin
11-13 . . . . Beloit
14-16 . . at Quad Cities
17-19 . . at Cedar Rapids
21-24 . . . Bowling Green
25-27 . . . . Fort Wayne
28-30 . . at Lake County

MAY
1 . . . . . at Lake County
2-4 . . . . at Lansing
5-7 . . . . . Lake County
8-10 . . . . Lansing
12-14 . . at Great Lakes
15-18 . . . Lake County
19-21 . . . . . South Bend
22-24 . . . . . at Dayton
25-27 . . at Bowling Green
28-30 . . . . . Dayton
31 . . . . . at Fort Wayne

JUNE
1-2 . . . . at Fort Wayne
4-6 . . . . Great Lakes
7-9 . . . . . South Bend
10-12 . . at Great Lakes
13-15 . . at South Bend

19 . . . . Fort Wayne
21-22 . . . . Fort Wayne
24-26 . . . . at Lansing
27-30 . . . Bowling Green

JULY
1-3 . . . . . . Lansing
4-6 . . . . . at Fort Wayne
8-10 . . . at Bowling Green
11-14 . . . . . at Dayton
16-18 . . . . Peoria
19-21 . . . . Burlington
23-25 . . . . at Clinton
26-28 . . at Kane County
29-31 . . . . . Lake County

AUGUST
1-3 . . . . . . Fort Wayne
4-6 . . . at Lake County
7-10 . . . . . at Lansing
12-14 . . . . South Bend
15-17 . . at Great Lakes
18-20 . . . . . Lansing
21-23 . . . . . . Dayton
24-26 . . . at South Bend
27-29 . . at Fort Wayne
30-31 . . . . . Great Lakes

SEPTEMBER
1 . . . . Great Lakes

WISCONSIN TIMBER RATTLERS

APRIL
3-6 . . . . Peoria
8-10 . . at West Michigan
11-13 . . at South Bend
14-16 . . . . . Lansing
17-19 . . . . Great Lakes
21-24 . . . at Burlington
25-27 . . at Kane County
28-30 . . . . . . Burlington

MAY
1 . . . . Burlington
2-4 . . . . Clinton
5-7 . . . at Kane County
8-10 . . . Cedar Rapids
12-14 . . . Quad Cities
15-18 . . . . . Peoria
19-21 . . . Kane County
22-24 . . . . at Beloit
25-27 . . . . at Clinton
28-30 . . at Cedar Rapids
31 . . . . Quad Cities

JUNE
1-2 . . . . . Quad Cities
4-6 . . . . . Cedar Rapids
7-9 . . . . . . at Clinton
10-12 . . . . . Beloit
13-15 . . at Quad Cities
19-22 . . . at Burlington
24-26 . . at Kane County
27-30 . . . . . Burlington

JULY
1-3 . . . . . Cedar Rapids
4-6 . . . . at Quad Cities
8-10 . . at Cedar Rapids
11-14 . . . Quad Cities
16-18 . . . Bowling Green
19-21 . . . . . Dayton
23-25 . . at Lake County
26-28 . . at Fort Wayne
29-31 . . . Kane County

AUGUST

1-3	Peoria
4-6	at Cedar Rapids
7-10	at Peoria
12-14	Clinton
15-17	Kane County
18-20	at Clinton

21-23	at Peoria
24-26	Beloit
27-29	Burlington
30-31	at Beloit

SEPTEMBER

1	at Beloit

SOUTH ATLANTIC LEAGUE

ASHEVILLE TOURISTS

APRIL

3-6	Delmarva
7-9	West Virginia
10-13	at Hickory
14-16	at West Virginia\
17-19	Hickory
21-23	at Greenville
24-27	at Augusta
29-30	Rome

MAY

1	Rome
2-5	Lakewood
7-9	at Lexington
10-13	at Rome
14-16	Lexington
17-20	Greenville
22-25	at Hagerstown
26-28	Lexington
29-31	at Charleston

JUNE

1	at Charleston
2-4	at Savannah
5-8	Kannapolis
9-11	at Lexington
12-15	Rome

19-22	at Augusta
23-26	Greenville
27-30	Greensboro

JULY

1-3	at Greenville
4-6	Lexington
7-9	Rome
10-13	at Kannapolis
15-17	Savannah
18-21	at Greenville
23-25	Greensboro
26-29	Charleston
30-31	at Greensboro

AUGUST

1-2	at Greensboro
3-5	at Lakewood
7-10	West Virginia
11-13	at Savannah
14-17	Augusta
19-21	at Kannapolis
22-24	at Delmarva
26-28	at Hagerstown
29-31	at West Virginia

SEPTEMBER

1	at West Virginia

AUGUSTA GREENJACKETS

APRIL

3-6	Charleston
7-9	at Savannah
10-13	at Charleston
14-16	Savannah
17-19	at Lexington
21-23	Hagerstown
24-27	Asheville
29-30	at Charleston

MAY

1	at Charleston
2-5	Greenville
7-9	at Delmarva
10-13	at Hickory
14-16	West Virginia
17-20	Greensboro
22-25	at Greenville
26-28	Savannah
29-31	at Lexington

JUNE

1	at Lexington
2-4	Rome
5-8	Lexington
9-11	at Rome
12-15	at Savannah

19-22	Asheville
23-26	Rome
27-30	at Lexington

JULY

1-3	at Rome
4-6	Greenville
7-9	at Savannah
10-13	at Greenville
15-17	Kannapolis
18-21	at Charleston
23-25	Savannah
26-29	Greensboro
31	at Kannapolis

AUGUST

1-3	at Kannapolis
4-6	at Greenville
7-10	Savannah
11-13	at West Virginia
14-17	at Asheville
19-21	Hickory
22-24	Lexington
26-28	at Savannah
29-31	Charleston

SEPTEMBER

1	Charleston

CHARLESTON RIVERDOGS

APRIL

3-6	at Augusta
7-9	Greenville
10-13	Augusta
14-16	at Greenville

17-19	Rome
21-23	at Lakewood
24-27	at Delmarva
29-30	Augusta

MAY

1	Augusta
2-5	Delmarva
7-9	at Rome
10-13	Savannah
14-16	Hickory
17-20	at Savannah
22-25	at Hickory
26-28	Greenville
29-31	Asheville

JUNE

1	Asheville
2-4	at Hickory
5-8	Savannah
9-11	at Greenville
12-15	at Lexington
19-22	Kannapolis
23-26	Savannah
27-30	at Kannapolis

JULY

1-3	at Savannah

DELMARVA SHOREBIRDS

APRIL

3-6	at Asheville
7-9	at Hagerstown
10-13	Greensboro
14-16	Hagerstown
17-19	at Greensboro
21-23	Savannah
24-27	Charleston
29-30	at Savannah

MAY

1	at Savannah
2-4	at Charleston
7-9	Augusta
10-13	Lakewood
14-16	at Kannapolis
17-20	at West Virginia
22-25	Kannapolis
26-28	Hagerstown
29-31	at Lakewood

JUNE

1	at Lakewood
2-4	at Hagerstown
5-8	Lakewood
9-11	Hickory
12-15	at West Virginia

19-22	Lexington
23-26	West Virginia
27-30	at Hagerstown

JULY

1-3	at Kannapolis
4-6	Lakewood
7-9	West Virginia
10-13	at Lakewood
15-17	at Greensboro
18-21	Hagerstown
23-25	at Rome
26-29	at Hickory
30-31	Lakewood

AUGUST

1-2	Lakewood
3-5	Greensboro
7-10	at Lakewood
11-13	Hagerstown
14-17	at Hickory
18-20	at Lexington
22-24	Asheville
26-28	at Greensboro
29-31	Hickory

SEPTEMBER

1	Hickory

GREENSBORO GRASSHOPPERS

APRIL

3-6	Hickory
7-9	Lakewood
10-13	at Delmarva
14-16	at Lakewood
17-19	Delmarva
21-23	at Rome
24-27	at Hickory
29-30	Greenville

MAY

1	Greenville
2-5	West Virginia
7-9	at Greenville
10-13	Lexington
14-16	Rome
17-20	at Augusta
22-25	at Rome
26-28	Lakewood
29-31	West Virginia

JUNE

1	West Virginia
2-4	at Lakewood

5-8	Hagerstown
9-11	at West Virginia
12-15	at Kannapolis
19-22	Hagerstown
23-26	Lakewood
27-30	at Asheville

JULY

1-3	at Lexington
4-6	West Virginia
7-9	Kannapolis
10-13	at West Virginia
15-17	Delmarva
18-21	Hickory
23-25	at Asheville
26-29	at Augusta
30-31	Asheville

AUGUST

1-2	Asheville
3-5	at Delmarva
7-10	at Hickory
11-13	Lakewood
14-17	Kannapolis

19-21 . . . . . at Hagerstown
22-24 . . . . . . at Lakewood
26-28 . . . . Delmarva
29-31 . . . . . at Kannapolis

GREENVILLE DRIVE

APRIL
3-6. . . . . . .at Kannapolis
7-9. . . . . . at Charleston
10-13 . . . . . . Kannapolis
14-16 . . . . . . Charleston
17-19 . . . . . .at Savannah
21-23 . . . . .Asheville
24-27 . . . . . . Lexington
29-30 . . . . . at Greensboro

MAY
1 . . . . . . at Greensboro
2-5. . . . . . . at Augusta
7-9. . . . . . . Greensboro
10-13 . . . . . West Virginia
14-16 . . . . .at Savannah
17-20 . . . . . . at Asheville
22-25 . . . . Augusta
26-28 . . .at Charleston
29-31 . . . . .Hickory

JUNE
1 . . . . .Hickory
2-4. . . . . Lexington
5-8. . . . . at Rome
9-11 . . . . . . Charleston
12-15 . . . at Hagerstown

HAGERSTOWN SUNS

APRIL
3-6. . . . . .Rome
7-9. . . . . Delmarva
10-13 . . . . . at Lakewood
14-16 . . . . .at Delmarva
17-19 . . . at Lakewood
21-23 . . . . . at Augusta
24-27 . . . . at West Virginia
29-30 . . . . .Hickory

MAY
1 . . . . .Hickory
2-5. . . . . Lexington
7-9. . . . . . . at Hickory
10-13 . . . . . . Kannapolis
14-16 . . . . . . Lakewood
17-20 . . . . . at Lexington
22-25 . . . . Asheville
26-28 . . . . .at Delmarva
29-31 . . . . .at Kannapolis

JUNE
1 . . . . . . .at Kannapolis
2-4. . . . . Delmarva
5-8. . . . . at Greensboro
9-11 . . . . . . at Lakewood
12-15 . . . . . . Greenville

HICKORY CRAWDADS

APRIL
3-6. . . . . . at Greensboro
7-9. . . . . .at Kannapolis
10-13 . . . . . . .Asheville
14-16 . . . . . . Kannapolis
17-19 . . . . . at Asheville
21-23 . . . . . Lexington
24-27 . . . . . . Greensboro
29-30 . . . . at Hagerstown

SEPTEMBER
1 . . . . .at Kannapolis

19-22 . . . . Savannah
23-26 . . . . . . at Asheville
27-30 . . . . at Hickory

JULY
1-3. . . . . .Asheville
4-6. . . . . at Augusta
7-9. . . . . .at Charleston
10-13 . . . . Augusta
15-17 . . . . . . at Rome
18-21 . . . . .Asheville
23-25 . . . . . at Lakewood
26-29 . . . at Hagerstown
31 . . . . .Rome

AUGUST
1-3. . . . . .Rome
4-6. . . . . Augusta
7-10 . . . . . at Lexington
11-14 . . . . .Rome
14-17 . . . . .at Savannah
19-21 . . . . . Charleston
22-24 . . . . Savannah
26-28 . . . .at Charleston
29-31 . . . . . Lexington

SEPTEMBER
1 . . . . Lexington

19-22 . . . . at Greensboro
23-26 . . . . Lexington
27-30 . . . . Delmarva

JULY
1-3. . . . . . . at Lakewood
4-6. . . . . . . Kannapolis
7-9. . . . . Lakewood
10-13 . . . . at Lexington
15-17 . . . . . West Virginia
18-21 . . . . . .at Delmarva
23-25 . . . . . Kannapolis
26-29 . . . . Greenville
31 . . . . . . .at Charleston

AUGUST
1-3. . . . . . . .at Charleston
4-6. . . . . at West Virginia
7-10 . . . . . . Kannapolis
11-13 . . . . . .at Delmarva
14-17 . . . . at Lakewood
19-21 . . . . . Greensboro
22-24 . . . . at Hickory
26-28 . . . . at Asheville
29-31 . . . . Lakewood

SEPTEMBER
1 . . . . Lakewood

MAY
1 . . . . at Hagerstown
2-5. . . . . . .at Kannapolis
7-9. . . . . . .Hagerstown
10-13 . . . . Augusta
14-16 . . . .at Charleston
17-20 . . . .at Kannapolis
22-25 . . . . . . Charleston
26-28 . . . . . . Kannapolis
29-31 . . . . . at Greenville

JUNE

JUNE
1 . . . . at Greenville
2-4. . . . . Charleston
5-8. . . . . . . West Virginia
9-11 . . . . . . .at Delmarva
12-15 . . . . . at Lakewood
19-22 . . . . at Rome
23-26 . . . . . . Kannapolis
27-30 . . . . . . Greenville

JULY
1-3. . . . . at West Virginia
4-6. . . . . . . Savannah
7-9. . . . . . . Lexington
10-13 . . . . . . at Rome
15-17 . . . . . . Lakewood
18-21 . . . . at Greensboro

KANNAPOLIS INTIMIDATORS

APRIL
3-6. . . . . . . Greenville
7-9. . . . . .Hickory
10-13 . . . . . at Greenville
14-16 . . . . . at Hickory
17-19 . . . . West Virginia
21-23 . . . at West Virginia
24-27 . . . . . . at Rome
29-30 . . . . West Virginia

MAY
1 . . . . West Virginia
2-4. . . . . .Hickory
7-9. . . . . . at Lakewood
10-13 . . . . at Hagerstown
14-16 . . . . Delmarva
17-20 . . . . .Hickory
22-25 . . . . . .at Delmarva
26-28 . . . . . at Hickory
29-31 . . . . . .Hagerstown

JUNE
1 . . . . .Hagerstown
2-4. . . . . . at West Virginia
5-8. . . . . at Asheville
9-11 . . . . Savannah
12-15 . . . . . . Greensboro

19-22 . . . . . .at Charleston
23-26 . . . . at Hickory
27-30 . . . . . . Charleston

JULY
1-3. . . . . Delmarva
4-6. . . . . . .at Hagerstown
7-9. . . . . . at Greensboro
10-12 . . . . . . .Asheville
15-17 . . . . . at Augusta
18-21 . . . . .Lakewood
23-25 . . . .at Hagerstown
26-29 . . . . at Lakewood
31 . . . . Augusta

AUGUST
1-3. . . . . Augusta
4-6. . . . . .Hickory
7-10 . . . . . at Hagerstown
11-13 . . . . Lexington
14-17 . . . . at Greensboro
19-21 . . . . . . .Asheville
22-24 . . . . at West Virginia
26-28 . . . . .Rome
29-31 . . . . . Greensboro

SEPTEMBER
1 . . . . Greensboro

LAKEWOOD BLUECLAWS

APRIL
3-6. . . . . .at Savannah
7-9. . . . . at Greensboro
10-13 . . . . . .Hagerstown
14-16 . . . . . . Greensboro
17-19 . . . at Hagerstown
21-23 . . . . . . Charleston
24-27 . . . . Savannah
29-30 . . . . at Lexington

MAY
1 . . . . at Lexington
2-5. . . . . at Asheville
7-9. . . . . . . Kannapolis
10-13 . . . . . .at Delaware
14-16 . . . . at Hagerstown
17-20 . . . . .Rome
22-25 . . . at West Virginia
26-28 . . . . at Greensboro
29-31 . . . . Delmarva

JUNE
1 . . . . Delmarva
2-4. . . . . Greensboro
5-8. . . . . .at Delmarva
9-11 . . . . . . .Hagerstown
12-15 . . . . .Hickory

19-22 . . . . . West Virginia
23-26 . . . . at Greensboro
27-30 . . . . at West Virginia

JULY
1-3. . . . . .Hagerstown
4-6. . . . . .at Delmarva
7-9. . . . . . at Hagerstown
10-13 . . . . Delmarva
15-17 . . . . . . at Hickory
18-21 . . . .at Kannapolis
23-25 . . . . . . Greenville
26-29 . . . . . Kannapolis
30-31 . . . . .at Delmarva

AUGUST
1-2. . . . . . . .at Delmarva
3-5. . . . . .Asheville
7-10 . . . . Delmarva
11-13 . . . . . at Greensboro
14-17 . . . . .Hagerstown
19-21 . . . . at West Virginia
22-24 . . . . . . Greensboro
26-28 . . . . .Hickory
29-31 . . . at Hagerstown

SEPTEMBER
1 . . . . at Hagerstown

SEPTEMBER
1 . . . . .at Kannapolis

LEXINGTON LEGENDS

APRIL
3-6 . . . . West Virginia
7-9 . . . . Rome
10-13 . . . . at West Virginia
14-16 . . . . at Rome
17-19 . . . . Augusta
21-23 . . . . at Hickory
24-27 . . . . at Greenville
29-30 . . . . . Lakewood

MAY
1 . . . . Lakewood
2-5 . . . . . at Hagerstown
7-9 . . . . Asheville
10-13 . . . . . at Greensboro
14-16 . . . . at Asheville
17-20 . . . Hagerstown
22-25 . . . . Savannah
26-28 . . . . at Asheville
29-31 . . . . Augusta

JUNE
1 . . . . Augusta
2-4 . . . . . . at Greenville
5-8 . . . . at Augusta
9-11 . . . . . . Asheville
12-15 . . . . . . Charleston

19-22 . . . . . .at Delmarva
23-26 . . . . at Hagerstown
27-30 . . . . Augusta

JULY
1-3 . . . . Greensboro
4-6 . . . . at Asheville
7-9 . . . . at Hickory
10-13 . . . . . Hagerstown
15-17 . . . . at Charleston
18-21 . . . . . .at Savannah
23-25 . . . . . Charleston
26-29 . . . . . Savannah
31 . . . . . at West Virginia

AUGUST
1-3 . . . . . at West Virginia
4-6 . . . . Rome
7-10 . . . . Greenville
11-13 . . . . .at Kannapolis
14-17 . . . . . West Virginia
18-20 . . . . . . Delmarva
22-24 . . . . . . at Augusta
26-28 . . . . West Virginia
29-31 . . . . . at Greenville

SEPTEMBER
1 . . . . at Greenville

SAVANNAH SAND GNATS

APRIL
3-6 . . . . Lakewood
7-9 . . . . Augusta
10-13 . . . . at Rome
14-16 . . . . . . at Augusta
17-19 . . . . . . Greenville
21-23 . . . . . .at Delmarva
24-27 . . . . at Lakewood
29-30 . . . . . Delmarva

MAY
1 . . . . Delmarva
2-4 . . . . Rome
7-9 . . . . at West Virginia
10-13 . . . . .at Charleston
14-16 . . . . . Greenville
17-20 . . . . . Charleston
22-25 . . . . at Lexington
26-28 . . . . at Augusta
29-31 . . . . Rome

JUNE
1 . . . . .Rome
2-4 . . . . .Asheville
5-8 . . . . . at Charleston
9-11 . . . . . .at Kannapolis
12-15 . . . . . Augusta

19-22 . . . . . at Greenville
23-26 . . . at Charleston
27-30 . . . . Rome

JULY
1-3 . . . . Charleston
4-6 . . . . at Hickory
7-9 . . . . Augusta
10-13 . . . . . Charleston
15-17 . . . . at Asheville
18-21 . . . . . Lexington
23-25 . . . . at Augusta
26-29 . . . at Lexington
31 . . . . .Hickory

AUGUST
1-3 . . . . Hickory
4-6 . . . . . Charleston
7-10 . . . . at Augusta
11-13 . . . . . Asheville
14-17 . . . . . Greenville
19-21 . . . . . at Rome
22-24 . . . at Greenville
26-28 . . . . . Augusta
29-31 . . . . . at Rome

SEPTEMBER
1 . . . . at Rome

ROME BRAVES

APRIL
3-6 . . . . . . at Hagerstown
7-9 . . . . . . at Lexington
10-13 . . . . Savannah
14-16 . . . . . Lexington
17-19 . . . . .at Charleston
21-23 . . . . . Greensboro
24-27 . . . . . Kannapolis
29-30 . . . . at Asheville

MAY
1 . . . . at Asheville
2-5 . . . . .at Savannah
7-9 . . . . Charleston
10-13 . . . . . . Asheville
14-16 . . . . at Greensboro
17-20 . . . . at Lakewood
22-25 . . . . . . Greensboro
26-28 . . . . West Virginia
29-31 . . . .at Savannah

JUNE
1 . . . . .at Savannah
2-4 . . . . at Augusta
5-8 . . . . . . Greenville
9-11 . . . . Augusta
12-15 . . . . . at Asheville

19-22 . . . . .Hickory
23-26 . . . . at Augusta
27-30 . . . . . .at Savannah

JULY
1-3 . . . . Augusta
4-6 . . . . . . .at Charleston
7-9 . . . . . . at Asheville
10-13 . . . . . . .Hickory
15-17 . . . . . Greenville
18-21 . . . . at West Virginia
23-25 . . . . . . Delmarva
26-29 . . . . . West Virginia
31 . . . . at Greenville

AUGUST
1-3 . . . . . at Greenville
4-6 . . . . . . at Lexington
7-10 . . . . . . Charleston
11-13 . . . . at Greenville
14-17 . . . . .at Charleston
19-21 . . . . . Savannah
22-24 . . . . . Charleston
26-28 . . . . .at Kannapolis
29-31 . . . . . Savannah

SEPTEMBER
1 . . . . Savannah

WEST VIRGINIA POWER

APRIL
3-6 . . . . at Lexington
7-9 . . . . .at Asheville
10-13 . . . . Lexington
14-16 . . . . . . .Asheville
17-19 . . . . .at Kannapolis
21-23 . . . . . Kannapolis
24-27 . . . .Hagerstown
29-30 . . . .at Kannapolis

MAY
1 . . . . .at Kannapolis
2-5 . . . . . at Greensboro
7-9 . . . . Savannah
10-13 . . . . at Greenville
14-16 . . . . . at Augusta
17-20 . . . . . Delmarva
22-25 . . . . . . Lakewood
26-28 . . . . at Rome
29-31 . . . . at Greensboro

JUNE
1 . . . . at Greensboro
2-4 . . . . Kannapolis
5-8 . . . . . . at Hickory
9-11 . . . . . . Greensboro
12-15 . . . . . Delmarva

19-22 . . . . . at Lakewood
23-26 . . . . .at Delmarva
27-30 . . . . . Lakewood

JULY
1-3 . . . . .Hickory
4-6 . . . . . at Greensboro
7-9 . . . . . .at Delmarva
10-13 . . . . . Greensboro
15-17 . . . . at Hagerstown
18-21 . . . . . . Rome
23-25 . . . . at Hickory
26-29 . . . . at Rome
31 . . . . Lexington

AUGUST
1-3 . . . . Lexington
4-6 . . . . . . .Hagerstown
7-10 . . . . . . at Asheville
11-13 . . . . Augusta
14-17 . . . . at Lexington
19-21 . . . . . . Lakewood
22-24 . . . . Kannapolis
26-28 . . . at Lexington
29-31 . . . . . .Asheville

SEPTEMBER
1 . . . . .Asheville

SHORT SEASON

NEW YORK-PENN LEAGUE

ABERDEEN IRONBIRDS

JUNE
13-16 . . . .at Hudson Valley
17-19 . . . . at Staten Island
20-22 . . . . Brooklyn
23-24 . . . . . Staten Island
25-26 . . . . . at Brooklyn
27-29 . . . . Hudson Valley

JULY
1-3 . . . . Staten Island

4-6 . . . . at Brooklyn
7-8 . . . . . at Staten Island
9-11 . . . . Batavia
12-14 . . . . Auburn
16-18 . . . . . . at Tri-City
19-21 . . at Mahoning Valley
22-23 . . . . Brooklyn
24-26 . . . . . . .Connecticut
27-29 . . . . .Tri-City
30-31 . . . . at State College

AUGUST
1 . . . . at State College
2-4 . . . . . .at Williamsport
6-8 . . . . Vermont
9-11 . . . . Jamestown
12-14 . . . . . at Vermont
15-17 . . . . at Connecticut

AUBURN DOUBLEDAYS

JUNE
13 . . . . Batavia
14 . . . . at Batavia

20-21 . . . . . Hudson Valley
22-24 . . . . Lowell
25-27 . . . .at Hudson Valley
28-30 . . . . . . .at Lowell
31 . . . . . . Hudson Valley

SEPTEMBER
1 . . . . Hudson Valley

15 . . . . Batavia
16 . . . . at Batavia
17-19 . . at Mahoning Valley

20-21 . . . . . . Williamsport
22-23 . . . .Mahoning Valley
24-25 . . . .at Williamsport
26 . . . . .Batavia
27 . . . . at Batavia
28 . . . . .Batavia
29 . . . . at Batavia

JULY
1-3 . . . . .Mahoning Valley
4-6 . . . .at Williamsport
7-8 . . . . State College
9-11 . . . . at Connecticut
12-14 . . . . at Aberdeen
16-18 . . . . Hudson Valley
19-21 . . . . Lowell
22-23 . . . . . at Jamestown
24-26 . . . . at State College
27-29 . . . . . . Jamestown

30-31 . . . . at Brooklyn

AUGUST
1 . . . . at Brooklyn
2-4 . . . . . at Staten Island
6-8 . . . . Tri-City
9-11 . . . . .Vermont
12-14 . . . . at Jamestown
15-17 . . . . State College
20-21 . . at State College
22-24 . . . . . Williamsport
25-26 . . . . . . Jamestown
27 . . . . at Batavia
28 . . . . .Batavia
29-30 . . at Mahoning Valley
31 . . . . at Batavia

SEPTEMBER
1 . . . . .Batavia

BATAVIA MUCKDOGS

JUNE
13 . . . . at Auburn
14 . . . . .Auburn
15 . . . . at Auburn
16 . . . . .Auburn
17-19 . . . at State College
20-21 . . .Mahoning Valley
22-23 . . . . . State College
24-25 . . at Mahoning Valley
26 . . . . at Auburn
27 . . . . .Auburn
28 . . . . at Auburn
29 . . . . .Auburn

JULY
1-3 . . . . State College
4-6 . . . .at Mahoning Valley
7-8 . . . . Jamestown
9-11 . . . . . . at Aberdeen
12-14 . . . .at Hudson Valley
16-18 . . . . Lowell
19-21 . . . .Connecticut
22-23 . . . . .at Williamsport

24-25 . . . . . . Jamestown
26 . . . . . . at Jamestown
27-29 . . . . . Williamsport
30-31 . . . . . at Vermont

AUGUST
1 . . . . at Vermont
2-4 . . . . at Tri-City
6-8 . . . . Staten Island
9-11 . . . . .Brooklyn
12-14 . . . .at Williamsport
15 . . . . . at Jamestown
16 . . . . . . Jamestown
17 . . . . . at Jamestown
20-21 . . . at Jamestown
22-24 . . .Mahoning Valley
25-26 . . . . Williamsport
27 . . . . .Auburn
28 . . . . at Auburn
29-30 . . at State College
31 . . . . .Auburn

SEPTEMBER
1 . . . . at Auburn

BROOKLYN CYCLONES

JUNE
13 . . . . . at Staten Island
14 . . . . Staten Island
15 . . . . at Staten Island
16 . . . . . . Staten Island
17 . . . . . . Hudson Valley
18-19 . . . .at Hudson Valley
20-22 . . . . at Aberdeen
23 . . . . . . Hudson Valley
24 . . . . .at Hudson Valley
25-26 . . . . . Aberdeen
27 . . . . . Staten Island
28 . . . . at Staten Island
29 . . . . . Staten Island

JULY
1 . . . . . .at Hudson Valley
2 . . . . Hudson Valley
3 . . . . . .at Hudson Valley
4-6 . . . . Aberdeen
7-8 . . . . . . Hudson Valley
9-11 . . . . . at State College
12-14 . . . . at Connecticut

16-18 . . . . . . Jamestown
19-21 . . . . . Williamsport
22-23 . . . . . at Aberdeen
24-26 . . . . .Vermont
27-29 . . . . .at Lowell
30-31 . . . . .Auburn

AUGUST
1 . . . . .Auburn
2-4 . . . . . . .Connecticut
6-8 . . . .at Mahoning Valley
9-11 . . . . . at Batavia
12-14 . . . . Lowell
15-17 . . . . . at Vermont
20 . . . . . at Staten Island
21 . . . . . . Staten Island
22-24 . . . . . . Tri-City
25-26 . . . . at Staten Island
27 . . . . Staten Island
28-30 . . . . . . at Tri-City
31 . . . . Staten Island

SEPTEMBER
1 . . . . at Staten Island

CONNECTICUT TIGERS

JUNE
13-15 . . . . at Tri-City
16-17 . . . . . at Vermont
18-19 . . . . Lowell
20-22 . . . . . at Vermont
23-24 . . . . .at Lowell
25-26 . . . . . Vermont
27-29 . . . . . . Tri-City

JULY
1-3 . . . . .at Lowell
4-6 . . . . .Vermont
7-8 . . . . . . at Tri-City
9-11 . . . . .Auburn
12-14 . . . . .Brooklyn
16-18 . . at Mahoning Valley
19-21 . . . . at Batavia
22-23 . . . . Tri-City

24-26 . . . . . . at Aberdeen
27-29 . . . . Staten Island
30-31 . . .at Williamsport

AUGUST
1 . . . . . . .at Williamsport
2-4 . . . . . . at Brooklyn
6-8 . . . . Jamestown
9-11 . . . . . . State College
12-14 . . . . at Staten Island
15-17 . . . . . . Aberdeen
20-21 . . . . . . .at Lowell
22-24 . . . . Hudson Valley
25-27 . . . . Lowell
28-30 . . .at Hudson Valley
31 . . . . Lowell

SEPTEMBER
1 . . . . Lowell

HUDSON VALLEY RENEGADES

JUNE
13-16 . . . . Aberdeen
17 . . . . at Brooklyn
18-19 . . . . .Brooklyn
20 . . . . . . Staten Island
21 . . . . at Staten Island
22 . . . . . . Staten Island
23 . . . . . . at Brooklyn
24 . . . . .Brooklyn
25 . . . . at Staten Island
26 . . . . . . Staten Island
27-29 . . . . . at Aberdeen

JULY
1 . . . . .Brooklyn
2 . . . . at Brooklyn
3 . . . . .Brooklyn
4 . . . . . at Staten Island
5 . . . . . . Staten Island
6 . . . . at Staten Island
7-8 . . . . . . at Brooklyn
9-11 . . . . .Mahoning Valley
12-14 . . . . Batavia

16-18 . . . . at Auburn
19-21 . . . . . . at Vermont
22 . . . . . Staten Island
23 . . . . at Staten Island
24-26 . . . . . .at Lowell
27-29 . . . . . .Vermont
30-31 . . . . at Jamestown

AUGUST
1 . . . . at Jamestown
2-4 . . . . . at State College
6-8 . . . . Williamsport
9-11 . . . . Tri-City
12-14 . . . . at Tri-City
15-17 . . . . Lowell
20-21 . . . . at Aberdeen
22-24 . . . at Connecticut
25-27 . . . . . Aberdeen
28-30 . . . .Connecticut
31 . . . . at Aberdeen

SEPTEMBER
1 . . . . at Aberdeen

JAMESTOWN JAMMERS

JUNE
13-16 . . .Mahoning Valley
17-19 . . .at Williamsport
20-21 . . . . State College
22-23 . . . . Williamsport
24-25 . . . at State College
26-29 . . at Mahoning Valley

JULY
1-3 . . . . Williamsport
4-6 . . . . at State College
7-8 . . . . . at Batavia
9-11 . . . . .Tri-City
12-14 . . . . . .Vermont
16-18 . . . . at Brooklyn
19-21 . . . at Staten Island
22-23 . . . . . .Auburn
24-25 . . . .at Batavia
26 . . . . .Batavia
27-29 . . . . . . at Auburn

30-31 . . . . . Hudson Valley

AUGUST
1 . . . . Hudson Valley
2-4 . . . . Lowell
6-8 . . . . . . at Connecticut
9-11 . . . . . . at Aberdeen
12-14 . . . . .Auburn
15 . . . . Batavia
16 . . . . at Batavia
17 . . . . Batavia
20-21 . . . . Batavia
22-24 . . . . State College
25-26 . . . . . .at Auburn
27-28 . . at Mahoning Valley
29-30 . . . . .at Williamsport
31 . . . . .Mahoning Valley

SEPTEMBER
1 . . . . . .Mahoning Valley

LOWELL SPINNERS

JUNE
13-15 . . . . .Vermont
16-17 . . . . at Tri-City

18-19 . . . . .at Connecticut
20-22 . . . . Tri-City
23-24 . . . . . .Connecticut

25-26 . . . . Tri-City
27-29 . . . . at Vermont
JULY
1-3 . . . . .Connecticut
4-6 . . . . at Tri-City
7-8 . . . . at Vermont
9-11 . . . . . . Staten Island
12-14 . . . .Mahoning Valley
16-18 . . . . . at Batavia
19-21 . . . . . . at Auburn
22-23 . . . . Vermont
24-26 . . . . . Hudson Valley
27-29 . . . . .Brooklyn
30-31 . . . . at Staten Island

AUGUST
1 . . . . at Staten Island
2-4 . . . . . . at Jamestown
6-8 . . . . State College
9-11 . . . . . . Williamsport
12-14 . . . . . . at Brooklyn
15-17 . . .at Hudson Valley
20-21 . . . . . .Connecticut
22-24 . . . . . at Aberdeen
25-27 . . . .at Connecticut
28-30 . . . . . . Aberdeen
31 . . . . . . at Connecticut
SEPTEMBER
1 . . . . . . .at Connecticut

MAHONING VALLEY SCRAPPERS

JUNE
13-16 . . . . . at Jamestown
17-19 . . . . .Auburn
20-21 . . . . . at Batavia
22-23 . . . . . at Auburn
24-25 . . . . Batavia
26-29 . . . . . Jamestown
JULY
1-3 . . . . at Auburn
4-6 . . . . Batavia
7-8 . . . . . . Williamsport
9-11 . . . .at Hudson Valley
12-14 . . . . . .at Lowell
16-18 . . . . . .Connecticut
19-21 . . . . . . Aberdeen
22-23 . . . . at State College
24-26 . . . .at Williamsport

27-29 . . . . . State College
30-31 . . . . at Tri-City
AUGUST
1 . . . . at Tri-City
2-4 . . . . at Vermont
6-8 . . . . .Brooklyn
9-11 . . . . . . Staten Island
12-14 . . . . at State College
15-17 . . . . Williamsport
20-21 . . . .at Williamsport
22-24 . . . . . at Batavia
25-26 . . . . . State College
27-28 . . . . . Jamestown
29-30 . . . . .Auburn
31 . . . . . . at Jamestown
SEPTEMBER
1 . . . . at Jamestown

STATE COLLEGE SPIKES

JUNE
13 . . . . . .at Williamsport
14 . . . . . . Williamsport
15 . . . . . .at Williamsport
16 . . . . . . Williamsport
17-19 . . . . . . .Batavia
20-21 . . . . . at Jamestown
22-23 . . . . . . .at Batavia
24-25 . . . . . . Jamestown
26 . . . . . .at Williamsport
27 . . . . . . Williamsport
28 . . . . . .at Williamsport
29 . . . . . . Williamsport
JULY
1-3 . . . . at Batavia
4-6 . . . . Jamestown
7-8 . . . . at Auburn
9-11 . . . . .Brooklyn
12-14 . . . . . Staten Island
16-18 . . . . . . at Vermont

19-21 . . . . at Tri-City
22-23 . . .Mahoning Valley
24-26 . . . . . . .Auburn
27-29 . . at Mahoning Valley
30-31 . . . . Aberdeen
AUGUST
1 . . . . Aberdeen
2-4 . . . . . . Hudson Valley
6-8 . . . . .at Lowell
9-11 . . . . . at Connecticut
12-14 . . .Mahoning Valley
15-17 . . . . . . at Auburn
20 21 . . . . .Auburn
22-24 . . . . at Jamestown
25-26 . .at Mahoning Valley
27-28 . . . . . Williamsport
29-30 . . . . Batavia
31 . . . . . . at Williamsport
SEPTEMBER
1 . . . . . . .at Williamsport

STATEN ISLAND YANKEES

JUNE
13 . . . . .Brooklyn
14 . . . . . . at Brooklyn
15 . . . . .Brooklyn
16 . . . . . . at Brooklyn
17-19 . . . . Aberdeen
20 . . . .at Hudson Valley
21 . . . . . Hudson Valley
22 . . . .at Hudson Valley
23-24 . . . . . at Aberdeen
25 . . . . . Hudson Valley
26 . . . . .at Hudson Valley

27 . . . . at Brooklyn
28 . . . . .Brooklyn
29 . . . . at Brooklyn
JULY
1-3 . . . . at Aberdeen
4 . . . . Hudson Valley
5 . . . . . .at Hudson Valley
6 . . . . Hudson Valley
7-8 . . . . Aberdeen
9-11 . . . . .at Lowell
12-14 . . . . at State College

16-18 . . . . . Williamsport
19-21 . . . . . . Jamestown
22 . . . . .at Hudson Valley
23 . . . . . . Hudson Valley
24-26 . . . . . at Tri-City
27-29 . . . . at Connecticut
30-31 . . . . Lowell
AUGUST
1 . . . . Lowell
2-4 . . . . .Auburn
6-8 . . . . at Batavia
9-11 . . . at Mahoning Valley

TRI-CITY VALLEYCATS

JUNE
13-15 . . . . . .Connecticut
16-17 . . . . . . Lowell
18-19 . . . . . at Vermont
20-22 . . . . . . .at Lowell
23-24 . . . . . . Vermont
25-26 . . . . . . .at Lowell
27-29 . . . . at Connecticut
30 . . . . at Vermont
JULY
1-2 . . . . at Vermont
4-6 . . . . Lowell
7-8 . . . . .Connecticut
9-11 . . . . . at Jamestown
12-14 . . . . .at Williamsport
16-18 . . . . . . Aberdeen
19-21 . . . . State College
22-23 . . . . .at Connecticut

24-26 . . . . . . Staten Island
27-29 . . . . . at Aberdeen
30-31 . . . .Mahoning Valley
AUGUST
1 . . . . .Mahoning Valley
2-4 . . . . Batavia
6-8 . . . . at Auburn
9-11 . . .at Hudson Valley
12-14 . . . . . Hudson Valley
15-17 . . . . at Staten Island
20-21 . . . . . . .Vermont
22-24 . . . . . . at Brooklyn
25-27 . . . . . . .Vermont
28-30 . . . . . . .Brooklyn
31 . . . . at Vermont
SEPTEMBER
1 . . . . at Vermont

VERMONT LAKE MONSTERS

JUNE
13-15 . . . . .at Lowell
16-17 . . . . .Connecticut
18-19 . . . . .Tri-City
20-22 . . . . . . .Connecticut
23-24 . . . . . at Tri-City
25-26 . . . . at Connecticut
27-29 . . . . . . Lowell
30 . . . . Tri-City
JULY
1-2 . . . . .Tri-City
4-6 . . . . . . at Connecticut
7-8 . . . . Lowell
9-11 . . . . .at Williamsport
12-14 . . . . at Jamestown
16-18 . . . . . State College
19-21 . . . . Hudson Valley
22-23 . . . . . . .at Lowell

24-26 . . . . . . at Brooklyn
27-29 . . .at Hudson Valley
30-31 . . . . Batavia
AUGUST
1 . . . . .Batavia
2 4 . . . . . .Mahoning Valley
6-8 . . . . at Aberdeen
9-11 . . . . at Auburn
12-14 . . . . Aberdeen
15-17 . . . . . . .Brooklyn
20-21 . . . . . . at Tri-City
22-24 . . . . Staten Island
25-27 . . . . Vermont
28-30 . . . . at Staten Island
31 . . . . Tri-City
SEPTEMBER
1 . . . . Tri-City

WILLIAMSPORT CROSSCUTTERS

JUNE
13 . . . . State College
14 . . . . . at State College
15 . . . . . . State College
16 . . . . . at State College
17-19 . . . . . . Jamestown
20-21 . . . . . . at Auburn
22-23 . . . . at Jamestown
24-25 . . . . . . .Auburn
26 . . . . . . State College
27 . . . . . at State College
28 . . . . . . State College
29 . . . . . at State College
JULY
1-3 . . . . . . at Jamestown
4-6 . . . . .Auburn

7-8 . . . . at Mahoning Valley
9-11 . . . . .Vermont
12-14 . . . . Tri-City
16-18 . . . . at Staten Island
19-21 . . . . . . at Brooklyn
22-23 . . . . .Batavia
24-26 . . . .Mahoning Valley
27-29 . . . . at Batavia
30-31 . . . . . . .Connecticut
AUGUST
1 . . . . .Connecticut
2-4 . . . . Aberdeen
6-8 . . . . .at Hudson Valley
9-11 . . . . .at Lowell
12-14 . . . . .Batavia
15-17 . . at Mahoning Valley

20-21	Mahoning Valley	29-30	Jamestown	7-9	Eugene	20-24	Spokane

20-21 . . . .Mahoning Valley
22-24 . . . . at Auburn
25-26 . . . . at Batavia
27-28 . . . . at State College

29-30 . . . . . . Jamestown
31 . . . . State College

SEPTEMBER
1 . . . . State College

7-9 . . . . .Eugene
10 . . . . . . at Salem-Keizer
11-12 . . . . at Salem-Keizer
13-15 . . . . Boise
16-18 . . . . at Eugene

20-24 . . . . .Spokane
25-29 . . . . at Tri-City
30-31 . . . . .Eugene

SEPTEMBER
1 . . . . .Eugene

NORTHWEST LEAGUE

BOISE HAWKS

JUNE
13-17 . . . . Tri-City
18-20 . . . . at Eugene
21-25 . . . . . . at Spokane
26-29 . . . . .Hillsboro
29-30 . . . . at Tri-City

JULY
1-3 . . . . at Tri-City
4-6 . . . . .Eugene
8-10 . . . . .Hillsboro
11-13 . . . . at Eugene
14-18 . . . . Spokane
19-21 . . . . . Salem-Keizer
22-26 . . . . . . at Everett

27-29 . . . . . . at Hillsboro
30-31 . . . . .Vancouver

AUGUST
1-3 . . . . .Vancouver
7-9 . . . . . at Salem-Keizer
10-12 . . . . .Eugene
13-15 . . . . . . at Hillsboro
16-18 . . . . at Salem-Keizer
19-23 . . . . . at Vancouver
25-29 . . . . Everett
30-31 . . . . . Salem-Keizer

SEPTEMBER
1 . . . . Salem-Keizer

SALEM-KEIZER VOLCANOES

JUNE
13-17 . . . . . . .Vancouver
18-20 . . . . . . at Hillsboro
21-25 . . . . Everett
26-28 . . . . . . at Eugene
29-30 . . . . . at Vancouver

JULY
1-3 . . . . at Vancouver
4-6 . . . . .Hillsboro
8-10 . . . . .Eugene
11-12 . . . . . at Hillsboro
13 . . . . .Hillsboro
14-18 . . . . . . at Everett
19-21 . . . . at Boise
22-26 . . . . .Spokane

27-29 . . . . .Eugene
30-31 . . . . at Tri-City

AUGUST
1-3 . . . . at Tri-City
7-9 . . . . Boise
10 . . . . at Hillsboro
11-12 . . . . .Hillsboro
13-15 . . . . . . at Eugene
16-18 . . . . Boise
20-24 . . . . Tri-City
25-29 . . . . . . at Spokane
30-31 . . . . at Boise

SEPTEMBER
1 . . . . at Boise

EUGENE EMERALDS

JUNE
13-17 . . . . . . at Spokane
18-20 . . . . Boise
21-25 . . . . at Tri-City
26-28 . . . . . Salem-Keizer
29-30 . . . . Spokane

JULY
1-3 . . . . Spokane
4-6 . . . . at Boise
8-10 . . . . at Salem-Keizer
11-13 . . . . Boise
14-18 . . . . . at Vancouver
19-21 . . . . .Hillsboro
22-26 . . . . Tri-City

27-29 . . . . at Salem-Keizer
30-31 . . . . Everett

AUGUST
1-3 . . . . Everett
7-9 . . . . at Hillsboro
10-12 . . . . at Boise
13-15 . . . . . Salem-Keizer
16-18 . . . . .Hillsboro
19-23 . . . . . . at Everett
25-29 . . . . . . .Vancouver
30-31 . . . . . . at Hillsboro

SEPTEMBER
1 . . . . at Hillsboro

SPOKANE INDIANS

JUNE
13-17 . . . . .Eugene
18-20 . . . . . at Vancouver
21-15 . . . . Boise
26-28 . . . . . . at Everett
29-30 . . . . . . at Eugene

JULY
1-3 . . . . at Eugene
4-6 . . . . . . .Vancouver
8-10 . . . . Tri-City
11-13 . . . . . . at Tri-City
14-18 . . . . at Boise
19-21 . . . . Everett
22-26 . . . . at Salem-Keizer

27-29 . . . . . . .Vancouver
30-31 . . . . .Hillsboro

AUGUST
1-3 . . . . .Hillsboro
7-9 . . . . Everett
10-12 . . . . . . at Everett
13-15 . . . . . . at Tri-City
16-18 . . . . Tri-City
20-24 . . . . . at Hillsboro
25-29 . . . . . Salem-Keizer
30-31 . . . . . at Vancouver

SEPTEMBER
1 . . . . at Vancouver

EVERETT AQUASOX

JUNE
13-17 . . . . .Hillsboro
18-20 . . . . at Tri-City
21-25 . . . . at Salem-Keizer
26-28 . . . . Spokane
29-30 . . . . . . at Hillsboro

JULY
1-3 . . . . at Hillsboro
4-6 . . . . Tri-City
8-10 . . . . . . .Vancouver
11-13 . . . . . at Vancouver
14-18 . . . . . Salem-Keizer
19-21 . . . . . . at Spokane
22-26 . . . . Boise

27-29 . . . . Tri-City
30-31 . . . . at Eugene

AUGUST
1-3 . . . . at Eugene
7-9 . . . . at Spokane
10-12 . . . . Spokane
13-15 . . . . . at Vancouver
16-18 . . . . . .Vancouver
19-23 . . . . .Eugene
26-29 . . . . . . at Boise
30-31 . . . . . . at Tri-City

SEPTEMBER
1 . . . . at Tri-City

TRI-CITY DUST DEVILS

JUNE
13-17 . . . . at Boise
18-20 . . . . Everett
21-25 . . . . .Eugene
26-28 . . . . at Vancouver
29-30 . . . . Boise

JULY
1-3 . . . . Boise
4-6 . . . . . . at Everett
8-10 . . . . . at Spokane
11-13 . . . . Spokane
14-18 . . . . . . at Hillsboro
19-21 . . . . . . .Vancouver
22-26 . . . . . at Eugene

27-29 . . . . at Everett
30-31 . . . . . Salem-Keizer

AUGUST
1-3 . . . . Salem-Keizer
7-9 . . . . .Vancouver
10-12 . . . . . at Vancouver
13-15 . . . . Spokane
16-18 . . . . . at Spokane
20-24 . . . . at Salem-Keizer
25-29 . . . . .Hillsboro
30-31 . . . . Everett

SEPTEMBER
1 . . . . Everett

HILLSBORO HOPS

JUNE
13-17 . . . . . . at Everett
18-20 . . . . . Salem-Keizer
21-25 . . . . . . .Vancouver
26-28 . . . . at Boise
29-30 . . . . Everett

JULY
1-3 . . . . Everett
4-6 . . . . . at Salem-Keizer

8-10 . . . . at Boise
11-12 . . . . . Salem-Keizer
13 . . . . . at Salem-Keizer
14-18 . . . . Tri-City
19-21 . . . . . . at Eugene
22-26 . . . . at Vancouver
27-29 . . . . Boise
30-31 . . . . . . at Spokane

AUGUST
1-3 . . . . at Spokane

VANCOUVER CANADIANS

JUNE
13-17 . . . . at Salem-Keizer
18-20 . . . . Spokane
21-15 . . . . . . at Hillsboro
26-28 . . . . Tri-City
29-30 . . . . . Salem-Keizer

JULY
1-3 . . . . . Salem-Keizer
4-6 . . . . at Spokane
8-10 . . . . at Everett

11-13 . . . . Everett
14-18 . . . . at Eugene
19-21 . . . . . . at Tri-City
22-26 . . . . . . .Hillsboro
27-29 . . . . . at Spokane
30-31 . . . . . . at Boise

AUGUST
1-3 . . . . at Boise
7-9 . . . . at Tri-City
10-12 . . . . Tri-City

13-15 . . . . Everett	19-23 . . . . Boise	30-31 . . . . .Spokane
16-18 . . . . at Everett	25-29 . . . . at Eugene	

1 . . . . .Spokane

ROOKIE

APPALACHIAN LEAGUE

BLUEFIELD BLUE JAYS

JUNE	
19-21 . . . . . Johnson City	22-24 . . . . . Elizabethton
22-24 . . . . . at Kingsport	25-27 . . . . Danville
25-27 . . . . Pulaski	28-30 . . . at Johnson City
28-30 . . . . . . .at Danville	31 . . . . .at Bristol

JULY	AUGUST
1 . . . . Princeton	1-2 . . . . .at Bristol
3-5 . . . .at Elizabethton	3-5 . . . . . . at Burlington
6-8 . . . . .Burlington	7-9 . . . . Princeton
9-11 . . . . Bristol	10-12 . . . . Danville
12-14 . . . . . .at Princeton	13-16 . . . . . .at Princeton
16-18 . . . . Greenville	17-19 . . . . at Burlington
19-21 . . . . . at Pulaski	21-23 . . . . Kingsport
	24-26 . . . . . at Greenville
	27-29 . . . . at Pulaski

BRISTOL PIRATES

JUNE	
19-21 . . . . . .at Princeton	25 . . . . at Greenville
22-24 . . . . . . .Burlington	26 . . . . Greenville
25-27 . . . . . Johnson City	27 . . . . at Greenville
28-30 . . . .at Elizabethton	28-30 . . . . Princeton
	31 . . . . .Bluefield

JULY	AUGUST
1 . . . . at Pulaski	1-2 . . . . .Bluefield
3-4 . . . . at Pulaski	3-5 . . . . . . at Greenville
5 . . . . Pulaski	7-9 . . . . . . at Kingsport
6 . . . . at Greenville	10-12 . . . . . Elizabethton
7-8 . . . . Greenville	13-15 . . . . at Kingsport
9-11 . . . . at Bluefield	16 . . . . Pulaski
12-14 . . . . . . Kingsport	17-19 . . . . . Johnson City
16-18 . . . .at Danville	21-23 . . . . at Burlington
19-21 . . . at Johnson City	24-16 . . . . . Elizabethton
22-23 . . . . Pulaski	27-29 . . . . Danville
24 . . . . at Pulaski	

BURLINGTON ROYALS

JUNE	
19-21 . . . . at Pulaski	24 . . . . Danville
22-24 . . . . .at Bristol	25-27 . . . . Kingsport
25-27 . . . . . Elizabethton	28-30 . . . . Pulaski
28-30 . . . . . Greenville	31 . . . . .at Princeton

JULY	AUGUST
1 . . . . .at Danville	1-2 . . . . .at Princeton
3 . . . . .at Danville	3-5 . . . . .Bluefield
4-5 . . . . Danville	7-9 . . . . . at Johnson City
6-8 . . . . at Bluefield	10-12 . . . . at Greenville
9-11 . . . . Princeton	13 . . . . .at Danville
12-14 . . . . . Johnson City	14 . . . . Danville
16-18 . . . . . at Kingsport	15-16 . . . . . .at Danville
19-21 . . . .at Elizabethton	17-19 . . . . .Bluefield
22-23 . . . . .at Danville	21-23 . . . . Bristol
	24-26 . . . . . at Pulaski
	27-29 . . . . . . Princeton

DANVILLE BRAVES

JUNE	
19-21 . . . . . at Kingsport	28-30 . . . . .Bluefield
22-24 . . . at Johnson City	
25-27 . . . . Greenville	JULY
	1 . . . . .Burlington
	3 . . . . .Burlington

4-5 . . . . at Burlington	AUGUST
6-8 . . . . .at Princeton	1-2 . . . . Pulaski
9-11 . . . . at Pulaski	3-5 . . . . Princeton
12-14 . . . . . Elizabethton	7-9 . . . .at Elizabethton
16-18 . . . . Bristol	10 12 . . . . . at Bluefield
19-21 . . . . . at Greenville	13 . . . . .Burlington
22-23 . . . . . . .Burlington	14 . . . . . . at Burlington
24 . . . . . . at Burlington	15-16 . . . . . . .Burlington
25-27 . . . . . . at Bluefield	17-19 . . . . Pulaski
28-30 . . . . Kingsport	21-23 . . . . . Johnson City
31 . . . . Pulaski	24-26 . . . . . .at Princeton
	27-29 . . . . at Bristol

ELIZABETHTON TWINS

JUNE	
19-21 . . . . . at Greenville	25-27 . . . . at Johnson City
22-24 . . . . Pulaski	28-30 . . . . Greenville
25-27 . . . . . at Burlington	31 . . . . at Kingsport
28-30 . . . . Bristol	

JULY	AUGUST
1 . . . . . . at Johnson City	1-2 . . . . . . at Kingsport
3-5 . . . . .Bluefield	3-5 . . . . . . Johnson City
6-8 . . . . . at Johnson City	7-9 . . . . Danville
9-11 . . . . Kingsport	10-12 . . . . at Bristol
12-14 . . . . . . .at Danville	13-15 . . . . . Greenville
16-18 . . . . .at Princeton	16 . . . . . Johnson City
19-21 . . . . . . .Burlington	17-19 . . . . . . Princeton
22-24 . . . . at Bluefield	21-23 . . . . . at Pulaski
	24-26 . . . . . .at Bristol
	27-29 . . . . . Kingsport

GREENVILLE ASTROS

JUNE	
19-21 . . . . . Elizabethton	25 . . . . Bristol
22-24 . . . . . . Princeton	26 . . . . .at Bristol
25-27 . . . . . . at Danville	27 . . . . Bristol
28-30 . . . . . at Burlington	28-30 . . . .at Elizabethton
	31 . . . . Johnson City

JULY	AUGUST
1 . . . . at Kingsport	1-2 . . . . . . Johnson City
3 . . . . at Kingsport	3-5 . . . . Bristol
4-5 . . . . Kingsport	7-9 . . . . . . at Pulaski
6 . . . . Bristol	10-12 . . . . . .Burlington
7-8 . . . . .at Bristol	13-15 . . . .at Elizabethton
9-11 . . . . . Johnson City	16 . . . . . at Kingsport
12-14 . . . . Pulaski	17 . . . . Kingsport
16-18 . . . . at Bluefield	18-19 . . . . at Kingsport
19-21 . . . . . . Danville	21-23 . . . .at Princeton
22-23 . . . . . at Kingsport	24-26 . . . . .Bluefield
24 . . . . Kingsport	27-29 . . . . at Johnson City

JOHNSON CITY CARDINALS

JUNE	
19-21 . . . . at Bluefield	25-27 . . . . . Elizabethton
24-24 . . . . Danville	28-30 . . . . . .Bluefield
25-27 . . . . .at Bristol	31 . . . . at Greenville
28-30 . . . . . Kingsport	

JULY	AUGUST
1 . . . . Elizabethton	1-2 . . . . . . at Greenville
3-5 . . . . Princeton	3-5 . . . . . .at Elizabethton
6-8 . . . . . . Elizabethton	7-9 . . . . .Burlington
9-11 . . . . . . at Greenville	10-12 . . . . . Kingsport
12-14 . . . . at Burlington	13-15 . . . . . at Pulaski
16-18 . . . . Pulaski	16 . . . . . .at Elizabethton
19-21 . . . . Bristol	17-19 . . . . . . .at Bristol
22-24 . . . . . .at Princeton	21-23 . . . . .at Danville
	24-26 . . . . at Kingsport
	27-29 . . . . . . Greenville

KINGSPORT METS

JUNE	
19-21	Danville
22-24	Bluefield
25-27	at Princeton
28-30	at Johnson City

JULY	
1	Greenville
3	Greenville
4-5	at Greenville
6-8	Pulaski
9-11	at Elizabethton
12-14	at Bristol
16-18	Burlington
19-21	Princeton
22-23	Greenville

24	at Greenville
25-27	at Burlington
28-30	at Danville
31	Elizabethton

AUGUST	
1-2	Elizabethton
3-5	at Pulaski
7-9	Bristol
10-12	at Johnson City
13-15	Bristol
16	Greenville
17	at Greenville
18-19	Greenville
21-23	at Bluefield
24-26	Johnson City
27-29	at Elizabethton

PRINCETON RAYS

JUNE	
19-21	Bristol
22-24	at Greenville
25-27	Kingsport
28-30	at Pulaski

JULY	
1	at Bluefield
3-5	at Johnson City
6-8	Danville
9-11	at Burlington
12-14	Bluefield
16-18	Elizabethton
19-21	at Kingsport

22-24	Johnson City
25-27	at Pulaski
28-30	at Bristol
31	Burlington

AUGUST	
1-2	Burlington
3-5	at Danville
7-9	at Bluefield
10-12	Pulaski
13-16	Bluefield
17-19	at Elizabethton
21-23	Greenville
24-26	Danville
27-29	at Burlington

PULASKI MARINERS

JUNE	
19-21	Burlington
22-24	at Elizabethton
25-27	at Bluefield
28-30	Princeton

JULY	
1	Bristol
3-4	Bristol
5	at Bristol
6-8	at Kingsport
9-11	Danville
12-14	at Greenville
16-18	at Johnson City
19-21	Bluefield
22-23	at Bristol

24	Bristol
25-27	Princeton
28-30	at Burlington
31	at Danville

AUGUST	
1-2	at Danville
3-5	Kingsport
7-9	Greenville
10-12	at Princeton
13-15	Johnson City
16	at Bristol
17-19	at Danville
21-23	Elizabethton
24-26	Burlington
27-29	at Bluefield

PIONEER LEAGUE

BILLINGS MUSTANGS

JUNE	
16-18	Great Falls
19-20	at Helena
21-24	at Great Falls
25-26	Missoula
27-30	Helena

JULY	
1-4	at Missoula
5-6	at Helena
8-11	Idaho Falls
12-14	Ogden
16-18	at Idaho Falls
19-22	at Ogden
23-24	Missoula
25-27	Great Falls
28-29	Helena

30-31	at Helena

AUGUST	
1-2	at Great Falls
4-7	Grand Junction
8-10	Orem
12-14	at Grand Junction
15-18	at Orem
20-23	Missoula
24-25	at Helena
26-27	at Great Falls
28-31	at Missoula

SEPTEMBER	
1-2	Great Falls
3-4	Helena

GRAND JUNCTION ROCKIES

JUNE	
16-19	at Ogden
20-23	Idaho Falls
24-25	Ogden
26-29	at Idaho Falls
30	at Orem

JULY	
1-3	at Orem
4-6	Orem
8-11	Missoula
12-14	Helena
16-18	at Missoula
19-22	at Helena
24-25	Ogden
26-27	Orem
28-29	at Orem

30-31	Idaho Falls

AUGUST	
1-2	Idaho Falls
4-7	at Billings
8-10	at Great Falls
12-14	Billings
15-18	at Great Falls
19-22	at Idaho Falls
23-24	at Ogden
25-28	Ogden
29-30	at Ogden
31	Orem

SEPTEMBER	
1-2	Orem
3-4	at Orem

GREAT FALLS VOYAGERS

JUNE	
16-18	at Billings
19-20	at Missoula
21-24	Billings
25-26	at Helena
27-30	Missoula

JULY	
1-2	at Helena
3-4	Helena
5-6	at Missoula
8-11	Ogden
12-14	Idaho Falls
16-18	at Ogden
19-22	at Idaho Falls
23-24	Helena
25-27	at Billings

28-31	at Missoula

AUGUST	
1-2	Billings
4-7	Orem
8-10	Grand Junction
12-14	at Orem
15-18	at Grand Junction
20-21	Helena
22-23	at Helena
24-25	Missoula
26-27	Billings
28-29	Helena
30-31	at Helena

SEPTEMBER	
1-2	at Billings
3-4	Missoula

HELENA BREWERS

JUNE	
16-18	Missoula
19-20	Billings
21-24	at Missoula
25-26	Great Falls
27-30	at Billings

JULY	
1-2	Great Falls
3-4	at Great Falls
5-6	Billings
8-11	at Orem
12-14	at Grand Junction
16-18	Orem
19-22	Grand Junction
23-24	at Great Falls
25-27	Missoula

28-29	at Billings
30-31	Billings

AUGUST	
1-2	at Missoula
4-7	at Idaho Falls
8-10	at Ogden
12-14	Idaho Falls
15-18	Ogden
20-21	at Great Falls
22-23	Great Falls
24-25	Billings
26-29	at Great Falls
30-31	Great Falls

SEPTEMBER	
1-2	Missoula
3-4	at Billings

IDAHO FALLS CHUKARS

JUNE	
16-19	Orem
20-23	Grand Junction
24-25	at Orem
26-29	Grand Junction
30	at Ogden

JULY	
1-2	at Ogden
3-6	Ogden
8-11	at Billings
12-14	at Great Falls
16-18	Billings
19-22	Great Falls
24-25	at Orem

26-27	at Ogden
28-29	Ogden
30-31	at Grand Junction

AUGUST	
1-2	at Grand Junction
4-7	Helena
8-10	Missoula
12-14	at Helena
15-18	at Missoula
19-22	Grand Junction
23-26	at Orem
27-30	Orem
31	at Ogden

SEPTEMBER
1-2 . . . . at Ogden

3-4 . . . . Ogden

MISSOULA OSPREY

JUNE
19-20 . . . . . . Great Falls
21-24 . . . . Helena

JULY
1-4 . . . . Billings
5-6 . . . . Great Falls
16-18 . . . . Grand Junction

19-22 . . . . Orem
28-31 . . . . . . Great Falls

AUGUST
1-2 . . . . Helena
12-14 . . . . Ogden
15-18 . . . . . Idaho Falls
26-27 . . . . Helena
28-31 . . . . Billings

OGDEN RAPTORS

JUNE
16-19 . . . . Grand Junction
20-21 . . . . at Orem
22-23 . . . . Orem
24-25 . . . at Grand Junction
26-27 . . . . Orem
28-29 . . . . at Orem
30 . . . . Idaho Falls

JULY
1-2 . . . . Idaho Falls
3-6 . . . . at Idaho Falls
8-11 . . . . . . at Great Falls
12-14 . . . . at Billings
16-18 . . . . . . Great Falls
19-22 . . . . Billings
24-25 . . . at Grand Junction
26-27 . . . . . . Idaho Falls

28-29 . . . . at Idaho Falls
30-31 . . . . at Orem

AUGUST
1-2 . . . . at Orem
4-7 . . . . Missoula
8-10 . . . . Helena
12-14 . . . . . at Missoula
15-18 . . . . . at Helena
19-22 . . . . Orem
23-24 . . . Grand Junction
25-28 . . at Grand Junction
29-30 . . . Grand Junction
31 . . . . Idaho Falls

SEPTEMBER
1-2 . . . . Idaho Falls
3-4 . . . . . . at Idaho Falls

OREM OWLZ

JUNE
16-19 . . . . . at Idaho Falls
20-21 . . . . Ogden
22-23 . . . . . . at Ogden
24-25 . . . . . Idaho Falls
26-27 . . . . . at Ogden
28-29 . . . . . . Ogden
30 . . . . . Grand Junction

JULY
1-3 . . . . . Grand Junction
4-6 . . . at Grand Junction
8-11 . . . . Helena
12-14 . . . . . . Missoula
16-18 . . . . . . at Helena
19-22 . . . . . at Missoula
24-25 . . . . . Idaho Falls

26-27 . . at Grand Junction
28-29 . . . Grand Junction
30-31 . . . . Ogden

AUGUST
1-2 . . . . Ogden
4-7 . . . . . at Great Falls
8-10 . . . . . . at Billings
12-14 . . . . . Great Falls
15-18 . . . . Billings
19-22 . . . . . at Ogden
23-26 . . . . . Idaho Falls
27-30 . . . . at Idaho Falls
31 . . . . at Grand Junction

SEPTEMBER
1-2 . . . at Grand Junction
3-4 . . . . . Grand Junction

ARIZONA LEAGUE   * HOME GAMES ONLY

ANGELS

JUNE
21 . . . . Athletics
23 . . . . Cubs
25 . . . . Giants
29 . . . . . Diamondbacks

JULY
1 . . . . Padres
4 . . . . Cubs
5 . . . . Rangers
8 . . . . Mariners
10 . . . . Dodgers
14 . . . . . Diamondbacks
17 . . . . Athletics
19 . . . . White Sox
22 . . . . Reds
24 . . . . Brewers

26 . . . . Athletics
30 . . . . Cubs

AUGUST
1 . . . . . . Diamondbacks
3 . . . . Giants
5 . . . . Padres
8 . . . . Indians
11 . . . . White Sox
14 . . . . Giants
16 . . . . Dodgers
18 . . . . Indians
19 . . . . . Diamondbacks
24 . . . . Cubs
26 . . . . Brewers
28 . . . . Mariners

ATHLETICS

JUNE
20 . . . . Angels
22 . . . . Giants
25 . . . . . Diamondbacks
28 . . . . Cubs

JULY
1 . . . . Rangers
2 . . . . Brewers
5 . . . . Padres
8 . . . . White Sox
10 . . . . Reds
13 . . . . Dodgers
16 . . . . Giants
18 . . . . Mariners
21 . . . . Indians

24 . . . . Cubs
27 . . . . Angels
29 . . . . Giants

AUGUST
1 . . . . Cubs
2 . . . . . Diamondbacks
5 . . . . Rangers
8 . . . . Brewers
11 . . . . Padres
12 . . . . White Sox
16 . . . . Reds
17 . . . . Dodgers
21 . . . . Angels
23 . . . . Mariners
26 . . . . . Diamondbacks
28 . . . . Cubs

BREWERS

JUNE
21 . . . . Reds
22 . . . . Indians
25 . . . . Dodgers
28 . . . . Padres
30 . . . . Mariners

JULY
3 . . . . Angels
6 . . . . Reds
8 . . . . Giants
11 . . . . White Sox
13 . . . . Rangers
17 . . . . Indians
18 . . . . Cubs
22 . . . . Padres

23 . . . . Athletics
26 . . . . Reds
29 . . . . Indians

AUGUST
1 . . . . Dodgers
2 . . . . Rangers
6 . . . . Mariners
7 . . . . Athletics
10 . . . . Reds
12 . . . . Giants
15 . . . . White Sox
17 . . . . . Diamondbacks
20 . . . . Indians
23 . . . . Cubs
25 . . . . . Diamondbacks
27 . . . . Dodgers

CUBS

JUNE
21 . . . . . Diamondbacks
24 . . . . Angels
26 . . . . Athletics
29 . . . . Giants

JULY
1 . . . . Reds
2 . . . . Padres
8 . . . . Indians
9 . . . . . Diamondbacks
11 . . . . Mariners
13 . . . . White Sox
19 . . . . Brewers
20 . . . . Angels
22 . . . . Dodgers

25 . . . . Giants
28 . . . . . Diamondbacks
29 . . . . Angels

AUGUST
2 . . . . Giants
3 . . . . Athletics
8 . . . . Padres
9 . . . . Angels
11 . . . . Rangers
12 . . . . Indians
17 . . . . White Sox
19 . . . . Giants
21 . . . . . Diamondbacks
22 . . . . Brewers
27 . . . . Athletics
29 . . . . . Diamondbacks

DIAMONDBACKS

JUNE
20 . . . . Giants
22 . . . . Cubs
26 . . . . Angels
27 . . . . Athletics

JULY
1 . . . . Dodgers
2 . . . . Indians
4 . . . . Giants
5 . . . . Mariners
10 . . . . Rangers
12 . . . . Brewers
16 . . . . Angels
17 . . . . Cubs
22 . . . . White Sox
23 . . . . Reds

25 . . . . Angels
27 . . . . Cubs
30 . . . . Giants
31 . . . . Athletics

AUGUST
4 . . . . Angels
5 . . . . Reds
11 . . . . Mariners
12 . . . . Padres
14 . . . . Cubs
16 . . . . Rangers
20 . . . . Athletics
22 . . . . White Sox
24 . . . . Giants
27 . . . . Padres

DODGERS

JUNE
20 . . . . Indians
23 . . . . Reds
26 . . . . Brewers
28 . . . . White Sox
30 . . . . Giants

JULY
3 . . . . Mariners
5 . . . . Indians
8 . . . . Padres
11 . . . . Angels
12 . . . . Athletics
17 . . . . Reds
19 . . . . Rangers
21 . . . . . Diamondbacks

23 . . . . White Sox
27 . . . . Indians
28 . . . . Reds
31 . . . . Brewers

AUGUST
2 . . . . White Sox
6 . . . . . . Diamondbacks
7 . . . . Mariners
11 . . . . Indians
12 . . . . Rangers
15 . . . . Angels
18 . . . . Athletics
20 . . . . Reds
22 . . . . Padres
26 . . . . Cubs
28 . . . . Brewers

PADRES

JUNE
21 . . . . Rangers
22 . . . . White Sox
26 . . . . Mariners
27 . . . . Brewers
30 . . . . Angels

JULY
3 . . . . Cubs
6 . . . . Athletics
7 . . . Diamondbacks
10 . . . . Indians
12 . . . . Mariners
17 . . . . Rangers
18 . . . . Dodgers
21 . . . . Brewers

24 . . . . Giants
26 . . . . Rangers
29 . . . . White Sox
31 . . . . Mariners

AUGUST
2 . . . . Reds
6 . . . . Angels
7 . . . . Cubs
10 . . . . Athletics
13 . . . . Dodgers
16 . . . . Indians
18 . . . . Mariners
20 . . . . White Sox
23 . . . . Reds
25 . . . . Dodgers
28 . . . . Rangers

GIANTS

JUNE
23 . . . . Athletics
24 . . . . . . Diamondbacks
27 . . . . Cubs
28 . . . . Angels

JULY
3 . . . . Rangers
5 . . . . White Sox
7 . . . . Brewers
9 . . . . Angels
12 . . . . Reds
14 . . . . Cubs
18 . . . . Indians
20 . . . . . Diamondbacks
23 . . . . Padres

26 . . . . . Diamondbacks
28 . . . . . . Athletics
31 . . . . Angels

AUGUST
4 . . . . Cubs
5 . . . . Dodgers
7 . . . . Rangers
9 . . . Diamondbacks
13 . . . . Brewers
15 . . . . Mariners
18 . . . . Reds
20 . . . . Angels
23 . . . . Indians
25 . . . . . . Athletics
28 . . . . White Sox
29 . . . . Angels

RANGERS

JUNE
20 . . . . Padres
22 . . . . Mariners
25 . . . . . . White Sox
28 . . . . Indians
30 . . . . Athletics

JULY
2 . . . . Giants
6 . . . . Cubs
7 . . . . Dodgers
11 . . . Diamondbacks
12 . . . . Indians
16 . . . . Padres
17 . . . . Reds
21 . . . . Mariners

23 . . . . Cubs
27 . . . . Padres
29 . . . . Mariners

AUGUST
1 . . . . White Sox
3 . . . . Brewers
6 . . . . Athletics
8 . . . . Giants
10 . . . . Angels
13 . . . . Reds
15 . . . Diamondbacks
18 . . . . Brewers
21 . . . . Padres
23 . . . . Dodgers
26 . . . . Mariners
27 . . . . . . White Sox

INDIANS

JUNE
21 . . . . Dodgers
23 . . . . Brewers
25 . . . . Reds
27 . . . . Mariners

JULY
1 . . . . White Sox
3 . . . . Athletics
6 . . . . Dodgers
7 . . . . Cubs
11 . . . . Padres
13 . . . . Angels
16 . . . . Brewers
19 . . . . Giants
22 . . . . . . Athletics

24 . . . . Rangers
26 . . . . Dodgers
28 . . . . Brewers

AUGUST
1 . . . . Reds
3 . . . . Mariners
5 . . . . . . White Sox
7 . . . Diamondbacks
10 . . . . Dodgers
13 . . . . Cubs
15 . . . . Padres
17 . . . . Rangers
21 . . . . Brewers
22 . . . . Giants
25 . . . . Angels
28 . . . . Reds

REDS

JUNE
20 . . . . Brewers
22 . . . . Dodgers
26 . . . . Indians
27 . . . . Rangers
30 . . . . . Diamondbacks

JULY
3 . . . . . White Sox
5 . . . . Brewers
8 . . . . Rangers
11 . . . . . . Athletics
13 . . . . Giants
16 . . . . . . Dodgers
19 . . . . Padres
21 . . . . Angels

24 . . . . . . Mariners
27 . . . . . . Brewers
29 . . . . . . Dodgers
31 . . . . Indians

AUGUST
3 . . . . Padres
6 . . . . Cubs
7 . . . . . White Sox
11 . . . . . . Brewers
12 . . . . . Mariners
15 . . . . . . Athletics
17 . . . . Giants
21 . . . . . . Dodgers
22 . . . . . . Rangers
26 . . . . . . Indians
27 . . . . . . Indians

MARINERS

JUNE
21 . . . . White Sox
23 . . . . Rangers
25 . . . . Padres
28 . . . . Reds

JULY
1 . . . . Brewers
2 . . . . Dodgers
6 . . . Diamondbacks
7 . . . . Reds
10 . . . . Giants
13 . . . . . . Padres
17 . . . . . White Sox
19 . . . . . Athletics
22 . . . . . . Rangers
23 . . . . . . Indians

26 . . . . . . White Sox
28 . . . . . . Rangers

AUGUST
1 . . . . Padres
2 . . . . Indians
5 . . . . . . Brewers
8 . . . . . . Dodgers
10 . . . Diamondbacks
13 . . . . . . Angels
16 . . . . Cubs
17 . . . . . . Padres
20 . . . . . . Rangers
22 . . . . . Athletics
25 . . . . Reds
27 . . . . . . Giants

WHITE SOX

JUNE
20 . . . . . . Mariners
23 . . . . . . Padres
26 . . . . . . Rangers
27 . . . . . . Dodgers
30 . . . . . . Indians

JULY
2 . . . . Reds
6 . . . . . . Angels
7 . . . . . Athletics
10 . . . . . . Brewers
12 . . . . . . Cubs
16 . . . . . Mariners
18 . . . Diamondbacks
21 . . . . . Giants
24 . . . . . Dodgers

27 . . . . . Mariners
28 . . . . . Padres
31 . . . . . Rangers

AUGUST
3 . . . . . . Dodgers
6 . . . . . . Indians
8 . . . . Reds
10 . . . . . Giants
13 . . . . . Athletics
16 . . . . . Brewers
18 . . . . . . Cubs
21 . . . . . Mariners
23 . . . . . Angels
25 . . . . . Rangers
26 . . . . . Padres

GULF COAST LEAGUE   * HOME GAMES ONLY

ASTROS

JUNE	
20	Braves
23	Tigers
26	Yankees 2
28	Pirates

JULY	
1	Phillies
3	Yankees 1
5	Blue Jays
8	Braves
10	Tigers
11	Yankees 2
14	Pirates
16	Phillies
18	Yankees 1
22	Blue Jays

23	Braves
26	Tigers
29	Yankees 2
31	Pirates

AUGUST	
2	Phillies
5	Yankees 1
6	Blue Jays
8	Braves
12	Tigers
13	Yankees 2
15	Pirates
18	Phillies
20	Yankees 1
23	Braves
25	Tigers
28	Yankees 2

BLUE JAYS

JUNE	
20	Phillies
24	Pirates
25	Yankees 1
28	Braves

JULY	
1	Tigers
2	Yankees 2
4	Astros
8	Phillies
9	Pirates
12	Yankees 1
14	Braves
16	Tigers
19	Yankees 2
21	Astros

24	Phillies
26	Pirates
28	Yankees 1
31	Braves

AUGUST	
2	Tigers
4	Yankees 2
7	Astros
8	Phillies
11	Pirates
14	Yankees 1
15	Braves
18	Tigers
21	Yankees 2
22	Phillies
26	Pirates
27	Yankees 1

BRAVES

JUNE	
21	Astros
24	Yankees 2
25	Tigers
27	Blue Jays
30	Yankees 1

JULY	
2	Phillies
4	Pirates
7	Astros
9	Yankees 2
12	Tigers
15	Blue Jays
17	Yankees 1
18	Phillies
22	Pirates

24	Astros
26	Yankees 2
28	Tigers
30	Blue Jays

AUGUST	
1	Yankees 1
4	Phillies
6	Pirates
8	Astros
11	Yankees 2
14	Tigers
16	Blue Jays
19	Yankees 1
21	Phillies
22	Astros
26	Yankees 2
28	Tigers

CARDINALS

JUNE	
21	Marlins
23	Nationals
25	Nationals
27	Mets

JULY	
1	Marlins
4	Nationals
7	Mets
9	Mets
10	Marlins
12	Marlins
14	Nationals
16	Nationals
18	Mets
22	Marlins
25	Nationals

28	Mets
30	Mets
31	Marlins

AUGUST	
2	Marlins
4	Nationals
6	Nationals
8	Mets
12	Marlins
15	Nationals
18	Mets
20	Mets
21	Marlins
23	Marlins
26	Mets
28	Nationals

MARLINS

JUNE	
20	Cardinals
24	Mets
27	Nationals
30	Cardinals

JULY	
2	Cardinals
3	Mets
5	Mets
7	Nationals
9	Nationals
11	Cardinals
15	Mets
18	Nationals
21	Cardinals
23	Cardinals

24	Mets
26	Mets
28	Nationals
30	Nationals

AUGUST	
1	Cardinals
5	Mets
7	Nationals
9	Nationals
11	Cardinals
13	Cardinals
14	Mets
16	Mets
19	Nationals
22	Cardinals
25	Nationals
27	Mets

METS

JUNE	
20	Nationals
23	Marlins
25	Marlins
26	Cardinals
28	Cardinals

JULY	
1	Nationals
4	Marlins
8	Cardinals
10	Nationals
12	Nationals
14	Marlins
16	Marlins
17	Cardinals
19	Cardinals

22	Nationals
25	Marlins
29	Cardinals
31	Nationals

AUGUST	
2	Nationals
4	Marlins
6	Marlins
7	Cardinals
9	Cardinals
12	Nationals
15	Marlins
19	Cardinals
21	Nationals
23	Nationals
25	Cardinals
28	Marlins

NATIONALS

JUNE	
21	Mets
24	Cardinals
26	Marlins
28	Marlins
30	Mets

JULY	
2	Mets
3	Cardinals
5	Cardinals
8	Marlins
11	Mets
15	Cardinals
17	Marlins
19	Marlins
21	Mets

23	Mets
24	Cardinals
26	Cardinals
29	Marlins

AUGUST	
1	Mets
5	Cardinals
8	Marlins
11	Mets
13	Mets
14	Cardinals
16	Cardinals
18	Marlins
20	Marlins
22	Mets
26	Marlins
27	Cardinals

ORIOLES

JUNE	
20	Rays
23	Twins
25	Twins
28	Rays
30	Red Sox

JULY	
2	Red Sox
4	Rays
8	Twins
10	Twins
12	Rays
15	Red Sox
17	Red Sox
18	Rays
21	Twins
23	Twins

26	Rays
28	Red Sox
30	Red Sox

AUGUST	
1	Rays
5	Twins
7	Twins
9	Rays
12	Red Sox
14	Red Sox
15	Rays
18	Twins
20	Twins
23	Rays
25	Red Sox
27	Red Sox

PHILLIES

JUNE	
21	.Blue Jays
23	Yankees 1
26	Pirates
27	.Tigers
30	.Astros

JULY	
3	Braves
4	Yankees 2
7	.Blue Jays
10	Yankees 1
12	Pirates
15	.Tigers
17	.Astros
19	Braves
22	Yankees 2

23	.Blue Jays
25	Yankees 1
29	Pirates
30	.Tigers

AUGUST	
1	.Astros
5	Braves
6	Yankees 2
9	.Blue Jays
12	Yankees 1
13	Pirates
15	.Tigers
19	.Astros
20	Braves
23	.Blue Jays
25	Yankees 1
28	Pirates

PIRATES

JUNE	
20	Yankees 1
23	.Blue Jays
25	Phillies
27	.Astros

JULY	
1	Yankees 2
3	.Tigers
5	Braves
8	Yankees 1
10	.Blue Jays
11	Phillies
15	.Astros
16	Yankees 2
19	.Tigers
21	Braves

23	Yankees 1
25	.Blue Jays
28	Phillies
30	.Astros

AUGUST	
2	Yankees 2
4	.Tigers
7	Braves
8	Yankees 1
12	.Blue Jays
14	Phillies
16	.Astros
18	Yankees 2
20	.Tigers
23	Yankees 1
25	.Blue Jays
27	Phillies

RAYS

JUNE	
21	Orioles
24	Red Sox
26	Red Sox
27	Orioles

JULY	
1	Twins
3	Twins
5	Orioles
7	Red Sox
9	Red Sox
11	Orioles
14	Twins
16	Twins
19	Orioles
22	Red Sox

24	Red Sox
25	Orioles
29	Twins
31	Twins

AUGUST	
2	Orioles
4	Red Sox
6	Red Sox
8	Orioles
11	Twins
13	Twins
16	Orioles
19	Red Sox
21	Red Sox
22	Orioles
26	Twins
28	Twins

RED SOX

JUNE	
20	Twins
23	.Rays
25	.Rays
28	Twins

JULY	
1	Orioles
3	Orioles
4	Twins
8	.Rays
10	.Rays
12	Twins
14	Orioles
16	Orioles
18	Twins
21	.Rays

23	.Rays
26	Twins
29	Orioles
31	Orioles

AUGUST	
1	Twins
5	.Rays
7	.Rays
9	Twins
11	Orioles
13	Orioles
15	Twins
18	.Rays
20	.Rays
23	Twins
26	Orioles
28	Orioles

TIGERS

JUNE	
21	Yankees 2
24	.Astros
26	Braves
28	Phillies
30	.Blue Jays

JULY	
2	Pirates
5	Yankees 1
7	Yankees 2
9	.Astros
11	Braves
14	Phillies
17	.Blue Jays
18	Pirates
21	Yankees 1

24	Yankees 2
25	.Astros
29	Braves
31	Phillies

AUGUST	
1	.Blue Jays
5	Pirates
7	Yankees 1
9	Yankees 2
11	.Astros
13	Braves
16	Phillies
19	.Blue Jays
21	Pirates
22	Yankees 2
26	.Astros
27	Braves

TWINS

JUNE	
21	Red Sox
24	Orioles
26	Orioles
27	Red Sox
30	.Rays

JULY	
2	.Rays
5	Red Sox
7	Orioles
9	Orioles
11	Red Sox
15	.Rays
17	.Rays
19	Red Sox
22	Orioles

24	Orioles
25	Red Sox
28	.Rays
30	.Rays

AUGUST	
2	Red Sox
4	Orioles
6	Orioles
8	Red Sox
12	.Rays
14	.Rays
16	Red Sox
19	Orioles
21	Orioles
22	Red Sox
25	.Rays
27	.Rays

YANKEES 1

JUNE	
21	Pirates
24	Phillies
26	.Blue Jays
27	Yankees 2
28	Yankees 2

JULY	
1	Braves
2	.Astros
4	.Tigers
7	Pirates
9	Phillies
11	.Blue Jays
14	Yankees 2
15	Yankees 2
16	Braves
19	.Astros
22	.Tigers

24	Pirates
26	Phillies
29	.Blue Jays
30	Yankees 2
31	Yankees 2

AUGUST	
2	Braves
4	.Astros
6	.Tigers
9	Pirates
11	Phillies
13	.Blue Jays
15	Yankees 2
16	Yankees 2
18	Braves
21	.Astros
22	Pirates
26	Phillies
28	.Blue Jays

YANKEES 2

JUNE	
20	.Tigers
23	Braves
25	.Astros
28	Yankees 1
30	Pirates

JULY	
3	.Blue Jays
5	Phillies
8	.Tigers
10	Braves
12	.Astros
15	Yankees 1
17	Pirates
18	.Blue Jays
21	Phillies

23	.Tigers
25	Braves
28	.Astros
30	Yankees 1

AUGUST	
1	Pirates
5	.Blue Jays
7	Phillies
8	.Tigers
12	Braves
14	.Astros
16	Yankees 1
19	Pirates
20	.Blue Jays
23	.Tigers
25	Braves
27	.Astros

INDEPENDENT

AMERICAN ASSOCIATION

AMARILLO SOX

MAY	
15-18	Winnipeg
19-21	Fargo-Moorhead
26-28	Trois-Rivieres
29-31	Grand Prairie

JUNE	
1	Grand Prairie
9-11	Laredo
13-15	Wichita
23-26	Kansas City

27-29	Sioux City

JULY	
4-6	Laredo
14-16	Quebec
25-27	Wichita

AUGUST	
3-6	Sioux Falls
12-14	Kansas City
15-17	Laredo
21-24	Grand Prairie

FARGO-MOORHEAD REDHAWKS

MAY	
26-28	Sioux Falls
29-31	Sioux City

JUNE	
1	Sioux City
6-8	Winnipeg
10-12	Lincoln
17-19	Rockland
23-26	St. Paul

JULY	
4-6	Winnipeg

8-10	Gary SouthShore
18-20	Sioux Falls
25-27	St. Paul

AUGUST	
3-6	Wichita
7-10	Gary SouthShore
22-24	Sioux City
26-28	Kansas City
29-31	Sioux Falls

SEPTEMBER	
1	Sioux Falls

GARY SOUTHSHORE RAILCATS

MAY	
22-25	Wichita
26-28	Kansas City

JUNE	
6-8	Sioux Falls
9-11	Sioux City
20-22	Lincoln
23-26	Sioux Falls

JULY	
4-6	St.Paul

14-16	Fargo-Moorhead
18-20	Amarillo
25-27	Winnipeg
30-31	Kansas City

AUGUST	
1-2	Kansas City
3-6	Lincoln
11-13	Sioux City
18-20	St.Paul
21-24	Kansas City

GRAND PRAIRIE AIRHOGS

MAY	
19-21	Lincoln
22-25	Laredo

JUNE	
2-5	Trois-Rivieres
6	Wichita
8	Wichita
16-18	Gary SouthShore
20-22	Amarillo
30	Sioux City

JULY	
1-2	Sioux City

4-6	Lincoln
15-17	Wichita
18-20	Quebec

AUGUST	
3-6	Laredo
7-10	Amarillo
18-20	Laredo
25-27	Wichita
29-31	Amarillo

SEPTEMBER	
1	Amarillo

KANSAS CITY T-BONES

MAY	
15-18	Lincoln
22-25	Fargo-Moorhead

JUNE	
2-5	Wichita
6-9	Laredo
17-19	Sioux City

20-22	Laredo
27-29	Gary SouthShore

JULY	
4-6	Sioux Falls
8-10	Grand Prairie
18-20	Winnipeg
21-23	Grand Prairie

LAREDO LEMURS

MAY	
15-18	Fargo-Moorhead
19-21	Winnipeg
30-31	Trois-Rivieres

JUNE	
1	Trois-Rivieres
2-4	Amarillo
13-15	Kansas City
16-18	Wichita
27-29	Grand Prairie

JULY	
1-3	Lincoln
11-13	Quebec
25-27	Grand Prairie
30-31	Amarillo

AUGUST	
1-2	Amarillo
8-11	Kansas City
12-14	Grand Prairie
21-24	Wichita
25-28	Amarillo

LINCOLN SALTDOGS

MAY	
23-25	Winnipeg
26-27	Grand Prairie

JUNE	
3-5	Fargo-Moorhead
6-8	Amarillo
13-15	Gary SouthShore
23-25	Laredo
27-29	Wichita

JULY	
7-9	Laredo

22-24	Amarillo
25-27	Kansas City
30-31	Grand Prairie

AUGUST	
1-2	Grand Prairie
7-10	Sioux Falls
11-13	Wichita
21-24	St. Paul
29-31	Sioux City

SEPTEMBER	
1	Sioux City

SIOUX CITY EXPLORERS

MAY	
17	Sioux Falls
19-21	St. Paul
22-25	Amarillo

JUNE	
2-5	Gary SouthShore
13-15	Grand Prairie
20-22	Sioux Falls
23-26	Rockland
27-29	St. Paul

JULY	
3-5	Wichita
11-13	Fargo-Moorhead
14-16	Kansas City
21-24	Gary SouthShore
30-31	Fargo-Moorhead

AUGUST	
1-2	Fargo-Moorhead
3-6	Winnipeg
14-17	Lincoln
26-28	Gary SouthShore

SIOUX FALLS CANARIES

MAY	
15-16	Sioux City
18	Sioux City
19-20	Gary SouthShore
29-31	Kansas City

JUNE	
1	Kansas City
2-5	Winnipeg
13-15	Fargo-Moorhead
17-19	Amarillo
30	Gary SouthShore

JULY	
1-3	Gary SouthShore
11-13	Grand Prairie
15-17	Laredo
25-27	Sioux City
30-31	Winnipeg

AUGUST	
1-2	Winnipeg
12-14	New Jersey
15-17	Winnipeg
19-20	Sioux City
26-28	Lincoln

ST. PAUL SAINTS

MAY	
15-18	Gary SouthShore
22-25	Sioux Falls

JUNE	
6-8	Sioux City
9-11	Sioux Falls
16-19	Lincoln

29-31	St. Paul

SEPTEMBER	
1	St. Paul

AUGUST	
3-6	St. Paul
15-17	Gary SouthShore
18-20	Amarillo

MINOR LEAGUES

20-22 . . . . Rockland

JULY
1-3 . . . . . .Fargo-Moorhead
8-10 . . . . Amarillo
11-13 . . . . Kansas City
18-20 . . . . Laredo
21-24 . . . . Sioux Falls

WICHITA WINGNUTS

MAY
15-18 . . . . . Grand Prairie
19-21 . . . . . . Kansas City
26-29 . . . . Laredo
30-31 . . . Gary SouthShore

JUNE
1 . . . . . Gary SouthShore
10-12 . . . . . . Kansas City
20-22 . .Fargo-Moorhead
23-26 . . . Grand Prairie
30 . . . . Amarillo

WINNIPEG GOLDEYES

MAY
26-28 . . . . Sioux City
29-31 . . . . .Lincoln

JUNE
1 . . . . .Lincoln
10-12 . . . . . Grand Prairie
13-15 . . . . St. Paul
27-30 . . .Fargo-Moorhead

JULY
1-3 . . . . Kansas City
8-10 . . . . Sioux City

ATLANTIC LEAGUE

BRIDGEPORT BLUEFISH

APRIL
30 . . . . Sugar Land

MAY
1 . . . . Sugar Land
2-5 . . . .Southern Maryland
13-15 . . . . . . Long Island
16-18 . . . . .York
27-29 . . . . . . Sugar Land
30-31 . . . . Camden

JUNE
1 . . . . Camden
6-9 . . . . Somerset
14-16 . . . . Lancaster
17-20 . . . . .York
26-29 . . . . Camden

CAMDEN RIVERSHARKS

MAY
2-5 . . . . Sugar Land
9-10 . . . . Bridgeport
19-22 . . . . Somerset
23-26 . . . . . . Bridgeport

JUNE
3-5 . . . .Southern Maryland
11-13 . . . . .York
17-20 . . . . . . Long Island
21-24 . . . . Lancaster

JULY
7-9 . . . . Lancaster

31 . . . . .Wichita

AUGUST
1-2 . . . . .Wichita
7-10 . . . . Sioux City
15-17 . . . . . . New Jersey
26-28 . . . . Winnipeg

JULY
1-2 . . . . Amarillo
7-9 . . . . Sioux Falls
11-13 . . . . Amarillo
18-20 . . . . Sioux City
21-24 . . . . Laredo

AUGUST
15-17 . . . . . Grand Prairie
18-20 . . . . Lincoln
29-31 . . . . Laredo

SEPTEMBER
1 . . . . Laredo

11-13 . . . Gary SouthShore
15-17 . . . . .St. Paul
21-23 . . .Fargo-Moorhead

AUGUST
7-10 . . . . .Wichita
12-14 . . . . .St. Paul
18-20 . . . . . . New Jersey
21-24 . . . . . . .Sioux Falls
29-31 . . . Gary SouthShore

SEPTEMBER
1 . . . . . . Gary SouthShore

JULY
7-9 . . .Southern Maryland
18-20 . . . . Somerset
27 29 . . . . . . Long Island

AUGUST
6-8 . . . . Lancaster
9-11 . . . . Camden
18-20 . . . . . . Long Island
21-24 . . . . Lancaster
29-31 . . . . . . Sugar Land

SEPTEMBER
1 . . . . Sugar Land
2-4 . . . . .York
10-11 . . . . Somerset
12-14 . .Southern Maryland

18-20 . .Southern Maryland
24-26 . . . . . . Long Island
27-29 . . . . . . Sugar Land
30-31 . . . . . . Long Island

AUGUST
1 . . . . Long Island
2-3 . . . . Somerset
12-14 . . . . .York
21-24 . . . . .York
26-28 . . . . . . Sugar Land

SEPTEMBER
2-4 . . . .Southern Maryland

5-7 . . . . Lancaster
12-14 . . . . Somerset

LANCASTER BARNSTORMERS

MAY
1 . . . . .York
2-5 . . . . Somerset
9-11 . . . . Long Island
13-15 . . . . .York
19-22 . . . . . . Bridgeport
27-29 . . . . . . Long Island
30-31 . . . . . . Sugar Land

JUNE
1 . . . . Sugar Land
6-9 . . . . Camden
17-20 . . . . . . Sugar Land
26-29 . .Southern Maryland

JULY
4-6 . . . . .York

LONG ISLAND DUCKS

MAY
2-4 . . . . .York
6-8 . . . . Lancaster
16-18 . . . . Camden
19-22 . .Southern Maryland
30-31 . . . . Somerset

JUNE
1 . . . . Somerset
2-5 . . . . Lancaster
11-13 . . . . . . Bridgeport
21-23 . . . . . . Sugar Land
30 . . . . Bridgeport

JULY
1-3 . . . . Bridgeport

SOMERSET PATRIOTS

APRIL
25-27 . . . . . . Long island
29-30 . . . . Camden

MAY
1 . . . . Camden
13-15 . . . . Camden
16-18 . . . . . . Sugar Land
23-26 . .Southern Maryland

JUNE
2-5 . . . . .York
11-13 . . . . Lancaster
14-16 . . . . . . Long Island
21-24 . . . . . . Bridgeport
30 . . . . Lancaster

SOUTHERN MARYLAND BLUE CRABS

APRIL
24-27 . . . . . . Bridgeport
29-30 . . . . . . Long Island

MAY
1 . . . . Long Island
6-8 . . . . Camden
13-15 . . . . . . Sugar Land
16-18 . . . . . . Lancaster
27-29 . . . . Camden
30-31 . . . . .York

JUNE
1 . . . . .York

16-18 . . . . . . Bridgeport

AUGUST
2-4 . . . .Southern Maryland
12-14 . . . . Somerset
15-17 . .Southern Maryland
26-28 . . . . . . Bridgeport

SEPTEMBER
2-4 . . . . Somerset
9-11 . . . . Camden
12-14 . . . . . . Sugar Land
19-21 . . . . Camden

4-6 . . . . Camden
7-9 . . . . Sugar Land
18-20 . . . . .York
21-23 . . . . . . Bridgeport

AUGUST
2-4 . . . . .York
12-14 . . . . . . Sugar Land
15-17 . . . . Somerset
21-24 . . . . Somerset
29-31 . . . . Camden

SEPTEMBER
1 . . . . Camden
9-11 . .Southern Maryland
16-18 . . . . Lancaster
19-21 . .Southern Maryland

JULY
1-3 . . . . Lancaster
4-6 . . . . Bridgeport
10-13 . . . . . . Sugar Land
24-26 . . . . .York
27-29 . .Southern Maryland
30-31 . . . . Lancaster

AUGUST
1 . . . . Lancaster
5-8 . . . . Camden
9-11 . . . . Sugar Land
18-20 . .Southern Maryland
26-28 . . . . . . Long Island

SEPTEMBER
5-7 . . . . .York
19-21 . . . . . . Bridgeport

6-9 . . . . Long Island
17-20 . . . . Somerset
21-24 . . . . .York

JULY
4-6 . . . . Sugar Land
10-13 . . . . Camden
21-23 . . . . Somerset
24-26 . . . . . . Sugar Land

AUGUST
6-8 . . . . Long Island
9-11 . . . . Lancaster
12-14 . . . . . . Bridgeport

26-28 . . . . York
29-31 . . . . Lancaster

SEPTEMBER
1 . . . . Lancaster
5-7 . . . . Bridgeport
16-18 . . . . Somerset

SUGAR LAND SKEETERS

APRIL		JULY	
24-27 . . . . Lancaster		1-3 . . . . Camden	
MAY		18-23 . . . . Lancaster	
6-11 . . . . Somerset		30-31 . . . . Bridgeport	
19-22 . . . . York		**AUGUST**	
23-26 . . . . . . Long Island		1-4 . . . . Bridgeport	
JUNE		15-20 . . . . Camden	
2-5 . . . . Bridgeport		21-24 . . Southern Maryland	
11-16 . . Southern Maryland		**SEPTEMBER**	
26-29 . . . . Somerset		2-7 . . . . Long Island	
30 . . . . Camden		16-21 . . . . York	

YORK REVOLUTION

APRIL		7-9 . . . . Somerset	
24-27 . . . . Camden		10-13 . . . . . Bridgeport	
29-30 . . . . Lancaster		21-23 . . . . Camden	
MAY		30-31 . . Southern Maryland	
6-8 . . . . Bridgeport		**AUGUST**	
9-11 . . . Southern Maryland		1 . . . . . Southern Maryland	
23-26 . . . . . . Lancaster		5 . . . . Lancaster	
27-29 . . . . Somerset		6-8 . . . . . . Sugar Land	
JUNE		9-11 . . . . . . Long Island	
6-9 . . . . Sugar Land		15-17 . . . . . . Bridgeport	
14-16 . . . . Camden		18-20 . . . . . . Lancaster	
26-29 . . . . . . Long Island		29-31 . . . . Somerset	
30 . . . . Southern Maryland		**SEPTEMBER**	
JULY		1 . . . . Somerset	
1-3 . . . Southern Maryland		9-11 . . . . . . Sugar Land	
		12-14 . . . . . . Long Island	

FRONTIER LEAGUE

EVANSVILLE OTTERS

MAY		JULY	
9 . . . . . . Southern Illinois		2-3 . . . . Frontier	
21-22 . . . . Rockford		9-10 . . . . . . Traverse City	
23-25 . . . . Frontier		11-13 . . . . . . Lake Erie	
JUNE		18-20 . . . Southern Illinois	
4-5 . . . . Normal		27-28 . . . . . Washington	
11-12 . . . . Gateway		**AUGUST**	
13-15 . . . . Rockford		7-8 . . . . Joliet	
24-26 . . . . Florence		9-11 . . . . River City	
27-29 . . . . . Schaumburg		15-17 . . . . . Washington	
		27-28 . . . . . Windy City	
		29-31 . . . . . . Florence	

FLORENCE FREEDOM

MAY		9-10 . . . . Frontier	
15-17 . . . . . Washington		22-23 . . . . . Schaumburg	
20-22 . . . . . Traverse City		24-26 . . . . . Rockford	
30-31 . . . . . Evansville		30-31 . . . . . . Gateway	
JUNE		**AUGUST**	
1 . . . . Evansville		1 . . . . Gateway	
4-5 . . . . Lake Erie		2-4 . . . . . Traverse City	
11-12 . . . . Windy City		9-10 . . . . Normal	
13-15 . . . Southern Illinois		15-17 . . . . . . Joliet	
20-22 . . . . . . Frontier		19-21 . . . . Windy City	
27-29 . . . . . River City		**SEPTEMBER**	
JULY		2-4 . . . . River City	
4-6 . . . . Washington			

GATEWAY GRIZZLIES

MAY		24-26 . . . . . Schaumburg	
7 . . . . . Southern Illinois		**JULY**	
9 . . . . Frontier		1-3 . . . . Florence	
10 . . . . Wichita		4-5 . . . . River City	
16-18 . . . . Traverse City		11-13 . . . Southern Illinois	
20-22 . . . . Joliet		24-26 . . . . . Evansville	
26 . . . . Frontier		27 . . . . Frontier	
30-31 . . . . . . Frontier		29 . . . . Frontier	
JUNE		**AUGUST**	
1 . . . . Frontier		6-8 . . . . Normal	
3-5 . . . . Rockford		9-11 . . . Windy City	
13-15 . . . . . Lake Erie		15-17 . . . Schaumburg	
17-19 . . . Southern Illinois		26-28 . . . . . Frontier	
21 . . . . . . River City		29-31 . . . . . Washington	

JOLIET SLAMMERS

MAY		21-23 . . . . Traverse City	
16-18 . . . Southern Illinois		30-31 . . . . . Frontier	
23-25 . . . . . . Normal		**AUGUST**	
27-29 . . . . . Washington		1 . . . . Frontier	
JUNE		2-4 . . . . . Schaumburg	
6-8 . . . . River City		9-11 . . . Southern Illinois	
10-12 . . . . Traverse City		12-14 . . . . . Lake Erie	
17-19 . . . . . . Normal		19-21 . . . . . Rockford	
27-29 . . . . . Gateway		26-28 . . . . . Florence	
JULY		29-31 . . . . . Frontier	
4-6 . . . . Evansville		**SEPTEMBER**	
18-20 . . . . Windy City		2-4 . . . . Gateway	

LAKE ERIE CRUSHERS

MAY		18-20 . . . . . . Florence	
16-18 . . . . . Schaumburg		21-23 . . . . . Frontier	
27-29 . . . . Traverse City		30-31 . . . . Windy City	
30-31 . . . . . . Joliet		**AUGUST**	
JUNE		1 . . . . Windy City	
1 . . . . Joliet		2-4 . . . . . Evansville	
6-8 . . . . Evansville		9-11 . . . . . . Frontier	
10-12 . . . . . . Normal		19-21 . . . . . Gateway	
17-19 . . . . Washington		22-24 . . . . . River City	
24-26 . . . . . Rockford		**SEPTEMBER**	
27-29 . . . . Washington		2-4 . . . . Southern Illinois	
JULY			
4-6 . . . . Frontier			

NORMAL CORNBELTERS

MAY		18-20 . . . . . . Frontier	
16-18 . . . . . Evansville		22-23 . . . . . Washington	
20-22 . . . . . River City		24-26 . . . . . Lake Erie	
27-29 . . . . . Evansville		30-31 . . . Southern Illinois	
JUNE		**AUGUST**	
6-8 . . . . Florence		1 . . . . . Southern Illinois	
13-15 . . . . . Frontier		2-3 . . . . Rockford	
24-26 . . . . Windy City		12-14 . . . . . Gateway	
27-29 . . . . . Frontier		19-21 . . . Schaumburg	
JULY		22-24 . . . . Traverse City	
8-10 . . . . Joliet		26-28 . . . . . Lake Erie	

RIVER CITY RASCALS

MAY		JUNE	
9 . . . . Wichita		1 . . . . Schaumburg	
11 . . . . Frontier		10-12 . . . . . Rockford	
23-25 . . . . . Gateway		13-15 . . . . Traverse City	
30-31 . . . . . Schaumburg		20-22 . . . . . Gateway	
		24-26 . . . . Joliet	

JULY		AUGUST	
8-10	Schaumburg	1	Evansville
11-13	Windy City	6-8	Florence
24-26	Frontier	12-14	Frontier
27-29	Normal	15-17	Southern Illinois
30-31	Evansville	26-28	Washington
		29-31	Lake Erie

ROCKFORD AVIATORS

MAY			
16-18	River City	8-10	Gateway
27-29	Florence	11-13	Frontier
30-31	Traverse City	17-19	Schaumburg
JUNE		21-23	River City
1	Traverse City	27-29	Windy City
6-8	Washington	**AUGUST**	
17-19	Frontier	6-8	Lake Erie
20-22	Joliet	12-14	Southern Illinois
JULY		15-17	Normal
1-3	Lake Erie	22-24	Evansville
		SEPTEMBER	
		3-4	Frontier

SCHAUMBURG BOOMERS

MAY			
23-25	Florence	11-13	Joliet
27-29	Gateway	24-26	Traverse City
JUNE		27-29	Lake Erie
3-5	Frontier	**AUGUST**	
6-8	Southern Illinois	6-8	Washington
17-19	River City	9-11	Rockford
20-22	Windy City	12-14	Evansville
JULY		22-24	Frontier
1-3	Joliet	26-28	Rockford
4-6	Normal	**SEPTEMBER**	
		2-4	Normal

SOUTHERN ILLINOIS MINERS

MAY			
6	Gateway	20-22	Evansville
13	Evansville	24-26	Frontier
20-22	Schaumburg	27-29	Traverse City
23-25	Lake Erie	**JULY**	
30-31	Normal	4-6	Rockford
JUNE		8-10	Windy City
1	Normal	21-13	Gateway
3-5	Joliet	24-26	Washington
10-12	Frontier	27-29	Florence

AUGUST			
2-4	River City	19-21	Frontier
6-8	Windy City	22-24	Florence
		29-31	Normal

TRAVERSE CITY BEACH BUMS

MAY			
23-25	Windy City	18-20	Gateway
JUNE		27-29	Joliet
3-5	Washington	30-31	Schaumburg
6-8	Frontier	**AUGUST**	
18-19	Evansville	1	Schaumburg
20-22	Lake Erie	6-8	Frontier
JULY		12-14	Florence
1-3	River City	15-17	Lake Erie
4-6	Windy City	20-21	Evansville
11-13	Normal	26-28	Southern Illinois
		29-31	Rockford

WASHINGTON WILD THINGS

MAY			
20-22	Frontier	9-10	Lake Erie
23-25	Rockford	11-13	Florence
30-31	Windy City	18-20	River City
JUNE		30-31	Normal
1	Windy City	**AUGUST**	
11-12	Schaumburg	1	Normal
13-15	Joliet	2-3	Frontier
20-22	Normal	9-10	Traverse City
24-26	Traverse City	20-21	River City
JULY		22-24	Gateway
2-4	Southern Illinois	**SEPTEMBER**	
		2-4	Evansville

WINDY CITY THUNDERBOLTS

MAY			
16-18	Frontier	21-23	Evansville
20-22	Lake Erie	24-26	Joliet
27-29	Southern Illinois	**AUGUST**	
JUNE		2-4	Gateway
3-5	River City	12-14	Washington
6-8	Gateway	15-17	Frontier
13-15	Schaumburg	22-24	Joliet
17-19	Florence	29-31	Schaumburg
27-29	Rockford	**SEPTEMBER**	
JULY		2-4	Traverse City
1-3	Normal		

SPRING TRAINING SCHEDULES

ARIZONA CACTUS LEAGUE

ARIZONA DIAMONDBACKS

FEBRUARY			
26	Los Angeles (NL)	7	at Oakland
27	at Chicago (NL)	8	at Los Angeles (AL)
27	at Los Angeles (NL)	8	at Chicago (AL)
28	Colorado	9	San Diego
MARCH		10	Seattle
1	Milwaukee	11	Cleveland
1	Chicago (NL)	12	at Colorado
2	at San Francisco	12	at Los Angeles (NL)
3	Los Angeles (AL)	13	Seattle
3	Colorado	14	at Milwaukee
4	at San Diego	15	at Cleveland
5	Kansas City	16	Milwaukee
6	Oakland	26	Chicago (NL)
		27	at Cincinnati
		27	Cleveland

CHICAGO CUBS

FEBRUARY			
27	Arizona	12	at Seattle
28	at Los Angeles (AL)	14	Los Angeles (NL)
MARCH		15	at Kansas City
1	San Francisco	16	Cleveland
1	at Arizona	17	at Oakland
2	Kansas City	17	Los Angeles (AL)
3	at Milwaukee	18	at Texas
4	Oakland	19	at Colorado
5	Colorado	20	Seattle
6	at Cleveland	21	at Chicago (AL)
7	at Los Angeles (AL)	22	Cincinnati
7	Cleveland	23	at Oakland
8	at Cincinnati	24	San Diego
9	Milwaukee	25	at San Diego
10	at San Francisco	25	Los Angeles (AL)
11	Colorado	26	at Arizona
		27	Chicago (AL)

CHICAGO WHITE SOX

FEBRUARY
28 . . . . at Los Angeles (NL)

MARCH
1 . . . . Cleveland
2 . . . . at Texas
3 . . . . Kansas City
4 . . . . at Cleveland
5 . . . . San Diego
6 . . . . Seattle
6 . . . . at Kansas City
7 . . . . at Cincinnati
8 . . . . .Arizona
9 . . . . at Oakland
10 . . . . . at Milwaukee
11 . . . . Texas

12 . . . . . at San Francisco
13 . . . . at Los Angeles (AL)
14 . . . . Cleveland
15 . . . . .Los Angeles (NL)
16 . . . . at Texas
17 . . . . . .at Milwaukee
18 . . . . Oakland
19 . . . . .Los Angeles (NL)
21 . . . . . Chicago (NL)
22 . . . . . . .San Francisco
22 . . . . . at San Diego
23 . . . . . . at Colorado
24 . . . . at Seattle
25 . . . . .Colorado
26 . . . . Cincinnati
27 . . . . .at Chicago (NL)

CINCINNATI REDS

FEBRUARY
26 . . . . at Cleveland
27 . . . . Cleveland
28 . . . . at Cleveland

MARCH
1 . . . . .Colorado
2 . . . . . . at San Diego
3 . . . . Seattle
4 . . . . . . at Kansas City
5 . . . .Los Angeles (NL)
6 . . . . . at San Francisco
7 . . . . Chicago (AL)
7 . . . . at Seattle
8 . . . . . Chicago (NL)
9 . . . . at Los Angeles (AL)
10 . . . . at Texas

11 . . . . . . .San Francisco
12 . . . . at Colorado
13 . . . . at Los Angeles (NL)
14 . . . . Texas
15 . . . . Milwaukee
16 . . . . Oakland
17 . . . . Cleveland
19 . . . . at Kansas City
20 . . . . Texas
21 . . . . Kansas City
22 . . . .at Chicago (NL)
23 . . . . Milwaukee
24 . . . . Cleveland
25 . . . . . . at Oakland
26 . . . .at Chicago (AL)
27 . . . . . .at Milwaukee
27 . . . . .Arizona

CLEVELAND INDIANS

FEBRUARY
26 . . . . Cincinnati
27 . . . . . . at Cincinnati
28 . . . . Cincinnati

MARCH
1 . . . .at Chicago (AL)
2 . . . . Seattle
3 . . . . at Texas
4 . . . . . . Chicago (AL)
5 . . . . at Seattle
6 . . . . . . Chicago (NL)
7 . . . .at Chicago (NL)
8 . . . . . at San Diego
9 . . . . Milwaukee
10 . . . . .Los Angeles (AL)
11 . . . . at Arizona

12 . . . . San Diego
13 . . . . Kansas City
14 . . . . . .at Chicago (AL)
15 . . . . .Arizona
16 . . . . at San Francisco
16 . . . .at Chicago (NL)
17 . . . . . at Cincinnati
18 . . . . .San Francisco
19 . . . . Oakland
21 . . . . . . at Colorado
22 . . . . .Colorado
23 . . . at Los Angeles (AL)
24 . . . . . . at Cincinnati
25 . . . . Texas
26 . . . . Milwaukee
27 . . . . at Arizona

COLORADO ROCKIES

FEBRUARY
28 . . . . at Arizona

MARCH
1 . . . . at Cincinnati
2 . . . . Milwaukee
3 . . . . at Arizona
3 . . . . at Seattle
4 . . . . . .San Francisco
5 . . . .at Chicago (NL)
5 . . . . at Texas
6 . . . . . at Milwaukee
7 . . .Los Angeles (AL)
8 . . . . Oakland
9 . . . . . at Kansas City
10 . . . . San Diego

11 . . . . . .at Chicago (NL)
12 . . . . Cincinnati
12 . . . . .Arizona
13 . . . . . . at Oakland
14 . . . . Seattle
14 . . . . . at San Francisco
15 . . . . .Los Angeles (AL)
16 . . . at Los Angeles (NL)
17 . . . . . at San Diego
19 . . . . . Chicago (NL)
20 . . . . Milwaukee
21 . . . . Cleveland
22 . . . . Seattle
22 . . . . . at Cleveland
23 . . . . . Chicago (AL)
24 . . . . Kansas City

KANSAS CITY ROYALS

FEBRUARY
27 . . . . Texas
28 . . . . at Texas

MARCH
1 . . . . San Diego
2 . . . .at Chicago (NL)
3 . . . .at Chicago (AL)
4 . . . . Cincinnati
5 . . . . at Arizona
6 . . . . . . Chicago (AL)
7 . . . . .San Francisco
8 . . . . . .at Milwaukee
9 . . . . .Colorado
10 . . . . at Seattle
11 . . . . .Los Angeles (NL)

12 . . . . at Oakland
13 . . . . . at Cleveland
14 . . . . Oakland
15 . . . . . Chicago (NL)
16 . . . . at San Diego
17 . . . . Texas
19 . . . . Cincinnati
20 . . . .Los Angeles (AL)
21 . . . at Los Angeles (AL)
21 . . . . . at Cincinnati
22 . . . . Texas
23 . . . . at San Francisco
24 . . . . . . at Colorado
25 . . . . Seattle
26 . . . . . at San Diego

LOS ANGELES ANGELS

FEBRUARY
28 . . . . . . Chicago (NL)

MARCH
1 . . . . at Seattle
2 . . . . Oakland
3 . . . . . at Arizona
4 . . . . Texas
5 . . . . at San Francisco
6 . . . .Los Angeles (NL)
7 . . . . . . Chicago (NL)
7 . . . . . at Colorado
8 . . . . .Arizona
9 . . . . Cincinnati
10 . . . . . at Cleveland
11 . . . . Seattle

12 . . . . Milwaukee
12 . . . . . . at Texas
13 . . . . . Chicago (AL)
14 . . . . at San Diego
15 . . . . . at Colorado
16 . . . . Seattle
17 . . . .San Francisco
17 . . . . .at Chicago (AL)
19 . . . . .at Chicago (AL)
20 . . . . at Kansas City
21 . . . . . Kansas City
22 . . . .at Milwaukee
23 . . . . . . Cleveland
24 . . . . .San Francisco
25 . . . .at Chicago (NL)
26 . . . . . at Oakland

LOS ANGELES DODGERS

FEBRUARY
26 . . . . . at Arizona
27 . . . . . .Arizona
28 . . . . . Chicago (AL)

MARCH
1 . . . . . .at Milwaukee
2 . . . . San Diego
3 . . . . . . at Oakland
4 . . . . Seattle
5 . . . . . . at Cincinnati
6 . . . . at Los Angeles (AL)

7 . . . . Texas
8 . . . . Seattle
8 . . . . at Texas
9 . . . .San Francisco
10 . . . . Oakland
11 . . . . at Kansas City
12 . . . . . . .Arizona
13 . . . . . . Cincinnati
14 . . . .at Chicago (NL)
15 . . . .at Chicago (AL)
15 . . . . San Diego
16 . . . . . . .Colorado

MILWAUKEE BREWERS

FEBRUARY
27 . . . . at Oakland
28 . . . . . at San Francisco

MARCH
1 . . . .Los Angeles (NL)
1 . . . . at Arizona
2 . . . . . . at Colorado
3 . . . . . . Chicago (NL)
4 . . . . . . at Oakland
5 . . . . Oakland
6 . . . . .Colorado
7 . . . . San Diego
8 . . . . . Kansas City
9 . . . . . .at Chicago (NL)
9 . . . . . at Cleveland

10 . . . . . . Chicago (AL)
12 . . . at Los Angeles (AL)
13 . . . . . at San Diego
14 . . . . .Arizona
15 . . . . Cincinnati
16 . . . . . at Arizona
17 . . . . . Chicago (AL)
18 . . . . Texas
19 . . . . . . at Seattle
20 . . . . at Colorado
21 . . . . at Texas
22 . . .Los Angeles (AL)
23 . . . . . at Cincinnati
25 . . . . .San Francisco
26 . . . . . at Cleveland
27 . . . . Cincinnati

25 . . . . .at Chicago (AL)
26 . . . . . at San Francisco

28 . . . . . . at Seattle
29 . . . . Seattle

OAKLAND ATHLETICS

FEBRUARY
26 . . . . . at San Francisco
27 . . . . Milwaukee
28 . . . . San Francisco

MARCH
1 . . . . Texas
2 . . . . at Los Angeles (AL)
3 . . . . . .Los Angeles (NL)
4 . . . . Milwaukee
5 . . . . . . .at Milwaukee
6 . . . . at Arizona
7 . . . . .Arizona
8 . . . . at Colorado
9 . . . . Chicago (AL)
10 . . . at Los Angeles (NL)
11 . . . . at San Diego
12 . . . . Kansas City
13 . . . . .Colorado
14 . . . . at Kansas City
15 . . . . Texas
15 . . . . . at San Francisco
16 . . . . at Cincinnati
17 . . . . Chicago (NL)
18 . . . . . .at Chicago (AL)
19 . . . . at Cleveland
21 . . . at San Francisco
22 . . . . Seattle
23 . . . . Chicago (NL)
23 . . . . at Seattle
24 . . . . at Texas
25 . . . . Cincinnati
26 . . . . .Los Angeles (AL)

SAN DIEGO PADRES

FEBRUARY
27 . . . . at Seattle
28 . . . . Seattle

MARCH
1 . . . . at Kansas City
2 . . . . at Los Angeles (NL)
2 . . . . Cincinnati
3 . . . at San Francisco
4 . . . . .Arizona
5 . . . . .at Chicago (AL)
6 . . . . Texas
7 . . . . . . .at Milwaukee
8 . . . . Cleveland
9 . . . . at Arizona
10 . . . . at Colorado
11 . . . . Oakland
12 . . . . at Cleveland
13 . . . . . . Milwaukee
14 . . . . .Los Angeles (AL)
15 . . at Los Angeles (NL)
16 . . . . Kansas City
17 . . . . .Colorado
18 . . . . at Seattle
20 . . . . . .San Francisco
21 . . . . . . at Seattle
22 . . . . . . Chicago (AL)
23 . . . . at Texas
24 . . . .at Chicago (NL)
25 . . . . . . Chicago (NL)
26 . . . . . . Kansas City

SAN FRANCISCO GIANTS

FEBRUARY
26 . . . . Oakland
28 . . . . at Oakland
28 . . . . Milwaukee

MARCH
1 . . . . . . .at Chicago (NL)
2 . . . . .Arizona
3 . . . . San Diego
4 . . . . at Colorado
5 . . . . .Los Angeles (AL)
6 . . . . Cincinnati
7 . . . . . . at Kansas City
8 . . . . Seattle
9 . . . . at Los Angeles (NL)
10 . . . . . . Chicago (NL)
11 . . . . at Cincinnati
12 . . . . Chicago (AL)
13 . . . . at Texas
14 . . . . .Colorado
15 . . . . Oakland
15 . . . . at Seattle
16 . . . . Cleveland
17 . . at Los Angeles (AL)
18 . . . . . . at Cleveland
20 . . . . . at San Diego
21 . . . . Oakland
22 . . . . . .at Chicago (AL)
23 . . . . Kansas City
24 . . . at Los Angeles (AL)
25 . . . . . .at Milwaukee
26 . . . . .Colorado

SEATTLE MARINERS

FEBRUARY
27 . . . . San Diego
28 . . . . . at San Diego

MARCH
1 . . . . . .Los Angeles (AL)
2 . . . . at Cleveland
3 . . . . at Cincinnati
3 . . . . .Colorado
4 . . . . at Los Angeles (NL)
5 . . . . Cleveland
6 . . . . . .at Chicago (AL)
7 . . . . Cincinnati
8 . . . at Los Angeles (AL)
8 . . . . . . at San Francisco
9 . . . . Texas
10 . . . . at Arizona
10 . . . . Kansas City
11 . . . at Los Angeles (AL)
12 . . . . Chicago (NL)
13 . . . . at Arizona
14 . . . . at Colorado
15 . . . . . . .San Francisco
16 . . . at Los Angeles (AL)
18 . . . . San Diego
19 . . . . Milwaukee
20 . . . .at Chicago (AL)
21 . . . . San Diego
22 . . . . . . at Oakland
22 . . . . . at Colorado
23 . . . . Oakland
24 . . . . Chicago (AL)
25 . . . . . at Kansas City
26 . . . . at Texas
28 . . . . .Colorado
29 . . . . . . at Colorado

TEXAS RANGERS

FEBRUARY
27 . . . . . . at Kansas City
28 . . . . Kansas City

MARCH
1 . . . . at Oakland
2 . . . . Chicago (AL)
3 . . . . Cleveland
4 . . . . at Los Angeles (AL)
5 . . . . .Colorado
6 . . . . . . at San Diego
7 . . . .at Los Angeles (NL)
8 . . . . .Los Angeles (NL)
9 . . . . at Seattle
10 . . . . Cincinnati
11 . . . .at Chicago (AL)
12 . . . . .Los Angeles (AL)
13 . . . . . . .San Francisco
14 . . . . . . at Cincinnati
15 . . . . at Oakland
16 . . . . Chicago (AL)
17 . . . . at Kansas City
18 . . .at Milwaukee
18 . . . . Chicago (NL)
20 . . . . . . at Cincinnati
21 . . . . Milwaukee
22 . . . . at Kansas City
23 . . . . . .San Diego
24 . . . . Oakland
25 . . . . . at Cleveland
26 . . . . Seattle

FLORIDA GRAPEFRUIT LEAGUE

ATLANTA BRAVES

FEBRUARY
26 . . . . Detroit
27 . . . . at Detroit
28 . . . . Houston

MARCH
1 . . . . . . at Washington
2 . . . . Detroit
2 . . . . at Houston
3 . . . . . . New York (NL)
4 . . . . .Washington
5 . . . .at Philadelphia
6 . . . . .Washington
7 . . . . at Boston
8 . . . . . at Washington
8 . . . . Miami
9 . . . . . .at New York (NL)
10 . . . . . at Philadelphia
11 . . . . Philadelphia
12 . . . . .at Miami
12 . . . . .Washington
13 . . . . . . at St. Louis
14 . . . . Tampa Bay
15 . . . . St. Louis
16 . . . .at New York (AL)
17 . . . . . . at Houston
19 . . . . . . New York (AL)
20 . . . .at New York (NL)
21 . . . . Detroit
21 . . . . . .at Baltimore
22 . . . . Boston
23 . . . . . . New York (NL)
24 . . . . Houston
25 . . . . at Detroit
26 . . . . Miami
27 . . . . at Detroit

BALTIMORE ORIOLES

FEBRUARY
28 . . . . . . at Tampa Bay

MARCH
1 . . . . Toronto
2 . . . . at Boston
3 . . . . .Minnesota
4 . . . . . .at New York (AL)
5 . . . . at Minnesota
6 . . . . Tampa Bay
7 . . . . . . Philadelphia
8 . . . . Boston
8 . . . . at Boston
9 . . . . .Pittsburgh
10 . . . . . at Pittsburgh
11 . . . . Boston
12 . . . . . . Philadelphia
13 . . . . .at New York (AL)
14 . . . . . at Minnesota
15 . . . . . New York (AL)
16 . . . . at Toronto
17 . . . . . .at Philadelphia
17 . . . . .Minnesota
19 . . . . Tampa Bay
20 . . . . . at Pittsburgh
21 . . . . Atlanta
22 . . . . . at Tampa Bay
23 . . . . .Pittsburgh
24 . . . . Boston
25 . . . . . at Minnesota
26 . . . .at Tampa Bay
26 . . . . at Boston
27 . . . . Tampa Bay

BOSTON RED SOX

FEBRUARY
28 . . . . .Minnesota

MARCH
1 . . . . at Minnesota
2 . . . . Baltimore
3 . . . . at Pittsburgh
4 . . . . . . Tampa Bay
5 . . . . . . at St. Louis
6 . . . . .at Miami
7 . . . . .Atlanta
8 . . . .at Baltimore
8 . . . . Baltimore
9 . . . . at Pittsburgh
10 . . . . Tampa Bay
11 . . . . . .at Baltimore
11 . . . . Miami
13 . . . . . . at Minnesota
14 . . . . . . .at Toronto
15 . . . . . . Philadelphia
16 . . . .at Tampa Bay
17 . . . . St. Louis
18 . . . .at New York (NL)
19 . . . . .Pittsburgh
20 . . . . . New York (AL)
21 . . . . . .at Philadelphia

22 . . . . at Atlanta
23 . . . . Tampa Bay
24 . . . . at Baltimore
25 . . . . at Tampa Bay

26 . . . . Baltimore
27 . . . . .Minnesota
28 . . . . at Minnesota
29 . . . . .Minnesota

18 . . . . Detroit
20 . . . . Atlanta
21 . . . . . . at Minnesota
22 . . . . at Miami
23 . . . . . . .Washington

23 . . . . at Atlanta
24 . . . . St. Louis
25 . . . . . at Washington
26 . . . . at Houston
27 . . . . . . .Washington

DETROIT TIGERS

FEBRUARY
26 . . . . at Atlanta
27 . . . . Atlanta
28 . . . . . . New York (AL)
28 . . . at Philadelphia

MARCH
1 . . . . Houston
2 . . . . at Atlanta
3 . . . . St. Louis
4 . . . . .Pittsburgh
5 . . . . at Houston
6 . . . . Philadelphia
7 . . . . at New York (AL)
8 . . . . . New York (NL)
9 . . . . at Miami
10 . . . . . at St. Louis
11 . . . . Toronto

12 . . . . .at New York (AL)
13 . . . . Miami
14 . . . . . . .Washington
15 . . . . Houston
16 . . . . at Washington
17 . . . . . . .Washington
18 . . . . Toronto
18 . . . .at New York (NL)
20 . . . . . at Washington
21 . . . . . . at Atlanta
22 . . . . . . at Toronto
23 . . . . Miami
24 . . . . . . at Pittsburgh
25 . . . . Atlanta
26 . . . .at Philadelphia
27 . . . . Atlanta
28 . . . . . Tampa Bay

HOUSTON ASTROS

FEBRUARY
28 . . . . at Atlanta

MARCH
1 . . . . at Detroit
2 . . . . Atlanta
3 . . . . at Miami
4 . . . .at New York (NL)
5 . . . . Detroit
6 . . . . . New York (NL)
7 . . . . at Washington
8 . . . . . . New York (AL)
8 . . . .at Philadelphia
9 . . . . Toronto
10 . . . . . at Washington

12 . . . . . .Washington
13 . . . . at Toronto
14 . . . . St. Louis
15 . . . . . . at Detroit
16 . . . . . . .Washington
17 . . . . .Atlanta
18 . . . . at Miami
19 . . . . at Washington
20 . . . . . . Philadelphia
21 . . . . Miami
22 . . . . St. Louis
23 . . . . . at St. Louis
24 . . . . . . at Atlanta
26 . . . . . New York (NL)

MIAMI MARLINS

FEBRUARY
28 . . . . at St. Louis

MARCH
1 . . . . St. Louis
1 . . . . .at New York (NL)
2 . . . . at Washington
3 . . . . Houston
4 . . . . .Minnesota
5 . . . .at New York (NL)
6 . . . . Boston
7 . . . . . . at St. Louis
8 . . . . . . at Atlanta
9 . . . . Detroit
10 . . . .at New York (NL)
11 . . . . . . at Boston
12 . . . . .Atlanta

13 . . . . at Detroit
14 . . . . New York (NL)
15 . . . . .Washington
16 . . . . . . at Minnesota
17 . . . . . New York (NL)
18 . . . . Houston
20 . . . . St. Louis
21 . . . . . . at Houston
22 . . . . . New York (NL)
22 . . . . at Washington
23 . . . . . . at Detroit
24 . . . . . . .Washington
25 . . . . St. Louis
26 . . . . . . at Atlanta
27 . . . . . at St. Louis
28 . . . . .at New York (AL)
29 . . . . .at New York (AL)

NEW YORK METS

FEBRUARY
28 . . . . .Washington

MARCH
1 . . . . Miami
2 . . . . . . at St. Louis
3 . . . . . at Atlanta
4 . . . . Houston
5 . . . . Miami
5 . . . . . at Washington
6 . . . . . . at Houston

7 . . . . St. Louis
8 . . . . at Detroit
9 . . . . Atlanta
10 . . . . Miami
11 . . . . . . at St. Louis
12 . . . . St. Louis
13 . . . . . at Washington
14 . . . . at Miami
15 . . . . . . .Minnesota
16 . . . . . . at St. Louis
17 . . . . . . at Miami

MINNESOTA TWINS

FEBRUARY
28 . . . . at Boston

MARCH
1 . . . . Boston
2 . . . . . at Tampa Bay
3 . . . .at Baltimore
3 . . . . Toronto
4 . . . . . . at Miami
5 . . . . Baltimore
6 . . . . St. Lois
7 . . . . . at Pittsburgh
8 . . . . . . at Toronto
9 . . . . . . Philadelphia
11 . . . at Tampa Bay
12 . . . . . . .Pittsburgh
13 . . . . Boston

14 . . . .at New York (AL)
14 . . . . Baltimore
15 . . . .at New York (NL)
16 . . . . Miami
17 . . . .at Baltimore
18 . . . . . Tampa Bay
19 . . . . . at St. Louis
20 . . . .at Tampa Bay
21 . . . . . New York (NL)
22 . . . . . New York (AL)
23 . . . .at Phladelphia
24 . . . . . . Tampa Bay
25 . . . . Baltimore
26 . . . . . . .Pittsburgh
27 . . . . at Boston
28 . . . . Boston
29 . . . . at Boston

NEW YORK YANKEES

FEBRUARY
26 . . . . . . at Pittsburgh
27 . . . . . . .Pittsburgh
28 . . . . . . at Detroit

MARCH
1 . . . . Philadelphia
2 . . . . . . at Toronto
3 . . . .Washington
4 . . . . Baltimore
5 . . . . at Tampa Bay
6 . . . .at Philadelphia
7 . . . . Detroit
8 . . . . . . at Houston
9 . . . . Tampa Bay
11 . . . . at Washington
12 . . . . Detroit

13 . . . . Baltimore
13 . . . .at Philadelphia
14 . . . . .Minnesota
15 . . . .at Baltimore
16 . . . . Atlanta
17 . . . . at Pittsburgh
18 . . . . Boston
19 . . . . . . at Atlanta
20 . . . . . . at Boston
21 . . . . .Pittsburgh
22 . . . . at Minnesota
23 . . . . Toronto
25 . . . . . Philadelphia
26 . . . . . . at Toronto
27 . . . . at Pittsburgh
28 . . . . Miami
29 . . . . Miami

PHILADELPHIA PHILLIES

FEBRUARY
26 . . . . Toronto
27 . . . . . . at Toronto
28 . . . . Detroit

MARCH
1 . . . . .at New York (AL)
2 . . . . .Pittsburgh
3 . . . . at Tampa Bay
4 . . . . Toronto
5 . . . . .Pittsburgh
6 . . . . at Detroit
6 . . . . New York (AL)
7 . . . .at Baltimore
8 . . . . Houston
9 . . . . . . at Minnesota
10 . . . . Atlanta

11 . . . . at Atlanta
12 . . . .at Baltimore
13 . . . . . New York (AL)
14 . . . . . at Pittsburgh
15 . . . . . . at Boston
16 . . . . .Pittsburgh
17 . . . . Baltimore
19 . . . . . . at Toronto
20 . . . . . at Houston
20 . . . . Toronto
21 . . . . Boston
22 . . . . at Pittsburgh
23 . . . . .Minnesota
24 . . . . . . at Toronto
25 . . . .at New York (AL)
26 . . . . Detroit
27 . . . . Toronto

PITTSBURGH PIRATES

FEBRUARY
26 . . . . . . New York (AL)
27 . . . .at New York (AL)
28 . . . . . . at Toronto

MARCH
1 . . . . Tampa Bay
2 . . . .at Philadelphia
3 . . . . Boston

4 . . . . at Detroit
5 . . . . . . at Toronto
6 . . . . Toronto
7 . . . . . . .Minnesota
8 . . . .at Tampa Bay
9 . . . . Boston
9 . . . .at Baltimore
10 . . . . Baltimore

MINOR LEAGUES

12 . . . . at Minnesota
13 . . . . at Tampa Bay
14 . . . . Philadelphia
15 . . . . . Tampa Bay
16 . . . . . .at Philadelphia
17 . . . . . . New York (AL)
19 . . . . at Boston
20 . . . . Baltimore

21 . . . . . .at New York (AL)
22 . . . . Philadelphia
23 . . . . .at Baltimore
24 . . . . Detroit
25 . . . . Toronto
26 . . . . at Minnesota
27 . . . . . . New York (AL)

23 . . . . at Boston
24 . . . . . . at Minnesota
25 . . . . Boston

26 . . . . Baltimore
27 . . . . .at Baltimore
28 . . . . at Detroit

ST. LOUIS CARDINALS

FEBRUARY	
28 . . . . Miami	

MARCH	
1 . . . . at Miami	
2 . . . . New York (NL)	
3 . . . . at Detroit	
5 . . . . Boston	
6 . . . . . . at Minnesota	
7 . . . . Miami	
7 . . . .at New York (NL)	
8 . . . . .Washington	
9 . . . . . at Washington	
10 . . . . .Detroit	
11 . . . . . . New York (NL)	

12 . . . . . .at New York (NL)
13 . . . . Atlanta
14 . . . . at Houston
15 . . . . at Atlanta
16 . . . . . . New York (NL)
17 . . . . at Boston
19 . . . . .Minnesota
20 . . . . at Miami
21 . . . . .Washington
22 . . . . at Houston
23 . . . . Houston
24 . . . . .at New York (NL)
25 . . . . at Miami
26 . . . . .Washington
27 . . . . Miami

TAMPA BAY RAYS

FEBRUARY	
28 . . . . Baltimore	

MARCH	
1 . . . . at Pittsburgh	
2 . . . . .Minnesota	
3 . . . . Philadelphia	
4 . . . . at Boston	
5 . . . . . . New York (AL)	
6 . . . . . .at Baltimore	
7 . . . . .at Toronto	
8 . . . . .Pittsburgh	
9 . . . . . at New York (AL)	

10 . . . . at Boston
11 . . . . .Minnesota
12 . . . . at Toronto
13 . . . . .Pittsburgh
14 . . . . at Atlanta
15 . . . . . at Pittsburgh
15 . . . . Toronto
16 . . . . Boston
18 . . . . . at Minnesota
19 . . . .at Baltimore
20 . . . . .Minnesota
21 . . . . Toronto
22 . . . . Baltimore

TORONTO BLUE JAYS

FEBRUARY	
26 . . . . . . .at Philadelphia	
27 . . . . Philadelphia	
28 . . . . .Pittsburgh	

MARCH	
1 . . . . .at Baltimore	
2 . . . . . . New York (AL)	
3 . . . . . . at Minnesota	
4 . . . .at Philadelphia	
5 . . . . .Pittsburgh	
6 . . . . . . at Pittsburgh	
7 . . . . . . Tampa Bay	
8 . . . . .Minnesota	
9 . . . . at Houston	
11 . . . . . . at Detroit	

12 . . . . Tampa Bay
13 . . . . Houston
14 . . . . Boston
15 . . . . . at Tampa Bay
16 . . . . Baltimore
18 . . . . at Detroit
19 . . . . . . Philadelphia
20 . . . .at Philadelphia
21 . . . .at Tampa Bay
22 . . . . Detroit
23 . . .at New York (AL)
24 . . . . . . Philadelphia
25 . . . . . at Pittsburgh
26 . . . . . New York (AL)
27 . . . .at Philadelphia

WASHINGTON NATIONALS

FEBRUARY	
28 . . . . . .at New York (NL)	

MARCH	
1 . . . . .Atlanta	
2 . . . . Miami	
3 . . . .at New York (AL)	
4 . . . . at Atlanta	
5 . . . . . New York (NL)	
6 . . . . at Atlanta	
7 . . . . Houston	
8 . . . . . . at St. Louis	
8 . . . . Atlanta	
9 . . . . St. Louis	
10 . . . . Houston	
11 . . . . . . New York (AL)	
12 . . . . at Atlanta	

12 . . . . at Houston
13 . . . . . New York (NL)
14 . . . . at Detroit
15 . . . . .at Miami
16 . . . . Detroit
16 . . . . at Houston
17 . . . . at Detroit
19 . . . . Houston
20 . . . . Detroit
21 . . . . . . at St. Louis
22 . . . . Miami
23 . . . .at New York (NL)
24 . . . . .at Miami
25 . . . . . New York (NL)
26 . . . . . . at St. Louis
27 . . . . .at New York (NL)

COLLEGES

COLLEGE ORGANIZATIONS

NATIONAL COLLEGIATE ATHLETIC ASSOCIATION

Mailing Address: P.O. Box 6222, Indianapolis, IN 46206. **Telephone:** (317) 917-6222. **Fax:** (317) 917-6826 (championships), 917-6710 (baseball). **E-Mail Addresses: Division I Championship:** dleech@ncaa.org (Damani Leech), rlbuhr@ncaa.org (Randy L. Buhr), ctolliver@ncaa.org (Chad Tolliver), thalpin@ncaa.org (Ty Halpin), jhamilton@ncaa.org (JD Hamilton), (kgiles@ncaa.org) Kim Giles; **Division II Championship:** kwillard@ncaa.org (Keith Willard). **Division III:** jpwilliams@ncaa.org (J.P. Williams). **Websites:** www.ncaa.org, www.ncaa.com.

President: Dr. Mark Emmert. **Managing Director, Division I Baseball/Football:** Damani Leech. **Assistant Director, Division I Baseball/Football:** Chad Tolliver. **Division II Assistant Director, Championship and Alliances:** Keith Willard. **Division III Assistant Director, Championships:** J.P. Williams. **Media Contact, Division I Championship and College World Series:** J.D. Hamilton. **Playing Rules Contact:** Ty Halpin. **Statistics Contacts:** Jeff Williams (Division I and RPI); Mark Bedics (Division II); Sean Straziscar (Division III).

Chairman, Division I Baseball Committee: Dennis Farrell (Commissioner, Big West Conference). **Division I Baseball Committee:** Patrick Chunn (Athletics Director, Fla. Atlantic); Joel Erdmann (Athletics Director, South Alabama); Larry Gallo Jr (Senior Associate Athletic Director, North Carolina); Robert Goodman (Senior Associate Commissioner, Colonial Athletic Association); Dan Guerrero (Athletics Director, UCLA); Dave Heeke (Athletics Director, Central Michigan); Eric Hyman (Athletics Director, Texas A&M);Ron Prettyman (Athletics Director, Indiana St.); Ed Scott (Associate Director of Athletics, Binghamton). **Chairman, Division II Baseball Committee:** Doug Jones (Head Baseball Coach, Tusculum). **Chairman, Division III Baseball Committee:** Ben Shipp (Head Baseball Coach, Mary Hardin-Baylor).

2015 National Convention: Jan. 14-17 at Washington D.C.

2013 CHAMPIONSHIP TOURNAMENTS

NCAA DIVISION I
68th College World Series . . . . .Omaha, June 14-24/25
Super Regionals (8) . . . . .Campus sites, June 6-9
Regionals (16). . . . . .Campus sites, May 30-June 2

NCAA DIVISION II
47th annual World Series . . . USA Baseball National Training
Complex, Cary, N.C., May 24-May 31
Regionals (8) . . . . Campus sites, May 15-18

NCAA DIVISION III
39th annual World Series . . . . Times Warner Cable Field
at Fox Cities Stadium, Appleton, Wis., May 23-27
Regionals (8) . . . . Campus sites, May 14-18

NATIONAL ASSOCIATION OF INTERCOLLEGIATE ATHLETICS

Mailing Address: 1200 Grand Blvd., Kansas City, MO 64106. **Telephone:** (816) 595-8000. **Fax:** (816) 595-8200. **E-Mail Address:** cwaller@naia.org. **Website:** www.naia.org.

President/CEO: Jim Carr. **Manager, Championship Sports:** Jason Ford. **Director, Sports Information:** Chad Waller. **President, Coaches Association:** Boyd Pitkin (Briar Cliff College, Iowa).

2014 NATIONAL CHAMPIONSHIP

Opening round: . . . . May 12-15, campus locations
Avista-NAIA World Series . . . . .May 23-30, Lewiston, ID

NATIONAL JUNIOR COLLEGE ATHLETIC ASSOCIATION

Mailing Address: 1631 Mesa Ave., Suite B, Colorado Springs, CO 80906.

Telephone: (719) 590-9788. **Fax:** (719) 590-7324.

E-Mail Address: mkrug@njcaa.org. **Website:** www.njcaa.org.

Executive Director: Mary Ellen Leicht.

Director, Division I Baseball Tournament: Jamie Hamilton. **Director, Division II Baseball Tournament:** Billy Mayberry. **Director, Division III Baseball Tournament:** Tim Drain. **Director Media Relations:** Mark Krug.

2014 CHAMPIONSHIP TOURNAMENTS

DIVISION I
World Series. . . . . Grand Junction, CO, May 24-31

DIVISION II
World Series. . . . . Enid, OK, May 24-31

DIVISION III
World Series. . . . . .Tyler, TX, May 24-30

CALIFORNIA COMMUNITY COLLEGE ATHLETIC ASSOCIATION

Mailing Address: 2017 O St., Sacramento, CA 95811. **Telephone:** (916) 444-1600. **Fax:** (916) 444-2616. **E-Mail Addresses:** ccarter@cccaasports.org, jboggs@cccaasports.org. **Website:** www.cccaasports.org.

Executive Director: Carlyle Carter. **Director, Membership Services:** Unavailable. **Director, Championships:** George Mategakis. **Assistant Director, Sports Information/Communications:** Jason Boggs.

2014 CHAMPIONSHIP TOURNAMENT

State Championship . . . . Fresno, CA, May 24-26

NORTHWEST ATHLETIC ASSOC. OF COMMUNITY COLLEGES

Mailing Address: Clark College TGB 121, 1933 Fort Vancouver Way, Vancouver, WA 98663.

Telephone: (360) 992-2833. **Fax:** (360) 696-6210. **E-Mail Address:** nwaacc@clark.edu. **Website:** www.nwaacc.org.

Executive Director: Marco Azurdia. **Executive Assistant:** Carol Hardin. **Sports Information Director:** Tracy Swisher. **Director of External Operations:** Scott Archer. **Compliance Manager:** Jim Jackson.

2014 CHAMPIONSHIP TOURNAMENT

NWAACC Championship. . . . . Lower Columbia CC
Longview, WA, May 22-26

AMERICAN BASEBALL COACHES ASSOCIATION

Office Address: 108 S. University Ave., Suite 3, Mount Pleasant, MI 48858. **Telephone:** (989) 775-3300. **Fax:** (989) 775-3600. **E-Mail Address:** abca@abca.org. **Website:** www.abca.org.

Executive Director: Dave Keilitz. Assistant to Executive Director: Betty Rulong. Membership/Convention Coordinator: Nick Phillips. Marketing Director: Juahn Clark. Associate Membership/Convention Coordinator: Jeff Franklyn.

Chairman: Mark Johnson. President: Scott Berry (Mayville, N.D., State).

2015 National Convention: Jan. 2-5 at Marriott World Center in Orlando, FL.

NCAA DIVISION I CONFERENCES

AMERICA EAST CONFERENCE

Mailing Address: 215 First St., Suite 140, Cambridge, MA 02142. Telephone: (617) 695-6369. Fax: (617) 695-6380. E-Mail Address: hager@americaeast.com. Website: www.americaeast.com.

Baseball Members (First Year): Albany (2002), Binghamton (2002), Hartford (1990), Maine (1990), Maryland-Baltimore County (2004), Massachusetts-Lowell (2014), Stony Brook (2002).

Director, Strategic Media/Baseball Contact: Jared Hager.

2014 Tournament: Four teams, double-elimination, May 21-23 at LeLacheur Park, Lowell, Mass.

AMERICAN ATHLETIC CONFERENCE

Mailing Address: 15 Park Row West, Providence, RI 02903. Telephone: (401) 453-0660. Fax: (401) 751-8540. E-Mail Address: csullivan@theamerican.org. Website: www.theamerican.org.

Baseball Members (First Year): Central Florida (2014), Cincinnati (2014), Connecticut (2014), Houston (2014), Louisville (2014), Memphis (2014), Rutgers (2014), South Florida (2014), Temple (2014).

Director, Communications: Chuck Sullivan.

2014 Tournament: Eight teams, pool play, May 21-25 at Clearwater, Fla.

ATLANTIC COAST CONFERENCE

Mailing Address: 4512 Weybridge Ln., Greensboro, NC 27407. Telephone: (336) 851-6062. Fax: (336) 854-8797. E-Mail Address: sphillips@theacc.org. Website: www.theacc.com.

Baseball Members (First Year): Boston College (2006), Clemson (1954), Duke (1954), Florida State (1992), Georgia Tech (1980), Maryland (1954), Miami (2005), North Carolina (1954), North Carolina State (1954), Notre Dame (2014), Pittsburgh (2014), Virginia (1955), Virginia Tech (2005), Wake Forest (1954).

Associate Director, Communications: Steve Phillips.

2014 Tournament: Eight teams, group play. May 20-25 at NewBridge Bank Park, Greensboro, N.C.

ATLANTIC SUN CONFERENCE

Mailing Address: 3370 Vineville Ave., Suite 108-B, Macon, GA 31204. Telephone: (478) 474-3394. Fax: (478) 474-4272. E-Mail Addresses: pmccoy@atlanticsun.org. Website: www.atlanticsun.com.

Baseball Members (First Year): East Tennessee State (2006), Florida Gulf Coast (2008), Jacksonville (1999), Kennesaw State (2006), Lipscomb (2004), Mercer (1979), North Florida (2006), Northern Kentucky (2013), South Carolina-Upstate (2008), Stetson (1986).

Director, Sports Information: Patrick McCoy.

2014 Tournament: Eight teams, double-elimination. May 21-25 at FGCU.

ATLANTIC 10 CONFERENCE

Mailing Address: 11827 Canon Blvd., Suite 200, Newport News, VA 23606. Telephone: (757) 706-3059. Fax: (757) 706-3042. E-Mail Address: ckilcoyne@atlantic10.org. Website: www.atlantic10.com.

Baseball Members (First Year): Dayton (1996), Fordham (1996), George Mason (2014), George Washington (1977), La Salle (1996), Massachusetts (1977), Rhode Island (1981), Richmond (2002), St. Bonaventure (1980), Saint Joseph's (1983), Saint Louis (2006), Virginia Commonwealth (2013).

Commissioner: Bernadette V. McGlade. Director, Communications: Drew Dickerson. Assistant Director, Communications/Baseball Contact: Chris Kilcoyne.

2014 Tournament: Seven teams, double elimination. May 21-24 at Billikens Sports Center (Saint Louis).

BIG EAST CONFERENCE

Mailing Address: Big East Conference/Proskauer, 11 Times Square (41st St. & 8th Ave.), 24th Floor, New York, NY 10036-8299. Telephone: (212) 969-3181. Fax: (212) 969-2900. E-Mail Address: jgreene@bigeast.com. Website: www.bigeast.com.

Baseball Members (First Year): Butler (2014), Creighton (2014), Georgetown (1985), St. John's (1985), Seton Hall (1985), Villanova (1985), Xavier (2014).

Assistant Director, Olympic Sports Media Relations: James Greene.

2014 Tournament: Four teams, modified double-elimination. May 22-25 at MCU Park, Brooklyn, N.Y.

BIG SOUTH CONFERENCE

Mailing Address: 7233 Pineville-Matthews Rd., Suite 100, Charlotte, NC 28226. Telephone: (704) 341-7990. Fax: (704) 341-7991. E-Mail Address: nicb@bigsouth.org. Website: www.bigsouthsports.com.

Baseball Members (First Year): Campbell (2012), Charleston Southern (1983), Coastal Carolina (1983), Gardner-Webb (2009), High Point (1999), Liberty (1991), Longwood (2013), UNC Asheville (1985), Presbyterian (2009), Radford (1983), Virginia Military Institute (2004), Winthrop (1983).

Assistant Director, Public Relations/Baseball Contact: Nic Bowman.

2014 Tournament: Eight teams, double-elimination. May 20-24 Rock Hill, S.C. (Winthrop University).

BIG TEN CONFERENCE

Mailing Address: 5440 Park Place, Rosemont, IL 60018. Telephone: (847) 696-1010. Fax: (847) 696-1110. E-Mail Addresses: dmihalik@bigten.org. Website: www.bigten.org.

Baseball Members (First Year): Illinois (1896), Indiana (1906), Iowa (1906), Michigan (1896), Michigan State (1950), Minnesota (1906), Nebraska (2012), Northwestern (1898), Ohio State (1913), Penn State (1992), Purdue (1906).

Assistant Director, Communications: Stephen Villatoro. 2014 Tournament: Six teams, double-elimination. May 21-25 at TD Ameritrade Park, Omaha.

BIG 12 CONFERENCE

Mailing Address: 400 E. John Carpenter Freeway, Irving, TX 75062. Telephone: (469) 524-1009. E-Mail Address: lrasmussen@big12sports.com. Website: www.big12sports.com.

Baseball Members (First Year): Baylor (1997), Kansas

(1997), Kansas State (1997), Oklahoma (1997), Oklahoma State (1997), Texas Christian (2013), Texas (1997), Texas Tech (1997), West Virginia (2013).

Assistant Director, Communications: Laura Rasmussen.

2014 Tournament: Double-elimination division play. May 21-25 at Chickasaw Bricktown Ballpark, Oklahoma City.

BIG WEST CONFERENCE

Mailing Address: 2 Corporate Park, Suite 206, Irvine, CA 92606. **Telephone:** (949) 261-2525. **Fax:** (949) 261-2528. **E-Mail Address:**jstcyr@bigwest.org. **Website:** www.bigwest.org.

Baseball Members (First Year): Cal Poly (1997), UC Davis (2008), UC Irvine (2002), UC Riverside (2002), UC Santa Barbara (1970), Cal State Fullerton (1975), Cal State Northridge (2001), Hawaii (2013), Long Beach State (1970).

Director, Communications: Julie St. Cyr.
2014 Tournament: None.

COLONIAL ATHLETIC ASSOCIATION

Mailing Address: 8625 Patterson Ave., Richmond, VA 23229. **Telephone:** (804) 754-1616. **Fax:** (804) 754-1973. **E-Mail Address:** rwashburn@caasports.com. **Website:** www.caasports.com.

Baseball Members (First Year): College of Charleston (2014), Delaware (2002), Hofstra (2002), James Madison (1986), UNC Wilmington (1986), Northeastern (2006), Towson (2002), William & Mary (1986).

Associate Commissioner/Communications: Rob Washburn.

2014 Tournament: Six teams, double-elimination. May 21-24 at Wilmington, N.C. (UNCW).

CONFERENCE USA

Mailing Address: 5201 N. O'Connor Blvd., Suite 300, Irving, TX 75039. **Telephone:** (214) 774-1300. **Fax:** (214) 496-0055. **E-Mail Address:** rdanderson@c-usa.org. **Website:** www.conferenceusa.com.

Baseball Members (First Year): Alabama-Birmingham (1996), Charlotte (2014), East Carolina (2002), Florida Atlantic (2014), Florida International (2014), Louisiana Tech (2014), Marshall (2006), Middle Tennessee State (2014), Old Dominion (2014), Rice (2006), Southern Mississippi (1996), Tulane (1996), Texas-San Antonio (2014).

Assistant Commissioner, Baseball Operations: Russell Anderson.

2014 Tournament: Eight teams, double-elimination. May 21-25 at Hattiesburg, Miss. (Southern Miss).

HORIZON LEAGUE

Mailing Address: 201 S. Capitol Ave., Suite 500, Indianapolis, IN 46225. **Telephone:** (317) 237-5604. **Fax:** (317) 237-5620. **E-Mail Address:** chammel@horizon-league.org. **Website:** www.horizonleague.org.

Baseball Members (First Year): Illinois-Chicago (1994), Oakland (2014), Valparaiso (2008), Wright State (1994), Wisconsin-Milwaukee (1994), Youngstown State (2002).

Assistant Director, Communications: Craig Hammel.
2014 Tournament: Six teams, double-elimination. May 21-24 at Kapco Park, Milwaukee (UW-Milwaukee).

IVY LEAGUE

Mailing Address: 228 Alexander Rd., Second Floor, Princeton, NJ 08544. **Telephone:** (609) 258-6426. **Fax:**

(609) 258-1690. **E-Mail Address:** trevor@ivyleaguesports.com. **Website:** www.ivyleaguesports.com.

Baseball Members (First Year): Rolfe—Brown (1948), Dartmouth (1930), Harvard (1948), Yale (1930). **Gehrig**—Columbia (1930), Cornell (1930), Pennsylvania (1930), Princeton (1930).

Assistant Executive Director, Communications/ Championships: Trevor Rutledge-Leverenz.

2013 Tournament: Best-of-three series between division champions. May 3-4 at team with best Ivy League record.

METRO ATLANTIC ATHLETIC CONFERENCE

Mailing Address: 712 Amboy Ave., Edison, NJ 08837. **Telephone:** (732) 738-5455. **E-Mail Address:** john.wooding@maac.org. **Website:** www.maacsports.com.

Baseball Members (First Year): Canisius (1990), Fairfield (1982), Iona (1982), Manhattan (1982), Marist (1998), Monmouth (2014), Niagara (1990), Quinnipiac (2014), Rider (1998), Saint Peter's (1982), Siena (1990).

Assistant Commissioner, External Relations: Whitney Swab. **Director, New Media-Communications (Baseball Contact):** John Wooding.

2014 Tournament: Six teams, double-elimination. May 21-25 at FirstEnergy Park, Lakewood, N.J.

MID-AMERICAN CONFERENCE

Mailing Address: 24 Public Square, 15th Floor, Cleveland, OH 44113. **Telephone:** (216) 566-4622. **Fax:** (216) 858-9622. **E-Mail Address:** jguy@mac-sports.com. **Website:** www.mac-sports.com.

Baseball Members (First Year): Akron (1992), Ball State (1973), Bowling Green State (1952), Buffalo (2001), Central Michigan (1971), Eastern Michigan (1971), Kent State (1951), Miami (1947), Northern Illinois (1997), Ohio (1946), Toledo (1950), Western Michigan (1947).

Director, Communications: Jeremy Guy.
2014 Tournament: Eight teams (top three in each division and two teams with the next-best overall records, regardless of division), double-elimination. May 21-24 at All Pro Freight Stadium (Avon, Ohio).

MID-EASTERN ATHLETIC CONFERENCE

Mailing Address: 2730 Ellsmere Ave., Norfolk, VA 23513. **Telephone:** (757) 951-2055. **Fax:** (757) 951-2077. **E-Mail Address:** brian.howard@themeac.com; porterp@themeac.com. **Website:** www.meacsports.com.

Baseball Members (First Year): Bethune-Cookman (1979), Coppin State (1985), Delaware State (1970), Florida A&M (1979), Maryland Eastern Shore (1970), Norfolk State (1998), North Carolina A&T (1970), North Carolina Central (2012), Savannah State (2012).

Assistant Director, Media Relations/Baseball Contact: Brian Howard.

2014 Tournament: Eight teams, double-elimination. May 15-18 at Norfolk State.

MISSOURI VALLEY CONFERENCE

Mailing Address: 1818 Chouteau Ave., St. Louis, MO 63103. **Telephone:** (314) 444-4300. **Fax:** (314) 444-4333. **E-Mail Address:** kbriscoe@mvc.org. **Website:** www.mvcsports.com.

Baseball Members (First Year): Bradley (1955), Dallas Baptist (2014), Evansville (1994), Illinois State (1980), Indiana State (1976), Missouri State (1990), Southern Illinois (1974), Wichita State (1945).

Asst. Commissioner, Communications: Kelli Briscoe.
2014 Tournament: Eight-team tournament with two

four-team brackets mirroring the format of the College World Series, with the winners of each four-team bracket meeting in a single championship game. May 20-24 at Bob Warn Field (Indiana State).

MOUNTAIN WEST CONFERENCE

Mailing Address: 10807 New Allegiance Dr., Suite 250, Colorado Springs, CO 80921. **Telephone:**(719) 488-4052. **Fax:** (719) 487-7241. **E-Mail Address:** jwillson@themw.com. **Website:** www.themw.com.
Baseball Members (First Year): Air Force (2000), Fresno State (2013), Nevada (2013), Nevada-Las Vegas (2000), New Mexico (2000), San Diego State (2000), San Jose State (2014).
Associate Director, Communications: Judy Willson.
2014 Tournament: Seven teams; play-in game, followed by six-team double-elimination. May 21-25 at UNLV.

NORTHEAST CONFERENCE

Mailing Address: 399 Campus Dr., Somerset, NJ 08873. **Telephone:** (732) 469-0440. **Fax:** (732) 469-0744. **E-Mail Address:** rventre@northeastconference.org. **Website:** www.northeastconference.org.
Baseball Members (First Year): Bryant (2010), Central Connecticut State (1999), Fairleigh Dickinson (1981), Long Island (1981), Mount St. Mary's (1989), Sacred Heart (2000), Wagner (1981).
Director, Communications/Social Media: Ralph Ventre.
2013 Tournament: Four teams, double-elimination. May 22-25 at Dodd Stadium, Norwich, Conn.

OHIO VALLEY CONFERENCE

Mailing Address: 215 Centerview Dr., Suite 115, Brentwood, TN 37027. **Telephone:** (615) 371-1698. **Fax:** (615) 371-1788. **E-Mail Address:** kschwartz@ovc.org. **Website:** www.ovcsports.com.
Baseball Members (First Year): Austin Peay State (1962), Belmont (2013), Eastern Illinois (1996), Eastern Kentucky (1948), Jacksonville State (2003), Morehead State (1948), Murray State (1948), Southeast Missouri State (1991), Southern Illinois-Edwardsville (2012), Tennessee-Martin (1992), Tennessee Tech (1949).
Assistant Commissioner: Kyle Schwartz.
2014 Tournament: Six teams, double-elimination. May 21-25 at Jackson, Tenn.

PACIFIC-12 CONFERENCE

Mailing Address: 1350 Treat Blvd., Suite 500, Walnut Creek, CA 92597. **Telephone:** (925) 932-4411. **Fax:** (925) 932-4601. **E-Mail Address:** sjennings@pac-12.org. **Website:** www.pac-12.com.
Baseball Members (First Year): Arizona (1979), Arizona State (1979), California (1916), UCLA (1928), Oregon (2009) Oregon State (1916), Southern California (1923), Stanford (1918), Utah (2012), Washington (1916), Washington State (1919).
Public Relations Contact: Sarah Jennings.
2014 Tournament: None.

PATRIOT LEAGUE

Mailing Address: 3773 Corporate Pkwy., Suite 190, Center Valley, PA 18034. **Telephone:** (610) 289-1950. **Fax:** (610) 289-1951. **E-Mail Address:** mdougherty@patriot-league.com. **Website:** www.patriotleague.org.
Baseball Members (First Year): Army (1993), Bucknell

(1991), Holy Cross (1991), Lafayette (1991), Lehigh (1991), Navy (1993).
Assistant Executive Director for Communications: Matt Dougherty.
2013 Tournament: Four teams, May 10-11 and May 17-18 at site of higher seeds.

SOUTHEASTERN CONFERENCE

Mailing Address: 2201 Richard Arrington Blvd. N., Birmingham, AL 35203. **Telephone:** (205) 458-3000. **Fax:** (205) 458-3030. **E-Mail Address:** cdunlap@sec.org. **Website:** www.secsports.com.
Baseball Members (First Year): East—Florida (1933), Georgia (1933), Kentucky (1933), Missouri (2013), South Carolina (1992), Tennessee (1933), Vanderbilt (1933). **West**—Alabama (1933), Arkansas (1992), Auburn (1933), Louisiana State (1933), Mississippi (1933), Mississippi State (1933), Texas A&M (2013).
Director of Communications: Chuck Dunlap.
2014 Tournament: 12 teams, modified single/double-elimination. May 20-25 at Hoover, Ala.

SOUTHERN CONFERENCE

Mailing Address: 702 N. Pine St., Spartanburg, SC 29303. **Telephone:** (864) 591-5100. **Fax:** (864) 591-4282. **E-Mail Address:** pperry@socon.org. **Website:** www.soconsports.com.
Baseball Members (First Year): Appalachian State (1972), The Citadel (1937), Davidson (1992), Elon (2004), Furman (1937), Georgia Southern (1992), UNC Greensboro (1998), Samford (2009), Western Carolina (1977), Wofford (1998).
Media Relations: Phil Perry.
2014 Tournament: Ten teams, single-game play-in for bottom four seeds, then double-elimination followed by a single-elimination championship game. May 20-25 at Joseph P. Riley, Jr. Park, Charleston, S.C.

SOUTHLAND CONFERENCE

Mailing Address: 2600 Network Blvd, Suite 150, Frisco, Texas 75034. **Telephone:** (972) 422-9500. **Fax:** (972) 422-9225. **E-Mail Address:** chipp@southland. **Website:** www.southland.org.
Baseball Members (First Year): Abilene Christian (2014/Transitioning), Central Arkansas (2007), Houston Baptist (2014), Incarnate Word (2014/Transitioning), Lamar (1999), McNeese State (1973), New Orleans (2014), Nicholls (1992), Northwestern State (1988), Oral Roberts (2013), Sam Houston State (1988), Southeastern Louisiana (1998), Stephen F. Austin State (2006), Texas A&M-Corpus Christi (2007).
Baseball Contact/Assistant Commissioner: Calhoun Hipp.
2014 Tournament: Two four-team brackets, double-elimination. May 21-24 at Bear Stadium, Conway, Ark. (Central Arkansas Host).

SOUTHWESTERN ATHLETIC CONFERENCE

Mailing Address: 2101 6th Ave. North, Suite 700, Birmingham, AL 35203. **Telephone:** (205) 251-7573. **Fax:** (205) 297-9820. **E-Mail Address:** z.lewis@swac.org. **Website:** www.swac.org.
Baseball Members (First Year): East Division—Alabama A&M (2000), Alabama State (1982), Alcorn State (1962), Jackson State (1958), Mississippi Valley State (1968). **West Division**—Arkansas-Pine Bluff (1999), Grambling State (1958), Prairie View A&M (1920), Southern (1934), Texas Southern (1954).

Director, Media Relations: Zena Lewis.

2014 Tournament: Eight teams, double-elimination. May 14-18 at LaGrave Field, Fort Worth, Texas.

SUMMIT LEAGUE

Mailing Address: 340 W. Butterfield Rd., Suite 3D, Elmhurst, IL 60126.
Telephone: (630) 516-0661. **Fax:** (630) 516-0673.
E-Mail Address: mette@thesummitleague.org. **Website:** www.thesummitleague.org.

Baseball Members (First Year): Indiana Purdue-Fort Wayne (2008), Nebraska-Omaha (2013), North Dakota State (2008), South Dakota State (2008), Western Illinois (1984).

Associate Director, Communications (Baseball Contact): Greg Mette.

2014 Tournament: Four teams, double-elimination. May 22-24 at Sioux Falls, S.D. (South Dakota State).

SUN BELT CONFERENCE

Mailing Address: 1500 Sugar Bowl Dr., New Orleans, LA 70112. **Telephone:** (504) 556-0884. **Fax:** (504) 299-9068. **E-Mail Address:** nunez@sunbeltsports.org. **Website:** www.sunbeltsports.org.

Baseball Members (First Year): Arkansas-Little Rock (1991), Arkansas State (1991), Georgia State (2014), Louisiana-Lafayette (1991), Louisiana-Monroe (2007), South Alabama (1976), Texas-Arlington (2014), Texas State (2014), Troy (2006), Western Kentucky (1982).

Assistant Director, Communications: Keith Nunez.

2014 Tournament: Eight teams, double-elimination. May 21-25 at South Alabama.

WEST COAST CONFERENCE

Mailing Address: 1111 Bayhill Dr., Suite 405, San Bruno, CA 94066. **Telephone:** (650) 873-8622. **Fax:** (650) 873-7846. **E-Mail Addresses:** rmccrary@westcoast.org (primary), jtourial@westcoast.org (secondary). **Website:** www.wccsports.com.

Baseball Members (First Year): Brigham Young (2012), Gonzaga (1996), Loyola Marymount (1968), Pacific (2014), Pepperdine (1968), Portland (1996), Saint Mary's (1968), San Diego (1979), San Francisco (1968), Santa Clara (1968).

Senior Director, Communications: Ryan McCrary.
Associate Commissioner, Broadcast Administration/Strategic Communications: Jeff Tourial.

2014 Tournament: Four teams, May 21-24 at Banner Island Ballpark, Stockton, Calif.

WESTERN ATHLETIC CONFERENCE

Mailing Address: 9250 East Costilla Ave., Suite 300, Englewood, CO 80112. **Telephone:** (303) 799-9221. **Fax:** (303) 799-3888. **E-Mail Address:** jerickson@wac.org. **Website:** www.wacsports.com.

Baseball Members (First Year): Cal State Bakersfield (2013), Chicago State (2014), Grand Canyon (2014), New Mexico State (2006), North Dakota (2014), Northern Colorado (2014), Sacramento State (2006), Seattle (2013), Texas-Pan American (2014), Utah Valley (2014).

Interim Commissioner: Jeff Hurd. **Associate Commissioner:** Dave Chaffin. **Director, Media Relations:** Jason Erickson.

2014 Tournament: Six teams, double-elimination, May 21-25 at Cubs Park, Mesa, Ariz.

NCAA DIVISION I TEAMS

* Denotes recruiting coordinator

ABILENE CHRISTIAN WILDCATS

Conference: Southland.
Mailing Address: Athletics, 163 Teague Special Events Center, ACU Box 27916, Abilene, TX 79699. **Website:** www.acusports.com.
Head Coach: Britt Bonneau. **Telephone:** (325) 674-2325. **Baseball SID:** Jared Mosley. **Telephone:** (325) 674-2353.
Assistant Coaches: Josh Scott, *Brandon Stover, Sean Winston. **Telephone:** (325) 674-2817.
Home Field: Crutcher Scott Field. **Seating Capacity:** 4000.

AIR FORCE FALCONS

Conference: Mountain West.
Mailing Address: 2169 Field House Dr., USAFA, CO 80840. **Website:** www.goairforcefalcons.com.
Head Coach: Mike Kazlausky. **Telephone:** (719) 333-5334. **Baseball SID:** Nick Arseniak. **Telephone:** (719) 333-9251. **Fax:** (719) 333-3798.
Assistant Coaches: *Toby Bicknell, Blake Miller. **Telephone:** (719) 333-7914.
Home Field: Falcon Field. **Seating Capacity:** 1,000. **Outfield Dimensions: LF**—340, **CF**—410, **RF**—315. **Press Box Telephone:** (719) 333-3472.

AKRON ZIPS

Conference: Mid-American (East).
Mailing Address: University of Akron, Rhodes Arena, Akron, OH 44325. **Website:** www.gozips.com.
Head Coach: Rick Rembielak. **Telephone:** (330) 972-7290. **Baseball SID:** Sam Baldwin. **Telephone:** (330) 972-6584. **Fax:** (330) 374-8844.
Assistant Coaches: Kyle Smith*, Fred Worth. **Telephone:** (330) 972-2393.
Home Field: Lee R. Jackson Field. **Seating Capacity:** 1500. **Outfield Dimensions: LF**—330, **CF**—400, **RF**—330. **Press Box Telephone:** (419) 769-3544.

ALABAMA CRIMSON TIDE

Conference: Southeastern (West).
Mailing Address: 1201 Coliseum Dr. Suite 205, Tuscaloosa, AL 35487. **Website:** www.rolltide.com.
Head Coach: Mitch Gaspard. **Telephone:** (205) 348-4029. **Baseball SID:** Rich Davi. **Telephone:** (205) 348-3550. **Fax:** (205) 348-8841.
Assistant Coaches: *Dax Norris, Andy Phillips. **Telephone:** (205) 348-4029.
Home Field: Sewell-Thomas Stadium. **Seating Capacity:** 6,541. **Outfield Dimensions: LF**—325, **CF**—400, **RF**—325. **Press Box Telephone:** (205) 348-4927.

ALABAMA A&M BULLDOGS

Conference: Southwestern Athletic.
Mailing Address: 4900 Meridian St., Normal AL 35762. **Website:** www.aamusports.com.
Head Coach: Mitch Hill. **Telephone:** (256) 372-4004. **Baseball SID:** Brandon Willis. **Telephone:** (256) 372-4005. **Fax:** (256) 372-5919.
Assistant Coaches: LaDale Hayes, *Mitch Hill. **Telephone:** (256) 372-4004.
Home Field: Alabama A&M Baseball Field. **Seating Capacity:** 500. **Outfield Dimensions: LF**—315, **CF**—405, **RF**—315.

ALABAMA STATE HORNETS

Conference: Southwestern Athletic.
Mailing Address: 915 S. Jackson St., Montgomery,
Alabama 36104. **Website:** www.bamastatesports.com.
Head Coach: Mervyl Melendez. **Telephone:** (334)
229-5600. **Baseball SID:** Ed Nicholson. **Telephone:** (334)
229-5600. **Fax:** (334) 262-2971.
Assistant Coaches: Drew Clark, *Jose Vazquez.
Telephone: (334) 229-5607.
Home Field: Wheeler-Watkins Complex. **Seating
Capacity:** 500. **Outfield Dimensions: LF**—330, **CF**—400,
RF—330. **Press Box Telephone:** (334) 229-8899.

ALABAMA-BIRMINGHAM BLAZERS

Conference: Conference USA.
Mailing Address: 1212 University Blvd., U236,
Birmingham, AL 35294. **Website:** www.uabsports.com.
Head Coach: Brian Shoop. **Telephone:** (205) 934-
5181. **Baseball SID:** Anthony Prisco. **Telephone:** (205)
996-2576. **Fax:** (205) 934-7505.
Assistant Coaches: Josh Hopper, *Perry Roth.
Telephone: (205) 934-5182.
Home Field: Regions Field. **Seating Capacity:** 8,500.
Outfield Dimensions: LF—320, **CF**—400, **RF**—325.
Press Box Telephone: (205) 934-0200.

ALBANY GREAT DANES

Conference: America East.
Mailing Address: 1400 Washington Ave., Albany, NY
12222. **Website:** www.ualbanysports.com.
Head Coach: Jon Mueller. **Telephone:** (518) 442-3014.
Baseball SID: Lizzie Barlow. **Telephone:** (518) 442-3359.
Fax: (518) 442-3139.
Assistant Coaches: Jeff Kaier, *Drew Pearce.
Telephone: (518) 442-3337.
Home Field: Varsity Field. **Seating Capacity:** 1,500.
Outfield Dimensions: LF—346, **CF**—400, **RF**—325.

APPALACHIAN STATE MOUNTAINEERS

Conference: Southern.
Mailing Address: 225 Broyhill Inn Ln., Boone, NC
28608. **Website:** www.goasu.com.
Head Coach: Billy Jones. **Telephone:** (828) 262-6097.
Baseball SID: Mike Flynn. **Telephone:** (828) 262-2845.
Fax: (828) 262-6106.
Assistant Coaches: Matt Payne, *Michael Rogers.
Telephone: (828) 262-7165.
Home Field: Beaver Field at Jim and Bettie Smith
Stadium. **Seating Capacity:** 1,000. **Outfield Dimensions:
LF**—330, **CF**—400, **RF**—330. **Press Box Telephone:** (828)
262-2016.

ARIZONA WILDCATS

Conference: Pacific-12.
Mailing Address: 1 National Championship Dr.,
Tuscon, AZ 85721. **Website:** www.arizonaathletics.com.
Head Coach: Andy Lopez. **Telephone:** (520) 621-4102.
Baseball SID: Blair Willis. **Telephone:** (520) 621-0914.
Fax: (520) 621-2681.
Assistant Coaches: *Shaun Cole, Matt Siegel.
Telephone: (520) 621-4714.
Home Field: Hi Corbett Stadium. **Seating Capacity:**
9,500. **Outfield Dimensions: LF**—366, **CF**—392,
RF—349. **Press Box Telephone:** (520) 621-4440.

ARIZONA STATE SUN DEVILS

Conference: Pacific-12.
Mailing Address: 500 E. Veterans Way #301, Tempe,
AZ 85287. **Website:** www.thesundevils.com.
Head Coach: Tim Esmay. **Telephone:** (480) 965-1904.
Baseball SID: Thomas Lenneberg. **Telephone:** (480) 965-
6594. **Fax:** (480) 965-5408.
Assistant Coaches: Mike Benjamin, *Ken Knutson.
Telephone: (480) 965-3677.
Home Field: Packard Stadium. **Seating Capacity:**
4,000. **Outfield Dimensions: LF**—338, **CF**—395,
RF—338. **Press Box Telephone:** (480) 727-7253.

ARKANSAS RAZORBACKS

Conference: Southeastern (West).
Mailing Address: 1255 S. Razorback Rd., Fayetteville,
AR 72701. **Website:** www.arkansasrazorbacks.com.
Head Coach: Dave Van Horn. **Telephone:** (479) 575-
3655. **Baseball SID:** Chad Crunk. **Telephone:** (479) 575-
2753. **Fax:** (479) 575-7481.
Assistant Coaches: Dave Jorn, *Tony Vitello.
Telephone: (479) 575-3552.
Home Field: Baum Stadium at George Cole Field.
Seating Capacity: 10,737. **Outfield Dimensions:
LF**—320, **CF**—400, **RF**—320. **Press Box Telephone:** (479)
575-4141.

ARKANSAS STATE RED WOLVES

Conference: Sun Belt.
Mailing Address: P.O. Box 1000, State University, AR
72467. **Website:** www.astateredwolves.com.
Head Coach: Tommy Raffo. **Telephone:** (870) 972-
2700. **Baseball SID:** Chris Graddy. **Telephone:** (870) 972-
2707. **Fax:** (870) 972-3367.
Assistant Coaches: Tighe Dickinson, *Anthony
Evermann. **Telephone:** (870) 972-2700.
Home Field: Tomlinson Stadium/Kell Field. **Seating
Capacity:** 1200. **Outfield Dimensions: LF**—335,
CF—400, **RF**—335. **Press Box Telephone:** (870) 972-
2541.

ARKANSAS-LITTLE ROCK TROJANS

Conference: Sun Belt.
Mailing Address: 2801 S. University Ave., Little Rock,
AR 72204. **Website:** www.ualrtrojans.com.
Head Coach: Scott Norwood. **Telephone:** (501) 663-
8095. **Baseball SID:** Patrick Newton. **Telephone:** (501)
683-7003. **Fax:** (501) 683-7002.
Assistant Coaches: Cole Gordon, *Chris Marx.
Telephone: (501) 280-0759.
Home Field: Gary Hogan Field. **Seating Capacity:**
1,000. **Outfield Dimensions: LF**—315, **CF**—390,
RF—305. **Press Box Telephone:** (501) 859-4537.

ARKANSAS-PINE BLUFF GOLDEN LIONS

Conference: Southwestern Athletic.
Mailing Address: 1200 N. University Dr., Mail Slot
4891, Pine Bluff, AR 71601. **Website:** www.uapblionsroar.
com.
Head Coach: Carlos James. **Telephone:** (870) 575-
8995. **Baseball SID:** Cameo Stokes. **Telephone:** (870)
575-7949. **Fax:** (870) 575-4655.
Assistant Coaches: *Marc MacMillan, Jon Tatum.
Telephone: (870) 575-8995.
Home Field: Torii Hunter Baseball Complex. **Seating
Capacity:** 1500. **Outfield Dimensions: LF**—330,
CF—400, **RF**—330.

ARMY BLACK KNIGHTS

Conference: Patriot League.
Mailing Address: 639 Howard Rd., West Point, NY 10996. **Website:** www.goarmysports.com.
Interim Head Coach: Matt Reid. **Telephone:** (845) 938-4939. **Baseball SID:** Ryan Yanoshak. **Telephone:** (845) 938-7197. **Fax:** (845) 938-1725.
Assistant Coaches: *Anthony DeCicco, Eric Folmar. **Telephone:** (845) 938-5877.
Home Field: Johnson Stadium. **Seating Capacity:** 880. **Outfield Dimensions: LF**—327, **CF**—400, **RF**—327. **Press Box Telephone:** (845) 938-3430.

AUBURN TIGERS

Conference: Southeastern (West).
Mailing Address: 392 S. Donahue Dr., Auburn, AL 36849. **Website:** www.auburntigers.com.
Head Coach: Sunny Golloway. **Telephone:** (334) 844-4922. **Baseball SID:** Wes Todd. **Telephone:** (334) 844-9182. **Fax:** (334) 844-9807.
Assistant Coaches: *Scott Foxhall, Greg Norton. **Telephone:** (334) 844-4910.
Home Field: Samford Stadium-Hitchock Field at Plainsman Park. **Seating Capacity:** 4,096. **Outfield Dimensions: LF**—315, **CF**—385, **RF**—331. **Press Box Telephone:** (334) 844-4138.

AUSTIN PEAY STATE GOVERNORS

Conference: Ohio Valley.
Mailing Address: APSU Baseball, Box 4515, Clarksville, TN 37044. **Website:** www.letsgopeay.com.
Head Coach: Gary McClure. **Telephone:** (931) 221-6266. **Baseball SID:** Cody Bush. **Telephone:** (931) 221-7561. **Fax:** (931) 221-7562.
Assistant Coaches: *Joel Mangrum, Derrick Dunbar. **Telephone:** (931) 221-7902.
Home Field: Raymond C. Hand Park. **Seating Capacity:** 2000. **Outfield Dimensions: LF**—325, **CF**—392, **RF**—320. **Press Box Telephone:** (931) 221-7406.

BALL STATE CARDINALS

Conference: Mid-American (West).
Mailing Address: 2000 W. University Ave., Muncie, IN 47306. **Website:** www.ballstatesports.com.
Head Coach: Rich Maloney. **Telephone:** (765) 285-8911. **Baseball SID:** Joe Hernandez. **Telephone:** (765) 285-8242. **Fax:** (765) 285-8929.
Assistant Coaches: *Scott French, Todd Linklater. **Telephone:** (765) 285-2862.
Home Field: Ball Diamond. **Seating Capacity:** 1,700. **Outfield Dimensions: LF**—330, **CF**—400, **RF**—330. **Press Box Telephone:** (765) 285-8932.

BAYLOR BEARS

Conference: Big 12.
Mailing Address: Baylor Ballpark, 1612 S. University Parks Dr., Waco, TX 76706. **Website:** www.baylorbears.com.
Head Coach: Steve Smith. **Telephone:** (254) 710-3029. **Baseball SID:** Zach Peters. **Telephone:** (254) 710-3784. **Fax:** (254) 710-1369.
Assistant Coaches: *Steve Johnigan, Trevor Mote. **Telephone:** (254) 710-3044.
Home Field: Baylor Ballpark. **Seating Capacity:** 5,000. **Outfield Dimensions: LF**—330, **CF**—400, **RF**—330. **Press Box Telephone:** (254) 754-5546.

BELMONT BRUINS

Conference: Ohio Valley.
Mailing Address: 1900 Belmont Blvd., Nashville, TN 37212. **Website:** www.belmontbruins.com.
Head Coach: Dave Jarvis. **Telephone:** (615) 460-6165. **Baseball SID:** Kristen Litchfield. **Telephone:** (615) 460-8023. **Fax:** (615) 460-5584.
Assistant Coaches: Matt Barnett, *Aaron Smith. **Telephone:** (615) 460-6165.
Home Field: E.S. Rose Park. **Seating Capacity:** 800. **Outfield Dimensions: LF**—330, **CF**—400, **RF**—330.

BETHUNE-COOKMAN WILDCATS

Conference: Mid-Eastern Athletic.
Mailing Address: 640 Mary McLeod Bethune Blvd., Daytona Beach, FL 32114. **Website:** www.bccathletics.com.
Head Coach: Jason Beverlin. **Telephone:** (386) 481-2224. **Baseball SID:** Michael Stambaugh. **Telephone:** (386) 481-2278. **Fax:** (386) 481-2238.
Assistant Coaches: Jason Bell, Keith Morrisroe, *Barrett Shaft. **Telephone:** (386) 481-2242. **Home Field:** Jackie Robinson Ballpark. **Seating Capacity:** 4800. **Outfield Dimensionss: LF**—317, **CF**—400, **RF**—325.

BINGHAMTON BEARCATS

Conference: America East.
Mailing Address: Binghamton University, Events Center Office #110, Binghamton, NY 13902. **Website:** www.bubearcats.com.
Head Coach: Tim Sinicki. **Telephone:** (607) 777-2525. **Baseball SID:** John Hartrick. **Telephone:** (607) 777-6800. **Fax:** (607) 777-4597.
Assistant Coaches: *Ryan Hurba. **Telephone:** (607) 777-5808, (607) 777-4552.
Home Field: Varsity Field. **Seating Capacity:** 500. **Outfield Dimensions: LF**—325, **CF**—390, **RF**—325. **Press Box Telephone:** (607) 777-3600.

BOSTON COLLEGE EAGLES

Conference: Atlantic Coast (Atlantic).
Mailing Address: 140 Commonwealth Ave., Chestnut Hill, MA 02467. **Website:** www.bceagles.cstv.com.
Head Coach: Mike Gambino. **Telephone:** (617) 552-2674. **Baseball SID:** Zanna Ollove. **Telephone:** (617) 552-2004. **Fax:** (617) 552-4903.
Assistant Coaches: *Scott Friedholm, Greg Sullivan. **Telephone:** (617) 552-3092.
Home Field: Eddie Pellagrini Diamond. **Seating Capacity:** 1,000. **Outfield Dimensions: LF**—330, **CF**—400, **RF**—320. **Press Box Telephone:** (978) 828-9221.

BOWLING GREEN STATE FALCONS

Conference: Missouri Valley.
Mailing Address: Bowling Green State University, Sebo Athletic Center–Baseball, Bowling Green, OH 43403. **Website:** www.bgsufalcons.com.
Head Coach: Danny Schmitz. **Telephone:** (419) 372-7065. **Baseball SID:** Scott Swegan. **Telephone:** (419) 372-7105. **Fax:** (419) 372-6969.
Assistant Coaches: *Rick Blanc, Mike Huling. **Telephone:** (419) 372-7641.
Home Field: Warren E. Steller Field. **Seating Capacity:** 1100 seats. **Outfield Dimensions: LF**—345, **CF**—400, **RF**—345. **Press Box Telephone:** (419) 372-1234.

BRADLEY BRAVES

Conference: Missouri Valley.
Mailing Address: 1501 W. Bradley Ave., Peoria IL 61625. **Website:** www.bradleybraves.com.
Head Coach: Elvis Dominguez. **Telephone:** (309) 677-2684. **Baseball SID:** Bobby Parker. **Telephone:** (309) 677-2624. **Fax:** (309) 677-2626.
Assistant Coaches: *John Corbin, Sean Lyons. **Telephone:** (309) 677-4583.
Home Field: Dozer Park. **Seating Capacity:** 7,500. **Outfield Dimensions: LF**—310, **CF**—400, **RF**—310. **Press Box Telephone:** (309) 680-4045.

BRIGHAM YOUNG COUGARS

Conference: West Coast.
Mailing Address: 30 SFH, BYU, Provo, UT 84602. **Website:** www.byucougars.com.
Head Coach: Mike Littlewood. **Telephone:** (801) 422-5049. **Baseball SID:** Ralph Zobell. **Telephone:** (801) 422-9769. **Fax:** (801) 422-0633.
Assistant Coaches: *Brent Haring, Trent Pratt. **Telephone:** (801) 422-5064.
Home Field: Miller Park. **Seating Capacity:** 2,500. **Outfield Dimensions: LF**—330, **CF**—410, **RF**—330. **Press Box Telephone:** (801) 422-4041.

BROWN BEARS

Conference: Ivy League (Rolfe).
Mailing Address: Brown University Baseball, 235 Hope St., Box 1932, Providence, RI 02912. **Website:** www.brownbears.com.
Head Coach: Marek Drabinski. **Telephone:** (401) 863-3090. **Baseball SID:** Eric Peterson. **Telephone:** (401) 863-7014. **Fax:** (401) 863-1463.
Assistant Coaches: *Grant Achilles, Mike McCormack. **Telephone:** (401) 863-2032.
Home Field: Murray Stadium. **Seating Capacity:** 1500. **Outfield Dimensions: LF**—340, **CF**—405, **RF**—325. **Press Box Telephone:** (401) 863-9427.

BRYANT BULLDOGS

Conference: Northeast.
Mailing Address: 1150 Douglas Pike, Smithfield, RI 02917. **Website:** www.bryantbulldogs.com.
Head Coach: Steve Owens. **Telephone:** (401) 232-6397. **Baseball SID:** Tristan Hobbes. **Telephone:** (401) 232-6558, ext. 2. **Fax:** (401) 319-5158.
Assistant Coaches: *Ryan Fecteau, Mike Gedman. **Telephone:** (401) 232-6967.
Home Field: Conaty Park. **Seating Capacity:** 500. **Outfield Dimensions: LF**—330, **CF**—400, **RF**—330. **Press Box Telephone:** (401) 531-6610.

BUCKNELL BISON

Conference: Patriot League.
Mailing Address: Langone Athletics and Recreation Center, Bucknell University, 1 Dent Dr., Lewisburg, PA 17837. **Website:** www.bucknellbison.com.
Head Coach: Scott Heather. **Telephone:** (570) 577-1059. **Baseball SID:** Todd Merriot. **Telephone:** (570) 577-3488. **Fax:** (570) 577-1660.
Assistant Coaches: *Jason Neitz. **Telephone:** (570) 577-1059.
Home Field: Depew Field. **Seating Capacity:** 500. **Outfield Dimensions: LF**—330, **CF**—400, **RF**—330. **Press Box Telephone:** (570) 428-5393.

BUFFALO BULLS

Conference: Mid-American (East).
Mailing Address: 21 Alumni Arena, Buffalo, NY 14260. **Website:** www.buffalobulls.com.
Head Coach: Ron Torgalski. **Telephone:** (716) 645-6834. **Baseball SID:** Joe Kepler. **Telephone:** (716) 645-5523. **Fax:** (716) 645-5523.
Assistant Coaches: *Brad Cochrane, Steve Ziroli. **Telephone:** (716) 645-3437.
Home Field: Amherst Audubon Field. **Seating Capacity:** 500. **Outfield Dimensions: LF**—330, **CF**—400, **RF**—330. **Press Box Telephone:** (716) 867-1908.

BUTLER BULLDOGS

Conference: Big East.
Mailing Address: 510 West 49th St., Indianapolis, IN 46208. **Website:** www.butlersports.com.
Head Coach: Steve Farley. **Telephone:** (317) 940-9721. **Baseball SID:** Kit Stetzel. **Telephone:** (317) 940-9994. **Fax:** (317) 940-9808.
Assistant Coaches: Pat Casey, *Miles Miller. **Telephone:** (317) 940-6536.
Home Field: Bulldog Park. **Seating Capacity:** 1,000. **Outfield Dimensions: LF**—330, **CF**—400, **RF**—330. **Press Box Telephone:** (317) 940-9817.

CALIFORNIA GOLDEN BEARS

Conference: Pacific-12.
Mailing Address: Haas Pavilion, Berkeley, CA 94720. **Website:** www.calbears.com.
Head Coach: David Esquer. **Telephone:** (510) 642-9026. **Baseball SID:** Scott Ball. **Telephone:** (510) 643-1741. **Fax:** (510) 643-6333.
Assistant Coaches: Tony Arnerich, *Mike Neu. **Telephone:** (510) 643-6006.
Home Field: Evans Diamond. **Seating Capacity:** 2,500. **Outfield Dimensions: LF**—320, **CF**—395, **RF**—320. **Press Box Telephone:** (510) 334-0793.

UC DAVIS AGGIES

Conference: Big West.
Mailing Address: One Shields Ave., Davis, CA, 95616. **Website:** www.ucdavisaggies.com.
Head Coach: Matt Vaughn. **Telephone:** (530) 752-7513. **Baseball SID:** Jason Spencer. **Telephone:** (530) 752-2663. **Fax:** (530) 752-6681.
Assistant Coaches: Brett Lindgren, *Tony Schifano. **Telephone:** (530) 752-7513.
Home Field: Dobbins Baseball Complex. **Seating Capacity:** 4,500. **Outfield Dimensions: LF**—310, **CF**—410, **RF**—310. **Press Box Telephone:** (530) 752-3673.

UC IRVINE ANTEATERS

Conference: Big West.
Mailing Address: Intercollegiate Athletics Building, 625 Humanities Quad, Irvine, CA 92697. **Website:** www.ucirvinesports.com.
Head Coach: Mike Gillespie. **Telephone:** (949) 824-4292. **Baseball SID:** Fumi Kimura. **Telephone:** (949) 751-7798. **Fax:** (949) 824-5260.
Assistant Coaches: Bob Macaluso, *Ben Orloff. **Telephone:** (949) 824-9521.
Home Field: Anteater Ballpark. **Seating Capacity:** 3200. **Outfield Dimensions: LF**—335, **CF**—405, **RF**—335. **Press Box Telephone:** (949) 824-9905.

UCLA BRUINS

Conference: Pacific-12.
Mailing Address: 325 Westwood Plaza, Los Angeles, CA 90095. **Website:** www.uclabruins.com.
Head Coach: John Savage. **Telephone:** (310) 794-2470. **Baseball SID:** Mike Leary. **Telephone:** (310) 206-7873. **Fax:** (310) 206-6831.
Assistant Coaches: *T.J. Bruce, Rex Peters. **Telephone:** (310) 794-8210.
Home Field: Jackie Robinson Stadium. **Seating Capacity:** 1,820. **Outfield Dimensions:** LF—330, CF—395, RF—330. **Press Box Telephone:** (310) 794-8213.

CAL POLY MUSTANGS

Conference: Big West.
Mailing Address: 1 Grand Ave., San Luis Obispo, CA 93407. **Website:** www.gopoly.com.
Head Coach: Larry Lee. **Telephone:** (805) 756-6367. **Baseball SID:** Eric Burdick. **Telephone:** (805) 756-6550. **Fax:** (805) 756-2650.
Assistant Coaches: Thomas Eager, *Teddy Warrecker. **Telephone:** (805) 756-1201.
Home Field: Baggett Stadium. **Seating Capacity:** 1,734. **Outfield Dimensions:** LF—335, CF—405, RF—335. **Press Box Telephone:** (805) 756-7456.

UC RIVERSIDE HIGHLANDERS

Conference: Big West.
Mailing Address: 900 University Ave., Riverside, CA 92521. **Website:** www.gohighlanders.com.
Head Coach: Doug Smith. **Telephone:** (951) 827-5441. **Baseball SID:** John Maxwell. **Telephone:** (951) 827-5438. **Fax:** (951) 827-3569.
Assistant Coaches: *Bobby Applegate, Bryson LeBlanc. **Telephone:** (951) 827-5441.
Home Field: Riverside Sports Complex. **Seating Capacity:** 2,227. **Outfield Dimensions:** LF—330, CF—405, RF—330. **Press Box Telephone:** (951) 827-6415.

UC SANTA BARBARA GAUCHOS

Conference: Big West.
Mailing Address: 552 University Rd., Santa Barbara, CA 93106. **Website:** www.ucsbgauchos.com.
Head Coach: Andrew Checketts. **Telephone:** (805) 893-3690. **Baseball SID:** Andrew Wagner. **Telephone:** (805) 893-8603. **Fax:** (805) 893-5477.
Assistant Coaches: *Eddie Cornejo, Jason Hawkins. **Telephone:** (805) 893-2021.
Home Field: Caesar Uyesaka Stadium. **Seating Capacity:** 1,000. **Outfield Dimensions:** LF—335, CF—400, RF—335. **Press Box Telephone:** (805) 893-4671.

CAL STATE BAKERSFIELD ROADRUNNERS

Conference: Western Athletic.
Mailing Address: 9001 Stockdale Highway, Bakersfield, CA 93311. **Website:** www.gorunners.com.
Head Coach: Bill Kernen. **Telephone:** (661) 335-1058. **Baseball SID:** Matt Turk. **Telephone:** (661) 654-3071. **Fax:** (661) 654-6978.
Assistant Coaches: Brandon Boren, Richie Escalera, Jody Robinson. **Telephone:** (661) 654-2678. **Home Field:** Hard Field. **Seating Capacity:** 2000. **Outfield Dimensionss:** LF—325, CF—390, RF—325. **Press Box Telephone:** (515) 240-0483).

CAL STATE FULLERTON TITANS

Conference: Big West.
Mailing Address: 800 N. State College Blvd., Fullerton, CA 92834. **Website:** www.fullertontitans.com.
Head Coach: Rick Vanderhook. **Telephone:** (657) 278-3780. **Baseball SID:** Andria Wenzel. **Telephone:** (657) 278-3970. **Fax:** (657) 278-3970.
Assistant Coaches: Jason Dietrich, *Mike Kirby. **Telephone:** (657) 278-2492.
Home Field: Goodwin Field. **Seating Capacity:** 3,500. **Outfield Dimensions:** LF—330, CF—400, RF—330. **Press Box Telephone:** (657) 278-5327.

CAL STATE NORTHRIDGE MATADORS

Conference: Big West.
Mailing Address: 18111 Nordhoff St., Northridge, CA 91330. **Website:** www.gomatadors.cstv.com.
Head Coach: Greg Moore. **Telephone:** (818) 256-5224. **Baseball SID:** Kevin Strauss. **Telephone:** (818) 677-3860. **Fax:** (818) 677-4950.
Assistant Coaches: Chris Hom, *Jordon Twohig. **Telephone:** (925) 864-4734.
Home Field: Matador Field. **Seating Capacity:** 1,000. **Outfield Dimensions:** LF—325, CF—395, RF—326. **Press Box Telephone:** (909) 730-2076.

CAMPBELL FIGHTING CAMELS

Conference: Big South.
Mailing Address: P.O. Box 10, Buies Creek, NC 27506. **Website:** www.gocamels.com.
Head Coach: Greg Goff. **Telephone:** (910) 893-1354. **Baseball SID:** Jason Williams. **Telephone:** (910) 814-4367. **Fax:** (910) 893-1330.
Assistant Coaches: *Justin Haire, Rick McCarty. **Telephone:** (910) 893-4335.
Home Field: Jim Perry Stadium. **Seating Capacity:** 1500. **Outfield Dimensions:** LF—337, CF—395, RF—328. **Press Box Telephone:** (910) 814-4781.

CANISIUS GOLDEN GRIFFINS

Conference: Metro Atlantic.
Mailing Address: 2001 Main St., Buffalo, NY 14208. **Website:** www.gogriffs.com.
Head Coach: Mike McRae. **Telephone:** (716) 888-8485. **Baseball SID:** Matt Lozar. **Telephone:** (716) 888-8266. **Fax:** (716) 888-8444.
Assistant Coaches: Frank Jagoda, *Matt Mazurek. **Telephone:** (716) 888-8478. **Home Field:** Demske Sports Complex. **Seating Capacity:** 1,000. **Outfield Dimensions:** LF—325, CF—405, RF—315. **Press Box Telephone:** (440) 477-3777.

CENTRAL ARKANSAS BEARS

Conference: Southland.
Mailing Address: P.O. Box 5004, Conway, AR 72034. **Website:** www.ucasports.com.
Head Coach: Allen Gum. **Telephone:** (501) 450-3147. **Baseball SID:** Steve East. **Telephone:** (501) 450-5743. **Fax:** (501) 450-5740.
Assistant Coaches: Nick Harlan, Trent Kline. **Telephone:** (501) 339-0101.
Home Field: Bear Stadium. **Seating Capacity:** 2,000. **Press Box Telephone:** (501) 450-5972.

CENTRAL CONNECTICUT STATE BLUE DEVILS

Conference: Northeast.

Mailing Address: 16151 Stanley St., New Britain, CT 06050. **Website:** www.ccsubluedevils.com.

Head Coach: Charlie Hickey. **Telephone:** (860) 832-3074. **Baseball SID:** Tom Pincince. **Telephone:** (860) 832-3089. **Fax:** (860) 832-3754.

Assistant Coaches: *Patrick Hall, Jim Ziogas. **Telephone:** (860) 832-3075.

Home Field: Balf Savin Baseball Field.

CENTRAL FLORIDA KNIGHTS

Conference: American Athletic.

Mailing Address: 4000 Central Florida Boulevard, Orlando, FL 32816. **Website:** www.ucfathletics.com.

Head Coach: Terry Rooney. **Telephone:** (407) 823-0141. **Baseball SID:** Andrew Jennette. **Telephone:** (407) 823-0994. **Fax:** (407) 823-5266.

Assistant Coaches: Ryan Klosterman, *Kevin Schnall. **Telephone:** (407) 823-4320.

Home Field: Jay Bergman Field. **Seating Capacity:** 3900. **Outfield Dimensions: LF**—320, **CF**—390, **RF**—320. **Press Box Telephone:** (407) 823-4487.

CENTRAL MICHIGAN CHIPPEWAS

Conference: Mid-American (West).

Mailing Address: 100 Rose Center, Mount Pleasant, MI 48859. **Website:** www.cmuchippewas.com.

Head Coach: Steve Jaksa. **Telephone:** (989) 774-4392. **Baseball SID:** Kyle Kelley. **Telephone:** (989) 774-1128. **Fax:** (989) 774-5391.

Assistant Coaches: *Jeff Opalewski, Doug Sanders. **Telephone:** (989) 774-2123.

Home Field: Theunissen Stadium. **Seating Capacity:** 2500. **Outfield Dimensions: LF**—330, **CF**—400, **RF**—330. **Press Box Telephone:** (989) 774-3579.

CHARLESTON SOUTHERN BUCCANEERS

Conference: Big South.

Mailing Address: 9200 University Blvd., North Charleston, SC 29406. **Website:** www.csusports.com.

Head Coach: Stuart Lake. **Telephone:** (843) 863-7591. **Baseball SID:** Zeke Beam. **Telephone:** (843) 863-7687. **Fax:** (843) 863-7695.

Assistant Coaches: Adam Vrable, *Adam Ward. **Telephone:** (843) 863-7764.

Home Field: CSU Ballpark. **Seating Capacity:** 1,500. **Outfield Dimensions: LF**—320, **CF**—400, **RF**—320. **Press Box Telephone:** (843) 863-7591.

CHARLOTTE 49ERS

Conference: Conference USA.

Mailing Address: 9201 University City Blvd., Charlotte, NC 28223. **Website:** www.charlotte49ers.com.

Head Coach: Loren Hibbs. **Telephone:** (704) 687-0726. **Baseball SID:** Ryan Rose. **Telephone:** (704) 687-1023. **Fax:** (704) 687-4918.

Assistant Coaches: *Brandon Hall, Kris Rochelle. **Telephone:** (704) 687-0728.

Home Field: Robert and Mariam Hayes Stadium. **Seating Capacity:** 1,100. **Outfield Dimensions: LF**—335, **CF**—390, **RF**—335. **Press Box Telephone:** (704) 687-5959.

CHICAGO STATE COUGARS

Conference: Western Athletic.

Mailing Address: 9501 S. Michigan Ave., Chicago, IL. **Website:** www.goscucougars.com.

Head Coach: Steve Joslyn. **Telephone:** (773) 995-

3637. **Baseball SID:** Derrick Sloboda. **Telephone:** (773) 995-3637. **Fax:** (773) 995-3656.

Assistant Coaches: *Ray Napientek, Dan Pirillo. **Telephone:** (773) 995-2817.

Home Field: Cougar Stadium. **Seating Capacity:** 500. **Outfield Dimensions: LF**—325, **CF**—385, **RF**—325.

CINCINNATI BEARCATS

Conference: American Athletic.

Mailing Address: 2751 O'Varsity Way, Suite 764, Richard E. Lindner Center, Cincinnati, OH 45221. **Website:** www.gobearcats.com.

Head Coach: Ty Neal. **Telephone:** (513) 556-1577. **Baseball SID:** Alex Lange. **Telephone:** (513) 556-5145. **Fax:** (513) 556-0619.

Assistant Coaches: Adam Bourassa, *J.D. Heilmann. **Telephone:** (513) 556-1577.

Home Field: Marge Schott Stadium. **Seating Capacity:** 3085. **Outfield Dimensions: LF**—325, **CF**—400, **RF**—325. **Press Box Telephone:** (513) 556-9645.

CITADEL BULLDOGS

Conference: Southern.

Mailing Address: 171 Moultrie St., Charleston, SC 29409. **Website:** www.citadelsports.com.

Head Coach: Fred Jordan. **Telephone:** (843) 953-5901. **Baseball SID:** Mike Hoffman. **Telephone:** (843) 953-5353. **Fax:** (843) 953-6727.

Assistant Coaches: *David Beckley, Britt Reames. **Telephone:** (843) 953-7265.

Home Field: Riley Park. **Seating Capacity:** 6,000. **Outfield Dimensions: LF**—305, **CF**—398, **RF**—337. **Press Box Telephone:** (843) 302-6193.

CLEMSON TIGERS

Conference: Atlantic Coast (Atlantic).

Mailing Address: 100 Perimeter Rd., Clemson, SC 29633. **Website:** www.clemsontigers.com.

Head Coach: Jack Leggett. **Telephone:** (864) 656-1947. **Baseball SID:** Brian Hennessy. **Telephone:** (864) 656-1921. **Fax:** (864) 656-0299.

Assistant Coaches: *Bradley LeCroy, Dan Pepicelli. **Telephone:** (864) 656-1948.

Home Field: Doug Kingsmore Stadium. **Seating Capacity:** 6,016. **Outfield Dimensions: LF**—320, **CF**—400, **RF**—330. **Press Box Telephone:** (864) 656-7731.

COASTAL CAROLINA CHANTICLEERS

Conference: Big South.

Mailing Address: P.O. Box 261954, Conway, SC 29528. **Website:** www.goccusports.com.

Head Coach: Gary Gilmore. **Telephone:** (843) 349-2524. **Baseball SID:** Mike Cawood. **Telephone:** (843) 349-2822. **Fax:** (843) 349-2819.

Assistant Coaches: *Joe Hastings, Drew Thomas. **Telephone:** (843) 349-2849.

Home Field: TicketReturn.com Field at Pelicans Ballpark (for 2013). **Seating Capacity:** 5,200. **Outfield Dimensions: LF**—308, CF—400, RF—328. **Press Box Telephone:** (843) 234-3474.

COLLEGE OF CHARLESTON COUGARS

Conference: Colonial Athletic.

Mailing Address: 301 Meeting St., Charleston, SC 29401. **Website:** www.cofcsports.com.

Head Coach: Monte Lee. Telephone: (843) 513-9642. Baseball SID: Will Bryan. Telephone: (843) 953-3683. Fax: (843) 953-6534.
Assistant Coaches: Matt Heath, *Chris Morris. Telephone: (843) 953-7013.
Home Field: Patriots Point. Seating Capacity: 2,000. Outfield Dimensions: LF—300, CF—400, RF—330. Press Box Telephone: (843) 819-7429.

COLUMBIA LIONS

Conference: Ivy League (Gehrig).
Mailing Address: 3030 Broadway, Mail Code 1930, New York, NY 10027. Website: www.gocolumbialions.com.
Head Coach: Brett Boretti. Telephone: (212) 854-8448. Baseball SID: Brock Malone. Telephone: (212) 854-9870. Fax: (212) 854-8168.
Assistant Coaches: *Pete Maki, Dan Tischler. Telephone: (212) 854-7772.
Home Field: Hal Robertson Field at Satow Stadium. Seating Capacity: 600. Press Box Telephone: (917) 678-3621.

CONNECTICUT HUSKIES

Conference: American Athletic.
Mailing Address: 2095 Hillside Rd., Storrs, CT 06269. Website: www.uconnhuskies.com.
Head Coach: Jim Penders. Telephone: (860) 486-1496. Baseball SID: Robert Mullen. Telephone: (860) 486-1496. Fax: (860) 486-5085.
Assistant Coaches: *Jeff Hourigan, Joshua MacDonald, Chris Podeszwa. Telephone: (860) 486-5771.
Home Field: J.O. Christian Field. Seating Capacity: 2,000. Outfield Dimensions: LF—337, CF—400, RF—325. Press Box Telephone: (203) 415-5381.

COPPIN STATE EAGLES

Conference: Mid-Eastern Athletic.
Mailing Address: 2500 W. North Ave., Baltimore, MD 21216. Website: www.coppinstatesports.com.
Head Coach: Sherman Reed. Telephone: (410) 951-3723. Baseball SID: Robert Knox. Telephone: (410) 951-3724. Fax: (410) 951-3724.
Assistant Coaches: *Gregory Beckman. Telephone: (410) 951-6941.
Home Field: Joe Cannon Stadium. Seating Capacity: 2,000. Outfield Dimensions: LF—325, CF—425, RF—325. Press Box Telephone: (410) 222-6652.

CORNELL BIG RED

Conference: Ivy League (Gehrig).
Mailing Address: Cornell Baseball, Teagle Hall, 512 Campus Rd., Ithaca, NY 14853. Website: www.cornellbigred.com.
Head Coach: Bill Walkenbach. Telephone: (607) 255-3812. Baseball SID: Brandon Thomas. Telephone: (607) 255-5627. Fax: (607) 255-9791.
Assistant Coaches: Tom Ford, *Scott Marsh. Telephone: (607) 255-6604.
Home Field: Hoy Field. Seating Capacity: 1,000. Outfield Dimensions: LF—315, CF—405, RF—325.

CREIGHTON BLUEJAYS

Conference: Big East.
Mailing Address: Creighton Athletics, 2500 California Plaza, Omaha, NE 68178. Website: www.gocreighton.com.

Head Coach: Ed Servais. Telephone: (402) 280-2483. Baseball SID: Glen Sisk. Telephone: (402) 280-2433. Fax: (402) 280-2495.
Assistant Coaches: *Spencer Allen, Thomas Lipari. Telephone: (402) 280-5545.
Home Field: TD Ameritrade Park. Seating Capacity: 24,000. Outfield Dimensions: LF—335, CF—408, RF—335. Press Box Telephone: (402) 546-0702.

DALLAS BAPTIST PATRIOTS

Conference: Missouri Valley.
Mailing Address: 3000 Mountain Creek Pkwy., Dallas, TX 75211. Website: www.dbu.edu.
Head Coach: Dan Heefner. Telephone: (214) 333-5327. Baseball SID: Reagan Ratcliff. Telephone: (214) 333-5942. Fax: (214) 333-5306.
Assistant Coaches: *Dan Fitzgerald, Wes Johnson. Telephone: (214) 333-6957.
Home Field: Horner Ballpark. Seating Capacity: 2,000. Outfield Dimensions: LF—330, CF—390, RF—330. Press Box Telephone: (214) 333-5542.

DARTMOUTH BIG GREEN

Conference: Ivy League (Rolfe).
Mailing Address: 6083 Alumni Gym, Hanover, NH 03755. Website: www.dartmouthsports.com.
Head Coach: Bob Whalen. Telephone: (603) 646-2477. Baseball SID: Rick Bender. Telephone: (603) 646-1030. Fax: (603) 646-3348.
Assistant Coaches: *Jonathan Anderson, Evan Wells. Telephone: (603) 646-9775.
Home Field: Red Rolfe Field at Biondi Park. Seating Capacity: 2,000. Outfield Dimensions: LF—325, CF—403, RF—340. Press Box Telephone: (603) 646-6937.

DAVIDSON WILDCATS

Conference: Southern.
Mailing Address: Box 7158, Davidson College, Davidson, NC 28035. Website: www.davidsonwildcats.com.
Head Coach: Dick Cooke. Telephone: (704) 894-2368. Baseball SID: Mark Brumbaugh. Telephone: (704) 894-2931. Fax: (704) 894-2636.
Assistant Coaches: Andy Carter, *Rucker Taylor. Telephone: (704) 894-2772.
Home Field: Wilson Field. Seating Capacity: 700. Outfield Dimensions: LF—325, CF—385, RF—325. Press Box Telephone: (704) 894-2740.

DAYTON FLYERS

Conference: Atlantic 10.
Mailing Address: 300 College Park, Dayton, OH 45469. Website: www.daytonflyers.com.
Head Coach: Tony Vittorio. Telephone: (937) 229-4456. Baseball SID: Ross Bagienski. Telephone: (937) 229-4431.
Assistant Coaches: Jim Roberson, *Matt Talarico. Telephone: (937) 229-4788. Home Field: Time Warner Cable Stadium. Seating Capacity: 500.

DELAWARE FIGHTIN' BLUE HENS

Conference: Colonial Athletic.
Mailing Address: 621 South College Ave., Newark, DE 19716. Website: www.bluehens.com.
Head Coach: Jim Sherman. Telephone: (302) 831-8596. Baseball SID: Jessica Calderone. Telephone: (302)

831-6519. **Fax:** (302) 831-8653.
Assistant Coaches: Dan Hammer, *Brian Walker.
Telephone: (302) 831-2723.
Home Field: Bob Hannah Stadium. **Seating Capacity:**
1,300. **Outfield Dimensions:** LF—320, CF—410,
RF—330.

DELAWARE STATE HORNETS

Conference: Mid-Eastern Athletic.
Mailing Address: 1200 N. Dupont Hwy, Dover, DE
19901. **Website:** www.dsuhornets.com.
Head Coach: J.P. Blandin. **Telephone:** (302) 857-6035.
Baseball SID: Dennis Jones. **Telephone:** (302) 857-6068.
Fax: (302) 857-6069.
Assistant Coaches: *Chris Barker, Tom Riley.
Telephone: (302) 857-7815.
Home Field: Soldier Field. **Seating Capacity:** 500.
Outfield Dimensions: LF—320, CF—385, RF—320.

DUKE BLUE DEVILS

Conference: Atlantic Coast (Coastal).
Mailing Address: 118 Cameron Indoor Stadium, Box
90555, Durham, NC 27708. **Website:** www.goduke.com.
Head Coach: Chris Pollard. **Telephone:** (919) 668-
0255. **Baseball SID:** Ashley Wolf. **Telephone:** (919) 668-
4393. **Fax:** (919) 668-0256.
Assistant Coaches: *Josh Jordan, Andrew See.
Telephone: (919) 668-5735.
Home Field: Jack Coombs Field. **Seating Capacity:**
2,500. **Outfield Dimensions:** LF—325, CF—400,
RF—335. **Press Box Telephone:** (603) 325-2225.

EAST CAROLINA PIRATES

Conference: Conference USA.
Mailing Address: East Carolina University, 102 Clark-
LeClair Stadium, Greenville, NC 27858. **Website:** www.
ecupirates.com.
Head Coach: Billy Godwin. **Telephone:** (252) 737-
1985. **Baseball SID:** Malcolm Gray. **Telephone:** (252) 737-
4523. **Fax:** (252) 737-1467.
Assistant Coaches: Dan Roszel, *Ben Sanderson.
Telephone: (252) 737-1467.
Home Field: Clark-LeClair Stadium. **Seating Capacity:**
5,000. **Outfield Dimensions:** LF—320, CF—400,
RF—320. **Press Box Telephone:** (252) 328-0068.

EAST TENNESSEE STATE BUCCANEERS

Conference: Atlantic Sun.
Mailing Address: P.O. Box 70707, Johnson City, TN
37614. **Website:** www.etsubucs.com.
Head Coach: Tony Skole. **Telephone:** (423) 439-4496.
Baseball SID: Kevin Brown. **Telephone:** (423) 439-5263.
Fax: (423) 439-6138.
Assistant Coaches: Xan Barksdale, *Kyle Bunn.
Telephone: (423) 439-5727.
Home Field: Thomas Stadium. **Seating Capacity:**
1,000.

EASTERN ILLINOIS PANTHERS

Conference: Ohio Valley.
Mailing Address: 600 Lincoln Ave., Charleston, IL
61920. **Website:** www.eiupanthers.com.
Head Coach: Jim Schmitz. **Telephone:** (217)
581-2522. **Baseball SID:** Gregory A. Lautzenheiser.
Telephone: (217) 581-7020. **Fax:** (217) 581-6434.
Assistant Coaches: *Jason Anderson. **Telephone:**
(217) 581-8510.

Home Field: Coaches Stadium. **Seating Capacity:**
500. **Outfield Dimensions:** LF—340, CF—380, RF—340.
Press Box Telephone: (419) 605-8512.

EASTERN KENTUCKY COLONELS

Conference: Ohio Valley.
Mailing Address: 115 Alumni Coliseum, 521 Lancaster
Ave., Richmond, KY 40475. **Website:** www.ekusports.com.
Head Coach: Jason Stein. **Telephone:** (859) 622-2128.
Baseball SID: Kevin Britton. **Telephone:** (859) 622-2006.
Fax: (859) 622-5108.
Assistant Coaches: *John Peterson. **Telephone:** (859)
622-4996.
Home Field: Turkey Hughes Field. **Seating Capacity:**
500. **Outfield Dimensions:** LF—340, CF—410, RF—330.
Press Box Telephone: (859) 358-8359.

EASTERN MICHIGAN EAGLES

Conference: Mid-American (West).
Mailing Address: 799 Hewitt Rd., Ypsilanti, MI 48197.
Website: www.emueagles.com.
Head Coach: Jay Alexander. **Telephone:** (734) 487-
0315. **Baseball SID:** Adam Kuffner. **Telephone:** (734) 487-
0317. **Fax:** (734) 485-3840.
Assistant Coaches: *Andrew Maki, Eric Peterson.
Telephone: (734) 487-8660.
Home Field: Oestrike Stadium. **Seating Capacity:**
1,200. **Outfield Dimensions:** LF—340, CF—390,
RF—325. **Press Box Telephone:** (731) 481-9328.

ELON PHOENIX

Conference: Southern.
Mailing Address: 2500 Campus Box, 100 Campus
Drive, Elon, NC 27244. **Website:** www.elonphoenix.com.
Head Coach: Mike Kennedy. **Telephone:** (336) 278-
6741. **Baseball SID:** Chris Rash. **Telephone:** (336) 278-
6712. **Fax:** (336) 278-6768.
Assistant Coaches: Robbie Huffstetler, *Greg Starbuck.
Telephone: (336) 278-6794.
Home Field: Latham Park. **Seating Capacity:** 2,000.
Outfield Dimensionss: LF—326, CF—385, RF—327.
Press Box Telephone: (336) 278-6788.

EVANSVILLE PURPLE ACES

Conference: Missouri Valley.
Mailing Address: 1800 Lincoln Ave., Evansville, IN
47722. **Website:** www.gopurpleaces.com.
Head Coach: Wes Carroll. **Telephone:** (812) 488-2059.
Baseball SID: Dustin Hall. **Telephone:** (812) 488-1152.
Fax: (812) 488-2199.
Assistant Coaches: Cody Fick, *Andy Pascoe.
Telephone: (812) 488-1027.
Home Field: Charles H. Braun Stadium. **Seating
Capacity:** 1200. **Outfield Dimensions:** LF—330,
CF—400, RF—330. **Press Box Telephone:** (812) 479-
2587.

FAIRFIELD STAGS

Conference: Metro Atlantic.
Mailing Address: 1073 N. Benson Rd., Fairfield, CT
06824. **Website:** www.fairfieldstags.com.
Head Coach: Bill Currier. **Telephone:** (203) 254-4000.
Baseball SID: Kelly McCarthy. **Telephone:** (203) 254-
4000. **Fax:** (203) 254-4117.
Assistant Coaches: *Trevor Brown. **Telephone:** (203)
254-4000, Ext. 3178.
Home Field: Alumni Baseball Diamond. **Outfield

Dimensions: LF—330, CF—400, RF—330.

FAIRLEIGH DICKINSON KNIGHTS

Conference: Northeast.
Mailing Address: 1000 River Rd., Teaneck, NJ 07666.
Website: www.fduknights.com.
Head Coach: Gary Puccio. **Telephone:** (201) 692-2245.
Baseball SID: Chris Strauch. **Telephone:** (201) 692-2499.
Fax: (201) 692-9361.
Assistant Coaches: Ryan Kresky, *Ray Skjold.
Telephone: (201) 692-2245.
Home Field: Naimoli Family Baseball Complex.
Outfield Dimensions: LF—321, CF—387, RF—321.

FLORIDA GATORS

Conference: Southeastern (East).
Mailing Address: University Athletic Association,
P.O. Box 14485, Gainesville, FL 32604. **Website:** www.
gatorzone.com.
Head Coach: Kevin O'Sullivan. **Telephone:** (352) 375-4683. **Baseball SID:** John Hines. **Telephone:** (352) 375-4683. **Fax:** (352) 375-4809.
Assistant Coaches: *Craig Bell, Brad Weitzel.
Telephone: (352) 375-4683.
Home Field: Alfred A. McKethan Stadium at Perry
Field. **Seating Capacity:** 5,500. **Outfield Dimensions:**
LF—326, CF—400, RF—321. **Press Box Telephone:** (352)
375-4683.

FLORIDA A&M RATTLERS

Conference: Mid-Eastern Athletic.
Mailing Address: 1835 Wahnish Way, Tallahassee, FL
32307. **Website:** www.famuathletics.com.
Head Coach: *Jamey Shouppe. **Telephone:** (850) 599-3202. **Baseball SID:** Vaughn Wilson. **Telephone:** (850)
599-3849. **Fax:** (850) 599-3810.
Assistant Coaches: Kevin Clethen. **Telephone:** (850)
412-7391.
Home Field: Moore-Kittles Field. **Seating Capacity:**
2500. **Outfield Dimensions:** LF—325, CF—410,
RF—325.

FLORIDA ATLANTIC OWLS

Conference: Conference USA.
Mailing Address: 777 Glades Rd., Boca Raton, FL
33431. **Website:** www.fausports.com.
Head Coach: John McCormack. **Telephone:** (561) 297-1055. **Baseball SID:** Brandon Goodwin. **Telephone:** (561)
756-0653. **Fax:** (561) 291-3956.
Assistant Coaches: Dickie Hart, *Jason Jackson.
Telephone: (561) 297-1055.
Home Field: FAU Baseball. **Seating Capacity:** 2,000.
Outfield Dimensions: LF—330, CF—400, RF—330.
Press Box Telephone: (561) 756-0653.

FLORIDA GULF COAST EAGLES

Conference: Atlantic Sun.
Mailing Address: Florida Gulf Coast University, 10501
FGCU Blvd. S., Fort Myers, FL 33965. **Website:** www.
fgcuathletics.com.
Head Coach: Dave Tollett. **Telephone:** (239) 590-7051.
Baseball SID: Matt Moretti. **Telephone:** (230) 590-1327.
Fax: (239) 590-7014.
Assistant Coaches: Chris Berry, *Rusty McKee.
Telephone: (239) 590-7059.
Home Field: Swanson Stadium. **Seating Capacity:**
1,500. **Outfield Dimensionss:** LF—330, CF—400,

RF—330. **Press Box Telephone:** (239) 357-2390.

FLORIDA INTERNATIONAL PANTHERS

Conference: Conference USA.
Mailing Address: 11200 SW 8th St., Miami, FL 33199.
Website: www.fiusports.com.
Head Coach: Turtle Thomas. **Telephone:** (305) 348-3166. **Baseball SID:** Greg Kincaid. **Telephone:** (305) 348-1496. **Fax:** (305) 348-2963.
Assistant Coaches: *Frank Damas, Sam Peraza.
Telephone: (305) 348-2145.
Home Field: FIU Stadium. **Seating Capacity:** 2000.
Outfield Dimensions: LF—325, CF –400, RF –325. **Press
Box Telephone:** (786) 972-1299.

FLORIDA STATE SEMINOLES

Conference: Atlantic Coast (Atlantic)
Mailing Address: 403 Stadium Dr. West, Room D0107
Tallahassee, FL 32306. **Website:** www.seminoles.com.
Head Coach: Mike Martin. **Telephone:** (850) 644-1073. **Baseball SID:** Jason Leturmy. **Telephone:** (850)
644-3920. **Fax:** (850) 644-3820.
Assistant Coaches: Mike Bell, *Mike Martin, Jr.
Telephone: (850) 644-1072.
Home Field: Dick Howser Stadium. **Seating Capacity:**
6700. **Outfield Dimensions:** LF—340, CF—400,
RF—320. **Press Box Telephone:** (850) 644-1553.

FORDHAM RAMS

Conference: Atlantic 10.
Mailing Address: 441 E. Fordham Rd., Bronx, NY
10458. **Website:** www.fordhamsports.com.
Head Coach: Kevin Leighton. **Telephone:** (718) 817-4292. **Baseball SID:** Scott Kwiatkowski. **Telephone:** (718)
817-4219. **Fax:** (718) 817-4244.
Assistant Coaches: Rob DiToma, *Jimmy Jackson.
Telephone: (718) 817-4290.
Home Field: Houlihan Park. **Seating Capacity:** 500.
Outfield Dimensions: LF—338, CF—400, RF—338.
Press Box Telephone: (718) 817-3373.

FRESNO STATE BULLDOGS

Conference: Mountain West.
Mailing Address: 5305 N. Campus Dr., NG 27, Fresno,
CA 93740. **Website:** www.gobulldogs.com.
Head Coach: Mike Batesole. **Telephone:** (559) 278-2178. **Baseball SID:** Matt Burkholder. **Telephone:** (559)
278-6186. **Fax:** (559) 278-4689.
Assistant Coaches: *Ryan Overland, Steve Rousey.
Telephone: (559) 278-2178.
Home Field: Beiden Field. **Seating Capacity:** 5,757.
Outfield Dimensions: LF—330, CF—400, RF—330.
Press Box Telephone: (559) 278-7678.

FURMAN PALADINS

Conference: Southern.
Mailing Address: 3300 Poinsett Hwy. Greenville, SC
29613. **Website:** www.furmanpaladins.com.
Head Coach: Ron Smith. **Telephone:** (864) 294-2146.
Baseball SID: Hunter Reid. **Telephone:** (864) 294-2000.
Fax: (864) 294-3061.
Assistant Coaches: Michael Ranson, *Jeff Whitfield.
Telephone: (864) 294-2243.
Home Field: Latham Stadium. **Seating Capacity:**
1,500. **Outfield Dimensions:** LF—330, CF—395,
RF—330. **Press Box Telephone:** (864) 294-3066.

GARDNER-WEBB RUNNIN' BULLDOGS

Conference: Big South.
Mailing Address: P.O. Box 877, Boiling Springs, NC 28017. **Website:** www.gwusports.com.
Head Coach: Rusty Stroupe. **Telephone:** (704) 406-4421. **Baseball SID:** Marc Rabb. **Telephone:** (704) 406-4355. **Fax:** (704) 406-4739.
Assistant Coaches: *Kent Cox, Ray Greene. **Telephone:** (704) 406-3557.
Home Field: John Henry Moss Stadium. **Seating Capacity:** 1,000. **Outfield Dimensions: LF**— 330, **CF—**390, **RF—**330.

GEORGE MASON PATRIOTS

Conference: Atlantic 10.
Mailing Address: 4400 University Dr., Ms3A5, Fairfax, VA 22030. **Website:** www.gomason.com.
Head Coach: Bill Brown. **Telephone:** (703) 993-3282. **Baseball SID:** TBD.
Assistant Coaches: *Steve Hay, Tag Montague. **Telephone:** (703) 993-3281.
Home Field: Hap Spuhler Field. **Seating Capacity:** 1,000. **Outfield Dimensions: LF—**320, **CF—**400, **RF—**320.

GEORGE WASHINGTON COLONIALS

Conference: Atlantic 10.
Mailing Address: Charles E. Smith Center, 600 22nd St., NW Washington, DC 20052. **Website:** www.gwsports.cstv.com.
Head Coach: Gregg Ritchie. **Telephone:** (202) 994-7399. **Baseball SID:** Dan DiVeglio. **Telephone:** (202) 994-0339. **Fax:** (202) 994-2713.
Assistant Coaches: *Dave Lorber, Tom Sheridan. **Telephone:** (202) 994-0327.
Home Field: Barcroft Park. **Seating Capacity:** 1,000. **Outfield Dimensions: LF—**330, **CF—**380, **RF—**330. **Press Box Telephone:** (202) 578-2652.

GEORGETOWN HOYAS

Conference: Big East.
Mailing Address: 37th & O St., NW, Washington, DC 20057. **Website:** www.guhoyas.com.
Head Coach: Pete Wilk. **Telephone:** (202) 687-2462. **Baseball SID:** Brendan Thomas. **Telephone:** (202) 687-6783. **Fax:** (202) 687-2491.
Assistant Coaches: *Curtis Brown, Phil Disher. **Telephone:** (202) 687-6406.
Home Field: Shirley Povich Field. **Seating Capacity:** 1,500. **Outfield Dimensions: LF—**330, **CF—**375, **RF—**330. **Press Box Telephone:** (917) 576-7445.

GEORGIA BULLDOGS

Conference: Southeastern (East).
Mailing Address: P.O. Box 1472, Athens, GA 30603. **Website:** www.georgiadogs.com.
Head Coach: Scott Stricklin. **Telephone:** (706) 542-7971. **Baseball SID:** Christopher Lakos. **Telephone:** (706) 542-7994. **Fax:** (706) 542-9339.
Assistant Coaches: Fred Corral, *Scott Daeley. **Telephone:** (706) 542-8379.
Home Field: Foley Field. **Seating Capacity:** 3,291. **Outfield Dimensions: LF—**350, **CF—**404, **RF—**314. **Press Box Telephone:** (706) 542-6161.

GEORGIA SOUTHERN EAGLES

Conference: Southern.
Mailing Address: 2480 Southern Dr. Statesboro, GA 30458. **Website:** www.georgiasoutherneagles.com.
Head Coach: Rodney Hennon. **Telephone:** (912) 478-7360. **Baseball SID:** Barrett Gilham. **Telephone:** (912) 478-5448. **Fax:** (912) 478-1063.
Assistant Coaches: *B.J. Green, Chris Moore. **Telephone:** (912) 478-5188.
Home Field: J.I. Clements Stadium. **Seating Capacity:** 3,000. **Outfield Dimensions: LF—**330, **CF—**385, **RF—**330. **Press Box Telephone:** (912) 478-5764.

GEORGIA STATE PANTHERS

Conference: Sun Belt.
Mailing Address: P.O. Box 3975, Atlanta, GA 30302. **Website:** www.georgiastatesports.com.
Head Coach: Greg Frady. **Telephone:** (404) 413-4153. **Baseball SID:** Allison George. **Telephone:** (404) 413-4032. **Fax:** (404) 413-4035.
Assistant Coaches: *Willie Stewart, Edwin Thompson. **Telephone:** (404) 413-4077.
Home Field: GSU Baseball Complex. **Seating Capacity:** 1,092. **Outfield Dimensions: LF—**334, **CF—**385, **RF—**338. **Press Box Telephone:** (678) 595-7728.

GEORGIA TECH YELLOW JACKETS

Conference: Atlantic Coast (Coastal).
Mailing Address: 150 Bobby Dodd Way NW, Atlanta, GA 30332. **Website:** www.ramblinwreck.com.
Head Coach: Danny Hall. **Telephone:** (404) 894-5471. **Baseball SID:** Mike DeGeorge. **Telephone:** (404) 894-5467. **Fax:** (404) 894-1248.
Assistant Coaches: Jason Howell, *Bryan Prince. **Telephone:** (404) 894-5081.
Home Field: Russ Chandler Stadium. **Seating Capacity:** 4167. **Outfield Dimensions: LF—**328, **CF—**400, **RF—**334. **Press Box Telephone:** (404) 894-3167.

GONZAGA BULLDOGS

Conference: West Coast.
Mailing Address: 502 E. Boone, Spokane, WA 99258. **Website:** www.gozags.com.
Head Coach: Mark Machtolf. **Telephone:** (509) 313-4209. **Baseball SID:** Chris Standiford. **Telephone:** (509) 313-4210. **Fax:** (509) 313-5730.
Assistant Coaches: Steve Bennett, *Danny Evans. **Telephone:** (509) 313-3597. **Home Field:** Patterson Baseball Complex. **Seating Capacity:** 2,500. **Outfield Dimensions: LF—**330, **CF—**385, **RF—**330. **Press Box Telephone:** (509) 279-1005.

GRAMBLING STATE TIGERS

Conference: Southwestern Athletic.
Mailing Address: 403 Main St., P.O. Box 4252, Grambling, LA 71245. **Website:** www.gsutigers.com.
Head Coach: James Cooper. **Telephone:** (318) 274-6566. **Baseball SID:** Santoria Black. **Telephone:** (318) 274-6562.
Assistant Coaches: *Davin Pierre. **Telephone:** (318) 274-2416.
Home Field: Jones Field at Ellis Park. **Seating Capacity:** 3,000. **Outfield Dimensions: LF—**315, **CF—**400, **RF—**350.

GRAND CANYON ANTELOPES

Conference: Western Athletic.
Mailing Address: 3300 W. Camelback Rd., Phoenix, AZ 85017. **Website:** www.gculopes.com.
Head Coach: Andy Stankiewicz. **Telephone:** (602) 639-6042. **Baseball SID:** Steve Heath. **Telephone:** (602) 639-6514.
Assistant Coaches: *Nathan Choate, Gregg Wallis. **Telephone:** (602) 639-7467.
Home Field: Brazell Stadium. **Seating Capacity:** 1,500. **Outfield Dimensions: LF**—320, **CF**—390, **RF**—328.

HARTFORD HAWKS

Conference: America East.
Mailing Address: 200 Bloomfield Ave., West Hartford, CT 06117. **Website:** www.hartfordhawks.com.
Head Coach: Justin Blood. **Telephone:** (860) 768-5760. **Baseball SID:** Dan Ruede. **Telephone:** (860) 768-4501. **Fax:** (860) 768-5047.
Assistant Coaches: *Steve Malinowski, Mike Nemeth. **Telephone:** (860) 768-4972.
Home Field: Fiondella Field. **Seating Capacity:** 1,000. **Outfield Dimensions: LF**—325, **CF**—405, **RF**—325.

HARVARD CRIMSON

Conference: Ivy League (Rolfe).
Mailing Address: Murr Center, 65 North Harvard St., Boston, MA -2163. **Website:** www.gocrimson.com.
Head Coach: Bill Decker. **Telephone:** (617) 495-2629. **Baseball SID:** Michael Black. **Telephone:** (617) 495-2206. **Fax:** (617) 495-2130.
Assistant Coaches: *Jeff Calcaterra, Mike Zandler. **Telephone:** (617) 496-1435.
Home Field: O'Donnell Field. **Seating Capacity:** 1,000. **Outfield Dimensions: LF**—335, **CF**—410, **RF**—335.

HAWAII RAINBOW WARRIORS

Conference: Big West.
Mailing Address: 1337 Lower Campus Rd., Honolulu, HI 96822. **Website:** www.hawaiiathletics.com.
Head Coach: Mike Trapasso. **Telephone:** (808) 956-6247. **Baseball SID:** John Barry. **Telephone:** (808) 956-7506. **Fax:** (808) 956-4470.
Assistant Coaches: Carl Fraticelli, *Rusty McNamara. **Telephone:** (808) 956-6247.
Home Field: Les Murakami Stadium. **Seating Capacity:** 4,312. **Outfield Dimensions: LF**—325, **CF**—385, **RF**—325.

HIGH POINT PANTHERS

Conference: Big South.
Mailing Address: 884 Montlieu Ave., High Point, NC 27262. **Website:** www.highpointpanthers.com.
Head Coach: Craig Cozart. **Telephone:** (336) 841-9190. **Baseball SID:** Joe Arancio. **Telephone:** (336) 841-4638. **Fax:** (336) 841-9182.
Assistant Coaches: Kenny Smith, *Rich Wallace. **Telephone:** (336) 841-4614.
Home Field: Williard Stadium. **Seating Capacity:** 550. **Outfield Dimensions: LF**—325, **CF**—400, **RF**—330. **Press Box Telephone:** (336) 841-9192.

HOFSTRA PRIDE

Conference: Colonial Athletic.
Mailing Address: 240 Hofstra University, PFC 232, Hempstead, NY 11549. **Website:** www.gohofstra.com.
Head Coach: John Russo. **Telephone:** (516) 463-3759. **Baseball SID:** Len Skoros. **Telephone:** (516) 463-4602. **Fax:** (516) 463-7514.
Assistant Coaches: *Kelly Haynes, Chris Johns. **Telephone:** (516) 463-5065.
Home Field: University Field. **Seating Capacity:** 600. **Outfield Dimensions: LF**—322, **CF**—382, **RF**—337. **Press Box Telephone:** (516) 463-1896.

HOLY CROSS CRUSADERS

Conference: Patriot League.
Mailing Address: 1 College St., Worcester, MA, 01601. **Website:** www.goholycross.com.
Head Coach: Greg DiCenzo. **Telephone:** (508) 793-2753. **Baseball SID:** Jim Sarkisian. **Telephone:** (508) 793-2583. **Fax:** (508) 793-2753.
Assistant Coaches: *Jeff Kane, Ron Rakowski. **Telephone:** (508) 793-2753.
Home Field: Fitton Field. **Seating Capacity:** 3,000. **Outfield Dimensions: LF**—332, **CF**—385, **RF**—313.

HOUSTON COUGARS

Conference: American Athletic.
Mailing Address: 3100 Cullen Blvd., Houston, TX 77204. **Website:** www.uhcougars.com.
Head Coach: Todd Whitting. **Telephone:** (713) 743-9406. **Baseball SID:** Allison McClain. **Telephone:** (713) 743-9406. **Fax:** (713) 743-9411.
Assistant Coaches: Frank Anderson, *Trip Couch. **Telephone:** (713) 743-9415.
Home Field: Cougar Field. **Seating Capacity:** 3,500. **Outfield Dimensions: LF**—330, **CF**—390, **RF**—330. **Press Box Telephone:** (713) 743-0840.

HOUSTON BAPTIST HUSKIES

Conference: Southland.
Mailing Address: 7502 Fondren, Houston, TX 77074. **Website:** www.hbuhuskies.com.
Head Coach: Jared Moon. **Telephone:** (281) 649-3332. **Baseball SID:** Russ Reneau. **Telephone:** (281) 649-3098. **Fax:** (281) 649-3496.
Assistant Coaches: *Xavier Hernandez, Russell Stockton. **Telephone:** (281) 649-3264.
Home Field: Husky Field. **Seating Capacity:** 500. **Outfield Dimensions: LF**—340, **CF**—400, **RF**—340. **Press Box Telephone:** (281) 923-0813.

ILLINOIS FIGHTING ILLINI

Conference: Big Ten.
Mailing Address: 1700 S. Fourth St., Champaign, IL 61820. **Website:** www.fightingillini.com.
Head Coach: Dan Hartleb. **Telephone:** (217) 244-8144. **Baseball SID:** Matt Wille. **Telephone:** (217) 300-9155. **Fax:** (217) 333-5540.
Assistant Coaches: Drew Dickinson, *Eric Snider. **Telephone:** (217) 244-5539.
Home Field: Illinois Field. **Seating Capacity:** 1,500. **Outfield Dimensions: LF**—330, **CF**—400, **RF**—330. **Press Box Telephone:** (217) 333-1227.

ILLINOIS STATE REDBIRDS

Conference: Missouri Valley.
Mailing Address: 211 Horton Field House, Campus Box 7130. **Website:** www.goredbirds.com.
Head Coach: Mark Kingston. **Telephone:** (309) 438-5709. **Baseball SID:** Ronan O'Shea. **Telephone:** (309)

438-5746. **Fax:** (309) 438-5634.
Assistant Coaches: *Bo Durkac, Billy Mohl.
Telephone: (309) 438-5151.
Home Field: Duffy Bass Field. **Seating Capacity:**
2,000. **Outfield Dimensions: LF**—330, **CF**—400,
RF—330.

ILLINOIS-CHICAGO FLAMES

Conference: Horizon.
Mailing Address: 839 W. Roosevelt Rd., Chicago, IL
60608. **Website:** www.uicflames.cstv.com.
Head Coach: Mike Dee. **Telephone:** (312) 996-8645.
Baseball SID: Mike Laninga. **Telephone:** (312) 996-5881.
Fax: (312) 996-8349.
Assistant Coaches: *John Flood, Sean McDermott.
Telephone: (312) 355-1757.
Home Field: Curtis Granderson Stadium at Les Miller
Field. **Seating Capacity:** 3,000. **Outfield Dimensions:**
LF—330, **CF**—401, **RF**—330. **Press Box Telephone:** (312)
355-1190.

INCARNATE WORD CARDINALS

Conference: Southland.
Mailing Address: 4301 Broadway, San Antonio, TX
78209. **Website:** www.cardinalathletics.com.
Head Coach: Danny Heep. **Telephone:** (210) 829-
3830. **Baseball SID:** Shane Meling. **Telephone:** (210) 805-
3071. **Fax:** (201) 805-3574.
Assistant Coaches: John Maley, *Russell Raley.
Telephone: (210) 805-3025.
Home Field: Sullivan Field. **Seating Capacity:** 500.
Outfield Dimensions: LF—335, **CF**—405, **RF**—335.
Press Box Telephone: (903) 399-0455.

INDIANA HOOSIERS

Conference: Big Ten.
Mailing Address: 1001 E. 17th St., Bloomington, IN
47401. **Website:** www.iuhoosiers.com.
Head Coach: Tracy Smith. **Telephone:** (812) 855-1680.
Baseball SID: Kyle Kuhlman. **Telephone:** (812) 855-4770.
Fax: (812) 855-9401.
Assistant Coaches: *Ben Greenspan, Fred Nori.
Telephone: (812) 855-9790.
Home Field: Bart Kaufman Field. **Seating Capacity:**
2,500. **Outfield Dimensions: LF**—330, **CF**—400,
RF—330. **Press Box Telephone:** (419) 308-8292.

INDIANA STATE SYCAMORES

Conference: Missouri Valley.
Mailing Address: 401 N 4th St., ISU Arena, Terre Haute,
IN 47809. **Website:** www.gosycamores.com.
Head Coach: Mitch Hannahs. **Telephone:** (812) 237-
4051. **Baseball SID:** Kevin Jenison. **Telephone:** (812) 237-
4073. **Fax:** (812) 237-4157.
Assistant Coaches: *Ronnie Prettyman, Brian Smiley.
Telephone: (812) 237-4630.
Home Field: Bob Warn Field. **Seating Capacity:** 2,000.
Outfield Dimensions: LF—335, CF—395, RF—335. **Press
Box Telephone:** (812) 237-4187.

IONA GAELS

Conference: Metro Atlantic.
Mailing Address: 715 North Ave., New Rochelle, NY
10801. **Website:** www.icgaels.com.
Head Coach: Pat Carey. **Telephone:** (914) 633-2319.
Baseball SID: Brian Beyrer. **Telephone:** (914) 633-2334.
Fax: (914) 633-2072.

Assistant Coaches: Scott McGrath, Matt Perper.
Telephone: (914) 633-2319.
Home Field: Salesian Field. **Seating Capacity:** 450.
Press Box Telephone: (914) 497-3136.

IOWA HAWKEYES

Conference: Big Ten.
Mailing Address: N411 Carver-Hawkeye Arena, Iowa
City, IA 52242. **Website:** www.hawkeyesports.com.
Head Coach: Rick Heller. **Telephone:** (319) 335-9743.
Baseball SID: James Allan. **Telephone:** (319) 335-6439.
Fax: (319) 335-9417.
Assistant Coaches: Scott Brickman, *Marty
Sutherland. **Telephone:** (319) 335-9743.
Home Field: Duane Banks Field. **Seating Capacity:**
3,000. **Outfield Dimensions: LF**—329, **CF**—395,
RF—329. **Press Box Telephone:** (319) 335-9520.

IPFW MASTODONS

Conference: Summit.
Mailing Address: 2101 E. Coliseum Blvd, Fort Wayne,
IN 46805. **Website:** www.gomastodons.com.
Head Coach: Bobby Pierce. **Telephone:** (260) 481-
5480. **Baseball SID:** Bill Salyer. **Telephone:** (260) 481-
0729. **Fax:** (260) 481-6002.
Assistant Coaches: *Grant Birely, Scott Micinski.
Telephone: (260) 481-0710.
Home Field: Mastodon Field. **Seating Capacity:**
1,000. **Outfield Dimensions: LF**—330, **CF**—405,
RF—330. **Press Box Telephone:** (260) 402-6599.

JACKSON STATE TIGERS

Conference: Southwestern Athletic.
Mailing Address: JSU Box 18060, Jackson, MS 39217.
Website: www.jsutigers.com.
Head Coach: Omar Johnson. **Telephone:** (601) 979-
3930. **Baseball SID:** Wesley Peterson. **Telephone:** (601)
979-5899.
Assistant Coaches: Christopher Stamps. **Telephone:**
(601) 979-3928.
Home Field: Jackson State University Baseball
Stadium. **Seating Capacity:** 800. **Outfield Dimensions:**
LF—365, **CF**—400, **RF**—365.

JACKSONVILLE DOLPHINS

Conference: Atlantic Sun.
Mailing Address: 2800 University Blvd. N.,
Jacksonville, FL 32211. **Website:** www.judolphins.com.
Head Coach: Tim Montez. **Telephone:** (904) 256-7414.
Baseball SID: Todd Vatter. **Telephone:** (904) 256-7402.
Fax: (904) 256-7424.
Assistant Coaches: Chris Hayes, *Chuck Jeroloman.
Telephone: (904) 256-7367.
Home Field: John Sessions Stadium. **Seating
Capacity:** 3,200. **Outfield Dimensions: LF**—340,
CF—405, **RF**—340. **Press Box Telephone:** (904) 256-
7588.

JACKSONVILLE STATE GAMECOCKS

Conference: Ohio Valley.
Mailing Address: 700 Pelham Road N., Jacksonville,
AL 36265. **Website:** www.jsugamecocksports.com.
Head Coach: Jim Case. **Telephone:** (256) 782-5362.
Baseball SID: Greg Seitz. **Telephone:** (256) 782-5279.
Fax: (256) 782-5958.
Assistant Coaches: Michael Murphree, *Brandon
Romans. **Telephone:** (256) 782-8141.

Home Field: Rudy Abbott Field. **Seating Capacity:** 1,500. **Outfield Dimensions: LF**—330, **CF**—400, **RF**—330. **Press Box Telephone:** (256) 782-5533.

JAMES MADISON DUKES

Conference: Colonial Athletic.
Mailing Address: 395 South High St., Memorial Hall, Harrisonburg, VA 22801. **Website:** www.jmusports.com.
Head Coach: Joe "Spanky" McFarland. **Telephone:** (540) 568-5510. **Baseball SID:** Kevin Warner. **Telephone:** (540) 568-4263. **Fax:** (540) 568-3703.
Assistant Coaches: Brandon Cohen, *Ted White. **Telephone:** (540) 568-3630.
Home Field: Eagle Field at Veterans Memorial Park. **Seating Capacity:** 1,200. **Outfield Dimensions: LF**—340, **CF**—400, **RF**—320. **Press Box Telephone:** (540) 568-6545.

KANSAS JAYHAWKS

Conference: Big 12.
Mailing Address: 1651 Naismith Dr., Lawrence, KS 66045. **Website:** www.kuathletics.com.
Head Coach: Ritch Price. **Telephone:** (785) 864-7907. **Baseball SID:** D.J. Haurin. **Telephone:** (785) 864-3575. **Fax:** (785) 864-7944.
Assistant Coaches: Ryan Graves, *Ritchie Price. **Telephone:** (785) 864-7908.
Home Field: Hoglund Ballpark. **Seating Capacity:** 2,500. **Outfield Dimensions: LF**—330, **CF**—400, **RF**—330. **Press Box Telephone:** (785) 864-4037.

KANSAS STATE WILDCATS

Conference: Big 12.
Mailing Address: West Stadium Center, 1800 College Ave., Manhattan, KS 66502. **Website:** www.kstatesports.com.
Head Coach: Brad Hill. **Telephone:** (785) 532-5723. **Baseball SID:** Chris Kutz. **Telephone:** (785) 532-7976. **Fax:** (785) 532-6093.
Assistant Coaches: Mike Clement, *Josh Reynolds. **Telephone:** (785) 532-7714.
Home Field: Tointon Family Stadium. **Seating Capacity:** 2,331. **Outfield Dimensions: LF**—340, **CF**—400, **RF**—325. **Press Box Telephone:** (785) 532-5801.

KENNESAW STATE OWLS

Conference: Atlantic Sun.
Mailing Address: 1000 Chastain Rd., MB 0201, Kennesaw, GA 30144. **Website:** www.ksuowls.com.
Head Coach: Mike Sansing. **Telephone:** (770) 423-6264. **Baseball SID:** Brandon Scardigli. **Telephone:** (678) 797-2562. **Fax:** (770) 423-6665.
Assistant Coaches: Kevin Erminio, *Derek Simmons. **Telephone:** (678) 797-2099.
Home Field: Stillwell Stadium. **Seating Capacity:** 1,200. **Outfield Dimensions: LF**—320, **CF**—405, **RF**—330.

KENT STATE GOLDEN FLASHES

Conference: Mid-American (East).
Mailing Address: 1025 Risman Dr., Kent, OH 44242. **Website:** www.kentstatesports.com.
Head Coach: Jeff Duncan. **Telephone:** (330) 672-8432. **Baseball SID:** Mollie Radzinski. **Telephone:** (330) 672-8419. **Fax:** (330) 672-2112.
Assistant Coaches: Mike Birkbeck, *Alex Marconi.

Telephone: (330) 672-8433.
Home Field: Schoonover Stadium. **Seating Capacity:** 1,200. **Outfield Dimensions: LF**—320, **CF**—415, **RF**—320. **Press Box Telephone:** (330) 672-2110.

KENTUCKY WILDCATS

Conference: Southeastern (East).
Mailing Address: 720 Sports Center Dr., Lexington, KY 40506. **Website:** www.ukathletics.com.
Head Coach: Gary Henderson. **Telephone:** (859) 257-8988. **Baseball SID:** Brent Ingram. **Telephone:** (859) 257-3838. **Fax:** (859) 323-4310.
Assistant Coaches: *Brad Bohannon, Brian Green. **Telephone:** (859) 257-3013.
Home Field: Cliff Hagan Stadium. **Seating Capacity:** 3,000. **Outfield Dimensions: LF**—340, **CF**—390, **RF**—310. **Press Box Telephone:** (859) 257-9011.

LA SALLE EXPLORERS

Conference: Atlantic 10.
Mailing Address: 1900 W. Olney Ave., Philadelphia, PA 19141. **Website:** www.goexplorers.com.
Head Coach: Mike Lake. **Telephone:** (215) 951-1995. **Baseball SID:** Paul Hembekides. **Telephone:** (215) 991-2886. **Fax:** (215) 951-1694.
Assistant Coaches: Scott Grimes, Michael McCarry. **Telephone:** (215) 951-1995.
Home Field: Hank DeVincent Field. **Seating Capacity:** 1,000

LAFAYETTE LEOPARDS

Conference: Patriot League.
Mailing Address: Kirby Sports Center, Easton, PA 18042. **Website:** www.goleopards.com.
Head Coach: Joe Kinney. **Telephone:** (610) 330-5476. **Baseball SID:** Mark Mohrman. **Telephone:** (610) 330-5003. **Fax:** (610) 330-5519.
Assistant Coaches: *Ian Law. **Telephone:** (610) 330-5945.
Home Field: Kamine Stadium. **Seating Capacity:** 500. **Outfield Dimensions: LF**—332, **CF**—403, **RF**—335.

LAMAR CARDINALS

Conference: Southland.
Mailing Address: 211 Redbird Ln., Beaumont, TX 77713. **Website:** www.lamarcardinals.com.
Head Coach: Jim Gilligan. **Telephone:** (409) 880-8315. **Baseball SID:** Clay Trainum. **Telephone:** (409) 880-7845. **Fax:** (409) 880-2338.
Assistant Coaches: Scott Hatten, *Jim Ricklefsen. **Telephone:** (409) 880-8135.
Home Field: Vincent-Beck Stadium. **Seating Capacity:** 3,500. **Outfield Dimensions: LF**—325, **CF**—380, **RF**—325. **Press Box Telephone:** (409) 880-8135.

LEHIGH MOUNTAIN HAWKS

Conference: Patriot League.
Mailing Address: 641 Taylor St., Bethlehem, PA, 18015. **Website:** www.lehighsports.com.
Head Coach: Sean Leary. **Telephone:** (610) 758-4315. **Baseball SID:** Chelsea Vielhauer. **Telephone:** (610) 758-5101. **Fax:** (610) 758-4407.
Assistant Coaches: John Bisco, *John Fugett. **Telephone:** (610) 758-4315.
Home Field: Baseball Field on Goodman Campus. **Seating Capacity:** 500. **Outfield Dimensions: LF**—320, **CF**—400, **RF**—320.

LIBERTY FLAMES

Conference: Big South.
Mailing Address: 1971 University Blvd., Lynchburg, VA 24515. **Website:** www.libertyflames.com.
Head Coach: Jim Toman. **Telephone:** (434) 582-2103. **Baseball SID:** Ryan Bomberger. **Telephone:** (434) 582-2292. **Fax:** (434) 582-2076.
Assistant Coaches: *Jason Murray, Garrett Quinn. **Telephone:** (434) 582-2119.
Home Field: Liberty Baseball Stadium. **Seating Capacity:** 2,500. **Outfield Dimensions:** LF—325, CF—395, RF—325. **Press Box Telephone:** (434) 582-2914.

LIPSCOMB BISONS

Conference: Atlantic Sun.
Mailing Address: 1 University Park Dr., Nashville, TN 37204. **Website:** www.lipscombsports.com.
Head Coach: Jeff Forehand. **Telephone:** (615) 966-5716. **Baseball SID:** Jamie Gilliam. **Telephone:** (615) 966-5166. **Fax:** (615) 966-1806.
Assistant Coaches: *Brian Ryman. **Telephone:** (615) 966-5879.
Home Field: Dugan Field. **Seating Capacity:** 1,500. **Outfield Dimensions:** LF—330, CF—405, RF—330. **Press Box Telephone:** (615) 479-6133.

LONG BEACH STATE DIRTBAGS

Conference: Big West.
Mailing Address: 1250 Bellflower Blvd., Long Beach, CA 90840. **Website:** www.longbeachstate.com.
Head Coach: Troy Buckley. **Telephone:** (562) 985-8215. **Baseball SID:** Steven Olveda. **Telephone:** (562) 985-7797. **Fax:** (562) 985-1549.
Assistant Coaches: Shawn Gilbert, *Jesse Zepeda. **Telephone:** (562) 985-7548.
Home Field: Blair Field. **Seating Capacity:** 3,000. **Outfield Dimensions:** LF—348, CF—400, RF—348. **Press Box Telephone:** (562) 433-8605.

LONG ISLAND-BROOKLYN BLACKBIRDS

Conference: Northeast.
Mailing Address: 1 University Plaza, Brooklyn, NY 11201. **Website:** www.LIUAthletics.com.
Head Coach: Donald Maines. **Telephone:** (718) 488-1538. **Baseball SID:** Casey Snedecor. **Telephone:** (718) 488-1307. **Fax:** (718) 780-4128.
Assistant Coaches: *Craig Noto. **Telephone:** (718) 488-1000.
Home Field: LIU Field. **Seating Capacity:** 1,000. **Outfield Dimensions:** LF—310, CF—416, RF—310.

LONGWOOD LANCERS

Conference: Big South.
Mailing Address: 201 High Street Farmville, VA 23901. **Website:** www.longwoodlancers.com.
Head Coach: Brian McCullough. **Telephone:** (434) 395-2843. **Baseball SID:** Greg Prouty. **Telephone:** (434) 395-2097. **Fax:** (434) 395-2568.
Assistant Coaches: *Jon Benick. **Telephone:** (434) 395-2351.
Home Field: Charles Buddy Bolding Stadium. **Seating Capacity:** 500. **Outfield Dimensions:** LF—335, CF—400, RF—335. **Press Box Telephone:** (434) 395-2710.

LOUISIANA STATE FIGHTING TIGERS

Conference: Southeastern (West).
Mailing Address: Athletic Administration Bldg., Baton Rouge, LA 70803. **Website:** www.lsusports.net.
Head Coach: Paul Mainieri. **Telephone:** (225) 578-4148. **Baseball SID:** Bill Franques. **Telephone:** (225) 578-2527. **Fax:** (225) 578-1861.
Assistant Coaches: Alan Dunn, *Javi Sanchez. **Telephone:** (225) 578-4148.
Home Field: Alex Box Stadium, Skip Bertman Field. **Seating Capacity:** 10,326. **Outfield Dimensions:** LF—330, CF—405, RF—330. **Press Box Telephone:** (225) 578-4149.

LOUISIANA TECH BULLDOGS

Conference: Conference USA.
Mailing Address: Louisiana Tech University, P.O. Box 3166, Ruston, LA 71272. **Website:** www.latechsports.com.
Head Coach: Wade Simoneaux. **Telephone:** (318) 257-5318. **Baseball SID:** Anna Claire Thomas. **Telephone:** (318) 257-5314. **Fax:** (318) 257-3757.
Assistant Coaches: Olen Parker, *Brian Rountree. **Telephone:** (318) 257-5312.
Home Field: J.C. Love Field at Pat Patterson Park. **Seating Capacity:** 3,000. **Outfield Dimensions:** LF—315, CF—385, RF—325. **Press Box Telephone:** (318) 257-3144.

LOUISIANA-LAFAYETTE RAGIN' CAJUNS

Conference: Sun Belt.
Mailing Address: 201 Reinhardt Dr., Lafayette, LA, 70508. **Website:** www.ragincajuns.com.
Head Coach: Tony Robichaux. **Telephone:** (337) 262-5189. **Baseball SID:** Jeff Schneider. **Telephone:** (337) 482-6332. **Fax:** (337) 482-6529.
Assistant Coaches: Anthony Babineaux, *Matt Deggs. **Telephone:** (337) 482-6093.
Home Field: ML Tigue Moore Field. **Seating Capacity:** 4,000. **Outfield Dimensions:** LF—330, CF—400, RF—330. **Press Box Telephone:** (337) 851-2255.

LOUISIANA-MONROE WARHAWKS

Conference: Sun Belt.
Mailing Address: 308 Warhawk Way, Monroe, LA 71209. **Website:** www.ulmwarhawks.com.
Head Coach: Jeff Schexnaider. **Telephone:** (318) 342-5396. **Baseball SID:** Tony Jones. **Telephone:** (318) 342-5461.
Assistant Coaches: *Bruce Peddie, Larry Thomas. **Telephone:** (318) 342-3589.
Home Field: Warhawk Field. **Seating Capacity:** 2,000. **Outfield Dimensions:** LF—330, CF—405, RF—330. **Press Box Telephone:** (318) 342-5476.

LOUISVILLE CARDINALS

Conference: American Athletic.
Mailing Address: 215 Central Ave., Louisville, KY 40292. **Website:** www.uoflsports.com.
Head Coach: Dan McDonnell. **Telephone:** (502) 852-0103. **Baseball SID:** Garett Wall. **Telephone:** (502) 852-3088. **Fax:** (502) 852-7401.
Assistant Coaches: *Chris Lemonis, Roger Williams. **Telephone:** (502) 852-3929.
Home Field: Jim Patterson Stadium. **Seating Capacity:** 4,000. **Outfield Dimensions:** LF—330, CF—402, RF—330. **Press Box Telephone:** (502) 852-3700.

LOYOLA MARYMOUNT LIONS

Conference: West Coast.
Mailing Address: 1 LMU Dr., Los Angeles, CA 90045.
Website: www.lmulions.com.
Head Coach: Jason Gill. **Telephone:** (310) 338-2949.
Baseball SID: Tyler Geivett. **Telephone:** (310) 338-7638.
Fax: (310) 338-2703.
Assistant Coaches: Danny Ricabal, *Bryant Ward.
Telephone: (310) 338-4511.
Home Field: Page Stadium. **Seating Capacity:** 600.
Outfield Dimensions: LF—326, **CF**—406, **RF**—321.
Press Box Telephone: (310) 338-3046.

MAINE BLACK BEARS

Conference: America East.
Mailing Address: 5747 Memorial Gym, Orono, ME
04469. **Website:** www.goblackbears.com.
Head Coach: Steve Trimper. **Telephone:** (207) 581-
1090. **Baseball SID:** Laura Reed. **Telephone:** (207) 581-
3646. **Fax:** (207) 581-3297.
Assistant Coaches: Nick Derba, *Jason Spaulding.
Telephone: (207) 581-1097.
Home Field: Mahaney Diamond. **Seating Capacity:**
4,400. **Outfield Dimensions: LF**—330, **CF**—400,
RF—330. **Press Box Telephone:** (207) 581-1049.

MANHATTAN JASPERS

Conference: Metro Atlantic.
Mailing Address: 4513 Manhattan College Pkwy.,
Riverdale, NY 10471. **Website:** www.gojaspers.com.
Head Coach: Jim Duffy. **Telephone:** (718) 862-7821.
Baseball SID: Pete McHugh. **Telephone:** (718) 862-7228.
Fax: (718) 862-8020.
Assistant Coaches: Elvys Quezada, *Rene Ruiz.
Telephone: (718) 862-7218.
Home Field: Van Cortlandt Park. **Seating Capacity:**
1,000. **Outfield Dimensions: LF**—330, **CF**—400,
RF—330.

MARIST RED FOXES

Conference: Metro Atlantic.
Mailing Address: 3399 North Road, Poughkeepsie, NY
12601. **Website:** www.goredfoxes.com.
Head Coach: Chris Tracz. **Telephone:** (845) 575-3000
Ext 2570. **Baseball SID:** Mike Ferraro. **Telephone:** (845)
575-3321.
Assistant Coaches: Justin Haywood, *Thomas Seay.
Telephone: (845) 575-3000 Ext 7583.
Home Field: McCann Field. **Seating Capacity:** 1,000.
Press Box Telephone: (914) 456-3447.

MARSHALL THUNDERING HERD

Conference: Conference USA.
Mailing Address: One John Marshall Way,
Huntington, WV 25755. **Website:** www.herdzone.com.
Head Coach: Jeff Waggoner. **Telephone:** (304) 696-
6454. **Baseball SID:** Caitie Smith. **Telephone:** (304) 696-
5276. **Fax:** (304) 696-2325.
Assistant Coaches: *Tim Donnelly, Josh Newman.
Telephone: (304) 696-7146.
Home Field: Appalachian Power Park. **Seating
Capacity:** 4,500. **Outfield Dimensions: LF**—330,
CF—400, **RF**—320.

MARYLAND TERRAPINS

Conference: Atlantic Coast (Atlantic).

Mailing Address: 1 Terrapin Trail, College Park, MD,
20742. **Website:** www.umterps.com.
Head Coach: John Szefc. **Telephone:** (301) 314-1845.
Baseball SID: Matt Bertram. **Telephone:** (301) 314-8093.
Fax: (301) 314-9094.
Assistant Coaches: Jim Belanger, *Rob Vaughn.
Telephone: (301) 314-9772.
Home Field: Bob "Turtle" Smith Stadium. **Seating
Capacity:** 2,500. **Outfield Dimensions: LF**—320,
CF—380, **RF**—325. **Press Box Telephone:** (301) 314-0379.

MARYLAND-BALTIMORE COUNTY RETRIEVERS

Conference: America East.
Mailing Address: Department of Athletics, RAC
Arena, 1000 Hilltop Circle, Baltimore, MD 21250. **Website:**
www.umbcretrievers.com.
Head Coach: Bob Mumma. **Telephone:** (410) 455-
2239. **Baseball SID:** Daniel LaHatte. **Telephone:** (410)
455-1530. **Fax:** (410) 455-3994.
Assistant Coaches: *Liam Bowen. **Telephone:** (410)
455-5845.
Home Field: Alumni Field. **Seating Capacity:** 1,000.
Outfield Dimensions: LF—330, **CF**—360, **RF**—340.
Press Box Telephone: (443) 928-3343.

MARYLAND-EASTERN SHORE HAWKS

Conference: Mid-Eastern Athletic.
Mailing Address: 1 College Backbone Rd., Princess
Anne, MD 21853. **Website:** www.umeshawks.com.
Head Coach: Pedro Swann. **Telephone:** (410) 651-
8158. **Baseball SID:** Stan Bradley. **Telephone:** (410) 621-
1108. **Fax:** (410) 651-7514.
Assistant Coaches: *John O'Neil, James Starling.
Telephone: (410) 651-8908.
Home Field: Hawks Stadium. **Seating Capacity:**
1,000.

MASSACHUSETTS MINUTEMEN

Conference: Atlantic 10.
Mailing Address: 131 Commonwealth Ave., Amherst,
MA 01003. **Website:** umassathletics.com.
Head Coach: Mike Stone. **Telephone:** (413) 545-3120.
Baseball SID: Jillian Jakuba. **Telephone:** (413) 577-0053.
Fax: (413) 577-0053.
Assistant Coaches: Mitchell Clegg, *Mike Sweeney.
Telephone: (413) 545-3766.
Home Field: Earl Lorden Field. **Seating Capacity:**
2,000. **Outfield Dimensions: LF**—330, **CF**—400,
RF—330. **Press Box Telephone:** (413) 420-3116.

MASSACHUSETTS-LOWELL RIVER HAWKS

Conference: America East
Mailing Address: 100 Pawtucket St., Lowell, MA
01854. **Website:** goriverhawks.com.
Head Coach: Ken Harring. **Telephone:** (978) 934-
2344. **Baseball SID:** Chris O'Donnell. **Telephone:** (979)
934-2306.
Assistant Coaches: *Brendan Monaghan, Eric
Pelletier. **Telephone:** (978) 934-2138.
Home Field: LeLacheur Park. **Seating Capacity:** 5,000.

MCNEESE STATE COWBOYS

Conference: Southland.
Mailing Address: 700 E. McNeese St., Lake Charles, LA
70607. **Website:** www.mcneesesports.com.
Head Coach: Justin Hill. **Telephone:** (337) 475-5484.
Baseball SID: Hunter Bower. **Telephone:** (337) 475-5207.

Fax: (337) 475-5202.
Assistant Coaches: *Cory Barton, Matt Collins.
Telephone: (337) 475-5904.
Home Field: Cowboy Diamond. **Seating Capacity:** 2,000. **Outfield Dimensions: LF**—330, **CF**—400, **RF**—330. **Press Box Telephone:** (337) 475-8007.

MEMPHIS TIGERS

Conference: American Athletic.
Mailing Address: 570 Normal, Room 207, Memphis, TN 38152. **Website:** www.gotigersgo.com.
Head Coach: Daron Schoenrock. **Telephone:** (901) 678-4137. **Baseball SID:** Mark Taylor. **Telephone:** (901) 678-5108. **Fax:** (901) 678-4134.
Assistant Coaches: *Clay Greene, Russ McNickle.
Telephone: (901) 678-4139.
Home Field: FedEx Park. **Seating Capacity:** 2,000. **Outfield Dimensions: LF**—318, **CF**—379, **RF**—317. **Press Box Telephone:** (901) 678-1301.

MERCER BEARS

Conference: Atlantic Sun.
Mailing Address: 1400 Coleman Ave., Macon, GA 31207. **Website:** www.mercerbears.com.
Head Coach: Craig Gibson. **Telephone:** (478) 301-2396. **Baseball SID:** Jason Farhadi. **Telephone:** (478) 301-5218. **Fax:** (478) 301-5350.
Assistant Coaches: Ty Megahee, *Brent Shade.
Telephone: (478) 301-2738.
Home Field: Claude Smith Field. **Seating Capacity:** 500. **Outfield Dimensions: LF**—330, **CF**—400, **RF**—320. **Press Box Telephone:** (478) 301-2339.

MIAMI HURRICANES

Conference: Atlantic Coast (Coastal).
Mailing Address: 6201 San Amaro Dr., Coral Gables, FL 33146. **Website:** www.hurricanesports.com.
Head Coach: Jim Morris. **Telephone:** (305) 284-4171. **Baseball SID:** Camron Ghorbi. **Telephone:** (305) 284-3230. **Fax:** (305) 284-2807.
Assistant Coaches: J.D. Arteaga, *Gino DiMare.
Telephone: (305) 284-4171.
Home Field: Alex Rodriguez Park at Mark Light Field. **Seating Capacity:** 4,999. **Outfield Dimensions: LF**—330, **CF**—400, **RF**—330. **Press Box Telephone:** (305) 284-8192.

MIAMI (OHIO) REDHAWKS

Conference: Metro Atlantic.
Mailing Address: 120 Withrow Court, Oxford, OH 45056. **Website:** www.muredhawks.com.
Head Coach: Danny Hayden. **Telephone:** (513) 529-6631. **Baseball SID:** Chad Twaro. **Telephone:** (513) 529-1601. **Fax:** (513) 529-6729.
Assistant Coaches: Matt Davis, *Jeremy Ison.
Telephone: (513) 529-6746.
Home Field: McKie Field at Hayden Park. **Seating Capacity:** 1,000. **Press Box Telephone:** (513) 529-4331.

MICHIGAN WOLVERINES

Conference: Big Ten.
Mailing Address: 1000 S. State St., Ann Arbor, MI 48103. **Website:** www.mgoblue.com.
Head Coach: Erik Bakich. **Telephone:** (734) 763-1957. **Baseball SID:** Kent Reichert. **Telephone:** (734) 647-1726. **Fax:** (734) 647-1188.
Assistant Coaches: Sean Kenny, *Nick Schnabel.

Telephone: (734) 647-4585.
Home Field: Wilpon Complex/Ray Fisher Stadium. **Seating Capacity:** 3,500. **Outfield Dimensions: LF**—312-395-320, **CF**—395, **RF**—320. **Press Box Telephone:** (734) 647-1283.

MICHIGAN STATE SPARTANS

Conference: Big Ten.
Mailing Address: 304 Jenison Field House, East Lansing, MI 48824. **Website:** www.msuspartans.com.
Head Coach: Jake Boss. **Telephone:** (517) 355-4486. **Baseball SID:** Jeff Barnes. **Telephone:** (517) 355-2271. **Fax:** (517) 353-9636.
Assistant Coaches: *Graham Sikes, Mark Van Ameyde.
Telephone: (517) 355-3419.
Home Field: McLane Baseball Stadium. **Seating Capacity:** 2,500. **Outfield Dimensions: LF**—305, **CF**—400, **RF**—301. **Press Box Telephone:** (517) 353-3009.

MIDDLE TENNESSEE STATE BLUE RAIDERS

Conference: Sun Belt.
Mailing Address: P.O. Box 90, Murfreesboro, TN 37132. **Website:** www.goblueraiders.com.
Head Coach: Jim McGuire. **Telephone:** (615) 898-2961. **Baseball SID:** Leslie Wilhite. **Telephone:** (615) 904-8115. **Fax:** (615) 898-5626.
Assistant Coaches: *Scott Hall, Skylar Meade.
Telephone: (615) 904-8796.
Home Field: Reese Smith Jr. Field. **Seating Capacity:** 2,300. **Outfield Dimensions: LF**—330, **CF**—390, **RF**—330. **Press Box Telephone:** (615) 898-2117.

MINNESOTA GOLDEN GOPHERS

Conference: Big Ten.
Mailing Address: 516 15th Ave. SE, Minneapolis, MN 55455. **Website:** www.gophersports.com.
Head Coach: John Anderson. **Telephone:** (612) 625-4057. **Baseball SID:** Justine Buerkle. **Telephone:** (612) 624-4345. **Fax:** (612) 626-1069.
Assistant Coaches: *Rob Fornasiere, Todd Oakes.
Telephone: (612) 625-3568.
Home Field: Siebert Field. **Seating Capacity:** 2,000. **Outfield Dimensions: LF**—330, **CF**—390, **RF**—330. **Press Box Telephone:** (612) 203-3028.

MISSISSIPPI REBELS

Conference: Southeastern (West).
Mailing Address: 908 All-America Dr., University, MS 38677. **Website:** www.olemisssports.com.
Head Coach: Mike Bianco. **Telephone:** (662) 915-6643. **Baseball SID:** Bill Bunting. **Telephone:** (662) 915-1083. **Fax:** (662) 915-7006.
Assistant Coaches: Cliff Godwin, *Carl Lafferty.
Telephone: (662) 915-6643.
Home Field: Swayze Field. **Seating Capacity:** 10,323. **Outfield Dimensions: LF**—330, **CF**—390, **RF**—330. **Press Box Telephone:** (662) 915-7858.

MISSISSIPPI STATE BULLDOGS

Conference: Southeastern (West).
Mailing Address: MSU Baseball Media Relations, Box 5308, Mississippi State, MS 39762. **Website:** www.mstateathletics.com.
Head Coach: John Cohen. **Telephone:** (662) 325-3597. **Baseball SID:** Kyle Niblett. **Telephone:** (662) 325-8040. **Fax:** (662) 325-2563.

Assistant Coaches: *Nick Mingione, Butch Thompson. **Telephone:** (662) 325-3597.
Home Field: Dudy Noble Field. **Seating Capacity:** 15,000. **Outfield Dimensions: LF**—330, **CF**—390, **RF**—326. **Press Box Telephone:** (662) 325-3776.

MISSISSIPPI VALLEY STATE DELTA DEVILS

Conference: Southwestern Athletic.
Mailing Address: 14000 Hwy. 82 West, Itta Bena, MS 38941. **Website:** www.mvsusports.com.
Head Coach: Doug Shanks. **Telephone:** (662) 254-3834. **Baseball SID:** Kenneth Mister. **Telephone:** (662) 254-3011. **Fax:** (662) 254-3639.
Assistant Coaches: Aaron Stevens, *Luke Walker. **Telephone:** 662-254-3342.
Home Field: Shanks Field. **Seating Capacity:** 300. **Outfield Dimensions:** LF—334, CF—410, RF—347.

MISSOURI TIGERS

Conference: Southeastern (East).
Mailing Address: 600 Stadium Blvd., Columbia, MO 65211. **Website:** www.mutigers.com.
Head Coach: Tim Jamieson. **Telephone:** (573) 882-1917. **Baseball SID:** Shawn Davis. **Telephone:** (573) 882-0711.
Assistant Coaches: Matt Hobbs, *Kerrick Jackson. **Telephone:** (573) 882-4783.
Home Field: Simmons Field at Taylor Stadium. **Seating Capacity:** 3,031. **Outfield Dimensions: LF**—330, **CF**—400, **RF**—330. **Press Box Telephone:** (573) 884-8912.

MISSOURI STATE BEARS

Conference: Missouri Valley.
Mailing Address: 901 S. National, Springfield, MO 65897. **Website:** www.missouristatebears.com.
Head Coach: Keith Guttin. **Telephone:** (417) 836-4497. **Baseball SID:** Eric Doennig. **Telephone:** (417) 836-4586. **Fax:** (417) 836-4868.
Assistant Coaches: Paul Evans, *Brent Thomas. **Telephone:** (417) 836-4496.
Home Field: Hammons Field. **Seating Capacity:** 8,000. **Outfield Dimensions: LF**—315, **CF**—400, **RF**—330. **Press Box Telephone:** (417) 832-3029.

MONMOUTH HAWKS

Conference: Metro Atlantic.
Mailing Address: 400 Cedar Ave., West Long Branch, NJ. **Website:** www.gomuhawks.com.
Head Coach: Dean Ehehalt. **Telephone:** (732) 263-5186. **Baseball SID:** Gary Kowal. **Telephone:** (732) 263-5387. **Fax:** (732) 571-3535.
Assistant Coaches: George Brown, *Rick Oliveri. **Telephone:** (732) 263-5347.
Home Field: Monmouth University Baseball Field. **Seating Capacity:** 1,500. **Outfield Dimensions: LF**—315, **CF**—390, **RF**—315. **Press Box Telephone:** (732) 263-5401.

MOREHEAD STATE EAGLES

Conference: Ohio Valley.
Mailing Address: 156 Academic Athletic Center, Morehead, KY 40351. **Website:** www.msueagles.com.
Head Coach: Mike McGuire. **Telephone:** (606) 783-2882. **Baseball SID:** Brent Fritzemeier. **Telephone:** (606) 783-5481. **Fax:** (606) 783-5035.
Assistant Coaches: Adam Brown, *Jeff Stanek.

Telephone: (606) 783-2881.
Home Field: Allen Field. **Seating Capacity:** 1,000. **Outfield Dimensions: LF**—315, **CF**—365, **RF**—320. **Press Box Telephone:** (606) 783-5000.

MOUNT ST. MARY'S MOUNTAINEERS

Conference: Northeast.
Mailing Address: 16300 Old Emmitsburg Rd., Emmitsburg, MD 21727. **Website:** www.mountathletics.com.
Head Coach: Scott Thomson. **Telephone:** (301) 447-3806. **Baseball SID:** Mark Vandergrift. **Telephone:** (301) 447-5384. **Fax:** (301) 447-5300.
Assistant Coaches: Ben Leonard, Dustin Pease. **Telephone:** (301) 447-3806.
Home Field: ET Straw Family Stadium.

MURRAY STATE TOUROUGHBREDS

Conference: Ohio Valley.
Mailing Address: 217 Stewart Stadium, Murray, KY. **Website:** goracers.com.
Head Coach: Rob McDonald. **Telephone:** (270) 809-4892. **Baseball SID:** John Brush. **Telephone:** (270) 809-7044. **Fax:** (270) 809-6814.
Assistant Coaches: Larry Scully, *Dan Skirka. **Telephone:** (270) 809-4192.
Home Field: Johnny Regan Field. **Seating Capacity:** 1,140. **Outfield Dimensions: LF**—335, **CF**—400, **RF**—330. **Press Box Telephone:** (270) 809-5650.

NAVY MIDSHIPMEN

Conference: Patriot League
Mailing Address: 566 Brownson Rd., Annapolis, MD 21402. **Website:** www.navysports.com.
Head Coach: Paul Kostacopoulus. **Telephone:** (410) 293-5571. **Baseball SID:** Alex Lumb. **Telephone:** (410) 293-8771. **Fax:** (410) 293-8954.
Assistant Coaches: *Ryan Mau, Matt Reynolds. **Telephone:** (410) 293-5585.
Home Field: Terwilliger Brothers Field at Max Bishop Stadium. **Seating Capacity:** 1500. **Outfield Dimensions:** LF—322, CF—397, RF—304. **Press Box Telephone:** (410) 293-5430.

NEBRASKA CORNHUSKERS

Conference: Big Ten.
Mailing Address: 403 Line Dr. Circle, Suite B, Lincoln, NE 68588. **Website:** www.huskers.com.
Head Coach: Darin Erstad. **Telephone:** (402) 472-2269. **Baseball SID:** Jeremy Foote. **Telephone:** (402) 472-7778. **Fax:** (402) 472-2003.
Assistant Coaches: Will Bolt, *Ted Silva. **Telephone:** (402) 472-1445.
Home Field: Hawks Field. **Seating Capacity:** 8,486. **Outfield Dimensions: LF**—335, **CF**—395, **RF**—325. **Press Box Telephone:** (402) 434-6861.

NEBRASKA-OMAHA MAVERICKS

Conference: Summit.
Mailing Address: 6001 Dodge St., Omaha, NE 68182. **Website:** www.omavs.com.
Head Coach: Robert Herold. **Telephone:** (402) 554-3388. **Baseball SID:** Bonnie Ryan. **Telephone:** (402) 554-3267. **Fax:** (402) 554-2555.
Assistant Coaches: Chris Gadsden, *Evan Porter. **Telephone:** (402) 554-2141.
Home Field: Ballpark at Boys Town.

NEVADA WOLF PACK

Conference: Mountain West.
Mailing Address: 1664 N. Virginia, Reno, NV 89557.
Website: www.nevadawolfpack.com.
Head Coach: Jay Johnson. **Telephone:** (775) 682-6978. **Baseball SID:** Jack Kuestermeyer. **Telephone:** (775) 684-6883. **Fax:** (775) 784-4387.
Assistant Coaches: *Mark Kertenian, Dave Lawn. **Telephone:** (775) 682-6979.
Home Field: Peccole Park. **Seating Capacity:** 3,000.
Outfield Dimensions: LF—340, CF—401, RF—340.
Press Box Telephone: (775) 784-1585.

UNLV REBELS

Conference: Mountain West.
Mailing Address: 4505 S. Maryland Parkway, Las Vegas, NV 89154. **Website:** www.unlvrebels.com.
Head Coach: Tim Chambers. **Telephone:** (702) 895-3499. **Baseball SID:** Sage Sammons. **Telephone:** (702) 895-3764. **Fax:** (702) 895-0989.
Assistant Coaches: Kevin Higgins, *Stan Stolte. **Telephone:** (702) 895-3802.
Home Field: Earl Wilson Stadium. **Seating Capacity:** 3,000. **Outfield Dimensions:** LF—335, CF—400, RF—335. **Press Box Telephone:** (702) 739-1595.

NEW JERSEY TECH HIGHLANDERS

Conference: Great West.
Mailing Address: NJIT University Heights, Newark, NJ 07102. **Website:** www.njithighlanders.com.
Head Coach: Brian Guiliana. **Telephone:** (973) 596-5827. **Baseball SID:** Tim Camp. **Telephone:** (973) 596-8461. **Fax:** (973) 596-8295.
Assistant Coaches: *Robbie McClellan, Grant Neary. **Telephone:** (973) 596-8396.
Home Field: Riverfront Stadium. **Seating Capacity:** 6,500.

NEW MEXICO LOBOS

Conference: Mountain West.
Mailing Address: Colleen J. Maloof Administration Building, 1 University of New Mexico, MSC04 2680, Albuquerque, NM 87131. **Website:** www.golobos.com.
Head Coach: Ray Birmingham. **Telephone:** (505) 925-5725. **Baseball SID:** Terry Kelly. **Telephone:** (505) 925-5520. **Fax:** (505) 925-5609.
Assistant Coaches: *Ken Jacome, Dan Spencer. **Telephone:** (505) 925-5725.
Home Field: Lobo Field. **Seating Capacity:** 1,000.
Outfield Dimensions: LF—350, CF—420, RF—350.

NEW MEXICO STATE AGGIES

Conference: Western Athletic.
Mailing Address: P.O. Box 30001, Dept 3145, Las Cruces NM 88003. **Website:** www.nmstatesports.com.
Head Coach: Rocky Ward. **Telephone:** (575) 646-5813. **Baseball SID:** Eddie Morelos. **Telephone:** (575) 646-1885. **Fax:** (575) 646-2425.
Assistant Coaches: *Mike Evans, Nate Shaver. **Telephone:** (575) 646-7693.
Home Field: Presley Askew Field. **Seating Capacity:** 1,000. **Outfield Dimensions:** LF—335, CF—400, RF—335. **Press Box Telephone:** (575) 646-5100.

NEW ORLEANS PRIVATEERS

Conference: Independent.

Mailing Address: Lakefront Arena, Baseball Office, 2000 Lakeshore Dr., New Orleans, LA 70148. **Website:** www.unoprivateers.com.
Head Coach: Ron Maestri. **Telephone:** (504) 280-7253. **Baseball SID:** Jason Plotkin. **Telephone:** (504) 280-6284.
Assistant Coaches: A.J. Battisto, *James Jurries.
Home Field: Maestri Field. **Seating Capacity:** 600.

NEW YORK TECH BEARS

Conference: Independent.
Mailing Address: P.O. Box 8000, Old Westbury, NY 11568. **Website:** www.nyitbears.com.
Head Coach: Bob Malvagna. **Telephone:** (516) 686-7513. **Baseball SID:** Sabrina Polidoro. **Telephone:** (516) 686-7504. **Fax:** (516) 686-1168.
Assistant Coaches: Stephen Malvagna, *Chris Rojas. **Telephone:** (516) 686-1315.
Home Field: President's Field. **Seating Capacity:** 500. **Outfield Dimensions:** LF—315, CF—395, RF—315. **Press Box Telephone:** (516) 351-7664.

NIAGARA PURPLE EAGLES

Conference: Metro Atlantic.
Mailing Address: P.O. Box 2009, UL Gallagher Center, Niagara University, NY 14109. **Website:** www.purpleea-gles.com.
Head Coach: Rob McCoy. **Telephone:** (716) 286-7361. **Baseball SID:** Bob Vail. **Telephone:** (716) 286-8586. **Fax:** (716) 286-8609.
Assistant Coaches: *Matt Spatafora. **Telephone:** (716) 286-8624.
Home Field: Sal Maglie Stadium. **Seating Capacity:** 3,000. **Outfield Dimensions:** LF—320, CF—408, RF—330.

NICHOLLS STATE COLONELS

Conference: Southland.
Mailing Address: P.O. Box 2032, Thibodaux, LA 70310. **Website:** www.geauxcolonels.com.
Head Coach: Seth Thibodeaux. **Telephone:** (985) 449-7149. **Baseball SID:** Clyde Verdin. **Telephone:** (985) 448-4282. **Fax:** (985) 448-4814.
Assistant Coaches: Blaze Lambert, *Chris Prothro. **Telephone:** (985) 448-4808.
Home Field: Ray E. Didier Field. **Seating Capacity:** 2,200. **Outfield Dimensions:** LF—330, CF—405, RF—330. **Press Box Telephone:** (985) 448-4794.

NORFOLK STATE SPARTANS

Conference: Mid-Eastern Athletic.
Mailing Address: 700 Park Ave., Norfolk, VA 23504. **Website:** www.nsuspartans.com.
Head Coach: Claudell Clark. **Telephone:** (757) 676-3082. **Baseball SID:** Matt Michalec. **Telephone:** (757) 823-2628. **Fax:** (757) 823-8218.
Assistant Coaches: *Joey Seal. **Telephone:** (757) 812-2409.
Home Field: Marty L. Miller Field. **Seating Capacity:** 1,500. **Outfield Dimensions:** LF—330, CF—404, RF—318. **Press Box Telephone:** (757) 823-8196.

NORTH CAROLINA TAR HEELS

Conference: Atlantic Coast.
Mailing Address: P.O. Box 2126, Chapel Hill, NC 27515. **Website:** www.tarheelblue.com.
Head Coach: Mike Fox. **Telephone:** (919) 962-2351. **Baseball SID:** Bobby Hundley. **Telephone:** (919) 843-

5678. **Fax:** (919) 962-6002.
Assistant Coaches: Scott Forbes, *Scott Jackson.
Telephone: (919) 962-5451.
Home Field: Boshamer Stadium. **Seating Capacity:**
5,000. **Outfield Dimensions:** LF—335, CF—400,
RF—340. **Press Box Telephone:** (919) 843-5709.

NORTH CAROLINA A&T AGGIES

Conference: Mid-Eastern Athletic.
Mailing Address: 1601 E. Market St., Greensboro, NC
27411. **Website:** www.ncataggies.com.
Head Coach: Joel Sanchez. **Telephone:** (336) 285-
4272. **Baseball SID:** Brian Holloway. **Telephone:** (336)
285-3608. **Fax:** (336) 334-7272.
Assistant Coaches: Franciso Saurez, *Wes Timmons.
Telephone: (336) 285-4272.
Home Field: War Memorial Stadium. **Seating Capacity:**
2,000. **Outfield Dimensions:** LF—336, CF—401, RF—336.
Press Box Telephone: (336) 328-6719.

NORTH CAROLINA CENTRAL EAGLES

Conference: Mid-Eastern Athletic.
Mailing Address: 1801 Fayetteville St., Durham, NC
27707. **Website:** www.nccueaglepride.com.
Head Coach: Jim Koerner. **Telephone:** (919) 530-6723.
Baseball SID: Chris Hooks. **Telephone:** (919) 530-6017.
Fax: (919) 530-5426.
Assistant Coaches: Tyler Hanson, *Jerry Shank.
Telephone: (919) 530-5268.
Home Field: Durham Athletic Park. **Seating Capacity:**
2,000. **Outfield Dimensions:** LF—330, CF—395,
RF—290.

NORTH CAROLINA STATE WOLFPACK

Conference: Atlantic Coast.
Mailing Address: 1081 Varsity Dr., Raleigh, NC 27606.
Website: www.gopack.com.
Head Coach: Elliott Avent. **Telephone:** (919) 515-
3613. **Baseball SID:** Cavan Fosnes. **Telephone:** (919) 896-
1863. **Fax:** (919) 515-3624.
Assistant Coaches: *Chris Hart, Tom Holliday.
Telephone: (919) 515-3613.
Home Field: Doak Field at Dail Park. **Seating
Capacity:** 3,051. **Outfield Dimensions:** LF—320,
CF—400, RF—330. **Press Box Telephone:** (919) 896-
1863.

UNC ASHEVILLE BULLDOGS

Conference: Big South.
Mailing Address: Justice Center, CPO #2600, 1
University Heights, Asheville, NC 28804. **Website:** www.
uncabulldogs.com.
Head Coach: Tom Smith. **Telephone:** (828) 251-6920.
Baseball SID: Mike Gore. **Telephone:** (828) 251-6923.
Fax: (828) 251-6386.
Assistant Coaches: *Jeremy Plexico, Brent Walsh.
Telephone: (828) 250-2309.
Home Field: Greenwood Field. **Seating Capacity:**
500. **Outfield Dimensions:** LF—330, CF—400, RF—330.

UNC GREENSBORO SPARTANS

Conference: Southern.
Mailing Address: 337 Health and Human
Performance Building, UNCG, Greensboro, NC 27403.
Website: www.uncgspartans.com.
Head Coach: Link Jarrett. **Telephone:** (336) 334-3247.
Baseball SID: Chip Welch. **Telephone:** (336) 334-5615.

Fax: (336) 334-3182.
Assistant Coaches: *Matt Boykin, Jerry Edwards.
Telephone: (336) 334-3247.
Home Field: UNCG Baseball Stadium. **Seating
Capacity:** 3,500. **Outfield Dimensions:** LF—340,
CF—405, RF—340. **Press Box Telephone:** (336) 420-6342.

UNC WILMINGTON SEAHAWKS

Conference: Colonial Athletic.
Mailing Address: 601 South College Rd., Wilmington,
NC 28403. **Website:** www.uncwsports.com.
Head Coach: Mark Scalf. **Telephone:** (910) 962-3570.
Baseball SID: Tom Riordan. **Telephone:** (910) 962-4099.
Fax: (910) 962-3001.
Assistant Coaches: *Randy Hood, Matt Williams.
Telephone: (910) 962-7471.
Home Field: Brooks Field. **Seating Capacity:** 3,500.
Outfield Dimensions: LF—340, CF—380, RF—340.
Press Box Telephone: (910) 395-5141.

NORTH DAKOTA

Conference: Western Athletic.
Mailing Address: Hyslop Sports Center Room 120,
2751 2nd Ave. N., Stop 9013, Grand Forks, ND 58202.
Website: www.fightingsioux.com.
Head Coach: Jeff Dodson. **Telephone:** (701) 777-
4038. **Baseball SID:** Witch Wigness. **Telephone:** (701)
777-4210. **Fax:** (701) 777-2285.
Assistant Coaches: *Brian DeVillers, J.C. Field.
Telephone: (701) 777-2352.
Home Field: Kraft Field. **Seating Capacity:** 2,000.
Outfield Dimensions: LF—330, CF—410, RF—330.
Press Box Telephone: (701) 746-2762.

NORTH DAKOTA STATE BISON

Conference: Summit.
Mailing Address: NDSU Dept 1200, P.O. Box 6050,
Fargo, ND 58108. **Website:** www.gobison.com.
Head Coach: Tod Brown. **Telephone:** (701) 231-8853.
Baseball SID: Ryan Perreault. **Telephone:** (701) 231-
8331. **Fax:** (701) 231-8022.
Assistant Coaches: Tyler Oakes, *David Pearson.
Telephone: (701) 231-7817.
Home Field: Newman Outdoor Field. **Seating
Capacity:** 4,419. **Outfield Dimensions:** LF—318,
CF—408, RF—314. **Press Box Telephone:** (701) 235-5204.

NORTH FLORIDA OSPREYS

Conference: Atlantic Sun.
Mailing Address: UNF Baseball, 1 UNF Dr.,
Jacksonville, FL 32224. **Website:** www.unfospreys.com.
Head Coach: Smoke Laval. **Telephone:** (904) 620-
1566. **Baseball SID:** Brian Morgan (interim). **Telephone:**
(904) 620-4029. **Fax:** (904) 620-2836.
Assistant Coaches: *Judd Loveland, Tim Parenton.
Telephone: (904) 620-2556.
Home Field: Harmon Stadium. **Seating Capacity:**
2,500. **Outfield Dimensions:** LF—330, CF—400,
RF—330. **Press Box Telephone:** (904) 620-2556.

NORTHEASTERN HUSKIES

Conference: Colonial Athletic.
Mailing Address: 360 Huntington Ave., Boston, MA
02115. **Website:** www.gonu.com.
Head Coach: Neil McPhee. **Telephone:** (617) 373-
3657. **Baseball SID:** Michael Black. **Telephone:** (617) 373-
4252. **Fax:** (617) 373-3152.

Assistant Coaches: Kevin Cobb, *Mike Glavine.
Telephone: (617) 373-5256.
Home Field: Friedman Diamond. **Seating Capacity:** 3,000. **Outfield Dimensions: LF**—330, **CF**—435, **RF**—342.

NORTHERN COLORADO BEARS

Conference: Great West.
Mailing Address: 270D Butler-Hancock Athletic Center, Greeley, CO 80639. **Website:** www.uncbears.com.
Head Coach: Carl Iwasaki. **Telephone:** (970) 351-1714. **Baseball SID:** Heather Kennedy. **Telephone:** (970) 351-1065. **Fax:** (970) 351-2018.
Assistant Coaches: Patrick Perry, *R.D. Spiehs.
Telephone: (970) 351-1203.
Home Field: Jackson Field. **Seating Capacity:** 1,500. **Outfield Dimensions: LF**—348, **CF**—416, **RF**—356. **Press Box Telephone:** (970) 978-0675.

NORTHERN ILLINOIS HUSKIES

Conference: Mid-American (West).
Mailing Address: Convocation Center 224, 1525 W. Lincoln Hwy., Dekalb IL 60115. **Website:** www.niuhuskies.com.
Head Coach: Ed Mathey. **Telephone:** (815) 753-2225. **Baseball SID:** Matt Scheerer. **Telephone:** (815) 753-1708. **Fax:** (815) 753-7700.
Assistant Coaches: Tom Carcione, *Todd Corell.
Telephone: (815) 753-0147.
Home Field: Ralph McKinzie Field. **Seating Capacity:** 1,000. **Outfield Dimensions: LF**—312, **CF**—395, **RF**—322. **Press Box Telephone:** (815) 753-8094.

NORTHERN KENTUCKY NORSE

Conference: Atlantic Sun.
Mailing Address: 133 The Bank of Kentucky Center, 500 Nunn Dr., Highland Heights, KY 41099. **Website:** nkunorse.com.
Head Coach: Todd Asalon. **Telephone:** (859) 572-6474. **Baseball SID:** Kelli Marksbury. **Telephone:** (859) 572-7850. **Fax:** (859) 572-7956.
Assistant Coaches: Dizzy Peyton, Kent Shartzer.
Telephone: (859) 572-5940.
Home Field: Bill Aker Baseball Complex. **Seating Capacity:** 500. **Outfield Dimensions: LF**—320, **CF**—365, **RF**—320.

NORTHWESTERN WILDCATS

Conference: Big Ten.
Mailing Address: 1501 Central St., Evanston, IL 60208. **Website:** www.nusports.com.
Head Coach: Paul Stevens. **Telephone:** (847) 491-4652. **Baseball SID:** Dan Yopchick. **Telephone:** (847) 467-3418. **Fax:** (847) 491-8818.
Assistant Coaches: *Jon Mikrut, Tim Stoddard.
Telephone: (847) 491-4651.
Home Field: Rocky Miller Park. **Seating Capacity:** 1,000. **Outfield Dimensions: LF**—350, **CF**—400, **RF**—350. **Press Box Telephone:** (847) 491-4200.

NORTHWESTERN STATE DEMONS

Conference: Southland.
Mailing Address: 468 Caspari St., Natchitoches, LA 71457. **Website:** www.nsudemons.com.
Head Coach: Lane Burroughs. **Telephone:** (318) 357-4139. **Baseball SID:** Matt Fowler. **Telephone:** (318) 357-6467. **Fax:** (318) 357-4515.

Assistant Coaches: Chris Curry, *Andy Morgan.
Telephone: (318) 357-4176.
Home Field: Brown-Stroud Field. **Seating Capacity:** 1,500. **Outfield Dimensions: LF**—320, **CF**—400, **RF**—330. **Press Box Telephone:** (318) 357-4606.

NOTRE DAME FIGHTING IRISH

Conference: Atlantic Coast (Atlantic).
Mailing Address: C113 Joyce Center, Notre Dame, IN 46556. **Website:** www.und.com.
Head Coach: Mik Aoki. **Telephone:** (574) 631-8466. **Baseball SID:** Russell Dorn. **Telephone:** (574) 631-4780. **Fax:** (574) 631-7941.
Assistant Coaches: Chuck Ristano, *Jesse Woods.
Telephone: (574) 631-6366.
Home Field: Frank Eck Stadium. **Seating Capacity:** 2,500. **Outfield Dimensions: LF**—330, **CF**—400, **RF**—330. **Press Box Telephone:** (574) 631-9018.

OAKLAND GOLDEN GRIZZLIES

Conference: Horizon.
Mailing Address: 201 Athletics Center, Rochester, MI 48309. **Website:** www.ougrizzlies.com.
Head Coach: John Musachio. **Telephone:** (248) 370-4059. **Baseball SID:** Dan Gliot. **Telephone:** (248) 370-3123. **Fax:** (248) 370-4056.
Assistant Coaches: Jacke Healey. **Telephone:** (248) 370-4228.
Home Field: OU Baseball Field. **Seating Capacity:** 500. **Press Box Telephone:** (248) 688-7646.

OHIO BOBCATS

Conference: Mid-American (East).
Mailing Address: N117 Convocation Center, Athens, OH 45701. **Website:** www.ohiobobcats.com.
Head Coach: Rob Smith. **Telephone:** (740) 593-1180. **Baseball SID:** Tom Symonds. **Telephone:** (740) 593-1298.
Assistant Coaches: Larry Day, *Craig Moore.
Telephone: (740) 593-1207.
Home Field: Bob Wren Stadium. **Seating Capacity:** 5,000. **Press Box Telephone:** (740) 593-0526.

OHIO STATE BUCKEYES

Conference: Big Ten.
Mailing Address: 650 Borror Dr., Columbus, OH 43210. **Website:** www.ohiostatebuckeyes.com.
Head Coach: Greg Beals. **Telephone:** (614) 292-1075. **Baseball SID:** Brett Rybak. **Telephone:** (614) 292-1112. **Fax:** (614) 292-8547.
Assistant Coaches: *Chris Holick, Mike Stafford.
Telephone: (614) 292-1075.
Home Field: Nick Swisher Field at Bill Davis Stadium. **Seating Capacity:** 4,450. **Outfield Dimensions: LF**—330, **CF**—400, **RF**—330. **Press Box Telephone:** (614) 292-0021.

OKLAHOMA SOONERS

Conference: Big 12.
Mailing Address: McClendon Center for Intercollegiate Athletics, 180 W. Brooks, Norman, OK 73019. **Website:** www.soonersports.com.
Head Coach: Pete Hughes. **Telephone:** (405) 325-8354. **Baseball SID:** Brendan Flynn. **Telephone:** (405) 325-6449. **Fax:** (405) 325-7623.
Assistant Coaches: Mike Anderson, Jamie Pinzino.
Telephone: (405) 325-8354.
Home Field: L. Dale Mitchell Park. **Seating Capacity:**

3,180. **Outfield Dimensions: LF**—335, **CF**—411, **RF**—335. **Press Box Telephone:** (405) 325-8363.

OKLAHOMA STATE COWBOYS

Conference: Big 12.
Mailing Address: 220 Athletics Center, Stillwater, OK 74078. **Website:** www.okstate.com.
Head Coach: Josh Holliday. **Telephone:** (405) 744-7141. **Baseball SID:** Wade McWhorter. **Telephone:** (405) 744-7853. **Fax:** (405) 744-7754.
Assistant Coaches: *Marty Lees, Rob Walton. **Telephone:** (405) 744-7141.
Home Field: Allie P. Reynolds Stadium. **Seating Capacity:** 4,000. **Outfield Dimensions: LF**—330, **CF**—398, **RF**—330. **Press Box Telephone:** (405) 744-5757.

OLD DOMINION MONARCHS

Conference: Conference USA.
Mailing Address: 4509 Elkhorn Ave., Norfolk, VA 23529. **Website:** www.odusports.com.
Head Coach: Chris Finwood. **Telephone:** (757) 683-5371. **Baseball SID:** Carol Hudson. **Telephone:** (757) 683-3395. **Fax:** (757) 683-3119.
Assistant Coaches: Tim LaVigne, *Karl Nonemaker. **Telephone:** (757) 683-4331.
Home Field: Bud Metheny Baseball Complex. **Seating Capacity:** 2,000. **Outfield Dimensions: LF**—325, **CF**—395, **RF**—325. **Press Box Telephone:** (757) 683-5036.

ORAL ROBERTS GOLDEN EAGLES

Conference: Southland.
Mailing Address: 7777 S. Lewis Ave., Tulsa, OK 74147. **Website:** www.orugoldeneagles.com.
Head Coach: Ryan Folmar. **Telephone:** (918) 495-7130. **Baseball SID:** Eric Scott. **Telephone:** (918) 495-6646. **Fax:** (918) 495-7142.
Assistant Coaches: *Ryan Neill, Sean Snedeker. **Telephone:** (918) 495-7205.
Home Field: JL Johnson Stadium. **Seating Capacity:** 2,500. **Outfield Dimensions: LF**—330, **CF**—400, **RF**—330. **Press Box Telephone:** (918) 495-7165.

OREGON DUCKS

Conference: Pacific-12.
Mailing Address: Len Casanova Center, 2727 Leo Harris Parkway, Eugene, OR 97401. **Website:** www. goducks.com.
Head Coach: George Horton. **Telephone:** (541) 346-5235. **Baseball SID:** Todd Miles. **Telephone:** (541) 346-0962. **Fax:** (541) 346-5449.
Assistant Coaches: Jay Uhlman, *Mark Wasikowski. **Telephone:** (541) 346-5768.
Home Field: PK Park. **Seating Capacity:** 4,000. **Outfield Dimensions: LF**—335, **CF**—400, **RF**—325. **Press Box Telephone:** (541) 346-6309.

OREGON STATE BEAVERS

Conference: Pacific-12.
Mailing Address: 114 Gill Coliseum, Corvallis, OR 97331. **Website:** www.osubeavers.com
Head Coach: Pat Casey. **Telephone:** (541) 737-3072. **Baseball SID:** Hank Hager. **Telephone:** (541) 737-7472. **Fax:** (541) 737-3072.
Assistant Coaches: Pat Bailey, Nate Yeskie. **Telephone:** (541) 737-7484.

Home Field: Goss Stadium at Coleman Field. **Seating Capacity:** 3248. **Outfield Dimensions: LF**—330, **CF**—400, **RF**—330. **Press Box Telephone:** (541) 737-7475.

PACIFIC TIGERS

Conference: West Coast.
Mailing Address: 3601 Pacific Ave., Stockton, CA 95211. **Website:** www.pacifictigers.com.
Head Coach: Ed Sprague. **Telephone:** (209) 946-2709. **Baseball SID:** Benjamin Laskey. **Telephone:** (209) 946-2730. **Fax:** (209) 946-2757.
Assistant Coaches: *Don Barbara, Mike McCormick. **Telephone:** (209) 946-2386.
Home Field: Klein Family Field. **Seating Capacity:** 2,500. **Outfield Dimensions: LF**—317, **CF**—405, **RF**—325. **Press Box Telephone:** (209) 946-2722.

PENN STATE NITTANY LIONS

Conference: Big Ten.
Mailing Address: Medlar Field at Lubrano Park, Suite 230, University Park, State College, PA 16801. **Website:** www.gopsusports.com.
Head Coach: Rob Cooper. **Telephone:** (814) 863-0239. **Baseball SID:** Robby Hamman. **Telephone:** (814) 865-1757. **Fax:** (814) 863-3165.
Assistant Coaches: *Brian Anderson, Ross Oeder. **Telephone:** (814) 863-0230.
Home Field: Medlar Field at Lubrano Park. **Seating Capacity:** 5,700. **Outfield Dimensions: LF**—325, **CF**—399, **RF**—320. **Press Box Telephone:** (814) 865-2552.

PENNSYLVANIA QUAKERS

Conference: Ivy League (Gehrig).
Mailing Address: 235 S. 33rd St., Philadelphia, PA 19104. **Website:** www.pennathletics.com.
Head Coach: John Yurkow. **Telephone:** (215) 898-6282. **Baseball SID:** Paul Seiter. **Telephone:** (215) 898-1748. **Fax:** (215) 898-1747.
Assistant Coaches: *Mike Santello, Josh Schwartz. **Telephone:** (215) 746-2325.
Home Field: Meiklejohn Stadium. **Seating Capacity:** 850. **Outfield Dimensions: LF**—330, **CF**—380, **RF**—330.

PEPPERDINE WAVES

Conference: West Coast.
Mailing Address: 24255 Pacific Coast Highway, Malibu, CA 90263. **Website:** www.pepperdinesports.com.
Head Coach: Steve Rodriguez. **Telephone:** (310) 506-4371. **Baseball SID:** Jacob Breems. **Telephone:** (310) 506-4333. **Fax:** (310) 506-4322.
Assistant Coaches: Rick Hirtensteiner, *Jon Strauss. **Telephone:** (310) 506-4404.
Home Field: Eddy D. Field Stadium. **Seating Capacity:** 1,800. **Outfield Dimensions: LF**—330, **CF**—400, **RF**—330. **Press Box Telephone:** (310) 506-4598.

PITTSBURGH PANTHERS

Conference: Atlantic Coast (Coastal).
Mailing Address: 212 Fitzgerald Fieldhouse, Pittsburgh, PA 15261. **Website:** www.pittsburghpanthers. com.
Head Coach: Joe Jordano. **Telephone:** (412) 648-8208. **Baseball SID:** Matt Haas. **Telephone:** (412) 648-8845. **Fax:** (412) 648-8246.

Assistant Coaches: *Jerry Oakes, Bryan Peters. **Telephone:** (412) 648-8238.
Home Field: Charles L. Cost Field. **Seating Capacity:** 900. **Outfield Dimensions: LF**—330, **CF**—405, **RF**—330. **Press Box Telephone:** (412) 624-6813.

PORTLAND PILOTS

Conference: West Coast.
Mailing Address: 5000 N. Willamette Blvd., Portland, OR 97203. **Website:** www.portlandpilots.com.
Head Coach: Chris Sperry. **Telephone:** (503) 943-7707. **Baseball SID:** Adam Linnman. **Telephone:** (503) 943-7731. **Fax:** (503) 943-8082.
Assistant Coaches: Tucker Brack, *Larry Casian. **Telephone:** (503) 943-7732.
Home Field: Joe Etzel Field. **Seating Capacity:** 1,000. **Outfield Dimensions: LF**—350, **CF**—390, **RF**—340. **Press Box Telephone:** (503) 943-7253.

PRESBYTERIAN BLUE HOSE

Conference: Big South.
Mailing Address: 105 Ashland Ave., Clinton, SC 29325. **Website:** www.gobluehose.com.
Head Coach: Elton Pollock. **Telephone:** (864) 833-8236. **Baseball SID:** Ryan Real. **Telephone:** (864) 833-7095. **Fax:** (864) 833-8323.
Assistant Coaches: *Mark Crocco, Jamie Serber. **Telephone:** (864) 833-7164.
Home Field: P.C. Baseball Complex. **Seating Capacity:** 500. **Outfield Dimensions: LF**—375, **CF**—400, **RF**—375. **Press Box Telephone:** (864) 833-8527.

PRINCETON TIGERS

Conference: Ivy League (Gehrig).
Mailing Address: P.O. Box 71, Princeton University, Princeton, NJ 08544. **Website:** www.goprincetontigers.com.
Head Coach: Scott Bradley. **Telephone:** (609) 258-5059. **Baseball SID:** Diana Chamorro. **Telephone:** (609) 258-2630. **Fax:** (609) 258-4477.
Assistant Coaches: *Lloyd Brewer, Hank Coogan. **Telephone:** (609) 258-5684.
Home Field: Clarke Field. **Seating Capacity:** 1,000. **Outfield Dimensions: LF**—335, **CF**—400, **RF**—320. **Press Box Telephone:** (609) 462-0248.

PURDUE BOILERMAKERS

Conference: Big Ten.
Mailing Address: Ross-Ade Pavilion Room 6031, 850 Beering Dr., West Lafayette, IN 47907. **Website:** www.purduesports.com.
Head Coach: Doug Schreiber. **Telephone:** (765) 494-3998. **Baseball SID:** Ben Turner. **Telephone:** (765) 494-3198. **Fax:** (765) 494-5447.
Assistant Coaches: Wally Crancer, *Tristan McIntyre. **Telephone:** (765) 494-9360.
Home Field: Alexander Field. **Seating Capacity:** 2,000. **Outfield Dimensions: LF**—340, **CF**—408, **RF**—330. **Press Box Telephone:** (217) 549-7965.

QUINNIPIAC BOBCATS

Conference: Metro Atlantic.
Mailing Address: 275 Mount Carmel Ave., Hamden, CT. **Website:** www.quinnipiacbobcats.com.
Head Coach: Dan Gooley. **Telephone:** (203) 582-8966. **Baseball SID:** Ken Sweeten. **Telephone:** (203) 582-8625. **Fax:** (203) 582-5385.

Assistant Coaches: Brett Conner, *John Delaney. **Telephone:** (203) 582-6546.
Home Field: Quinnipiac Field. **Seating Capacity:** 1,000. **Press Box Telephone:** (203) 859-8529.

RADFORD HIGHLANDERS

Conference: Big South.
Mailing Address: 801 E. Main St., Radford, VA 24141. **Website:** www.ruhighlanders.com.
Head Coach: Joe Raccuia. **Telephone:** (540) 831-5881. **Baseball SID:** Tom Galbraith. **Telephone:** (540) 831-5726. **Fax:** (540) 831-6095.
Assistant Coaches: *Alex Guerra, Mark McQueen. **Telephone:** (540) 831-6513.
Home Field: RU Baseball Stadium. **Seating Capacity:** 1,000. **Outfield Dimensions: LF**—335, **CF**—400, **RF**—335. **Press Box Telephone:** (540) 831-6062.

RHODE ISLAND RAMS

Conference: Atlantic 10.
Mailing Address: 3 Keaney Rd., Suite 1, Kingston, RI 02881. **Website:** www.gorhody.com.
Head Coach: Jim Foster. **Telephone:** (401) 874-4550. **Baseball SID:** Jodi Pontbriand. **Telephone:** (401) 874-5356. **Fax:** (401) 874-5354.
Assistant Coaches: *Raphael Cerrato, Luke Demko. **Telephone:** (401) 874-4888.
Home Field: Bill Beck Field. **Seating Capacity:** 1,000. **Outfield Dimensions: LF**—330, **CF**—400, **RF**—330. **Press Box Telephone:** (401) 481-6648.

RICE OWLS

Conference: Conference USA.
Mailing Address: 6100 Main St., Houston, TX 77251. **Website:** www.riceowls.com.
Head Coach: Wayne Graham. **Telephone:** (713) 348-8864. **Baseball SID:** John Sullivan. **Telephone:** (713) 348-5636. **Fax:** (713) 348-6019.
Assistant Coaches: *Patrick Hallmark, Clay Van Hook. **Telephone:** (713) 348-8859.
Home Field: Reckling Park. **Seating Capacity:** 5,368. **Outfield Dimensions: LF**—335, **CF**—400, **RF**—335. **Press Box Telephone:** (713) 348-4931.

RICHMOND SPIDERS

Conference: Atlantic 10.
Mailing Address: 28 Westhampton Way, Richmond, VA 23173. **Website:** www.richmondspiders.com.
Head Coach: Tracy Woodson. **Telephone:** (804) 289-8391. **Baseball SID:** Scott Burns. **Telephone:** (804) 287-6313. **Fax:** (804) 289-8820.
Assistant Coaches: Josh Davis, *Matt Tyner. **Telephone:** (804) 289-8391.
Home Field: Pitt Field. **Seating Capacity:** 1,000. **Outfield Dimensions: LF**—328, **CF**—390, **RF**—328. **Press Box Telephone:** (804) 289-8363.

RIDER BRONCS

Conference: Metro Atlantic.
Mailing Address: 2083 Lawrenceville Rd., Lawrenceville, NJ 08648. **Website:** www.gobroncs.com.
Head Coach: Barry Davis. **Telephone:** (609) 896-5055. **Baseball SID:** Bud Focht. **Telephone:** (609) 896-5138. **Fax:** (609) 896-0341.
Assistant Coaches: Lou Proietti, Jaime Steward. **Telephone:** (609) 895-5703.
Home Field: Sonny Pittaro Field. **Seating Capacity:**

2,000. **Outfield Dimensions: LF**—330, **CF**—405, **RF**—330.

RUTGERS SCARLET KNIGHTS

Conference: American Athletic.
Mailing Address: 83 Rockafeller Rd., Piscataway NJ, 08854. **Website:** www.scarletknights.com.
Head Coach: Joe Litterio. **Telephone:** (732) 445-7833.
Baseball SID: Jimmy Gill. **Telephone:** (732) 445-8103.
Fax: (732) 445-3063.
   Assistant Coaches: Casey Gaynor, *Tim Reilly.
Telephone: (732) 445-7833.
   Home Field: Bainton Field. **Seating Capacity:** 1,500.
Outfield Dimensions: LF—330, **CF**—410, **RF**—320.
Press Box Telephone: (732) 921-1067.

SACRAMENTO STATE HORNETS

Conference: Western Athletic.
Mailing Address: 6000 J. St., Sacramento, CA 95819.
Website: www.hornetsports.com.
   Head Coach: Reggie Christiansen. **Telephone:** (916) 278-4036. **Baseball SID:** Andrew Tomsky. **Telephone:** (916) 278-6896. **Fax:** (916) 278-5429.
   Assistant Coaches: *Jake Angier, Steve Holm.
Telephone: (916) 278-2018.
   Home Field: John Smith Field. **Seating Capacity:** 1,200. **Outfield Dimensions: LF**—333, **CF**—400, **RF**—333. **Press Box Telephone:** (916) 889-6643.

SACRED HEART PIONEERS

Conference: Northeast.
Mailing Address: 5151 Park Ave., Fairfield, CT 06825.
Website: www.sacredheartpioneers.com.
   Head Coach: Nick Giaquinto. **Telephone:** (203) 365-7632. **Baseball SID:** Jim Sheehan. **Telephone:** (203) 365-4813. **Fax:** (203) 371-7889.
   Assistant Coaches: *Wayne Mazzoni, Alex Trezza.
Telephone: (203) 365-4469.
   Home Field: Ballpark at Harbor Yard. **Seating Capacity:** 5,500.

ST. BONAVENTURE BONNIES

Conference: Atlantic 10.
Mailing Address: P.O. Box G., Reilly Center, St. Bonaventure, NY 14778. **Website:** www.gobonnies.com.
   Head Coach: Larry Sudbrook. **Telephone:** (716) 375-2641. **Baseball SID:** Corey Dietman. **Telephone:** (716) 375-4019. **Fax:** (716) 375-2383.
   Assistant Coaches: Eddie Gray, *B.J. Salerno.
Telephone: (716) 375-2699.
   Home Field: Fred Handler Park at McGraw Jennings Field. **Seating Capacity:** 500. **Outfield Dimensions: LF**—330, **CF**—403, **RF**—330.

ST. JOHN'S RED STORM

Conference: Big East.
Mailing Address: 8000 Utopia Parkway, Queens, NY 11439. **Website:** www.redstormsports.com.
   Head Coach: Ed Blankmeyer. **Telephone:** (718) 990-6148. **Baseball SID:** Tim Brown. **Telephone:** (718) 990-1521. **Fax:** (718) 969-8468.
   Assistant Coaches: *Mike Hampton, Corey Muscara.
Telephone: (718) 990-7523.
   Home Field: Jack Kaiser Stadium. **Seating Capacity:** 3,500. **Outfield Dimensions: LF**—325, **CF**—400, **RF**—325. **Press Box Telephone:** (718) 990-2724.

ST. JOSEPH'S HAWKS

Conference: Atlantic 10.
Mailing Address: 5600 City Ave., Philadelphia, PA 19131. **Website:** www.sjuhawks.com.
   Head Coach: Fritz Hamburg. **Telephone:** (610) 660-1718. **Baseball SID:** Joe Greenwich. **Telephone:** (610) 660-1738. **Fax:** (610) 660-1724.
   Assistant Coaches: Matt Allison, *Kyle Werman.
Telephone: (610)660-1704.
   Home Field: Smithson Field. **Seating Capacity:** 400.
Outfield Dimensions: LF—327, **CF**—400, **RF**—331.

SAINT LOUIS BILLIKENS

Conference: Atlantic 10.
Mailing Address: 3330 Laclede Ave., St. Louis, MO 63103. **Website:** www.slubillikens.com.
   Head Coach: Darin Hendrickson. **Telephone:** (314) 977-3172. **Baseball SID:** Jake Gossage. **Telephone:** (314) 977-2524. **Fax:** (314) 977-7193.
   Assistant Coaches: Will Bradley, *Kevin Moulder.
Telephone: (314) 977-3260.
   Home Field: Billiken Sports Center. **Seating Capacity:** 500. **Outfield Dimensions: LF**—330, **CF**—403, **RF**—330.
Press Box Telephone: (314) 956-1265.

ST. MARY'S GAELS

Conference: West Coast.
Mailing Address: 1928 St. Mary's Rd., Moraga, CA 94856. **Website:** www.smcgaels.com.
   Head Coach: Eric Valenzuela. **Telephone:** (925) 631-4637. **Baseball SID:** Ben Enos. **Telephone:** (925) 631-4950. **Fax:** (925) 631-4405.
   Assistant Coaches: Matt Fonteno, *Mark Viramontes.
Telephone: (925) 631-4637.
   Home Field: Louis Guisto Field. **Seating Capacity:** 500. **Outfield Dimensions: LF**—330, **CF**—400, **RF**—330.
Press Box Telephone: (925) 376-3906.

ST. PETER'S PEACOCKS

Conference: Metro Atlantic.
Mailing Address: 2641 Kennedy Blvd., Jersey City, NJ 07306. **Website:** www.spc.edu.
   Head Coach: Sean Cashman. **Telephone:** (201) 761-7319. **Baseball SID:** Lily Rodriguez. **Telephone:** (201) 761-7301. **Fax:** (201) 761-7301.
   Assistant Coaches: T.J. Baxter, Ed Moskal, Matt Owens. **Telephone:** (201) 761-7318.
   Home Field: Jaroshack Field. **Outfield Dimensions: LF**—318, **CF**—405, **RF**—310.

SAM HOUSTON STATE BEARKATS

Conference: Southland.
Mailing Address: 620 Bowers Blvd., Huntsville, TX 77341. **Website:** www.gobearkats.com.
   Head Coach: David Pierce. **Telephone:** (936) 294-1731. **Baseball SID:** Kevin Rodriguez. **Telephone:** (963) 294-1764. **Fax:** (936) 294-3538.
   Assistant Coaches: *Sean Allen, Philip Miller.
Telephone: (936) 294-4435.
   Home Field: Don Sanders Stadium. **Seating Capacity:** 1,163. **Outfield Dimensions: LF**—330, **CF**—400, **RF**—330. **Press Box Telephone:** (936) 294-4132.

SAMFORD BULLDOGS

Conference: Southern.
Mailing Address: Samford Baseball, 800 Lakeshore

Dr., Birmingham, AL 35229. **Website:** www.samford-sports.com.

Head Coach: Casey Dunn. **Telephone:** (205) 726-2134. **Baseball SID:** Joey Mullins. **Telephone:** (205) 726-2799. **Fax:** (205) 726-2132.

Assistant Coaches: Mathew Addison, *Tony David. **Telephone:** (205) 726-4330.

Home Field: Joe Lee Griffin Field. **Seating Capacity:** 1,000. **Outfield Dimensions: LF**—335, **CF**—390, **RF**—330. **Press Box Telephone:** (205) 532-3477.

SAN DIEGO TOREROS

Conference: West Coast.
Mailing Address: 5998 Alacala Park, San Diego, CA 92110. **Website:** www.usdtoreros.com.
Head Coach: Rich Hill. **Telephone:** (619) 260-5953. **Baseball SID:** Chris Loucks. **Telephone:** (619) 260-7930. **Fax:** (619) 260-7990.
Assistant Coaches: *Tyler Kincaid, Rasmon Orozco. **Telephone:** (619) 260-7486.
Home Field: Fowler Park. **Seating Capacity:** 1,700. **Outfield Dimensions: LF**—312, **CF**—395, **RF**—329. **Press Box Telephone:** (619) 260-8829.

SAN DIEGO STATE AZTECS

Conference: Mountain West.
Mailing Address: Athletic Dept., 5302 55th St., San Diego, CA 92182. **Website:** www.goaztecs.com. **Head Coach:** Tony Gwynn. **Telephone:** (619) 594-6889. **Baseball SID:** Dave Kuhn. **Telephone:** (619) 594-5242. **Fax:** (619) 582-6541.
Assistant Coaches: *Mark Martinez, John Pawlowski. **Telephone:** (619) 594-6889.
Home Field: Tony Gwynn Stadium. **Seating Capacity:** 2,500. **Outfield Dimensions: LF**—330, **CF**—410, **RF**—330. **Press Box Telephone:** (619) 594-4103.

SAN FRANCISCO DONS

Conference: West Coast.
Mailing Address: 2130 Fulton St., San Francisco, CA 94117. **Website:** www.usfdons.com.
Head Coach: Nino Giarratano. **Telephone:** (415) 422-2934. **Baseball SID:** Zack Farmer. **Telephone:** (415) 422-5248. **Fax:** (415) 422-2510.
Assistant Coaches: Seth Etherton, *Troy Nakamura. **Telephone:** (415) 422-2393.
Home Field: Benedetti Diamond. **Seating Capacity:** 1,000. **Outfield Dimensions: LF**—315, **CF**—415, **RF**—321. **Press Box Telephone:** (415) 422-2919.

SAN JOSE STATE SPARTANS

Conference: Mountain West.
Mailing Address: 1393 S. 7th St., San Jose, CA 95112. **Website:** www.sjsuspartans.com.
Head Coach: Dave Nakama. **Telephone:** (408) 924-1255. **Baseball SID:** Dominic Urrutia. **Telephone:** (408) 924-1211. **Fax:** (408) 924-1291.
Assistant Coaches: Nicholas Enriquez, *Brad Sanfilippo. **Telephone:** (408) 924-1262.
Home Field: Municipal Stadium. **Seating Capacity:** 5,200. **Outfield Dimensions: LF**—320, **CF**—390, **RF**—320. **Press Box Telephone:** (408) 924-7276.

SANTA CLARA BRONCOS

Conference: West Coast.
Mailing Address: 500 El Camino Real, Santa Clara, CA 95050. **Website:** www.santaclarabroncos.com.

Head Coach: Dan O'Brien. **Telephone:** (408) 554-4882. **Baseball SID:** David Gentile. **Telephone:** (408) 554-4670. **Fax:** (408) 554-6969.
Assistant Coaches: Keith Beauregard, *Gabe Ribas. **Telephone:** (408) 554-4151.
Home Field: Stephen Schott Stadium. **Seating Capacity:** 2,200. **Outfield Dimensions: LF**—340, **CF**—400, **RF**—335. **Press Box Telephone:** (408) 554-5587.

SAVANNAH STATE TIGERS

Conference: Mid-Eastern Athletic.
Mailing Address: 3219 College St., Savannah, GA 31404. **Website:** www.ssuathletics.com.
Head Coach: Carlton Hardy. **Telephone:** (912) 358-3082. **Baseball SID:** Opio Mashariki. **Telephone:** (912) 358-3430. **Fax:** (912) 353-5287.
Assistant Coaches: Anthony Macon. **Telephone:** (912) 358-3161.
Home Field: Tiger Field. **Seating Capacity:** 800. **Outfield Dimensions: LF**—330, **CF**—400, **RF**—330. **Press Box Telephone:** (912) 358-3082.

SEATTLE REDHAWKS

Conference: Western Athletic.
Mailing Address: 901 12th Ave., P.O. Box 222000, Seattle, WA 98122. **Website:** www.goseattleu.com.
Head Coach: Donny Harrel. **Telephone:** (206) 398-4399. **Baseball SID:** Jason Behenna. **Telephone:** (206) 296-5915. **Fax:** (206) 296-2154.
Assistant Coaches: *Elliott Cribby, Mike Nadeau. **Telephone:** (206) 398-4396.
Home Field: Bannerwood Park. **Seating Capacity:** 1,000. **Outfield Dimensions: LF**—330, **CF**—410, **RF**—330.

SETON HALL PIRATES

Conference: Big East.
Mailing Address: 400 South Orange Ave., South Orange, NJ 07079. **Website:** www.shupirates.com.
Head Coach: Rob Sheppard. **Telephone:** (973) 761-9557. **Baseball SID:** Matt Sweeney. **Telephone:** (973) 761-9493. **Fax:** (973) 761-9061.
Assistant Coaches: *Phil Cundari, Mark Pappas. **Telephone:** (973) 275-6437.
Home Field: Owen T. Carroll Field. **Seating Capacity:** 1,000. **Outfield Dimensions: LF**—318, **CF**—400, **RF**—325. **Press Box Telephone:** (973) 943-8434.

SIENA SAINTS

Conference: Metro Atlantic.
Mailing Address: 515 Loudon Rd., Loudonville, NY 12211. **Website:** www.sienasaints.com.
Head Coach: Tony Rossi. **Telephone:** (518) 786-5044. **Baseball SID:** Jason Rich. **Telephone:** (518) 783-2411. **Fax:** (518) 783-2992.
Assistant Coaches: Elliot Glynn, *Mike Kellar. **Telephone:** (518) 782-6875.
Home Field: Siena Field. **Seating Capacity:** 1,000. **Outfield Dimensions: LF**—300, **CF**—400, **RF**—325. **Press Box Telephone:** (518) 542-7240.

SOUTH ALABAMA JAGUARS

Conference: Sun Belt.
Mailing Address: 171 Jaguar Dr., HPELS Room 1105, Mobile, AL 36688. **Website:** www.usajaguars.com.
Head Coach: Mark Calvi. **Telephone:** (251) 414-8243.

Baseball SID: Charlie Nichols. **Telephone:** (251) 414-8017. **Fax:** (251) 460-7297.
Assistant Coaches: Bob Keller, *Jerry Zulli. **Telephone:** (251) 414-8209.
Home Field: Stanky Field. **Seating Capacity:** 3,775. **Outfield Dimensions: LF**—330, **CF**—400, **RF**—330. **Press Box Telephone:** (251) 461-1842.

SOUTH CAROLINA GAMECOCKS

Conference: Southeastern (East).
Mailing Address: 431 Williams St., Columbia, SC 29208. **Website:** www.gamecocksonline.com.
Head Coach: Chad Holbrook. **Telephone:** (803) 777-0116. **Baseball SID:** Andrew Kitick. **Telephone:** (803) 777-5257. **Fax:** (803) 777-2967.
Assistant Coaches: *Sammy Esposito, Jerry Meyers. **Telephone:** (803) 777-7913.
Home Field: Carolina Stadium. **Seating Capacity:** 8,242. **Outfield Dimensions: LF**—320, **CF**—390, **RF**—320. **Press Box Telephone:** (803) 777-6648.

SOUTH CAROLINA-UPSTATE SPARTANS

Conference: Atlantic Sun.
Mailing Address: 800 University Way, Spartanburg, SC 29303. **Website:** www.upstatespartans.com.
Head Coach: Matt Fincher. **Telephone:** (864) 503-5135. **Baseball SID:** Jay D'Abramo. **Telephone:** (864) 503-5166. **Fax:** (864) 503-5127.
Assistant Coaches: *Grant Rembert, Drew Saberhagen. **Telephone:** (864) 503-5164.
Home Field: Cleveland S. Harley Park. **Seating Capacity:** 500. **Outfield Dimensions: LF**—335, **CF**—402, **RF**—305. **Press Box Telephone:** (864) 503-5815.

SOUTH DAKOTA STATE JACKRABBITS

Conference: Summit.
Mailing Address: 2820 HPER Center, Brookings, SD 57006. **Website:** www.gojacks.com.
Head Coach: Dave Schrage. **Telephone:** (605) 688-5027. **Baseball SID:** Jason Hove. **Telephone:** (605) 688-4623. **Fax:** (605) 688-5999.
Assistant Coaches: *Brian Grunzke, Ben Norton. **Telephone:** (605) 688-5778.
Home Field: Ery Heuther Field. **Seating Capacity:** 1,500. **Outfield Dimensions: LF**—330, **CF**—400, **RF**—330. **Press Box Telephone:** (605) 695-1827.

SOUTH FLORIDA BULLS

Conference: American Athletic.
Mailing Address: 4202 E. Fowler Ave., ATH 100, Tampa, FL 33620. **Website:** www.gousfbulls.com.
Head Coach: Lelo Prado. **Telephone:** (813) 974-2504. **Baseball SID:** TBA. **Telephone:** (813) 974-0415. **Fax:** (813) 974-4029.
Assistant Coaches: Lance Carter, *Chris Heintz. **Telephone:** (813) 974-2995.
Home Field: Red McEwen Field. **Seating Capacity:** 3,211. **Outfield Dimensions: LF**—330, **CF**—400, **RF**—330. **Press Box Telephone:** (813) 410-1194.

SOUTHEAST MISSOURI STATE REDHAWKS

Conference: Ohio Valley.
Mailing Address: One University Plaza, Cape Girardeau, MO 63701. **Website:** www.gosoutheast.com.
Head Coach: Steve Bieser. **Telephone:** (573) 982-6002. **Baseball SID:** Sean Stevenson. **Telephone:** (573) 651-2294. **Fax:** (573) 651-2810.

Assistant Coaches: Dillon Lawson, *Lance Rhodes. **Telephone:** (573) 982-6002.
Home Field: Capaha Field. **Seating Capacity:** 2,000. **Outfield Dimensions: LF**—330, **CF**—400, **RF**—330. **Press Box Telephone:** (573) 335-8895.

SOUTHEASTERN LOUISIANA LIONS

Conference: Southland.
Mailing Address: 800 Galloway Dr. Hammond, LA 70402. **Website:** www.lionsports.net.
Head Coach: Matt Riser. **Telephone:** (985) 549-3566. **Baseball SID:** Damon Sunde. **Telephone:** (985) 549-3774. **Fax:** (985) 549-3495.
Assistant Coaches: Daniel Latham, *Zack Zulli. **Telephone:** (985) 549-2896.
Home Field: Pat Kenelly Field at Alumni Stadium. **Seating Capacity:** 2630. **Outfield Dimensions: LF**—330, **CF**—400, **RF**—330. **Press Box Telephone:** (985) 549-2431.

SOUTHERN JAGUARS

Conference: Southwestern Athletic.
Mailing Address: P.O. Box 10850, Baton Rouge, LA 70813. **Website:** www.gojagsports.com.
Head Coach: Roger Cador. **Telephone:** (225) 771-2513. **Baseball SID:** Chris Jones. **Telephone:** (225) 771-3495.
Assistant Coaches: Chris King, *Fernando Puebla. **Telephone:** (225) 771-3712.
Home Field: Lee-Hines Stadium. **Seating Capacity:** 1,500. **Outfield Dimensions:** LF—360, CF—395, RF—325.

SOUTHERN CALIFORNIA TROJANS

Conference: Pacific-12.
Mailing Address: 1021 Childs Way, Los Angeles, CA 90089. **Website:** www.usctrojans.com.
Head Coach: Dan Hubbs. **Telephone:** (213) 740-8446. **Baseball SID:** Rachel Caton. **Telephone:** (213) 740-3809. **Fax:** (213) 740-7584.
Assistant Coaches: *Gabe Alvarez, Matt Curtis. **Telephone:** (213) 740-8447.
Home Field: Dedeaux Field. **Seating Capacity:** 2,500. **Outfield Dimensions: LF**—335, **CF**—395, **RF**—335. **Press Box Telephone:** (213) 748-3449.

SOUTHERN ILLINOIS SALUKIS

Conference: Missouri Valley.
Mailing Address: Baseball Clubhouse, Mailcode 6702, Southern Illinois University, Carbondale, IL 62901. **Website:** www.siusalukis.com.
Head Coach: Ken Henderson. **Telephone:** (618) 453-3794. **Baseball SID:** Scott Gierman. **Telephone:** (618) 453-5470. **Fax:** (618) 453-2648.
Assistant Coaches: *P.J. Finigan, Ryan Strain. **Telephone:** (618) 453-7646.
Home Field: Itchy Jones Stadium. **Seating Capacity:** 2,000. **Outfield Dimensions: LF**—330, **CF**—390, **RF**—330. **Press Box Telephone:** (618) 751-3400.

SOUTHERN ILLINOIS-EDWARDSVILLE COUGARS

Conference: Ohio Valley.
Mailing Address: Box 1129 Edwardsville, IL 62026. **Website:** www.siuecougars.com.
Head Coach: Tony Stoecklin. **Telephone:** (618) 650-2331. **Baseball SID:** Joe Pott. **Telephone:** (618) 650-2860. **Fax:** (618) 650-3369.
Assistant Coaches: *Danny Jackson. **Telephone:** (618) 650-2032.

Home Field: Roy E. Lee Field at Simmons Baseball Complex. **Seating Capacity:** 1,000. **Outfield Dimensions: LF**—330, **CF**—390, **RF**—330. **Press Box Telephone:** (314) 707-1712.

SOUTHERN MISSISSIPPI GOLDEN EAGLES

Conference: Conference USA.
Mailing Address: 118 College Dr., Hattiesburg, MS 39402. **Website:** www.southernmiss.com.
Head Coach: Scott Berry. **Telephone:** (601) 266-6542. **Baseball SID:** Jack Duggan. **Telephone:** (601) 266-5947. **Fax:** (601) 266-4507.
Assistant Coaches: *Chad Caillet, Michael Federico. **Telephone:** (601) 266-5891.
Home Field: Pete Taylor Park. **Seating Capacity:** 6,600. **Outfield Dimensions: LF**—340, **CF**—400, **RF**—340. **Press Box Telephone:** (601) 266-5684.

STANFORD CARDINAL

Conference: Pacific-12.
Mailing Address: 641 E. Campus Dr., Stanford, CA 94305. **Website:** www.gostanford.com.
Head Coach: Mark Marquess. **Telephone:** (650) 723-4528. **Baseball SID:** Brett Moore. **Telephone:** (650) 725-2959. **Fax:** (650) 725-2957.
Assistant Coaches: *Rusty Filter, Ryan Garko. **Telephone:** (650) 723-9528.
Home Field: Klein Field at Sunken Diamond. **Seating Capacity:** 4,000. **Outfield Dimensions: LF**—335, **CF**—400, **RF**—335. **Press Box Telephone:** (650) 723-4629.

STEPHEN F. AUSTIN STATE LUMBERJACKS

Conference: Southland.
Mailing Address: P.O. Box 13010, SFA Station, Nacogdoches, TX 75962. **Website:** www.sfajacks.com.
Head Coach: Johnny Cardenas. **Telephone:** (936) 468-5982. **Baseball SID:** Ben Rikard. **Telephone:** (936) 468-5801. **Fax:** (936) 468-4593.
Assistant Coaches: *Chris Connally, Chad Massengale. **Telephone:** (936) 468-7796.
Home Field: Jaycees Field. **Seating Capacity:** 1,000. **Outfield Dimensions:** LF—320, CF—400, RF—320. **Press Box Telephone:** (936) 559-8344.

STETSON HATTERS

Conference: Atlantic Sun.
Mailing Address: 421 N. Woodland Blvd., DeLand, FL 32723. **Website:** www.gohatters.com.
Head Coach: Pete Dunn. **Telephone:** (386) 822-8106. **Baseball SID:** Cris Belvin. **Telephone:** (386) 822-8937. **Fax:** (386) 822-7486.
Assistant Coaches: *Mark Leavitt, Chris Roberts. **Telephone:** (386) 822-8733.
Home Field: Melching Field at Conrad Park. **Seating Capacity:** 2,500. **Outfield Dimensions: LF**—335, **CF**—403, **RF**—335. **Press Box Telephone:** (386) 736-7360.

STONY BROOK SEAWOLVES

Conference: America East.
Mailing Address: Indoor Sports Complex, Stony Brook, NY 11794. **Website:** goseawolves.org.
Head Coach: Matt Senk. **Telephone:** (631) 632-9226. **Baseball SID:** Thomas Chen. **Telephone:** (631) 632-7289. **Fax:** (631) 632-8841.
Assistant Coaches: Mike Marron, *Joe Pennucci.

Telephone: (631) 632-4755.
Home Field: Joe Nathan Field. **Seating Capacity:** 1,000. **Outfield Dimensions: LF**—330, **CF**—390, **RF**—330. **Press Box Telephone:** (914) 843-7185.

TEMPLE OWLS

Conference: American Athletic.
Mailing Address: 1800 N. Broad St., Philadelphia, PA 19121. **Website:** www.owlsports.com.
Head Coach: Ryan Wheeler. **Telephone:** (215) 204-8639. **Baseball SID:** Korey Blucas. **Telephone:** (215) 204-7446. **Fax:** (215) 933-5257.
Assistant Coaches: *Brian Pugh, Kevin Small. **Telephone:** (215) 204-8640.
Home Field: Skip Wilson Field. **Seating Capacity:** 1,000. **Press Box Telephone:** (609) 969-0975.

TENNESSEE VOLUNTEERS

Conference: Southeastern (East).
Mailing Address: 1551 Lake Loudoun Blvd., Knoxville, TN 37996. **Website:** www.utsports.com.
Head Coach: Dave Serrano. **Telephone:** (865) 974-2057. **Baseball SID:** Brian Bruce. **Telephone:** (865) 974-8876. **Fax:** (865) 974-1269.
Assistant Coaches: Greg Bergeron, *Aric Thomas. **Telephone:** (865) 974-2057.
Home Field: Lindsey Nelson Stadium. **Seating Capacity:** 3,800. **Outfield Dimensions: LF**—320, **CF**—404, **RF**—330. **Press Box Telephone:** (865) 974-3376.

TENNESSEE TECH GOLDEN EAGLES

Conference: Ohio Valley.
Mailing Address: 1100 McGeen Blvd., Box 5057, Cookeville, TN 38505. **Website:** www.ttusports.com.
Head Coach: Matt Bragga. **Telephone:** (931) 372-6546. **Baseball SID:** Larry Bragga. **Telephone:** (931) 372-6546. **Fax:** (931) 372-6145.
Assistant Coaches: Cody Church, *Brandon Turner. **Telephone:** (931) 372-6546.
Home Field: Quillen Field. **Seating Capacity:** 1,000. **Outfield Dimensions: LF**—331, **CF**—400, **RF**—329.

TENNESSEE-MARTIN SKYHAWKS

Conference: Ohio Valley.
Mailing Address: 15 Mt. Pelia Rd., 1022 Elam Center, Martin, TN 38237. **Website:** www.utmsports.com.
Head Coach: Brad Goss. **Telephone:** (731) 881-7337. **Baseball SID:** Ryne Rickman. **Telephone:** (731) 881-7632. **Fax:** (731) 881-7624.
Assistant Coaches: *Eric Ebers. **Telephone:** (731) 881-3691.
Home Field: Skyhawk Park. **Seating Capacity:** 500. **Outfield Dimensions: LF**—330, **CF**—385, **RF**—330. **Press Box Telephone:** (270) 703-2601.

TEXAS LONGHORNS

Conference: Big 12.
Mailing Address: 2139 San Jacinto Blvd., Austin, TX 78712. **Website:** www.texassports.com.
Head Coach: Augie Garrido. **Telephone:** (512) 471-5732. **Baseball SID:** Justin Moore. **Telephone:** (512) 232-9438. **Fax:** (512) 471-6040.
Assistant Coaches: Skip Johnson, *Tommy Nicholson. **Telephone:** (512) 471-5732.
Home Field: UFCU Disch-Falk Field. **Seating Capacity:** 6,756. **Box Telephone:** (512) 471-1146.

TEXAS A&M AGGIES

Conference: Southeastern (West).
Mailing Address: P.O. Box 30017, College Station, TX 77842. **Website:** www.aggieathletics.com.
Head Coach: Rob Childress. **Telephone:** (979) 845-4810. **Baseball SID:** Thomas Dick. **Telephone:** (979) 862-5486. **Fax:** (979) 845-6825.
Assistant Coaches: Andy Sawyers, *Justin Seely. **Telephone:** (979) 845-4810.
Home Field: Olsen Field at Blue Bell Park. **Seating Capacity:** 6,100. **Outfield Dimensions: LF**—330, **CF**—400, **RF**—330. **Press Box Telephone:** (979) 458-3604.

TEXAS A&M-CORPUS CHRISTI ISLANDERS

Conference: Southland.
Mailing Address: Islanders Athletics, 6300 Ocean Dr., Unit 5719, Corpus Christi, TX 78412. **Website:** www.goislanders.com.
Head Coach: Scott Malone. **Telephone:** (361) 825-3218. **Baseball SID:** Brett Winegarner. **Telephone:** (361) 825-3411. **Fax:** (361) 825-3218.
Assistant Coaches: *Brett Gips, Marty Smith. **Telephone:** (361) 825-3252.
Home Field: Chapman Field. **Seating Capacity:** 1,200. **Outfield Dimensions: LF**—335, **CF**—399, **RF**—325. **Press Box Telephone:** (337) 302-4722.

TEXAS CHRISTIAN HORNED FROGS

Conference: Big 12.
Mailing Address: 2900 Stadium Dr., Fort Worth, TX 76129. **Website:** www.gofrogs.com.
Head Coach: Jim Schlossnagle. **Telephone:** (817) 257-5354. **Baseball SID:** Brandie Davidson. **Telephone:** (817) 257-7479. **Fax:** (817) 257-7962.
Assistant Coaches: Bill Mosiello, *Kirk Saarloos. **Telephone:** (817) 257-5588.
Home Field: Lupton Stadium. **Seating Capacity:** 4,500. **Outfield Dimensions: LF**—330, **CF**—390, **RF**—325. **Press Box Telephone:** (817) 257-7966.

TEXAS SOUTHERN TIGERS

Conference: Southwestern Athletic.
Mailing Address: 3100 Cleburne Street, Houston, TX 77004. **Website:** www.tsu.edu.
Head Coach: Michael Robertson. **Telephone:** (713) 313-4315. **Baseball SID:** Rodney Bush. **Telephone:** (713) 313-7603. **Fax:** (713) 313-1045.
Assistant Coaches: *Marqus Johnson, Ehren Moreno. **Telephone:** (713) 313-4315.
Home Field: Macgregor Park. **Seating Capacity:** 500. **Outfield Dimensions:** LF—315, CF—390, RF—315.

TEXAS STATE BOBCATS

Conference: Sun Belt.
Mailing Address: Darren B. Casey Athletic Administration Complex, 601 University Dr., San Marcos, TX 78666. **Website:** www.txstatebobcats.com.
Head Coach: Ty Harrington. **Telephone:** (512) 245-3383. **Baseball SID:** Joshua Flanagan. **Telephone:** (512) 245-4387. **Fax:** (512) 245-8387.
Assistant Coaches: *Jeremy Fikac, Mike Silva. **Telephone:** (512) 245-8387.
Home Field: Bobcat Ballpark. **Seating Capacity:** 2,500. **Outfield Dimensions: LF**—335, **CF**—404, **RF**—335. **Press Box Telephone:** (940) 390-6853.

TEXAS TECH RED RAIDERS

Conference: Big 12.
Mailing Address: 2901 Drive of Champions, Lubbock, TX 79409. **Website:** www.texastech.com.
Head Coach: Tim Tadlock. **Telephone:** (806) 742-2770. **Baseball SID:** Scott Lacefield. **Telephone:** (806) 742-2770. **Fax:** (806) 742-1970.
Assistant Coaches: Ray Hayward, *J-Bob Thomas. **Telephone:** (806) 742-2770.
Home Field: Dan Law Field at Rip Griffin Park. **Seating Capacity:** 4,368. **Outfield Dimensions:** LF—330, CF—404, RF—330. **Press Box Telephone:** (817) 691-3786.

TEXAS-ARLINGTON MAVERICKS

Conference: Western Athletic.
Mailing Address: 1309 West Mitchell St., Arlington, TX 76019. **Website:** www.utamavs.com.
Head Coach: Darin Thomas. **Telephone:** (817) 272-2542. **Baseball SID:** Art Garcia. **Telephone:** (817) 272-2239. **Fax:** (817) 272-9524.
Assistant Coaches: *Jay Sirianni, Fuller Smith. **Telephone:** (817) 272-0111.
Home Field: Clay Gould Ballpark. **Seating Capacity:** 1,600. **Outfield Dimensions: LF**—330, **CF**—400, **RF**—330. **Press Box Telephone:** (817) 462-4225.

TEXAS-PAN AMERICAN BRONCS

Conference: Western Athletic.
Mailing Address: 1201 W. University Dr., Edinburg, TX 78539. **Website:** www.utpabroncs.com.
Head Coach: Manny Mantrana. **Telephone:** (956) 665-2235. **Baseball SID:** Jonah Goldberg. **Telephone:** (956) 665-2240. **Fax:** (956) 665-2261.
Assistant Coaches: Robert Clayton, *Norberto Lopez. **Telephone:** (956) 665-2891.
Home Field: Edinburg Baseball Stadium. **Seating Capacity:** 5,500. **Outfield Dimensions:** LF—325, CF—405, RF—325.

TEXAS-SAN ANTONIO ROADRUNNERS

Conference: Conference USA.
Mailing Address: One UTSA Circle, San Antonio, TX 78249. **Website:** www.goutsa.com.
Head Coach: Jason Marshall. **Telephone:** (210) 458-4811. **Baseball SID:** Brett Damaskos. **Telephone:** (210) 458-6460. **Fax:** (210) 458-4569.
Assistant Coaches: *Jim Blair, Brett Lawler. **Telephone:** (210) 458-4195.
Home Field: Roadrunner Field. **Seating Capacity:** 800. **Outfield Dimensions: LF**—335, **CF**—405, **RF**—340. **Press Box Telephone:** (210) 458-4612.

TOLEDO ROCKETS

Conference: Mid-American (West).
Mailing Address: 2801 West Bancroft St., MS-408, Toledo, OH 43606. **Website:** www.utrockets.com.
Head Coach: Cory Mee. **Telephone:** (419) 530-6263. **Baseball SID:** Brian Debenedictis. **Telephone:** (419) 530-4919. **Fax:** (419) 530-4428.
Assistant Coaches: *Josh Bradford, Nick McIntyre. **Telephone:** (419) 530-3097.
Home Field: Scott Park. **Seating Capacity:** 1,000. **Outfield Dimensions: LF**—330, **CF**—400, **RF**—330. **Press Box Telephone:** (419) 530-3089.

TOWSON TIGERS

Conference: Colonial Athletic.
Mailing Address: 8000 York Rd., Towson, MD 21152.
Website: www.towsontigers.com.
Head Coach: Mike Gottlieb. **Telephone:** (410) 704-3775. **Baseball SID:** Dan O'Connell. **Telephone:** (410) 704-3102. **Fax:** (410) 704-3861.
Assistant Coaches: Eric Franc, Scott Roane. **Telephone:** (410) 704-4587.
Home Field: John B. Schuerholz Park. **Seating Capacity:** 500. **Press Box Telephone:** (410) 704-5810.

TROY TROJANS

Conference: Sun Belt.
Mailing Address: 5000 Veterans Stadium Dr., Troy, AL 36082. **Website:** www.troytrojans.com.
Head Coach: Bobby Pierce. **Telephone:** (334) 670-3489. **Baseball SID:** Wes Johnson. **Telephone:** (334) 670-5655. **Fax:** (334) 670-5655.
Assistant Coaches: Brad Phillips, *Mark Smartt. **Telephone:** (334) 670-5705.
Home Field: Riddle-Pace Field. **Seating Capacity:** 2,200. **Outfield Dimensions:** LF—340, CF—400, RF—310. **Press Box Telephone:** (334) 670-5701.

TULANE GREEN WAVE

Conference: Conference USA.
Mailing Address: Tulane Athletics, Ben Weiner Dr., New Orleans, LA 70118. **Website:** www.tulanegreenwave.com.
Head Coach: Rick Jones. **Telephone:** (504) 862-8238. **Baseball SID:** Curtis Akey. **Telephone:** (504) 314-7271. **Fax:** (504) 862-8554.
Assistant Coaches: *Jake Gautreau, Chad Sutter. **Telephone:** (504) 314-7203.
Home Field: Greer Field at Turchin Stadium. **Seating Capacity:** 5,000. **Outfield Dimensions:** LF—325, CF—400, RF—325. **Press Box Telephone:** (504) 862-8244.

UTAH UTES

Conference: Pacific-12.
Mailing Address: 1825 E. South Campus Dr., Salt Lake City, UT 84112. **Website:** www.utahutes.com.
Head Coach: Bill Kinneberg. **Telephone:** (801) 581-3526. **Baseball SID:** Brooke Frederickson. **Telephone:** (801) 581-8302.
Assistant Coaches: *Mike Crawford, Bryan Kinneberg. **Telephone:** (801) 581-3024.
Home Field: Spring Mobile Ballpark. **Seating Capacity:** 15,500. **Outfield Dimensions:** LF—345, CF—420, RF—315.

UTAH VALLEY WOLVERINES

Conference: Western Athletic.
Mailing Address: 800 W. University Pkwy., Orem, UT 84058. **Website:** www.wolverinegreen.com.
Head Coach: Eric Madsen. **Telephone:** (801) 863-6509. **Baseball SID:** Clint Burgi. **Telephone:** (801) 863-8644. **Fax:** (801) 863-8813.
Assistant Coaches: Dave Carter, *Cooper Fouts. **Telephone:** (801) 863-8647.
Home Field: Brent Brown Ballpark. **Seating Capacity:** 5,000. **Outfield Dimensions:** LF—312, CF—408, RF—305. **Press Box Telephone:** (801) 362-1548.

VALPARAISO CRUSADERS

Conference: Horizon.
Mailing Address: 1009 Union St., Valparaiso, IN 46383. **Website:** www.valpoathletics.com.
Head Coach: Brian Schmack. **Telephone:** (219) 464-6117. **Baseball SID:** Brad Collignon. **Telephone:** (219) 464-5396. **Fax:** (219) 464-5762.
Assistant Coaches: Mike Stalowy, *Ben Wolgamot. **Telephone:** (219) 464-5239.
Home Field: Emory G. Bauer Field. **Seating Capacity:** 500. **Outfield Dimensions:** LF—330, CF—400, RF—330. **Press Box Telephone:** (219) 464-6006.

VANDERBILT COMMODORES

Conference: Southeastern (East).
Mailing Address: 2601 Jess Neely Dr., Nashville, TN 37212. **Website:** www.vucommodores.com.
Head Coach: Tim Corbin. **Telephone:** (615) 322-6594. **Baseball SID:** Kyle Parkinson. **Telephone:** (615) 343-0020. **Fax:** (615) 343-7064.
Assistant Coaches: Scott Brown, *Travis Jewett. **Telephone:** (615) 322-6594.
Home Field: Hawkins Field. **Seating Capacity:** 3,626. **Outfield Dimensions:** LF—310, CF—400, RF—330. **Press Box Telephone:** (615) 320-0436.

VILLANOVA WILDCATS

Conference: Big East.
Mailing Address: 800 E. Lancaster Ave., Jake Nevin Field House, Villanova, PA 19085. **Website:** www.villanova.com.
Head Coach: Joe Godri. **Telephone:** (610) 519-4529. **Baseball SID:** David Berman. **Telephone:** (610) 519-4122. **Fax:** (610) 519-7323.
Assistant Coaches: Kevin Mulvey, *Derek Shunk. **Telephone:** (610) 519-5520.
Home Field: Villanova Ballpark at Plymouth. **Seating Capacity:** 750. **Outfield Dimensions:** LF—330, CF—405, RF—330. **Press Box Telephone:** (860) 490-6398.

VIRGINIA CAVALIERS

Conference: Atlantic Coast (Coastal).
Mailing Address: P.O. Box 400853, Charlottesville, VA 22904. **Website:** www.virginiasports.com.
Head Coach: Brian O'Connor. **Telephone:** (434) 982-5131. **Baseball SID:** Andy Fledderjohann. **Telephone:** (434) 982-5131. **Fax:** (434) 982-5525.
Assistant Coaches: Karl Kuhn, *Kevin McMullan. **Telephone:** (434) 982-5776.
Home Field: Davenport Field. **Seating Capacity:** 4980. **Outfield Dimensions:** LF—332, CF—404, RF—332. **Press Box Telephone:** (434) 244-4071.

VIRGINIA COMMONWEALTH RAMS

Conference: Atlantic 10.
Mailing Address: 1300 W. Broad St., P.O. Box 842003, Richmond, VA 23284. **Website:** www.vcuathletics.com.
Head Coach: Shawn Stiffler. **Telephone:** (804) 828-4822. **Baseball SID:** Scott Day. **Telephone:** (804) 828-1727. **Fax:** (804) 828-4938.
Assistant Coaches: Kurt Elbin, *Jeff Palumbo. **Telephone:** (804) 828-4820.
Home Field: The Diamond. **Seating Capacity:** 9,689. **Outfield Dimensions:** LF—330, CF—405, RF—330. **Press Box Telephone:** (804) 263-6769.

VIRGINIA MILITARY INSTITUTE KEYDETS

Conference: Big South.
Mailing Address: Cameron Hall, Lexington, VA 24450.
Website: www.vmikeydets.com.
Head Coach: Marlin Ikenberry. **Telephone:** (540) 464-7609. **Baseball SID:** Brad Salois. **Telephone:** (540) 464-7015. **Fax:** (540) 464-7853.
Assistant Coaches: Travis Beazley, *Jonathan Hadra. **Telephone:** (540) 464-7605.
Home Field: Gray-Minor Stadium. **Seating Capacity:** 1,000. **Outfield Dimensions: LF**—330, **CF**—400, **RF**—330. **Press Box Telephone:** (940) 642-9865.

VIRGINIA TECH HOKIES

Conference: Atlantic Coast (Coastal).
Mailing Address: 460 Jamerson Athletic Center, Blacksburg, VA 24061. **Website:** www.hokiesports.com.
Head Coach: Patrick Mason. **Telephone:** (540) 231-3671. **Baseball SID:** Marc Mullen. **Telephone:** (540) 231-1894. **Fax:** (540) 231-6984.
Assistant Coaches: *Mike Kunigonis, Robert Woodard. **Telephone:** (540) 231-0398.
Home Field: English Field. **Seating Capacity:** 4,000. **Outfield Dimensions: LF**—330, **CF**—400, **RF**—330. **Press Box Telephone:** (540) 231-8974.

WAGNER SEAHAWKS

Conference: Northeast.
Mailing Address: Spiro Sports Center, 1 Campus Rd., Staten Island, NY 10301. **Website:** www.wagnerathletics.com.
Head Coach: Jim Carone. **Telephone:** (718) 390-3154. **Baseball SID:** Kevin Ross. **Telephone:** (718) 390-3215. **Fax:** (718) 420-4015.
Assistant Coaches: *Chris Collazo, Joe Mercurio. **Telephone:** (718) 420-4121.
Home Field: Richmond County Bank Ballpark. **Seating Capacity:** 7,171. **Outfield Dimensions: LF**—320, **CF**—390, **RF**—318. **Press Box Telephone:** (716) 969-6126.

WAKE FOREST DEMON DEACONS

Conference: Atlantic Coast (Atlantic).
Mailing Address: 1834 Wake Forest Dr., Winston-Salem, NC 27103. **Website:** www.wakeforestsports.com.
Head Coach: Tom Walter. **Telephone:** (336) 758-5570. **Baseball SID:** Nick Sebesta. **Telephone:** (336) 758-5842. **Fax:** (336) 758-5840.
Assistant Coaches: Bill Cilento, *Dennis Healy. **Telephone:** (336) 758-5645.
Home Field: Wake Forest Baseball Park. **Seating Capacity:** 6,000. **Outfield Dimensions: LF**—325, **CF**—400, **RF**—315. **Press Box Telephone:** (336) 759-7373.

WASHINGTON HUSKIES

Conference: Pacific-12.
Mailing Address: Graves Building, Box 354070, Seattle, WA 98021. **Website:** www.gohuskies.com.
Head Coach: Lindsay Meggs. **Telephone:** (206) 616-4335. **Baseball SID:** Brian Tom. **Telephone:** (206) 897-1742. **Fax:** (206) 543-5000.
Assistant Coaches: *Taylor Johnson, Jason Kelly. **Telephone:** (206) 685-7016.
Home Field: Husky Ballpark. **Seating Capacity:** 2,000. **Outfield Dimensions: LF**—327, **CF**—395, **RF**—317. **Press Box Telephone:** (206) 455-5361.

WASHINGTON STATE COUGARS

Conference: Pacific-12.
Mailing Address: Bohler Athletic Complex Room M40, P.O. Box 641602, Pullman, WA 99164. **Website:** www.wsucougars.com.
Head Coach: Donnie Marbut. **Telephone:** (509) 335-0368. **Baseball SID:** Craig Lawson. **Telephone:** (509) 335-0265. **Fax:** (509) 335-0267.
Assistant Coaches: Gregg Swenson, *Pat Waer. **Telephone:** (509) 335-0216.
Home Field: Bailey-Brayton Field. **Seating Capacity:** 3,500. **Outfield Dimensions: LF**—330, **CF**—400, **RF**—330. **Press Box Telephone:** (509) 432-9063.

WEST VIRGINIA MOUNTAINEERS

Conference: Big 12.
Mailing Address: P.O. Box 0877, Morgantown, WV 26507. **Website:** www.wvusports.com.
Head Coach: Randy Mazey. **Telephone:** (304) 293-9881. **Baseball SID:** Grant Dovey. **Telephone:** (304) 293-2821. **Fax:** (304) 293-4105.
Assistant Coaches: *Derek Matlock, Steven Trout. **Telephone:** (304) 293-0067.
Home Field: Hawley Field. **Seating Capacity:** 1,500. **Outfield Dimensions: LF**—325, **CF**—390, **RF**—325. **Press Box Telephone:** (304) 293-6480.

WESTERN CAROLINA CATAMOUNTS

Conference: Southern.
Mailing Address: 92 Catamount Rd., Cullowhee, NC 28723. **Website:** www.catamountsports.com.
Head Coach: Bobby Moranda. **Telephone:** (828) 227-2021. **Baseball SID:** Daniel Hooker. **Telephone:** (828) 227-2339. **Fax:** (828) 227-7688.
Assistant Coaches: *Alan Beck, Bruce Johnson. **Telephone:** (828) 227-2022.
Home Field: Hennon Stadium. **Seating Capacity:** 1,500. **Outfield Dimensions: LF**—325, **CF**—395, **RF**—325. **Press Box Telephone:** (828) 227-7020.

WESTERN ILLINOIS FIGHTING LEATHERNECKS

Conference: Summit.
Mailing Address: 209 Western Hall, 1 University Circle, Macomb, IL 61455. **Website:** www.wiuathletics.com.
Head Coach: Ryan Brownlee. **Telephone:** (309) 298-1521. **Baseball SID:** Sean Ingrassia. **Telephone:** (309) 298-1133. **Fax:** (309) 298-1960.
Assistant Coaches: *Shane Davis, Dusty Napoleon. **Telephone:** (309) 298-1521.
Home Field: Alfred D. Boyer Stadium. **Seating Capacity:** 500. **Outfield Dimensions: LF**—330, **CF**—400, **RF**—330. **Press Box Telephone:** (309) 298-3492.

WESTERN KENTUCKY HILLTOPPERS

Conference: Sun Belt.
Mailing Address: 1605 Ave. of Champions, Bowling Green, KY 42101. **Website:** www.wkusports.com.
Head Coach: Matt Myers. **Telephone:** (270) 745-2493. **Baseball SID:** Jeremy Brown. **Telephone:** (270) 745-5388. **Fax:** (270) 745-2573.
Assistant Coaches: *Blake Allen, Brendan Dougherty. **Telephone:** (270) 745-2274.
Home Field: Nick Denes Field. **Seating Capacity:** 1,500. **Outfield Dimensions: LF**—330, **CF**—400, **RF**—330. **Press Box Telephone:** (270) 745-6941.

WESTERN MICHIGAN BRONCOS

Conference: Mid-American (West).
Mailing Address: 1903 W. Michigan Ave., Kalamazoo, MI 49008. **Website:** www.wmubroncos.com.
Head Coach: Billy Gernon. **Telephone:** (269) 276-3205. **Baseball SID:** Kristin Keirns. **Telephone:** (269) 387-4123. **Fax:** (269) 387-7063.
Assistant Coaches: Blaine McFerrin, *Adam Piotrowicz. **Telephone:** (269) 276-3208.
Home Field: Robert J. Bobb Stadium at Hyames Field. **Seating Capacity:** 1,500. **Outfield Dimensions:** LF—310, CF—395, RF—335.

WICHITA STATE SHOCKERS

Conference: Missouri Valley.
Mailing Address: 1845 Fairmount, Wichita, KS 67260. **Website:** www.goshockers.com.
Head Coach: Todd Butler. **Telephone:** (316) 978-3636. **Baseball SID:** Tami Cutler. **Telephone:** (316) 978-5559. **Fax:** (316) 978-3336.
Assistant Coaches: Brent Kemnitz, *Brian Walker. **Telephone:** (316) 978-5302.
Home Field: Eck Stadium. **Seating Capacity:** 7,851. **Outfield Dimensions:** LF—330, CF—390, RF—330. **Press Box Telephone:** (316) 978-3390.

WILLIAM & MARY TRIBE

Conference: Colonial Athletic.
Mailing Address: 751 Ukrop Way, Williamsburg, VA 23185. **Website:** www.tribeathletics.com.
Head Coach: Brian Murphy. **Telephone:** (757) 221-3492. **Baseball SID:** Andrew Phillips. **Telephone:** (757) 221-3344. **Fax:** (757) 221-2048.
Assistant Coaches: *Brian Casey. **Telephone:** (757) 221-3475.
Home Field: Plumeri Park. **Seating Capacity:** 1,000. **Outfield Dimensions:** LF—325, CF—400, RF—325. **Press Box Telephone:** (757) 221-3998.

WINTHROP EAGLES

Conference: Big South.
Mailing Address: 1162 Eden Terrace, Rock Hill, SC 29733. **Website:** www.winthropeagles.com.
Head Coach: Tom Riginos. **Telephone:** (803) 323-2129. **Baseball SID:** Rick Rogers. **Telephone:** (803) 323-6067. **Fax:** (803) 323-2303.
Assistant Coaches: *Clint Chrysler, Ben Hall. **Telephone:** (803) 323-2129.
Home Field: Winthrop Ballpark. **Seating Capacity:** 1,800. **Outfield Dimensions:** LF—325, CF—390, RF—325. **Press Box Telephone:** (803) 323-2155.

WISCONSIN-MILWAUKEE PANTHERS

Conference: Horizon.
Mailing Address: 3409 N. Downer Ave., Milwaukee, WI 53211. **Website:** www.uwmpanthers.com.
Head Coach: Scott Doffek. **Telephone:** (414) 229-5670. **Baseball SID:** Chris Zills. **Telephone:** (414) 229-4593. **Fax:** (414) 229-5749.
Assistant Coaches: Cory Bigler. **Telephone:** (414) 229-2433.
Home Field: Henry Aaron Field. **Outfield Dimensions:** LF—315, CF—390, RF—315. **Press Box Telephone:** (414) 750-2090.

WOFFORD TERRIERS

Conference: Southern.
Mailing Address: 429 N. Church St., Spartanburg, SC 29303. **Website:** www.athletics.wofford.edu.
Head Coach: Todd Interdonato. **Telephone:** (864) 597-4497. **Baseball SID:** Brent Williamson. **Telephone:** (864) 597-4093. **Fax:** (864) 597-4129.
Assistant Coaches: *Jason Burke, J.J. Edwards. **Telephone:** (864) 597-4499.
Home Field: Russell C. King Field. **Seating Capacity:** 1,600. **Outfield Dimensions:** LF—325, CF—395, RF—325. **Press Box Telephone:** (864) 597-4487.

WRIGHT STATE RAIDERS

Conference: Horizon.
Mailing Address: 3640 Colonel Glenn Hwy., Dayton, OH 45435. **Website:** www.wsuraiders.com.
Head Coach: Greg Lovelady. **Telephone:** (937) 775-3668. **Baseball SID:** Matt Zircher. **Telephone:** (937) 775-2831. **Fax:** (937) 775-2368.
Assistant Coaches: *Jeff Mercer, Justin Parker. **Telephone:** (937) 775-4188.
Home Field: Nischwitz Stadium. **Seating Capacity:** 750. **Outfield Dimensions:** LF—330, CF—400, RF—330. **Press Box Telephone:** (937) 304-6586.

XAVIER MUSKETEERS

Conference: Big East.
Mailing Address: 3800 Victory Pkwy., Cincinnati, OH 45207. **Website:** www.goxavier.com.
Head Coach: Scott Googins. **Telephone:** (513) 745-2891. **Baseball SID:** Bryan McEldowney. **Telephone:** (513) 745-3388. **Fax:** (513) 745-2825.
Assistant Coaches: Billy O'Conner, *Nick Otte. **Telephone:** (513) 745-2890.
Home Field: Hayden Field. **Seating Capacity:** 500. **Outfield Dimensions:** LF—310, CF—380, RF—310. **Press Box Telephone:** (937) 478-5027.

YALE BULLDOGS

Conference: Ivy League (Rolfe).
Mailing Address: 20 Tower Parkway, New Haven, CT 06511. **Website:** yalebulldogs.com.
Head Coach: John Stuper. **Telephone:** (203) 432-1466. **Baseball SID:** Jon Erickson. **Telephone:** (203) 432-4747.
Assistant Coaches: *Tucker Frawley, Ray Guarino. **Telephone:** (203) 432-1467.
Home Field: Yale Field. **Seating Capacity:** 6,000.

YOUNGSTOWN STATE PENGUINS

Conference: Horizon.
Mailing Address: Youngstown State Baseball, 1 University Plaza, Youngstown, OH 44555. **Website:** www.ysusports.com.
Head Coach: Steve Gillispie. **Telephone:** (330) 941-3485. **Baseball SID:** John Vogel. **Telephone:** (330) 941-1480. **Fax:** (330) 941-3191.
Assistant Coaches: *Jason Neal, Kevin Smallcomb. **Telephone:** (304) 633-8150.
Home Field: Eastwood Field. **Seating Capacity:** 6,000. **Outfield Dimensions:** LF—335, CF—380, RF—335. **Press Box Telephone:** (330) 505-0000, Ext. 229.

AMATEUR
& YOUTH

INTERNATIONAL ORGANIZATIONS

INTERNATIONAL BASEBALL FEDERATION

Headquarters: Maison du Sport International—54, Avenue de Rhodanie, 1007 Lausanne, Switzerland. **Telephone:** (+41-21) 318-82-40. **Fax:** (41-21) 318-82-41. **Website:** www.ibaf.org. **E-Mail:** office@ibaf.org. **Year Founded:** 1938.
President: Riccardo Fraccari.
1st Vice President: Alonso Perez Gonzalez. **2nd Vice President:** Tom Peng. **3rd Vice President:** Antonio Castro. **Secretary General:** Israel Roldan. **Treasurer:** Angelo Vicini. **Members at Large:** Masaaki Nagino, Paul Seiler, Luis Melero. **Continental VP, Africa:** Ishola Williams. **Continental VP, Americas:** Jorge Otsuka. **Continental VP, Asia:** Byung-Suk Lee. **Continental VP, Europe:** Jan Esselman. **Continental VP, Oceania:** Rob Finlay. **Executive Director:** Michael Schmidt.
Assistant to the President: Oscar Lopez. **Media Relations Coordinator:** Riccardo Schiroli. **Global Marketing:** International Events Manager: Masaru Yokoo Chief Public Relations Officer: Oscar Lopez. **Operations/National Federation Relations:** Francesca Fabretto. **Antidoping Officer:** Victor Isola. **Administration/Finance:** Sandrine Pennone.

CONTINENTAL ASSOCIATIONS

CONFEDERATION PAN AMERICANA DE BEISBOL (COPABE)

Mailing Address: Calle 3, Francisco Filos, VIsta Hermosa, Edificio 74, Planta Baja Local No. **1, Panama City, Panama. Telephone:** (507) 229-8684. **Fax:** Unavailable. **Website:** www.copabe.net. **E-Mail:** copabe@sinfo.net.
Chairman: Eduardo De Bello (Panama). **Secretary General:** Hector Pereyra (Dominican Republic).

AFRICAN BASEBALL/SOFTBALL ASSOCIATION

Mailing Address: Paiko Road, Changaga, Minna, Niger State, PMB 150, Nigeria. **Telephone:** (234-66) 224-555. **Fax:** (234-66) 224-555. **E-Mail Address:** absasecretariat@yahoo.com.
President: Ishola Williams (Nigeria). **Vice President/Baseball:** Etienne N'guessan. **Vice President/Softball:** Fridah Shiroya.

BASEBALL FEDERATION OF ASIA

Mailing Address: No. 946-16 Dogok-Dong, Kangnam-Gu, Seoul, 135-270 Korea. **Telephone:** (82-2) 572-8413. **Fax:** (82-2) 572-8416.
President: Tom Peng. **Vice Presidents:** Suzuki Yoshinobu, Kim Jong-Up, Shen Wei (China). **Secretary General:** Hua-Wei Lin. **Members At Large:** Allan Mak, Tom Navasero, Vutichai Udomkarnjananan.

EUROPEAN BASEBALL CONFEDERATION

Mailing Address: Otto-FleckSchneise 12, D—60528 Frankfurt, Germany. **Telephone:** +49-69-6700-284. **Fax:** +49-69-67724-212. **E-Mail Address:** office@baseballeurope.com. **Website:** baseballeurope.com.
President: Jan Esselman (Netherlands). **1st Vice President:** Peter Kurz (Israel). **2nd Vice President:** Jürgen Elsishans (Germany). **3rd Vice President:** Petr Ditrich (Czech Republic). **Secretary General:** Lars Sundin Treasurer: Rene Laforce (Belgium). **Vocals:** Mick Manning (Ireland), Mats Fransson (Sweden), Monique Schmitt (Switzerland), Didier Seminet (France), Valentinas Bubulis (Lithuania).

BASEBALL CONFEDERATION OF OCEANIA

Mailing Address: 48 Partridge Way, Mooroolbark, Victoria 3138, Australia. **Telephone:** 613 9727 1779. **Fax:** 613 9727 5959. **E-Mail Address:** bcosecgeneral@basebal' loceania.com. **Website:** www.baseballoceania.com.
President: Bob Steffy (Guam). **1st Vice President:** Laurent Cassier (New Caledonia). **2nd Vice President:** Victor Langkilde (American Samoa). **Secretary General:** Chet Gray (Australia). **Executive Committee:** Rose Igitol (CNMI), Temmy Shmull (Palau), Innoke Niubalavu (Fiji).

ORGANIZATIONS

INTERNATIONAL GOODWILL SERIES, INC.

Mailing Address: 982 Slate Drive, Santa Rosa, CA 95405. **Telephone:** (707) 538-0777. **E-Mail Address:** bobw.24@goodwillseries.org. **Website:** www.goodwillseries.org.
President, Goodwill Series, Inc.: Bob Williams.

INTERNATIONAL SPORTS GROUP

Mailing Address: 3135 South Vermont Ave., Milwaukee, WI 53207. **Telephone:** (541) 882-4293. **E-Mail Address:** isgbaseball@yahoo.com. **Website:** www.isg-baseball.com.
President: Tom O'Connell. **Vice President:** Peter Caliendo.
Secretary/Treasurer: Randy Town. **Board Members:** Jim Jones, Rick Steen, Bill Mathews, Pat Doyle. **Founder/Senior Consultant:** Bill Arce.

NATIONAL ORGANIZATIONS

USA BASEBALL

Mailing Address, Corporate Headquarters: 403 Blackwell St., Durham, NC 27701. **Telephone:** (919) 474-8721. **Fax:** (919) 474-8822. **Email Address:** info@usabaseball.com. **Website:** www.usabaseball.com.
President: Mike Gaski. **Treasurer:** Jason Dobis. **Board of Directors:** Jenny Dalton-Hill, John McHale, Jr. (Major League Baseball), Wes Skelton (Dixie Baseball), Steve Keener (Little League), Steve Tellefsen (Babe Ruth), Damani Leech (NCAA); John Gall (Recent Athlete), George Grande (At Large).
Executive Director/Chief Executive Officer: Paul Seiler. **Director, National Team Development Programs/Women's National Team:** Ashley Bratcher. **General Manager, National Teams:** Eric Campbell. **Chief Financial Officer:** Ray Darwin. **Director, Travel Services:** Jocelyn Fern. **Assistant Director, Operations:** Tom Gottlieb. **Director, Digital/Social Media:** Kevin Jones. **Assistant Director, Accounting/Finance:** Cicely

Lopez. **Chief Operating Officer:** David Perkins. **Director, Development:** Rick Riccobono. **Director, Community Relations:** Lindsay Robertson. **Director, 18U National Team/Alumni:** Brant Ust.

National Members: Amateur Athletic Union (AAU), American Amateur Baseball Congress (AABC), American Baseball Coaches Association (ABCA), American Legion Baseball, Babe Ruth Baseball, Dixie Baseball, Little LeagueBaseball, National Amateur Baseball Federation (NABF), National Association of Intercollegiate Athletics (NAIA), National Baseball Congress (NBC), National Collegiate Athletic Association (NCAA), National Federation of State High School Athletic Associations, National High School Baseball Coaches Association (BCA), National Junior College Athletic Association (NJCAA), Police Athletic League (PAL), PONY Baseball, T-Ball USA, United States Specialty Sports Association (USSSA), YMCAs of the USA.

Events: www.usabaseball.com/events/schedule.jsp.

BASEBALL CANADA

Mailing Address: 2212 Gladwin Cres., Suite A7, Ottawa, Ontario K1B 5N1. **Telephone:** (613) 748-5606. **Fax:** (613) 748-5767. **Email Address:** info@baseball.ca. **Website:** www.baseball.ca.

Director General: Jim Baba. **Head Coach/Director, National Teams:** Greg Hamilton. **Manager, Baseball Operations:** Andre Lachance. **Program Coordinator:** Kelsey McIntosh. **Manager, Media/Public Relations:** Adam Morissette. **Administrative Coordinator:** Denise Thomas. **Administrative Assistant:** Penny Baba.

NATIONAL BASEBALL CONGRESS

Mailing Address: 300 S. Sycamore, Wichita, KS 67213. **Telephone:** (316) 264-6887. **Fax:** (316) 264-2129. **Website:** www.nbcbaseball.com. **Year Founded:** 1931.

General Manager: Josh Robertson. **Tournament Director:** Casey Walkup.

ATHLETES IN ACTION

Mailing Address: 651 Taylor Dr., Xenia, OH 45385. **Telephone:** (937) 352-1000. **Fax:** (937) 352-1245. **Email Address:** baseball@athletesinaction.org. **Website:** www.aiabaseball.org.

Director, AIA Baseball: Chris Beck. **General Manager, Alaska:** Chris Beck. **General Manager, Great Lakes:** John Henschen. **General Manager, New York Collegiate League:** Chris Rainwater. **International Teams Director:** John McLaughlin. **Youth Baseball Director:** Matt Richter.

SUMMER COLLEGE LEAGUES

NATIONAL ALLIANCE OF COLLEGE SUMMER BASEBALL

Telephone: (508) 404-7403. **E-Mail Address:** pgalop@comcast.net. **Website:** www.nacsb.org

Executive Directors: Bobby Bennett (Sunbelt Baseball League), Jeff Carter (Southern Collegiate Baseball League). **Assistant Executive Director:** David Biery (Valley Baseball League). **Treasurer:** Larry Tremitiere (Southern Collegiate Baseball League). **Director, Public Relations/Secretary:** Stefano Foggi (Florida Collegiate Summer League). **Compliance Officer:** Kim Lance (Great Lakes Summer Collegiate League).

Member Leagues: Atlantic Collegiate Baseball League, Cal Ripken Collegiate Baseball League, Cape Cod Baseball League, Florida Collegiate Summer League, Great Lakes Summer Collegiate League, New England Collegiate Baseball League, New York Collegiate Baseball League, Southern Collegiate Baseball League, Sunbelt Baseball League, Valley Baseball League.

ALASKA BASEBALL LEAGUE

Mailing Address: PO Box 318, Kenai, AK, 99611. **Telephone:** (907) 283-6186. **Fax:** (907) 746-5068. **E-Mail Address:** mikebaxter@acsalaska.net.

Year Founded: 1974 (reunited, 1998).

President: James Clark (Peninsula Oilers). **1st VP, Rules/Membership:** Chris Beck (Chugiak-Eagle River Chinooks). **2nd VP, Umpiring:** Pete Christopher (Mat-Su Miners). **3rd VP, Marketing:** Jon Dyson (Anchorage Glacier Pilots). **4th VP, Scheduling:** Todd Dennis (Goldpanners). **5th VP, Secretary:** Shawn Maltby (Anchorage Bucs). **League Spokesperson:** Mike Baxter.

Regular Season: 40 league games and approximately 5 non-league games. **2014 Opening Date:** June 8. **Closing Date:** July 31.

Playoff Format: Regular season league champion qualifies for National Baseball Congress World Series if desired. Also, a round robin end-of-season tournament with a best 2-of-3 final determines playoff champion.

Roster Limit: 26 plus exemption for Alaska residents. **Player Eligibility:** Open except drafted college seniors.

ANCHORAGE BUCS

Mailing Address: PO Box 240061, Anchorage, AK 99524-0061. **Telephone:** (907) 561-2827. **Fax:** (907) 561-2920. **E-Mail Address:** gm@anchoragebucs.com. **Website:** anchoragebucs.com. **General Manager:** Shawn Maltby. **Head Coach:** Tony Cappuccilli (UNLV). **Field:** Mulcahy Field—Turf infield, grass outfield, lights.

ANCHORAGE GLACIER PILOTS

Mailing Address: 435 West 10th Avenue, Suite A, Anchorage, AK 99501. **Telephone:** (907) 274-3627. **Fax:** (907) 274-3628. **E-Mail Address:** gpilots@alaska.net. **Website:** glacierpilots.com. **General Manager:** Jon Dyson. **Head Coach:** Conor Bird (CC of Marin, Calif.). **Field:** Mulcahy Field—turf infield, grass outfield, lights.

CHUGIAK-EAGLE RIVER CHINOOKS

Mailing Address: 651 Taylor Dr, Xenia, OH 45385. **Telephone:** (937) 352-1237. **Fax:** (937) 352-1245. **E-Mail Address:** chris.beck@athletesinaction.org. **Website:** www.aiabaseball.org. **Additional Website:** www.cerchinooks.com. **General Manager:** Chris Beck. **Head Coach:** Jon Groth (Tyler, Texas, CC). **Field:** Loretta French Field—grass, no lights.

FAIRBANKS ALASKA GOLDPANNERS

Mailing Address: 1747 Crosson Ave., Fairbanks, AK, 99707. **Telephone:** (907) 451-0095, (619) 561-4581. **Fax:** (907) 456-6429, (619) 561-4581. **E-Mail Address:** todd@

goldpanners.com. **Website:** goldpanners.com. **General Manager:** Todd Dennis. **Head Coach:** Mike Grahovac (Concordia Irvine, Calif.). **Field:** Growden Memorial Park – turf infield, grass outfield, lights.

MAT-SU MINERS

Mailing Address: PO Box 2690, Palmer, AK 99645-2690. **Telephone:** (907) 746-4914; (907) 745-6401. **Fax:** (907) 746-5068. **E-Mail Address:** generalmanager@matsuminers.org. **Website:** matsuminers.org. **General Manager:** Pete Christopher. **Assistant GM:** Bob Plumley. **Head Coach:** Ben Taylor (Chandler-Gilbert, CC).

PENINSULA OILERS

Mailing Address: 601 S Main St, Kenai, AK 99611. **Telephone:** (907) 283-7133. **Fax:** (907) 283-3390. **E-Mail Address:** gm@oilersbaseball.com. **Website:** oilersbaseball.com. **General Manager:** James Clark. **Head Coach:** Kyle Richardson (Yuba, Calif., CC). **Field:** Coral Seymour Memorial Park—grass, no lights.

ALL AMERICAN COLLEGIATE BASEBALL LEAGUE

Mailing Address: 8442 Sandowne Ln, Huntersville NC 28078. **Website:** www.allamericanleague.com. **VP/CFO:** Joseph Finch. **Telephone:** 304-685-3532. **Commissioner:** Paul Busa. **Telephone:** 617-543-4247. **Email Address:** coachbusa@gmail.com.

Founded: 2013.

Participating Teams: Mooresville All Americans (Mooresville, NC), Carolina Freedom (Morganton, NC), North Carolina Liberty (Salisbury, NC), Rowan Patriots (Spencer, NC), Stanly Pioneers (Oakboro, NC), Mt Pleasant Militia (Mt Pleasant, NC), Caldwell Warriors (Lenoir, NC).

ATLANTIC COLLEGIATE BASEBALL LEAGUE

Mailing Address: 1760 Joanne Drive, Quakertown, PA 18951. **Telephone:** (215) 536-5777. **Fax:** (215) 536-5777. **E-Mail:** tbonekemper@verizon.net. **Website:** www.acbl-online.com.

Year Founded: 1967.

Commissioner: Ralph Addonizio. **President:** Tom Bonekemper. **Assistant Commissioner:** Doug Cinella. **Vice Presidents:** Brian Casey, Ben Smookler. **Secretary:** Nick Rizzacasa. **Treasurer:** Bob Hoffman.

Regular Season: 40 games. **2014 Opening Date:** Unavailable. **Closing Date:** Unavailable. **All-Star Game:** Unavailable. **Roster Limit:** 25.

ALLENTOWN RAILERS

Mailing Address: Suite 202, 1801 Union Blvd, Allentown, PA 18109. **E-Mail Address:** ddando@lehighvalleybaseballacademy.com. **Field Manager:** Dylan Dando.

JERSEY PILOTS

Mailing Address: 401 Timber Dr, Berkeley Heights, NJ 07922. **Telephone:** (908) 464-8042. **E-Mail Address:** bensmookler@aol.com. **President/General Manager:** Ben Smookler. **Field Manager:** Aaron Kalb.

LEHIGH VALLEY CATZ

Mailing Address: 103 Logan Dr, Easton, PA 18045. **Telephone:** (610) 533-9349. **Website:** www.lvcatz.com. **General Manager:** Tom Lisinicchia. **Field Manager:** Dennis Morgan.

NORTH JERSEY EAGLES

Mailing Address: 107 Pleasant Avenue, Upper Saddle River, NJ 07458. **General Manager:** Brian Casey. **Field Manager:** Jorge Hernandez.

QUAKERTOWN BLAZERS

Telephone: (215) 679-5072. **E-Mail Address:** gbonekemper@yahoo.com. **Website:** www.quakertownblazers.com. **General Manager:** Jerry Mayza. **Field Manager:** Mark Angelo.

SOUTH JERSEY GIANTS

Website: www.southjerseygiants.com. **Field Manager:** Greg Manco (gmanco@sju.edu).

STATEN ISLAND TIDE

Website: www.statenislandtide.com. **General Manager:** Gary Sutphen. **Field Manager:** Tommy Weber.

TRENTON GENERALS

E-Mail Address: gally22@aol.com. **General Manager:** Dave Gallagher. **Field Manager:** Jim Maher.

CALIFORNIA COLLEGIATE LEAGUE

Mailing Address: 806 W Pedregosa St, Santa Barbara, CA 93101. **Telephone:** (805) 680-1047. **Fax:** (805) 684-8596. **Email Address:** burns@calsummerball.com. **Website:** www.calsummerball.com.

Founded: 1993.

Commissioner: Pat Burns.

Division Structure: North Division—Bakersfield Sound, Conejo Oaks, San Luis Obispo Blues, Santa Barbara Foresters. South—Academy Barons, Los Angeles Brewers, Southern California Catch, Team Vegas Baseball Club.

Regular Season: 36 games (24 divisional games, 12 inter-divisional games). **2014 Opening Date:** June 1. **Closing Date:** July 31. **Playoff Format:** Divisional champions meet in a best two-out-of-three championship series. **Roster Limit:** 33.

ACADEMY BARONS

Address: 901 E. **Artesia Blvd, Compton, CA 90221.** **Telephone:** (310) 635-2967. **Website:** www.academybarons.org. **Email Address:** tavelli08@gmail.com. **Director:** Don Buford. **Field Manager:** Tip Lefebvre.

BAKERSFIELD SOUND

Address: PO Box 20760, Bakersfield, CA 93390. **Telephone:** (661) 343-2616. **Website:** www.calsummerball.com. **Email Address:** bakersfieldsound.baseball@yahoo.com. **General Manager:** Dave Packer. **Field Manager:** Rob Paramo.

CONEJO OAKS

Address: 1710 N. Moorpark Rd., #106, Thousand Oaks, CA91360. **Telephone:** (805) 797-7889. **Fax:** (805) 529-9862. **Email Address:** oaksbaseball@roadrunner.com. **Website:** www.oaksbaseball.org. **General Managers:** Randy Riley, Verne Merrill. **Field Manager:** David Soilz.

LOS ANGELES BREWERS

Address: 2312 Park Ave., #413, Tustin CA 92626. **Telephone:** (949) 278-2458. **Email Address:** jwicks@labrewersbaseball.com. **Website:** www.labrewersbase-

ball.com. **General Manager/Field Manager:** Jameson Wicks.

SAN LUIS OBISPO BLUES

Address: 241-B Prado Rd., San Luis Obispo, CA 93401. **Telephone:** (805) 215-6660. **Fax:** (805) 528-1146. **Email Address:** chal@bluesbaseball.com. **Website:** www.blues-baseball.com. **General Manager:** Adam Stowe. **Field Manager:** Chal Fanning.

SANTA BARBARA FORESTERS

Address: 4299 Carpinteria Ave., Suite 201, Carpinteria, CA 93013. **Telephone:** (805) 684-0657. **Email Address:** foresters19@dock.net. **Website:** www.sbforesters.org. **General Manager/Field Manager:** Bill Pintard.

SOUTHERN CALIFORNIA CATCH

Address: 14830 Grayville Drive, La Mirada, CA 90638. **Telephone:** (562) 686-8262. **Email Address:** borr@fca.org. **Website:** www.socalcatch.com. **General Manager:** Ben Orr.

TEAM VEGAS BASEBALL CLUB

Address: 9265 Euphoria Rose Ave., **Las Vegas NV 89166. Telephone:** (702) 575-9394. **Email Address:** rangerbuck2002@yahoo.com. **Website:** www.teamvegasbaseball.com. **General Manager/Field Manager:** Buck Thomas.

CAL RIPKEN COLLEGIATE LEAGUE

Address: 4006 Broadstone St, Frederick, MD 21704. **Telephone:** 301-693-2577. **E-Mail:** jwoodward@calripkenleague.org or brifkin@calripkenleague.org. **Website:** www.calripkenleague.org.

Year Founded: 2005.

Commissioner: Jason Woodward. **League President:** Brad Rifkin. **Deputy Commissioner:** Jerry Wargo.

Regular Season: 40 games. **2014 Opening Date:** June 4. **Closing Date:** July 26. **All-Star Game:** July 16. **LCS Format:** same as last year, July 28 to August 3.

Roster Limit: 30 (college-eligible players 22 and under).

ALEXANDRIA ACES·

Address: 600 14th Street NW, Suite 400, Washington, DC 20005. **Telephone:** (202) 255-1683. **E-Mail:** ddinan@ralaw.com. **Website:** www.alexandriaaces.org. **Chairman/CEO:** Donald Dinan. **VP Operations/GM:** Don Kaniewski. **Head Coach:** David DeSilva. **Ballpark:** Frank Mann Field at Four Mile Run Park.

BALTIMORE REDBIRDS

Address: 2208 Pine Hill Farms Lane, Cockeysville, MD 21030. **Telephone:** (410) 802-2220. **Fax:** (410) 785-6138. **E-Mail:** johntcarey@hotmail.com. **Website:** www.baltimoreredbirds.org. **President:** John Carey. **Head Coach:** Michael Carter. **Ballpark:** Carlo Crispino Stadium at Calvert Hall High School.

BETHESDA BIG TRAIN

Address: 5420 Butler Road, Bethesda, MD 20816. **Telephone:** 301-365-1076. **Fax:** 301- 229-8362. **E-Mail:** faninfo@bigtrain.org. **Website:** www.bigtrain.org. **General Manager:** Adam Dantus. **Head Coach:** Sal Colangelo. **Ballpark:** Shirley Povich Field.

D.C. GRAYS

Address: 900 19th Street NW, 8th floor, Washington, DC 20006. **Telephone:** (202) 327-8116. **Fax:** (202) 327-8101. **Website:** www.dcgrays.com. **E-Mail Address:** barbera@acg-consultants.com. **President/Chairman:** Michael Barbera. **General Manager:** Antonio Scott. **Head Coach:** Arlan Freeman. **Ballpark:** Hoy Field at Gallaudet University.

GAITHERSBURG GIANTS

Address: 10 Brookes Avenue, Gaithersburg, MD 20877. **Telephone:** (240) 888-6810. **Fax:** (301) 355-5006. **E-Mail:** alriley13@gmail.com. **Website:** www.gaithersburggiants.org. **General Manager:** Alfie Riley. **Head Coach:** Jeff Rabberman. **Ballpark:** Criswell Automotive Field at Kelley Park.

FCA HERNDON BRAVES

Address: 1305 Kelly Court, Herndon, VA 20170-2605. **Telephone:** (702) 909-2750. **Fax:** (703) 783-1319. **E-Mail:** fcaherndonbraves@yahoo.com. **Website:** www.herndon-braves.com. **President & General Manager:** Todd Burger. **Head Coach:** Justin Janis. **Ballpark:** Alan McCullock Field at Herndon High School.

PRESSTMAN CARDINALS

Address: 10441 Hickory Ridge Road L, Columbia, MD 21044. **Telephone:** 410-300-7059. **Fax:** (410) 730-4620. **E-Mail:** presstmancards@hotmail.com. **Website:** www.presstmancardinals.org. **President/Head Coach:** Reginald Smith. **General Manager:** Ray Hale. **Ballpark:** Joe Cannon Stadium.

ROCKVILLE EXPRESS

Address: PO Box 10188, Rockville, MD 20849. **Telephone:** 301-367-9435. **E-Mail:** info@rockvilleexpress.org. **Website:** www.rockvilleexpress.org. **President/GM:** Jim Kazunas. **Email:** jameskazunas@rockvilleexpress.org. **Head Coach:** Rick Price. **Ballpark:** Knights Field at Montgomery College-Rockville.

SILVER SPRING-TAKOMA T-BOLTS

Address: 906 Glaizewood Court, Takoma Park, MD 20912. **Telephone:** (301) 270-0794. **E-Mail:** tboltsbaseball@gmail.com. **Website:** www.tbolts.org. **General Manager:** David Stinson. **Head Coach:** Doug Remer. **Ballpark:** Blair Stadium at Montgomery Blair High School.

VIENNA RIVER DOGS

Address: 12703 Hitchcock Ct, Reston, VA 20191. **Telephone:** (703) 615-4396. **Fax:** (703) 904-1723. **E-Mail Address:** tickets@brucehallsports.com. **Website:** www.viennariverdogs.org. **President/General Manager/Head Coach:** Bruce Hall. **Ballpark:** James Madison High School.

YOUSE'S ORIOLES

Address: 3 Oyster Court, Baltimore, MD 21219. **Telephone:** (410) 477-3764. **E-Mail:** tnt017@comcast.net. **Website:** www.youseorioles.com. **General Manager/Head Coach:** Tim Norris. **Ballpark:** Bachman Park.

CAPE COD LEAGUE

Mailing Address: PO Box 266, Harwich Port, MA 02646. **Telephone:** (508) 404-8597. **E-Mail:** info@capecodbaseball.org. **Website:** www.capecodbaseball.org.

Year Founded: 1885.
Commissioner: Paul Galop. **President:** Judy Walden Scarafile. **Treasurer/Webmaster:** Steven Wilson. **Secretary:** Kim Wolfe. **Senior Vice President:** Jim Higgins. **VP/Deputy Commissioner:** Bill Bussiere. **VP:** Peter Ford. **Senior Deputy Commissioner/Director of Officiating:** Sol Yas. **Deputy Commissioner, West:** Jim McNally. **Deputy Commissioner, East:** Peter Hall. **Deputy Commissioner Emeritus:** Dick Sullivan.
Director, Public Relations/Broadcasting: John Garner Jr. **Director, Communications:** Jim McGonigle. **Director, Publications:** Lou Barnicle. **Director, Memorabilia:** Dan Dunn. **Editor, Publications:** Rich Plante. **Assistant to the Officers:** Bill Watson. **Assistants, Marketing:** Melissa Ellis, Sue Pina. **Director, Social Media:** Ashley Crosby. **Coordinator, Special Events/Projects:** Joe Sherman. **Website Editor:** Victoria Martin.
Division Structure: East—Brewster, Chatham, Harwich, Orleans, Yarmouth-Dennis. West—Bourne, Cotuit, Falmouth, Hyannis, Wareham. **Regular Season:** 44 games. **2014 Opening Date:** June 11. **Closing Date:** August 13. **All-Star Game:** July 26. **Playoff Format:** Top four teams in each division qualify. Three rounds of best-of-three series.
Roster Limit: 25 (college-eligible players only).

BOURNE BRAVES

Mailing Address: PO Box 895, Monument Beach, MA 02553. **Telephone:** (508) 345-1013. **E-Mail Address:** bournebravesgm@hotmail.com. **Website:** www.bournebraves.org. **President:** Nicole Norkevicius. **General Manager:** Chuck Sturtevant. **Head Coach:** Harvey Shapiro.

BREWSTER WHITECAPS

Mailing Address: PO Box 2349, Brewster, MA 02631. **Telephone:** (508) 896-8500, ext. **147. Fax:** (508) 896-9845. **E-Mail Address:** cagradone@comcast.net. **Website:** www.brewsterwhitecaps.com. **President:** Claire Gradone. **General Manager:** Ned Monthie. **Head Coach:** John Altobelli.

CHATHAM ANGLERS

Mailing Address: PO Box 428, Chatham, MA 02633. **Telephone:** (508) 241-8382. **Fax:** (508) 430-8382. **Website:** www.chathamas.com. **President:** Doug Grattan. **General Manager:** Bob Sherman. **Head Coach:** John Schiffner.

COTUIT KETTLEERS

Mailing Address: PO Box 411, Cotuit, MA 02635. **Telephone:** (508) 428-3358. **Fax:** (508) 420-5584. **E-Mail Address:** Info@kettleers.org. **Website:** www.kettleers.org. **President:** Paul Logan. **General Manager:** Bruce Murphy. **Head Coach:** Mike Roberts.

FALMOUTH COMMODORES

Mailing Address: PO Box 808 Falmouth, MA 02541. **Telephone:** (508) 472-7922. **Fax:** (508) 862-6011. **Website:** www.falcommodores.org. **President:** Steve Kostas. **General Manager:** Eric Zmuda. **Head Coach:** Jeff Trundy.

HARWICH MARINERS

Mailing Address: PO Box 201, Harwich Port, MA 02646. **Telephone:** (508) 432-2000. **Fax:** (508) 432-5357. **E-Mail Address:** mehendy@comcast.net. **Website:** www.harwichmariners.org. **President:** Mary Henderson. **General Manager:** Ben Layton. **Head Coach:** Steve Englert.

HYANNIS HARBOR HAWKS

Mailing Address: PO Box 852, Hyannis, MA 02601. **Telephone:** (508) 364-3164. **Fax:** (508) 534-1270. **E-Mail Address:** bbussiere@harborhawks.org. **Website:** www.harborhawks.org. **President:** Brad Pfeifer. **General Manager:** Tino DiGiovanni. **Head Coach:** Chad Gassman.

ORLEANS FIREBIRDS

Mailing Address: PO Box 504, Orleans, MA 02653. **Telephone:** (508) 255-0793. **Fax:** (508) 255-2237. **Website:** www.orleansfirebirds.com. **President:** Steven Garran. **General Manager:** Sue Horton. **Head Coach:** Kelly Nicholson.

WAREHAM GATEMEN

Mailing Address: PO Box 287, Wareham, MA 02571. **Telephone:** (508) 748-0287. **Fax:** (508) 880-2602. **E-Mail Address:** sheri.gay4gatemen@comcast.net. **Website:** www.gatemen.org. **President/General Manager:** Thomas Gay. **Head Coach:** Cooper Farris.

YARMOUTH-DENNIS RED SOX

Mailing Address: PO Box 814, South Yarmouth, MA 02664. **Telephone:** (508) 394-9387. **Fax:** (508) 398-2239. **E-Mail Address:** jimmartin321@yahoo.com. **Website:** www.ydredsox.org. **President:** Steve Faucher. **General Manager:** Jim Martin. **Head Coach:** Scott Pickler.

CENTRAL VALLEY COLLEGIATE LEAGUE

Mailing Address: P.O. Box 144, Kingsburg, CA 93631. **E-mail:** cvcl@hotmail.com. **Website:** www.cvclbaseball.webs.com. **Twitter:** @CVCL1.
Year Founded: 2013. **President:** Jamie Cederquist. **Vice-President:** Jon Scott. **Regular Season:** 30 games. **2014 Opening Date:** June 5. **Closing Date:** July 27. **All-Star Game:** July 9 at 7:15pm in Kingsburg, CA. **Roster Limit:** 35 (college-eligible players only).

CALIFORNIA EXPOS

Mailing Address: P.O. Box 561, Fowler, CA 93625. **E-mail:** exposcv@aol.com. **Website:** www.californiaexpos.webs.com. **Twitter:** @cvexpos. **General Manager:** Jamie Cederquist. **Field Manager:** Thomas Raymundo/Jake Martinez.

CENTRAL VALLEY VIPERS

Mailing Address: P.O Box 144, Kingsburg, CA 93631. **E-mail:** j_scot25@hotmail.com. **Website:** www.cvipers.webs.com. **Twitter:** @centralvalleyvi. **General Manager:** Jon Scott Field. **Manager:** Jon Scott/Kolton Cabral.

CENTRAL VALLEY KNIGHTS

Mailing Address: Kerman, CA.
E-mail: esco35@yahoo.com. **Website:** www.cvknights.weebly.com. **General Manager:** Paul Valenzuela III. **Field Manager:** Paul Valenzuela III.

TEAM AVENUE ACES

Mailing Address: 9786 N. Woodward Street, Fresno, CA 93720. **E-mail:** teamavenue@gmail.com. **Website:** teamavenuebaseball.us. **Twitter:** @teamavenuebase. **General Manager:** Thomari Story-Harden. **Field Manager:** Thomari Story-Harden.

CENTRAL VALLEY MUD HENS

Mailing Address: Reedley, CA E-mail: jfranco@immanuelschools.com. **Website:** Unavailable. **General Manager:** Josh Franco.. **Field Manager:** Josh Franco.

VISALIA LIGHTNING

Mailing Address: Visalia, CA. **E-mail:** d.dominguez@att.net. **Website:** Unavailable. **General Manager:** Dereck Dominguez. **Field Manager:** Dereck Dominguez.

VALLEY STORM

Mailing Address: PO Box 144, Kingsburg, CA 93631. **Email Address:** valleystormbaseball@aol.com. **Website:** www.californiaexpos.webs.com. **Twitter:** @valleystorm1. **General Manager:** Jamie Cederquist. **General Manager:** Jon Scott. **Field Manager:** Unavailable.

COASTAL PLAIN LEAGUE

Mailing Address: 125 Quantum Street, Holly Springs, NC27540. **Telephone:** (919) 852-1960. **Fax:** (919) 516-0852. **Email Address:** justins@coastalplain.com. **Website:** www.coastalplain.com.

Year Founded: 1997.

Chairman/CEO: Jerry Petitt. **President:** Pete Bock. **Commissioner:** Justin Sellers. **Director, On-Field Operations:** Jeff Bock.

Division Structure: East—Edenton, Fayetteville, Morehead City, Peninsula, Petersburg, Wilmington, Wilson. West—Asheboro, Columbia, Florence, Forest City, Gastonia, Martinsville, Thomaville.

Regular Season: 56 games (split schedule). **2014 Opening Date:** May 27. **Closing Date:** August 16. **All-Star Game:** July 14. **Playoff Format:** Three rounds, best of three in each round (August 7-17).

Roster Limit: 30 (college-eligible players only).

ASHEBORO COPPERHEADS

Mailing Address: PO Box 4006, Asheboro, NC 27204. **Telephone:** (336) 460-7018. **Fax:** (336) 629-2651. **E-Mail Address:** info@teamcopperhead.com. **Website:** www.teamcopperhead.com. **Owners:** Ronnie Pugh, Steve Pugh, Doug Pugh, MIke Pugh. **General Manager:** David Camp. **Head Coach:** Donnie Wilson (Cal State - Dominguez Hills).

COLUMBIA BLOWFISH

Mailing Address: PO Box 1328, Columbia, SC 29202. **Telephone:** (803) 254-3474. **Fax:** (803) 254-4482. **E-Mail Address:** info@blowfishbaseball.com. **Website:** www.blowfishbaseball.com. **Owner:** HWS Baseball V (Michael Savit, Bill Shanahan). **General Manager:** Skip Anderson. **Head Coach:** Unavailable.

EDENTON STEAMERS

Mailing Address: PO Box 86, Edenton, NC 27932. **Telephone:** (252) 482-4080. **Fax:** (252) 482-1717. **E-Mail Address:** edentonsteamers@hotmail.com. **Website:** www.edentonsteamers.com. **Owner:** Edenton Steamers Inc. **President:** Wallace Evans. **General Manager:** Chip Pruden. **Head Coach:** Dan Pirillo (Chicago State).

FAYETTEVILLE SWAMPDOGS

Mailing Address: PO Box 64691, Fayetteville, NC 28306. **Telephone:** (910) 426-5900. **Fax:** (910) 426-3544. **E-Mail Address:** info@fayettevilleswampdogs.com. **Website:** www.goswampdogs.com. **Owners:** Lew Handelsman,

Darrell Handelsman. **General Manager:** Jeremy Aagard. **Head Coach:** Darrell Handelsman.

FLORENCE REDWOLVES

Mailing Address: PO Box 809, Florence, SC 29503. **Telephone:** (843) 629-0700. **Fax:** (843) 629-0703. **E-Mail Address:** jamie@florenceredwolves.com. **Website:** www.florenceredwolves.com. **Owners:** Kevin Barth, Donna Barth. **General Manager:** Jamie Young. **Head Coach:** Jared Barkdoll (Francis Marion).

FOREST CITY OWLS

Mailing Address: PO Box 1062, Forest City, NC 28043. **Telephone:** (828) 245-0000. **Fax:** (828) 245-6666. **E-Mail Address:** forestcitybaseball@yahoo.com. **Website:** www.forestcitybaseball.com. **Owner/President:** Ken Silver. **Managing Partner:** Jesse Cole. **General Manager:**Jeremy Boler. **Head Coach:** David Tufo (Menlo College).

GASTONIA GRIZZLIES

Mailing Address: PO Box 177, Gastonia, NC 28053. **Telephone:** (704) 866-8622. **Fax:** (704) 864-6122. **E-Mail Address:** jesse@gastoniagrizzlies.com. **Website:** www.gastoniagrizzlies.com. **President:** Ken Silver. **Managing Partner/General Manager:** Jesse Cole. **Head Coach:** Jason Wood (Southeastern C.C.).

MARTINSVILLE MUSTANGS

Mailing Address: PO Box 1112, Martinsville, VA 24114. **Telephone:** (276) 403-5250. **Fax:** (276) 403-5387. **E-Mail Address:** jesse@teamcoleandassociates.com. **Website:** www.martinsvillemustangs.com. **Owner:** City of Martinsville. **GeneralManager:** Unavailable. **Head Coach:** Matt Duffy.

MOREHEAD CITY MARLINS

Mailing Address: 1921 Oglesby Road, Morehead City, NC 28557. **Telephone:** (252) 269-9767. **Fax:** (252) 727-9402. **E-Mail Address:** mitch@mhcmarlins.com. **Website:** www.mhcmarlins.com. **President:** Buddy Bengel.**General Manager:** Mitch Kluver. **Head Coach:** Jamie Sheetz (Missouri State).

PENINSULA PILOTS

Mailing Address: PO Box 7376, Hampton, VA 23666. **Telephone:** (757) 245-2222. **Fax:** (757) 245-8030. **E-Mail Address:** jeffscott@peninsulapilots.com. **Website:** www.peninsulapilots.com. **Owner:** Henry Morgan. **General Manager:** Jeffrey Scott. **Head Coach/Vice President:** Hank Morgan.

PETERSBURG GENERALS

Mailing Address: 1981 Midway Ave, Petersburg, VA 23803. **Telephone:** (804) 722-0141. **Fax:** (804) 733-7370. **E-Mail Address:** petggenerals@earthlink.net. **Website:** www.generals.petersburgsports.com. **Owner:** City of Petersburg. **General Manager:** Ryan Massenburg. **Head Coach:** Bob Smith.

THOMASVILLE HI-TOMS

Mailing Address: PO Box 3035, Thomasville, NC 27361. **Telephone:** (336) 472-8667. **Fax:** (336) 472-7198. **E-Mail Address:** info@hitoms.com. **Website:** www.hitoms.com. **Owner:** Richard Holland. **President:** Greg Suire. **Director, Business Relations:** Nick Gaski. **Head Coach:** Zach Brown (Furman).

WILMINGTON SHARKS

Mailing Address: PO Box 15233, Wilmington, NC 28412. **Telephone:** (910) 343-5621. **Fax:** (910) 343-8932. **E-Mail Address:** info@wilmingtonsharks.com. **Website:** www.wilmingtonsharks.com. **Owners:** Lew Handelsman, Darrell Handelsman. **President:** Greg Suire (<--DELETE PLEASE). **General Manager:** TBD. **Head Coach:** Ryan McCleney (UNC Pembroke).

WILSON TOBS

Mailing Address: PO Box 633, Wilson, NC 27894. **Telephone:** (252) 291-8627. **Fax:** (252) 291-1224. **E-Mail Address:** wilsontobs@gmail.com. **Website:** www.wilson-tobs.com. **Owner:** Richard Holland. **President:** Greg Suire. **General Manager:** Thomas Webb. **Head Coach:** Austin Love.

FLORIDA COLLEGIATE SUMMER LEAGUE

Mailing Address: 2410 N Rio Grande Ave, Orlando, FL 32804. **Telephone:** (321) 206-9174. **Fax:** (407) 574-7926. **E-Mail Address:** info@floridaleague.com. **Website:** www.floridaleague.com.

Year Founded: 2004.

President: Rob Sitz. **Vice President:** Stefano Foggi. **League Operations Director:** Phil Chinnery. **Marketing Director:** Jay Hatch.

Regular Season: 45 games. **2014 Opening Date:** June 3. **Closing Date:** August 3. **All-Star Game:** Unavailable. **Playoff Format:** Five teams, No. 4 and No. 5 seed play-in game. Second round features two best-of-three series, with winners meeting in winner-take-all championship game.

Roster Limit: 27 (college-eligible players only).

COLLEGE PARK FREEDOM

Operated by the league office. Email Address: orlandofreedom@floridaleague.com. **Head Coach:** Scott Makarewicz. **General Manager:** Jay Hatch.

DELAND SUNS

Operated by the league office. E-Mail Address: delandsuns@floridaleague.com. **Head Coach:** Rick Hall. **General Manager:** Unavailable.

LEESBURG LIGHTNING

Mailing Address: 318 South 2nd St, Leesburg, FL 34748. **Telephone:** (352) 728-9885. **E-Mail Address:** leesburglightning@floridaleague.com. **Head Coach:** Dave Therneau. **General Manager:** Dave Therneau.

SANFORD RIVER RATS

Operated by the league office. E-Mail Address: sanfordriverrats@floridaleague.com. **Head Coach:** Ken Kelly. **General Manager:** Ken Kelly. **Assistant GM:** Phil Chinnery.

WINTER PARK DIAMOND DAWGS

Operated by the league office. E-Mail Address: winterparkdiamonddawgs@floridaleague.com. **Head Coach:** Kevin Davidson. **General Manager:** Mitchell Adams.

WINTER GARDEN

Operated by the league office. Email Address: info@floridaleague.com. **Head Coach:** Ruben Felix. **General Manager:** Adam Bates.

FUTURES COLLEGIATE LEAGUE OF NEW ENGLAND

Mailing Address: 46 Chestnut Hill Rd, Chelmsford, MA 01824. **Telephone:** (617) 593-2112. **E-Mail Address:** futuresleague@yahoo.com. **Website:** www.thefuturesleague.com.

Year Founded: 2010.

Commissioner: Chris Hall.

Member Clubs (team contact): Brockton Rox (Mike Canina: mcanina@brocktonrox.com), Martha's Vineyard Sharks (Jerry Murphy: jerry.murphy@mvsharks.com), Nashua Silver Knights (Tim Bawmann: tbawmann@lowellspinners.com), North Shore Navigators (Bill Terlecky: navigatorsgm@gmail.com), Old Orchard Beach Raging Tide (Taylor McCarthy: taylor@oobragingtide.com), Pittsfield Suns (Jeff Goldklang: jgoldklang@goldklanggroup.com), Seacoast Mavericks (Dave Hoyt: dave@usamavs.com), Torrington Titans (Sander Stotland: sander.stotland@torringtontitans.com), Wachusett Dirt Dogs (John Morrison: lefty@dirtdawgsball.com).

Regular Season: 54 games. **Playoff Format:** Top six teams make playoffs. Top two teams get byes. No. 3 seed plays No. 6 seed and No. 4 seed plays No. 5 seed in one-game playoffs. Winners play top two seeds in best-of-three semifinal series. Winners meet in best-of-three championship series.

Roster Limit: 30. Half must be from New England or play collegiately at a New England college.

GREAT LAKES SUMMER COLLEGIATE LEAGUE

Mailing Address: 133 W Winter St, Delaware, OH 43015. **Telephone:** (740) 368-3527. **Fax:** (740) 368-3999. **E-Mail Address:** kalance@owu.edu. **Website:** www.greatlakesleague.org.

Year Founded: 1986.

President/Commissioner: Kim Lance.

Regular Season: 40 games. **Playoff Format:** Top six teams meet in playoffs.

Roster Limit: 30 (college-eligible players only).

CINCINNATI STEAM

Mailing Address: 2745 Anderson Ferry Rd, Cincinnati, OH 45238. **Telephone:** (513) 922-4272. **Website:** www.cincinnatisteam.com. **GeneralManager:** Max McLeary. **Head Coach:** Billy O'Connor.

DAYTON DOCS

Mailing Address: Dayton Docs Baseball Club, PO Box 773, Greenville, OH 45331. **Telephone:** (937) 423-3053. **Website:** www.docsbaseball.com. **President/General Manager:** Joe Marker. **Head Coach:** Burt Davis.

GRAND LAKE MARINERS

Mailing Address: 1460 James Drive, Celina, OH 45822. **Telephone:** (419) 586-3187. **Website:** www.grandlakemariners.com. **General Manager:** Betty Feliciano. **Head Coach:** Mike Goldschmidt.

HAMILTON JOES

Mailing Address: 6218 Greens Way, Hamilton, OH 45011. **Telephone:** (513) 267-0601. **E-mail address:** darrelgrissom@fuse.net. **Website:** www.hamiltonjoes.com.

General Manager: Josh Manley. Head Coach: Darrel Grissom.

LAKE ERIE MONARCHS

Mailing Address: 2220 West Sigler Road, Carleton, MI 48117. Telephone: (734) 626-1166. Website: www.lakeeriemonarchs.com. General Manager: Jim DeSana. Head Coach: Brian Lewis

LEXINGTON HUSTLERS

Mailing Address: 2061 Lexington Road, Nicholasville, KY 40356. Telephone: (859) 335-0928. Fax: (859) 881-0598. Website: lexingtonhustlers.wordpress.com. Email Address: lexigntonhustlers@gmail.com. General Manager: Jeff Adkins. Head Coach: Kyle Medley

LICKING COUNTY SETTLERS

Mailing Address: 958 Camden Dr, Newark, OH 43055. Telephone: (678) 367-8686. Website: www.settlersbaseball.com. General Manager: Sean West. Head Coach: Andy Levell.

LIMA LOCOS

Mailing Address: 3588 South Conant Rd, Spencerville, OH 45887. Telephone: (419) 647-5242. Website: www.limalocos.com. General Manager: Steve Meyer. Head Coach: Dan Furuto.

SOUTHERN OHIO COPPERHEADS

Mailing Address: PO Box 442, Athens, OH 45701. Telephone: (740) 541-9284. Website: www.copperheadsbaseball.com. General Manager: David Palmer. Head Coach: Chris Moore.

XENIA SCOUTS

Mailing Address: 651 Taylor Dr, Xenia, OH 45385. Telephone: (937) 352-1000. E-Mail Address: john.henschen@athletesinaction.org Website:www.aiabaseball.org. General Manager: John Henschen. Head Coach: J.D. Arndt.

JAYHAWK LEAGUE

Mailing Address: 865 Fabrique, Wichita, KS 67218. Telephone: (316) 942-6333. Fax: (316) 942-2009. Website: www.jayhawkbaseballleague.org. Year Founded: 1976. Commissioner: Jim Foltz. President: J.D. Schneider. Vice President: Frank Leo. Public Relations/Statistician: Gary Karr. Secretary: Cheryl Kastner.

Regular Season: 32 games. Playoff Format: Top two teams qualify for National Baseball Congress World Series. Roster Limit: 30 to begin season; 28 at midseason.

DERBY TWINS

Mailing Address: 1245 N. Pine Grove, Wichita, KS 67212. Telephone: (316) 992-3623. E-mail Address: jwells@riadatrading.com, jwells53@att.net. Website: www.derbytwins.com. General Manager: Jeff Wells. Head Coach: Billy Hall.

DODGE CITY A'S

Mailing Address: 1715 Central Ave., Dodge City, KS 67801. Telephone: 620-225-0238. Website: www.dodgecityas.com. General Manager/Head Coach: Phil Stevenson.

EL DORADO BRONCOS

Mailing Address: Box 168, El Dorado, KS 67042. Telephone: (316) 323-5098. Website: www.360eldorado.com. General Manager: Doug Bell. Head Coach: Pat Hon.

HAYS LARKS

Mailing Address: 2715 Walnut, Hays, KS 67601. Telephone: (785) 259-1430. Fax: (630) 848-2236. Website: www.hdnews.net/larks. General Manager/Head Coach: Frank Leo.

LIBERAL BEE JAYS

Mailing Address: PO Box 793, Liberal, KS 67901. Telephone: (620) 629-1162. Fax: (620) 624-1906. Head Coach: Mike Silva. Website: beejays.net.

WELLINGTON HEAT

Mailing Address: Unavailable. Telephone: (928) 854-4092. Website: www.wellingtonheat.com. Email Address: wellingtonheat@yahoo.com. General Manager/Owner/Head Coach: Rick Twyman.

MIDWEST COLLEGIATE LEAGUE

Mailing Address: PO Box 172, Flossmoor, IL 60422. E-Mail Address: commissioner@midwestcollegiateleague.com. Website: www.midwestcollegiateleague.com. Year Founded: 2010.

President/Commissioner: Don Popravak.

Regular Season: 46 games. 2014 Opening Date: May 27. Closing Date: Aug. 4. All-Star Game: July 9. Playoff Format: Top four teams meet in best-of-three series. Winners meet in best-of-three championship series.

Roster Limit: 28.

CHICAGO SOUTHLAND VIKINGS

Mailing Address: PO Box 172, Flossmoor, IL 60422. Telephone: (312) 420-1268. E-Mail Address: don@southlandvidings.com. Website: www.southlandvikings.com. General Manager: Don Popravak. Head Coach: Chris Cunningham.

CHICAGO ZEPHYRS

Mailing Address: 3 S 517 Winfield Road, Suite B, Warrenville, IL 60555. Telephone: (630) 327-9295. E-Mail Address: chicagozephyrs@gmail.com. Website: www.zephyrs-baseball.com. General Manager/Head Coach: Marco Fajardo.

DUPAGE COUNTY HOUNDS

Mailing Address: 17-8 Squirrel Trail, Cary, IL 60013. Telephone: (815) 704-3839. E-Mail Address: tickets@dupagehounds.com. Website: www.DuPageHounds.com. General Managers: Joe Stevani, Josh VanSwol. Head Coach: Sean Osborne.

LEXINGTON SNIPES

Mailing Address: 216 Prairie Ridge Drive, Lexington, IL 61753. Telephone: (309) 287-1668. E-Mail Address: billyd_73@yahoo.com. Website: www.lexingtonsnipes.com. General Manager/Head Coach: Billy Dubois.

NORTHWEST INDIANA OILMEN

Mailing Address: 1500 119th Street, Whiting, IN 46394. Telephone: (219) 659-1000. E-Mail Address: info@

nwioilmen.com. **Website:** www.nwioilmen.com. **General Manager:** Unavailable. **Head Coach:** Justin Huisman.

JOLIET ADMIRALS

Mailing Address: 1450 S New Wilke Rd, Suite 205, Arlington Heights, IL 60005. **Telephone:** 815-704-3839. **Email Address:** joe@dupagehounds.com. **Website:** Unavailable. **General Manager:** Joe Stefani. **Head Coach:** Jorge Garza.

M.I.N.K. LEAGUE
(Missouri, Iowa, Nebraska, Kansas)
Mailing Address: PO Box 601, Nevada, MO 64772. **Telephone:** (417) 667-6159. **Fax:** (417) 667-4210. **E-mail Address:** jpost@morrisonpost.com. **Website:** www.minkleaguebaseball.com.
Year Founded: 1995.
Commissioner: Bob Steinkamp. **President:** Jeff Post. **Vice President:** Arden Rakosky. **Secretary:** Edwina Rains.
Regular Season: 42 games. **Playoff Format:** Top team in North and South divisions play best-of-three series for league championship. Top team in each division qualifies for National Baseball Congress World Series.
Roster Limit: 30.

CHILLICOTHE MUDCATS

Mailing Address: 426 E Jackson, Chillicothe, MO 64601. **Telephone:** (660) 247-1504. **Fax:** (660) 646-6933. **E-Mail Address:** doughty@greenhills.net. **Website:** www.chillicothemudcats.com. **General Manager:** Doug Doughty. **Head Coach:** Eric Peterson.

CLARINDA A'S

Mailing Address: 225 East Lincoln, Clarinda, IA 51632. **Telephone:** (712) 542-4272. **E-Mail Address:** m.everly@mchsi.com. **Website:** www.clarindaiowa-as-baseball.org. **General Manager:** Merle Eberly. **Head Coach:** Ryan Eberly.

JOPLIN OUTLAWS

Mailing Address: 5860 North Pearl, Joplin, MO 64801. **Telephone:** (417) 825-4218. **E-Mail Address:** merains@mchsi.com. **Website:** www.joplinoutlaws.com. **President/General Manager:** Mark Rains. **Head Coach:** Rob Vessell.

NEVADA GRIFFONS

Mailing Address: PO Box 601, Nevada, MO 64772. **Telephone:** (417) 667-6159. **E-Mail Address:** jpost@morrisonpost.com. **Website:** www.nevadagriffons.org. **President:** Bob Hawks. **General Manager:** Jeff Post. **Head Coach:** Ryan Mansfield.

OMAHA DIAMOND SPIRIT

Mailing Address: 4618 N 135th Ave, Omaha, NE 68164. **Telephone:** (402) 679-0206. **E-Mail Address:** arden@omahadiamondspirit.com. **Website:** www.omahadiamondspirit.com. **General Manager:** Arden Rakosky. **Head Coach:** Adam Steyer.

OZARK GENERALS

Mailing Address: 1336 W Farm Road 182, Springfield, MO 65810. **Telephone:** (417) 832-8830. **Fax:** (417) 877-4625. **E-Mail Address:** rda160@yahoo.com. **Website:** www.generalsbaseballclub.com. **General Manager/Head Coach:** Rusty Aton.

ST. JOSEPH MUSTANGS

Mailing Address: 2600 SW Parkway, St. **Joseph, MO 64503. Telephone:** (816) 279-7856. **Fax:** (816) 749-4082. **E-Mail Address:**rmuntean717@gmail.com. **Website:** www.stjoemustangs.com. **President:** Dan Gerson. **General Manager:** Rick Muntean. **Manager/Director, Player Personnel:** Matt Johnson.

SEDALIA BOMBERS

Mailing Address: 2205 S Grand, Sedalia, MO 65301. **Telephone:** (660) 287 4722. **E-Mail Address:** jkindle@knobnoster.k12.mo.us. **Website:** www.sedaliabombers.com. **President/General Manager/Head Coach:** Jud Kindle. **Vice President:** Ross Dey.

MOUNTAIN COLLEGIATE LEAGUE
E-mail Address: info@mcbl.net. **Website:** www.mcbl.net. **Year Founded:** 2005. **Directors:** Kurt Colicchio, Ron Kailey, Aaron McCreight, Ryan Kolo, Paul Birge. **Commissioner:** Karl Holden. **Director of Umpires:** Gary Weibert.
Regular Season: 48 games. **Playoff Format:** Second-place and third-place teams meet in one-game playoff; winner advances to best-of-three league championship series against first-place team. **All-Star Game:** Unavailable.
Roster limit: 31 total, 25 active (college-eligible players only).

CASPER CUTTHROATS

Telephone: (307) 277-9159. **Email Address:** aaron@caspercutthroats.com. **Website:** www.caspercutthrpoats.com **Owner/General Manager:** Aaron McCreight. **Head Coach:** Steve Stutzman.

CHEYENNE GRIZZLIES

Telephone: (307) 631-7337. **E-Mail Address:** rkaide@aol.com. **Website:** www.cheyennegrizzlies.com. **Owner/General Manager:** Ron Kailey. **Head Coach:** Jared Franklin.

COLORADO BOBCATS

Telephone: 575-779-0928. **E-Mail Address:** pcbirge@gmail.com. **Website:** coloradobobcats.com. **Owner/General Manager:** Paul Birge. **Head Coach:** Kellen Mitts.

COLORADO SPRINGS BLUE SOX

Telephone: (719) 200-5692. **E-Mail Address:** steven@coloradobaseballacademy.com. **Website:** www.csbluesox.com. **General Manager:** Steven Locket. **Head Coach:** Lou Trujillo.

FORT COLLINS FOXES

Telephone: (970) 225-9564. **E-Mail Address:** info@fortcollinsfoxes.com. **Website:** www.fortcollinsfoxes.com. **Owner/General Manager:** Kurt Colicchio. **Head Coach:** Brad Averitte.

NORTHERN COLORADO TOROS

Telephone: 970-775-3676. **E-Mail Address:** onefifteenbaseballclub@yahoo.com. **Website:** onefifteenbaseball.com. **Owner/General Manager:** Ryan Kolo. **Head Coach:** Steve Gerrard.

NEW ENGLAND COLLEGIATE LEAGUE

Mailing Address: 122 Mass Moca Way, North Adams, MA 01247. **Telephone:** (413) 652-1031. **Fax:** (413) 473-0012. **E-Mail Address:** smcgrath@necbl.com. **Website:** www.necbl.com.

Year founded: 1993.

President: John DeRosa. **Commissioner:** Sean McGrath. **Deputy Commissioner:** Gregg Hunt. **Secretary:** Max Pinto. **Treasurer:** Brigid Schaffer.

Regular Season: 42 games. **2014 Opening Date:** June 5. **Closing Date:** Aug. **12. All-Star Game:** July 20 in Holyoke, MA.

Roster Limit: 30 (college-eligible players only).

DANBURY WESTERNERS

Mailing Address: 9 Pleasant View, New Milford, CT 06776. **Telephone:** (203) 502-9167. **E-Mail Address:** jspitser@msn.com. **Website:** www.danburywesterners.com. **President:** Paul Schaffer. **General Manager:** Jon Pitser. **Field Manager:** Jamie Shevchik.

HOLYOKE BLUE SOX

Mailing Address: 100 Congress St, Springfield, MA 01104. **Telephone:** (413) 652-9014. **E-Mail Address:** Barry@Holyokesox.com Website: www.holyokesox.com. **President:** Clark Eckhoff. **General Manager:** Hunter Golden. **Field Manager:** Darryl Morhardt.

KEENE SWAMP BATS

Mailing Address: PO Box 160, Keene, NH 13431. **Telephone:** (603) 357-5464. **Fax:** (603) 357-5090. **E-Mail Address:** kwatterson@ne.rr.com. **Website:** www.swampbats.com. **President:** Kevin Watterson. **VP/General Manager:** Walt Kilburn.

LACONIA MUSKRATS

Mailing Address: 134 Stevens Rd, Lebanon, NH 03766. **Telephone:** (864) 380-2873. **E-Mail Address:** noah@laconiamuskrats.com. **Website:** www.laconiamuskrats.com. **President:** Jonathan Crane. **General Manager:** Noah Crane. **Field Manager:** Matt Alison.

MYSTIC SCHOONERS

Mailing Address: PO Box 432, Mystic, CT 06355. **Telephone:** (860) 608-3287. **E-Mail Address:** dlong@mysticbaseball.org. **Website:** www.mysticbaseball.org. **Executive Director:** Don Benoit. **General Manager:** Dennis Long. **Field Manager:** Phil Orbe.

NEW BEDFORD BAY SOX

Mailing Address: 427 John St, New Bedford, MA 02740. **Telephone:** 802-578-9935. **Email Address:** poconnor@nbbaysox.com. **Website:** www.nbbaysox.com. **President:** Pat O'Connor. **General Manager:** Jim Periera. **Field Manager:** Rick Miller.

NEWPORT GULLS

Mailing Address: PO Box 777, Newport, RI 02840. **Telephone:** (401) 845-6832. **E-Mail Address:** gm@newportgulls.com. **Website:** www.newportgulls.com. **President/General Manager:** Chuck Paiva. **Field Manager:** Mike Coombs.

NORTH ADAMS STEEPLECATS

Mailing Address: PO Box 540, North Adams, MA 01247. **Telephone:** (413) 884-4100. **E-Mail Address:** dan.bosley@verizon.net. **Website:** www.steeplecats.com. **President:** Dan Bosley. **General Manager:** Johno Hinkell. **Field Manager:** Chris Cates.

OCEAN STATE WAVES

Mailing Address: 1174 Kingstown Rd, Wakefield, RI 02879. **Telephone:** (401) 360-2977. **E-Mail Address:** matt@oceanstatewaves.com. **Website:** www.oceanstatewaves.com. **President:** Jeff Sweenor. **General Manager:** Matt Finlayson. **Field Manager:** Eric Cirella.

PLYMOUTH PILGRIMS

Mailing Address: 134 Court Street, Plymouth, MA 02360. **Telephone:** (401) 862-3711. **Fax:** (508) 830-1621. **E-Mail Address:** chris@pilgrimsbaseball.com. **Website:** www.pilgrimsbaseball.com. **President:** Dave Dittmann. **General Manager:** Chris Patsos. **Field Manager:** Greg Zackrison.

SANFORD MAINERS

Mailing Address: PO Box 26, 4 Washington St, Sanford, ME 04073. **Telephone:** (207) 324-0010. **Fax:** (207) 324-2227. **E-Mail Address:** jwebb@nicholswebb.com. **Website:** www.sanfordmainers.com. **CEO:** Steve Cabana. **General Manager:** John Webb. **Field Manager:** Aaron Izaryk.

VERMONT MOUNTAINEERS

Mailing Address: PO Box 57, East Montpelier, VT 05651. **Telephone:** (802) 223-5224. **E-Mail Address:** gmvtm@comcast.net. **Website:** www.thevermontmountaineers.com. **President:** Katheran Thayer. **General Manager:** Brian Gallagher. **Field Manager:** Joe Brown.

NEW YORK COLLEGIATE BASEBALL LEAGUE

Mailing Address: 4 Creekside Ln, Rochester, NY 14624-1059. **Telephone:** (585) 314-1122. **E-Mail Address:** slehman@nycbl.com. **Website:** www.nycbl.com.

Year founded: 1978.

President/Commissioner/Executive Director: Stan Lehman. **Vice President:** Cal Kern. **Treasurer:** Dan Russo. **Secretary:** Paul Welker. **Director, Baseball Operations:** Jake Dennstedt. **Franchise Development:** Cal Kern.

Franchises: Cortland Crush, Genesee Rapids, Geneva Red Wings, Geneva Twins, Hornell Dodgers, Niagara Power, Olean Oilers, Oneonta Outlaws, Rochester Ridgemen, Sherrill Silversmiths, Syracuse Junior Chiefs, Syracuse Salt Cats, Wellsville Nitros.

2014 Opening Date: June 1. **Season Ends:** July 26. **All-Star Game/Scout Day:** July 8 at Kerr-Pegula Athletic Complex, Houghton, New York. **Playoff Format:** Three rounds beginning on July 27; the first round will feature the #1 seeded team vs. #4 seeded and the #2 seeded team vs. #3 seeded team in a best-of-three series. The winners of these series will advance to play in the Division Championship Series in a best-of-three series. The winners of those two series will play for the NYCBL championship in a best-of-three series.

Roster Limit: 30 (college-eligible players only).

CORTLAND CRUSH

Mailing Address: 2745 Summer Ridge Rd, LaFayette, NY 13084. **Telephone:** 315-391-8167. **Email Address:** wmmac4@aol.com. **Website:** unavailable. **President:** Bill

McConnell. **Field Manager:** Bill McConnell.

GENESEE RAPIDS

Mailing Address: 9726 Rt. **19 Houghton, NY 14474. Telephone:** 716-969-0688. **Email Address:** rkerr@frontiernet.net. **Email Address:** unavailable. **President:** Ralph Kerr. **Field Manager:** Unavailable.

GENEVA RED WINGS

Mailing Address: PO BOX 17624, Rochester, NY 14617. **Telephone:** 585-342-5750. **Fax:** 585-342-5155. **E-Mail Address:** gwings@rochester.rr.com. **Website:** genevaredwings.com. **President:** David Herbst. **Executive GM:** John Oughterson.

GENEVA TWINS

Mailing Address: PO BOX 17624, Rochester, NY 14617. **Telephone:** 585-342-5750. **Fax:** 585-342-5155. **E-Mail Address:** gwings@rochester.rr.com. **Website:** genevaredwings.com. **President:** David Herbst. **Executive GM:** John Oughterson.

HORNELL DODGERS

Mailing Address: PO Box 235, Hornell, NY 14843. **Telephone:** (607) 661-4173. **Fax:** (607) 661-4173. **E-Mail Address:** gm@hornelldodgers.com. **Website:** www.hornelldodgers.com. **General Manager:** Paul Welker. **Field Manager:** Tom Kenney.

NIAGARA POWER

Mailing Address: 2905 Staley Road, Grand Island, NY 14072. **Telephone:** (716) 773-1748. **Fax:** (716) 773-1748. **E-Mail Address:** ckern@fca.org **Website:** www.niagarapower.org. **General Manager:** Cal Kern. **Field Manager:** Josh Rebandt.

OLEAN OILERS

Mailing Address: 126 N 10th, Olean, NY 14760. **Telephone:** 716-378-0641. **E-Mail Addresses:** baseball@oleanoilers.com, Bellr41@yahoo.com. **General Manager:** Bobby Bell. **Field Manager:** Bobby Bell.

ONEONTA OUTLAWS

Mailing Address: PO Box 608, Oneonta, NY 13820. **Telephone:** (607) 432-6326. **Fax:** (607) 432-1965. **E-Mail Address:** stevepindar@oneontaoutlaws.com. **Website:** www.oneontaoutlaws.com. **General Manager:** Steve Pindar. **Field Manager:** Joe Hughes.

ROCHESTER RIDGEMEN

Mailing Address: 651 Taylor Dr, Xenia, OH 45385. **Telephone:** (937) 352-1225. **E-Mail Addresses:** baseball@athletesinaction.org, chris.rainwater@athletesinaction.org. **Website:** www.aiabaseball.org. **General Manager:** Chris Rainwater. **Field Manager:** Unavailable.

SHERRILL SILVERSMITHS

Mailing Address: PO Box 111, Sherrill, NY 13440. **Telephone:** (315) 264-4334. **E-Mail Address:** sherrillsilversmiths@hotmail.com. **Website:** www.leaguelineup.com/silversmiths. **General Manager:** Matthew Rafte. **Field Manager:** Unavailable.

SYRACUSE JR CHIEFS

Mailing Address: 227 Walters Dr, Liverpool, NY 13088.

Telephone: (315) 263-3777. **E-Mail Address:** perfect.practice@yahoo.com. **General Manager:** Mike DiPaulo. **Field Manager:** Unavailable.

SYRACUSE SALT CATS

Mailing Address: 208 Lakeland Ave, Syracuse, NY 13209. **Telephone:** (315) 727-9220. **Fax:** (315) 488-1750. **E-Mail Address:** mmarti6044@yahoo.com. **Website:** www.leaguelineup.com/saltcats. **General Manager:** Manny Martinez. **Field Manager:** Mike Martinez.

WELLSVILLE NITROS

Mailing Address: 2848 O'Donnell Rd, Wellsville, NY 14895. **Telephone:** 585-596-9523. **Fax:** 585-593-5260. **E-Mail Address:** ackley8122@roadrunner.com. **Website:** www.nitros baseball.com. **General Manager:** Steven J. Ackley. **Assistant Manager:** Shelley Butler.

NORTHWOODS LEAGUE

Office Address: 2900 4th St SW, Rochester, MN 55902. **Telephone:** (507) 536-4579. **Fax:** (507) 536-4597. **E-Mail Address:** info@northwoodsleague.com. **Website:** www.northwoodsleague.com.

Year Founded: 1994.

President: Dick Radatz Jr. **Vice President, Business Development:** Matt Bomberg, Vice President, Operations: Glen Showalter.

Division Structure: North—Alexandria, Duluth, Mankato, Rochester, St. Cloud, Thunder Bay, Waterloo, Willmar. South—Battle Creek, Eau Claire, Green Bay, La Crosse, Lakeshore, Madison, Rochester, Wisconsin, Wisconsin Rapids.

Regular Season: 70 games (split schedule).

2014 Opening Date: May 27. **Closing Date:** August 10. **All-Star Game:** July 22 at Lakeshore. **Playoff Format:** First-half and second-half division winners meet in best-of-three series. Winners meet in best-of-three series for league championship.

Roster Limit: 30 (college-eligible players only).

ALEXANDRIA BLUE ANCHORS

Mailing Address: PO Box 517, Alexandria, MN 56308. **Telephone:** 320-492-9025. **E-Mail Address:** info@northwoodsleague.com. **Website:** www.blueanchors.com. **General Manager:** Kendall Hughson. **Field:** Knute Nelson Memorial Stadium.

BATTLE CREEK BOMBERS

Mailing Address: 189 Bridge Street, Battle Creek, MI 49017. **Telephone:** (269) 962-0735. **Fax:** (269) 962-0741. **Email Address:** info@battlecreekbombers.com. **Website:** www.battlecreekbombers.com. **General Manager:** Tony Iovieno. **Field:** C.O. Brown Stadium.

DULUTH HUSKIES

Mailing Address: PO Box 16231, Duluth, MN 55816. **Telephone:** (218) 786-9909. **Fax:** (218) 786-9001. **E-Mail Address:** huskies@duluthhuskies.com. **Website:** www.duluthhuskies.com. **Owners:** Andy Karon, Michael Rosenzweig. **General Manager:** Craig Smith. **Field Manager:** Daniel Hersey (Central Florida CC). **Field:** Wade Stadium.

EAU CLAIRE EXPRESS

Mailing Address: 108 E Grand Ave, Eau Claire, WI 54701. **Telephone:** (715) 839-7788. **Fax:** (715) 839-7676.

E-Mail Address: info@eauclaireexpress.com. Website: www.eauclaireexpress.com. Owner: Bill Rowlett. General Manager: Andy Neborak. Director of Operations/Field Manager: Dale Varsho. Field: Carson Park.

GREEN BAY BULLFROGS

Mailing Address: 1306 Main Street, Green Bay, WI 54302. Telephone: (920) 497-7225. Fax: (920) 437-3551. Email Address: info@greenbaybullfrogs.com. Website: www.greenbaybullfrogs.com. General Manager: Liz Kern. Field: Joannes Stadium.

KALAMAZOOO GROWLERS

Mailing Address: 251 Mills St, Kalamazoo, MI 49048. Telephone: 555-555-1212. Website: www.kzoobaseball. com. General Manager: Brian Colopy. Field: Homer Stryker Field.

KENOSHA KINGFISH

Mailing Address: 7817 Sheridan Rd, Kenosha, WI 53143. Telephone: 262-653-0900. Website: www.king-fishbaseball.com. General Manager: Jake McGhee. Field: Simmons Field.

LA CROSSE LOGGERS

Mailing Address: 1223 Caledonia St, La Crosse, WI 54603. Telephone: (608) 796-9553. Fax: (608) 796-9032. E-Mail Address: info@lacrosseloggers.com. Website: www.lacrosseloggers.com. Owner: Dan Kapanke. General Manager: Chris Goodell. Assistant General Manager: Ben Kapanke. Field Manager: Jason Nell (Iowa Lakes CC). Field: Copeland Park.

LAKESHORE CHINOOKS

Mailing Address: 995 Badger Circle, Grafton, WI 53024. Telephone: (262) 618-4659. Fax: (262) 618-4362. E-Mail Address: info@lakeshorechinooks.com. Website: www. lakeshorechinooks.com. Owner: Jim Kacmarcik. General Manager: Dean Rennicke. Assistant GM: Chad Bauer. Field Manager: Eddy Morgan (Wisconsin-Superior). Field: Kapco Park.

MADISON MALLARDS

Mailing Address: 2920 N Sherman Ave, Madison, WI 53704. Telephone: (608) 246-4277. Fax: (608) 246-4163. E-Mail Address: conor@mallardsbaseball.com. Website: www.mallardsbaseball.com. Owner: Steve Schmitt. President: Vern Stenman. General Manager: Conor Caloia. Field Manager: Donnie Scott (ProBound Baseball Academy, Clearwater). Field: Warner Park.

MANKATO MOONDOGS

Mailing Address: 1221 Caledonia Street, Mankato, MN 56001. Telephone: (507) 625-7047. Fax: (507) 625-7059. E-Mail Address: office@mankatomoondogs.com. Website: www.mankatomoondogs.com. Owner: Mark Ogren. Vice President: Kyle Mrozek. General Manager: Greg Weis. Director of the MoonDogs: Scott Ogren. Field Manager: Mike Orchard (Central Arizona JC). Field: Franklin Rogers Park.

ROCHESTER HONKERS

Mailing Address: 307 E Center St, Rochester, MN 55904. Telephone: (507) 289-1170. Fax: (507) 289-1866. E-Mail Address: honkers@rochesterhonkers.com. Website: www.rochesterhonkers.com. Owner/General

Manager: Dan Litzinger. Field Manager: Brian Aguilar (Oral Roberts). Field: Mayo Field.

ST. CLOUD ROX

Mailing Address: 5001 8th St N, St. Cloud, MN 56303. Telephone: (320) 240-9798. Fax: (320) 255-5228. E-Mail Address: info@stcloudrox.com. Website: www.stcloud-rox.com. President: Scott Schreiner. GM: Wes Sharp. Field Manager: Augie Rodriguez (Augusta State, Ga.). Field: Joe Faber Field.

THUNDER BAY BORDER CATS

Mailing Address: PO Box 29105, Thunder Bay, ON P7B 6P9. Telephone: (807) 766-2287. Fax: (807) 345-8299. E-Mail Address: baseball@tbaytel.net. Website: www. bordercatsbaseball.com. President/General Manager: Brad Jorgenson. Field Manager: Andy Judkins (Central Arizona JC). Field: Port Arthur Stadium.

WATERLOO BUCKS

Mailing Address: PO Box 4124, Waterloo, IA 50704. Telephone: (319) 232-0500. Fax: (319) 232-0700. E-Mail Address: waterloobucks@waterloobucks.com. Website: www.waterloobucks.com. General Manager: Dan Corbin. Field Manager: Travis Kiewiet. Field: Riverfront Stadium.

WILLMAR STINGERS

Mailing Address: PO Box 201, Willmar, MN, 56201. Telephone: (320) 222-2010. E-Mail Address: ryan@will-marstingers.com. Website: www.willmarstingers.com. Owners: Marc Jerzak, Ryan Voz. General Manager: Nick McCallum. Field Manager: Matt Hollod (Southern Utah). Field: Bill Tauton Stadium.

WISCONSIN RAPIDS RAFTERS

Mailing Address: 521 Lincoln St, Wisconsin Rapids, WI 54494. Telephone: (715) 424-5400. E-Mail Address: info@raftersbaseball.com. Website: www.raftersbaseball.com. Owner/President: Vern Stenman. General Manager: John Fanta. Field: Witter Field.

WISCONSIN WOODCHUCKS

Mailing Address: PO Box 6157, Wausau, WI 54402. Telephone: (715) 845-5055. Fax: (715) 845-5015. E-Mail Address: info@woodchucks.com. Website: www.wood-chucks.com. Owner: Mark Macdonald. General Manager: Ryan Treu. Field Manager: Erik Supplee (Wake Forest). Field: Athletic Park.

PACIFIC INTERNATIONAL LEAGUE

Mailing Address: 4400 26th Ave W, Seattle, WA 98199. Telephone: (206) 623-8844. Fax: (206) 623-8361. E-Mail Address: spotter@potterprinting.com. Website: www. pacificinternationalleague.com.

Year Founded: 1992.

President: Unavailable. Vice President: Unavailable. Commissioner: Brian Gooch. Secretary: Steve Potter. Treasurer: Mark Dow. Member Clubs: Northwest Honkers, Everett Merchants, Kamloops Sundevils, Kelowna Jays, Langley Blaze, Seattle Studs, Trail (BC) franchise, Burnaby Collegiate.

Regular Season: 20 league games. 2014 Opening Date: Unavailable. Playoff Format: The top team is invited to NBC World Series. Roster Limit: 30; 25 eligible for games (players must be at least 18 years old).

PERFECT GAME COLLEGIATE BASEBALL LEAGUE

Mailing Address: 8 Michaels Lane, Old Brookville, NY 11545. **Telephone:** (516) 521-0206. **Fax:** (516) 801-0818. **E-Mail Address:** valkun@aol.com. **Website:** www.pgcbl. org. **Year Founded:** 2010.

President: Jeffrey Kunion. **Executive Committee:** Tom Hickey (Cooperstown Hawkeyes), Bob Ohmann (Newark Pilots), Paul Samulski (Albany Dutchmen).

Member Teams: East Division—Albany Dutchmen, Amsterdam Mohawks, Cooperstown Hawkeyes, Glens Falls Golden Eagles, Mohawk Valley DiamondDawgs. West Division—Adirondack Trail Blazers, Elmira Pioneers, Newark Pilots, Utica Brewers, Watertown Wizards.

Regular Season: 48. **2014 Opening Date:** June 4. **Closing Date:** August 30. **All-Star Game:** July 15. **Playoff Format:** Top three teams in each division qualify for the three-round postseason; Second and third-place finishers have a one-game playoff; next two series are best-of-three. **Roster Limit:** 30 (maximum of two graduated high school players per team).

PROSPECT LEAGUE

Mailing Address: 10011 Woodland Birth Drive, Arlington, TN 38002. **Telephone:** (901) 218-3386. **Fax:** (480) 247-5068. **E-Mail Address:** commissioner@ prospectleague.com. **Website:** www.prospectleague. com.

Year Founded: 1963 as Central Illinois Collegiate League; 2009 as Prospect League.

Commissioner: Dave Chase.

Regular Season: 60 games. **2014 Opening Date:** May 27. **Closing Date:** August 5. **Championship Series:** Aug 8-11. **Roster Limit:** 28.

BUTLER BLUESOX

Mailing Address: 6 West Diamond Street, Butler, PA 16001. **Telephone:** (724) 282-2222 or (724) 256-9994. **Fax:** (724) 282-6565. **E-Mail Address:** frontoffice@butler-bluesox.net. **Website:** www.butlerbluesox.com. **League Director:** Wink Robinson. **General Manager:** Matt Cunningham. **Field Manager:** Anthony Rebyanski.

CHILLICOTHE PAINTS

Mailing Address: 59 North Paint Street, Chillicothe, OH 45601. **Telephone:** (740) 773-8326. **Fax:** (740) 773-8338. **E-Mail Address:** paints@bright.net. **Website:** www.chilli-cothepaints.com. **League Director/General Manager:** Bryan Wickline. **Field Manager:** Unavailable.

DANVILLE DANS

Mailing Address: 138 East Raymond, Danville, IL 61832. **Telephone:** (217) 918-3401. **Fax:** (217) 446-9995. **E-Mail Address:** danvilledans@comcast.net. **Website:** www.danvilledans.com. **League Director:** Jeannie Cooke. **Co-General Managers:** Jeanie Cooke, Rick Kurth. **Field Manager:** Jamie Sailors.

HANNIBAL CAVEMEN

Mailing Address: 403 Warren Barrett Drive, Hannibal, MO 63401. **Telephone:** (573) 221-1010. **Fax:** (573) 221-5269. **E-Mail Address:** hannibalbaseball@sbcglobal.org. **Website:** www.hannibalcavemen.com. **President:** Robert Hemond. **League Director/General Manager:** John Civitate. **Field Manager:** Jay Hemond.

LORAIN COUNTY IRONMEN

Mailing Address: 2840 Meister Road, Lorain, OH 44052. **Telephone:** (440) 752-0372. **Email Address:** info@ lcironmen.com. **Website:** loraincountyironmen.com. **League Director:** Kevin Rhomberg. **General Manager:** Unavailable. **Field Manager:** Unavailable.

QUINCY GEMS

Mailing Address: 300 Civic Center Plaza, Suite 237, Quincy, IL 62301. **Telephone:** (217) 223-1000. **Fax:** (217) 223-1330. **E-Mail Address:** rebbing@quincygems.com. **Website:** www.quincygems.com. **League Director:** Rob Ebbing. **General Manager:** Terry Martin. **Field Manager:** Chris Martin.

RICHMOND RIVERRATS

Mailing Address: 201 NW 13th Street, Richmond, IN 47374. **Telephone:** (765) 935-7287. **Fax:** (765) 935-7529. **E-Mail Address:** dbeaman@richmondriverrats.com. **Website:** www.richmondriverrats.com. **League Director:** Duke Ward. **General Manager:** Deanna Beaman. **Field Manager:** Tyler Lairson.

SLIPPERY ROCK SLIDERS

Mailing Address: PO Box 496, Slippery Rock, PA 16057. **Telephone:** (724) 458-8831. **Fax:** (724) 458-8831. **E-Mail Address:** mbencic@zoominternet.net. **Website:** www. theslipperyrocksliders.com. **League Director/General Manager:** Mike Bencic. **Field Manager:** Brad Neffendorf.

SPRINGFIELD SLIDERS

Mailing Address: 1415 North Grand Avenue East, Suite B, Springfield, IL 62702. **Telephone:** (217) 679-3511. **Fax:** (217) 679-3512. **E-Mail Address:** slidersfun@ springfieldsliders.com. **Website:** www.springfieldsliders. com. **League Director:** Shane Martin. **General Manager:** Dennis Martin. **Field Manager:** Pete Romero.

TERRE HAUTE REX

Mailing Address: 30 North 5th Street, Terre Haute, IN 47807. **Telephone:** (812) 514-8557. **Fax:** (812) 514-8551. **E-mail Address:** threxbaseball@indianastatefoundation. org. **Website:** www.threxbaseball.com. **League Director:** Roland Shelton. **General Manager:** Casey DeGroote. **Field Manager:** Ronnie Prettyman.

WEST VIRGINIA MINERS

Mailing Address: 476 Ragland Road, Suite 1, Beckley, WV 25801. **Telephone:** (304) 252-7233. **Fax:** (304) 253-1998. **E-mail Address:** wvminers@wvminersbaseball. com. **Website:** www.wvminersbaseball.com. **President:** Doug Epling. **League Director/General Manager/Field Manager:** Tim Epling.

SOUTHERN COLLEGIATE BASEBALL LEAGUE

Mailing Address: 9723 Northcross Center Court, Huntersville, NC 28078. **Telephone:** (704) 635-7126. **Fax:** (704) 234-8448. **E-Mail Address:** SCBLCommissioner@aol. com. **Website:** www.scbl.org.

Year Founded: 1999.

Commissioner: Bill Capps. **President:** Jeff Carter. **Executive Vice President:** Brian Swords. **VP, Marketing/Development:** Dave Collins. **Secretary:** James Bradley. **Treasurer:** Brenda Templin. **League Historian:** Larry

Tremitiere. **Umpire in Chief:** Tom Haight.

Regular Season: 40 games. **Playoff Format:** Seven-team single-elimination tournament with best-of-three championship series between final two teams. **Roster Limit:** 30 (College-eligible players only).

BALLANTYNE SMOKIES

Mailing Address: 31014 Executive Point, Fort Mill, SC 29708. **Telephone:** (704) 996-1367. **Email Address:** jspencer@ballantynesmokies.com. **General Manager:** John Spencer. **Head Coach:** JD Vidal.

CAROLINA CHAOS

Mailing Address: 142 Orchard Drive, Liberty, SC 29657. **Telephone:** (864) 843-3232, (864) 901-4331. **E-Mail Address:** brian_swords@carolinachaos.com. **Website:** www.carolinachaos.com. **General Manager:** Brian Swords. **Head Coach:** Guy Howard.

LAKE NORMAN COPPERHEADS

Mailing Address: PO Box 9723, Northcross Center Court, Huntersville, NC 28078. **Telephone:** (704) 892-1041, (704) 564-9211. **E-Mail Address:** jcarter@copperheadsports.org. **Website:** www.copperheadsports.org. **General Manager:** Jeff Carter. **Head Coach:** Derek Shoe.

MORGANTON AGGIES

Mailing Address: PO Box 3448, Morganton, NC 28680. **Telephone:** (828) 438-5351. **Fax:** (828) 438-5350. **E-Mail Address:** gleonhardt@ci.morganton.nc.us. **General Manager:** Gary Leonhardt. **Head Coach:** Travis Howard.

PINEVILLE PIONEERS

Mailing Address: 10229 Rodney Street, Pineville, NC 28134. **Telephone:** (704) 889-2287. **E-Mail Address:** brian.hoop96@gmail.com. **General Manager:** Garry Hill. **Assistant GM:** Brian Hoop. **Head Coach:** Terry Brewer.

STATESVILLE OWLS

Mailing Address: PO Box 17637, Asheville, NC 28816. **Telephone:** (828) 320-5100. **Email Address:** brian.suarez@statesvilleowls.com. **General Manager:** Brian Suarez. **Head Coach:** Ryan Smith.

CAROLINA VIPERS

Mailing Address: 10800 Sikes Place, Suite 225, Charlotte, NC 28277. **Telephone:** (704) 246-8620. **E-Mail Address:** mpolito@tprsolutions.com. **General Manager:** Keith Bray. **Head Coach:** Aaron Bray.

SUNBELT BASEBALL LEAGUE

Mailing Address: 3022 Liberty Way, Atlanta, GA 30318. **Telephone:** (770) 490-7912. **E-mail Address:** info@sunbeltleague.com. **Website:** www.sunbeltleague.com. **Year Founded:** 2006.

Commissioner: Bobby Bennett. **Email:** bobbybennett27@me.com. **Executive Director:** Marty Kelly. **Director of Player Development:** Todd Pratt. **Director, Operations:** Karl Garcia. **Regular Season:** 28 games. **Playoff Format:** division championship series and league championship series, best of 3. **Roster Limit:** 30 (college-eligible players 22 and under).

ATLANTA CRACKERS

Telephone: (770) 380-1461. **E-Mail:** kmeistickle@gmail.com. **General Manager:** Steve Autry. **Head Coach:** Kevin Meistickle.

BERKLEY LAKE TIDES

Telephone: (678) 409-3977. **E-Mail:** kgarcia10@hotmail.com. **General Manager:** Karl Garcia. **Head Coach:** Scott Ward.

BROOKHAVEN BUCKS

Telephone: (404) 840-0039. **E-Mail:** jdbravo@bellsouth.net. **General Manager:** John Davis. **Head Coach:** Nick Hogan.

DOUGLASVILLE BULLS

Telephone: (770) 990-6686. **E-Mail:** tpratt2829@bellsouth.net. **General Manager:** Todd Pratt. **Head Coach:** Austin Janowski.

643DP COUGARS

Telephone (678) 883-4629. **E-Mail:** coachroy10@hotmail.com. **General Manager:** Jay Andrews. **Head Coach:** Roy Anderson.

SOUTH ATLANTA BEARCATS

Telephone: (404) 291-0094. **Email:** dilowe@comcast.net. **General Manager:** Scott Fletcher. **Head Coach:** Dion Lowe.

PEACHTREE CITY CHUKARS

Telephone: (404) 245-3580. **Email:** homeplate318@bellsouth.net. **General Manager:** Lloyd Thompson. **Head Coach:** Rodney Dickenson.

WINDWARD BRAVES

Telephone: (404) 403-0812. **E-Mail:** rube@windwardbaseball.com. **General Manager:** Eric Ruben. **Head Coach:** Davis May.

TEXAS COLLEGIATE LEAGUE

Mailing Address: 735 Plaza Blvd, Suite 200, Coppell, TX 75019. **Telephone:** (979) 985-5198. **Fax:** (979) 779-2398. **E-Mail Address:** info@tclbaseball.com. **Website:** www.texascollegiateleague.com.

Year Founded: 2004.
President: Uri Geva.
Regular Season: 60 games (split schedule). **Playoff Format:** The first- and second-half champions will be joined in the TCL playoffs by two wild card teams. Winners of the one-game divisional round meet in the best-of-three championship series. **Roster Limit:** 30 (College-eligible players only)

ACADIANA CANE CUTTERS

Telephone: (337) 451-6582. **Fax:** (337) 451-6581. **E-Mail Address:** info@canecuttersbaseball.com. **Website:** www.canecuttersbaseball.com. **Owners:** Richard Chalmers, Sandi Chalmers. **General Manager:** Jacob Andrews. **Head Coach:** Lonny Landry.

ALEXANDRIA ACES

Mailing Address: 1 Babe Ruth Dr, Alexandria, LA 71301. **Telephone:** (318) 473-2273. **Website:** www.myacesbaseball.com. **President/Chief Executive Officer:** Eric Moran.

BRAZOS VALLEY BOMBERS

Mailing Address: 405 Mitchell St, Bryan, TX 77801. **Telephone:** (979) 799-7529. **Fax:** (979) 779-2398. **E-Mail Address:** info@bvbombers.com. **Website:** www.bvbombers.com. **Owners:** Uri Geva, Chris Clark. **General Manager:** Chris Clark. **Head Coach:** Curt Dixon.

EAST TEXAS PUMP JACKS

Mailing Address: PO Box 2369, Kilgore, TX 75663. **Telephone:** (903) 218-4638. **Fax:** (866) 511-5449. **E-mail Address:** info@pumpjacksbaseball.com. **Website:** www.pumpjacksbaseball.com. **Owners:** Alan Poff, Brett Cox, Mike Lieberman. **General Manager:** Mike Lieberman. **Head Coach:** Mark Kertenian.

TEXAS MARSHALS

Mailing Address: 7920 Beltline Rd, Suite 1005 Dallas, TX 75254. **Telephone:** (214) 578-4388. **E-Mail Address:** info@texasmarshals.com. **Website:** www.texasmarshals.com. **Owner:** Marc Landry. **General Manager:** Kendrick Moore. **Head Coach:** Dax Powell.

WOODLANDS STRYKERS

Mailing Address: 25009 OakHurst Dr, Spring, TX 77386. **Telephone:** (713) 724-9825. **Fax:** (281) 465-0748. **Owner/General Manager:** Ramiro Lozano. **Head Coach:** Freddy Rodriguez.

VICTORIA GENERALS

Mailing Address: 1307 E Airline Road, Suite H, Victoria, TX 77901. **Telephone:** (361) 485-9522. **Fax:** (361) 485-0936. **E-Mail Address:** info@baseballinvictoria.com, tkyoung@victoriagenerals.com. **Website:** www.victoriagenerals.com. **President:** Tracy Young. **VP/General Manager:** Blake Koch. **Head Coach:** Stephen Flora.

VALLEY BASEBALL LEAGUE

Mailing Address: Valley Baseball League, 3006 Preston Lake Boulevard, Harrisonburg, VA 22801. **Telephone:** (540) 810-9194. **Fax:** (540) 434-5083. **E-Mail Addresses:** don@lemish.com & baseball@shentel.net. **Website:** www.valleyleaguebaseball.com.

Year Founded: 1923.

President: Donald L. Lemish. **Assistant to the President:** Don Harper. **Executive Vice President:** Bruce Alger. **Media Relations Director:** Lauren Jefferson. **Secretary:** Megan Smith. **Treasurer:** Gene Davis.

Regular Season: 44 games. **2014 Opening Date:** May 30. **Closing Date:** August 9. **All-Star Game:** North vs South, July 6 at Harrisonburg. **Playoff Format:** Eight teams; best-of-three each in quarterfinals and semifinals, and finals.

Roster Limit: 28 (college eligible players only)

COVINGTON LUMBERJACKS

Mailing Address: PO Box 30, Covington, VA 24426. **Telephone:** (540) 969-9923, (540) 962-1155. **Fax:** (540) 962-7153. **E-Mail Address:** covingtonlumberjacks@valleyleaguebaseball.com. **Website:** www.lumberjacksbaseball.com. **President:** Dizzy Garten. **Head Coach:** Dan Scott.

ALDIE SENATORS

Mailing Address: 42020 Village Center Plaza, Suite 120-50, Stoneridge, VA 20105. **Telephone:** (703) 542-2110, (703) 989-5009. **Fax:** (703)327-7435. **E-Mail Address:** haymarketsenators@valleyleaguebaseball.com. **Website:** www.haymarketbaseball.com. **President:** Scott Newell. **General Manager:** BernieSchaffler. **Head Coach:** Justin Aspegren.

CHARLES TOWN (WV) CANNONS

Mailing Address: 2862 Northwestern Pike, Capon Bridge, WV 26711.. **Telephone:** (540) 743-3338, (540) 843-4472. **Fax:** (304) 856-1619. **E-Mail Address:** bigdaddy432@verizon.net. **Website:** www.charlestowncannons.com. **President:** Brett Fuller. **Recruiting Coordinator:** Brett Fuller. **General Manager:** Steve Sabins.

FRONT ROYAL CARDINALS

Mailing Address: 382 Morgans Ridge Road, Front Royal, VA 22630. **Telephone:** (703) 244-6662, (540) 905-0152. **E-Mail Address:** DonnaSettle@centurylink.net-frontroyalcardinals@valleyleaguebaseball.com. **Website:** www.valleyleaguebaseball.com. **President:** Donna Settle. **Head Coach:** Jake Weghorst.

HARRISONBURG TURKS

Mailing Address: 1489 S Main St, Harrisonburg, VA 22801. **Telephone:** (540) 434 5919. **Fax:** (540) 434-5919. **E-Mail Address:** turksbaseball@hotmail.com. **Website:** www.harrisonburgturks.com. **Operations Manager:** Teresa Wease. **General Manager/Head Coach:** Bob Wease.

NEW MARKET REBELS

Mailing Address: PO Box 902, New Market, VA 22844. **Telephone:** (304) 856-1623. **Fax:** (540) 740-9486. **E-Mail Address:** nmrebels@shentel.net. **Website:** www.rebels-baseball.biz. **President/General Manager:** Bruce Alger. **Head Coach:** C.J. Rhodes.

STAUNTON BRAVES

Mailing Address: 14 Shannon Place, Staunton, VA 24401.**Telephone:** (540) 886-0987, (540) 885-1645. **Fax:** (540) 886-0905. **E-Mail Address:** sbraves@hotmail.com. **Website:** www.stauntonbravesbaseball.com. **General Manager:** Steve Cox. **Head Coach:** George Laase.

STRASBURG EXPRESS

Mailing Address: PO Box 417, Strasburg, VA 22657. **Telephone:** (540) 325-5677, (540) 459-4041. **Fax:** (540) 459-3398. **E-Mail Address:** neallaw@shentel.net. **Website:** www.strasburgexpress.com. **General manager:** Jay Neal. **Head coach:** Butch Barnes.

WAYNESBORO GENERALS

Mailing Address: 435 Essex Ave., Suite 105, Waynesboro VA 22980. **Telephone:** (540) 932-2300. **Fax:** (540) 932-2322. **E-Mail Address:** waynesborogenerals@valleyleaguebaseball.com. **Website:** www.waynesborogenerals.com. **Chairman:** David T Gauldin II. **Head Coach:** Mike Bocock.

WINCHESTER ROYALS

Mailing Address: PO Box 2485, Winchester, VA 22604. **Telephone:** (540) 539-8888, (540) 664-3978. **Fax:** (540) 662-1434. **E-Mail Addresses:** winchesterroyals@valleyleaguebaseball.com, jimphill@shentel.net.**Website:** www.winchesterroyals.com. **President:** Todd Thompson.

Operations Director: Jimmie Shipp. Coach: Kyle Phelps

WOODSTOCK RIVER BANDITS

Mailing Address: P.O. Box 227, Woodstock, VA 22664. Telephone: (540) 481-0525. Fax: (540) 459-8227. E-Mail Address: woodstockriverbandits@valleyleaguebaseball.com. Website: www.woodstockriverbandits.org. General Manager: R.W. Bowman Jr. Head Coach: Phil Betterly.

WEST COAST LEAGUE

Mailing Address: PO Box 8395, Portland, OR 97207. Telephone: (503) 764-9510. E-Mail Address: wilson@westcoastleague.com. Website: www.westcoastleague.com.

Year Founded: 2005.

President: Ken Wilson. Vice President: Eddie Poplawski. Secretary: Jerry Walker. Treasurer: Tony Bonacci. Supervisor, Umpires: Tom Hiler.

Division Structure: North—Bellingham, Kelowna, Walla Walla, Wenatchee, Victoria. South—Bend, Corvallis, Cowlitz, Kitsap, Klamath Falls, Medford.

Regular Season: 54 games. 2014 Opening Date: June 6. Closing Date: August 10. Playoff Format: First- and second-place teams in each division meet in best-of-three semifinal series; winners advance to best-of-three championship series.

Roster Limit: 25 (college-eligible players only).

BELLINGHAM BELLS

Mailing Address: 1221 Potter Street, Bellingham, WA 98229. Telephone: (360) 746-0406. E-Mail Address: info@bellinghambells.com. Website: www.bellinghambells.com. Owner: Eddie Poplawski. General Manager: Nick Caples. Head Coach: Gary Hatch.

BEND ELKS

Mailing Address: PO Box 9009, Bend, OR 97708. Telephone: (541) 312-9259. E-Mail Address: richardsj@bendcable.com. Website: www.bendelks.com. Owner/General Manager: Jim Richards. Head Coach: Joe Dominiak.

CORVALLIS KNIGHTS

Mailing Address: PO Box 1356, Corvallis, OR 97339. Telephone: (541) 752-5656. E-Mail Address: dan.segel@corvallisknights.com. Website: www.corvallisknights.com. President: Dan Segel. General Manager: Bre Kerkvliet. Head Coach: Brooke Knight.

COWLITZ BLACK BEARS

Mailing Address: PO Box 1255, Longview, WA 98632. Telephone: (360) 703-3195. E-Mail Address: gwilsonagm@gmail.com. Website: www.cowlitzblackbears.com. Owner/ General Manager: Tony Bonacci. Head Coach: Tim Matz (Santa Ana, Calif., JC).

KELOWNA FALCONS

Mailing Address: 201-1014 Glenmore Dr, Kelowna, BC, V1Y 4P2. Telephone: (250) 763-4100. E-Mail Address: mark@kelownafalcons.com. Website: www.kelownafalcons.com. Owner: Dan Nonis. General Manager: Mark Nonis. Head Coach: Geoff White.

KITSAP BLUEJACKETS

Mailing Address: PO Box 68, Silverdale, WA 98383. Telephone: (360) 692-5566.

E-Mail Address: rsmith@kitsapbluejackets.com. Website: www.kitsapbluejackets.com. Managing Partner/General Manager: Rick Smith. Head Coach: Ryan Parker (Olympic, Wash., JC).

KLAMATH FALLS GEMS

Mailing Address: 2001 Crest Street, Klamath Falls, Oregon 97603. Telephone: (541) 883-4367. E-Mail Address: grant@klamathfallsgems.com. Website: www.klamathfallsgems.com. Owners: Jerry and Lisa Walker. General Manager:

Grant Wilson. Head Coach: Mitch Karraker (Oregon).

MEDFORD ROGUES

Mailing Address: PO Box 699, Medford, Oregon 97501. Telephone: (541) 973-2883. E-Mail Address: chuck@medfordrogues.com. Website: www.medfordrogues.com. Owner: CSH International. General Manager: Chuck Heeman. Head Coach: Josh Hogan (Lane, Ore., CC).

VICTORIA HARBOURCATS

Mailing Address: 1014 Caledonia Avenue, Victoria, BC, V8T 1G1. Telephone: (250) 216-0006. E-Mail Address: holly@harbourcats.com. Website: www.harbourcats.com. Owner: John McLean. General Manager: Holly Jones. Head Coach: Dennis Rogers (Riverside, Calif., CC).

WALLA WALLA SWEETS

Mailing Address: 109 E Main Street, Walla Walla, WA 99362. Telephone: (509) 522-2255. E-Mail Address: Zachary.Fraser@pacificbaseballventures.com. Website: www.wallawallabaseball.com. Owner: Pacific Baseball Ventures, LLC. General Manager: Zachary Fraser. Head Coach: JC Biagi (Walla Walla, Wash., CC).

WENATCHEE APPLESOX

Mailing Address: PO Box 5100, Wenatchee, WA 98807. Telephone: (509) 665-6900. E-Mail Address: sales@applesox.com. Website: www.applesox.com. Owner/General Manager: Jim Corcoran. Head Coach: Ed Knaggs.

WCL PORTLAND

Mailing Address: 2811 NE Holman, Portland, Oregon 97211. Telephone: (503) 280-8691. E-Mail Address: rvance@cu-portland.edu. Website:www.wccbl.com/portland.

Year Founded: 2009.

Commissioner: Rob Vance.

Regular Season: 30 games. Playoff Format: First-place team faces fourth-place team and second-place team faces third-place team in first round. Winners advance to championship game.

Roster Limit: 24 (college-eligible players only). Teams: Bucks, Dukes, Lobos, Ports, Stars, Toros.

HIGH SCHOOL BASEBALL

NATIONAL FEDERATION OF STATE HIGH SCHOOL ASSOCIATIONS

Mailing Address: P.O. Box 690, Indianapolis, IN 46206. **Telephone:** (317) 972-6900. **Fax:** (317) 822-5700. **E-Mail Address:** baseball@nfhs.org. **Website:** www.nfhs.org.

Executive Director: Bob Gardner. **Chief Operating Officer:** James Tenopir. **Assistant Director:** Elliot Hopkins. **Director, Publications/Communications:** Bruce Howard.

NATIONAL HIGH SCHOOL BASEBALL COACHES ASSOCIATION

Mailing Address: P.O. Box 12843, Tempe, AZ 85284. **Telephone:** (602) 615-0571. **Fax:** (480) 838-7133. **E-Mail Address:** rdavini@cox.net. **Website:** www.baseball-coaches.org. **Executive Director:** Ron Davini. **Executive Secretary:** Robert Colburn (St. Andrews's School, New Castle, Del.). **President:** John Lowery Sr. (Jefferson HS, Shepherdstown, W.Va.). **First Vice President:** Tim Saunders (Dublin Coffman HS, Dublin, Ohio). **Second Vice President:** Steve Vickery (El Capitan HS, Lakeside, Calif.).

2014 National Convention: Dec. 4-7, at Nashville, Tenn.

NATIONAL TOURNAMENTS

IN-SEASON

HORIZON NATIONAL INVITATIONAL

Mailing Address: Horizon High School, 5653 Sandra Terrace, Scottsdale, AZ 85254. **Telephone:** 602-291-1952. **E-mail:** huskycoach1@yahoo.com. **Website:** www.horizonbaseball.com.

Tournament Director: Eric Kibler.
2014 Tournament: March 24-28.

INTERNATIONAL PAPER CLASSIC

Mailing Address: 4775 Johnson Rd., Georgetown, SC 29440. **Telephone:** (843) 527-9606. **Fax:** (843) 546-8521. **Website:** www.ipclassic.com.

Tournament Director: Alicia Johnson.
2014 Tournament: March 6-9 (eight teams).

LIONS INVITATIONAL

Mailing Address: 8281 Walker Street, La Palma, CA 90623. **Telephone:** 714-220-4101x502. **Fax:** (619) 239-3539. **Email:** Pascal_C@AUHSD.US. **Website:** www.anaheimlionstourney.com

Tournament Director: Chris Pascal.
2014 Tournament: March 29- April 2 (78 teams).

NATIONAL CLASSIC BASEBALL TOURNAMENT

Mailing Address: P.O. Box 338, Placentia, CA 92870. **Telephone:** (714) 993-2838. **Fax:** (714) 993-5350. **E-Mail**

Address: placentiamustang@aol.com. **Website:** www.national-classic.com

Tournament Director: Marcus Jones.
2014 Tournament: April 14-17 (78 teams).

USA BASEBALL NATIONAL HIGH SCHOOL INVITATIONAL

Mailing Address: 403 Blackwell St., Durham, NC 27701. **Telephone:** (919) 474-8721. **Fax:** (919) 474-8822. **Email:** rickriccobono@usabaseball.com. **Website:** www.usabaseball.com.

Tournament Director: Rick Riccobono.
2014 Tournament: March 26-29 at USA Baseball National Training Complex, Cary, NC (16 teams).

USA CLASSIC NATIONAL HIGH SCHOOL INVITATIONAL

Mailing Address: P.O. Box 247, Millington, TN 38043. **Telephone:** (901) 873-5880. **Fax:** (901) 873-5885. **Email:** jwaits@cityofmillington.org. **Website:** www.millingtontn.gov.

Tournament Organizers: Jeff Waits, Johnny Ray.
2014 Tournament: Unavailable.

POSTSEASON

SUNBELT BASEBALL CLASSIC SERIES

Mailing Address: 505 North Blvd., Edmond, OK 73034. **Telephone:** (405) 348-3839. **Fax:** (405) 340-7538. **Email:** lyngor@aol.com. **Website:** www.sunbeltclassicbaseball.com.

Chairman: John Schwartz.
2014 Senior Series: Unavailable.
2014 Junior Series: Unavailable.
2014 Sophomore Series: Unavailable.

ALL-STAR GAMES/AWARDS

PERFECT GAME ALL-AMERICAN CLASSIC

Mailing Address: 1932 Wynnton Road, Columbus, Georgia 31999. **Telephone:** (706) 763-2827. **Fax:** (706) 320-2288. **Event Organizer:** Blue Ridge Sports & Entertainment. **Vice President, Events:** Lou Lacy. **2014 Game:** San Diego Petco Park, August 10th.

UNDER ARMOUR ALL-AMERICA GAME, POWERED BY BASEBALL FACTORY

Mailing Address: 9212 Berger Rd., Suite 200, Columbia, MD 21046. **Telephone:** 410-715-5080. **E-Mail Address:** jason@baseballfactory.com. **Website:** baseballfactory.com. **Event Organizers:** Baseball Factory, Team One Baseball. **2014 Game:** Aug 16.

GATORADE CIRCLE OF CHAMPIONS (National HS Player of the Year Award)

Mailing Address: The Gatorade Company, 321 N. Clark St., Suite 24-3, Chicago, IL, 60610. **Telephone:** 312-821-1000. **Website:** www.gatorade.com.

SHOWCASE EVENTS

ALL-AMERICAN BASEBALL TALENT SHOWCASES

Mailing Address: 333 Preston Ave., Unit 1, Voorhees, NJ 08043. **Telephone:** (856) 354-0201. **Fax:** (856) 354-0818. **Email Address:** hitdoctor@thehitdoctor.com. **Website:** thehitdoctor.com. **National Director:** Joe Barth.

ARIZONA FALL CLASSIC

Mailing Address: 6102 W. Maui Lane, Glendale, AZ 85306. **Telephone:** (602) 978-2929. **Fax:** (602) 439-4494. **Email Address:** azbaseballted@msn.com.

Website: www.azfallclassic.com.
Directors: Ted Heid, Tracy Heid.

2014 Events

Four Corner Classic . . . . .Peoria, AZ, May 29-June 1
Classic Qualifier . . . . Peoria, AZ, June 13-June 15
Arizona Summer Classic . . . . Peoria, AZ, July 10-13
Arizona Summer Classic (16U) . . . . .July 17-20
AZ Sophomore Fall Classic. . . . . Oct. 2-5
All Academic Tryout & Game . . . . .Oct. 9
AZ Senior Fall Classic (HS seniors) . . . . Peoria, AZ, Oct. 9-12
AZ Junior Fall Classic (HS juniors) . . . . Peoria, AZ, Oct. 16-19
Mizuno Universal Classic. . . . . Peoria, AZ, Oct. 24-29

BASEBALL FACTORY

Office Address: 9212 Berger Rd., Suite 200, Columbia, MD 21046. **Telephone:** (800) 641-4487, (410) 715-5080. **Fax:** (410) 715-1975. **Email Address:** info@baseball factory.com. **Website:** www.baseballfactory.com.

Chief Executive Officer & Founder: Steve Sclafani. **President:** Rob Naddelman. **Executive VP & Chairman of the Under Armour All-America Game Selection Committee:** Steve Bernhardt. **Senior VP, Marketing/ Brand:** Jason Budden. **Senior VP, Baseball Operations:** Jim Gemler. **Senior VP, Player Development:** Dan Forester. **VP, Creative:** Matt Kirby. **VP, Youth Baseball:** Jeff Brazier. **VP, Finance:** Gene Mattingly. **Senior Director, Player Development/Scouting:** Andy Ferguson. **Senior Director, College Recruiting:** Dan Mooney. **Senior Director, Event Marketing/Partnerships:** Dave Lax. Senior Multimedia Producer: Brian Johnson. Senior Director, Youth Baseball: Joe Lake. Senior Director, Web Development: Wei Xue.

Executive Player Development Coordinator: Steve Nagler. **Senior Player Development Coordinators:** Dave Packer, John Perko. **Regional Player Development Coordinators:** Patrick Wuebben, Chris Brown, Adam Darvick, Will Bach, Rob Onolfi, Ryan Schweikert, Scott Ritter, Jesse Tome, Drew Baldwin, Ed Bach, Mark Lemon, Christian Culicerto, Josh Hippensteel. **Director of Client/ Staff Logistics:** Cecile Banas. **Director, PVP Program/ National Tryouts:** Bryan Dunkel. **Director, Social Media:** Becky Oldham. **Director, College Recruiting Operations:** Dan Rollins.

Under Armour All-America Pre-Season Tournament: January 17-19 in Tucson, AZ (Kino Sports Complex).

Under Armour All-America Game: August 16, in Chicago, IL (Wrigley Field).

2014 Under Armour Baseball Factory National Tryouts/Premium Video Program: Various locations across the country. Year round. Open to high school players, ages 14–18 and a separate division for pre-high school players, ages 12–14. For full schedule, visit www.baseballfactory.com/tryouts.

BLUE-GREY CLASSIC

Mailing address: 68 Norfolk Road, Mills MA 02054. **Telephone:** (508) 376-1250. **Email Address:** impact-prospects@comcast.net. **Website:** www.impactprospects.com.

2014 Events: Various dates, locations June-Sept 2014.

BOBBY VALENTINE ALL-AMERICAN CAMPS

Address: 52 Mason Street, Greenwich, CT 06830. **Telephone:** (203) 517-1277. **Fax:** (203) 517-1377. **Website:** www.allamericanfoundation.com

EAST COAST PROFESSIONAL SHOWCASE

Website: www.eastcoastproshowcase.com. **Tournament Directors:** John Castleberry. **2014 Showcase:** July 30-Aug 2, Syracuse, N.Y.

IMPACT BASEBALL

Mailing Address: P.O. Box 47, Sedalia, NC 27342. **Email Address:** andypartin@aol.com. **Website:** impactbaseball. com. **Operator:** Andy Partin.

2014 Events: Various dates, May-Aug 2014.

NEW BALANCE BASEBALL GAMES

Mailing Address: 23954 Madison Street, Torrance, CA 90505. **Telephone:** 310-791-1142 x 4426. **Website:** newbalancegames.com

Event Organizer: Kirsten Leetch.

2014 Area Code Games: Aug 4-9 at Blair Field in Long Beach, Calif.

PACIFIC NORTHWEST CHAMPIONSHIPS

Mailing Address: 9849 Fox Street, Aumsville, OR 97325. **Telephone:** 503-385-8019. **Email Address:** mckay@baseballnorthwest.com. **Website:** www.baseball-northwest.com. **Tournament Organizer:** Jeff McKay.

PERFECT GAME USA

Mailing Address: 1203 Rockford Road SW, Cedar Rapids, IA 52404. **Telephone:** (319) 298-2923 Fax: (319) 298-2924. **Email Address:** jerry@perfectgame.org. **Website:** www.perfectgameusa.com.

President/Director: Jerry Ford. **Vice Presidents:** Andy Ford, Jason Gerst, Tyson Kimm, Steve Griffin. **VP, Business Development:** Brad Clement. **International Scouting Director:** Kentaro Yasutake. **National Showcase Director:** Jim Arp. **National Tournament Director:** Taylor McCollough. **National Scouting Director:** Greg Sabers. **National BCS Director:** Ben Ford. **Director, Crosscheckers:** Allan Simpson. **League Director:** Steve James. **Director, College Baseball:** Kendall Rogers. **Northeast Director:** Dan Kennedy. **Western Tournament Director:** Matt Bliven. **Scouting Coordinators:** Kirk Gardner, Todd Gold, Frankie Pilleire, Jheremy Brown, Jason Piddington, Kenny Gardner, Justin Hlubek, Justin Amidon. **Super25 Director:** Drake Browne. **National Spokesman:** Daron Sutton. **All American Spokesman:** Trevor Hoffman.

2014 Showcase/Tournament Events: Sites across the United States, Jan 9-Nov. 7.

PROFESSIONAL BASEBALL INSTRUCTION—BATTERY INVITATIONAL

(for top high school pitchers and catchers)

Mailing Address: 107 Pleasant Avenue, Upper Saddle River N.J. 07458. **Telephone:** (800) 282-4638. **Fax:** (201) 760-8720. **Email Address:** info@baseballclinics.com. **Website:** www.baseballclinics.com/battery-invitational/.

President: Doug Cinnella.

Senior Staff Administrator: Greg Cinnella. **General Manager/PR/Marketing:** Jim Monaghan.

SELECTFEST BASEBALL

Mailing Address: 60 Franklin Pl., Morris Plains, NJ 07950. **Telephone:** (862) 222-6404. **Email Address:** selectfest@optonline.net. **Website:** www.selectfestbaseball.org. **Camp Directors:** Bruce Shatel.

2014 Showcase: Unavailable.

TEAM ONE BASEBALL (A DIVISION OF BASEBALL FACTORY)

Office Address: 1000 Bristol Street North, Box 17285, Newport Beach, CA 92660. **Telephone:** (800) 621-5452. **Fax:** (949) 209-1829. **Email Address:** jroswell@teamonebaseball.com. **Website:** www.teamonebaseball.com.

Senior Director: Justin Roswell. **Executive VP:** Steve Bernhardt. **Senior VP, Baseball Operations:** Jim Gemler. **VP, Player Development:** Dan Forester.

2014 Under Armour Showcases: Team One National East: July 11-12 in Peachtree City, GA (The Chuck at Homeplate)**; Team One National West:** July 29–30 in Azusa, CA (Azusa Pacific University); **Team One Futures Series East:** September 20 in Jupiter, FL (Roger Dean Stadium); **Team One Futures Series West:** October 25 in Azusa, CA (Azusa Pacific University); **Team One Futures Series Texas:** November 1 in Plano, TX (John Paul II High School).

2014 Under Armour Tournaments: Under Armour Memorial Day Classic: May 23-26 in Jupiter, FL (Roger Dean Sports Complex), **Under Armour Southeast Championships:** June 6–10 in Jupiter, FL (Roger Dean Sports Complex), **Under Armour Firecracker Classic:** June 30 – July 4 in Jupiter, FL (Roger Dean Sports Complex), **Under Armour Southwest Championships 16U:** July 25-29 in Azusa, CA (Azusa Pacific University/Citrus College), **Under Armour Southwest Championships 18U:** July 31 – August 4 in Azusa, CA (Azusa Pacific University/Citrus College), **Under Armour Fall Classic:** September 19–21 in Jupiter, FL (Roger Dean Sports Complex), **Under Armour Invitational:** October 11 12 in St. Petersburg, FL (Walter Fuller Complex), **Under Armour SoCal Classic:** October 24–26 in Azusa, CA (Azusa Pacific University/Citrus College).

TOP 96 COLLEGE COACHES CLINICS

Mailing Address: 6 Foley Dr. Southboro, MA 01772. **Telephone:** 508-481-5935.

Email Address: doug.henson@top96.com. **Website:** www.top96.com. **Directors:** Doug Henson, Dave Callum.

2014 Prospect Camps: 70-plus camps throughout the US; 15-30 college coaches guaranteed; see website for details, dates and locations.

YOUTH BASEBALL

ALL AMERICAN AMATEUR BASEBALL ASSOCIATION

Mailing Address: 331 Parkway Dr., Zanesville, OH 43701. **Telephone:** (740) 453-8531. **Email Address:** clw@aol.com. **Website:** www.aaaba.us.

Year Founded: 1944.

President: George Arcurio, III. **Executive Director/Secretary:** Bob Wolfe.

2014 Events: AAABA National Tournament—Aug 4 10, Johnstown, Pa..

AMATEUR ATHLETIC UNION OF THE UNITED STATES, INC.

Mailing Address: P.O. Box 22409, Lake Buena Vista, FL 32830. **Telephone:** (407) 828-3459. **Fax:** (407) 934-7242. **Email Address:** debra@aausports.org. **Website:** www.aaubaseball.org.

Year Founded: 1982. **Sports Manager, Baseball:** Debra Horn.

AMERICAN AMATEUR BASEBALL CONGRESS

National Headquarters: 100 West Broadway, Farmington, NM 87401. **Telephone:** (505) 327-3120. **Fax:** (505) 327-3132. **Email Address:** aabc@aabc.us. **Website:** www.aabc.us.

Year Founded: 1935.

President: Richard Neely.

AMERICAN AMATEUR YOUTH BASEBALL ALLIANCE

Mailing Address: 1703 Koala Drive, Wentzville, MO 63385. **Telephone:** (636) 332-2803. **Email Address:** clwjr28@aol.com. **Website:** www.aayba.com.

President, Baseball Operations: Carroll Wood. **President, Business Operations:** Greg Moore.

AMERICAN LEGION BASEBALL

National Headquarters: American Legion Baseball, 700 N Pennsylvania St., Indianapolis, IN 46204. **Telephone:** (317) 630-1213. **Fax:** (317) 630-1369. **Email Address:** baseball@legion.org. **Website:** www.legion.org/baseball.

Year Founded: 1925.

Program Coordinator: Mike Buss.

2014 World Series (19 and under): Aug 15-19. At Veteran's Field, Shelby, N.C. **2014 Regional Tournaments (Aug 7-11): Northeast**—Middletown, Conn; **Mid-Atlantic**—Brooklawn, NJ; **Southeast**—Asheboro NC; **Mid-South**—North Little Rock, Ark; **Great Lakes**—Terre Haute, Ind; **Central Plains**—Fargo, N.D.; **Northwest**—Eugene, Ore; **Western**—Surprise, Ariz.

BABE RUTH BASEBALL

International Headquarters: 1770 Brunswick Pike, P.O. Box 5000, Trenton, NJ 08638. **Telephone:** (609) 695-1434. **Fax:** (609) 695-2505. **Email Address:** info@baberuthleague.org. **Website:** www.baberuthleague.org.

Year Founded: 1951.

President/Chief Executive Officer: Steven Tellefsen.

CONTINENTAL AMATEUR BASEBALL ASSOCIATION

Mailing Address: P.O. Box 1684 Mt. Pleasant, SC 29465. **Telephone:** 843-860-1568. **Fax:** 843-856-7791. **Email Address:** Diamonddevils.org. **Website:** www.cababaseball.com.

Year Founded: 1984.

Chief Executive Officer: Larry Redwine. **President/COO:** John Rhodes. **Executive Vice President:** Fran Pell.

DIXIE YOUTH BASEBALL

Mailing Address: P.O. Box 877, Marshall, TX 75671. **Telephone:** (903) 927-2255. **Fax:** (903) 927-1846. **Email Address:** dyb@dixie.org. **Website:** www.dixie.org.
Year Founded: 1955.
Commissioner: Wes Skelton.

DIXIE BOYS BASEBALL

Mailing Address: P.O. Box 8263, Dothan, Alabama 36304. **Telephone:** (334) 793-3331. **Email Address:** jjones29@sw.rr.com. **Website:** http://baseball.dixie.org.
Commissioner/Chief Executive Officer: Sandy Jones.

DIZZY DEAN BASEBALL

Mailing Address: P.O. Box 856, Hernando, MS 38632. **Telephone:** (662) 429-4365, (423) 596-1353. **Email Address:** DPhil10513@aol.com, jimmywahl@bellsouth.net, Bdunn39270@comcast.net, hsuggsdizzydean@aol.com. **Website:** www.dizzydeanbbinc.org.
Year Founded: 1962.
Commissioner: Danny Phillips. **President:** Jimmy Wahl. **VP:** Bobby Dunn. **Secretary:** Donnie Stone. **Treasurer:** Houston Suggs.

HAP DUMONT YOUTH BASEBALL (A DIVISION OF THE NATIONAL BASEBALL CONGRESS)

Email Address: bruce@prattrecreation.com,gbclev@hapdumontbaseball.com. **Website:** www.hapdumont-baseball.com.
Year Founded: 1974.
President: Bruce Pinkall

LITTLE LEAGUE BASEBALL

International Headquarters: 539 US Route 15 Hwy, P.O. Box 3485, Williamsport, PA 17701-0485. **Telephone:** (570) 326-1921. **Fax:** (570) 326-1074. **Website:** www.littleleague.org.
Year Founded: 1939.
Chairman: Dr. Davie Jane Gilmour.
President/Chief Executive Officer: Stephen D. Keener. **Chief Financial Officer:** David Houseknecht. **Vice President, Operations:** Patrick Wilson. **Treasurer:** Melissa Singer. **Senior Communications Executive:** Lance Van Auken.

NATIONAL AMATEUR BASEBALL FEDERATION

Mailing Address: P.O. Box 705, Bowie, MD 20718. **Telephone:** (410) 721-4727. **Fax:** (410) 721-4940.
Email Address: nabf1914@aol.com.
Website: www.nabf.com.
Year Founded: 1914.
Executive Director: Charles Blackburn.

NATIONAL ASSOCIATION OF POLICE ATHLETIC LEAGUES

Mailing Address: 1662 N. US Highway 1 Suite C, Jupiter, FL 33469. **Telephone:** (561) 745-5535. **Fax:** (561) 745-3147. **Email Address:** copnkid@nationalpal.org. **Website:** www.nationalpal.org.
Year Founded: 1914.
President: Christopher Hill.

PONY BASEBALL AND SOFTBALL

International Headquarters: P.O. Box 225, Washington, PA 15301. **Telephone:** (724) 225-1060. **Fax:** (724) 225-9852. **Email Address:** info@pony.org.
Website: www.pony.org.
Year Founded: 1951.
President: Abraham Key.

REVIVING BASEBALL IN INNER CITIES

Mailing Address: 245 Park Ave., New York, NY 10167. **Telephone:** (212) 931-7800. **Fax:** (212) 949-5695. **Year Founded:** 1989. **Director, Reviving Baseball in Inner Cities:** David James (David.James@mlb.com). **Vice President, Community Affairs:** Thomas C Brasuell. **Email:** rbi@mlb.com. **Website:** www.mlb.com/rbi.

SUPER SERIES BASEBALL OF AMERICA

National Headquarters: 3449 East Kael St., Mesa, AZ 85213-1773. **Telephone:** (480) 664-2998. **Fax:** (480) 664-2997. **Email Address:** info@superseriesbaseball.com. **Website:** www.superseriesbaseball.com.
President: Mark Mathew.

TRIPLE CROWN SPORTS

Mailing Address: 3930 Automation Way, Fort Collins, CO 80525. **Telephone:** (970) 223-6644. **Fax:** (970) 223-3636. **Websites:** www.triplecrownsports.com. **Email:** john@triplecrownsports.com.
Director, Baseball Operations: John Casale.

U.S. AMATEUR BASEBALL FEDERATION

Mailing Address: 1222 Innovative Dr Suite 130, San Diego, CA 92154. **Telephone:** (619) 934-2551. **Fax:** (619) 271-6659. **Email Address:** usabf@cox.net. **Website:** www.usabf.com.
Year Founded: 1997.
Senior Chief Executive Officer/President: Tim Halbig.

UNITED STATES SPECIALTY SPORTS ASSOCIATION

Executive Vice President, Baseball: Don DeDonatis III, 33600 Mound Rd., Sterling Heights, MI 48310. **Telephone:** (810) 397-6410. **Email Address:** michussa@aol.com.
Executive VP, Baseball Operations: Rick Fortuna, 6324 N. Chatham Ave., #136, Kansas City, MO 64151. **Telephone:** (816) 587-4545. **Email Address:** rick@kcsports.org. **Website:** www.usssabaseball.org. **Year Founded:** 1965/Baseball 1996.

WORLD WOOD BAT ASSOCIATION (A DIVISION OF PERFECT GAME USA)

Mailing Address: 1203 Rockford Road SW, Cedar Rapids, IA 52404. **Telephone:** (319) 298-2923. **Fax:** (319) 298-2924. **Email Address:** taylor@perfectgame.org. **Website:** www.perfectgame.org.
Year Founded: 1997.
President: Jerry Ford. **National Director:** Taylor McCollough. **Scouting Director:** David Rawnsley.

BASEBALL USA

Mailing Address: 2626 West Sam Houston Pkwy. N., Houston, TX 77043. **Telephone:** (713) 690-5055. **Email Address:** info@baseballusa.com. **Website:** www.baseballusa.com.

Tournament Director: Steve Olson

CALIFORNIA COMPETITIVE YOUTH BASEBALL

Mailing Address: P.O. Box 338, Placentia, CA 92870. **Telephone:** (714) 993-2838. **Email Address:** ccybnet@aol.com. **Website:** www.ccyb.net.

Tournament Director: Todd Rogers.

COCOA EXPO SPORTS CENTER

Mailing Address: 500 Friday Road, Cocoa, FL 32926. **Telephone:** (321) 639-3976. **Fax:** (407) 390-9435. **Email Address:** brad@cocoaexpo.com. **Website:** www.cocoaexpo.com.

Athletic Director: Brad Traina.

Activities: Spring training program, spring & fall leagues, instructional camps, team training camps, youth tournaments.

COOPERSTOWN BASEBALL WORLD

Mailing Address: P.O. Box 646, Allenwood, NJ 08723. **Telephone:** (888) CBW-8750. **Fax:** (888) CBW-8720. **Email:** cbw@cooperstownbaseballworld.com. **Website:** www.cooperstownbaseballworld.com.

Complex Address: Cooperstown Baseball World, SUNY-Oneonta, Ravine Parkway, Oneonta, NY 13820.

President/Chairman: Eddie Einhorn. **Vice President:** Debra Sirianni.

2014 Tournaments (15 Teams Per Week): Open to 12U, 13U, 14U, 15U, 16U

COOPERSTOWN DREAMS PARK

Mailing Address: 330 S. Main St., Salisbury, NC 28144. **Telephone:** (704) 630-0050. **Fax:** (704) 630-0737. **Email Address:** info@cooperstowndreamspark.com. **Website:** www.cooperstowndreamspark.com.

Complex Address: 4550 State Highway 28, Milford, NY 13807.

Chief Executive Officer: Louis Presutti. **Director, Baseball Operations:** Geoff Davis.

2014 Tournaments: Weekly May 21–Aug 28.

COOPERSTOWN ALL STAR VILLAGE

Mailing Address: P.O. Box 670, Cooperstown, NY 13326. **Telephone:** (800) 327-6790. **Fax:** (607) 432-1076. **Email Address:** Info@cooperstownallstarvillage.com. **Website:** www.cooperstownallstarvillage.com.

Team Registrations: Jim Rudloff. **Hotel Room Reservations:** Shelly Yager. **Presidents:** Martin and Brenda Patton.

ESPN WIDE WORLD OF SPORTS

Mailing Address: P.O. Box 470847, Celebration, FL 34747. **Telephone:** (407) 938-3802. **Fax:** (407) 938-3442. **Email address:** wdw.sports.baseball@disneysports.com. **Website:** www.disneybaseball.com.

Manager, Sports Events: Aaron Hudson. **Senior Sports Manager:** Kyle Cantrell. **Tournament Director:** Al Schlazer.

KC SPORTS TOURNAMENTS

Mailing Address: KC Sports, 6324 N. Chatham Ave., No. 136, Kansas City, MO 64151.

Telephone: (816) 587-4545. **Fax:** (816) 587-4549. **Email Address:** info@kcsports.org. **Website:** www.kcsports.org.

Activities: USSSA Youth tournaments (ages 6-18).

U.S. AMATEUR BASEBALL FEDERATION

Mailing Address: P.O. Box 531216, San Diego, CA 92153. **Telephone:** (619) 934-2551. **Fax:** (619) 271-6659. **Email Address:** usabf@cox.net. **Website:** www.usabf.com.

Year Founded: 1997. **Senior Chief Executive Officer/President:** Tim Halbig.

INSTRUCTIONAL SCHOOLS/PRIVATE CAMPS

ACADEMY OF PRO PLAYERS

Mailing Address: 140 5th Avenue, Hawthorne, NJ 07506. **Telephone:** (973) 304-1470. **Fax:** (973) 636-6375. **Email Address:** taylor@akademapro.com. **Website:** www.academypro.com. **Camp Director:** Taylor Bargiacchi.

ALL-STAR BASEBALL ACADEMY

Mailing Addresses: 223 Wilmington Pike, Suite 301 Chadds Ford, PA 19317. **Telephone:** (484) 770-8350. **Fax:** (484)-770-8336 . **Email Address:** basba@allstarbaseballacademy.com. **Website:** www.allstarbaseballacademy.com. **Directors:** Mike Manning, Jim Freeman.

AMERICAN BASEBALL FOUNDATION

Mailing Address: 2660 10th Ave. South, Suite 620, Birmingham, AL 35205. **Telephone:** (205) 558-4235. **Fax:** (205) 918-0800. **Email Address:** abf@asmi.org. **Website:** http://americanbaseballfoundation.com/. **Executive Director:** David Osinski.

AMERICA'S BASEBALL CAMPS

Mailing Address: 3020 ISSQ Pine Lake Road #12, Sammamish, WA 98075. **Telephone:** (800) 222-8152. **Fax:** (888) 751-8989. **Email Address:** info@baseballcamps.com. **Website:** www.baseballcamps.com.

CHAMPIONS BASEBALL ACADEMY

Mailing Address: 5994 Linneman Street Cincinnati, OH 45230. **Telephone:** (513) 831-8873. **Fax:** (513) 247-0040. **Email Address:** championsbaseball@ymail.com. **Website:** www.championsbaseball.net.

DOYLE BASEBALL ACADEMY

Mailing Address: P.O. Box 9156, Winter Haven, FL 33883. **Telephone:** (863) 439-1000. **Fax:** (863) 294-8607. **Email Address:** info@doylebaseball.com. **Website:** www.doylebaseball.com. **President:** Denny Doyle. **CEO/CFO:** Blake Doyle.

ELEV8 SPORTS INSTITUTE

Mailing Address: 490 Dotterel Road, Delray Beach, FL 33444. **Telephone:** (800) 970-5896. **Fax:** (561) 278-6679. **Email Address:** info@elev8si.com. **Website:** http://elev8sportsinstitute.com/

FROZEN ROPES TRAINING CENTERS

Mailing Address: 24 Old Black Meadow Rd., Chester, NY 10918. **Telephone:** (845) 469-7331. **Fax:** (845) 469-6742. **Email Address:** info@frozenropes.com. **Website:** www.frozenropes.com.

IMG ACADEMY

Mailing Address: IMG Academies, 5500 34th St. W., Bradenton, FL 34210. **Telephone:** 941-739-7480. **Fax:** 941-739-7484. **Email Address:** acad_baseball@img.com. **Website:** www.imgacademy.com.

MARK CRESSE BASEBALL SCHOOL

Mailing Address: P.O. Box 1596 Newport Beach, CA 92659. **Telephone:** (714) 892-6145. **Fax:** (714) 890-7017. **Email Address:** info@markcresse.com. **Website:** www.markcresse.com.
Owner/Founder: Mark Cresse.

US SPORTS CAMPS/NIKE BASEBALL CAMPS

Mailing Address: 750 Lindaro Street, Suite 220, San Rafael, CA 94901. **Telephone:** (415) 479-6060. **Fax:** (415) 479-6061. **Email Address:** baseball@ussportscamps.com. **Website:** www.ussportscamps.com/baseball/.

MOUNTAIN WEST BASEBALL ACADEMY

Mailing Address: 389 West 10000 South, South Jordan, UT 84095. **Telephone:** (801) 561-1700. **Fax:** (801) 561-1762. **Email Address:** kent@utahbaseballacademy.com. **Website:** www.mountainwestbaseball.com. **Director:** Bob Keyes

NORTH CAROLINA BASEBALL ACADEMY

Mailing Address: 1137 Pleasant Ridge Road, Greensboro, NC 27409. **Telephone:** (336) 931-1118. **Email Address:** info@ncbaseball.com. **Website:** www.ncbaseball.com.
Owner/Director: Scott Bankhead.

PENNSYLVANIA DIAMOND BUCKS

Mailing Address: 2320 Whitetail Court, Hellertown, PA 18055. **Telephone:** (610) 838-1219, (610) 442-6998. **Email Address:** janciganick@yahoo.com. **Camp Director:** Jan Ciganick. **Head of Instruction:** Chuck Ciganick.

PROFESSIONAL BASEBALL INSTRUCTION

Mailing Address: 107 Pleasant Ave., Upper Saddle River, NJ 07458. **Telephone:** (800) 282-4638 (NY/NJ), (877) 448-2220 (rest of U.S.). **Fax:** (201) 760-8820. **Email Address:** info@baseballclinics.com. **Website:** http://www.baseballclinics.com/battery-invitational/. **President:** Doug Cinnella.

RIPKEN BASEBALL CAMPS

Mailing Address: 1427 Clarkview Rd., Suite 100, Baltimore, MD 21209. **Telephone:** (410) 823-0808. **Fax:** (410) 823-0850. **Email Address:** information@ripkenbaseball.com. **Website:** www.ripkenbaseball.com.

SHO-ME BASEBALL CAMP

Mailing Address: P.O. Box 2270, Branson West, MO 65737. **Telephone:** (417) 338-5838. **Fax:** (417) 338-2610. **Email Address:** info@shomebaseball.com. **Website:** www.shomebaseball.com.

COLLEGE CAMPS

Almost all of the elite college baseball programs have summer/holiday instructional camps. Please consult the college section for listings.

SENIOR BASEBALL

MEN'S SENIOR BASEBALL LEAGUE

(25 and Over, 35 and Over, 45 and Over, 55 and Over)
Mailing Address: One Huntington Quadrangle, Suite 3N07, Melville, NY 11747. **Telephone:** (631) 753-6725. **Fax:** (631) 753-4031.
President: Steve Sigler. **Vice President:** Gary D'Ambrisi.
E-Mail Address: info@msblnational.com.
Website: www.msblnational.com.

MEN'S ADULT BASEBALL LEAGUE

(18 and Over)
Mailing Address: One Huntington Quadrangle, Suite 3N07, Melville, NY 11747. **Telephone:** (631) 753-6725. **Fax:** (631) 753-4031.
E-Mail Address: info@msblnational.com. **Website:** www.msblnational.com.
President: Steve Sigler. **Vice President:** Gary D'Ambrisi.

NATIONAL ADULT BASEBALL ASSOCIATION

Mailing Address: 5944 S. Kipling St., Suite 200, Littleton, CO 80127. **Telephone:** (800) 621-6479. **Fax:** (303) 639-6605. **E-Mail:** nabanational@aol.com. **Website:** www.dugout.org.
President: Shane Fugita.

NATIONAL AMATEUR BASEBALL FEDERATION

Mailing Address: P.O. Box 705, Bowie, MD 20718. **Telephone:** (410) 721-4727. **Fax:** (410) 721-4940.
Email Address: nabf1914@aol.com.
Website: www.nabf.com.
Year Founded: 1914.
Executive Director: Charles Blackburn.

ROY HOBBS BASEBALL

Open (18-over), Veterans (38-over), Masters (48-over), Legends (55-over); Classics (60-over), Seniors (65-over), Timeless (70-over), Women's open.
Mailing Address: 2048 Akron Peninsula Rd., Akron, OH 44313. **Telephone:** (330) 923-3400. **Fax:** (330) 923-1967. **E-Mail Address:** rhbb@royhobbs.com.
Website: www.royhobbs.com.
President: Tom Giffen. **Commissioner:** Rob Giffen.

DIRECTORIES

- **AGENT**
- **SERVICE**

AGENT DIRECTORY

ACES INC
188 Montague St.
Brooklyn, NY 11201
Phone: (718)-237-2900
Fax: (718)-522 Agent Robert Garber-3906
Web: www.acesincbaseball.com
E-mail: aces@acesinc1.com
Agents: Seth Levinson, Esq., Sam Levinson,
Keith Miller, Peter Pedalino, Esq., Mike
Zimmerman, Jamie Appel, Brandon
O'Hearn, Josh Yates

METIS SPORTS MANAGEMENT, LLC
132 North Old Woodward Ave.
Birmingham, MI 48009
Phone: (248)-594-1070
Fax: (248)-281-5150
Web: www.metissports.com
E-mail: marketing@metissports.com
Agents: Storm T. Kirschenbaum, Esq.,
Hector Faneytt, Jack Fang

ONYX SPORTS MANAGEMENT
60 E. Rio Salado Pkwy. Suite 900
Tempe, AZ 85281
Phone: (480)-643-9112, (480)-213-2421
Fax: (480)-696-5474
Web: www.onyxsm.com
E-mail: jcook@onyxsm.com,
zprice@onyxsm.com
Agents: Jesse D. Cook, Esq., Zacahary I.
Price, Esq.

PRO STAR MANAGEMENT, INC
1600 Scripps Center, 312 Walnut Street
Cincinnati, OH 45202
Phone: (513)-762-7676
Fax: (513)-721-4628
Web: www.prostarmanagement.com
E-mail: prostar@fuse.net
Joe Bick, President; Brett Bick, Executive
Vice President; Ryan Bick, Vice President

RMG BASEBALL
445 W. Erie Street, Suite 205
Chicago, IL 60654
Phone: (312)-907-3500
Web: www.rmgbaseball.com
Robert M. Garber

SOSNICK COBBE SPORTS
712 Bancroft Rd., #510
Walnut Creek, CA 94598
Phone: (925)-890-5283
Fax: (925)-476-0130
Web: www.sosnickcobbesports.com
E-mail: Mattsoz@aol.com,
PaulCobbe@me.com
Agents: Matt Sosnick, Paul Cobbe, Adam
Karon, John Furmaniak, Matt Hofer, Tripper
Johnson, Jonathan Pridie

THE L. WARNER COMPANIES, INC
9690 Deereco Rd., Ste. 650
Timonium, MD 21093
Phone: (410)-252-0808
Fax: (443)-281-5554
Web: www.lwarner.com/baseball
E-mail: roliver@lwarner.com
Agents: Rick Oliver, President; Jay Witaskis,
Vice President; Joe Gaza, Director of
Baseball Operations; Lee Warner, Chairman
and CEO

THE LEGACY AGENCY
1500 Broadway, 25th floor
New York, NY 10036
Phone: (212)-334-6880
Fax: (212)-334-6895
Web: www.legacy-agency.com
E-mail: info@legacy-agency.com
Agents: Peter E. Greenberg, Esq., Edward L.
Greenberg, Chris Leible

THE LEGACY AGENCY
500 Newport Center Dr., Ste. 800
Newport Beach, CA 92660
Phone: (949)-720-8700
Fax: (949)-720-1331
Web: www.legacy-agency.com
E-mail: info@legacy-agency.com
Agents: Greg Genske, Brian Peters, Brodie
Scoffield, R.J. Hernandez, Kenny Felder,
Joe Brennan, Joe Mizzo, Hiram Bocachica,
Mike Maulini

SERVICE DIRECTORY

ACCESSORIES

WILSON SPORTING GOODS
8750 West Bryn Mawr Ave., 13th Floor
Chicago, IL 60631
Phone: (800)-333-8326
Fax: (773)-714-4565
Web: www.wilson.com
E-mail: askwilson@wilson.com

THE BENCHCOACH
912 Bristlewood Dr.
McKinney, TX 75070
Phone: (972)-740-5417
Fax: (866)-447-6572
Web: www.TheBenchCoach.com
E-mail: dcarney@thebenchcoach.com

APPAREL

DEMARINI
6435 NW Croeni Rd.
Hillsboro, OR 97124
Phone: (800)-937-BATS (2287)
Fax: (503)-531-5506
Web: www.demarini.com

MINOR LEAGUES, MAJOR DREAMS
P.O. Box 6098
Anaheim, CA 92816
Phone: (800)-345-2421
Fax: (714)-939-0655
Web: www.minorleagues.com
E-mail: mlmd@minorleagues.com

BAGS

DEMARINI
6435 NW Croeni Rd.
Hillsboro, OR 97124
Phone: (800)-937-BATS (2287)
Fax: (503)-531-5506
Web: www.demarini.com

DIAMOND SPORTS
1880 E. St. Andrew Place
Santa Ana, CA 90720
Phone: (714)-415-7600
Fax: (714)-415-7601
Web: www.diamond-sports.com
E-mail: info@diamond-sports.com

LOUISVILLE SLUGGER
800 W. Main St.
Louisville, KY 40202
Phone: (800)-282-2287
Fax: (502)-585-1179
Web: www.slugger.com
E-mail: customer.service@slugger.com

THE BENCHCOACH
912 Bristlewood Dr.
McKinney, TX 75070
Phone: (972)-740-5417
Fax: (866)-447-6572
Web: www.TheBenchCoach.com
E-mail: dcarney@thebenchcoach.com

WILSON SPORTING GOODS
8750 West Bryn Mawr Ave., 13th Floor
Chicago, IL 60631
Phone: (800)-333-8326
Fax: (773)-714-4565
Web: www.wilson.com
E-mail: askwilson@wilson.com

BASEBALLS

DIAMOND SPORTS
1880 E. St. Andrew Place
Santa Ana, CA 90720
Phone: (714)-415-7600
Fax: (714)-415-7601
Web: www.diamond-sports.com
E-mail: info@diamond-sports.com

WILSON SPORTING GOODS
8750 West Bryn Mawr Ave., 13th Floor
Chicago, IL 60631
Phone: (800)-333-8326
Fax: (773)-714-4565
Web: www.wilson.com
E-mail: askwilson@wilson.com

BASES

BEAM CLAY
One Kelsey Park
Great Meadows, NJ 07838
Phone: (800)-247-BEAM (2326)
Fax: (908)-637-8421
Web: www.beamclay.com
E-mail: sales@beamclay.com

See our ad on page 312!

BATS

B45 - THE ORIGINAL YELLOW BIRCH BAT COMPANY
281 Rue Edward-Assh
Ste-Catherine-de-la-J.C., QC G3N 1A3
Phone: (888)-669-0145
Fax: (418)-875-3535
Web: www.b45online.com
E-mail: info@b45online.com

DEMARINI
6435 NW Croeni Rd.
Hillsboro, OR 97124
Phone: (800)-937-BATS (2287)
Fax: (503)-531-5506
Web: www.demarini.com

LOUISVILLE SLUGGER
800 W. Main St.
Louisville, KY 40202
Phone: (800)-282-2287
Fax: (502)-585-1179
Web: www.slugger.com
E-mail: customer.service@slugger.com

OLD HICKORY BAT COMPANY
P.O. Box 588
White House, TN 37188
Phone: (866)-PROBATS
Fax: (615)-285-0512
Web: www.oldhickorybats.com
E-mail: mail@oldhickorybats.com

PHOENIX BATS
7801 Corporate Blvd., Ste. E
Plain City, OH 43064
Phone: (614)-873-7776
Fax: (614)-932-2313
Web: www.phoenixbats.com
E-mail: customercare@phoenixbats.com

SAM BAT
110 Industrial Ave.
Carleton Place, ON K7C 3T2
Phone: (613)-257-3060
Fax: (613)-257-8577
Web: www.sambat.com
E-mail: bats@sambat.com

TRINITY BAT COMPANY
2493 E. Orangethorpe Ave.
Fullerton, CA 92831
Phone: (714)-449-1275
Fax: (714)-449-1285
Web: www.trinitybats.com
E-mail: bats@trinitybats.com

DINGER BATS
109 S. Kimbro St.
Ridgway, IL 62979
Phone: (618)-272-7250
Fax: (618)-272-7253
Web: www.dingerbats.com
E-mail: Info@dingerbats.com

COOPERSTOWN BAT COMPANY
118 Main Street, PO Box 415
Cooperstown, NY 13326
Phone: (607)-547-2415
Fax: (607)-547-6156
Web: www.cooperstownbat.com
E-mail: cobatco@cooperstownbat.com

BATTING CAGES

See our ad on page 312!

BEAM CLAY
One Kelsey Park
Great Meadows, NJ 07838
Phone: (800)-247-BEAM (2326)
Fax: (908)-637-8421
Web: www.beamclay.com
E-mail: sales@beamclay.com

WEST COAST NETTING
5075 Flightline Dr.
Kingman, AZ 86401
Phone: (928)-692-1144
Fax: (928)-692-1501
Web: www.westcoastnetting.com
E-mail: info@westcoastnetting.com

C&H BASEBALL, INC
10615 Technology Terrace, #100
Bradenton, FL 34211
Phone: (800)-248-5192
Fax: (941)-727-0588
Web: www.chbaseball.com
E-mail: info@chbaseball.com

SPI NETS
2001 Amistad Dr.
San Benito, TX 78586
Phone: (866)-243-6387
Fax: (956)-276-9691
Web: www.spinets.net
E-mail: info@spinets.net

AALCO MANUFACTURING
1650 Avenue H
St. Louis, MO 63125
Phone: (800)-537-1259
Web: www.aalcomfg.com
E-mail: tim@aalcomfg.com

NATIONAL SPORTS PRODUCTS
3441 S 11th Ave.
Eldridge, IA 52807
Phone: (800)-478-6497
Web: www.nationalsportsproducts.com
E-mail: sales@nationalsportsproducts.com

MASTER PITCHING MACHINE, INC
4200 NE Birmingham Rd.
Kansas City, MO 64117
Phone: (800)-878-8228
Fax: (816)-452-7581
Web: www.masterpitch.com
E-mail: joeg@masterpitch.com

JUGS SPORTS
11885 S.W. Herman Rd.
Tualatin, OR 97062
Phone: (800)-547-6843
Fax: (503)-691-1100
Web: www.jugssports.com

BATTING GLOVES

DEMARINI
6435 NW Croeni Rd.
Hillsboro, OR 97124
Phone: (800)-937-BATS (2287)
Fax: (503)-531-5506
Web: www.demarini.com

BUNTING/PLEATED FANS/FLAGS

INDEPENDENCE BUNTING & FLAG CORP
44 West Jefryn Blvd.
Deer Park, NY 11729
Phone: (800)-995-9129
Fax: (888)-824-1060
Web: www.independence-bunting.com
E-mail: independencebunting@gmail.com

CAMPS/SCHOOLS

PROFESSIONAL BASEBALL INSTRUCTION
107 Pleasant Ave.
Upper Saddle River, NJ 07458
Phone: (201)-760-8720
Fax: (201)-760-8820
Web: www.baseballclinics.com
E-mail: info@baseballclinics.com

CAPS/HEADWEAR

MINOR LEAGUES, MAJOR DREAMS
P.O. Box 6098
Anaheim, CA 92816
Phone: (800)-345-2421
Fax: (714)-939-0655
Web: www.minorleagues.com
E-mail: mlmd@minorleagues.com

OC SPORTS
1201 Melissa Drive
Bentonville, AR 72712
Phone: (866)-776-6774
Fax: (866)-776-1010
Web: www.ocsports.com
E-mail: customsports@ocsports.com

CONCESSION OPERATIONS

FUTURE POS
10979 Reed Hartman Hwy., Suite 117
Cincinnati, OH 45242
Phone: (513) 464 6804
Fax: (513)-530-9546
Web: www.fposman.com
E-mail: futurepos@fuse.net

CONFETTI/STREAMERS

PYROTECNICO
P.O. Box 149
New Castle, PA 16103
Phone: (724)-652-9555
Fax: (724)-652-1288
Web: www.pyrotecnico.com
E-mail: mkillingsworth@pyrotecnico.com

DUGOUT ORGANIZERS

THE BENCHCOACH
912 Bristlewood Dr.
McKinney, TX 75070
Phone: (972)-740-5417
Fax: (866)-447-6572
Web: www.TheBenchCoach.com
E-mail: dcarney@thebenchcoach.com

EMBROIDERED PATCHES

THE EMBLEM SOURCE, LLC
4575 Westgrove #500
Addison, TX 75001
Phone: (972)-248-1909
Web: www.theemblemsource.com
E-mail: larry@theemblemsource.com

ENTERTAINMENT

BIRDZERK!
P.O. Box 36061
Louisville, KY 40233
Phone: (502)-458-4020
Fax: (502)-458-0867
Web: www.birdzerk.com
E-mail: info@theskillvillegroup.com

BREAKIN' BBOY MCCOY
P.O. Box 36061
Louisville, KY 40233
Phone: (502)-458-4020
Fax: (502)-458-0867
Web: www.bboymccoy.com
E-mail: info@theskillvillegroup.com

THE SKILLVILLE GROUP
P.O. Box 36061
Louisville, KY 40233
Phone: (502)-458-4020
Fax: (502)-458-0867
Web: www.theskillvillegroup.com
E-mail: info@theskillvillegroup.com

RB3-RUSSIAN BAR TRIO
P.O. Box 36061
Louisville, KY 40233
Phone: (502)-458-4020
Fax: (502)-458-0867
Web: www.rb3usa.com
E-mail: info@theskillvillegroup.com

ZOOPERSTARS!
P.O. Box 36061
Louisville, KY 40233
Phone: (502)-458-4020
Fax: (502)-458-0867
Web: www.zooperstars.com
E-mail: info@theskillvillegroup.com

FIELD COVERS/TARPS

BEAM CLAY
One Kelsey Park
Great Meadows, NJ 07838
Phone: (800)-247-BEAM (2326)
Fax: (908)-637-8421
Web: www.beamclay.com
E-mail: sales@beamclay.com

See our ad on page 312!

C&H BASEBALL, INC
10615 Technology Terrace, #100
Bradenton, FL 34211
Phone: (800)-248-5192
Fax: (941)-727-0588
Web: www.chbaseball.com
E-mail: info@chbaseball.com

COVERMASTER, INC
100 Westmore Dr., 11-D
Rexdale, ON M9V 5C3
Phone: (800)-387-5808
Fax: (416)-745-1811
Web: www.covermaster.com
E-mail: info@covermaster.com

SPI NETS
2001 Amistad Dr.
San Benito, TX 78586
Phone: (866)-243-6387
Fax: (956)-276-9691
Web: www.spinets.net
E-mail: info@spinets.net

FIELD EQUIPMENT

DIAMOND SPORTS
1880 E. St. Andrew Place
Santa Ana, CA 90720
Phone: (714)-415-7600
Fax: (714)-415-7601
Web: www.diamond-sports.com
E-mail: info@diamond-sports.com

FIELD WALL PADDING

AALCO MANUFACTURING
1650 Avenue H
St. Louis, MO 63125
Phone: (800)-537-1259
Web: www.aalcomfg.com
E-mail: tim@aalcomfg.com

BEAM CLAY
One Kelsey Park
Great Meadows, NJ 07838
Phone: (800)-247-BEAM (2326)
Fax: (908)-637-8421
Web: www.beamclay.com
E-mail: sales@beamclay.com

See our ad on page 312!

C&H BASEBALL, INC
10615 Technology Terrace, #100
Bradenton, FL 34211
Phone: (800)-248-5192
Fax: (941)-727-0588
Web: www.chbaseball.com
E-mail: info@chbaseball.com

COVERMASTER, INC
100 Westmore Dr., 11-D
Rexdale, ON M9V 5C3
Phone: (800)-387-5808
Fax: (416)-745-1811
Web: www.covermaster.com
E-mail: info@covermaster.com

NATIONAL SPORTS PRODUCTS
3441 S 11th Ave.
Eldridge, IA 52807
Phone: (800)-478-6497
Web: www.nationalsportsproducts.com
E-mail: sales@nationalsportsproducts.com

PROMATS ATHLETICS
1455 Harrison Road
Salisbury, NC 28147
Phone: (800)-617-7125
Fax: (704)-603-4138
Web: www.promatsathletics.com
E-mail: dnance@promatsathletics.com

SPI NETS
2001 Amistad Dr.
San Benito, TX 78586
Phone: (866)-243-6387
Fax: (956)-276-9691
Web: www.spinets.net
E-mail: info@spinets.net

FIREWORKS

PYROTECNICO
P.O. Box 149
New Castle, PA 16103
Phone: (724)-652-9555
Fax: (724)-652-1288
Web: www.pyrotecnico.com
E-mail: mkillingsworth@pyrotecnico.com

FOAM HANDS & NOVELTY GIFTS

RICO INDUSTRIES, INC
7000 N. Austin
Niles, IL 60714
Phone: (855)-608-4618
Fax: (312)-427-0190
Web: www.ricoinc.com
E-mail: jimz@ricoinc.com

GIVEAWAY ITEMS

RICO INDUSTRIES, INC
7000 N. Austin
Niles, IL 60714
Phone: (855)-608-4618
Fax: (312)-427-0190
Web: www.ricoinc.com
E-mail: jimz@ricoinc.com

GLOVES

DINGER BATS
109 S. Kimbro St.
Ridgway, IL 62979
Phone: (618)-272-7250
Fax: (618)-272-7253
Web: www.dingerbats.com
E-mail: info@dingerbats.com

FRANK'S SPORT SHOP
430 E. Tremont Ave.
Bronx, NY 10457
Phone: (718)-299-5223/(212)-945-0020
Fax: (718)-583-1653
Web: www.frankssportshop.com

See our ad on the insert!

LOUISVILLE SLUGGER
800 W. Main St.
Louisville, KY 40202
Phone: (800)-282-2287
Fax: (502)-585-1179
Web: www.slugger.com
E-mail: customer.service@slugger.com

WILSON SPORTING GOODS
8750 West Bryn Mawr Ave., 13th Floor
Chicago, IL 60631
Phone: (800)-333-8326
Fax: (773)-714-4565
Web: www.wilson.com
E-mail: askwilson@wilson.com

GRAPHIC DESIGN

AALCO MANUFACTURING
1650 Avenue H
St. Louis, MO 63125
Phone: (800)-537-1259
Web: www.aalcomfg.com
E-mail: tim@aalcomfg.com

INSURANCE

K&K INSURANCE
1712 Magnavox Way
Fort Wayne, IN 46804
Phone: (800)-637-4757
Fax: (260)-459-5120
Web: www.kandkinsurance.com
E-mail: kk-sports@kandkinsurance.com

See our ad on the inside front cover!

MUSIC/SOUND EFFECTS

CLICK EFFECTS
2408 Felts Ave.
Nashville, TN 37211
Phone: (615)-460-7330
Fax: (615)-460-7331
Web: www.clickeffects.com
E-mail: info@clickeffects.com

SOUND DIRECTOR, INC
2918 SW Royal Way
Gresham, OR 97080
Phone: (503)-665-6869
Fax: (503)-914-1812
Web: www.sounddirector.com
E-mail: jj@sounddirector.com

NETTING/POSTS

AALCO MANUFACTURING
1650 Avenue H
St. Louis, MO 63125
Phone: (800)-537-1259
Web: www.aalcomfg.com
E-mail: tim@aalcomfg.com

PROMATS ATHLETICS
1455 Harrison Road
Salisbury, NC 28147
Phone: (800)-617-7125
Fax: (704)-603-4138
Web: www.promatsathletics.com
E-mail: dnance@promatsathletics.com

BEAM CLAY
One Kelsey Park
Great Meadows, NJ 07838
Phone: (800)-247-BEAM (2326)
Fax: (908)-637-8421
Web: www.beamclay.com
E-mail: sales@beamclay.com

See our ad on page 312!

C&H BASEBALL, INC
10615 Technology Terrace, #100
Bradenton, FL 34211
Phone: (800)-248-5192
Fax: (941)-727-0588
Web: www.chbaseball.com
E-mail: info@chbaseball.com

NATIONAL SPORTS PRODUCTS
3441 S 11th Ave.
Eldridge, IA 52807
Phone: (800)-478-6497
Web: www.nationalsportsproducts.com
E-mail: sales@nationalsportsproducts.com

SPI NETS
2001 Amistad Dr.
San Benito, TX 78586
Phone: (866)-243-6387
Fax: (956)-276-9691
Web: www.spinets.net
E-mail: info@spinets.net

NUTRITION

RAPID PERFORMANCE PRODUCTS
229 E. Main Street
Forestville, WI 54213
Phone: (920)-856-6767
Fax: (920)-856-6989
Web: www.rapidperform.com
E-mail: jeremy@countryovens.com

PENNANTS

RICO INDUSTRIES, INC
7000 N. Austin
Niles, IL 60714
Phone: (855)-608-4618
Fax: (312)-427-0190
Web: www.ricoinc.com
E-mail: jimz@ricoinc.com

PITCHING AIDS/SHOWCASES

PROFESSIONAL BASEBALL INSTRUCTION
107 Pleasant Ave.
Upper Saddle River, NJ 07458
Phone: (201)-760-8720
Fax: (201)-760-8820
Web: www.baseballclinics.com
E-mail: info@baseballclinics.com

PITCHING MACHINES

C&H BASEBALL, INC
10615 Technology Terrace, #100
Bradenton, FL 34211
Phone: (800)-248-5192
Fax: (941)-727-0588
Web: www.chbaseball.com
E-mail: info@chbaseball.com

JUGS SPORTS
11885 S.W. Herman Rd.
Tualatin, OR 97062
Phone: (800)-547-6843
Fax: (503)-691-1100
Web: www.jugssports.com

SPORTS TUTOR, INC
3300 Winona Ave.
Burbank, CA 91504
Phone: (818)-972-2772
Fax: (818)-972-9651
Web: www.sportsmachines.com
E-mail: orders@sportstutorinc.com

ATHLETIC TRAINING EQUIPMENT COMPANY - ATEC
655 Spice Island Dr.
Sparks, NV 89431
Phone: (800)-998-ATEC (2832)
Fax: (800)-959-ATEC (2832)
Web: www.atecsports.com
E-mail: askATEC@wilson.com

MASTER PITCHING MACHINE, INC
4200 NE Birmingham Rd.
Kansas City, MO 64117
Phone: (800)-878-8228
Fax: (816)-452-7581
Web: www.masterpitch.com
E-mail: joeg@masterpitch.com

PLAYING FIELD PRODUCTS

BEAM CLAY
One Kelsey Park
Great Meadows, NJ 07838
Phone: (800)-247-BEAM (2326)
Fax: (908)-637-8421
Web: www.beamclay.com
E-mail: sales@beamclay.com

See our ad on page 312!

C&H BASEBALL, INC
10615 Technology Terrace, #100
Bradenton, FL 34211
Phone: (800)-248-5192
Fax: (941)-727-0588
Web: www.chbaseball.com
E-mail: info@chbaseball.com

DIAMOND PRO
1112 East Copeland Rd., Suite 500
Arlington, TX 76011
Phone: (800)-228-2987
Fax: (800)-640-6735
Web: www.diamondpro.com
E-mail: diamondpro@diamondpro.com

PROMATS ATHLETICS
1455 Harrison Road
Salisbury, NC 28147
Phone: (800)-617-7125
Fax: (704)-603-4138
Web: www.promatsathletics.com
E-mail: dnance@promatsathletics.com

RAIN OUT
2780 S. Jones Blvd.
Las Vegas, NV 89146
Phone: (888)-609-1163
Web: www.rainoutproducts.com
E-mail: mbaker@rainoutproducts.com

SPI NETS
2001 Amistad Dr.
San Benito, TX 78586
Phone: (866)-243-6387
Fax: (956)-276-9691
Web: www.spinets.net
E-mail: info@spinets.net

STALKER RADAR (APPLIED CONCEPTS)
2609 Technology Dr.
Plano, TX 75074
Phone: (888)-stalker
Web: www.stalkerradar.com
E-mail: sales@stalkerradar.com

See our ad on page 2!

POINT OF SALE ITEMS

COOPERSTOWN BAT COMPANY
118 Main Street, PO Box 415
Cooperstown, NY 13326
Phone: (607)-547-2415
Fax: (607)-547-6156
Web: www.cooperstownbat.com
E-mail: cobatco@cooperstownbat.com

FUTURE POS
10979 Reed Hartman Hwy., Suite 117
Cincinnati, OH 45242
Phone: (513)-464-6804
Fax: (513)-530-9546
Web: www.fposman.com
E-mail: futurepos@fuse.net

STADIUM1 SOFTWARE, LLC
13479 Polo Trace Drive
Delray Beach, FL 33446
Phone: (561)-779-4040
561-498-8358
Web: www.stadium1.com
E-mail: tim.mcdulin@stadium1.com

PROMOTIONAL ITEMS

C&H BASEBALL, INC
10615 Technology Terrace, #100
Bradenton, FL 34211
Phone: (800)-248-5192
Fax: (941)-727-0588
Web: www.chbaseball.com
E-mail: info@chbaseball.com

RICO INDUSTRIES, INC
7000 N. Austin
Niles, IL 60714
Phone: (855)-608-4618
Fax: (312)-427-0190
Web: www.ricoinc.com
E-mail: jimz@ricoinc.com

PROTECTIVE EQUIPMENT

BEAM CLAY
One Kelsey Park
Great Meadows, NJ 07838
Phone: (800)-247-BEAM (2326)
Fax: (908)-637-8421
Web: www.beamclay.com
E-mail: sales@beamclay.com

See our ad on page 312!

C&H BASEBALL, INC
10615 Technology Terrace, #100
Bradenton, FL 34211
Phone: (800)-248-5192
Fax: (941)-727-0588
Web: www.chbaseball.com
E-mail: info@chbaseball.com

DIAMOND SPORTS
1880 E. St. Andrew Place
Santa Ana, CA 90720
Phone: (714)-415-7600
Fax: (714)-415-7601
Web: www.diamond-sports.com
E-mail: info@diamond-sports.com

JUGS SPORTS
11885 S.W. Herman Rd.
Tualatin, OR 97062
Phone: (800)-547-6843
Fax: (503)-691-1100
Web: www.jugssports.com

PROMATS ATHLETICS
1455 Harrison Road
Salisbury, NC 28147
Phone: (800)-617-7125
Fax: (704)-603-4138
Web: www.promatsathletics.com
E-mail: dnance@promatsathletics.com

WILSON SPORTING GOODS
8750 West Bryn Mawr Ave., 13th Floor
Chicago, IL 60631
Phone: (800)-333-8326
Fax: (773)-714-4565
Web: www.wilson.com
E-mail: askwilson@wilson.com

RADAR EQUIPMENT

JUGS SPORTS
11885 S.W. Herman Rd.
Tualatin, OR 97062
Phone: (800)-547-6843
Fax: (503)-691-1100
Web: www.jugssports.com

STALKER RADAR (APPLIED CONCEPTS)
2609 Technology Dr.
Plano, TX 75074
Phone: (888)-stalker
Web: www.stalkerradar.com
E-mail: sales@stalkerradar.com

See our ad on page 2!

SCOREBOARD

CLICK EFFECTS
2408 Felts Ave.
Nashville, TN 37211
Phone: (615)-460-7330
Fax: (615)-460-7331
Web: www.clickeffects.com
E-mail: info@clickeffects.com

SHOES

FRANK'S SPORT SHOP
See our ad on the insert!
430 E. Tremont Ave.
Bronx, NY 10457
Phone: (718)-299-5223/(212)-945-0020
Fax: (718)-583-1653
Web: www.frankssportshop.com

SPECIAL EFFECTS & LASERS

PYROTECNICO
P.O. Box 149
New Castle, PA 16103
Phone: (724)-652-9555
Fax: (724)-652-1288
Web: www.pyrotecnico.com
E-mail: mkillingsworth@pyrotecnico.com

SPORTING GOODS

PROFESSIONAL BASEBALL INSTRUCTION
107 Pleasant Ave.
Upper Saddle River, NJ 07458
Phone: (201)-760-8720
Fax: (201)-760-8820
Web: www.baseballclinics.com
E-mail: info@baseballclinics.com

SPORTS VISION

20OVER8
Suite 592, Village Shoppes
95 Washington Street
Canton, MA 02021
Phone: (781)-769-4797
Fax: (781)-769-4794
Web: www.20over8.com
E-mail: DRL@20over8.com

TICKETS

PATRON MANAGER CRM
850 Seventh Ave., Ste. 1201
New York, NY 10019
Phone: (212)-271-4328
Fax: (212)-271-4327
Web: www.patrontechnology.com
E-mail: info@patrontechnology.com

WORLDWIDE TICKETCRAFT
3606 Quantum Blvd.
Boynton Beach, FL 33426
Phone: (877)-426-5754
Fax: (954)-426-5761
Web: www.worldwideticketcraft.com
E-mail: erikc@wwticket.com

TRAINING EQUIPMENT

ATHLETIC TRAINING EQUIPMENT COMPANY - ATEC
655 Spice Island Dr.
Sparks, NV 89431
Phone: (800)-998-ATEC (2832)
Fax: (800)-959-ATEC (2832)
Web: www.atecsports.com
E-mail: askATEC@wilson.com

JUGS SPORTS
11885 S.W. Herman Rd.
Tualatin, OR 97062
Phone: (800)-547-6843
Fax: (503)-691-1100
Web: www.jugssports.com

LOUISVILLE SLUGGER
800 W. Main St.
Louisville, KY 40202
Phone: (800)-282-2287
Fax: (502)-585-1179
Web: www.slugger.com
E-mail: customer.service@slugger.com

TRAVEL

BROACH BASEBALL TOURS
3235 South Blvd.
Charlotte, NC 28209
Phone: (800)-849-6345
Fax: (704)-365-3800
Web: www.baseballtoursusa.com
E-mail: info@broachsportstours.com

TROPHIES/AWARDS

COOPERSTOWN BAT COMPANY
118 Main Street, PO Box 415
Cooperstown, NY 13326
Phone: (607)-547-2415
Fax: (607)-547-6156
Web: www.cooperstownbat.com
E-mail: cobatco@cooperstownbat.com

UNIFORMS

WILSON SPORTING GOODS
8750 West Bryn Mawr Ave., 13th Floor
Chicago, IL 60631
Phone: (800)-333-8326
Fax: (773)-714-4565
Web: www.wilson.com
E-mail: askwilson@wilson.com

VIDEO/AUDIO CONTENT DELIVERY SYSTEMS

CLICK EFFECTS
2408 Felts Ave.
Nashville, TN 37211
Phone: (615)-460-7330
Fax: (615)-460-7331
Web: www.clickeffects.com
E-mail: info@clickeffects.com

WINDSCREENS

BEAM CLAY
See our ad on page 312!
One Kelsey Park
Great Meadows, NJ 07838
Phone: (800)-247-BEAM (2326)
Fax: (908)-637-8421
Web: www.beamclay.com
E-mail: sales@beamclay.com

C&H BASEBALL, INC
10615 Technology Terrace, #100
Bradenton, FL 34211
Phone: (800)-248-5192
Fax: (941)-727-0588
Web: www.chbaseball.com
E-mail: info@chbaseball.com

COVERMASTER, INC
100 Westmore Dr., 11-D
Rexdale, ON M9V 5C3
Phone: (800)-387-5808
Fax: (416)-745-1811
Web: www.covermaster.com
E-mail: info@covermaster.com

NATIONAL SPORTS PRODUCTS
3441 S 11th Ave.
Eldridge, IA 52807
Phone: (800)-478-6497
Web: www.nationalsportsproducts.com
E-mail: sales@nationalsportsproducts.com

SPI NETS
2001 Amistad Dr.
San Benito, TX 78586
Phone: (866)-243-6387
Fax: (956)-276-9691
Web: www.spinets.net
E-mail: info@spinets.net

YOUR NAME HERE. Make sure the baseball community can find you in 2015
Call 919-213-7924 or e-mail advertising@baseballamerica.com

INDEX

MAJOR LEAGUE TEAMS

MINOR LEAGUE TEAMS

INDEPENDENT TEAMS

OTHER ORGANIZATIONS